UNDERSTANDING COLONIAL NIGERIA

In this landmark new history, Toyin Falola analyzes the impact of Britain's colonization of Nigeria from the late nineteenth century to 1960, when the country regained independence. Falola covers major events in depth, from the initial conquest and denial of Indigenous sovereignty to the emergence and functioning of the colonial state and later nationalist movements, offering fascinating insights into labor and trade relations, regionalism and nationalism, and Nigeria's role during World Wars I and II. *Understanding Colonial Nigeria* assesses the economic, political, social, and cultural changes that culminated in the emergence of a coalition of diverse groups agitating for the end of colonial rule from the 1940s – from labor coalitions and politicians to youth groups and market women. From the country's borders and state structure to the present conflicts, Falola powerfully reflects on the lasting consequences of British intervention in the affairs of Nigerian states and communities.

TOYIN FALOLA is Professor of History, University Distinguished Teaching Professor, and the Jacob and Frances Sanger Mossiker Chair in the Humanities at the University of Texas at Austin. He served as General Secretary of the Historical Society of Nigeria, President of the African Studies Association, Vice-President of the UNESCO Slave Route Project, and Kluge Chair of the Countries of the South, Library of Congress. He was a member of the Scholars' Council, Kluge Center, the Library of Congress. He has received more than thirty lifetime career awards and over twenty honorary doctorates. He has written extensively on African knowledge systems, including *Religious Beliefs and Knowledge Systems in Africa* (2021), *African Spirituality, Politics and Knowledge Systems: Sacred Words and Holy Realm* (2021), and *Decolonizing African Studies: Knowledge Production, Agency and Voice* (2022). He is also the series coeditor for Cambridge University Press's African Identities series.

UNDERSTANDING COLONIAL NIGERIA

British Rule and Its Impact

TOYIN FALOLA

University of Texas at Austin

Shaftesbury Road, Cambridge CB2 8EA, United Kingdom

One Liberty Plaza, 20th Floor, New York, NY 10006, USA

477 Williamstown Road, Port Melbourne, VIC 3207, Australia

314–321, 3rd Floor, Plot 3, Splendor Forum, Jasola District Centre, New Delhi – 110025, India

103 Penang Road, #05–06/07, Visioncrest Commercial, Singapore 238467

Cambridge University Press is part of Cambridge University Press & Assessment, a department of the University of Cambridge.

We share the University's mission to contribute to society through the pursuit of education, learning and research at the highest international levels of excellence.

www.cambridge.org
Information on this title: www.cambridge.org/9781009337182

DOI: 10.1017/9781009337205

© Toyin Falola 2025

This publication is in copyright. Subject to statutory exception and to the provisions of relevant collective licensing agreements, no reproduction of any part may take place without the written permission of Cambridge University Press & Assessment.

When citing this work, please include a reference to the DOI 10.1017/9781009337205

First published 2025

A catalogue record for this publication is available from the British Library.

A Cataloging-in-Publication data record for this book is available from the Library of Congress.

ISBN 978-1-009-33718-2 Hardback
ISBN 978-1-009-33722-9 Paperback

Cambridge University Press & Assessment has no responsibility for the persistence or accuracy of URLs for external or third-party internet websites referred to in this publication and does not guarantee that any content on such websites is, or will remain, accurate or appropriate.

For Professors Yemi Akinwumi, Sati Fwatshak, and Zack Gundu
Change agents of Central Nigeria

CONTENTS

List of Figures *page* ix
List of Maps xi
Preface xiii
Acknowledgments xvi
Timeline of Events xviii

PART I **Introduction** 1

1 The Colonial Archives and Alternative Voices 3

2 Narrating Colonial Nigeria 25

PART II **Conquest and Colonization** 45

3 Peoples and States in the Nineteenth Century 47

4 Prelude to Colonization: Trade and Missions 75

5 Lagos and the Niger Area 98

6 Conquest and Reactions 120

7 Administrative Experimentation, Boundary Formation, and Colonial Consolidation, 1900–1914 142

PART III **Colonial Societies** 171

8 World War I and Its Aftermath 173

9 The Interwar Years 196

10 Indirect Rule and the Native Administration 215

11 The Legal System and Law Enforcement 235

12	Colonial Economy	254
13	Western Education	276
14	Social Changes	303
15	Women	321
16	Religions	347
17	Health and Medicine	369
18	Cultures	388
19	Urbanization	405
20	Creativity and Aesthetics	423

PART IV **Nationalism and Independence** 453

21	Reform Movements Before 1940	455
22	World War II and Its Aftermath	474
23	Trade Unions and Politics	494
24	Party Politics and Personalities	510
25	Constitutions and Emerging Federalism	530
26	Regionalism and Ethnic Politics in the 1950s	548

PART V **Conclusion** 571

27	Colonial Legacies	573

Bibliography 593
Index 683

FIGURES

1.1 Light was produced from an *atupa* (lamp), depicting a knowledge-based solution. *page* 18
2.1 Colonial Nigeria illustrates the conquest and full colonization of the geographical and territorial areas of the country officially incorporated as part of the British Empire in West Africa. 28
3.1 The presentation of bride price, tubers of yam, and a gallon of palm oil by a suitor to a would-be in-law was a cherished tradition across several Nigerian communities in the nineteenth century. 71
4.1 The development of Lagos seaport wharf was a contributing factor to the development of Lagos in the nineteenth century. 92
5.1 The West African Frontier Force mounted by the British colonial government was pivotal in the penetration and subsequent conquest of the Niger area by the first decade of the twentieth century. 102
6.1 Britain's penetration and conquest of Nigeria was fierce, bloody, and met with diverse forms of resistance by the Indigenous population across the country. 135
7.1 Frederick Lugard, the first High Commissioner (1900–6), Governor of Southern and Northern Nigeria Protectorate (1912–14), last Governor of the Northern Protectorate, and first Governor-General of Nigeria (1914–19). 143
7.2 Lugard's Rest House, Lokoja. 147
12.1 A Yoruba family removing seeds from cocoa pods. 261
16.1 The First Storey Building in Badagry, Nigeria. 349
16.2 The Central Mosque, Ode Omu, built in 1948. 359
20.1 Creativity and aesthetics were at the height of colonial Nigeria's developmental phase as locals weaved mats and produced ceramics, fine pots, and other traditional crafts as part of the age-long skills for economic and communal growth. 425
22.1 Mrs. Funmilayo Ransome-Kuti (b. 1900) strongly advocated women's rights and was one of the strongest forces for a pan-Nigerian constitution and Nigerian independence. 484
24.1 Herbert Macaulay (1864–1946), foremost politician, political activist, journalist, and architect, is regarded as Nigeria's father of modern nationalism. 517

26.1 Abubakar Tafawa Balewa, Northern Nigerian politician, legislator, founder of the Northern People's Party, and the first and only Prime Minister of Nigeria at independence. 565
26.2 Renowned nationalists, politicians, and premiers of Nigeria's Eastern, Northern, and Western regions. 565
26.3 Representative of Queen Elizabeth II, Princess Alexandra of Kent, in a friendly smile with two female hosts during her three-week official state visit. 567
26.4 Princess Alexandra of Kent and Nigerian prime minister Sir Abubakar Tafawa Balewa, together at the opening of the First Session of the First Parliament as part of the independence ceremonies in October 1960. 567
26.5 Rosemary Anieze, wearing the sash, crowned Miss Independence on September 28, 1960. 568
26.6 Queen Elizabeth II and Prince Philip in a royal visit to the Emir of Kano, Muhammadu Sanusi I, on February 16, 1956. 569
27.1 A sprawling street in Lagos in the 1960s hosts one of its most important and iconic colonial structures, and the first cathedral building in Nigeria, the Cathedral Church of Christ, completed in 1946. 579

MAPS

7.1 Colonial Nigeria in Phases (1881–1922)   *page* 144
7.2 Northern Nigeria Protectorate and Colony and Protectorate of Southern Nigeria (1887 and 1900)   146
7.3 Provincial Divisions of Nigeria in Phases (1926–61)   165

PREFACE

This is the second volume of three interrelated books, each on a distinctive era of Nigeria's history: the first is on precolonial Nigeria; this one is about the colonial era; and the third discusses the postcolonial and contemporary life of the nation. The annals of history contain narratives that greatly influence how people understand their world. The story of British colonial rule in Nigeria is a captivating and intricate narrative of conquest, colonization, social transformation, and the fight for independence. Within the pages of this comprehensive and meticulously researched book, I embarked on a journey to unravel the intricacies of a pivotal period in Nigerian history. Although no one can fully master the complicated history of Nigeria in all its various historical eras, events, and thematic dimensions, I aim to shed light on the multifaceted layers that make up the history of a complex nation.

Part I of the journey starts with Chapter 1, "The Colonial Archives and Alternative Voices," which explores the archives and spaces where alternative voices that affirm and challenge the prevailing narratives are discovered. By carefully studying all relevant published materials, I attempt to create a nuanced understanding of the events from the mid-nineteenth century to the early 1960s. In the opening of Chapter 2, "Narrating Colonial Nigeria," I explain my sources and approaches. Presenting these from a critical perspective, I aim to provide readers with a deeper understanding of the intricate nature of the colonial experience.

Continuing the exploration in Part II, I delve into the intricacies of the nineteenth century, a time when numerous peoples and states coexisted, each possessing distinct identities, cultures, and political systems. Chapter 3, "Peoples and States in the Nineteenth Century," invites readers to understand the rich and varied history of precolonial Nigeria by providing a backdrop for significant encounters that defined the nation's colonial history. The discussion on colonization was dominated by trade and missions, establishing the basis for European regional interests. In Chapter 4, "Prelude to Colonization: Trade and Missions," I explore the complex networks of trade and religious impact before the arrival of colonial powers. In Chapter 5, "Lagos and the Niger Area," the attention turns to Lagos and the Niger area, which were historical crossroads that came together, influencing the future path of the region.

The conquest of Nigeria and the subsequent reactions are an important chapter in the nation's history. In Chapter 6, "Conquest and Reactions," I analyze the intricate dynamics of power, resistance, and adaptation that unfolded when colonial forces met various Indigenous populations. Chapter 7, "Administrative Experimentation, Boundary Formation, and Colonial Consolidation, 1900–1914," focuses on the period from 1900 to 1914, which involved administrative experimentation, boundary formation, and colonial consolidation, and sheds light on the mechanisms utilized to strengthen colonial control.

Part III of the book provides an overview of the changes and continuities in Nigerian society during colonial rule. Chapter 8, "World War I and Its Aftermath," explores the consequences of World War I and its aftermath, examining the significant changes that followed this worldwide conflict. Chapter 9, "The Interwar Years," delves into the social, political, and economic changes that influenced Nigerian society between the two World Wars. As explained in Chapter 10, "Indirect Rule and the Native Administration," indirect rule and native administration played crucial roles in colonial governance. The chapter explores how the colonial authorities maintained control while respecting and incorporating existing Indigenous governance systems.

Chapter 11, "The Legal System and Law Enforcement," examines this era's legal system and law enforcement mechanisms, providing insight into the complex relationship between justice and power. Chapter 12, "Colonial Economy," analyzes the colonial economy, which is crucial in facilitating imperial exploitation. It reveals the intricate dynamics of trade, labor, agriculture, and resource extraction, seeking to unravel the complex relationship between the colonizer and the colonized. Chapter 13, "Western Education," examines the introduction of Western education and its profound impact on the nation. It sheds light on how knowledge can bring about transformation, as well as its far-reaching implications on individuals and communities.

Chapter 14, "Social Changes," discusses various changes, such as shifts in gender roles, family structures, and social hierarchies. In Chapter 15, "Women," the focus is on the voices and experiences of women, who have often been marginalized in historical narratives. This chapter highlights their resilience, agency, and significant contributions to Nigerian society. Chapter 16, "Religions," delves into the complex relationship between various religions, including Indigenous religions, Islam, and Christianity. It sheds light on how these religions significantly shaped belief systems, cultural practices, and social cohesion. Chapter 17, "Health and Medicine," explores these vital components of societal well-being, including the intricate dynamics of health care in colonial Nigeria, ranging from traditional healing practices to the introduction of Western medical systems.

Chapter 18, "Cultures," celebrates Nigeria's rich and diverse heritage, exploring the various cultural expressions and artistic traditions that thrived during this period. Chapter 19, "Urbanization," examines the process of urbanization and its significant effects on social structures, demographics, and economic activities. Chapter 20, "Creativity and Aesthetics," invites readers to delve into the realms of literature, music, visual arts, and performance. It shines a spotlight on the remarkable creative expressions that emerged despite the limitations imposed by colonial rule.

Part IV is on the emergence of nationalism and the arduous fight for independence. Chapter 21, "Reform Movements Before 1940," analyzes the reform movements that emerged before 1940 and the crucial role they played in setting the stage for the ensuing transformative events. Chapter 22, "World War II and Its Aftermath," explores the impact of World War II and its repercussion on the trajectory of Nigerian nationalism.

Trade unions and politics have played a crucial role in shaping the aspirations of the Nigerian people. Accordingly, Chapter 23, "Trade Unions and Politics," explores the origins of labor movements and how they interacted with the wider political environment. In Chapter 24, "Party Politics and Personalities," consideration turns to the influential political figures and their ideologies, shedding light on the convoluted dynamics of the nationalist struggle.

The emergence of constitutions and the evolution of federalism, the themes in Chapter 25, "Constitutions and Emerging Federalism," are integral to Nigeria's path toward independence. The chapter explores the legal and political structures that established the groundwork for a nation capable of governing itself. Chapter 26, "Regionalism and Ethnic Politics in the 1950s," considers regionalism and politics during that era and insights into the complex dynamics that influenced the journey toward independence. The concluding chapter, "Colonial Legacies," makes up Part V of the book and assesses the lasting effects of colonial rule on present-day Nigerian society, politics, and institutions. This is significant because comprehending the present requires confronting and coming to terms with the lingering effects of the past.

Notably, the book is set out in a way that allows you to read it in its entirety; however, you can also focus on a specific chapter of choice, presented as integral, which explains a few instances of repetition. As we embark on this intellectual journey through the pages of *Understanding Colonial Nigeria*, our knowledge may deepen, our empathy may expand, and our commitment to justice and equality will be strengthened. By understanding our collective history, we can uncover valuable insights into the intricacies of our current situation and shed light on how we can create a fair and inclusive future for all.

ACKNOWLEDGMENTS

Writing a book cannot be done alone; it requires collaboration and the support of many people who contribute to its creation. As I contemplate the conclusion of *Understanding Colonial Nigeria*, I am overwhelmed with profound gratitude for the numerous individuals who have played a crucial part in making this project a reality.

My heartfelt gratitude goes to my family. Their unwavering love and encouragement have always been tremendous sources of inspiration for me. I am incredibly grateful for their firm belief in me, especially for their understanding throughout the extensive hours of research and writing. Their support has been truly invaluable.

I also want to express my sincere appreciation to my academic advisors and friends, Dr. Bola Dauda and Dr. Michael Afolayan. Their guidance, expertise, and constructive feedback have significantly shaped this book. I am most thankful for their commitment to academic excellence and genuine passion for the subject matter. Their dedication played a critical role in refining my ideas and expanding my knowledge.

I am grateful for the support and assistance provided by the archival staff at Ibadan, various libraries in different parts of the world, and the University of Texas at Austin. I am truly impressed by their tireless dedication to preserving historical documents and their willingness to assist me in navigating the extensive collection of resources. Their efforts are truly commendable. I also appreciate the scholars and researchers whose pioneering works provided the basis for my study. Their meticulous research and insightful analyses have greatly contributed to our understanding of colonial Nigeria. I owe a debt of gratitude to the interviewees who graciously shared their stories and personal experiences. Their willingness to do so helped me to gain a more comprehensive and nuanced understanding of the historical events discussed in this book. Your contributions have greatly enhanced the richness and depth of the narrative.

I thank my colleagues and friends for their invaluable support, intellectual engagement, and stimulating discussions throughout the entire process. I have been motivated by your enthusiasm and camaraderie during the challenging moments. 'Tayo Keyede, my devoted consultant, I am grateful. Peter M. J. Gross, you are the best copy editor. Adebukola Bassey, you are super-efficient. I thank an army of fact-checkers and proofreaders: Wale Luqman, Wale Ghazal, Dr. Oluwafunminiyi Raheem, Damilola Osunlakin, Damilare Ajiboye, Adanna Ogbonna, Miriam Odeyemi, Jacob Keiser, Adisa Habeeb, Mihir Msgokhale, Hetty ter Haar, Abidogun Jamaine, Claire Ayelotan, Matthew Alugbin, Christian Obinna, Oyeleke Joanna Oreoluwa, Anuoluwapo Enilolobo, Kareem Shamusudeen, Ahmed Adisa, Yahaya Halidu, Wale Olaogun, Theophilus Femi Alawonde, and many more. Jacob Keiser was asked to read the entire work from the point of view of someone who knew little to nothing about Nigerian history. His questions were many and, as I answered them, the improvements became substantial. I must mention Dr. Oluwafunminiyi Raheem, who prepared the bibliography, and my assistant, Vasah Revandkar, who prepared the manuscript according to the publication guidelines. Mike Efionayi and Dr. Kazeem Ekeolu assisted with the images. I am very grateful to you all.

I would also like to express my appreciation to the publishing team at Cambridge University Press for their exceptional expertise and commitment to bringing the publication of this book to fruition. Their attention to detail in editing, design, and production has resulted in a final product of the utmost quality. I am deeply grateful to all those who have directly or indirectly contributed to the creation of this book.

In conclusion, this book is a testament to the collaborative efforts of individuals, each of whom has played a significant role in its production. I appreciate your efforts and constant support throughout this journey. Thank you for coming along with me.

TIMELINE OF EVENTS

Date	Event
1861	Britain establishes a colony at the port of Lagos.
1877	Englishman George Goldie makes his first exploration of the Nigerian interior.
1884–5	European leaders discuss their interests in specific African territories at the West Africa Conference, held in Berlin. Some historians contend that the great European powers, in effect, "partitioned" Africa at the conference.
1885	The establishment of the Oil Rivers Protectorate in Southeastern Nigeria; renamed the Niger Coast Protectorate in 1893.
1886	Formation of the Royal Niger Company (RNC), which monopolizes trade in the Niger basin until the revocation of its charter in 1900. In the same year, a peace treaty is signed, ending the prolonged war among the Yoruba-speaking people of the southwest.
1887	King Jaja of Opobo is exiled to the West Indies for the abrogation of the Treaty of Protection.
1893	Establishment of a British protectorate over Yoruba territories in the southwest.
1894	Revolt of Brassmen against the RNC. In the same year, Nana Olomu, an Itsekiri leader, "Governor of the River," is deposed and deported for hindering British access to interior markets.
1898–1909	The Ekumeku underground resistance movement fights against the RNC and British colonial rule.
1899	Frederick Lugard is appointed High Commissioner of Britain's Nigerian territory. He sometimes uses force to bring natives under English dominion.
1900	Creation of the Protectorate of Northern Nigeria. The extension of the Northern Protectorate ends in 1903 when British forces conquer the Sokoto Caliphate and kill the sultan.
1902–3	The Aro Expedition was part of Britain's effort to "pacify" the hinterlands of Eastern Nigeria.

TIMELINE OF EVENTS

1908	Protests in Lagos against the water rate were fueled by the reporting of Nigerian journalists such as Herbert Macaulay, who used newspapers to report on and critique the performance of the colonial government.
1912	The establishment of the Southern Nigeria Civil Service Union, which is later renamed the Nigerian Civil Servants' Union.
1914	Great Britain unifies its Lagos Colony and its Northern and Southern "Protectorates" in the Nigerian basin. Lagos is named the colony's capital city.
1914–18	Nigerian troops aid the British cause in World War I.
1920s	A growing spirit of nationalism begins to take root in Nigeria. The National Congress of British West Africa (NCBWA) is founded.
1923	The establishment of the Clifford Constitution allows for elected representation in the governance of Nigeria for the first time.
1925	The British government initiates improvements in the mission schools of the Niger basin. The West African Students' Union (WASU) is founded.
1929	The "Women's War," or Aba Riots, was a major protest against British indirect rule in Southeastern Nigeria.
1931	The Nigerian Union of Teachers (NUT) is established.
1936	The Nigerian Youth Movement (NYM), a political organization of young nationalists in the Lagos area, is founded.
1944	Nnamdi Azikiwe establishes the National Council of Nigeria and the Cameroons (later Nigerian Citizens) (NCNC), which quickly becomes an influential political party pushing for Nigerian independence from British colonial rule. Mrs. Olufunmilayo Ransome-Kuti founds the Abeokuta Ladies' Club, later renamed the Abeokuta Women's Union (AWU), to lobby against the injustices of indirect colonial rule.
1945	The Nigerian Labour Union organizes a general strike, bringing work and business to a standstill. The strike precipitates important economic changes in the form of the first Ten Year Plan, which is adopted later the same year.
1946	The Richards Constitution is enacted, providing a central legislature and dividing Nigeria into three regions: the North, West, and East.
1948	The first university in Nigeria is established in Ibadan, the University of Ibadan.
1949	Northern People's Congress (NPC) is founded under the leadership of Tafawa Balewa, Aminu Kano, and Ahmadu Bello, the Sardauna of Sokoto.
1951	The MacPherson Constitution amends the Richards Constitution, moving Nigeria closer to independence. The Action Group (AG), a Yoruba-dominated political party in the southwest, is founded under the leadership of Obafemi Awolowo.

1953	Anthony Enahoro, for the first time, moves a motion for Nigeria's independence. It suffers a setback in the parliament.
1954	The Lyttleton Constitution establishes a federal system of government for Nigeria.
1956	American and British oil companies discover vast oil reserves in Nigeria.
1957	Regional self-government is attained in the East and West. The Willink Minorities Commission is instituted to look into the fears of the ethnic minority in Nigeria. Samuel L. Akintola, for the second time, moves a motion for Nigeria's independence, which is passed by parliament but rejected by the British colonial government.
1958	The Willink Minorities Commission submits its report. Remi Fani-Kayode revisits the independence motion successfully passed in parliament and to be granted on April 2, 1960, but it is rejected again by the colonial government.
1959	Regional self-government is attained in the North. Sir Tafawa Balewa proposes a motion on independence to the parliament. It is passed but had to wait until 1960.
1960	Nigeria becomes independent on October 1, after a three-year transition period.

PART I

Introduction

1

The Colonial Archives and Alternative Voices

Introduction

The development of society is an ongoing process, creating records and materials that either describe that development or the influences that have stalled it. As time passes, additional records accumulate to describe that time. Record keeping positions archives as not only important but also necessary.[1] Archived history can exist in individual fragments before it is gathered in an architectural structure.

An archive is often described as the set of materials created or received by a person or organization – in a personal or official capacity – highlighting important information about events, actions, orders, and decisions.[2] The materials and their provenance are carefully controlled to be preserved in their original state.[3] Archives are distinguished from other sources of history by "collective control, principle of provenance and original order."[4] Provenance refers to the originality and the authentication of the materials' origins, and it emphasizes the fact that archival maintenance requires different materials to be preserved differently.[5] An archival record needs to be stored in connection with the events it describes, which explains the principle of collective control. Materials with similar historiography need to be preserved jointly in the same record. These records must also be preserved in their original order.

The definition of an archive transcends the realm of materials or records to include the building that stores the materials. This includes the preservation mechanisms that are used inside the structure. The buildings and institutions

---

[1] Elisabeth Kaplan, "We Are What We Collect, We Collect What We Are: Archives and the Construction of Identity," *American Archivist* 63 (2000): 126–151.

[2] Francis X. Blouin Jr. and William G. Rosenberg, eds., *Archives, Documentation, and Institutions of Social Memory: Essays from the Sawyer Seminar* (Ann Arbor: University of Michigan Press, 2006).

[3] Richard Pearce-Moses, *A Glossary of Archival and Records Terminology* (Chicago: The Society of American Archivists, 2005).

[4] Kate Theimer, "Archives in Context and as Context," *Journal of Digital Humanities* 1, no. 2 (2012): 1–2.

[5] Pearce-Moses, *A Glossary*.

that hold information are as important as the records and materials they retain.[6] The archivists who maintain such records are equally important.[7] They decide which materials are relevant, and that influences the kinds of stories that archive records. Despite the guiding principles of provenance, collective control, and original order, archival facts can be aligned to support a subjective viewpoint.[8]

Different scholars have examined the extent of archival appraisal and how their voices explain reality.[9] The colonial archives, in particular, have been challenged based on the anachronistic manner in which early colonial scholars appraised them. Their work did not describe the true state and intent of Africa and Nigeria.[10] It has been described as intellectual imprisonment and the colonization of the African thinking process, shaping African views of their colonial history. After Nigerian intellectual efforts developed an increasing consciousness of their history, these records were scrutinized. Nigerian-oriented accounts of events and appraisals of archival records were examined and explained in their fixed "native" natures.[11] To set the record straight, examining differences in these stories and the perspectives of African writers is expedient.

The Creation of the Nigerian National Archives

The preservation of historical records is essential.[12] Past events and exchanges must be retained to serve as reference points. Archives enable the proper documentation and preservation of national values, cultures, and history for reference in the present and the future. The usefulness of archives is not confined to an appreciation of the past; they can also provide insights into current and developing situations.[13] This requires a proper recording of

---

[6] Achille Mbembe, "The Power of the Archive and Its Limits," in *Refiguring the Archive*, ed. Carolyn Hamilton, Verne Harris, Michèle Pickover, et al. (Dordrecht: Kluwer Academic Publishers, 2002), 19–27.

[7] Evgenia Vassilakaki and Valentini Moniarou-Papaconstantinou, "Beyond Preservation: Investigating the Roles of Archivist," *Library Review* 66, no. 3 (2017): 110–126.

[8] Pearce-Moses, *A Glossary*.

[9] Luciana Duranti, "The Concept of Appraisal and Archival Theory," *The American Archivist* 57, no. 2 (1994): 328–344.

[10] Stephanie Newell, "Life Writing in the Colonial Archives: The Case of Nnamdi Azikiwe (1904–1996) of Nigeria," *Life Writing* 13, no. 3 (2016): 307–321.

[11] Mahmood Mamdani, *Define and Rule: Native as Political Identity* (Cambridge: Harvard University Press, 2012).

[12] George M. Cunha, Frazer G. Poole, and Clyde C. Walton, "The Conservation and Preservation of Historical Records," *The American Archivist* 40, no. 3 (1977): 321–324.

[13] Gabriel B. O. Alegbeleye, "Archives Administration and Records Management in Nigeria: Up the Decades from Amalgamation," *Information Management* 22, no. 3 (1998): 26.

current developments alongside the records of the past.[14] Nigerian authorities, beginning with the colonial government, have made efforts to retain old records and preserve materials from the present.

The late introduction of writing skills complicated recordkeeping in precolonial Nigeria. Instead, most memories and records were maintained through other methods. The most widely recognized archival records from precolonial Nigeria are the old Arabic records and collections that can be traced back to around the eleventh century AD.[15] These came from early interactions between the Arab world and residents in the territory now known as Nigeria, which was facilitated through the trans-Saharan trade.[16] Unfortunately, most of these records were maintained privately and have not been preserved in modern archives.[17] S. S. Waniko[18] was an early archivist who successfully retrieved some of these Arabic manuscripts, ensuring they were adequately preserved.[19]

Aside from older records, which have been difficult to collect, Nigeria's archival activities to document ongoing events increased with the advent of the British colonial administration. After the 1914 amalgamation, Nigeria was officially recognized as an entity, and records of its existence and activities were collated in earnest.[20] The 1914 amalgamation marked the start of archival recordkeeping and its administration as an entity and a state.[21] The Colonial Office initially performed the functions of archival administration, and it was interested in keeping accurate records. From the amalgamation onward, the Colonial Office was interested in protecting current and historical records. In 1914, the colonial dispatch requested an organized structure for the preservation of early and contemporary documents, asserting that these records should

---

[14] Joan M. Schwartz and Terry Cook, "Archives, Records, and Power: The Making of Modern Memory," *Archival Science* 2, no. 1 (2002): 1–19.

[15] F. O. Babalola, "The Future of Arabic Manuscripts in Nigeria," *The Nigerian Archives* 1, no. 4 (1993): 9–26.

[16] Ali A. Mazrui, Patrick M. Dikirr, Robert Ostergard Jr., Michael Toler and Paul Macharia, eds., *Africa's Islamic Experiences: History, Culture, and Politics* (New Delhi: Sterling Publishers Private Ltd., 2009).

[17] A. O. Umar, "The Origin, Development and Utilization of Arabic Manuscripts in the National Archives, Kaduna." Paper presented at the workshop on *Exploring Nigeria's Arabic/Ajami Manuscript Resources for the Development of New Knowledge*, held at Arewa House, Kaduna, Nigeria, May 7–8, 2009.

[18] S. S. Waniko, *Arrangement and Classification of Nigerian Archives* (Lagos: Nigerian Archives Services, 1958).

[19] Folarin Shyllon, "The Poverty of Documentary Heritage Management in Nigeria," *International Journal of Cultural Property* 9, no. 1 (2000): 23–48.

[20] A. H. Lafinhan, "1st January and the Birth of a Nation," *Nigerian Tribune*, January 1, 2008.

[21] Alegbeleye, "Archives Administration and Records."

be kept in colonial custody.[22] The Secretary of State asked Sir Frederick Lugard to send records of the arrangement to the Colonial Office.

In 1936, the Colonial Office sent two different circular dispatches.[23] The first dispatch concerned the office's interest in keeping and preserving records, reminding colonial officers of the matter's importance. The second dispatch concerned the preservation of contemporary records, which included treasury records and account books. Through the Colonial Secretary, it made suggestions regarding when it was considered unnecessary to retain these records, along with guidance on which records to destroy and which to keep.[24] The final dispatch of 1948 was of great importance, and it included a memorandum from Sir Hilary Jenkinson, the well-known archivist, issuing directions for appropriate recording.[25]

Nigeria's colonial officials responded with assurances that records were being kept adequately and appropriately. Lord Lugard stated that the records were "in a very fair state of preservation and that the current arrangements were adequate for their safe-keeping,"[26] finding no notable challenges to obstruct recordkeeping in colonial Nigeria, especially in the early stages. In 1937, one Mr. J. A. M. Maybin circulated an internal memorandum to all officials, requesting that they send reports to the Chief Secretary Officer stating how their records were being kept and preserved. Unfortunately, the heads of various units and departments responded with statements explaining that they lacked the staff and facilities to assist with recordkeeping and the preservation of documents.[27]

Kenneth Dike also conducted a public record survey of all governmental bodies from 1951 to 1953. He strongly advocated the creation of a public record office in Nigeria, which was established on April 1, 1954, and was later appointed as the first Supervisor of Public Records.[28] In 1949, Dike was awarded the Colonial Social Science Research Fellowship, which authorized him to conduct comprehensive research on Nigeria's history. During that research, he discovered that many records had been inadvertently destroyed by neglect. Official records and documents had decayed or suffered damage from water and insects. Dike began working pro bono to retrieve the remaining

---

[22] C. A. Ukwu, "The Archives in Nigeria: Its Mission and Vision," *The Nigerian Archives* 2, no. 1 (1995): 1–44.
[23] Alegbeleye, "Archives Administration and Records."
[24] Alegbeleye, "Archives Administration and Records," 26.
[25] Abiola Abioye, "Fifty Years of Archives Administration in Nigeria: Lessons for the Future," *Records Management Journal* 17, no. 1 (2007): 52–62.
[26] Abioye, "Fifty Years of Archives Administration," 53.
[27] Kenneth O. Dike, *Report on the Preservation and Administration of Historical Records and the Establishment of a Public Record Office in Nigeria* (Lagos: Government Printer, 1954).
[28] Dike, *Report on the Preservation*.

records and care for them, which led to his appointment as head of a survey to identify and gather all available historical records and documentation. This work led Dike to issue the recommendation for the establishment of the Nigerian Record Office.[29]

The Nigerian Record Office was established at the University College Ibadan, in 1954, in a small two-room apartment under the supervision of the Federal Ministry of Works.[30] The office was legally recognized after its name was changed to the National Archives of Nigeria on November 14, 1957, with the promulgation of Public Archives Ordinance No. 43. The National Archives of Nigeria moved to its permanent site at the University College Ibadan in 1958, occupying its first official building.[31] The building was the first archive in tropical Africa, and its ongoing development continued.

The National Archives was instrumental in establishing a local interest in historical scholarship and encouraging a nationalistic consciousness among scholars. As the relevance of the archives became more visible, they expanded to serve the nation better. The Kaduna and Enugu branches of the National Archives were established in 1962 and 1963, respectively. These archives have maintained federal, regional, and state records and documents to preserve Nigeria's historical heritage. Each region's colonial administration records, official publications, newspapers, and other documents are stored in their relevant archives. The archives in Ibadan still retain records of the oldest newspaper in Nigeria, Ìwé Ìròhìn, which began operating in 1859.

Nigeria's archives still function, and their facilities have expanded to include repair and binding rooms, repository rooms, processing rooms, and search rooms. Branches were established in Sokoto and Benin in 1982; Ilorin and Akure in 1985; Calabar in 1986; Port Harcourt and Owerri in 1989; and Abeokuta, Jos, and Maiduguri in 2005. Offices in Ibadan, Enugu, and Kaduna now hold authority over other archives within their regions.[32]

Kenneth Dike was head of the National Archives, as supervisor of records, from 1954 to 1963. He had also headed the effort before the archives were officially established. The 1957 Public Archives Ordinance changed Dike's role to that of Director on a part-time basis, although this decision was criticized.[33] Lloyd C. Gwam, appointed to succeed Dike in 1964, was respected for his scholarship and understanding of the archive. His book, *Archive Memoranda*, is regarded to date as orientation material and a guideline for newly appointed

---

[29] Dike, *Report on the Preservation*.
[30] Simon Heap, "The Nigerian National Archives, Ibadan: An Introduction for Users and a Summary of Holdings," *History in Africa* 18 (1991): 159–172.
[31] Abioye, "Fifty Years of Archives Administration."
[32] Abioye, "Fifty Years of Archives Administration."
[33] S. O. Sowoolu, "The Problem of Archival Development in Nigeria." Paper presented at the Seminar for Directors of Archival Institutions from Developing Countries, Moscow, August 28–September 5, 1972.

archivists,[34] but his tenure was cut short by his early death. S. O. Sowoolu took over responsibility for the archives after Gwam's death, and many new ideas were adapted to develop the archive during his eighteen-year tenure. One of Sowoolu's many reputable achievements was how he protected records from the East during the 1967–70 Nigerian civil war.[35]

The Use of the Archives to Write on Colonial Nigeria

Thomas Richard describes imperial or colonial archives as not only a building, or the books it keeps, "but the collectively imagined junction of all that was known or knowable, a fantastic representation of an epistemological master pattern, a virtual focal point for the heterogeneous local knowledge of metropolis and empire."[36] In most cases, colonial archives were evidence of controlled information supporting a dictated line of thought. At the inception of the British colonization of Nigeria, colonial officials controlled most of the information about their activities in Nigeria and some information from the precolonial era.[37] Their control over these materials determined which resources were available to scholars studying early Nigeria. Many scholars have observed that colonialism extended to the fortification of power through the use and control of knowledge. Early studies of African history could only be conducted with the materials made available by colonial officers.

Dike's work to create the National Archives of Nigeria was instrumental in developing a native African interest in African history. It laid a firm foundation to aid the trajectory of a paradigm shift that brought African history from colonial narration to African inquiry. The limitations of the colonial archives and their influence on African colonial history had an overbearing tendency to narrate the African experience from colonial and British perspectives. Dike fought against these artificially imposed constraints. As other activists and nationalists rose against colonialism, Dike inspired others to tell African stories from African perspectives; this approach was seen in his criticism of Margery Perham's written work on Nigeria's independence.[38] Perham was an important political figure who influenced the Colonial Office.[39] Perham's argument opposed independence for West Africans based on claims

---

[34] Patricia C. Franks, ed., *The International Directory of National Archives* (Lanham: Rowan & Littlefield, 2018), 277.
[35] Ukwu, "The Archives in Nigeria."
[36] Thomas Richards, *The Imperial Archive: Knowledge and the Fantasy of Empire* (London: Verso, 1993), 11.
[37] Tim Livsey, "Open Secrets: The British 'Migrated Archives,' Colonial History, and Postcolonial History," *History Workshop Journal* 93, no. 1 (2022): 95–116.
[38] Thomas P. Ofcansky, "Margery Perham: A Bibliography of Published Work," *History in Africa* 15 (1988): 339–350.
[39] The Colonial Office was in charge of colonial records in Nigeria.

of technological underdevelopment, "incapability," "primitiveness," and other imagined shortcomings.[40] Dike opposed this denigration and stated that every society has a background and a culture in which its values and orientations are built.

Dike's criticism of Perham noted that Africa came from a long stretch of unexplored history, and that making assumptions about African history and statehood based on "slender evidence" was illogical at best.[41] This was a clarion call for Africans – and Nigerians in particular – to conduct research and emphasize self-knowledge through available materials. Dike asserted that anything else would encourage European slander against African history, distorting it "to justify the continent's colonization."[42] Dike's urging, and his knowledge of the Nigerian archival material, shifted the course of African history.

Dike's studies, research, and knowledge gathered from examining the archives allowed him to take different positions, issue new affirmations, and mount alternative criticisms of earlier claims and narratives about the British colony in Nigeria. One of his several rebuttals opposing the anachronistic viewpoint of British scholars disagreed with the justification of the British invasion of Lagos. Britain deposed King Kosoko as the Oba of Lagos and installed Oba Akitoye in 1851, claiming that Kosoko was undemocratic and alleging that he promoted the slave trade that Britain opposed.[43] Dike countered these claims, suggesting that Lagos was invaded like any other territory, as Kosoko's removal may have been caused by his past efforts at preventing European traders from accessing Lagos's trade with other Yoruba communities.[44] Oba Akitoye's replacement was regarded as flexible and willing to accommodate British interests. These allegations were supported by the fact that the British deposed Bonny's king, Dappa Pepple, who was confrontational and defended his territory against colonial imperialists.[45]

After the Lander brothers launched their historical exploration of the Niger in 1830,[46] the British government partnered with missionaries and commercial

---

[40] Margery Perham, "The British Problem in Africa," *Foreign Affairs* 29, no. 4 (1951): 637–650.
[41] Kenneth O. Dike, "African History and Self-Government," *West Africa*, February 28, 1953, 177–178; March 14, 225–226 and March 21, 251.
[42] Kenneth O. Dike, "African History Twenty-Five Years Ago and Today," *Journal of The Historical Society of Nigeria* 10, no. 3 (1980): 13–22.
[43] Robert S. Smith, *The Lagos Consulate 1851–1861* (Berkeley: University of California Press, 1979).
[44] Kenneth O. Dike, *Trade and Politics in the Niger Delta 1830–1835: An Introduction to the Economic and Political History of Nigeria* (London: Oxford University Press, 1955), 244.
[45] Julius O. Ihonvbere and Timothy M. Shaw, *Illusions of Power: Nigeria in Transition* (Trenton: Africa World Press, 1998), 11.
[46] Robin Hallett, ed., *The Niger Journal of Richard and John Lander* (London: Routledge & Kegan Paul, 1965).

entities. Their ventures allegedly focused on developing the Niger Valley, especially after contracting it to Macgregor Laird in 1857, hoping to replace Europeans with educated Africans. Dike offered an alternative explanation: The interest in expanding the Niger Delta was to extend colonial trade and commerce, not to advance scientific or missionary endeavors.[47]

Nigeria was amalgamated in 1914,[48] and a central legislative council was formed for its administration through the 1946 Richards Constitution.[49] The decision to amalgamate different British-controlled areas with their protectorate had been seen as a positive development and the beginning of the nation.[50] However, Dike provided a different perspective on the amalgamation, framing it as driven by the British need for more resources. Dike asserted that the decision was premeditated, intending to use resources from the Southern Protectorate to exploit the Northern Protectorate, which was less capable of supporting colonial administration on its own. This decision was calculated to reduce Britain's financial commitments.

Dike also pointed out that extractive infrastructure, like roads and railways, was also more easily constructed under a centralized administration. Dike opposed the notion put forward by Lord Frederick Lugard, who asserted that the amalgamation and indirect rule were focused on economic development and the advancement of civilization.[51] Instead, Dike considered the colonial endeavor and the amalgamation of Nigeria to be exploitative and undertaken to benefit the British administration.[52] This intent was apparent in the British manner of approach, the administration's use of force, and the discriminatory attitudes toward Nigerians.[53]

Dike and other early historians, such as Professors Jacob F. Ade Ajayi and Saburi O. Biobaku, contributed materials for the foundation of African historiography.[54] This enabled other historians to draw from the archives' pool of knowledge to write about Nigerian colonial history. It laid the

---

[47] Kenneth O. Dike, *Origins of the Niger Mission 1841–1891* (Ibadan: Ibadan University Press, 1962).

[48] Fola Fagbule and Feyi Fawehinmi, *Formation: The Making of Nigeria from Jihad to Amalgamation* (Abuja: Cassava Republic Press, 2021).

[49] Benjamin O. Nwabueze, *A Constitutional History of Nigeria* (London: C. Hurst & Company, 1982), 42–46.

[50] Lord Lugard, *The Dual Mandate in British Tropical Africa* (London: Frank Cass, 1970).

[51] Lugard, *Dual Mandate*.

[52] Moses Ochonu, *Colonial Meltdown: Northern Nigeria in the Great Depression* (Athens: Ohio University Press, 2009).

[53] Toyin Falola, *Colonialism and Violence in Nigeria* (Bloomington: Indiana University Press, 2009).

[54] Olufunke Adeboye, "J. F Ade Ajayi, 1929–2014," *Africa* 85, no. 4 (2015): 741–744.

foundation for the institution known as the Ibadan School of History.[55] The school was developed at the University of Ibadan, Nigeria's first university and the first to form a dedicated history department. The Department of History at the University of Ibadan was instrumental in developing the local school of history because of its high quality of teaching. The very first set of Nigerian historians emerged from these efforts, and they shared the school's philosophies.[56] The Ibadan School of History was credited as the first coordinated school, having a profound influence on the telling of Nigeria's history until the 1970s.[57]

The Ibadan School of History's primary assignment was to retell the history of Nigerian colonialism, oppose the way that it had been recorded and told by colonial records, and create a national consciousness for postcolonial Nigeria.[58] The National Archives at the University of Ibadan provided access to colonial records, enabling the global visibility of the work of people like Dike and encouraging the development of the school. The school emphasized the consideration of historical sources and the use of a multidisciplinary approach to collect data. Aside from decolonizing the narration of African history, it also reconciled historical facts to promote national unity.[59]

Within the Ibadan School of History, Dike made several significant contributions to the reconstruction of African and Nigerian history. His book, *Trade and Politics in the Niger Delta*,[60] was outstanding for its retelling of African history using knowledge gained from orally recorded sources. In relying on oral accounts, Dike drew attention to the conceptualization of African perspectives for African history, appraising the roles of major African historical actors and examining different events from new viewpoints.[61]

Martin Klein provided a comprehensive review of works written by scholars identified with the Ibadan School, examining their orientation.[62] The first collection of views from African historians was Ajayi and Crowder's volume on the history of West Africa,[63] wherein two-thirds of the writers identified

---

[55] Paul E. Lovejoy, "The Ibadan School of Historiography and its Critics," in *African Historiography: Essays in Honour of Jacob Ade Ajayi*, ed. Toyin Falola (Harlow: Longman, 1993), 195–202.

[56] Adiele E. Afigbo, "The Flame of History Blazing at Ibadan," *Journal of The Historical Society of Nigeria* 7, no. 4 (1975): 715–720.

[57] John D. Omer-Cooper, "The Contribution of the University of Ibadan to the Spread of the Study and Teaching of African History within Africa," *Journal of the Historical Society of Nigeria* 10, no. 3 (1980): 23–31.

[58] Omer-Cooper, "The Contribution of the University of Ibadan."

[59] Adeboye, "J. F. Ade Ajayi."

[60] Dike, *Trade and Politics in the Niger Delta*.

[61] Martin A. Klein, "Review of The Decolonization of West African History," *The Journal of Interdisciplinary History* 6, no. 1 (1975): 111–125.

[62] Klein, "Review of The Decolonization."

[63] Jacob F. A. Ajayi and Michael Crowder, *History of West Africa*, Vol. 1 (New York: Columbia University Press, 1972).

with the Ibadan School of History.[64] Ebiegberi J. Alagoa, one of the writers included in the volume, discussed the precolonial Niger Delta from 1600 to 1800, giving a new explanation for the slave trade during that period. Alagoa found fault with Horton's arguments about the veracity, uselessness, and incredulousness of oral tradition. He established that other data, apart from colonial records, could explain the past, especially the slave trade activities in the Niger Delta from 1600 to 1700.[65]

Abdullahi Smith,[66] making inquiries outside of the colonial boundaries of the Ibadan School, reconstructed and changed the view of history in old Central Sudan. He explained how the country's Kanuri and Hausa groups emerged from Central Sudan, supporting his assertions with linguistics, geography, archeology, and other documents. Smith traced the origin of the Kanuri kingship system to relationships between the old nomads and the stable agriculturalists, identifying the links that joined the Hausa monarchs to society's economic systems. His work took an African view of institutions and identified diversity at work in the process of Islamization for society and general systems.[67] Philip Curtin was another historian aligned with the Ibadan School, and his historical exploration of Africa's slave trade belongs in the echelon of top scholars on the subject.[68] Curtin's radical opinion asserted that the slave trade in African society was more social than economic, opposing views emphasizing the economic intent of the transatlantic slavers.[69]

The Ibadan School of the 1950s and 1960s has received criticism because the scope of its work was largely confined to colonialism and the events that preceded it.[70] This restriction has not allowed for much expansion of the school and the subject matter that it discusses.[71] Some scholars have also criticized the Ibadan School's apparent preference for written records, like those in the archives, and their traditional nature of understanding subjects.[72] The school has excluded or unconsciously omitted oral history.[73] However, the

---

[64] Klein, "Review of The Decolonization."
[65] Jan Vansina, Hope M. Wright, Selma Leydesdorff, and Elizabeth Tonkin, *Oral Tradition: A Study in Historical Methodology* (New York: Routledge, 2017).
[66] Ajayi and Crowder, *History of West Africa*.
[67] Mahdi Adamu, "The Hausa and their Neighbours in the Central Sudan," in *General History of Africa, 4: Africa from the Twelfth to Sixteenth Century*, ed. Djibril T. Niane (Paris: UNESCO, 1984), 266–300.
[68] Eric Williams is a distinguished author who wrote *Capitalism and Slavery* (North Carolina: University of North Carolina Press Books, 2021).
[69] Ajayi and Crowder, *History of West Africa*.
[70] Lovejoy, "The Ibadan School of Historiography."
[71] Peter P. Ekeh, "Colonialism and Social Structure." An Inaugural Lecture (Ibadan: University of Ibadan, 1983).
[72] Olutayo C. Adesina, "The Future of the Past." An Inaugural Lecture (Ibadan: Ibadan University Press, 2012).
[73] Klein, "Review of The Decolonization."

school enjoyed intellectual success by producing scholars who identified with its philosophy.[74] The first set of academic gladiators from the University of Ibadan included Kenneth Dike, Tekena Tamuno, Saburi Biobaku, Jacob F. Ade Ajayi, Emmanuel A. Ayandele, Joseph C. Anene, and Henry F. C. Smith. They ensured the torch was passed to others who extended the school's engagements. Scholars such as Obaro Ikime, Ebiegberi J. Alagoa, Rowland A. Adeleye, Benjamin O. Oloruntimehin, and Okon Uya became the new Ibadan scholars, raising the standard for African history.[75] In 1955, the pioneer scholars formed the Historical Society of Nigeria.[76]

In its early formation, the Ibadan School of History inspired other writings that refocused scholarly works to interpret African history through African lenses and voices. One example is Meillassoux's discussion of different studies presented at the International African Seminar at Fourah Bay College, tracking the development of trade and markets in West Africa.[77] He examined studies of African trade routes and how they came to be, studying the problems discussed by Abner Cohen, the different types of routes discussed by Jean-Louis Boutillier, and African efforts to maintain those routes.[78] Scholars also considered the social impact of Nigeria's older trade systems and the relationships between European traders and West African traders.

The scholarship that refocused African history, removing it from the ethnocentric and colonized constraints of early narratives, was not solely an African effort. European scholars also used records to criticize colonial narratives of African history.[79] Jean Suret-Canale, a Marxist and a strong pro-African activist, was one of these scholars who worked to view Africa from an African perspective.[80] Suret-Canale embarked on a project correcting colonial writings and records to create a more comprehensive and aggregated perspective.[81] He linked the African occupation and invasion with the economic interests of European colonial officers.[82]

---

[74] Adesina, "The Future of the Past."
[75] Michael Omolewa, "The Education Factor in the Emergence of the Modern Profession of Historian in Nigeria, 1926–1956," *Journal of The Historical Society of Nigeria* 10, no. 3 (1980): 41–62.
[76] Christopher B. N. Ogbogbo, "Historical Society of Nigeria: The Study of History and the Nigerian Nation. Address by the President of the Historical Society of Nigeria," *Journal of The Historical Society of Nigeria* 24 (2015): 4.
[77] Claude Meillassoux, ed., *The Development of Indigenous Trade and Markets in West Africa* (London: Oxford University Press, 1971).
[78] Meillassoux, *The Development of Indigenous Trade.*
[79] Klein, "Review of The Decolonization."
[80] Richard W. Johnson, "Forever on the Wrong Side," *London Review of Books*, September 27, 2012, 27.
[81] Klein, "Review of The Decolonization."
[82] Jean Suret-Canale, "Les Sociétés Traditionnelles En Afrique Noire ET Le Concept De Mode De Production Asiatique'," *La Pensée* no. 117 (1964): 19–42.

The Limitations of the Colonial Archives in Writing About Colonial Nigeria

The first and most obvious limitation of the colonial archives is its control over the voices that are included in and the stories that are told by its documents. Archival records are not necessarily objective and devoid of interpretations. However, the acquisition of records exerts control over these voices; therefore, colonial archives rely on voices that might have been distorted by control over resources. Clearly defined objectives have to be established to recognize and claim the hidden voices.

European colonial governments did not compromise on their need for detailed and deliberate recordkeeping, which was also the case with Nigeria.[83] The Colonial Office in England sent a memo that asked British officials about the state of records in Nigeria and suggested that Dike should be given the power to conduct a coordinated survey. This points to the structural imbalance of power and suggests that voices are missing from the state archives.[84] Despite this, they maintain a veneer of objectivity.[85]

Another shortcoming is that Nigerian archival records were incomplete, leaving postcolonial writers with remnants of documents that show colonial administrations in a positive light.[86] Some scholars assert that Britain divided public and colonial records into groups to be elevated, transferred, or left behind.[87] In Northern Nigeria, four months were spent removing and destroying documents.[88] According to the Malayan Report on Nigeria, an estimated 747 files were tagged as classified, 79 were moved to the Colonial Office, and 480 were destroyed. Only a carefully compiled set of documents was passed

---

[83] Jacob Soll, *The Information Master: Jean-Baptiste Colbert's Secret State Intelligence System* (Ann Arbor: University of Michigan Press, 2009).

[84] Nichola Dirks, "Annals of the Archive: Ethnographic Notes on the Sources of History," in *From the Margins: Historical Anthropology and its Future*, ed. Brian K. Axel (Durham: Duke University Press, 2002), 47–65.

[85] Jordanna Bailkin, "Where Did the Empire Go? Archives and Decolonization in Britain," *The American Historical Review* 120, no. 3 (2015): 884–899.

[86] Mandy Banton, "'Expatriate' or 'Migrated' Archives: The Role of the UK Archivist," *Archives* 34, no. 121 (2009): 14–24. See also Mandy Banton, "Destroy? 'Migrate'? Conceal? British Strategies for the Disposal of Sensitive Records of Colonial Administrations at Independence," *Journal of Imperial and Commonwealth History* 40, no. 2 (2012): 321–335.

[87] Mandy Banton's Examination of Letter sent from the Office of The British High Commission in Nigeria, by S. J. G. Fingland, 28 Feb. 1961, in TNA CO 822/2935, Disposal of Files in Tanganyika, 1960–1962. A sixth category related to files concerning the mandated territory of Cameroon, which were to be sent to the High Commissioner there. See also Banton, "Destroy? 'Migrate'? Conceal?"

[88] A. T. Weatherhead, Governor's Office, Kaduna, to M. P. Preston, Governor-General's Office, Lagos, July 14, 1959, In TNA DO 186/17, Disposal of Nigerian Government Archives, 1959–62. As examined by Banton.

down to the incoming government after independence, while most of the files that were moved to London concerned constitutional and administrative issues. The affected documents included records relating to the separation and amalgamation of Nigeria, reports on Nnamdi Azikiwe and fund management, and reports on the Minority Commission and the African Continental Bank.[89] Why were archival and official documents transferred or destroyed, and why were not all documents passed down to the incoming government? This underscores the limits of the documentation available to Nigerian officials and scholars, leaving many of the British colonial officials' activities and intentions obscured.[90] The archives and remaining documents have left Nigerians with an incomplete understanding of their colonial past, especially when relying on colonial records.[91]

The National Archives in Nigeria are arguably more of a colonial archive, despite the time between the realization of independence and the present. This is largely due to the limited acquisition of public records, which makes the colonial records about 90 percent of the material that it preserves.[92] These records and other colonial archives have received criticism, encouraging scholarly efforts to address the imbalance.

Moses Ochonu, examining the archives' current problems and their influence on postcolonial discussions of postcolonial history, has outlined and explained different problems that could affect historical scholarship.[93] Ochonu's perspective was shaped by his experience with the Nigerian Archives. His concerns included "archival fragmentation, the politicization of historical data, the boom in memoirs and autobiographies, and the question of sensing Africa outside the oral, written, and ethnographic templates."[94]

Fragmentation is a notorious problem for colonial archives and their records. The scattering of sources and materials on similar subjects compels scholars to undertake a monumental task of assembly.[95] This has been viewed as a defining feature of the archives, subject to disorganization

---

[89] H. A. F. Rumbold, Chairman of Committee on Territorial Questions, To N. D. Watson, Central Africa Office, 23 Oct. 1963 In TNA DO 183/508, Dissolution of The Federation: Archives, 1963. As examined by Mandy Banton.
[90] Banton, "Destroy? 'Migrate'? Conceal?"
[91] Philip D. Curtin, "The Archives of Tropical Africa: A Reconnaissance," *The Journal of African History* 1, no. 1 (1960): 129–147.
[92] Amodu O. Solomon, "National Archives Ibadan and Archival Management in Nigeria: Challenges and Prospects," *Kashere Journal of Humanities, Management and Social Sciences* 3, no. 2 (2019): 47–62.
[93] Moses E. Ochonu, "Elusive History: Fractured Archives, Politicized Orality, and Sensing the Postcolonial Past," *History in Africa* 42 (2015): 287–298.
[94] Ochonu, "Elusive History," 228.
[95] Ochonu, "Elusive History."

resulting from political anxiety.[96] The fragmentation of colonial archives reflects the uncoordinated colonial government and the manifestation of a "dysfunctional bureaucracy." Fragmentation can be advantageous in some situations, but for the archives it means more time spent researching with less effective results.

Colonial archives have also been shaped by the politicization of the materials and records that they hold. The retained information and records had been selected to support colonial or national interests in the present day. This filters their collections and excludes materials that could have historical value. These efforts can distort the voices of the past, and present-day historians are left negotiating their way through skewed records to access the truth amidst documents buried by politicization. The Malayan Report suggests what kinds of information, files, and documents were destroyed or moved to the United Kingdom. The remaining documents are unlikely to condemn colonial officials or their actions. This postcolonial limitation has left historians desperate for those materials.[97]

Another phenomenon that shapes archival records is the glorification of individuals who had the resources to publish or center themselves in biographies. The personal accounts of these people tend to become public history, shaping how official records present them. By publishing their perceptions of incidents, these accounts can become part of archives and be embraced by society.[98] A typical example of this dynamic can be seen in the life of Nnamdi Azikiwe, who partly shaped what public records would say about him by what he published about himself in his newspapers.[99] Newell has claimed that Azikiwe deliberately made himself politically visible in the colonial archives. His anticolonial opposition to British colonial authorities and records of activities in Nigeria were obvious in London. Azikiwe used his *West African Pilot* and *African Morning Post* newspapers (based in Lagos and Accra, respectively) to criticize the racist, capitalist, and colonial activities in the British colony. The Colonial Office in London kept records of this criticism.[100] The editorials, columns, and critical opinions from the newspapers formed parallel official records around the 1930s, and some of the material was tagged as "top secret."[101]

---

[96] Ann L. Stoler, *Along the Archival Grain: Epistemic Anxieties and Colonial Common Sense* (Princeton: Princeton University Press, 2010).
[97] Lyn Schumaker, *Africanizing Anthropology: Fieldwork, Networks, and the Making of Cultural Knowledge* (Durham: Duke University Press, 2001).
[98] Neil Genzlinger, "The Problem with Memoirs," *New York Times*, January 28, 2011.
[99] Newell, "Life Writing in the Colonial Archives," 307–321.
[100] Stephanie Newell, *The Power to Name: A History of Anonymity in Colonial West Africa* (Athens: Ohio University Press, 2013).
[101] Newell, *The Power to Name*.

One factor that made Azikiwe's work notable and popular was the emergence of different nationalist movements agitating for independence. The environment encouraged increased unionism, petitions, riots, and strikes, and the creation of a public relations department by the colonial officials provided many opportunities to criticize the administration of the British colony in the 1930s. Azikiwe's motives were studied for around three decades. After examining his publications, bank transactions, and other details, colonial officials could only arrive at speculative conclusions.[102] Azikiwe's activities, and the colonial scrutiny of his tendency to dominate archival documentation, have created a substantial biography of a single person. Some colonial officials and African scholars believe this to be intentional.[103]

Colonial archives are challenged by the anachronistic approach to acquiring documents and the struggle for control over material that should qualify as public records. Records and reports detail intentional interference with documentation that has created a lacuna of knowledge. In appraising these records, voices are distorted by missing or only partially available information. The colonial archives in Nigeria ended at the point of decolonization, and the expected amount of postcolonial documentation has not been acquired. Colonial records still compose the bulk of the National Archives, with few postcolonial governmental activities included.

Alternative Voices to the Archives

Nigeria's historiography has not been primarily based on archival documents and records. The weaknesses of the colonial archives have encouraged writers to tap into other historical knowledge through alternative sources. Their work has exposed a massive amount of information about the precolonial, colonial, and postcolonial eras in Nigeria. Sources have included local chronicles, oral traditions, objects, rituals, performances, and festivals. Objects such as *atupa* (lamps) are important materials produced by Nigerians to light their homes at night. Gourds from plants and pots made of clay were used for storage and to refrigerate water. As Figure 1.1 suggests, knowledge-based solutions to everyday problems were designed prior to British rule, and through these objects or materials one could easily draw superior historical knowledge and alternative sources to sufficiently understand the different phases of the Nigerian past.

Nigeria's history transcends the advent of colonialism in Africa. Africans are not people without history or historical records. European explorers and

---

[102] (PRO CO 583/317/4, March 1946).
[103] Ochonu, "Elusive History."

Figure 1.1 Light was produced from an *atupa* (lamp), depicting a knowledge-based solution. Behind the *atupa* is a gourd filled with water for preservation and as a coolant.

scholars failed to appreciate how Africans conceptualized that history.[104] Chronicles have explained the existence of African history outside of colonial archives, and their distinguishing features are their originality and their resistance to biased interpretation. Kanem-Borno, for instance, was one of the earliest areas to develop teaching and scholarly traditions[105] due to its interactions through the trans-Saharan trade and relationships with the Amazigh (Berbers) and Arab traders. This tradition developed throughout the eighteenth century, and Fulani scholars were among the predominant scholars putting history into records. Islamic schools, especially in Gazargamu and among Sufi communities, had large amounts of writing and chronicles of events,[106] although many of them have not survived to the present day. The calligraphy

[104] Joseph C. Miller, "History and Africa/Africa and History," *The American Historical Review* 104, no. 1 (1999): 1–32.
[105] John Hunwick, "The Arabic Literary Tradition of Nigeria," *Research in African Literatures* 28, no. 3 (1997): 210–223.
[106] Dmitry Bondarev, "Multiglossia in West African Manuscripts: The Case of Borno, Nigeria," in *Manuscript Cultures: Mapping the Field*, ed. Jörg B. Quenzer, Dmitry Bondarev and Jan-Ulrich Sobisch (Berlin: De Gruyter, 2014), 113–158.

schools and learning traditions of the Borno still provide credible historical sources, offering alternative voices for inquiries into Nigeria's history.[107]

Scholars such as Shaykh Ibrahim Salih have used these sources most effectively. Scholarship in the North extended to Kano. The Tijaniyya school, at the height of its influence in the twentieth century, became a major center of scholarship.[108] One of its distinguished scholars was 'Abd Allah Suka, who wrote poems on praxis and piety in Islam, known as *'Atiyyat al-mu'ti*. Some of his works have been preserved for contemporary historians.[109]

Documentation and scholarly writing were also present during the establishment of the Sokoto Caliphate.[110] Usman Dan Fodio, his son Muhammad Bello, and his brother 'Abd Allah have been credited with more than 300 written works. His family was renowned for its writing during the early nineteenth century.[111] Despite colonial rule, these efforts continued into the twentieth century, nurtured in reputable Islamic schools in Zaria, Kwara, and elsewhere. Some of the earliest chronicles of the region have survived to the present day, despite being written in the sixteenth century or earlier. This includes the anonymous "Kano Chronicles,"[112] which Herbert R. Palmer translated into English in 1908.[113]

The *Kano Chronicles* established lines of succession for the kings of Kano from about 1000 CE to the reign of Mohammed Bello,[114] showing how precolonial Nigeria can be studied through the records maintained by established institutions. Another chronicle was Ahmad B. Furtuwa's recording of the first twelve years of Mai Idris Aloma's reign in Borno. These records covered his activities in Kanem and other wars, along with a chronicle of Mai Idris Katakamarbe's war in Kanem, which allegedly inspired the former.[115] The chronicling was not restricted to these areas but extended to other parts, including those inhabited by the Yoruba. Adam 'Abd Allah

---

[107] Hamidu Bobboyi, "The Ulama of Borno: A Study of the Relations between Scholars and State under the Sayfawa, 1470–1808," unpublished PhD dissertation, Northwestern University, 1992.

[108] Alaine S. Hutson, "Women, Men, and Patriarchal Bargaining in an Islamic Sufi Order: The Tijaniyya in Kano, Nigeria, 1937 to the Present," *Gender & Society* 15, no. 5 (2001): 734–753.

[109] John Hunwick, "The Arabic Literary Tradition of Nigeria."

[110] Murray Last, "The Nature of Knowledge in Northern Nigeria," in *The Trans-Saharan Book Trade, Manuscript Culture, Arabic Literacy and Intellectual History in Muslim Africa*, ed. Graziano Krätli and Ghislaine Lydon (Leiden: Brill, 2011), 178–211.

[111] 'Abd Allah b. Muhammad Fodiye, *Diya' al-ta'wil*. 2 Volumes, 1815.

[112] John Hunwick, "A Historical Whodunit: The So-Called 'Kano Chronicle' and its Place in the Historiography of Kano," *History in Africa* 21 (1994): 127–146.

[113] Murray Last, "Historical Metaphors in the Intellectual History of Kano before 1800," *History in Africa* 7 (1980): 161–178.

[114] Hunwick, "A Historical Whodunit."

[115] Hunwick, "The Arabic Literary Tradition of Nigeria."

was credited with writing history chronicles that touched on several Nigerian groups.[116]

Another alternative to a reliance on colonial archives is the use of oral tradition to reconstruct the history of precolonial and colonial Nigeria. The absence of extensive written records in many places in precolonial Nigeria meant that historical accounts were frequently maintained as oral traditions.[117] Many historical objects, artifacts, and performances are given historical context through oral traditions passed from generation to generation.[118] Oral tradition is a set of verbal information transmitted from eyewitness accounts, hearsay, memories, and stories to retrieve memories of the past.[119] These traditions do not need to involve interviews with elderly African men or women since they can exist as proverbs or idioms describing past events. One example is the reenactment of Abeokuta's war stories, expressed as a proverb: *kógun mája Iléwó, kógun mája Ìbàrà, ogún ja Iléwó, ogún ja Ìbàrà, ólé ará Aké dà séyìn odi* (Ilewo and Ibara should not be faced by war, they were attacked and the Ake's indigenes have been exiled).[120] Another example is *Láyé Abíódún afi igbá won owó, Láyé Àólé adi àdìkalè* (During the reign of Abiodun, money was weighed by calabash, and during the reign of Aole, the people fled).[121] Poetry, praise, and other renditions create a comprehensive oral record of Nigeria's history.

Oríkì, popular among the Yoruba, has been a common way of telling the stories of people, institutions, families, and kings.[122] The Yoruba are well known for developing the strong oral tradition exhibited in their cultures and laws, but this technique of recording the past extends beyond their borders. In Igala, accounts from different oral traditions have been combined with a study of past kings' burial grounds to place their reigns in chronological order and link them with specific dates. The tradition allowed Clifford to reconstruct the genealogy of Abutu Eje, tracing a link to the contemporary monarch.[123] Oral tradition was also used to record the history of precolonial Igbo peoples in the territory that is currently Southeast Nigeria. These traditions recounted the activities of their ancestors and the construction of their

---

[116] Muhammad Fodiye, *Diya' al-ta'wil*.
[117] Patrick Nunn, *The Edge of Memory: Ancient Stories, Oral Tradition and the Post-Glacial World* (New York: Bloomsbury Sigma, 2019).
[118] Olukoya Ogen, "Exploring the Potential of Praise Poems for Historical Reconstruction among the Idepe-Ikale in Southeastern Yorubaland," *History in Africa* 39 (2012): 77–96.
[119] Jan M. Vansina, *Oral Tradition as History* (Oxford: James Currey, 1985).
[120] Toyin Falola, "Indigenous Knowledge and Oral Traditions in Nigeria," in *The Oxford Handbook of Nigerian History*, ed. Toyin Falola and Mathew Heaton (Oxford: Oxford University Press, 2022), 28.
[121] Falola, "Indigenous Knowledge," 28.
[122] Ọlátúndé O. Ọlátúnjí, *Features of Yoruba Oral Poetry* (Ibadan: University Press, 1984).
[123] John S. Boston, "Oral Tradition and the History of Igala," *The Journal of African History* 10, no. 1 (1969): 29–43.

society's political structures.[124] They also reflected on the motivations behind their egalitarian society and the scattered settlements of different Igbo villages, which had similarities in cultures and beliefs, including the worship of Aro. Songs, stories, and tales from elders established chronological accounts for different villages and their people.[125]

The establishment of Arabic scholarship, which brought writing and specific learning modes, has meant that oral traditions are not the only sources of precolonial history in the Northern region of Nigeria. Many historical events in regions such as Borno and the territories occupied by the Hausa/Fulani have been recorded in written records. The region's early exposure to trans-Saharan trade formed a foundation for accepting the Islamic religion. Many political leaders before Usman Dan Fodio practiced Islam, and they may have performed pilgrimages to Mecca and other Islamic states.[126] The North depended on Arabic writing, and its records have survived the test of time. The Sokoto Caliphate emphasized Islamic doctrines at the beginning of the nineteenth century, and scholars felt that oral traditions were less important.

The reliance on oral accounts and memories has challenged the credibility of these historical resources. Some of the details they provide may be false or have failed to capture full and true accounts of the events they intend to record. Many oral traditions are premised on mythological beliefs and legends, which can defy logical conclusions in the present day. Figures such as Sango, Ògún, and Obàtálá were painted as Yoruba gods who possessed unearthly power.[127] Sango was popularly believed to control thunder and embody mythological bravery.[128] However, he was an Alaafin of Oyo who had a human brother. The legend of Ògún is often told by Yoruba hunters, revered for his supernatural control over iron and the fate of hunters.[129] Many legends that try to explain the past of the Yoruba people have details that cannot be verified. In Ilaro, an old Yoruba settlement had an oral tradition claiming that its fourth king did not die but stated that he would enter the ground and become immortal.

---

[124] John N. Oriji, *Traditions of Igbo Origin: A Study of Pre-colonial Population Movements in Africa* (New York: Peter Lang, 1990).

[125] Adiele E. Afigbo, "Oral Tradition and History in Eastern Nigeria," *African Notes: Bulletin of the Institute of African Studies* 3, no. 3 (1966): 12–20.

[126] Attahiru A. Sifawa, "The Role of Kanem Borno 'Ulama' in the 20 Intellectual Development of the Bilad al-Sudan." Paper presented at a conference on Impact of "Ulama" in the Central Bilad al-Sudan, organized by the Centre for Trans-Saharan Studies, University of Maiduguri, 1991.

[127] Alex Cuoco, *African Narratives of Orishas, Spirits and other Deities: Stories from West Africa and the African Diaspora: A Journey into the Realm of Deities, Spirits, Mysticism, Spiritual Roots and Ancestral Wisdom* (Parker: Outskirts Press, 2014).

[128] Iya Afin Ayobunmi Sangode, *Sango: The Cult of Kingship* (Scotts Valley: CreateSpace Publishing, 2014).

[129] Sandra T. Barnes, ed. *Africa's Ogun: Old World and New* (Indianapolis: Indiana University Press, 1997).

However, archaeological evidence from that location has failed to confirm the story.[130]

In the royal courts of African monarchies, an official historian was often appointed to maintain the oral accounts of history that were shared with the public.[131] These historians celebrated their kings' victories and influenced public sentiment.[132] Faseke, emphasizing the reported experience of Kunle Afolayan at the Egbado palace, noted that a palace historian had described the victories of an Egbado Oba in 1840. Many other historical reports contradicted this account, which may have been intended to claim accolades for the Oba's lineage.[133]

Another challenge for oral tradition is the fact that the accounts frequently fail to note specific dates.[134] There is a heavy reliance on the reigns of kings, or sequences of events, to compensate for the fact that there was no established consensus for recording time. It can also be difficult to separate exaggerations from statements of fact since many oral accounts tell their stories with "condensed or poetic language."[135] Finally, oral records of the invasion and the occupation of Nigerian societies are less reliable when tracking the establishment of the British administration. This information was recorded more thoroughly in the colonial archives because societal preferences shifted away from oral traditions. Western civilization encouraged a more logical, scientific approach to history. The shortcomings of oral traditions are undeniable, but they served as primary sources of history in Nigerian communities.[136] Oral traditions are true to Africa and represent the African approach to recounting African history. They have been the most reliable and readily available sources of information from the continent's antiquity.

African societies have diverse historical sources for scholars, including rituals and festivals. The polytheistic origins of Nigerian societies have encouraged them to worship different deities that serve different purposes, with different stories attached to them. In most cases, the *Orisa* were human, worshipped as deities that established ways of living in African societies. Some of these gods have different appellations, in the form of *Oríkì*, that also

---

[130] Modupeolu M. Faseke, "Oral History in Nigeria: Issues, Problems, and Prospects," *The Oral History Review* 18, no. 1 (1990): 77–92.
[131] Paulo D. M. Farias, "History and Consolation: Royal Yorùbá Bards Comment on their Craft," *History in Africa* 19 (1992): 263–297.
[132] Francis West, "Review of Oral Tradition: A Study in Historical Methodology," *History and Theory* 5, no. 3 (1966): 348–352; and Wande Abimbola, *Ifa: An Exposition of Ifa Literary Corpus* (Ibadan: Oxford University Press, 1976).
[133] Faseke, "Oral History in Nigeria."
[134] David P. Henige, "Oral Tradition and Chronology," *The Journal of African History*, 12, no. 3 (1971): 371–389.
[135] Faseke, "Oral History in Nigeria," 80.
[136] Wande Abimbọla, *Yoruba Oral Tradition* (Ile-Ife: University of Ife, 1975).

tell the people's history.[137] *Oríkì* is often rendered in the dialectic format of their corresponding societies. In some instances, they include people from different settlements. The eulogies and tributes sung to many of these gods also retell African histories.[138] *Ifá*, the god of divination, is consulted with different enchantments and poetry, including songs. The *Babaláwo* may say *adífá fún Obàtálá nígbà tín ó ti òde òrun bòwáyé* (cast divination for *Obàtálá* when he journeyed from heaven to the earthly realm), referencing Obàtálá when he descended into the world.[139]

Yoruba mythology made Ile-Ife look like the center of the world, serving as an origin point from which everyone migrated.[140] The historical sanctity of this town protected it from attack and made it a point of reference for many Yoruba kingdoms. Rituals in Africa are performed by consulting the gods and, in so doing, worshippers state the powers and supremacy of the god by chanting stories of what the said god had achieved in the past. Many festivals honoring these deities involve historical details.

Voices from outside the colonial archives play a major role in reconstructing Nigerian history. Nationalist writers and scholars have advocated traditional sources of history to protect African history's integrity and purity. These goals cannot be accomplished through the colonial archives because of the biases in their curatorial decisions.

Conclusion

The colonial archives served as a trigger for the development of Nigerian historiography. The creation of the National Archives at the University College Ibadan, under the pioneering leadership of Kenneth Dike, was instrumental in encouraging the study of history. The National Archives also marked the conceptualization of African history and a growing consciousness around its approach and scope of discussion. The Ibadan School of History carved out a niche for restating colonial and precolonial Nigerian history from Nigerian perspectives devoid of colonial influence. The Ibadan School criticized anachronistic and ethnocentric accounts of African history.

However, the archives are plagued by deficiencies. The colonial acquisition of materials about precolonial and colonial history was politically influenced, and many records were destroyed, while few were turned over to Nigeria after

---

[137] Lindon Thomas, "Oriki Orisa: The Yoruba Prayer of Praise," *Journal of Religion in Africa* 20, no. 2 (1990): 205–224.

[138] Pierre Verger, "Oral Tradition in the Cult of the Orishas and Its Connection with the History of the Yoruba," *Journal of the Historical Society of Nigeria* 1, no. 1 (1956): 61-63.

[139] Wande Abimbola, *Ifá Will Mend Our Broken World: Thoughts on Yoruba Religion and Culture in Africa and the Diaspora* (Massachusetts: Aim Books, 1997).

[140] Adelegan Adegbola, *Ile-Ife: The Source of Yoruba Civilization* (Ketu: Oduduwa International Communications, 2009).

independence. The archive faces other challenges that encourage scholars to look elsewhere when reconstructing African history. These other resources can be referred to as other voices, historical sources that are specific to Nigeria, which are continuous modes of transmitting history across generations. They include local chronicles, like the *Kano Chronicles*, along with oral traditions from Western and Eastern Nigeria, rituals and festivals, and different historical objects. Some of these sources face challenges in retaining their credibility over time, rendering many unreliable.

Understandably, the colonial archives might face limitations in preserving African and Nigerian history, which is why all voices must be heard. Other sources must be considered through a comprehensive, methodological approach to access the full construction of Nigerian colonial history.

2

Narrating Colonial Nigeria

Nigeria's history is often viewed from three distinct eras, examined and re-examined by scholars on their unending quest to understand each era's key events.[1] Extensive research, discovery, and writings have provided detailed scholarship on the country's historical trajectory.[2] In the long precolonial era, Nigeria's indigenous polities were free to develop their societies. It was a period when the territory was viewed as neither a body of nations nor a single country. It comprised different independent kingdoms, empires, nations, caliphates, and sovereign entities involved in survival, war, domination, defeat, and renewal to identify the systems of government that worked best to meet their needs. These independent political entities never considered unification under a single government.[3] The heritage and definition of the things considered African or Pan-African have roots in this period of Nigerian history. This was the state of Africa when the British colonial government arrived, which brought in a new historical era.[4]

The colonial era is not only the second component of Nigeria's historical partitioning but also the cause of that partitioning. Without the intervention of British imperialists,[5] Nigeria's history would have developed at its own rate, retaining enduring systems and convictions from the precolonial era. The British colonial administration was built on the preceding efforts of Christian missionaries, established over four decades, and its political and administrative systems were finally completed in the second decade of British

---

[1] Jacob F. A. Ajayi, *Milestones in Nigerian History* (Ibadan: Ibadan University Press, 1962).

[2] Kamilu S. Fage and David O. Alabi, *Political and Constitutional Development in Nigeria: From Pre-colonial to Post-colonial Era* (Kano: Northern Printers Limited, 2003); Cornelius O. Ejimofor, *British Colonial Objectives and Policies in Nigeria: The Roots of Conflict* (Onitsha: Africana-FEP, 1987); and Adeshina Afolayan, *Identities, Histories and Values in Postcolonial Nigeria* (Lanham: Rowman & Littlefield, 2021).

[3] Joseph A. Atanda, "Government of Yorubaland in the Pre-Colonial Period," *Tarikh* 4, no. 2 (1973): 1–2.

[4] Robin Horton, "Stateless Societies in the History of West Africa," in *History of West Africa*, Vol. 1, ed. Jacob F. A. Ajayi and Michael Crowder (London: Longman, 1976), 72–113.

[5] Efiong I. Utuk, "Britain's Colonial Administrations and Developments, 1861–1960: An Analysis of Britain's Colonial Administrations and Developments in Nigeria," Master of Science in Teaching, Portland State University, 1975.

rule in the 1920s.[6] The colonial era, which is responsible for the division of Nigeria's history, has left a lasting impact on every sector of the country. It is the foundation of present-day Nigerian governance, and many economic sectors were developed during the colonial period. This underscores the importance of subjecting that era to a proper critical analysis, narrating its cogent periods and events.

The third historical era, extending into the present day, is the postcolonial period. It began on October 1, 1960, after a century of occupation, when Nigeria's inhabitants regained control over their governance and affairs, but it has been characterized by inconsistency and enduring challenges. Different systems, interventions, and challenges have threatened democracy and peace within the nation.[7] As Nigeria's history develops, different scholars have attempted to analyze, critique, and explain the present era.[8]

Dialogue and Conquest

Colonialism was a logical extension of European efforts to replace the outlawed and heavily criticized slave trade.[9] The practice drained the African continent of resources, treating its population as forced labor to serve European businesses and plantations. The British government officially outlawed the slave trade in 1807 after extensive pressure from different human rights activists and resistance by the enslaved.[10]

After the British abolished slavery, they urged other European countries to follow their example and end the slave trade in Africa. Britain's royal navy was deployed, and the British Empire and its allies became an antislavery force.[11] Economic interests, which had been a guiding force in the British Empire's decisions, led to the replacement of the slave trade as Europe and Britain were to be supplied with raw materials through "legitimate trade."[12]

---

[6] Niels Kastfelt, "Christianity, Colonial Legitimacy and the Rise of Nationalist Politics in Northern Nigeria," in *Legitimacy and the State in Twentieth-Century Africa*, ed. Terence Ranger and Olufemi Vaughan (London: Palgrave Macmillan, 1993), 191–209.

[7] Imoh Imoh-Itah, Luke Amadi, and Roger Akpan, "Colonialism and the Post-Colonial Nigeria: Complexities and Contradictions 1960–2015: A Post–Development Perspective," *International Journal of Political Science* 2, no. 3 (2016): 9–21.

[8] For instance, Razaq A. Adefulu, *Reflections on Politics, Democratic Governance and Development in Post-colonial Nigeria* (Ilishan-Remo: Faculty of Management and Social Sciences, Babcock University, 2003).

[9] Seymour Drescher, *Pathways from Slavery: British and Colonial Mobilizations in Global Perspective* (New York: Routledge, 2018).

[10] Roger Anstey, *The Atlantic Slave Trade and British Abolition, 1760–1810* (London: Macmillan, 1975).

[11] Matthew Wyman-McCarthy, "British Abolitionism and Global Empire in the Late 18th Century: A Historiographic Overview," *History Compass* 16, no. 10 (2018): 1–12.

[12] Robin Law, ed. *From Slave Trade to "Legitimate" Commerce: The Commercial Transition in Nineteenth-Century West Africa* (Cambridge: Cambridge University Press, 1995).

Africa was a place to source raw materials for Europe, and Europeans began extracting raw materials instead of human beings. Europe's constant demand for agricultural products drove European powers to occupy African nations, kingdoms, and villages. They established their authority in the region to support their continuing exploitation of raw materials and developed new markets for European products.[13]

Legitimate trade transited to the European invasion of Africa, which was described as "the Scramble for Africa."[14] Historians have described it as such to characterize the aggressive and rapid European expansion into African regions in pursuit of economic interests.[15] After the scramble encouraged increasing conflict among European powers, they agreed to regulate their activities on the continent. This was managed through the Berlin Conference, organized in 1884–5, dividing Africa among European countries to avoid open conflict. During this process, the region, now known as Nigeria, fell under British conquest, control, and colonization as part of the British Empire in West Africa.[16] Its people, as depicted in Figure 2.1, became "colonial subjects."

The advent of Christianity and the creation of missions in Southern Nigeria were instrumental in establishing the British colonial government in the country. Christian missionaries had opened up Badagry through to Abeokuta in 1846. Their creation of educational institutions made locals more receptive to European ideas of "civilization."[17] The British facilitated their invasion of Lagos by exploiting rivalries between royal families in the region.[18] King Kosoko had deposed King Akitoye, who fled to Badagry and solicited support that divided Lagos further. Kosoko supported the slave trade, did not tolerate Christian missionaries, and rejected the British and their traders in Lagos.[19] John Beecroft, the British Consul for Benin and Biafra, responded in 1848 by joining forces with missionaries and other interests who had worked to develop Abeokuta as a nexus of trade. Their goal was to overthrow the existing authorities in Lagos.[20]

Beecroft took Akitoye into British custody, which destabilized Badagry. With assistance from the Egba, Beecroft sent four warships to invade Lagos and

---

[13] William E. B. Du Bois, "The Realities in Africa: European Profit or Negro Development?" *Foreign Affairs* 21, no. 4 (1943): 721–732.

[14] M. E. Chamberlain, *The Scramble for Africa* (London: Routledge, 2013).

[15] Robin Brooke-Smith, ed., *The Scramble for Africa* (London: Macmillan International Higher Education, 1987).

[16] Brooke-Smith, *The Scramble for Africa*.

[17] Emmanuel A. Ayandele, *The Missionary Impact on Modern Nigeria 1842–1914* (London: Longmans, 1966).

[18] Jacob F. A. Ajayi, "The British Occupation of Lagos, 1851–61: A Critical Review," *Nigeria Magazine* 69 (1961): 96–105.

[19] Preye Adekoya, "The Succession Dispute to the Throne of Lagos and the British Conquest and Occupation of Lagos," *African Research Review* 10, no. 3 (2016): 207–226.

[20] Adekoya, "The Succession Dispute to the Throne."

Figure 2.1 Colonial Nigeria illustrates the conquest and full colonization of the geographical and territorial areas of the country officially incorporated as part of the British Empire in West Africa.

offered Kosoko an agreement to abolish the slave trade and ally with Britain.[21] As expected, Kosoko rejected the offer: this was a pretext for attempts to install Akitoye as ruler of Lagos. Beecroft's initial efforts were unsuccessful, and the full bombardment of Lagos began in December 1851 with the assistance of Commodore Bruce. Kosoko fended off the invasion with a defiance that surprised British officials. When Lagos was finally taken after Kosoko had fled to Epe, around seventy-five British fighters had been wounded and around sixteen were dead.[22] After the conquest of Lagos, Akitoye was installed as Oba and made to sign a treaty that opposed the slave trade. As Oba, Akitoye was required to support all British decisions, trading his freedom to attain the throne.[23] A power struggle followed his death, and Dosumu, also controlled by the British, eventually succeeded him. The acquisition of Lagos, and its official recognition as a crown colony in 1861, made it easier for Britain to gradually access the hinterlands of the Yorubaland and Nigeria's greater southwest.[24]

---

[21] Kristin Mann, *Slavery and the Birth of an African City: Lagos, 1760–1900* (Bloomington: Indiana University Press, 2007).

[22] Jacob F. A. Ajayi, *Christian Missions in Nigeria 1841–1891: The Making of a New Elite* (London: Longman, 1965).

[23] Obaro Ikime, "Colonial Conquest and Resistance in Southern Nigeria," *Journal of the Historical Society of Nigeria* 6, no. 3 (1972): 251–270.

[24] Anthony G. Hopkins, "Property Rights and Empire Building: Britain's Annexation of Lagos, 1861," *The Journal of Economic History* 40, no. 4 (1980): 777–798.

The Yoruba city of Ijebu Ode defied British officials and imposed a £50 passage fee for using their trade routes. In 1891, the Ijebu refused to discuss trade negotiations with Acting Governor Denton. This continued until Sir Gilbert Thomas Carter took a more radical approach as Governor and Commander-in-Chief of the Colony of Lagos. In 1892, Carter demanded an apology from the *Awujale*, king of the Ijebu, for insulting the British crown, insisting that representatives should be sent to Lagos, where they would admit their stubbornness and tender their apologies. Once the representatives were in Lagos, Carter began new discussions with them at gunpoint.[25] Carter demanded that the Ijebu open their trade routes in exchange for an annual subsidy of £500, which would replace the £50 passage fees. The delegates refused. Carter responded by gathering the Ijebu who were staying in Lagos, forcing them to sign, and declaring that the agreement now applied to all Ijebu people. After claiming that the Ijebu defaulted on this "agreement," Carter attacked in 1892.[26]

Between 1861 and 1893, the majority of Yorubaland – up to the Ilorin region – had been claimed by the British colonial government. Some smaller areas were conquered later.[27] The Alaafin of Oyo signed a few treaties, such as the peace treaty of 1886. This was before the 1893 treaty with Governor Moloney that put the Oyo Empire under British control. In 1895, Oyo was bombarded by the British, who had accused the Alaafin of punishing one of his subjects through outlawed local traditions.[28] Similar methods were applied to King Pepple of Bonny, who stubbornly refused to compromise the sovereignty of his people. In refusing to surrender to British officials, Pepple blocked trade roots and attacked the Amakiri of Kalabari, affecting British activities at the Oil River in 1853. He was eventually deported from his kingdom and sent to Fernando Po until 1861, while his subjects were placed under British control.[29] Pepple's son, Prince Dappo, was controlled by British officials after Pepple's death. He was forced to sign a treaty that surrendered his authority.[30]

[25] Gabriel O. Oguntomisin, "The Impact of the Ijebu Expedition of 1892 on Politics in Epe, 1892–1925," *African Notes: Bulletin of the Institute of African Studies* 19, nos. 1–2 (1995): 1–12.
[26] Adeyemi B. Aderibigbe, "The Ijebu Expedition, 1892: An Episode in the British Penetration of Nigeria Reconsidered," Proceedings of the Leverhalme Inter-Collegiate History Conference, University College of Rhodesia and Nyasaland, 1960, 267–282.
[27] Anthony I. Asiwaju, "The Western Provinces under Colonial Rule," in *Groundwork of Nigerian History*, ed. Obaro Ikime (London: Heinemann Educational Book, 1980), 429–445.
[28] Tunde Oduwobi, "From Conquest to Independence: The Nigerian Colonial Experience," *Historia Actual Online* 25 (2011): 20.
[29] Godwin C. Ezeh, *Contemporary Issues in Nigerian History* (Nsukka: Mike Social Publishers, 2004), 128.
[30] K. B. C. Onwubiko, *School Certificate History of West Africa: AD 1800–Present Day [Book Two]* (Aba: Africana Educational Publishers Co., 1973).

British efforts to subdue the Igbo faced strong resistance, especially from the Arochukwu, who held influence over their society's trade and commerce.[31] The British Empire needed to overcome Arochukwu's opposition to expand its trading operations in the region. In 1901, British officials launched the Anglo–Aro War and a series of other military expeditions in Arochukwu territory.[32] Despite the British victories, some areas continued to defy them, especially in Mbano.[33] After the British established control in Northern Nigeria, they placed the region under the administration of the Royal Niger Company (RNC) led by George Taubman Goldie.[34] Britain retained authority over the areas controlled by the company in 1887, but the British government needed to formalize its occupation to prevent other European countries from claiming the territory. In 1900, the region became the Northern Protectorate.[35]

Governance

The British administration began formalizing its governing structure for Nigeria on January 1, 1900. Southern Nigeria was unified under a single administrative structure, and the Northern region, formerly under the control of the RNC, became "Northern Nigeria."[36] Military expeditions continued until 1919, but Britain had established a governing presence in most territories. The Northern region became the Northern Protectorate,[37] and the Colony of Lagos, the Northern Protectorate, and the Southern Protectorate were amalgamated under a single administrative system in 1914.[38]

The British administration encountered problems in attempting to impose its authority on a diverse group of people who had divergent traditions for political administration and trade. This challenge, which was often called the "Native Question,"[39] needed to be solved to maintain the colonial administration's control without demanding an excessive amount of resources from the British.

---

[31] Ogechi E. Anyanwu, *The Making of Mbano: British Colonialism, Resistance, and Diplomatic Engagements in Southeastern Nigeria, 1906–1960* (Lanham: Rowman & Littlefield, 2021).

[32] Adiele E. Afigbo, *The Abolition of the Slave Trade in Southeastern Nigeria, 1885–1950* (New York: University of Rochester Press, 2006), 44–46.

[33] Anyanwu, *The Making of Mbano*.

[34] Bruce Vandervort, *Wars of Imperial Conquest* (London: Routledge, 1998), 189–191.

[35] Abubakar Saad, "The Northern Province under Colonial Rule," in *Groundwork of Nigeria History*, ed. Obaro Ikime (London: Heinemann Educational Books, 1980).

[36] Utuk, "Britain's Colonial Administrations."

[37] Adiele E. Afigbo, "The Consolidation of British Imperial Administration in Nigeria: 1900–1918," *Civilisations* 21, no. 4 (1971): 436–459.

[38] A. O. Anjorin, "The Background to the Amalgamation of Nigeria in 1914," *Odù: Journal of Yoruba and Related Studies* 3, no. 2 (1967): 72–86.

[39] Mahmood Mamdani, "Indirect Rule, Civil Society, and Ethnicity: The African Dilemma," *Social Justice* 23, no. 1/2 (1996): 145–150.

Britain lacked the personnel necessary for a full-scale bureaucracy, leading the administration to adopt the principle of indirect rule.[40] This concept, which was largely introduced by Lord Lugard, exploited pre-existing systems and authorities to benefit the colonial administration. Native authorities were initially the most important element of the indirect rule system.

In Southern Nigeria, and in Oyo in particular, the Council of Chiefs was amended to recognize the British Resident Officer as president of the council, which comprised the Alaafin and other chiefs like the Balogun, Otun, and Osi. This system was extended to Ilesa, Ekiti, and other Yoruba towns. The Native Councils Ordinance of 1901 allowed other towns and villages to establish their councils. These groups became the core administrative bodies of their communities, performing all major government functions.[41] British reforms made the Alaafin more powerful than any other regional authority apart from British officials. This overturned local systems that had developed to apply checks and balances, like the authority of the *Oyomesi*. The Alaafin's court became a Grade A court, and authorities under him, including the Bale of Ibadan, were considered Grade B.[42] Regional appeals could be sent to the Alaafin's court for adjudication, making him the supreme authority beneath the British. The British government also adopted the taxation system already in place in Oyo and other Yoruba areas, placing the Native authorities in important roles.

In Northern Nigeria, colonial officials enforced indirect rule through advisory roles.[43] The Sultan and the Emirs held power over other institutions within their respective emirates. The old emirates, which had fallen under the sultan's control after the 1807 Jihad, regained their independence under emirs distributed throughout the provinces.[44] Native chiefs, their governance mechanisms, and existing institutions were largely retained by the colonial administration.[45] Only the Waziri was left with the sultan for administrative purposes, while other native chiefs and dignitaries who ruled precolonial Northern Nigeria headed their respective districts. The Native Authority Ordinance of 1916 gave the sultan and the emirs the authority to appoint chiefs and councilors, but

---

[40] Obaro Ikime, "Reconsidering Indirect Rule: The Nigerian Example," *Journal of the Historical Society of Nigeria* 4, no. 3 (1968): 421–438.
[41] Joseph A. Atanda, "The New Oyo Empire A Study of British Indirect Rule in Oyo Province, 1894–1934," unpublished PhD dissertation, University of Ibadan, 1967.
[42] Margery Perham, *Lugard: The Years of Authority, 1898–1945* (London: Collins, 1956), 445.
[43] Obaro Ikime, "The Establishment of Indirect Rule in Northern Nigeria," *Tarikh* 3, no. 3 (1971): 1–15.
[44] Peter K. Tibenderana, "The Administration of Sokoto, Gwandu and Argungu Emirates under British Rule, 1900–1946," unpublished PhD dissertation, University of Ibadan, 1974.
[45] Lewis H. Gann and Peter Duignan, eds., *Colonialism in Africa, 1870–1960: The History and Politics of Colonialism, 1914–1960*, Vol. 2. (Cambridge: Cambridge University Press, 1970).

every appointment had to be approved by British officials. Islamic principles of justice were retained under the indirect rule system, and the emir applied the rules of the Quran.[46]

Indirect rule encountered difficulties in Eastern Nigeria among the Igbo people.[47] Most Igbo societies did not have a centralized political system, as their acephalous societies resolved issues through village assemblies. The British disregarded existing systems and appointed Warrant Chiefs and District Officers.[48] The arbitrary selection process for these local officials made it difficult for them to establish legitimacy among local communities. This led to public unrest and uprisings that included the Aba Women's War of 1929.[49]

The colonial government redefined Nigeria's political make-up by promulgating several constitutions.[50] It began with the 1922 Clifford Constitution, which applied to Southern Nigeria, while the Northern Protectorate continued to be governed by proclamation. This constitution introduced legislative principles and councils to recommend laws for the Southern Protectorate. The increasing political consciousness among Nigeria's inhabitants, and their experience in World War II, encouraged the promulgation of the 1946 Richards Constitution. The 1946 constitution merged the legislative administrations of the Northern and Southern Protectorates, dividing Nigeria into three regions to simplify administration for British officials.

The constitution encouraged the direct participation of Nigerians, introducing elective principles and promoting national unity. It was seen as a huge step toward democracy and independence, but it deepened divisions between the Northern and Southern Protectorates. These disagreements played out in various constitutional conferences held before 1951, and the suggested amendments failed to diffuse ethnic tensions. The 1954 constitution laid the foundation for federalism in Nigeria, giving Nigerians the authority to govern themselves within their respective regions. This developed into the 1960 independence constitution, which ushered in a new political era.[51]

---

[46] Noel James Coulson, *A History of Islamic Law* (London: Routledge, 2017).
[47] Adiele E. Afigbo, *The Warrant Chiefs: Indirect Rule in Southeastern Nigeria, 1891–1929* (London: Longman, 1972).
[48] Afigbo, *The Warrant Chiefs*.
[49] Judith Van Allen, "'Sitting on a Man': Colonialism and the Lost Political Institutions of Igbo Women," *Canadian Journal of African Studies* 6, no. 2 (1972): 165–181.
[50] Benjamin O. Nwabueze, *A Constitutional History of Nigeria* (London: C. Hurst & Company, 1982).
[51] Matthew E. Egharevba, "Constitutional Development and Inter-Group Relations in Nigeria: The Unending Dilemma," *Biudiscourse Journal of Arts & Education* 2, no. 1 (2007): 174–187.

Trade and Economy

The occupation of Nigeria was driven by economic and commercial interests. During the scramble for Africa, the British sought to retain their advantage in Europe by finding raw materials and new markets in Nigeria. The British administration's activities, including the 1914 amalgamation, were not philanthropic but had economic motives.[52] In the 1870s and 1880s, the National African Company carried out military operations to open up trade routes.[53] Toward the end of the nineteenth century, the RNC, Unilever, and other British companies were granted permission to carry out trading and activities that included governance in sub-Saharan regions.[54] Under the persuasion of Sir George Goldie, the British government permitted the RNC to operate in most parts of the Niger Delta.[55] Other companies were also granted rights to establish trading activities in the region.

To coordinate their activities and enable the establishment of a British government, British companies founded the Lagos Chamber of Commerce in 1886.[56] After colonial rule was established, especially before World War I, government policies favored these companies and deferred to their judgment in guiding the British colony's core economic activities. These companies continued to advance their interests through their positions as special legislative council members.[57]

The oil palm, a primary source of trade goods in the Niger Delta, attracted the interest of the colonial government.[58] During the colonial administration, British officials and companies exported palm oil, palm kernels, and other palm products from the interior regions. Technological developments and the abolition of the slave trade drove the increasing demand for palm products. The Industrial Revolution in Europe and the British construction of local railways required palm oil for lubrication.[59] Palm oil was also useful for cooking and producing candles, soap, pharmaceutical products, and livestock feed. British officials were well aware of palm oil's value in the late nineteenth

---

[52] Lord Lugard, *Dual Mandate in British West Africa* (London: Thomas and Nelson, 1922).
[53] Obaro Ikime, *The Fall of Nigeria: The British Conquest* (London: Heinemann, 1981).
[54] John E. J. Flint and Robert Cornevin, "Lettres Aux Éditeurs/Correspondence," *Canadian Journal of African Studies* 9, no. 1 (1975): 157–159.
[55] Colin Newbury, "Trade and Technology in West Africa: The Case of the Niger Company, 1900–1920," *The Journal of African History* 19, no. 4 (1978): 551–575.
[56] Anthony G. Hopkins, "An Economic History of Lagos, 1880–1914," unpublished PhD dissertation, University of London, 1964.
[57] Olakunle A. Lawal, "British Commercial Interests and the Decolonization Process in Nigeria, 1950–60," *African Economic History* 22 (1994): 93–110.
[58] Samuel Ovete Aghalino, "British Colonial Policies and the Oil Palm Industry in the Niger Delta Region of Nigeria, 1900–1960," *African Study Monographs* 21, no. 1 (2000): 19–33.
[59] Gerald K. Helleiner, *Peasant Agriculture, Government, and Economic Growth in Nigeria* (Homewood: R. D. Irwin, 1966).

century.[60] These products formed about 89 percent of all exports from Nigeria by 1900 until they were replaced by other products such as cocoa and rubber. Demand was also affected by the development of oil palm plantations in other parts of the world.[61] The British administration's most active involvement in processing Nigeria's oil palm products occurred in 1910.

Economic pressure from other countries and the need for human and material resources encouraged the British administration to develop Nigeria's agricultural sector for growing cash crops. Farmers began producing crops based on market demands,[62] changing local societies' social dynamics. Many local businesses and trades ended up being run by women who did not hold the same status as their male counterparts.

British officials were also interested in animal hides and skin, especially in Northern Nigeria. Due to their long history of raising livestock, the Hausa had an advantage in providing these goods.[63] The Hausa had dominated the precolonial production of hides and skin in markets throughout the Northern region and up to the Sahara. After the invasion of the British, northern routes were disrupted by the United African Company (UAC). The UAC later transferred its interests to the RNC, which increased the flow of goods to the south. The RNC controlled northern trade and reduced its emphasis on trade in hides and skin until Britain revoked the company's charter and consolidated the Northern region in 1903. The colonial administration rekindled interest in these products around 1907, when the sales of raw hides had climbed from £500 to around £12,937. By 1914, £500,000 worth of hides had been exported to other countries.[64]

During the colonial period, Nigeria supported the global economy, especially through both World Wars. Britain and other European countries relied on Nigerian goods, and the country was a major center for producing food. It was also important for recruiting and enlisting soldiers, with about 50,000 Nigerian men in the Royal Army during World War I.[65] The recruitment into the army meant that some rural areas lost labor to cultivate agricultural products that were the backbone of Nigeria's economy. Those who remained in the villages had incentives to produce cash crops, which led to temporary shortages in food production in Nigeria.[66] Many more Nigerians

---

[60] Kenneth O. Dike, *Trade and Politics in the Niger Delta, 1830–1885: An Introduction to the Economic and Political History of Nigeria* (London: Clarendon Press, 1956).
[61] Helleiner, *Peasant Agriculture*.
[62] Anthony G. Hopkins, *An Economic History of West Africa* (London: Longman, 1973).
[63] Edward C. Hopen, *The Pastoral Fulbe Family in Gwandu* (London: Routledge, 2018).
[64] Akanmu G. Adebayo, "The Production and Export of Hides and Skins in Colonial Northern Nigeria, 1900–1945," *The Journal of African History* 33, no. 2 (1992): 273–300.
[65] Albert T. Nzala, I. I. Potekhin, and Aleksandr Z. Zusmanovich, *Forced Labour in Colonial Africa* (London: Zed Press, 1977).
[66] Michael Watt, *Silent Violence: Food, Famine and Peasantry in Northern Nigeria* (London: Berkeley, 1983).

were recruited to fight in World War II,[67] which had similarly disastrous effects on the nation's economy. Less food was produced and many Nigerian men were sent to the mines to produce tin for the war effort.[68] The British government increased its revenue substantially from Nigeria's commercial activities during the war. Some profits were sent to Britain, and some of the revenue was used to address Nigerian agitation for workers' compensation and related political challenges.[69]

The taxation system of the colonial government was different from precolonial systems. Taxation was a major source of funding for colonial imperialism, and it was applied without considering local traditions or practices. In the North, immediately after the conquest of Usman Dan Fodio's Sokoto Caliphate, the British government outlawed tribute payments. Instead, the colonial administration imposed the payment of land revenues and other taxes in 1904, which residents found incomprehensible.[70] After the successful completion of the Sokoto conquest in 1903, the British administration imposed direct taxes on all areas originally occupied by the Sokoto Caliphate. They also transferred the right to collect these taxes from native leaders to the British administration. To avoid conflict with local religious beliefs, the taxes were called "capitation fees." This was to assist with collection from Northerners who were familiar with the payment of *Zakat*.[71] In 1909, the payments were described as compound taxes. These unfamiliar taxes were also introduced to the Eastern and Western regions, meeting strong resistance from the Igbo.

In 1905, British taxation was assessed based on the number of adults residing in a household. This expanded to land use and products in 1908 and 1909, respectively. Local inhabitants were eventually expected to pay 10 percent of their income earned from production for land use taxes. Many people, especially among the lowest tiers of society, resisted these edicts.[72] Women in the North were not taxed directly, and attempts to tax them in Eastern Nigeria were met with serious confrontations that threatened to develop into full-scale revolt.

---

[67] Oluwafunminiyi Raheem and Oluyemisi A. Disu, "Fighting for Britain: Examining British Recruitment Strategies in Nigeria," in *Unknown Conflicts of the Second World War: Forgotten Fronts*, ed. Christopher Murray (London: Routledge, 2019), 8–22.
[68] A. Ahmed, "Jos: Class and Ethnicity," *The Analyst* III, no. 3 (1988).
[69] Emmanuel O. Akubor, "From Hinterland Trade to International Commerce: Historicizing Nigeria's Contributions to World Economy from 1914," *JORAS-Nigerian Journal of Religion and Society* 4 (2014): 134–151.
[70] NAK/SNP 15 Acc. 374, Memorandum on Land Tenure and Taxation, 1, see also NAK/SNP 6 C.162/1907, Land tenure and land revenue in Northern Nigeria, 63–69.
[71] NAK/Sokoto Province Annual Report (henceforth NAK/Sokprof) 2/285/1906.
[72] NAK/Sokprof 2/9, 985/1908, Report no. 36 for half year ending 30 June 1908, by E.J. Stanley.

Impacts and Developments

Colonialism is an important part of Nigeria's history that has impacted every area and sector.[73] The colonial administration left its mark on new social constructs and developmental influences as part of an enduring legacy. The primary drivers of these developments were not philanthropic interests. Instead, the British were guided by economic and commercial concerns.

The British colonial administration is widely credited with developing Nigeria's transportation infrastructure.[74] Nigeria's earliest advanced transport systems involved the construction of waterways and ports that allowed larger amounts of goods to be imported into Nigerian markets. This infrastructure also facilitated the extraction of raw materials, which was the main justification for British colonial efforts. Rivers were carefully monitored to ensure that shipments could easily travel from coastal ports to the interior regions. The Roads and Rivers Ordinance, made by Governor Moor in 1903, made village heads and other leaders responsible for maintaining local transportation routes.[75]

Waterways alone could not reach every part of the interior. The colonial administration built major railways across the country that linked strategic points with coastal regions. This project and its subsequent investment were considered to be the administration's most important investment in Nigeria.[76] By the end of the nineteenth century, rails were laid in Lagos. The British had high expectations for economic growth in their Nigerian territories, and railways quickly turned those expectations into a reality. The opening of the Lagos–Ibadan railway in 1901 allowed access to new Yoruba settlements and towns in the southwest.[77] The construction of the Baro–Kano rail lines in 1912 opened new markets in Northern Nigeria, increasing the flow of merchants, raw materials, and finished products.

Ilorin and Ibadan had previously been linked by rail lines constructed in 1908 linking the north and south. After coal was discovered in Udi, the colonial administration constructed a railway into Eastern Nigeria to access more remote areas.[78] The 1924 Enugu–Makurdi–Kafanchan construction linked

---

[73] Toyin Falola, ed., *Britain and Nigeria: Exploitation or Development?* (London: Zed Books, 1987).

[74] Tokunbo Ayoola, "Colonial Inheritance, Postcolonial Neglect, and the Management of Nigerian Railway by Rail India Technical and Economic Services (RITES)," *Lagos Notes and Records* 14, no. 1 (2008): 60–85.

[75] Solomon D. Neumark, "Transportation in Sub-Saharan Africa," in *An Economic History of Tropical Africa*, ed. Zbigniew A. Konczacki and Janina M. Konczacki (New Jersey: Frank Cass, 1977), 40.

[76] Michael Crowder, *West Africa under Colonial Rule* (London: Hutchinson, 1976), 273.

[77] Olufemi Omosini, "Background to Railway Policy in Nigeria, 1877–1901," in *Topics on Nigerian Economic and Social History*, ed. Isaac A. Akinjogbin and Segun O. Osoba (Ife: University of Ife Press, 1980), 147.

[78] Olasiji Oshin, "Road Transport and the Declining Fortunes of the Nigerian Railway, 1901–1950," *The Journal of Transport History* 12, no. 1 (1991): 11–36.

coal production in Enugu and tin mining in Bauchi, followed by additional Kafanchan–Kaduna, Kafanchan–Jos, Zaria–Gusau, and Kano–Nguru railways in 1924, 1927, 1927, 1929, and 1930, respectively. Rails connected every major settlement in the country, transferring finished products to the interior and bringing raw materials to ports.[79] Despite this massive investment, navigable roads were still necessary to feed the railway terminals. The colonial government focused on this need for road transport in 1904, establishing the Department of Roads to monitor and regulate their use. Governor Egerton led the construction of roads for "trunk lines" that fed the railways, especially in Lagos. Local footpaths were transformed into properly constructed roads.[80] Other major roads were built to connect with train stations across the country.

The colonial government also developed educational institutions. Christian missionaries were the main force behind Nigerian education during the second half of the nineteenth century, and their efforts extended into the post-1900 era, as the colonial government was not involved until 1877.[81] The missionary interest in education was linked with their desire to teach the gospel since early educational institutions were built to convert students to Christianity and to teach religious values. The colonial government and Christian missionaries collaborated on developing an organized system for primary and secondary education in Nigeria.

The colonial government had a stronger commitment to tertiary education due to economic reasons. The British initially preferred to create vocational and technical schools that delivered obvious benefits, teaching medicine, surveying practices, and pharmacology.[82] The government established Yaba College in 1930 due to its need for skilled individuals with advanced knowledge and to train medical personnel at the initial King's College, Lagos site.[83] Additional structures were built for the college in 1932.[84] However, the scope of the college's curriculum was too limited, and graduates had to travel to Europe and the United Kingdom for additional training. Ongoing demands prompted the construction of additional tertiary institutions in the country.[85]

After the Asquith and Elliot Commissions evaluated the possibility of creating a Nigerian university, the British created University College, Ibadan,

---

[79] Omosini, "Background to Railway Policy."
[80] Oshin, "Road Transport and the Declining Fortunes."
[81] Immaculata N. Enwo-Irem, "Colonialism and Education: The Challenges for Sustainable Development in Nigeria," *Mediterranean Journal of Social Sciences* 4, no. 5 (2013): 163.
[82] Jacob F. A. Ajayi, "Higher Education in Nigeria," *African Affairs* 74, no. 297 (1975): 420–426.
[83] Aliyu B. Fafunwa, *History of Education in Nigeria* (London: Allen & Unwin, 1974).
[84] Ade Fajana, "Colonial Control and Education: The Development of Higher Education in Nigeria 1900-1950," *Journal of the Historical Society of Nigeria* 6, no. 3 (1972): 323–340.
[85] Fajana, "Colonial Control and Education."

in 1948.[86] It was intended to be an extension of University College, London, with other institutions constructed in its wake. The colonial government laid the foundation for the University of Nigeria, the University of Ife, and Ahmadu Bello University.[87] These educational institutions and systems were responsible for the growth of nationalist sentiment in Nigeria and local requests for self-governance.

The narrative arc of healthcare services in Nigeria also changed during the colonial period. Christian missionaries were the first to provide Western healthcare, but the colonial government eventually provided its services with various restrictions. The colonial government's earliest healthcare efforts involved converting a military facility into a public hospital, creating an infectious disease hospital in 1873, and converting debtors' prisons into hospitals and psychiatric treatment facilities.[88] The colonial administration's creation of Yaba College was not completely philanthropic, as it exalted Western medical concepts to the detriment of local healthcare practices. Nigeria's pharmaceutical sector relied on – and continues to rely on – Western treatments that subsumed African medical services. The current healthcare system in Nigeria is mainly modeled after British practices.

The colonial administration in Nigeria brought modern infrastructure and new institutions, but it also had negative consequences. British cultural influences opposed the existing African values that had maintained Nigeria's social institutions. Nigerians were taught that their previous ways of life were inferior, and foreign approaches were exalted as superior practices. Cultural imperialism taught African minds to be biased against their communities. The introduction of Western medicine linked traditional healthcare practices with paganism, barbarism, and irrationality, dismissing effective treatments as dangerous and unscientific. These cultural shifts, introduced during the colonial era, persist to the present day.

Nigeria during the World Wars

The narration of Nigeria's colonial experience must include the country's participation in both World Wars, which shaped the first half of the twentieth century. The British Empire, at the height of its colonial activity, established itself as an international force that could exert control over vast distances. Britain's massive economic and political interests compelled it to involve colonial territories in its clashes with other world powers. Africa – and Nigeria in particular – was

---

[86] Fafunwa, *History of Education in Nigeria*.
[87] Kenneth Mellanby, *The Birth of Nigeria's University* (London: Methuen and Company Limited, 1958), 25–27.
[88] Dennis A. Ityavyar, "Background to the Development of Health Services in Nigeria," *Social Science & Medicine* 24, no. 6 (1987): 487–499.

directly involved in both World Wars via the exploitation of agricultural products, raw materials, and human resources. Britain and other European countries needed massive armies drawn from all over the world.[89]

Nigerians were enlisted in World War I to fight a war that was not their own. After Britain declared war in 1914, it called up large numbers of Africans and dispatched them to different posts. The Nigerian colony already faced social unrest, instability, and economic challenges, which meant that the loss of Nigerian lives and the ongoing exportation of local products had devastating effects on the country.[90] British requirements for food, tin, and other Nigerian products granted special concessions to large businesses that could produce these items in the quantities demanded. Many small businesses run by Nigerians ended up closing.

Other projects and developments in Nigeria were affected by the secondary effects of World War I. The development of roadways, the Port Harcourt railway terminal, Lagos Harbor, and the Eastern railway to Kaduna were put on hold. Government parastatals and other organizations also suspended their work. Many Nigerians in cities were left jobless, either enlisting in the army or enduring hardship as they searched for alternative employment.[91] Nigeria's import shortage increased the cost of items that Nigerians depended on for survival, and the limited availability of silver currency exacerbated the situation. The colonial government introduced paper currency as a substitute, but the situation worsened and commodity prices continued to increase. Rising inflation in cities led to protests and demands for wage increases. In 1918, Sir Wood Renton evaluated the situation and recommended that a war bonus be paid in Nigeria and the Gold Coast. The government ignored these recommendations, and employees threatened strikes and industrial labor action. These were the first proposals for such collective action, and the government conceded to their demands. This motivated additional protests against the government.

The war effort increased demand for palm kernel, palm oil, and other palm products in Europe, especially to support soldiers. In 1915 and 1916, the discovery of additional applications increased the consumption of these products: they could be used to make lauric acid, which was used to produce margarine; glycerin, which was used for explosives; and soap, along with other products. Oil palm products became one of the most important exports during World War I.[92]

---

[89] David Killingray and James Matthews, "Beasts of Burden: British West African Carriers in the First World War," *Canadian Journal of African Studies* 13, no. 1–2 (1979): 5–23.

[90] Jide Osuntokun, "Post–First World War Economic and Administrative Problems in Nigeria and the Response of the Clifford Administration," *Journal of the Historical Society of Nigeria* 7, no. 1 (1973): 35–48.

[91] C. O. 583/74/23397: G. M. Bland to D. C. Cameron 26.

[92] Peter J. Yearwood, "The Expatriate Firms and the Colonial Economy of Nigeria in the First World War," *The Journal of Imperial and Commonwealth History* 26, no. 1 (1998): 49–71.

From 1939 to 1945, World War II had even greater effects on Nigeria. Britain faced intense attacks from German forces, and the British government once again asked Africans to fight in a war they did not start. A massive drive for human and material resources across Nigeria drained a substantial amount of resources and citizens. The British Empire relied on its colonies to support the war, and Nigerians were exploited.[93] When Japanese blockades stopped the exports of palm oil and other products from Britain's eastern colonies, Nigeria was seen as a replacement to meet the needs of Britain and other parts of Europe.[94] Palm kernel was in high demand, and Nigerian exports increased in later years. Eastern Nigeria increased its output from 157,715 tons in 1940 to 170,096 tons in 1941 and 170,451 tons in 1942.[95]

Nigerians and their elites – including traditional leaders – supported Britain in World War II. British propaganda had convinced them of Hitler's evilness, and educated elites, such as Herbert Macaulay, used mass media and public discussion to publicly present the war as a fight for freedom and democracy.[96] These arguments fueled Nigerian nationalists' early demands for independence, encouraging them to argue for greater participation in Nigeria's governance. World War II triggered an aggressive social change in Nigeria. War returnees had experienced Western culture and introduced alternatives to the previously accepted practices of their hometowns. Nigerian society shifted, and public opinion changed regarding concepts such as collectivist social ideologies. After Nigerians fought alongside Europeans, the illusion of white supremacy was dispelled and they were encouraged to view the colonizers from a new perspective.[97]

Political Consciousness, Nationalism, and Negotiation for Sovereignty

Political consciousness and nationalism in Nigeria can be traced to the start of colonialism. Cultural nationalists and Native authorities worked alongside other civil groups, like the Arochukwu in Eastern Nigeria, to oppose the British colonial administration's dominance. This opposition ultimately shaped the government's response. Nationalism and political consciousness before 1914 focused on the survival of cultures and institutions as the colonial assault was seen as an attempt to erase valuable parts of history. Colonialists

---

[93] Onwuka N. Njoku, "Export Production Drive in Nigeria during the Second World War," *Transafrican Journal of History* 10, no. 1/2 (1981): 11–27.
[94] Evans Harold, "Studies in War-Time Organization: The Resident Ministry of West Africa," *African Affairs* 173, no. 43 (1944): 52–58.
[95] Njoku, "Export Production Drive."
[96] Crowder, *West Africa under Colonial Rule*.
[97] Gabriel Olusanya, *The Second World War and Politics in Nigeria, 1939–1953* (London: Evans Brothers, 1973).

overcame this opposition through conquest and one-sided treaties that subordinated Nigerian political and economic institutions.[98]

After the two World Wars, Nigerians recognized that their counterparts in other parts of the world, especially Europe, were not inherently superior. Educational institutions encouraged Nigerians to complete their studies in Europe, further developing a native political consciousness in Nigeria. The development of mass media, including publicly and privately owned newspapers and radio stations, motivated Nigerians to become more involved in their country's political issues.[99]

The actions of the colonial administration also sparked opposition through oppressive policies that exploited Nigerians. Many policies were outright discriminatory, asserting that Nigerians could not carry out administrative duties or hold political office in their own country. European residential neighborhoods excluded Africans, who were treated as second-class citizens in many African countries, including Nigeria.[100] Unfamiliar taxation policies, such as capitation taxes and land use taxes, were strongly opposed by the people. The Nigerian political consciousness and nationalist movements became more clearly defined, ideologically and conceptually, after students in Nigeria and abroad established activist groups. The National Congress for British West Africa (NCBWA), created in 1920, was an early political body that pressured the government to create a legislative council that included Africans. These agitations and others were instrumental in introducing elective principles, especially in the colonial government's 1922 constitution.[101]

Herbert Macaulay's Nigerian National Democratic Party of 1923 was another political body composed of Nigerians. It challenged the colonial government's income taxes, judicial system, and general administration. Macaulay was largely regarded as the father of Nigerian nationalism. The West African Students Union (WASU) was another activist organization led by Ladipo Solanke in 1925. WASU became a platform for African students agitating for freedom, inclusiveness, and equal consideration. It also promoted pan-African ideologies to demonstrate the relevance of African cultures and systems.[102] The Lagos Youth Movement, which became the National Youth Movement in 1938, promoted unity in Nigeria and clamored for good governance across the nation. The movement also used its newspapers, like the *Lagos Daily News*, to promote political consciousness in Nigeria.

---

[98] Kelechi C. Ubaku, Chikezie A. Emeh, and Chinenye N. Anyikwa, "Impact of Nationalist Movement on the Actualization of Nigerian Independence, 1914–1960," *International Journal of History and Philosophical Research* 2, no. 1 (2014): 54–67.

[99] Olusanya, *The Second World War*.

[100] Michael Omolewa, *Certificate History of Nigeria* (Harlow: Longman Group, 1986).

[101] James S. Coleman, *Nigeria: Background to Nationalism* (Berkeley: University of California Press, 1958).

[102] Ubaku, Emeh, and Anyikwa, "Impact of Nationalist Movement."

Herbert Macaulay and Nnamdi Azikiwe formed the National Council of Nigeria and the Cameroons in 1944. Their goals were to establish a political structure for Nigeria's elections and demand self-governance and independence. In 1959, after Cameroon and Nigeria separated, the political group became the National Council of Nigerian Citizens (NCNC), and continued to make demands and promote its ideology in Nigeria's political arena. The NCNC relied heavily on the *Comet* newspaper and the *West African Pilot* to share its ideologies and viewpoints.[103] It engaged with the government regarding constitutional proposals for ensuring proper representation.

Different constitutional amendments, and the introduction of new constitutions after the 1946 Richards Constitution, introduced political positions for Nigerians. The Macpherson Constitution – and subsequent constitutions, especially the Lyttleton Constitution – regionalized the political construction of the colony to promote inclusiveness. This developed Nigeria's political consciousness along regional lines while political efforts became regionally focused. As a result, the Action Group political party was created to represent the interests of Western Nigeria,[104] and the Northern People's Congress represented the North.[105] Educated elites participated in several activities and agitations, expressed through different meetings and conferences. These nationalist activities and other external pressures ultimately drove the British government to concede self-governance to Nigeria, which ended more than a century of colonial occupation and rule.[106]

Nigeria had begun agitating for independence well before 1960; Nigerian demands for political independence were guided by nationalist activities that date back to 1922. These demands took many forms and led to the enactment of several constitutions that addressed Nigerian political concerns. Ghana's 1957 independence strengthened Nigerian demands for self-governance, and the colonial government faced increasing calls to transfer power to Nigeria's native residents. Nigeria's House of Representatives, which constituted its central legislative body, sent delegates to London to participate in a constitutional review conference. Their major assignment was to demand independence for Nigeria.[107] However, the issue of independence was not the primary

---

[103] Stephanie Newell, "Life Writing in the Colonial Archives: The Case of Nnamdi Azikiwe (1904–96) of Colonial Nigeria," *Life Writing* 33, no. 3 (2016): 307–321.
[104] John A. A. Ayoade, "Party and Ideology in Nigeria: A Case Study of the Action Group," *Journal of Black Studies* 16, no. 2 (1985): 169–188.
[105] Richard L. Sklar, *Nigerian Political Parties: Power in an Emergent African Nation* (Trenton: Africa World Press, 2004), 381–383.
[106] Gabriel O. Olusanya, "The Zikist Movement – A Study in Political Radicalism, 1946–50," *The Journal of Modern African Studies* 4, no. 3 (1966): 323–333.
[107] Oluwatoyin Oduntan and Kemi Rotimi, "Tensional Decolonization and Public Order in Western Nigeria, 1957–1960," *Decolonization: Indigeneity, Education & Society* 4, no. 2 (2015): 103–122.

focus of conference discussions: delegates focused on the issue of ethnic minorities and their concerns about the potential for large ethnic groups to monopolize government control after independence.[108]

Leaders of the three major delegate groups raised the issue of attaining independence by 1959, and the Colonial Secretary, Alan Lennox Boyd, stated that it would not be possible for the government to grant such a request. The secretary cited concerns over the potential for political instability and agitation stemming from minority ethnic groups. The colonial government attempted to resolve these issues with the Sir Henry Willink Commission. The colonial government eventually granted political freedom to the Western and Eastern Regions, and by 1959 the Northern Region was granted a similar opportunity.[109]

The colonial government's willingness to eventually grant independence was seen in the Lyttleton Constitution, which provided more freedom for regional governments and restructured the central government. Regional government activities and commitments became the responsibility of party leaders in the individual regions, who would be recognized as premiers. By September 1957, the central government was also headed by a Nigerian prime minister. By that time, representatives on the executive council were largely Nigerians, but the council was headed by the Governor-General, who was not a Nigerian. After the December 1959 elections, Tafawa Balewa was named Prime Minister of Nigeria.[110] In January 1960, the Federal House of Representatives passed another appeal to request independence for Nigeria by October 1, 1960. The British parliament responded by passing the Independence Act, which later received assent from the British crown. On October 1, 1960, the Charter of Freedom was delivered to the Speaker, Jaja Wachukwu, presented by Princess Alexandra of Kent in place of Her Majesty Queen Elizabeth II. The charter served as a legal document declaring Nigeria as a free and independent country.[111]

Conclusion

Nigeria's colonial history was built on the rich cultural heritage of its regions and the social constructs that identified them. Change is constant and

---

[108] Lexington Izuagie, "The Willink Minority Commission and Minority Rights in Nigeria," *EJOTMAS: Ekpoma Journal of Theatre and Media Arts* 5, no. 1–2 (2015): 206–223.

[109] Kalu Ezera, "Nigeria's Constitutional Road to Independence," *The Political Quarterly* 30, no. 2 (1959): 131–140.

[110] Larry Diamond, *Class, Ethnicity, and Democracy in Nigeria: The Failure of the First Republic* (New York: Syracuse University Press, 1988).

[111] Robert L. Tignor, *Capitalism and Nationalism at the End of Empire: State and Business in Decolonizing Egypt, Nigeria, and Kenya, 1945–1963* (Princeton: Princeton University Press, 2015), 261–290.

inevitable, but the social changes intended to bring "civilization" to Nigeria brought serious consequences. Colonialism resulted in the denigration of Nigerian cultures and values that had been developed over a long period.[112] The British government did not support local practices that did not promote its ability to control the country. The colonial government would not have been as successful without help from Christian missionaries. Missionaries provided healthcare services and other developmental infrastructure as part of their religious efforts, and the colonial administration built on these activities to establish a presence in Nigeria.[113] Many government projects were also completed with cooperation from Christian missionaries. After 1945, the process to terminate the colonial era officially began, with a new generation of Nigerian politicians who set the stage for the ethnic politics that culminated in the civil war a few years after independence in 1960.

---

[112] Merima Ali, Odd–Helge Fjeldstad, Boqian Jiang, and Abdulaziz B. Shifa, "Colonial Legacy, State-Building and the Salience of Ethnicity in Sub-Saharan Africa," *The Economic Journal* 129, no. 619 (2019): 1048–1081.

[113] Mario J. Azevedo, *Historical Perspectives on the State of Health and Health Systems in Africa*, Vol. I (Cham: Palgrave Macmillan, 2017), 331–366.

PART II

Conquest and Colonization

3

Peoples and States in the Nineteenth Century

This chapter provides an overview of the sociopolitical and economic conditions among various polities in the area that later became Nigeria. It works from the common understanding that the sequences preceding an event, seen as causes, are as important as the event itself, which is usually seen as an effect.[1] The chapter studies the evolution of practices, culture, political developments, and economic aspects among these societies before 1900. Like other nation-states that emerged from the ashes of colonialism in Africa, Nigeria did not develop from a homogenous culture or people described as a nation, either in the concrete or loose meanings of the word. The polities that were melded into a nation had been transformed by Western modernity, effected through the introduction of Western education, missionary activities, colonial administrators, and the advent of writing culture. Nigerian groups of the nineteenth century consisted of hundreds of ethnicities, some of which shared mutually intelligible languages with many dialectic variations.[2]

The exact number of these groups cannot be ascertained today. Some figures claim that more than 450 ethnic groups existed, while others cite a number closer to 250. Regardless of the framing, these counts are always established as a minimum that suggests the existence of additional entities. The degree of intermingling that existed among cultures through cultural exchanges and events such as war, migration, trade, and politics bonded people together before colonial domination.[3] These activities make it somewhat easier to navigate the historical developments of this period.[4] Events during this epoch are particularly interesting because they culminated in an entity that

---

[1] William H. Walsh, *An Introduction to Philosophy of History* (London: Hutchinson, 1967).

[2] Jacob F. A. Ajayi and Ebiere J. Alagoa, "Nigeria before 1800: Aspects of Economic Development and Inter-Group Politics," in *Groundwork of Nigeria History*, ed. Obaro Ikime (London: Heinemann Educational Book, 1980), 227.

[3] Apollos O. Nwauwa, "The Foundation of the Aro Confederacy: A Theoretical Analysis of State Formation in Southeastern Nigeria," *ITAN: Bensu Journal of Historical Studies* 1 (1990): 93–108.

[4] E. Z. Obata, "Patterns of Political System in Pre-colonial Nigeria," in *Foundations of Nigerian Federalism: Pre-Colonial Antecedents*, ed. Jonah I. Elaigu and Erim O. Erim (Abuja: National Council on Intergovernmental Relations, 1996).

was supported by several polities and political actors of the time. However, this was done through external imposition and not through the development of an internal consensus.

Interactions among Nigerian Cultures

At various times before the eighteenth century, several groups migrated from different parts of Africa to settle in the area eventually known as Nigeria. Arable land and security were essential for forming human society and establishing civilization. They became the reason why this West African space attracted multiple waves of migration that developed into the more than 250 language groups currently present in Nigeria.[5] These groups shared farming traditions and other features connected with their geophysical locations, such as fishing (in coastal and riverine communities), hunting, net-making, blacksmithing, weaving, cloth dying, trading, boat-making, and healing practices, among others.[6]

Some groups also maintained livestock, with various degrees of success, usually at the domestic level, but the nomadic nature of Fulani migrants easily met the larger socioeconomic requirements of this practice.[7] The Lake Chad basin was a flourishing field of habitation for the people, but at various times around the fifteenth century this population migrated from different parts of Africa into the area later known as Northern Nigeria. Unlike other migrant groups, due to their specific nature as an itinerant population, they frequently settled among Hausa communities without establishing any political formation or power.[8]

Between the eighteenth and nineteenth centuries, political entities in the Niger area underwent a major transformation to consolidate existing hegemonies. Events of this period recalibrated extant political formations in a way that demonstrated how war became a harbinger of societal transformation and change. Two basic units of analysis have been developed over time to understand how these polities were organized and governed: centralized and acephalous states. By the nineteenth century, some of these polities had evolved broader, sophisticated political systems and structures that were analogous to their European counterparts, and others existed as pockets of independent

---

[5] Jacob F. A. Ajayi, "Africa at the Beginning of the Nineteenth Century: Issues and Prospects," in *General History of Africa – VI: Africa in the Nineteenth Century until the 1880s*, ed. Jacob F. A. Ajayi (Oxford: Heinemann Educational Publishers, 1995), 1–24.

[6] Richard O. Ekundare, *An Economic History of Nigeria 1860–1960* (London: Methuen & Co Ltd., 1973).

[7] Derrick J. Stenning, "Transhumance, Migratory Drift, Migration: Patterns of Pastoral Fulani Nomadism," *The Journal of the Royal Anthropological Institute of Great Britain and Ireland* 87, no. 1 (1957): 57–73.

[8] Frank L. Lambrecht, "The Pastoral Nomads of Nigeria," *Expedition Magazine* 18, no. 3 (1976): 26–31.

ministates governed through different political morphologies to suit their environment.[9] A few factors can be attributed to these developments, but their geophysical surroundings were a primary cause. These fixtures dictated the economic activities that were fundamental to their military and political behavior, and they also shaped the population of these polities and their relationships with neighbors.

Acephalous states were never excluded from political dynamics, especially the military and diplomatic interactions that often gave rise to centralized states. As with the centralized states, these entities survived years of conflict and cooperation with close and distant neighbors.[10] However, only some of them came close to developing a centralized state before the nineteenth century. Many of these polities were found in the modern Nigerian state's creeks, swamps, and mountainous regions. Dozens, if not hundreds, of independent ministates existed in locations that ranged from the plateau regions north of the Niger River to the spaces inhabited by the Igbo (or Ugbo) and O-kun communities to its south. These groups were ruled either by dynasties or conferences of elders. Their geographic locations protected them from being annexed by more powerful neighbors with more sophisticated political cultures. Such neighbors would have needed to conquer hundreds of small villages, and it was difficult to administer these settlements from a remote location as hundreds of local representatives would have been necessary.

The composition and geography of these polities reduced their economic value to the campaigns that Obaro Ikime has described as "overlapping Imperialism,"[11] due to their dramatic and ubiquitous manifestation. In the nineteenth century, in place of bringing these polities under a political canopy, powerful neighbors turned them into reserve pools of slave labor. In Oyo, Nupe, the Hausa states of Katsina and Kano, Benin, and others, and much later, Ibadan and Ilorin in the nineteenth century, these communities became areas of influence within larger states.

The arrangements developed among powerful states are best understood from the standpoint of contemporary relations between powerful and weak states. The latter becomes a proxy to be manipulated in ways that advance the geopolitical interests of the former. For example, deals were occasionally made between Old Oyo and Benin to determine the fate of acephalous communities in the Ekiti region of what became known as Yorubaland.[12] By similar measures of authority, the O-kun region was shared by different military factions

---

[9] Sati U. Fwatshak, "Reconstructing the Origins of the People of Plateau State: Questioning the 'We are all Settlers' Theory," *Journal of the Historical Society of Nigeria* 16 (2005/2006): 122–140.

[10] Philip T. Ahire, ed., *The Tiv in Contemporary Nigeria* (Zaria: Tiv Studies Project, 1993).

[11] Obaro Ikime, *Can Anything Good Come Out of History?* (Ibadan: Bookcraft, 2019), 89.

[12] Peter Morton-Williams, "The Oyo and the Atlantic Trade 1670–1830," *Journal of the Historical Society of Nigeria* 3, no.1 (1964): 25–45.

and groups from Ibadan, Nupe, and Ilorin in the nineteenth century. Most of the slaves sold into the transatlantic trade in the Nigerian area before the nineteenth century's general political implosions were drawn from weaker groups, either from the north or south of the Niger. These settlements were small and easy to raid. For instance, this realization led the polities known as the Egba to cluster together in one location, Abeokuta, to protect themselves. This was an exceptional development because cooperation among these polities rarely took place to oppose a formidable force that threatened their existence. Instead, such alliances were normally created as acts of retribution against neighbors with unresolved issues.

Culture and civilization were contagious, and cultural exchanges perpetually circulated among polities around the Niger area, regardless of their system of political organization. Some resulted from conquest, and others took place as diplomatic gestures aimed to forge alliances for purposes that ranged from security to prestige.[13] When a small polity is linked with a larger one, it serves as a deterrent to others – territorial integrity was secured, at least until the collapse of the more powerful entity due to a new challenger that had become strong enough to supplant it.

Some affiliations developed to claim the prestige that came from sharing the heritage of a powerful neighbor. In other cases, it had nothing to do with relationships or dichotomies between weaker and stronger states. Cultural exchanges and political links occurred between two powerful states to enhance their geopolitical interests and consolidate the political positions of the ethnic groups in the region. In place of tapping into other cultures to demonstrate loyalty and receive protection and shared glory, they engaged with those cultures to reinforce their authority and status in relation to the culture they borrowed from.

Trade and political relations provided a concrete basis for intermingling among Nigerian peoples and cultures, influencing their shared fate and history before the advent of colonialism.[14] Scholars such as Jacob F. A. Ajayi and Kenneth Dike have emphasized the significance of these dynamics for the creation of modern Nigeria, many of which have been considered to be more of a problem than an advantage throughout their careers.[15] Ile-Ife traditions are invariably linked to Benin, Benin to Eastern Yoruba settlements and the delta states, Hausa states to Tiv, Jukun to Igala, Nupe to Oyo, Borno to cultures

---

[13] Gabriel A. Akinola, "The Origin of the Eweka Dynasty of Benin: A Study in the Use and Abuse of Oral Traditions," *Journal of the Historical Society of Nigeria* 8, no.3 (1976): 21–36.

[14] Dawood O. Egbefo and Hadizat A. Salihu, "The Impact of Trade and Commercial Activities in Pre-colonial Esan Economy up to 1900," *SAU Journal of Humanities* 2, no. 1&2 (2014): 164–175.

[15] Jacob F. A. Ajayi, "Towards a More Enduring Sense of History," Being a Tribute to K. O. Dike on Behalf of the Historical Society of Nigeria, October, 1983.

around the Lake Chad basin, Idoma to Igbo, and hosts of others whose history and evolution are intertwined. At one time, the Oba of Benin was required to receive his royal insignia and legitimacy from the Ooni of Ife.[16] In a similar vein, the Attah of Idah was responsible for the authority and legitimacy of the Chief of Panda, serving as the custodian for his staff of office.[17] Similar relationships existed between the Idoma from Wukari, the Tiv from Jukun, some Eastern Yoruba states like Akure, Owo, Akoko, and others from Benin.[18] This interaction level led to transferring one community's political office and title to a different community.[19] None of these arrangements was static as they often evolved and revolved within the reality of overlapping imperialism that modified them.

In the second half of the eighteenth century, the bubble burst for many of the strong polities in the Niger area of West Africa. Gradual consolidation culminated in vast structures and territories controlled by the empires and kingdoms of this period.[20] Many of these states had trouble administering their acquisitions, and they became an albatross as one century continued into the next. Vassal states had been making constant demands for independence, and a clamor for political reform was on the horizon.[21]

Developments during the period examined in this chapter were shaped by five principal events: the slave trade abolition and the switch to legitimate trade; the Sokoto Jihad; the decline and collapse of the Old Oyo Empire; freed captives returning from Sierra Leone, along with the arrival of missionaries; and the advent of colonial rule.[22] The political developments connected with Oyo and the Uthman dan Fodio jihad in the north should not suggest that other polities were politically irrelevant during the same period. This classification represents key developments affecting small and powerful polities in the Niger area. Their effect on the dynamics of political development in the region

---

[16] Alan F. C. Ryder, "A Reconsideration of the Ife–Benin Relationship," *Journal of African History* 6, no. 1 (1965): 25–37.

[17] James R. Wilson-Haffenden, "Ethnological Notes on the Kwottos of Toto (Panda) District, Keffi Division, Benue Province, Northern Nigeria," *Journal of the Royal African Society* 27, no. 108 (1928): 380–393.

[18] Uwomano Benjamin Okpevra, "The Dynamics of Intergroup Relations in Pre-Colonial Nigeria up to 1800: A Reappraisal of a Lopsided Historiography," *LWATI: A Journal of Contemporary Research* 11, no. 1 (2014): 126–143.

[19] Stephen A. Akintoye, "The North-Eastern Yoruba Districts and the Benin Kingdom," *Journal of the Historical Society of Nigeria* 4, no. 4 (1969): 539–553.

[20] Yusuf B. Usman, *The Transformation of Katsina, 1400–1883: The Emergence and Overthrow of the Sarauta System and Establishment of the Emirate* (Zaria: Ahmadu Bello University Press, 1981).

[21] Joseph A. Atanda, "The Fall of the Old Oyọ Empire: A Re-consideration of Its Cause," *Journal of the Historical Society of Nigeria* 5, no. 4 (1971): 477–490.

[22] A. Orugbani, *Nigeria Since the 19th Century* (Port Harcourt: Paragraphics, 2005).

provided a ready pretext for the colonial administration to establish its political authority.

The weakening of the Old Oyo polity and its eventual collapse in the 1830s meant that hundreds of communities from the former empire became newly independent.[23] These changes began in the late eighteenth century and continued for most of the following century. By the late eighteenth century the Alaafin already controlled a political entity that covered almost the entire region of modern Southwestern Nigeria.[24] When its political bubble burst, the Old Oyo Empire stretched across an area bigger than many contemporary European states.

Some of the newly independent states attempted to fill the power vacuum that Old Oyo left behind, leading to another sequence of important events during this period.[25] By 1810, Uthman dan Fodio and his Muslim forces had seized almost every major polity except Borno in the northern Niger region.[26] The political formation that followed joined communities under the Borno Empire that stretched from this area down to the Niger basin. It swept up large polities like Kano, Katsina, Nupe, and parts of the Old Oyo vassal states, particularly Ilorin, that had caused trouble for others in the northeastern region of the empire.[27] During this same period, the great Benin Empire was another large polity across the Niger and far to the east of Oyo.[28] It underwent the same purge that occurred in Oyo and the Hausa states. Similar events unfolded in Nupe[29] and Borgu,[30] two other prominent polities in precolonial West Africa.

The magnitude of political eruption in West Africa from the late eighteenth century through most of the nineteenth century suggests a significant moment for the evolution and formation of states in the region. And this was only

---

[23] Atanda, "The Fall of the Old Oyọ Empire."
[24] Robin Law, "A West African Cavalry State: The Kingdom of Oyo," *The Journal of African History* 16, no. 1 (1975): 1–15.
[25] Bolanle Awe, "The Rise of Ibadan as a Yoruba Power in the Nineteenth Century," unpublished PhD dissertation, University of Oxford, 1964.
[26] Ibraheem Sulaiman, *A Revolution in History: The Jihad of Usman Dan Fodio* (London: Mansell Publishing, 1987).
[27] Stephanie Zehnle, *A Geography of Jihad: Sokoto Jihadism and the Islamic Frontier in West Africa* (Berlin: De Gruyter, 2020).
[28] Jacob Egharevba, *A Short History of Benin* (Ibadan: Ibadan University Press, 1968).
[29] Femi J. Kolapo, "The Dynamics of Early 19th Century Nupe Wars," *Scientia Militaria – South African Journal of Military Studies* 31, no. 2 (2012): 14–35; and Femi J. Kolapo, "Military Turbulence, Population Displacement and Commerce on a Southern Frontier of the Sokoto Caliphate: Nupe c.1810–1857," unpublished PhD dissertation, York University, 1999.
[30] Marjorie H. Stewart, "The Borgu People of Nigeria and Benin: The Disruptive Effect of Partition on Traditional Political and Economic Relations," *Journal of the Historical Society of Nigeria* 12, no. 3–4 (1985): 95–120.

a microcosm of events in other parts of Africa.[31] The foreign policy of the Benin Empire was unlike that of Old Oyo, taking on a more benign form of soft imperialism.[32] Benin's decline during the same period did little to affect larger polities, and it did not have the same ripple effects seen in Old Oyo.[33] The empire had refused overtures from early European merchants looking to trade in human cargo, concentrating instead on farm products and expecting similar tribute from its outlying states, although this did not prevent it from taking slaves as its political power increased.[34] Coastal states under its influence were given substantial leeway to control their ports and trade, which meant that the empire's decline and the independence of its component polities resulted in few changes.

All through the history of the Old Oyo polity, Nupe stood as a formidable counterpart.[35] Sometimes Old Oyo collected tributes from Nupe to ensure its loyalty, and sometimes it served as a tributary entity to the Oyo empire. Nupe constituted a larger, central polity for pockets of communities. The coming of Tsoede in the fifteenth century made it even more powerful.[36] However, when the polity declined in the nineteenth century, this coincided with the continuous spread of the jihad from the North that took over its political affairs and saved it from the political disintegration suffered by Oyo.[37] These frames, which qualify as signifiers for nineteenth-century developments in the Niger area, triggered waves of change in every aspect of society.

Political Developments

The nineteenth century was significant and strategic for the evolution of states across West Africa and the entire continent. Developments of this period were similar to the creation of states in the fifteenth century, especially in the West African region. Events from that period resulted in the formation and expansion of polities that would be reconstituted in the nineteenth century. This trend repeated even as time and circumstances brought different changes

---

[31] John B. Webster and Albert A. Boahen, *The Revolutionary Years: West Africa Since 1800* (London: Longman, 1967).

[32] Ebiuwa Aisien and Felix O. U. Oriakhi, "Great Benin on the World Stage: Re-assessing Portugal–Benin Diplomacy in the 15th and 16th Centuries," *IOSR Journal of Humanities and Social Science* 11, no. 1 (2013): 107–115.

[33] Philip A. Igbafe, "The Fall of Benin: A Reassessment," *The Journal of African History* 11, no. 3 (1970): 385–400.

[34] H. M. Feinberg, "Review of Benin and the Europeans 1485–1897," *African Historical Studies* 4, no. 2 (1971): 405–410.

[35] Robert Smith, "The Alafin in Exile: A Study of the Igboho Period in Oyo History," *The Journal of African History* 6, no. 1 (1965): 57–77.

[36] Smith, "The Alafin in Exile."

[37] Idris S. Jimada, *The Historical Background to the Establishment of Patigi Emirate: c. 1810–1898* (Zaria: Ahmadu Bello University, 2016).

within the same polities. The rise and fall of polities in the fifteenth century around Central Sudan brought new social systems and political developments that characterized the subsequent period.[38] The fall of polities such as Ife and Mali coincided with the opening of trade across the Atlantic.

These developments brought remarkable societal changes by introducing new items and practices to signify modernity and status. Changes to regional currency systems altered the economic morphologies of societies to the point where colonial rule was merely the icing on a previously baked cake. The factors at play during the decline of local empires influenced the specific forms of colonial administration.

The aftereffects of a polity collapsing due to natural disasters, climate change, or related economic decline differ from those present when religious and political wars drive the collapse. The fall of the Mali Empire was significant for the spread of Islam in West Africa. By the eighteenth century, the Tuaregs and the nomadic Fulani population were founding and leading reformist movements locally referred to as the *Qadiriyya* brotherhood.[39] The first such movement to link its philosophy of Islam with militarization and political action was in the Futa Jallon region of Senegambia in 1727. The campaign ended the following year, although pockets of insurrection remained active. The following campaign ended with the death of Abd al-Qadi in the Futa Toro region in the 1770s.[40]

During this same period, dan Fodio had developed a substantial following among the Hausa, Fulani, and Tuareg populations of major Hausa states. Most of these people were peasants and members of the lowest rungs of society. A campaign for change gathered substantial momentum among these groups. Neither the Tuaregs nor the Fulani formed sovereign political entities of their own. The nature of their economic activities as nomads and traders made it easier for them to settle within states formed by other groups who had migrated into the Niger area. The Tuareg and Fulani were valued for their Islamic knowledge and Arabic education, which they brought to their host communities. The *Ulama* were close to the Hausa rulers and their elite classes, although they held different views on the nature of Islam to be practiced in these states. They also disagreed over what constituted true Islam in the views of the time.

The changes proposed by dan Fodio's Islamic reformists, starting in the 1770s, were ignored by states for economic and political reasons. In Gobir, dan Fodio assisted King Yunfa in claiming the throne, and it was hoped that they

---

[38] Akinwunmi Ogundiran, *The Yoruba: A New History* (Bloomington: Indiana University Press, 2020).

[39] Roland Oliver and Anthony Atmore, *Africa since 1800* (Cambridge: Cambridge University Press, 2005), 63–77.

[40] Toyin Falola and Matthew M. Heaton, *A History of Nigeria* (New York: Cambridge University Press, 2008), 73.

could work together to implement reforms. However, Yunfa was unwilling to implement key elements of the reformists' campaign, and he antagonized them with the full force of the state. This was a prelude to events that would follow the end of the first campaign, which ran between 1804 and 1808, shaping Islam's subsequent spread and form across the Niger.[41]

In Hausaland, Islam was co-opted into the traditional belief system of the people, which made it easier for its ideas to spread across society.[42] The religion was adopted as a state religion in the great Borno Empire in the eleventh century, and it has played major roles in social and political systems since then, bringing Arab culture and civilization along with it.[43] However, it had little influence over economic transactions in the region. Although Islam was fundamental for state systems of administration, it had little or no effect on the adjudication of cases, economic transactions, or financial systems. It was unable to change the legal scope of enslavement. These differences formed points of departure between regional establishments and Muslims who wished to reform them.

Fashion, clothing styles, and cultural attitudes toward dress in Nigerian societies were influenced by Arabs, the Christian missionaries that followed, freed captives, and other agents of Western taxonomic modernity. Dan Fodio's demands for "true" Islam included a dress code that adhered to his ideas of modesty. Another traditional practice that dan Fodio opposed was the exchange of tokens for favors. Colonial records would later describe these activities as bribes that had permeated the socioeconomic behavior of the people, influencing the administration of justice in exchange for favors. Peasants paid bribes to the ruling elites and nobles – either willingly or under coercion – to gain favor in the court and other administrative matters. It was believed that the implementation of a Shari'a justice system would purge society of these practices.

Reformists also opposed slavery. The slave trade was the bedrock of economic growth for the major Hausa states, as it had been in Old Oyo since Borno rose to prominence. Borno's rise brought the spread of Islam to the population of this region, opening markets in North Africa and the Arab world from which Islam originated. Many victims of the slave trade in Hausa territory were Muslims. Reformists denounced these practices. They stated that under true Islamic belief it is prohibited for a Muslim to enslave a fellow Muslim or for a non-Muslim to enslave a Muslim. As Muslims, they were to stand apart from society's social ladder, and this dignifying doctrine cemented

---

[41] Samuel N. Nwabara, "The Fulani Conquest and Rule of the Hausa Kingdom of Northern Nigeria (1804–1900)," *Journal des Africanistes* 33, no. 2 (1963): 231–242.

[42] Mahdi Adamu, *The Hausa Factor in West African History* (Zaria: Ahmadu Bello University Press, 1978).

[43] Hamsatu Z. Laminu, *Scholars and Scholarship in the History of Borno* (Zaria: Open Press, 1993).

the fate of Oyo in the first half of the nineteenth century, during the 1817 Muslim uprising. These views limited the revenues that could be collected by the palace, the royal family, nobles, and those who participated in the slave trade. Only society's wealthiest and most influential members could profit from investments in slavery.

The opposition to slavery remained a point of contention between the Islamic advocacy of the reformists and that of Borno state. Borno's scholars accused the reformists of hypocrisy because their invasion of Borno territory was an attack on fellow Muslims.[44] However, the jihadists saw them as infidels who practiced syncretic Islam. The campaign's focus on a review of the tax regime in the states it targeted suggests that their goals involved deconstructing the elite class.

Concerns over polytheism and dress codes had no real economic effects, but many reformist demands disproportionately affected the ruling elite. They meant to transform the status quo and build a new society based on what they considered authentic Islam. Their desires pitted Hausa rulers against the reformists, framed as a struggle between cultural traditions and the "civilization" that Islam brought.[45] Those who preferred the status quo aligned with the establishment, and others organized around the resistance. Although Yunfa promised that his ascension to the throne would bring reforms, he reinforced restrictions that his predecessor in Gobir had placed on the practice of Islam and Islamic culture. Men were prohibited from wearing turbans, and women were forbidden from wearing hijabs or other clothing associated with Islam. Yunfa also refused to allow his subjects to convert to Islam. Some of dan Fodio's followers responded by fleeing their settlements in Gobir.

At this point, it was clear to Yunfa and other northern elites that dan Fodio had acquired substantial influence in the sociopolitical atmosphere of the state. In 1804, he was expelled from the kingdom while his followers refused to return after their new homes were subjected to a deadly invasion from Yunfa's forces. This led to dan Fodio's acclaimed holy journey, which parallels the Prophet's journey from Mecca to Medina in the seventh century. Dan Fodio moved from Degel in Gobir to Gudu in Gwandu. His political reform campaign was militarized there, and his supporters mobilized as dan Fodio realized that the ruling elites had manipulated his campaign for their gain since reforms that threatened the existing status quo would never be willingly implemented. Within six years, principal Hausa kingdoms from Gwandu, Katsina, Kano, Zaria, Gobir, Zamfara, Kebbi, and parts of the Borno Empire came under the

[44] Aziz A. Batran, "The Nineteenth Century Islamic Revolution in West Africa," in *General History of Africa VI: Africa in the Nineteenth Century until the 1880s*, ed. Jacob F. A. Ajayi (Berkeley: University of California, 1989), 539–554.

[45] Murray Last, "The Sokoto Caliphate and Borno," in *General History of Africa – VI: Africa in the Nineteenth Century until the 1880s*, ed. Jacob F. A. Ajayi (Paris: UNESCO Publishing, 1998), 558.

reformists' newly established political order.[46] New polities were also created, including Fombina, the largest emirate established by the reformists, with its capital in Yola.[47] Borno's charges of hypocrisy were validated during the years of the jihad and the following establishment of the caliphate. Not only were Muslims displaced and enslaved during the unrest that preceded the establishment of the caliphate in 1810, despite the claims that true Islam opposed slavery, but these people were also subjected to the same indignities under the new political order.[48]

Although its power and influence were at their lowest ebb during this time, Borno managed to stave off the jihadist forces until the British occupation of the area in 1903 that incorporated both of them into the colonial state.[49] The jihad continued through "flag bearers" who operated through different cells at various times. Dan Fodio returned to teaching and other spiritual activities, taking the title of caliph and leaving the new order's administration to his two sons and others.[50]

Dan Fodio's caliphate, now headquartered in Sokoto, was divided and ruled from two axes: east and west.[51] Both entities provided authority and support to flag bearers operating within their administrative spheres. Muhammad Bello, the eldest son of dan Fodio, took charge of the larger entity and claimed the seat of power in Sokoto. Bello's brother, Abdullahi, controlled the remaining territory.[52] Reforms were effected to influence clothing and fashion, introduce Shari'a law, and reconstitute the defense system. The new administration also increased the spread of Arabic education and training of *ulamas*, and adopted the *Kofa* system of royal representation.[53] However, the new order faced fundamental challenges that impaired its campaign for complete social transformation.

Using a *Ribat* security network, the leadership of the caliphate built garrisons that reassured the population, demonstrating that the caliphate could ensure their security.[54] Compared with the spread of Islamic teaching and

---

[46] Zehnle, *A Geography of Jihad*.
[47] Alkasum Abba, *History of Yola, 1809-1914: The Establishment and Evolution of a Metropolis* (Zaria: Ahmadu Bello University, 2003).
[48] Thomas Hodgkin, "Islam and National Movements in West Africa," *The Journal of African History* 3, no. 2 (1962): 323-327.
[49] Marc-Antoine Pérouse de Montclos, "Boko Haram and 'Sahelistan' Terrorism Narratives: A Historical Perspective," *Afrique contemporaine* 255, no. 3 (2015): 18-39.
[50] Zehnle, *A Geography of Jihad*.
[51] Zehnle, *A Geography of Jihad*.
[52] Hamza M. Maishanu and Isa M. Maishanu, "The Jihād and the Formation of the Sokoto Caliphate," *Islamic Studies* 38, no. 1 (1999): 119-131.
[53] Sarah Eltantawi, *Shari'ah on Trial: Northern Nigeria's Islamic Revolution* (Berkeley: University of California Press, 2017), 40-65.
[54] Mohammed B. Salau, "Ribats and the Development of Plantations in the Sokoto Caliphate: A Case Study of Fanisau," *African Economic History* 34 (2006): 23-43.

Arabic education, this network was also more successful at preventing revolt and muting dissenting voices within the caliphate. As its territory expanded, the situation worsened, especially after the death of dan Fodio in 1817. That same year, Abd al-Salam began a revolt against the caliphate.[55] Al-Salam was one of dan Fodio's compatriots who had led the earlier emigration of peasants and other *Kadirawas* (the local name of the resistance) from Gobir to Kebbi in the formative years of the jihad. He felt that his political authority was not substantial enough after the importance of his role in the jihad. Others started their respective opposition movements for various reasons revolving around political decisions and the administration of the caliphate. Similar complaints fueled the Buhari uprising and the Kano civil war that lasted for a few years.

Despite this ongoing turmoil, the caliphate's endurance can be attributed to its decentralized administrative system. Emirs had the autonomy to administer their emirates at their discretion, in compliance with Islamic tenets. The sultan could only assent to the decisions made by emirates in selecting their emirs, except on rare occasions, such as the events leading to the Kano civil war. This limited the sultan's control to a supervisory role and assisted the operations of flag bearers who seized control of captured territories. Under the flag bearers, the jihadists moved into the Niger River basin and became instruments of power, counterpower, and the balance of power in state politics from 1810 onward.[56] From Rabba, where the Islamic State had been established, they became a major force in internal struggles for power between Nupe princes.[57]

Jihadists swayed political developments in the Niger basin through military strength; wealth acquired through raids, tributes, trade, and war booty; and reformist ideas that strengthened the political currency of any faction seeking power. This continued until the colonial invasion. Igalaland, Lafiagi, Shonga, and many other areas were incorporated into the caliphate.[58] By 1850, the western border of the caliphate stretched from Nupe, under the rule of Etsu Masaba, to encompass Koton Karfe, Lokoja, and surrounding communities in the Igala area.[59] The Yoruba garrison town of Ilorin was also brought under the

---

[55] Mukhtar U. Bunza, "The Application of Islamic Law and the Legacies of Good Governance in the Sokoto Caliphate, Nigeria (1804–1903): Lessons for the Contemporary Period," *Electronic Journal of Islamic and Middle Eastern Law* 1 (2013): 94.

[56] Marc-Antoine Pérouse de Montclos, "The Spread of Jihadist Insurrections in Niger and Nigeria: An Analysis Based on the Case of Boko Haram," in *Transnational Islam: Circulation of Religious Ideas, Actors and Practices between Niger and Nigeria*, ed. Elodie Apard (Ibadan: IFRA-Nigeria, 2020), 152–179.

[57] Jimada, *The Historical Background*.

[58] Kolapo, "The Dynamics of Early 19th Century Nupe," 17.

[59] Audu Jacob, "Precolonial Political Administration in the North Central Nigeria: A Study of the Igala Political Kingdom," *European Scientific Journal* 10, no. 19 (2014): 401.

caliphate's banner around 1817 after the death of Afonja, the Yoruba warlord who controlled the town.[60]

While the jihadists' movement swept across northern states, power was shifting in the region to the south of the Niger. Old Oyo had been the dominant force in the area, but it experienced a major decline after the sixteenth-century consolidation of the polity. Internal divisions among Oyo chiefs and military leaders were exacerbated by the actions of Basorun Gaha in the second half of the eighteenth century.[61] Around this time, dan Fodio was gaining ground in major northern states. For the Nupe, this period marked the end of peaceful administration. Internal tussles followed, and the Fulani minority acquired most of the polity's political power through their influence in commanding jihadist soldiers.[62]

Benin also witnessed a major political purge during this time. Polities such as those in the Warri delta area began to claim independence by exploiting political weaknesses. After its rise to prominence in the second part of the eighteenth century, the people of Old Oyo had grown weary of the Alaafin. They felt subjected to increasing despotism under successive leaders, and Basorun Gaha used his role as prime minister to usurp power from the Alaafin.[63] In theory, the Alaafin was the king who issued commanding orders and exercised state power but in practice, it was the prime minister who held the power. Basorun Gaha came to be feared for his atrocities, but the people had no means of removing him. After installing and deposing four successive Alaafins between the 1750s and 1774, the fifth Alaafin found a way to turn the tables: Alaafin Abiodun discreetly mobilized support to oppose the prime minister, which led to an attack on Basorun Gaha's home in which he was killed.[64] The peaceful rule of Alaafin Abiodun was the end of an era in Oyo politics.[65]

Nupe and Old Oyo were plagued by similar internal wrangling. Arguments over who would become the Alaafin, and Afonja's decision to render the throne irrelevant, meant struggles between different political blocs in the empire. The empire's major decline led to the 1817 Muslim insurrection and the capital's movement to the South after the original site was brought to ruin

---

[60] Aliyu A. Idress, "Ilorin Factor in the 19th Century Nupe Politics: A Study in the Inter-Emirate Relations within Sokoto Caliphate, Nigeria," *Transafrican Journal of History* 20 (1991): 181–189.

[61] Robin C. C. Law, "The Constitutional Troubles in Oyo in the Eighteenth Century," *The Journal of African History* 12, no. 1 (1971): 25–44.

[62] Idris S. Jimada, *The Nupe and the Origins and Evolution of Yoruba c.1275–1897* (Zaria: The Abdullahi Smith Centre for Historical Research, 2005).

[63] Samuel Johnson, *The History of the Yorubas from the Earliest Times to the Beginning of the British Protectorate* (Lagos: CSS Press, 1921).

[64] Johnson, *The History of the Yorubas*.

[65] Robin Law, *The Oyo Empire c.1600–c.1836: A West African Imperialism in the Era of the Atlantic Slave Trade* (London: Oxford University Press, 1977).

in the 1830s. The trade network between Old Oyo and its northern neighbors had brought a proliferation of the Hausa population in the empire's capital and its component polities.[66] Hausa captives in Oyo were valued for their Arabic and Islamic education skills. Their knowledge earned them positions at the top of the empire's administrative structure, and their other responsibilities outside the royal court integrated the Hausa into Oyo society. Islam and Islamic culture had spread so widely through the empire that by 1817, when the uprising rallied around the idea of repelling an infidel state, it gathered significant support from the Yoruba population. Others joined these Hausa and Yoruba Muslims from Ilorin.

After the reign of Alaafin Abiodun around 1789, Afonja formed a team to reduce Old Oyo's influence by weakening the Alaafin's office. Afonja could not mount a legitimate claim to the throne, especially not from his location in Ilorin. Two important allies of Afonja were Solagbreu, a wealthy Muslim friend and convert, and Alimi, an Islamic scholar and warlord of Fulani origin.[67] These pragmatic choices represented both sides of the conflict in Afonja's strategic alliance. Their collaboration also signaled Afonja's commitment to subverting the authority of Old Oyo to claim the throne for the Ilorin. Solagbreu was expected to use his financial resources to sustain and enhance the army, prosecuting military campaigns. Alimi's strengths included a formidable number of soldiers and nuanced military expertise. He was believed to have possessed traditional powers, and he was known to command skilled cavalry forces.

Afonja's soldiers and allies were largely Muslims, but he remained a "pagan" who hoped to use these forces for his agenda. This suggests that he had a limited understanding of geopolitical developments in the Niger area, especially on the other side of the Niger, even as jihadists there were advancing and steadily expanding their base. Internal discord and discontent among the lower classes allowed the jihadists to gain support for their opposition to the ruling bodies in many of these polities.

Alimi was part of the wave of Fulani warlords who migrated to the Niger and Benue areas after the establishment and spread of the caliphate after 1810. In the name of Islam, they took control of territories that ranged from Nupe to Ilorin. Afonja, who had refused to convert to Islam, was surrounded by individuals with divergent interests during his campaign to topple Old Oyo and reinforce Ilorin. Their common goal was to bring down Oyo, which served as the modus operandi of the jihadists. Beyond this, it remained to be seen how Alimi and the jihadist forces would support an "infidel" in his bid for political power.

---

[66] Olatunji Ojo, "The Organization of the Atlantic Slave Trade in Yorubaland, Ca. 1777 to Ca.1856," *The International Journal of African Historical Studies* 41, no. 1 (2008): 77–100.

[67] Johnson, *The History of the Yorubas*.

After the implosion of Old Oyo, during which Hausa slaves repaid the injustices that they had suffered under their former masters, this conflict became clear. Afonja was accused of excesses ranging from stealing and dispossession of people's properties to heavy-handedness. Some questioned whether he was fit to hold power and consolidate the different elements of the former Yoruba garrison town. He was eventually executed in a serious conflict between his tiny faction and the larger reformist group. After the first phase of the jihad ended in 1810, the reformist flag bearers transformed the movement's religious drive and messaging into political currency.

After the fall of the Old Oyo, Ibadan organized mercenaries into military expeditions led by different warlords. Their methods were similar to those of the Fulani Jihadists, the Hausa, the Tuareg, and compatriots from other cultures. Military networks established to maintain a balance of power had reinforced the presence of the Fulani elements across many parts of the Niger's northern end. This eventually took form in Yorubaland as well. As Old Oyo was gradually brought to ruin, Alimi became its former garrison town's political and spiritual leader. Like dan Fodio, he turned its administration over to his son, Abdul-Salam.[68]

With Ilorin as the new center of jihadist activity, and because of its close location to Yorubaland, it planned a campaign to spread Islam from the western end of the caliphate while the southern wave of the movement from Gwandu was to be launched from here. Ilorin's role was similar to that of Nupe in the north-central region of the Niger. The weakening of Oyo's hegemony had seen increasing military raids to claim captives that would be sold to the Atlantic market. Other maneuvers suggested that the cat was away and the mice were out to play. Ilorin was not the sole power seeking to supplant Oyo. At the former empire's western border, the towns of Ijebu, Owu, and, eventually, Abeokuta, Ijaiye, and Ibadan emerged to claim power.

The activities of Ijebu and Ife slave merchants in the popular Apomu market led to two wars in Ife territory, fought by the country's various political factions seeking to control trade and competition.[69] Conflict over the market town became a proxy war to assert power over the region. The Alaafin lent authority to Ijaiye, Owu, and Ogbomoso, which meant that whichever belligerent faction prevailed would have ongoing implications for the Alaafin's role in the unfolding future of the country.[70] Around 1817, the allied forces of Ife and

---

[68] Abdullahi Smith, "A Little New Light on the Collapse of the Alafinate of Yoruba," in *Studies in Yoruba History and Culture*, ed. Gabriel O. Olusanya (Ibadan: University Press, 1983), 42–71.

[69] Isaac A. Akinjogbin, ed., *War and Peace in Yorubaland, 1793–1893* (Ibadan: Heinemann Educational Books, 1998).

[70] Earlier in the century, the town of Apomu was established by the joint forces of Ooni Otutubiosun, Alaafin Majeogbe, and the Awujale of Ijebu, settling a rift that developed after accusations that Majeogbe was illegally trading slaves. The establishment of the

Ijebu – later reinforced by the fleeing Oyo population – displaced Owu. The ripple effects of this schism's major fallout included Egba towns and villages being displaced from their forest areas.[71] More than 100 small and large polities were dissolved, and their people were enslaved as the spoils of war. They were brought to the Ibadan camp of the allied forces, which was established in the territory previously occupied by this displaced population.

The camp transformed into a strong political entity in West Africa and subsequently vanquished its rivals – Ijaiye, Ijebu, and the Egba – in their newly constituted town of Abeokuta. By capturing the heart of the Yoruba country, it became the incarnation of Old Oyo's maneuverings in the Ijaiye war of 1860-5. About two decades before this decisive faceoff, Ibadan had established its authority in the evolving politics of Yoruba territory when it repelled the forceful incursion of jihadist forces from Ilorin.[72] The military confrontation pushed the latter group from Osogbo to Offa, where they met their final defeat in 1840.[73] Around this same period, the Egba people of Ibadan escaped to new homes that were protected by hills and rocks. They arrived at these locations in small groups and rebuilt their lost culture. The Egba nation had formed about a century earlier, premised on the need for common security among a loose collection of polities led by Lisabi.[74] Security and safety had implicitly dominated the subconscious politics of the nation, which was at the root of their response to the allied siege on Owu. Their concerns grew stronger after the enslavement of the people from Ibadan.

The successful Egba escape from the Ibadan camp to arrive in Abeokuta was followed by a political organization based on a military structure. Sodeke led these efforts until his demise,[75] and in the 1850s, after years of interregnum, the system transformed into the modern experiments initiated by freed captives from Sierra Leone. Security consciousness generally supplanted the system of

---

market was an effort to restore the balance of power between these Yoruba populations, with each planting a tree at the location and calling it Apimo, a place of consensus. Isaac A. Akinjogbin, "The Growth of Ife from Oduduwa to 1800," in *The Cradle of a Race: Ife from the Beginning to 1980*, ed. Isaac A. Akinjogbin (Port Harcourt: Sunray Publications Ltd., 1978), 112.

[71] Jacob F. A. Ajayi and Robert S. Smith, *Yoruba Warfare in the 19th Century* (London: Cambridge University Press, 1964).

[72] Hakeem O. Danmole and Toyin Falola, "Ibadan–Ilorin Relations in the Nineteenth Century: A Study in Imperial Struggles in Yorubaland," *Transafrican Journal of History* 14 (1985): 21–35.

[73] Stephen A. Akintoye, *Revolution and Power Politics in Yorubaland 1840-1893: Ibadan Expansion and the Rise of Ekitiparapo* (Ibadan: Longman, 1971).

[74] Saburi Biobaku, *The First 150 Years of the Egba at Abeokuta (1830-1980)* (Ibadan: Institute of African Studies, 1983).

[75] Hakeem B. Harunah, "Sodeke: Hero and Statesman of the Egba," *Journal of the Historical Society of Nigeria* 12, no.1/2 (1984): 109–131.

divine royalty that had survived for about nine centuries in the region since the reign of Oduduwa in Ile-Ife around the tenth to eleventh centuries.[76]

Not only did Ibadan paradoxically become a military–republican state, it also influenced the activities and actions of communities that retained royal leaders. Although Ife was spared from military overthrow, the acclaimed cradle of civilization remained unsafe due to obligations imposed on its kinsmen in the newly constituted town of Modakeke.[77] This Modakeke population had refused to fight their kinsmen in Ibadan and abstained from getting involved in proxy wars with Ife. In response, attempts were made to reclaim the land originally given to them in the 1840s by Ooni Abeewala to secure their support.

By this time, the entire region had become militarized, and military skills became a valuable currency for navigating the social ladder of evolving polities. Military lords supported towns and kingdoms that were not organized around military leadership within or outside the polity.[78] Cells of military leaders in Ibadan developed so much independence and power that they could claim vassal states that answered to them through Ibadan's emblematic authority.

This same process permeated the polities of Hausa states and other northern entities during this period, including the Tiv and other polities in the Benue-Plateau valleys.[79] Several parts of Ekiti, an acephalous state, fell under the rule of these military lords. Their imperial adventures continued into the O-kun region of the Niger basin, which contained a plethora of small polities that included Ijumu, Ikiri, and Oworo. These communities were raided for slaves and war booty.[80] The defeat of the Ilorin forces at Offa failed to stop their ongoing incursions into Yorubaland whenever they saw an opportunity. By the 1850s, Ibadan occupied Oyo's former area of influence in the northeastern part of the country, claiming Igbomina, Ibolo, Ekiti, Akoko, and other areas that included the Ijesa and Ife communities to the south.[81]

Confrontations between Ibadan and Ilorin in these vassal states, especially those in the northeast, shaped the major events of this period until the 1886

---

[76] Toyin Falola and Dare Oguntomisin, *The Military in Nineteenth Century Yoruba Politics* (Ile-Ife: University of Ife Press, 1984).
[77] Isaac A. Akinjogbin, "Ife Years of Travail 1793–1893," in *The Cradle of a Race: Ife from the Beginning to 1980*, ed. Isaac. A. Akinjogbin (Port Harcourt: Sunray Publications Ltd., 1978), 153.
[78] Akanmu G. Adebayo, "Iwo: The Case Study of a Non-Belligerent Yoruba State in the 19th Century," in *War and Peace in Yorubaland, 1793–1893*, ed. Adeagbo Akinjogbin (Ibadan: Heinemann Educational Books, 1998), 91–98.
[79] Tesemchi Makar, *The History of Political Change among the Tiv in the 19th and 20th Centuries* (Enugu: Fourth Dimension Publishers, 1994).
[80] Ade Obayemi, "The Sokoto Jihad and the 'O-kun' Yoruba: A Review," *Journal of the Historical Society of Nigeria* 9, no. 2 (1978): 61–87.
[81] Olawale B. Salami, "Slaves, Government and Politics in Ibadan, 1835–1893," *IOSR Journal Of Humanities and Social Science* 3, no. 6 (2012): 13–17.

British intervention.[82] Just as the jihad and events in Old Oyo had shaped the Niger area's political landscape, the British government's abolition of slavery in 1807 – to support its vested interests – had dramatic effects on the flow of trade.[83] Human cargo was replaced by agricultural products that were described as "legitimate" trade, although the events and factors persisted that had driven the tremendous rise in the slave trade during this period. The jihad continued, Oyo's hegemony could no longer shape trade flow, and Oyo's vassal states gradually claimed independence.

The difference between legitimate and illegitimate trade was a matter of law, but both types of trade continued simultaneously until the second half of the nineteenth century. Ships loaded slaves and palm oil together until effective measures were taken to boost agricultural trade at the slave coast. The shift toward emphasizing palm oil and other produce posed challenges to communities that lacked the necessary resources, which, for instance, contributed to the decline of the Igala kingdom in the nineteenth century.[84] Igala had grown through its trade in human captives and had difficulty meeting the demand for palm oil. Other groups also had difficulty providing the commodities demanded by European merchants. However, these shifting priorities benefited Bonny, Old Calabar, Benin, and other delta states that could participate in this period's export economy.[85] This socioeconomic shift transformed the social fabric of societies from this point on.

The continued practice of slavery impeded farming and other economic activities that would support West African markets. The first step for increased production and economic growth, therefore, was to stop the slave trade. Antislavery patrols were strengthened, and Lagos, the most prominent slave port in West Africa, was bombarded by British naval forces in 1851.[86] The long-range assault demonstrated the power of modern technology, and half of Kosoko's men had fallen to the invasion before the British army landed. The decisive victory had palpable effects on the coastal city's political development for the rest of the century. The British government had become as influential in the area as the Fulani-led jihadists were in the northern states.

By putting their weight behind Akitoye, the British government established indirect control over the polity. Lagos had lost its sovereignty to the British government, which continued until its formal annexation and designation as a British protectorate in 1861. It was incorporated into the Nigerian

---

[82] Danmole and Falola, "Ibadan–Ilorin Relations," 21–35.
[83] Philip D. Curtin, *The Atlantic Slave Trade: A Census* (Madison: The University of Wisconsin Press, 1967), 224.
[84] Jacob, "Precolonial Political Administration."
[85] Obaro Ikime, *Niger Delta Rivalry: Itsekiri-Urhobo Relations and the European Presence, 1884–1926* (London: Longmans, 1969).
[86] Robert S. Smith, *The Lagos Consulate, 1851–1861* (Lagos: University of California Press, 1979).

colony in 1900.[87] Early control of Lagos was necessary for effectively coordinating British businesses interested in the Niger area as the leading export market.

The British government's presence in Lagos made it a key player in the political atmosphere of the Niger area. In 1886, when the government intervened in the Yorubaland crisis, it was able to stabilize the Oyo polity. Its intervention in Northern Nigeria, which sacked Sokoto and deposed Sultan Attahiru I in 1903, brought some sense of balance to the region as Borno's authority dwindled. The intervention of the British government, through the Royal Niger Company (RNC), decided the fate of many northern polities. Unfortunately for these polities, the British only removed political elites who resisted their colonial adventure, replacing them with more compliant ones. The same systems and structures of government expanded into areas unconquered by the caliphate.[88] In Abeokuta, the return of the freed captives began in the 1830s, and the presence of Christian missionaries, pioneered by Henry Townsend of the Church Missionary Society in the 1840s, engineered a new form of government. It was known as the Egba United Government.[89]

The Egba United Government instituted a constitutional monarchy, and returnees played a decisive role. The system was preferred to better engage the British government, which was the polity's major economic partner until it lost its independence to the Lagos government following the 1914 Ijemo massacre.[90] In Lagos and Abeokuta, Herbert Macaulay, Adegboyega Edun, and other returnees and their descendants shaped political currents within the emerging society.

Socioeconomic Transformations

Mongo Park and his team arrived at the base of the Niger River in 1795 as part of an expedition led by the African Association for the Promotion of Scientific Knowledge about Africa.[91] This was only one of many "scientific" explorations launched across the Niger by various Western imperial states. The scientific aspect of this enterprise was concerned with identifying locations in the

---

[87] Smith, *The Lagos Consulate*.
[88] Maiyaki M. Mejida, "Anthropological and Ethnographical Work on Bassa and Her Neighbours in the Nigeria Benue Valley: A Critical Assessment of Historical Reconstruction," *Journal of the Historical Society of Nigeria* 25 (2016): 61–79.
[89] Agneta Pallinder-Law, "Aborted Modernization in West Africa? The Case of Abeokuta," *The Journal of African History* 15, no. 1 (1974): 65–82.
[90] Harry A. Gailey, *Lugard and the Abeokuta Uprising: The Demise of Egba Independence* (New York: Routledge, 1982).
[91] Mungo Park, *Travels in the Interior of Africa* (Dublin: P. Hayes, 1825).

Niger area that could be exploited for trade, communications, and military movements following the abolition of the slave trade.[92]

Park's expedition opened trade routes for various Western imperial states from the "west to the eastern extremity of Africa."[93] Clapperton, Denham, Barth, the Lander brothers, and others furthered this exploration and established trading routes across the Niger area. Although the trade routes for transporting slaves had remained open during the transition to legitimate trade, new routes were needed to access the hinterlands where legitimate goods were produced. These scientific explorations were accompanied by trade and Christian missionaries.[94] Missionaries in the area commonly used the phrase "Bible and Plough" to describe their efforts. They encouraged people to participate in legitimate trade by teaching them modern farming practices and introducing new seeds.

In 1849, Beecroft was appointed British Consul for the Bight of Benin and Biafra to effectively manage trade around this area.[95] This was followed by the annexation of Lagos about a decade later, in 1861. It became the Oil Rivers Protectorate in 1887 and the Niger Coast Protectorate in 1894. As part of its efforts to capture this West African market, the British government gave the RNC the concession to trade on its behalf in the northern parts of the Niger. This continued until 1898, when the concession was revoked.[96] This structure of trade and administration, which was absent from previous trading relations in the area, placed the economic morphology of Africans in the hands of their European counterparts. It was a precursor to losing political power for local rulers,[97] although it boosted trade volume and strengthened trading relations with European merchants. Europeans controlled the price and the volume of trade while societies focused their economic production on exports.[98] Economic engagements of this period were shaped by Europe's Industrial

---

[92] Mungo Park, *The Journal of a Mission to the Interior of Africa: In the Year 1805* (Philadelphia: Edward Earle, 1815).

[93] Abiodun Adetugbo, "The Development of English in Nigeria up to 1914: A Socio-Historical Appraisal," *Journal of the Historical Society of Nigeria* 9, no. 2 (1978): 96.

[94] Philip D. Curtin, *The Image of Africa: British Ideas and Action, 1780–1850* (London: Palgrave Macmillan, 1964), 289–317.

[95] Anthony I. Asiwaju, "Dahomey, Yorubaland, Borgu and Benin in the Nineteenth Century," in *General History of Africa VI: Africa in the Nineteenth Century until the 1880s*, ed. Jacob F. A. Ajayi (Berkeley: University of California, 1989), 716.

[96] Ahmed M. Mohammed, *European Trade, Imperialism and Under Development in Northern Nigeria 19th and 20th Centuries* (Zaria: Ahmadu Bello University Press Limited, 2016).

[97] Michael Crowder and Obaro Ikime, eds., *West African Chiefs: The Changing Status under Colonial Rule and Independence* (New York: Africana Publishing, 1970); and Olufemi Vaughan, *Nigerian Chiefs: Traditional Power in Modern Politics, 1890s–1990s* (Rochester: University of Rochester Press, 2006).

[98] Melville J. Herskovits and Mitchell Hurwitz, *Economic Transition in West Africa* (London: Routledge, 1964), 77–88.

Revolution, with pronounced shifts in trading patterns; volumes increased to meet the growing demand of European industries, and those industries created new products for the markets.

The abolition of the slave trade increased the proportion of agricultural products involved in transatlantic trade, and it liberalized African economies that participated. Societies saw increased prosperity as slaves gained the opportunity to secure their freedom and join economic activities. The social order of societies was reconfigured through this economic system: slaves and others on the lowest rungs of society could ascend to the highest levels. Fictive filial relations expanded to provide more hands for economic production.

Manifestations of this period's prosperity became apparent in developments like the establishment of *Egbe Mafowoku* (Never be in dearth of money) among the Ijebu people, an age-grade system assumed by everyone born between 1845 and 1848.[99] The age-grade system came into being during a period when the prosperity of this industrious and enterprising population is believed to have reached its peak.[100] They produced clothes sold in local and transatlantic markets which were popular among the Yoruba population in Brazil.[101] Like many of the items traded during this period, their production had been a long-standing tradition that stretched back to the time of the slave trade. The major transformation was the magnitude of demand for such items and the administrative reorganization of trade. The guns and gunpowder that had circulated through Gold Coast markets for centuries, originally brought by European merchants, became a decisive factor in post-1830 politics after the fall of Old Oyo.[102]

The coordination and stability required to improve agricultural production became a necessity, and this prompted a restructuring of the activities of these trading companies. The slave trade had no such requirements – increasing instability meant greater profits for the slave merchants, making slavery and instability mutually reinforcing elements. To underscore the specific requirements of agricultural trade, it is notable that the participants on both sides of the Atlantic remained the same. Their trading structures and systems changed as resources and networks shifted to accommodate the new flow of goods.

The establishment of protectorates and the annexation of polities were instrumental in regulating and later monopolizing trade. Different polities in the Niger area reacted to the changing economic conditions with the increased use of slave labor. Nobles attempted to dominate trade through the magnitude

---

[99] AbdulGafar O. Fahm, "Ijebu Ode's Ojude Oba Festival: Cultural and Spiritual Significance," *SAGE Open* 5, no. 1 (2015): 1–11.

[100] Emmanuel A. Ayandele, *The Ijebu of Yorubaland 1850–1950: Politics, Economy, and Society* (Ibadan: Heinemann, 1992), 5.

[101] Stanley B. Alpern, "What Africans Got for Their Slaves: A Master List of European Trade Goods," *History in Africa* 22 (1995): 10.

[102] Alpern, "What Africans Got for Their Slaves," 19.

of their participation and their control over local markets. In Igboland, the Aro cult used religious manipulation to discourage local participation in European trade.[103] Aro priests described Europeans as strange beings from the gods who could only be dealt with through their spiritual power. Many Igbo and Ibibio communities steered clear of the new, legitimate trade and preferred to supply slave labor to delta states, constrained by the sanctions and military activities of Aro priests.[104]

Capital became an essential consideration for participating in markets, and the evolving economy led to the increased use of loan systems such as pawnship.[105] Umbrellas, European gin, firearms, rum, pendants, bracelets, earrings, flashlights, and other European products proliferated in society as global trade gained influence. Cotton, pepper, cocoa, palm oil, palm kernel, ivory, and other products from interior regions were produced and transported for export in quantities that far surpassed previous practices. Participants began neglecting the cultivation of food crops to focus on cash crops for participation in this trade in order to access the trendy Western products that had become status symbols in society. Regional trade also expanded significantly through networks of kinsmen that crossed the regions of Sierra Leone and Senegambia to circulate Western products.[106] The ranks of the caravan traders also swelled in response to the abolition of slavery, accommodating the surging amount of goods in transit.[107]

In the fifteenth century, the fall of Mali changed the influence of Islam and Islamic culture in the region.[108] Jihadists declared that the "animist" clothing culture of people in Hausa states, to the north of the Niger, was antithetical to Islamic doctrines of modesty. The use of wraps worn around the neck, with no aesthetic tailoring, was common among these societies until the late nineteenth century when British occupation forces captured the Oba of Benin.[109] However, contact with Arabs from the sub-Saharan route leading to the Maghreb region and Europeans from across the Atlantic brought some

---

[103] Ndu L. Njoku, "The Dual Image of the Aro in Igbo Development History: An Aftermath of their Role in the Slave Trade," *Journal of Retracing Africa* 2, no. 1 (2016): 29–48.
[104] Adiele E. Afigbo, "The Eclipse of the Aro Slaving Oligarchy of South–Eastern Nigeria 1901–1927," *Journal of the Historical Society of Nigeria* 6, no. 1 (1971): 3–24.
[105] Paul E. Lovejoy and Toyin Falola, *Pawnship in Africa: Debt Bondage in Historical Perspective* (Boulder: Westview, 1994).
[106] Cecil Magbialy Fyle, "The Yoruba Diaspora in Sierra Leone's Krio Society," in *The Yoruba Diaspora in the Atlantic World*, ed. Toyin Falola and Matt D. Child (Indianapolis: Indiana University Press, 2005), 367–369.
[107] Toyin Falola, "The Yoruba Caravan System of the Nineteenth Century," *The International Journal of African Historical Society of Nigeria* 24, no. 1 (1991): 111–132.
[108] David C. Conrad, *Empires of Medieval West Africa: Ghana, Mali, and Songhay* (New York: Chelsea House, 2010).
[109] Philip A. Igbafe, *Benin under British Administration, 1897–1938: The Impact of Colonial Rule on an African Kingdom* (London: Longman, 1979).

nuances to these material cultures. New fabrics, cowries, beads, ornaments, and clothing styles were introduced to these groups.[110] Arab-style clothing proliferated in Niger-area cultures from the northern states of Katsina, Gobir, Kano, and Zazzau. One example is the male style of dress that the Yoruba refer to as *agbada*, which various cultures in the Niger area have given different names.[111]

The use of *agbada* in these cultures, which was usually an indication of wealth and social status, proliferated during the nineteenth century's seismic economic and political shocks. Evidence from praise poems indicates that Arab-style clothing culture also became influential during the nineteenth century, especially among the elite class in Yorubaland. Most praise lines from this period include this aspect of the social transformation.[112] The style and dignity of the clothes are woven into the praise poems. These materials were imported commodities from northern neighbors.

As the jihadist argument indicates, the spread of Islam among the Hausa population did not translate into a major alteration of their clothing culture. By 1804, clothing in Arab culture was limited due to Bunu's imposition until later in the century. The ban on Arab clothing in Gobir was lifted after the success of the jihad. The Rabba garrison security network built by the caliphate effectively spread Islamic doctrine among the population. The distribution and displacement of the Hausa population also brought a diffusion of the language, consolidating its use in Northern Nigeria as the caliphate's language of communication alongside Arabic.[113]

Garrisons also hosted *Ulama* who taught in Quranic schools. This method of teaching and the *Ulama*'s loyalty to the caliphate ensured that the use of hijab and turbans, the practice of purdah, and other Islamic injunctions prevailed in society.[114] The establishment of a political structure premised on Shari'a also contributed to the social changes that took place north of the Niger River. Some of these cultures, such as the *agbada* tradition, spread across the Niger area as the jihad gained ground. Britain's abolition of the slave trade and slavery also resulted in a wave of Western culture brought to West Africa

---

[110] Akinwunmi Ogundiran, "Material Life and Domestic Economy in a Frontier of the Oyo Empire during the Mid-Atlantic Age," *International Journal of African Historical Studies* 42, no. 3 (2009): 351–385.

[111] Tunde M. Akinwunmi, "Oral Traditions and the Reconstruction of Yoruba Dress," in *Yoruba Identity and Power Politics*, ed. Toyin Falola and Ann Genova (Rochester: Rochester University Press, 2006), 49–73.

[112] Akinwunmi, "Oral Traditions and the Reconstruction."

[113] Fulani conquistadors, rather than imposing their own language, adopted the widely spoken Hausa. Adekunle Adeniran, "Personalities and Policies in the Establishment of English in Northern Nigeria during the British Colonial Administration, 1900–1943," *Journal of the Historical Society of Nigeria* 9, no. 2 (1978): 109–113.

[114] Oluwakemi Adesina, "Women, Shari'ah, and Zina in Northern Nigeria," *African Nebula* 2 (2010): 43–56.

through the returnees. Some of them had been returned forcefully by the colonial governments of Bahia in Brazil and elsewhere due to fears of a slave uprising.[115] The returned population primarily came to reinforce the Muslim community in places like Lagos, while their Christian counterparts migrated out from Badagry, Lagos, Calabar, Bonny, and Abeokuta to Ilesha in particular.[116] New items of trade flowed in from European capitals and cities to become luxury items,[117] and this new population also affected the socioeconomic transformation of this period.

The arrival of Christian missionaries had additional effects on the social changes of this period. They emphasized the importance of modest dress, which led to the proliferation of *iro* and *buba* – traditional upper wrappings – among Yoruba women. This style of dress included headgear and a small piece of cloth used to cover the neck or simply flank it on either of the shoulders. This tradition transcended religious communities to become a cultural tradition. Even adherents of traditional belief systems joined the trend. It was later modified during colonial rule with the introduction of Western clothing.

The displacement of the Old Oyo population, which spread across Yorubaland, had its effects on the social forms of the nineteenth century. The masquerade tradition already existed among several Yoruba communities before the nineteenth century, mostly through the influence of Oyo, but the arrival of Oyo migrants transformed the tradition in these communities. Masquerades shifted away from grass outfits to adopt more fashionable fabrics.[118] Although some masquerades retained grass garments decorated with palm fronds, the influence of Oyo encouraged a new style for this ritual practice.

The Sango cult also became more established across regional communities, along with Oyo preferences for food and social life. Oyo traditions became so integrated into various local practices that the missionaries and returnees

---

[115] Jao J. Reis, Flavio dos Santos Gomes, and Marcus J.M. de Carvalho, trans. by H. Sabrina Gledhill, *The Story of Rufino: Slavery, Freedom, and Islam in the Black Atlantic* (New York: Oxford University Press, 2020).

[116] Akinjide Osuntokun and Tunji Oloruntimehin, "J. F. Ade Ajayi and His Intellectual Contribution to the Study of History," in *J. F. Ade Ajayi: His Life and Career*, eds. Michael Omolewa and Akinjide Osuntokun (Ibadan: Bookcraft, 2014), 300; and Kristin Mann, "Gendered Authority, Gendered Violence: Family, Household and Identity in the Life and Death of Brazilian Freed Woman in Lagos," in *African Women in the Atlantic World: Property, Vulnerability and Mobility, 1660–1880*, ed. Mariana P. Candido and Adam Jones (London: James Currey, 2019), 148–170.

[117] Buttressing the situation from the position of Edna Bay, Ogundiran explained that "these imports were tied to the political economy of power in the sense that they provided a means by which old and new monarch(s) and powerful persons ... solidified their patronage and their control of clients, dependents, or followers." Akinwunmi Ogundiran, "Of Small Things Remembered: Beads, Cowries, and Cultural Translations of the Atlantic Experience in Yorubaland," *The International Journal African Historical Studies* 35, no. 2/3 (2002): 428.

[118] Falola and Heaton, *A History of Nigeria*, 77.

noted the cultural similarities and shared history of people in the region.[119] The nineteenth century saw centuries of cultural circulation and exchange consolidated among these cultures. One particular example included gifts such as yam and palm oil given by a suitor as part of the bride price tradition across several Nigerian communities during this period (see Figure 3.1).

Figure 3.1 The presentation of bride price, tubers of yam, and a gallon of palm oil by a suitor to a would-be in-law was a cherished tradition across several Nigerian communities in the nineteenth century.

---

[119] Through his 1825–1827 travels, Clapperton referred to these people as Yarriba due to their immense cultural similarities.

These interactions led to a formative moment for the syntax and language of different cultures in present-day Nigeria. New words were added to Indigenous vocabularies, which were recorded in the writing culture shaped by Christian missionaries and returnees. Loan words had already been present from other cultures as distant as the Middle East, but the process that continued across the Longue Durée of external relations for peoples and cultures around the Niger River was encapsulated and standardized through the activities of missionaries and returnees. These agents of Western civilization developed a writing culture by creating a literate society and sorting the language practices of different cultural communities to create a body and structure of communication that was intelligible to all within the larger group.[120] Previously independent language and dialect groups were fused into a single entity that reinforced the Old Oyo language.

Control over Yoruba words and expressions was established through Christian instructional books and other literature produced by returnees, and material produced later by educated members of society. There is now a standard Yoruba, which is largely Oyo in nature, and others represent each of the dozens of dialect groups constituting the Yoruba community.[121] The printing press played a significant role in this process.[122] As the local language underwent these reforms, a new language was introduced. Centuries of Oyo relations with Europeans had not previously led to the adoption of languages such as English or Portuguese, but the nineteenth century was a time of transformation. Relations between delta states such as Bonny and the Old Calabar had changed their social systems to include record keeping and communication. However, the magnitude of the Old Oyo's engagements with the Portuguese and the British did not affect this social aspect of Yorubaland until the returnees and the Christian missionaries promoted it through their works. This shaped the evolving social milieu of that period.[123]

Once Western imperialists were involved, relations between many communities across the Niger developed into unbridled competition and rivalry to establish a monopoly on trade.[124] The Portuguese opened trading relations with these polities, and the British and French dominated the market in the eighteenth century. At this stage, Portuguese guides were employed to navigate

---

[120] Jacob F. A. Ajayi, "How Yoruba Was Reduced to Writing," *Odu* 8 (1960): 49–58.
[121] Francis O. Egbokhare and S. Oluwole Oyetade, *Harmonization and Standardization of Nigerian Languages* (Cape Town: CASAS, 2002).
[122] John D. Y. Peel, *Religious Encounter and the Making of the Yoruba* (Bloomington: Indiana University Press, 2003).
[123] Peel, *Religious Encounter*.
[124] Albert A. Boahen, ed. *General History of Africa: VII Africa under Colonial Domination 1880–1935* (Paris: UNESCO, 1990), 6.

the terrain. Increasing trade between the British and the delta states developed a hybridized English language used in commercial and social interactions.

Hope Waddell's official report notes that records of state affairs were kept in intelligible journals dating back to 1767. During this same period, Bonny and Old Calabar nobles sent their children to European schools. After their return, their education enabled them to perform bureaucratic functions in state administrations. Kings, including the Oba of Benin, are said to have been fluent in English by the late eighteenth century. This was common among the highest echelons of society, while others communicated in local languages and used the hybridized language – popularly known as pidgin English – in the markets.

These practices changed substantially in the nineteenth century with the establishment of schools and the immense success of missionaries. Communication between the British and various groups in the Niger area reached a crescendo when the British began intervening in the internal politics of coastal states and others in the interior. The shift from the slave trade and the increase in legitimate trade crippled export and import markets. Large foreign companies now traded directly with the people, diminishing the role of middlemen and limiting the role of coastal communities such as the Urhobo and Itsekeri, who had previously acted as a buffer between Europeans and inland markets.[125] The British built forts and factories in strategic locations, which were usually coastal for easier transport, while their trade agents circulated through villages to collect goods. Increasing contact with these traders made English more attractive as a common language for bridging communication barriers. In Yorubaland and the delta states, these trends were accelerated by the return of kinsmen from the Americas and Sierra Leone. Before the end of the nineteenth century, elementary and secondary schools were established in various locations throughout the region that would become the largest British colony in Africa.

The education ordinances of 1882 and 1896 reinforced the role that language would play in the emerging society, passing grants to fund schools for the advancement of education and the English language.[126] Composition, spelling, grammar, and dictation were learning structures that missionaries and colonial administrators used to impose Western education and communication systems. English became the official language of state communication, while official correspondence from the second half of the century invariably involved the British government and its representatives. Students were also taught arithmetic and other subjects necessary to function as clerks, messengers, interpreters, stock-keepers, and in similar roles. However, these transformations were not as pronounced across the Niger. They were less dramatic in Northern Nigeria, where Islamic culture and literacy had taken root.

---

[125] Ikime, *Niger Delta Rivalry*.
[126] Adetugbo, "The Development of English," 98.

Local dietary patterns, especially in the south, were also modified during this period. The early adoption of Western culture in Bonny and Old Calabar meant that their inhabitants were acquainted with the table etiquette of their Western counterparts before the nineteenth century. These habits were reintroduced by returnees in Yorubaland and subsequently adopted by educated members of society. The introduction of new crops also changed dietary patterns as different varieties of food became available.

Conclusion

These major events characterized and shaped the historical narrative of the area that would become known as Nigeria in the year 1900. Two significant periods dictated the form and structure of the society that the colonizers met on the ground when they arrived to establish their enterprise. One of them was the fifteenth-century displacement of polities in West Africa that precipitated their later displacement in the nineteenth century. Between the nineteenth and twentieth centuries, it is difficult to say which was more influential in the making of modern Nigeria. The latter century consolidated the processes that had begun in the previous century, baptized in political crises and recalibrations that occurred in every corner of the Niger area. The ongoing process of state reformation did not readily make room for invading colonial forces. The year 1900 became a popular benchmark for Nigerian historians only because it notes the official period of British occupation in the lands and polities formed around the Niger River and Lake Chad. The effective colonialization of these polities did not occur until the Northern and Southern Protectorates were amalgamated along with the Oil Rivers and Lagos. This renewed the traditional prestige of the Old Oyo Empire and Borno, even though their influence – and that of other Indigenous governing bodies in the area – would be submerged under the new administration that controlled the trajectory of their decline.[127]

---

[127] Vincent Hiribarren, "A European and African Joint-Venture: Writing a Seamless History of Borno (1902–1960)," *History in Africa* 40 (2013): 77–98.

4

Prelude to Colonization

Trade and Missions

A single chapter does not seem sufficient to do justice to the period that preceded the colonial era. Nineteenth-century events had a remarkable impact on the modern Nigerian state, which is why this chapter focuses on specific themes and activities during that time frame. Three important influences were Christian missionaries' activities, the intricate changes in trading relations between Africans and their European counterparts, and the shifting relationships between different groups of Africans.[1] These factors had indelible effects on the sociopolitical and economic formation of societies.

Missionary activities and trading relationships prepared Africa's cultures and polities for colonial rule. The colonial transformation occurred not as a sudden shock but as a long metamorphosis enabled by trade, the introduction of Western education, the advent of Christianity, returning freed slaves, and the trickle of social changes that accompanied these developments.[2] The British and French governments made frantic efforts to change trade dynamics in Africa between 1807 and the 1850s, focusing intently on the West and Central regions of the continent. Trade in human cargo had transformed European societies in many respects, and at the end of the previous century Britain's Industrial Revolution accelerated those shifts.[3] Africanist scholars who study the transatlantic slave trade and conditions of slavery in the Americas and the Caribbean have documented the changing dynamics that influenced policy and the direction of slavery and the slave trade in Europe.[4] They steered similar changes in the "farm-states" in the Americas and the Caribbean.[5]

---

[1] Richard Reid, "Africa's Revolutionary Nineteenth Century and the Idea of the 'Scramble'," *The American Historical Review* 126, no. 4 (2021): 1424–1447.

[2] Catherine Coquery-Vidrovitch, *Africa and the Africans in the Nineteenth Century: A Turbulent History* (London: Routledge, 2009).

[3] Philip D. Curtin, ed., *Africa Remembered: Narratives by West Africans from the Era of the Slave Trade* (Madison: The University of Wisconsin Press, 1967).

[4] Ibrahima Thiaw and Deborah L. Mack, "Atlantic Slavery and the Making of the Modern World: Experiences, Representations, and Legacies," *Current Anthropology* 61, no. S22 (2020): 145–158.

[5] David B. Davis, *Inhuman Bondage: The Rise and Fall of Slavery in the New World* (Oxford: Oxford University Press, 2006).

After this chapter reconsiders these conditions, it examines the transformation of the emergent global trading relations, facilitated by those activities described as "legitimate" trade. The chapter examines the social upheaval brought by the slave trade and its transmutation into legitimate trade, along with the activities of Christian missionaries who were instrumental in introducing Western education and Western civility.

Trade

In 1794, Toussaint L'Ouverture successfully led a slave revolt in Santo Domingo, (Haiti) during which hundreds of slave owners died. Most of the survivors fled to the United States where their gory tales terrified their counterparts. This was before the Thirteenth Amendment of the United States Constitution in 1865. A similar riot in Brazil failed. Edward Rossiter explained how fear also grew in England of a similar event in a British Caribbean colony. Prior to these developments, a wind of change was already gusting across the United States where about 200,000 slaves had regained freedom because of either the death or the decisions of their masters.[6]

The late eighteenth century and the following century were remarkable periods, not just in the history of West African societies and the whole of Africa but for Atlantic history more generally.[7] As the Sokoto Jihad and the weakening of the Old Oyo polity took shape in the late eighteenth century – spurred on by those who could be called "antiestablishment" – Africans who had been sold into slavery in the Americas and the Caribbean also prepared this period for its historic moment.[8] The changing situation in the Atlantic farm plantations, cities, and capitals would transform Atlantic history from pure mercantilism and commercial relations to a mix of forces that included resistance and a drive toward social reordering. These developments unfolded as both sides of the Atlantic were at the peak of their participation in trading human cargo and its financial and related gains.[9] About 12.5 million Africans were enslaved to lay the foundation of modern European states and their economies.[10] This activity continued until the 1860s, when the transatlantic slave trade effectively came to an end. A significant amount of this

---

[6] Akpojevbe Omasanjuwa and Junisa Phebean, "Acrimony in Colonial Liberia," *Journal of Universal History Studies* 3, no. 1 (2020): 2.
[7] Frank W. Thackeray and John E. Findling, ed., *Events that Changed the World in the Eighteenth Century* (Santa Barbara: ABC–CLIO, 1998).
[8] Adaye Orugbani, *Nigeria Since the 19th Century* (Port Harcourt: Paragraphics, 2005).
[9] Toyin Falola and Matt D. Child, ed., *The Yoruba Diaspora in the Atlantic World* (Bloomington: Indiana University Press, 2005).
[10] Andrew Kahn and Jamelle Bouie, "The Atlantic Slave Trade in Two Minutes," *Slate*, September 16, 2021, https://slate.com/news-and-politics/2021/09/atlantic-slave-trade-history-animated-interactive.html.

population was enslaved while the slave revolt occurred in Santo Domingo, continuing until the mid-nineteenth century.[11]

Chapter 3 examined the Sokoto Jihad, the weakening and collapse of the Old Oyo Empire, and the general instability across the Niger area. These trends had two major implications: greater profits for slave traders, and increasing organization among the enslaved population as part of a quest for identity. The enslaved population developed sophisticated beliefs and doctrines, especially regarding the institution of slavery. Many who identified with Islam also adopted the religion's views on enslavement. The slave revolt in Haiti, for instance, triggered a series of responses from slave owners in Europe and the Americas.[12] There were growing fears of slave revolts that could destroy the wealth that had taken years to build. The notion of a racial hierarchy, which developed in the sixteenth century, gained impetus during the twilight of the eighteenth century and the better part of the nineteenth century.[13] This period coincided with European technological and industrial breakthroughs led by Britain.

The Abolition Act of 1807 was a response to the threat of slave revolts.[14] The culture that wielded the most advanced technology and science during a particular period had the greatest influence over geopolitical development and world politics. The British Empire occupied that position during the early nineteenth century, which was influential in the abolition of the slave trade and the activities of Western imperial powers in Africa.[15] France was Britain's only major rival, but had lost its advantage after the Napoleonic wars and the events that followed. The British government – newly strengthened by the Industrial Revolution, a booming economy, and the weakening of France – dominated the transition to "legitimate" trade that supplanted the importation of slaves into Europe.[16] However, it did not have complete authority, and some concessions were made, such as the continuation of the slave trade in Brazil and Cuba.

After the passage of the Slave Trade Act in 1807, slave communities in the Portuguese colony of Brazil organized pockets of resistance.[17] Many captives

---

[11] Olatunji Ojo, "The Slave Ship Manuelita and the Story of a Yoruba Community, 1833-1834," *Revista Tempo* 23, no. 2 (2017): 361-382.

[12] Laurent Dubois, *Avengers of the New World: The Story of the Haitian Revolution* (Cambridge: The Belknap Press, 2004).

[13] A glimpse of this is discussed in a critique of Bylden's notion of race and racism, by Valentin-Yves Mudimbe, *The Invention of Africa: Gnosis, Philosophy, and the Order of Knowledge* (Bloomington: Indiana University Press, 1998), 98-134.

[14] Richard Anderson and Henry B. Lovejoy, eds., *Liberated Africans and the Abolition of the Slave Trade, 1807-1896* (New York: University of Rochester Press, 2020).

[15] William R. Johnston, *Great Britain Great Empire: An Evaluation of the British Imperial Experience* (St. Lucia: University of Queensland Press, 1981).

[16] Angus E. Dalrymple-Smith, *Commercial Transitions and Abolition in West Africa 1630-1860* (Leiden: Brill, 2020).

[17] Stuart B. Schwartz, *Slaves, Peasants, and Rebels: Reconsidering Brazilian Slavery* (Urbana: University of Illinois Press, 1992).

had been taken there during the massive nineteenth-century implosion, and their resistance culminated in the Male revolt of 1835 in Bahia.[18] The palpable threat posed by trading enslaved humans, which Ayandele referred to as "living tools,"[19] made alternative, more efficient means of economic production more attractive for trade with Europe. The change in financial incentives encouraged governments in countries such as Britain and the United States to adopt repatriation policies.

The American Colonization Society, supported by the US government, laid the basis for this repatriation act. It negotiated the selection of Liberia for repatriating the slave population.[20] British efforts followed in Sierra Leone, applying a different model that would prove to be more successful than the Liberian project.[21] Efforts to repatriate these populations increased after the Male revolt, increasing the number of returnees in Sierra Leone. The Abolition Act and the massive repatriation schemes significantly affected trade and missionary activities in the Niger area. Over the longer term, they shaped European activities in Africa from this period onward.

By the turn of the nineteenth century, European interest in Africa had shifted from a narrow focus on trade to encompass other areas that included governance and social formation. The rapidly growing scale of European industry and its accompanying markets required new methods for promoting trade. The sociopolitical state of African societies had to be altered so that they could generate enough demand to match Europe's expanding production capacity. Although the nineteenth century brought trade liberalization, cross-cultural exchange has always been a key component of African societies.[22] Commerce was a thriving means of mutual communication between communities. Urban centers such as the Old Oyo capital, Kano, Benin, the Old Calabar, and Bonny existed before the nineteenth century, populated by traders of different origins and dominated by trading contacts. Mahdi Adamu and Anthony Hopkins have documented the complex market networks operated by Hausa merchants in various parts of West Africa before the nineteenth century.[23] These markets were expanded by growing numbers of

---

[18] Joao Jose Reis, "Slave Resistance in Brazil: Bahia, 1807–1835," *Luso–Brazilian Review* 25, no.1 (1988): 111–144.

[19] Emmanuel A. Ayandele, *Nigerian Historical Studies* (London: Frank Cass, 1979), 44.

[20] Omasanjuwa and Phebean, "Acrimony in Colonial Liberia," 1–38.

[21] Richard Anderson, "The Diaspora of Sierra Leone's Liberated Africans: Enlistment, Forced Migration, and 'Liberation' at Freetown, 1808–1863," *African Economic History* 41 (2013): 101–138.

[22] Melville J. Herskovits and Mitchell Harwits, eds., *Economic Transition in Africa* (London: Routledge, 1964); Robin Law, *Contemporary Source Material for The History of the Old Oyo Empire, 1627–1824* (Toronto: York University, 2001).

[23] Mahdi Adamu, *The Hausa Factor in West African History* (Zaria: Ahmadu Bello University Press, 1978), 116–122. In particular reference to this period, see Anthony G. Hopkins, *An Economic History of West Africa* (New York: Routledge, 2020).

participants and the flow of European goods. Igbo women were usually known for engaging in short-distance trading excursions around their communities, and the international flow of trade positioned them to produce palm oil and kernels. They also traded local and imported products.[24]

By the mid-nineteenth century, Dogon-Dawa had replicated the economic development of other polities around the Niger, transforming into a large cotton plantation in Katsina operated by slave labor purchased through West African markets.[25] Maska transformed during this same period through the diversification of local skills, craftsmanship, and entrepreneurial investments.[26] The same was true for Ibadan, the Yoruba city-state that emerged from the collapse of the Old Oyo Empire. It became a collection point for palm oil produced in the interior, drawing a larger population of migrants in pursuit of the economic opportunities that a cross-cultural market location could provide.[27]

Regional, inter-, and intracountry migration, driven by political upheavals during this period, contributed significantly to the transformation of societies and economies in states around the Niger area. The collapse of large empires and kingdoms had propelled the rise of other entities with even more sophisticated political organizations. By this time, Yoruba and Fulani warriors in the region had organized themselves into mercenary groups that undertook military actions for economic motives. The interplay between military, economic, political, and religious powers profoundly influenced the organization of states and social mobility in ways that were not seen in previous centuries.[28] Even newly emerging states and power blocs had to navigate this terrain.[29]

Trade had expanded rapidly on the eve of colonial rule such that extant West African currency could not accommodate market transactions, especially for export trade. Hopkins reports that a one-ton bag of cowries, containing 400,000 shells, was valued at less than £13.[30] Previous transactions, which were dominated by nobles and members of the royal class, valued cowries

---

[24] Gloria Ifeoma Chuku, "From Petty Traders to International Merchants: A Historical Account of Three Igbo Women of Nigeria in Trade and Commerce, 1886 to 1970," *African Economic History* 27 (1999): 1–22.

[25] Paul E. Lovejoy, "Plantations in the Economy of the Sokoto Caliphate," *The Journal of African History* 19, no. 3 (1978): 341–368.

[26] Yusufu Bala Usman, *The Transformation of Katsina, 1400–1883: The Emergence and Overthrow of the Sarauta System and the Establishment of the Emirate* (Zaria: Ahmadu Bello University Press, 1981), 199.

[27] Robert Smith, *Kingdoms of the Yoruba* (London: Methuen, 1969), 158.

[28] Idris S. Jimada, *The Historical Background to the Establishment of Patigi Emirate: c1810–1898* (Zaria: Ahmadu Bello University, 2016).

[29] Hakeem B. Harunah, "Sodeke: Hero and Statesman of the Egba," *Journal of the Historical Society of Nigeria* 12, no.1/2 (1984): 109–131.

[30] Anthony G. Hopkins, "The Currency Revolution in South–West Nigeria in the Late Nineteenth Century," *Journal of the Historical Society of Nigeria* 3, no. 3 (1966): 472.

imported from the West Indies – and, much later, from East Africa. European merchants met this demand and transformed the shell pieces into status symbols in the material and spiritual worlds.[31] As larger numbers of participants exchanged goods, they preferred a lighter and more portable currency. Various studies on the use of cowries and the evolution of currency in the Niger area suggest that a clear transition in the system of exchange is difficult to identify among precolonial Nigerian people. Silver, gold, iron, and copper coins regularly circulated alongside cowries, used in barter systems before the nineteenth century.[32] Barter systems and the use of cowrie shells gradually faded from the market before the currency act of 1880 because neither was well suited for emerging markets.

In Lagos, the 1880 monetary legislation only recognized British coins, silver, gold, and a few foreign gold coins as legal tender. This only affected Lagos but had larger implications for the hinterlands and general trade in the region.[33] The transition to new units of exchange was far from seamless, considering the many competing interests at work.

The old merchant class prioritized their existing contacts, looking to expand into the interior after many years of trading engagements in the region. The West African market also drew new entrants, seeking opportunities brought by the advent of the so-called legitimate trade.[34] The former group wanted to maintain existing systems of exchange – cowries and the barter system – hoping it would block new entrants who needed to learn how such systems operated in the region. New market participants recognized that the transition to modern currency would be essential for promoting trade. Old systems of market exchange operated simultaneously with transactions that used British silver coins and dollars until the 1880s. They began accounting for smaller volumes of trade as the century drew close.

Technological advancements in mobility and transportation, along with shifts in demography and politics, heavily influenced this transition. Older sailing ships were replaced by newly developed steamships. By the middle of the nineteenth century, shipping companies employed steam-powered vessels that were faster and more efficient than previous "analog locomotives."[35] The

---

[31] Akinwunmi Ogundiran, "Of Small Things Remembered: Beads, Cowries, and Cultural Translations of the Atlantic Experience in Yorubaland," *The International Journal of African Historical Studies* 35, no. 2/3 (2002): 427–457.

[32] Walter I. Ofonagoro, "The Currency Revolution in Southern Nigeria 1880–1948," Occasional Paper No. 14, African Studies Center: University of California, Los Angeles, 1976, 4.

[33] Ofonagoro, "The Currency Revolution," 7.

[34] Hopkins, "The Currency Revolution," 471–483.

[35] Juan C. Villa, Maria Boile, and Sotirios Theofanis, *International Trade and Transportation Infrastructure Development: Experiences in North America and Europe* (Amsterdam: Elsevier, 2020), 6.

African Steamship Company, the British and African Steam Navigation Company, and the Fabre-Fraissinet line began operating in the Niger area in 1851, 1868, and 1889, respectively, and other companies followed close behind.[36] The greatly reduced shipping times brought by this technological revolution allowed more perishable goods to be shipped over larger distances.

Trade in "legitimate goods" revolutionized the banking and financial systems on both sides of the Atlantic. Capital and insurance became key factors for trade that was developing on a larger scale, and big merchant groups diversified into banking to provide credit and regulate trade. The Bank of West Africa, incorporated in London under the Joint Stock Companies Acts of 1862, extended its offices to Lagos and Sierra Leone in 1867. The African Banking Corporation was created in Lagos in 1891 and was responsible for importing British coins into the West African province of the British Empire. After the bank was involved in a crisis – related to its owner's alleged conflicts of interest – the Bank of British West Africa emerged eight years later.[37]

Scholars have had difficulty quantifying the impact of the abolition of the slave trade on Nigeria's demographics. However, even without evidence of any exponential population increase, it is widely accepted that the population stabilized in the second half of the nineteenth century. Working together with the liberalization of trade and missionary activity meant more people exchanging goods in emerging markets. The production and distribution of wealth became more concentrated among private market participants, as opposed to the state interests that controlled assets in the previous century.

The redistribution of wealth from nobles to ordinary people changed the political and socioeconomic landscape. Increased participation in emerging markets and greater volumes of trade produced new wealth, creating a new set of elites that included freed slaves – this group included Oko Jumbo, Oshodi Tapa, and Jack Jaja Annie Pepple. Some became so powerful that they claimed traditional titles to match their new economic status. In 1870, political maneuvering led to the emergence of Opobo as the sovereign enclave of Jack Jaja Annie Pepple, a freed slave from the Bonny, later known as Amachachi Jaja.[38] This event, which focused traders' attention on the new settlement in the delta area, showed that private individuals had become more important to commercial dynamics.[39]

---

[36] Martin Lynn, *Commerce and Economic Change in West Africa: The Palm Oil Trade in the Nineteenth Century* (Cambridge: Cambridge University Press, 1997), 108.

[37] Chibuike Ugochukwu Uche, "Foreign Banks, Africans, and Credit in Colonial Nigeria, c.1890–1912," *The Economic History Review Series* 52, no. 4 (1999): 671.

[38] Walter I. Ofonagoro, "Notes on the Ancestry of Mbanaso Okwaraozurumba otherwise known as King Jaja of Opobo, 1821–1891," *Journal of the Historical Society of Nigeria* 9, no. 3 (1978): 145–156.

[39] Solomon O. Jaja, *Opobo Since 1870: A Documentary Record with an Introduction* (Ibadan: University of Ibadan, 1991).

In the nineteenth century, the fiscal regime of the Niger area was shaped by questions of compatibility. The extant mediums of exchange were no longer compatible with the evolving market structure and system; cowries and other failed economic schemes could no longer provide the flexibility required by new market dynamics. The British government was also interested in the evolution of the region's fiscal system to exert absolute control over local markets. The dollar was demonetized in 1897 following a ban on cowrie imports from East Africa and the promulgation of the Currency Act in Lagos.

Studies have shown that the transformation of economic power had opposing effects. The economic and political positions of European countries were strengthened, but it was an unmitigated disaster for African states. The market expanded as economic power was concentrated in private hands, but the benefits were unevenly distributed. Western imperial powers framed their interest in altering the trading dynamics of the Niger area as a quest to improve the socioeconomic landscape and uplift the lives of newly civilized people.

Until the mid-nineteenth century, trading activities took place on the shores of coastal communities that had shelters and barracoons for processing slaves. Markets were dominated by those who occupied African society's highest echelons, and they maintained their advantage by rigging the market in their favor. Kings and their representatives enjoyed many privileges under this regime. They had the first pick of any goods European merchants brought to the community for trade. Captives sold to European merchants by the king and his representatives received a 31 percent premium.[40]

Kings enjoyed the right of first contact with willing merchants from Europe, and commodities produced by nobles were always priority purchases for merchants who wanted to continue trading in the region. This explains the tremendous wealth accumulated by West African chiefs and royals between the late seventeenth and mid nineteenth centuries. Royal palaces in coastal communities and settlements with easy access to Atlantic trade, such as Bonny, Brass, the Old Calabar, Benin, Oyo, and Dahomey (now the Republic of Benin), were decorated with European furniture and materials. European merchants who sought royal favor gave many of these items as gifts. This set a precedent for the materialism that society's elites would exhibit, and that trend continued as trade expanded and markets were liberalized.

Textiles, mirrors, umbrellas, shoes, biscuits, sugar, tobacco, gin, and other items from Europe quickly spread through markets due to their influence as status symbols, and they easily became signifiers of importance based on who could access them before the liberalization of trade. They were initially the exclusive property of kings, and later they were accumulated by returnees and the emerging educated class. Britain championed this liberalization of trade in

---

[40] Kristin Mann, *Slavery and the Birth of an African City: Lagos 1760–1900* (Bloomington: Indiana University Press, 1997), 55.

Africa, which gradually eroded the economic authority of African leaders and Africans, undermining their ability to control prices and regulate markets.[41] The competitive nature of these emerging markets undid attempts to regain influence over local economies. However, aristocrats held positions in society that allowed them to retain control over the production of goods that were most prized by European markets.

The slave trade in West Africa did not end until Lagos was annexed in 1861. Even then, slave production and circulation continued among several polities around the Bights of Benin and Biafra until late in the century, when a protectorate was established in those areas.[42] In the early nineteenth century, Dahomey raided Oyo towns for slave labor used on farm plantations to produce export crops. Other slaves sold around the Bight of Benin and Biafra were sold by Hausa, Yoruba, Nupe, and Bariba merchants – along with traders from elsewhere in the region – who traded in various goods.[43] During this period, the use of farm labor doubled in response to market demands. The circulation of "living tools," traded in markets for local production, increased substantially. Many were retained to cultivate new commodities for trade.[44]

Some Hausa captives were returned to Dahomey near the end of the eighteenth century, at the onset of repatriation policies enacted by Western imperial powers. They dominated the developing trade patterns, like others that followed them elsewhere in the West African region. After rejoining local societies, they traded European wares and human captives with the king's blessing. This was when Dahomey gained an advantage over Old Oyo in the Niger area's geopolitical dynamics. Hausa merchants had access to various trading commodities from throughout the kingdom. They bought captives from Dahomey and sold them to Yoruba merchants, who then sold them in European markets or within local markets. Captives included the Bayin

---

[41] Terence Ranger and Olufemi Vaughan, eds., *Legitimacy and the State in Twentieth Century Africa: Essays in Honour of A. H. M. Kirk-Greene* (Oxford: Palgrave Macmillan, 1993).

[42] Philip D. Curtin, *The Atlantic Slave Trade: A Census* (Madison: The University of Wisconsin Press, 1967).

[43] This market's meeting point remained a central market for the cities of Kishi, Shaki, Raka, Ikoyi, Igboho, Ilorin, and Lagos. Ibadan and Abeokuta joined this marketplace toward the middle of the nineteenth century.

[44] Newbury has argued, in his work on the abolition of the slave trade in West Africa, that Europeans in the region were engaging in wishful thinking when they expected moral arguments (humanitarian grounds) and trade in "legitimate goods" to abolish the market for slaves and end the operation of slave squadrons on the West African coast. As stated, "Only by encouraging the production of a new cash crop – and thus an alternative use for captives – can it be said that 'legitimate' trade diminished the number of those who were otherwise destined" to be enslaved in Atlantic cities. Colin W. Newbury, *The Western Slave Coast and Its Rulers: European Trade and Administration among the Yoruba and Adja-Speaking Peoples of South-Western Nigeria, Southern Dahomey, and Togo* (London: Oxford University Press, 1961), 42.

Gwandu (slaves of the estate), who were used to produce farm products in Hausaland, such as groundnuts.

Hausa merchants traded commodities such as handkerchiefs from Manchester; Silesias (a sturdy twill-weave cotton fabric) from Germany; linens, silk handkerchiefs, and tobacco from Brazil; and snuff, iron, and beads.[45] After the first phase of the jihad, their number multiplied in the area around Dahomey. They thrived in the kingdom, and by the time it was incorporated into the French West African colony its cultural link with Oyo was a distant memory. The instability caused by the jihad devastated their homes and shattered their livelihoods, but it propelled their migration, resettlement, and participation in local, regional, and global trade. The nineteenth-century crisis in the region followed a similar pattern to other cultures across the Niger area, affecting the Hausa distribution across West Africa and the types of states that emerged afterwards. As with the Yoruba dispersion described in Chapter 3, the reconstitution of these displaced polities never quite replicated their previous forms. The same process occurred in Itsekiri, Bonny, and elsewhere.

The migration patterns of Indigenous people and the returnees from the Americas and Sierra Leone changed the land tenure system in some societies, especially in the emerging urban centers of Lagos, Badagry, Ibadan, Abeokuta, and Ilesa. These places attracted migrants during this period, and the mixed migration of the nineteenth century advanced the developing process of job specialization from the previous centuries.

Hausa migrants and Yoruba traders, known for their itinerant trading activities, flooded West African markets with local and European goods. The massive displacement of the population around the Niger, which coincided with the abolition of the slave trade, had implications for regional settlement patterns and the overall economy of the West African region. Candido and Jones have explained that mobility and economic transformation during this period enhanced the "integration of women in urban activities such as the production and commercialization of food, as well as the commercialization of services such as washing and sewing. New economic activities facilitated the social mobility of African women."[46]

Due to the intensity of their economic participation in the Gold Coast colony and surrounding settlements, the Hausa community installed their regional chief before the colonial period. They constituted a large percentage of runaway slaves and became an instrument of conquest in the British West African colony due to encouragement from British imperial agents. The British government promoted legitimate trade as a replacement for the slave trade. This

---

[45] Adamu, *Hausa Factor*, 117–118.
[46] Mariana P. Candido and Adam Jones, "Introduction," in *African Women in the Atlantic World: Property, Vulnerability and Mobility, 1660–1880*, ed. Mariana P. Candido and Adam Jones (Rochester: James Currey, 2019), 13.

meant that the slave trade had to be abolished on an international level and among the local economies of West African states – this required intervention in the local politics of West African societies. Missionaries played an important role in the implementation of this policy. Whenever European merchants began operating in a region, nearby slaves escaped their masters to secure their "freedom." Kings and chiefs could do little in response. Some escaped slaves joined the pool of traders, commercial farmers, and artisans of the period. Others, particularly among the Hausa population, enlisted in the imperial army. They were also recruited into the armies of various West African states, such as Lagos and the Gold Coast. They became instrumental in executing economic policy for Western imperial powers in West Africa, either fighting for them or the local authorities.

Botanical farms were established in Lagos and Sierra Leone to experiment with new seeds, such as rice, maize, cocoa, and new strains of palm kernel and cotton. Palm oil dominated West African trade with Europe from the start of the nineteenth century.[47] Hopkins has shown that Britain imported about 1,000 tons of palm oil from West Africa in 1810.[48] Between 1810 and 1855, the trade volume increased to 40,000 tons. By the second half of the nineteenth century, trade had grown to include groundnut oil. A technique was discovered for extracting oil from palm kernels and using the waste to prepare livestock feed. Ivory, pepper, and other trade items that had been insignificant in the previous century were also found in this emerging economy. The liberalization of trade did little to remove the control and regulation of trade as it merely transferred it from local kings to European merchants. However, many saw them as champions for freedom. The allegiance of Africans shifted from the divinity of rulers to the materialism of their marketplaces.

Missionaries

European societies and their counterparts in America responded to the slave threat because it menaced the ultracapitalist societies being constructed under their tutelage. This response included forming so-called humanitarian bodies for the civilization of Africa. Mamdani's critique rightly places these groups – which emerged from the humanist school formed in Europe in the late sixteenth and early seventeenth centuries – at the center of efforts to reproduce the old racial taxonomy.[49] They promoted Western universalism and entrenched processes that asphyxiated local production.

---

[47] Martin Lynn, "Change and Continuity in the British Palm Oil Trade with West Africa, 1830–55," *The Journal of African History* 22, no. 3 (1981): 331–348.
[48] Hopkins, *An Economic History*, 177.
[49] Mahmood Mamdani, *Neither Settler Nor Native: The Making and Unmaking of Permanent Minorities* (London: Harvard University Press, 2020), 8–9.

The goal of foreign missions was to recreate socioeconomic dynamics and political morphologies from their own countries. However, these foreign missions created second-class participants in the global world order. Their appeals and propaganda gained waves of support in different parts of the West as the eighteenth century advanced into the nineteenth and slave revolts became incessant in the Americas. The Male revolt was due to the remarkable strength of the Muslim slave population among the many thousands that had been smuggled across the Atlantic after the abolition of the slave trade. Events in Cuba and elsewhere during this same period sent a clear signal to slave owners in and around the colony of Brazil, showing the danger of continuing to trade in human labor.

Sections of the Muslim population, which cut across the cultural and language demography of the slave community, argued to overthrow the existing order and colonize the land. Islamic doctrine could twist the practice of slavery in favor of its adherents, which was one of the demands of the jihadists confronting the collapsed Hausa kingdoms and leadership of the late eighteenth century. The same doctrine was involved in the collapse of Old Oyo following its implosion, due partly to Muslim revolt among Hausa captives and Yoruba Muslim incursions from Ilorin and Oyo. This population, ostensibly taken from the "dark continent," where people were said to be illiterate and lacking a viable means of historical documentation, communicated through pamphlets, letters, and other means. Their communication used a language, such as Ajami, that slave owners could not decode, and this was a key source of concern regarding the institution of slavery in Europe and the Americas. Reis and his colleagues have documented these dynamics in Rufino's ordeal in Brazil.[50]

Rufino was a Muslim in the Salvador province of Brazil, and his magico-spiritual potency made him a target of the colonial government. Another man in Cuba named Prieto was on trial for similar reasons.[51] The difference is that Prieto was put to death, whereas Rufino survived to thrive in cross-cultural trade. The Lucumi revolt in Cuba occurred the same year as the Male uprising in Bahia. The threats embedded in the institution of slavery under the old order could not have been clearer to nobles, political elites, and other stakeholders. The nineteenth century became a time of persecution of the slave population in the Americas and the Caribbean, hoping to deter further escalation from enslaved communities. Repatriation was another option for scattering the slave resistance and thinning the population that had come to be seen as a threat.

---

[50] Jao Jose Reis, Flavio dos Santos Gomes, and Marcus J. M. de Carvalho, *The Story of Rufino: Slavery, Freedom, and Islam in the Black Atlantic*, trans. H. Sabrina Gledhill (New York: Oxford University Press, 2020).

[51] Henry Lovejoy, *Prieto: Yoruba Kingship in Colonial Cuba during the Age of Revolutions* (Chapel Hill: University of North Carolina Press, 2019).

To suggest that Christian churches changed their perspectives on racial hierarchy and the institution of slavery in response to the events of this period would distort the trajectory of Christian missions in the Nigerian area. Instead, this series of events, from the late eighteenth century to the middle of the nineteenth century, increased the vigor with which different missions pursued the Christianization of Africans. Their enterprise also gained wider acceptance among the Western population. Embarking on a foreign mission to transform the social and economic fabric of another culture is no easy task, and these efforts required adequate finances to staff the missions and support their activities.[52]

The production, importation, and distribution of religious materials were impossible without funding, which meant that none of the missions was purely motivated by religious interest. Rather, they all involved some level of economic consideration. An intricate relationship developed between missionaries, large mercantile firms, and colonial governments, although colonial administrators would eventually sever their relationship due to conflicts between their secularism and the missions' ecclesiasticism.[53] The split occurred after religious networks within and outside the colonies had been used as part of the colonization process.

Earlier in the sixteenth century – when the Portuguese and the Spanish held sway as the imperial lords of Europe – the Portuguese government attempted to spread its Catholicism among coastal communities around the Bight of Benin.[54] During this early contact, Christianity was introduced to Benin, the dominant state in the region, and Warri, its tributary state. Apart from some relics and artifacts, this mission did not see lasting success for the same reasons that limited trade and trading relations.

During the sixteenth century, trade was limited to the coast. Venturing into the hinterlands was unwise, not because of any resistance from local authorities but because the delicate health of Europeans made them highly vulnerable to malaria.[55] Africa was largely fatal for white explorers until the discovery and application of quinine in the first half of the nineteenth century. Black returnees from Europe and America also died in large numbers when they returned

---

[52] Steven Maughan, "'Mighty England Do Good': The Major English Denominations and Organisation for the Support of Foreign Missions in the Nineteenth Century," in *Missionary Encounters: Sources and Issues*, ed. Robert A. Bickers and Rosemary Seton (London: Curzon Press, 1996), 11–37.

[53] Emmanuel A. Ayandele, "The Missionary Factor in Northern Nigeria, 1870-1918," *Journal of the Historical Society of Nigeria* 3, no. 3 (1966): 514–522.

[54] J. O. Ijoma, "Portuguese Activities in West Africa before 1600: The Consequences," *Transafrican Journal of History* 11 (1982): 136–146.

[55] Benjamin Diara, Johnson C. Diara, and Nche G. Christian, "The 19th Century European Missionaries and the Fight Against Malaria in Africa," *Mediterranean Journal of Social Sciences* 4, no. 16 (2013): 89–96.

to Liberia before quinine was widely available. Early Catholic missions had no catechists among the people, and they could not find priests in Europe to lead their missions and coordinate their volunteers.

The sixteenth century was also the period in which the Catholic Church and its doctrine were the primary authority for Christianity and religion in Europe. However, its religious tenets were incompatible with African societies' philosophy and cultural values. The Church saw itself as a civilization, offering the only road to salvation and redemption. Africans felt that some communal matters could transcend the authority of the Church. Personal beliefs and the concept of personal commitment advanced by the Church were also difficult to reconcile with the communal cosmology of Africans. Without any viable structure on the ground to promote the cause of the Catholic mission, the few elites who had allegedly converted quickly lapsed and resumed native practices. Christianity lasted for some time in Warri, where many royal family members were Christian converts between 1570 and 1733.[56]

Many of the obstacles that thwarted early missions were subtly – and occasionally overtly – removed by the missions that followed in the nineteenth century. The 1789 incident in Haiti could be interpreted as part of the winds of change that blew through European capitals and America during the eighteenth century. The war in America, the Revolution in France, the Industrial Revolution in Britain, and the rise of the Protestants in America and Europe are examples of how political and social landscapes were changing in the West. Semmel described this period as the Methodist Revolution in England – a sort of liberal version of the French Revolution that cut across the entire superstructure of the British Empire[57] to affect its presence in foreign lands. Slave uprisings and government responses brought this wave to Africa, where returnees played a major role. In sixteenth-century Warri and Benin, no Indigenous population identified with Christianity or Western civilization as transatlantic trade was in its early stages. The abolition of the slave trade and the return of former slaves to Africa strengthened Christian missions and regional trade. This relationship can be seen in an 1838 letter written by Buxton to Melbourne while canvassing for the Niger Expedition:

> We must elevate the minds of her people and call forth the resources of her soil ... Let missionaries and school masters, the plough and the spades, go together and agriculture will flourish; the avenues to legitimate commerce will be opened; confidence between man and man will be inspired; whilst civilization will advance as the natured effect and Christianity operate as the proximate cause of this happy change.[58]

[56] Jacob F. A. Ajayi, *Christian Missions in Nigeria, 1841–1891* (London: Longman, 1965), 9.
[57] Bernard Semmel, *The Methodist Revolution* (London: Heinemann Educational Books, 1974), 6–7.
[58] Quoted in Ajayi, *Christian Missions*, 10–11.

PRELUDE TO COLONIZATION: TRADE AND MISSIONS   89

The Niger Expedition was launched in 1841, consisting of professionals from different fields, including medicine, anthropology, geography, and evangelism.[59] Its goal was to learn about the people and land that would be exploited for commercial and religious goals. The mission cost about £100,000, and Buxton died two years later. He was disappointed by his expedition's outcome and expense, but it sent a clear message to emerging entrepreneurs in Europe. The idea resonated even more among business leaders interested in expanding trade and trading networks in the Nigerian area and the rest of West Africa.

Earlier in the nineteenth century, various explorers had traversed the River Niger area and coastal region to prepare for the expansion of the market in this "new age" of trade. The routes and waterways mapped by explorers, such as Mungo Park and the Lander brothers, allowed Christian missions to access the hinterlands.[60] The Buxton expedition and returnee captives added to their knowledge of the local terrain. In 1842, the Badagry mission was established as a launching point for expeditions into the hinterlands.[61] Henry Townsend visited Abeokuta in the same year, but its mission was not established until around four years later.[62]

Egba returnees were among the freed captives in Sierra Leone. Their migration to their new homeland began in the 1830s, and they arrived in the town of Abeokuta, where they acted as agents of social change.[63] For various reasons, such as their acculturation with Western taxonomic modernity and an evolving social milieu that demanded fundamental social changes, some of this returning population retained their Christian identities. By 1846, continuous demands for priests to oversee their spirituality and represent the Christian faith were finally heeded by the colonial government in Sierra Leone. This resulted in the return of Henry Townsend.[64]

The period from the 1830s until about 1897 was considered the height of missionary activity and imperial interest that culminated in the invasion of

---

[59] Howard Temperley, *White Dreams, Black Africa: The Antislavery Expeditions to the River Niger 1841–1842* (New Haven: Yale University Press, 1991).

[60] William H. Clarke, *Travels and Explorations in Yorubaland, 1856–1858*, ed., Joseph A. Atanda (Ibadan: Ibadan University Press, 1972).

[61] William H. Taylor, *Mission to Educate: A History of the Educational Work of the Scottish Presbyterian Mission in East Nigeria 1846–1960* (Leiden: E. J. Brill, 1996), 51.

[62] This date is given as 1843 in other accounts, which adds to the disagreement over whether this followed the visitation of the British missionary agent, Thomas Birch Freeman, to the town in 1842. See S. A. Dada, *A History of the African Church* (Ibadan: Aowa Printers, 1986), 2; Harunah, "Sodeke: Hero and Statesman," 109; and Harry A. Gaily, *Lugard and the Abeokuta Uprising: The Demise of Egba Independence* (London: Routledge, 1982), 9.

[63] John D. Y. Peel, *Religious Encounter and the Making of the Yoruba* (Bloomington: Indiana University Press, 2003).

[64] Saburi O. Biobaku, *The First 150 Years of the Egba at Abeokuta: 1830–1980* (Lagos: Nelson Publishers Limited, 1990).

multiple sovereign entities in parts of Southern Nigeria.[65] It sealed the fate of southern polities that might be called recalcitrant: six different missionary bodies operated in this area, including the Anglican Church Missionary Society (CMS), The Wesleyan Society, the Methodist Missionary Society, the French mission committee of the United Presbyterian Church of Scotland, the Foreign Mission Board of the Southern Baptist Convention of the United States, and the Catholic Society of African Missions of France.[66] Scottish missionaries entered Calabar in 1846; the Southern Baptist Convention laid their station in Badagry and Ijaiye in 1850 and 1851, respectively; the Catholics in 1867; and the Holy Ghost Fathers in 1884, among others.

The arrival of these missionary bodies was well-timed for the politics of the Nigerian area and its advancement in science and technology. These groups were instrumental in restoring political balance, building political power, and maintaining political hegemony from the middle of the nineteenth century to 1900 when the colonial state swiftly imposed control. They usurped this role from groups and emerging powers, including the Fulani, the Ibadan, and the Dahomey. In the locations where they were allowed to establish stations, local rulers focused more on the political advantage gained from a missionary presence, dismissing the ecclesiastical component as a minor concern.

These alliances were similar to the one between Afonja and Alimi: the former remained indifferent to Islam while forging political ties with the latter. Ayandele referred to earlier attempts to Christianize the Bight of Benin as "feeble and spasmodic." During that time, the Olu of Warri had aligned with Augustinian Missionaries from São Tomé to end Benin's imperialism. In this later stage, when missionaries had the backing of their home governments – including access to their military capabilities – Egba chiefs welcomed the arrival of the Church Missionary Society in Abeokuta. The mid-nineteenth century saw geopolitical power in the region shift against their neighbors: Ibadan, Dahomey, and Ijebu.[67]

Abeokuta had previously played defense against its strong neighboring polities. By the mid-nineteenth century, it went on the offensive with its access to British-supplied weapons. Mahadi has explained that the Egba's defeat of the Dahomey Army during this period led the king to view his Hausa mallams with mistrust. This population had been migrating across the West African region on an unprecedented scale since the late eighteenth century. They assumed roles where royals, nobles, and commoners valued their magico-spiritual responsibilities in their new locations. This contributed to the spread of Islam in the Old Oyo Empire and the rest of the Yoruba territory during the

---

[65] Ogbu U. Kalu, ed., *Christianity in West Africa: The Nigerian Story* (Ibadan: Daystar, 1978).
[66] Ajayi, *Christian Missions*, 13–15.
[67] Saburi Biobaku, *The Egba and Their Neighbors 1842–1872* (London: Oxford University Press, 1965).

late eighteenth century.[68] These migrations also occurred during the empire's decline in the following century. Their spiritual practices, along with the literacy and elitism of the religion typified by the clothing culture among Dahomey's Hausa population, attracted the population to the religion brought by Hausa migrants and merchants.

Although the king's mallams had promised him victory in his confrontation with Abeokuta, he was disappointed. He had not expected the missionaries to intervene on behalf of their mission in Abeokuta and the Christian converts there. The presence of missionaries typically transformed a location into a British-protected zone, later called a protectorate. Abeokuta leaders used the influence of the missionaries to advance their geopolitical interests, until this relationship broke down during the Ifole crisis of 1867.[69] The history of this expulsion began in Lagos. This strategic Atlantic city, riddled with political shenanigans, was dominated by two parties: the Kosoko and the Akitoye. The British government had primarily been concerned with enacting the full abolition of slavery and promoting legitimate trade in its place. This interest allied them with the missionaries, who were themselves promoting their home countries' imperial interests.[70] Britain's growing industry and an alliance between the Akitoye faction and the missionaries triggered the invasion of Lagos in 1851.

Others had hoped to follow the path of Akitoye and the Egba chiefs, which led to the defeat of the Dahomey army, but the annexation of Lagos in 1861 was an unpleasant shock for local leaders, including the Egba chiefs. They had wanted the British government to support their (imperialistic) goals in local geopolitical developments and had not sought the political imposition of an alien ruler. As Afonja learned in Ilorin, these relationships can be difficult to manage. The resulting 1861 action took control of Lagos away from the coastal city's traditional rulers and transferred it to the British Empire. This began the decline of missionary activities in the Nigerian area. Various missions left Yorubaland, moving to Lagos or returning to Europe. One enduring legacy of British control of Lagos was the development of the seaport that heralded the city's growth in the nineteenth century (see Figure 4.1).

Kings and chiefs feared the loss of their sovereignty, but the evolving social milieu meant that their suspicion of the missionaries was not enough to deter

---

[68] Tajudeen G. O. Gbadamosi, *The Growth of Islam among the Yoruba, 1841–1908* (New Jersey: Humanities Press, 1978).
[69] Gaily, *Lugard and the Abeokuta Uprising*, 17.
[70] The Holy Ghost Fathers, for the French government; the Christian Missionary Society, for the British; and the Foreign Mission Board of the Southern Baptist Convention of the United States, for American interest. Before the final demarcation of colonial boundaries, these missionary bodies competed for stations in West Africa with the added interest of promoting their home countries' trading interests. Newbury, *The Western Slave Coast*.

Figure 4.1 The development of Lagos seaport wharf was a contributing factor to the development of Lagos in the nineteenth century.

them from forging political alliances. Despite changing attitudes after the Lagos incident, missionaries were integral to the peace treaty signed by different parties to end Yorubaland's protracted political crisis in 1886. The Akitoye and Kosoko case in Lagos was typical of events that led to invasion or the threat of invasion. The same theme is common in delta polities such as Warri, Itsekiri, and Opobo. Polities on the northern plains of the Niger were mostly under Sokoto rulership, such as Nupe, Sokoto, and Kano. These polities, including those in the Muslim north, had called for the presence of the missionaries at various times after the missionaries resumed their activities in the Nigerian area. From 1842 onwards, missionaries were invited into various domains by leaders who sought to increase their political standing and counteract powerful regional authorities or usurp, retain, or consolidate power within a polity.

Examples included the relationship between Zaria and the Sokoto caliphate in the second half of the nineteenth century and the struggle between Nana Olomu, who succeeded his father in Itsekiri, and Dogho, his rival.[71] Ayandele has shown how the literacy of the northern polities under the Sokoto caliphate led the missionaries to the mistaken assumption that this population would be the most receptive to their missionary work. It was assumed that Islam had

---

[71] Obaro Ikime, "Colonial Conquest and Resistance in Southern Nigeria," *Journal of the Historical Society of Nigeria* 6, no. 3 (1972): 267–268.

prepared these communities for a monotheistic worldview, which would allow for a smooth transition to the cosmological view propagated by missionaries. In reality, this population was the most difficult to engage.

The year 1888 was recognized as the termination of enthusiastic missionary activities in the north. Many of the efforts resulted in no converts.[72] Those who engaged with the missionaries were mostly preaching Islam, hoping to convert the new arrivals, and some diviners and practitioners of traditional belief systems did the same.[73] This experience is seen in the case of Bishop Samuel Ajayi Crowther during the tour of his upper Niger mission. He encountered Muslim converts in places like Ilorin, Ibadan, and the Middle-Belt region, who engaged him in theological arguments.[74]

Missionaries sought to convert this population to spread Western civilization and knowledge. The military strength and the imperial network the missionaries could access endeared them to polities around the River Niger and the Lake Chad region. The delta states of Bonny, Itsekeri, Old Calabar, and Brass benefited from a more literate population that was able to manage their emerging economies, which was of particular interest to the trading elites. Like others, they would blend this with their traditional structures and systems.

The missionaries also jostled the established political order as they influenced the evolution of the polities in many of these areas. This often culminated in establishing protectorates led by individuals selected by their political leadership. The limited effectiveness of missionary activities in the northern part of the country led the population in the south to migrate northwards. This was not done for trade, as in previous decades, but to administer the imperial structure that was put in place. This migration continued during the colonial era, affecting the social demography of the colony and the subsequent independent state.

The return of freed captives revitalized missionary efforts in the Niger area. The British and Foreign Bible Society was established in 1804, aiming to subsidize the production, importation, and distribution of religious texts through missionary efforts. This did little to gain converts until the Bible was translated into local languages for the cultures and peoples in some parts of the country in the second half of the century. Samuel Ajayi Crowther, S. F. Schon, G. P. Bargoy, A. W. Banfield, Miller, and other local and foreign missionaries

---

[72] Emmanuel A. Ayandele, *The Missionary Factor in Northern Nigeria, 1870–1918* (New York: Routledge, 1979), 519.

[73] John D. Y. Peel, "Problems and Opportunities in an Anthropologist's Use of a Missionary Archive," in *Missionary Encounters: Sources and Issues*, ed. Robert A. Bickers and Rosemary Seton (Hove: Psychology Press, 1996), 75.

[74] Femi J. Kolapo, *Christian Missionary Engagement in Central Nigeria, 1857–1891: The Church Missionary Society's All African Mission on the Upper Niger* (Cham: Palgrave Macmillan, 2019).

deployed their linguistics skills to create a body of letters and words in local languages as they began documenting them in religious instructional books and dictionaries.[75] Their work would become the standard characterization of Nigerian languages, including Hausa, which had earlier been recorded in the Ajami form of the Arabic language.

Like Crowther, Allakura Sharp was determined to "liberate" his brethren in the North by converting them to Christianity.[76] Sharp was a freed Kanuri captive from Borno. James Johnson, a descendant of returnee blacks in Sierra Leone, was posted to the CMS mission in the Niger area.[77] Like others, he believed in transforming African minds and societies through Christianity and Christian civilization. Racial discrimination within the Church resulted in a confrontation with religious authorities, which led to his promotion of other African clerics of the time and the propagation of the idea of Ethiopianism.[78]

In subsequent years, Mojola Agbebi, William E. Cole, Jacob K. Coker, and other emerging cultural nationalists in Yorubaland responded to the situation with the Church and its treatment of James Johnson and Samuel Ajayi Crowther. They created new denominations from existing churches.[79] These were the Native Baptist Church, the United Native African Church, the African Church, and others that became the harbingers of African Christianity.[80] Although they were kaleidoscopic in doctrine and tenets, which created some divisions among them, their central theme was "Africa for the African."[81] This shared bond allowed them to collaborate productively. Many of these denominations, known as the Aladura group in Yorubaland, have since become the globalized African Christianity, which incorporates several cultural elements into its system and practices.[82]

During the first phase of this missionary activity, missionaries gained most of their followers from common people and those who had fled their masters to receive British protection. This was a change from efforts in the sixteenth

---

[75] Kolapo, *Christian Missionary Engagement*.
[76] Henry Barth, *Travels and Discoveries in North and Central Africa: Including Accounts of Tripoli, the Sahara, the Remarkable Kingdom of Bornu, and the Countries around Lake Chad* (London: Ward, Lock, 1890), 286–310.
[77] Graham A. Duncan, "Ethiopianism in Pan-African Perspective, 1880–1920," *Studia Historiae Ecclesiasticae* 41, no. 2 (2015): 198–218.
[78] Albert A. Boahen, "New Trends and Processes in Africa in the Nineteenth Century," in *General History of Africa: VI Africa in the Nineteenth Century until the 1880s*, ed. Jacob F. A. Ajayi (Paris: UNESCO Publishing, 1998), 55–56.
[79] Oluwafunminiyi Raheem, "Martin Luther versus Us: Assessing the Reformation through the Perspectives of an African Class," *African Diaspora Discourse – ADD* 2, no. 2 (2020): 66–67.
[80] Dada, *A History of the African Church*.
[81] Raheem, "Martin Luther versus Us," 66.
[82] Vicki Brennan, *Singing Yoruba Christianity: Music, Media and Morality* (Bloomington: Indiana University Press, 2018).

century when missionary attention was focused on the elite class. The renewed efforts hoped to create a middle-class population that would be consumers and carriers of Western civilization and advocates for imperial interests. This social class was used in the transformation of England, France, and other Western cultures from the middle of the eighteenth century to the solidification of the revolutions in the centuries that followed. This focus on society's lower class was enabled by the socioeconomic dictates of the time: the expansion of trade and the abolition of slavery.

These forces transformed Brass, Old Calabar, Lagos, Warri, Bonny, and other coastal settlements into trading city-states. They had formerly been known as slave-trading outposts or small fishing villages, but Christianity and Christian civilization quickly spread through these coastal cities and they developed into important economic centers. It became difficult for polities such as Itsekiri to maintain relevance as legitimate trade became more entrenched and larger amounts of private wealth were created. This social and political upheaval advanced the interests of the missionaries and supported their imperial objectives.

No local authority could question missionary activities while they were promoting free trade. In many cases, the missionaries and their governments held "free trade" to be synonymous with "monopoly of trade" as long as Western interests monopolized that trade. This was a major contention between missionaries and many polities; traditional rulers had expected to maintain the trade dynamics that existed during the slave trade, allowing them to wield formidable clout. Constraints on whom they were allowed to trade with and which goods were permissible for trading undermined their traditional authority as sovereign leaders.

Some political leaders who sought to retain their status, such as those in Kano, insisted that their royal houses received preferential treatment in trading engagements with Europeans. These demands reflected the dynamics in Lagos during the slave trade, mirroring the privileges held by monarchs, royal households, and their affiliates in the past. This attempt to restore such privileges informed the establishment of Opobo (bombarded about a decade later by the British navy), along with other polities that had attempted to maintain these rights and privileges in the new era of trade.[83]

The socioeconomic milieu of the time prevented European missionaries and traders from accepting the terms proposed by local rulers. The latest infiltration of European influence sought to reach ordinary Africans, not just the elites engaged by the previous trade regime. The more these missionaries and traders were able to undermine the political authority of Indigenous rulers, the more latitude they had to pursue their goals.

---

[83] Jaja, *Opobo Since 1870*, XIX.

Missionaries either followed trade, working through the trading outposts established by their home countries, or vice versa, opening local markets and areas of trade through missionary activities.[84] This explains the relative failure of missionary work in Northern Nigeria, where trade and profits were limited compared to the south.[85] Differences between the terrain and climate in the two regions also determined what they produced for the export market. The combination of an unreceptive audience and insufficiently profitable trade meant that this population could not fulfill the aspiration of spreading missionary work throughout the Nigerian area.

The education system, training programs, trade incentives, and other humanitarian activities of missionaries triggered a rural–urban migration. Coastal cities and important neighboring polities witnessed swift expansion during these years, which increased in the early part of the twentieth century. Missionary projects that had been proposed earlier – for the civilization of African societies and the promotion of European technological advancement – were commissioned along with other infrastructural developments to support the Pax Britannica project.

Buxton's letter explains that the mission's success would hinge on the provision of medical facilities, the introduction of Western education, the facilitation of trade and commerce, and the cultivation of lands. This combination influenced the posting and activities of the missionaries. In 1899, when the Foreign Board of London considered extending its mission to the northern end of the River Niger, staff were assigned based on their medical and industrial skills. The Catholic Church, possibly due to its earliest experiences in the area, pursued a vigorous health campaign that was unmatched. They built schools, and in a few places they created the only modern health facility available in the area. Through schools and hospitals, they gained converts.

The role of Catholic missionaries during the 1914 Ijemo massacre in Abeokuta shows this dynamic at work.[86] The Catholic priest, Father Sounde, treated many of the people injured in the massacre, and they became Christian converts. The humanitarian gestures of missionaries during this period, either by educating people or by treating their illnesses and injuries, created a sense of gratitude that made conversion easier.[87] The Church established training schools for artisans, teaching masonry, carpentry, tailoring, and welding skills. They also established plans to support these trades after completion of their

---

[84] This was the case with the delta states of Bonny, Itsekiri, and others, such as Abeokuta, Lokoja, and the northern states.
[85] Chinedu N. Ubah, "Problems of Christian Missionaries in the Muslim Emirates of Nigeria, 1900–1928," *Journal of African Studies* 3, no. 3 (1976): 351–371.
[86] John L. Ausman, "The Disturbances in Abeokuta in 1918," *Canadian Journal of African Studies* 5, no. 1 (1971): 45–60.
[87] Akinjide Osuntokun, "Disaffection and Revolts in Nigeria during the First World War, 1914–1918," *Canadian Journal of African Studies* 5, no. 2 (1971): 171–192.

training. The distribution of European goods and capital assisted traders by facilitating greater amounts of trade. Farmers had access to improved versions of their existing crops, such as palm kernel and cotton, and they were introduced to new crops, such as rice, maize, and cocoa. This combination of economic and religious activities gave Africans the impression that Christianity was the path to civilization.

Conclusion

The Queen of England, during her speech on Great Britain's cotton shortage in the late nineteenth century, identified the role that residents of the Nigerian area would play. Her words triggered the events that preceded the colonial era:

> The insufficiency of the supply of raw materials upon which the great cotton industry depends has inspired me with deep concern, I trust that the efforts which are being made in various parts of the Empire to increase the area under cultivation may be attended with a large measure of success![88]

Mamdani added to these remarks as he attempted to make sense of the European situation that led to this speech. He stated that Europe's evolving socioeconomic ambience did not position manufacturers and laborers in opposition to the trade in slaves, the "living tools." Instead, it drove the colonization of global trade through the expansion of foreign production estates in the form of colonies. As the eighteenth century closed, this became the dominant discourse in Europe's political climate, especially in Britain, "so that Africans who yesterday were transported to the New World could now stay at home – in both instances to produce cotton for the 'satanic mills.'"[89]

A remarkable consequence of this role, which has persisted through subsequent eras, was the transformation of a society's means of production without a corresponding change in its mode of production. Production increased, but the processes of production did not develop accordingly. The free flow of European goods into the Nigerian area weakened local competition and industries. Kano textiles and Ijebu cloth that was once sold widely in the Maghreb and Atlantic cities and towns, up to the better part of the nineteenth century, paved the way for European materials to flood these markets at lower prices.

---

[88] The Queen, quoted in Mahmood Mamdani, *Citizens and Subjects: Contemporary Africa and the Legacy of Late Colonialism* (Princeton: Princeton University Press, 1996), 37.

[89] Mamdani, *Citizens and Subjects*, 37.

5

Lagos and the Niger Area

In the years before Portugal's and Spain's incursions into Africa – and even after their arrival and the eventual intrusion of other European imperial powers – the trans-Saharan route was a key component of regional trade.[1] It linked people and products to the Maghreb and other parts of the world. This trade route linked Africa with the rest of the world through cultural practices and elements that circulated between this region and the Arab world.[2] States located along the trans-Saharan route were regional supercultures and superpowers.[3]

In the fifteenth century, European powers arrived at the coast with cargo ships. After trade was diverted to coastal cities, this led to the collapse of several polities that had grown powerful from the trans-Saharan trade. The old routes were neither closed nor obsolete, but they began to lose significance. Dominant routes and trading markets for cross-cultural Atlantic trade were under political pressure from within and outside their polities. New commodities from Europeans that arrived through the transatlantic route were highly valued. Subsequent political wrangling within polities culminated in political disintegration for some and the waning of political hegemony for others.

Trade is an essential fixture in state formation, as seen in events from the fifteenth century in the Niger area[4] and the entire West African region.[5] Developments in the nineteenth century reinforced this idea. As Biafra and the Bight of Benin grew busier, so did the polities along their trade routes. Slave trade was essential in West and Central Africa until the nineteenth century, but the great Benin Empire's direct involvement was ceded to other coastal polities, such as Allada, Weme, Little Adra, Dahomey, Badagry, and, much

---

[1] Klaus Braun and Jacqueline Passon, ed. *Across the Sahara: Tracks, Trade and Cross-Cultural Exchange in Libya* (Cham, Switzerland: Springer, 2020).

[2] Ghislaine Lydon, *On Trans-Saharan Trails: Islamic Law, Trade Networks, and Cross-Cultural Exchange in Nineteenth-Century Western Africa* (New York: Cambridge University Press, 2009).

[3] M. Elfasi and I. Hrbek, *General History of Africa III: Africa from the Seventh to the Eleventh Century* (Oxford: Heinemann Publishers, 1995).

[4] The use of the "Niger Area" refers to most of the geographical space later named Nigeria.

[5] Philip D. Curtin, *The Atlantic Slave Trade: A Census* (Madison: Wisconsin Press, 1969).

later, Lagos. Trade in this region was largely controlled by Benin,[6] while Oyo was one of the largest and most powerful polities close to this market.[7]

European ships left the Benin port of Ughoton after finding a shortage of human bodies to trade, and Benin extended its political influence into coastal states to the west. The empire followed the European presence in West African markets, continuing to trade in meager supplies of slaves and other commodities and maintaining its access to European goods.[8] Benin imperialism had spread into the eastern region of Yorubaland during this period, and some of these commodities were collected as tributes there.[9] Events toward the end of the eighteenth century and the early nineteenth century saw power shifting to Lagos, Ijebu, and Dahomey.

The Nupe[10] and Hausa states[11] were conspicuously involved in the slave trade while they undertook major purges that led to the massive displacement of their populations across the Niger area. By the nineteenth century, trade and politics had become so decentralized that many powerful states competed in political consolidations, from the creeks of the delta states to the savanna and forest regions around the River Niger. These disruptions and other displaced populations of the period fed markets in Lagos and other coastal settlements in the Niger area. This chapter discusses the nineteenth-century development of Lagos and coastal politics in the Niger area.[12]

Lagos: The Making of an Atlantic City

Extant texts and data contain little information about the early history of Lagos, which is a common problem for many polities in precolonial Africa's past. Instead, the city's history is clouded by different versions of origin traditions and shrouded in contradictions, uncertainties, and extrapolations

---

[6] Philip A. Igbafe, "Slavery and Emancipation in Benin, 1897–1945," *The Journal of African History* 16, no. 3 (1975): 409–429.
[7] Adesina A. Raji, "Revisiting Oyo Empire within the Confine of the Atlantic Age," *Humanus Discourse* 1, no 4 (2021): 1–17.
[8] Alan F. C. Ryder, *Benin and the Europeans 1485–1897* (New York: Humanities Press, 1970).
[9] Stephen A. Akintoye, "The North-Eastern Yoruba Districts and the Benin Kingdom," *Journal of the Historical Society of Nigeria* IV, no. 4 (1969): 539–553.
[10] Mohammed L. Salawu, "Slave Factor in the Development of Bida Emirate: 1857–1900," *African Research Review* 11, no. 47 (2017): 13–22.
[11] Philip Burnham, "Raiders and Traders in Adamawa: Slavery as a Regional System," in *Asian and African Systems of Slavery*, ed. James L. Watson (Oxford: Blackwell, 1980), 43–72.
[12] Michael J. C. Echeruo, "The Lagos Scene in the 19th Century," *Présence Africaine* no. 82 (1972): 77–93.

regarding periods and dates.[13] Otunba Payne, in his 1893 almanac of events in Yorubaland, commenced a chronology of the Kings of Lagos with Addo in 1630.[14] Kristin Mann's chronology starts earlier, with Asipa, indicating that Addo took over during the time he is said to have reigned.[15] It is important to note that, in terms of periodic accuracy, Payne's work is less reliable, and many of his submissions are countered or redefined by other texts from professional historians and anthropologists.

Despite the contradictions and extrapolations, the history of Lagos as an Atlantic city becomes clearer as one delves into the history of trade in "living tools" in the Bight of Benin and Biafra.[16] The history of Lagos is woven together with the history of the slave trade such that it is possible to describe the evolution of Lagos as the history of the transatlantic slave trade.[17] The chronology of the kings of Lagos begins with the town's political evolution during the period of Benin's imperialism in the area. To the south of Lagos was the region known as the Bight of Benin and the Atlantic Ocean. Port cities and polities like Dahomey, Alladah, Whydah, and, later, Badagry were to the west. To the east of Lagos were Ijebu (another coastal state), Ondo, Benin, Ekiti, and Ilesa. The great Oyo Empire was to the north, along with Egbado and Egba.[18]

Lagos was a fishing community in West Africa that continuously drew migrants from across the region after the Atlantic trade route opened.[19] Its flow of migrants increased in the late eighteenth century. Similar polities, which were factions in the delta and Yoruba states, were in contact with Lagos as a coastal population center. Other settlements in Nupe and Hausa countries, as well as other West African states, also established communication with Lagos at various times in a dynamic manner that boosted their trade in human commodities, crafts, and industrial or agricultural products.[20] Lagos was constructed *ab initio* as an island group of independent polities under the

---

[13] Michael J. C. Echeruo, *Victorian Lagos: Aspects of Nineteenth Century Lagos Life* (London: Macmillan, 1977); Rasheed O. Ajetunmobi, *The Evolution and Development of Lagos State* (Lagos: A-Triad Associates, 2003); and Takiu Folami, *A History of Lagos, Nigeria: The Shaping of an African City* (New York: Exposition Press, 1982).

[14] John Augustus Otunba Payne, *Table of Principal Events in Yoruba History: With Certain Other Matters of General Interest, Compiled Principally for Use in the Court within the British Colony of Lagos, West Africa* (Lagos: Andrew M. Thomas, 1883), 6.

[15] Kristin Mann, *Slavery and the Birth of an African City Lagos 1760–1900* (Bloomington: Indiana University Press, 1997), 45.

[16] Hakeem B. Harunah, *Nigeria's Defunct Slave Ports: Their Cultural Legacies and Touristic Value* (Lagos: First Academic Publishers, 2000), 125.

[17] David Armitage and Michael J. Braddick, eds., *The British Atlantic World, 1500–1800* (New York: Palgrave Macmillan, 2002).

[18] Akin Mabogunje, "Lagos: A Study in Urban Geography," unpublished PhD dissertation, University of London, 1962.

[19] Robert Smith, "The Lagos Consulate, 1851–1861: An Outline," *The Journal of African History* 15, no. 3 (1974): 393–416.

[20] Anthony G. Hopkins, *An Economic History of West Africa* (New York: Routledge, 2020).

rulership of the Olofin, located at Iddo, the largest of the polities that dotted the lagoon area.[21]

The history and role of Lagos in West Africa, as mentioned earlier, were shaped by migrant forces, especially the military and diplomatic forces dispatched from the great Benin Empire around the sixteenth century. Other migrants, who had shaped the morphology of Lagos earlier (before the Benin impact), were mostly from locations scattered around the Old Oyo Empire and other principal Yoruba towns around the fifteenth century. The earliest migrants included the Awori from Iseri, the Ijebu, Aja, and other groups from the Gbe-speaking community.[22] All of these groups searched for the amenities and shelter provided by the lagoon. The pattern of migration and the coastal geophysical attributes had a remarkable impact on the role of Lagos in the Niger area as a collection, distribution, and market center. Environmental fixtures and the heterogeneity of its polity spurred entrepreneurial activity. It would soon be seen by Oba Akinsemoyin, who reigned between 1760 and 1775, as the center of its civilization.[23]

The formidable polity of Lagos was built around trade and commerce. After the decline of the Old Oyo Empire, different emerging and existing powers – Dahomey, Abeokuta, Ibadan, and Ijebu – scrambled to "conquer" trade routes and port cities. Lagos stood apart from these struggles, and its royals and political elites forged alliances with warring factions to safeguard their interests or act as imperial aggressors. It stood shoulder to shoulder with emerging powers in the Niger area and even arbitrated between the Egba and the Ijebu at its Ogboni house. Events in the subsequent years of the nineteenth century show that the military, commercial, and diplomatic strength of Lagos would only be subdued by the mighty British fleet, acting under the West African Anti-slavery Squadron to invade and subdue the local chiefs and king.[24] As Figure 5.1 shows, the squad mounted by the British was crucial in its overall colonization of the Niger Area at the beginning of the twentieth century.

The principal history of Lagos' influence and role it would play in the mid-nineteenth century began with Akinsemoyin.[25] He had returned from exile around the Bight of Benin, in territory that some scholars have identified as Apa or Badagry, around the middle of the eighteenth century. Akinsemoyin had encountered European slave traders, believed to be either Portuguese or

---

[21] Robert S. Smith, *Kingdoms of the Yoruba* (London: Methuen, 1969).
[22] Ade Adefuye, Babatunde Agiri, and Akinjide Osuntokun, *History of the Peoples of Lagos State* (Ikeja: Lantern Books, 1987).
[23] Mann, *Slavery and the Birth*.
[24] Adekunle Alli, *Lagos from the Earliest Times to British Occupation* (Festac-Town: Adeniran Ogunsanya College of Education, 2002).
[25] Adewale Onagbesan, Account for the Life and Times of Oba Akinsemoyin, *Academia*, www.academia.edu/30839962/ACCOUNT_OF_OBA_AKINSEMOYIN.

Figure 5.1 The West African Frontier Force mounted by the British colonial government was pivotal in the penetration and subsequent conquest of the Niger area by the first decade of the twentieth century.

Dutch, that he invited to Lagos after the demise of Erelu Kuti.[26] Traditions of this period indicate that the royal machinations that plagued the town's political system from the early nineteenth century – ultimately resulting in its invasion and annexation during the second half of the century – resembled the political activity of its early years. Ologun Kutere's reign has been characterized as the most favorable for the people of Lagos, which suggests that political stability and strong state institutions enabled unparalleled prosperity and development within the polity.[27]

Akinsemoyin was banished from Lagos after protesting against perceived injustice on behalf of Gbabaru, his uncle. Gbabaru had tampered with the town's succession plans to favor a friend who had helped save both his life and his political power. These events marked the beginning of exile politics in the history of the coastal state. This remained an integral part of the history of Lagos up until the time of the British invasion in 1851. Attacks, counterattacks, sabotage, and other underhanded tactics characterized its royal struggles for power.[28] A central theme in their traditions is that of an exiled party who

---

[26] Robin Law, "Trade and Politics Behind the Slave Coast: The Lagoon Traffic and the Ruse of Lagos, 1500–1800," *Journal of African History* 24, no. 3 (1983): 321–348.

[27] Preye Adekoya, "The Succession Dispute to the Throne of Lagos and the British Conquest and Occupation of Lagos," *African Research Review* 10, no. 42 (2016): 207–226.

[28] Adekoya, *The Succession Dispute*.

became even more powerful than the reigning king of Lagos.[29] In such cases, the king was deposed and the formerly exiled rival claimed the throne. These events showed how highly the polity regarded its economic health since the town was a conglomeration of migrants who sought trading opportunities and social stability. Lagos might be the only polity with a tradition of princes or kings returning from exile to rule. This tradition was often associated with decisions made by local chiefs, comprised of representatives from different groups within the town, who protected the polity's socioeconomic interests.

Akinsemoyin returned to Lagos with European merchants, where he sold about 269 slaves to them from 1761–5.[30] This figure showed the town's relative weakness when compared to the likes of Oyo, selling far less than the 800 slaves brought to the same market by the Alaafin in his first attempts at the trade around three decades earlier.[31] Lagos was less significant for West African trade in human cargo for many years. The region's largest buyers focused on other ports in the Bight of Benin, which consisted of several port cities and towns. Jakin, Little Popo, Alladah, Ouidah, Offra, and Apa were the most popular. Badagry and Porto Novo became relevant much later, arising from the ruins of these polities. Lagos did not become a dominant force in the regional slave trade until the eighteenth century when Dahomey gained political influence and European merchants attempted to boycott its market. Before Akinsemoyin's encounter with European merchants, Lagos was an insignificant fishing village. It was barely recognized in European lists of coastal states around the Niger area.

The Portuguese led the European infiltration of the Niger area, and their first port of call was the coastal, isolated, and sophisticated "Yoruba" polity of Ijebu in the late 1400s.[32] The traders were searching for slaves to work their new farmlands in the Americas and goods to be exchanged elsewhere along the coast. This took them to Benin, the most powerful state along the coast by the turn of the fifteenth century.[33] Because of Benin's level of development, the Portuguese named it the Bight of Benin and Biafra. Benin was the focus of European cartographers who wanted to map the West African markets, making it a global brand that received attention from virtually every European trader in the region.[34] However, Benin would not become West Africa's Liverpool or Sicily.

---

[29] On the politics of Kosoko and Akitoye, see, for instance, Obafemi Oladimomi Ayantuga, *Ijebu and its Neighbors, 1851–1914* (London: University of London, 1965).
[30] Mann, *Slavery and the Birth*, 38.
[31] Samuel Johnson, *The History of the Yorubas from the Earliest Times to the Beginning of the British Protectorate* (Lagos: CMS Bookshops, 1921), 168.
[32] Smith, *Kingdoms of the Yoruba*, 61–63.
[33] Kit Elliott, *Benin: An African Kingdom and Culture* (Minneapolis: Lerner Publications Company, 1979), 45.
[34] Alan F. C. Ryder, *Benin and the Europeans, 1485–1897* (London: Longmans, 1969).

Although it was a large and powerful entity, the Benin Empire could not meet the increasing Portuguese demands for living tools. Other European arrivals at this time, such as the Dutch, increased the market demands. Trade was initiated based on available goods, which included a small number of slaves along with pepper, ivory, and cloth that were traded for gold and gold dust at Minna. By the middle of the sixteenth century, the Portuguese empire's expansion into foreign colonies in the Americas and the Caribbean marked a complete change in trading relations.[35] Slaves were now needed on plantations in places like São Tomé, but Benin would not meet the traders' demands for healthy men taken in battle or enslaved from within the empire. This had nothing to do with humanitarian considerations; indeed, the empire was renowned for massive rituals that involved human sacrifice.[36] Instead, it needed to meet its farm plantations' need for slaves. In Minna, elites rejected Portuguese demands for slaves due to similar reasons.

When European ships initially sailed to the West African coast, they were on equal footing with the region's powerful states and dominant powers. Benin's stature led bewildered merchants to give its name to a large swath of Atlantic waters. Along with Benin, areas such as Old Oyo, Borgu, and powers far to the landlocked interior, such as Borno and Kano, sustained a massive trade network, making them comparable to Amsterdam. Over time, inequalities developed between the Europeans and Africans, and the balance of trade shifted decisively in favor of the Europeans in the nineteenth century.[37] By the second part of that century, this became a point of contention for educated natives who spoke out in the nascent press. An excerpt from a 1904 article in the *Lagos Weekly* painted a graphic picture:

> As to its effects materially by which we imply the material prosperity or advancement of the native – European civilization has only tended to make us poor. Poor because there is nothing that we produce which we offer to the world as a commodity and for which there is any demand ... It has created in us wants which it cannot supply and excited tastes which it furnishes no means of gratifying except at the expense and very often detriment of our so-called uncivilized brethren. If all the natives were civilized after the fashion of those in the civilized communities on the West Coast, all trade with the continent would be extinguished for there would be no producers. The trade now carried on the activities and industries which bring the large fleet of steamers to our shores – is supplied altogether by the natives who have not been under European

---

[35] Philip W. Porter, *Benin to Bahia: Portuguese Empire in the South Atlantic* (Saint Paul: North Central Publishing, 1959).
[36] James D. Graham, "The Slave Trade, Depopulation and Human Sacrifice in Benin History: The General Approach," *Cahiers d'Études Africaines* 5, no. 18 (1965): 317–334.
[37] Ahmed Modibbo, *European Trade, Imperialism and Under-Development in Northern Nigeria 19th and 20th Centuries* (Zaria: Ahmadu Bello University Press Limited, 2016).

training, either secular or religious. Those natives who have been under such training have lost the productive power of their fathers and have become useless drones – an incubus upon the momentum of the activities of life.[38]

This led to the primacy of external trade in economic considerations and social tastes among West African states. Trade among these polities had not been introduced by the Portuguese or the opening of the Atlantic route, but it was a well-established activity in the region. Trading networks within and outside the West African region had transported products before the dominance of Atlantic trade. However, the vast resources desperately required by Western imperial powers were ubiquitous in Africa.[39] Their arrival presented multiple trade networks that offered a variety of choices. This was most evident after the 1807 abolition of the slave trade, when the promotion and politics of "legitimate trade" culminated in the total transfer of bargaining power from African polities to European merchants in the middle of the century.

During the long period of history before the European arrivals, Benin expanded its realm of influence to Lagos.[40] Its army invaded the island, reconfigured the political culture of Lagos, infused a new social form, and attempted to expand its economy.[41] Although no sources are provided, Mann puts this event in the middle of the sixteenth century.[42] Robin Law has suggested that it occurred between the sixteenth and seventeenth centuries, using notes from his earlier work, "The Dynastic Chronology of Lagos," published in 1968 in the *Lagos Notes and Records*.[43]

Benin's occupation of Lagos came before the reign of Oba Akinsemoyin – the first ruler to be recorded in the chronology of the kings – at around 1760. Mann's postulation, placing the reign of Asipa at around 1550, is a separate question regarding the construction of the list. The key fact is that the basis of the island city's formation is rooted in a struggle for control over Atlantic markets. From Lagos, Benin maintained its trading relations with Europeans.[44] Local chiefs in Lagos, now representatives of Benin, promoted and coordinated the collection of goods from across the island and the surrounding polities.

---

[38] Cited in Echeruo, *Victorian Lagos*, 117.
[39] Bethwell A. Ogot, ed., *General History of Africa V: Africa from the Sixteenth to the Eighteenth Century* (Paris: UNESCO Publishing, 2000).
[40] Paula Ben-Amos Girshick and John Thornton, "Civil War in the Kingdom of Benin, 1689–1721: Continuity or Political Change?" *The Journal of African History* 42, no. 3 (2001): 365.
[41] Bashir O. Animashaun, "Benin Imperialism and the Transformation of Idejo Chieftaincy Institution in Lagos, 1603–1850," *Journal of the Historical Society of Nigeria* 25 (2016): 37–52.
[42] Mann, *Slavery and the Birth*, 27.
[43] Robin Law, "The Career of Adele at Lagos and Badagry," *Journal of the Historical Society of Nigeria* III, no. 2 (1978): 37.
[44] Ajetunmobi, *The Evolution and Development*, 48.

Akinsemoyin's return to the island was another historic development that made Lagos a focal point for Atlantic markets. Lagos had depended on its neighbors to maintain its food security – the topography is mostly sand. The surrounding waters were used for fishing activities that encouraged the development of other skills, such as boat-building and net-making, to manage and maximize their economic potential.[45] Lagos also developed the capacity to produce salt and smoked fish. The limited opportunities for farming encouraged the population to engage in activities that primarily involved trading, fishing, and the afore-noted boat-making, and net-making. As Atlantic trade expanded, trade networks were used to collect goods and develop new routes to meet the increasing demand.[46] These routes saw fundamental changes in what they transported and how often they were used after they became linked to the Atlantic market.

Lagos in the Atlantic Trade

Coastal navigation presented major challenges for opening up communication among coastal states in the Niger area. The principal methods of transportation used by people of the Bight of Benin and Biafra had restricted their ability to access specific regions. Bridges, fords, and flotation devices such as calabashes, canoes, tubs, and rafts could not survive passage across deep water. This obscured Lagos from European merchants in the early years of trade. Most activities occurred in local markets until the late eighteenth century, although European ships had successfully navigated the estuaries of the Niger Delta.

Communication among societies was stronger between groups linked by shallow waters.[47] Coastal communities around the Niger, including Lagos, brought in *revenue* by providing transportation services to the traders and migrants traveling through their territory.[48] They also collected tolls for goods that traveled through their domain. Indigenous structures to collect tolls, which many saw as exorbitant exploitation of merchants, remained in place until late in the nineteenth century. Attempts to counter the excesses of the toll collectors, who often doubled as gatekeepers for their communities and had sole authority over the imposition of tolls, were thwarted by civil wars, interethnic conflict, and the general political maneuverings of that century.

Lagos collected its revenue in cowries, farm goods, and the newly introduced British currency. Toll collectors demanded as much as £5.25 from traders,

---

[45] Adefuye, Agiri, and Osuntokun, *History of the Peoples of Lagos State*.
[46] Adefuye, Agiri, and Osuntokun, *History of the Peoples of Lagos State*.
[47] Rasheed O. Ajetunmobi, "Theories and Concepts in Migration and Settlement Studies: The Case of the Coastal Yoruba," *The Social Sciences*, 7, no. 2 (2012): 289–296.
[48] Ayodeji Olukoju, "Making Sense of the Yoruba Littoral," *Yoruba Studies Review* 2, no. 1 (2017): 45–60.

which explains the city's rapid advancement during the eighteenth century. The sudden rise of Lagos during this period has been attributed to the transatlantic slave trade shifting westward, away from the influence of Dahomey. The value of slaves exported from Lagos was immeasurable due to the city's political, military, and economic clout, which shows the developmental domino effect of trade flows during this period. During the two-decade reign of Ologun Kutere, who saw Lagos' military prowess expand to play an influential role in the Badagry debacle of the late eighteenth century, about 50,000 slaves were shipped across the Atlantic from Lagos port.[49] This number was distributed unevenly throughout his reign. The largest recorded number of slaves (21,412) were shipped around the turn of the nineteenth century.

Lagos had barely increased its participation in West Africa's trading of human cargo before intervening in geopolitical developments around the Niger area. It began with Badagry in the 1780s, using a standing army filled with captives from Hausaland, Nupe, and others from the interior. This suggests that Lagos had previously been increasing its participation in the slave trade through other markets around the Bight of Benin. The city's ability to construct larger, more efficient transportation systems to navigate the surrounding waters contributed substantially to its increasing participation. More efficient boats saved time while navigating the island, increasing trade volume. The volume and frequency of trips to collect goods from around the Bight of Benin had gradually improved since the 1760s when merchants were first invited to the port city. European goods became regular trading items in Lagos during this period, particularly among nobles and the royal family. European goods were also used for diplomatic gestures, and European weapons were used for defense and aggression. Not only did the economic and social value of these goods boost the material wealth of the elites in Lagos, they also enabled a population increase that expanded the economic base and collection of revenue for the king and chiefs. Ologun Kutere used these advantages to maintain political stability during his reign.

Competition among royalty had plagued Lagos since the time of Gbabaru and Akinsemoyin, and Ologun Kutere's immediate predecessor, Eletu Kekere, reigned for less than four years. Ologun Kutere took the throne in 1780, when around 2,000 slaves were shipped from Lagos. By distributing the slave trade's benefits among influential families and trusted slaves, he maintained his hold on power in a way that was not seen during the period that preceded his reign or the subsequent administrations until the 1861 annexation. Trade, especially in imported goods, had become the single most important aspect of society. Political stability and economic expansion established Lagos as a formidable coastal polity from the late eighteenth century. Around 50,000 slaves were shipped from its port from 1780 to 1803, and its population increased from

---

[49] Mann, *Slavery and the Birth*, 60.

5,000 to around 20,000 over roughly the same period. Its restructured economy enabled new social forms that affected the organization of labor, economic structures, and familial relations, making Lagos a power bloc in West African trade and geopolitics.[50] This period overlapped Oyo's constitutional crisis, leading to political turbulence in regions where most of its trading goods, including slaves, originated. That had tremendous implications for Lagos's economic growth, market consolidation, and political exactitude. Unlike Dahomey, Old Oyo's policy toward the Atlantic did not include control over ports. The weakening of the empire during this time offered a decentralized market base for Yoruba territory.[51]

The liberalization of markets in the Niger area, heralded by the transition from the slave trade to the so-called "legitimate trade," began with the decline of different monarchical structures in the area starting at the turn of the eighteenth century.[52] The breaking of royal trade monopolies weakened royal control over trade and commerce in their domains. This happened across many Niger states as years of political instability and turmoil began.[53] It was later evident that the transition to the liberal economic regime in the delta region and other parts of the Bight of Benin and Biafra was effectively an act of rebellion against state authorities in these areas. In Itsekiri, this relegated the local kingship tradition to irrelevance. In other places, it meant that people colluded with European merchants and merchant companies to undermine the ruling powers.

In the context of Old Oyo's decline and the rise of Lagos, this began with other state actors engaging in greater amounts of trade, especially in the slave trade. Old Oyo had previously dominated this market, but emerging powers opposed it.[54] The empire left a power vacuum that encouraged raids and kidnapping to acquire slaves that could be sold. As more players became involved in the market, more slaves were captured, and cargo ships moved westward to conduct business from the port of Lagos, which meant that the city saw increasing traffic in its domain. Even after the slave trade became illegal, thousands of victims were smuggled aboard cargo ships to avoid

---

[50] Sandra Barnes, *Patrons and Power: Creating A Political Community in Metropolitan Lagos* (Indianapolis: Indiana University Press, 1986).

[51] Robin Law, *The Oyo Empire c.1600–c.1836: A West African Imperialism in the Era of the Atlantic Slave Trade* (London: Oxford University Press, 1977); Peter Morton-Williams, "The Oyo and the Atlantic Trade 1670–1830," *Journal of the Historical Society of Nigeria* III, no. 1 (1964): 25–45.

[52] Gabriel O. Oguntomisin, "Political Change and Adaptation in Yorubaland in the Nineteenth Century," *Canadian Journal of African Studies* 15, no. 2 (1981): 225–228.

[53] Olatunji Ojo, "The Organization of the Atlantic Slave Trade in Yorubaland, Ca. 1777 to Ca.1856," *The International Journal of African Historical Studies* 41, no. 1 (2008): 77–100.

[54] Jacob F. A. Ajayi and Robert Smith, *Yoruba Warfare in the 19th Century* (London: Cambridge University Press, 1964).

detection by antislavery squads.[55] The decentralized nature of this traffic allowed Lagos to accumulate power in ways that were not possible for the devastated towns of Whydah and Ouidah from earlier in the seventeenth century into the eighteenth century.[56]

With absolute control over trade, internal political stability, and the other dynamics previously mentioned, Ologun Kutere strengthened the institution of government and built a strong economy that made Lagos a central focus of trade, migration, commerce, and European activity. This institution had been on a steady footing since Benin's imperial conquest – another reason for this period's advancements. The island's heterogeneous composition and the hegemony of Benin before the nineteenth century ensured that the distribution of power and respect was maintained through the king, vis-à-vis the institution of government. The latter was so strong that, even after the royal struggles for power characterizing the years that followed the reign of Ologun Kutere, the town maintained its political autonomy. Apart from its own exiled princes, Lagos faced no real threat from emerging regional powers.

The administration of Lagos established checks and balances that were strengthened by the demographics of the town's residents. There was no Gaha[57] figure among the chiefs, like the one found in the Old Oyo Empire, especially among the Idejo class. Neither the chiefs nor the king became more powerful than the entire institution of government. When a powerful chief had issues with Kosoko in the years after Kutere's demise, that chief had to leave the town in self-exile, losing the support of other chiefs in keeping the prince away from town. However, when that chief returned to town, it led to a civil war that unseated Kosoko after he lost his faction's support.

As war raged in the hinterlands, revenue continued accumulating in Lagos.[58] Its neighbor, the Egba, also saw an advantage from its position on the Ogun River, allowing it to collect tolls on goods and products that moved through its emergent town of Abeokuta. As the volume and frequency of trade sharply increased during this period, ferry stations became potential markets in their own right. Transportation through deep water remained challenging, and trips to port were daunting for traders during the rainy season when routes

---

[55] Olatunji Ojo, "The Slave Ship Manuelita and the Story of a Yoruba Community, 1833–1834," *Tempo* 23, no. 2 (2017): 361–382.

[56] Robin Law, "A Lagoonside Port on the Eighteenth-Century Slave Coast: The Early History of Badagri," *Canadian Journal of African Studies* 28, no. 1 (1994): 32–59.

[57] Robin Law, "Making Sense of a Traditional Narrative: Political Disintegration in the Kingdom of Oyo," *Cahiers d'Études Africaines* 22, no. 87/88 (1982): 387–401.

[58] Ann O'Hear, "The Enslavement of Yoruba," in *The Yoruba Diaspora in the Atlantic World*, ed. Toyin Falola and Matt D. Child (Bloomington: Indiana University Press, 2005), 56–76.

were slippery and could be filled with bush ants.[59] Environmental conditions defined trade patterns across the region for the better part of the nineteenth century until the colonial government constructed trade routes and built up the region's transportation industry. Before that time, trade was mostly organized during the dry season.

Water travel was the dominant navigation method between towns around the Bight of Benin and Biafra. The water route was considered faster and more efficient for carrying loads than travel by land, although such trade routes were plagued by pirates who hijacked goods and took captives to sell in slave markets. An account from Osifekunde, a Yoruba trader, describes being kidnapped by Ijo pirates and sold to the slave market in Warri during one of his trips.[60]

Slaves for the Atlantic market mostly came from landlocked hinterlands, and the coastal states were usually small polities that relied on larger interior powers to ensure a supply of slaves. The European slave trade was affected by the limitations of water transport. Hausa captives were taken through the Nupe territory, which also produced substantial amounts of slaves, and their journey to reach slave markets across the Niger River was regularly delayed. After arriving in places such as Ijakin, Ilorin, and Ibadan, they were taken to Lagos port. As the trade network along these routes increased with the spread of the jihad, Hausa and Nupe merchants began to boycott these markets. Instead, they preferred to sell captives and other commodities directly to the Lagos market.[61] Coastal states of the delta mostly produced agricultural products, and trade through coastal networks was a significant part of their normal experience.

Trade and commerce provided an opportunity to overcome an environment's material limitations. Onitsha women, like their counterparts in Ijebu and elsewhere in Yorubaland, organized their trade activities around their Omu (Queen) under the protection of the king and his chiefs. Beyond the borders of delta states and coastal communities, where traders needed protection from pirates, security was provided. They mostly moved in caravans, due to security risks and as protection from thieves, marauders, and bandits. Trade brought Onitsha women to the fore of their society and its administration as their interest was protected by their Omu patron. Gloria Chuku explained that "before 1900, Oguta women were carrying their trading activities over the

---

[59] Gabriel O. Ogunremi, *Counting the Camels: The Economics of Transportation in Pre-Industrial Nigeria* (New York: Nok Publishers International, 1982), 53–54.

[60] Peter C. Lloyd, "Osifekunde of Ijebu," in *Africa Remembered: Narratives by West Africans from the Era of the Slave Trade*, ed. Phillip D. Curtin (Madison: University of Wisconsin Press, 1967), 217–288.

[61] Mahadi Adamu, *The Hausa Factor in West African History* (Zaria: Ahmadu Bello University Press, 1978).

Oguta Lake and along Niger River by canoe to Ossomari, Aboh, and Onitsha."[62] Ikosi, Ode Omi, Ikorodu, Ikosi, Ijebu, Mahin, Maku, and Eko (Lagos) were linked by the lagoon through which their traders traveled, and this network would later include Badagry, Epe, and others. From Maku, traders traveled as far as the Ughoton to reach Benin, Warri, and other delta states. In an account that mirrors the traders' experience, Osifekunde notes that it could take up to two days to travel from Kuramo to Ode Omi by sea, while the trip from Ode Omi to Mahin took around nine hours.[63]

When slaves had to be moved over land with farm products and other goods, they acted as porters and took on the role of the camels, horses, and donkeys that usually carried the items. The wars, raids, and invasions that produced slaves until the 1900s were carried out during the dry season when harvests had been gathered for the year and residents relaxed until the next season for planting.[64] This gave three advantages to the invaders: they could loot the harvests of these communities, put the captives to work in domestic and commercial activities during and after the dry season, and easily transport their loot to other locations. In the rainy season, these polities concentrated on cultivating their farmlands, supporting the revenue derived from the sale of human captives. Their agricultural products were sold alongside looted goods in the local markets, and intermediaries sold those items to the Atlantic market.

During the abolition of the slave trade, these dynamics shifted. Human captives were sold mainly within the West African market, and agricultural produce became the primary commodities traded in Atlantic markets. This development both amplified and extended the intervention of Western imperial states in the Niger polities. It affected the internal dynamics of trade and relationships with the forces of production along with trade networks and transportation systems. This increased the volume of trade, participation in trade, and the frequency of trading activities in ways that substantially affected transportation networks. The colonial government began to develop these networks even before its official declaration of the Nigerian colony.

Lagos existed at the center of the transportation network, continuing to act as the nerve center for West African trade in the Niger, which had begun with the arrival of European slave ships in the 1780s. Bohannan and Dalton have identified three market structures in the Niger area based on their supporting states: societies without markets, societies with peripheral markets, and

---

[62] Gloria I. Chuku, "From Petty Traders to International Merchants: A Historical Account of Three Igbo Women of Nigeria in Trade and Commerce, 1886 to 1970," *African Economic History* 27 (1999): 2.

[63] Lloyd, "Osifekunde of Ijebu," 242.

[64] Jacob F. A. Ajayi and Stephen A. Akintoye, "Yorubaland in the Nineteenth Century," in *Groundwork of Nigerian History*, ed. Obaro Ikime (Ibadan: Heinemann Educational Books, 1999), 276–290.

societies dominated by markets and commercial transactions.[65] Lagos fell into the third category, which scholars have described as among the states impacted by trade and market principles. The city occupied a significant position in cross-cultural trade, which characterized the Niger-area politics from the late eighteenth century. Its various transportation options made it an attractive destination for traders and migrants from all over the area, even migrants from the diaspora during the years of repatriation.[66] Neighbors like Mahin and Ugbo never transformed into market states.

Lagos and the Imperial Politics of Colonization

Figures that track the sale of human cargo indicate that the Portuguese were the lead European buyers until the market's collapse in the late 1860s.[67] Portugal was the first European country to trade in African slaves and one of the last countries to comply with the Abolition Act.[68] After the Tordesillia treaty of 1494, which supposedly divided the world between Spain and Portugal, the two countries acquired influence over a vast area of land.[69] Their rivalry was like that of France and Britain. The Pope supervised and sanctioned the treaty to resolve the two empires' scramble to expand and acquire foreign territories. Similar dynamics played out in the Berlin Conference of 1884–5.

To cultivate its newly acquired lands, Portugal sought to acquire African laborers. Its economy relied on this slave labor, an example that other European powers followed. Portugal expanded its political influence in Europe through its foreign farm colonies, which meant that its transformation into an industrial economy was slower than that of Britain. It actively participated in the slave trade even after it had become "illegal." From 1601 to 1867, the Portuguese took more than a million captives from the Bight of Benin – around 1,134,714[70] – while the British acquired a total of 358,410 over the same period.[71] Spain, Portugal's main rival when the West African market was opened, only took 138,845 captives from 1676 to 1775. Spain had ceased its

---

[65] Paul Bohannan and George Dalton, eds., *Markets in Africa* (Evanston: North Western University Press, 1965).
[66] Mariana P. Candido and Adam Jones, *African Women in the Atlantic World: Property, Vulnerability and Mobility, 1660–1880* (London: James Currey, 2019), 148–170.
[67] Emilia Viotti da Costa, "The Portuguese–African Slave Trade: A Lesson in Colonialism," *Latin American Perspectives* 12, no. 1 (1985): 41–61.
[68] Charles Boxer, *The Portuguese Seaborne Empire, 1415–1825* (New York: A.A. Knopf, 1969).
[69] Samuel Edward Dawson, *The Lines of Demarcation of Pope Alexander VI and the Treaty of Tordesillas A. D. 1493 and 1494* (Ottawa: Hope & Sons, 1899).
[70] da Costa, "The Portuguese–African Slave Trade."
[71] David Richardson, *Principles and Agents: The British Slave Trade and Its Abolition* (Yale: Yale University Press, 2022).

participation in the market before resuming trade in 1776.[72] Its participation in the market was similar to Dutch, Danish, and US activity, which recorded between 3,937 and 124,974 humans traded over the same period. These figures, which track captives taken by national carriers for these countries, suggest that Britain was never a dominant slave trader or exporter in the Bight of Benin. By 1867, when official records were terminated, the French had taken the lead by accumulating 3,652,86 captives from the area.[73] Britain's marginal position in the market made it much easier to transition into agricultural trade. Its role in establishing the Abolition Act was related to these dynamics.

The number of slaves imported into Britain by British merchants was dramatically reduced after the Abolition Act. In the roughly two decades before the act, the British had taken 46,751 captives from the Bight of Benin. In the following two decades, only 13,791 were taken. British merchants had already been trading agricultural commodities in West African markets during their years of involvement in the slave trade. Trade in these commodities intensified shortly before the termination of their involvement in the slave trade in 1825. The Industrial Revolution and the empire's economic needs substantially influenced this process.

British, Dutch, Danish, and American merchants terminated their participation in the slave trade during the first half of the nineteenth century.[74] The Dutch were the first to leave the market, taking their last trips to West African ports between 1776 and 1800.[75] Despite the British government's position, the French continued their participation in the slave trade until it officially ended in 1867, when records of their involvement showed a considerable decline.[76] After European slave merchants decided to avoid economic regulation in the 1780s in Dahomey, which they considered to be draconian, Lagos recorded its largest numbers of exported slaves as its port became a magnet for slavers. These numbers fluctuated, though they were paltry compared to the volume of trade during the years of abolition up to 1850. The greatest sales of this period, from the opening of Lagos to slavers in 1761 to 1800 – a few years before the Abolition Act – were a mere 14,077 slaves recorded in 1786–90.

After the Abolition Act, "illegal" slave traders exported 37,715 slaves from 1846 to 1850. This occurred during the rivalry between Akitoye and Kosoko, and the two alternated control from 1841 to 1851 until the antislavery British

---

[72] Mann, *Slavery and the Birth*, 33.
[73] Robert L. Stein, *The French Slave Trade in the Eighteenth Century: An Old Regime Business* (Madison: University of Wisconsin Press, 1979).
[74] Richard Anderson and Henry B. Lovejoy, eds., *Liberated Africans and the Abolition of the Slave Trade, 1807–1896* (New York: University of Rochester Press, 2020).
[75] Kwame Nimako and Glenn Willemsen, *The Dutch Atlantic: Slavery, Abolition and Emancipation* (London: Pluto Press, 2011).
[76] Daniel P. Resnick, "The Societe des Amis des Noirs and the Abolition of Slavery," *French Historical Studies* 7, no. 4 (1972): 558–569.

government formally reinstated Akitoye. Despite their substantial participation in the region's slave markets, the Portuguese never gained a solid political foothold among the people and polities of this area. The French, who had also been heavily involved in the trade, were less influential than the British in West African politics. The British Empire's influence in West Africa had more to do with its role in promoting "legitimate" trade and the geopolitical developments of eighteenth-century Europe, which enabled its political ascendancy and hegemony. As trade volume in West Africa increased, Lagos, Kalabari (the new Calabar), the Old Calabar, Brass, Bonny, Warri, Itsekri, and other coastal states were transformed from fishing villages into trading hubs and market-based city-states. The expansion of trade and the nature of the goods traded affected the regional organization of trade.[77]

As the market for legitimate trade intensified, it led to the emergence of new peasant, commercial, and industrial classes.[78] The latter two groups formed the basis of the new social strata, known as the middle class. In the north, the production of indigo, cotton, groundnut, and leather increased to meet growing market demands, while tobacco was cultivated later, which drove societal changes. Developmental advancement in any territory around the Niger and the West African coast had a domino effect on the others.[79] Cross-cultural trade had never had a better social, political, or economic environment than it enjoyed during this period.

The spread of Islam and the continued relevance of traditional belief systems faced challenges due to the expansion of trade and the Christian missionaries and other British agents of civilization that would arrive later. The Abolition Act of 1807 coincided with the decline of pre-nineteenth-century West African hegemonic powers such as the Old Oyo Empire. These developments meant that Lagos became less dependent on the struggling Benin Empire's political hegemony in the early part of the nineteenth century. Benin was dismantling its traditional links with the rest of Yorubaland during that period, especially with what was left of the Ife hegemony. The political reordering of this period affected the entire Niger area from the turn of the century until the British colonial government officially claimed sovereignty.[80] These events began the

---

[77] Kenneth Dike, *Trade and Politics in the Niger Delta, 1830–1885: An Introduction to the Economic and Political History of Nigeria* (London: Clarendon Press, 1956).

[78] David Imhonopi, Ugochukwu M. Urim, and Charles T. Iruonagbe, "Colonialism, social Structure and Class Formation: Implication for Development in Nigeria," in *A Panoply of Readings in Social Sciences: Lessons for and from Nigeria*, ed. David Imhonopi and Ugichukwu M. Urim (Otta: Covenant University, 2013), 107–122.

[79] Melville J. Herskovits and Mitchell Harwit, *Economic Transition in West Africa* (London: Routledge, 1964); Isaac A. Akinjogbin, *Dahomey and Its Neighbours 1708–1818* (New York: Cambridge University Press, 1967).

[80] Joseph A. Atanda, "Kings in Nigerian Society Through the Ages," Inaugural Lecture (Ibadan: University of Ibadan, 1991).

formation of the new states that comprise modern Nigeria, and the relationships among them have persisted.

During this time, vassal states gained their independence and made early attempts to establish their geopolitical presence. They then lost this sovereignty to foreign powers, for various reasons connected to geopolitical developments and their internal political dynamics. The region's newly independent states and emerging powers posed geopolitical threats to each other as they fought to secure a larger share of the region's markets and trading networks. Incessant wars were waged to expand their spheres of influence, raids were conducted to acquire human cargo that could be sold to illicitly docked cargo ships, and the conflicting interests of emerging states caused general political instability.[81]

Internally, royal succession conflicts left many of the polities weakened from within. In the Northern states, under the Sokoto caliphate, some of the emirates opposed their central ruler. The British government seized critical roles in each of these situations. It paid particular attention to areas important for exporting local products, such as the fishing communities of the delta states, Lagos, and others around the Bight of Benin and Biafra. The attention transformed these areas into city-states dominated by mercantilism and the regulation of West African markets.

Early efforts at foreign rule were first attempted in the city-states that had embraced mercantilism. They became incubation centers for Western civilization, intending to increase the flow of trade and remove potential barriers, and their progress would later characterize the evolution of the states in the Niger area.[82] The Queen's government had established an official presence in Lagos by 1849 when Agent Beecroft was appointed the Consul for the Bights of Benin and Biafra.[83] This occurred after the 1845 agreement in London between Britain and France to terminate the trade in human cargo. The 1851 invasion of Lagos by British naval forces, which the locals called *Ija Agidingbi*, was ostensibly to end the slave traffic from the Bight of Benin and Biafra.

As the British Empire made deals with European powers to abolish the slave market in West Africa, it strengthened its hold on the region's agricultural markets. Trading stations were built around coastal states to collect and transport goods from the interior, and the British government's representatives regulated these markets. A treaty ceded the territories of Lagos and its people to the Queen of England on January 1, 1852, in a deal that was

---

[81] Saburi Biobaku, *The Egba and Their Neighbors 1842–1872* (London: Oxford University Press, 1965).

[82] Toyin Falola, *Cultural Modernity in a Colonized World: The Writings of Chief Isaac Oluwole Delano* (Austin: Pan-African University Press, 2020).

[83] Kenneth O. Dike, "John Beecroft, 1790–1854: Her Brittanic Majesty's Consul to the Bights of Benin and Biafra 1849–1854," *Journal of the Historical Society of Nigeria* 1, no. 1 (1956): 5–14.

particularly humiliating for the king and chiefs of Lagos. The treaty contained nine articles that referenced the Queen's desire to promote agricultural products, and although it did not expressly declare Lagos to be a protectorate of the Queen this was implied through the wording of the treaty.[84]

Lagos authorities, under the leadership of Akitoye, were to dismantle every structure that was in place for trafficking slaves in their domains and areas of influence. Christian missionaries and British merchants were to be allowed to carry out their activities freely. The appointment of a Consul to oversee the region sent a clear message regarding the status of local communities and the loss of sovereignty for traditional authorities, especially regarding the regulation of trade. Two years later, Benjamin Campbell, Her Britannic Majesty's Consul for the Bight of Benin, and Thomas Miller, Commander of H. M. Sloop "Crane" and Senior Officer in the Bights of Benin and Biafra, sailed to Epe to sign the same treaty with Kosoko. He had escaped into exile to build that coastal settlement following the 1851 invasion, where he lost his throne to the British and their protégé, Akitoye.[85]

In exchange for an annual stipend of around $1,000, or 2,000 heads of cowry, accompanied by the "opportunity" to collect tolls on goods traded around his area of influence, Kosoko opened Epe for legitimate trade and agreed to end the slave trade.[86] Lagos was promised a similar stipend. Agreements were also established to open all viable ports for European activities. Kosoko agreed to these terms barely three years after resisting Britain's earlier dictate – for which he lost his position to his uncle – and his changed attitude was most likely due to his first-hand experience with British military power. To protect Lagos, he was also required to promise that he would not invade its territory in any guise. These concessions were granted to recognize and enhance trade within his sphere of influence.

The sovereign rulers of Lagos were limited by the administrative structure put in place under the Consul to ensure the free flow of trade and commerce through a Treaty of Cessation signed on August 6, 1861.[87] Under the treaty, they renounced their authority, retaining the "privilege" to adjudicate native cases. This was subject to appeal under British law if either of the parties so desired. The treaty, supposedly drafted on behalf of the Lagos people, asserted that Dosunmu, king of Lagos, was ceding Lagos to the Queen of England due to the activities of Dahomey and other raiding kingdoms in the Bight of Benin. The treaty declared that Lagos would be under the Queen's protection, and the

---

[84] Jacob F. A. Ajayi, *Christian Missions in Nigeria, 1841–1891: The Making of a New Elite* (London: Longmans Green, 1965), 76–77.
[85] Adekoya, "The Succession Dispute," 219.
[86] Smith, "The Lagos Consulate."
[87] Adeoye A. Akinsanya and Rafiu A. Akindele, "Legitimate Trade, Annexation and Cession of Lagos and International Law," *Journal of Management and Social Sciences* 7, no. 1 (2018): 266–278.

subsequent regime was called the Protectorate of Lagos.[88] The terms of the 1852 agreement are considered humiliating, including Dosunmu's purported statement of resignation that abdicates the island and territory of Lagos to the *Pax Britannica*:

> ... I, Docemo, do, with the consent and advice of my Council, give, transfer, and by these presents grant and confirm unto the Queen of Great Britain, her heirs and successors forever, the port and Island of Lagos, with all the rights, profits, territories, and appurtenances whatsoever thereunto belonging, and as well the profits and revenue as the direct, full, and absolute dominion and sovereignty of the said port, island, and premises, with all the royalties thereof, freely, fully, entirely, and absolutely. I do also covenant and grant that the quiet and peaceable possession thereof shall with all possible speed, be freely and effectually delivered to the Queen of Great Britain, or such person as Her Majesty shall thereunto appoint for her use in the performance of this grant; the inhabitants of the said island and territories, as the Queen's subjects, and under her sovereignty, Crown, jurisdiction, and government, being still suffered to live there.[89]

This proclamation established the Queen's formal presence in the Niger area, embodied by the British government, and gave it a major administrative boost. It was a final step in the formal abolition of the slave trade. The Lagos governance structure was replicated elsewhere in the 1880s, starting with the 1887 proclamation of the Oil Rivers Protectorate that became the Niger Coast Protectorate seven years later.[90] Otunba Payne provides the following description:

> The Colony of Lagos with the adjoining Protectorate include the islands of Lagos and Iddo, the Northern Districts of Ebute Metta, and Igbessa on the N.W., the Western District comprising Badagry, Appa, Pokia, Illaro and Addo; the Eastern Districts with Palma and Leckie, Mahin, Ogbo and Jakiri extending from the French Settlement at Kutpnu to the Benin River where the British Protectorate of the Niger or Oil Rivers commences, and is situated on the 9th parallel North Latitude, and between 2° and 6° East Longitude.[91]

---

[88] Augustus A. A. B. Aderibigbe, "Expansion of the Lagos Protectorate 1863–1900," unpublished PhD dissertation, University of London, 1959.

[89] The Treaty of Cessation, August 6, 1861. Treaty between Norman B. Bedingfeld, Commander of Her Majesty's ship Prometheus, and Senior Officer of the Bights Division, and William McCoskry, Esquire, Her Britannic Majesty's Acting Consul, on the part of Her Majesty the Queen of Great Britain, and Docemo, King of Lagos, on the part of himself and Chiefs.

[90] Michael Lobban, *Imperial Incarceration: Detention without Trial in the Making of British Colonial Africa* (Cambridge: Cambridge University Press, 2021), 198–237.

[91] Payne, *Table of Principal Events*, 1.

These areas were gradually incorporated into the Protectorate in a way that reflected the incremental extension of British influence across the lagoon and the interior. By 1874, following the Ashantee war, this area had become part of the Gold Coast colony.[92] It became the eastern province of the West African colonial administrative unit. In another "Letter of Patent," issued in 1886, Lagos and its dependencies were proclaimed to be a colony that was separate from the Gold Coast colony. In 1874, the Lagos government intervened in interethnic wars among the Yoruba. From Lagos, the administration entered Ijebu, Abeokuta, Ibadan, and Oyo. They signed treaties with various chiefs, such as the Amity and Commerce agreement with Oyo.[93]

Conclusion

Before the abolition of the cowry system and the 1880 introduction of monetary reforms, trade had expanded across the Niger area and in Lagos. Despite the existence of other mediums of exchange, cowries accounted for about 60 million units of traded cloth or about 300 camel loads in the Kano market.[94] Around 120–150 million units were exchanged for about 5,000 slaves in the same market during the same year.[95] This expansion continued until the colonial era, gradually eroding traditions and social values that had been in place before the nineteenth century.[96]

European gin, firearms, gunpowder, tobacco, and other wares circulated through the Niger area, mainly from Lagos, as trade shifted westward. This increased the Ijebu people's involvement in trade. These merchants began acting as intermediaries that distributed European goods through the hinterlands. In a bid to reclaim this trade and its associated revenue, Lagos asserted its influence over traders mostly from rival states such as Ibadan. This led to the Lagos government's invasion of Ibadan based on allegations that a previous agreement between the two had been violated.[97]

Although Ibadan did not immediately fall under the Protectorate of Lagos or the control of its government, this action reinforced the need to control the administration of polities and states in the hinterlands. In subsequent years, as

---

[92] Alan Lloyd, *The Drums of Kumasi: The Story of the Ashanti Wars* (London: Longmans, 1964).
[93] Toyin Falola, "The Ibadan Conference of 1885: Diplomacy and Conflict Resolution in Mid-Nineteenth Century Yorubaland," *Geneva Africa* 23, no. 2 (1985): 37–56.
[94] James B. Odunbaku, "Importance of Cowrie Shells in Pre-colonial Yoruba land South Western Nigeria: Orile-Keesi as a Case Study," *International Journal of Humanities and Social Science* 2, no. 18 (2012): 234–241.
[95] Ogunremi, *Counting the Camels*, 38.
[96] Anthony G. Hopkins, "The Currency Revolution in South-West Nigeria in the Late Nineteenth Century," *Journal of the Historical Society of Nigeria* 3, no. 3 (1966): 471–483.
[97] Tunde Oduwobi, *Ijebu under Colonial Rule, 1892–1960: An Administrative and Political Analysis* (Lagos: First Academic Publishers, 2004).

modern transportation systems were introduced, waterways lost their significance among coastal communities. Routes along the lagoon were abandoned as the colonial government neglected their development. Lagos maintained its grip on trade and administration in the Niger area throughout the colonial period,[98] which had concomitant effects on its demography and social structure.[99]

[98] Olakunle A. Lawal and Oluwasegun M. Jimoh, "Missiles from 'Kirsten Hall': Herbert Macaulay versus Hugh Clifford, 1922–1931," *Lagos Historical Review* 12 (2012): 41–62.

[99] For a coverage of the Victorian hypotheses that adumbrate these changes, see Echeruo, *Victorian Lagos*, 112–113.

6

Conquest and Reactions

European/Western powers in the modern era have overcome their differences to find a shared interest: an ambition to conquer the world. To achieve this goal, they have worked together through the 1494 Treaty of Tordesillas, the formation of the United Nations, and beyond.[1] After European powers saw that internecine wars and general instability in the Niger area showed no signs of ending – which had palpable effects on their interests and investments in overseas trade during their unbridled scramble for African markets – they called a conference in Berlin, Germany. This meeting discussed the terms and conditions for occupying and dividing Africa among themselves like so many slices of a pie.[2] The most important agreement made at the meeting was the principle of "effective occupation" in any potential colony. The "sphere of influence" was premised on this principle, and territorial claims had to be confirmed in written documents and agreements that were ratified by signatories to the Berlin Act.[3]

European powers had two methods of acquiring territory: one involved force, the other used "diplomacy."[4] The domination of African polities through either method ensured law and order to facilitate trade and economic growth. By 1900, many parts of the Niger area had been incorporated under British colonial rule.[5] Western imperial powers pursued a kaleidoscopic process of conquest among precolonial African societies, making it challenging to generalize the process.[6] Such a generalization remains challenging even within the nation-states that emerged afterward. Less force and more diplomacy were

---

[1] Philip T. Hoffman, *Why Did Europe Conquer the World?* (Princeton: Princeton University Press, 2017).

[2] Thomas Pakenham, *Scramble for Africa: The White Man's Conquest of the Dark Continent from 1876–1912* (New York: Random House, 1991).

[3] Sybil E. Crowe, *The Berlin West African Conference, 1884–1885* (New York: Longman, 1942).

[4] Mieke van der Linden, *The Acquisition of Africa (1870–1914): The Nature of International Law* (Leiden: Brill, 2017).

[5] Obaro Ikime, *The Fall of Nigeria: The British Conquest* (London: Heinemann Educational Books, 1977).

[6] John M. Mackenzie, *The Partition of Africa* (London: Methuen, 1983).

used in the conquest of Yorubaland.[7] The acquisition of Hausaland, and other parts of the area later known as Northern Nigeria, was largely a military affair.[8] States in the delta region – Benin, Opobo, and Okrika – were also overcome by force after mounting fierce resistance against British incursion.[9] Their kings were either killed or sent into exile.[10]

Strategies and Processes of Colonization

The Western processes and strategies for colonizing African economies and states, especially in West Africa, cannot be separated from the exploratory missions led through the area. The Association for the Promotion of Scientific Knowledge About Africa was the vanguard of such efforts, starting in the late eighteenth century.[11] The commission, given to Mungo Park in 1795, laid the precedent for subsequent exploration, opening up the coasts of West Africa and polities beyond those waters, which were referred to as the hinterlands.[12] This was an attempt to increase trade and strengthen European interests in the region. During this process, explorers disseminated the ideals of Western civilization that have become the standard for knowledge production in European universities and institutions.[13] However, Africans of that period were not recognized by European philosophies of humanism. To be recognized, Africans needed to be brought into the fold upon which this standard was made.[14]

Exploratory missions involved geographers, ethnologists, anthropologists, missionaries, merchants, and other interested parties who undertook the "scientific mapping" of West Africa. In 1807, less than a decade after Mungo Park reached the Niger basin, the British condemned the slave trade through the Abolition Act. As Yuval Harari, an Israeli Professor of History, noted in his discussion of human evolution and state formation:

> If they really wanted to control the vast new territories, they had to gather enormous amount of new data about the geography, climate, flora, fauna,

---

[7] Joseph C. Anene, *Southern Nigeria in Transition, 1885–1906* (Cambridge: Cambridge University Press, 1966).
[8] Samson C. Ukpabi, "The Beginning of the British Conquest of Northern Nigeria," *Bulletin de l'Institut Fondamental d'Afrique Noire* 35, no. 3 (1973): 593–613.
[9] Don Ohadike, *The Ekumeku Movement: Western Igbo Resistance to the British Conquest of Nigeria, 1883–1914* (Athens: Ohio University Press, 1991).
[10] Emmanuel Adagogo Jaja, *King Jaja of Opobo (1821–1891): A Sketch History of the Development and Expansion of Opobo* (Lagos: Opobo Action Council, 1977).
[11] Otu Abam Ubi, *The Yakurr of the Middle Cross River Region (Nigeria)* (Lulu.com, 2019).
[12] Mungo Park, *Travels in the Interior of Africa* (London: Eland, 2012).
[13] Hugh Clapperton, *Hugh Clapperton into the Interior of Africa: Records of the Second Expedition, 1825–1827* (Leiden: Brill, 2005).
[14] Mokwugo Okoye, *African Responses* (London: Arthur H. Stockwell, 1964), 164–186 and 330–362.

language, culture, and history of the continent ... For modern Europeans, building an empire was a scientific project, while setting up a scientific discipline was an imperial project.[15]

Western activities transitioned into an era of "legitimate" trade in which agricultural products were encouraged and dominated the trading relations between West African and European markets. Exploration evolved to serve different, multilayered interests and to begin the colonization process. The Abolition Act itself was influenced by developments in Europe and the Americas, and by allegedly humanitarian groups such as the Association for the Scientific Knowledge About Africa and others that pursued interests that were shaped by Europe's technological and scientific advancements from the first Industrial Revolution.[16] Machine labor was replacing human labor, and excess production was exported overseas. Other groups were reacting to the threats that an increasing slave population posed to their societies.[17]

Before these developments, various European powers were solely interested in locating a lucrative slave market along the coast of West Africa. An exploration of this vast coastline, and knowledge of its geophysical landscape for inland exploration, was out of the question. Ongoing developments changed the mission and the intent of Western imperial powers in West Africa and their relations with the region's traditional authorities.[18] Events on both sides of the Atlantic facilitated the process of colonization, shaping strategies for conquest and resistance. The nineteenth century has been described as a chaotic and destabilizing time in the history of societies across the Niger–Benue area.[19] It is also characterized as a transformative time for the history and evolution of state formation in the region.[20]

Several factors led established authorities in West Africa to rely on European powers. Different polities in the region were plagued by internal rivalry, powerful states had begun weakening and disintegrating in the late eighteenth century, and warfare was pursued with crude technology and ineffective scientific models. An external force was necessary to break the stalemate of

---

[15] Yuval Noah Harari, *Sapiens: A Brief History of Humankind* (London: Hervill Secker, 2014), 247 and 255.

[16] Paul Langford, "The Eighteenth Century (1688–1789)," in *The Oxford Illustrated History of Britain*, ed. Kenneth O. Morgan (New York: Oxford University Press, 1984), 352–418.

[17] Manuel Barcia, *West African Warfare in Bahia and Cuba: Soldier Slaves in the Atlantic World 1807–1844* (London: Oxford University Press, 2016); and Akpojevbe Omasanjuwa and Junisa Phebean, "Acrimony in Colonial Liberia," *Journal of Universal History Studies* 3, no. 1 (2020): 1–5.

[18] Robert I. Rotberg, *Africa and Its Explorers: Motives, Methods, and Impact* (Cambridge: Harvard University Press, 1970).

[19] Paul C. Dike, *Confluence Nigerians: Man, History & Culture in the Niger/Benue Confluence Region* (Abuja: National Gallery of Art, Nigeria, 2005).

[20] Richard J. Reid, *A History of Modern Africa: 1800 to the Present* (London: Blackwell Publishing Ltd., 2009).

geopolitical development among West African polities. By the mid-nineteenth century, Western imperial states and their representatives had accumulated substantial political and economic capital in West Africa. Traditional African elites needed political capital to strengthen their hegemony or counter other hegemonic forces, and their subjects had similar needs for economic capital.[21] Shortly after the abolition of slavery, new and improved seedlings were introduced, botanical gardens and farms were established, and farmers were encouraged to cultivate particular sets of crops. The sale of these commodities, the introduction of currency, and other reforms had led the states of West Africa to rely on foreign trade.[22]

The West African economy became beholden to the whims of imperial states in Europe and their syndicated merchant companies. This crippled local traders, businesses, and industries, while the successful economic conquest led to the gradual revocation of the authority held by traditional leaders.[23] This began in earnest with the British naval bombardment of Lagos in 1851. Their goal was to end the flourishing, clandestine slave market in the area. Akitoye and the ruler of Epe were offered a deal by the British government that would establish a local consulate and cede the authority to regulate trade in their territories. In exchange, they would receive an annual stipend of £1,000.[24] Epe had the option to rebuff this lopsided treaty, but Lagos did not. It was one of the earliest attempts to reduce the Niger area's traditional authorities and societies to the status of British subjects.

A few years before the bombardment of Lagos, Britain had appointed a representative named Beecroft to serve as Consul for the Bight of Benin and Biafra. This responsibility was too ambiguous, given the vast array of polities that the role encompassed and the administrative structure that would be required. Around five years later, T. J. Hutchinson wrote one of many

---

[21] Gloria Ifeoma Chuku, "From Petty Traders to International Merchants: A Historical Account of Three Igbo Women of Nigeria in Trade and Commerce, 1886 to 1970," *African Economic History* 27 (1999): 1–22; and Saburi Biobaku, *The Egba and their Neighbors 1842–1872* (London: Oxford University Press, 1965).

[22] Anthony G. Hopkins, "The Currency Revolution in South-West Nigeria in the Late Nineteenth Century," *Journal of the Historical Society of Nigeria* 3, no. 3 (1966): 471–483; Chibuike Ugochukwu Uche, "Foreign Banks, Africans, and Credit in Colonial Nigeria, C.1890-1912," *The Economic History Review Series* 52, no. 4 (1999): 669–691; and Adebayo A. Lawal, *Nigeria Culture, Politics, Governance and Development* (Ibadan: Connel Publications, 2015), 165–194.

[23] Kenneth Dike, *Trade and Politics in the Niger Delta, 1830–1885: An Introduction to the Economic and Political History of Nigeria* (London: Clarendon Press, 1956).

[24] Treaty of Epe, 28 September 1854. Agreement entered to this 28th Day of September 1854 between Kosoko his Caboceers and Chiefs, and Benjamin Campbell Esquire Her Britannic Majesty's Consul for the Bight of Benin, and Thomas Miller Esquire Commander H. M. Sloop "Crane" Senior Officer in the Bights of Benin and Biafra; Treaty Between Great Britain and Lagos, January 1, 1852.

appeals to the British government, imploring it to increase the official British presence in the area. "If the government do not step in to put an end to the lawlessness of the Filatahs," he wrote, "all ideas of a successful trade with the Niger, Tshadda and Binue countries may be given up."[25] Despite these shortcomings, the British government initiated its direct involvement in the Niger–Benue region from a foothold in Calabar. Humanitarian idealism laid a foundation that supported every other process and strategy that engineered the colonial project. This included the justification for dubious treaties and military actions that went a long way toward the conquest and consolidation of the area that became the Nigerian colony under British rule.[26]

Campaigns launched from Europe by various merchants and groups sought to transition West African societies to so-called legitimate trade. The steady encroachment of these interest groups, moving further into the hinterlands, sparked a seismic shift in the sociopolitical and economic landscape of communities, kingdoms, and empires that would become the Nigerian colony. Once these interest groups, merchants, explorers, missionaries, scientists, and administrators had come to a unanimous agreement on the future shape of trade, society, and politics in the Niger area, they worked in concert.[27]

Slavery and its institutions within local societies were targeted by the British, especially through missionary efforts. The traditional religious aspect of local institutions was of paramount concern for them, and it was tightly intertwined with every other aspect of the states in which they operated. The missionary interest overlapped with institutions that were involved in educational, political, and commercial activities. Missionaries built schools and constructed modern healthcare facilities and churches. They taught different crafts, such as masonry, carpentry, plumbing, and tailoring. At the same time, missionaries introduced and encouraged farmers to cultivate new sets of improved crops. Their activities aided the transition into modernity and an emergent economy that was based on legitimate trade.

The British army needed to shore up its military and moral support in the regions where missionaries operated. Meanwhile, dissidents and slaves now had places where they could seek sanctuary. As slave exports were condemned, so were the use of slave labor and the institution of slavery in society. This was ostensibly to extend the idea of humanism to this population, but the colonial government itself used forced labor in its drive to develop the infrastructure of the colony, which was literally their industrial complex. Western imperial

---

[25] Quoted in Idris Sha'aba Jimada, *The Historical Background to the Establishment of Patigi Emirate: C.1810–1898* (Zaria: Ahmadu Bello University Press, 2016), 208.

[26] Robert A. Bickers and Rosemary Seton, *Missionary Encounters: Sources and Issues* (London: Curzon Press, 1996).

[27] Femi J. Kolapo, *Christian Missionary Engagement in Central Nigeria, 1857–1891: The Church Missionary Society's All African Mission on the Upper Niger* (Cham: Palgrave Macmillan, 2019).

powers dictated the direction of trade in Africa through the abolition of slavery, which was notable for its role in the process that led to the revocation of local sovereignty. It put traditional authorities at odds with their European counterparts, for the two groups could only find common ground when it enhanced their political capital. Traditional leaders that were not sidelined, forced to flee, captured, killed, or exiled became completely subservient to a foreign authority.[28]

Emerging entrepreneurs, traders, and the returnee population were the earliest political supporters of the colonial enterprise, and military support was provided by local enslaved and dissident populations. The interests of the traders and returnees occasionally clashed with those of the prevailing *Pax Britannica*, which increasingly sought to reduce their political, social, and economic influence. They all supported the idea of transition, especially returnees and emerging entrepreneurs, but they opposed Western powers in a few important areas. They criticized the politics of racial supremacy in the church, as seen in responses from James Johnson and Mojola Agbebi,[29] and they challenged the Royal Niger Company (RNC)'s monopolization of trade, which was most notable in the reactions of the Brass and Bonny populations.

As advocates of change, returnees and their descendants – who constituted society's educated class – believed that the Western colonization of states around the Niger was a way to achieve the region's next stage of evolution. Following the logic of Edward Blyden and other returnees in places like Liberia, they believed that they would be at the forefront of this evolution due to their indoctrination in these two civilizations.[30]

When Ilorin and Bida were attacked in 1897, the mission involved 500 British soldiers who were Yoruba and Hausa.[31] These fighters had been drawn from the slaves and dissidents who escaped from cruel masters and unjust societies, and they worked to demolish the institution of slavery and change the status quo across the Niger. The colonial mission not only exploited rivalries among various regional authorities but also used sympathizers and allies among the local population to weaken local resistance.

When European and African authorities are compared, one exhibits coherence of purpose, and the other embodies disarray. The former entered into several multi- and bilateral treaties, while the latter continued jockeying for

---

[28] Obaro Ikime, "Colonial Conquest and Resistance in Southern Nigeria," *Journal of the Historical Society of Nigeria* 6, no. 3 (1972): 267–268.

[29] Iheanyi M. Enwerem, *A Dangerous Awakening: The Politicization of Religion in Nigeria* (Ibadan: IFRA-Nigeria, 1995), 49.

[30] Emmanuel A Ayandele, *The Educated Elite in the Nigerian Society* (Ibadan: Ibadan University Press, 1974); and Agneta Pallinder-Law, "Aborted Modernization in West Africa? The Case of Abeokuta," *The Journal of African History* 15, no. 1 (1974): 65–82.

[31] Rowland A. Adeleye, *Power and Diplomacy in Northern Nigeria, 1804–1906: The Sokoto Caliphate and Its Enemies* (London: Longman, 1971).

European arms and support into the colonial era. Their intent to sabotage their neighbors and perceived enemies played out in a paradigm that Uzoigwe has described as a classic exhibition of game theory.[32] The strategies of traditional authorities in this area were effective from the sixteenth century until the late nineteenth century. In the beginning, traditional African authorities dictated the terms of trade, playing European powers against each other while maintaining an advantage through trade that was tightly under their control.[33] Polities like Nupe, Bida, Dahomey, and Abeokuta could ask the French to support their opposition to British influence until around the mid-nineteenth century. From 1885 onward, this was no longer possible. When the German Chancellor convened the Berlin Conference – addressing Portugal's concerns vis-à-vis Belgium in Central Africa, which had been engaged in a prolonged campaign of attrition since King Leopold I's 1876 moves in the region – Britain had already established a formidable presence in the Niger area. Articles 34 and 35, the essentials of the Berlin Act, laid the legal groundwork for claiming colonies in occupied territories and having them acknowledged by other European powers. One article related to spheres of influence and the other to their supporting evidence, even as both were mapped across the Niger.

The 1849 Consulate of the Bight of Benin and Biafra, along with the 1852 and 1861 Lagos treaties, provided major opportunities for Britain to infiltrate the Niger area. By the time the year-long Berlin Conference had ended, the British government had declared the Oil Rivers Protectorate as its sphere of influence. In the following year, the British government in Lagos intervened in the Yoruba wars, which led to the treaty of trade and friendship that opened up the country to European trade and activities. It also transferred the polities' powers of arbitration to the Lagos government. The British government remained hesitant to establish foreign colonies out of concerns regarding their cost and management. Instead, George Goldie's RNC was granted a Royal Charter to conduct trade and administer the Niger–Benue area on behalf of the empire.[34] In the preceding years, Goldie had pursued a radical drive for monopolization, buying off French merchants in the area and putting local traders at a disadvantage.[35] As its reach and presence in the Bight of Benin and Biafra expanded, the Oil Rivers Protectorate became the Niger Coast Protectorate in 1893 and the Southern Province in 1900.

The evolution of the Niger area accelerated between 1886 and 1900. The principles of the Berlin Conference prevented clashes among Western powers

---

[32] Godfrey N. Uzoigwe, *Britain and the Conquest of Africa: The Age of Salisbury* (Ann Arbor: The University of Michigan Press, 1974), 91.
[33] Peter J. M. McEwan, ed., *Africa from Early Times to 1800* (London: Oxford University Press, 1968), 244–289.
[34] Uzoigwe, *Britain and the Conquest of Africa,* 41.
[35] Ike Okonta and Oronto Douglas, *Where Vultures Feast: Shell, Human Rights, and Oil in the Niger Delta* (London: Verso, 2003), 12.

while recognizing the colonial enterprise as a legal and political construct. No sovereign authority would readily cede its authority to another, which meant that colonizers expanded their enterprise through two strategies. One involved a dubious treaty where colonial powers exaggerated their claims, and the other involved feigned or willful ignorance of local authorities.[36] Some treaties were signed under threat of violence, which was described as "gunboat diplomacy."

After the British Empire intervened in Yoruba politics in the late nineteenth century, and after it invaded Ijebu in 1892, it compelled Yoruba lords to sign a treaty in 1893.[37] Before the Berlin Conference, treaties had given equal opportunities to British interests and other European traders in the Niger area, but the 1893 treaty insisted on British exclusivity. The British government remained reluctant to become fully involved in the colonial enterprise, but its merchants and economic interests in West Africa made arguments for containing the massive encroachment of France and Germany in the region. After the 1886 intervention in Yoruba politics, gunboat diplomacy continued in Opobo in 1887.[38] Jaja was forced to leave the town, boarding a British naval warship that transported him to the West Indies, where he died in 1891.[39] Between 1892, when Ijebu was invaded, and 1904, when the British expanded their reach to Borno, the expansion across the Niger area was conducted under an administrative framework. In 1897, Nupe and Ilorin were added to the expanding protectorate. After the West African Frontier Force was formed in 1898, Sokoto was invaded in 1902.[40]

Arms Race, Diplomacy, and the Niger Delta

The transition to agricultural trade as a replacement for human cargo led to increased occurrences of war, intra- and intercommunity crises, and general political instability in the Niger area.[41] The military became the single most important institution in society during this period. Cotton, ivory, pepper, palm products, and other agricultural commodities were exchanged for an

---

[36] Anietie A. Inyang and Manasseh E. Bassey, "Imperial Treaties and the Origins of British Colonial Rule in Southern Nigeria, 1860–1890," *Mediterranean Journal of Social Sciences* 5, no. 20 (2014): 1946–1953.

[37] Johnson U. J. Asiegbu, *Nigeria and Its British Invaders, 1851–1920: A Thematic Documentary History* (New York: NOK Publishers, 1984).

[38] Robert V. Kubicek, "The Colonial Steamer and the Occupation of West Africa by the Victorian State, 1840–1900," *The Journal of Imperial and Commonwealth History* 18, no. 1 (1990): 9–32.

[39] Solomon O. Jaja, *Opobo Since 1870: A Documentary Record with an Introduction* (Ibadan: University of Ibadan, 1991).

[40] Chinedu N. Ubah, "The British Occupation of the Sokoto Caliphate: The Military Dimension, 1897–1906," *Paideuma* 40 (1994): 81–97.

[41] Melville J. Herskovits and Mitchell Harwits, *Economic Transition in West Africa* (London: Routledge, 1964).

abundance of gin and European weapons. These became dominant commodities for exchange while farmers and traders in the Niger area produced commodities that supported European economies and fueled their new industries.[42] The European imports led to the destruction of local industries and regional polities.[43] It was more important for these communities, kingdoms, and empires to acquire European items than it was to apply them effectively for personal or collective/communal use.

The accumulation of weapons was seen as a deterrent that offered protection from external aggression and internal uprisings. The Ijebu were the first to use these modern weapons due to their geographic location.[44] Many of the states that acquired this technology could barely use it. Dane guns required sufficient time for reloading, and their precision was questionable in untrained hands. These shortcomings allowed the archers and cavalry soldiers of the Old Oyo Empire to defeat Dahomey forces armed with advanced weapons. It was doubtful that these various kingdoms and empires could resist the British colonial encroachment into their territories when those forces possessed even more sophisticated weapons. Imperial British forces were led by well-trained military officers who commanded experienced troops.

By the late nineteenth century, significant improvements in Europe's military-industrial complex left local African authorities armed with obsolete technology that they could not maintain. However, most of their revenue was dedicated to accumulating these weapons.[45] European merchants encouraged this trend and continued to sell obsolete weapons to states in the Niger area, leading to the proliferation of such weapons in West African markets.[46] To maintain their advantage over this population and to minimize the potential for resistance, Western imperial powers met in Brussels in 1892 and restricted the sale of advanced weapons to Africans.[47] Meanwhile, these powers were producing repeater rifles, steamboats, Gatling and Maxim guns, rockets, and the heavy artillery of naval forces.[48] Some of these weapons,

---

[42] Ahmed M. Mohammed, *European Trade, Imperialism and Underdevelopment in Northern Nigeria 19th and 20th Centuries* (Zaria: Ahmadu Bello University Press Limited, 2016).

[43] Okwudiba Nnoli, "A Short History of Nigeria Underdevelopment," in *Path to Nigeria Development*, ed. Okwudiba Nnoli (Dakar: CODESRIA, 1981).

[44] Akin Adejuwon, "'Art' of War: Analysis of Weapons of the 19th Century Yoruba Civil Wars," *Revista Universitaria de Historia Militar* 8, no. 17 (2019): 183.

[45] Joseph P. Smaldone, *Warfare in the Sokoto Caliphate: Historical and Sociological Perspectives* (Cambridge: Cambridge University Press, 1977).

[46] Paul Mmegha Mbaeyi, *British Military and Naval Forces in West African History 1807–1874* (New York: NOK Publishers, 1978), 35.

[47] M'baye Gueye and Albert Adu Boahen, "African Initiatives and Resistance in West Africa, 1880–1914," in *General History of Africa: VII Africa under Colonial Domination 1880–1935*, ed. Albert Adu Boahen (Paris: UNESCO, 1990), 147.

[48] Mbaeyi, *British Military and Naval Forces*.

especially the repeater rifles, made their way to the arsenals of Niger area states such as Kano.

Before the restriction of the arms trade, the desire to possess European weaponry and the hope for protection through European political capital had informed relations between local authorities and European powers. The diffusion of the Christian missionary presence and free trade within these territories provided few direct benefits for local rulers, but it assisted in acquiring supplies of ammunition and securing these polities through access to foreign military prowess.[49] When missionary activities occurred within a territory, local authorities could persuade European powers to prevent neighbors or regional enemies from accessing advanced weaponry. However, trouble ensued when local authorities and foreign missionaries had conflicting interests. This most often took the form of ideological differences due to their divergent worldviews and cosmologies. In the delta states, local practices like human sacrifice and other rituals were considered barbaric and pagan. The use of slave labor, which was at the core of local cultures, was the exact practice that Christian missionaries sought to eradicate in the Niger area and the rest of Africa in their quest to transform societies.

Basic ideological differences often resulted in missionaries inviting the British army to invade polities that were led by unyielding local authorities. Such was the case with Calabar, but it required more than weaponry to conquer these territories. Military strategy and tactics that included diplomacy and alliances would also determine who won the wars that would occur in these territories. None of the regional powers or states could match the capabilities of the British. Fundamental changes altered the political landscape of the Niger area, and these sociopolitical reformations played into the newly discovered interests of Western imperial powers in Africa.[50] Every powerful state in the region was faced with resentment and a deficit of legitimacy from their vassal states, which encouraged political skirmishes within their polities.[51] These divisions were exploited by the British government for its benefit.

Local populations provided British forces with food, soldiers, information, and moral support. They also acted as saboteurs to undermine the ongoing efforts of states that attempted to counter colonial incursion into their territories. The region's emerging power blocs had been successful conquerors up until the time of their conquest when they were still expanding their political

---

[49] Emmanuel A. Ayandele, *Missionary Impact in Modern Nigeria 1842–1914* (London: Longman Group, 1966).

[50] Daryll Forde and Phyllis M. Kaberry, eds., *West African Kingdoms in the Nineteenth Century* (London: Oxford University Press, 1967).

[51] Idrees Aliyu, "Collaboration and the British Conquest of Bida in 1798: The Role and Achievement of the Indigenous Interest Groups," *African Study Monographs* 10, no. 2 (1989): 69–82.

reach across the region.[52] However, they lacked the diplomatic expertise to maintain their expanded territories or secure the respect of the imperial agents.

Sokoto had become the Northern region's seat of power in the early nineteenth century, following the first successful phase of the jihad.[53] By the mid-nineteenth century, it controlled virtually all the polities in the Benue–Niger area, with few exceptions, mostly in the Plateau–Benue and southern regions. However, Sokoto did not maintain a firm grip on these territories. Its gradual disintegration had been slowed by the Islamic doctrine that laid the basis for the establishment of the caliphate.[54] The lands that they controlled did not provide them with much diplomatic capital, which left huge gaps for imperial powers to exploit.

This tension between the consolidation of established powers and the continuing expansion of new challengers exacerbated the arms race. Private individuals were forbidden from accessing the increasing amounts of weaponry that circulated through the Niger. Zaria, Nasarawa, Yola, and others within the emirate forged alliances with imperial agents at various times for political advantage. In the twilight of the nineteenth century, when Benin attempted to regain its formerly dependent territories to the southeast of the Niger River, it was invaded by British forces.[55] These former territories played a decisive role in the conquest of Benin, possibly even more so than the gunboats, repeater rifles, and other sophisticated resources assembled for the expedition, including the skilled and well-trained soldiers.[56] The spread of weaponry and the competition to acquire it in emerging states and among the region's emerging powers increased after the establishment of Lokoja as a regional operational base for British activities in the Benue–Middle-Niger area. It was not only a noteworthy moment in the British colonial enterprise, it was also a significant milestone for the distribution of European goods and services.

European "services" included the various diplomatic roles that they played in the region, forming alliances and instigating rebellions within vassal states, as well as encouraging slaves to rise against their masters. Arms and logistics were provided to weaker powers to advance these interests. Many polities and cultures that encountered these services, including those in Australia, South

---

[52] Robert E. Bradbury, "The Kingdom of Benin," in *West African Kingdoms in the Nineteenth Century*, ed. Robert E. Bradbury (Oxford: Oxford University Press, 1967), 7.

[53] Rowland A. Adeleye, "The Sokoto Caliphate in the 19th Century," in *History of West Africa*. Vol. II, ed. Jacob F. A. Ajayi and Michael Crowther (London: Longman, 1974), 60–69.

[54] Alkasum Abba, *History of Yola, 1809–1914: The Establishment and Evolution of a Metropolis* (Zaria: Ahmadu Bello University, 2003).

[55] Paddy Docherty, *Blood and Bronze: The British Empire and the Sack of Benin* (London: Hurst, 2021).

[56] Alan F. C. Ryder, *Benin and the Europeans 1485–1897* (London: Longmans, 1969).

and Central America, and the Caribbean, had hoped that their support for the invading parties would bolster their influence in regional political developments. Various factions supported the diplomatic gestures that resulted in the invasion and defeat of their overlords, justifying their actions as a way to overthrow existing tyrants. The freed slaves and vassal states within Africa saw oppressive regimes that needed to be replaced. However, their diplomatic naiveté and limited knowledge of geopolitical developments meant that they could not see how their British allies abhorred such goals, which were outside of their normal mercantile interests. These alliances successfully toppled regimes throughout the region, but British administrators quickly replaced their dethroned predecessors.

Conquest and Responses

Regional polities were not passive observers while Lugard and other colonial officials led imperial armies to their borders. Despite the assertions from Alan Barnes and colonial historiographers, these polities met their conquerors with neither applause nor a total lack of resistance.[57] Some people, such as those in Yorubaland, did welcome the transition to a regime that protected them from surprise attacks, bandit raids, and marauding warlords. Asiwaju has described how taxes were referred to as *owo orun* (fee paid for rest).[58] Toward the mid-twentieth century, with demonstrations like those from the Abeokuta Women's Union, such was no longer the case. Even before the social unrest, the relatively peaceful colonial incursion into Yorubaland met some difficulties. When the colonial government in Lagos made its full intentions known to local Yoruba lords, many of them had already grown weary of going to war, aside from the invasion of Ijebu or the fate of Jaja of Opobo.

The colonial army's activity in places like Itsekiri, Nupe, Ilorin, Kano, and Sokoto showed the need for caution. The British had displayed their military capabilities with the 1861 invasion of Lagos, and the event sparked major resistance across Yorubaland directed at Christian missionaries. By the time of the 1886 intervention, all parties involved in the Ekitiparapo War, or every major power and alliance in Yorubaland, were already exhausted.[59] The war had cost lives, revenue, and time.

After the trade in slaves became less active and agricultural production had been drastically reduced, people feared to journey to farms, economic activities were paralyzed, while war became unprofitable for any of the belligerents. They

---

[57] Alan Burns, *History of Nigeria* (London: Allen & Unwin, 1929).
[58] Anthony I. Asiwaju, *Western Yorubaland under Colonial Rule 1889–1945* (London: Longman Group Limited, 1976).
[59] Isaac A. Akinjogbin, *War and Peace in Yorubaland, 1793–1893* (Ibadan: Heinemann Educational Books, 1998).

could neither trade in a lucrative market for human cargo nor participate in the ongoing exchange of agricultural products. With the French activities in the Niger area, the British government's failure to provide arbitration in the Yoruba wars could have given an advantage to the former. The Ijebu allegedly violated the arbitration agreement, which resulted in the 1892 expedition.[60] The Ijebu saga was only one of the events following the 1886 treaty suggesting an ongoing rivalry among Yoruba kingdoms. Instead of reinforcing Old Oyo's supremacy by giving it the authority to conduct arbitration between different parties, this responsibility was transferred to the Lagos government. This left Yorubaland without a coordinating power that was equivalent to the Old Oyo Empire. If anything, this treaty exacerbated the scramble for control over the flow of trade, especially with European products. The proliferation of powerful, independent lords meant a greater number of factions also scrambled for European arms and goods to maintain or expand their reach.[61]

This instability led the Ijebu to close their borders to all traffic. This decision was made for various reasons, including the desire to block Ibadan, its historic enemy, from accessing European goods and ammunition. This blockade affected a major route that linked Lagos to the hinterlands, which not only altered the flow of trade but also disrupted missionary activities in the country. The situation forced the government in Lagos to take military action after it received pressure from missionaries, merchants, and residents. Attempts to prevent the intervention were unsuccessful.[62]

As in Lagos and elsewhere, the attack on Ijebu was reinforced by local mercenaries – especially freed Hausa slaves – that were led by trained European soldiers. The British antislavery act and Kosoko's refusal to toe the British government's line were reasons for the 1851 bombardment. Two wars of conquest in Yorubaland were imperial rather than colonial, and the difference lay in the intent behind the invasions. The former was concerned with opening new routes and promoting "legitimate" trade, while the latter sought to incorporate territories around the Niger under a British protectorate. Local authorities were not asked to sign a treaty that protected their lands and people under the British government; rather, they were ordered to abolish the slave trade, promote legitimate trade, and open up their territories to the free flow of goods. Similar tactics were adopted for the delta areas.

These two conquests produced similar results because free trade was a tool for usurping local authorities, but the intent behind the bombardment of Lagos

---

[60] Robert Smith, "Nigeria–Ijebu," in *West African Resistance: The Military Response to Colonial Occupation*, ed. Michael Crowder (London: Hutchinson & Co., 1971), 175–184.

[61] Isaac A. Akinjogbin, "Dahomey and Yoruba in the Nineteenth Century," in *Africa in the Nineteenth and Twentieth Centuries*, ed. Joseph C. Anene and Godfrey N. Brown (Ibadan: Ibadan University Press, 1966), 255–269.

[62] Obafemi Oladimomi Ayantuga, *Ijebu and Its Neighbors, 1851–1914* (London: University of London, 1965).

and Ijebu was slightly different from that of Nupe, Sokoto, Itsekiri, and elsewhere. From this period onward, each of the British government's military expeditions came with colonial intent. It was clear that effective control over the flow of trade and maximum production from the hinterlands required a certain measure of political authority. By this time, the British government had also shifted its policy on acquiring African colonies, starting with Egypt, which explains its rapacious acquisition of territory in the twilight of the nineteenth century.[63] Yorubaland's incorporation under the expanding protectorate in 1893 was not complete until the end of 1896 when eastern Yorubaland was taken from Bida, a vast emirate that emerged from Nupe's 1857 jihadist reforms.[64]

These events show how private companies were involved in the colonization process, in the West African colonies, and as part of the global imperial project. After George Goldie's company received a Royal Charter in 1886, he accelerated his stake in the Niger area under the authority of the Queen for the British Empire. The company repelled foreign competitors and reduced the influence of local merchants so that it could collect taxes and customs duties, regulating the flow of trade in the vast and expanding area that fell under its control. State authorities in the Niger area challenged the RNC's influence, so the company sought to diminish their strength and political hegemony. The most efficient method of neutralizing this resistance was to exploit tensions within local power structures. None of the great powers was eager to surrender their authority to binding treaties that restricted their conduct and trading activities in areas under the supposed protection of the Queen.

Two polities were major obstacles for the RNC: the Sokoto Caliphate and the Bida Emirate. The former served as the Caliphate's central administrative headquarters, but by the latter part of the nineteenth century Bida was the most powerful and the largest of the emirates. This was especially true when Gwandu was established as the Southern headquarters of the Caliphate. Despite its size, the Bida Emirate made remarkable advances across the Niger, reaching eastern Yorubaland and aiming to capture Benin, the delta, and Igbo states. The Bida Emirate was considered to be the richest in the caliphate, which made it a significant prize for the British colonial project.[65] Curbing its continued expansion would diminish its revenue, reduce its political capital, and incorporate its hundreds of polities under the British protectorate. However, the Berlin Conference required valid, proven agreements with local authorities before other imperial powers recognized claims of colonial

---

[63] A. J. Christopher, *The British Empire at Its Zenith* (London: Croom Helm, 1988).
[64] Jimada, *The Historical Background*, 205.
[65] Michael Mason, "Captive and Client Labor and the Economy of the Bida Emirate: 1857–1901," *The Journal of African History* 14, no. 3 (1973): 453–471.

occupation within the region. The situation in the Benue–Niger area made these prospects look very dim.

In his desperation to secure an agreement that proved British occupation of the area, Goldie produced a dubious deal that was questioned by other imperial powers. Etsu Maliki, ruler of the emirate at the time, responded by calling for a public assembly of all European merchants in 1887. He refuted Goldie's claim and implied that all merchants operating in the region, regardless of their country of origin, could trade and conduct activities in the emirate to oppose Goldie's monopolization.[66] Goldie insisted that his "agreement" was obtained from Gwandu, not Bida, and used it as a legal basis for activities in the emirate and its territories. The lines of battle were drawn between the two forces. Following the precedent set with Lagos and Epe, the company offered to pay up to £2,000 as an annual stipend for Etsu Maliki. The rivalry gained intensity in 1895 when the RNC responded to the grievances of its southern province by stationing a military garrison at Jebba and Gbajibo, which was meant to reinforce a possible uprising against Bida. The emirate answered by marching a large army, numbering about 12,000 troops, to Ogidi.

The atmosphere was tense, and so were the actors. Things never escalated into full-blown war, but Goldie's army confronted the Etsu's forces in June 1896, and the clash resulted in a humiliating defeat for the former. Goldie then sought help from several dissenting forces in the emirate, including the northeastern Yoruba states, the traditional leaders of Nupe before the usurpation of power by Fulani forces (the *Yissazhi*), and the strategically located coastal town of Kyadiya. A second clash resulted in the collapse of the Bida Emirate in 1897. As expected, it was incorporated into the British protectorate.[67] Authority was transferred to the traditional leaders of Nupe, who ruled under the newly established Patigi Emirate. From Bida, colonial forces swept through the Middle-Niger polities and those of the Niger–Benue basin, including Ilorin. Its fierce resistance held out for two days with about 1,000 cavalry soldiers and 5,000 infantry troops. By 1903, the entire caliphate had fallen to the colonial project.

After the collapse of Bida, the strongest resistance came from Adamawa, Kano, and Sokoto. The geographic location of these polities was an important component of their resistance to the colonial incursion. In a bid to claim effective occupation of territories in West Africa and comply with the Berlin Conference, the French, German, and British forces intensified their scramble for an established area of influence. The invasions, attacks, and threats executed by the RNC were not isolated incidents in West Africa. Similar attacks were simultaneously carried out by France, especially around Lake Chad, which bordered the northern states. In its attempts to acquire as much land

---

[66] Jimada, *The Historical Background*, 212.
[67] Aliyu, "Collaboration and the British Conquest," 69–82.

Figure 6.1 Britain's penetration and conquest of Nigeria was fierce, bloody, and met with diverse forms of resistance by the Indigenous population across the country.

as possible and threaten British interests in the region, France rapidly made massive waves in polities around Lake Chad, creating a torrent of displaced persons from the region who flowed into the caliphate and its emirates, such as Kano and Adamawa, from the late nineteenth century.[68]

The displaced population included deposed kings and their subjects, along with thousands of warriors and their weapons. This enhanced the military capacity of the caliphate and its emirates, and it bought more time for them to prepare for the colonial army. The threat of attack was inevitable since they had witnessed the collapse of polities that were their southern and western neighbors. Unlike Nupe, Ilorin, and Bida, they had the time to study the military tactics and strategies of invading British forces. The Emir of Kano sent his men to enlist in the West African Frontier Force in Lokoja and the French military in Chad. After learning the rudiments of modern warfare, they would desert their posts and apply their new knowledge as commanders and trainers in the emir's army.

The geography around the emirates also had disadvantages. They were squeezed between two powerful invaders with identical intent: colonization of their land and their people. If they were not being threatened by the British, then a French attack was imminent. This reinforced their military discipline and kept them prepared for the eventuality of war. The civil wars and political

---

[68] Smaldone, *Warfare in the Sokoto Caliphate,* 105.

turmoil in the caliphate, which reached a crescendo near the end of the nineteenth century, also contributed to the military atmosphere. It weakened the caliphate's collective resolve to oppose the invading forces, but it also strengthened their military capacity as they increased their stores of arms and ammunition to suppress internal crises.

In the northern Niger area, arms proliferation was prevalent in the final decade of the nineteenth century. The caliphate and its emirates in Kano and Adamawa outnumbered the colonizing forces, but they could not match the effectiveness of the invaders. The subsequent clashes demonstrated that greater numbers of weapons and fighters do not always guarantee victory. The British forces had the advantage of strategy merged with effective technology. British forces launched long-distance attacks on cities under siege, weakening defensive forces or causing them to flee. Adamawa fell in 1901,[69] and the expedition was carried on to Kano and Sokoto in 1903. As seen in Ilorin, Nupe, Bida, and elsewhere, massive amounts of ammunition and arms were claimed as spoils of war even as many of the weapons had never been deployed to the front because none of the soldiers could use them. Kano's efforts to train a modern army were never completed.

These victories created the Northern Protectorate that was prematurely declared by Lugard in 1900. The proclamation had been issued before the effective occupation of either the Sokoto Caliphate, the central political body in the region, or Kano, its economic nerve center. This shows the desperation of the colonial enterprise at that point, along with the machinations of Goldie's RNC, which wanted European powers to believe that it had the area under its complete control. Even after the successful invasion of Sokoto and the powerful northern states, resistance continued for the better part of colonial rule elsewhere.[70]

The Colonial Office in London rejected Goldie's claims of control and coordination in the Middle-Niger area, recognizing the magnitude of the task ahead and the strength of the caliphate, as well as its strategic position in forging the Northern Protectorate. Instead of granting the request for military reinforcements, the Colonial Office revoked the RNC's charter and appointed Lugard as Governor-General of the Northern Protectorate in January 1900.[71] The British government's presence and activities in the Niger moved into its final stage, transitioning from a private chartered

---

[69] Sa'ad Abubakar, *The Lamibe of Fombina: A Political History of Adamawa 1809–1901* (Zaria: Ahmadu Bello University Press, 1977).

[70] Adiele E. Afigbo, "The Eclipse of the Aro Slaving Oligarchy of South-Eastern Nigeria 1901–1927," *Journal of the Historical Society of Nigeria* 6, no.1 (1971): 3–24.

[71] George Nwangwu, "The Influence of Companies on the Legal, Political and Economic History of Nigeria," *Journal of Economics and Sustainable Development* 9, no. 12 (2018): 118.

company to official colonial administration.[72] This was supported by the establishment of the West African Frontier Force in 1898.[73]

These developments should not be mistaken for the failure of Goldie's "government." The Royal Charter was only granted after considering every option available for the administration of the newly declared Oil Rivers Protectorate. The charter was a way for the British government to assert its presence and "effective occupation" in the Bight of Benin and Biafra, where it had been dominant since the transition to legitimate trade. Goldie's business was meant to bear the costs of complying with the Berlin Conference, protecting the Queen and her empire from any financial risk. At that point, the British government still had doubts about the profitability of the enterprise. These private sentiments ran counter to the public messaging of flourishing foreign colonies and capital in the West. Britain had already taken its share of the economic pie in other parts of Africa, Asia, and America.[74]

The exploratory efforts of the various teams that followed Park's adventure across the Niger, including those that followed the land routes such as Richard and John Lander (the Lander brothers), Hugh Clapperton, Heinrich Barth, and William Balfour Baikie, had been undertaken as scientific inquiries meant to aid the imperial project. These explorations established the richness and sophistication of cultures and societies from the caliphates through the Yoruba country and elsewhere.[75] In Yorubaland and many of the delta states, colonial rule was gradually established after various systems of administration integrated them more tightly with British interests and authority. This culminated in the declaration of the Oil Rivers Protectorate, which expanded to include the Niger Coast and the Southern Protectorate.

British trade flourished early in these regions as local authorities saw the value in pursuing commercially viable products instead of the illegal slave trade. The intensity of British activity in this area challenges the idea that the British government would have adopted a company model for its area of influence in the Niger region before 1900 due to concerns about the project's profitability. As Afigbo has observed, the British government unfailingly selected the cheapest and most profitable model for establishing dominance and administering foreign territories.[76] Flint adds that "the policy of 'legitimate commerce' was opposed to colonial activity, except in extreme

---

[72] David C. Somervell, *The British Empire* (London: Christophers, 1945), 286.

[73] Samson C. Ukpabi, "The Origins of the West African Frontier Force," *Journal of the Historical Society of Nigeria* 3, no. 3 (1966): 485–501.

[74] Somervell, *The British Empire*.

[75] William H. Clarke, *Travels and Explorations in Yorubaland, 1856–1858* (Ibadan: Ibadan University Press, 1972).

[76] Adiele E. Afigbo, *The Abolition of the Slave Trade in Southeastern Nigeria 1885–1950* (New York: University of Rochester Press, 2006).

circumstances."[77] Existing knowledge shows that the British government understood that this region was as rich and had as much economic potential as Uganda, where Lugard had earlier been posted. The British government in Lagos largely overlooked the atrocities and excesses of Goldie's exploitative rule in the Middle-Niger area.

The RNC's policies were markedly different from those of the Oil Rivers Protectorate, involving heavy taxes and a rapacious, monopolistic drive. People of the Middle-Niger states were held hostage for years, leading to starvation and anger directed at the company and its activities. Among the autochthonous western Igbo communities, the company's predations resulted in the formation of the Ekumeku resistance group, which operated in three phases that lasted well into colonial rule.[78] The first phase of Ekumeku activities lasted from 1883 to 1900 when they smuggled arms and other illicit goods to oppose the RNC's draconian rule. This morphed into outright resistance to colonial domination from 1900 to 1902 after the revocation of the RNC's charter left them facing new oppressors cut from the same cloth. The movement, described as an Asaba affair and known today as Anioma in the hinterlands, reformed at different times between 1904 and 1914.[79] The Ekumeku movement also staged an invasion of the RNC headquarters in 1898, inflicting major damage on the company.[80] This development was allegedly one of the reasons why the British government decided to revoke the company's charter.

In parts of Igboland, where the Arochukwu maintained some political capital as a central social authority, the government faced both passive and violent resistance.[81] The Ekumeku was organized as a mutual trust and social justice organization, but the Aro was rooted in spiritualism. This perspective influenced their operations as they managed to resist and survive the colonial onslaught. Although the Aro cult promoted slavery and "paganism," which were criminal activities in the emerging British colony, it was widely distributed and capable of being re-established in any suitable community or

---

[77] These extreme circumstances saw the intermittent intervention of the British government in the Niger area, followed by trading companies handling the administration of areas until 1900, when the government finally took over. See John E. Flint, "Chartered Companies and the Scramble for Africa," in *Africa in the Nineteenth and Twentieth Centuries*, ed. Joseph C. Anene and Godfrey N. Brown (Ibadan: Ibadan University Press, 1966), 112.

[78] Philip A. Igbafe, "Western Ibo Society and Its Resistance to British Rule: The Ekumeku Movement 1898–1911," *The Journal of African History* 12, no. 3 (1971): 441–459.

[79] Tony Eluemunor, "Ekumeku War: Anioma Uprising against British Rule," *Vanguard*, March 30, 2019.

[80] Don C. Ohadike, *The Ekumeku Movement: Western Igbo Resistance to the British Conquest of Nigeria, 1883–1914* (Athens: Ohio University Press, 1991).

[81] Diana Rosenberg, "Ibo Resistance to British Colonial Power," *Ufahamu* 19, no. 1 (1991): 3–21.

location.[82] It survived several offensives from the British government largely through passive resistance that relied on decoy activities.[83] Colonial forces might hear about Aro cult activities in a specific community only to be welcomed there with open arms. The invaders were fed, given gifts, and assured that the cult had never existed in such a place. This subterfuge was enabled by networks of Aro communities, cults, sympathizers, and informants who tracked the invading forces through their communities. The cult was so powerful that it survived the demystification of its practices and the claims that white intruders had made to gain a larger share of trading activities in the region.[84] The Aro cult remained a dominant force among people who relied on its spiritual guidance and those who could not trust the justice of the modern British system.

A similar dimension can be seen among the resistance mounted by some autochthonous communities in the Plateau region, which suggests that the colonial enterprise had more difficulties capturing and administering acephalous societies in the Niger area than it did with larger, centralized states. The key difference was a lack of central authority structures. Villages with populations organized in compounds and clans are prone to make independent decisions that could impair the massive colonial project and its relentless pursuit of resources.

In Sokoto, Kano, and the emirates, the fall of the caliphate meant the establishment of foreign rule over a vast expanse of towns, villages, and territories.[85] In smaller, distributed communities without a central authority, the British forces needed to conquer each polity individually. The exceptions were those who willingly gave up sovereignty, for one reason or the other, through peaceful diplomatic means. This included communities that collaborated with British forces to enable the invasion of their neighbors and perceived enemies. The Plateau region remained largely neglected in the colonial scramble until a need developed for tin and mining sites.[86] Once the British colonial government in Bauchi discovered these resources, it became another area to be brought under colonial rule by diplomacy or military force.

---

[82] John N. Oriji, "The Slave Trade, Warfare and Aro Expansion in the Igbo Hinterland," *Transafrican Journal of History* 16 (1987): 151–166.

[83] Afigbo, "The Eclipse of the Aro Slaving Oligarchy."

[84] Ndu Life Njoku, "The Dual Image of the Aro in Igbo Development History: An Aftermath of Their Role in the Slave Trade," *Journal of Retracing Africa* 2, no. 1 (2015): 29–48.

[85] Aliyu S. Alabi, "Voices after the Maxim Gun: Intellectual and Literary Opposition to Colonial Rule in Northern Nigeria," in *Resurgent Nigeria: Issues in Nigerian Intellectual History: A Festschrift in Honour of Dahiru Yahya*, ed. Sa'idu Babura Ahmad and Ibrahim Khaleel Abdussalam (Ibadan: University Press, 2011), 124–146.

[86] Yakiban Mangvwat, *A History of Class Formation in the Plateau Province of Nigeria, 1902-1960: The Genesis of a Ruling Class* (Durham: Carolina Academic Press, 2013).

The arrival of Europeans was not recognized as the advent of colonial rule until the process was complete. Communities could only resist with less effective weapons such as clubs, machetes, spears, and poisonous arrows that stood no chance against machine guns and repeating rifles. They were dazed by explosive shells as the white man "with his bizarre physical appearance and monstrous weapons" invaded and entered their lands.[87] In Benin, before it fell to British forces in 1897, local magic and rituals could not prevent their defeat. The RNC stationed its regional headquarters in Ibi in 1883, which signaled the first British presence in the area after the scramble that had begun in the early part of the century. Wase was invaded in 1898, and Goemailand in the following year.[88] Across the Niger area, scattered resistance movements devised various ways to oppose the intrusion throughout the colonial period.

Conclusion

The colonization of the Niger area was a gradual, systemic process that penetrated the socioeconomic and sociopolitical fabric of society through imperial agents. The so-called explorers in this enterprise played their role alongside European missionaries, merchants, and returnees. These colonial agents engaged in scientific exploration and study within the Niger area, which created the basis for modern academic study and its methodologies, theories, and perspectives.[89] However, the colonization process in this region was far from uniform, affected by the geographic location of states along with their political morphology and economic viability. The experiences of the delta states and the entire Bight of Benin, along with the Yoruba states, were very different from those of the Middle-Niger states. Autochthonous states in the Plateau–Benue areas and others in the Igbo states and elsewhere had their own experiences with this process.

The recovery of massive amounts of weaponry from the arsenal of invaded polities, the military reorganization of the states, and the instability that plagued the region due to political expansion were only beginning at the time of colonial conquest. Without European intervention, these weapons and the military preparations, alongside the alliances and disruptive forces operating in the area, would have written a different history for the Niger area. With or without colonial incursion, this region's political recalibration along

---

[87] Elizabeth Isichei, "Colonialism Resisted," in *Studies in the History of Plateau State, Nigeria*, ed. Elisabeth Isichei (London: Macmillan Press, 1982), 207.
[88] Isichei, "Colonialism Resisted."
[89] Achille Mbembe, *On the Post-Colony* (London: University of California Press, 2001); Linda Tuhiwai Smith, *Decolonizing Methodologies: Research and Indigenous Peoples* (London: Zed Books, 2012); and Toyin Falola and Christian Jennings, eds., *Africanizing Knowledge: African Studies across Disciplines* (New Brunswick: Transaction Publishers, 2002).

the lines of modern nation-states was imminent. In the twentieth century, the effective colonization of this area brought reforms in currency, fiscal regimes, judicial systems, economic systems, political morphologies, and communication and transportation networks, especially after the 1914 amalgamation.

By this time, many resistance movements had been suppressed, with a few exceptions that included the Aro cult in Igboland. However, new forms of resistance developed to oppose the colonial state as the struggle shifted from opposing colonial intrusion to challenging its policies. By the end of World War I, these efforts focused on demanding inclusion in the government and better remuneration for "native" workers. Toward the end of World War II, resistance against colonial rule gained new momentum.[90] It took on a global dimension to demand the creation of a modern nation-state for Nigeria to be ruled through self-government.[91]

---

[90] Rudolf von Albertini, "The Impact of Two World Wars on the Decline of Colonialism," *Journal of Contemporary History* 4, no. 1 (1969): 17–35.

[91] James S. Coleman, *Nigeria: Background to Nationalism* (Berkeley: University of California Press, 1958).

7

Administrative Experimentation, Boundary Formation, and Colonial Consolidation, 1900–1914

In January 1900, the British colonial government proclaimed the birth of the Nigerian colony.[1] This was divided into two parts: the Southern and Northern colonies. These two administrative units were to be governed differently despite the intention of the colonial establishment to govern both as a single entity for administrative efficiency.[2] This arrangement continued even after the amalgamation of the two regions in 1914, following several piecemeal reforms and policies from both sides.[3] The amalgamation process itself, in terms of structure and institutional harmony, continued till late in the colonial administration.[4] And, as was evident in what later became the Nigerian state, this process was not completed by the time the British handed it over to the nationalist politicians.

Additional to these two administrative units was the Lagos Protectorate, which oversaw the affairs of the coastal city where the colonial government made the headquarters of its activities in Nigeria.[5] Apart from Lagos, these administrative units were further broken into three structures: the provinces, which later served as the postcolonial regions and states; the division; and the districts, the equivalent of local government administration. This experiment also involved the reordering of the political and administrative power of traditional rulers in the colony. In 1906, the Lagos Colony was administratively merged with the Southern Protectorate,[6] and this recalibration of the polity was expanded to the Northern colony in 1914.[7] The 1914 amalgamation

---

[1] Tunde Oduwobi, "From Conquest to Independence: The Nigerian Colonial Experience," *Historia Actual Online* 25 (2011): 19–29.
[2] Oduwobi, "From Conquest to Independence," 21.
[3] Obaro Ikime, *The Fall of Nigeria: The British Conquest* (London: Heinemann, 1977).
[4] Jeremy J. White, *Central Administration in Nigeria, 1914–1948* (Dublin: Irish Academy Press, 1981).
[5] Adeyemi A. B. Aderibigbe, "Expansion of the Lagos Protectorate, 1863–1900," unpublished PhD dissertation, University of London, 1959.
[6] Joseph C. Anene, *Southern Nigeria in Transition, 1885–1906* (Cambridge: Cambridge University Press, 1966).
[7] Mary Bull, "Indirect Rule in Northern Nigeria, 1906–1911," in *Essays in Imperial Government*, ed. Kenneth Robinson and Frederick Madden (Oxford: Basil Blackwell, 1963), 47–87.

Figure 7.1 Frederick Lugard, the first High Commissioner (1900–6), Governor of Southern and Northern Nigeria Protectorate (1912–14), last Governor of the Northern Protectorate, and first Governor-General of Nigeria (1914–19). Lugard initiated the indirect rule system, oversaw the Amalgamation of the Southern and Northern Protectorates in 1914, and laid the foundation for the modern Nigerian state.

often alluded to the need for a Northern colony free of the financial support of the taxpayers' money in Britain, grants from the South, and the need to harmonize colonial policies for effective communication across the divides and, in consequence, an easy administration.[8] Yet, institutional, structural, and ideological harmonization of the two divides remained the Achilles heel of the amalgamation, thus putting nation-building efforts after independence in serious jeopardy.[9] The administrative experiments were primarily a function of imperial considerations and not the prospect of nation-building.

After Lord Lugard (illustrated in Figure 7.1) retired from his controversial role as the Governor-General of Nigeria (1914–19) where he championed the indirect rule system and amalgamation of the Southern and Northern Protectorates, serving previously as the first High Commissioner (1900–6) and Governor of the two Protectorates (1912–14), several reforms trickled in. This culminated in the introduction of a representative government, a phase that had slowly commenced from around 1881 and formally began in 1922 (as represented in Map 7.1), with regionalization of the colony in 1946, regional government in 1951, and eventual independence in 1960.[10]

---

[8] Lord Lugard, *The Dual Mandate in British Tropical Africa* (New York: Routledge, 1965).
[9] Emmanuel O. Ojo, "Nigeria, 1914–2014: From Creation to Cremation?" *Journal of the Historical Society of Nigeria* 23 (2014): 67–91.
[10] Ian F. Nicolson, *The Administration of Nigeria, 1900–1960: Men, Method and Myths* (Oxford: Oxford University Press, 1969).

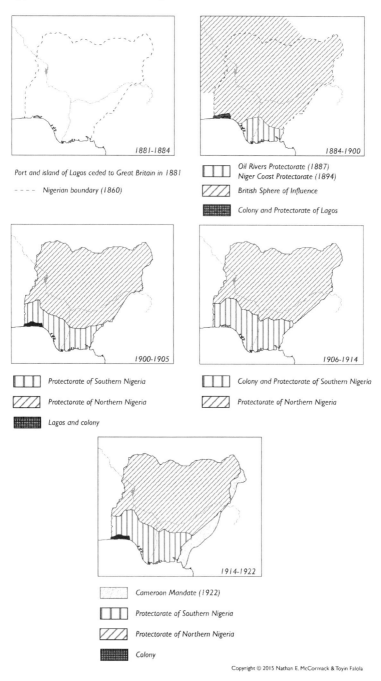

Map 7.1 Colonial Nigeria in Phases (1881–1922).

The Political Economy of Power

A cursory look at the history of precolonial Nigerian societies reveals kaleidoscopic structures, systems, frames, and cultures of administration.[11] This, as well as the political situation in each region of the colony, shaped the changes and transformations injected into the system by the colonial government. Several parts of previous chapters point to the complexity of the political developments that resulted in the colonial episode on the eve of 1900 in the Niger area. Among their peculiarities was the discovery that the colonial experience of these cultures differed to varying degrees. The colonial experience and experimentation in the area that largely became the Southern Protectorate in 1900 began with the establishment and operation of the Court of Equity in Bonny in 1854.[12] Also significant was the 1852 British imperial treaty with Akitoye in Lagos, ceding trade coordination in the area to the British Consul for an annual remuneration of £1,000.[13] The same cannot be said of the area that largely became the Northern Protectorate, which was administered after the Queen appointed Sir Gorge Goldie to represent her interest in the area which covered the Bight of Biafra, Nupe, Middle-Niger, and the Hausa states – the Niger and Benue area – in 1886.[14] In other words, between 1887 and 1900, the British government successfully amalgamated different parts into the Northern Nigeria Protectorate and the Protectorate of Southern Nigeria, with the Colony of Lagos merged with the latter (see Map 7.2).

Even then, apart from the diplomatic game Goldie played in Bida, which gave him the dubious right to coordinate the economic activities of the emirate, the political coordination of this region remained as it had been under the caliphate system headquartered in Sokoto, with the sultan as the supreme head until 1903 when the caliphate collapsed to the British forces. By this time, Goldie had left his position, and the colonial project was already in full swing with the January 1, 1900 declaration by Lugard.[15] For ease of his administrative duties, recreational purposes, and the need for an apparent view of the Rivers Niger and Benue confluence, a rest house (shown in Figure 7.2) was constructed at Mount Patii in present-day Kogi State, Nigeria. In this way, the colonial experimentation in the Northern Protectorate started

---

[11] Obaro Ikime, *Can Anything Good Come Out of History?* (Ibadan: BookCraft, 2018); and Colin W. Newbury, *The Western Slave Coast and Its Rulers: European Trade and Administration among Adja–Speaking Peoples of South Western Nigeria, Southern Dahomey, and Togo* (London: Oxford University Press, 1961).

[12] John O. Asein, *Introduction to Nigerian Legal System* (Lagos: Ababa Press Ltd., 2005), 153.

[13] Preye Adekoya, "The Succession Dispute to the Throne of Lagos and the British Conquest and Occupation of Lagos," *African Research Review* 10, no. 42 (2016): 207–226.

[14] John Flint, *Sir George Goldie and the Making of Nigeria* (London: Oxford University Press, 1960).

[15] Flint, *Sir George Goldie.*

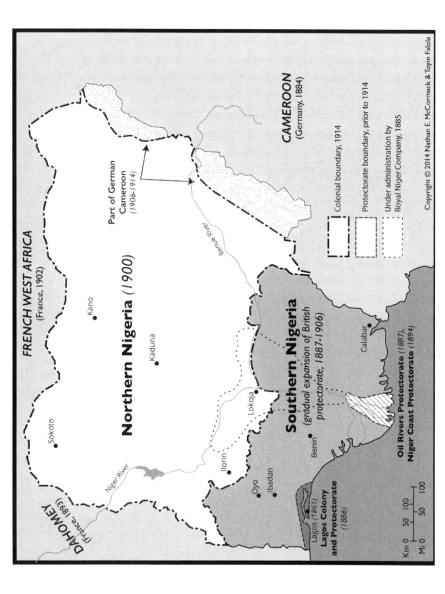

Map 7.2 Northern Nigeria Protectorate and Colony and Protectorate of Southern Nigeria (1887 and 1900).

Figure 7.2 Lugard's Rest House, Lokoja.

later than that of the South, which commenced with the British private companies' administration in the mid-nineteenth century. This attests to the role of the structure and political situation in each region in their colonial experiences noted earlier.

The British government had no misgivings and expressed its readiness to use the local authorities in their area of influence for various reasons.[16] Where this authority was weak, the government sought to strengthen it under its supervision. On the other hand, when this proved too strong for the trading and economic interests of its merchants and other agents of *Pax Britannica* and the colonial project, the polity was invaded and the power hierarchy was forcefully restructured.[17]

With the enthronement of the Sokoto Caliphate and the Fulani hegemony in the north in the early nineteenth century, this region largely represented the latter. This was also common with others in the south, such as Opobo, Lagos, Ijebu, Benin, and the acephalous states in the Bight of Biafra. As noted in Chapter 6, British influence in the government of the polities around the Bight

---

[16] Lord Lugard, *Political Memoranda*. 3rd ed. (London: Frank Cass, 1970).
[17] John D. Hargreaves, "West African States and the European Conquest," in *Colonialism in Africa 1870–1960 Volume One: The History and Politics of Colonialism 1870–1914*, ed. Lewis H. Gann and Peter Duignan (New York: Cambridge University Press, 1969), 199–219.

of Benin and Biafra had begun earnestly even before the deal was sealed with Akitoye in 1852. In the same name and spirit of promoting legitimate trade in this area, Beecroft was appointed as the British Consul to the Bights of Benin and Biafra in 1849. The implication is that, steadily, the political structure of these states began to take on a new form.[18] In a similar situation that led to the intervention of the British government in Lagos politics, following the 1886 treaty that ended the Ekitiparapo War,[19] the decline in the political authority in the Delta states in the first half of the nineteenth century led to the pursuit of an alternative political authority to administer the emerging commercial relations in the states. In this light, the political heads of this area consented to establish the Court of Equity in 1854.

From 1891, when Sir Claude Macdonald took over the charge of this region for effective colonial occupation, the court multiplied from Bonny, Warri, Opobo, and other polities in the region.[20] The court, which appeared two years after the treaty between Great Britain and Lagos, would become the first local institution for alien rule in the Niger area and the template for subsequent administrative reviews, particularly in the Bight of Benin and Biafra. This judicial system, which equally held political and economic powers and later transformed into the Native Council under McDonald, with a subsequent effect on the traditional institution of arbitration and power in the region, did not surface in the north until 1903 with the introduction of Lugard's Native Authority System.[21]

Ultimately, the political dynamics in these regions on the eve of the official colonial presence in 1900 determined how the indirect colonial rule system panned out in these polities. Similarly, the complications of executing this system in its various forms across the Niger area resulted in the complexity of the experimentations and reforms, which saw multiple modifications dictated by the need to address developing political, social, and economic challenges. Details of these developments have been studied extensively by Adiele Afigbo, Kenneth Dike, Mahdi Adamu, Joseph Atanda, and other scholars. And from these extensive studies, only a review that considers the fundamentals of this alien administration across the Niger area could be

---

[18] Adiele E. Afigbo, *The Abolition of the Slave Trade in Southeastern Nigeria 1885–1950* (Rochester: Rochester University Press, 2006).

[19] Document extracted from lecture delivered by Chief Oladiran Ajayi, The Otun Asiwaju of Modakeke on July 15, 1989, at Modakeke High School Hall in a Special Commemorative/Mid-year Lecture to Mark the Creation of Ife North Local Government Area, 8; and Anthony I. Asiwaju, *Western Yorubaland under European Rule 1889–1945: A Comparative Analysis of French and British Colonialism* (London: Longman Group Limited, 1976).

[20] Adiele E. Afigbo, *The Warrant Chiefs: Indirect Rule in Southeastern Nigeria, 1891–1929* (London: Longman Group, 1972).

[21] Arthur N. Cook, *British Enterprise in Nigeria* (London: Oxford University Press, 1943), 67.

attempted here. That said, it is worth reiterating at this point that the political economy of power that characterized the colonial episodes came from both sides of the colonial enterprise: the people of the Niger area and their British counterparts.[22] In David Fieldhouse's study on this, the whole text provides a graphic image of the political economy of the colonial enterprise inside and outside Africa. It also reflects on several factors leading to the colonial project, the gradual evolution of this process in Africa, and the transplantation of the colonial experience in the Americas and the Caribbean to the new colonies in Africa.[23]

On the latter's part, they debated various permutations of the best possible system of administration for the effective exploitation and spread of Western civilization in the area. On the side of the former, this signaled the different responses of the local authorities in the area to the systemic infusions injected into their political frames for this purpose.[24] In their various correspondences and comments, all the colonial officers, including those in the Colonial Office in Britain, agreed on the logic of using local authorities in this area for an efficient colonial enterprise.[25] The reasons for this included the cost of administration, continuity of government, health care, available trained British officers, maintenance of peace with the local authorities, and, by implication, the traditions of the people and diffusion of Western civilization at all levels.[26] The success of the Christian missionaries in adopting this model in their ecumenical mission, which Henry Hamilton Johnston, one of the colonial High Commissioners to the South, described as constituting an essay on colonization,[27] gave a ready-made precedent to this consensus.

From the return of the freed slaves from the Americas and Sierra Leone in the mid-nineteenth century, they became agents of social transformation and dissemination of the Gospel to their kinsmen. Their position gave them the latitude to act as intermediaries between the old and the new in society.[28] In the context of the colonial administration, the only question that remained was

---

[22] David K. Fieldhouse, *The Colonial Empires: A Comparative Survey from the Eighteenth Century* (London: Macmillan Press), 177-206.

[23] Fieldhouse, *The Colonial Empires*.

[24] John E. Flint, "Nigeria: The Colonial Experience from 1880 to 1914," in *Colonialism in Africa 1870-1960 Volume One: The History and Politics of Colonialism 1870-1914*, ed. Lewis H. Gann and Peter Duignan (New York: Cambridge University Press, 1969), 220-260.

[25] Godfrey N. Uzoigwe, *Britain and the Conquest of Africa: The Age of Salisbury* (Ann Arbor: University of Michigan Press, 1974).

[26] Adiele E. Afigbo, "The Consolidation of British Imperial Administration in Nigeria: 1900-1918," *Civilizations* 21, no. 4 (1971): 438.

[27] Adiele E. Afigbo, "The Warrant Chief System in Eastern Nigeria: Direct or Indirect Rule?" *Journal of the Historical Society of Nigeria* 3, no. 4 (1967): 449.

[28] Toyin Falola, ed., *Tradition and Change in Africa: The Essays of J.F. Ade Ajayi* (Trenton: Africa World Press, 2000): 55-129.

the extent to which the central government held by British personnel should be involved in the administration of these local authorities that became officially and collectively known as the Native Authority. The local authorities were referred to as Warrant Chiefs in Igboland, Ibibio, Ogoja, and Ijo, where the precolonial political systems were more fluid.[29]

By this, the colonial government also recognized the significance of peace and order in the exploitation of the tropical resources of this vast region. They knew that the abrupt disruption of the extant political culture of the people would not achieve this, but, rather, put them in confrontation with the local authorities with the support of their subjects. However, systematic obstruction of this institution could, in the main, lead to confrontation between the ruling elite and their subjects, a situation in which the colonial government could claim intervention and bring about peace and order. The case of the Abeokuta government in 1914, following the introduction of direct taxation in the town by the Lagos government through the Alake and the consequent revocation of the independence of the Egba nation following the government's intervention, comes to mind.[30] This way, the administration of the colony was to alternate between the central government held by the British and the local government system held by the local authorities, with varying degrees of supervision from the former.

Further to this is that, in some cases, such as payment of tax and tributes, construction of roads, clearing of creeks, erection of public facilities such as trenches and palaces, and other matters of subject–ruler relationship, the colonial enterprise shared some political boundaries with the traditional power structure and dynamics of the people. If anything, this structure and the system only needed to be rehabilitated using the same traditional institutions of the people. In this way, for instance, the Indigenous institution of justice of the people gradually lost its power to the Native Council in Igbo and the Delta states, and the Native Authorities in Yorubaland and the Northern states.[31] Also, the local institutions, such as slavery, payment of tributes and revenue generation, human sacrifice, security, and the religious institution of the people, were reordered or disrupted.[32] In this process of transforming the local structure using the local authority, they were also believed to be training these authorities for modern government. In this respect, for instance, Lugard went a step further, attempting an early education program for the sons of the

---

[29] Gwilym Iwan Jones, "From Direct to Indirect Rule in Eastern Nigeria," *Odù: Journal of Yoruba and Related Studies* 2, no. 2 (1965): 72–80.

[30] See Oluwatoyin Oduntan, *Power, Culture and Modernity in Nigeria: Beyond the Colony* (New York: Routledge, 2018).

[31] Margery Perham, *Native Administration in Nigeria* (London: Oxford University Press, 1937).

[32] Michael Crowder and Obaro Ikime, eds., *West African Chiefs: The Changing Status under Colonial Rule and Independence* (Ile-Ife: University of Ife Press, 1970).

chiefs and nobles to prepare them for taking up their parents' role in the colony's local administration. The diffusion and penetration of Western civilization thus influenced the hope of the indirect rule system adopted in the Niger area.

Furthermore, the environmental condition of this region affected the health condition of the British officers and policy consistency. This also affected the number of British officers available for colonial service in the tropical region, and contributed to the cost of administration. Until the late nineteenth century, when quinine was developed against malaria, Africa was regarded as the "white man's grave."[33] Even after the discovery of quinine, the white man was still vulnerable to this condition caused by mosquitoes. An infected colonial officer, whose tenure was officially limited to a particular period, would require a disruptive period to attend to his health and recuperate.[34] This would require the posting of a new officer, even if in an acting capacity, resulting in none of the officers getting to know their administrative units well enough to make effective policy toward colonial subjugation before being transferred or going on compulsory leave.

Meanwhile, the colonial enterprise relied heavily on information and data to execute its project. The cost of maintaining such a notorious system could make the colonial enterprise unprofitable. Therefore, at best, what the colonial government hoped to achieve with indirect rule was to exploit the resources of the people and, in the process, civilize their political, economic, and social behavior through modifications that suited their purpose.[35]

As the colonial agents were scheming on this and weighing their options, the political situation in the Niger area provided grounds for the political economy of power on the part of the local authorities. The narratives that go with this, from the Niger Coast to the interior polities, have been examined in previous chapters. It should be reiterated that the scramble for the political capital of the British government took a different shape in the internal political dynamics of this area. Even though communities were fond of sabotaging one another in the conquest efforts of the British government, they detested the overlordship of their polities by these forces. This informed their early response to working with the colonial government. Particularly in the Southern Protectorate, exempting the Western province, Warrant Chiefs and native colonial officers, such as court clerks and messengers, were conscripted into the colonial service, as the people feared being stigmatized as colonial collaborators.[36] Where house

---

[33] Phillip D. Curtin, "The 'White Man's Grave': Image and Reality, 1780–1850," *Journal of British Studies* 1 (1961): 94–110.

[34] Phillip D. Curtin, "The End of the 'White Man's Grave'? Nineteenth-Century Mortality in West Africa," *The Journal of Interdisciplinary History* 21, no. 1 (1990): 63–88.

[35] Olufemi Vaughan, *Nigerian Chiefs: Traditional Power in Modern Politics, 1890s–1990s* (Rochester: University of Rochester Press, 2006).

[36] Adiele E. Afigbo, "Anthropology and Colonial Administration in South-Eastern Nigeria, 1891–1939," *Journal of the Historical Society of Nigeria* 8, no. 1 (1975): 19–35.

heads and village heads could not be coerced into the system, new sets of men were appointed to represent such a unit. The major criterion, then, was not strictly maintaining the people's traditions but to reinforce the colonial enterprise.

The situation thus ensured the security of tenure for the early Warrant Chiefs and other natives in the colonial service, as their positions were not enviable but contemptuous in the eyes of the people they governed on behalf of the colonial government.[37] In some areas where the Native Court was established, its operation was obstructed by the absence of clerks to conduct their activities, and others were too remote for the keen supervision of the British officers from the central government. This, however, changed following the 1914 amalgamation process as the political expediency and potency of these positions became clearer to the people and the imposition of the northern version of the indirect rule system in the area.

The local authorities in Yorubaland, Benin, and the Sokoto Caliphate could not have followed the same conscription process, given the already established structure of power in the polities. Their role in the colonial enterprise reinforced the authority of some among them, like the headmen around the Bights of Benin and Biafra. The headmen, court clerks, and messengers wielded political powers beyond what traditions, colonial ordinances, and proclamations allowed them.

It became increasingly difficult for British officers to effectively tour the administrative units as the colonial area expanded through further conquests that lasted till the first decade of 1900. Cases of corruption and abuse of office thus abounded in the Native Authority and Warrant Chief systems.[38] As they sought to consolidate their newly formed power, the local authorities became more powerful and were resisted by the people. During the early stage of colonization, people feared them as much as they detested them as the people saw them in the light of the colonizers. But during the latter stage, starting from 1914, while still being detested, they were seldom feared. This encouraged a series of uprisings against their authority from this period onward.[39] The fear they enjoyed in the early years was keenly in tune with – or, rather, served as a reminder of – the horror the British military shelling of their communities and neighboring communities left in their psyche. In places like the Delta states and Igboland, where the local authorities, including the court messengers, were sometimes beaten up by the people or harassed,

---

[37] Afigbo, *The Warrant Chiefs*.
[38] Enyi J. Egbe, "Native Authorities and Local Government Reforms in Nigeria since 1914," *IOSR Journal of Humanities and Social Science* 19, no. 3 (2014): 118.
[39] Michael Crowder, *Colonial West Africa: Collected Essays* (New York: Routledge, 2012), 140.

the colonial government intervened promptly to restore and ensure the dignity of the native institution through which they served the colonial enterprise.

In an attempt to make the indirect rule system effective, the government developed legal provisions to shore up the power of the local authorities, which in many parts of the South had been sagging since the abolition of the slave trade.[40] Many of these states sustained their political dominance through the slave trade. Society was intensively woven with the institution of slavery, and the social fabric was lined with the hierarchical order that recognized this power structure. Coupled with the dwindling revenue from this market, the increased British presence in the Bight of Benin and Biafra from the time of the abolition brought about the disruption of the role of the middlemen in the distribution of goods in the interior of the coastal states.[41] This, in a way, sapped the coastal states from additional revenue derived from their strategic location as distribution centers.

The increase in the implementation of legitimate trade in this region, which led to the gradual decline of traditional relations in the societies, soon became an obstacle to the indirect rule system. The British government, which soon realized that breaking the communal or traditional ties of the people would be counterproductive to their enterprise, quickly reversed such policies as the 1901 Slave Proclamation.[42] If the slaves become free from their masters and individuals in society are given the freedom to pursue their economic activities independent of the existing authorities, as earlier envisaged for the promotion of the so-called legitimate trade, there would be no traditional authority with which they could enthrone and perpetuate colonial rule. Consequent to this, the first step was taken in the proclamation for "the better maintenance and guidance of the trade system of the new Calabar people" in 1899 to strengthen the house head system in the Bight of Benin and Biafra.[43] This, alongside others such as the 1903 Roads and Creeks (Rivers) proclamation, redeemed the collapsing house head system as a viable political unit in this area.[44] Yet, this institution, serving as an integral part of the socioeconomic formation and political power composition of the society, was used to coerce or pressurize the local elite and local authorities into submission to colonial rule and the wishes of the colonial officers.[45]

---

[40] Afigbo, "The Consolidation of British Imperial Administration," 436–459.
[41] Kenneth O. Dike, *Trade and Politics in the Niger Delta, 1830–1885: An Introduction to the Economic and Political History of Nigeria* (London: Oxford at the Clarendon Press, 1966).
[42] Afigbo, *The Warrant Chiefs*.
[43] Afigbo, "The Warrant Chief System," 688.
[44] Ifi Amadiume, *Male Daughters, Female Husbands: Gender and Sex in an African Society* (London: Zed Books Ltd., 2015).
[45] Uyilawa Usuanlele, "Pawnship in Edo Society: From Benin Kingdom to Benin Province Under Colonial Rule," in *Pawnship, Slavery, and Colonialism in Africa*, ed. Paul E. Lovejoy and Toyin Falola (Trenton: Africa World Press, 2003), 232.

The political structure of the states in the Niger area has been described as one that oscillates between a central and an acephalous system of village or house units. Afigbo argues against the popular notion that the Warrant Chief system was adopted in the Delta and Igbo states because there was no viable traditional political structure or local authority to be located for indirect rule. The British government in the area adopted it [46] because they thought the house head system and small centralized polities across the coasts where they traded were widely spread to the interior.[47] This belief, and the fact that for centuries they had been trading with these chiefs and their agents or boys along the coast, had overblown the extent of their political authority. It was this form of authority they were looking for in the interior as they endeavored to put a joint Native–British government in place in the area. The warrant issued to these chiefs was in recognition of their dwindling authority and significance, which could render ineffective their appointment to the Native Council. In this way, unlike their counterparts in Yorubaland and the Hausa states, their authority was not inherent in their position but in the warrant issued to them in a letter of appointment by the colonial government.

Therefore, instead of further eroding their remaining prestige by supporting the collapse of the traditional structure that had sustained them in the past, the colonial government slowed its position on the slavery institution. One of the ways it ensured this was to prohibit harassment or any form of resistance to the order and authority of the house heads by their subjects. In addition, no house member was allowed to work independently without the permission of the house head, and any slave caught fleeing his master faced persecution from the government. In turn, the house heads were to maintain law and order in their areas of jurisdiction. The 1903 Roads and Creeks Proclamation strengthened this position when it accorded the chiefs the power to mobilize their people, including using force, in the construction of road networks. In 1912, the law was reviewed to accommodate how slaves could purchase their freedom from their masters. The law was, however, repealed by 1915.

Nevertheless, the slave population in this area became more active in the administration of the colony from this period onward as they dominated trade in the area due to the lethargy of the house heads, who were already feeding off the exploitation of the system and their position, to the discontent of the colonial government. The political economy of power during this period, as is generally known, equally prioritized the transformation of the political structure and governance system of the colony to accord with modernity as much as it was positioned to keep its traditional flavor. In bringing this to administrative reality, the indirect rule system was implemented in such a way that the measure of involvement of the central government in the local administration of the Native

---

[46] Afigbo, "The Warrant Chief System."
[47] Usuanlele, "Pawnship in Edo Society," 683–700.

Authority and the Native Council formed the fundamental basis of the dichotomy between the administration of the Southern and the Northern Protectorates. This became even more evident within the Southern Protectorate until 1914.

Before this period, five major systems of indirect administration operated in the Nigerian colony from 1900: the independence granted to the Egba United Government in Abeokuta in 1893,[48] with unique relations with Lagos, and the administration of the Colony of Lagos with such body as the Legislative House; the three others were found in the Native Council in Igboland and the Delta states (Eastern and Central provinces under the Southern Protectorate), and the variations in the Native Authority systems in Yorubaland (Western province of the Southern Protectorate), and the Northern Protectorate. This kaleidoscopic picture, which shows the nature of the political power wielded by the local authorities in these areas in the new political dispensation, is presented in the following section.

Additionally, these all emerged as a result of the proclivity of the colonial administration to work with the regional peculiarities in the colony, at least in accordance with the best of their knowledge, the available data, the circumstance(s) of the time, and the extent to which reason could prevail on powerful colonial figures like Lugard. In light of these clauses, the boundaries within and without the colonial state were haphazardly drawn.[49] The Yoruba, for instance, suffered immensely in this regard as they lost their Western polities of Ketu, Sabe, and others to the French colony, later known as Bénin, during the partition of the colonial boundary between the two imperial states in the twilight of the nineteenth century.[50] This was accompanied by the tactful legalization of the Fulani occupation of its Eastern polities earlier in the century, particularly in Kabba and Ilorin, by Lugard's Northern government. All reasoning for a broader administrative spread across the second-largest British colony following India was rebuffed by Lugard, who amalgamated the two provinces, north and south, under the same administrative spread that imposed the latter structure on others.

The Harmonization of the Indirect Rule System in Northern and Southern Protectorates

Discourses on the political development around this period have shown that, but for the communication barrier, several colonial administrators preceding

---

[48] Saburi O. Biobaku, "The Egba Council, 1899–1918," *ODU: Journal es* 22, no. 2 (1952): 35–49.

[49] John D. Hargreaves, "The Making of the Boundaries: Focus on West Africa," in *Partitioned Africans: Ethnic Relations across Africa's International Boundaries 1884–1984*, ed. Anthony I. Asiwaju (Lagos: Lagos University Press, 1984), 19–28.

[50] Anthony I. Asiwaju and Ogunsola John Igue, eds., *The Nigeria–Benin Transborder Cooperation: Proceedings of a Bilateral Workshop, Topo, Badagry, May 1988* (Lagos: University of Lagos Press, 1994).

Lugard, such as Sir McDonald and Ralph Moor, had realized the suitability of a united colony of Nigeria divided into the Maritime and Sudan provinces. This emerged with disparate administrative structures within each protectorate to reflect their cultural and traditional ties and boundaries. It was on this matter that the Niger Committee, comprising senior British administrators in Nigeria and Britain, was set up in 1898 by the Colonial Office in London, which came up with recommendations on how to tackle these disparate challenges.[51] Whereas this was most desirable, the poor means of effective communication via road, rail, and water networks, as well as telegraphy and the postal services, the health and climatic condition of the area, and the availability of adequate staff members, altered their decision to apply this "unification" principle in piecemeal fashion and, rather, to proceed as soon as practicable.[52] To this effect, colonial narratives have shown how the transportation industry, especially the railway, the resulting political dynamics that ensued on both sides of the administrative divide, and the infrastructural developments of the time culminated in the 1914 amalgamation.[53]

Before this time, revenue from the Southern Protectorate had already contributed substantially to the infrastructural developments in the North, especially in the railway and communication sectors. The colonial government gave these sectors serious consideration and earnestly kept up the developmental efforts of infrastructure in the early days of the administration. By 1912, a railway link had been established between the Southern and Northern Protectorates, thereby increasing communication between the two parts of the colony.[54] Besides the administrative advantage of the massive infrastructural projects the government embarked on in this sector, it also facilitated trade and commerce. Efforts were consciously directed at linking the areas of production to the points of consumption and distribution within and outside the colony.[55] This way, in addition to the incentives for encouraging farmers to grow certain crops (usually cash crops), farmers could produce more as they produced beyond the subsistence level. The commercial market had expanded, and so had the production and varieties of crops in this commercial cycle.[56]

---

[51] Godfrey N. Uzoigwe, "The Niger Committee of 1898: Lord Selbourn's Report," *Journal of the Historical Society of Nigeria* 4, no. 3 (1968): 467–476.
[52] Uzoigwe, "The Niger Committee of 1898," 467–476.
[53] Afigbo, "The Consolidation of British Imperial Administration," 444–446.
[54] Wale Oyemakinde, "Railway Construction and Operation in Nigeria, 1895–1911: Labour Problems and Socio-economic Impact," *Journal of the Historical Society of Nigeria* 7, no. 2 (1974): 303–324.
[55] Olufemi R. Ekundare, *An Economic History of Nigeria 1860–1960* (London: Methuen & Co., 1973).
[56] Paul E. Lovejoy and Jan S. Hogendorn, *Slow Death for Slavery: The Course of Abolition in Northern Nigeria, 1897–1936* (New York: Cambridge University Press, 1993).

Indigo, groundnut, leather and leather works, livestock, rice, millet, cotton, potatoes, tobacco, clothes, and other industrial and farm products from the North complemented the cocoa, palm oil and palm products, cassava, and other products from the South in a greater measure that built on the precolonial exchanges. The harmonization of the two administrations became even more important besides the intensity of the trading and commercial activities on the north–south corridor when the two regions' geophysical fixtures were considered for harmonization. A waterlogged southern region that largely covered the Bight of Benin and Biafra was undoubtedly indispensable to the landlocked Northern Protectorate for trade and administrative convenience. Dispatches from the two units to the Colonial Office in London (and vice versa) were communicated through the Lagos port. This was likewise the case for other communication items between the home office and the colony, such as farm products and raw materials for the British industry – the primary reason for the occupation in the first place. Considering these administrative units' geographical conditions, Lagos took the form of the administrative center of the British colony in Nigeria.[57] And it was only by building closer and more efficient links with this administrative unit that the colonial government could maximize its presence in the Niger area.

The colonial administrative experiments in the colony transformed the political landscape of the Niger area in a measure clear enough to quantify but too complex to qualify in certain terms. The argument continues among scholars of chieftaincy institutions and political evolution in the region and the rest of Africa, as to whether the colonial administrative experiments of these years lowered the institution's status or gave it impetus.[58] The other side of this debate remains the extent to which this was altered or shored up. The dilemma of an absolute characterization in this matter is not so distant from the challenges an objective observer of the nineteenth-century developments and the eventual colonial incursion of these polities in the following century faced when measuring their effects in absolute terms. This was a period in which Western humanitarianism, philanthropy, science, and capitalism were conjured to engineer a collective transformation of "barbarian" society.[59] The social, economic, political, and cultural contexts that defined these civilizations were to be systematically altered.

Yet, as noted, this process saw some local authorities wielding enormous influence over how this was executed. It was to this extent that notable differences could be seen in the indirect rule system of the colony. Basically,

---

[57] Jean Herskovits, "Liberated Africans and the History of Lagos Colony to 1886," Ph.D. diss., University of Oxford, 1960.
[58] Crowder and Ikime, *West African Chiefs*.
[59] Robert A. Bickers and Rosemary Seton, *Missionary Encounters: Sources and Issues* (London: Curzon Press, 1996).

at the upper echelon of the colonial administrative pyramid was the Colonial Office in London, where final decisions regarding important developments in the colony's administration were made.[60] Such decisions included the system and structure of administration, policy developments, major infrastructural development, the posting and management of staff, and other issues that may affect the colony's general management. Before 1914, the British colonial mission in Nigeria was headed by a High Commissioner and a Consul-General in the two provinces. Also, before the amalgamation of 1906, which saw Lagos and the Southern Protectorate synched within the same administrative unit, the British colonial mission in Lagos was headed by an administrator. This individual shared the same secretariat with the High Commissioner and the Consul-General of the Southern Protectorate.

By 1903, when Sir Walter Egerton was appointed to oversee the administrations of the Southern Protectorate in preparation for the amalgamation of the Southern Protectorate and the Colony of Lagos, this title and position were upgraded to that of a Governor of Lagos and High Commissioner of Southern Nigeria. Similarly, Lugard was brought back to the colony in 1912 after his exit from the mission in 1906 to Hong Kong to prepare for the 1914 amalgamation of the two protectorates. In this way, the Colonial Office in London ensured they brought competent hands into the colony's administration at strategic times. Both officers could achieve their missions given that they had been advocates of such transformation before and during the early years of the colonial episode. Both mapped out the strategy through which these mergers could be achieved promptly upon their arrival with the passion they had advocated an elaborate colonial administration for efficiency in the Niger area. By the time Lugard succeeded in his mission, the position, the title of head of the colonial mission, and the nomenclature of the administration had also evolved.

As a single administrative unit, at least in theory, the head of the mission became known as the Governor-General, and was assisted or deputized by two officers referred to as Lieutenant-Governors – one heading the Northern mission and the other the Southern mission. They were also referred to as the Colonial Secretary. With this evolution, power devolved from the Colonial Office in London to the Governor-General, and from there to his assistants, who put this power into effect in their regions. From these officers, power was further diffused to other levels on the administrative ladder. These were the residents, district officers, and local authorities. Owing to the magnitude of his assignment, an assistant district officer supported the district officer. As briefly noted, the local authorities were either referred to as Warrant Chiefs, as in the decentralized states in Igboland and the Niger Delta, or as paramount chiefs, as

---

[60] As Fieldhouse wrote, "Colonial affairs were never entirely insulated from domestic agencies of government." *The Colonial Empires*, 243.

in the case of Benin, both of which operated through the Native Council or the Native Authority, as operated differently in the North and Yorubaland. The role which the assistant district officer came to occupy was one formerly administered by the colonial traveling commissioners who performed the same functions as these commissioners.

As the lowest in the rank of these officers, they, as the name suggests, traversed their designated administrative spheres to collect taxes and check the activities of the local authorities, acting as a direct link between the provincial government and the local authorities. This is because they carried messages between these two and helped execute government policies at the local government level.[61] The local government system, it is essential to draw from the foregoing, was the nerve of the colonial administration.[62] Whatever decision was made in London, Lagos, Oyo, Enugu, Calabar, Kaduna, or other administrative headquarters had no effect whatsoever unless the buy-in of this unit was secured, hence the importance the government attached to its relations with this unit and the local authorities. This was to the extent that Lugard's government and subsequent administrators in the Northern Protectorate were committed to preserving and expanding the area of influence and capacity of these local authorities. This was carried out by introducing the sole authority system across the colony following the amalgamation. This, unlike what was at play in the South, had been the hallmark of the native administrative system in the North since the fall of the Sokoto Caliphate.[63] Under this system, the government preserved the extant political structure of the people with modifications that further empowered local authorities beyond their traditional reach.

Lugard perceived indirect rule as a system in which a strong local authority with a cross- and interterritorial sphere of influence was essential. As in other Islamic states, this was the ready-made template he encountered in the evolving Sokoto Caliphate under the Fulani hegemony and Islamic rule.[64] The emirate system in this region had structured the society in some form of feudalistic frame in which land and access to it were central to the accumulation and characterization of wealth and status. Simply put, the relationship between an individual and the land had become an instrument of power.[65] This way, the society was organized among powerful nobles, fief-holders, and

---

[61] Perham, *Native Administration in Nigeria*.
[62] Egbe, "Native Authorities and Local Government Reforms," 113–127.
[63] Joseph P. Smaldone, *Warfare in the Sokoto Caliphate: Historical and Sociological Perspectives* (London: Cambridge University Press, 1977).
[64] Jürgen Osterhammel, *Colonialism: A Theoretical Overview*, trans. Shelley L. Frisch (Jamaica: Ian Randle Publishers, 1970), 97–100.
[65] Yusuf Bala Usman, *The Transformation of Katsina, 1400–1883: The Emergence and Overthrow of the Sarauta System and Establishment of the Emirate* (Zaria: Ahmadu Bello University Press, 1981).

peasants. The structure was such that it already operated on a hierarchy of power and entitlement envisaged by the colonial enterprise. Also, as in centralized states like Yorubaland and Benin, but unlike the acephalous states such as Benue-Plateau and the Delta states, political power was divinely inspired. This gave the local authorities in the colony varying degrees of political legitimacy and authority.[66] In using and modifying these existing structures, the government introduced a judicial system through which they continued to build their political capital among their people.

This came, except in the North, where the caliphate system already had an effective structure that this modern institution was to serve, such as collecting taxes and revenue and executing elite projects. Adjudication was a common practice which was dispensed accordingly and came in different forms, regardless of size and morphology. As noted in the caliphate, the rest also took their idiosyncratic form in Old Oyo, Benin, Ilesha, and other powerful central states in the region up until the nineteenth century.[67] However, the peculiarity of the caliphate resided in the recession of these structures in other states in the Niger area, many of which were only just recovering from the decades of wars in the region. Some of them were, interestingly, taking their convalescence under the caliphate. Thus, the caliphate became the epitome of good local governance, admirably and relatively equal to emerging modern European nation-states. Since Islam was the basis of this political consolidation and hegemony, the institution was protected to the extent that some of its practices were repealed, as in the Southern states and their traditional institutions. Among these were the decapitation of offenders and tax practices prescribed by the Shari'a.[68]

Certainly, paying taxes was not alien to polities around the Niger area. Rather, this had existed in various forms among the people and other forms of revenue generation, such as tolls, which traders paid as a tribute to the local authority of the space where they conducted their trade before the colonial masters arrived. Tributes were paid by those who relied on the protection of the local authorities, of which the king or emir was the embodiment, to the state to symbolize, inter alia, their continued loyalty to the authority.[69] Share of war booty and occasional visitations from Western imperial agents, neighbors, and subjects also constituted areas where these polities generated revenue to

---

[66] Yakiban Mangvwat, *A History of Class Formation in the Plateau Province of Nigeria, 1902-1960: The Genesis of a Ruling Class* (North Carolina: Carolina Academic Press, 2013); Bolanle Awe, "The Ajele System: A Study of Ibadan Imperialism in the Nineteenth Century," *Journal of the Historical Society of Nigeria* 3, no. 1 (1964): 47–60.

[67] Peter J. M. McEwan, ed., *Africa from Early Times to 1800* (London: Oxford University Press, 1968).

[68] Lovejoy and Hogendorn, *Slow Death for Slavery,* 161.

[69] Isaac A. Akinjogbin, *Dahomey and Its Neighbours 1708-1818* (New York: Cambridge University Press, 1967); and Alkasum Abba, *History of Yola, 1809-1914: The Establishment and Evolution of a Metropolis* (Zaria: Ahmadu Bello University, 2003).

run their governments and reward their administrators. Added to this in the caliphate was the payment of alms in the form of Zakat used to promote Islam, such as the construction of mosques and aiding the poor. Largely in the South, the palace of the king, the village square, or the council of elders was the Alkali court as it existed in the caliphate. Through traditions, norms, and cultural precedence, cases were adjudged, with designated fees paid to the state's coffers to be shared between the king and his chiefs, as in the centralized states. The magnitude of the case determined whether this was taken to the king and his chiefs or remained within the jurisdiction of the family, compound, clan, village, or district heads.[70]

The colonial administrative experiment took the same form, with some nuances. By virtue of the developments during the period under study, as rooted in the expositions in the previous chapters that prepared the ground for the administration, these polities receded their right of tributary and other associated privileges for the right of taxation by the Queen.[71] In one instance, Moor, the British High Commissioner and Consular-General to the Niger Coast Protectorate, was recorded to have pointedly told a meeting of Benin aristocrats, after the empire's conquest in 1897, "There is only one king in the country and that is the white man . . . The Ovonrnwen is no longer king of the country; the white man is the only man who is king in this country and to him only service is due."[72] This was followed by the abolition of tribute and the proclamation of land revenue, as well as various land policies that transferred the right of land from the community and centralized it with the state. In this way, the Queen could exert her authority in her new sphere of influence and, at the same time, generate adequate revenue to run the colony and develop the metropolitan state.[73]

Additionally, there was the signification of *Pax Britannica* in the states' superstructure. For instance, owing to the instrument of taxation, the government further entrenched the legitimate trade and the diversification of occupations independent of farming as the system promoted a cash-based economy.[74] Expressed differently, farmers acquired British currency and used it to pay for things, as did railway workers, clerks, messengers, traders,

---

[70] Adedayo E. Afe, "Indegenous Judicial System and Governance in the Old Ondo Province, Southwestern Nigeria," *Journal of Law, Policy and Globalization* 20 (2013): 100–105.

[71] Philip Igbafe, "British Rule in Benin 1897–1920: Direct or Indirect?" *Journal of the Historical Society of Nigeria* 3, no. 4 (1967): 701.

[72] CSO 1/13,7. P.29. Moor to F.O.7 September, 1897 quoted in Igbafe, "British Rule in Benin 1897–1920," 701.

[73] Ibrahim M. Jumare, "Colonial Taxation in the Capital of Northern Nigeria," *African Economic History* 26 (1998): 83–97.

[74] Abiodun Afolabi, "The Colonial Taxation Policy Among the Yoruba of Southwestern Nigeria and Its Implications for Socio–Economic Development," *Journal of the Historical Society of Nigeria* 19 (2010): 63–92.

artisans, and owners of other businesses, such as clubs, restaurants, and showrooms. And with the age of paid labor and cash economy came the promotion of cash crops and job specialization, the development and creation of urban centers, and the increasing dichotomy between urban and rural development.

As mentioned earlier, the government also believed that, with this system, they were schooling the local authorities in modern government. Speaking to the difficulties noted in Chapter 6 regarding the colonization of autochthonous states in this area, the direct taxation that had been integral to the conduct of the Northern colonial government since the reforms that followed the fall of Sokoto in 1903 could not find expression in the South until 1914 in light of the Native Revenue Ordinance.[75] From McDonald to Egerton, administrators in the South were still grappling with the reality of bringing the thousands of villages and autochthonous communities in this region under the colonial order since they had to be conquered. In addition, they were short of staff members who would take a wider tour of the area for effective colonization. Therefore, while Lugard was able to settle into the administration of the North on the wings of the caliphate, the administrators in the South were working under a series of conquests, resistance, and attempts at devising means of bringing these small polities under a single administrative unit.

Meanwhile, direct taxation could only be advanced where effective colonial administration had taken root.[76] To this extent, the colonial administration in the South, Yorubaland in particular, did not take effective root until the dramatic years that followed the 1914 amalgamation. Pointing briefly to the dynamics of implementing this policy is the amount of data required in this process.[77] Field agents from local structures such as the *Jakada* in the North, and British Traveling Commissioners and Assistant District Officers, both from the local and central governments, were assigned to comb every ward, the smallest unit of the colonial structure, for estimates of the land and property of the people with a view to mapping their potential production and ascertaining their tax rate.[78]

In accordance with standard practice, this was reviewed intermittently as it was expected that the economic condition of the people would not be static but dynamic, and usually upwards.[79] The available data suggests that women were

---

[75] Joseph A. Atanda, *The New Oyo Empire: Indirect Rule and Change in Western Nigeria 1894–1934* (London: Longman, 1973).
[76] Isaac Tarus, "A History of the Direct Taxation of the African Peoples of Kenya, 1895–1973," unpublished PhD dissertation, Rhodes University, Grahamstown, 2004.
[77] H. A. R. J. Wilson, *Income Tax* (London: H. F. L. Publishers, 1950).
[78] Jumare, "Colonial Taxation in the Capital of Northern Nigeria," 88–89.
[79] Ahmed M. Mohammed, *European Trade, Imperialism and Under-Development in Northern Nigeria 19th and 20th Centuries* (Zaria: Ahmadu Bello University Press Limited, 2016).

exempted from the system. Against this, however, the structure through which such data was collected in the caliphate was blurred. Following the caliphate's conquest of the larger part of the North, the region was divided between the Muslim and non-Muslim populations, both of which were found in the caliphate.

As in the British colonial state, the laws that governed them were different under the protection the state afforded them. For instance, while the non-Muslim population was to pay for protection, among other levies under the caliphate, the Muslim population was exempted. With the British conquest, all units collapsed under the legal and political principles governing colonial subjects, thus the tax payment by all under the Native Revenue Ordinance also collapsed.[80] Resistance against some of the changes Lugard effected in the north, it should be added, was eased by the manner of colonial conquest, which saw the flight of potential dissenters, including the *Ulama*.[81] The alternative drive for sustaining the economy of the South came from customs duty, court charges, and the collection of dues different from the direct taxation practiced in the North. Part of this was the water rate introduced by the Lagos government in 1908.[82]

The practice of the indirect tax collection system in the South also operated upon the local template of governance, again with modifications.[83] The Warrant Chiefs and their boys in the Niger Delta and Igboland, the Obas (kings), chiefs, and their messengers in Yorubaland, Benin, and other centralized states in the area that later constituted the Southern Protectorate, were co-opted into the administration of the colonial state. The Warrant Chiefs and some of their boys were used in the execution of the policies of the colonial government, including collecting taxes, constructing roads, and clearing creeks for viable waterways. It was in the process of the involvement of the boys under the house heads (among which were the Warrant Chiefs) in carrying out the functions of their masters, including in the area of their commercial engagements, that they usurped the role of the latter and began to wield equal power as Warrant Chiefs. The colonial government worked so well with the local power structure among the people that the form of government became more important than the principles guiding the structure.[84] For

---

[80] Obaro Ikime, "The British and Native Administration Finance in Northern Nigeria, 1900–1934," *Journal of the Historical Society of Nigeria* 7, no. 4 (1975): 673–692.

[81] Aliyu S. Alabi, "Voices after the Maxim Gun: Intellectual and Literary Opposition to Colonial Rule in Northern Nigeria," in *Resurgent Nigeria: Issues in Nigerian Intellectual History: A Festschrift in Honour of Dahiru Yahya*, ed. Sa'idu Babura Ahmad and Ibrahim Khaleel Abdussalam (Ibadan: University Press, 2011), 124–146.

[82] Olakunle A. Lawal and Oluwasegun M. Jimoh, "Missiles from 'Kirsten Hall': Herbert Macaulay versus Hugh Clifford, 1922–1931," *Lagos Historical Review* 12 (2012): 45.

[83] Afolabi, "The Colonial Taxation Policy," 63–92.

[84] Falola, *Tradition and Change in Africa*, 158–163.

instance, with the colonial incursion, many practices, especially those that held Yoruba kings sacred, were demystified.[85] This was the case with the house heads and selection into the Native Council in the East and the Niger Delta.

These local powers were given to work with the colonial government mainly through the court system. In Igboland and the Niger Delta, the government upgraded the Courts of Equity to the Native Council, which consisted of two grades: the Minor and the Native Courts. As the names suggest, the former was to oversee minor cases, usually characterized as cases not exceeding a certain amount (£20 at a time) and mainly constituted by local chiefs without the supervision of the British officials. On the other hand, the latter had as its president the High Commissioner and Consul-General, with the vice-president as his deputy, and some Warrant Chiefs among the members. The court's president was empowered to transfer cases from the Minor Court to the Supreme Court or review cases from the Minor Court.[86] The structure that took hold here, though, could not be said to be in tune with the local hierarchy of power, as none existed in the precolonial days besides measures of social stratification at family and communal levels. Its logic lies in the proximity and accessibility of the polities that made up the Native Court to the Colonial Office and officers.

In the other part of the Southern Protectorate, as in the caliphate, the local hierarchy of power was pursued by the government. The hierarchy of power in the Native Authority System in the caliphate remained within the precolonial power structure that flowed from the emir at the top of the pyramid to the village heads in non-Muslim communities at the lowest level. Equally, in the centralized states of the South, at the local level, power devolved from the kings, according to their traditional hierarchies, to their chiefs. The elaborate version of this administration, it should be recalled, had been dismantled during the nineteenth-century crises, part of which the colonial government sought to resuscitate. This was achieved through the administration of the polities in larger clusters described as provinces, divisions, and districts, all of which were created in phases from 1926 up until 1961, as illustrated in Map 7.3.[87] Power was distributed through this structure according to the traditional potency of the communities, which, in turn, was supposedly meant to guarantee their authority to ensure peace and order in their sphere of influence. In reality, this would only be enforced at the whim of the

---

[85] It was not until this period, for instance, that Yoruba kings began to travel and conduct functions in public glare, a practice which began with the invitation of the traditional rulers by the colonial officers. Samuel Johnson, *The History of the Yorubas from the Earliest Times to the Beginning of the British Protectorate* (Lagos: CSS Press, 1921).

[86] Obaro Ikime, "Reconsidering Indirect Rule: The Nigerian Example," *Journal of the Historical Society of Nigeria* 4, no. 3 (1968): 421–438.

[87] Cook, *British Enterprise*.

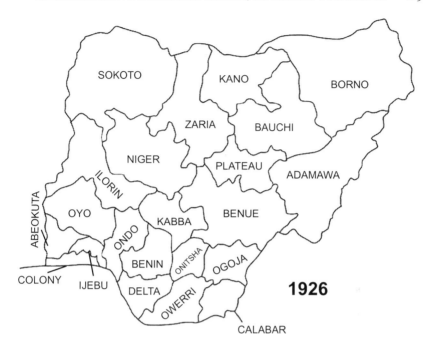

Map 7.3 Provincial Divisions of Nigeria in Phases (1926–61).

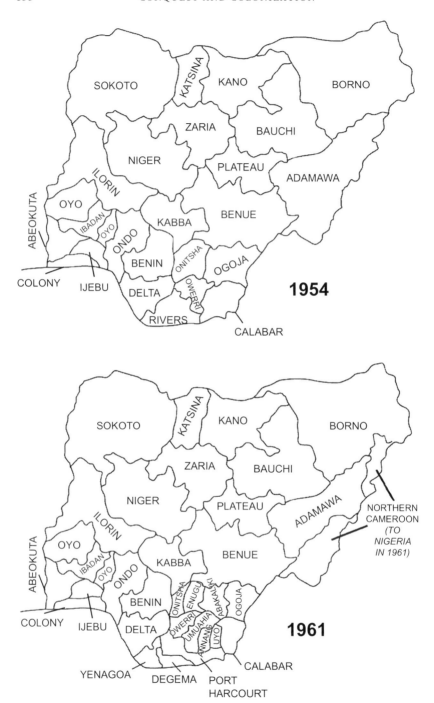

Map 7.3 (cont.)

intervention of the central government because the distribution of power could not operate within the seismic reorganization of the nineteenth century.

This resulted in protests in the likes of Ibadan against what later became the New Oyo, which was made a provincial headquarter. Each district, the lowest in the Native Authority structure, consisted of an average of five communities and was headed by the traditional ruler, considered to wield supreme authority among them. In cases where the ruler could not be ascertained, the government appointed one of the traditional rulers anyway, reinforcing their traditional authority based on colonial administrative imperative and not the traditional principle of power distribution. In light of the traditional dynamics of power in these cultures, it goes without saying that throughout the colonial period, as well as in recent times, this became a major albatross in the administration of chieftaincy institutions in Nigeria.[88] The court system here followed this administrative distribution and consisted of four grades, ranging from A to D. As in other regions, the power of the courts was determined by intertwined and multilayered factors such as their location, the maximum punishment they could adjudge to a case, the magnitude of the case, and the hierarchy of the officials in the colonial administration.[89]

All over the colony, the court, as constituted in its various forms, was responsible for collecting taxes, constructing local projects, and the general administration of their localities. Half of their collected revenue was given to the central government, while they retained the remaining half for other purposes as well as for the payment of the administrators, including the chiefs or local authorities.[90] Although this arrangement had assuaged the fears of the local authorities in Yorubaland about the Native Court System and the Native Revenue Ordinance, which effectively took the administration of their polities and means of generating revenue away from them, the returns they derived through it were considerably limited compared to what had usually been accruable to them in the previous era. Hence, in all the colony's regions, the local authorities devised ways to assuage their losses through clandestine court processes, collection of private gifts, and manipulation of cases and accounts of the local treasury. Such cases often resulted in the dismissal of the officials involved and, ultimately, as regards manipulation of the local treasury, the introduction of the Native Revenue Ordinance to keep the authorities' activities in check.

In the case of the latter, rather than having the chief in charge of the area's revenue, it was centrally monitored by the council with periodic auditing by the district, provincial, and central governments. Europeans residing in the

---

[88] Terrence Ranger and Olufemi Vaughan, *Legitimacy and the State in the Twentieth Century Africa: Essays in Honor of A. H. M. Kirk-Greene* (London: St Antony's, 1993).
[89] Atanda, *The New Oyo Empire*.
[90] Ikime, "The British and Native Administration," 673–692.

colony were tried by the Supreme Court, which also served as the land's highest court, where appeals from the local courts were held. On the part of the people, they also devised ways to evade tax payments. In the North, peasants migrated to other villages at the time of tax collection – until the government introduced an interterritorial collection of taxes which mandated all male adults to pay or show evidence of tax payment to the tax collectors, regardless of their location. In other places, men manipulated the system by setting up businesses in the names of their wives since women were exempted from the practice.[91] The introduction of direct taxation to the South disrupted the house head system British administrators sought to protect for colonial use even before the official declaration of colonial rule in 1900. With the law, as for the slaveholders in the North, the house heads had the responsibility of paying the taxes meant to be paid by their boys or granting them the liberty to work or earn a living on their own from which their taxes could be paid. The latter liberated the slavery institution in the whole colony as it appeared to be the best option for protecting the interests of the elites.[92]

Conclusion

The eminent role played by Lugard in the colonial administration of Nigeria, as Gaily averred,[93] and as mirrored in his diaries accounting for his time in East Africa, should be understood from his experience in the British colonial enterprise in other parts of the world, East Africa in particular.[94] In this way, British colonial administrative experiments in Nigeria, as in its conquest of the polities that constituted the colony, came in different dimensions that took the form of local peculiarities until 1914 when Lugard made the necessary readjustment. The disruptions caused by the 1914 act of amalgamation and Lugard's policy of direct taxation could be measured by the multiple strings of protests and uprisings staged from the North to the South at various times by the people.[95] Also, in executing indirect rule as practiced in the North, the colonial government reinforced the authority of some local authorities while others were (in)advertently relegated. Such was the relationship between the district and provincial heads and members of their council, on the one hand, and the recognized paramount ruler of a polity and other traditional

---

[91] Afolabi, "The Colonial Taxation Policy," 76–77.
[92] Lovejoy and Hogendorn, *Slow Death for Slavery*, 159–198.
[93] Harry A. Gaily, *Lugard and the Abeokuta Uprising: The Demise of Egba Independence* (London and New York: Routledge, 1982).
[94] Margery Perham and May Bull, eds., *The Diaries of Lord Lugard*, Vol. I–III (London: Faber and Faber, 1958).
[95] Toyin Falola, *Colonialism and Violence in Nigeria* (Bloomington: Indiana University Press, 2009).

authorities within the polity, on the other.[96] It could also be deduced from the foregoing that the government considered important the supervision of the traditional institutions of the people in their administrative conduct and the spread of the same traditional institutions elsewhere. The 1914 amalgamation harmonized the terms and principles of this intervention. In subsequent years, the government began to increase the participation of Indigenous educated elements in the administration of the colony as a way of meeting the demands of this community, triggered by various methods of protests.[97]

---

[96] Anthony Kirk-Greene, *Britain's Imperial Administrators, 1858–1966* (London: Palgrave Macmillan Press, 1999).

[97] Emmanuel A. Ayandele, *The Educated Elite in the Nigerian Society: University Lecture* (Ibadan: Ibadan University Press, 1974).

PART III

Colonial Societies

8

World War I and Its Aftermath

The period from 1914 to 1939 signified a remarkable moment in the relationship between local authorities in Nigeria and the British government, as well as between these authorities and their subjects. From the outbreak of World War I to the economic depression that followed the interwar years of economic recovery, a series of dramatic events followed. In some ways, these events signaled a departure from the prewar years; in others, things remained much the same. For example, the events transformed the economy into one of labor and wage earning while, by extension of previous practices, they further diversified and entrenched the raw material export economy. In combination, as this chapter argues, these two issues triggered the decline, if not the death, of local innovations in industrial production.

The war catalyzed massive investment in infrastructure even with the economic depression of the postwar years, expanded trade and markets, as well as the consumption pattern of the "native" population. Motorways, railways, waterways, and airways were expanded and developed throughout the postwar years as the colonial government made an intensive effort to contribute to the reconstruction and rehabilitation efforts in London. These measures expanded the market not only through local consumption but also via the export of raw materials as well as the surging interest of investors. Furthering the creation of a labor economy at this time required the activities of large trading and shipping conglomerates, which pushed local traders and competitors out of the market.

Even after the return of German traders and markets to the colony after the war, the local population could not return to the prewar level of participation in the colonial economy. Earlier, the suspension of the German market had contributed substantially to the economic woes and marginalization of the people as British merchants and the government monopolized the market.

Colonial Rule and World War I

The massive wave of social, economic, and political eruptions of this period in the history of Nigeria followed the sporadic reforms injected into the colonial system by the central colonial administration and implemented by local authorities at the local government level. Going by the economic and imperial motives of the colonial enterprise, many of these reforms were undertaken without proper appreciation of the peculiar extant social structure that existed among the peoples and cultures in the colony. With the outbreak of World War I in 1914 and the economic depression that followed from 1929 to 1939, resulting in unemployment, production, and export deficits,[1] the colonial government and the British empire were recalibrated. This was to respond to even more dire existential threats that dwarfed the exigencies of the prewar rivalry and competition among Western imperial powers. For more than a century up to the outbreak of the war, Britain had dominated the maritime industry in Europe with the strongest naval power and best maritime facilities.[2]

It was in this light that the British empire overran Spain and Portugal, the early modern superpowers of Europe, and, at the same time, outpaced France, Germany, the Netherlands, Belgium, and Italy, her contemporaries in the imperial project, especially after the eighteenth century. The late eighteenth-century Industrial Revolution that began in England propelled this maritime advantage so that Britain became the arbiter of global trade and politics.[3] This was epitomized in the empire's transition from the slave trade to the so-called legitimate trade.[4] No doubt, the transition to and promotion of legitimate trade (i.e., transaction in any product but slaves) and technological advancements are mutually reinforcing. Attempts to encourage free trade, expand participation, and enlarge the market base in Africa, Asia, the Caribbean, and the Americas, as well as the need to improve the traffic between these territories and European capitals, stimulated the revolutions in the maritime industry in Europe.[5]

Possessing new maritime technologies such as steam power meant the acceleration of trade and more efficient trading activities as the ships were faster and more durable on the sea.[6] These technological features multiplied the prospect of merchant companies and ship owners attracting investors and a better insurance policy since the risk of the foreign trade upon which the economy of the metropolitan states had primarily depended earlier had been

---

[1] Murray N. Rothbard, *America's Great Depression* (Auburn: The Ludwig von Mises Institute, 2000).
[2] Paul M. Mbaeyi, *British Military and Naval Forces in West African History 1807–1874* (New York: NOK Publishers, 1978).
[3] Jeremy Black and Philip Woodfine, *The British Navy and the use of Naval Power in the Eighteenth Century* (Leicester: Leicester University Press, 1988).
[4] Robin Law, ed., *From Slave Trade to "Legitimate" Commerce: The Commercial Transition in Nineteenth-Century West Africa* (Cambridge: Cambridge University Press, 1995).
[5] Meluille J. Herskovits and Mitchell Harwit, *Economic Transition in West Africa* (London: Routledge, 1964).
[6] Daniel Headrick, *The Tools of Empire: Technology and European Imperialism in the Nineteenth Century* (New York: Oxford University Press, 1981).

minimized. In addition to owning this technology, Britain was brought to the fore of the imperial pursuit in Europe through its naval power and technology as its maritime prowess combined to transform its military.[7] Being a water-locked empire, Britain invested heavily in securing its waters and using this to expand its reach beyond Europe.[8] Expectedly, the leading position of Britain in Europe that was heralded by the course of the eighteenth-century developments in the region was not without some rivalry and schematics from other competing powers, such as France, and later, Germany.

By the turn of the twentieth century, through a common interest, virtually every corner of Africa had come directly or indirectly under foreign rule by these western powers.[9] This completed the earlier stage of imperial rivalry and competition among European powers. But what followed was World War I. By the turn of the twentieth century, Britain had continued to step up the scale of its maritime prowess and German naval power was expanding at a speed that assured the security of its men and interest on the high seas.[10] The wealth guaranteed by owning slices of the African pie and colonies elsewhere ramped up the competition and rivalry among these Western imperial powers. This followed attempts at consolidating their hold on these territories with military expansionism, a continuation of efforts to secure strategic locations on the sea for the control of trade and geopolitical clout.[11]

The role of the military in the Western imperial expansionist drive of the nineteenth century cannot be quickly forgotten. In the arms race that followed, there was no Berlin Conference to avert the impending doom as various powers increased their military spending and strengthened their arsenals. This was driven by new technology and technological enthusiasm in which raw materials from Africa played a major role. All through the years leading to World War I in 1914, Britain and Germany alternately surpassed one another in naval power.[12]

In a way, the steamship facilitated trade in the so-called legitimate market and the colonization of Africa, just as the HMS *Dreadnought* propelled the reorganization of these two epochal moments. Contrary to the view by scholars such as Rathbone that the eventual outbreak of World War I had no significant

---

[7] Black and Woodfine, *The British Navy*.
[8] Mbaeyi, *British Military and Naval Forces*.
[9] Prosser Giford and William R. Louis, eds., *France and Britain in Africa: Imperial Rivalry and Colonial Rule* (New Haven: Yale University Press, 1971).
[10] Dirk Nottelman, "From Ironclads to Dreadnoughts: The Development of the German Navy 1864–1918," *Warship international* 49, no. 4 (2012): 317–355.
[11] David W. Sweet, "The Baltic in British Diplomacy before the Frist World War," *The Historical Journal* 13, no. 3 (1970): 451–490.
[12] Thomas Hoerber, "Prevail or Perish: Anglo–German Naval Competition at the Beginning of the Twentieth Century," *European Security* 20, no. 1 (2011): 65–79.

impact on Africa and Africans,[13] the impact of this single event reverberated across the region, especially in Nigeria where it coincided with the implementation of the Lugardian administrative reforms.[14] Indeed, the whole of the attributes that characterize World War II as a significant moment in Africa in this argument can be traced to – or rather, are well-rooted in – the events heralded by World War I.[15] The latter changed the course of history in Africa and the whole world in a way that far outstripped the former.[16] The primary significance of the former in African history resides, however, in the administrative measures injected into the colonial system by the colonial powers in response to the crisis, with concomitant effects on the living conditions of the people and their social formation. Higher taxes, a trade monopoly by European merchants, increased white settlers in settler colonies in Southern and East Africa, increased forced labor, and systemic and institutional swindling of the people all came together to reframe the network of relations and organization among Africans living under the colonial condition.[17]

The introduction of the cash economy recalibrated the socioeconomic landscape of the Nigerian colony. A few ways this was made possible could be seen in the proliferation of professional specialization, wage earners, and wage labor. The success of this transition itself is not unconnected to the new tax and fiscal regime that prevailed in the system as the people scrambled to meet their tax obligations under the new system. With paid labor and the rise of wage earners came the breakdown of filial and communal relations and the structure of social relations to economic entanglement.[18] Economic communities and networks supplanted filial and communal networks as rings of mobilization were formed around the former and not the latter.[19] During this period, it became imperative for workers to form a close association with coworkers, especially through unions, since they now shared a common fate that transcended traditional political boundaries. Indeed, under the

---

[13] Richard Rathbone, "World War I and Africa: Introduction," *The Journal of African History* 19, no. 1 (1978): 1–9.

[14] Oliver Coates, "Nigeria and the World: War, Nationalism, and Politics, 1914–60," in *The Oxford Handbook of Nigerian Politics*, ed. Carl Levan and Patrick Ukata (Oxford: Oxford University Press, 2018), 699–713.

[15] E. C Ejiogu and Nneka L. Umego, "Africans and the Two Great Wars: A General Overview," *Journal of Asian and African Studies* 57, no. 1 (2022): 3–10.

[16] E. C. Ejiogu and Adaoma Igwedibia, "The World Wars and Their Legacies in Africa and in the Affairs of Africans: The Case of East Africa – Kenya," *Journal of Asian and African Studies* 57, no. 1 (2022): 113–130.

[17] Anne Samson, *World War I in Africa: The Forgotten Conflict among the European Powers* (London: I.B. Tauris, 2013).

[18] Peter C. Lloyd, "Class Consciousness among the Yoruba," in *The New Elites of Tropical Africa*, ed. Peter C. Lloyd (London: Oxford University Press, 1966), 330.

[19] Martin L. Kilson, Jr., "Nationalism and Social Classes in British West Africa," *The Journal of Politics* 20, no. 2 (1958): 368–387.

colonial project and in the colonial state, one of the ways to measure the presence of the colonial administration was the breakdown of these old formations.

None of these, however, became well-entrenched in the whole of the Nigerian colony until World War I when Lugard implemented his version of the indirect rule system from the North to the Southern Colony and Protectorate in 1914. Synonymous with effective colonial experience, as unequivocally stated at various times by colonial administrators like Lugard, is the collection of taxes from the "native" population.[20] Herbert Symonds Goldsmith, the Lieutenant-Governor of Northern Nigeria in 1917, expressed this view in one of his addresses, in that the payment of tax was the keynote of the administration of the colony.[21] Direct taxation pedals the cash economy and, ultimately, the cash economy sparks the establishment of new socioeconomic communities. For the first time in the history of the people, they had to contend with protecting their economic interests through unions connected by common economic interests.

From coal workers to market traders, artisans to teachers, railway workers to farmers, protecting the interests of members mostly of different polities, cultures, and backgrounds, against the oppression and exploitation of the colonial state, colonial subjects began to operate through biosocial networks. This was aimed at fulfilling their aspirations in a way that launched society into modernity. Moreover, studies conducted on the role of peasants and the middle class in the production of events during the colonial period mirror the significant contribution of the cash economy in the creation of a new social order and social class in the emergence of African nationalism.[22] The entrenchment of this system during World War I meant a significant impact in the Nigerian colony and was a turning point in the history of the colony. This created the basis for the post–World War II demands for independence and the revolutionary ideas and actions that followed.[23]

In response to the economic hardship that arose from the increasing marginalization of the native population in the economy, the new Lagos elite, led by Herbert Macaulay, demanded Indigenous representation in the legislative body of the colonial state and led protests against the government.[24] This

---

[20] Leigh Gardner, *Taxing Colonial Africa: The Political Economy of British Imperialism* (Oxford: Oxford University, 2012).
[21] Toyin Falola, *Colonialism and Violence in Nigeria* (Bloomington: Indiana University Press, 2009), 83.
[22] James S. Coleman, *Nigeria: Background to Nationalism* (Berkeley: University of California Press, 1958).
[23] Ajibola A. Abdulrahman, "Nationalism and Decolonization in Africa, 1918–1975," in *Africa in Global History: A Handbook*, ed., Toyin Falola and Mohammed Bashir Salau (Berlin: De Gruyter Oldenbourg, 2021), 185–202.
[24] Coleman, *Nigeria: Background to Nationalism*.

marked the first major shift from the pre–World War I demands focused on specific government policies and acts, leading to the establishment of the first political party in Nigeria: the Nigerian National Democratic Party (NNDP).[25] By this time, the level of literacy among the people, especially in the South, had greatly improved since the nineteenth century, expanding the community of potential nationalists and easing communication flow among the native population.[26] Already, newspapers, pamphlets, tracts, and other literature had surfaced as viable media of communication among the native population through the emergence of the printing press.[27] With the remarkable efforts of the missionaries and Indigenous communities, the audience base of this media had expanded during the interwar years. If effective communication were of any significance in the mobilization of the people against the government and annexing their grievances into collective action, the secret lies in these media and the literacy of the people.

Through his involvement in Lagos politics, Macaulay, like the nationalist movement that sprang up after him, especially in the post–World War II years, became the nemesis of the colonial administrators.[28] It was as a result of this that Sir Hugh C. Clifford, described by the Secretary of State for the Colonies as the doyen of his Service generation, yielded ground and began the process of Indigenous representation in the colony. All through this period, he was the face of "Nigeria's" nationalism even though his activities were primarily based in Lagos.[29] Regardless, implications vibrated across the colony that he was as the "gadfly" of the British administration in Nigeria.[30] This role he played until after the end of World War II, as well as contributing to Nigerian nationalism, and the break from the traditional to the modern government, to the days of World War I, and its aftermath. This occurred both as a culmination of his previous engagements with the British government in Lagos and London and as a fundamental structural frame for subsequent political mobilization and political formation. The fundamental breaks the post–World War II heralded in this formation and the structure of political mobilization was the frame of identity used for negotiating this space.

---

[25] Samuel O. Arifalo, "The Rise and Decline of the Nigerian National Democratic Party (NNDP) 1923–1938," *Odu: A Journal of West African Studies* 24 (1983): 89–110.

[26] James S. Coleman, "Nationalism in Tropical Africa," *The American Political Science Review* 48, no. 2 (1954): 404–426.

[27] Emmanuel T. Babalola, "Newspaper as Instrument for Building Literate Communities: The Nigerian Experience," *Nordic Journal of African Studies* 11, no. 3 (2002): 403–410.

[28] Olakunle A. Lawal and Oluwasegun M. Jimoh, "Missiles from 'Kirsten Hall': Herbert Macaulay versus Hugh Clifford, 1922–1931," *Lagos Historical Review* 12 (2012): 421–62.

[29] Tekena Tamuno, *Herbert Macaulay, Nigerian Patriot* (London: Heinemann Educational, 1976).

[30] Lawal and Jimoh, "Missiles from 'Kirsten Hall.'"

Whereas the pre–World War II political space was based primarily on access to western education, a situation that brought about the domination of returnees and their descendants, the latter epoch was based around affiliation to a community and sociocultural formation such as an ethnic group. The effect of World War I reverberated across the social spectrum. Both the old and new social classes in the colony and the educated elites mobilized the mechanism of the media to continually bite the colonial government. Before Clifford agreed to the 1922 constitutional amendments that gave the local population three seats to Lagos and one to Calabar in the Legislature[31] – which technically translates to mean the educated middle class – Macaulay had been accumulating the attributes that conferred on him many nicknames. These include *Ejo n gboro* ("the one who throws fear into people as a snake would if seen in the city"), "master of Mischief Making," "the Wizard of Kirsten," and many more, inspired by his acerbic writings and activities in protest against the colonial administration.[32] It was in response to this that the events leading to the creation of the NNDP occurred. It was similarly this momentum that was sustained by Nnamdi Azikiwe, Obafemi Awolowo, Anthony Enahoro, and others in their nationalist activities in the latter days.

The period of World War I and its aftermath in the Nigerian colony can be discussed either in terms of the responses and activities of peasants, traders, artisans, and individuals at the lower level of society, or it can be examined through the lens of those in the middle class with western education but in close collaboration with every other group, including the former.[33] Aside from this were the Mahdists and magico-religious movements such as the one led by prophet Yesu in Satiru, one of the villages of Sokoto.[34] The style and frame of protest adopted on both sides were different, but ultimately they both served the same, intertwined course, even though, in their fluctuating variables, this same period could be explained entirely in terms of trade growth as well as from the scene of the massive protests and social eruption that pervaded the period due to an unfavorable economic context. All of these speak to the dynamism and intricacies of events during this twenty-five-year period, which defined the roots of the modern Nigerian state. As was mentioned in Chapter 7, the general transformation in the transportation industry, mainly the railway system, ushered in the amalgamated Nigerian colony in the years of the war.

This communication loop was expanded in the subsequent years, with a significant impact on the distribution of goods and development of trade

[31] Tekena N. Tamuno, "Governor Clifford and Representative Government," *Journal of the Historical Society of Nigeria* 4, no. 1 (1967): 117–124.
[32] Lawal and Jimoh, "Missiles from 'Kirsten Hall,'" 42.
[33] Lloyd, *The New Elites of Tropical Africa*.
[34] Rowland A. Adeleye, "Mahdist Triumph and British Revenge in Northern Nigeria: Satiru 1906," *Journal of the Historical Society of Nigeria* 6, no. 2 (1972): 193–214.

until the outbreak of World War II disrupted the process as efforts and resources were again diverted to building the military industry in its entirety – personnel and weapons, among others.[35] The opening of the Kano–Zaria–Zungeru–Baro–Jebba–Ilorin–Osogbo–Ibadan–Lagos railway routes, which spurred trade and administrative communication, was threatened by infrastructural developments on the road network. Both projects, as in others in the colonial state, were considered in terms of their economic value, as roads and routes that could not serve the purpose of the colonial state were ignored for more economically productive projects.[36] This came at the expense of the limited resources at the disposal of the colony since the bulk of the revenue went into the prosecution of the war, recuperating the economy of the metropolitan state, and serving the economic purpose of the European merchants and merchant companies. Hence, the construction of the Bauchi light railway, which went as far as Bukuru in 1914 after three years of work, became important in serving the tin-mining area of Northern Nigeria. This was also the same way Osogbo–Ibadan–Lagos served the purpose of transporting agricultural goods from the interior of the Western Province of the Southern Protectorate to a viable terminal for onward distribution.[37]

In opening alternative routes from the railway system, the government embarked on a massive project that linked the whole colony by motorable roads.[38] From Port Harcourt, Enugu, Kaduna, Lagos, Ibadan, Ijebu Ode, Ilesha Akure, Ondo, Benin, and Sapele, the south was linked to the north by road. The Western Province was joined to the Eastern province through Asaba and Onitsha. As these changes in the transportation industry were ongoing,[39] harbors also expanded by enhancing custom revenue and flow of trade in the same way that frantic efforts were made to establish the airways industry. Before the establishment of Lagos, Kano, Osogbo, Minna, and Maiduguri as the "all seasons" aerodromes in 1935 by the Air Services Development Committee, Lagos, Forcados, Yola, Kano, Maiduguri, Kano, Calabar, Katsina, Lokoja, Jos, Minna, Makurdi, Jebba, Onitsha, Port Harcourt, and other locations were designated as landing sites cleared for the occasional landing of airlines flying into the colony.[40] It is in light of all

---

[35] Anthony G. Hopkins, *An Economic History of West Africa* (New York: Routledge, 2020).
[36] Hopkins, *An Economic History*.
[37] Richard Olufemi Ekundare, *An Economic History of Nigeria 1860–1960* (London: Methuen & Co Ltd., 1973), 145.
[38] Ayodeji O. Olukoju, "Transportation in Colonial West Africa," in *An Economic History of West Africa since 1750*, ed. Gabriel O. Ogunremi and E. K. Faluyi (Ibadan: Rex Charles Publishers, 1996), 144–156.
[39] Edward K. Hawkins, *Road Transportation in Nigeria: A Study of an African Enterprise* (London: Africana University Press, 1958).
[40] Tunde Decker, *A History of Aviation in Nigeria, 1925–2005* (Lagos: Dele-Davis Publishers, 2008).

these that one can begin to reflect on the magnitude of administrative and technical efforts put in place by the colonial British government in managing the war as well as the postwar situation in her colonies.

Since the economy of the empire, as in other western colonial powers in Africa had, by the virtue of colonial clauses, become intertwined with London, the two economies existed largely in a metropolitan–colony relationship wherein the cause and effects of developments vibrated across the boundaries of the colonial empire.[41] Africanist scholars argue that the relations birthed during this period animated and shaped the current pattern of global relations.[42] Nigeria was being promoted through the exhibition of the Nigerian colony's natural potential and major agricultural products of possible interest to investors. This was carried out at the Canadian National Exhibition in Toronto in 1928 and at the International Maritime and Colonial Exhibition at Antwerp during the celebration of the centenary of Belgium's independence two years later. While this was ongoing, the British government was building and, at the same time, securing her economic interest in both the metropolitan and the colonial state.[43] This is more so since the wealth of the latter was expected to be transferred to the former. On display at the exhibitions, therefore, was the culmination of the natural wealth of the people. These included:

> cocoa, beans, palm kernels, palm oil, copra, coconut oil, cotton and cottonseed; and a few minor agricultural products including kolanuts, benniseed and maize. There were exhibits of various qualities of mahogany and samples of such Nigerian woods as iroko and ebony. Some exhibits of mineral resources were also on display: these included tin ore, refined tin ore and samples of coal from the coal fields of Enugu.[44]

The participation of the colonial government in these exhibitions is best seen as the foreign engagement of the "national" policy of the government, which was to promote and expand the agricultural base as well as the extractive industry of the colony. Products from both ends were showcased at the exhibitions with the implication that the economy of the state was dominated by macroeconomic actors to the further detriment of the peasant class and

---

[41] R. J. Gavin and Wale Oyemakinde, "Economic Development in Nigeria since 1800," in *Groundwork of Nigerian History*, ed. Obaro Ikime (Ibadan: Heinemann, 1980), 482–517.

[42] Walter Rodney, *How Europe Underdeveloped Africa* (Kingston: Bogle-Louverture, 1972); Achille Mbembe, *On the Post-Colony* (London: University of California Press, 2001); and Samir Amin, *Eurocentrism: Modernity, Religion, and Democracy: A Critique of Eurocentrism and Culturalism*, trans. Russel Moore and James Membrez (New York: Monthly Review Press, 1989).

[43] Ekundare, *An Economic History of Nigeria*, 127.

[44] Ekundare, *An Economic History of Nigeria*, 118.

local industry.[45] It was also during this period that greater efforts were put in motion to develop the extractive industry in Nigeria as a replica of the agricultural industry where raw materials found their way to the metropolitan capital to be made into finished products.

World War I and Sociopolitical Developments

The outbreak of World War I in 1914 – the same year that the amalgamation process of the two colonies and protectorates of Nigeria was initiated – and the economic conditions that followed through the years of economic depression spelled the end of colonial rule. In a frantic effort to prosecute the war and rebuild the economy of the metropolitan state, the Colonial Office in London, as well as the colonial administration in Nigeria, launched a series of economic and administrative reforms that further alienated the local population.[46] As in their responses to certain government policies in the past, and a greater magnitude of organizational and structural form, the local population protested against the introduction and implementation of some of these administrative and economic measures as they affected their economic well-being. Protests took different organizational and structural forms, and included individuals, groups, unions, and political movements/parties. Some were lone protests, such as the refusal of individuals to pay tax; others were hierarchically structured with leading actors; yet others maintained an acephalous posture of networks of cells.[47] In most cases, they were inflamed by the conduct of the local authorities in the implementation of the ordinances and other government policies and the execution of their powers in the process. The 1927 Native Revenue Ordinance was introduced to address this by way of close supervision of the local authorities through the Native Authority System that had been established by the central government.[48]

In the following years, protests continued in the colony, with the south as the epicenter.[49] From the violent resistance and protests in Warri, Owerri, Oyo, Calabar, Ibadan, Kano, and other provinces on both sides of the amalgamated colonies and protectorates between 1914 and 1930, to the establishment and

---

[45] Ahmed M. Mohammed, *European Trade, Imperialism and Underdevelopment in Northern Nigeria 19th and 20th Centuries* (Zaria: Ahmadu Bello University Press Limited, 2016).

[46] Lewis H. Gann and Peter Duignan, eds., *Colonialism in Africa 1870–1960*, Vol. 1 (London: Cambridge University Press, 1977).

[47] Moses E. Ochonu, *Colonial Meltdown: Northern Nigeria in the Great Depression* (Athens: Ohio University Press, 2009).

[48] Joseph A. Atanda, *The New Oyo Empire: Indirect Rule and Change in Western Nigeria 1894–1934* (London: Longman, 1973).

[49] For instance, Chike P. Dike, ed., *The Women's Revolt of 1929: Proceedings of a National Symposium to Mark the Sixtieth Anniversary of the Women's Uprising in South–Eastern Nigeria* (Lagos: Nelag & Co., 1995).

proliferation of trade unions, leading to the post–World War II demands, the recurring message of the people was centered on the economy of the colony. This was particularly so in the mechanisms of exploitation deployed by the colonial state through instruments such as tax, disparate remuneration for Black and White officers in the service of the colonial state, and the unfavorable trading conditions to which the local population were subjected. There is no doubting the extent to which the colonial state disrupted the socioeconomic and political morphology of the precolonial Nigerian societies and cultures. This is more so when one considers the sequence and intensity of events during these years. As mentioned in Chapter 7, the colonial governance of Yorubaland in particular did not take structure or effect until the 1914 amalgamation. It should be added here, however, that the effective colonial administration of this area, as in the rest of the Southern province, was one heralded by violence and instability, resulting in the second phase of the people's resistance against colonial rule.[50] The first phase was characterized by resistance of the people against colonial incursion, conquest, and appropriation of their sovereignty, while the latter was defined by resistance against colonial consolidation.

The impact of the introduction of direct taxation on the people reverberated among both rural and urban dwellers. The poor remuneration and conditions of service of railway workers, clerks, miners, teachers, and other "colonial subjects" in the colonial service, and the marginalization of this local population in the trading and commercial activities in the colony through the monopolistic practices of British merchant companies, aided and abetted by the colonial government, impacted the local population. By implication, the purchasing power of this population was limited as tax rates and tax payments rose. These years molded public opinion among the people, which was ignited into collective action in the post–World War II years as the experience of being under the yoke of the economic burden of London was aggravated by the same old mechanisms of exploitation.[51]

Making matters worse, the economic depression that spanned about a decade from 1929–39 also impacted the new world emerging from imperial and colonial territories.[52] The change in public opinion in Western European capitals from the promotion of humanitarian services through legitimate trade in sub-Saharan Africa to humanitarianism through colonization is a telltale sign of the obstruction and obfuscation of the role these spheres of influence were to play in the economies of

---

[50] Albert Adu Boahen, ed., *General History of Africa: VII Africa under Colonial Domination 1880–1935* (Paris: UNESCO, 1990).
[51] Jean Suret-Canale and Albert Adu Boahen, "West Africa 1945–60," in *Africa Since 1935*, ed. Ali A. Mazrui and C. Wondji (Paris: UNESCO Publishing, 1999), 161–191.
[52] Moses Ochonu, "Conjoined to Empire: The Great Depression and Nigeria," *African Economic History* 34 (2006): 103–145.

these imperial powers.[53] Like a conquered appendage of these imperial states, the economic burdens of this western population devolved on these African polities through the devolution of power in the administration of the colonial empire.[54] As seen in Chapter 7, this readily linked the imperial capital in London to different polities in Africa, with Nigeria being the largest of all. The Colonial Office in London, which emerged in the late nineteenth century due to the change in public opinion concerning the activities of British merchants and missionaries in Africa and which headed the colonial mission, was a revenue-generating ministry, insofar as it was established to see that the colonial project did not run at loss or at the expense of the British taxpayers' money. If the ministry ever had a motto, goal, or modus operandi, it would be "for the profitability of the colonial enterprise." This is considering that before the British government finally agreed to administer her foreign colonies and revoke the royal charter given to the merchant companies, profitability became the prime condition and purpose for which the Colonial Office was established thereafter.

This role, the effective administrative occupation of the Nigerian colony through the 1914 amalgamation, the Great Depression, and the economic ambivalence in London during and after World War I and subsequent events that culminated in the independence of the colony in 1960 came to define the colonial experience as being as effective as it was practical. In a way, it took the colonial state more than a decade to conquer and consolidate its sphere of influence in the Niger area that became the Nigerian colony in 1900. The 1914 amalgamation became the potential project of the colonial state imagined by the Niger Committee in 1899, even though popular thoughts among the colonial administrators considered it defective during and after this period.[55] This explains the sporadic turn of events during these years. In executing its responsibilities, the Colonial Office in London increased pressure on the colonial economies in various parts of Africa and elsewhere under its jurisdiction. The situation in Nigeria was further complicated by Lugard's insubordination toward the Colonial Office. The amalgamation of the colony and the protectorates of Southern and Northern Nigeria thus created a more effective means of going about this in Nigeria, administratively.[56] The centralization of the administration of the colonial empire was at this time taking both on local and global dimensions. As Kirk-Greene explained:

---

[53] Godfrey N. Uzoigwe, *Britain and the Conquest of Africa: The Age of Salisbury* (Ann Arbor: The University of Michigan Press, 1974).

[54] David K. Fieldhouse, *The Colonial Empires: A Comparative Survey from the Eighteenth Century* (London: Macmillan Press, 1966).

[55] Godfrey N. Uzoigwe, "The Niger Committee of 1898: Lord Selbourne's Report," *Journal of the Historical Society of Nigeria* IV, no. 3 (1968): 467–476.

[56] Anthony Kirk-Greene, *Britain's Imperial Administrators, 1858–1966* (London: Palgrave Macmillan Press, 1999), 39.

The First World War brought fundamental administration reform to the Colonial Office in its wake. What a long-time Colonial Office official like Sir Charles Jeffries acknowledges as the pre-war "convenience" of the geographical departmental structure, whereby each maintained its own coherent set of files and correspondence dealing with single territories as a self-contained entity and where "experience, precedent and common sense prevailed," was quickly found to be inadequate for the post-war extension and complexity of Empire.[57]

Even though Lugard's time in office was to end after the amalgamation, the outbreak of the war in this year of an administrative merger would prolong his mandate in office. According to the Colonial Office in London, an administrator like Lugard was needed for the consolidation of this administrative amendment because of the difficult terrain presented by the outbreak of war. Lugard left Nigeria in 1918, the year the war ended, after twenty years as colonial governor, and proceeded to greater capacities in the British Empire, part of which included the position of British Delegate to the Permanent Mandates Commission of the League of Nations.[58] Subsequent administrators in the colony would come to build on the foundations and structures he had laid in the colony.

As mentioned in Chapter 7, the amalgamation process continued until the independence of Nigeria in 1960. Paradoxically, as the colonial state was evolving through the years of the amalgamation to the other integrative efforts of subsequent years, such as the 1927 Native Revenue Ordinance and the 1947 legislative tie, the colony was disintegrating. Tellingly, as colonial rule became entrenched, so too did the exploitation of the people and their resources. The response of the people engendered wider and collective mobilization across the colony. With the resources of the empire and its dependencies diverted into prosecuting the war, there was much strain on the economy and on the well-being of the people, particularly those in the periphery – those colonial subjects who produced the raw materials needed to prosecute the war.

In the same way that this population was made to contribute manpower to fight the war, mostly through conscription,[59] British officers in the colonial service were also transferred to fill strategic posts in the prosecution of the war. In terms of human labor, this created certain damage to the colonial state and the administration of the colony. On the part of the people, it added to the pressure on economic production. For the colonial government, it meant that the administrative attention of the state had been diverted to the war, thus causing a shortage of British administrative staff to supervise the activities of

---

[57] Kirk-Greene, *Britain's Imperial Administrators*, 39.
[58] Margery Perham and May Bull, eds., *The Diaries of Lord Lugard*, Vol. I (London: Faber and Faber, 1958).
[59] Oluwafunminiyi Raheem and Oluyemisi A. Disu, "Fighting for Britain: Examining British Recruitment Strategies in Nigeria," in *Unknown Conflicts of the Second World War: Forgotten Fronts*, ed. Chris Murray (London: Routledge, 2019), 1–15.

the Native Authorities and Councils. This development gave greater power to the local authorities, who used the opportunity to unleash terror on their people in the form of exploitation through the letters of the Native Authority System – the first of the Lugardian form of indirect rule to be introduced to the south after the amalgamation. This was particularly the case with the *edimani* (the Igbo rendition of the English word "headman") and the *udamani* ("headmen in charge of the wards"), who traditionally had no legitimacy to their newly acquired political power and relevance but had the support of the colonial government.[60] Their roles in the events of this period were mainly in the collection of taxes from the people. They were also used in the conscription of this population.

Generally, they were resented in their role, and were viewed as agents of exploitation by the colonial state as well as the structure of government and the power they occupied within it, all of which were strange to the societies in this area. It should be recalled that the practice of using the *edimani* and the *udamani* in the administration of the local government in the colonial state in this area was an old initiative in itself that began with various administrative experiments instigated in the Courts of Equity. This later culminated in the declaration of the Southern protectorate in 1900 and the establishment of the Native Administrative Council. This role was, however, fortified by the creation of paramount chiefs, sole Native Authorities, and permanent presidents of the Native Courts through the Lugardian rule.[61] The implication of the paramountcy of these authorities and the reconfiguration of the court system where many of their powers were derived is that, fundamentally, the sociopolitical landscape of the people had effectively been distorted along with the structure that sustained this new administrative system. Coming with increasing power for the holders of the government warrant or certificate of recognition, and the preference of Lugard to limit the number of members of the court and the Native Authority/Council, it gradually became more intensely competitive to occupy this position. Hence, applicants other than headmen and house heads vied for roles within the Native Administrative warrant.[62]

To keep the position, then, would be to accede to the instructions of the colonial government even when this seemed impractical. As the warrant chiefs were perpetrating their exploitation of the people in the absence of close supervision during the war, the court messengers and clerks also wielded overbearing powers beyond their roles.[63] The latter took advantage of

[60] Adiele E. Afigbo, *The Warrant Chiefs: Indirect Rule in Southeastern Nigeria 1891–1929* (London: Longman Group, 1972).
[61] Afigbo, *The Warrant Chiefs*, 169.
[62] Afigbo, *The Warrant Chiefs*, 174–175.
[63] Adiele E. Afigbo, "Revolution and Reaction in Eastern Nigeria: 1900–1929: (The Background to the Women's Riot of 1929)," *Journal of the Historical Society of Nigeria* 3, no. 3 (1966): 539–557.

the illiteracy of the chiefs in the court to assume a de facto role as president of the court. Officially, the clerks were to act in the capacity of a protocol officer, ensuring order and smooth proceedings in the court in many ways, including record keeping. In what the educated elites successfully fought in the second decade of the twentieth century, the use of local authorities in the modern administration of the colony, aside from the "legitimacy" it granted the alien rule, was, to say the least, manipulative. It was a sort of continuation of the devious diplomatic deception that supposedly handed over their lands and sovereignty to the Queen. These chiefs saddled the local administration of the colonial state and had limited initiative of their own in the system, and at best, would only accept the decisions reached by informed members of the cabinet. This placed the court clerks and British officials in the court at an advantage to influence the proceedings and conduct of the court. Since the war had sapped the colonial government of its staff and Lugard had insisted that, as was the practice in the north, Native Authorities and Councils should be solely manned by the local authorities with limited supervision from the central government, the clerks were at this time empowered to lead the court.[64] This intention was factored into the structure of the government as well as the titles of the British administrative officers and members of the Native Authority. Therefore, district officers headed the mission at the district level, and residents at the provincial level, in place of the "standard Colonial Service ranks of Provincial Commissioner and District Commissioner to emphasize the advisory and less executive role of the administrative officer in the system of indirect rule."[65] Convinced that the authority and power of the local authorities must be upheld at all times for an effective direct rule system, Lugard gave such titles as Paramount Rulers, Sole Authorities, and President of the Native Court (an important institution in the administration of justice and the making of executive and legislative decisions) to them.

Disparate and obnoxious charges and miscarriages of justice thus prevailed in the system, with the clerks combining their former role with that of the president and judge in the court. The leadership vacuum was not limited to the Eastern province of the Southern protectorate; rather, it was a Pandora's Box that the Lugardian rule had unleashed across the colony. In Yorubaland, attempts by the Alake to assert authority over the people through the whims of the colonial government in Lagos, in light of the special status of the polity under colonial rule, sparked massive protests and historically unprecedented chaos in the town in 1929.[66] The issue with leadership here was even more intriguing, in that the structure of the political authority of the polity remained

---

[64] Kirk–Green, *Britain's Imperial Administrators*, 147.
[65] Kirk-Greene, *Britain's Imperial Administrators*, 147.
[66] Judith A. Byfield, "Taxation, Women, and the Colonial State: Egba Women's Tax Revolt," *Meridians: Feminism, Race, Transnationalism* 3, no. 2 (2003): 250–277.

disrupted by the composition of the town. Up until the events that resulted in the Ijemo Massacre of 1914,[67] and even in the subsequent years to varying degrees, the authority of the Alake remained questioned by many in the polity. The history and trajectory of groups that made up the polity have been well documented by historians.[68] The town is made up of dozens of independent polities, among which were the 1830s and post-1830s migrants propelled by the nineteenth-century instability in Yorubaland. Others, such as the Ijemo, Itoko, and Ikopa, could be regarded as the aboriginals of the large mountainous forest. The arrival of the returnees and their descendants into the nascent polity initiated the process of organizing the town along a modern line of governance by the mid-nineteenth century.[69]

This arrangement, which recognized the authority of the Alake as a paramount ruler, was supported by the missionaries and the subsequent colonial government in Lagos. However, all extant polities in the town maintained their political and administrative sphere of influence, a position which they would under no circumstances accede to the Alake and the new central government he occupied. Thus, when the colonial officer from Lagos, Mr. Johnson, and the secretary to the Egba United Government, Mr. Adegboyega Edun, visited Ponlade village sometime around 1914 for inspection, the village head – an old man whose name became the name of the village: Chief Ponlade – refused to recognize either the authority of the former or that of the Alake. His refusal to carry out Johnson's order to clear a bush path that linked the village to Ijebu, a neighboring town, to increase the network of communication between the two led to major cancerous effects on the administration of Abeokuta. Firstly, the arrest of the old chief and his incarceration in the palace of the Alake sparked protests by the people of Ijemo; his death under the care of the Alake further exacerbated this.[70] The inability of the Alake to contain the situation prompted the issuance of an invitation to the colonial government in Lagos to be present at the scene – a situation interpreted by Lugard to imply the inability of the local authorities headed by Alake to rule their people through law and order and at the same time maintain their quasi-independence under the 1893 treaty with the Egba United Government.

---

[67] Lanre Davies, "The Political Economy of the Egba Nation: A Study in Modernisation and Diversification, 1830–1960," *African Nebula* no. 7 (2014): 87.

[68] Saburi O. Biobaku, "Historical Sketch of Egba Traditional Authorities," *Africa: Journal of the International African Institute* 22, no. 1 (1952): 35–49; Hakeem B. Harunah, "Sodeke: Hero and Stateman of the Egba," *Journal of the Historical Society of Nigeria* 12, no. 1/2 (1983–1984): 109–131; and Oluwatoyin Oduntan, *Power, Culture and Modernity in Nigeria: Beyond the Colony* (New York: Routledge, 2018).

[69] Agneta Pallinder-Law, "Aborted Modernization in West Africa? The Case of Abeokuta," *The Journal of African History* 15, no. 1 (1974): 65–82.

[70] Harry A. Gaily, *Lugard and the Abeokuta Uprising: The Demise of Egba Independence* (London: Routledge, 1982).

The situation here resembled the process by which Yoruba governments, including Oyo led by the Alaafin, lost their authority, power, and sovereignty to the British government in the twilight of the nineteenth century. On the other hand, the recognition of the paramountcy of the Alake among equals by the British colonial government, largely through the influence of the missionaries, was also an instrument of indirect rule, which the Lugardian rule later made popular across the colony. To this extent, even when the intervention of the Lagos government led to the revocation of the independence of the Egba United Government, the position of the Alake was retained for the administration of the town through the Native Authority System. In the penultimate event that resulted in this, the government had called for a meeting with the people of Ijemo to appease them regarding the demise of their chief and the need to return peace to the polity. Even though there are conflicting historical reports regarding precisely what transpired between the people and the British official who had come to a peace meeting with armed men, what remained certain is that the outcome of the meeting occasioned the mutiny of the people, including the Oluwo and Arinmokunrin Barabara, the traditional political head of the people. Earlier in the northern protectorate of the colony, the Satiru revolt of 1906 gave a certain bearing to subsequent discontentment, as depicted in the Ijemo incident, for instance, with the British rule.[71]

The effect of this event, which took a heavy toll on the people and their future in the political morphology of Abeokuta, was still very apparent when, in 1918, the government attempted to impose direct taxation on them. Added to this was the forced labor arrangement in which the government mandated the use of people in public works for a set number of days. While the use of free labor on public works was part of the Indigenous labor system of the people – a custom that had allowed the practice to go relatively well through mobilization by the same old channel of authority – taxing those whose time for personal economic production had been cut short by the same government was both alien and insensitive. Besides, what sense could a poor farmer make of the relevance of projects such as the construction of communication networks via larger roads, railways, and telecommunications, when the old means of communication through minor roads, waterways, interpersonal communications, and other traditional means were still considered efficient for the level of his socioeconomic and political engagements?

As was the case in other polities in the colony, the use of forced labor in public works, even when presented as the continuation of the old practice of communal labor, was conceived differently by the people. They saw these projects less in terms of serving their purpose than that of the colonizers. The local authorities had also been seen as puppets of the colonial officers who had come to exploit them. Thus, the projects were considered to encompass

---

[71] Adeleye, "Mahdist Triumph and British Revenge," 193–214.

the interests of the local authorities as well. Generally, as the social structure of cultures that made up the Nigerian colony was being transformed, so too were the relations between the people and the traditional authorities. At no other time was this more pronounced than during the period under study, with resounding effects on the subsequent years through to contemporary times. It was in such a stifling condition that the people of Abeokuta, like others in various locations in the Eastern provinces, such as Calabar, Warri, and Owerri, took to violent protest against both governments. This manifested in the destruction of railway lines, telecommunication infrastructure, and government properties. The sociopolitical situation in the South was so readily apparent that even Lugard, who had thrown reason in the bin during his administration of the colony, understood the necessity of a piecemeal implementation of his version of the indirect rule system in the region.

Consequently, this policy was implemented in each of the administrative units as the political atmosphere portends. Even then, the political landscape here was different from that of the North where Lugard had once administered through the system wherein, going by the turn of events, there was never a perfect time for the implementation of his indirect rule. To this extent, from Iseyin to Okeiho, Abeokuta to Ibadan, Calabar to Owerri, Warri to Itsekiri, Urhobo to Igbudu, Isoko to Onitsha, Isin to Igbomina, and many other spots in the administrative stretch of the colonial state, varying degrees of protest were organized from 1914 to the late 1930s. These protests all revolved around the introduction of the direct tax system. Some of these protests took their organizational form within a community, while others cut across communities to other areas within the new administrative units: province, division, and district. Significant in the case of the latter was the coordination among the Itsekiri, Isoko, and Urhobo under the Igbudu resolutions, a sort of national conference convened by Osheu and Edna Otuedon from Itsekiri and Urhobo, and the rural Igbo women's protests in Owerri and Calabar provinces popularly known as the Aba Women's War.[72]

A couple of factors can be identified as possible reasons why there could never be a perfect time for the full implementation of Lugardian rule in the Southern protectorate. Aside from the traditional sociopolitical morphology of the people that contradicted some of these practices, the evolving economic milieu in the region was a major challenge. From 1914, attempts by the colonial government to maximize the resources of the colony had increased tremendously, leading to various policies that further skewed the economic landscape of the colony against the people on several fronts. On the one hand there was the monopolization of trade against international actors, especially the Germans, in the Nigerian market; on the other, there was the monopolization of trade against local actors. On the whole, the Nigerian market was to be

---

[72] Falola, *Colonialism and Violence*, 95.

owned and controlled by the British. Both issues had significant consequences on the socioeconomic context of the society, which the colonial government had thought to tax further. Whereas the decision to ban the Germans in the Nigerian colonial market was part of the war effort to neutralize the economic base and political strength of Berlin, the monopolization of trade against local merchants aimed to shore up the economic stake of British merchants in the Nigerian market to assuage losses during the war.

Not only was production slowed during the war years, but the purchasing power of the people had also been reduced drastically, and the transportation of goods through international waters had become even riskier due to the possibility of German attacks on British trading ships. From every indication, the market on both sides had been reduced and, to maximize profit, economic actors in this loop were also reduced. This gave British merchants an unfair advantage as local merchants were sacrificed for this purpose, with retailers and middlemen among them losing their advantages in the chain of supply and demand in the colony. Additional to this was the huge gap left in the market during the war with the suspension of German ships, goods, and merchants whose products were considered more valuable due to their quality and favorable price in parts of the colony. The war measures did not end there, as they also affected the processes of customs duty in the colony. To promote the British market, the government increased import tariffs on goods from other countries. The activities of the British shipping company Elder Dempster[73] and the United African Company,[74] in Nigeria are typical of the monopolistic conduct of the colonial government. Due to their unchallenged position, like the Royal Niger Company that preceded them, they could fix both purchase and sale prices of goods in the region. In all, these measures alone resulted in economic depression among the people even before the Great Depression of the late 1920s to the late 1930s.

Increasingly, the people who were expected to pay taxes and, in some cases, as in Abeokuta and other places, provide free labor for projects they did not much understand were at the same time driven out of the economic space in the polity. As the monopolization drive was raging under the supervision of the government, the financial sector of the state was skewed against them.[75] The expansion of trade and the liberalization of the market created more room for the big players in an economy where they could use their capital and war chest to capture a larger share of the market. The intensification of this process

---

[73] Ayodeji Olukoju, "Elder Dempster and the Shipping Trade of Nigeria during the First World War," *The Journal of African History* 33, no. 2 (1992): 255–271.
[74] David K. Fieldhouse, *Merchant Capital and Economic Decolonization: The United Africa Company 1929-1987* (Oxford: Clarendon Press, 1994).
[75] Adebayo A. Lawal, *Nigeria Culture, Politics, Governance and Development* (Ibadan: Connel Publications, 2015).

during World War I and in subsequent years marked a disastrous development for the local population as their competing powers against their foreign partners became increasingly limited.[76] The United African Company, Elder Dempster, and other British companies that dominated trade in the colony during this period were all conglomerations of various merchant companies in London and other investors. In addition to this, these companies had on their boards members who wielded great influence in government. For instance, the board of directors of the British West African Bank were at the same time directors in the firms that combined to become the Elder Dempster Shipping Company.[77] Owing to the enormous power enjoyed by the directors of these companies, all protests from the people and other British merchants who felt short-changed in the arrangement were ignored by the colonial government.

Here began the trend in which the economic growth in the state does not always correspond to better living conditions for the people or general developments in public space and well-being. Dominated by large foreign companies, profits made from the market were expatriated to London, thereby expanding the transference of the wealth of the colonial state to the metropolitan state. In the economic growth that followed this trend, therefore, market and production might have expanded but with no commensurate impact on those whose labor was engaged in this process or on other local actors with limited capital. It was also within this mix that local industries took their final hit leading to the collapse of local production. The majority of people who were meant to be actors in this sector preferred to work as wage earners. Among other things, this would at least allow them to pay their taxes and survive under colonial rule.

In this way, the colonial government created an economic structure which established and expanded the means for wage labor while it created limited room for the growth and expansion of local industrial production. The period thus signified what would become of the relationship between the metropolitan and the colonial state. Even Indians and Syrians in the colony were given more attention and greater priority than the local population by the government and banks. Summarily, in a situation where the local merchants could not access loans and grants to expand their businesses, British merchants as well as other foreign actors in the local market were aided in their economic pursuits. The conditions under which the colonial government conducted its activities in the British West African colonies could at best be seen as another version of the settler economy system in Southern and East Africa, where the

---

[76] Benjamin O. Oloruntimehin, "African Politics and Nationalism, 1919–35," in *General History of Africa: VII Africa under Colonial Domination 1880–1935*, ed. Albert Adu Boahen (Paris: UNESCO, 1990), 565–579

[77] Olukoju, "Elder Dempster and the Shipping Trade," 262.

lands of the people were taken from them and transferred to the European settlers.[78] In the two colonial zones, the intention was clear: take the resources of the locals, exploit the people, and use their wealth to accumulate resources in London. Big companies and macroeconomic actors played a decisive role in this process as they began to take control of the people's increasingly limited share of the market.

Within this paradigm, it was not enough for the government to substitute the creation and expansion of wage labor for industrial development; the labor needed to be cheap to further maximize profit, and British merchants needed to secure a larger share of the market. It was this situation that added to the occurrence of the Aba Women's War in which the women used the opportunity of the introduction of the objectionable Native Revenue Ordinance to protest against the working conditions of their husbands in the mines as well as their condition in the colonial economy.[79] In the same way that British merchants exploited the labor of the people, the government was scheming as regards the railways, coal mines, and other government establishments. On the part of the government, this was a way of cutting its recurrent expenditure of the colonial state to have enough to rebuild the devastated economy and structures in the metropolitan state and execute projects for the transition of the colony into modernity. But the reality on the ground pointed to a sinister motive by the British colonial government.

In a situation that would explode after World War II, union bodies also began to spring up to protect the interest of their members – usually the Indigenous workers. By 1931, the Nigerian Union of Teachers was established for this purpose,[80] and in subsequent years others followed, from the railway to the mining industry and beyond.[81] By the end of World War II, virtually all occupations in the colonial state had been organized into unions, including tailors, carpenters, transport workers, farmers, and produce buyers.[82] During the interwar years, cocoa producers used this to effect a cocoa "hold-up" in a collective response to the price-fixing by British conglomerates. To be clear, not all these unions were necessarily organized to protest against the government. Primarily, they were to protect the interest of their members against any

---

[78] Martin H. Y. Kaniki, "The Colonial Economy: The Former British Zones," in *General History of Africa: VII Africa under Colonial Domination 1880–1935*, ed. Albert Adu Boahen (Paris: UNESCO, 1990), 382–419.
[79] Afigbo, "Revolution and Reaction," 550–557.
[80] Ade Fajana, "The Nigerian Union of Teachers: A Decade of Growth, 1931–40," *West African Journal of Education* 3 (1973): 383.
[81] Baba Thomas Bingel, "Understanding Trade Unionism in Nigeria: Historical Evolution and Prospects for Future Development," in *Trade Unionism in Nigeria: Challenges for the 21st Century*, ed. Funmi Adewumi (Lagos: Frederick Ebert Foundation, 1997).
[82] Wogu Ananaba, *The Trade Union Movement in Nigeria* (Benin City: Ethiope Publishing, 1969).

threat to their collective interest either from the government or from another entity. This was the case with the Railway Workers Union, known initially as the Nigerian Railway Worker Union,[83] and the Road Transport Union officially referred to as the Nigerian Motor Transport Union. Before the former was transformed into a federated entity in the year World War II began in 1939, both sectors of the Nigerian transportation industry established their union bodies. This was in the wake of the existential threat posed by road transportation, which was progressively preferred by the people and reduced the profit and relevance of the railway. Both unions were thus meant to regulate, coordinate, and strengthen the operation of their members, and engage with the government, along with the networks of transportation now available in the colony.

The introduction and promotion of new cash crops and the enhancement of the extant ones was how the colonial government encouraged wage labor as well as a wage and consumption economy as a substitute for the local industry during this period. Artisans who had lost in the competition for a market with their European counterparts and others unemployed by the nature of the colonial economy followed the trail of arable lands for the production of these products. In most cases, this population engaged in labor on cocoa farms in the forest region of Yorubaland, cotton in the north, palm products in the Niger Delta, mining in the Plateau and Eastern areas, and various economic opportunities outside of the colony. In the process, this resulted in a changing demography in the colony, with concomitant effects on the social relations and form of the society.[84]

Conclusion

The general economic policy of the colonial government during this period was exhibited in tax and trading policies that created a stifling atmosphere within which the people competed with other economic actors in the colonial state, and mounted palpable pressure on the local population. Colonial historiography is replete with accounts that illustrate the general increase in taxation and unfavorable economic ambience in which "colonial subjects" survived rising demands and burdens on rural producers who were at the lowest, but yet most important, rung of the socioeconomic ladder in the colonial state. But Kirk-Greene reminds us of the basic imperial and colonial logic that guided these practices and upon which they were justified. As he explains,

---

[83] Wale Oyemakinde, "The Railway Workers and Modernization in Colonial Nigeria," *Journal of the Historical Society of Nigeria* 10, no. 1 (1979): 113–124.

[84] William A. Shack and Elliot P. Skinner, eds., *Strangers in African Societies* (Berkeley: University of California Press, 1979).

Two powerful imperial influences were also in play in the 1920s. Lugard's frank thesis of a reciprocal mandate, "that Europe is in Africa for the mutual benefit of her own industrial classes and of the native races in their profess to a higher plane" ... echoes ... Joseph Chamberlain's vision a quarter of a century earlier of developing new territory as "trustees for civilization, for the commerce of the world ..."[85]

This view was expressly supported by the League of Nations that emerged after the end of World War I, and its view on this became the second powerful imperial influence that shaped the colonial narrative of this period. In its argument, it charged the administering authorities in the colonial empires to be accountable and look after the well-being and development of their subjects who are not yet able to stand by themselves.[86] The United Nations, which succeeded this body after World War II, supported the decolonization of the colonies, even though this was replaced by another system of exploitation between these powers and their colonies. In all respects, therefore, the colonial government established a system in which the promise and mandate of civilization which begat the imperial Niger mission shortly after the abolition of the slave trade and transmutation to the so-called legitimate trade continued to be the basis for the exploitation of the people, their lands, and their resources.

This way – in the face of the marginalization, systemic discrimination, worsening economic conditions, and increased economic burden symbolized by higher and multiple taxes and other stifling measures – the people were expected to be content with the reciprocating western civilization that brought modernization and modern government to them. They were also expected to show appreciation of this by way of loyalty to the Queen and her empire. In this conflicting worldview, one believed to be spreading civilization, even through exploitation, to support the economic system of the "mother culture" that birthed this civilization, although this civilization would have no root without the colonized people. Others, however, conceived of the war and postwar measures as nothing more than exploitative and oppressive. Hence, the kind of relationship that existed between the government and the people was characterized by mutual suspicion and a trust deficit which the postcolonial government have since inherited, together with the structure of the economy as outlined in the foregoing discussion.

---

[85] Kirk-Greene, *Britain's Imperial Administrators*, 39.
[86] Kirk-Greene, *Britain's Imperial Administrators*.

9

The Interwar Years

Nigeria's interwar years were characterized by a decade-long economic depression that afflicted almost half of the twenty-one-year period of colonial history.[1] Instability, social unrest, and political mobilization strained societies that were already challenged by postwar recovery efforts.[2] The previous chapters considered the political economy of this period, viewed through the lens of World War I and its aftermath in Nigeria. This chapter, however, highlights events that defined the interwar epoch in Nigerian history, including the economic crisis, political oppression, protests, and political concessions from the colonial government. These events and developments – especially during the aftermath of World War I and the years that immediately preceded World War II – are important not only for Nigeria's colonial history but also for understanding its postcolonial situation. Terms such as "Imperial Preference," "Empire Solidarity," "Recovery through Empire," and similar perspectives drove protectionist government policies during this period, leading to the economic implosion that wounded the colonial state and came to define postcolonial politics.[3]

Bauer described the economic environment of the interwar years, which was the result of government policies and responses to declining revenues and increasing expenditures, as one that "increased the prizes of political power and the intensity of the struggle for them."[4] By the second half of the period, these changes resulted in greater demands for political power from educated and commercial elites, who were joined by peasants, traders, and other inhabitants of the colonial state.

---

[1] Chima J. Korieh, *Nigeria and World War II: Colonialism, Empire, and Global Conflict* (Cambridge: Cambridge University Press, 2020), 33–71.

[2] Judith A. Byfield, "Taxation, Women, and the Colonial State: Egba Women's Tax Revolt," *Meridians* 3, no. 2 (2003): 250–277.

[3] Moses E. Ochonu, *Colonial Meltdown: Northern Nigeria in the Great Depression* (Athens: Ohio State University Press, 2009); and Olufemi R. Ekundare, *An Economic History of Nigeria 1860–1960* (London: Methuen & Co Ltd., 1973), 103–217.

[4] Quoted in Peter C. Lloyd, ed., *The New Elites of Tropical Africa* (London: Oxford University Press, 1966), 330.

The discourse around colonial Nigeria's interwar years exhibits a uniquely kaleidoscopic and paradoxical frame, speaking to economic decline and growth occurring within a simultaneously restricted and expanded political space.[5] The colony's infrastructure was improved while local participation in the economic space was marginalized. A greater number of laws and ordinances were accompanied by an increase in crime, and many other contradictions were at work.[6] These forces shaped the colonial narrative of the time.

Trade and Commerce in the Interwar Years

A new set of educated elites emerged in various parts of Africa during the colonial period, especially as it drew to a close.[7] They played critical roles in the decolonization and nationalist development of their countries.[8] On a fundamental level, they opened the debate and public discourse about the nature of the colonial state and its impact on the postcolonial state.

Two schools of thought emerged to interpret what constituted the colonial state, and what the colonial state was made of, vis-à-vis the contemporary evolution of the postcolonial states. This discussion, led by Ali Mazrui, Bethwell A. Ogot, Jacob F. Ade Ajayi, and many others, has shaped our understanding and interpretation of events during this period.[9] Whenever this narrative is mentioned, the interwar years occupy cogent evolutionary decades. At individual and institutional levels of scholarship, these educated elites began to dissect, understand, and teach Africa's colonial history either as an epic or an epochal moment.[10] The period was as epochal as it was epic for the evolution of thousands of cultural groups arbitrarily clustered into Africa's modern states.

The epochal narrative, championed by Kenneth Dike and Jacob F. Ajayi at the Ibadan School of History, observed this period as one of both evolution and continuation. Previous practices before 1900 were modified to suit the colonial enterprise and its conception of government and society. The epic school, led by Makerere University in Tanzania, viewed it as a clean break from the old

---

[5] Judith Byfield, "Innovation and Conflict: Cloth Dyers and the Interwar Depression in Abeokuta, Nigeria," *The Journal of African History* 38, no. 1 (1997): 77–99.

[6] Adiele E. Afigbo, "Revolution and Reaction in Eastern Nigeria: 1900–1929: The Background to the Women's Riot of 1929," *Journal of the Historical Society of Nigeria* 3, no. 3 (1966): 539–557.

[7] Jim C. Harper, *Western-Educated Elites in Kenya, 1900–1963: The African American Factor* (New York: Routledge, 2016).

[8] Emmanuel A. Ayandele, *The Educated Elite in the Nigerian Society* (Ibadan: Ibadan University Press, 1974).

[9] Sabelo J. Ndlovu-Gatsheni, "Decoloniality as the Future of Africa," *History Compass* 13, no. 10 (2015): 485–496.

[10] Ndlovu-Gatsheni, "Decoloniality as the Future."

practices of people now described as colonial subjects.[11] The former considers this period as evolutionary, and the latter perceives it as revolutionary. Drawing a clear distinction between these two is tantamount to finding a clear view of the colonial institution's impact on the state's institution of chieftaincy – an exercise that has been described as intricate enough on its own.[12]

An examination of trade and commerce shows that pre-1900 commodities continued to sustain Nigeria's local markets and exports. Millet, palm products, rice, yam, cassava, groundnut, cocoa, cotton, rubber, livestock, craft works, clothes, kola nuts, and other products remained actively traded throughout the colonial period. The period tracks the changing value of these commodities: first as a means of currency, and second as items for consumption. Various developments contributed to the changing values of this period. There was a population explosion, the advent of a cash economy, and increasing urban migration and job specialization. Western education and ideas of modernity became prevalent, bringing an immense liberalization of trade into a kaleidoscopic economic landscape. A revolution in local modes of production also accounted for the cash economy that was previously mentioned.

These developments can be viewed as evolutionary because many of these practices and phenomena had already existed in societies that were moving toward colonial rule, especially in the second half of the nineteenth century. They were revolutionary in the way that the colonial state concretized and defined them. In this changing social milieu, it became difficult for yam farmers to continually search for fertile land where they could cultivate crops. In the Benue-Plateau region, land was the recurring cause of violent conflict between neighboring communities, especially among the Tiv, who were known for yam cultivation, and their neighbors.[13]

The British government did not invoke the odious Land Apportionment Act that it had implemented in Eastern and South African colonies. Instead, the epistemology of land and ownership was modified for political reasons in Nigeria and other West African colonies, accompanied by the breakdown of society's remaining communal inclinations. The government did not need to exert any special effort as merely introducing a cash economy and paid labor created a domino effect that established the new order. Nigeria recalibrated its demographics through labor, trade, and other migration patterns.[14]

---

[11] Jacob F. A. Ajayi, *History and the Nation and Other Addresses* (Ibadan: Spectrum Books, 1991); and Walter Rodney, *How Europe Underdeveloped Africa* (Kingston: Bogle–Louverture, 1972).

[12] Olufemi Vaughan, *Nigerian Chiefs: Traditional Power in Modern Politics, 1890s–1990s* (Rochester: University of Rochester Press, 2006).

[13] Tesemchi Makar, *The History of Political Change among the Tiv in the 19th and 20th Centuries* (Enugu: Fourth Dimension Publishers, 1994).

[14] William A. Shack and Elliot P. Skinner, *Strangers in African Societies* (Berkeley: University of California Press, 1979).

Worsening economic conditions in the interwar years led people to consume more cassava and cassava products, eroding the market share held by yams. Decisions to cultivate either crop were based on the amount of labor required, the expected time to harvest, and the demands of the market. Studies of this period show that people resorted to various measures, including illegal ones, to survive the colonial state. The economic picture of that time shows a population with declining purchasing power that affected its consumption patterns.

In previous years, more European consumer goods found their way to the colony, flooding local markets and crippling local industries. Urban migration, Western education, the specialization of labor, and foreign cultural influences changed the social demography of the state, putting pressure on land and the economic production of the peasant class. These interwar years saw the lingering effects of World War I compounded by health hazards, local economic decline, and market fluctuations culminating in the Great Depression of the late 1920s and 1930s.[15] Unemployment and underemployment were introduced into the public lexicon, along with a changing epistemology of poverty.[16]

World War I had massive effects on Nigeria's entire population, felt directly by the people drawn to fight and indirectly by colonial subjects who endured the colonial state's economic recovery measures.[17] Among the Igbo and the Niger Delta population, men who had been conscripted into the British army had to be replaced by local women laborers. These women began to cultivate the land, becoming the primary earners in many families from the war period onward. The socioeconomic situation of the interwar years concretized these changing economic roles for women. After the war, the military skills and training of the conscripted population became useless. Their hopes of engaging the colonial state in different capacities went unfulfilled.[18] A return to farming, or producing goods to be exported, was neither encouraged nor permissible in their situation. The prices of exported goods from Nigeria had declined, influenced by reduced purchasing power and low industrial output from postwar Europe. Although the prices of food crops had improved considerably while the shortage of trade and scarce resources had led to inflation, there was little they could do to enhance production in an arena dominated by women. Industries that could provide

---

[15] Moses Ochonu, "Conjoined to Empire: The Great Depression and Nigeria," *African Economic History* 34 (2006): 103–145.

[16] Tunde Decker, "Aini – An African Indigenous Template of Poverty and the Task for Neo-Monetary Modules of Interventions," in *Development from Below and Above in Africa*, ed. Maurice Amutabi (Nairobi: Centre for Democracy, Research and Development, 2018), 83–91.

[17] George N. Njung, "Victims of Empire: WWI Ex-servicemen and the Colonial Economy of Wartime Sacrifices in Postwar British Nigeria," *First World War Studies* 10, no. 1 (2019): 49–67.

[18] Dónal Hassett and Michelle Moyd, "Introduction: Writing the History of Colonial Veterans of the Great War," *First World War Studies* 10, no. 1 (2019): 1–11.

alternative employment were recuperating from the war, and colonial postwar economic policies limited their capacity to participate.

This unemployed population was soon joined by workers who had been laid off from government positions and roles at private companies. Unemployment numbers reached their peak in the 1930s as the effect of the great economic depression began to bite harder.[19] The colonial state's "Recovery through Empire" policy was no mere rhetoric. The British government sought to centralize and annex resources from its foreign territories as part of a collective reconstruction and rehabilitation effort to benefit the metropolitan state. Restrictions were placed on local economic actors, and many roles in government institutions, the civil service, corporate bodies, and private companies were eliminated.

Colonial policies and lost jobs prevented large numbers of people from participating in Nigeria's economy. The administrators of the colony regularly bemoaned its fiscal position in every meeting until the end of the depression. The prevailing idea was that the government needed to reduce costs and save its resources for infrastructure that could enable the exploitation and exportation of goods and products from the colony to the metropolitan capital.[20] Many indigenous jobs in the administration were terminated. Those who remained needed to exist on reduced salaries while their taxes either stayed the same or increased. This lack of job security affected food security and patterns of living. The economic displacement and disruption redistributed social value without creating any new benefits. People responded to economic hardship by resorting to illegal activities.[21] Armed robbery had been common in the previous century when Borgu princes became highwaymen to divert trade and political power to Nikki. Banditry now saw a resurgence, along with increased activity from pirates and other criminal elements along waterways and caravan routes.

Additional crimes evolved over the interwar years. Organized crime became prevalent in the abandoned mines and factories of the Plateau region. Other individuals, primarily in the South, created counterfeit British currency and engaged in kidnapping.[22] The phenomenon of youth delinquency and poverty generally became more widespread over this period, especially in urban locations.[23] A major difference existed between the criminal elements. One

---

[19] Axel Harneit-Sievers, "African Business, 'Economic Nationalism,' and British Colonial Policy: Southern Nigeria, 1935-1954," *African Economic History* 24 (1996): 25-68; and Tunde Decker, "Colonial Memories and Emotions in Southwestern Nigeria: How 'Good' were the 'Bad' Old' Days?," *Ife Journal of History* 8, no. 1 (2016/2017): 5-25.

[20] Ochonu, "Conjoined to Empire," 103-145.

[21] Paul Osifodunrin, *Escapee Criminals and Crime Control in Colonial Southwestern Nigeria, 1861-1945* (Ibadan: IFRA-Nigeria, 2005), 57-77.

[22] Ayodeji Olukoju, "Self-Help Criminality as Resistance?: Currency Counterfeiting in Colonial Nigeria," *International Review of Social History* 45, no. 3 (2000): 385-407.

[23] Tunde Decker, "Social Welfare Strategies in Colonial Lagos," *African Nebula* 1, no. 1 (2010): 56-62.

group recognized its criminality, often citing hunger, strife, and obligations to their families, states, communities, and selves as the motive for their activity. The other group seldom saw their acts as crimes. Their illegal survival outside of state regulation determined their mode of operation. A previous study notes that "there seems to be no correlation between the performance of the economy ... and counterfeiting,"[24] but this does not entirely exclude the economic milieu of the time.

Wealth, social status, and political power were entwined before the colonial epoch. Nineteenth-century political developments in the Niger area, more than at any time in the past, had restructured the basis of society through social relations, political formation, and economic morphology. This reached a crescendo within the region due to the expanded availability of status symbols and the link between wealth and political power as both were secured with military prowess and economic acumen.[25]

In the oral cultural artifacts of different cultures within the colony, the elements of power, wealth, and status have always occupied a central position.[26] When, by the turn of the twentieth century, the new colonial currency system and fiscal policies supplanted previous economic practices, people responded by engaging with the economy outside of state regulation.[27] It was a way to participate in a colonial economy that remained alien and incomprehensible. For blacksmiths and goldsmiths in Ilaro, Abeokuta, Ijebu, and elsewhere, it was a small task to melt, process, and corrugate French coins from neighboring communities and colonies, transforming them into "British" coins for legitimate transactions. If the alien state could make value out of nickel, brass, steel, and other metals, then so could these artisans. By blurring the logic of the Weberian state, after which the colony was modeled, they had retained their traditional knowledge of refashioning material into objects of value within society.

By the end of World War I, this practice had become commonplace across the colony. Blacksmiths and goldsmiths had been joined by traders and workers who had been made redundant by either the government or the unbridled competition from large British conglomerates. The counterfeit currency, along

---

[24] Toyin Falola, "'Manufacturing Trouble': Currency Forgery in Colonial Southwestern Nigeria," *African Economic History* 25 (1997): 124.

[25] Anthony G. Hopkins, *An Economic History of West Africa* (New York: Routledge, 2020); and Hakeem O. Danmole and Toyin Falola, "Ibadan–Ilorin Relations in the Nineteenth Century: A Study in Imperial Struggles in Yorubaland," *Transafrican Journal of History* 14 (1985): 21–35.

[26] Robin Law, "Horses, Firearms, and Political Power in Pre-colonial West Africa," *Past & Present* 72, no. 1 (1976): 112–132.

[27] Walter I. Ofonagoro, "From Traditional to British Currency in Southern Nigeria: Analysis of a Currency Revolution, 18801948," *The Journal of Economic History* 39, no. 3 (1979): 623–654.

with the colonial administration's postwar measures, accelerated the monetization of Nigerian societies.[28] The introduction of taxes, levies, and dues, along with market transactions that occurred over longer distances through improved transportation networks, meant that the colony's socioeconomic landscape was increasingly centered around modern currency. Government regulation and changing patterns of behavior led to the increased value of British coins.[29] These coins largely supplanted other symbols of wealth, such as the ownership of slaves or having a large family, which were the primary units of labor. Labor could be acquired and other symbols of wealth could be created with this new currency. These economic developments were responsible for the division of society based on labor, production, and wealth.

This currency, manifesting and being spent in different ways, became synonymous with the industrious and enterprising Yoruba population of the Ijebu nation. This dynamic partially explains the new currency phenomenon.[30] The correlation between the Ijebu and counterfeit currency cannot be divorced from the group's prominent role in clandestine activities in Ilesa, Ife, Ibadan, Osogbo, Abeokuta, Kano, and elsewhere. Counterfeit money was used for bank transactions, market exchanges, court dues, levies, taxes, and other payments. Counterfeit currency was supposed to be seized and destroyed by the authorities, but the government's instructions suggest that some coins may have been accepted as valid due to their level of craftsmanship. Regulations stated that "counterfeit coins received in remittances for which no claim against the government is likely to be preferred should be broken or mutilated and then destroyed. Any especially good specimens should be sent to the Treasury for inspection."[31] It is difficult to tell whether these "good specimens" were destroyed or retained by the state, but the latter is a possibility when considering the costs that such counterfeits imposed on banks, the government, and colonial officials.

Apart from currency counterfeiting, labeled the "owo Ijebu" phenomenon, which endured for several years and caused immense concern for the colonial state, there were also pressures introduced by ongoing migration patterns. Regional migration facilitated anticolonial and nationalist networks. The history of West Africa clearly shows the regional integration among cultures and peoples enabled by migration across boundaries. Clothes, kola nuts, millet, leatherwork, livestock, and other commodities moving along West African precolonial trading corridors largely remained traded with European commodities during the colonial period. Colonial states created borders along trade routes, but local

---

[28] Robin Hermann, "Empire Builders and Mushroom Gentlemen: The Meaning of Money in Colonial Nigeria," *The International Journal of African Historical Studies* 44, no. 3 (2011): 393–413.
[29] Anthony G. Hopkins, "The Currency Revolution in South–West Nigeria in the Late Nineteenth Century," *Journal of the Historical Society of Nigeria* 3, no. 3 (1966): 471–483.
[30] Olukoju, "Self-Help Criminality as Resistance?" 385–407.
[31] Falola, "Manufacturing Trouble," 139.

inhabitants continued to observe traditional boundaries that were navigable by social design.[32] The colonial economy, its attendant crisis, and the incentive to pursue cash labor altered patterns of regional migration.

Many realized that although they were under colonial rule in British or French territories, the idiosyncrasies of the colonial administrators and their specific socioeconomic conditions provided some nuances for the political economy of each colony. These economic and social drives, which had shaped waves of migration and migrants in precolonial times, continued to influence movements in colonial times, especially from the interwar years onward.[33] The economies of these colonies never really stabilized until independence, continuing into the postcolonial order. Rouch has explained that "at one end are migrants who form only segmented, temporary, tribal groupings. At the other end are migrants who form autonomous, multi-purpose tribal communities."[34] Migration patterns evolved from itinerant trading camps and began to support permanent settlements that developed into ethnic communities. These were the origins of Yoruba, Hausa, and Igbo communities in places like Ghana and Cote d'Ivoire.

Politics and Social Transformations

Wienner, Mamdani, Mudimbe, and other scholars of colonial and postcolonial Africa have studied the contradictions of notions of humanitarianism, liberalism, social justice, and the rule of law that supposedly drove the colonial enterprise in many parts of the colonial world.[35] These forces regularly came into conflict with economic pursuits and the administration of justice, affected by the distribution of power in these colonies. The exigencies of the postwar efforts led the Colonial Office in London to alter its policies of humanitarianism and civilization for its "primitive" colonial subjects, choosing instead to pursue developmentalism.

During this period, the new approach recast any marks of civilization that could be attributed to Africans as successful developmental policies enacted by

---

[32] Jacob F. A. Ajayi, "Towards an African Economic Community: A Historical Perspective," Lecture Presented at the Discussion of the Lagos Plan of Action, 1970, 2298-299; and John D. Hargreaves, "The Making of the Boundaries: Focus on West Africa," in *Partitioned Africans: Ethnic Relations across Africa's International Boundaries 1884-1984*, ed. Anthony I. Asiwaju (Lagos: Lagos University Press, 1984), 19-28.

[33] Antoine Pecoud and Paul de Guchteneire, *Migration Without Borders: Essays on the Free Movement of People* (New York: Berghahn Books, 2007).

[34] Jean Rouch, *Migrations au Ghana, Gold Coast, enquêtes 1953-1955* (Paris: Société des Africanistes, 1956).

[35] Martin J. Wiener, *An Empire on Trial: Race, Murder, and Justice under British Rule, 1870-1935* (New York: Cambridge University Press, 2009); Mahmood Mamdani, *Neither Settler Nor Native: The Making and Unmaking of Permanent Minorities* (London: Harvard University Press, 2020); and Valentin-Yves Mudimbe, *The Invention of Africa: Gnosis, Philosophy, and the Order of Knowledge* (Bloomington: Indiana University Press, 1998).

the colonial state. To enhance the dividends of these encounters, people reformed the precolonial mutual aid institutions and social networks of mobility from what Przerworski and Teune described as a "cooperative and development perspective."[36] Railways, electricity, telegraphs, ports, and other projects advancing the colony's modernization were not necessarily undertaken for the public good. Instead, they were designed for the exploration and exploitation of natural resources. This imperative was so strong that not even pandemics such as the bubonic plague and smallpox could slow the developmental drive of the colonial state.[37]

The British government retained its lofty ideals as the basis of European civilization. Terms such as "human rights" saturated the global discourse after World War II. The formation of modern states and the facilitation of international relations was meant to be the legacy of the colonial powers.[38] These views divided African societies into colonial subjects and the European population – settlers, as seen in the settler economies of Central, South and East Africa.[39] Not only did the white population enjoy different laws and rules, but they also existed in a social echelon that was higher than that of their Black counterparts.

The ideals of liberalism, human rights, humanitarianism, and the rule of law were conceived as European privileges. From the perspective of the colonizers, Africans and other colonial subjects had been granted these benefits through their contact with European civilization. These rights were only available to the extent that colony administrators allowed. A court proceeding involving Nigerian women protesting economic conditions in the colony during this period graphically emphasized the limitations of equality and social justice as espoused by Western powers. A legal representative of the women questioned a British Officer whose answer shows the intents and designs of the colonial state:

A. Irondi, Lagos: Do the British use tear gas on their women? If not why do they apply gas on our women?

> Answer: I have not known of any occasion when British police opened tear gas on British women. But how dare you draw a parallel? Do Nigerians rule Britain? Do Nigerians make and own tear gas or rifles? Why dare you draw a parallel? He who rules another does so only by might of his arms and diplomacy.[40]

---

[36] Quoted in Anthony I. Asiwaju, "The Co-Operative Movement in the Colonial Context: A Comparison of the French and British Rural West African Experience to 1960," *Journal of the Historical Society of Nigeria* 11, no. 1/2 (1981–June 1982): 89.

[37] Olukayode A. Faleye, "Plague and Trade in Lagos, 1924–1931," *The International Journal of Maritime History* 30, no. 2 (2018): 287–301.

[38] Mamdani, *Neither Settler Nor Native*.

[39] Kenneth Good, "Settler Colonialism: Economic Development and Class Formation," *The Journal of Modern African Studies* 14, no. 4 (1976): 597–620.

[40] Nnamdi Azikiwe, *My Odyssey: An Autobiography* (London: C. Hurst and Company, 1970), 332.

Undoubtedly, this statement emphasizes the position of several colonial administrators. From Benin to Sokoto, in Yorubaland, and elsewhere, the colonial state had dissolved the traditional authority of local rulers. These individuals were informed that their rights and sovereignty had been transferred to the British by conquest.[41]

Tributes, tolls, levies, and other sources of revenue were administered and regulated by the British colonial government. The colonial officer quoted earlier reiterates the legal view that established the authority of colonial rulers. Legally, politically, socially, and economically, the people were considered inferior to the European population. Mamdani described their role in the colony as that of a "permanent minority." This condition influenced the organization of nationalist movements during the interwar years. It was responsible for the shifting dimensions of the movements and actors from the second decade of this period, which resulted in the movement's radical phase toward the end of this period into World War II and its aftermath.[42]

Connivance between the colonial government and British merchant companies marginalized indigenous economic actors. The practice of favoring the British above other actors, including foreign and local competitors, continued throughout this period. It compounded the existing negative effects imposed by postwar recovery programs and the Great Depression.[43] Contracts between shipping companies, metropolitan banks, insurance companies, industrial firms, and British trading agents allowed British stakeholders to capture all the benefits of the Nigerian economy's growth. Chambers of commerce and their agents from Liverpool, Manchester, and London became entrenched in the economies of British West African colonies. They controlled the banking and finance sectors, along with export, shipping, and distribution networks. The largest purchase and distribution network was the United African Company, anchoring the affairs of chambers of commerce and their agents in these territories. Such networks regulated the prices of goods from 1937 to 1938, causing Nigeria's infamous "cocoa pool" crisis.[44]

The marginalization of local economic actors resonated throughout the colony's political space during this period, and it influenced the establishment of the Yaba Higher College in 1934. Other significant developments included the road transport worker strike action, organized in response to government policies that favored railway workers and introduced double licensing. These

---

[41] Philip Igbafe, "British Rule in Benin 1897–1920: Direct or Indirect?" *Journal of the Historical Society of Nigeria* 3, no. 4 (1967): 701.

[42] James S. Coleman, *Nigeria: Background to Nationalism* (Berkeley: University of California Press, 1958.).

[43] Dan O. Chukwu, "The Economic Impact of Pioneer Indigenous Banks in Colonial Nigeria, 1920–1960," *Journal of the Historical Society of Nigeria* 19 (2010): 93–100.

[44] Adebayo A. Lawal, *Nigeria: Culture, Politics, Governance and Development* (Ibadan: Connel Publications, 2015), 165–194.

incidents set the stage for the 1930s to see the beginnings of sociopolitical eruption in the colony, which would be fully unleashed by the Nigerian experience in World War II.[45]

The organizational power of people across the British West African colonies had greatly improved by the end of the war. By 1920 they had established the National Congress of British West Africa in the Gold Coast.[46] In 1925 Ladipo Solanke, a Nigerian student studying in Britain, established the West African Students Union (WASU) in London.[47] Both organizations advocated people who lived under colonial rule, especially in opposition to the racial hierarchical structure that governed colonies. They aimed to enhance the sociopolitical and economic capital of people within and beyond the colonies.

Winifred Tete-Ansa was a businessman and a subject of the British colonial empire in Ghana who resided in the United States. By the time he began his massive 1920s campaign for Indigenous collective efforts in the British West African colony, political activism had resulted in the establishment of banks, corporate bodies, and other economic and political interest groups, such as the British West African Corporation.[48] These organizations, especially the West African Student Union, had gained tremendous momentum among the people of British West Africa. Altogether, the political awareness of the people within the colonial state had been steadily increasing. From the United Kingdom to various parts of British West Africa, Solanke made several tours to galvanize the energy and consciousness of local youth, informing them about their condition and how the WASU, as a body, planned to protect their interests.[49] The work of WASU became instrumental in organizing British West African youth for action, encouraging them to acquire Western education and pursue nationalist goals and a Pan-African consciousness. The National Congress of British West Africa coordinated a collective trading network as a response to colonial rule across the West African British colonial estates.[50]

Cross-regional networks, established in response to colonial rule, were a direct response to the changes made by the Colonial Office in London during the war. The office had standardized the administration of its colonies, which was a shift from the previous self-contained entities, facilitating its shift to the

---

[45] Martin L. Kilson, "Nationalism and Social Classes in British West Africa," *The Journal of Politics* 20, no. 2 (1968): 368–387.

[46] Gabriel I. C. Eluwa, "The National Congress of British West Africa: A Study in African Nationalism," *Présence Africaine* 77 (1971): 131–149.

[47] James S. Coleman, "Nationalism in Tropical Africa," *The American Political Science Review* 48, no. 2 (1954): 404–426.

[48] Chukwu, "The Economic Impact," 93–100.

[49] Julius O. Adekunle, "Yoruba Factor in Nigerian Politics," in *Yoruba Identity and Power Politics*, ed. Toyin Falola and Ann Genova (Rochester: University of Rochester Press, 2006), 273–276.

[50] Toyin Falola and Matthew M. Heaton, *A History of Nigeria* (New York: Cambridge University Press, 2008), 139.

developmental approach to governance. These changes were the beginnings of a closer collective experience among colonized people. The collective ambience in the colonies made the interwar period significant for the sociopolitical evolution of West African states. Economic conditions were deteriorating, eroded by the activities of British merchant companies and conglomerates and also by political subjugation and ruinous economic policies and programs imposed by the colonial state. The demand for West African resources, which included industrial and agricultural products, witnessed dramatic fluctuations during this time. This was partly due to the unstable capacity of British industries during the postwar era, and also due to the Great Depression that followed. Clifford Geertz described the economic situation in the colonies as "involution" – the agricultural economy of the colonies was feeding on itself, rather than expanding through profit and surplus investment.[51]

The extractive economy established and promoted by the colonial government, designed to assist the economic recovery of London, was shrinking or retaining similar levels and modes of production in the colonies, starving producers of the capital that would have been necessary to expand production. The British conglomerates controlling the colony's economy further limited the opportunities to generate capital for economic expansion. Local economic actors were not only marginalized, they were also subject to discrimination in the allocation of freight space from the Association of West African Merchants (AWAM). The organization was ostensibly created to manage economic fluctuations at the time, but it prevented colonial subjects from receiving the full value for their goods. In the early 1930s, various political actors in Lagos argued that at least 28,000 indigenous market actors had been driven out of business due to the activities of the United African Company and other organizations at work in the colony's interior. During the same period, the Elder Dempster Shipping Company boasted in its 1928 report:

> One cannot help being impressed, unfavorably, by the disappearance of the big Native Merchants, shrewd, active, and highly esteemed, and it is regrettable that for some reason or other, native partnerships and combinations have proved successful and are practically non-existent today.[52]

This period's economy largely involved the export of raw materials. Many of the political actors who thrived as anticolonial leaders, pursuing factional interests framed along with national narratives, were second-grade civil service functionaries and business owners. Prominent figures, like Chief Obafemi Awolowo and his kinsman Samuel Akinsanya, applied their intellectual acumen to the cocoa trade. They benefited from the 1935–6 boom and felt the bite of the crisis that followed.

---

[51] Quoted in Ochonu, "Conjoined to Empire," 105.
[52] Quoted in Harneit-Sievers, "African Business," 30.

Socioeconomic disruption from the war years spilled over into the 1920–1 economic crisis, which preceded the 1929–39 Great Depression. The creation of infrastructure in emerging cities, as a result of the colonialist government's developmental framework, created a steady flow of migrants from rural to urban spaces.[53] Some of those who migrated to the cities at this time included the anticolonial leaders who reduced the clout and authority of Herbert Macaulay's Nigerian National Democratic Party (NNDP) in the 1930s. Macaulay had been described as the father of Nigerian nationalism due to his trailblazing role in the Lagos political space from the late nineteenth century. His popularity and anticolonial activities had gained great momentum in Lagos by the start of the twentieth century and soon inspired subsequent political actors with his organizational efforts.[54] Tete-Ansa, Theophilus A. Doherty, H. A. Subair, and other vibrant economic actors attempted to rekindle the hopes and aspirations of local traders who sought to engage the colonial market from a stronger, collective position. After their failure, the focus of the emerging elites shifted from economic issues to political demands.[55] This revived the leading political organization of the time: the NNDP. The colonial administration allowed the party to be active in the political space after the 1922 concession by Clifford. Many of those involved in its political revitalization had been directly affected by economic conditions in the interwar years – particularly during the Great Depression – and they took broader measures to address commercial implications.

Tete-Ansa did not belong to the same social class as most political activists, but he provided some nuance to this broader framework, inspiring other collective efforts. The large amounts of capital available to British conglomerates and large merchant companies had increased their role in local markets and constrained the activities of other participants, which is why Tete-Ansa started a bank in an effort to finance African trade cooperatives. These groups sought to pool the resources and capital of local economic actors so that they could be applied more effectively. Like other measures taken by British West African colonial subjects, these groups soon lost their purpose and faded into obscurity.

Cooperatives were created to export West African cocoa directly to America, boycotting European companies. The National Bank of Nigeria (NBN) was established in 1933 to function as a financial institution that represented the interests of farmers, traders, and other local economic actors.[56] Other initiatives,

---

[53] Insa Nolte, *Obafemi Awolowo and the Making of Remo: The Local Politics of a Nigerian Nationalist* (Edinburgh: Edinburgh University Press, 2009).
[54] Olakunle A. Lawal and Oluwasegun M. Jimoh, "Missiles from 'Kirsten Hall': Herbert Macaulay versus Hugh Clifford, 1922–1931," *Lagos Historical Review* 12 (2012): 41–62.
[55] Kilson, "Nationalism and Social Classes," 379.
[56] Chukwuemeka Okoye and Amon Okpala, "The History of Community Banking and its Role in Nigerian Rural Economic Development," *The Review of Black Political Economy* 28, no. 3 (2001): 73–87.

such as Ansa's 1929 formation of the Industrial and Commercial Bank Ltd in Lagos, were the evolution of smaller communal schemes that many within colonial society had depended on for collective action and financial assistance. They offered microcredit facilities to members and helped form a close relationship among members in the colonial economy.[57]

The colonial economy changed the socioeconomic landscape of society and created nascent forms of saving among its subjects. In precolonial times, savings and the generation of capital were unheard of. Systems of financial assistance and responsibilities were resolved through practices such as pawnship, family or communal contributions, and purchases made with credit.[58] By the turn of the twentieth century, these networks were augmented by cooperative organizations such as microfinance banks like the NBN, deposit money banks, *esusu* (rotating credit associations), daily contribution collectors, and communal contributions that were made to ethnocultural union bodies. Slavery and the practice of pawnship were abolished by the colonial government.

In Ghana and Nigeria, social networks of financial responsibility and assistance were engaged all through the colonial epoch, and they metamorphosed in the postcolonial era. From Itsekiri, Benin, Yorubaland, Ibibio, Warri, Onitsha, Asaba, and various other places in the interior of the Southern protectorate and colony, people began to converge on the Lagos metropolis. These migrants pursued Western education, trade, and other commercial opportunities. In Lagos and elsewhere, they organized around ethnic and communal networks that were described as kinship assistance unions. Apart from their economic potency, these unions also served as political conduits between urban and rural areas – linking a group's urban homes with townships that were often referred to as homesteads. These dynamics led to rivalry and contention within the sociocultural structure that transformed into the Action Group after World War II. The unions informed their rural members about unfolding political developments within the colony, and they contributed to the development of their kinsmen and communities.

Such groups acted as intermediaries between the traditional and the modern in their communities. Leadership roles were often occupied by the mid-nineteenth-century returnees and their descendants. Macaulay was an example of this later phase. The WASU and other ethnocommunal unions of this period show that the forms of biosociality deconstructed by colonial forces were replaced by a litany of socioeconomic bodies created to navigate the colonial cash economy.[59] Although it deconstructed some older networks for

---

[57] W. M. Warren, "Urban Real Wages and the Nigerian Trade Union Movement, 1939–60: Rejoinder," *Economic Development and Cultural Change* 17, no. 4 (1969): 618–633.
[58] Paul E. Lovejoy and Toyin Falola, *Pawnship, Slavery, and Colonialism in Africa* (Trenton: Africa World Press, 2003).
[59] Asiwaju, "The Co-Operative Movement," 97–102.

social mobility, the colonial economy also expanded parts of these structures. The WASU created a home for West African students in London, similar to the assistance that ethnocommunal bodies provided for their kinsmen migrating to Lagos, Ibadan, and other cities.

Ethnocommunal bodies in the cities, like WASU, the National Congress of British West Africa, British West African Cooperatives, and other "transnational" bodies were forms that the colonial state simultaneously deconstructed and reconstructed. Africans used these bodies to mobilize and organize boycotts and other opposition to the government. This was most noticeable during the cocoa pool crisis, in which organizers informed their members of plans made by British merchant companies.

British companies provided credit to local actors due to the amount of capital necessary to participate in the cocoa market, especially for traders who conveyed produce to the cities and forwarded it to ports. Competition between British companies created favorable conditions for traders to acquire capital. In the late 1930s, ten of these companies disrupted the relationship. Traders refused to sell their products, which resulted in the 1937 cocoa pool crisis.[60] Although there were attempts to organize a boycott of the British companies largely organized by Samuel Akinsanya's Nigeria Produce Traders Union (NPTU) and other cooperative societies of Nigerian cocoa farmers, it did not see much success. The farmers' direct participation created a porous market structure that made it difficult to engage in collective action.[61] Farmers and indigenous produce buyers formed different associations and societies or organized into unions and collective bodies, to maximize their gains in the colonial economy. Their strength was weakened by government actions and interventions in the organization and operation of collective structures. The events of this period showed that collective action to oppose British economic interests would achieve little if the people lacked political power.

The four seats in the Lagos legislative house that had been reserved for Indigenous representation were entirely ceremonial. There was little that four nonofficial members of a 46-member legislative house could do to affect government policy. These seats were only meant to neutralize anticolonial "missiles" from the likes of Macaulay. By the time policies were presented to the house, an invocation of the Colonial Office's authority often ended the discussion. This became even more pronounced under Cameron and Bourdillon during the Great Depression and the World War II years.[62] The apparent romance between the NNDP and the colonial government, who were

---

[60] Harneit-Sievers, "African Business," 32–35.
[61] Asiwaju, "The Co-Operative Movement," 97–102.
[62] Stephen O. Arifalo, "The Rise and Decline of the Nigerian Youth Movement, 1934–1941," *The African Review: Journal of African Politics, Development and International Affairs* 13, no. 1 (1986): 59–76.

perceived to be ignoring the needs of ordinary people, prompted action. The resulting 1934 mobilization created the Lagos Youth Movement (LYM).[63] This organization expanded its scope and objectives to become the Nigerian Youth Movement (NYM) in 1936.

Shortcomings in the colony's educational processes had adverse effects on its economy. Many communities had been investing in the education of their people since the turn of the century, creating infrastructure and scholarship projects, particularly in the South. By the time Yaba College – the colony's first institution of higher education – was established in 1934, dozens of secondary schools had been operating in various parts of the interior. Lagos alone had Igbobi, Kings College, CMS Grammar School, Methodist Boys High School, St. Gregory, and many others ready to send their graduates to the new institution of higher learning.[64] The first class, numbering around 500 students, was trained in diverse disciplines that included liberal arts and the sciences, teacher training, human and veterinary medicine, surveying, commerce, and forestry.[65]

Admissions into Yaba College were highly competitive, such that a large number of applicants and the limited number of spaces made it more competitive than British universities. However, the colonial administration had designed the school's degrees to be inferior to those from similar institutions in Britain and elsewhere. Certifications from Yaba College were only relevant within the Nigerian colony.[66] The school's staff and administrators were also paid lower salaries than their counterparts at other institutions. Colonial educational policy was designed to create a population that was politically loyal to London and subordinate to the British Empire.[67]

In March of 1934, three months after the opening of Yaba College, students and the newly emerging political actors of Lagos organized a rally to oppose the idea of alien imposition by the NNDP. The recently created LYM (subsequently the NYM) began engaging with all of the colony's raging political disputes, from transport union actions to the cocoa pool crisis. This had resounding effects within the colony. By the 1938 elections, the movement had become a political party that put up candidates for the legislative council and the Lagos Town Council, claiming all available seats and signaling the demise of the NNDP. During this period, Nnamdi Azikwe returned from his studies in the United States for a brief stint in Accra, Ghana, where the colonial

---

[63] F. O. E. Okafor, *The Nigerian Youth Movement, 1934-44: A Re-appraisal of the Historiography* (Onitsha: Etukokwu Publishers, 1989).

[64] Ade Fajana, "Colonial Control and Education: The Development of Higher Education in Nigeria 1900-1950," *Journal of the Historical Society of Nigeria* 6, no. 3 (1972): 323-340.

[65] Festus Ogunlade, "Post-Secondary Education Years, 1947-1958," in *J. F. Ade Ajayi: His Life and Career*, ed. Michael Omolewa and Akinjide Osuntokun (Ibadan: Bookcraft, 2014), 58.

[66] Arifalo, "The Rise and Decline," 63.

[67] Fajana, "Colonial Control and Education."

government accused him of treason for incendiary editorials and publications. Azikwe submitted several job applications to the colonial government and private companies and went on to experience the unemployment crisis firsthand. His submissions went unanswered, which resulted in his foray into journalism in Ghana. Like other political actors during this period, Azikwe needed to protect his investments within the colonial economy, along with his dignity. After 1937, he divested his resources from Ghana to invest in Nigerian media and other businesses in Nigeria.[68] This led to his showdown with NYM leadership when the *Daily Service* newspaper was launched as the official mouthpiece of the movement, in opposition to his own *West African Pilot*.

Anticolonial leaders and actors were not paid for their activism, which led them to pursue what sociologists describe as the advancement of elite interest in the collective.[69] Azikiwe established a presence in the NYM and served as a bridge between old and new generations of political actors. Together with Akinsanya, Hezekiah O. Davies, and Ernest Ikoli, he constructed what Awolowo described as a "volcanic nationalist quartet." Leading political actors of the time all had access to the media in various capacities. This had been the case since Macaulay, who was trained as an engineer but practiced journalism. More followed his example, including Awolowo, Azikwe, Okoli, and others who either owned publishing companies or worked in their highest echelons.

The access to media explained the prominence and characterization of the "volcanic nationalists' quartet" in Nigeria. Information was being distributed more rapidly across the colonial space during this time, and its audience was growing rapidly. In the period that followed, the NYM fragmented into the National Council of Nigerian Citizens (NCNC) and the Action Group (AG), which were leading political parties in the South. The media was used as a platform for the decolonization of the Nigerian colony. Gifford has explained that the drive for decolonization began during the interwar years, originally in the French colonies. The political and economic emancipation of colonial subjects was at the core of the debate.[70] This conflict and aspects of its psychological and cultural liberation became central to the engagements of later anticolonial leaders. This was a fundamental departure from the older generation of local actors in the political space, using the currency of Western education and Western ideology.

New political actors wore traditional cultural attire, acting as ambassadors for their ethnocultural leaning. They doubled as cultural and political "nationalists" in their activism, using their ethnocultural networks and

---

[68] Azikiwe, *My Odyssey*, 286–353.
[69] Abner Cohen, *The Politics of Elite Culture: Explorations in the Dramaturgy of Power in a Modern African Society* (Berkeley: University of California Press, 1981).
[70] Prosser Gifford and William Roger Louis, *Decolonization and African Independence: The Transfer of Power, 1960–1980* (London: Yale University Press, 1988), 10.

identities to build political clout and negotiate the notions of modernity and development in the political space.[71] This allowed them to modify and redefine the changing nature of local agitation that had already been transformed by Macaulay and his compatriots in the years that immediately followed the war.

Conclusion

Administrative reforms during this period were significant measures that often followed government policies and ordinances. The fundamental reforms injected into the colonial administration, especially during the period studied in this chapter, allowed the colonial state to continue promoting a policy of two protectorates in one country.[72] The contradictions of colonial rule are most evident in the administrative and political reforms of 1914, which were supposedly aimed at creating a Nigerian state.

As Tamuno has observed, the nineteenth century's historic rivalries and wars of conquest delayed the evolution of common political institutions before the colonization of polities in the Niger area. The "well known cultural diversity made more acute the resolution of political conflicts,"[73] and the British colonial enterprise institutionalized these intricacies in the structure, system, and policies of the colonial state. The North continued to be administered through ordinances until around two years after World War II, when anticolonial and "nationalist" agitations in the colony were at a crescendo. The Northern area was seen as a "self-contained Native state" in which the representation of the Emir in the legislative house would be tantamount to an insult to his person.[74]

While the South had been represented in legislative processes and modern government, encouraging the cultural and political evolution of its people, the North remained structured and administered through the Emirate system. British colonial administrators further distorted the ability to build institutions for forging consensus among the people. Several scholars have examined these dynamics in detail. Ikime states that "actions like Clifford's and later Bourdillon's make it look like the British had certain vested interests in the

---

[71] Mufutau Oluwasegun Jimoh, "A Study in Spatial Focal Points and Social Contestation of Urban Life in Lagos: A History of Glover Memorial Hall, 1889–1960," *Ife Journal of History* 8, no. 1 (2016/2017): 124–149.

[72] The National Conference, "National Conference: Final Draft of the Conference Report," August 2014, 4.

[73] Tekena N. Tamuno, "Introduction: The Search for Viable Policies," in *Nigeria Since Independence: The First Twenty-Five Years*, Vol. IV, ed. Tekena Tamuno and Jospeh A. Atanda (Ibadan: Heinemann Educational Books Ltd., 1989), 3.

[74] O. E. Udofia, "Nigerian Political Parties: Their Role in Modernizing the Political System, 1920–1966," *Journal of Black Studies* 11, no. 4 (1981): 435–447.

North which they were eager to protect."[75] This references the further breakdown of the Southern protectorate and colony in 1939; the North was left intact to preserve its oligarchy despite the diversity of its people. Ajayi and Ekoko explain that when colonial administrators left the North unchanged, "they regarded the Islamic leaders as an essential conservative and stabilizing influence on Nigeria as a whole."[76]

During his time in Nigeria, Lugard did not hide his admiration for the Northern Emirate system. Subsequent administrators also embraced this view. This had additional consequences for the Southern region as the colonial economy created waves of destitute and displaced persons in the North who migrated to the South, usually begging for alms. The colonial system was grounded in the precolonial caliphate framework. Because the administration reinforced Islamic doctrines and tenets, and the tools of nationalism and decolonization were embedded in Judeo-western philosophy, the winds of political action were most active in the South during the interwar years. Young men who migrated from their villages to the emerging cities – where they received secondary and higher education, becoming the leaders in the drive for decolonization – were mainly from this region.

Although early nationalists advocated the entire country of Nigeria, many of their activities remained in the South. Agitations also occurred in the North during this period, but they largely took the form of commercial and economic demands via petitions and similar activities. Beginning in the 1930s, the nature of protest and anticolonial demands began to change. Previously fragmented bodies, unions, organizations, and groups began to harness their demands and political participation through political parties. Market women, trade unions, community groups, farmers' unions, mass movements, and other organizations exerted more influence over the political process. Western education was crucial to this process, which explains the strength of "nationalist" anticolonial demands in the South.

---

[75] Obaro Ikime, *Can Anything Good Come Out of History?* (Ibadan: Bookcraft, 2018), 139.

[76] Jacob F. A. Ajayi and Abednego E. Ekoko, "Transfer of Power in Nigeria: Its Origin and Consequences," in *Decolonization and African Independence: The Transfer of Power, 1960–1980*, ed. William Roger Louis and Ronald Robinson (London: Yale University Press, 1988), 245–270.

10

Indirect Rule and the Native Administration

Britain's indirect rule policy was adapted to suit the preferences of colonial administrators and the specific circumstances of different Nigerian societies. It was difficult to impose a minority-oriented reorganization in societies with established, precolonial systems of organization, especially when local majorities believed that the existing systems were successful. In Nigeria, which had an established history of indigenous administration and governance,[1] colonizers attempted to implement radical changes. This assertion of British dominance, acting to reorganize local systems, was met with resistance from groups who preferred their methods of governance. Plans to overcome this resistance were described as "the native question."[2]

A systemic answer to the native question was needed to account for the intellectual resilience of African societies. Different recommendations shaped the new proposals for governance. First, Lord Lugard examined local attitudes toward British officials and their ability to influence the local population.[3] The results informed his adoption of the indirect rule system, which he saw as the most effective choice for establishing a successful colonial system.[4] Indirect rule was not an independent system in its own right. Rather, it described the British government's approach to pre-existing institutions within the colony. The colonizers planned to exploit these institutions for more effective governance within the territories.[5] The system adapted native authority to suit the British system of government, allowing them to be administered as a unit within the British colonial system.[6]

---

[1] Victor O. Edo, "The Practice of Democracy in Nigeria: The Pre-colonial Antecedent," *Lumina: An Interdisciplinary Research Journal* 21, no. 2 (2010): 1–7.
[2] Mahmood Mamdani, "Indirect Rule, Civil Society, and Ethnicity: The African Dilemma," *Social Justice* 23, no. 1/2 (1996): 145–150.
[3] John Gerring, Daniel Ziblatt, Johan Van Gorp, and Julián Arévalo, "An Institutional Theory of Direct and Indirect Rule," *World Politics* 63, no. 3 (2011): 377–433.
[4] Leslye M. Murray, "Indirect Rule: Lugardian Style," MA thesis, Morehead State University, 1973.
[5] Margery Perham, "A Re-statement of Indirect Rule," *Africa* 7, no. 3 (1934): 321–334.
[6] Sir William Geary, *Nigeria under British Rule* (London: Frank Cass, 1965).

Lord Lugard and the Introduction of Indirect Rule

The indirect rule system developed from what Lord Lugard described as a "dual mandate," which were plans to make Africa accessible to the self-described forces of civilization and to teach local inhabitants to accept them.[7] Critics have described this mandate as "selfish ethnocentrism." The imposition of indirect rule was bloody, and African polities were accessed in an extremist, ruthless fashion.[8] The introduction of the indirect rule system was a pretext for justifying colonial adventures, supported by flimsy rhetoric about civilizing people, which could not be defended with reasoned, conscionable arguments.[9]

The indirect rule system was not restricted to Nigeria, and it was applied by other colonizing powers.[10] The Portuguese adopted it in Mozambique and Angola, the French applied it in Tunisia and Algeria, the Belgians used it in Burundi and Rwanda, and the Dutch brought the system to the East Indies.[11] In these regions, native administrations often took on an advisory role that subjected them to the dictates and absolutism of colonial governments.[12] Although the full complexities of the indirect rule system were conceptually developed in Nigeria and West Africa with the involvement of Lord Lugard, the British colonial administration had previously applied it in other colonies.[13] From 1757, British dominance in the Indian subcontinent consisting of Pakistan, Burma, and Bangladesh involved direct and indirect rule, especially in India, which lasted until India's independence in 1947.[14] In Nigeria, Lugard introduced policies and regulations that formed a corpus of requirements for the operation of indirect rule.[15]

Lugard defended this system as a necessity, especially in territories where decentralized states needed continuity in governing large expanses of land. However, he emphasized that it was not the system that was important, but how it was applied. Despite its different applications, each component needed

---

[7] Lord Lugard, *The Dual Mandate in British Tropical Africa* (United Kingdom: Frank Cass Publishers, 1965); and Barbara Harlow and Mia Carter, *Imperialism and Orientalism: A Documentary Sourcebook* (Massachusetts: Blackwell Publishers, 1999).
[8] David E. Apter, *Ghana in Transition* (Princeton: Princeton University Press, 2015), 119–130.
[9] Aimé Césaire, *Discourse on Colonialism*. Trans. Joan Pinkham (New York: Monthly Review Press, 1972).
[10] Michael Crowder, "Indirect Rule: French and British Style," *Africa: Journal of the International African Institute* 34, no. 3 (1964): 197–205.
[11] Mieke van der Linden, *The Acquisition of Africa (1870–1914): The Nature of International Law* (Leiden: Brill, 1987).
[12] Perham, "A Re-statement of Indirect Rule."
[13] Michael H. Fisher, *Indirect Rule in India: Residents and the Residency System, 1764–1858* (New York: Oxford University Press, 1991).
[14] Lakshmi Iyer, "Direct versus Indirect Colonial Rule in India: Long-Term Consequences," *The Review of Economics and Statistics* 92, no. 4 (2010): 693–713.
[15] Perham, "A Re-statement of Indirect Rule."

to reference the central system.[16] Lugard developed three concepts that formed the elements of the indirect rule system – decentralization, cooperation, and continuity – and he argued for their existence in the colony's administration.[17] His book later became a guide for applying the indirect rule system.[18] He stated:

> If continuity and decentralization are, as I have said, the first and most important conditions in maintaining an effective administration, cooperation is the keynote of success in its application-continuous co-operation between every link in the chain, from the head of the administration to its most junior member, co-operation between the Government and the commercial community, and, above all, between the provincial staff and the native rulers. Every individual adds their share not only to the accomplishment of the ideal but to the ideal itself. Its principles are fashioned by his quota of experience; its results are achieved by his patient and loyal application of these principles, with as little interference as possible with native customs and modes of thought.[19]

Lugard's strategy required a decentralized government that remained supported by a solid, fortified central government that allowed African officials and institutions to function. Powers were delegated to Native Chiefs and Warrant Chiefs across the colony. The system also required cooperation between the native administration and the colonial government, due to the nature of societies before colonialism.[20] Direct rule involved the creation and maintenance of a chain of cooperative authorities as everyone's relevance was necessary. If this system was successful, which is an argument made mostly by apologists of British dominance, the success was due to the cooperative relationships established with native authorities. Nigerians were more inclined to obey their native rulers, which supported the continuity of native authorities. The powers of local leaders were considered to be unquestionable. Nigerians (Yoruba people, in this case) interestingly referred to their native kings as *Kabiyesi*, loosely translated to mean "questioning you is not an option."

Indirect Rule in Practice

Nigerians believed in their pre-existing systems of government, and indirect rule exploited existing power structures to encourage compliance. To understand the mechanisms and practice of indirect rule, it is vital to understand the

---

[16] Lugard, *The Dual Mandate*.
[17] Lugard, *The Dual Mandate*, 113.
[18] Lugard, *The Dual Mandate*.
[19] Lugard, *The Dual Mandate*.
[20] Umar Bello, "Colonial Essentialism in Lord Lugard's 'The Dual Mandate,' a Critical Textual Analysis," *Advances in Social Sciences Research Journal* 4, no. 6 (2017): 73–90.

influence of the native authorities. The history and the make-up of administrative powers in Nigerian states have anachronistically been described as precolonial, and they have received relatively little analytical inspection. Native systems in Nigeria passed through different stages, dating back to the earliest discovered evidence of their existence in about 9000 BC that was found in southern Nigeria's rocky Iwo Eleru.[21] Some of these states, empires, caliphates, and kingdoms employed administrative systems that could rival the strength of many European systems. In precolonial Nigeria, these centralized and decentralized administrative structures existed in different states across the country.

Despite the claims that precolonial eastern Nigerian societies were "stateless,"[22] they existed as distributed fragments of decentralized states. The extant structures were different from Western norms in that there was no distinct head or centralized governing body. The highest authorities in these decentralized societies were most likely the leaders of village groups. A typical example is the Igbo society, which was based on a patrilineal age-group system where elders and other age-based groups divided up responsibilities for the peaceful functioning of society.[23] Village assemblies also existed, wherein members of society could address issues and contribute to matters that required their attention.

Direct democracy was moderately effective at caring for every member of society within these small groups. Despite the prevalence of autonomous societal orientation within the scattered Igbo states, their customs, cultures, languages, and economic systems were similar.[24] Societies like the Ibibio, Isoko, Tiv, and Urhobo operated comparable systems in the south-south region of Nigeria. Scholars have asserted that this system formed the foundation of many other political structures in the country, including its centralized systems, and it has been posited that centralized systems initially arise from decentralized systems.[25] Centralized states and empires also existed before the advent of colonialism in Nigeria.[26] Some widely renowned examples include

---

[21] Philip Allsworth-Jones, Katerina Harvati, and Christopher Stringer, "Archaeological Context of the Iwo Eleru Cranium from Nigeria and Preliminary Results of New Morphometric Studies," in *West African Archaeology: New Developments, New Perspectives*, ed. Philip Allsworth-Jones (Oxford: Archaeopress, 2010), 29–42.

[22] Robin Horton, "Stateless Societies in the History of West Africa," in *History of West Africa*, Vol. 1, ed. Jacob F. A. Ajayi and Michael Crowder (London: Longman, 1971), 72–81.

[23] John Middleton and David Tait, eds., *Tribes without Rulers: Studies in African Segmentary Systems* (London: Routledge & Kegan Paul, 1958).

[24] Daryll Forde and G. I. Jones, *The Ibo and Ibibio Speaking Peoples of Southeastern Nigeria* (London: Oxford University Press, 1950).

[25] Toyin Falola and Mathew M. Heaton, *A History of Nigeria* (Cambridge: Cambridge University Press, 2008).

[26] Joseph A. Atanda, *Political Systems of Nigerian Peoples up to 1900* (Ibadan: John Archers Publishers Limited, 2006), 4–16.

the Oyo, Kanem-Borno, Hausaland, Kwararafa, Benin, and other kingdoms that had been annihilated or conquered by them.[27] These centralized states were run by individual leaders who wielded ultimate political authority, and their roles were largely hereditary. Although executive, legislative, and judiciary powers were centralized, some provincial appointees or chiefs were also appointed to regional leadership positions. These roles could also be determined through hereditary lines. This system developed additional complexities over time. In Hausa societies, the monarchical system was overthrown during the jihad.[28] This was replaced by an Islamic-based system of government that followed Shari'a laws under Islamic tenets.[29] As Nigerian societies became more complex and politically powerful, it became more difficult to remove them. These societies had grown so influential that colonialism would be unable to eradicate them. Some examples include the Sokoto Caliphate, the Oyo Empire, and acephalous Igbo societies.

The Sokoto Caliphate began as a small, centralized empire.[30] The spread of Islam assisted with the caliphate's expansion, and support from Usman dan Fodio further strengthened its position. The caliph became a religious and political leader, appointed by the consent of the people, which resembled the office of Emperor Pontifex Maximus in Rome.[31] Some emirs served the caliph as regional heads, but they depended on the religious and political supremacy of the caliph's office. The caliphate was strong enough to demand military support from the emirs whenever the need arose, which was the case with the invasions of Borno and Eastern Kano.[32] Emirs were also expected to rule based on the principles of Islam, upholding Islamic beliefs and practices. Many of them were accused of corruption, like the Hausa leaders and kings before the jihad.[33] The caliphate's administration ran smoothly throughout its territory. It was respected for its taxation system and its economic activity, which flourished during this period.[34] The caliphate's Shari'a legal system gained

---

[27] Joseph A. Atanda, "Government of Yorubaland in the Pre-colonial Period," *Tarikh* 4, no. 2 (1971): 1–12.

[28] S. A. Albasu, "The Jihad in Hausaland and the Kano Fulani," *Nigeria Magazine* 53, no. 1 (1985): 52–54.

[29] Ehiedu E. G. Iweriebor, "State Systems in Pre-colonial, Colonial and Post-Colonial Nigeria: An Overview," *Africa: Rivista Trimestrale Di Studi e Documentazione Dell'Istituto Italiano per l'Africa e l'Oriente* 37, no. 4 (1982): 507–513.

[30] Murray Last, *The Sokoto Caliphate* (London: Longmans, Green and Co. Ltd., 1967).

[31] Joseph R. Strayer, "The State and Religion: Greece and Roine, the West, Islam," in *The Decline of Empires*, ed. S. N. Eisenstadt (Englewood Cliffs: Prentice-Hall, 1967), 129.

[32] Rowland A. Adeleye, *Power and Diplomacy in Northern Nigeria, 1804–1906: The Sokoto Caliphate and Its Enemies* (New York: Humanities Press, 1971.)

[33] Sa'ad Abubakar, "The Emirate-Type of Government in the Sokoto Caliphate," *Journal of the Historical Society of Nigeria* 7, no. 2 (1974): 211–229.

[34] Sule A. Gusau, "Economic Ideas of Shehu Usman dan Fodio," *Journal Institute of Muslim Minority Affairs* 10, no. 1 (1989): 139–151.

support in the region, and this native system spread throughout the Northern societies.[35]

The Oyo Empire was another large political authority, and its society practiced a form of constitutional monarchy.[36] Nigeria was familiar with democratic practices, and they were even present among the acephalous communities of the Igbo. It is difficult to claim that Europeans brought democracy to Nigeria. As Claude Ake noted, "You cannot be a colonizer and a democrat."[37] The Oyo Empire was one of West Africa's largest empires, and it began to draw attention during the sixteenth century, around the time that the Moroccans broke up the Songhai Empire.[38] Around 1698, the Oyo Empire became more expansive than other Yoruba kingdoms.[39] It had different tributaries and provinces, including the Nupe and the Bariba. Its authority was exercised by the *Ajele* (resident representatives) who served in these regions, and they ensured that tributes were paid to the central government in Oyo-Ile.[40] Oyo's military strength was almost at its peak, which fortified the supremacy of its supreme leader, the Alaafin.[41]

The Oyo Empire ruled over thirteen large polities and additional smaller ones.[42] Democratic principles were present in the way that the Alaafin was chosen. The ruler was appointed by the Oyo Mesi council, and certain actions could not be taken without their approval.[43] Prominent figures, such as Basorun Gaa, demonstrated how the Alaafin's power could be limited through a system of checks and balances.[44] Before the advent of colonialism, the Yoruba political systems were self-sustaining. However, the empire suffered from a dramatic loss of influence at the end of the eighteenth century and the beginning of the nineteenth century.[45] The political mistakes of Alaafin Awole cost him his life and led to the empire's gradual demise.

---

[35] Mukhtar U. Bunza, "The Application of Islamic Law and the Legacies of Good Governance in the Sokoto Caliphate, Nigeria (1804–1903): Lessons for the Contemporary Period," *EJIMEL* 1 (2013): 84–101.

[36] Yunusa K. Salami, "The Democratic Structure of Yoruba Political-Cultural Heritage," *The Journal of Pan African Studies* 1, no. 6 (2006): 67–78.

[37] Claude Ake, *Revolutionary Pressures in Africa* (London: Zed Press, 1978), 86.

[38] Robin Law, "A West African Cavalry State: The Kingdom of Oyo," *The Journal of African History* 16, no. 1 (1975): 1–15.

[39] Samuel Johnson, *The History of the Yorubas from the Earliest Times to the Beginning of the British Protectorate* (Lagos: CSS Press, 1921).

[40] Bolanle Awe, "The Ajele System: A Study of Ibadan Imperialism in the Nineteenth Century," *Journal of the Historical Society of Nigeria* 3, no. 1 (1964): 47–60.

[41] Isaac A. Akinjogbin, "The Oyo Empire in the 18th Century – A Reassessment," *Journal of the Historical Society of Nigeria* 3, no. 3 (1966): 449–460.

[42] Isaac A. Akinjogbin, *Dahomey and its Neighbours 1708–1818* (Cambridge: Cambridge University Press, 1967), 3.

[43] Salami, "The Democratic Structure of Yoruba," 72.

[44] Salami, "The Democratic Structure of Yoruba," 72.

[45] Joseph A. Atanda, "The Fall of the Old Oyọ Empire: A Re-consideration of Its Cause," *Journal of the Historical Society of Nigeria* 5, no. 4 (1971): 477–490.

The same strengths seen in the Sokoto Caliphate's centralized system were present in other centralized states outside of the Oyo Empire. These entities had developed sustainable and robust systems independently, over hundreds of years. This was also the case with the acephalous Igbo societies, which employed stable, decentralized systems that lasted for many years. The political systems of precolonial Igbo society were regarded as less complex than those of the Sokoto Caliphate and the Oyo Empire. Society was primarily divided into age-based groups, but it also acknowledged individual achievements.[46] Without a king or monarch, the largest and most influential political structure was the village group.[47] The most basic groups were organized around families. Governmental powers were exercised by the Oha-na-Eze, the head of the village's council of elders, who presided over family structures and led age-based groups along with the Umuada. Some scholars have categorized Igbo levels of government as the family, the extended families, the village, and the town, ordered by increasing importance.[48] Women participated in the decision-making processes of these societies through different women's assemblies and other groups. Many scholars have cited this system as a reason to consider precolonial Igbo societies to be dual-sex societies.[49]

Village administration consisted of Ofo titleholders from the villages' founding families; these individuals were referred to as "elders." Diversified, age-based groups performed many functions. These included the implementation of policies, economic activity, construction, and military service.[50] Igbo society was a reflection of the direct democracy exhibited in early forms of democratic systems. Decisions were reached by consensus, and every part of society was represented. Individuals were recognized for significant accomplishments, which was frequently done by bestowing the Ozo title.[51] These titleholders had the right to convene and lead meetings to discuss important village matters.

In Igbo society, judicial responsibilities normally resided with family heads. More serious issues would be discussed by either the Amala or the Council of

---

[46] Emmanuel C. Onyeozili and Obi N. I. Ebbe, "Social Control in Precolonial Igboland of Nigeria," *African Journal of Criminology and Justice Studies* 6, no. 1&2 (2012): 40.

[47] Godfrey N. Uzoigwe, "Evolution and Relevance of Autonomous Communities in Precolonial Igboland," *Journal of Third World Studies* 21, no. 1 (2004): 139–150.

[48] Jonah Onuoha and Tochukwu J. Omenma, "The Seniority Ideology and Governance in Igbo Culture," *Ikenga International Journal of African Studies* 9, no. 1&2 (2007): 145–153.

[49] Kamene Okonjo, "The Dual-Sex Political System in Operation: Igbo Women and Community Politics in Midwestern Nigeria," in *Women in Africa: Studies in Social and Economic Cange*, ed. Nancy J. Hafkin and Edna G. Bay (Stanford: Stanford University Press, 1976), 45–58.

[50] Ikpechukwuka E. Ibenekwu, "Igbo Traditional Political System and the Crisis of Governance in Nigeria," *Ikoro: Journal of the Institute of African Studies* 9 (2010): 3–10.

[51] Innocent O. Nweke, "Ozo Title Institution in Igboland in Relation to Politics in Nigeria: A Comparative Analysis," *OGIRISI: A New Journal of African Studies* 15, no. 1 (2019): 96–108.

Elders, depending on the situation. There was a strong belief that gods like Ala would administer justice for issues such as homicides and abnormal births. Every group held judicial, executive, and legislative power over their areas of focus. The collective participation in their society's governance encouraged relative peace and tranquility. These functional systems explain why the colonial government contemplated the native question and attempted to resolve it with an indirect rule system. The strength of extant native authorities, their systems, and local institutions were well established. These unquestionable and indispensable mechanisms of governance posed a threat to the establishment of British rule. Instead of taking an assimilative approach, the colonial administration adopted an associative system to control the territory comprising modern-day Nigeria.

Indirect Rule Applied

The four West African colonies – Gambia, Sierra Leone, Gold Coast, and Nigeria – were ruled as "Crown colonies" that were administered by a governor, under the appointment of the Crown, with the Royal Order in Council. The governor served with an executive council and an advisory legislative council for the colony's day-to-day administration. The governor's supremacy and authority were often backed by a Letter Patent or Royal Instruction that grant the authority to lead the British colony.[52]

Nigeria's colonization process had begun with the agreement between Akitoye, the deposed Oba of Lagos, and Britain's John Beecroft. As explained in earlier chapters, this led to the overthrow of Oba Kosoko, who supported the practice of slavery. Akitoye sought to regain power, and Beecroft was working to extend British dominance and end the formal practice of slavery. Their mutual interests created the Lagos Treaty of Cession in 1861, which proclaimed that Lagos was a Crown Colony.[53]

The processes for the direct control of Nigeria began in 1897 when the rules and guidelines used to govern Nigeria were created by the Niger Committee, headed by the Earl of Selborne.[54] Lord Lugard was appointed to serve a six-year term at the High Commission of the Northern Nigeria Protectorate. Based on the recommendation of the Niger Committee, the Colony of Lagos and the Southern Protectorate were amalgamated on May 1, 1906. By 1913, after Lugard returned from a posting as Governor of Hong Kong, he recommended the amalgamation

---

[52] K. A. Korsah, "Indirect Rule – A Means to an End," *African Affairs* 43, no. 173 (1944): 177–82.
[53] Giles D. Short, "Blood and Treasure: The Reduction of Lagos, 1851," *ANU Historical Journal* 13 (1977): 11–19.
[54] John M. Carland, *The Colonial Office and Nigeria, 1898–1914* (Stanford: Hoover Institution Press, 1985), 2–5.

of the Northern and Southern Protectorates under the central administration of the Governor-General. This recommendation was approved in 1914.[55]

The campaign to bring "civilization" to Africans and teach them proper governance was not immediately implemented across the entire region now known as Nigeria. The many kingdoms that existed before colonialism had built strong regional spheres of influence through different methods, and each community needed to be addressed in its own right. The general principle of the indirect rule system should be considered, along with how it was gradually introduced to these regions.

In northern Nigeria, the British administration encountered difficulties implementing indirect rule due to the local belief that non-Muslims held no authority as rulers. The North was largely taken by conquest, and new emirs were appointed by Lugard afterward. It was difficult to govern an aggrieved and conquered population.[56] The indirect rule system in the North became a system of "pacification" or "tension management."[57] Lugard's appointment in 1899 to hold authority over the Northern Protectorate was largely because of his bravery and military experience. His role as High Commissioner was regarded as more of a military assignment.[58] He disregarded the Niger Committee's advice to merge the Northern region under "Sudan Province," deciding instead to separate them into five provinces that were grouped into two units. The "civil province" consisted of Benue, Middle-Niger, and Kano, while the "military province" had Borgu and Borno. Provinces were classified based on the extent of the British administration's influence in the area.

Six stable officers were recruited to assist Lugard with his administration. William Wallace headed the Middle-Niger Province, with the assistance of Dr. D. W. Carnegie and H. Cummings. W. P. Hewby and Major A. Burdon were in charge of the Benue Province. Lt. Col. G. V. Kemball was assigned to head the "military province." Colonial administration in the region was tenuous because the local population only recognized the authority of the Sokoto Caliphate.[59] The vast expanse of the Northern region led William Wallace to make a formal complaint that resulted in the creation of more provinces; British Residents were expected to supervise large amounts of territory.[60] Seven additional provinces were created, and sixteen existed by 1904.

---

[55] Johnson U. J. Asiegbu, *Nigeria and Its British Invaders, 1851–1920: A Thematic Documentary History* (New York: NOK Publishers International, 1984), xxxi.

[56] Obaro Ikime, "The Establishment of Indirect Rule in Northern Nigeria," *Tarikh* 3, no. 3 (1971): 1–15.

[57] Wilbert E Moore, *Social Change* (Englewood Cliffs: Prentice–Hall, 1963), 10–11 and 70–84.

[58] Z. O. Apata, "Lugard and the Creation of Provincial Administration Northern Nigeria 1900 – 1918," *Transafrican Journal of History* 21 (1992): 111–123.

[59] Apata, "Lugard and the Creation of Provincial Administration."

[60] Colonial Office Record 446/1 1898.

Northern rulers were initially treated respectfully, with the colonial government serving as advisers. Some have claimed that the advent of colonial authority initially provided more powers to the Native Administrators by reducing the authority of existing bodies that had served as checks and balances. Under the indirect rule system, the authority of the emirs was only challenged when it was considered to be necessary and appropriate.[61] Despite this deferential approach, it never represented the true nature and intent of the British administration. Northern protectorates had been conquered forcefully, and the administration had deposed the existing leaders of the Sokoto Caliphate. No native authority retained independent powers since their offices would be conferred by the British administration, which held supreme authority.[62] Lugard made this clear in an address to the new heads of Sokoto, including its new sultan.[63] The emirs were to consider their powers as being held in trust for the British state, and they would be subject to the preferences and instructions of the governor and his subordinates.[64]

When imposing the indirect rule system on Northern Nigeria, the colonial administrator retained the emirate system and discarded the caliphate system. After the appointment of Muhammad Attahiru II, following the seizure of the caliphate, the sultan no longer held the power to appoint emirs of other emirates. The emirs would never again be subordinate to the sultan's authority, and Sokoto itself was reduced to a mere emirate. The councils of the sultan and those of the emirs, like the Majalisar Sarki, continued to be weakened. Their authority went unrecognized after the conquest of the Sokoto Caliphate.[65] All the sultans' councilors, like *Magajin Rafi*, *Magajin Gari*, *Ubandoma*, and *Geladima*, became district heads. All of them were sent from the capital to their new districts, except for the *Waziri*, who was considered administratively relevant as the most senior council member. This led to the erosion of societal institutions that had depended on counselors.

The Native Authority Ordinance of 1916 gave the emir the right to appoint his council officials to assist with the dispensation of his duties, but it was

---

[61] Lewis H. Gann and Peter Duignan, eds., *Colonialism in Africa, 1870–1960: The History and Politics of Colonialism, 1914–1960*, Vol. 2 (Cambridge: Cambridge University Press, 1970).

[62] Peter K. Tibenderana, "The Irony of Indirect Rule in Sokoto Emirate, Nigeria, 1903–1944," *African Studies Review* 31, no. 1 (1988): 67–92.

[63] Anthony H. M. Kirk-Greene and Margery Perham, *The Principles of Native Administration in Nigeria: Selected Documents, 1900–1947* (London: Oxford University Press, 1965).

[64] Frederick D. Lugard, *Political Memoranda Revision of Instructions to Political Officers on Subjects Chiefly Political and Administrative*, 2nd ed. (London: Frank Cass and Company, Ltd. 1970).

[65] Peter Kazenga Tibenderana, "The Administration of Sokoto, Gwandu and Argungu Emirates under British Rule, 1900–1946," unpublished PhD dissertation, University of Ibadan, 1974.

largely superficial.[66] In practice, they held no such power. Lugard had clearly stated that the power to appoint any chief belonged to the governor and the British administration. The British appointment of officials meant additional control over the emir.

The indirect rule system also affected the judicial system of the Northern Protectorate. The sultan headed the judicial council and applied principles from the Qur'an. However, his authority only extended to matters that were not documented in Shari'a law.[67] Alkali judges supplemented these decisions by exercising powers that the sultan had delegated. However, the Native Court Proclamation of 1906 and the Native Court Ordinance of 1914 concentrated judicial powers in the hands of the British Colonial Administration.[68] British Residents became responsible for appointing Alkali judges to the Native Courts. The decisions of customary and Shari'a courts were amended by British administrators, and all rulings were expected to align with the principles of natural justice and public policy. Although the sultan served as president of the Sokoto Judicial Council, British Residents held greater judicial powers. They could transfer cases from Native Courts to Provincial Courts and carry out appellate functions. Residents could use the rationalizations of transparency and unadulterated justice to suspend or dismiss any Alkali judge who violated administrative rules.[69]

Pre-existing taxation systems in the Sokoto Caliphate and other emirates made it easier for the British to collect revenue. Native authorities held some relevance for revenue and expenditure in the emirates. They were entitled to 60 percent of the total revenue generated from local government, and the remaining 40 percent was submitted to the central authority. Native authorities did not enjoy financial independence since they had to acquire the colonial administrator's approval before undertaking development projects, and they were subject to oversight from the central government.[70] After the 1912 establishment of the Baituma Native Treasury, the sultan's control over the treasury was diminished.[71] British Residents prepared the budget and assumed a more direct role in finances.

British officials also applied the indirect rule system in Oyo and other Yoruba territories in Western Nigeria.[72] Native Chiefs held authority within their territories, but only under British oversight. The system was adopted in

---

[66] Raymond L. Buell, *The Native Problem in Africa* (New York: The Macmillan Company, 1928).

[67] Noel James Coulson, *A History of Islamic Law* (London: Routledge, 2017).

[68] Takehiko Ochiai, "The Application of Sharia and the Evolution of the Native Court System in Colonial Northern Nigeria (1900–1960)," *Asian Journal of African Studies* 49 (2020): 77–110.

[69] D. Kingdom, ed., *The Laws of Nigeria* (Lagos: Government Printers, 1923).

[70] Michael Crowder and Obaro Ikime, eds., *West African Chiefs: Their Changing Status under Colonial Rule and Independence* (Ile-Ife: University of Ife Press, 1970).

[71] Peter K. Tibenderana, "The Irony of Indirect Rule in Sokoto Emirate, Nigeria, 1903–1944," *African Studies Review* 31, no. 1 (1988): 67–92.

[72] Joseph A. Atanda, "Indirect Rule in Yorubaland," *Tarikh* 3, no. 3 (1970): 16–28.

Western Nigeria and the Oyo Empire under circumstances that were similar to those of Northern Nigeria. The British Empire's lack of personnel and its difficulties in governing a conquered people increased the system's attractiveness and served as one-sided justifications for its adoption. The system appealed to Major Henry E. McCallum, appointed Governor of Lagos in 1897, largely due to his experience in Asia.[73]

The earliest reflection and manifestation of indirect rule in Yorubaland was the operation of the Council of Chiefs, which consisted of the British Resident, serving as president, and about twelve other chiefs, including the *Baales* and the *Balogun*, *Otun*, and *Osi*. Oyo's Council of Chiefs was also led by the Resident, and it included the Alaafin and seven of his chiefs, possibly the most revered Oyomesi. Ibadan Council's jurisdiction extended to the Ife–Ilesha division, and the Oyo Council predominantly governed Oyo. Its establishment extended northeast of Yorubaland, into the Ilesha and Ekiti provinces, with councils of chiefs that were established in 1900. The *Owa* of Ilesa served with his chiefs, and fifteen top-tier kings were members of the council on the Ekiti side. These councils initially performed all the duties of the executive, judiciary, and legislative branches.[74]

Atanda has observed that indirect rule's development in Yorubaland underwent additional changes.[75] Sir William MacGregor observed that the inclusion of a British official in their council was belittling for the chiefs, and he was concerned that it might undermine their authority. The native authorities were given additional powers as a result of these concerns. The Native Councils Ordinance of 1901 established similar councils in villages and towns that had the structures to support them. The Alaafin was also allowed to install chiefs and kings that he controlled. Chiefs regained some strength and popularity, such that the increased authority that paramount chiefs held over their subjects eased the requirements of British colonial administration. However, British officials retained supervisory powers over kings, influencing their decisions without interfering too directly in court matters. These developments continued up to 1931.

In 1914, District Officer William Alston Ross repositioned the Alaafin and helped him regain his supremacy, especially in the area that had been under the old Oyo Empire. Lugard's introduction of the system followed the pattern that played out in the North. Attempts were made to consolidate the powers of the Alaafin up to Ibadan, whose office was considered to have authority over the Bale of Ibadan. Outlying regions on the outskirts of Oyo and Ibadan fell under the authority of headmen who were loyal to and under the authority of

---

[73] Joseph A. Atanda, *The New Oyo Empire: Indirect Rule and Change in Western Nigeria* (London: Longman, 1973).
[74] Atanda, *The New Oyo Empire*.
[75] Atanda, "Indirect Rule in Yorubaland."

the Alaafin.[76] In judicial matters, the Alaafin's court was considered to be primary, and courts maintained by others, such as the Bale of Ibadan, were considered secondary. The Alaafin's court was given appellate jurisdiction over courts in Ibadan, Ila, Ife, and Ilesha. This did not affect appellate jurisdiction as cases did not generally move from the lower courts to the court of the Alaafin.

In 1918, Lugard also adopted the taxation systems in Oyo and the Yoruba districts that had been predominant in the North.[77] By that time, Lugard had ensured that the institutions for native authorities, courts, and revenue collection were established in Oyo Province. Some of the precolonial systems had been excluded from these new processes. The Alaafin gained power once institutions of the Oyo Empire were no longer capable of countering his authority.

The principles of indirect rule were applied differently to suit various individuals and situations, but the acephalous societies in Nigeria, especially among the Igbo of southeastern Nigeria, did not have extant systems that could easily be exploited. These societies had independent village groups, decentralized powers, and no hereditary leadership.[78] They practiced direct democracy, emphasizing leadership through age groups and village assemblies. The exceptions were mostly trading societies, including Oguta and Onitsha,[79] along with the "holy city" of Nri.[80]

To control these societies, the British administration issued warrants to individuals who became the Warrant Chiefs presiding over Native Courts in different provinces.[81] The appointment of Warrant Chiefs was plagued by irregularities in the criteria for their selection. Sometimes they were chosen due to popularity; in other instances they were people of low social standing or those who were from different societal structures.[82] The process paid no attention to the traditions of precolonial existence. Many Warrant Chiefs could not establish their legitimacy. Some applied their powers arbitrarily, drawing authority from the British colony and its control over Native Courts and the supervision of labor.[83] The abuses and excesses of Warrant Chiefs

---

[76] Margery Perham, *Lugard: The Years of Authority, 1898–1945* (London: Collins, 1956), 445.
[77] Abiodun Afolabi, "The Colonial Taxation Policy among Yoruba of Southwestern Nigeria and Its Implications for Socio-economic Development," *Journal of the Historical Society of Nigeria* 19 (2010): 63–92.
[78] Margherita Goltzsche, *Gesellschaft und Politik bei den Ibo um 1900: die Rolle völkerkundlicher Studien als Quellen zur afrikanischen Geschichte* (Bern: Herbert Lang, 1976).
[79] Ikenna Nzimiro *Studies in Ibo Political Systems: Chieftaincy and Politics in Four Niger States* (London: Frank Cass. 1972).
[80] Adiele E. Afigbo, *Ropes of Sand: Studies in Igbo History* (Nsukka: AP Express Publishers, 1981).
[81] Adiele E. Afigbo, *The Warrant Chiefs: Indirect Rule in Southeastern Nigeria, 1891–1929* (London: Longman, 1972).
[82] Afigbo, *The Warrant Chiefs*.
[83] Walter I. Ofonagoro, "An Aspect of British Colonial Policy in Southern Nigeria: The Problems of Forced Labour and Slavery, 1895–1928," in *Studies in Southern Nigerian History*, ed. Boniface I. Obichere (London: Frank Cass, 1982), 219–243.

gradually became intolerable and resulted in the Aba Women's War, which spread through the whole of the southeast region and some Ibibio-speaking areas.[84] An uprising of women, fighting against an unfamiliar taxation system, attacked the Warrant Chiefs for disrespecting their traditions.[85]

The riots prompted the investigation of local traditional institutions in 1929. By 1930, elders and traditionally influential individuals composed councils and courts that resembled institutions from the precolonial era. However, these councils now held authority over a wider range of territory. These changes and other arbitrary decisions set off a new round of public criticism directed at colonial institutions.[86]

The requirements for joining councils gradually relaxed to favor educated elites and to adopt the "best man policy" popularly known as *Okacha Mma*.[87] Larger numbers of younger, educated individuals were recommended as members, which was the direct result of agitations from the emerging educated elites. Their nationalistic focus was redirected away from the idea of more representation within colonial structures; instead, their efforts accumulated to become pressure for full Nigerian independence.[88] As the twentieth century progressed, educated elites attained more relevance in every region, serving on different councils across all three branches of government. Educated elites also participated in different conferences and committees that promoted ideas of independence and national consciousness.[89] The relevance of traditional rulers and native authorities had begun to wane.

Resistance and Challenges

Native authorities and their associated institutions existed before colonialism, and they had become too integrated with local identities to be given up easily. The caliphates, empires, and other kingdoms of Nigeria had developed long before the British arrival, and their subjects maintained a sense of loyalty that stemmed from a sense of pride. Jaja of Opobo, Nana of Ebriohioni, Kosoko of

---

[84] Misty L. Bastian, "'Vultures of the Marketplace': Southeastern Nigeria Women and Discourses of the Ogu Umunwanyi (Women's War) of 1929," in *Women in African Colonial Histories*, ed. Jean Allman, Susan Geiger, and Nakanyike Musisi (Bloomington: Indiana University Press, 2002), 260–281.

[85] Judith Van Allen, "'Sitting on a Man': Colonialism and the Lost Political Institutions of Igbo Women," *Canadian Journal of African Studies/La Revue canadienne des études africaines* 6, no. 2 (1972): 165–181.

[86] Afigbo, *Ropes of Sand*.

[87] Chinedu N. Ubah, "Changing Patterns of Leadership among the Igbo, 1900–1960," *Transafrican Journal of History* 16 (1987):167–184.

[88] Robert D. Pearce, *The Turning Point in Africa: British Colonial Policy 1938–48* (London: Frank Cass, 1982).

[89] Olisanwuche P. Esedebe, "The Educated Elite in Nigeria Reconsidered," *Journal of the Historical Society of Nigeria* 10, no. 3 (1980): 111–130.

Lagos, and others resisted the British invasion directly. Other groups and individuals maintained their resistance after the imposition of indirect rule. The British administration seized various parts of Nigeria through diplomacy and conquest. However, the Egba enjoyed freedom and limited independence from the British colony due to their 1893 Treaty of Friendship and Commerce.[90] The Alake of Egbaland became head of the Egba region, wielding authority over the Owu and other groups who became part of the Egba United Government.[91] However, disputes arose over Alake's actions and the conduct of his assistant, Mr. Edun. A departure from traditional approaches to taxation sparked civil unrest among the Ijemo, which led the British government to exert more authority over the Egba and abrogate the 1893 treaty.

The Egba people were familiar with the concept of taxation, but direct taxation was imposed at a time when people were already upset by the application of the indirect rule system and the Alake's newly defined powers through the Egba United Government. Residents also objected to compulsory labor policies, and the unrest culminated in the Adubi Uprising of 1918 after the British government had introduced 5 percent and 2/6 taxation rates on men and women, respectively.[92] In addition to taxes, the British administration demanded free labor to construct roads and other infrastructure, which left people with little time to focus on their enterprises. The situation deteriorated into open revolt and, as the labor situation worsened, people went hungry and failure to comply risked fines and imprisonment. These objections could not be resolved through judicial means, because the Native Courts were filled with unprofessional and incompetent staff.

Adubi, a leader of the Abule-Owu, demonstrated his frustration with forced labor, the unfamiliar taxation system, and the biased, unprofessional Native Courts that issued arbitrary and unjust fines. He encouraged resistance against the British administration, their indirect rule system, and the Alake, who was seen as an agent of the British.[93] These sentiments were shared by the people of Egbaland and the Eleri farmers of Itori. Adubi led them in a collective protest against the British government, which responded with violence and additional restrictions.[94] Resistance did not stop at the borders of Egbaland, as serious incidents occurred elsewhere too, including Ilorin, which mounted strenuous resistance against the indirect rule system.[95]

---

[90] Tekena N. Tamuno, *The Evolution of the Nigerian State: The Southern Phase, 1898–1914* (London: Longman, 1972), 353.
[91] Tamuno, *The Evolution of the Nigerian State*.
[92] NAI. CSO 26/3, File no. 21790, Assessment Report, Imala District, Abeokuta Province. 4th of January 1928–2nd of March 1928.
[93] NAI. C. 92/1918. Appointment of Commission of Enquiry into the Abeokuta Disturbances–Re. P. 91.
[94] Commission of Enquiry Report called him Adubi of Eleri.
[95] Bashir O. Ibrahim, "Agitation and Protest against the British Colonial Policies in Ilorin 1923–1936," *Alore: Ilorin Journal of the Humanities* 13 (2003): 142–154.

Precolonial Ilorin was controlled by the Sokoto Caliphate and ruled by the Emir.[96] Different councils existed to govern the affairs of the Ilorin people, which included the Council of the Ulama, the Council of the Emir, the Daudu's Council, and the Balogun's Council. The Emir headed the main council, followed by the Balogun, the Magaji Geri, and the Chief Imam of Ilorin. These groups performed legislative and executive functions. Under the indirect rule system, they supported British dominance, unusual policies, and increasing taxation. The British administration initially supported Emir Sulayman, who welcomed an indirect rule system that positioned him above his subordinate chiefs. This gave the Emir a sense of freedom from the Balogun Agba, who held a powerful office and was considered to have been instrumental in the Emir's installation.[97] The Emir's new powers allowed for the appointment of district heads that were expected to report to the British Resident in charge of the province. The power dynamics between the Emir and the colonial authority had eroded the office of the Balogun, and these individuals noted their pronounced lack of respect under the new system. The riot of 1907 was linked to Balogun Inakoju Ali, who was deposed and fled to Jebba, later ending up in Lokoja. His exile encouraged an enduring sense of dissatisfaction that lingered in the minds of the public.[98]

Taxation under the colonial administration also emerged as a concern for the Ilorin people. They had grown accustomed to a taxation system that allowed them to pay taxes with agricultural products and to determine their own schedule of payments. British Residents widened the scope of taxation after they were charged with the duty of tax and tribute assessment. The implementation of licenses caused additional friction, especially for brewers, servers, and sellers of alcohol. Hunters were particularly upset by the new licensing policies because they were charged multiple times and were required to hold different licenses due to the diversification of trade.[99] Hunters and farmers organized protests in Ilorin, which were met with force; around twenty people were estimated to have been killed.[100] Other hunters and farmers elsewhere in the emirate joined in the protest.

The 1907 agitations continued despite the British administration's show of force. The Emir was granted additional authority, and subordinates like the Babakekere became inordinately powerful due to support from the Emir and the colonial administration. They began abusing judicial powers and engaging in corrupt practices. People grew frustrated with the Emir's habit of appointing

---

[96] C. O. O. Agboola, "The Jihad and the Islamization Ideal: A Reconsideration of the Case of Ilorin Emirate, c. 1823–1900," *Global Journal of Humanities* 6, no. 1&2 (2007): 45–49.

[97] Rowland A. Adeleye, *Power and Diplomacy in Northern Nigeria, 1804–1906: The Sokoto Caliphate and Its Enemies* (London: Longman, 1971), 219.

[98] Adeleye, *Power and Diplomacy in Northern Nigeria*, 219.

[99] Obaro Ikime, "The British and Native Administration Finance in Northern Nigeria, 1900–1934," *Journal of the Historical Society of Nigeria* 7, no. 4 (1975): 673–692.

[100] Ibrahim, "Agitation and Protest against the British."

relatives to important government roles, and they objected to increasing taxes that they could not afford to pay. Mallams from Oke-Imole organized a demonstration after their opposition to tax increases went unheard. The British Resident attempted to resolve this by requesting a formal complaint through the Emir, which caused another demonstration. Although the series of demonstrations persisted, reaching a crescendo in 1913, it was diplomatically resolved following intervention on both sides.[101]

Other actions that opposed indirect rule came from regions in Eastern Nigeria dominated by the Igbo. The Igbo and the Ibibio had difficulties adjusting to indirect rule, and its imposition was harsh and unforgiving. The majority of British policies were incomprehensible to them, and they considered their systems to have been perfected before the advent of colonial administration. British officials committed a series of missteps in Eastern Nigeria. They burned any villages that attempted to resist their authority. Village heads, who also functioned as spiritual leaders within their communities, were openly disrespected. Local shrines were desecrated and destroyed. One example was the Aro expedition of 1901–2, which destroyed the ancient sacred site of Aro Chukwu. Ongoing disrespect for local traditions was met with anger and discontent.[102]

After many such atrocities, colonial officials introduced the alien concept of Warrant Chiefs, which was a direct contradiction of acephalous local customs and traditions. Warrant Chiefs ran Native Courts according to their whims, and many villages that had previously been independent were now merged under the new system.[103] Even though their authority was questioned, these Warrant Chiefs appointed headmen who acted as their agents to assess taxes. The Aba Women's War is one of the most notable responses to the Warrant Chiefs and their headmen. Okuego, the Warrant Chief, had sent Mark Emereuwa to conduct a census for the proper assessment of taxes. While carrying out his duties, Emereuwa arrived at the residence of Nwanyereuwa and asked for a count of her livestock and the number of people who resided with her. An angry Nwanyereuwa realized that everything counted would be taxed.[104] She doused Emereuwa with palm oil and demanded to know whether his grandmother had been counted. Nwanyereuwa gathered other women for her cause, and their protests spread across the Eastern Region, including the Ibibio.[105]

---

[101] E. Torday, "Gazetteer of Ilorin Province. Compiled by the Hon. H. B. Hermon Hodge, George Allen & Unwin, Ltd. pp. 301 and map. 21," *Africa* 3, no. 3 (1930): 378–378.

[102] Adiele E. Afigbo, "Revolution and Reaction in Eastern Nigeria: 1900–1929 (The Background to the Women's Riot of 1929)," *Journal of the Historical Society of Nigeria* 3, no. 3 (1966): 539–557.

[103] Afigbo, *The Warrant Chiefs*.

[104] Afigbo, *The Warrant Chiefs*.

[105] Caroline Ifeka-Moller, "Female Militancy and Colonial Revolt: The Women's War of 1929, Eastern Nigeria," in *Perceiving Women*, ed. Shirley Ardener (New York: John Wiley and Sons, Inc., 1975), 127–157.

Consequences and Reforms

The imposition of indirect rule in Nigeria was a paradigm shift, abandoning collaborative native establishments to implement a hierarchical structure led by colonial officials. In the new administrative era, many traditional, cultural, and historical values were disrespected or lost. The democratic structure of the Alaafin's territory was disrupted. He received unprecedented power and authority that overturned previous checks and balances within the Oyo Empire. The Oyomesi became increasingly irrelevant as they lost their authority in the Alaafin's court. The Alaafin became accountable only to colonial officials; he was free to do anything without consulting the Oyomesi. The Sultan's influence was drastically reduced. The emirates, which Usman dan Fodio's jihad had united under a single caliphate after a long period of amalgamation, disintegrated into independent parts that only answered to the British. Similar events occurred elsewhere in Nigeria, and the sole native authorities became too powerful to be challenged.

The introduction of the indirect rule system set limits on the cultural absolutism of existing monarchs and native authorities. The Alaafin had been regarded as *Alase Ikeji Orisa*, second only to the gods. The Kabiyesi, above question among the Yoruba, now needed approval from colonial officials before taking action. Both offices were now appointed by the British Governor. The British administration would later be the template for forming a government based on native authorities after independence. Under Nigeria's current chieftaincy laws, the existence and authority of these offices are subject to the will of state governors.[106] This has eroded the importance of these traditional institutions.

Indirect rule restructured laws and judicial systems within the colonies. The Colonial Law Validation Act of 1865 stated that the British Crown could make laws on behalf of its colonies by Royal Order in Council.[107] This enshrined British law as the supreme legislation under the indirect rule system. Different proclamations and ordinances defined the powers held by every governing body within the Nigerian colony, including the native authorities. Laws that had previously been implemented by local administrations were dismissed as customary, and they now needed to pass "repugnancy tests."[108] The powers of native authorities and their chiefs were diminished or transferred to the governor's councils. The Nigerian judiciary also underwent a remodeling. Native authorities were initially the heads of Native Courts, where their controversial actions generated discontent. Many native heads amassed power and abused their offices to make

---

[106] Victor Iyanya, "Traditional Rulers and Crisis of Legitimacy in the Post-colonial Nigeria: The Case of the Igede of Central Nigeria." Paper read at the ASAUK 2018 Conference, Aston Webb – Senate Chamber, University of Birmingham, September 12, 2018.

[107] Robert Watt and Francis Johns, *Concise Legal Research* (Annandale: Federation Press, 2009), 33.

[108] *Laoye v. Oyetunde* (1944) A.C 170.

arbitrary decisions. Later, their jurisdiction became customary law, and their authority was weakened or transferred to legislative bodies. The native authorities' ability to preside over criminal matters, which allowed them to impose heavy punishments at their discretion, was removed. Native authorities currently serve, at best, as ceremonial leaders without any serious authority.

The indirect rule system also encouraged the development of national consciousness and the Nigerian quest for independence. As the influence of native authorities waned in colonial Nigeria, there were more opportunities for educated elites to become involved in government. These individuals were elected to different legislative councils, where they became cogent and important parts of the colony. They developed their demands for independence after experience taught them that the British were not racially superior.[109]

It is evident that the precolonial governance systems of Nigeria, which were exploited by the indirect rule system under different native authorities, had been suited to the specific needs of different societies. These systems had developed locally. The Sultan's authority was recognized within the Sokoto Caliphate, and the egalitarian, acephalous societies of Eastern Nigeria functioned well for residents of those communities. It is essential for Nigeria's current government to study the country's past, using it to develop a system of government that accommodates Nigeria's historical development. This will support the inherent diversity of the country's citizens.

Conclusion

Nigeria's indirect rule system was not applied because the territory's established systems of governance were weak. Rather, it was imposed for the sake of administrative convenience. This fact has been established through discussions on the mode, strength, and implementation of governance across societies. The strength of local institutions meant that British officials could not completely discard Nigeria's native forms of government.

In using pre-existing systems, the indirect rule system shifted each local government's mode of operation to become subordinate units under the British colonial structure. The absolute authority of native heads was undermined as they became subject to the decisions of colonial administrators. This loss of power and influence marked the beginning of the native institutions' decline.[110] Under the current political dispensation, they hold almost none of their previous influence.

---

[109] Hamza A. Garba, Hafiz Jibril, Khalil A. Abba, and Tasiu A. Sani, "Role of Nigerian Educated Elites towards Anti-Colonial Struggle in Nigeria, 1930s–1960," *International Journal for Social Studies* 3, no. 6 (2017): 83–98.

[110] A. M. Yakubu, "The Demise of Indirect Rule in the Emirates of Northern Nigeria," in *Legitimacy and the State in Twentieth-Century Africa*, ed. Terence Ranger and Olufemi Vaughan (London: Palgrave Macmillan, 1993), 162–190.

The indirect rule system has also contributed to present-day Nigeria's different challenges and successes. Many of the contemporary practices in the country originated from the colonial period – administrative systems that impact the economy, technology, education systems, and mode of governance. Some have argued that indirect rule is the foundation of many political problems in the country. The failure to recognize Nigeria's diverse groups and societies and convert them to a workable federal system has continued to disturb the country's peace.

11

The Legal System and Law Enforcement

Previous chapters of this book provide a constellation of background details in support of this chapter's narrative. The British colonial enterprise, in Nigeria and elsewhere, was an economic and political project on an imperial scale.[1] Further components of "civilization" were added to this project, including Western education, modern infrastructure, and urbanization. Others include economic expansion, the fusion of culturally distinct polities, and the creation of modern sovereign states through the administrative decisions later known as "Imperial Priority and Empire Recovery" policies from the Colonial Office in London.[2] Before the development of these policies and their entrenchment in the colonial system, British imperial activities in the Niger area were organized around the notion of a "Pax Britannica."[3] This included ideas of white supremacy and racial hierarchy that protected the interests of British merchants, missionaries, explorers, and other actors above any "native" interests. These ideas evolved as markets in the Niger area transitioned from trade in slaves to agricultural production.

Colonial policies were significant for the evolution of states, not only in this area but in all of West Africa and elsewhere in Africa, because they altered the sociopolitical and economic landscapes of the affected polities.[4] Political and economic power in the region was steadily ceded to foreign forces, and the advent of Christianity and the spread of Christian missions influenced the social frame of these cultures.[5]

The emergence of legitimate trade initiated the effective occupation of polities in this region as Western imperial powers scrambled to control markets in the

---

[1] Tiyambe Zeleza, "The Political Economy of British Colonial Development and Welfare in Africa," *Transafrican Journal of History* 14 (1985): 139–161.
[2] Lord Lugard, *The Dual Mandate in British Tropical Africa* (New York: Routledge, 1965).
[3] François Crouzet, "Outside the Walls of Europe – The Pax Britannica," *European Review* 7, no. 4 (1999): 447–453.
[4] Anthony G. Hopkins, *An Economic History of West Africa* (New York: Routledge, 2020).
[5] Kanayo L. Nwadialor and Nwachukwu J. Obiakor, "The Gospel and the Flag: The Missionary Strands in the British Colonial Enterprise in Nigeria, 1841–1960," *Academic Journal of Interdisciplinary Studies* 4, no. 3 (2015): 249–258.

area.[6] Around three decades after the abolition of the slave trade, toward the mid-nineteenth century, it was clear to British imperial agents in the Bight of Benin and Biafra that regional economic access and expansion could only be secured with political power. As a tool, political power would serve several purposes, especially for establishing law and order in politically unstable areas. These included the Bight of Benin and Biafra, Benue-Plateau, the Sudanic region, and other parts of the Niger area in that century.[7] In 1848, about three years before the invasion of Lagos, John Beecroft was appointed as Consul-General of the newly created sphere of influence for the British government in the Bight of Benin and Biafra.[8] This primarily included the delta states of Bonny, Old and New Calabar, Warri, and others, but its administrative reach soon encompassed the coastal city of Lagos after it was invaded in 1851. British influence was further strengthened after the eventual annexation of Lagos in 1861.[9] By 1885, when the Berlin Conference concluded, the British administrative unit encompassed the larger part of the area designated as the Bight of Benin and Biafra. Its name was changed to the Oil Rivers Protectorate as a reflection of its changing scope.[10] Less than a decade later, it became the Niger Coast Protectorate. The strategic incorporation of polities in this area continued unabated, ignoring all military or diplomatic resistance from the native population.

By 1893, the whole of Yorubaland had been brought under the British Empire, excluding areas subject to imperial control through the Northern emirate system.[11] These places included Ilorin, Kabba, and northeastern Yoruba towns such as Owo and Akoko.[12] The territory became known as the Southern Protectorate in 1900, which signaled the effective occupation of

---

[6] John E. Flint, "Chartered Companies and the Scramble for Africa," in *Africa in the Nineteenth and Twentieth Centuries*, ed. Joseph C. Anene and Godfrey N. Brown (Ibadan: Ibadan University Press, 1966), 110–117; and Jacob F. A. Ajayi, ed., *General History of Africa: VI Africa in the Nineteenth Century until the 1880s* (Paris: UNESCO Publishing, 1998).

[7] Toyin Falola and Matthew M. Heaton, *A History of Nigeria* (New York: Cambridge University Press, 2008).

[8] Kenneth O. Dike, "John Beecroft, 1790–1854: Her Britannic Majesty's Consul to the Bight of Benin and Biafra, 1849–1854," *Journal of the Historical Society of Nigeria* 1, no. 1 (1956): 5–14.

[9] Robert Sydney Smith, *The Lagos Consulate, 1851–1861* (Berkeley: University of California Press, 1979).

[10] Mary Kingsley, *West African Studies* (Cambridge: Cambridge University Press, 2010), 443–566.

[11] Siyan Oyeweso and Olasiji Oshin, "British Conquest and Administration of Yoruba," in *Culture and Society in Yorubaland*, ed. Deji Ogunremi and Biodun Adediran (Ibadan: Rex Charles, 1998), 31–35.

[12] Idris Sha'aba Jimada, *The Historical Background to the Establishment of Patigi Emirate: C.1810–1898* (Zaria: Ahmadu Bello University Press, 2016).

a large expanse of land, territories, and peoples in the Niger area.[13] Given the complexity of the colonial project and the intricacies of cultural imperialism necessary to institutionalize colonial rule, the 1900 pronouncement was less effective than the 1914 amalgamation of colonial administrative units.[14]

British territories included the Southern Protectorate, the Lagos Colony (still within the southern sphere), and the Northern Protectorate.[15] The Northern Protectorate's history of colonial rule took a different course due to its position along the Sahara and its distance from ports. After the Berlin Conference, Sir George Goldie of the Royal Niger Company (RNC) received a charter to conduct trade on behalf of the British Empire in the Niger coast area.[16] The company's activities caused the steady decline of the caliphate's authority in the Northern Region, and it undermined local authorities in parts of Igboland that were beyond the influence of Lagos and the Oil Rivers government.[17] This charter was withdrawn before the area became a British colony in 1900, signaling a change in the principles and objectives driving the administration of the area. All of these processes eroded various aspects of the host societies, but primarily their structures for law and governance were weakened. The administration of justice and the attendant political morphology were quite different, for they had been carefully shaped to follow extant sociocultural formations. This chapter examines the contours of this system in the Nigerian colony.

Administration of Justice and the Legal System

Establishing law and order is an essential feature and manifestation of power and authority in a geographic area. However, law and order are concepts meant to be applied through established institutions recognized and supported by the people.[18] Public support is needed to legitimize authority and avoid the mockery of the system. That is why the administration of justice is sacrosanct:[19] It must be seen as fair by everyone, regardless of their social status in the polity.

---

[13] Joseph C. Anene, *Southern Nigeria in Transition, 1885–1906: Theory and Practice in a Colonial Protectorate* (Cambridge: Cambridge University Press, 1966).
[14] Joseph A. Atanda, *The New Oyo Empire: Indirect Rule and Change in Western Nigeria 1894–1934* (London: Longman Group Limited, 1973).
[15] Ian F. Nicolson, *The Administration of Nigeria, 1900–1960: Men, Methods and Myths* (Oxford: Clarendon Press, 1969).
[16] Barbara Harlow and Mia Carter, *Archives of Empire: Vol. 2. The Scramble for Africa* (New York: Duke University Press, 2003), 380–388.
[17] John Flint, *Sir George Goldie and the Making of Nigeria* (London: Oxford University Press, 1960).
[18] John Lea and Jock Young, *What Is to Be Done about Law and Order?* (Harmondsworth: Penguin Books, 1984).
[19] Vernon Rich, *Law and the Administration of Justice* (New York: Wiley & Sons, 1979).

Various local authorities exercised political authority in the Niger Area long before the arrival of the colonizers.[20] Monarchs and their chiefs applied power through the administration of justice, affecting local inhabitants, traders, and strangers in the polity.[21] Family heads and compound heads administered justice within their enclaves. The administration of society's justice existed in the realm of the collective.[22] Laws were drawn from local customs, history, and practices that were accessible to everyone. In these preliterate societies, the laws were reinforced in the people's minds through daily activities, festivals, rituals, apprenticeships, and other social engagements.[23] Rules and norms were collectively defined for social control, peacekeeping, and justice.[24] In the Niger area, the troubles of the nineteenth century eroded this legal system and created an opening for the British government. In the Hausa states, Kanuri, Nupe, and elsewhere, Islamic doctrine had guided the evolution of legal systems and the administration of justice.[25] By the nineteenth century, virtually every colonial administrator after Goldie found the Northern areas maintaining a sophisticated system and structure that could be adapted to suit the colonial enterprise.

Although compatible legal systems and other forms of sociopolitical organization existed in other parts of the colony, the British viewed Northern institutions with something like veneration. This was not so much admiration for the emirs and local authorities in the region as this system's effects on the civilization and culture of colonial subjects that prepared these powerful precolonial institutions for exploitation. From 1848, when the first Consul-General was appointed to the Bight of Benin and Biafra, continuing through the establishment of the Courts of Equity across this administrative space in 1854, the British legal system influenced the local administration of justice.[26] By the twentieth century, the inclusion of Pax Britannica in the legal frame of colonized societies had caused trouble for colonial administrators. English laws, English lawyers, and the accompanying English culture had brewed

---

[20] Okechukwu Ikeanyibe, "History of Pre-colonial Southern Nigeria," in *Nigerian Peoples and Culture*, ed. S. A. Idahosa et al. (Benin City: Benson Idahosa University, 2007), 44–62.

[21] Taslim O. Elias, Samuel N Nwabara, and Chuma O Akpamgbo, *African Indigenous Laws* (Enugu: Government Printer, 1975).

[22] Alfred B. Ellis, *The Yoruba Speaking Peoples of the Slave Coast of West Africa: Their Religion, Manners, Customs, Laws, Language, etc.* (Lagos: Pilgrims Books, 1974).

[23] Idahosa O. Ojo, "The Nature of Laws and Law Making in Precolonial Benin," *POLAC Historical Review* 4, no. 1 (2020): 89–103.

[24] Toyin Falola, *The Power of African Cultures* (New York: University of Rochester Press, 2003).

[25] Kota Kariya, "Muwālāt and Apostasy in the Early Sokoto Caliphate," *Islamic Africa* 9, no. 2 (2018): 179–208.

[26] Adiele E. Afigbo, *The Warrant Chiefs: Indirect Rule in Southeastern Nigeria 1891–1929* (London: Longman Group, 1972).

a sophisticated modern population in the city of Lagos.[27] Many were returnees, and their descendants were familiar with Western civilization through education and trade.[28] These elements and the work of Christian missionaries continued to introduce Western ideas to the local population.

Only two years after Lugard's 1906 proclamation institutionalizing the colonization of the Northern Protectorate, Lagos erupted in chaos as the population protested the introduction of water rates.[29] During this same period, traders and Lagos intelligentsia fought British land policies, successfully altering the colonial trajectory of the area so that it avoided the fate of Central, East, and Southern African colonies that implemented settler economies. These events showed the British government what might happen if its legal system and supporting social formations were extended from the South to the North.[30]

The colonial Nigerian legal system and its administration of justice were drawn from three primary sources: Islamic law (Shari'a), customary law, and the Crown law, which served as civil law.[31] These laws did not adhere to class lines, unlike the developments that Mamdani tracked in Uganda.[32] Civil law was applied in the High Court and the Supreme Court whenever the decisions of Native Courts were appealed, usually for issues brought by natives without indoctrination in Western civilization. Civil law was also adopted in cases where customary law seemed to lack a fundamental basis for the administration of justice to the extent that it applied to the local experience.

After Lugard's 1914 amalgamation of Southern and Northern Nigeria, the native administration enjoyed increased power and expanded authority; these administrators included local chiefs, kings, and titleholders such as court messengers and clerks.[33] The massive disruption of World War I, coinciding with local reforms, played a significant role in this process. The war left the colonial administration with a shortage of workers. British officers were integral to the administration of justice in the South, particularly among the Igbo, Ibibio, and delta states. The exigencies of war had demanded their service

[27] Michael J. C. Echeruo, *Victorian Lagos: Aspects of Nineteenth Century Lagos Life* (London: Macmillan, 1977).
[28] Lisa A. Lindsay, "'To Return to the Bosom of Their Fatherland': Brazilian Immigrants in Nineteenth-Century Lagos," *Slavery & Abolition* 15, no. 1 (1994): 26–27.
[29] Olakunle A. Lawal and Oluwasegun M. Jimoh, "Missiles from 'Kirsten Hall': Herbert Macaulay versus Hugh Clifford, 1922–1931," *Lagos Historical Review* 12 (2012): 41–62.
[30] Adiele E. Afigbo, "Background to Nigerian Federalism: Federal Features in the Colonial State," *Publius* 21, no. 4 (1991): 13–29.
[31] Noel Otu, "Colonialism and the Criminal Justice System in Nigeria," *International Journal of Comparative and Applied Criminal Justice* 23, no. 2 (1999): 293–306.
[32] Mahmood Mamdani, *Politics and Class Formation in Uganda* (New York: Monthly Review Press, 1976).
[33] Adiele E. Afigbo, "The Consolidation of British Imperial Administration in Nigeria: 1900–1918," *Civilizations* 21, no. 4 (1971): 434–446.

elsewhere, and local government had to be managed by native authorities. Native authorities were expected to use their new powers to ensure the implementation of wartime economic policies and later recovery efforts. Afigbo has explained that the involvement of illiterate local chiefs and authorities in a modern bureaucratic government, especially one reliant on communication through the English language, gave new importance to the role of the court clerk. These individuals took over from district officers, serving as the court's president, albeit in a de facto capacity.[34]

The Chief Justice and judges, magistrates, registrars, clerks, interpreters, messengers, sheriffs, the director of prisons and his men, and other native authorities were essential to the administration of justice during this period. However, a larger number of cases were referred to British courts, to the detriment of the native system. This was due to ongoing migration from the interior to the emerging cities and the burgeoning diffusion of Western civilization, particularly in the South. British law was considered universal, and customary laws were viewed through the lens of natural justice, fairness, and equity. Any customary law that opposed these values was considered repugnant.[35]

Notions of rationality were conceived in Western frameworks. Lord Chief Justice Hewart explained to an audience that rationality remained the prerogative of the British officers, and they needed no comprehension of native law so long as it was just.[36] In the colony, this logic meant that the universality of British law prevented the judges and the administration of justice from being subject to opposing principles. One example is the treatment of divorce and custody rights. In a native court, a man would be denied custody of children in a dissolved marriage due to local customs and traditions. He would be prohibited from taking custody of the child if he had failed to pay his wife's dowry. Such decisions could be repealed by the British court using the Crown law's principles of equity, fairness, and universality. Slavery, pawnship, infanticide (specifically, the killing of twins), human sacrifice, burial rites, and other practices were considered barbaric and repugnant. Meanwhile, the colonial government's attitude was ambivalent at best regarding the powerful, secret organizations that set the basic norms of precolonial society and engaged in these practices. As David Pratten puts it, "Colonial perspectives of the Ekpo

---

[34] Adiele E. Afigbo, "Revolution and Reaction in Eastern Nigeria: 1900–1929: The Background to the Women's Riot of 1929," *Journal of the Historical Society of Nigeria* 3, no. 3 (1966): 539–557.

[35] Derek Asiedu–Akrofi, "Judicial Recognition and Adoption of Customary Law in Nigeria," *The American Journal of Comparative Law* 37, no. 3 (1989): 578.

[36] Sidney Abrahams, "The Colonial Legal Service and the Administration of Justice in Colonial Dependencies," *Journal of Comparative Legislation and International Law* 30, no. 3/4 (1948): 10.

society placed it in an ambiguous space between being essential to the fabric of the society and being an 'armed and lawless constabulary.'"[37]

The colonial government and Christian missionary activities besieged the Aro, Ekpo, and Ogboni groups in the South. Colonial administrators continued to restrict the operations of these groups, especially regarding the sale of human beings. The 1914 amalgamation prompted Lugard to scrutinize the Southern Protectorate's administration through his loyalists in government. The Aro and other secret societies in the Igbo–Ibibio area were identified as potential authorities with enough traditional influence to implement colonial policies. The government's subsequent dealings with the Long Juju and others changed from militarism and destruction to collaboration and diplomacy.[38]

The situation with the Aro demonstrates how the colonial state's political economy influenced the application of Crown law in developing the colony's legal system. Many of these reforms were met with various types of resistance. One example was the traditional burial practices for those who were destitute, people who died of suicide, and deaths that were due to infectious diseases or unusual circumstances. These people were normally buried in the forest, distant from any towns. The practice was meant to prevent their souls from returning to afflict the community. Under British law, this was also done with celebrated ancestors who would normally have been buried near their homes. Despite the government's official policy, the practice continued in places like Benin, the delta states, and prominently in Yorubaland.[39]

Burial practices and other customs related to marriage and sacrifice continued to cause friction between the missionaries, who were agents of Western civilization and modernization, and the secret societies that were arbiters of the old traditions. In many places, British civil law accompanied the rest of Western civilization, in which Judeo-Christian motifs were integral. This explains the transitions to civilization and modernization in the northern and southern parts of the colony. These differences became more distinct in the mid-nineteenth century, consolidated under the rule of Lugard. Aspects of Islamic law were repealed if they were considered repugnant by colonial administrators. This was the case with amputation imposed as a criminal punishment and with the distribution of taxation among subjects of the caliphate.[40]

---

[37] David Pratten, *The Man–Leopard Murders: History and Society in Colonial Nigeria* (London: Edinburgh University Press, 2007), 91.
[38] Pratten, *The Man–Leopard Murders*, 90–95.
[39] Robin Poynor, "Ako Figures of Owo and Second Burials in Southern Nigeria," *African Arts* 21, no. 1 (1987): 82–90.
[40] John E. Flint, "Nigeria: The Colonial Experience from 1800 to 1914," in *Colonialism in Africa 1870–1960*, Vol. 1, ed. Lewis H. Gann and Peter Duignan (Cambridge: Cambridge University Press, 1977), 229.

As part of its imperialist cultural drive, the colonial government transformed the social status of offenders, and by extension, it changed the epistemic reality of the people. This transformation was reinforced through established institutions and laws. Prisons were used to confine offenders as part of the administration of justice in the Niger area starting in the nineteenth century.[41] However, their early presence was limited to a few polities, such as the Northern Caliphate and the Egba United Government in Abeokuta. The traditional administration of justice rarely resulted in the confinement of offenders.[42] Confinement was reserved for those with mental illness, people possessed by spirits, and leprosy victims or those suffering from other infectious diseases. Instead, the administration of traditional African justice involved banishment, curses, retribution for the victim, and other mechanisms specific to individual cultures.[43] In transforming these systems, the British government undertook a massive construction effort to distribute prisons throughout the colony's administrative units.[44]

The British government's earlier activities and gradual penetration of the social and political landscape meant that the prison construction process began long before the official occupation of the area. In 1872, the British government in Lagos completed the construction of Nigeria's first formal prison, on Broad Street, which could hold 300 prisoners.[45] The government introduced the Prison Ordinance of 1884, granting legal authority to the prison, and Agodi Prison was opened in the same year. Agodi Prison in Ibadan had only two cells: one for male and one for female prisoners. Abeokuta prison was built in 1900. Then Ewedo prison, which had originally been constructed by its traditional ruler, was rebuilt by the government in 1910. Kano Central Prison was opened in 1903, after the city's conquest in that same year, and the list continues, including Sapele, Abinsi, Ilaro, Owo, Ondo, Ibadan, and Lokoja.[46]

The traditional and modern means of administering justice in Africa fundamentally differed in their restoration and retribution approaches. When a justice system focuses on restoration, offenders can be reintegrated into society, and the victim can be compensated. A system focused on

---

[41] Johnson O. Ajayi, "Nigeria Prisons and the Dispensation of Justice," *AFRREV IJAH: An International Journal of Arts and Humanities*, 1, no. 3 (2012): 208–233.

[42] O. O. Wobasi, "Traditional System of Government and Justice in Ikwerre," in *Studies in Ikwerre History and Culture*, ed. Ontonti Nduka (Lagos: Kraft Books, 1993), 38–60.

[43] Andrew Novak, *The Death Penalty in Africa: Foundations and Future Prospects* (New York: Palgrave Pivot, 2014), 9–23.

[44] Etannibi E. O. Alemika and Emily I. Alemika, "Penal Crisis and Prison Management in Nigeria," *Lawyers Bi-Annual* 1, no. 2 (1995): 62–80.

[45] Viviane Saleh-Hanna and Chukwuma Ume, "An Evolution of the Penal System: Criminal Justice in Nigeria," in *Colonial Systems of Control: Criminal Justice in Nigeria*, ed. Viviane Saleh-Hanna (Ottawa: University of Ottawa Press, 2008), 58.

[46] Saleh-Hanna and Ume, "An Evolution of the Penal System," 55–68.

retribution emphasizes the offender – the criminal – and it can neglect reparation or relief for the victim other than prosecution of the offender. Under the restorative system, judgments ensure that both parties are reunited and can continue social relations. The traditional justice system's focus on restoration encouraged people to avoid the retribution-focused British system whenever possible.

British courts also required larger amounts of time and expense in the pursuit of justice. Despite the government's insistence on constructing its institutions, justice was still administered at various levels beyond the Native Courts and the British Courts. The Chief Judge administered justice in the entire colony, and the judges and magistrates under him were directly involved with running the bureaucracy of justice, assisted by the registrar and clerical staff. These activities, along with the regulation of their institution and the recruitment of judges and magistrates, were coordinated by the Colonial Judicial Service.[47]

After British officers were withdrawn from Native Courts in the Eastern provinces of the Southern colony, and because of the mixed migration driven by World War I, the role of interpreters in Native Courts became less influential. Instead, the British courts saw larger amounts of activity. The socioeconomic configuration and political economy of the colonial state ensured that the British courts had many cases to adjudicate. The proliferation of private property, wealth, businesses, union bodies, and protests against the colonial state led to incidents of arson, murders, violent sexual assaults, public disturbances, robberies, and incitements against colonial officials, which constituted the bulk of the cases flooding the British courts. These cases and related matters were often beyond the jurisdiction of the Native Authorities. Many of these issues had been absent from local norms and customs. They were created by the colonial economy and had no precedent in native judgments.

The administration of justice in the colonial state not only involved pronouncing verdicts on legal matters but was also essential for forming laws. The social upheaval caused by the colonial economy pervaded the entire social structure of society. Economic stress caused by World War I produced new realities for society, such as beggars and homeless persons, and more broadly, a greater spread of poverty. After the war, people flooded cities from the interior, especially from the Northern Protectorate, and the growing population of people suffering from economic hardship was a major concern for the colonial administrators in Lagos.[48] The colonial economy had produced a growing population of displaced people living on the streets, interfering

---

[47] Adetokunbo Ademola, "Personnel Problems in the Administration of Justice in Nigeria," *Law and Contemporary Problems* 27, no. 4 (1962): 578.
[48] Babatunde J. Decker, "A History of the Poor in Lagos, 1861–1960," (unpublished PhD dissertation, University of Lagos, 2012).

with traffic, and posing threats to public health. Three legal measures were taken in response: reparation, persecution, and rehabilitation. The last two were applied consecutively in some cases. Beggars and juveniles received training to develop job skills that could contribute to the economy.

Before British officers were withdrawn from the Native Authority bench in 1914, they acted as presidents for Native Courts while local chiefs acted as assessors who assessed the validity of plaintiff claims based on their customs and traditions. After the authority of their roles expanded, plans were made to teach modern governance and Western education to the sons of the chiefs so that they could serve as successors. The plan failed to materialize, but it became apparent that Western education was relevant for modern government structures and systems.

In some parts of the delta states, such as the Old Calabar and Warri, house heads and monarchs had used Western education to train their children since the eighteenth century.[49] By the start of World War II, educated individuals jostled for power at local government levels, especially in Yorubaland and Lagos. Traditional secret societies were also beginning to reorganize around goals best described as improvement unions. The idea of improvement in the colonial state primarily pertained to forms and aspects of Western civilization, such as literacy, etiquette, and family organization. This explains the prevalence of literature and pamphlets that taught people about Western norms during the early colonial period. Improvement unions were formed to address their members' socioeconomic challenges, including social mobility and the administration of justice. They functioned as kinship networks for self-help, including farmers' and traders' unions and cooperative societies. As these bodies gained increasing power, they were regulated more closely by the government through measures such as the 1935 Co-operative Ordinance.[50] The law provided a fundamental basis for establishing and operating unions, associations, and other biosocial bodies in the colony. Members could be subject to levies, seizure of property, or other punishments meted out to members based on the union's or association's rules.[51]

The hierarchical frame that dictated the administration of justice in precolonial times persisted during this period, although it was subject to modifications. The magnitude of cases determined where justice was administered: family, compound, community, union body, native court, provincial court, or central government (British) court. Native Courts handled cases related to

---

[49] Abiodun Adetugbo, "The Development of English in Nigeria up to 1914: A Socio-Historical Appraisal," *Journal of the Historical Society of Nigeria* 9, no. 2 (1978): 89–96.

[50] Okoro Okereke, *Co-operatives and the Nigerian Economy* (Nsukka: University of Nigeria Press, 1986), 220.

[51] Pratten, *The Man–Leopard Murders*, 99.

divorce, tax evasion, land disputes, and other petty cases. They were also used to prosecute native practices such as the Sopona (smallpox) cult, certain beliefs and forms of worship, slavery, trade disputes, and harassment.[52] British courts handled more serious crimes such as murder. British courts addressed cases that had originated in Native Courts, either through appeal or the preference of the appellant. Disputes over boundaries between communities were also taken to the British courts due to their possible implications for colonial administrative units. The limitation of this arrangement was that the interest of the native authorities was usually aligned with one of the parties involved in the case, making miscarriages of justice a common feature of Native Courts. This lack of impartiality encouraged residents to bring their grievances directly to the British courts.

British courts relied heavily on the validity of local customs and traditions when they were applicable. This brings anthropologists into the discourse concerning the administration of justice in the colonial state. The government had commenced its rule by deploying anthropologists and colonial administrators, dispatched to the interior to inquire about the history, customs, and traditions of the people to be colonized.[53] The collected results were used for assessing the local worldview and maintaining the law and order necessary for the exploitative mission of the colonial enterprise.

Anthropologists offered both contempt and praise for the natives' forms of civilization. Their work facilitated the creation of written records of local history among the emerging educated elite, especially in the South. History produced customs and traditions, and these were transmuted into laws to administer justice in the colonial state. These forces led to the proliferation of documented oral traditions.[54] As local authorities – paramount chiefs, permanent presidents of the Native Courts, and administrative heads (sole Native Authorities) – gained increasing relevance in the administration of an indirect rule system legitimized by extant traditions, history became a contested space for negotiating power.[55]

In 1958, a Chieftaincy Declaration was made regarding the colony's Western regional government.[56] The process was justified to prevent chieftaincy matters from being taken to court, which could demean the authority and prestige

---

[52] Atanda, *The New Oyo Empire*.
[53] Vincent Hiribarren, "A European and African Joint-Venture: Writing a Seamless History of Borno (1902–1960)," *History in Africa* 40 (2013): 77–98.
[54] Toyin Falola, *Yoruba Gurus: Indigenous Production of Knowledge in Africa* (Trenton: Africa World Press Inc., 1999).
[55] Anthony I. Asiwaju, "Political Motivation and Oral Historical Traditions in Africa: The Case of Yoruba Crowns, 1900–1960," *Journal of the International African Institute* 46, no. 2 (1976): 116–121.
[56] Wale Oyemakinde, "The Chiefs Law and the Regulation of Traditional Chieftaincy in Yorubaland," *Journal of the Historical Society of Nigeria* 9, no. 1 (1977): 63–74.

of such institutions. The declaration was the culmination of years of consultation between the government, native authorities, and individual members of administrative units. Many reforms were injected into the system toward the end of the colonial epoch, expanding and reforming the administrative spread. As more provinces, divisions, and districts were created, a reorganization was necessary, and new heads were needed in these newly established units. This meant that some chiefs were effectively "promoted" and given a suitable rank to lead these units. This triggered a scramble for political legitimacy through the documentation of oral traditions, which ultimately necessitated the 1958 government declaration to regulate such institutions.[57]

The government's declaration ended contested histories and established an official document that described the source, extent, and limits of power and political authority at the local government levels of the colonial state. Under this legal system, everyone within the state was more closely bound by state authority, with more depth than was seen in the precolonial period. Monarchs could be deposed based on accusations of infringing on the land's constitution. These charges could be brought by a consensus among chiefs, who could issue a vote of "no confidence" in the monarch.

Being deposed was the sole method of holding monarchs to account under the state's administration of justice, and they could not be sued or accused of wrongdoing in any other way. In the colonial legal system, monarchs were deposed for their inability to maintain law and order or for other offenses, such as corruption, that could warrant their detention and treatment as common criminals. The frame of societal norms had shifted away from these authorities and their institutions, investing their power in the new colonial administrators. As colonial subjects themselves, traditional leaders were no longer the arbiters of political power. Instead of establishing codes of conduct for social control and justice in their communities, they merely observed their development.

The British government promoted the idea of gender restrictions in its dealings with local authorities and the general population. This relegated the role of women in the colony to a status similar to that of European women who acted primarily as housewives and nursing mothers. Hellen Callaway has explained how damaging this notion was for British women who followed their husbands to administrative posts in the Nigerian colony.[58] The participation of women was limited in the colonial sociopolitical space, which ignored their prominent roles in protesting against marginalization in the colonial state. Men were prioritized and actively consulted in negotiating

---

[57] Tunde Oduwobi, *Ijebu under Colonial Rule, 1892–1960: An Administrative and Political Analysis* (Lagos: First Academic Publishers, 2004).

[58] Hellen Callaway, *Gender, Culture and Empire: European Women in Colonial Nigeria* (London: Macmillan Press, 1987).

political power, the establishment of agricultural policies and programs, which included the distribution of improved seeds for cultivation, and decisions regarding access to Western education. Within the frame of Pax Britannica, the colonial government only promoted the education of young women to the extent that they could comprehend and assist their husbands.

The hierarchy of rights in the colony was established along the lines of gender roles, sex, and racial principles, which had ongoing legal implications. The 1922 right of franchise was restricted to men who earned around £100 per annum. Social class considerations also affected the workings of the colonial legal system. Chapter 10's example of courtroom testimony from a British officer provides a vivid image of this hierarchy. The colonial administration of justice and its legal system also provided room for the chief legal officer, usually the Chief Justice, to affect government policies by providing them with a legal basis.

The transformation of African societies from traditional groups to the Weberian state reformed the institution of government. New administrative units and departments were established.[59] The office of the Chief Justice was created to unify the judicial and executive arms of the two protectorates, inter alia. The Prisons Service was established and headed by a director supported by a police force operating at local government and central levels. Constables from the central government were used to arrest the accused and other offenders, also protecting local authorities and other members of the Native Authority as they performed their duties.[60] Many members of this service were slaves, runaways, and other citizens of extremely low social status.

Given the role that police forces played in the colonial state, few voluntarily enlisted for the service. Young men with the right social status in this milieu pursued trade, cash labor, or civil positions in the colonial service. These men were integral to maintaining law and order to the extent that they reflected what later became indoctrinated in modernization theory. Their ideals would become unpopular in postcolonial communities of the intelligentsia in Third World countries – or *postcolonial states*, as it meant at the time.[61] Modernization theory conditioned citizens to oppose any form of protest within the state, seeing protests as signs of weakness or atavistic and inimical to the notion of progress and modernization. Modernization theory found its roots in the colonial project, and one of its many paradoxes was the idea that dissenting voices were unnecessary distractions in a democratic society. This influenced the public's view of

---

[59] Efiong I. Utuk, "Britain's Colonial Administrations and Developments, 1861–1960: An Analysis of Britain's Colonial Administrations and Developments in Nigeria," Master of Science in Teaching, Portland State University, 1975.
[60] Afigbo, *Warrant Chiefs*, 118–174.
[61] Mahmood Mamdani, Thandika Mkandawire, and Wamba-dia-Wamba, "Social Movements, Social Transformation and Struggle for Democracy in Africa," *Economic and Political Weekly* 23, no. 19 (1988): 973–981.

security forces and their role in the democratic administration of a state. Police forces were established with the sole intent of coercion, which can be seen in their roles in the Satiru Uprising in the North,[62] the Ijemo Massacre,[63] the Aba Women's War,[64] and many other protests against the colonial state.

Police forces were also used to investigate criminal matters such as murder, counterfeit currency, robbery, kidnapping, and rape. Officers acted as court officials when they transported suspects to the court. As with the Native Court, the police administration was plagued by corruption and incompetence that stemmed from insufficient training and inept personnel, which resulted from decisions made to serve the needs of the colonialists. There were also low numbers of police relative to the overall population. After several incidents where police officers were harassed and beaten by locals, their official role was attached to the institution of the Native Authority. This was one of the ways that the power of the local authorities was bolstered by the colonial government, especially in the Eastern provinces. These forces replaced the traditional police of societies which rulers had used to deliver messages, collect information, apprehend accused persons, and distribute or implement government policies. The state's need for these new police functions became more acute toward the end of colonial rule, mainly in their application as an instrument of force.

Kirk-Greene[65] and Ranger[66] have explained that the "thin white line" of the British colonial administration remained successful through coercion, collaboration, confidence, competence, and colonial ideology. These factors seldom operated independently, as the root of their actions resided in the colonial ideology of racial hierarchy and superiority. As the ideals of Pax Britannica and humanitarianism later transformed into developmentalism, the government's approach shifted from coercion to working with collaborators. This can be seen in Aro and Ekpo societies in Igboland and Ibibio and in the 1922 compromise made by the Clifford government to introduce some measure of democratic principles to the local polity. By working through collaborators, the colonial government sought to exploit larger amounts of local resources. The period following World War I saw a major break from the colonial practice of expansion to pursue a consolidation strategy. Afigbo has illustrated how the

---

[62] Rowland A. Adeleye, "Mahdist Triumph and British Revenge in Northern Nigeria: Satiru 1906," *Journal of the Historical Society of Nigeria* 6, no.2 (1972): 193–214.

[63] John L. Ausman, "The Disturbances in Abeokuta in 1918," *Canadian Journal of African Studies* 5, no. 1 (1971): 45–60.

[64] Monday E. Noah, "Aba Women's Riot: Need for a Re-Definition," in *The Women's Revolt of 1929: Proceedings of a National Symposium*, ed. C. Dike (Lagos: Nelag, 1995), 105–124.

[65] Anthony H. M. Kirk-Greene, "The Thin White Line: The Size of the British Colonial Service in Africa," *African Affairs* 79, no. 314 (1980): 25–44.

[66] Terence Ranger, "Making Northern Rhodesia Imperial: Variations on a Royal Theme, 1924–1938," *African Affairs* 79, no. 316 (1980): 349–373.

former played a role in the abolition of the slave trade in the Eastern provinces, characterized by the ruthless use of weapons, while the court and constables dominated the latter approach.[67]

Collaborators, including witnesses, were essential to this process. As the population increased, the administration expanded and the Native Courts struggled due to their limitations, thus larger numbers of collaborators were needed to maintain peace and order. This explains the government's changing attitude toward the secret societies and union bodies administering justice, especially among their members. However, the growing influence of such bodies and their secretive operations eventually encouraged the government to limit their power.

The neutralization of secret societies, especially ones with magico-religious functions, such as the Aro, Ekpo society, and the Ibini Ukpabi, was accomplished through the erosion of their traditional base. Their traditional adherents were undermined by new economic, administrative, social, religious, and cultural systems.[68] The organizations that sustained old socioeconomic practices were waning. Groups solely concerned with trade in legitimate commercial goods, such as the farmers' union, produce buyers, and other local traders, were driven out of business by the colonial government's postwar economic policies.[69] British trade and culture stifled local mobilization, organization, and collective action.

The Nigerian colony derived its legislation from two primary sources: local ordinances or proclamations, and Imperial legislation enacted by the British Parliament and applied to Nigeria. Through institutional and legal mechanisms, the colony's incorporation into the metropolitan government presented the colonialists with an effective means of controlling the colony's resources to serve the metropolitan state.[70] The imperial legislation that governed British colonies meant that the mood of the British politicians, commoners, and bourgeoisie affected the socioeconomic and political atmosphere of colonized areas. This became even more influential with postwar recovery efforts.

In 1932, the so-called Ottawa Agreement was reached to enhance the activities of British merchants in Africa, Asia, Australia, and other colonies that later formed the British Commonwealth of Nations.[71] The agreement focused on increasing the market share that British merchants enjoyed in these

---

[67] Adiele E. Afigbo, *The Abolition of the Slave Trade in Southeastern Nigeria 1885–1950* (New York: University of Rochester Press, 2006).
[68] Afigbo, *The Abolition of the Slave Trade*, 55.
[69] Moses E. Ochonu, *Colonial Meltdown: Northern Nigeria in the Great Depression* (Athens: Ohio State University Press, 2009).
[70] Anthony Kirk-Greene, *Britain's Imperial Administrators, 1858–1966* (London: Palgrave Macmillan Press, 1999).
[71] John E. Lattimer, "The Ottawa Trade Agreements," *Journal of Farm Economics* 16, no. 4 (1934): 565–581.

colonies, driving away competition from industrial competitors such as Japan and America. The Ottawa Agreement arrived a few years after the international trade fair exhibitions organized by the Canadian and Belgian governments in 1928 and 1930, respectively.[72] The Nigerian colonial government participated in these exhibitions to showcase its natural resources, drawing investors from extractive and agricultural industries.

The Ottawa Agreement appeared to be the government's anticipation of investments and improved markets resulting from the exhibition and closer ties between Britain and her colonial dependents. The goal was the formation of a single economic bloc, later described as the Commonwealth of Nations. It further legitimized the trade monopoly held by British merchants and other foreign actors, such as the Syrians and Lebanese, in the colonial economy. The Conference Shipping Lines operated by British shipping companies – including the Elder Dempster shipping company, which played a significant role – and the formation of British trading consortiums, such as the United African Company, had driven local actors from the market.[73] These actors responded by forming their unions and associations to reintegrate themselves into business activities.

The Ottawa Agreement neutralized the efforts of local economic actors by giving governmental preference to foreign traders acting within the prism of imperial priority. Winifred Tete-Ansa attempted to export cocoa from the British West African colony directly to the United States, forming a collective that could boycott British firms, but the government frustrated this effort.[74] Similar activities faced even greater challenges under the new agreement.

In 1930, the British government acted to protect its interests through imperial legislation under the pretext of international labor law and the League of Nations. The Secretary of State for the Colonies wrote to Nigeria's colonial government, asking for a review of the working conditions of labor vis-à-vis hours of work, rate of pay, terms and conditions of contracts, health, housing conditions, and other factors.[75] Ostensibly, this was to enhance the social welfare of labor forces in the Lagos colony and the provinces. The underlying value of the request can be seen in the latitude given for implementing the policy up until the outbreak of World War II and also in the activities and inclination of a government that created legal frameworks such

---

[72] Olufemi R. Ekundare, *An Economic History of Nigeria 1860–1960* (London: Methuen & Co Ltd., 1973), 215–218.
[73] Ahmed Modibbo, *European Trade, Imperialism and Under-Development in Northern Nigeria, 19th and 20th Centuries* (Zaria: Ahmadu Bello University Press Limited, 2016).
[74] Johnson O. Aremu, "Administration of British West African Colonies and the Furtherance of Nigeria–Gold Coast Relations, 1885–1960," *International Journal of Humanities and Cultural Studies* 1, no. 4 (2015): 3.
[75] Tunde Decker, "Social Welfare Strategies in Colonial Lagos," *African Nebula* 1, no. 1 (2010): 56–62.

as the Ottawa Agreement. Imperial instructions were never followed to the letter, and ongoing exploitation through imperial legal frameworks continued unabated. This occurred at least until the gradual nationalization of the people's resources that began in the 1950s – at the peak of the radical and organized response to social, economic, and political injustices occurring under colonial rule.

Colonial rule did not initially discriminate against any specific social group or class within the native population. Trade unions, male and female market actors, mass movements, community and sociocultural groups, professional bodies, improvement unions, and other entities in the colony's collective frame acted altogether to organize their demands through political parties.[76] These parties became collective vehicles for social justice and representation in the government.[77] After World War I ended, the responses to British colonial administration, policies, and laws began taking the form of organized political action through entities such as the Nigerian National Democratic Party (NNDP), and later the Nigerian Youth Movement (NYM) and subsequent political parties.[78] Union bodies, such as the People's Union in Lagos, were no longer organized in response to specific government policies. Instead, major intervention in the state's political economy was driven either by parties or by the parties working in concert with affected groups or unions. This was the case with the Road Transport Workers and the NYM in the latter group's early days.

The 1929 Aba Women's War signaled how the collaborative strategy of engaging the colonial government simultaneously succeeded and failed. On the one hand, it exposed the representative government established by Clifford as a cosmetic attempt to legitimize oppressive colonial policies, introducing tax reform to the Eastern provinces during an economic downturn. On the other hand, local collaborators were able to convince people that the government planned to take up their lands and products, as it had done in colonies elsewhere in Africa. Such claims were false as collaborators were only trying to retain their position and enhance their political strength, but they were taken seriously.[79] These events show how people were able to organize and resist the government with older structures of mobilization, outside of political parties.

The activities of the NNDP, the only political party of the time, were limited to Lagos and showed the limitations of political organization. This demonstrated

---

[76] Bola Ige, *People, Politics and Politicians of Nigeria (1940–1979)* (Ibadan: Heinemann Educational Books, 1995),
[77] O. E. Udofia, "Nigerian Political Parties: Their Role in Modernizing the Political System, 1920–1966," *Journal of Black Studies* 11, no. 4 (1981): 435–447.
[78] Udofia, "Nigerian Political Parties."
[79] Toyin Falola, *Colonialism and Violence in Nigeria* (Bloomington: Indiana University Press, 2009), 108–117.

how the British colonial government and its officials, as well as their local counterparts, sought to manipulate the legal frame of the state to their advantage. Local authorities relied on warrant documents issued by the government along with their conferred legal responsibilities in the Native Administration, while the government rationalized their actions through the power of conquest and ideals of a superior civilization.[80]

Conclusion

The basis of a state and its government, even under illegal colonial rule, is premised on the administration of justice and a legal system that confers public legitimacy. On this basis, several policies, promulgations, ordinances, agreements, treaties, and decrees were injected into the state at various times and stages of the colonial enterprise. Their expansive scope covered the most remote and commonplace aspects of society, from family to marriage, trade to industry, property to political participation, and every other aspect of life. Resentment against this extensive control fueled the nationalist movements that gained radical currency from the 1930s, gaining impetus in the years following World War II. As Kilson explains:

> Nationalism, in one of its aspects, clearly expresses the dissatisfaction of an emerging African middle class with a situation in which many of the recognized functions and rewards of a middle class – in the commercial, professional, administrative and ecclesiastical fields – are in the hands of "strangers" ... The demand for African control of state power is in part a demand for unrestricted access to these functions.[81]

By the time the LYM was established, it had become obvious that the "local representation" of the Clifford Constitution was superficial.[82] This realization drove subsequent political action demanding better representation and self-government.

Several constitutional conferences and debates were launched in Nigeria and London to discuss the legal basis of the Nigerian state, building on the constitutional developments that new administrators had heralded in the colony before the 1950s. Issues related to systems of government, state composition, interaction among political units, and aspects of the proposed independent state were ostensibly framed by public opinion – as interpreted by

---

[80] Philip Igbafe, "British Rule in Benin 1897–1920: Direct or Indirect?" *Journal of the Historical Society of Nigeria* 3, no. 4 (1967): 701–717.

[81] Martin L. Kilson, Jr., "Nationalism and Social Classes in British West Africa," *The Journal of Politics* 20, no. 2 (1958): 379.

[82] Stephen O. Arifalo, The Rise and Decline of the Nigerian Youth Movement, 1934–1941," *The African Review: A Journal of African Politics, Development and International Affairs* 13, no. 1 (1986): 59–76.

"nationalist" leaders. Despite their successes, Nigerian laws were drawn from sources that remained within the precedents set by the colonial state. One source was English common law, based on the doctrine of equity and statutes of general application in which, in the words of Lord Macmillan, justice acted on a common objective regardless of time and cultural space. Other sources included native customs and traditions, along with local legislation and interpretation derived from law reports, textbooks, and monographs on Nigerian laws and judicial precedent.[83]

---

[83] Maurice Ayodele Coker, "Law and Politics in Nigeria: The Political Functioning of the Judiciary in Colonial Nigeria, 1940–1960," *Mediterranean Journal of Social Sciences* 5, no. 20 (2014): 2085.

12

Colonial Economy

As the field of African studies developed from the early 1950s to the 1970s, it replaced colonial historiography's dominant narratives with a sizable amount of its nationalist historiography.[1] Debate raged at the time among the emerging social scientists and historians over the role of a society's economic and political landscape in shaping its internal dynamics and evolution.[2] The question of whether economic formation determines a group's political morphology or vice versa has remained similar to that of the chicken and the egg. This debate has been ongoing since the early formative years of Africanist scholars.[3]

In the later years, it became popular to consider how the political economy of these societies functioned in their internal workings and development, which embraced political and economic variables. A society's economic and political aspects are as indispensable as they are inseparable. From a society's formation and through its evolution, they reinforce each other in a complex, multilayered, and interrelated web.[4] The economic ramifications of the colonial encounter in Africa, and in Nigeria specifically, have received substantial attention from scholars and have been well documented over the years.[5]

This perspective considers the economic transformation and general ambience of the time, studies the commercial activities of traders and merchants, and assesses the impact of all their activities on the colonial subjects that comprise

---

[1] Christopher Fyfe, "The Emergence and Evolution of African Studies in the United Kingdom," in *Out of One, Many Africas: Reconstructing the Study and Meaning of Africa*, ed. William G. Martin and Michael O. West (Chicago: University of Illinois Press, 1999), 54–61.

[2] William G. Martin, "The Rise of African Studies (USA) and the Transnational Study of Africa," *African Studies Review* 54, no. 1 (2011): 59–83.

[3] Paul T. Zeleza, "Reckoning with the Past and Reimagining the Futures of African Studies for the 21st Century," Africa Peacebuilding Network Lecture Series No. 4, Keynote Address at the Social Science Research Council Training Workshop, United States International University-Africa, Nairobi, January 7, 2019, 7–8.

[4] Aminu I. Yandaki, *The State in Africa: A Critical Study in Historiography and Political Philosophy* (Zaria: Gaskiya Corporation, 2015).

[5] See, for instance, Thomas Bimberg and Stephen Resnick, *Colonial Development: An Econometric Study* (New Haven: Yale University Press, 1975).

society.[6] Preceding discussions have shown that this period's political and social narratives, like other epochs in history, can hardly be written without providing some sense of their economic incentives. A purely economic focus drove the entrenchment of colonial rule in Africa;[7] the addition of sociopolitical interests maximized the imperial enterprise in the region.[8] In the years preceding the colonial episode, the political landscape of African cultures, especially in the sub-Saharan region, had begun to mutate. Centrifugal and centripetal forces in regional politics and markets shaped the changes.[9] As the activities of European merchants intensified in a given area, especially among the British, additional English practices were integrated into the local sociopolitical environment. As European commercial interest expanded in the region, their political clout and influence grew, resulting in seismic changes in the sociopolitical morphology of these cultures.[10] The changing economic landscape of societies affects their political composition, which effectively adapts to manage these changes and transformations.[11] These alterations also show how the political morphology of culture embodies and unbundles its economic reality.

Africanist scholars, such as Jane Guyer and Jacob F. A. Ajayi, assert that Africa's integration into global markets should not be seen as a function of the colonial enterprise. Instead, they view it as a long-term process involving centuries of external contact and foreign relations, on the one hand, and continually evolving relations among social forces in the material reproduction of these polities, on the other, reaching a decisive moment in the Age of Atlanticism.[12] The economy was directed to serve a global network of markets

---

[6] Monday Yakiban Mangvwat, *A History of Class Formation in the Plateau Province of Nigeria, 1902–1960: The Genesis of a Ruling Class* (Durham: Carolina Academic Press, 2013); and Ahmed Modibbo Mohammed, *European Trade, Imperialism and Under Development in Northern Nigeria 19th and 20th Centuries* (Zaria: Ahmadu Bello University Press Limited, 2016).

[7] Barrie Ratcliffe, "The Economics of the Partition of Africa: Methods and Recent Research Trends," *Canadian Journal of African Studies* 15, no. 1 (1981): 3–31.

[8] John Flint, *Sir George Goldie and the Making of Nigeria* (London: Oxford University Press, 1960); and John E. Flint, "Chartered Companies and the Scramble for Africa," in *Africa in the Nineteenth and Twentieth Centuries*, ed. Joseph C. Anene and Godfrey N. Brown (Ibadan: Ibadan University Press, 1966), 109–120.

[9] Michael Crowder and Obaro Ikime, eds., *West African Chiefs: The Changing Status under Colonial Rule and Independence* (Ile-Ife: The University of Ife Press, 1970); and John B. Webster and Albert A. Boahen, *The Revolutionary Years: West Africa Since 1800* (London: Longman Group, 1980).

[10] Michael J. C. Echeruo, *Victorian Lagos: Aspects of Nineteenth Century Lagos Life* (London: Macmillan Education Limited, 1977).

[11] Kenneth Dike, *Trade and Politics in the Niger Delta, 1830–1885: An Introduction to the Economic and Political History of Nigeria* (London: Clarendon Press, 1956).

[12] Jacob F. A. Ajayi, "Africa at the Beginning of the Nineteenth Century: Issues and Prospects," in *General History of Africa – VI: Africa in the Nineteenth Century until the 1880s*, ed. Jacob F.A. Ajayi (Oxford: Heinemann Educational Publishers, 1995), 1–22.

more than at any other time in the region's history, and the intensification of free market laissez-faire doctrines culminated in the marginalization of local actors in the states' economic trajectories. This chapter examines the changes and transformations that affected colonial Nigeria's economy, outlining how the political landscape of societies affected their economic lives, and vice versa.

Cash Economy and Social Disruption

Cash labor, agricultural and industrial exploitation, and the distribution of transportable goods were the activities at the core of the colonial economy. Import and export markets expanded tremendously due to several factors: the arrival of new actors and the repositioning of extant ones; new products that were introduced and familiar products that were enhanced; and technological and industrial innovation and the accompanying developments in Europe, America, and Asia. Others include the advancement of transportation networks, the development of infrastructure in the colonies and metropolitan centers, and the successful introduction of Western taxonomic modernity to the native population.[13] All of these combined to shape and redefine the socioeconomic landscape of African cultures, and this had consequences for their political morphology.

One of the efforts that launched these changes and transformed societies from their precolonial past was the deconstruction of past modes of production.[14] Labor had previously been drawn from within the family, including the extended family, slaves, and other community members or, occasionally, outsiders within this structure.[15] Additional laborers could be added to this arrangement by sourcing them through pawnship or other circumstances linking an individual to a family.[16] These arrangements came under intense attack from agents of British imperial interests in the region, beginning in the mid-nineteenth century with the 1851 bombardment of Lagos. From the coastal city of Lagos, the campaign of conquest and exploitation was taken to several polities in the interior, especially in the Niger Delta and Igbo areas that later became the Niger Coast Protectorate – the practice of forced labor was prevalent there.[17] However, the government's position in this

---

[13] Toyin Falola, ed., *Tradition and Change in Africa: The Essays of J. F. Ade Ajayi* (Trenton: Africa World Press, 2000).

[14] Tunde Babawale, *Nigeria in the Crisis of Governance and Development: A Retrospective and Prospective Analyses of Selected Issues and Events*, Vol. 2 (Lagos: Political and Administrative Resource Center, 2007), 1.

[15] Klas Rönnbäck, *Labour and Living Standards in Pre-colonial West Africa: The Case of the Gold Coast* (New York: Routledge, 2016).

[16] Paul E. Lovejoy and Toyin Falola, *Pawnship in Africa: Debt Bondage in Historical Perspective* (Boulder: Westview Press, 1994).

[17] Adiele E. Afigbo, *The Abolition of the Slave Trade in Southeastern Nigeria 1885–1950* (Rochester: University of Rochester Press, 2006).

area was counterintuitive, issuing proclamations and ordinances either for or against the continuation of the institution of forced labor at various times. This was because the continuation of the practice was seen as a way of administering the societies that were often erroneously classified as stateless, owing to their acephalous and small, decentralized formations.[18]

The colonial government's position regarding forced labor was delegated to the "man on the spot," differing from one region to the next. In the Northern protectorate, elites could keep their slaves if they paid taxes and other levies. Arrangements were made for the emancipation of this population and their productive engagement in the economy, which involved paying a *mugun* fee to their masters for their commercial activities.[19] The system's flexibility in the area was linked to religious doctrine and the slow pace of Western modernity's encroachment. The institutions of labor were deeply embedded in social and cultural norms not only in the Niger area but also across Africa. Deconstructing these institutions was equivalent to reconfiguring the social strata of society. The rapid spread of Western education and Christianity in Yorubaland, including Lagos, meant that efforts to source labor from captives received less attention from the government. Converts to these new doctrines were seen as concrete signifiers of Western civilization, occupying several positions other than slavery in the colonial state.

The least prestigious new jobs in the colonial service that replaced slave labor in the new formal economy involved domestic tasks in the homes of the colonizers and work as messengers in the colonial service. People were paid to perform these tasks, and they were considered an emerging class in the social stratification of the evolving milieu. In the Native Courts of Igboland and the Niger Delta in the Southern protectorate, for instance, some messengers were considered above the average population and local authorities in the colonial state. Their positions allowed them to negotiate this space better than their kinsmen. Messengers and constables had access to the corridors of power through their ability and responsibility to uphold and enforce the law.[20]

Teachers, catechists, interpreters, clerks, secretaries, journalists, lawyers, doctors, and other professionals emerged from the local population to meet the needs of the colonial state. Christian missions trained carpenters, traders, masons, clerks, nurses, and others who learned how to read and write in English and local languages. These skills were necessary for navigating the evolving colonial economy. Concerted missionary efforts on the fringes of the

---

[18] Afigbo, *The Abolition of the Slave Trade*.
[19] Mahdi Adamu, *The Hausa Factor in West African History* (Zaria: Ahmadu Bello University Press, 1978); and Paul E. Lovejoy and Jan S. Hogendorn, *Slow Death for Slavery: The Course of Abolition in Northern Nigeria, 1897-1936* (New York: Cambridge University Press, 1993).
[20] Adiele E. Afigbo, *The Warrant Chiefs: Indirect Rule in Southeastern Nigeria 1891-1929* (London: Longman Group, 1972).

Northern protectorate and in the nooks and crannies of the Southern parts of the colony produced waves of migrants from all parts of the colony. These were mostly laborers in search of industries, construction sites, and farms where they could work to earn a living. This motive saw many of them converging in emerging urban centers and cities.[21] Women were not left out of these opportunities since new economic activities helped to facilitate the social mobility of African women. Migrants were also driven by the introduction of tax payments and financial reforms.[22] Taxation was not completely alien to local inhabitants, but the instrumentality of cash payments introduced major disruptions to older forms of the practice.

Migrant labor was prevalent during this period and was central to economic production, deviating from the enslaved modes of production previously applied to commerce.[23] Economic historians of African societies believe that the region's economy entered a capitalist stage, although various detours were involved on the way to this end. The liberalist school presents this stage as an entrenchment and expansion of previous practices, while Marxists identify this behavior as a fundamental break from the past.

Hopkins and other scholars have shown that this transition was subtle in West African economies, arriving as the result of systemic changes that included the introduction of portable currencies, such as copper and silver coins, especially in the nineteenth century.[24] New forms of market exchange replaced barter systems that had been predominant in distant centuries. By the end of the nineteenth century, the British government's rapid financial reforms and the massive expansion of trade volumes for agricultural and industrial products led to a decline in the value of cowries and other bartered goods in Nigerian markets.[25] This created a preference for the British coins that were managed and circulated by British merchant companies.[26] These coins would later be counterfeited, but the financial reforms and expanded transportation networks heralded the colonial epoch's arrival in Nigeria.

The production of counterfeit money during this period was only one manifestation of the gap between government policies and local practices, especially regarding communication and comprehension. Policies were used

---

[21] Mariana P. Candido and Adam Jones, eds., *African Women in the Atlantic World: Property, Vulnerability and Mobility, 1660–1880* (Rochester: James Currey, 2019), 13.

[22] Anthony G. Hopkins, "The Currency Revolution in South–West Nigeria in the Late Nineteenth Century," *Journal of the Historical Society of Nigeria* 3, no. 3 (1966): 471–483.

[23] Segun O. Osoba, "The Phenomenon of Labor Migration in the Era of British Colonial Rule: A Neglected Aspect of Nigeria's Social History," *Journal of the Historical Society of Nigeria* 4, no. 4 (1969): 515–538.

[24] Hopkins, "Currency Revolution."

[25] Olawoye-Mann Salewa, "Towards a Harmonious View of Money: The Nigerian Experience," *Journal of African Studies and Development* 13, no. 4 (2021): 115–123.

[26] Ayodeji Olukoju, "Self-Help Criminality as Resistance? Currency Counterfeiting in Colonial Nigeria," *International Review of Social History* 45, no. 3 (2000): 385–407.

to define these territories as colonial estates of the British imperial hegemony. This process integrated Nigeria and other British West African colonies into the British economic system. But the reforms were mere paperwork without accompanying infrastructure developments to link state policy with productive activities. The colonial state understood this relationship and earnestly combined financial reforms with ordinances and proclamations related to trade and commerce.[27] Its goal was the maximum exploitation of native resources, and the new transportation network formed a nerve center in its massive infrastructural development projects.

Vigorous efforts cleared creeks and waterways for navigation and communication among the coastal states, which also linked these states with their neighbors in other terrains, such as the forest and savannah regions.[28] Much of this work extended precolonial transportation networks that were already in use.[29] As Chuku explained in her study, "before 1900, Oguta women were carrying their trading activities over the Oguta lake and along the Niger River by canoe to Ossomari, Aboh, and Onitsha."[30] Some of these waterways were expanded and deepened, allowing bigger ships to visit the colony from international waters based on their importance to the colonial economy. Seafood and other products could easily find their way to interested markets, strengthening trade and commerce between coastal communities and those on the mainland.

The colonial government had also focused on developing a railway system before the interwar years.[31] Railways connected interior markets directly to the coast and vice versa. The railway industry became essential for transporting merchants, distributing products, and enabling communication between the two colonial administrations.[32] In 1914, when Lugard's proclamation came into effect, Northern and Southern parts of the colony had been integrated through a railway system that met at Jebba. Afigbo explained in his study of this industry that the fruition of the views and decisions from the 1898 Niger Committee and the 1914 amalgamation was largely made possible by the two

---

[27] Edwin G. Charle Jr., "English Colonial Policy and the Economy of Nigeria," *The American Journal of Economics and Sociology* 26, no. 1 (1967): 79–92.
[28] Olufemi R. Ekundare, *An Economic History of Nigeria 1860–1960* (London: Methuen & Co Ltd., 1973), 128–154.
[29] Gabriel Ogundeji Ogunremi, *Counting the Camels: The Economics of Transportation in Pre-Industrial Nigeria* (New York: Nok Publishers International, 1982).
[30] Gloria Ifeoma Chuku, "From Petty Traders to International Merchants: A Historical Account of Three Igbo Women of Nigeria in Trade and Commerce, 1886 to 1970," *African Economic History* 27 (1999): 1–22.
[31] Francis Jaekel, *The History of the Nigerian Railway, Vol. 2: Network and Infrastructures* (Ibadan: Spectrum Books Ltd., 1997).
[32] Joshua A. Odeleye, "Politics of Rail Transport Development in Developing Countries: Case of Nigeria," *Journal of Civil Engineering and Architecture* 6, no. 12 (2012): 1695–1702.

administrations reaching a consensus on the operation of the railways and their role in the integration and management of these areas.[33] After the occurrence of World War I, the government's attention shifted to the creation of road networks.[34] Its intense drive elicited concern among staff and authorities in the railway industry.

When the great economic depression began unfolding in the late 1920s, road networks had begun to supplant the rail system.[35] The campaign to expand the roads gained support from communities that recognized the value of wider roads as improvements over the narrow footpaths previously used for economic distribution, cultural exchange, and social interactions. They contributed heavily, offering financial support and labor attached to the notion of imperial responsibilities for the colonial state. The opening of these routes also introduced new transportation technology to travel via road. Lorries, cars, and bicycles came to represent a nascent social milieu that was incomprehensible to many in society.[36] Aerodromes were constructed to complement ships that now used steam engines, and bridges were built to improve transportation networks. The transportation industry's reforms became a significant indicator of market expansion. Upgraded transportation networks were accompanied by increasing volumes and frequency of trade, greater generation of revenue, easier transportation of goods and people, and the exploitation of native resources and wealth.

Cash labor and cash crops were mutually reinforcing in the colonial economy. Many migrants followed the colonial state's financial, industrial, commercial, and transportation developments to find themselves in and around the Ife, Ondo, and Ekiti territories in the Southern protectorate. Cocoa and palm products were cultivated on massive plantations in those areas to meet export demands (see Figure 12.1).[37] Other migrants relocated to mines in Bauchi, Jos, Warri, and elsewhere; railway stations in locations such as Ogbomoso, Kaduna, Osogbo, and Jebba; construction sites around the colony; and different government offices. Shipping firms took advantage of the colony's expansion and infrastructure developments, increasing their operations in the region. This further integrated the British West African Colonies and the metropolitan state.

---

[33] Adiele E. Afigbo, "The Consolidation of British Imperial Administration in Nigeria: 1900–1918," *Civilizations* 21, no. 4 (1971): 436–446.

[34] Oladipo Olubomehin, *Road Transportation in South Western Nigeria, 1900–1960* (Saarbrücken: LAP Lambert Academic Publishing, 2011).

[35] Oladipo O. Olubomehin, "Road Transportation as Lifeline of the Economy in Western Nigeria, 1920 to 1952," *African Journal of History and Culture* 4, no. 3 (2012): 37–45.

[36] Simon Heap, "Transport and Liquor in Colonial Nigeria," *Journal of Transport History* 21, no. 1 (2001): 28–53.

[37] Samuel O. Aghalino, "British Colonial Policies and the Oil Palm Industry in the Niger Delta Region of Nigeria, 1900–1960," *African Study Monographs* 21, no. 1 (2000): 19–33.

Figure 12.1 A Yoruba family removing seeds from cocoa pods. Cocoa was an important crop that flourished in Western Nigeria, becoming a source of revenue for the local population in the region in colonial times.

On November 1, 1906, Elder Dempster & Co. began a direct transport and shipping service on steam-powered ships traveling between Lagos and the Gold Coast.[38] During the same period, Woermann-Linie ran mailing and

[38] Marika Sherwood, "Elder Dempster and West Africa 1891–C.1940: The Genesis of Underdevelopment?" *The International Journal of African Historical Studies* 30, no. 2 (1997): 253–276.

transportation services from Lagos to Togo, the Gold Coast, Liberia, Las Palmas, Hamburg, Southampton, and Boulogne. The African Steamship Company Ltd. and the British and African Steam Navigation Company opened sailing services from Lagos through Accra, Cape Coast, Sekondi Axim, and Sierra Leone, where mail and passengers were collected for transport to Plymouth and Liverpool.[39]

These patterns of migration and their economic implications meant the proliferation of foreign firms across the region, from the coast to the interior.[40] These companies employed attendants and sales representatives, and so did the emerging Indigenous firms that were quickly driven out of business. Depending on their capacity, these companies employed clerks, secretaries, accountants, and other workers who sought alternative employment in the colonial state. This social disruption reinforced the specialization of labor that was promoted by the government and accepted by the public. The government encouraged job specialization in the economy through its trade, financial, and education policies, and the people encouraged job specialization through their resilience and adaptability to the socioeconomic environment of the colonial state. This would later develop into Guyer's theory of the political economy of everyday life in the postcolonial exacerbation of this economic condition.[41] This included food vendors in cities and urban centers and commodity suppliers, many of whom were Hausa migrants.

These new roles suggest an expanding economy that could serve the public, but the opposite was true. Despite the economic expansion and a greater number of options for earning a living in the colonial state – more than the farming and industrial occupations of precolonial times – poverty was increasing due to rising unemployment and the uneven distribution of resources in the colony.[42] The economic displacement of World War I, followed by the economic depression of the 1920s and the early 1930s before the outbreak of World War II, created difficult economic circumstances that were exacerbated by the British government's response. This gave rise to a substantial population of migrants and impoverished people.

Economic expansion and growth in the colony did not match the growth of either the local population or its needs. The lion's share of benefits from the economy was captured by imperial demands. Items of trade moving along newly opened and rejuvenated routes through the interior remained largely

---

[39] *The Lagos Standard*, "Hope for West Africa," *The Lagos Standard*, May 1, 1907.
[40] Adebayo A. Lawal, *Nigeria Culture, Politics, Governance and Development* (Ibadan: Connel Publications, 2015), 165–194.
[41] See Wale Adebanwi, ed., *The Political Economy of Everyday Life in Africa: Beyond the Margins* (London: James Currey, 2017).
[42] Babatunde J. Decker, "A History of the Poor in Lagos, 1861–1960," (unpublished PhD dissertation, University of Lagos, 2012).

unchanged from precolonial days, but the authority of the local rulers had been overshadowed by the colonizers.[43] Imperial conquest claimed all revenues from tributes, tolls, levies, and other payments within the region that had previously accrued to local authorities. These funds were now passed to the Queen through the colonial state. However, this policy was administered rather haphazardly, like many other government policies of the time.

The *Lagos Standard* reported on the activities of a constable in Ajilete village, in the Badagry district, who was found to be extorting tolls from traders. The merchants had been transporting fish from Porto Novo by daily caravan through the village, traveling to Abeokuta and returning with indigo and chewing sticks, and they were expected to provide goods and services in the form of tributes for the people of the village.[44] The exchange of livestock, kola nuts, indigo, leather, cotton, clothes, and other items continued alongside the European goods that frequently supplanted Indigenous products. The abuse of authority by individuals at the local government level, and the absence of adequate supervision from the colonial state, were not limited to a single region; they pervaded the colonial state's Native Administration and had a substantial effect on the economic condition and administration of the colony.[45] Conflicting views persisted between the state and various societies regarding colonial policies and implementation.

The colonial government continued its intense drive to maximize the extraction of local resources. As a precursor to international exhibitions arranged by the Belgian and Canadian governments between 1928 and 1932, in the early years of the Great Depression, Nigeria's colonial government proposed the organization of an agricultural show. The proposal would be implemented by the Lagos Agricultural Union in November 1906, raised in a meeting between the Colonial Secretary and other major stakeholders in the colonial economy and its administration in December 1905.[46] The planning committee expected the exhibition to attract potential investors from the area that would become the first Commonwealth of British Countries after World War I. A draft Preliminary Notice describing the plan was sent to chambers of commerce in Liverpool, Manchester, Sheffield, Glasgow, London, and other major British cities.

---

[43] Ibrahim M. Jumare, "Colonial Taxation in the Capital of Northern Nigeria," *African Economic History* 26 (1998): 83–97; and Philip Igbafe, "British Rule in Benin 1897–1920: Direct or Indirect?" *Journal of the Historical Society of Nigeria* 3, no. 4 (1967): 701.

[44] *The Lagos Standard*, "Badagry District (from a correspondent) Badagry," *The Lagos Standard*, May 1, 1907, 7.

[45] Adiele E. Afigbo, "Revolution and Reaction in Eastern Nigeria: 1900–1929: The Background to the Women's Riot of 1929," *Journal of the Historical Society of Nigeria* 3, no. 3 (1966): 539–557.

[46] *The Lagos Weekly Record*, "Lagos Agricultural Union," *The Lagos Weekly Record*, Vol. XVII-7, January 20, 1906.

Imperial Responsibilities and Preference

After the colonial enterprise transitioned from its humanitarian, liberal, and civilizing mission to adopt a developmental paradigm, public opinion was divided on the average conditions under which colonial subjects should exist. There was no question as to the Queen's basic role in these foreign territories, for she was "divinely mandated" to liberate inferior civilizations.[47] Whether the argument was for or against the colony, it informed the general belief that framed the experience of natives in the colonial state.

A member of the House of Commons questioned the Colonial Secretary, Bonar Law, on the steps taken by the Colonial Office to assuage the challenges of revenue generation two years into World War I. In response, Secretary Law expressed his regret for the necessity of such changes.[48] In every instance, the local population was pushed to the periphery of economic and political activity – contrary to the administration's supposed mission to boost trade and protect the interests of all subjects – since they were regarded as infants to be weaned on Western civilization. Sets of obligations and practices that were framed as imperial responsibilities became tantamount to civil responsibilities in the colonial state. The former encouraged loyalty to the Queen and the sustenance of her vast empire, but the latter appeared to be dedicated to the maintenance of the sovereign state. This included tax payments, mobilization for war efforts, and the maintenance of peace to enable trade. Kaniki has explained that taxation in the colonial state was "introduced or increased not only to raise revenue but to drive Africans to serve the interest of international capitalism."[49] These responsibilities began at different times in different parts of the colony. By 1914, they had become increasingly standardized, and imperial preference shaped the oppressive agreements that the British government forced on its colonies. The forging of closer economic ties through the 1932 Ottawa agreement following the economic depression was the culmination of ideas that had birthed the colonial project three decades earlier.

The Colonial Office played an integral part in the British Empire's rebuilding efforts through the mobilization of resources. This was arbitrarily enacted to limit native participation in local markets and export activity, but it became institutionalized and sanctioned by the London office. These two counterproductive notions characterized the local experience in the colonial state, for

---

[47] *The Lagos Weekly Record*, "Proposed Duty on Palm Kernels, Debate in the House of Commons," *The Lagos Weekly Record*, August 3, 1916; and Extracts from Official Report, Vol. 85, no. 81, *The Lagos Weekly Record*, Vol. XXVI–27, November 4 and 11, 1916.

[48] *The Lagos Weekly Record*, "Proposed Duty on Palm Kernels, Debate in the House of Commons," *The Lagos Weekly Record*, Vol. XXVI–27, August 3, 1916; and Extracts from Official Report, Vol. 85, no. 81, December 23–30, 1916.

[49] Martin H. Y. Kaniki, "The Colonial Economy: The Former British Zones," in *General History of Africa: VII Africa Under Colonial Domination 1880–1935*, ed. Albert Adu Boahen (Paris: UNESCO, 1990), 397.

imperial burdens were shouldered by people who saw diminishing returns from the commercial activities conducted in their region.[50] As the government galvanized local support, mobilizing people through conscription into the British army and forced labor on government projects, the reduction in available workers put pressure on rural producers. The remaining population was expected to contribute to war efforts even as their lives were made more difficult by famine, drought, restrictive government policies, and reduced productivity at different times and in the different regions of the colony.[51]

The 1905 annual report of major events shaping the colony's administration noted attempts to consolidate economic spheres of influence among Asian powers as well as America and other Western Imperial powers.[52] Japan's victory, for instance, in the Russo–Japanese war positioned it as an emerging power in Asia and swiftly determined its stake in global trade and politics. The desire to also assert itself economically, like Britain and France, increased Japan's participation in West African trade. Japanese merchants entered markets in the region and engaged in intense competition with other world powers. This attitude was based on the accumulation of decades of commercial and industrial reforms in the state under the Tokugawa dynasty, modeled through Western imperialism and economic morphology.[53] By the twentieth century, when colonial rule became the norm in Africa, the number of global imperial actors in the region had increased not only with the individuals but also with the states involved. Emerging and established imperial states had begun looking abroad to meet their economic needs and exert political hegemony. Increasing levels of foreign involvement in local markets created pressures that literally dictated the socio-economic landscape and well-being of the native population.

The school of thought following society's transition to capitalism during this period argues that change was driven by the introduction of capital and the pursuit of economic production and reproduction.[54] Capital was a real issue for merchants and traders on both sides of the Atlantic and Indian oceans. Local actors were at a disadvantage, while their foreign counterparts enjoyed robust credit and insurance facilities. When these services were available to local actors, the options were much more limited than those available to foreign actors.[55]

---

[50] *The Lagos Standard*, "A Question of the Moment," *The Lagos Standard*, Vol. XXII-49, August 9, 1916.

[51] Ochonu, *Colonial Meltdown*.

[52] *The Lagos Weekly Record*, "Lagos Agricultural Union," *The Lagos Weekly Record*, Vol. XVII-7, January 20, 1906.

[53] Gail Lee Bernstein and Haruhiro Fukui, eds., *Japan and the World: Essays on Japanese History and Politics in Honour of Ishida Takeshi* (London: Macmillan Press, 1998).

[54] Walter Rodney, *How Europe Underdeveloped Africa* (Kingston: Bogle-Louverture, 1972).

[55] Dan O. Chukwu, "The Economic Impact of Pioneer Indigenous Banks in Colonial Nigeria, 1920–1960," *Journal of the Historical Society of Nigeria* 19 (2010): 93–100.

British companies also operated almost seamlessly with the colonial government. From the nineteenth century, the role of the British Chambers of Commerce had increased substantially, claiming a larger stake of private interest and characterizing the elite consensus in British politics. From London, Liverpool, Manchester, and other British financial hubs, their influence extended into British colonies in West Africa and other parts of the world.[56] Their agents and conglomerates were in charge of currency distribution, price regulation, financial policies, the import and export of goods, and every other aspect of trade and commerce in the colonies.[57]

When the financial sector's dominant actors can exert so much control over the economy, it has clear implications for free markets and the government's laissez-faire doctrine. Arthur Young, quoted by Colonel Lord Henry Cavendish-Bentinck, described the colonial project as "entirely commercial, a traders project and the spirit of monopoly pervaded every step of its progress."[58] This statement, made during an impassioned session in the House of Commons, explains the reasoning behind every step of the British Empire's administration during this period. Local actors were increasingly shut out of the markets due to their inability to compete with access to either capital or government influence, starting with the commencement of colonial rule and worsening by the outbreak of World War I. An account of the Gold Coast mining industry, provided in the Finance and Insurance columns of *Public Opinion*, reported that "the west African market is enjoying a boom all on its own."[59] The benefits were not equally distributed as the same report noted that "Of the hundreds of (local) Companies formed, the bulk have lost every penny of their capital, some others will go through a process of reconstruction."[60]

Local actors shifted their focus to other, more favorable markets where they could compete fairly. They also formed unions and cooperative bodies that proliferated during the interwar years.[61] The boom was largely beneficial for foreign actors at the expense of their local counterparts, but a new class of elites

---

[56] Godfrey N. Uzoigwe, *Britain and the Conquest of Africa: The Age of Salisbury* (Ann Arbor: University of Michigan Press, 1974); and Toyin Falola and Matthew M. Heaton, *A History of Nigeria* (New York: Cambridge University Press, 2008).

[57] Chibuike Ugochukwu Uche, "Foreign Banks, Africans, and Credit in Colonial Nigeria, C.1890–1912," *The Economic History Review Series* 52, no. 4 (1999): 669–691.

[58] *The Lagos Weekly Record*, "Proposed Duty on Palm Kernels, Debate in the House of Commons," *The Lagos Weekly Record*, Vol. XXVI–27, August 3, 1916; and Extracts from Official Report, Vol. 85, no. 81, November 4 & 11, 1916.

[59] *The Lagos Weekly Record*, "Public Opinion," *The Lagos Weekly Record*, Vol. XVII–7, January 20, 1906.

[60] *The Lagos Weekly Record*, "Public Opinion."

[61] Anthony I. Asiwaju, "The Cooperative Movement in the Colonial Context: A Comparison of the French and British Rural West African Experience to 1960," *Journal of the Historical Society of Nigeria* 11, nos. 1/2 (1981–2): 89–108.

was produced from the local population. "Class of elites" is a collective term for a small group of indigenous, educated, and economic elites who emerged across Nigeria around the 1930s with a common political orientation informed by the need to play a dominant role in the country's development. Although the indigenous elites, a few of whom were nonliterate, were not as global in exposure, experience, or outlook, they held influential powers that made their interventions in the colonial state key. For the educated and economic power elites, the goals they set out to achieve were not different from those of the indigenous class since all three were directly affected by colonial policies that not only placed them as a second fiddle but also extricated their knowledge, experience, and expertise from colonial development agendas.

Many of these new classes of elites became influential in nationalist and anticolonial efforts, using their economic strength to finance mobilization and political activities.[62] Being involved in cocoa production and distribution became synonymous with wealth in the Yoruba region of the Southern protectorate.[63] The crop, which was introduced by the end of the nineteenth century, became widely cultivated in the Yoruba territory's forest plains. Its cultivation alongside other cash crops influenced the region's transformation and agricultural sophistication during this period.[64] The newfound wealth was channeled into the creation of new infrastructure, vehicles, and other Western products that signified a specific class in society.

The boom of the late 1930s boosted the social status of cocoa farmers and produce buyers. However, only a small number of these local actors were able to produce the crop on a commercial scale. Some of these wealthy elites also invested in the transportation industry and the distribution of foreign goods. Indian, Lebanese, and American companies placed advertisements seeking business partnerships. Meanwhile, Japanese clothes and fabrics, German liquor and textiles, and American manufactured goods competed intensely to gain a greater share of the African market. In the process, they eliminated many local industries and actors. Many of these imported products symbolized the modern period into which colonial society transitioned. These products dominated the pages of newspapers, periodicals, pamphlets, and other colonial literature.[65]

Foreign interests dominated the medical sector, displacing local doctors and treatments. Food consumption began to resemble Western patterns after the

---

[62] Martin L. Kilson, "Nationalism and Social Classes in British West Africa," *The Journal of Politics* 20, no. 2 (1968): 368–387.

[63] Aribidesi Usman and Toyin Falola, *The Yoruba from Prehistory to the Present* (Cambridge: Cambridge University Press, 2019), 321–358.

[64] Reuben K. Udo, *Geographical Regions of Nigeria* (Berkeley: University of California Press, 2020), 26–36.

[65] Joseph Rubenstein, "On Nigerian Pop Culture," *Dialectical Anthropology* 3 (1978): 261–267.

introduction of junk food and canned goods. Basic home appliances, furniture, and other objects were measured against Western standards. Changing local tastes created headwinds for local industries and actors, but the real damage was done by the affordable prices at which the competing products were sold. Japanese, German, American, and other products entering the colony were mass produced on an industrial scale. Their reduced manufacturing time and construction costs allowed them to dominate the Nigerian market. Ijebu textiles and other local clothing industries suffered substantial losses.[66] The extensive government projects to develop road transportation networks allowed these foreign products to be distributed easily to every corner of the colony. Leather and fabric industries in Kano were affected, along with other local industries, such as metalworking.

Merchants from the Levant region, commonly Syrians and Lebanese, were also formidable competition. They, along with other foreign actors, had more leverage over native markets, continuing to operate while native shops and businesses closed. The British government and imperial agents in the finance sector justified their bias against local actors by citing an inability to provide sufficient, quantifiable, and valuable collateral for loans. This lack of access to capital limited the role of local actors, who were largely involved in the production of raw materials that were exported by foreign actors and returned as finished goods. Even when these items came back as imported commodities, foreign actors continued to retain advantages by controlling distribution.[67]

Petty trading and the production of raw materials were the only available roles for the local population in this international division of labor. Foreign actors, especially from the British Chambers of Commerce, determined market rates for raw materials and set the prices of imported finished products. They also created economic incentives that determined which crops would be cultivated by local farmers, which was another way for the colonial state to dominate and exploit its subjects.

The production of cotton, palm kernel, cocoa, and rubber was promoted by the government to serve the industrial needs of the metropolitan state. Before 1900, when the entire Niger area was declared a British colony, the government in Lagos had established a botanical research center for the enhancement of these products. This was part of the imperial drive to promote "legitimate trade" and divert local resources to meet Britain's industrial needs – efforts that were led by missionaries and the British trading community. In 1906, the House

---

[66] Emmanuel A. Ayandele, *The Ijebu of Yorubaland 1850–1950: Politics, Economy, and Society* (Ibadan: Heinemann Educational Books Plc., 1992).

[67] Ayodeji Olukoju, "Elder Dempster and the Shipping Trade of Nigeria During the First World War," *The Journal of African History* 33, no. 2 (1992): 255–271; David K. Fieldhouse, *The Colonial Empires: A Comparative Survey from the Eighteenth Century* (New York: Delacorte Press, 1966); and Anthony G. Hopkins, *An Economic History of West Africa* (New York: Routledge, 2020).

Committee on Edible and Oil Producing Nuts and Seeds presented a report to the British House of Commons showing that efforts to increase local crop production had yielded results. The committee's submission to Parliament and the British government confirmed a 34 percent increase in milk fat produced by a species of palm kernel cultivated in the colony.[68] These efforts affected a variety of crop species, with varying degrees of success. It was not enough for farmers to cultivate these crops; the crops required processing to meet the import standards of the metropolitan market. The government provided guidance and resources to assist with these requirements.

This economic structure posed serious risks to farmers. If foreign demand for crops diminished, local farmers suffered major financial losses. During World War I, Arthur Young's description of the colonial project exposed its negative impacts of the colonial project in even more glaring terms. War broke out in the same year that the colonial administration of the Northern and Southern Nigerian colonies was centralized. As the central administration delegated power to the Native Authority units (local administrators), the Colonial Office in London granted more authority to British merchant companies. This process turned the empire's laissez-faire economic posture into a nationalist policy. British colonies were integrated into coordinating units that reported to the metropolitan capital. Their resources were dedicated to the pursuit of war and the recovery of the empire under the Imperial Responsibilities and Empire Recovery obligations.[69] Imperial explorers and geographers had exhaustively surveyed Africa to assess its mineral wealth and other resources, with the most notable mineralogical surveys dating back to this period.[70] This concerted effort culminated in the government's participation in international trade exhibitions in Belgium and Canada, while Nigeria considered its involvement as early as 1905.

In addition to establishing different committees in the British Parliament for various aspects of the resources and wealth of the colonies, including the Committee on Development of Empire Resources and the Committee on Edible and Oil Producing Nuts and Seeds, the centralization of the colonial administration led to the emergence of national departments to exploit local resources. These include Railway, the Army, Maritime, Forestry, Audit, Treasury, Public Works, Medical, Post and Telegraphs, Prisons, Judiciary, Agriculture, Education, Customs, Printing, Police, and Geological Survey, among others. They implemented government policies through force and diplomacy, extracting local resources and enabling effective communication

---

[68] *The Lagos Weekly Record*, "Proposed Duty on Palm Kernels."
[69] John E. Lattimer, "The Ottawa Trade Agreements," *Journal of Farm Economics* 16, no. 4 (1934): 565–581.
[70] Richard Rathbone, "World War I and Africa: Introduction," *The Journal of African History* 19, no. 1 (1978): 9.

across the colonized territory.[71] The administration's increased centralization and the imperial government's nationalist drive came simultaneously with the centralization of capital and the network of British merchants. Companies amalgamated into larger conglomerates that placed additional pressure on local markets.

Similar attempts at collaboration and centralization among local actors were impeded by many factors, and the government eventually played a decisive role.[72] These local actors included the emerging educated elites and influential figures mostly operating in the import and export sectors of the economy, buying produce and distributing goods.[73] Many of these individuals believed that they were better suited to represent the interests of their kinsmen in the nascent Weberian state, asserting that the conduct of government was less comprehensible to the minds of precolonial local authorities. By the turn of the twentieth century, this population included lawyers, engineers, and doctors that were going to London to represent the economic interests of their kinsmen.[74] The *Lagos Weekly Note Record* described their demand for local representation as a valid expression of "British Imperial statesmanship rather than the diabolical and destructive attitude of Empire-wreckers who are now moving heaven and earth to relegate the native to a condition of perpetual economic serfdom and social and moral degradation."[75] Similar sentiments were shared by British newspapers such as *African World* and politicians including Sir George Toulmin, along with the general population.

The colonial administration reversed its proposal to develop Nigeria into a settler colony that would have been similar to those in East and Southern Africa. Possibly, this was a response to resistance organized by colonial Nigeria's new class of educated elites, but the real reasons for the decision are best known to the Colonial Office and British administrators.[76] The elite population mediated relations between the state and the general population through mobilization, the organization of union bodies and movements, acerbic pieces published in newspapers and magazines, and other media outlets that gave voice to the public.[77] They were regarded as a danger to the

---

[71] Anthony Kirk-Greene, *Britain's Imperial Administrators, 1858–1966* (London: Palgrave Macmillan Press, 1999).
[72] Rathbone, "World War I and Africa," 6; and Asiwaju, "The Cooperative Movement in Colonial Context."
[73] Axel Harneit-Sievers, "African Business, 'Economic Nationalism,' and British Colonial Policy: Southern Nigeria, 1935–1954," *African Economic History* 24 (1996): 25–68.
[74] Emmanuel A. Ayandele, *The Educated Elite in the Nigerian Society* (Ibadan: Ibadan University Press, 1974).
[75] *The Lagos Weekly Note Record*, "Weekly Note," Vol. XXVI-29, August 5 and 12, 1916.
[76] Kaniki, "The Colonial Economy."
[77] James S. Coleman, *Nigeria: Background to Nationalism* (Berkeley: University of California Press, 1958).

colonial project, labeled subversive subjects and anarchists, and ultimately ignored in the administration of the state.

Authorities and agents of government at the local level became more powerful. In some cases, they engaged in authoritarian extortion through the court and tax systems. By supporting these authorities, the colonial government extended its influence in the interior while special arrangements were made with local authorities to expand the exploitation of resources.[78] The Native Revenue Proclamation of 1906, which established the structure and system of revenue generation and Native Administration in Northern Nigeria, allowed the colonial government to accomplish the same goals with precolonial fief-holders and the *Jakada* who assisted them. One-third of the collected taxes went to the district head, one-fifth to the village head, and one-half to the protectorate. The remaining revenue was for the "recognized chief," or emir, in the area, to distribute among agents and meet financial obligations.[79]

In Lagos, the educated population was instrumental in running the local government as advisers and even kingmakers.[80] However, this did not guarantee that they would be represented in the administration of either Lagos or the colony. C. L. Temple described Lagos as the "storm center of the administrative politics" and the "grave of reputations," due to the intensity of anticolonial agitation in the coastal city.[81] The declining economic environment and deteriorating living conditions brought by World War I, and the reforms and debates that followed within the colony and abroad, forced Governor Clifford to reckon with this elite class and their demands to represent their kinsmen in government.[82]

The Clifford Constitution eventually made some concessions to local representation in 1922. By that time, Japanese, American, German, and other foreign interests had been subdued by Colonial Office reforms. Its drive for centralization required the colony's annual budgets and expenditures to be examined and approved by the office. It also required Nigerian colonial administrators to impose export duties on goods that traveled to ports outside of those approved by the British government. Two years into the war, these duties dominated the discourse in British political space. Britain's surging economic interest in its Nigerian colony was evident from

---

[78] Obaro Ikime, "Reconsidering Indirect Rule: The Nigerian Example," *Journal of the Historical Society of Nigeria* 4, no. 3 (1968): 421–438.

[79] Obaro Ikime, "The British and Native Administration Finance in Northern Nigeria, 1900–1934," *Journal of the Historical Society of Nigeria* 7, no. 4 (1975): 673–692.

[80] Olakunle A. Lawal and Oluwasegun M. Jimoh, "Missiles from 'Kirsten Hall': Herbert Macaulay versus Hugh Clifford, 1922–1931," *Lagos Historical Review* 12 (2012): 41–62.

[81] *The Lagos Weekly Record*, "His Honor C. L. Temple–C. M. G. An Appreciation," *The Lagos Weekly Record*, Vol. XXVI-20, August 19 and 26, 1916.

[82] O. E. Udofia, "Nigerian Political Parties: Their Role in Modernizing the Political System, 1920–1966," *Journal of Black Studies* 11, no. 4 (1981): 435–447.

the introduction of a £2 minimum fee per shipment of palm kernels exported outside of British territories.

Similar restrictions were soon placed on cotton, cocoa, and other products, where British merchants sought to limit competition. These market manipulations greatly restricted the opportunities for local market actors. The Colonial Office, addressing the economic crisis, implemented Taxation by Order in Council, which allowed colonial administrators to repel foreign competition in the local trade of palm kernel by arbitrarily increasing export duties. The policy was fiercely contested by local educated and economic elites along with the Anti-Slavery and Aborigines Protection Society, which were supported by some members of the British Parliament. A deputation from the Parliamentary Committee of the Anti-Slavery Society led by Mr. J. W. Wilson protested the report from the House Committee on Edible and Oil Producing Nuts and Seeds. Wilson argued that "the native industry would be seriously depressed by this tariff, and that the natives would be disturbed having being taxed for the advantage of this country's [sic]."[83] Parliamentarians such as Sir Toulmin noted the policy's implications for monopolization, putting local actors at a disadvantage.[84]

Parliamentarians argued that the new policy failed to address problems with Britain's organization of the palm kernel industry. Germany's more advanced capabilities gave it a superior position in Nigerian markets. Instead of reorganizing British industry, policies attempted to cripple American, German, and other foreign competitors by restricting market access. Local workers were laid off by foreign companies at the same time that the colonial government retrenched local staff and conscripted the working population into the imperial army. A communiqué issued to colonial administrators in British West Africa, which was also published in the *Christian Science Monitor* on July 8, 1916, explained that the taxation policy was to be implemented during World War I and for the following five years.[85] Ideally, the measure would allow the British government and its imperial agents to catch up with Germany's industrial capabilities to claim a larger share of the market. The focus on palm kernel may reflect its importance in the production of major staple and industrial goods and materials.

Economic conditions during and after World War I drastically reduced the purchasing power of people living in the Nigerian colony. Firms that had previously made daily sales of £300 reported new sales figures from £4 to £9.[86] As the economic crisis hit harder and a larger share of the recovery efforts was

[83] *Daily News and Leader*, "Palm Oil Tariff," *Daily News and Leader*, July 20, 1916.
[84] *The Lagos Weekly Record*, "Proposed Duty on Palm Kernels."
[85] *The Christian Science Monitor*, "British Scheme to Keep Trade in Palm Kernel," *The Christian Science Monitor*, July 8, 1916, reproduced in *The Lagos Weekly Record*, Vol. XXVI–20, August 19 and 26, 1916.
[86] *The Lagos Weekly Record*, Vol. XXVI–21, September 2 and 9, 1916.

borne by residents, the government recorded £267,000 in savings from a reduction of capital and recurrent expenditures. That included the displacement of around 40 percent of the government's workforce.[87] The government and its imperial agents shored up their revenue by raiding Nigeria's people and its resources, driving local inhabitants into penury. Lugard summarized and justified the colonial exploitation of local resources as the right of a superior civilization.[88] Major Arthur G. Leonard furthered this view by asserting that colonial officers provided the British energy that drove the mobilization and exploitation of local resources.[89]

The debate in the House of Commons revealed an interesting relationship between West Africa's palm kernel industry and the distribution of liquor. As local societies were recalibrated by European influences, especially trade goods, European liquor replaced the local wines that were ordinarily produced by the destruction of palm trees. Concerns were raised over the newfound popularity of European liquor, but limiting its distribution could harm efforts to increase the production of palm kernel, a product that constituted one of the most widely distributed and revenue-generating commodities across the colony. The campaign to restrict the distribution of alcohol in the British West African colony was largely the responsibility of missionaries and humanitarians who felt it damaged the minds of the natives and impaired missionary activities. Humanitarians based their arguments for the prohibition on the hermitic characterization of people who were unable to act in a civilized manner.

Nigeria's colonizers considered imposing a policy of segregation similar to that which existed in British colonies elsewhere. The proposal was directly related to trade and the colony's economy, but its proponents were also concerned about the health of British officers and merchants. Segregation was considered a biopower project to support the exploitation of native wealth and resources. The educated elites of Lagos rigorously opposed this move, deploying mechanisms of resistance in protest letters and articles published by their ubiquitous newspapers and printing presses. This group of people and their British administrators had similar concerns about the policy's applications, but they arrived at different conclusions. Both sides were concerned about the extent to which the government would recalibrate existing power dynamics in matters such as land, property, security, and other incentives to deliver a seamless implementation of policy that did not disrupt trading activities. It was also thought that the policy could be most effective in the interior rather than in cities and urban centers.

---

[87] Ochonu, *Colonial Meltdown*, 112–113.
[88] Lord Lugard, *The Dual Mandate in British Tropical Africa* (New York: Routledge, 1965).
[89] *West African Mail*, March 28, 1907, reproduced in *The Lagos Standard*, "Hope for West Africa," May 1, 1907, 4.

The Secretary of the Manchester Chamber of Commerce, responding to Governor Lugard in 1916, concluded that the policy was desirable if the conditions were properly considered by the government. On the other hand, Lagos elites saw the conditions as reasons to discard the policy. The government's proposed land and settlement policy had been defeated earlier, and this new policy risked failure due to the costs and responsibilities that such a campaign would impose on the colonial administration. The 1904 Land Revenue Proclamation and the introduction of Direct Taxation in Northern Nigeria already meant that one-quarter of the proceeds from the land was taxed by the colonial government, and three-quarters went to the emir.[90] Ultimately, this paradigm of land regulation was sustained in place of transitioning to an era of spatial segregation and its attendant land policies.

As private property increased and larger numbers of migrants from different backgrounds traveled to cities and emerging urban centers, the ownership of land became a major form of investment and social security.[91] Apart from the government's intervention through land regulation, this was a departure from older practices that saw land as communally owned and collectively accessed by right of birth or acquaintance.[92] Land remained fixed capital due to its immobility, and its value was boosted by the fact that migrants had to rent land and apartments for urban economic ventures. Land ownership became increasingly contentious in the hinterlands as a continuation of precolonial rivalry and competition. The colonial economy remodeled the structure of the family, social relationships, and land ownership in a series of domino effects.[93]

Conclusion

The colonial economy consisted of actors who were grouped through racial hierarchies. These groups gave rise to anticolonial and nationalist agitations, and economic issues dominated the political space of the colonial state.[94] The colonial economy was also affected by global events and interactions between international markets and economic actors within the colony. The British government's drive for centralization increasingly jeopardized the interests

---

[90] Ikime, "The British and Native Administration," 674.
[91] Steven Pierce, "Pointing to Property: Colonialism and Knowledge about Land Tenure in Northern Nigeria," *Africa* 83, no. 1 (2013): 142–163.
[92] E. Omuojine, "The Land Use Act and the English Doctrine of Estate," *Journal of the Nigerian Institute of Surveyors and Valuers* 22, no. 3 (1999): 54–56.
[93] Namnso B. Udoekanem, David O. Adoga, and Victor O. Onwumere, "Land Ownership in Nigeria: Historical Development, Current Issues and Future Expectations," *Journal of Environment and Earth Science* 4, no. 2 (2014): 182–187.
[94] Olusola Olasupo, Isaac O. Oladeji, and E. O. C. Ijeoma, "Nationalism and Nationalist Agitation in Africa: The Nigerian Trajectory," *The Review of Black Political Economy* 44 (2017): 261–283.

of local inhabitants. The British government used Pax Britannica as an ideal justification for its actions and decisions in the colony. Official colonial rule immediately introduced a new blend of economic systems into the colony that was alien to the local population. Cash labor, as well as agricultural exploitation, were at the heart of Britain's colonial economy. The markets for import and export expanded drastically while infrastructure that would ease colonial Nigeria's industrial exploitation was built. One of the legacies of the colonial economy is the large transportation network that dots the Nigerian landscape today.

Nigeria's colonial economy during this period (1900–40s) faced serious stress occasioned by the effects and aftermath of World War II, where the Pax Britannica was no longer sufficient to maintain the empire's solidarity. Radical nationalist drives were amplified in the 1930s, displacing the old order dominated by Macaulay's Nigerian National Democratic Party. The nationalist doctrine was used against the colonial state, deployed in the political liberation of the colony and bringing British fears to life. This population's involvement in the war had shown that the concept of white superiority was irredeemably flawed.[95]

Efforts by cosmopolitan powers to promote imperial interests came at a huge cost. The displacement of conscripted natives in World War I continued after they were abandoned following World War II. Many of those who made it back to the colony had become amputees, and this population turned into anticolonial activists due to the government's failure to keep to its promises regarding the war. The mobilization and organization of people in the colonial state after World War II found a modus operandi that was largely limited to the political scene and concerned with the transition of power to local representation. Economic foundations laid by the British colonial administrators had become too entrenched to be disrupted without a systemic, concentrated effort. The local population remained constrained by a lack of access to capital, unable to compete with their foreign counterparts on equal footing. The activities of foreign companies continued with government support.

---

[95] *The Lagos Weekly Record*, "Weekly Note"; and *The Lagos Weekly Record*, Vol. XXVI-22, September 16–30, 1916.

13

Western Education

The history of Western education in Nigeria can be traced to the activities of the European missionaries who arrived to spread the gospel. In their attempts to win souls and get more converts, they introduced Western education/formal education. This type of education is described as "Western" because it largely reflects the ideas and ideologies of European formal education, although it could be argued that the type of education initiated by the Church was "missionary education" because the curriculum was solely based on Christian doctrines, and the goal was to produce people who would continue the process of evangelization. This, however, does not take away the fact that the missionaries should be credited with the development of Western education in Nigeria; after all, the only thin line of difference between missionary education and formal or Western education was the scope (as in the curriculum), as most of the pedagogical practices, as well as the principles of instructions, were similar. It can thus be argued that missionary education laid the foundation for Western education.

Western Education up till 1960

Both Onyerisara Ukeje and J. U. Asiku noted that the history of Western education in Nigeria could be traced to 1842 when missionaries like Reverend Thomas Birch Freeman of the Methodist Mission arrived in Nigeria.[1] They argued that the arrival of the Methodist Mission and other mission societies, such as the Church Missionary Society (CMS), the Baptist Church, and the Roman Catholic Church, set the stage for the development of Western education in the country. This was particularly so because these mission societies established schools wherever they went. While there is a scholarly consensus that Western education is tied to the arrival of the missionaries, it would be historically inaccurate to posit that the establishment of schools started in 1842, even when there were several denominations of missionary churches.

---

[1] Onyerisara Ukeje and J. U. Asiku, "Education in Nigeria," in *Education in Africa: A Comparative Survey*, ed. Babs Fafunwa and J. U Asiku (New York: George Alen and Unwin 1982), 206.

Babs Fafunwa traced the development of schools in Nigeria to the activities of the Portuguese missionaries in Benin, who, after the conversion of the Oba of Benin and some of the Benin chiefs, established primary schools for royalty.[2] According to Fafunwa, the Portuguese missionaries believed that sustainable trade with the Benin people would mean converting them to Christianity.[3] With this established, it could be considered that Western education became prominent only with the rapid number of missionary societies in the nineteenth century. The missionary societies believed the most potent way to penetrate the minds of the Indigenous people was to establish schools, which they believed was a viable means of propagation. The first mission school was established in 1843 by Mr. and Mrs. De Graft.[4]

In 1846, Reverends Samuel Ajayi Crowther, Charles Gollmer, and Henry Townsend founded two schools in Abeokuta: one for boys, the other for girls. Similarly, the Scottish Presbyterian Mission established a school in 1846. The Southern Baptist Convention also established schools at Ijaye, Ogbomoso, and Lagos in 1855. It should be noted that the scope of study in these mission schools was based on theology. This immediately created difficulties for the mission schools because there were no central laws to regulate the schools' affairs. However, the educational activities of the missionary schools facilitated the literacy of the Indigenous people, the orthography of the local languages, and the introduction of the English language as the official medium of communication, given that Nigeria as a country is both multilingual and multiethnic.

Furthermore, it is imperative to include that the British government was absent during missionary education. This explains why there were no major educational reforms during the period and how haphazard some educational policies were, especially as what was regarded as formal learning was the teaching of religious doctrines. It could also be posited that missionary education was not functional for society. Indeed, theological education was only needed by a specific set of people. Since most people were not yet fully convinced about Christianity, it appeared incongruous that the missionaries designed a Christian-based education. The sole mission of the missionaries as regards education was to "convert the 'heathen' or the benighted African to Christianity via education."[5]

The presence of the colonial government marked a milestone in the development of Western education in Nigeria. The British colonial government had initially penetrated Nigeria following the annexation of Lagos. Even when the British government, in a treaty with Oba Akitoye, had permitted education development, it had only taken up the responsibilities for around twenty years

[2] Babs Fafunwa, *History of Education in Nigeria* (New York: Routledge, 2018), 74.
[3] Fafunwa, *History of Education in Nigeria*, 74.
[4] Fafunwa, *History of Education in Nigeria*, 82.
[5] Fafunwa, *History of Education in Nigeria*, 82.

when the treaty was signed.[6] The British government only rolled out a paltry sum of £30 each to the mission societies of Church Missionary Society (CMS), the Wesleyan Methodist, and the Catholic Society as a form of support for their educational initiatives. One of the reasons the British government stayed out of missionary education was that it had no clear-cut policies for the education of people in its colonies. Despite the British being involved in West Africa, in earnest since the early 19th century, they only adopted their first clear educational ordinance in 1882, which is a really long time to go without any formal educational policies. This further explains why the 1882 Educational Ordinance, the first colonial educational policy, was administered to the colonies of Lagos, the Gold Coast (now Ghana), Sierra Leone, and Gambia. This ordinance provided for the establishment of an education board saddled with the responsibility of the development of government-owned schools as well as the provision of grants. The educational ordinance was a direct copy of the British Education Act of 1844, and it was not long before its inadequacies influenced another educational ordinance. Because the ordinance was largely copied from the British Educational Policy and even served to function for most of the British colonies in West Africa, it no longer lacked relevance to Nigerian society.

Folasade Suleiman noted that most of the goals of education in the 1882 Educational Ordinance were too narrow, most importantly because they were designed in the interest of the English child or learner.[7] Not much research was conducted to discover how the stated educational goals would fit Nigerian needs. The inadequacies of the 1882 Educational Ordinance led to the development of the 1887 Educational Ordinance. This slightly improved version of the former showed the colonial government's genuine interest in promoting education.[8] This ordinance empowered the colonial government to be directly involved in the affairs of the schools and provided grants for schools, teachers, and individual learners, among a host of others. Through this educational ordinance, the mission schools had a better vision for the ongoing education of the students. The colonial government further demanded that the mission schools shape up or shape out – that is, if they were to continue in the task of education, they must conform to the standards of education as determined by the government. Some mission schools eventually folded because they could not meet the standards. The 1887 Educational Ordinance was also largely effective and was widely regarded as a purely Nigerian education ordinance. This hinged on the fact that the colony of Lagos had been separated in 1886 from the Gold Coast to become the Colony and Protectorate of Lagos.

[6] Ukeje and Asiku, "Education in Nigeria," 207.
[7] Folasade R. Sulaiman, "Internationalization in Education: The British Colonial Policies on Education in Nigeria 1882–1926," *Journal of Sociological Research* 3, no. 2 (2012): 93.
[8] Sulaiman, "Internationalization in Education," 93.

It is imperative to note that the proliferation of the Christian mission schools under the full backing of the colonial government provoked the Muslim community in Lagos at that time, who had been convinced that the colonial government intentionally excluded them from their education policies. Thus, they pressured the colonial government, who created a government primary school in 1899 for Muslim children. It could be argued that the fact that the Muslim children were undergoing Qur'anic education was a factor that influenced the colonial government's reluctance to include them in their Western education. The colonial government's admiration of the mission schools was another factor. As Gbadebo O. Gbadamosi noted, the Muslim community operated an educational system that could be divided into three: "The first phase began at the early age of about five when the young Muslim children were sent down to piazza schools managed by some Mallams."[9] The second and third stages were concerned with the completion of the Qur'an, which included a near-perfect recitation and the interpretation of the Qur'an. The British government was concerned about the susceptibility of the Muslims to change and how the mission schools would fit in with the ideals of Islam and its adherents.[10] The colonial government had little difficulty with the Western education of Muslims in Lagos but faced much greater problems in the North, as most of the emirs rejected Western education, which was widely regarded as Christian education at the time. In general, Western education thrived in Lagos and most of what became the Southern Protectorate more so than in Northern Nigeria.

It is important to further discuss the development of postprimary or secondary education in Nigeria. Secondary education was already operational before the colonial government's interest in education. The CMS established the first secondary school in 1859 under the supervision of a Nigerian clergyman, Reverend Thomas B. Macaulay, who was the father of the nationalist Herbert Macaulay. The demand for postprimary education hinged on Nigerians' thirst for further education.[11] Unlike primary education, secondary education's scope was not based on theology. Rather, it was geared toward a literacy curriculum, wherein subjects such as Greek and Latin were taught. Other secondary schools after the Church Missionary Society Grammar School followed the same curriculum and instructional delivery pattern. The government even copied the model of this school in establishing government-owned secondary schools; thus, between 1859 and 1914, eleven secondary schools were established.[12]

However, secondary schools during this period did not reflect secondary education, especially as secondary school students took primary school

---

[9] Gbadebo O. Gbadamosi, "The Establishment of Western Education among Muslims in Nigeria 1896–1926," *Journal of the Historical Society of Nigeria* 4, no. 1 (1967): 90.
[10] Gbadamosi, "The Establishment of Western Education," 95.
[11] Oyewole Olayioye Ajala, "A Historical Review of Secondary Education in Western Nigeria: 1842–1976" (unpublished PhD dissertation, North Texas University, 1980), 67.
[12] Ajala, *A Historical Review*, 69.

subjects. Aside from the nomenclature and instructional delivery, in some cases there was not much difference between primary and secondary education. This could be attributed to the fact that, at this point, the colonial government had not intervened. This fueled multiple criticisms from various quarters. Particularly, Reverend Henry Carr, in one of his supervisions of the secondary schools in 1897, discovered that the scope of the curriculum was too advanced for the learners. He contended that the secondary students were not getting secondary school education and that most students had not been prepared for advanced studies in primary schools.[13] Henry Carr gave secondary schools and secondary education a sense of purpose before colonial intervention.

Jacob F. Ade Ajayi further noted that the mission societies that established the schools were aware of the defects but lacked the money to address them.[14] With a constrained budget, it was much more difficult for the mission schools to thrive according to adequate standards. Another factor Ajayi identified was that the missionaries did not exist to own schools; education development appeared to be an afterthought. This showed why most of the policies were irregular. Even the development of education seemed futile, as the people were not sold on the idea of education. They also did not understand the inherent value of European education spread across several communities. Ajayi noted thus:

> Each community had its traditional method of educating their children, to communicate and to count in the local language, and to understand the traditions, customs and religion of the community. It was futile and unnecessary for the European school to attempt to compete in this field.[15]

Additionally, the amalgamation of the Southern Protectorate and the Northern Protectorate by Lord Frederick Lugard gave more purpose to educational development in Nigeria. The British government was basically drawn into education planning in Nigeria through local demands. This led to the development of more education ordinances to address the country's education problems. There was also prompt intervention from the colonial authorities because they were not pleased with the education planning in Nigeria at the time. The first Governor-General of Nigeria in 1914, Lugard, was particularly dissatisfied with the existing education system in the new Nigerian territory and thus immediately set up plans to review educational policies. One major thing of note carried out by Lugard was the indigenization of instructors. The Governor-General directed that European teachers/instructors should step aside for their Nigerian counterparts. This directive could have been based on the fact that Nigerian teachers had a better understanding of Nigerian learners. They would also be able to localize the modes of teaching in order

---

[13] Ajala, *A Historical Review*, 78–79.
[14] Jacob F. A. Ajayi, "The Development of Secondary Grammar School Education in Nigeria," *Journal of the Historical Society of Nigeria* 2, no. 4 (1963): 521.
[15] Ajayi, "The Development of Secondary Grammar School," 521.

for the students to better understand what was being taught. Since both teachers and learners share the same background, this ultimately enhances classroom communication.

Lugard described Nigerian teachers as "a better supply of reliable natives to occupy posts of responsibility."[16] He further ensured a smooth working relationship between the government and the mission schools, and the government enjoyed full control over schools that fell within the non-assisted category.[17] Lugard's education reforms in Nigeria led to the development of the 1916 Education Ordinance. This ordinance covered the entirety of the Southern and Northern Protectorates, now called Nigeria, but the education code was specifically for the Southern Protectorate. The 1916 Education Ordinance allowed for the financial intervention of the colonial government because finances were a major stumbling block in the affairs of education. M. S. Jayeola-Omoyeni and J. O. Omoyeni posited that the education reforms chaired by Lugard enabled the functionality of education in the country. For the first time, education was relevant to society.[18] Education was also designed for all Nigerians. This facilitated the improvement of education in Northern Nigeria, specifically. However, the 1916 Education Ordinance was further amended in 1919.

The 1926 Phelps-Stokes Commission was a sequel to the 1916 Education Ordinance. This commission was set up to facilitate improved quality of education of African people. Even when it was argued that the previous education ordinance enabled a relevant educational system, the findings of the Phelps-Stokes Commission proved otherwise. It was discovered that most of the instructional deliveries and the textbooks, among a host of others, were not beneficial to the people. This was followed by recommendations that the educational plans in the country should be reviewed and that the local language should be employed as a medium of classroom instruction. During this period, there were proposals for the development of higher education in Nigeria and other parts of West Africa.

One major factor that contributed to the development of higher education in Nigeria was the development of nationalism. This is not to say that the colonial government was not interested in developing higher education in the country. Ade Fajana noted that the British colonialists saw education as a means through which the colonial powers and authority could be firmly established.[19] The nationalists, on the other hand, identified that tertiary education made achieving self-rule more realistic. Proposals for developing university education in the country began in the late nineteenth century, with actors such as James Johnson,

---

[16] Fafunwa, *History of Education in Nigeria*, 111.
[17] Sulaiman, "Internationalization in Education," 94.
[18] M. S. Jayeola-Omoyeni and J. O. Omoyeni, "Contributions of Western Education to the Making of Modern Nigeria during and after the First World War," *European Scientific Journal* 10, no. 31 (2014): 273.
[19] Ade Fajana, "Colonial Control and Education: The Development of Higher Education in Nigeria 1900–1950," *Journal of the Historical Society of Nigeria* 6, no. 3 (1972): 323.

Otunba Payne, and J. S. Leigh taking center stage.[20] These actors were all members of the Lagos Literary and Industrial Institute, a think tank that concerned itself with the intellectual sagacity of Lagos life. The mass media was also employed to force the colonial government's interest in higher education.

However, credit for developing higher education in Nigeria should also be given to Eric Hussey, the Director of Education. He was the one who proposed the three levels of education – primary, secondary, and higher education – which the country still follows now. One of his proposals for education reforms in Nigeria led to the development of Yaba Higher College in 1932.[21] While Yaba College was the country's first academic higher education institution, it is pertinent to note that there had been institutions, albeit vocational, that offered postsecondary education. These included the Central Agricultural Research Station and Moor Plantation at Ibadan. However, these institutions did not fill the gap in higher education, hence the establishment of Yaba College. While the college filled the vacuum, it was immediately noticeable that the curriculum did not reflect the national aspirations of Nigerians. There was an obvious disparity between Yaba College and higher institutions in the United Kingdom. This led to the development of commissions such as the Asquith Commission and the Elliot Commission, which considered how higher education could be well designed and effective. This led to the establishment of University College, Ibadan, in 1948.

The establishment of University College was also criticized. Again, the curriculum did not reflect nationalistic aspirations because it was modeled after University College London. The institution did not issue degrees. The Ashby Commission was set up to look into higher education reforms in the country,[22] which noted, among a host of other issues, that there was a disconnect in the transition between secondary and higher education in the country and recommended that more universities be established to make higher education accessible to all. The task of developing the system fell on Nigerians, who began to exercise power from the 1950s onward.

System and Values of Western Education

Civilizations educate their populations to inculcate belief systems and cultural practices, preparing individuals to sustain cultures and join communities.[23] These social rites provide relevant skills and knowledge for navigating the surrounding economic and political space. This information is described as a civilization's knowledge system. The nature and institutions of British

---

[20] Fajana, "Colonial Control and Education," 326.
[21] Fafunwa, *History of Education in Nigeria*, 134.
[22] Hamza Maiyeri, Yan Bin, and Weizheng Liu, "The Development of Higher Education in Nigeria," *IOSR Journal of Research and Methods in Education (IOSR–JRME)* 11, no. 4 (2021): 11.
[23] Fafunwa, *History of Education in Nigeria*.

colonial enterprise shaped Nigeria's systems and forms of education, which were infused into the fabric of society during the colonial period.

Like other civilizations and cultures, precolonial Nigerian societies had developed institutions and systems for educating new generations to reproduce cultures and traditions.[24] This knowledge system was not only intended to reproduce Nigerian cultures; it also provided information that was important for self-reliance. This system, through which civilizations had been preserved and animated, remains one of the most instructive institutions created by societies, which infused knowledge from every aspect into social outlets that include religion, art, politics, and economics.

Civilizations have always meticulously documented and transmitted their practices and belief systems. In precolonial Nigeria and elsewhere in sub-Saharan Africa, this was done through oral communication framed as narratives, poems, and other spoken art.[25] Education was a communal affair that transferred specific details of the civilization and its environment across generations. However, this practice has been transformed alongside other structures and systems of precolonial existence. It has grown beyond its communal origins and unique details after encountering Western education's proponents and their cause of cultural imperialism, which subjected it to universalism.[26]

In the universal frame, African education systems were detached from their traditional societies and attached to modern metropolitan states.[27] The new system was built as a fundamental structure of the colonial state, intending to transmute society from traditional to modern. In some quarters of society during and after this period, it was argued that this form of education produced an idle, lazy population furnished with information irrelevant to society's evolution. The system produced and sustained an educated population, some members of whom became detached from their broader society and culture.[28] Development experts and scholars have examined the diverse experience of modern states and ultimately recognized that a formal education system can provide the national cohesion needed for development.[29] With this in mind,

---

[24] David Imbua, Otoabasi Akpan, Ikechukwu Amadi, and Yakubu Ochefu, eds., *History, Culture, Diasporas and Nation Building: The Collected Works of Okon Edet Uya* (Bethesda: Arbi Press, 2012).

[25] Toyin Falola and Christian Jennings, eds., *Africanizing Knowledge: African Studies across Disciplines* (New Brunswick: Transaction Publishers, 2002).

[26] Linda Tuhiwai Smith, *Decolonizing Methodologies: Research and Indigenous Peoples* (London: Zed Books, 2012).

[27] Ngugi wa Thiong'o, *Decolonising the Mind: The Politics of Language in African Literature* (Harare: Zimbabwe Publishing House, 1981).

[28] *The Lagos Standard*, "Lagosian on Dits," *The Lagos Standard*, Vol. XIII-22, February 13, 1907.

[29] Archie Mafeje, "Culture and Development in Africa: The Missing Link," *CODESRIA Bulleting*, nos. 3 and 4 (2008): 61; and Robert J. Berg and Jennifer S. Whitaker, eds., *Strategies for African Development* (Berkeley: University of California Press, 1986).

colonial education was designed to produce a middle-class population that could sustain and reproduce the colonial legacy of Pax Britannica in all its contours.[30]

In many respects, Western education is appraised as colonial education.[31] The two ideas are often used interchangeably, conditioned by their history and trajectory in Africa. Their history has been traced to European activities in the region as part of a bid for imperial acquisitions. They were merged with elements of cultural imperialism, denigrating African people's traditions and cultural practices to deny their ingenuity and integral roles as components of civilization.[32] The dual motives of material accumulation and cultural imperialism went hand-in-glove throughout the nineteenth and twentieth centuries when different regions endured their colonial periods.[33] The encounter with Western education came piecemeal as trade, commerce, and missionary activities gradually encroached on cultures and societies. The process was engineered at different times and with varying degrees of intensity due to differences between the geography and cultural fixtures of different locations. The spread of Western education in Nigeria was uneven due to factors that included the concentration of returnees within a population, the presence of Christian missionaries, and the operations of government offices and merchant enterprises.[34]

In many parts of the Southern Protectorate, Christian missionaries and the concentration of returnees from the Americas and Sierra Leone reinforced the spread of Western education. The presence of government offices and business operations also shaped the value and content of education systems as their presence supported the spread of Western education through grants and increasing demand for graduates from the new schools. From the mid-nineteenth century, when liberated captives began populating Lagos, Calabar, Abeokuta, and other cities and towns in the hinterlands of the Southern Protectorate, society began an earnest transition into a new form that was influenced by Western civilization.

Sierra Leone had been designed by Western imperial powers to serve, alongside Liberia,[35] as an African home for liberated captives. The limited

---

[30] Godfrey N. Brown, "British Educational Policy in West and Central Africa," *Journal of Modern African Studies* 2, no. 3 (1964): 365–377.

[31] Michael Omolewa, "Educating the 'Native': A Study of the Education Adaptation Strategy in British Colonial Africa, 1910–1936," *Journal of African American History* 91, no. 3 (2006): 267–287.

[32] Azubike C. Onuora-Oguno, *Development and the Right to Education in Africa* (Cham: Palgrave Macmillan, 2019), 109–122.

[33] L. H. Gann and Peter Duignan, eds., *Colonialism in Africa 1870–1960*, Vol. 1 (Cambridge: Cambridge University Press, 1977).

[34] Gail P. Kelly and Philip G. Altbach, eds., *Education and the Colonial Experience* (New Brunswick: Transaction, 1984), 1–5.

[35] Akpojevbe Omasanjuwa and Junisa Phebean, "Acrimony in Colonial Liberia," *Journal of Universal History Studies* 3, no. 1 (2020): 1–38.

opportunities provided by the political economy of this space meant that they needed structures and systems transplanted from Europe to facilitate their return to West African homes. Many who returned to Sierra Leone at this time left the country, migrating to places like Gambia and the West Indies. Apart from Sierra Leone's economic condition, this population was also encouraged to migrate to West African towns due to family networks, which they hoped to strengthen for integration and social mobility.[36] During this period, society's socioeconomic landscape was transitioning from one that was dominated by crony capitalism to adopting a more laissez-faire, liberal form. This transformation was primarily driven by the abolition of the slave trade, the conditions of freedom experienced by this population in their Atlantic homes, and the population's return to Sierra Leone and Liberia.

The return of freed slaves was part of the strategy designed by abolitionists, including merchants, missionaries, and humanitarians, to recalibrate the social stratification of African cultures. By creating a middle-class population, this group could disrupt the monopoly that nobles and traditional elites held on economic power.[37] In the slave trade era, slaves and commodities such as palm products, cotton, and ivory were controlled solely by nobles: the chiefs, titleholders, and kings. Export trade was limited, putting the local population and regional economies at a disadvantage.

Returnees had received experience and training in their Atlantic homes. They also had an interest in going back to their homelands and transforming their societies.[38] This desire to implement an "advanced" civilization and redefine the social status in their home territories made them catalysts for imposing Western taxonomic modernity and disrupting the social order that supported existing political economies.[39] The implication of this trajectory was clear when the stakeholders in the colony's political economy began arguing over the system of colonial education. The dispute began in earnest in the late nineteenth century, when the administration remained confined to Lagos and parts of the delta states in the Bight of Benin and Biafra.[40]

---

[36] Mariana P. Candido and Adam Jones, *African Women in the Atlantic World: Property, Vulnerability and Mobility, 1660–1880* (London: James Currey, 2019), 148–170; and Kristin Mann, *Slavery and the Birth of an African City: Lagos 1760–1900* (Bloomington: Indiana University Press, 1997).
[37] Robert A. Bickers and Rosemary Seton, eds., *Missionary Encounters: Sources and Issues* (London: Curzon Press, 1996).
[38] Susan A. C. Rosenfeld, "Apparitions of the Atlantic: Mobility, Kinship, and Freedom among Afro-Brazilian Emigrants from Bahia to Lagos, 1850–1900" (unpublished PhD dissertation, University of California), 2020.
[39] *The Lagos Standard*, "British Influence in the Interior: Its Effect Upon Native Rule," *The Lagos Standard*, Vol. XII–9, January 23, 1907.
[40] F. O. Ogunlade, "Education and Politics in Colonial Nigeria: The Case of King's College Lagos (1906–1911)," *Journal of the Historical Society of Nigeria* 7, no. 2 (1974): 325–345.

Returnees invited and facilitated the work of missionaries in various locations.[41] The missionaries deployed education, health services, and other campaigns to improve public welfare as a way of gaining converts from the local population.[42] The presence of returnees in the Southern Niger region not only gave impetus to missionary activities but also supported Western education. Missionaries who invited the local population to maintain a Christian lifestyle through Sunday services, social conduct, and other engagements also equipped local children to function in the political economy of the evolving society. The returnees were already acquainted with European civilization, and in a society where European actors were becoming more influential in economic and political matters, this familiarity endeared them to foreign actors and local kin. They acted as a bridge between modernization and tradition.[43]

To some extent, returnees negotiated the form that Western civilization's inculcation took in society. This manifested alongside the transition of the returnees that Ade Ajayi described as a conversion from Anglophobes to Anglophiles.[44] This created the middle class that Britain's abolitionists needed, and the local population aspired to be like these new citizens. As agents of civilization, the new middle class began setting social standards for society, breaking down precolonial structures of learning and education.

At the start of the twentieth century, changing patterns of migration and settlement altered the social norms of society that constituted the processes and systems of education. Educated elites among the returnees, their descendants, and others within the missionary community and the colonial government wanted to retain some traditional elements within the new, Western education systems. This desire was inherited by nationalists in the post–World War II years, but it could not be implemented due to financial constraints. The precolonial education system, which involved community elders, instilled an ethos of self-reliance that was completely unfamiliar with the concept of unemployment.[45] Campaigns were launched to ensure that the education system covered industrial and agricultural skills alongside lessons in literary study, which had been the ubiquitous nucleus of the curriculum.[46] The

---

[41] Fafunwa, *History of Education*, 78 and 81, among others.

[42] Emmanuel A. Ayandele, *Missionary Impact in Modern Nigeria 1842–1914* (London: Longman Group, 1966).

[43] Philip S. Zachernuk, *Colonial Subjects: An African Intelligentsia and Atlantic Ideas* (Charlottesville: University of Virginia Press, 2000).

[44] Akinjide Osuntokun, "Professor Jacob F. Ade Ajayi and the Ibadan School of History," in *J. F. Ade Ajayi: His Life and Career*, ed. Michael Omolewa and Akinjide Osuntokun (Ibadan: Bookcraft, 2014), 300.

[45] Maurice Amutabi, ed., *Development from Below and Above in Africa* (Nairobi: Centre for Democracy, Research and Development, 2018); and Toyin Falola and Mike Odey, *Poverty Reduction Strategies in Africa* (New York: Routledge, 2018).

[46] Stafford Kay and Bradley Nystrom, "Education and Colonialism in Africa: An Annotated Bibliography," *Comparative Education Review* 15, no. 2 (1971): 240–259.

precolonial occupations of masonry, carpentry, tailoring, metalworking, and artistry were transformed during the colonial period.[47] Such skills had not been taught through the training institutions sustained by the political economy of the colonial state, but instead through communal, informal education systems that involved everyday learning in social interactions.[48]

During the colonial period, these occupations contributed vital industrial skills to the colony, and they were taught in training institutes such as the Hope Waddell Training Institute and others in Calabar, Abeokuta, and Lagos.[49] However, it was challenging to include these industrial skills in school curricula because colonial social stratification saw these skills as less valuable than literary knowledge. Clerks enjoyed a social status that was greater than that of carpenters or tailors. Regardless of their level of training, mechanics and other skilled laborers operated at the lowest rung of the formal sector of the colonial system. They had no prospects for advancement when compared with their white-collar peers who had a formal education.

The artisans, produced by the training institutions established by missionaries, earned less than doctors, lawyers, journalists, clerks, teachers, and others who had been educated in literary studies. The social stigma attached to practical skills, and the costs involved in applying them, deprived them of stakeholder funding. Educational curricula expanded to include more than the mere reading, writing, and arithmetic that were required for roles as clerks, bookkeepers, letter-writers, catechists, and teachers employed by the missionaries, merchant companies, and government offices. Lessons were added to teach Greek, Latin, English, algebra, geography, and other advanced subjects. Schools that produced graduates with primary education were joined by institutions providing secondary and tertiary education anchored by the colony's political economy.

Stakeholders during this period consisted of an extensive network formed by communities, missionaries, and the government, which drove the development of Western education in Nigeria. They desired an educational system that taught a mixture of industrial and agricultural skills, but they strongly supported literary programs. The ongoing demand for foreign goods, and the ability to access them, had formed the basis for new social classes. The social mobility of returnees was considered to be an archetype for the evolving civilization.

---

[47] John Michael Vlach, "Affecting Architecture of the Yoruba," *African Arts* 10, no. 1 (1976): 48–55; and Moses Akintunde Akintonde and Margaret Olugbemisola Areo, "Art and Craft of Old Oyo: It's Manifestation in the Present Oyo," *Journal of Humanities and Social Science* 15, no. 5 (2013): 50–59.

[48] Willie F. Page, ed., *Encyclopedia of African History and Culture*, Vol. 1: *Ancient Africa* (New York: Facts on File Inc., 2005).

[49] A. W. Wilkie and J. K. Macgregor, "Industrial Training in Africa," *International Review of Mission* 3, no. 4 (1914): 742–747.

Meanwhile, Japanese, German, French, English, American, Italian, and other imported goods dominated Nigerian markets while local industries suffered.

Missionary schools that could not meet their financial obligations relied on contributions from the government and the community. Community contributions were made by private individuals, paying grants and school fees, or through support from social groups.[50] The bulk of these contributions came from educated and emerging elites who prevented their children from learning industrial skills. Such knowledge could only be used to work as "servants" for contemporaries who had become professionals by receiving literary education.

The British government had begun to promote the idea of empire recovery and imperial priority after World War I. This gave it an institutional bias to protect its interests in the colony, which meant a lack of support for vocational or skills-based training. Local industries that were enhanced with skilled workers could compete with business interests outside the colony. The general condition of local industry and its inclusion in the education system reflected the role that the colony was to play in the global economy, which was expected to function as an appendage of the metropolitan state and produce cheap labor. By continuing to restrict the amount of skilled labor produced by the colony, the government kept local businesses operating at a disadvantage and aided the exploitation of society.

The colonial state created a middle class that was only capable of consumption, with an increasing taste for foreign commodities. The funding of industrial and agricultural education during this period was also affected by the limited availability of such roles, compared to the colonial state's ongoing recruitment of staff, including clerks, from Sierra Leone, the Gold Coast, and the West Indies. The colonial economy opened up various opportunities for individuals who had acquired basic literary knowledge.[51]

As the government centralized its administration, government departments enlarged and the administration of the colony required additional workers. Merchant companies were also centralizing and expanding, which increased their demand for clerks and bookkeepers. Two types of work were available to residents within the colony: administrative jobs in government offices and merchant companies or unskilled labor at construction sites and on commercial farms. The social conditioning of the colonial state promoted the idea that physical skills were primitive and less respectable than acquired literary knowledge. This developed into arrogance and criticism that was widely disseminated by colonial newspapers.

---

[50] Celestina I. Harry, "Development of Primary/Secondary Schools in Colonial Times and the Need for Sustainable Innovations, Growth and Value Creation: A Comparative Analysis," *International Journal of Humanities, Social Sciences and Education* 7, no. 3 (2020): 80–89.

[51] Moses Ochonu, "African Colonial Economies: Land, Labor, and Livelihoods," *History Compass* 11, no. 2 (2013): 91–103.

People like Rev'd Venn had hoped to integrate Western modernity with the social ambience and specific cultural properties of local Africans, but colonial education was geared toward the exact opposite. Venn demonstrated that his approach was possible by merging traditional medical treatments with modern science and recruiting students who had backgrounds in local medicine to continue advanced medical training in Britain.[52] The hope was that local medicine would remain relevant, allowing West African knowledge to make substantial contributions to modern science through Indigenous efforts. This would allow Western imperial powers to explore and exploit the region's resources and wealth while maintaining an active role for Africans. Venn's systemic approach to medicine could be applied to other fields, allowing society to transition into modernity while retaining its specific cultural heritage, as had been experienced in Japan, although under different circumstances.[53] In the Gold Coast, it was framed as the Basel model, and schools were expected to be self-sustaining by selling agricultural and industrial products produced by students under the supervision of school administrators.

Such schools had a marketing department that distributed school products; other departments handled different aspects of industrial and agricultural production. In most cases, products were drawn from practical examinations undertaken by students. The system allowed schools to experiment with new crops and conduct research to modify existing ones. It also meant the implementation of substantial technological advancements, moving from precolonial manual farming to more modern, mechanized practices. This system required specialized equipment and faculty to train students, but it cultivated industrial and agricultural knowledge among the population, growing the ranks of the middle class.

The colonial government only required a small middle class to disrupt the precolonial order and promote its interests. Western imperial powers initially used traditional authorities to exploit local resources, and during the colonial period they worked through the middle class.[54] Although this population gained no political power, their social and economic advancement made them much more influential than those who held traditional authority. As colonial occupation continued, they saw themselves as more similar to the colonizers than to their kinsmen, regarding the latter group with contempt.[55]

---

[52] Jacob F. A. Ajayi, "Henry Venn and the Policy of Development," *Journal of the Historical Society of Nigeria* 1, no. 4 (1959): 340.

[53] Robert O. Collins, ed., *African History: Text and Readings* (New York: Random House, 1971).

[54] Abner Cohen, *The Politics of Elite Culture: Explorations in the Dramaturgy of Power in a Modern African Society* (Berkeley: University of California Press, 1981).

[55] Frantz Fanon, *Black Skin, White Masks* (London: Pluto Press, 1967); and Emmanuel A. Ayandele, *The Educated Elite in the Nigerian Society* (Ibadan: Ibadan University Press, 1974).

Although the new middle class engaged in some political activism – the colonial economy subjected them to the same range of inequalities that oppressed their brethren – their ability to collaborate with groups outside of their social class was impaired by their social conditioning. This was another reason why the local population was reluctant to send their children to missionary schools for education. In many cases, children who acquired Western education lost contact with their local communities, even after they were no longer confined to boarding schools. Boarding schools hoped to accelerate the learning of their students by restricting contact with the local population. Pupils were expected to socialize exclusively with the missionaries, their teachers, and their schoolmates. The boarding school model also allowed missionaries to extend their influence into the more distant parts of administrative units because a district or division could share a single school to draw students from a large surrounding area.[56] Parents had some concerns about sending their children into these new learning environments, mostly due to the labor shortage that it would create on their farms but also because of the Christian indoctrination that occurred in such schools. These fears, which revolved around the maintenance of local traditions and culture, later gave way to the socioeconomic reality of the evolving milieu. The acquisition of Western education had become essential.[57]

The emergence of the community school model, marked by the establishment of Abeokuta Grammar School, resolved some parents' concerns. Newspapers were flooded with public notices of admission into Queen's College and King's College, alongside listings of European commodities, starting in the late nineteenth century. Before British examinations were offered in the colony, children were sent abroad to obtain secondary school certificates and higher education. In the 1891 publication of the *Lagos Weekly Record*, Queen's College called for "daughters of gentlemen" in Africa to enroll for adequate preparation to attend Cambridge, Oxford, and other institutions of higher learning, making a prospectus available at the office of the newspaper in Lagos and other locations within the city. King's College made similar announcements for prospective male students from the region.[58] The educational accomplishments of male children were prioritized. It was rare for emerging or traditional elites to send their daughters to institutions such as Queen's College.

The state of college admissions at the time can be inferred from a native resident's petition circulated in Bonny in 1906. It implored the government to

---

[56] Ezekiel O. Adeoti, *Alayande as Educationist 1948–1983: A Study of Alayande's Contribution to Education and Social Change* (Ibadan: Heinemann Educational Books, 1997).

[57] Toyin Falola, *Cultural Modernity in a Colonized World: The Writings of Chief Isaac Oluwole Delano* (Austin: Pan-African University Press, 2020).

[58] *The Lagos Weekly Record*, "The School Inspection of the Colony," *The Lagos Weekly Record*, Vol. II – no. 10, October 17, 1891.

promote female education in the area.[59] The petition asserted that when boys became more educated in comparison to their female counterparts, it would be harder for them to relate to each other. The implication was that such an approach to education might not be sustainable, and it was one of the earliest arguments in the colony to advance the idea that women sustain nations and reproduce civilizations. A complex mix of factors continued to limit the educational opportunities available to girls in various parts of the colony.[60]

Western education was seen as a golden ticket to providing social mobility in the colonial state. Educated natives deployed their literary knowledge in the pursuit of social justice and to make political demands. As trade expanded, parents saw that it was necessary to educate their children, especially the males, to advance their commercial and social activities with bookkeeping and letter writing. The colonial state also cultivated an aura of accomplishment around this population, leading parents to view the education of their children as a status symbol. The acceptance and spread of Western education followed the evolution of the colonial state – education became an important currency for social mobility. Communities made financial contributions to fund the education of their children. Parents risked labor shortages on their farms, preferring to have children that aspired to become lawyers and professionals in other fields outside of the industry. These children were also aware of the colony's socioeconomic condition and the high status enjoyed by such professions. All of the stakeholders involved were aware that industrial education was necessary, but the political economy of the colonial state discouraged anyone from acting on that knowledge. Instead, it promoted the production of more schools to provide literary education.

Parents were correct to fear that their children would become detached from their families and communities, and the process was systemic and deliberate in some areas. This included physical measures, such as the boarding schools, and the concepts that were introduced by the educational content and its attached value system. Pupils were compelled to convert to Christianity and studied the Bible daily. In geography, religious studies, history, language, and art classes, they learned about history, climate, languages, culture, ethics, and other ideas through European epistemologies and ontologies. Before the establishment of the government's teacher training institutes, many positions were held by Europeans. In an environment that confined students to European and Europeanized teachers, they began seeing themselves as different from other members of their native societies – and they knew little about the cultures within those societies.

---

[59] *The Lagos Standard*, "The Urgent Need for Female Education in Bonny," *The Lagos Standard*, Vol. XIII, no. 20, January 30, 1907.
[60] S. Bappa, J. Ibarahim, A. M. Imam, and F. J. A. Kamara, eds., *Women in Nigeria Today* (London: Zed Books, 1985).

The colonial state imposed a hierarchical, race-based classification of the population. In churches, schools, and government offices, this phenomenon was challenged by the emerging educated population. The situation in colonial schools is described in correspondence between a contributor known as Africanus and the editor of *The Lagos Standard* in 1907:

> The teaching staff engaged for the college shall consist of a Professor of English who would act as the principal/head of the college, at a salary of £600 to £700 by annual increments of £20 per annum and a duty allowance of £120 attached to the post; a Professor of Mathematics as a vice principal at £500 to £600 by increments of £20 per annum; a professor of Chemistry whose salary was not yet determined at the time of the publication; a Commercial Instructor from £300 to £400 by increments of £10 per annum; a chief native assistant at £120 to £150 by increments of £5 per annum; and a second native assistant at £80 to £120 by annual increment of £5 per annum.[61]

He further argued:

> From what one can most naturally infer from the quotation, if a Dr. Blyden, a Henry Carr, or a Dr. Abayomi Cole ... were to apply for a post in the College, they could elected [sic] only to one or other of the two posts of assistants, simply because they are native Africans; while a European because he happens to be a native of Europe may be elected [sic] to the higher offices.[62]

Agitations such as this, from inside and outside of the colony, led to the educated population's integration into positions of authority in schools. Their arguments were similar to Venn's, asserting that schools should be controlled by the educated population to domesticate the Western knowledge system that was being introduced locally.

The dynamics between the educated population and their kinsmen echoed the relationships between white colonizers and local residents. As the colonial state evolved, the educated population created a pool of subjects that depended on the government for their livelihood. Many of them became produce buyers and distributors, and increased participation in the colonial economy fueled their political activism, which developed into the campaign for self-governance during the post–World War II era.[63] Most of the educated elites received their higher education in distant locations, such as Sierra Leone, Britain, and the United States. This changed in 1948 when University College Ibadan was established as an annex of the University of London. Students from Yaba

---

[61] *The Lagos Standard*, "Correspondence between Africanus and the Editor of the Lagos Standard," January 12, 1907, published in *The Lagos Standard*, Vol. XIII, no. 20, January 30, 1907.
[62] *The Lagos Standard*, "Correspondence between Africanus and the Editor."
[63] Prosser Gifford and William Roger Louis, *Decolonization and African Independence: The Transfer of Power, 1960–1980* (London: Yale University Press, 1988).

College kick-started its operations, receiving university certificates that were equal to others obtained abroad.

The acquisition of Western education was confined within the premise of Victorian England and its Pax Britannica. This training led many to accept the position of Western imperialists who propagated the idea that African cultures were inferior. Western education displaced traditional knowledge systems and became so entrenched that attempts to challenge notions of Western superiority needed to be mounted from within a prison of concretized Western epistemologies and ontologies.[64] Like other government departments during this period, the Department of Education's reforms placed greater emphasis on the colonial government and the merchant class's needs, neglecting society's requirements. Before the twentieth century, the government regulated educational efforts and helped missionaries spread their message in the interior, providing school grants and organizing educational systems and structures.[65] The *Lagos Observer* of 1888 illustrated the intricacies of government intervention by noting that:

> The whole grant for 1888 amount to 711.12.6. pounds. As has been made known in the last issue on this paper, the Wesleyans had but a little. The CMS and Catholics were gainers. Before the "Education Ordinance" came in vogue, the yearly Grant for all three was 600 pounds. It is not impossible that though the Grant 1888 came over 700 pounds, and the Wesleyans received a small share, the Grant of 1889 may come down to 500 pounds and the Wesleyans be among those who would have larger share. Hence, gain or lose, the average Grant of the Government, will in a number of years amount to the same 600 pounds!!![66]

Divergent views between the government and the missionaries eventually led the former to establish its schools in place of funding and regulating those established by missionaries.

The primary differences in approaches to colonial education were secularism and the incorporation of local languages in pedagogy and school curricula. The government estimate for the year 1907 shows that it paid little attention to the education sector. Discussions of revenue generation and expenditures centered on railway lines and the transportation network, with general infrastructural developments to drive the exploration and exploitation of local resources.[67] In previous years, schools had made several complaints about

---

[64] Ozo-Mekuri Ndimele, ed., *Nigerian Languages, Literatures, Culture and Reforms: A Festschrift for Ayo Bamgbose* (Port Harcourt: M & J Grand Orbit Communications, 2016); and Bola Dauda and Toyin Falola, *Wole Soyinka: Literature, Activism, and African Transformation* (New York: Bloomsbury Academic, 2021).
[65] *The Lagos Observer*, "Jottings by 'Stet,'" *The Lagos Observer* VII, no. 20, December 29, 1888.
[66] *The Lagos Observer*, "Jottings by 'Stet'."
[67] *The Lagos Standard*, "The Governor's Message and the Colonial Estimates, 1907," *The Lagos Standard*, Vol. XI, no. 17, January 9, 1907.

the government's negligent approach to education in terms of legislature, grant provisions, inspections, and general regulation.[68] These concerns culminated in challenges to school calendars and curricula. In a meeting of managers of the various schools within the colony, "held at the Breadfruit School Room,"

> it was decided that a letter should be addressed to the Governor with the object of bringing to his notice the inconvenience and pecuniary loss that would be sustained by the schools if the inspection and examinations should be deferred to the beginning of the next year, as the inspector was not expected to out to the coast until then. And to invite the inconvenience they would respectfully ask for a resident inspector for the colony.[69]

The meeting was held in the early years of Western education in the Niger area, especially Lagos, when inspectors from the Office of the Colonial Secretary performed annual inspections. To improve the efficiency of schools and the colonial educational system, the inspector's two-week visit would involve an interschool competition: an exhibition in which the three best schools received £35 grants.[70] This arrangement placed undue stress on management, staff, and students, so the secretary approved a proposal to have a resident subinspector for schools in the colony.

Authority over school reform and regulation remained with the Colonial Office's control over the education sector. In addition to the inspector, it had an Advisory Committee on Native Education in Tropical Africa. This body recommended reforms for the British dependencies through meetings and conferences, which occasionally involved other stakeholders. The missionaries, who were significant for the spread and development of Western education in the Nigerian colony, conspicuously dominated the boards of education that were established by the government throughout this period.[71] In 1910, it was evident that schools were producing graduates who could not communicate well in English since they had studied languages such as Latin and Greek. In response to this limitation and other issues with school examinations, the government took action to improve the colony's education system. Cambridge examinations syndicates formed a partnership with the Department of Education in that year, later working with the Oxford Delegacy for Local Examinations in 1929.[72] The government took complete control of secondary education, restricting missionary activity to primary schools.

---

[68] *The Lagos Weekly Record*, "The School Inspection of the Colony," *The Lagos Weekly Record*, Vol. II – 10, October 17, 1891.
[69] *The Lagos Weekly Record*, "General News," *The Lagos Weekly Record*, Vol. II – 12, October 31, 1891.
[70] *The Lagos Weekly Record*, "General News."
[71] *The Lagos Observer*, Vol. VI, no. 14, January 7, 1888.
[72] Michael Omolewa, "The Cambridge University Local Examinations Syndicate and the Development of Secondary Education in Nigeria, 1910–1926," *Journal of the Historical Society of Nigeria* 8, no. 4 (1977): 111–130.

The Colonial Office had previously asserted that social services were not the government's responsibility. This could be interpreted to mean dispensable social services in the mobilization of state biopower for the colonial project.[73] By changing this position, it helped to internationalize and standardize Nigeria's colonial education system while promoting the Pax Britannica doctrine among its educated population. Educational syndicates, acting with the University of London School Examinations Board, determined which literature would be adopted in the schools, what subjects would be taught, and which educational pursuits were worthwhile. In Lagos, the syndicates conducted preliminary exams for junior and senior school certificates.[74] The boards that set the standards for examinations and helped the colonial government reform its education system also strengthened English elements of school curricula, to the detriment of Indigenous Knowledge Systems. These reforms democratized Western education – greater numbers of people could complete their secondary education in Nigeria and pursue study in higher institutions. Access to secondary education had previously been limited to those who had enough money to travel to Sierra Leone or Britain for their studies. Local exams determined what would be learned and what was forgotten while acquiring secondary education in Nigeria; students began preparing for their exams at the start of junior school.

Geographic concerns influenced the spread and development of Western education in the colony. Northern candidates did not have access to the Cambridge exams until 1937, at St. Bartholomew School, Wusasa, around three decades after the Southern region began producing graduates.[75] Missionary activities and the spread of Western education were mutually reinforcing influences in the colony, which supported the Lugardian policy, continued by later administrators, to preserve a "self-contained" caliphate.[76] Christian missionaries spent many years infiltrating and influencing Southern villages and communities in the interior of the Niger area, assisted by the presence of the British government, but their work in the North was mostly restricted to non-Muslim areas.[77]

Studies on the spread and development of Christianity in the Northern Niger River Basin have shown the complex dynamics influencing missionary activities in the region, which were exacerbated by colonial administrators.[78] Even before

---

[73] Fajana, "Colonial Control and Education," 327.
[74] Omolewa, "Educating the Native."
[75] Omolewa, "The Cambridge University Local Examinations," 126.
[76] Lord Lugard, *The Dual Mandate in British Tropical Africa* (New York: Routledge, 1965); and Adiele E. Afigbo, "Revolution and Reaction in Eastern Nigeria: 1900–1929: The Background to the Women's Riot of 1929," *Journal of the Historical Society of Nigeria* 3, no. 3 (1966): 539–557.
[77] Jacob F. A. Ajayi, *Christian Missionaries in Nigeria, 1841–1891: The Making of a New Elite* (London: Longman, 1965).
[78] Patrick E. Nmah and Chukwudi Ani Amunnadi, "Christianity in Northern Nigeria from 1841–2012: A Church under Persecution," *LWATI: A Journal of Contemporary Research* 9, no. 1 (2012): 309–324.

the incursion of colonial rule, the area was in disarray. Missions had difficulty identifying roles for African priests vis-à-vis their European counterparts. Ayandele and Kolapo have noted that the demise of Bishop Samuel Ajayi Crowther, the Niger mission meeting, and the frenzy in local missions had a tremendous impact on the bearing of the Niger mission.[79] The failure of the Niger mission, which was meant to spread Christianity to the Northern part of the Niger River, affected the spread and development of Western education in the area.[80] Colonial administrators also blocked attempts to revive the mission. Afigbo, who studied the root of Nigerian federalism, has explained that the colonial administration deliberately restricted the diffusion of Western ideals – including English laws and Western education – in the North.[81] They were reluctant to repeat the experience of introducing these concepts to the South, especially their experience of doing so in Lagos.

The government's administrative concerns were linked to those of the education system, which explains the spread of schools in the South and their limited presence in the North. Schools in the South produced graduates to meet the North's administrative needs in the same way that schools in the British Gold Coast colony and elsewhere fed the South during the early period of the administration. This exacerbated the proliferation of literary schools in the region to meet increasing needs.

In the Southern region, the emerging educated community created formidable challenges for colonial authorities in discussing and debating what was described as "adaptive education." The term was meant to describe proposals from the colonial government and bodies such as the Phelps-Stokes commission, which were supposed to incorporate local realities and environments into educational systems. Proponents of this system made arguments that were conspicuously analogous to those promoted by Venn and other African elites, although the new arguments took things to greater extremes.

Early campaigns had attempted a sort of educational hybridity in which literary education was combined with lessons in industrial and agricultural skills. Adaptive education was to be built exclusively on local knowledge and lessons that were based on everyday experiences within the colony. Opponents argued that the new approach would downgrade the colony's education system, preventing the locally educated community from competing fairly

---

[79] Femi J. Kolapo, *Christian Missionary Engagement in Central Nigeria, 1857–1891: The Church Missionary Society's All African Mission on the Upper Niger* (Cham: Palgrave Macmillan, 2019); and Emmanuel A. Ayandele, "The Missionary Factor in Northern Nigeria, 1870–1918," *Journal of the Historical Society of Nigeria* 3, no. 3 (1966): 514–522.

[80] Kenneth O. Dike, *Origins of the Niger Mission 1841–1891* (Ibadan: Ibadan University Press, 1962).

[81] Adiele E. Afigbo, "Background to Nigerian Federalism: Federal Features in the Colonial State," *Publius* 21, no. 4 (1991): 13–29.

with their foreign counterparts.[82] This position, advanced by members of the educated class, can be understood by comparing the courses and curriculum designed for adaptive education with the extant literary education of the time.

A report titled *Education in Africa* listed relevant subjects that included science, physiology, hygiene, sanitation, social studies, mathematics, languages, gardening, and rural economics. It explained further that "education should be adopted to the mentality, aptitudes, occupations, and traditions of the various peoples ... Its aim should be to ... promote the advancement of the community as a whole through the improvement of agriculture, the development of native industries, and the improvement of health."[83] On the other hand, extant secondary education at the time consisted of foreign languages, including Latin, Greek, and English, along with history, geography, chemistry, physics, biology, and algebra – all taught from a Eurocentric perspective. Both approaches to education represented opposite extremes for society's evolution, nationally and internationally.

Although the educated population was not completely averse to the adaptive approach, they were skeptical about its proponents, who were largely invested in the success of the imperial project. This included the European administrators.[84] The curriculum neglected the classics and other literary courses that were considered imperative for educational advancement. This omission showed how their approach was driven by the political economy of the colony.[85] Clifford anticipated the predicament faced by later colony administrators, drafting an ordinance that empowered the government to commission and decommission colony schools, ostensibly to improve their standards by way of curbing their proliferation. In the 1930s, it became evident that it was also meant to curb the increasing numbers of students enrolling in secondary education. Administrators began to reduce staffing positions during this period, and unemployment numbers climbed, especially among those with secondary education.[86]

The education system that encouraged Southerners to migrate North for work was reinforced by the region's sociocultural dynamics. The transition of Hausa states to Islamic rule, beginning in the eleventh century and reaching its crescendo in the nineteenth century, had shaped a society around Islamic laws

---

[82] This argument translated into protests and other actions by the native population in the 1930s, following the establishment of Yaba College. Stephen O. Arifalo, "The Rise and Decline of the Nigerian Youth Movement, 1934–1941," *The African Review: Journal of African Politics, Development and International Affairs* 13, no. 1 (1986): 59–76.

[83] Edward H. Berman, "American Influence on African Education: The Role of the Phelps-Stokes Fund's Education Commissions," *Comparative Education Review* 15, no. 2 (1971): 135–138.

[84] *The Lagos Standard*, "British Administration in Nigeria," *The Lagos Standard*, Vol. XIII, no. 19, Lagos, January 23, 1907.

[85] Berman, "American Influence on African Education," 137.

[86] Moses E. Ochonu, *Colonial Meltdown: Northern Nigeria in the Great Depression* (Athens: Ohio State University Press, 2009).

and treaties. Western powers brought a major change to the traditional education system by promoting literacy, that is, the basic ability to read and write.[87] It spread through the social strata of the South in the late nineteenth century due to missionary efforts, taking place centuries after Islamic knowledge was shared through Arabic scripts in the North.[88]

The North had produced enough scholars to reform the Arabic script itself, creating a West African version: the *Ajami* script. This dynamic shows how their education system formed the nucleus of their society and societal production.[89] This point was noted by colonial administrators, and Lugard himself discussed it in correspondence with his wife during his time as Nigeria's Governor-General.[90] Islamic culture was entrenched in the North through this system but not in the West or the South. Humans act and understand reality through their ontologies and epistemologies, which are the basis of every education.[91]

When colonial administrators obstructed the efforts of missionaries attempting to infiltrate the North, their decisions were linked with their desire to preserve the social ambience existing in the region, along with their fears of social disruption. In form and intent, colonial education was developed to maintain the extractive role of the colony and to reinforce the colonial project. However, Ajayi has argued that it still produced a class of people who would match and demystify the intellectual vibrancy of their European counterparts. The intellectual acumen shown in the efforts of Kenneth Dike and others at institutions such as University College Ibadan was able to restructure Nigeria's educational curriculum.[92]

Nigeria's educational system remained stubbornly colonial despite many reform efforts.[93] During one meeting in 1935 – held between the Advisory

---

[87] Akinwunmi Isola, "Making Culture Memorable: The Literary Contributions of Isaac Oluwole Delano," Lecture Delivered at the Isaac Oluwole Delano Inaugural Memorial Lecture, Muson Centre, Lagos, December 20, 2004.

[88] Yusufu Bala Usman, *The Transformation of Katsina, 1400–1883: The Emergence and Overthrow of the Sarauta System and the Establishment of the Emirate* (Zaria: Ahmadu Bello University Press, 1981); and Muhammad Sani Umar, "Muslims' Intellectual Responses to British Colonialism in Northern Nigeria, 1903–1945," (PhD dissertation, Northwestern University, 1997).

[89] Mukhtar U. Bunza, "Arabic Manuscripts as Alternative Sources in the Reconstruction of Northern Nigeria," in *Arabic/Ajami Manuscripts: Resources for the Development of New Knowledge in Nigeria*, ed. Yakubu Y. Ibrahim, I.M. Jumare, Mahomoud Hamman, and Salisu Bala (Kaduna: Arewa House Centre for Historical Documentation and Research, 2010).

[90] Lugard to Flora Lugard 2/2/16 cited in Fajana, "Colonial Control and Education," 323.

[91] Damilola Osunlakin, "Rethinking Cultural Diversity and Sustainable Development in Africa," in *Imagining Vernacular Histories: Essays in Honor of Toyin Falola*, ed. Mobolanle Ebunoluwa Sotunsa and Abikal Borah (Lanham: Rowman and Littlefield, 2020), 47–70.

[92] Jacob F. A. Ajayi, *History and the Nation and Other Addresses* (Ibadan: Spectrum Books, 1991).

[93] Philip G. Altbach and Gail Paradise Kelly, *Education and the Colonial Experience* (New York: Advent Books, 1991).

Committee on Native Education in Tropical Africa and the British Examinations Boards, which conducted external exams in Nigerian secondary schools – they discussed the replacement of local flora and fauna with European plants for botanical studies.[94] Meanwhile, the government expected examination boards to ask candidates about their local environment, listing natural resources and their expected value. This was an extension of the metropolitan state's drive for maximum exploration and exploitation of local wealth and resources.

Western education has greatly transformed the sociopolitical landscape of Nigerian society since the late nineteenth century, and it has been applied as an agency for animating local traditions and history.[95] Henry Townsend's *Iwe Iroyin* and subsequent newspapers such as *The Lagos Standard*, the *Lagos Weekly Review*, and the *West African Pilot* began to shape public opinion and government policies.[96] The new, educated elites wrote incisive newspaper columns, owned printing press companies, and shifted the editorial focus of newspapers to publicize conditions in the colony.[97] Traditional authorities were unable to work within the frame of Western epistemologies and ontologies, which brought the emerging educated elite to the fore of political debates from the second half of the nineteenth century.[98] These authorities consulted with them for letters and communications with the colonial authority. Lugard attempted to address this dynamic with a concerted effort to train the children of the Native Authorities.

Traditional authorities in the South and the North had pioneered attempts to train their children with Western education due to its proximity to political power. Colonial administrators in the North had established one such school by 1910. Its success was so limited that the government's recruiting efforts ultimately failed in the 1920s and 1930s. Children in non-Muslim areas, who had attended mission or Native Authority schools, returned home to continue farming and engage in other traditional activities. The schools were mostly administered by a single staff member, and education was limited to the primary level.

Scholars have studied how the liberal dispositions of the sultan and some emirs shaped their relationships with Christian missionaries and the development of Western education in their enclaves. However, this attitude was only shared

---

[94] Omolewa, "Educating the 'Native'," 270–271.
[95] Toyin Falola, *Yoruba Gurus: Indigenous Production of Knowledge in Africa* (Trenton: Africa World Press Inc., 1999).
[96] Nnamdi Azikiwe, *My Odyssey: An Autobiography* (London: C. Hurst and Company, 1970).
[97] Derek R. Peterson, Emma Hunter, and Stephanie Newell, eds., *African Print Cultures: Newspapers and Their Publics in the Twentieth Century* (Ann Arbor: University of Michigan Press, 2016).
[98] Adiele E. Afigbo, Emmanuel A. Ayandele, Robert J. Gavin, and Robin Plamer, eds., *The Making of Modern Africa*, Vol. 2: *The Twentieth Century* (London: Longman Group, 1992); and Terence Ranger and Olufemi Vaughan, eds., *Legitimacy and the State in Twentieth Century Africa: Essays in Honour of A. H. M. Kirk-Greene* (Oxford: Palgrave Macmillan, 1993).

among the aristocracy, especially regarding education for women.[99] In 1937, when students from the region began taking British examinations in the South, the North suffered from vast amounts of social inequality. In that same decade, two girls' schools were established in Kano and Katsina to bridge the gap. These institutions partially addressed the concerns raised in the letter from Bonny. Girls were to be trained in personal hygiene, welfare work, childcare, and domestic science subjects that would apply to housekeeping.[100] As the letter suggested, this would allow some level of interaction between male and female children.[101] Even this form of limited education was only available to the aristocratic class. The limited resources available to the missionaries, the government's inability to adequately fund the education sector, and the aristocracy's patronage of private, fee-based schooling strengthened local class divisions. Elites in the North followed the same logic as the larger population in the South, considering the colony's political and economic reality before other considerations when developing Western education in the region. As Ajayi wrote:

> Industrial education taught skills; literary education taught knowledge and knowledge was power. Literary education was therefore superior. It was such education that made it possible for Dr. Williams Ferguson, a black man, to be made the governor of Sierra Leone, and for Crowther to become a bishop.[102]

Education was a way for the ruling class to sustain their power and privileges. In this regard, the literary education system was largely conservative, reproducing imperial and elite interests. In addition to the responsibilities noted by Ajayi, it became instrumental in codifying local languages into letters and words. With the increasing presence of print media, literary graduates championed the documentation of local histories and traditions along with scripture reading.[103] Through these efforts, the diffusion of Christian ideals was given an immense lift, especially in the South.

---

[99] Peter Kazenga Tibenderana, "The Beginnings of Girls' Education in the Native Administration Schools in Northern Nigeria, 1930–1945," *The Journal of African History* 26, no. 1 (1985): 93–109.

[100] For the exact dynamics in the Belgian imperial estate of Congo, see Gertrude Mianda, "Colonialism, Education, and Gender Relations in the Belgian Congo: The Evolue Case," in *Women in African Colonial Histories*, ed. Jean Allman, Susan Geiger, and Nakanyike Musisi (Bloomington: Indiana University Press, 2002), 144–163.

[101] This was part of the marginal role traditionally assigned to European women of this period, and under the Ruskin model of sex (socialization for sex roles). A dimension of male chauvinism that was prevalent in European culture had been transplanted into colonial society as part of the Western taxonomic modernity imposed on the colony. See Hellen Callaway, *Gender, Culture and Empire: European Women in Colonial Nigeria* (London: The Macmillan Press Ltd., 1987).

[102] Ajayi, "The Development of Secondary Grammar School Education," 522.

[103] John D. Y. Peel, *Religious Encounter and the Making of the Yoruba* (Bloomington: Indiana University Press, 2003).

The political atmosphere in the South was more charged due to the awareness and consciousness supported by the population's literacy. After returning to the country from studies that usually took place in London and the United States, many of the new graduates radicalized the nationalist agitations of the time. They adapted Western knowledge systems to weaponize the colony's drive for decolonization.[104] These revolutionaries sought to break the status quo, but it did little to affect systems and structures that had been concretized by the colonial education system.

Conclusion

The spread and development of Western education in Nigeria were similar to its progress in British dependencies elsewhere. The connection between these colonies and London, maintained through the Colonial Office and the British Parliament, ensured that this would be the case. The evolution of Western education in Sierra Leone, which produced the earliest educated elites that aided the process in the Nigerian colony, was repeated elsewhere.

The increasing number of educated individuals who were not absorbed into the postcolonial state's political economy also began to emigrate to Europe and the Americas. The British administration had largely left the spreading of Western education to missionary efforts, but its specific interest in secondary education triggered its direct involvement. In 1907, the administration declared its intent to open the Lagos Government College. Following the advice of Chief Kitoye Ajasa, one of the Lagos elites serving on the committee for the institution's establishment, the proposed school was named King's College. It commenced operation in 1909.[105]

On January 30, 1907, Mr. Orisadipe Obasa of the Department of Education announced that the Lagos School for Girls would open at a temporary site located in Caxton House, Marina.[106] That same year, more than £10,000 was spent on the completion of school buildings for educational and industrial instruction in Bonny.[107] The government's intervention in the spread of Western education during this period was resisted by the missionaries as they took action to remain relevant and occasionally formed partnerships that departed from their past rivalries and competition.[108] In 1928, the CMS and the Wesleyan Methodist Mission established the United Mission College in Ibadan to train women

---

[104] Ali Mazrui and C. Wondji, *General History of Africa*, Vol. VIII: *Africa since 1935* (California: University of California Press, 1993).
[105] Ogunlade, "Education and Politics," 325–345.
[106] *The Lagos Standard*, Vol. XIII, no. 20, January 30, 1907.
[107] *The Lagos Standard*, "The Urgent Need for Female Education in Bonny," *The Lagos Standard*, XIII, no. 17, January 9, 1907.
[108] Felix K. Ekechi, *Missionary Enterprise and Rivalry in Igboland 1857–1914* (London: Frank Cass, 1972).

teachers. Their joint venture was followed by the establishment of Igbobi College in 1932. Catholic, Baptist, and other Christian missions also joined efforts to propagate secondary education in the colony. Schools including the Methodist Boys' High School (1876), the Methodist Girls' High School (1879), St. Gregory (1881), the Baptist Academy (1885), and King's College (1909) – which was adopted by Henry Carr as the model school for piloting the hybridized education system – advanced some regions within the colony, but all of them returned to literary education. Every other model for modern education in the colony followed the same path.[109]

---

[109] See, among others, Peter Kazenga Tibenderena, "The Beginnings of Girls Education in the Native Administration Schools in Northern Nigeria, 1930–1945," *The Journal of African History* 26, no. 1 (1985): 93–109; Ajayi, "Henry Venn and the Policy of Development," 331–342; and Cohen, *The Politics of Elite Culture.*

14

Social Changes

Societies reach an equilibrium of identity through a process of continuous change. However, evolutionary disturbances redirect the trajectory of a society's individual and institutional processes, systems, and convictions to attain a new equilibrium in an ongoing process.[1] Every society is gradually transforming into a new state, although change can be more radical when a new phenomenon is introduced. Change is constant, and societies cannot remain stagnant since they metamorphose through time and history.

Roots and Agents of Social Changes

Nigeria and other parts of Africa have undergone comprehensive social transformations over time, acquiring new faces, phases, systems, styles, and convictions. Nigeria's rich and diverse cultures have built a system and body of beliefs through observed and unobserved social engagement. Colonialism compelled Nigerian societies to undergo radical changes from their precolonial social systems. Juxtaposing the precolonial and colonial systems is useful for understanding the background and the extent of social changes in Nigeria. Barrington Moore traced the roots of social change and conceptualized comparative historical analysis to perform cross-sectional analyses of history and sociology, which identified signs of social change.[2] In every society, changes can only be studied and understood effectively through the lens of history. Jack Goldstone has defined the parameters of these changes as Existence/Absence, Convergence/Divergence, and Discrimination/Reconciliation.[3]

Nigeria's precolonial administration functioned through a system of local authorities that was quite different from the colonial administrators'

---

[1] Max Gluckman, "The Utility of the Equilibrium Model in the Study of Social Change," *American Anthropologist* 70, no. 2 (1968): 219–237.

[2] Barrington Moore, *Social Origins of Dictatorship and Democracy: Lord and Peasant in the Making of the Modern World* (Boston: Beacon Press, 1993).

[3] Jack A. Goldstone, "Comparative Historical Analysis and Knowledge Accumulation in the Study of Revolutions," in *Comparative Historical Analysis in the Social Sciences*, ed. James Mahoney and Dietrich Rueschemeyer (Cambridge: Cambridge University Press, 2003), 41–90.

approach.[4] The Sokoto Caliphate, which was led by the Sultan of Sokoto, expanded and conquered regions in Northern Nigeria, extending down to the Niger–Benue region and Kwara.[5] The Sultan's system of government built every stratum of society on loyalty to the central government's authority. The caliphate appointed emirs to manage conquered emirates, and these authorities were either loyalists or members of Usman Dan Fodio's movement.[6]

Among the Yoruba, Benin, and Nupe societies, political structures were based on a centralized kingship system. These groups placed confidence in the authority of the gods, and a few political structures existed as checks on powerful individuals in the community.[7] The Alaafin and other Yoruba kings were referred to as *Iku Baba yeye, Alase Ikeji Orisa* (one who decrees death, the second in command to the gods), which emphasized their authority and semidivinity status.[8] The Igbo precolonial system was formed on principles of egalitarianism and decentralization.[9] Igbo societies did not follow a king or a central leader, and political powers were divided by age groups within villages. Some of Nigeria's major societies were decentralized, and others followed a central leader.[10]

Goldstone's models and parameters for determining social change are based on the premise that influence within one sector of society will lead to development and change in other aspects of society. Nigeria's colonial administration wielded influence over society, and its authority diminished the traditional precolonial political systems and other social institutions within Indigenous communities. By 1900, the British had conquered and annexed the Northern Protectorate, introducing a new system of government.[11] Traditional political leaders were not completely removed by Lugard's Indirect Rule system, but the Sultan of Sokoto's absolute authority and totalitarianism were drastically reduced.

---

[4] Sam E. Oyovbaire, "Structural Change and Political Processes in Nigeria," *African Affairs* 82, no. 326 (1983): 3–28.

[5] Hamza M. Maishanu and Isa M. Maishanu, "The Jihad and the Formation of the Sokoto Caliphate," *Islamic Studies* 38, no. 1 (1999): 119–131.

[6] Sa'ad Abubakar, "The Emirate-type of Government in the Sokoto Caliphate," *Journal of the Historical Society of Nigeria* 7, no. 2 (1974): 211–229.

[7] Joseph R. Strayer, "The State and Religion: An Exploratory Comparison in Different Cultures," *Comparative Studies in Society and History* 1, no. 1 (1958): 38–43; and Shmuel N. Eisenstadt, "Religious Organizations and Political Process in Centralized Empires," *The Journal of Asian Studies* 21, no. 3 (1962): 271–294.

[8] Adeyemi J. Ademowo and Adedapo Adekunle, "Law in Traditional Yoruba Philosophy: A Critical Appraisal," *Caribbean Journal of Philosophy* 2, no. 1 (2013): 345–354.

[9] E. Nwaubani, "Igbo Political Systems," *Lagos Notes and Records* 12, no. 1 (2006): 1–27.

[10] Joseph A. Atanda, "Government of Yorubaland in the Pre-colonial Period," *Tarikh* 4, no. 2 (1971): 1–12.

[11] Colin Newbury, "Accounting for Power in Northern Nigeria," *The Journal of African History* 45, no. 2 (2004): 257–277.

The sultan's office lost its authority over other emirs within the caliphate, and those offices were subordinate to the colonial government. Many of the sultan's activities required approval from British officials. Similar situations unfolded in Yoruba societies and other precolonial traditional political systems.[12] The village assemblies and the age-grade systems in Igbo societies were replaced by colonial District Officers. Toward the end of the colonial administration, as citizens became more directly involved in democracy and the Legislative and Executive Councils, political power shifted to the educated elites and other individuals who had not traditionally held authority in the region.[13]

Political change in these social systems explains the convergence of two different systems that were previously foreign to Nigerian society. The imposition of Western political culture is one of several ways that social change was observed in Nigeria.[14] Nigerian societies initially resisted these impositions, and that resistance was overcome through British military conquest, especially in Northern Nigeria. Social change occurred through political institutions, but the political change was not confined to the state's political institutions. As colonial officers introduced changes to the Nigerian political system, this led to changes in other aspects of society, which is why the political system was the root of social change. This is supported by Myrdal's Circular Cumulative Causation explanation of social change, whereby a change in an institution or aspect of society will communicate the change to other areas.[15] Change starts within one institution and spreads to other institutions. A European example of this principle was the First Industrial Revolution of 1760–1830, which drove changes in almost every aspect of European society due to changes in industrial and economic orientation.[16]

In the Nigerian context, colonialism introduced radical political change and affected other aspects of the affected societies, compelling them to change. Nigeria's agricultural economy underwent radical shifts as people were incentivized to change from food crops to cash crops, driven by the constant need to export raw materials.[17] Under colonialism, Western civilization and culture

[12] Sylva M. Ngu, "The Amalgamation of Northern and Southern Protectorates of Nigeria: Issues and Challenges," *JORAS* 4 (2014): 1–13.
[13] Tola Odubajo and Bamidele Alabi, "The Elite Factor in Nigeria's Political-Power Dynamics," *Journal of Studies in Social Sciences* 8, no. 1 (2014): 121–139.
[14] Paul K. N. Ugboajah, "Culture–Conflict and Delinquency: A Case Study of Colonial Lagos," *Eras Edition* 10 (2008): 1–24.
[15] Gunnar Myrdal, *An American Dilemma: The Negro Problem and Modern Democracy* (New York: Harper, 1944).
[16] Jan De Vries, "The Industrial Revolution and the Industrious Revolution," *The Journal of Economic History* 54, no. 2 (1994): 249–270. See also Edward Anthony Wrigley, *Energy and the English Industrial Revolution* (Cambridge: Cambridge University Press, 2010).
[17] Eno J. Usoro, *The Nigerian Oil Palm Industry: Government Policy and Export Production, 1906–1965* (Ibadan: Ibadan University Press, 1974).

were also spread through educational institutions established by Christian missionaries and the British colonial administration. Within these schools, people adapted to new ideas and encouraged extensive changes in social constructs, styles, and convictions within their societies.[18] These changes happened in the context of colonial rule, which created policies that led to transformation. Thus, political change was at the root of social change.

The change in social institutions, described by British officials as the introduction of civilization, did not come from philanthropic urges to develop Nigerians' full potentials. Colonialism was partly driven by the radical changes that had been caused by the Industrial Revolution.[19] The capitalist economies led European countries to look elsewhere in a quest for raw materials and new markets.[20] In an attempt to compete with other European countries, the colonial government once banned the exportation of palm oil to any country other than England, and strict regulation controlled the palm oil industry within the colony.[21] To support its economic interests and overcome local challenges, the colonial government engaged in projects to promote the extraction and exportation of raw materials. Roads, railways, and other transportation facilities were constructed, and the colonial government created health facilities near coastal areas for the exclusive use of British officials and European traders.

The first healthcare institution to be built was a sick bay that treated members of the Royal Navy and other British officials. In 1873, the Infectious Disease Hospital was created in Lagos to benefit Europeans.[22] The healthcare system and its associated facilities eventually began treating Nigerians to ensure that people continued working, which prevented the interruption of British trade. Historical materialism, which Lenin described as the central pillar of Marxist theory for social development, explains these decisions whereby continuity in production must be maintained by continuity in productive forces, including labor.[23] If the colony's labor force had declined, Britain's industrial agenda would have suffered, and that threat guided decisions for social development in the Nigerian

---

[18] Anthony I. Nwabughuogu, *Problems of Nation Building in Africa* (Okigwe: Fasman Educational and Research Publications, 2009), 1–2.

[19] Umaru Abubakar Bala, "Colonialism and the Development in Nigeria: Effects and Challenges," *International Affairs and Global Strategy* 70 (2019): 9–20.

[20] Eno J. Usoro, "Colonial Economic Development Strategy in Nigeria 1919–1939: An Appraisal," *The Nigerian Journal of Economic and Social Studies* 19, no. 1 (1977): 121–141.

[21] Olusegun Adeyeri and Kehinde David Adejuwon, "The Implications of British Colonial Economic Policies on Nigeria's Development," *International Journal of Advanced Research in Management and Social Sciences* 1, no. 2 (2012): 1–16.

[22] Dennis A. Ityavyar, "Background to the Development of Health Services in Nigeria," *Social Science & Medicine* 24, no. 6 (1987): 487–499.

[23] Adam Schaff, "The Marxist Theory of Social Development," in *Readings in Social Evolution and Development*, ed. Shmuel N. Eisenstadt (New York: Pergamon Press, 1970): 71–94.

colony. The colonial administration's economic interests influenced the social development of Nigerian society.

In attempting to explain the origins of the social change process in colonial Nigeria, it is necessary to understand the agents of social change that were present. Christian missionaries were a prominent force for change during the colonial period.[24] Different religious missions spread their beliefs and taught Western values and ideals throughout Nigeria.[25] The introduction of Christianity challenged the belief that African gods held mysterious powers.[26] Traditional powers of punishment, vengeance, or salvation were dismissed as false, while different forms of *Juju* (so-called magic) attributed to religious and traditional beliefs were rendered irrelevant. As traditional religions and their beliefs lost respect, they equally lost their ability to uphold existing laws and social orders. Societies began adopting colonial and "modern" approaches to justice and punishment. The use of *Juju* in taking oaths or entering into contracts, which was widely practiced before colonialism, was abandoned among many of those who converted to foreign religions.[27]

Christianity and Islam changed existing social practices. Traditional initiation ceremonies marked individual life events, such as joining a society, becoming an adult, and entering into marriage. These ceremonies ceased to hold in many places. The practice of polygamy, and its effects on status in a community, were changed along with the age-grade system in the East and naming and funeral ceremonies. These social conventions were altered by the tenets of Christian teaching.[28] Nigerians who converted to Christianity renounced polygamy as sinful.[29] Christianity expanded the frontiers of Western education by creating schools in different locations. The earliest school providing basic education, the Nursery of Infant Church, was created by the Church Missionary Society in 1843.[30] Additional facilities were constructed by other missionaries, and they spread new ideas, orientations, and

---

[24] Emmanuel A. Ayandele, *The Missionary Impact on Modern Nigeria, 1842–1914: A Political and Social Analysis* (London: Longmans, 1966).

[25] Jacob F. A. Ajayi, *Christian Missions in Nigeria, 1841–1891: The Making of a New Élite* (London: Longmans, 1965).

[26] Chukwuma O. Okeke, Christopher N. Ibenwa, and Gloria Tochukwu Okeke, "Conflicts Between African Traditional Religion and Christianity in Eastern Nigeria: The Igbo Example," *SAGE Open* 7, no. 2 (2017): 1–10.

[27] Ayandele, *The Missionary Impact on Modern Nigeria*.

[28] James S. Coleman, *Nigeria: Background to Nationalism* (Berkeley: University of California Press, 1958).

[29] Edmund O. Egboh, "Polygamy in Iboland (South–Eastern Nigeria) with Special Reference to Polygamy Practice among Christian Ibos," *Civilisations* 22, no. 3 (1972): 431–444.

[30] Ajike F. Osanyin, *Early Childhood Education in Nigeria* (Shomolu: Concept Publishing Limited, 2002), 26.

values that affected all of society's systems. Christian missionaries also established the first healthcare facilities in the country, creating the foundation for medical services.[31] Social changes were arguably the core effects of Nigeria's interaction with Christian missionaries.[32]

Western education and educational facilities were instrumental in changing society's views and introducing new cultures. Anywhere in the world, education emancipates minds and extends imaginations. The introduction of Western education expanded Nigerian minds to receive new ideas, techniques, and cultural perspectives that would be reflected in various respects. The effects of education have alleviated poverty and promoted equality in society.[33] In Onitsha, Catholic missionaries established basic primary education to promote Christianity.[34] The Catholic doctrine, writing, English, reading, and basic mathematics were taught in missionary schools. By 1926, about 45,000 Nigerians had become Catholics. Education changed the religion and ideology of Nigerians.[35] Schools that had been established by missionaries and the colonial administration produced graduates who left farming occupations and abandoned local trades to secure formal jobs as clerks, secretaries, receptionists, interpreters, and foremen. These schools did not initially produce graduates who engaged in advanced professional activities like medicine or law, but they introduced the local population to new roles and occupations that could support their families.[36]

Educational institutions spread throughout Nigeria due to Christian missionaries and colonial administrators, and the curriculum reflected their preferences. This encouraged individuals to act in "civil" ways that modelled constructed ideal European character traits. People began dressing like the whites, emulating foreign speaking patterns, and acting in ways they considered European.[37] Nigerians had encountered foreign cultures through their experience in both World Wars, and some were able to travel to Britain to complete advanced education. Returnees from these journeys introduced new values to Nigerian cultures. Education and educational advancement,

---

[31] Ren Winnett, Rich Furman, Douglas Epps, and Greg Lamphear, eds., *Health Care Social Work: A Global Perspective* (Oxford: Oxford University Press, 2019).

[32] Dozie Okoye, "Things Fall Apart? Missions, Institutions, and Interpersonal Trust," *Journal of Development Economics* 148 (2021): 1–78.

[33] Kolawole Ogundari and Adebayo B. Aromolaran, "Impact of Education on Household Welfare in Nigeria," *International Economic Journal* 28, no. 2 (2014): 345–364.

[34] Felix K. Ekechi, "The Holy Ghost Fathers in Eastern Nigeria, 1885–1920: Observations on Missionary Strategy," *African Studies Review* 15, no. 2 (1972): 217–239.

[35] Celestine A. Obi, ed., *A Hundred Years of the Catholic Church in Eastern Nigeria 1885–1985* (Onitsha: Africana-Fep Publishers, 1985).

[36] Samuel N. Nwabara, *Iboland: A Century of Contact with Britain 1860–1960* (London: Hodder and Stoughton, 1977), 61–67.

[37] Emmanuel Johnson Ibuot, Cletus Johnson Ibuot, and Ibia E. Ibia, "Education, Ideology and Social Transformation," *Journal of the Historical Society of Nigeria* 27 (2018): 24–47.

especially when attained outside of Nigeria, were also responsible for the emergence of Nigerian nationalism. Herbert Macaulay and other Nigerians used their education to mobilize other elites in their struggle for independence.

Education introduced some changes in Northern Nigeria, which affected some of the values of the Hausa people, but it was less effective than in the South. The northern educational system already had children studying the Quran and other Islamic teachings under Mallams. The British initially introduced an educational system that respected local values and political beliefs.[38] The British government established its first educational institution in Kano in 1910: the Nasarawa Central Schools.[39] Educational efforts were organized into different structures. One structure was that of the Mallam School, teaching individuals from the ages of 18 to 30 from the surrounding provinces. These students would become Mallams, and they were trained as teachers who could administer and operate schools that would be established later. The Sons of Chiefs schools were separate structures that intended to educate prospective leaders of the North, training them in literacy by teaching them how to read and write. There was a Technical or Craft School to train servants of the emirs and their sons, which taught carpentry, leatherwork, weaving, blacksmithing, and other skills.[40] Finally, the Family Schools trained individuals to become clerks for government officials.[41]

The structure of the Nasarawa Central Schools was shaped by Northern cultural values and the region's Islamic beliefs. The government built a mosque near the school and allowed students to attend Quranic school after classes.[42] The intent was to develop a curriculum that could gradually educate Northern citizens in a way that did not directly conflict with local values. Although these educational efforts were successful, they were also more subtle. Many Northerners had received a Western education and had begun to embrace Western values by the time of independence, but to a lesser extent than elsewhere in Nigeria.

In 1914, the government created additional schools in each province, teaching primary education across the North. The administration also continued to train teachers. Subjects like geography, English, and history were taught alongside "the 3 Rs" of education (reading, writing, and arithmetic). By 1922, these schools had developed different specialties. Hugh Clifford transformed the Katsina Province School into the Katsina Teachers Training School, and the Sokoto Provincial School became a proper craft school that produced

---

[38] Alexander Thurston, "Islamic Modernism and Colonial Education in Northern Nigeria: Na'ibi Sulaiman Wali (1927–2013)," *Religion & Education* 44, no. 1 (2017): 101–117.
[39] Mahmud M. Tukur, *British Colonisation of Northern Nigeria, 1897–1914: A Reinterpretation of Colonial Sources* (Dakar: Amalion Publishing, 2016).
[40] Gbadebo O. Gbadamosi, "The Establishment of Western Education among Muslims in Nigeria 1896–1926," *Journal of the Historical Society of Nigeria* 4, no. 1 (1967): 89–115.
[41] Colonial Report Annual: Northern Nigeria 1909 and 1911.
[42] Colonial Report Annual: Northern Nigeria 1910–1911, 722.

motor parts, office fittings, shoes, and other objects.[43] These developments and other educational efforts spread Western values and realigned Northern Nigeria's social orientation.

The World Wars were another inseparable component of Nigeria's colonial experience. These wars, especially World War II, were major agents of social change. Nigerians were a major component of British forces in the war, providing 45,000 soldiers to serve in infantry regiments.[44] Those who returned from the conflict brought new ideas and worldviews that reshaped the perspectives of many people. The experience of World War II expanded the imagination of Nigerians who served in the conflict. For many of them, it was their first experience with new technologies that were common in other parts of the world. Nigerians who had been enlisted from remote regions saw the benefits of transportation infrastructure like rails, ferries, and other innovations. They encountered new languages, skills, foods, and urban cultures that engendered lifestyle changes when they returned to Nigeria.[45] Soldiers who visited officers or attended events were exposed to Western songs, along with plays, football, and boxing matches.

The adoption and dissemination of bread production can arguably be attributed to experience from the war. The use of alcohol and tobacco by Nigerians had been influenced by the attitudes of military officers that they encountered around the world. The postwar experiences among Nigerians and soldiers from other African countries encouraged a culture of sanitation. Soldiers at war were required to bury their refuse, use clean water, wear clean clothes, and generally remain as hygienic as possible. These values were transmitted to the families of soldiers after their return. The war also encouraged the acceptance of Western medicine as soldiers received medical examinations and Western drugs and injections.[46]

After World War II, coins became more widely adopted and used for local transactions. Currency not only became more widely accepted for payments and trade in Nigerian markets, which boosted the colonial economy, it also facilitated the administration's assessment and imposition of taxes. Colonial administrators issued currency payments to soldiers and other sectors of the colony in wartime, which increased the scope of transactions in which currency could be used.[47] Nigerian soldiers were eager to acquire new knowledge. Toward the end of the war, military service inspired soldiers to pursue

---

[43] Alan Peshkin, "Education and National Integration in Nigeria," *The Journal of Modern African Studies* 5, no. 3 (1967): 323–334.

[44] James R. Brennan, "The First Victory: The Second World War and the East Africa Campaign by Andrew Stewart," *Canadian Journal of History* 53, no. 1 (2018): 180–182.

[45] James K. Matthews, "World War I and the Rise of African Nationalism: Nigerian Veterans as Catalysts of Change," *The Journal of Modern African Studies* 20, no. 3 (1982): 493–502.

[46] David Killingray and Martin Plaut, *Fighting for Britain: African Soldiers in the Second World War* (London: Boydell & Brewer Ltd., 2012).

[47] Robert Kakembo, *An African Soldier Speaks* (London: Edinburgh House Press, 1946).

additional learning. Nigerian soldiers received additional technical training, receiving electrical and mechanical education, before returning home. These soldiers learned how to repair vehicles and fix electrical appliances. Some of them opened repair businesses for trucks, bicycles, and radiators, along with other appliances that were used regularly. Some returnees established transportation businesses, such as the Calabar Transport Service.

After World War II, many new businesses and trades were established, as in the case of the city of Onitsha, which became a commercial center.[48] Overall, wartime experiences encouraged Nigerians to learn more and acquire advanced knowledge. The war affected every aspect of Nigerian society and its war returnees, altering the foundations of the country's social constructs.[49] New nationalist groups emerged that understood how society was changing. These groups became agents of social change, especially in relation to political orientations that had been altered by colonial administrators.[50]

Social Changes: Manifestations and Reflections

Colonialism introduced massive changes to social orientation in every aspect and sector of society. The British colonial administration upset the traditional equilibrium in which precolonial Nigerians existed. The establishment of colonial authority changed industries, politics, societies, lifestyles, and the cultural identities of Nigerians before 1960 when the country became independent. The roots of these social changes developed during the colonial era, but these changes were translated, manifested, and reflected in the daily activities of Nigerians.

The colonial administration imposed radical changes that transformed the economy. This development served Britain's economic interests, but affected Nigeria's population and changed their perception of business and how it should be conducted. Nigeria's industry had three distinct phases: the period before the official establishment of Nigeria's colonial administration in 1900, the industrial developments that were evident during the colonial administration, and the Nigerian industry after independence.[51] Craftsmanship was a core value of precolonial society in Nigeria, and the various crafts were held in high regard.[52] Nigerians made artifacts that were traded locally and

---

[48] Killingray and Plaut, *Fighting for Britain*.
[49] Oliver Coates, "Nigeria and the World Wars," in *The Oxford Handbook of Nigerian History*, ed. Toyin Falola and Matthew M. Heaton (Oxford: Oxford University Press, 2022).
[50] Matthews, "World War I."
[51] J. O. C. Onyemelukwe, "Structural and Locational Characteristics of Manufacturing," in *A Geography of Nigerian Development*, 2nd ed., ed. J. S. Oguntoyinbo, O. O. Areola, and M. Filani (Ibadan: Heinemann Educational Books Ltd., 1983), 296–310.
[52] Oboh M. Yakubu, "Arts, Crafts and Indigenous Industries in Nigeria," *Journal of Cultural Studies* 4, no. 1 (2002): 215–234.

across different regions of the country. Wood carvings, leatherwork, textiles, brass, bronze, pottery, and ironwork formed the core of craft businesses.

The kingdom of Benin was notable for brilliant bronze and wooden artwork, and the Igbo societies specialized in blacksmithing, pottery, and woodcarving. The Ibibio–Efik region was famous for raffia embroidery and woodcarving. Oyo residents carved calabash and made dyed and woven textiles to be transported to other parts of the country.[53] In the Northern region, products were made from animal skins that were widely available in the area.[54] Crafting professions relied on raw materials and resources that were locally available.

The colonial administration and Western education modernized production processes in many industries. Modernization introduced new practices for adding value to raw materials, refining production processes and encouraging the more widespread distribution of goods within and beyond the country.[55] By 1920, oil mills had refined the production of palm oil, which was processed from local palm fruits. Mills made the production process faster, easier, and cleaner. Ginneries improved cotton yields, sawmills enhanced the production of lumber, and other methods were introduced for publishing, printing, furniture making, and baking to be exported.[56] These radical changes in industrial processes developed over time.

Precolonial Nigeria was largely structured around an agrarian economy.[57] Farming and other agricultural practices were found throughout the country. The distribution of natural features and their composition defined the dominant agricultural practices of specific areas. Places near rivers were occupied by fishermen who engaged in related businesses. Northern Nigeria produced grains and other crops for consumption. Agriculture was the main basis of income, and products like beans, maize, cassava, and plantains were grown for consumption and small-scale trading. The establishment of the colonial administration shifted the focus away from production for local consumption as people began to produce cash crops that could be exported.

The colonial administration encouraged the production of groundnuts, palm products, and cocoa for export, which boosted the colonial economy and allowed Nigeria to compete favorably with other countries. These three kinds of products comprised about 70 percent of the total products exported from

---

[53] For details on each area identified herein, see K. C. Murray, "Arts and Crafts of Nigeria: Their Past and Future," *Africa: Journal of the International African Institute* 14, no. 4 (1943): 155–164.

[54] Dickson 'Dare Ajayi, "Recent Trends and Patterns of Nigeria's Industrial Development," *African Journal for the Psychological Study of Social Issues* 9, no. 2 (2006): 135–151.

[55] Bola Ayeni, *Spatial Dimension of Manufacturing Activities in Nigeria* (Ibadan: Technical Report, Department of Geography, University of Ibadan, 1981).

[56] O. Teriba, E. C. Edosien, and M. O. Kayode, *The Structure of Manufacturing Industry in Nigeria* (Ibadan: University of Ibadan Press, 1981), 13–28.

[57] Meillassoux, *The Development of Indigenous Trade*.

Nigeria during colonial rule. Beginning from 1951, Nigeria was exporting 497,000 tons of palm products, 180,136 tons of groundnuts, and 97,000 tons of cocoa. Nigerian exports generated significant amount of money for the colonial administration. Machinery was also introduced to improve production efficiency.[58] Many Nigerians responded to financial incentives by investing in cash crops, changing the motives at work in agriculture.

The colonial administration changed the systems for transporting goods and individuals. Transportation infrastructure became a lifeline for the economy, and it remains an essential part of the country's economy to the present day.[59] After colonial authority was established, it became important to develop reliable methods of transportation.[60] The railway became the government's first major transportation project.[61] Tracks laid in 1898 connected Otta to Iddo in the present-day areas of the Ogun and Lagos states, respectively. Jebba, Ilorin, Gusau, Minna, Enugu, Port Harcourt, Zaria, Makurdi, and other towns were linked via railroads in 1930. Additional construction connected Borno to Maiduguri in 1964. The establishment and maintenance of railway systems enabled a huge transportation network between Nigeria's Northern and Southern Protectorates.[62] People relied on trains to transport goods across the country, and the migration of individuals encouraged cultural diffusion.[63]

By 1920, the colonial government had begun the construction of road networks that improved existing footpaths. The construction of new roads was assisted by missionaries, and free labor was exploited.[64] Construction occurred in Oyo and Abeokuta, and similar roads were developed in Ijebu, Ondo, and other areas of Western Nigeria, including the road that connected Agbowo to Ikorodu. Development continued across the country and expanded into the Northern region, which brought an economic boom. Connections between Nigeria's regions and communities brought substantial social change, exposing

---

[58] M. E. Abo, O. A. Fademi, G. O. Olaniyan, et al., "Evolution of Extension Strategies towards Sustainable Agriculture in Nigeria," *Journal of Agricultural & Food Information* 4, no. 4 (2002): 65–80.

[59] Lord Lugard, *The Dual Mandate in British Tropical Africa* (London: Frank Cass & Co., 1965).

[60] Oladipo O. Olubomehin, "Road Transportation as Lifeline of the Economy in Western Nigeria, 1920 to 1952," *African Journal of History and Culture* 4, no. 3 (2012): 37–45.

[61] Joshua A. Odeleye, "Politics of Rail Transport Development in Developing Countries: Case of Nigeria," *Journal of Civil Engineering and Architecture* 6, no. 12 (2012): 1695–1702.

[62] Francis Jaekel, *The History of the Nigerian Railway, Vol. 2: Network and Infrastructures* (Ibadan: Spectrum Books Ltd., 1997).

[63] Azalahu Francis Akwara, Joseph Effiong Udaw, and Gerald E. Ezirim, "Adapting Colonial Legacy to Modernism: A Focus on Rail Transport Development in Nigeria," *Mediterranean Journal of Social Sciences* 5, no. 6 (2014): 465.

[64] Ade Adefuye, John Gershion, and Joshua Ricketts, "Jamaican Contribution to the Socio-Economic Development of the Colony Province," in *Studies in Yoruba History and Culture*, ed. Gabriel O. Olusanya (Ibadan: Ibadan University Press, 1983), 135–152.

people to cultures and customs from other parts of Nigeria and Europe. Transportation drove social change because people and businesses no longer had to spend substantial time and energy trekking from village to village.

Another social change was the growing number of people who identified with Western culture. Nigerians began identifying with Christianity, and they adopted basic behaviors akin to those of the Christian church members.[65] Before 1960, Nigerians had begun speaking English, especially in the course of their duties. Western standards were adopted as the ideal way for "ladies" and "gentlemen" to act. The Western "nuclear family" was prioritized over the extended family that had previously been idealized.[66]

Social changes swept through lifestyles, daily routines, and cultures. New forms of entertainment emerged. Rich cultural practices like *Egelege* wrestling and the *Oze* of the *Odual* society in the Niger Delta were transformed into new performances. Many precolonial festivals existed to worship the gods, but re-enactments of these events became a point of interest for tourists. The early introduction of filmmaking later became localized. Images and settings for films were originally dominated by colonial imagery of Europeans and their achievements, which were not relatable to the Nigerian population. The settings and actors were neither African nor Black. Individuals who received preferential treatment from British officials had early opportunities to view imported films.[67] Much later in the 1970s, filmmaking in Nigeria underwent a developmental boost that made it more widely relatable.[68]

Returnees from the World Wars had also been exposed to other European customs, including football, music, and other activities. Western and local literature was more widely distributed during the 1940s, and people found it to be a fascinating method of relaxation.[69] Political stakeholders in Nigeria began developing a national consciousness, and agitations for independence became more widespread as individuals worked to end colonialism and discriminatory policies.[70] However, the prominence of Western education encouraged

---

[65] Oluwafunminiyi Raheem, "Martin Luther versus Us: Assessing the Reformation through the Perspectives of an African Class," *African Diaspora Discourse – ADD* 2, no. 2 (2020): 49–72.

[66] Dare Arowolo, "The Effects of Western Civilization and Culture on Africa," *Afro Asian Journal of Social Sciences* 1, no. 1 (2010): 1–13.

[67] Onookome Okome, "The Context of Film Production in Nigeria: The Colonial Heritage," *Ufahamu: A Journal of African Studies* 24, no. 2–3 (1996): 42–62.

[68] Steve Ogunsuyi, *African Theatre Aesthetics and Television Drama in Nigeria* (Abuja: Roots Books and Journal Ltd., 2007), 31.

[69] G. M. Brown and T. B. Michael, "Traditional Forms of Entertainment and their Implication on Socio–Economic Development in the Niger Delta: The Experience of Odual Kingdom in Rivers State, 1600–2015," *South–South Journal of Humanities and International Studies* 1, no. 3 (2015): 313–331.

[70] Gabriel O. Olusanya, "The Zikist Movement – A Study in Political Radicalism, 1946–50," *The Journal of Modern African Studies* 4, no. 3 (1966): 323–333.

Nigerians to travel outside their country to study in Europe. This exposure strengthened the continuous calls for independence. These new nationalists shared their political consciousness with the public through mass media and other efforts.

The elective principles introduced by the 1923 Clifford Constitution marked the beginning of a new political consciousness. Educated Nigerians formed political associations and unions to oppose, criticize, or run for political offices.[71] In 1923, Herbert Macaulay officially created Nigeria's first political party. It was known as the Nigerian National Democratic Party (NNDP), and similar parties contested the political offices that the government had made available.[72] Political parties brought new perspectives, and they participated in indirect democracy for the first time. The Nigerian Youth Movement (NYM)[73] and the National Council of Nigeria and the Cameroons[74] were formed in Lagos in 1934 and 1944, respectively. Different regions and ethnic groups eventually formed political parties. The *Egbe Omo Oduduwa* became the Yoruba Action Group in 1950, and the North formed the Northern People's Congress in 1951, aggregating the political interests of various regions.[75] This increase in nationalist activities contributed to social changes.

Mass media, especially radio and newspapers, were another source of social change.[76] Traditional and conventional methods for communicating and distributing information changed after the introduction of mass media in various parts of Nigeria. Henry Townsend's *Iwe Iroyin*, created by the Christian missionaries, was the first known newspaper in Nigeria.[77] Early missionary newspapers, such as *Iwe Iroyin,* were established to spread the gospel and educate Nigerians.[78] The *Iwe Iroyin* would later become a weapon for political advocacy that pitted Townsend against the colonial administration

---

[71] Richard L. Sklar, *Nigerian Political Parties: Power in an Emergent African Nation* (Princeton: Princeton University Press, 2015).

[72] O. E. Udofia, "Nigerian Political Parties: Their Role in Modernizing the Political System, 1920–1966," *Journal of Black Studies* 11, no. 4 (1981): 435–447.

[73] Stephen O. Arifalo, The Rise and Decline of the Nigerian Youth Movement, 1934–1941," *The African Review: A Journal of African Politics, Development and International Affairs* 13, no. 1 (1986): 59–76

[74] Kanu Omenukwa, "The National Council of Nigeria and the Cameroons (NCNC) and the British Administration, 1944–1960: A Study of Responses to Changing Political Situations" (BA project, University of Birmingham, 1967).

[75] Shola J. Omotola, "Nigerian Parties and Political Ideology," *Journal of Alternative Perspectives in the Social Sciences* 1, no. 3 (2009): 612–634.

[76] Luke U. Uche, *Mass Media, People, and Politics in Nigeria* (New Delhi: Concept Publishing Company, 1989), 94–96.

[77] Oluwatoyin B. Oduntan, "Iwe Irohin and the Representation of the Universal in Nineteenth-Century Egbaland," *History in Africa* 32 (2005): 295–305.

[78] Fred I. A. Omu, *Press and Politics in Nigeria, 1880–1937* (Atlantic Highlands: Humanities Press, 1978).

in 1867.[79] In Lagos, Robert Campbell's *Anglo-African* newspaper reported on local politics.[80] The majority of the pre-1900 newspapers were patronized by Europeans.

By 1882, newspapers like the *Lagos Observer* began operating independently from the influence of Christian missionaries. Other papers included the *Mirror* in 1887, *The Chronicle* in 1908, and the *Nigerian Pioneer* in 1914. The *Lagos Daily News* and *Nigerian Daily Times* were established in 1925 and 1926, respectively. In 1947, toward the end of the colonial administration, Dr. Nnamdi Azikiwe founded the *West African Pilot*, the *Daily Times*, and the *Daily Mirror*. Nigerians created these news outlets to increase local political consciousness and to promote the inclusion of the elites in the country's government.[81] Newspapers that criticized the colonial system were available to people who could afford them.[82]

The radio was another tool for distributing information. To promote colonial values and information, the British Broadcasting Service was introduced in 1932, which became the Nigerian Broadcasting Service in 1951.[83] Additional radio broadcast networks were built in Kaduna, Enugu, and Ibadan between 1952 and 1955. In 1956, Ordinance No. 39 declared that the Nigerian Broadcasting Corporation would begin operation in 1957.[84] Newspapers and radio were widely accessed by Nigerians, who received crucial political information and updates about the colonial society.

The fabric of society was originally woven from a collectivist orientation. The colonial government and Christian missionary activities redirected these attitudes to embrace individualism. Collectivism was based on principles of social integration and collective responsibilities to other individuals, while individualism promoted the successful growth of individuals at the expense of a collective relationship with society.[85] In precolonial society, which was characterized by collectivist social relationships, a child's upbringing was not merely a task for the child's parents: it was society's responsibility.[86] A Yoruba

---

[79] Omu, *Press and Politics in Nigeria*.

[80] Richard J. M. Blackett, "Return to the Motherland: Robert Campbell, a Jamaican in Early Colonial Lagos," *Journal of the Historical Society of Nigeria* 8, no. 1 (1975): 133–143.

[81] Lai Oso, "The Commercialization of the Nigerian Press: Development and Implications," *Africa Media Review* 5, no. 3 (1991): 41–51.

[82] Lai Oso and Umaru Pate, eds., *Mass Media and Society in Nigeria* (Lagos: Malthouse Press, 2011).

[83] Israel W. Udomisor, "Management of Radio and Television Stations in Nigeria," *New Media and Mass Communication* 10 (2013): 2.

[84] Udomisor, "Management of Radio and Television."

[85] Harry C. Triandis, Xiao Ping Chen, and Darius K.S. Chan, "Scenarios for the Measurement of Collectivism and Individualism," *Journal of Cross-cultural Psychology* 29, no. 2 (1998): 275–289.

[86] Omóbólá A. Aládésanmí and Ìbùkún B. Ògúnjìnmí, "Yorùbá Thoughts and Beliefs in Child Birth and Child Moral Upbringing: A Cultural Perspective," *Advances in Applied Sociology* 9 (2019): 569–585.

adage states "*Oju merin lo bi omo, Igba oju lonto*": parents give birth to a child, but many people are responsible for raising it. Family structures in those societies were organized around systems of extended families, which had political and social relevance.[87] The heads of extended families in Igbo societies, *Okpara*, led their families and represented them on the council of elders.[88] Similar roles existed in other areas and ethnic groups. The social orientation of Nigerian ethnic groups embraced the principles of humanism that were seen in their most highly valued social behaviors.

The collective and humanistic principles of communities were evident in their treatment of individuals, which showed concern for cooperation and collective growth.[89] Nigerian communities were concerned about the problems that individuals experienced, and thus they found collective solutions for them.[90] Societies recognized communal systems for land tenure, and the king held the land in trust for the community. Land was allocated to individuals and families depending on their needs. The community at large recognized concepts of social justice and hospitality.[91]

Precolonial social structures began disintegrating after contact with Europeans. Although Christian missionaries promoted goodwill and humanism, they undermined the collective attributes of African societies while providing Western education that promoted European values. The British government had similar effects, disrupting Nigerian political systems that were based on enduring family connections. British colonial rule introduced new political ideologies. The administration imposed Warrant Chiefs that undermined age groups and family systems in Igbo communities. As Western education developed and expanded, it became a necessity for anyone who wished to remain relevant in their community. The educational curriculum ridiculed some aspects of Indigenous systems and enshrined foreign-derived values.

Monogamy and nuclear families became important, replacing and complementing extended families. People in the cities began to take responsibility for themselves, ignoring the difficulties experienced by others. Christian teachings of individual salvation also promoted individualism.[92] Nigerians who fought

---

[87] Olanrewaju Abdul Shitta Bey, "The Family as Basis of Social Order: Insights from the Yoruba Traditional Culture," *International Letters of Social and Humanistic Sciences* 23 (2014): 79–89.

[88] John N. Oriji, "Sacred Authority in Igbo Society," *Archives de sciences sociales des religions* 68, no. 1 (1989): 113–123.

[89] Jones A. Akinpelu, "Values in Nigerian Society," in *New Perspectives in Moral Education*, ed. Otonti A. Nduka and E. O. Iheoma (Ibadan: Evans Bros, 1983), 33–56.

[90] Otonti Nduka, "Moral Education in the Changing Traditional Societies of Sub-Saharan Africa," *International Review of Education* 26, no. 2 (1980): 153–170.

[91] Jafotito A. Sofola, *African Culture and the African Personality* (Ibadan: African Resources Publ. Co., 1973).

[92] Eugene O. Iheoma, "Moral Education in Nigeria: Problems and Prospects," *Journal of Moral Education* 14, no. 3 (1985): 183–193.

in World War II saw Western values promoted by white soldiers, which reinforced British values of materialism and individualism.

The concepts of women's rights and responsibilities underwent social change. Indigenous cultures, especially in southern regions, gave women the right to trade and conduct transactions in markets. However, they had less political and social relevance than men. In the precolonial period, the social distribution of relevance for women was dynamic – many of them were seen as strong and influential, but within a patriarchal society. Precolonial Nigerian history included the influential Queen Amina of Zazzau, Queen Idia and Queen Emotan of the Benin Kingdom, and Queen Moremi of the Old Ife Kingdom, who influenced the political atmosphere of their cities.[93] Despite this, women were still seen as subordinate to men. In the Northern region, women had less freedom. In the South, women had more access to power.[94] The Northern region marginalized secluded women who lived in segregated parts of houses that were forbidden to strangers and men.[95] In some areas, women were under the supervision of their husbands, fathers, or other male relatives.[96]

Southern Nigerian concepts of widowhood emphasized the disparate treatment of women. In some cases, women were expected to prepare the dead for burial, some societies practiced levirate marriage, and other customs further undermined the dignity of women. Some cultures had a requirement to establish that the husband's death was not caused by the wife in any way, which was often done through trial by ordeal.[97] Women's rights, especially political rights, were not fully recognized during the colonial period, but the emancipation of women began during that time.

Education was one of the earliest tools for women's liberation, for men who held authority began to see women differently, especially after encountering the ideas of Christian missionaries. The commercial expansion under the colonial administration also placed greater burdens on women. They provided free labor for the benefit of their husbands, and men began crowding them out of occupations that had traditionally been dominated by women.[98] In the early years of the British administration, the colonial government also ignored the

---

[93] Kamene Okonjo, "Sex Roles in Nigerian Politics," in *Female and Male in West Africa*, ed. Christine Oppong (London: George Allen and Unwin Ltd., 1983), 211–222.

[94] Sunday Abraham Ogunode, "Kingship and Power Politics in Akokoland, 1900–1999" (Ph.D. diss., University of Ibadan, 2021).

[95] Rachel E. Yeld, "Islam and Social Stratification in Northern Nigeria," *The British Journal of Sociology* 11, no. 2 (1960): 112–128.

[96] Yeld, "Islam and Social Stratification."

[97] Alice Armstrong, Chaloka Beyani, Chuma Himonga, et al., "Uncovering Reality: Excavating Women's Rights in African Family Law," *International Journal of Law, Policy and the Family* 7, no. 3 (1993): 314–369.

[98] Ester Boserup, *Women's Role in Economic Development* (London: Allen & Unwin, 1970).

status and political roles of women in society, which contributed to the 1929 Aba Women's War.[99]

Women became more actively involved in commercial activities as the colonial era progressed. Men began producing cash crops and trading with Europeans, while women established themselves within local trade systems, seizing new opportunities that were provided by market expansion.[100] The colonial government also enacted legislation that gave women the right to challenge the actions and authority of men in specific situations.[101] The new concept of Christian marriage also redefined traditional views of marriage, wherein women were expected to serve their husbands.[102] Women were also encouraged to enroll in schools, where they built their political consciousness and gained opportunities to influence the colonial government at the grass-roots level.[103]

Adaptation and Resistance

Every society passes through periods of change that affect different groups. No matter how beneficial these changes may be, they are normally opposed by some members of society. Accordingly, the changes that were introduced to and imposed on Nigerian societies were met with some opposition. The earliest resistance came from Nigerian communities that refused to accept Christian missionaries. These missionaries brought education and aspects of Western culture, but their new religion ridiculed traditional Nigerian institutions. Some people were unwilling to accept this new religion's attacks on tradition and they expelled the missionaries from their communities. The Ijebu people in Southern Nigeria rejected the missionaries and refused missionary assistance in their conflict with the Egba.[104] In Northern Nigeria, Islam opposed the introduction of Christianity and its associated educational institutions. Lord Lugard supported the Islamic resistance and protected the Northern colony from missionary incursions.

---

[99] Ifi Amadiume, *Male Daughters, Female Husbands: Gender and Sex in an African Society* (London: Zed Books Ltd., 2015).

[100] George Brooks, "The Signares of Saint-Louis and Goree: Women Entrepreneurs in Eighteenth Century Senegal," in *Women in Africa, Studies in Social and Economic Change*, ed. Nancy Hafkin and Edna Bay (Stanford: Stanford University Press, 1976), 19–44.

[101] Martin Chanock, "Making Customary Law: Men, Women and Courts in Colonial Northern Rhodesia," in *African Women and the Law: Historical Perspectives*, ed. Margaret. J. Hay and Marcia Wright (Boston: Boston University, 1982), 53–67.

[102] Kristin Mann, *Marrying Well: Marriage, Status and Social Change among the Educated Elite in Colonial Lagos* (Cambridge: Cambridge University Press, 1985).

[103] Charmaine Pereira, "Domesticating Women? Gender, Religion and the State in Nigeria under Colonial and Military Rule," *African Identities* 3, no. 1 (2005): 69–94.

[104] Ayandele, *The Missionary Impact on Modern Nigeria*.

The British administration was also resisted by Nigeria's earliest cultural nationalists. These people fought the British to sustain their communities and values. Many of these societies had to be conquered in military campaigns before they accepted colonial control. The Mbano minority group mounted continuous resistance and endured violence from 1903 until the 1930s when they finally entered into diplomatic agreements.[105] Similar incidents occurred in many parts of the country. Local forces resisted the British to protect their interests, but European military forces had powerful, advanced weaponry. Societies like the Egba, who had been weakened in conflict with the Ijebu, could not afford to fight the colonial authorities and soon negotiated treaties.[106]

The administration's disregard for some aspects of cultural traditions created additional frictions. The women of Eastern Nigeria were slow to accept the new taxation system, which resulted in social unrest. British officials, through their Warrant Chief, sent an officer to conduct a census for assessing taxes. The concept of taxation and the idea of counting people as part of a survey were foreign concepts for the Igbo women. One specific woman, Nwanyiukwu of Oloko, was aggrieved and insulted the officials. The incident led to a mass protest in 1929, resulting in a review of the Warrant Chief system and a reform of the colonial taxation system that had been opposed by Igbo society.[107]

Many fabrics and fashions from precolonial Nigeria endured through the colonial period and served as a basic mode of dress. The *iro* (waist wrapper), *buba* (blouse), and *gele* (headgear) often accompanied foreign bags and shoes, illustrating the Afro-Western cultural mix of dressing among Yoruba women. Societies also continued to rely on traditional healthcare practices despite being rejected by Europeans. This knowledge was powerful enough to treat many of the ailments and diseases that afflicted the people.

Colonial rule was opposed by different ethnonationalists and cultural nationalists. Political parties emerged in 1923 after the Clifford Constitution introduced elective principles. Nationalists who had studied outside Nigeria saw first-hand that whites were not intellectually superior to them, despite the misconceptions that had proliferated through Western cultures. Soldiers who returned from World War II became convinced that Nigerians could run their own country. The influence of the British administration, which resulted in additional social changes and further damage to traditional values, was opposed by the new class of educated elite. This form of resistance ultimately led to Nigeria's independence.

---

[105] Ogechi E. Anyanwu, *The Making of Mbano: British Colonialism, Resistance, and Diplomatic Engagements in Southeastern Nigeria, 1906–1960* (Lanham: Lexington Books, 2021).

[106] Obaro Ikime, "Colonial Conquest and Resistance in Southern Nigeria," *Journal of the Historical Society of Nigeria* 6, no. 3 (1972): 251–270.

[107] Ihuoma Elizabeth Obienusi, "Aba Women Protest and the Aftermath 1929 till 1960," *COOU International Journal of Humanity, Social Sciences and Global Affairs* 1, no. 1 (2019): 126–145.

15

Women

Several scholars and researchers have engaged colonialism extensively, studying its impact in different areas and sectors of Nigeria, and their findings reveal a legacy that has affected the entire country.[1] Socioeconomic and political traditions, institutions, and systems existed to serve the people before British colonizers arrived.[2] However, colonial rule undermined many aspects of these Indigenous systems, ideologies, and institutions, while the installation of colonial arrangements opposed the core structures and realities of the Nigerian people.[3] One such reality was the Indigenous concept of gender and its expression. Varying cultural systems, ideologies, and institutions operated in different regions of the country. Perceptions of gender and femininity differed from region to region, and their diverse forms were affected by colonialism. The scholarship regarding gender and its expressions during Nigeria's colonial era is a collection of regional research depicting the various realities of different communities within Nigeria.[4]

---

[1] Max Siollun, *What Britain Did to Nigeria: A Short History of Conquest and Rule* (London: C. Hurst Publishers Limited, 2021); Abubakar Bala Umar, "Colonialism and the Development in Nigeria: Effects and Challenges," *International Affairs and Global Strategy* 70 (2019): 9–20; and Benjamin Maiangwa, "How the Colonial Enterprise Hard-wired Violence into Nigeria's Governance," *Quartz Africa*, October 21, 2020, https://qz.com/africa/1920769/the-british-colonial-enterprise-wired-violence-into-nigeria/.

[2] Sa'ad Abubakar, "Pre-colonial Government and Administration among the Jukun," Inaugural Lecture, University of Maiduguri, March 26, 1986; and Jacob F. A. Ajayi and Ebiegberi J. Alagoa, "Nigeria before 1800: Aspects of Economic Development and Inter-Group Relations," in *Groundwork of Nigerian History*, ed. Obaro Ikime (Ibadan: Heinemann Educational Books, 1980), 224–235.

[3] Benjamin Maiangwa, Muhammad Dan Suleiman, and Chigbo A. Anyaduba, "The Nation as Corporation: British Colonialism and the Pitfalls of Postcolonial Nationhood in Nigeria," *Peace and Conflict Studies* 25, no. 1 (2018): 2–23.

[4] See, for instance, Obioma Nnaemeka and Chima Korieh, "Long Journeys of Impediments and Triumphs," in *Shaping our Struggles: Nigerian Women in History, Culture and Social Change*, ed. Obioma Nnaemeka and Chima Korieh (Trenton: Africa World Press, 2010), vii–xxv; and Nina Mba, *Nigerian Women Mobilized: Women's Political Activity in Southern Nigeria, 1900–1965* (Berkeley: Institute of International Studies, 1982).

Writing about Nigerian women within the discourse of gender and colonialism is ongoing.[5] Historical and cultural diversity exist within the colonial experience of women in different parts of the country. Nigerian women are not a homogenous entity; the different cultural and historical realities of various regions have created diverse experiences with colonialism. This chapter explores the colonial creation of new gender ideologies and how they are responsible for the marginal position of women in different areas and sectors of the country. This chapter will also discuss notable Nigerian women and their impact on various communities during the colonial regime. It will examine the status and experiences of women from parts of present-day Eastern, Western, Southern, and Northern Nigeria during the precolonial and colonial eras, focusing on the participation of women in politics, culture, and the economy. Before delving into this discourse, it is necessary to understand the concepts and practices of colonialism as they pertain to the Nigerian experience.

Colonialism and Women

The word "colonialism" has historical significance in different regions of the world in relation to its impact on women. It describes either one country's experience of invading another country or the experience of being invaded by a stronger nation.[6] The Nigerian context uses the latter definition. Colonialism in Nigeria can be viewed as the extension of Western European power into less-powerful regions inhabited by people of diverse cultures, languages, and traditions. The nation of Nigeria is itself a colonial invention.[7] Women were part of that invasion, with imperial power extended to them. Colonialism is a process that birthed a historical era and experience that is crucial to the identity, history, and current status of various nations across the globe.[8] The British controlled the sociopolitical and economic affairs of the country during this time through the policy of indirect rule.[9] Lugard's creation of the indirect rule doctrine meant that the British colonial government would alter Indigenous ruling structures but not abolish them. The British asserted their authority through native chiefs.[10] These chiefs facilitated the colonial

---

[5] Durba Ghosh, "Gender and Colonialism: Expansion or Marginalization?" *The Historical Journal* 47, no. 3 (2004): 737-755.

[6] Jürgen Osterhammel, *Colonialism: A Theoretical Overview* (Princeton: Markus Wiener and Kingston Ian Randle Publishers, 1997).

[7] Tekena N. Tamuno, *The Evolution of the Nigerian State: The Southern Phase, 1898-1914* (New York: Humanities Press, 1972).

[8] Kenneth Twitchett, "Colonialism: An Attempt at Understanding Imperial, Colonial and Neo-colonial Relationships," *Political Studies* 13, no. 3 (1965): 300-323.

[9] Michael Crowder, "Indirect Rule: French and British Style," *Africa: Journal of the International African Institute* 34, no. 3 (1964): 197-205.

[10] Adiele E. Afigbo, *The Warrant Chiefs: Indirect Rule in Southeastern Nigeria, 1891-1929* (London: Longman, 1972).

exploitation of the country and a systematic imposition of Western ideologies and cultures on the Nigerian people. The process of invasion is important to this discourse because it provides practical illustrations of the experience of colonialism in parts of Nigeria.

British advancement into different regions of the country was met with varying degrees of resistance.[11] Women organized some of the resistance. It is noted that the toughest resistance came from the region presently known as Southeastern Nigeria.[12] Heavy-handed colonial governance was characterized by a disregard for Indigenous cultural and religious values – naturally, Indigenous people resisted. This resistance, which was a consequence of the blatant disregard for valued cultural and religious expressions, was met with brutal reactions from the colonial government.[13] In the northern part of Nigeria, Bergstrom has noted that colonization came with the imposition of new governing structures and borders dividing Hausa communities into two parts.[14] One part was incorporated into French territory, and the other became Nigerian territory. These changes altered the trajectory and history of the Hausa people.

An examination of colonial impositions is inadequate without discussion of the significant changes to the status of women in this region. Before the encroachment of colonial forces, the northern region of Nigeria experienced an Islamic jihad that established Islamic law and practices.[15] Before these successive invasions, the Hausa people had unique cultural and social structures as well as identities of their own.[16] As one would expect from invasion and colonial imposition, the Indigenous cultures, world views, and ideologies of the Hausa were relegated to the background, while Islamic and colonial doctrines and philosophies took center stage. It has been suggested that the colonial invasion in Northern Nigeria was met with much less resistance than in parts of the South.[17]

The status of Hausa women and their experiences were heavily impacted by Islam and colonialism, which justifies claims that the histories and heritages of women in these regions were complex. Coles and Mack have observed that in

---

[11] Obaro Ikime, "Colonial Conquest and Resistance in Southern Nigeria," *Journal of the Historical Society of Nigeria* 6, no. 3 (1972): 251–270.

[12] Diana Rosenberg, "Ibo Resistance to British Colonial Power," *Ufahamu: A Journal of African Studies* 19, no. 1 (1991): 3–21.

[13] Adiele E. Afigbo, "Revolution and Reaction in Eastern Nigeria: 1900–1929: The Background to the Women's Riot of 1929," *Journal of the Historical Society of Nigeria* 3, no. 3 (1966): 539–557.

[14] Kari Bergstrom, "Legacies of Colonialism and Islam for Hausa Women: An Historical Analysis, 1804–1960" (Working Paper, Michigan State University, 2002).

[15] Hamza M. Maishanu and Isa M. Maishanu, "The Jihād and the Formation of the Sokoto Caliphate," *Islamic Studies* 38, no. 1 (1999): 119–131.

[16] Finn Fuglestad, "A Reconsideration of Hausa History before the Jihad," *The Journal of African History* 19, no. 3 (1978): 319–339.

[17] Olufemi Vaughan, *Religion and the Making of Nigeria* (Durham: Duke University Press, 2017), 39–68.

parts of present-day Hausa communities in Northern Nigeria, the culture is predominantly Islamic, and a small fraction of the people are Christians or animists.[18] They also noted that women in these regions are some of the most secluded Muslim women in the African continent. This provides additional perspective on the effects of Islamic and colonial invasions on the status and experience of Nigerian Hausa women.

A closer examination of southern regions of Nigeria reveals a stark contrast in the experiences of women. Southern women had played very important roles in various resistance movements that opposed colonial rule. The Aba Women's War[19] and the Egba women's revolt[20] are prominent examples of opposition, illustrating how Nigerian women had the agency and autonomous opinions to engineer resistance activities. These events subvert postcolonial notions of endemic subordination and docility among Nigerian women.

Colonialism and the Formation of Gender Ideologies

Postcolonial notions of gender relations in Nigeria are built around the idea of a woman's subservience, docility, and dependence.[21] These ideas stem from conceptions of culturally prescribed roles for women as mere wives and mothers. Male domination and female subservience have been described as fundamental aspects of African and Nigerian traditions and culture.[22] Ideas of assertive, independent women have been framed as contaminations of westernization, or even as vestiges of colonialism. This opinion, which is popular among antifeminist theorists and their discourse, is uncritical at best. It fails to understand the paradigms of precolonial gender relations in many parts of the continent. However, this opinion has been loosely held by skeptics regarding global and intercontinental interactions.

Van Allen has noted that others consider British colonialism and missionary projects in Africa to have saved women who were supposedly suppressed and marginalized by their cultures.[23] Amaechi and Amaechi

---

[18] Catherine Coles and Beverley Mack, "Women in the Twentieth Century Hausa Society," in *Hausa Women in the Twentieth Century*, ed. Catherine Coles and Beverley Mack (Madison: The University of Wisconsin Press, 1991), 3–28.

[19] Marc Matera, Misty L. Bastian, and Susan Kingsley, *The Women's War of 1929: Gender and Violence in Colonial Nigeria* (London: Palgrave Macmillan, 2011).

[20] Judith A. Byfield, "Taxation, Women, and the Colonial State: Egba Women's Tax Revolt," *Meridians: Feminism, Race, Transnationalism* 3, no. 2 (2003): 250–277.

[21] Chinenye Anikwenze, "The Long Walk to Equality: Historical Influences on Women in Igbo Society," *The Republic*, January 20, 2021, https://republic.com.ng/december-20-january-21/the-long-walk-to-equality/.

[22] Adeyinka A. Aderinto, "Patriarchy and Culture: The Position of Women in a Rural Yoruba Community, Nigeria," *The Anthropologist* 3, no. 4 (2001): 225–230.

[23] Judith Van Allen, "'Sitting on a Man': Colonialism and the Lost Political Institutions of Igbo Women," *Canadian Journal of African Studies* 6, no. 2 (1972): 165–181.

corroborate this observation by noting that external influences – meaning invasive European ideologies – are considered to have liberated Nigerian women who were supposedly oppressed.[24] Outside of the discourse of gender, Van Allen summarizes this conception:

> In the conventional wisdom, Western influence has "emancipated" African women – through the weakening of kinship bonds and the provision of "free choice" in Christian monogamous marriage, the suppression of "barbarous" practices, the opening of schools, the introduction of modern medicine and hygiene, and, sometimes, of female suffrage.[25]

Oyewumi has challenged this weak thinking by noting that history and tradition are just as much the products of colonialism as states, ethnicity, and cash crops.[26] Stories about Nigeria's past and history can also be inventions of colonialism. Oyewumi explores history in the context of "history as lived experience, as a record of lived experience which is coded in the oral traditions; and finally, the recently constituted written history."[27]

Today's ideas of culture and tradition have been shaped by the ideological interests of colonial forces. Before extensive African scholarly engagement, Denzer found that the most consulted literature regarding the life and realities of the precolonial Yoruba woman included "Reverend Samuel Johnson's History of the Yoruba (completed in 1898, but not published until 1921), augmented by material from the nineteenth-century writings of explorers Hugh Clapperton, and Richard and John Lander, and missionaries Thomas Jefferson Bowen, William F. Clarke, and Anna Hinderer."[28] These works are extensive, but they are European reactions to African existence. The subject of European writings about Africa has been the focus of debates on decolonization as the full expression of colonialism is a strategic exercise in dominating less-powerful countries and regions. This process of domination is tangible and intangible. Its subtle infiltrations into the psychology of the colonized enabled Europeans to rewrite Africa's history and encouraged Africans to believe it as true.

Cultural references to gender relations in Nigeria frequently discuss the dominance of men and the silence and invisibility of women. In her study of Yoruba traditions, Oyewumi observes that historical reconstitutions of Yoruba culture have invented gendered traditions: the binaries of men and women as

---

[24] Chidi M. Amaechi and Edwin U. Amaechi, "Precolonial African Gender Cosmology and the Gender Equality Nexus: The Road Not Taken in Igboland, Nigeria," *Asian Women* 35, no. 3 (2019): 93–113.
[25] Van Allen, "Sitting on a Man," 165.
[26] Oyeronke Oyewumi, "Making History, Creating Gender: Some Methodological and Interpretive Questions in the Writing of Oyo Oral Traditions," in *African Gender Studies: A Reader*, ed. Oyeronke Oyewumi (New York: Palgrave Macmillan, 2005), 169–206.
[27] Oyewumi, "Making History," 169.
[28] LaRay Denzer, "Yoruba Women: A Historiographical Study," *The International Journal of African Historical Studies* 27, no. 1 (1994): 2–3.

social categories have been invented within Yoruba historical spaces.[29] Within these spaces, men occupy dominant and active positions while women receive little or no recognition. Awe corroborates this observation, stating that there is a dearth of information about the historical achievements of women.[30] She has suggested that the existence of a deep, gendered bias in the representation of history often leads to the achievements of women being attributed to men or to the mistaken idea that outstanding women were, indeed, men. Inventions of historical male dominance are directly responsible for the current perceptions and expressions of Nigeria's gender relations. Oyewumi notes further that the written histories of the Yoruba people are reflections of the creation of men and kings and these reflections were drawn from oral traditions that were formally lacking gender categories.[31] She has opined that occupations and kinship relations are devoid of gender categories while age and seniority are more relevant markers of status for the Yoruba people.

It can be inferred that Western contact and the imposition of Victorian gender relations must have affected the original conceptions of sociocultural relations in Africa. Oyewumi and Awe consider representations of history and culture, often in written form, as coconspirators that facilitate the invention of gender and the creation of male dominance and female subservience and invisibility. Coles and Mack have noted that – contrary to the prevalent belief system – precolonial Igbo women were fairly independent within their communities.[32] In predominantly polygamous households, women owned their own houses and controlled their household affairs. A woman needed to fend for herself and her children, which most women managed effectively. Igbo women engaged in trading activities on multiple levels, from small-scale trading and selling surplus produce to large-scale transactions involving agricultural products, cloth, and other commodities.[33] Women were dominant actors in commerce who could hold positions of respect and regard in their communities:

> Precolonial women's marketing activities played an important role in this respect. Some women who lived under the stigma of barrenness used their marketing abilities to make a place of honor for themselves in their husbands' households. According to the Hendersons, writing about women in Onitsha during the early 1960s, "the woman who has no children can build a position of status only by trading – there is no other legitimate route."[34]

---

[29] Oyewumi, "Making History."
[30] Bolanle Awe, ed., *Nigerian Women in Historical Perspective* (Ibadan: Bookcraft, 1992).
[31] Oyewumi, "Making History."
[32] See Coles and Mack, "Women in the Twentieth Century."
[33] Nwando Achebe, *Farmers, Traders, Warriors, and Kings: Female Power and Authority in Northern Igboland, 1900–1960* (Portsmouth: Heinemann, 2005).
[34] See Matera, Bastian, and Kingsley, *The Women's War of 1929*.

Van Allen also acknowledges the autonomy of precolonial Igbo women. Her exploration of the practice of "Sitting on a Man" finds that the autonomy of African women was heavily impacted by the process of westernization brought about by colonialism. She noted that Igbo women held traditionally significant political offices and played recognizable roles in their communities' sociocultural affairs. These women exercised power derived from the solidarity of their women's meetings, kinship groups, and market networks. One such exercise of independent power was the practice of "Sitting on a Man."[35] This is a form of protest or forceful action enforced by women against the behavior of men whereby they "sit on him" or wage war against him while adorning themselves with palm leaves, and dancing and singing protest songs.

Mutual interdependence was supported and promoted by Igbo worldviews, cultural systems, and institutions. Amaechi and Amaechi challenge the idea that men had always dominated the Igbo community and instead assert that the Igbo practiced gender complementarity.[36] This interdependence, which was believed to exist between the spirit world and the human world, was also expected to operate in gendered relationships among the Igbo. There were expectations of mutuality and cooperation. The following excerpt shows the Igbo view of gender relations, which implies that the domestic space in Igbo households was controlled by men and women:

> [I]n their domestic affairs, where the mundane practice of activities like cooking carried significant symbolic valence. Men supplied basic and highly valued foodstuffs, but women controlled their preparation and gave food savor through their use of condiments and extra vegetables from "women's crops." Just as no pounded yam, a great favorite among the Igbo, could be prepared without male input (i.e., the yam itself), the starch staple would not be good to eat without women's laborious pounding and the pepper sauce they created to pour over it.[37]

Van Allen further emphasizes that Igbo women were not absent from political circles and spaces. Political power within Igbo communities was more diffused than centralized, which implies that no person had a monopoly on authority. No individual could issue commands that people were expected to obey without question. The diffuse nature of power in that era meant various legitimate groups and institutions, composed either of men or women, were created to handle different political and community issues.

Ojiakor has found that women chiefs existed in communities like the *Ogbaru*, where they were referred to as *Ogene* and *Onowu*.[38] In Onitsha, dignified women

---

[35] Van Allen, "Sitting on a Man."
[36] Amaechi and Amaechi, "Precolonial African Gender."
[37] Matera, Bastian, and Kingsley, *The Women's War of 1929*, 19.
[38] Ikenna Nzimiro, *Family and Kinship in Ibo Land: A Study in Acculturation Process* (Cologne: Druck: G. Wasmund, 1962), 53.

chiefs were referred to as *Omu*.[39] Women, especially first daughters, could inherit, become titleholders, and serve as ritual elites.[40] Acholonu has shown that women were actively involved in sociopolitical offices and assumed or controlled religious and economic offices,[41] while Amaechi and Amaechi have explained that men and women were eligible to hold positions as priests and priestesses.[42] In their opinion, women even held more prominent positions, especially concerning the *Ala* deity recognized as the god of fertility.[43]

Different scholars of Igbo extraction have asserted that women exercised immense power and control as groups. Within Igbo communities, women's groups were formed to address different concerns and situations within the community. One such prominent group among the Igbo people is the *Umuada* or the *Umuokpu* group. These women were often directly involved in community politics and issues of peacekeeping, law and order, and conflict resolution.[44] They often enforced justice. And with inheritance among the *Umuada*, their involvement not only guaranteed the peaceful distribution of wealth but also ensured political and spiritual legitimacy.[45]

Scholars have provided a similar account regarding the place of Yoruba women in precolonial Nigeria. Awe and Denzer, in their efforts to provide more accurate historical representations of Yoruba women, have engaged with field research and oral historical sources to reveal that these women occupied prominent and significant positions in the precolonial economy, influencing politics, family, and religion.[46] Women were core actors in local market networks and long-distance trading activities.[47] In political spaces, women occupied prominent positions. In Ile-Ife, for instance, there was one female Ooni,[48] an office whose occupier is still considered the most prominent monarch and traditional authority of the Ife kingdom. In the Oyo kingdom,

---

[39] Ngozi E. Ojiakor, *Igbo Women in Nigerian Politics, 1929-1999* (New York: The Edwin Mellen Press, 2008).

[40] Ukachukwu D. Anyanwu, "Gender Question in Igbo Politics," in *The Igbo and the Tradition of Politics*, ed. Ukachukwu D. Anyanwu and Jude C. U. Aguwa (Enugu: Fourth Dimension, 1993), 113-120.

[41] Rose Acholonu, "Igbo Women in Political Limbo," in *The Igbo and the Tradition of Politics*, ed. Ukachukwu D. Anyanwu and Jude C. U. Aguwa (Enugu: Fourth Dimension, 1993), 289-297.

[42] Amaechi and Amaechi, "Precolonial African Gender."

[43] Amaechi and Amaechi, "Precolonial African Gender."

[44] Cletus O. Obasi and Rebecca G. Nnamani, "The Role of Umuada Igbo in Conflict Management and Development in Nigeria," *Open Journal of Political Science* 5, no. 4 (2015): 256-263.

[45] Amaechi and Amaechi, "Precolonial African Gender."

[46] Awe, *Nigerian Women*; and Denzer, "Yoruba Women."

[47] A. O. Y. Raji and T. S. Abejide, "The Guild System and Its Role in the Economy of Precolonial Yorubaland," *Arabian Journal of Business and Management Review* 3, no. 3 (2013): 14-22.

[48] M. A. Fabunmi, *An Anthology of Historical Notes on Ife City* (Lagos: John West Publications, 1985), 268 and 271.

records show that Orompoto was a woman who succeeded Egunogu in holding the office of Alaafin – a role that is to Oyo what the Ooni is to Ife.[49] Orompoto commanded a large army "with a rearguard numbering one thousand in the infantry and another thousand mounted on horses."[50]

Six women have been identified in the records of the Obas (kings) of Ilesa. Historical sources cite the participation of women in monarchies and traditional governance of the past. Denzer notes:

> In the political arena, traditions recall that women founded kingdoms and communities, occasionally wielded political authority as rulers, acted as regents, sat on the king's councils, held political offices, intrigued in palace politics, helped to make and unmake kings, served as go-betweens in diplomatic relations, and safeguarded their towns when their menfolk waged war elsewhere. They conducted key rituals to maintain the spiritual well-being of kings and kingdoms as well as of their own families and communities.[51]

Evidence shows that Nigerian women were neither silent nor docile in the affairs of the state. Among the Hausa of Northern Nigeria, historical submissions from prejihad and precolonial eras show that women were not as marginalized or secluded as they are in contemporary times but rather played active roles in the region's economics and politics. In the prejihad times, for instance, "femininity was no hindrance to a woman's political leadership and social mobility among the Hausa people."[52] Ingyroko, Sugh, and Terfa present extensive research materials that support this notion. In their opinion, the prejihad era was characterized by

> active involvement of women with political title designations as Magajiya (queen) Iya (queen mother), with as much power as the male ruling counterparts. Notable female historical names in Hausa land included Bazoa Turrunku, daurama of Daura and queen Amina of Zazzua a renowned political and military leader who expanded her territory.[53]

Korieh and Nnaemeka have explained that British colonizers who had followed an Islamic jihad in the region capitalized on recently established gender ideologies from Islam that suited their plans for dividing the population and implementing their process of indirect rule.[54] Nwankwo has consolidated various scholarly assertions establishing that northern leadership was practiced differently than in

---

[49] Franklin Ugobude, "Orompoto, the First Female Alaafin of Oyo," *The Guardian*, December 15, 2019.
[50] Denzer, "Yoruba Women," 8.
[51] Denzer, "Yoruba Women," 3.
[52] Denzer, "Yoruba Women."
[53] Margaret Ingyoroko, Elizabeth T. Sugh, and Terfa T. Alkali, "The Nigerian Woman and the Reformation of the Political System: A Historical Perspective," *Journal of Socialomics* 6, no. 2 (2017): 2–8.
[54] Nnaemeka and Korieh, "Long Journeys of Impediments."

the south.[55] In his opinion, Northern women were more removed from political leadership and authority in ways that suited colonial plans. Although these claims have merit, scholars such as Ifeka-Moller are concerned that these representations of precolonial African communities are overtly romanticized versions of Africa's past.[56] Critics are wary of creating a false utopia that disregards the reality of women kings and rulers that were the exceptions, not the norm. These challenges – questioning whether women held autonomy and authority in precolonial Nigeria – do not provide evidence that such claims should be dismissed. However, they are necessary for objective representations of history that effectively identify colonialism's influence on the current marginalized status of Nigerian women in different regions of the country.

The consensus among scholars is that colonialism created new gender ideologies, contributing to the marginalized status of Nigerian women in the present day. Korieh and Nnaemeka[57] and Pereira[58] agree that colonial gender ideologies contradicted the realities of precolonial Nigerian women. They assert that the extensive exploration of gender expressions in precolonial Nigeria shows that the resulting marginalization of Nigerian women is one of colonialism's many legacies.

Anunobi has noted that the ethos of nineteenth-century Victorian England, which held women to be separate, excluded them from visible, central positions in their communities.[59] This ideology was imported by colonialists and Christian missionaries, and it promoted the domesticity of women. Women were urged to stay home and tend to their families instead of "toiling" outside the house. Under the Victorian ethos, women who engaged in work outside the home were supposed to channel their efforts into church initiatives or other nonphysical activities that promoted social reform.[60] This ideology grew out of notions that women were pure and fragile. As custodians of religion, they were expected to pray for the family while upholding the values and morals of the community.[61]

---

[55] Chiedo Nwankwor, "Women's Protests in the Struggle for Independence," in *The Oxford Handbook of Nigerian Politics*, ed. Carl LeVan and Patrick Ukata (Oxford: Oxford University Press, 2018), 108.

[56] Caroline Ifeka-Moller, "'Sitting on a Man': Colonialism and the Lost Political Institution of Igbo Women: A Reply to Judith Van Allen," *Canadian Journal of African Studies* 7, no. 2 (1973): 317–318.

[57] Nnaemeka and Korieh, "Long Journeys of Impediments."

[58] Charmaine Pereira, "Domesticating Women? Gender, Religion and the State in Nigeria under Colonial and Military Rule," *African Identities* 3, no. 1 (2005): 69–94.

[59] Fredoline Anunobi, "Women and Development in Africa: From Marginalization to Gender Inequality," *African Social Science Review* 2, no. 1 (2002): 41–63.

[60] Judith R. Walkowitz, *Prostitution and Victorian Society: Women, Class, and the State* (Cambridge: Cambridge University Press, 1980).

[61] Richard D. Altick, *The Weaker Sex: Victorian People and Ideas* (New York: W.W. Norton & Company, 1973).

Pereira considers the introduction of the Christian religion in colonial Nigeria, with its gendered and male-centered messages, as an event that enabled male hegemony and the marginalization of women in southern parts of the country that were quick to adopt the religion and its views.[62] Given the solipsism of the British, it is little surprise that the idea of women kings and rulers was incomprehensible to them. It might even have appeared to be barbaric, which explains their decision to unilaterally appoint men as native chiefs. Anunobi consolidates previous opinions to state that colonialism was introduced when norms for nineteenth-century Victorian England enforced the separation of women and the restriction of their roles.[63] This explains the bias against women in Nigeria and the exclusion of women from political issues and offices. Amadiume supports this idea, stating that colonialists failed to see the political power that women already held in various institutions.[64]

Colonialism had visible impacts on Nigeria's economic systems.[65] The growth of international trade and the integration of local production with global markets created complex gender ideologies and stratifications in commerce and industry. It also strengthened capitalist approaches to economic organization. Hay and Stichter have suggested that the growth of international trade had negative effects on the economic condition of women in West Africa,[66] creating a gendered struggle for control of resources. During the introduction of cash crops and the growth of import and export activities, men dominated agricultural production and export activities. Mba has noted that new expansion in trade and commerce created new opportunities for Nigerian women, but these women were excluded from the most lucrative aspects of commerce and relegated to the activities of petty trading.[67] As colonialism progressed, economic growth was accompanied by an increase in private land ownership. The land became a tangible commodity that was used to secure loans from Europeans.[68] Men were able to use their positions as chiefs, appointed by Europeans, to access these sources of financing. Cultural attitudes regarding the inheritance of land in places like Southeastern Nigeria put

---

[62] Pereira, "Domesticating Women?"
[63] Anunobi, "Women and Development in Africa," 41–63.
[64] Ifi Amadiume, *Male Daughters, Female Husbands: Gender and Sex in an African Society* (London: Zed Books, 1987).
[65] John O. Aghahowa and E. E. M. Ukpebor, "The British Colonial Economic Policies and Nigeria's Underdevelopment," *Journal of Oriental and African Studies* 14 (2005): 193–210.
[66] Margaret Jen Hay and Sharon Stichter, *African Women South of the Sahara* (New York: Longman, 1995).
[67] Mba, *Nigerian Women Mobilized*.
[68] Namnso B. Udoekanem, David O. Adoga, and Victor O. Onwumere, "Land Ownership in Nigeria: Historical Development, Current Issues and Future Expectations," *Journal of Environment and Earth Science* 4, no. 21 (2014): 183–184.

women at a disadvantage.[69] Indigenous cultural expressions and European attitudes reinforced each other to marginalize women further.

Women in Colonial Nigeria

The process of colonialism engendered new political structures and systems that excluded women.[70] Olatunde has stated that the era of colonial rule in Nigeria was a time of political invisibility for Nigerian women.[71] Mba corroborates this idea by noting that women were considered to be unsuitable for the rigors of public life, a pretext that blocked women from voting, contesting elections, sitting in parliament, or working in the civil service.[72] Olatunde also emphasizes exclusion, observing that this was the norm until women began demanding their place in political spaces.

The British had adopted the indirect rule system in parts of Nigeria as a colonial policy which never truly considered women. The public protests and demonstrations from women, particularly the Aba Women's War, were quite unexpected.[73] Public opposition to colonial governance in the Southeastern part of Nigeria, as noted earlier, had started as early as 1925, following the Nwaobiala Dance movement,[74] which has received some scholarly attention. The event involved large gatherings of women's groups and dancers in marketplaces to express their grievances with the colonial government.[75] These women protested against colonial disregard for their traditions and values. Their list of demands included the following:

- That no dirt was to be allowed in houses and compounds and greater cleanliness was to be observed.
- That no nuisance should be committed in compounds or under breadfruit trees or palm tree, lest the falling fruit be contaminated.

---

[69] Elizabeth Achinewhu-Nworgu, Queen C. Nworgu, Shade Babalola, Chinuru C. Achinewhu, and Charles Nna Dikeh, "Exploring Land Ownership and Inheritance in Nigeria," in *Education Provision to Every One: Comparing Perspectives from Around the World*, ed. James Ogunleye (Sofia: Bulgarian Comparative Education Society, 2014), 354–361.

[70] Emmanuel O. Jaiyeola and Isaac Aladegbola, "Patriarchy and Colonization: The 'Brooder House' for Gender Inequality in Nigeria," *Journal of Research on Women and Gender* 10 (2020): 9–10.

[71] Diane Olatunde, "Women's Participation and Representation in Nigeria's Politics in the Last Decade (1999–2009)" (unpublished PhD dissertation, University of the Witwatersrand, 2010).

[72] Mba, *Nigerian Women Mobilized*.

[73] Matera, Bastian, and Kent, *The Women's War of 1929*.

[74] Kuumba M. Bahati, "African Women, Resistance Cultures and Cultural Resistances," *Agenda: Empowering Women for Gender Equity* 68, (2006): 112–121.

[75] Judith Lynne Hanna, "Dance and Women's Protest in Nigeria and the United States," in *Women and Social Protest*, ed. Guida West and Rhoda Lois Blumberg (New York: Oxford University Press, 1990), 333–345.

- That all the old roads were to be cleaned and reopened.
- That old customs should be observed and not allowed to lapse.
- That no girls or young married women should wear cloth until they were with first child, but go naked as in old days. (At Achi, the "dancers" had actually torn the clothes off some girls they encountered.)
- That men should not plant cassava, but leave this as the women's prerequisite. Cassava should not be mixed with yams in the farms, and Aro coco yams (the big, pointed-leaf colocasia) should not be planted at all.
- That women with child should not eat coco yams, cassava, or stock fish, as these resulted in the birth of twins.[76]

These demands reflected the women's concerns over the growing disregard for traditional values and culture. The sweeping of compounds and the denuding of young women, who were customarily forbidden from being fully clothed until they married and had their first child, were symbolic acts to cleanse their land and reclaim their culture. This 1925 movement, which has largely been disregarded by history, is considered to have culminated in the much more elaborate Women's War of 1929. A closer look at Nwaobiala shows that women protested gendered problems as a way of referencing changes in cultural patterns. Women were concerned about issues of fertility, the purity of the land, and the steep increase in bride prices that followed the introduction of foreign currency, and they demanded a return to precolonial payments for bride wealth.

These protests underscored a recognition of growing inflation and its socioeconomic effects on women. Matera, Bastian, and Kent have observed that these inflated bridewealth payments affected women's chances of getting married, and they made it more difficult for the bridewealth to be returned when marriages failed.[77] Given the disadvantaged economic position of women under colonial rule, mothers could not repay the bridewealth of their daughters if their marriages were dissolved. The Nwaobiala Dance was a precursor to the Aba Women's War that regularly features in the discourse concerning women's resistance to colonial rule and early forms of women's activism in Africa. As Matera, Bastian, and Kent have noted, the British government had failed to recognize that women could organize and demonstrate without the assistance of men. This ignorance was deliberate, given that women's organizations, age groups, and other gender-focused gatherings constituted the morphology of Igbo culture. Because of this failure, growing resentment among women culminated in the Women's War of 1929.

Historical sources and literature attribute the Aba Women's War to a list of factors that were considered to be undermining local customs. Afigbo has

---

[76] Matera, Bastian, and Kent, *The Women's War of 1929*, 117.
[77] Matera, Bastian, and Kent, *The Women's War of 1929*.

noted that the British imposition of taxes was culturally interpreted to connote British sovereignty, and the population census was seen as inviting death, which elicited outrage from Nigeria's inhabitants.[78] Afigbo discusses the cultural implications of taxation and the census:

> During the Government tax campaigns[,] bewildered interpreters who labored [to] translate 'taxation' into indigenous languages and dialects which had no word for the institution, rendered it in such a way that it came to the people as either "tax on head" or "tax on land" which with further amplification meant "ransom" or "land rent" respectively. Seen in this light taxation raised the question of how a free man could be required to pay a ransom on his head or how a stranger could ask for rent on land from the sons of the soil ... The second point which shocked many people was the census of population which accompanied the assessment of taxation. Throughout the four Eastern Provinces the counting of human beings, especially of free men, was contrary to custom ... Again the counting of human beings was believed to cause death.[79]

Despite these reactions, Nigeria's men were subjected to the British taxation policy. The 1929 Women's War was sparked by the misunderstanding that women would also be taxed. Some Warrant Chiefs alluded to a British desire to tax women, which would place greater financial stress on families where husbands already struggled to pay British-imposed taxes. Women rallied and made their way to the Native Courts, where they chased away local chiefs. These protesters made it clear that they had grievances with the changes imposed by colonial rule and its implications for local cultures and economies. According to Afigbo, "nine native courts were burnt, three destroyed and four damaged."[80] Historical records show that women looted European factories and establishments to demonstrate their unhappiness with the British.

This war and its precedent (the Nwaobiala Dance of 1925) can be viewed as continuous efforts by women seeking to quell the growing erasure of cultural values, using their bodies as symbols of the struggle. This perspective accounts for other anticolonial actions, like the denuding of young, unmarried women as an attempt to return to the cultural and moral standards of the precolonial period. Using different war songs and dances, as well as through the messages in their songs, these women worked to decolonize their region and expressed their anger at the ongoing colonial invasion.[81]

Nwanyeruwa is significant for the Women's War of 1929. As noted by scholars, Nwanyeruwa had resisted Mark Emeruwa, a tax collector and

---

[78] Afigbo, "Revolution and Reaction," 539–557.
[79] Afigbo, "Revolution and Reaction," 551.
[80] Afigbo, "Revolution and Reaction," 551.
[81] Tayo Agunbiade, "Remembering Margaret Ekpo and the Enugu Strike Massacre," *Aljazeera*, December 12, 2020, www.aljazeera.com/features/2020/12/12/remembering-margaret-ekpo-and-enugu-strike-massacre.

assessor employed by Warrant Chief Okugo Okezie. Emeruwa was attempting to count the family of Nwanyeruwa who had recently lost her daughter-in-law. Cultural misgivings among the Igbo people, in relation to the proposed counting, led the woman to resist Emeruwa's efforts. Verbal resistance turned into a scuffle and attracted the intervention of Nwanyeruwa's cowife. Additional reports show that Nwanyeruwa had relayed the incident to a group of women who proceeded to Emeruwa's compound to "sit on him." These women sang and danced traditionally to express their grievances, which forced Emeruwa and his family to flee to the mission church. The women later took their demonstration into the market square, attracting other women and proceeding to take their demonstration to Chief Okugo, the Warrant Chief that had ordered the count. Okugo did not attempt to contain the situation or appease the women but he permitted reprisals from his household that injured members of the women's group. Women from neighboring towns and villages learned of the situation and started their local protests. Okugo was eventually arrested, tried, convicted, and imprisoned for two years. However, the protests emboldened the women, who continued to resist counting and taxation.

The final straw was an incident where a colonial doctor accidentally ran down women who were protesting with a car. The already irate women channeled their anger toward colonial buildings and properties such as Native Courts and trading centers. Protestors demanded that Warrant Chiefs turn in their caps, which were symbols of their power and respect within the community. They also attacked Warrant Chiefs' properties, eating the yams in their storage barns and freeing their livestock. Perham's account reflects an intense group of women ready to do serious damage:

> At Utu-Etim-Ekpo appeared crowds of women scantily dressed in sackcloth, their faces smeared with charcoal, sticks wreathed with young palms in their hands, while heads were bound with young ferns. It is interesting to note that no Europeans understood the exact significance of these last symbols though nearly all the native witnesses assumed that they meant war. They burned the Native Court and sacked and looted the "factory" (European store) and clerks' houses. They declared that the District Officer was born of a woman, and as they were women they were going to see him. Police and troops were sent, and as, on two occasions, the women ran towards them with frenzied shouts, fire was opened with a Lewis gun as well as with rifles, and eighteen women were killed and nineteen wounded.[82]

Matera, Bastian, and Kent consider Perham's account to be skewed, but it shows the extent to which women fought for their status and position in their communities.[83] The killing of women at Utu-Etim-Ekpo did not deter their comrades as the number of women protesters multiplied, and they marched to

---

[82] Cited in Matera, Bastian, and Kent, *The Women's War of 1929*, 138–139.
[83] Matera, Bastian, and Kent, *The Women's War of 1929*.

the district office to demand official statements guaranteeing that women would not be taxed. Additional women were killed after they tried to push their way into district offices, and one of the British officers opened fire. These events are often referred to as a riot, which implies that they had neither strategy nor planning. Such a label contradicts the nature of the organization and does not demonstrate that theirs were deliberate efforts to improve their communities. These women did not attack people, but targeted objects that were symbols of colonial rule. The British, attempting to quell the "unruly" group, killed about fifty women and wounded many others.[84] This corresponds with scholarly analysis noting that colonizers adopt violence to suppress native voices and anticolonial activities.

Women in the Eastern region were not the only Nigerians exasperated by the colonial regime. The Egba women's revolt of 1947–8, which was led by Funmilayo Ransome-Kuti, is also a significant demonstration against colonial rule and the imposition of taxes.[85] This protest, which lasted for nine months, employed both traditional and modern methods. Women convened at the *Alake*'s palace to chant derogatory songs, and letters and petitions were also forwarded to the press.[86] The women's protest, popularly described as a revolt, resulted from the heavy-handedness of colonial officials and the steep fines levied against women. Payments were demanded for trivial issues, such as breaches of sanitation, in an attempt to compensate for a dwindling economy affected by World War II, which had affected the importation of goods and import duty payments.[87] As Byfield states:

> These summonses were given only to women. Court messengers went around collecting names and summoned those "who in their opinion, did not keep their compounds sufficiently clean." Specific charges included not sweeping the ground in front of their houses or keeping pots of water in which mosquito larvae could breed. Even in cases in which several women from one compound were named on one summons, each had to pay the fine. These prosecutions were primarily against women living in small farm villages, but market women were also subject to these excessive fines. The harassment was such that according to Ajisafe, a local Egba historian, Itori, one of the principal rural markets, closed as a result. Although it was later determined that these sanitation fees were illegal,

---

[84] Nwankwor, "Women's Protests in the Struggle."
[85] Alex A. Ugwuja and Jude E. Onyishi, "Female Political Protests in Colonial and Postcolonial Nigeria: The Abeokuta Women's Revolt as a Framework, 1945–1999," *PREORC Journal of Gender and Sexuality Studies* 1 (2020): 52–78.
[86] Byfield, "Taxation, Women, and the Colonial State," 250–277.
[87] Ayodeji Olukoju, "'Buy British, Sell Foreign': External Trade Control Policies in Nigeria during World War II and its Aftermath, 1939–1950," *The International Journal of African Historical Studies* 35, no. 2/3 (2002): 363–384.

their successful imposition in Abeokuta established for the architects of the tax scheme that women were an important source of revenue.[88]

The fines were imposed to increase colonial revenue. Regular taxation of Abeokuta residents, as suggested by Lugard, commenced on January 1, 1918, and was imposed on every adult. Although other regions enjoyed some economic autonomy, Egba women were taxed directly. This practice was encouraged by the government because it collected taxes from a larger number of adults, making men and women pay equal taxes. The imposition of heavy taxes on men and women raised serious concerns. The population did not oppose the idea of taxing men and women, especially when early measures only affected Igbo women, but there were concerns over the collection of exorbitant fees and exploitation through fines, excessive taxation, and the imposition of hard labor. These were not the only ways in which women were taxed. The state collected revenue from market fees which directly affected women as the primary traders of food and other items. Fines also generated opportunities for further penalties. Taxes imposed on market sheds led some women to create illegal market spaces in an attempt to avoid these fines. Not only were these women fined for breaking the law, they were also made to pay court fees.

British activities had positive and negative effects on women in Egba, and the lives of women before the Egbaland revolt provided some context for their ongoing protests. The town of Abeokuta, which had been created in the 1830s, had become the center of economic activity in Yoruba territory.[89] Abeokuta produced export commodities such as palm kernel, palm oil, and cocoa. It also imported items and produced dyed cloth and kola nuts, while the 1899 construction of a railway facilitated additional trade.[90] The attention from European traders greatly increased commercial activity among the Egba people, which meant that men and women alike benefited from improved living conditions. This supports Afigbo's assertion that the situation for women under colonial rule was not completely bad.[91] He states that Nigerian women gained and lost economic and legal rights during colonial administration, and some of the effects have continued into the postcolonial era. However, the gains and losses are heavily aligned to specific regions and their pre-existing gender structures, meaning that the experience of women under the colonial regime was neither completely good nor completely bad. As Byfield has noted, Egba women constituted about 50 percent of cocoa buyers and they "transported it to bulking

---

[88] Byfield, "Taxation, Women, and the Colonial State," 255.
[89] Saburi O. Biobaku, "An Historical Sketch of Egba Traditional Authorities," *Africa: Journal of the International African Institute* 22, no. 1 (1952): 35–49.
[90] Harry A. Gailey, *Lugard and the Abeokuta Uprising: The Demise of Egba Independence* (London: Routledge, 2014), 29.
[91] Afigbo, *Revolution and Reaction*.

centers."[92] Women dominated retail trade in the expanding kola nut market and trade in food and cloth. They were the dominant actors in retail sales of palm oil, and since women customarily owned palm kernels, they profited from its expanding market.

After the British extension of colonial power beyond the confines of Lagos, the Egba chiefs agreed to a treaty that would "open trade routes through Egba territory"[93] in exchange for the town's independence. This independence was compromised following Egba's political crisis in 1897, which led to a threat of intervention from the colonial governor of Lagos. The people of Egba formed the Egba United Government (EUG), which encouraged the development of local infrastructure. This led to the subjugation of Egba's men and women, who were compelled to perform forced labor so that construction could be completed.

Regional development and expansion had economic benefits for local women, but also provided avenues for their exploitation. Ajisafe has noted that the EUG's exploitation began as forced construction labor in 1905.[94] This was legitimized by the Order of Council rule permitting the Alake and his officials to demand free labor from rural citizens, excluding the residents of Abeokuta. Refusal meant paying a fine or undertaking three months of imprisonment while performing hard labor.[95] These demands sidestepped the system of checks and balances that constrained the Alake's office and prevented abuses of power.

Increasing labor demands and the demand for additional labor in cocoa production had gendered implications for women. To meet these demands, men acquired more wives. These women were exploited in a free labor scheme under the guise of marriage. The increasing number of marriages, regardless of the associated expenses, kept many women and girls from attending school. This was an issue that had greater implications for the future economic status of women in the country. The Egba women's revolt of 1947 was, hence, a response to forced labor, taxation, and the threat of further exploitation, along with other oppressive factors endured by the Egba people. The sustained economic crisis brought about by the two World Wars meant that the British continued to exploit the natives. Women responded to this ongoing exploitation by convening at the palace of the Alake and seeking an audience with him. Soyinka states that women adopted a deferential position that was suitable for consulting with the king, and they approached the palace to express their concerns. They shared their message thus:

> Kabiyesi, the message which I bring you today, is the message of all the women who have left their stall, their homes and children, their farms and petty affairs to come and visit you today. They are the suffering crowd who

[92] Byfield, "Taxation, Women, and the Colonial State," 252.
[93] Byfield, "Taxation, Women, and the Colonial State," 251.
[94] Ajayi K. Ajisafe, *History of Abeokuta* (Abeokuta: Fola Bookshops, 1924).
[95] Ajisafe, *History of Abeokuta*.

are gathered on your front lawn ... they are all the womanhood of Egba, and they have come to say – Enough is Enough.[96]

Women addressed the economic crisis by creating organizations and associations to fight for their interests. The Abeokuta Women's Union emerged in 1947 in affiliation with market women and Christian-educated women of the Abeokuta Ladies Club (ALC).[97] These groups, led by Funmilayo Ransome-Kuti, took up many societal issues and championed the cause of women in their communities. They were a huge part of the women's agitations and the revolt of 1947.

Women's organizations were common among the Yoruba at the time. As Hunt has noted, these organizations provided avenues for interactions and mobilization that dated back to the mid-1920s.[98] Following the creation of the Lagos Market Women's Association, the Nigerian Women's Party and the Abeokuta Women's Union were established in the 1940s.[99] Denzer has explained that these women's organizations eventually aligned with different political groups in the country.[100] As indicated earlier, in 1947 women organized protests to leave their stalls and homes and convene at the king's palace to express their concerns regarding the actions of tax collectors and the unfairness of taxes collected from young women, who were being taxed earlier than men. Byfield also notes that some tax collectors abused their powers to violate the dignity and privacy of young women, stripping them to confirm that they had breasts which meant they were old enough to be taxed.[101]

The women decried the economic implications of heavy taxation as they often paid their taxes along with other indirect taxes imposed by the government. Many of them assisted their husbands with additional taxes. They complained about the political marginalization of women under colonial governance, and they referenced the relegated responsibilities and positions of the *Iyalode* (female-constituted representative in the palace), who had constituted women leaders, and the *Erelu*, who was either a noblewoman or a princess during the precolonial period.[102] Women, therefore, demanded more female representation, since they were taxed alongside men and therefore believed they deserved to be equally represented. Women demanded greater investments in healthcare and education, two key issues that affected them directly at the time. The Egbaland women's protests of 1947 were as

---

[96] Wole Soyinka, *Ake: The Years of Childhood* (New York: Random House, 1981), 208.
[97] Cheryl Johnson, "Grass Roots Organizing: Women in Anticolonial Activity in Southwestern Nigeria," *African Studies Review* 25, no. 2/3 (1982): 148–155.
[98] Nancy Rose Hunt, "Placing African Women's History and Locating Gender," *Social History* 14, no. 3 (1989): 359–379.
[99] Hunt, "Placing African Women's History."
[100] Denzer, "Yoruba Women."
[101] Byfield, "Taxation, Women, and the Colonial State."
[102] Nwankwor, "Women's Protests in the Struggle," 108.

much in opposition to heavy taxation as they were in favor of greater female representation in local politics. It was an avenue for demanding recognition for the socioeconomic contributions that women had made and were making to the state. The women's revolt of 1947 contributed to the temporary removal of the Alake and led to the temporary abolition of taxes on women and the integration of women into the local council.[103] This was a huge feat and an important historical accomplishment for women at the time.

The impact of colonialism in different regions of the world largely depended on the strategies of the colonizers and the resistance adopted by the colonized. In examining the decolonization strategies of postcolonial Nigeria, it is necessary to understand the resistance and response of women under the colonial regime. Women's agitations in the late 1940s coincided with nationalist movements where women held equal positions as key actors fighting for the nation's political independence.[104] At the time, these women prioritized the need for national freedom over their occupation of political spaces. Johnson-Odum and Mba have noted that this sacrifice was detrimental to their place and status in postcolonial Nigeria.[105] The era of nationalist movements focused on anticolonial activities, encouraging women to sideline their grievances for the sake of the nation's independence.

The predilection for collective action meant that women convened and organized for and against different issues in the era of colonialism. Nwankwor has noted that women in southwestern Nigeria started organizing against colonial activities as early as 1908.[106] By 1940, these women's movements had become popular for their anticolonial and prowomen positions. In the same year, Madam Alimotu Pelewura led the Lagos Market Women's Association in protesting against the imposition of annual taxes on women.[107] Pelewura's group was known to have actively supported the Nigerian National Democratic Party (NNDP), a militant party that opposed colonial exploitation.[108]

As women organized and mobilized across Nigeria, nationalist sentiments and mobilizations were also developing. Although women aligned with nationalist movements and groups in the fight for collective Nigerian independence, their organizations emerged independently of nationalist movements.[109] Some

---

[103] Cheryl J. Johnson, "Nigerian Women and British Colonialism: The Yoruba Example with Selected Biographies" (unpublished PhD dissertation, Northwestern University, 1978).
[104] Nwankwor, "Women's Protests in the Struggle," 103–120.
[105] Cheryl Johnson-Odum and Nina Emma Mba, *For Women and the Nation: Funmilayo Ransome-Kuti of Nigeria* (Urbana: University of Illinois Press, 1997).
[106] Nwankwor, "Women's Protests in the Struggle," 103–120.
[107] Cheryl Johnson, "Madam Alimotu Pelewura and the Lagos Market Women," *Tarikh* 7, no. 1 (1981): 1–10.
[108] See Nwankwor, "Women's Protests in the Struggle," 111–112.
[109] Sara Panata, "Campaigning for Political Rights in Nigeria: The Women Movement in the 1950s," *Clio. Women, Gender, History* 43 (2016): 175–185.

of the women's movements were more concerned with women's issues than nationalist issues. Nwankwor has stated that "male-led nationalist parties eagerly partnered with acquiescent women's movement organizations that prioritized nationalist goals, while they shunned those that focused on women's agenda such as the Women's Party; it would die shortly thereafter."[110] This supports Johnson-Odum and Mba's statement that the marginal political status of women in postcolonial Nigeria can be attributed to the relegation of their concerns and needs in favor of nationalist agitations.[111] Women who worked in concert with nationalist parties and movements did not occupy central positions but rather served as background supporters. As was typical in such situations, they were sidelined in political negotiations and neglected when it was time to distribute the spoils of independence.[112]

Regardless of the current status of Nigerian women, several studies link various women's movements – including the Nwaobiala Dance, the Aba Women's War, and the Egba women's revolt – to the growth and development of nationalist movements in the country.[113] The Aba Women's War of 1929 is cited as the largest organized movement of citizens opposing colonial actions. These protests laid the groundwork for the articulation of nationalist concerns and sentiments, making immense contributions to shaping and structuring politics in the country.

Prominent Women Figures

Funmilayo Ransome-Kuti appears several times in discussions of agitations and demonstrations against colonial exploitation, particularly on the Abeokuta Women's Union and the Egba Women's Revolt of 1947.[114] Johnson describes her as the "mother of women's movements in Nigeria, and an inspiration to those in other parts of Africa."[115] She was born in Abeokuta in 1900, educated in England, and lived a large part of her life in Abeokuta. Ransome-Kuti considered herself to be not only a women's advocate but an advocate for human rights. She was actively involved in antiracist and anti-imperialist struggles for most

---

[110] Nwankwor, "Women's Protests in the Struggle."
[111] Johnson-Odum and Mba, *For Women and the Nation*.
[112] N. Nwankwo, "Women and a Challenge Dated in History (1914–2003)," in *Gender Audit 2003 Election; and Issues in Women's Political Participation*, ed. Abiola Akiyode Afolabi and Lanre Arogundade (Lagos: WARDC, 2006), 7–20.
[113] Toyin Falola and Adam Paddock, *The Women's War of 1929: A History of Anti-Colonial Resistance in Eastern Nigeria* (Durham: Carolina Academic Press, 2011).
[114] Cheryl Johnson-Odim, "On Behalf of Women and the Nation: Funmilayo Ransome-Kuti and the Struggles for Nigerian Independence," in *Expanding the Boundaries of Women's History: Essays on Women in the Third World*, ed. Cheryl Johnson-Odim and Margaret Strobel (Bloomington: Indiana University Press, 1992), 144–157.
[115] Cheryl Johnson, "'For Their Freedoms': The Anti-Imperialist and International Feminist Activity of Funmilayo Ransome-Kuti of Nigeria," *Women's Studies International Forum* 32 (2009): 51–59.

of her life.[116] After her studies and her marriage to Rev. Israel Oludotun Ransome-Kuti, she started women's organizations that were dedicated to teaching women different crafts and etiquette. In her fight for women's suffrage and economic empowerment, she established one of the first kindergartens in Nigeria.[117] She also educated market women and conducted classes to improve their literacy.[118]

Ransome-Kuti returned to Abeokuta when her husband became principal of the Abeokuta Grammar School and soon resumed her literacy classes for market women; shortly afterward, she established the ALC. Johnson-Odum and Mba have noted that the club's core principles were "to help in raising the standard of womanhood in Abeokuta ... to help in encouraging learning ... and thereby wipe out illiteracy."[119] Ransome-Kuti took an interest in the experiences of market women and interacted with them extensively. She became a trusted ally in their fight against colonial exploitation. Johnson-Odum and Mba note that she identified with the market women so fully that in her attempt to "make the women feel like I was one of them," she wore traditional Yoruba clothing and abandoned Western dresses and attire.[120] It was a symbolic expression of solidarity with ordinary women of her time.

Ransome-Kuti changed the ALC to the Abeokuta Women's Union (AWU) in 1946, signaling its shift to a more politically oriented agenda.[121] In a later fight against free labor and unjust taxation, the AWU worked with the market women of Abeokuta to conduct demonstrations and campaigns that employed traditional and modern strategies. These methods, as indicated earlier, temporarily led to the Alake's abdication and the abolition of taxation on women, along with better representation for women in the local government.[122] Nwankwor has stated that earlier women's protests in Southeastern Nigeria may have influenced protests in other regions.[123] The women's group adopted modern strategies such as the use of newsletters to express their concerns,[124] but they also adopted the traditional approach of "sitting on a man," which implies the occupation of a man's residence while

---

[116] Adam Mayer, *Naija Marxisms: Revolutionary Thought in Nigeria* (London: Pluto Press, 2016).
[117] Njideka Agbo, "Funmilayo Anikulapo-Kuti: The Education Game–Changer," *The Guardian*, October 25, 2018.
[118] Johnson, "For Their Freedoms."
[119] Johnson-Odum and Mba, *For Women and the Nation*, 64.
[120] Johnson-Odum and Mba, *For Women and the Nation*.
[121] Mutiat T. Oladejo, *The Women Went Radical: Petition Writing and Colonial State in Southwestern Nigeria, 1900–1953* (Ibadan: BookBuilders, 2018).
[122] Obioma Ofoego and Toyin Falola, *Funmilayo Ransome-Kuti and the Women's Union of Abeokuta* (Paris: UNESCO Publishing, 2015).
[123] See Nwankwor, "Women's Protests in the Struggle."
[124] Sara Panata, "'Dear Readers ... ': Women's Rights and Duties through Letters to the Editor in the Nigerian Press (1940s–1950s)," *Numéros* 1 (2020): 141–198.

singing derisive songs to insult him and protest his actions. This method was adopted in their 1947 protest that led to the temporary deposition of Alake Ademola.

Ransome-Kuti organized and led many protests in her time. Johnson-Odum and Mba note that she regularly challenged traditional practices that were intended to silence women.[125] There is an elaborate account of her rebellion against the *Oro* cult,[126] a force or power that compelled people to obey society's sanctions and commands. Only men were permitted to go outside their homes or be on the streets when the *Oro* was unleashed. However, when the *Oro* was released during the women's protests and demonstrations to silence them, Ransome-Kuti was said to have angrily seized it. This symbol – a wooden stick on the end of a rope that was whirled to make a whirring noise[127] – was later displayed in her home. It was an act of physical defiance and a metaphor for her opposition to the colonial and Indigenous systems that stifled the agency of women or prevented them from airing their grievances.

Ransome-Kuti and her husband were members of the Nigerian Union of Teachers (NUT), which advanced the cause of equality in education for women and men.[128] She was a huge supporter of education for the poor and needy, and, with her husband, she founded and participated in several unions and organizations to promote education and educational experiences for students. To meet the AWU's objectives of achieving the enfranchisement of Nigerian women, Ransome-Kuti took her organizational capacity to the national level. She established the Nigerian Women's Union (NWU) in 1949 and also organized a conference for various Nigerian women's organizations in 1953, drawing around 400 women delegates from provinces across the country. The event represented various women of different classes and ethnicities, one of which included the Federation of Nigerian Women's Societies (FNWS). The new organization, which had her as its president, was committed to achieving universal suffrage. It proposed the introduction of symbols to enhance the election experience and enfranchise nonliterate voters. She remained a formidable force in women's activism and the fight for human rights and universal suffrage until she passed away in 1978.[129]

Margaret Ekpo also holds a prominent position among influential women during the colonial regime.[130] She was born in Creek Town, Calabar, in 1916.

---

[125] See Johnson-Odum and Mba's *For Women and the Nation*.
[126] Johnson-Odum and Mba, *For Women and the Nation*, 82.
[127] Johnson, "For Their Freedoms," 35.
[128] Michael E. Veal, *Fela: Life and Times of an African Musical Icon* (Philadelphia: Temple University Press, 2000), 24.
[129] Stephanie Shonekan, "Fela's Foundation: Examining the Revolutionary Songs of Funmilayo Ransome-Kuti and the Abeokuta Market Women's Movement in 1940s Western Nigeria," *Black Music Research Journal* 29, no. 1 (2009): 127–144.
[130] Stella A. Effah–Attoe and Solomon O. Jaja, *Margaret Ekpo: Lioness in Nigerian Politics* (Abeokuta: ALF Publications, 1993).

She and her husband later moved to Aba, in the present-day Abia State. She was a strong advocate for anticolonial and feminist movements that encouraged women to demand civil rights, like their counterparts in Ireland, which she had encountered during a visit to their country in 1944. She also formed various women's organizations to improve the political consciousness of women.[131] Ekpo was a member of the NCNC along with Funmilayo Ransome-Kuti, leading the women's branch of the party in Aba while working as the national secretary for the NWU.[132] She founded the Aba Township Women's Association and was a member of the Eastern House of Chiefs. Ekpo eventually became vice-president of the party in 1959,[133] which provided her with a platform for mobilizing women and encouraging them to exercise their franchise to participate in political activities. Ekechi has noted that women voted in the election for Aba Urban District Council, which was held in December 1955, and they constituted the majority of the voters.[134] Following that election, women were voted into the Urban District Council.

Ekpo served as a member of the Caretaker Committee of the Urban District Council and was a member of the Eastern House of Assembly. She used her position to promote women's issues and concerns, taking a radical anticolonial approach. She opposed the employment of colonial officers' wives because she felt that they were taking jobs meant for Indigenous women.[135] Ekpo also spoke out against the underrepresentation of women in political office and opposed restrictions on women who sought to teach in Christian missions. She fought to improve women's socioeconomic and political status in the country and advocated the development of infrastructure, including the repair and improvement of rural roads.[136] She also opposed electoral corruption and voter fraud in the northern part of the country.

Oyinkan Abayomi was another notable figure from Nigerian women's sociopolitical history.[137] She was a British-educated Nigerian woman whose background and parental involvement in activism contributed to her interest in promoting the status of women and encouraging literacy. She was born in a house on Victoria Street, in Lagos, on March 6, 1897. She became actively involved in political and civic activities in colonial Nigeria, founding

---

[131] Margaret Ekpo, *Breaking Barriers: An Autobiography* (Calabar: Profiles & Biographies, 2003).
[132] Felix K. Ekechi, "Historical Women in the Fight for Liberation," in *The Feminization of Development Processes in Africa: Current and Future Perspectives*, ed. Valentine Udoh James and James S. Etim (New York: Praeger Publishers, 1999).
[133] Emeka Emmanuel Okafor and Monica Ewomazino Akokuwebe, "Women and Leadership in Nigeria: Challenges and Prospects," *Developing Country Studies* 5, no. 4 (2015): 1–11.
[134] See Ekechi, "Historical Women in the Fight."
[135] Ekpo, *Breaking Barriers*.
[136] Women In Nigeria, *Margaret Ekpo: A Political Biography* (Nigeria: Women in Nigeria, 1996).
[137] Cheryl Johnson-Odim, "Lady Oyinkan Abayomi: A Profile," in *Nigerian Women in Historical Perspective*, ed. Bolanle Awe (Lagos: Sankore Press, 1993), 149–163.

organizations such as the British West Africa Educated Girl's Club (BWAEGC), which raised funds for charity activities. Abayomi's BWAEGC was eventually renamed the Ladies Progressive Club (LPC), changing its focus to promoting education for girls and creating educational programs for women. The LPC raised funds to provide scholarships for young girls and mobilized adult women to participate in educational activities that promoted literacy for women. Abayomi's petitions were particularly instrumental in establishing Queen's College, Lagos, in 1927, the first government-supported secondary school for girls.[138]

On the political front, Abayomi contributed to the formation of the Lagos Youth Movement, which became the Nigerian Youth Movement.[139] She founded the Nigerian Women's Party in 1944 to create a space for Nigerian women to thrive politically because she believed that women were being marginalized not only by the British but also by their Nigerian counterparts.[140] She advocated women's literacy, adult women's learning, equality in the workplace, and larger numbers of women placed in the civil service.

Other women leaders, despite being nonliterate, also distinguished themselves as activist voices who opposed colonial repression and exploitation. Alimotu Pelewura, discussed earlier, was a Muslim nonliterate who organized demonstrations and opposition to the British.[141] Pelewura fought attempts to regulate market prices and monopolize the distribution of food during World War II. Colonialist price controls were a way of managing the economy and addressing the economic crisis that followed the War, and Pelewura condemned their artificial prices for ignoring market forces. She garnered support from the Lagos Women's League, which was founded in 1901, and the Women's Party founded in 1944, to oppose the imposition of price controls during World War II.[142]

Pelewura led a protest in 1940 that involved around 7,000 women who converged at the Glover Memorial Hall to lodge their grievances. Their complaints were tax-related, opposing the enormous burden placed on women who had to pay taxes for their unemployed spouses and male relatives. They complained that exorbitant taxes affected them both directly and indirectly. Pelewura and her supporters threatened to stop all trading activities if the government

---

[138] Cheryl Johnson-Odim, "Women and Gender in the History of Sub-Saharan Africa," in *Women's History in Global Perspective: Women and Gender in the History of Sub-Saharan Africa*, Vol. 3, ed. Bonnie G. Smith (Urbana: University of Illinois Press, 2005), 54.

[139] Omiko Awa, "Lady Oyinkansola Abayomi: An Amazon, Trailblazer," *The Guardian*, February 16, 2020.

[140] Awa, "Lady Oyinkansola Abayomi."

[141] Halimat T. Somotan, "Lagos Women in Colonial History: A Biographical Sketch of Alimotu Pelewura," *Vestiges: Traces of Record* 4 (2018): 72–74.

[142] See Denzer, "Yoruba Women."

failed to meet their demands. Oladejo has noted that Pelewura's group collaborated with farmers to boycott food sales to government agents.[143] She also sought and gained the support of the NCNC. Her influence among Nigerian women was so great that the government is said to have approached her in 1944, proposing to pay her a monthly salary if she stopped her mobilization efforts. However, Pelewura stayed true to her cause of improving the economic status of, and trading opportunities for, women. She refused the offer and continued mobilizing women from different parts of Yoruba land.[144]

Oladejo also found that Pelewura clearly displayed anticolonial sympathies and did not shy away from protests or demonstrations. She led and organized the market women's contributions to the workers' relief fund and organized a grand welcome for a labor leader who had been detained by the colonial administration. In 1947, she was honored as the Erelu of Lagos in recognition of her hard work and dedication to fighting for women's economic empowerment and social justice.[145] On her death in 1951, many women attended her funeral.

Conclusion

By exploring the place and history of women in colonial Nigeria, it is possible to gain a perspective that opposes the idea of endemic patriarchy and the continuous subjugation of women in various Nigerian cultures. This chapter has examined the gender inventions and redefinitions that were inspired by colonial contact, and it has followed women's anticolonial efforts by reviewing notable women's actions at various times in colonial history. An exploration of prominent Nigerian women in the colonial era shows how their respective impacts further emphasized the agency and influence of Nigerian women.[146]

---

[143] Mutiat Titilope Oladejo, "Women, Politics and Social Development in Colonial Yorubaland: Thematic Analysis of Selected Yoruba Women," *Journal of International Politics and Development* 8, no. 1&2 (2012): 113–127.

[144] Oladejo, "Women, Politics and Social Development."

[145] Cheryl Johnson-Odim, "Pelewura, Alimotu (188?–1951)," in *The Oxford Encyclopedia of Women in World History*, Vol. 1, ed. Bonnie G. Smith (Oxford: Oxford University Press, 2008), 429.

[146] Sara Panata, "Nigeria on the Move: The Place of Women's and Feminist Movements in National Socio—political Struggles (1944–1994)" (unpublished PhD dissertation, University of Paris 1 Panthéon—Sorbonne, 2020).

16

Religions

A plurality of religions is one of Nigeria's distinguishing features.[1] These religions address the social and psychological worldviews of Nigeria's citizens, going to the root of their existence.[2] Indigenous religious practices that existed before colonial conquest are described as "African Traditional Religion,"[3] and they were common in every part of Nigeria.[4] African traditional religions are evidence of local culture and a long-nourished history. They have an overarching effect on the lived experience of their practitioners. Doi has explained that there was no point in a Yoruba person's life without religious connection or association.[5] Religion affected their lives from birth to death, and many Nigerians understood their existence through traditional beliefs, especially before the spread of other religions.

Traditional Yoruba mythology was structured in a way that restricted individuals from accessing *Olodumare* or *Olorun* (the Yoruba Supreme Being) directly. Instead, practitioners used intermediaries like *Ogun*, *Sango*, *Obatala*, and others who were recognized as individual gods and goddesses.[6] Igbo mythology believed in *Chukwu*, the Supreme Being, and other subordinate deities that influenced different parts of their existence, such as *Ala*, the god of earth; *Idemili*, the god in charge of water; and *Agwu*, the god of health and divination.[7] Every individual had a personalized god called *Chi* similar to the Yoruba *Ori*.[8] The *Chi* was believed to be a personal deity that guided and

---

[1] Abiodun A. Oladiti, "Religion and Politics in Pre-Colonial Nigeria," *Cogito: Multidisciplinary Research Journal* 2 (2014): 72–84.
[2] Rosalind I. J. Hackett, *Religion in Calabar: The Religious Life and History of a Nigerian Town* (Berlin: Mouton De Gruyter, 1989).
[3] There is a lot of disagreement as the most appropriate label to characterize Indigenous religions. The most common, "traditional religion," is deployed here.
[4] Bolaji E. Idowu, *African Traditional Religion: A Definition* (London: S. C. M Press, 1973).
[5] Abdur Rahman I. Doi, *Islam in Multi-Religious Society. Nigeria: A Case Study* (Kuala Lumpur: A. S. Noordeen, 1984), 120–122.
[6] Bolaji E. Idowu, *Olodumare: God in Yoruba Belief* (London: Longmans, 1962).
[7] Chukwuma O. Okeke, Christopher N. Ibenwa, and Gloria Tochukwu Okeke, "Conflicts between African Traditional Religion and Christianity in Eastern Nigeria: The Igbo Example," *Sage Open* 7, no. 2 (2017): 1–10.
[8] Elizabeth Allo Isichei, *A History of the Igbo People* (London: Macmillan, 1976).

guarded individual Igbo on behalf of the *Chukwu*.[9] *Ikenga*, on the other hand, is an Igbo cult that exemplify individual achievement and personal success. They are two attributes highly valued among the Igbo. The influence of traditional religion in the Northern part of Nigeria began to wane with the introduction of Islam.[10]

Islam can be regarded as Nigeria's oldest foreign religion.[11] It arrived through the trade routes of old medieval empires in Kanem-Borno, Mali, and Songhai. Evidence of Islam in Nigeria dates back to the thirteenth century.[12] The religion spread across the Northern region, and it received an additional boost in the jihad of the nineteenth century. People became acclimated to Islam, adopting it into their culture in ways that influenced the religion's modes of practice.[13] To purify the practice of Shari'a and Islam in the North, Sheikh Usman Dan Fodio embarked on a jihad – a campaign that established the caliphate system and adopted strict practices of Islam and Shari'a.[14] Islam is also reported to have been practiced in Oyo-Ile in the Yoruba region from around the sixteenth century.[15]

Nigeria's first contact with Christianity was through the Portuguese during the search for materials and a sea route to India.[16] Missionary engagement began in 1515, undertaken by Roman Catholics. They built schools for royal princes and interested individuals.[17] The second phase of missionary activity occurred in September 1842 in Badagry where the First Storey building was erected by Reverend Hery Townsend (see Figure 16.1).[18] This was undertaken by the British Christian Mission, and it was followed by the spread of Christianity across the country.

Before the arrival of British colonizers, traditional religions had more adherents in the Western and Eastern regions, which contained Yoruba, Edo, Ijo, Igbo, and many other communities. Islam was predominant in Northern Nigeria, and some

---

[9] Francis A. Arinze, *Sacrifice in Igbo Religion* (Ibadan: University Press, 1974).
[10] Dean Stewart Gilliland, "African Traditional Religion in Transition: The Influence of Islam on African Traditional Religion in North Nigeria," unpublished PhD dissertation, Hartford Seminary, 1971.
[11] Abdur Rahman I. Doi, *Islam in Nigeria* (Zaria: Gaskiya Corporation, 1984).
[12] Par Y. Urvoy, *Histoire de l'Empire du Bornou* (Paris: Larose, 1949), 54.
[13] Humphrey J. Fisher, "Conversion Reconsidered: Some Historical Aspects of Religious Conversion in Black Africa," *Africa* 43, no. 1 (1973): 27–40.
[14] Murray Last, "Some Economic Aspects of Conversion in Hausaland (Nigeria)," in *Conversion to Islam*, ed. Nehemiah Levtzion (New York: Holmes & Meier, 1979), 237.
[15] Ahamad Faosiy Ogunbado, "Impacts of Colonialism on Religions: An Experience of South-Western Nigeria," *IOSR Journal of Humanities and Social Science* 5, no. 6 (2012): 51–57.
[16] Ayodeji Abodunde, *A Heritage of Faith: A History of Christianity in Nigeria* (Lagos: Pierce Watershed, 2016).
[17] Babatunde Fafunwa, *History of Education in Nigeria* (Ibadan: NPS Educational Publishers Ltd., 2002).
[18] Bengt Sundkler and Christopher Steed, *A History of the Church in Africa* (Cambridge: Cambridge University Press, 2000), 225.

Figure 16.1 The First Storey Building in Badagry, Nigeria, built by the Reverend Henry Townsend of the Church Missionary Society between 1842 and 1845.

adherents lived in Western Nigeria. Christian influence was most strongly established in Eastern and Western Nigeria. Yoruba communities were spaces in which all three religions met, mixing traditional believers, Christians, and Muslims.[19] The Nigerian population led lives that were heavily influenced by religious values when the missionaries arrived in the mid nineteenth century. The larger project of colonialism sought to change the lives of local inhabitants, which meant changing their religious values.[20] The colonial administration interacted with the different local religions on different occasions, applying different standards. These interactions, their progress, and colonialism's negative effects on these religions deserve scholarly examination.

The Colonial State and Religion

The British government's investigation of Nigerian polities probably suggested to them that "loyalty to religion is often more important than loyalty to the state among Nigerians."[21] Hugh Clapperton's visit in 1824 showed how

---

[19] John D. Y. Peel, *Christianity, Islam and Orisa Religion: Three Traditions in Comparison and Interaction* (Oakland: University of California Press, 2016).
[20] Ogunbado, "Impacts of Colonialism on Religions."
[21] Toyin Falola, *Violence in Nigeria: The Crisis of Religious Politics and Secular Ideologies* (Rochester: University Rochester Press, 1998), 50.

religious systems operated in the North, revealing the religious influence over the political and social structure of Nigerian societies.[22] After the British conquest reduced the caliph's authority, these religious–political structures were retained for colonial use. The colonial administration used an indirect rule system to exploit pre-existing political structures in Nigeria, which were based on religion. The Sultan of Sokoto, the sultan's emirs, and the traditional rulers of Yorubaland were integrated into the indirect rule system. In the North, the indirect rule system used Islamic religious–political systems from 1900 to 1906. These systems were imposed during the jihad of 1807, and few adjustments were necessary for the colonial administration. This approach was extended to the Southern Protectorate from 1912 to 1918.[23]

The religious component of Indigenous political institutions was actually understood and factored into consideration when it suited the colonial objectives. Indirect rule was applied more easily in the North, with a nodding reference to the powerful sultan, Allah's representative on earth.[24] The Alaafin and other Yoruba kings were referred to as "Kabiyesi alase ikeji orisa," which meant that they were understood, at least for some time, as second only to the gods.[25] The institutionalization of indirect rule was assisted by the religious–political systems of the North and similar systems in the Yoruba states of the South, but it was challenged by Igbo society. Although institutionalized religious bodies existed in traditional Igbo society, the Council of Elders also held religious and political authority.[26] The British disregard for these councils and their installation of District Officers as central authorities were unfamiliar and unwelcome concepts. Local resistance led to the abandonment of this approach in 1929.[27]

Christianity did not directly inspire the adoption of the indirect rule system, but its enduring history in the region had influenced local views. Colonialism was presented as the implementation of the civil society discussed in Christian teachings due to the political and social links between them. This is evident in the adoption of the Gregorian calendar, observances of Sunday and other holidays, and the use of the cross as a symbol in health institutions.[28]

---

[22] Jamie Lockhart and Paul Lovejoy, eds., *Hugh Clapperton into the Interior of Africa: Records of the Second Expedition, 1825–1827* (Leiden: Brill, 2005).
[23] Falola, *Violence in Nigeria*.
[24] Vernie Liebl, "The Caliphate," *Middle Eastern Studies* 45, no. 3 (2009): 373–391.
[25] Michael Oluwaleke Olayera, "Religion, Politics and Insecurity in Nigeria: Impact and Way Forward," *Trinitarian: International Journal of Arts and Humanities* 1, no. 1 (2021): 1–11.
[26] Chinwe Nwoye, "Igbo Cultural and Religious Worldview: An Insider's Perspective," *International Journal of Sociology and anthropology* 3, no. 9 (2011): 304–317.
[27] Falola, *Violence in Nigeria*.
[28] Jude C. Aguwa, "Religious Conflict in Nigeria: Impact on Nation Building," *Dialectical Anthropology* 22, no. ¾ (1997): 343.

Many Northern Muslims saw the period of colonialism as an era of Christianity. They called British officials *Nasara*, which meant Christians, rather than *Turawa*, which meant light-skinned Europeans.[29] Christians quickly and easily adapted to the colonial system. The religions and religious systems in place before colonialism influenced the effectiveness of indirect rule by either encouraging or opposing colonial efforts.

The colonial administration offered a controversial justification for its existence, seeing itself as bringing civilization and encouraging African development by expanding local minds. This motive was one of the duties discussed by Lord Lugard himself.[30] In Nigeria, the British government pursued this goal by attempting to establish a liberal political system.[31] This proposal was received differently by the various religious blocs. Northern Muslim leaders, for instance, were reluctant to accept a system that ceded political power to non-Muslims. They were not ready to accept a franchise that placed them on equal footing with non-Muslims.[32] Northern Muslim beliefs ascribed legitimacy to politics in an Islamic religious culture where Allah was head of state. Under their theocratic system, non-Muslims could reside in the state as long as they were subject to Shari'a and the principles of Islamic law. These beliefs were established in part by the outcome of the jihad of the nineteenth century, which had shaped the jurisprudential and political views of people in the region.[33] Alternative systems were met with resistance.

The religious orientation of Christians was a notable counterinfluence that supported the adoption of secularism since Christian teachings had encouraged this type of society. Nigerian groups were aware of this form of a secular government through previous contact with Europeans and Christians. During the colonial period, Christianity was prosecularism.[34] Followers of African traditional religions lost their voices, even if they were supportive of political secularism. This may have been because there were no recognizable bodies to project a unified stance on their behalf, and the predominance of Christianity and Islam had overshadowed their reactions.

---

[29] John N. Paden, *Religion and Political Culture in Kano* (Berkeley: University of California Press, 2020).

[30] Lord Lugard, *Dual Mandate in British Tropical Africa* (London: Frank Cass, 1970); Lord Lugard, *Political Memoranda: Revision of Instructions to Political Officers on Subjects Chiefly Political and Administrative 1913–1918* (London: Frank Cass, 1970).

[31] Ehiedu E. G. Iweriebor, "State Systems in Pre-Colonial, Colonial and Post-Colonial Nigeria: An Overview," *Africa: Rivista Trimestrale Di Studi e Documentazione Dell'Istituto Italiano per l'Africa e l'Oriente* 37, no. 4 (1982): 507–513.

[32] Mervyn Hiskett, *The Course of Islam in Africa* (Edinburgh: Edinburgh University Press, 1994).

[33] Hiskett, *The Course of Islam in Africa*.

[34] Azalahu Francis Akwara and Benedict O. Ojomah, "Religion, Politics and Democracy in Nigeria," *Canadian Social Science* 9, no. 2 (2013): 48–61.

Colonial policies initially favored the Islamic system that existed in the North, and Lord Lugard implemented political and economic systems that preserved the authority of local emirs. These religious leaders were permitted to keep their administrative systems intact because they could support the colonial system.[35] In maintaining existing religious and political structures, the colonial government created a feudal system that was compatible with Muslim beliefs in the North. In 1903, Lugard told Waziri, the Sultan of Sokoto, that the sultan and the emir would be partly selected by the High Commissioner. Beyond that, he promised that there would be no interference with the religious system that formed the basis of their political orientation.[36] In upholding his promise, Lugard's administration restricted Christian missionary activities in the North despite the administration's overall preference for Christianity. Crampton[37] has stated that Lugard felt it would be counterproductive to impose religious missions on people that resented them.

Indigenous Religion: Retention and Changes

African religions developed many of the symbols present in Nigerian culture and tradition. To a large extent, Indigenous religions influenced political cultures and structures. This was a major concern for a colonial government that promised to respect local religious structures. In the North, traditional religions had been suppressed by the jihad of Usman Dan Fodio.[38] In the Western and Southern Regions, the colonial administration needed to consider the traditional systems that had endured.

In the Yoruba religious system, the Oba had political power supported by the *Orisa*.[39] The checks and balances that were present under traditional principles were evident in the relationship between the Alaafin of Oyo and the Oyomesi. The Oyomesi were responsible for selecting the Alaafin, and they could oppose their ruler's most egregious actions.[40] However, the Alaafin's authority was respected,

---

[35] Rotgak I. Gofwen, *Religious Conflicts in Northern Nigeria and Nation Building: The Throes of Two Decades 1980–2000* (Kaduna: Human Rights Monitor, 2004).

[36] Emefie Ikenga-Metuh, "Two Decades of Religious Conflicts in Nigeria: A Recipe for Peace," *Bulletin of Ecumenical Theology* 6, no. 1 (1994): 69–93.

[37] Edmund P. T. Crampton, *Christianity in Northern Nigeria* (London: Geoffrey Chapman, 1979).

[38] Goriawala Mucizz, "Maguzawa: The Influence of the Hausa Muslims on the Beliefs and Practices of the Maguzawa, The Traditional Religionists of Kano and Katsina," in *The Gods in Retreat: Continuity and Change in African Religions*, ed. Emefie I. Metuh (Enugu: Fourth Dimension Publishers Co. Ltd., 1985), 47–58.

[39] Biodun Jekayinfa, *History of Hierarchy of Great Kings of Yorubaland* (Lagos: Lichfield Nigeria Limited, 2001).

[40] Jonah Isawa Elaigwu, Erim O. Erim, and Godfrey N. Uzoigwe, eds., *Foundations of Nigerian Federalism: Pre-colonial Antecedents* (Abuja: National Council on Intergovernmental Relations, 1996), 33.

and the office still had substantial power over its citizens. This system was retained and enhanced by the British administration as they built their indirect rule policies around it. Igbo communities had developed traditional systems of government that held religious significance, but they were decentralized. These systems were incapable of supporting the British government's plans. Instead, the British appointed a District Officer. Their decision led to the Aba Women's War in 1929, which compelled the government to rethink its approach.

Indigenous religion shaped many aspects of societies, including the justice system. In the Yoruba political structure, the Oba held judicial powers.[41] Issues outside of their authority, in some cases, were taken to religious cults for trial by ordeal. Ordeals involved drinking specific liquids, and the reaction to the mixtures would indicate whether a person was guilty or innocent. Kings could also instruct offenders to carry out rituals, usually at the recommendation of the *Awo*. Deities such as Sango, Ogun, and others in Yoruba society and the *Swamd* in the Tiv Society[42] were believed to oppose injustice or criminality, and oaths were taken to adjudicate issues before their supernatural courts.[43] The decentralized political structures of traditional Igbo society observed similar practices. The colonial government retained the system of adjudication dispensed by the communities' political leaders. However, these leaders no longer had jurisdiction over criminal matters, and trials by ordeal were forbidden.[44]

African religions struggled against widespread misconceptions and a substantial amount of prejudice during the colonial period. Collectively, Quarcoopome referred to these practices as the most misunderstood religion ever.[45] Local beliefs were dismissed as paganism, their major adherents were vilified, and Christians were taught that pagans would be sent to hell. Indigenous religion had been a major influence on the African people;[46] however, these beliefs faced criticism and condemnation after contact with Islam and Christianity.[47] Igbo communities encountered the Christian religion in 1841 after the failed missionary journey to Lokoja. Missionaries at Abo attempted to disseminate their religion, but it was

---

[41] Siyan Oyeweso and Olutayo C. Adesina, ed., *Oyo: History, Tradition and Royalty* (Ibadan: Ibadan University Press, 2021).

[42] Ezekiel Kehinde Akano and Jacob Olusola Bamigbose, "The Role of African Traditional Religion in Conflict Management in Nigeria," *Journal of Living Together* 6, no. 1 (2019): 246–258.

[43] Olufemi B. Olaoba, "The Traditional Judicial Organization and Procedure in Ekiti Palaces with Particular Reference to Ekiti North, 1830–1930," unpublished PhD dissertation, University of Ibadan, 1992.

[44] David Killingray, "The Maintenance of Law and Order in British Colonial Africa," *African Affairs* 85, no. 340 (1986): 411–37.

[45] Theophilus N. O. Quarcoopome, *West African Traditional Religion* (Ibadan: African Universities Press, 1987), 1.

[46] Joseph Omosade Awolalu, *Yoruba Beliefs and Sacrificial Rites* (London: Longman, 1979).

[47] John Allembillah Azumah, *The Legacy of Arab-Islam in Africa: A Quest for Inter-religious Dialogue* (Oxford: Oneworld, 2001).

not well received.[48] In 1857, Bishop Ajayi Crowther and John Christopher Taylor were sent to Igbo communities by the Church Missionary Society (CMS) and stationed themselves in Onitsha. In 1885, the CMS was joined by the Roman Catholic Mission (RCM), and Christian missionary activity took place near European trade centers and outposts. After the establishment of the colonial government opened Igbo communities to Christian missions, their religion began to gain prominence.[49]

African religions, believing in many different gods, were replaced by a monotheistic belief in a Christian god that was presented as more powerful. Igbo beliefs honoring the power of their ancestors were challenged with scientific criticism asserting that the dead could not wield supernatural forces. The historic *Osu* system of the Igbo,[50] which discriminated against some members of society, was opposed by Christian teaching. The condemnation of these beliefs did not sit well with the Igbos, and religious converts were met with criticism and discrimination. In Igbo communities, the shift from Indigenous beliefs to Christianity was encouraged by new practices and policies. Christian efforts built primary schools to impart new values and teach Christian principles, and the colonial government only employed people who had attended these schools.[51] During the colonial era, economic growth and changing social structures made Indigenous religious practices look outdated while Christianity became newly fashionable.[52] Urban immigration was another factor as migrants looking for work left villages where Indigenous religions were predominant to look for work in cities where Christianity and Islam were more common.[53]

Yoruba religion was affected by Christianity and Islam before and during the colonial era. Islam had successfully replaced traditional beliefs in some Yoruba societies through the Islamic principle of imposing structure on society from the family level to the national level, which was similar to Indigenous practices.[54] This approach continued to gain Islamic converts during the period of colonialism.[55] The link between Christianity and education also

---

[48] Felix K. Ekechi, *Missionary Enterprise and Rivalry in Igboland 1857–1914* (London: Frank Cass, 1972).

[49] Chinedu N. Ubah, "Religious Change among the Igbo during the Colonial Period," *Journal of Religion in Africa* 18, no. 1 (1988): 71–91.

[50] Victor E. Dike, "The Osu Caste System in Igboland: Discrimination Based on Descent." A paper presented to the Committee on Elimination of Racial Discrimination, 61st session of the International Dalit Solidarity Network, 2002, 5–23.

[51] Sylvia Leith-Ross, *African Women: A Study of the Ibo of Nigeria* (London: Faber & Faber, 1939), 297.

[52] Edmund O. Egboh, "The Beginning of the End of Traditional Religion in Iboland, South-Eastern Nigeria," *Civilisations* 21, no. 2/3 (1971): 269–279.

[53] Egboh, "The Beginning of the End."

[54] Siegfried Frederick Nadel, *Nupe Religion* (London: Routledge, 2018).

[55] Joachim Wach, *The Comparative Study of Religions* (New York: Columbia University Press, 1958).

made it attractive to the Yoruba people. While they attended school to pursue job opportunities, they were taught to question many Indigenous religious activities.[56]

The Spread of Islam and its Consequences

After the conquest of the Sokoto caliphate, British officials realized that Islam could be exploited in Nigeria. In the North, oaths were taken by African officials who were allowed to engage in Islamic practices while they remained loyal to the British Crown.[57] The British administration, especially under Lugard, encouraged the practice of Islam in Africa and Nigeria. This was due to his belief that Islam was the apex of spiritual engagement for Africans in Nigeria.[58] Lugard's ethnocentric perspective was driven by a specific logic: he saw Islam as inferior to the Christianity practiced by colonial officials. Africans were considered to be inferior to white colonizers, and so Islam was suitable as an inferior religion for an inferior set of people.[59] In believing that Islam's developmental limitations were complementary to the limitations of Africans, Lugard and other officials defended its proliferation.[60]

Islam had taken root in Nigeria as far back as the fourteenth century, becoming adapted with the Hausa/Fulani traditional system. Local cultures and practices mixed with Islamic beliefs over time. The 1807 jihad carried out by Usman Dan Fodio was intended to institutionalize the Islamic political system and purify the religion. This jihad marked the beginning of Islam spreading through Nigeria under a recognizable structure.

Islam had begun proliferating in earnest while the British established their colonial administration, but the religion's spread was more prominent in Nigeria's non-Muslim areas at the beginning of the British colonial government's invasion. Muslims were employed by the Royal Niger Company (RNC) in the Yoruba, Hausa, and Nupe areas. They had been drawn into the West African Frontier Force to serve as police and spies due to their comprehensive knowledge of local environments. They were used in the 1896 invasion of Igalaland, and personnel remained in the area until 1900 to assist with the

---

[56] William Bascom, "Urbanization among the Yoruba," *American Journal of Sociology* 60, no. 5 (1955): 446–454.

[57] Margery Perham, *Lugard: The Years of Authority 1898–1945* (London: Collins, 1960); Margery Perham, *Lugard: A Maker of Modern Africa – The Years of Adventure, 1858–1898* (London: Collins, 1956 and 1960).

[58] Jonathan Reynolds, "Good and Bad Muslims: Islam and Indirect Rule in Northern Nigeria," *The International Journal of African Historical Studies* 34, no. 3 (2001): 601–618.

[59] Lord Lugard, *The Dual Mandate in British Tropical Africa* (New York: Routledge, 1965), 8.

[60] Andrew E. Barnes, "'Evangelization where it is not Wanted': Colonial Administrators and Missionaries in Northern Nigeria during the First Third of the Twentieth Century," *Journal of Religion in Africa* 25, no. 4 (1995): 412–441.

dissemination and fortification of the colonial government in Idah and the rest of the Igala Land.[61] After Idah, the British garrison moved to Akwacha in 1900 to continue the British conquest and to Ankpa in 1904, where they maintained a presence until their 1933 move to Enugu.[62]

The use of Muslim personnel in non-Muslim areas encouraged the spread of Islam. Mosques were built in newly occupied regions, and transient Muslims married local non-Muslims. The process of Islamization grew more pronounced as Islamic culture and fashions were adopted in affected areas. A notable assimilation of Islam in the Igbo community was the settlement of Nupe Muslims from the Ankpa Igala region, arriving in the Ibo–Eze regions. Interreligious settlement and marriages also occurred in the Ibagwa-Nkwo areas.[63]

The construction of roads and railways in Nigeria, especially from 1913 to 1927, assisted the spread of Islam. These routes connected the North with other parts of the country. The Port Harcourt–Kaduna railway line enabled navigation between Jos and Bukuru, Kafachan, Jingere, and Naraguta in 1926, which made Jos attractive for settlement. Northern Muslims migrated to Jos looking for work in the mining industry. About 12,944 Muslims were recorded to have settled in Jos as of 1930 to work in the area. This led to interethnic and interreligious marriages, increasing the local presence of Islam.[64]

Different colonial policies encouraged the spread of Islam in the other non-Muslim areas of the North. Muslim Native Authority schools were established in the Northern region's Southern reaches, spreading Islamic principles and culture among the mostly non-Muslim attendees. The schools used Arabic as a primary means of communication until 1928 when it was changed to English. The British government further boosted Islam with financial assistance to construct and repair mosques in the region, along with grants given to individual Imams.[65] Lokoja town was important for the dissemination of Islam among non-Muslim Nigerians in the North during the colonial era. Lokoja served as a British headquarters and settlement for planning the activities of the RNC.[66] The emirs who had refused to concede were exiled to the town, and they brought their Muslim relatives and other scholars to the

---

[61] Mohammed S. Abdulkadir, "Colonial Conquest and African Resistance: The Case of Idah and Ankpa in Igalaland (1864–1904)," History Department Seminar, Bayero University, Kano, 1987, 16–21. See also Mohammed. S. Abdulkadir, "An Economic History of Igalaland: 1896–1939," unpublished PhD dissertation, Bayero University, Kano, 1990.
[62] Mohammed S. Abdulkadir, "Islam in the Non-Muslim Areas of Northern Nigeria, c. 1600–1960," *Ilorin Journal of Religious Studies* 1, no. 1 (2011): 1–20.
[63] Abdur Rahman I. Doi, "Islam in Ibo land," *Islam and the Modern Age* 7, no. 1 (1974): 3.
[64] Abdulkadir, "Islam in the Non-Muslim Areas."
[65] NAK/Lokoprof, 768/1935. Education in non-Muslim Areas.
[66] Adam A. Okene, "Colonial Conquest and Resistance: The Case of Ebiraland 1886–1917 AD," *Kano Studies* 1, no. 1 (2000): 23.

area, which encouraged Islamic activity in Lokoja.[67] More scholars from Borno, Kano, Sokoto, Katsina, and Bida also migrated to Lokoja, founding Islamic schools that taught Islamic tenets.[68]

Scholars have debated how Islam was introduced to Nigeria's Eastern regions. Some believe that Islam found its way down to the Southeast, where Christianity was dominant and seemed to be the only foreign religion. Islam's recorded presence in the Igbo society occurred in the Nsukka division during the eighteenth and nineteenth centuries.[69] Nsukka's proximity to Idoma and Igala, along with trade routes in the region, exposed the Igbos to the Islamic religion.[70] Uchendu asserted that proper evidence of Islam in the Igbo community dates to the 1930s, when Garba Oheme, the horseman of Enugu Ezike, converted in 1937 during his time in Calabar. Oheme was posited as the first person from the Igbo region to convert to Islam. An opposing account cites Aduku, an Amufie Muslim, as the first recorded convert. He was not originally an Igbo, but he naturalized and converted later, in 1918.[71]

The Igbo became more receptive to the Islamic religion around 1947 due to their activities with cattle traders at Afikpo. These Northern Muslims moved through Abakaliki down to Umuahia. The commercial relationship enhanced the spread of Islam and encouraged some Muslim settlements, especially in Afikpo.[72] By 1957, individuals were much more receptive to Islam. One renowned example is that of Okpani Egwani, who attended primary school in Afikpo. He served in the army in 1944, lived in Lagos, and later traveled to Egypt and other African countries. Okpani converted to Islam and became part of the Tijaniyya under the leadership of Ibrahim Niyas from Kaolek, Senegal. During his travels, Okpani learned Arabic and the tenets of Islam. He changed his name to Alhaji Ibrahim and returned to Afikpo, intending to convert the entire village to Islam. He became the head of the Anuohia Muslim body.[73] These events were substantiated by other scholars corroborating Ottenberg's reports.[74] The activities of "Ibrahim" accelerated the spread of

---

[67] Ahmed Rufai Mohammed, *History of the Spread of Islam in the Niger–Benue Confluence Area: Igalaland, Ebiraland and Lokoja c. 1900–1960* (Ibadan: Ibadan University Press, 2014).

[68] Ahmed Rufai Mohammed, "Lokoja as a Center of Islamic Scholarship and Radiation in the Niger–Benue Confluence Area: c.1970-1960s," *Kano Studies* 3, no. 1 (1987/88): 19–42.

[69] Egodi Uchendu, "Evidence for Islam in Southeast Nigeria," *The Social Science Journal* 47, no. 1 (2010): 172–188.

[70] Doi, *Islam in Nigeria*.

[71] Uchendu, "Evidence for Islam in Southeast Nigeria."

[72] Simon Ottenberg, "A Moslem Ibo Village," *Cahiers d'etudes Africaines* 11, no. 2 (1971): 231–243.

[73] Ottenberg, "A Moslem Ibo Village."

[74] Saheed Ahmad Rufai, "A Foreign Faith in a Christian Domain: Islam among the Igbos of Southeastern Nigeria," *Journal of Muslim Minority Affairs* 32, no. 3 (2012): 372–383.

Islam among Igbo communities, especially in Nsukka. When the Biafra war started in 1967, Islam spread to Enoha, Owerri Abakalili, and other places. Enoha had the highest percentage of Muslims due to Shaikh Ibrahim Nwagui's missionary activities in the region.[75]

Islam had existed in Yoruba regions since the sixteenth century without establishing a major presence. It was introduced to Yorubaland through itinerant Muslim scholars, preachers and traders from Northern Nigeria and other parts of West Africa and trade between Oyo-Ile and Mali in the fifteenth century. The first Yoruba mosque dated to around the sixteenth century.[76] From 1841 to 1908, Islam gained greater prominence and was widely practiced alongside Christianity and Yoruba Orisa religion.[77] During the colonial period, Ramadan activities and the Hajj ceremony, which conferred the titles of Alhaji and Alhaja on (Nigerian) pilgrims, were instrumental in the popularization of Islam and its acceptance in Nigeria. In 1927, a Madrasa was established in Lagos by the *Ansar-Ud-Deen* Society, which increased the religion's presence in the area.[78] The Ahmadiyya's missionary activities in the West encouraged the spread of Arabic and Western culture in the 1920s, creating a conduit for the spread of Islamic doctrine among the Yoruba.[79] Other Islamic societies, such as Anwar-ul-Deen, Anwar-ul-Islam in Abeokuta, and Ansar-ul-Islam in Ilorin, led to a collective movement for the spread of Islam in the region.[80] The impact can also be seen in architecture, notably in the building of impressive mosques, such as that of Ode Omu, built in 1948 (see Figure 16.2). In 1954, Islamic societies wielded national influence, and the Muslim Students Society was formed to extend their doctrines further.[81]

The colonial administration's tolerance of Islam, and its promise to avoid interfering with Northern practices, serviced its interest in maintaining domination. The calculation was that the culture and political structure could be adapted to suit the indirect rule system. The expectation was that Muslims would listen to their political leaders because they held religious authority over them. The Islamic practice of polygamy, similar to existing practices in African religions, was left as is. Households with multiple wives could easily convert to

---

[75] Uchendu, "Evidence for Islam in Southeast Nigeria."
[76] Ogunbado, "Impacts of Colonialism on Religions."
[77] Tajudeen G. O. Gbadamosi and Jacob F. A. Ajayi, "Islam and Christianity in Nigeria," in *Groundwork of Nigerian History*, ed. Obaro Ikime (Ibadan: Heinemann Educational Books, 1980), 152–161.
[78] Stefan Reichmuth, "Education and the Growth of Religious Associations among Yoruba Muslims: The Ansar-Ud-Deen Society of Nigeria," *Journal of Religion in Africa* 26 (1996): 367–368.
[79] Hassan A. B. Fasinro, *Ahmadiyya Achievements and Conflicts: As I See It* (Lagos: Irede Printers, 1995).
[80] Hakeem O. A. Danmole, "The Frontier Emirate: A History of Islam in Ilorin," unpublished PhD dissertation, University of Birmingham, 1981.
[81] Abdul Maliki, "Islam in Nigeria," *Islamic Quarterly* 9, no. 1 (1965): 30.

Figure 16.2 The Central Mosque, Ode Omu, built in 1948.

Islam without severing existing relationships. Polygamous marriages were widely accepted in Nigeria due to their religious backing. Islamic influences affected the social outlook and position of communities, bringing Islamic fashions to new regions of the country.

Christianity

Christianity is one of Nigeria's most widely accepted religions.[82] It has been an influential factor in many of Nigeria's historical developments. The region's earliest encounter with Christianity took place in 1477 when Portuguese traders made contact with the old Benin kingdom. Another encounter occurred with the Warri people in 1570–4.[83] By 1515, missionaries had converted princes from the Benin and Warri kingdoms, although the kings themselves could not embrace the religion publicly.[84] The spread of Christianity failed to gain momentum for several reasons, including the local climate and the fact that the religion was only observed within the palaces of the elites.

[82] Abodunde, *A Heritage of Faith*.
[83] Kanayo L. Nwadialor, "Christian Missionary Enterprise in Nigeria in Historical Perspective," in *Issues in Nigerian History and Socioeconomic Development*, ed. Nwachukwu J. Obiakor, Kanayo L. Nwadialor, and Bakky N. Adirika (Awka: Rity Printz, 2016), 1–22.
[84] S. I. Okoro, "The Igbo and Educational Development in Nigeria, 1846-2015," *International Journal of History and Cultural Studies* 4, no. 1 (2018): 65–80.

The British government's abolition of the slave trade encouraged a new wave of Christian missionaries traveling to Africa. This time, their motives were more than commercial. Their new goals were to spread Christianity, advance "civilization," and develop alternatives to the slave trade that involved "legitimate" products. The CMS came with the British government's 1841 naval expeditions, eventually arriving in the Yoruba region at Badagry in 1842. Missionaries founded a station there in 1847 before creating a station for the Igbo region in 1857.[85]

The second phase of Nigeria's Christian mission was driven by Protestant groups who sought to infiltrate new territories after finding little success among the Roman Catholics of Europe. Protestants intended to convert Africans to Christianity while establishing their "civilization" through schools and the expansion of the British government.[86] In 1842, shortly before the arrival of the CMS, Methodist missionaries arrived in Badagry. There, William De Graft and his wife established a nursery school for education.[87] Henry Townsend led the CMS to Abeokuta in 1843.[88] Other missionary groups began settling in rapidly. In January 1843, the Church of Scotland sent a mission to Calabar. The CMS established a presence in Onitsha in 1852. In 1885, the RCM arrived in Onitsha, continuing to Lagos by 1868. Northern Ireland's Qua Ibo joined in Uyo and Akso, and Eket in 1887. This continued until they extended too far into many parts of Northern Nigeria, including Bida, in 1910.[89]

Christian missionary activities were supported by former slaves who had returned to Nigeria to spread the gospel. Bishop Ajayi Crowther was particularly influential in spreading the religion. He became head of the Niger mission in 1857, and the first Anglican Bishop in 1864.[90] Crowther took a nonconfrontational approach to his work, using scriptural dialogue and African languages. His approach was respected because it presented opportunities for potential converts to discuss their beliefs openly.[91] Crowther's translation of the bible further facilitated the wider understanding of Christian beliefs.

---

[85] Okoro, "The Igbo and Educational Development in Nigeria."
[86] F. Deaville Walker, *A Hundred Years in Nigeria: The Story of the Methodist Mission in the Western Nigeria District 1842–1942* (London: Cargate Press, 1943).
[87] Magnus O. Bassey, *Missionary Rivalry and Educational Expansion in Nigeria, 1885–1945* (Lewston: E. Mellen Press, 1999), 34.
[88] Simon A. Ajayi, *Emmanuel Oyewole Akingbala: The Adventures of a Nigerian Baptist Pastor* (Ibadan: Hope Publications, 1999), 26.
[89] Martin Odidi, "The Church and Social Responsibilities: A Case Study of the Development of Church Schools in the Diocese of Kaduna, Church of Nigeria, Anglican Communion," unpublished PhD dissertation, University of the South, 2019.
[90] A. F. Wall, "Crowther, Samuel Ajayi: 1807–1891," *International Bulletin of Missionary Research* 16, no. 1 (1992): 15–21.
[91] John Azumah and Lamin Sanneh, eds., *The African Christian and Islam* (Carlisle: Langham Publishing, 2013).

Christian missionary activities intensified among the Igbo of the Eastern region. At the end of the colonial period, this religion was widely practiced by residents. After the colonial invasion, various missions arrived in the country. In 1903, Mary Slessor opened the Arochukwu station of the United Free Scotland Mission, and the CMS opened its Awka station.[92] In 1905, the CMS settled near Owerri at Egbu, and Father Dan Walsh established an RCM station in Emekuku.[93] The Primitive Methodist Missionary Society ventured deeper into Igboland, establishing a station in Bende, Uzuakoli, in 1910.[94] After the 1914 amalgamation, many missionaries established different stations and groups across Igboland, influencing local inhabitants with Christian doctrines.

Missionary teaching opposed the extant Igbo deities.[95] Indigenes were told that their insignificant gods had no power and should be abandoned. Igbo doctrine, which believed in the continuing influence of deceased ancestors in the world of the living, was ridiculed by Christian missionaries. Local rituals, festivals, and divination practices that had previously been performed to show respect to deities and ancestors were collectively dismissed as fetishes that should be stopped.[96] The Osu system and polygamous practices were also condemned by the Christians. Many Igbo refused to accept this ridicule and the calls for sudden cultural change in all aspects. They could not comprehend Christian assertions that opposed their lived experience with manifestations, interventions, and power wielded by the deities and their ancestors. To some category of Igbo, Christianity was received as an evil omen that had to be resisted through every possible method, which included assistance from supernatural allies. The people of Ahiazu and Obollo consulted with their deities to understand the intentions of the Christians, asking for divine intervention.[97] As a result, in the early years of contact missionaries were only allowed to settle in taboo sites, such as the "evil forest," where it was expected that demons would torment and intimidate them.

The indirect rule system and the appointment of Warrant Chiefs affected missionary activities under colonial authority. The local Warrant Chief determined which areas were open to missionary activities, and the location of new churches required approval from the District Officer.[98] The

---

[92] Edet A. Udo, "The Missionary Scramble for Spheres of Influence in Eastern Nigeria, 1900–1952," *Ikenga: Journal of African Studies* 1, no. 2 (1972): 22–36.
[93] Ubah, "Religious Change among the Igbo," 71–91.
[94] Ogbu U. Kalu, "Primitive Methodists on the Railroad Junctions of Igboland," *Journal of Religion in Africa* 16, no. 1 (1986): 44–66.
[95] Okeke, Ibenwa, and Okeke, "Conflicts between African Traditional Religion."
[96] Okeke, Ibenwa, and Okeke, "Conflicts between African Traditional Religion."
[97] Ubah, "Religious Change among the Igbo," 71–91.
[98] NAE Okidist 4090/11, Colonial Secretary to the Provincial Commissioner, Eastern Province, 20 June 1912. Also Okidist 20/1921, Resident of Owerre to District Officer, 4 Oct., 1921. "NAE" refers to the holding of the Nigerian National Archives, Enugu.

introduction of the Native Land Acquisition Ordinance required missionaries to secure colonial approval before occupying any land.[99] These rules and other colonial policies were intended to promote peaceful coexistence while upholding law and order. However, local Warrant Chiefs held the power to dismiss local missionaries and invite new groups at their discretion. For example, Chief Ike Nwaji of Aku invited the RCM after he dismissed the Primitive Methodist Mission.[100] Nevertheless, missionaries had access to the entire colony.

Christian missionary activities proceeded more smoothly among the Yoruba. After missionary efforts failed in the fifteenth century, missionaries made new contact with the Yoruba in the West. Records show that the Yoruba were more willing to tolerate Christianity than in several other parts of the country. Former Yoruba slaves also contributed to the spread of Christianity, giving missionaries the courage to establish themselves more assertively in the Yoruba region.[101] Some Christian missionaries claimed to have been invited by these former slaves.[102] Badagry received the first Pentecostal missionaries in the Yoruba region. Reverends Thomas Birch Freeman and Henry Townsend of the Methodist Mission Society and Church Mission Society arrived in 1842[103] to begin missionary work in the country. After their arrival, other missionary groups settled in various parts of the region.

Many of these groups settled in Abeokuta, which had a reputation for being open to Christianity. Abeokuta's prominence made it a focal point for Christian missions, and it soon became the "Citadel of Christianity" in Nigeria.[104] Local reactions from kings and chiefs generally followed the example set by Sodeke of Egbaland with his treatment of Freedman and Townsend in 1842 and 1843. Christianity was seen as a blessing that had previously been predicted by Ifa divination in 1830.[105] After much consultation with their Ifa divination practices, the Egba people celebrated the arrival of missionaries throughout the streets of Abeokuta.[106] Sodeke reportedly said "The white man's religion is

---

[99] See Section 3(a) Native Land Acquisition Ordinance.
[100] Ubah, "Religious Change among the Igbo."
[101] Samson Adetunji Fatokun, "Christian Missions in South-Western Nigeria, and the Response of African Traditional Religion," *International Review of Mission* 96, no. 380-381 (2007): 105–113.
[102] Modupe Oduyoye, *The Planting of Christianity in Yorubaland* (Ibadan: Day Star Press, 1969), 253–255.
[103] M. M. Familusi, *Methodism in Nigeria (1842–1992)* (Ibadan: N. P. S. Educational Publishers, 1992), 11.
[104] Toyin Falola and Biodun Adediran, *Islam and Christianity in West Africa* (Ile-Ife: University of Ife Press Ltd., 1983), 112.
[105] Fatokun, "Christian Missions in South-Western Nigeria."
[106] S. A. Adewale, "The Role of Ifa in the Work of the 19th Century Missionaries," *Orita: Ibadan Journal of Religious Studies* 12, no. 1 (1978): 26.

true, and both myself and you will have to follow it."[107] As foretold by prophecy, the missionaries facilitated the development of Abeokuta and built schools in the region.

In Yoruba territory, relations between Christian missionaries and African religions were relatively good, but some friction existed. Missionaries presented their Christian beliefs as superior to traditional beliefs, declaring that their preferred political and social systems were obvious improvements. The disparagement of systems based on traditional Yoruba practices fostered tension in society. The Ake church was destroyed in protest and burned down to oppose the heresies of the Christians in 1846.[108] Some Christians were arrested and tortured by Ogboni courts due to their affronts.

Christian missionaries originally met with a warm reception in Ibadan. The CMS mission in Ibadan was established in 1853 by Reverend David Hinderer and his wife.[109] Interactions were cordial; Yoruba leaders provided houses that were used as missionary schools.[110] As the indirect rule system was established, CMS missionaries built more schools to educate Ibadan residents. After the 1892 conquest of the Ijebu people, subdued by British colonial forces in the Imagbo War, missionary activities in the area increased. Ijebu's proximity to Lagos, and the agreement with the *Awujale* of Ijebu Ode, thus encouraged missionary efforts to spread Christianity in the region.[111]

Missionaries introduced many changes to Yoruba society, including the reformation of the Ogboni Confraternity. Historically, this group was a secret religious society that adjudicated specific conflicts. Christian converts were prohibited from engaging in Ogboni activities, which were seen as fetishistic practices that opposed the will of the Christian God. Reverend Thomas A. J. Ogunbiyi of the Anglican missionary group created the Christian Ogboni Society in 1914.[112] Its goal was to increase the status of Christian elites and encourage the practice of Christian doctrine.[113] However, the society was not accepted by other groups within the Anglican Church. Bishops Tugwell and

---

[107] Frank D. Walker, *The Romans of the Black River: The Story of the CMS Nigeria Mission* (London: Church Missionary Society, 1931), 46.

[108] Jare Adefemi, ed., *The History of the Cathedral of St. Peter, Ake, Abeokuta, 1843–1986* (Abeokuta: The Standing Committee, 1986), 3-4.

[109] Olufunke A. Adeboye, "Christianity and Traditional Life in Ibadan 1853–1940," in *Readings in Nigerian History and Culture: Essays in Memory of J. A. Atanda*, ed. Dare Oguntomisin and Samuel A. Ajayi (Ibadan: Hope Publications, 2002), 106–115.

[110] Olufemi Vaughan, *Religion and the Making of Nigeria* (Durham: Duke University Press, 2016).

[111] Vaughan, *Religion and the Making of Nigeria*.

[112] Toyin Falola, ed., *Tradition and Change in Africa: The Essays of J. F. Ade Ajayi* (Trenton: Africa World Press, 2000), 146.

[113] Geoffrey Parrinder, *Religion in an African City* (London: Oxford University Press, 1953), 178.

Oluwole banned any relations with the new society, and it became the Reformed Ogboni Fraternity, admitting people of other faiths in 1943.[114]

Despite the predominance of Islamic religion in the North and the restrictions that Lugard placed on missionary activity in the region, Christianity still found its way into Northern Nigeria. The colonial administration kept Lugard's prohibitions in place for as long as possible, which led Protestant missions to adopt new strategies. They began preaching in public, holding sermons along routes that would be used by Muslims in the North. It was hoped that interested Muslims would inquire about the sermons as they were preached.[115] By the 1930s, restrictions on missionary activities in the North were completely ineffective. Missionaries had begun providing social amenities and services for Nigerians, and they had become regular fixtures in the North. Workers began to identify themselves as Christians, and missionaries took every opportunity to preach the gospel at hospitals and other institutions that they had founded.[116]

In the colonial North, Christianity eventually became more pronounced among non-Muslim natives and migrants who considered themselves Christians. Although missionaries were not allowed to convert people in the North, they had approval to administer services and events for migrants who settled in the North. The migrants who settled in the *Sabon Gari* became a concentration of Christianity in the North during the colonial era. By 1930, Anglican and Catholic churches had been established in Kano, and the practice of Christianity was becoming more prominent.[117] Muslim outcasts who traditionally experienced discrimination found it appealing to embrace Christianity, and these conversions supported further mission activity in the North.

In Nigeria, Christianity was eventually accepted as part of the nation's cultural values. One example is the Ogboni confraternity system and its adoption of Christian practices in 1914, encouraged by Rev. Ogunbiyi and Yoruba elites in the African church. The society later allowed people of other faiths to join after it was denounced by the Anglican Church; it later became the Reformed Ogboni Fraternity.

In the 1920s, the Aladura church movement was another attempt to merge Christianity with Indigenous values. This movement interpreted the Indigenous idealism of native experiences in a Christian context, originating as a prayer group from the CMS that was concerned by the prevalence of famine and other social issues. They embraced Christian beliefs that included

---

[114] Akinbowale Akintola, *Reformed Ogboni Fraternity (ROF): Its Origin and Interpretation of its Doctrines and Symbolism* (Ogbomoso: Ogunniyi Printing Works, 1992).

[115] Andrew E. Barnes, " 'The Great Prohibition': The Expansion of Christianity in Colonial Northern Nigeria," *History Compass* 8, no. 6 (2010): 440–454.

[116] Chinedu N. Ubah, "Christian Missionary Penetration of the Nigerian Emirates, with Special Reference to the Medical Missions Approach," *The Muslim World* 77 (1987): 16–27.

[117] Crampton, *Christianity in Northern Nigeria*.

miracles and speaking in tongues.[118] The Aladura church, led by David Odubanjo, was initially associated with the Faith Tabernacle. These connections were later renounced due to the perceived spiritual ineffectiveness of the tabernacle. Churches adopted different Yoruba practices, songs, and musical instruments. One example of an Aladura church is the Christ Apostolic Church, which was created in 1920. This church believed that healing should occur through prayer, while Western and traditional medicines were rejected altogether. The second Aladura church was the Cherubim and Seraphim, founded in 1925 by Moses Orimolade Tunolase and Christiana Abiodun. They had received a vision from God directing them to open a church that began as a prayer group.[119] In 1934, Josiah Oshitelu was expelled from the Anglican Church and founded the Church of the Lord. He was popular for successfully predicting events that occurred in the 1920s, declaring that they were destined to happen because of local pagan practices.[120] The Celestial Church of Christ was the fourth major Aladura church, founded by Samuel Oshoffa in 1947.

Aladura churches attracted huge numbers of followers across the country because of the African manners and practices incorporated into church services.[121] They recognized the religious power of sorcerers, witches, spiritual forces, and visions.[122] These churches also focused on solving personal problems, such as health problems, rituals for conception and birth, and financial issues. Aladura churches became an alternative to the traditional religions' *Babalawo* in diagnosing spiritual problems.[123]

Other African cultures gradually accepted Christian churches, especially after the religious groups made some concessions. Rules against polygamy were relaxed as some Anglican and Baptist churches allowed polygamous converts, but they were not allowed to receive the sacrament of baptism. Later, these rules were ignored completely, especially among Aladura churches. The Ebenezer African Church was formed in the Yoruba region of Nigeria, and it recognized some traditional social positions.[124] This relaxation

---

[118] Kofi Johnson, "Aladura: The Search for Authenticity an Impetus for African Christianity," *AJPS* 14, no. 1 (2011): 149–165.

[119] Joseph Akinyele Omoyajowo, *Cherubim and Seraphim: The History of an African Independent Church* (New York: NOK Publishers Int., 1982).

[120] Peter Probst, "The Letter and the Spirit: Literacy and Religious Authority in the History of the Aladura Movement in Western Nigeria," *Africa* 59, no. 4 (1989): 478–495.

[121] Oluwafunminiyi Raheem, "Martin Luther versus Us: Assessing the Reformation through the Perspectives of an African Class," *African Diaspora Discourse – ADD* 2, no. 2 (2020): 65–69.

[122] Akintunde E. Akinade, "New Religious Movements in Contemporary Nigeria: Aladura Churches as a Case Study," *Asia Journal of Theology* 10, no. 2 (1996): 316–332.

[123] Bọlaji E. Idowu, *Towards an Indigenous Church* (London: Oxford University Press, 1965).

[124] Robert W. July, *The Origins of Modern African Thought: Its Development in West Africa During the Nineteenth and Twentieth Centuries* (Trenton: Africa World Press, 2004), 291.

of doctrines allowed traditional Nigerian rulers to be converted in ways that allowed them to hold their traditional positions while assuming roles in the Christian faith.

New Religious Movements

Other religions, in addition to the Islamic and Christian beliefs in Nigeria during the colonial period, also found their way into the country. The Bahá'í Faith was introduced during the 1920s.[125] Enoch Olinga was a popular Nigerian who facilitated the religion's growth in 1950, and a National Spiritual Assembly was selected in 1956.[126] The religion continued to develop from this point, preaching the relevance of other religions and protecting the unity of all humans.

Hinduism spread slowly, transmitted through interactions with Indians and Hare Krishnas.[127] The Rosicrucian (AMORC) became another popular religion, especially in Calabar.[128] It arrived in 1925. The AMORC worship center in Calabar is built in an Egyptian style. Their religion believes that it can assist individuals in discovering and understanding the secrets of existence, granting special powers to allow inner visions for personal development and success.[129]

The Brotherhood of the Cross and Star (BCS), popularly known as the Olumba, is a religious minority in Nigeria.[130] The BCS was established by Olumba Obu in the Niger Delta in the 1950s. He believed that he had received a message from God declaring that Olumba would lead all men. He was believed to have consecrated a stream close to his house, which later became a sacred site for Olumba's followers. They believed that ailing individuals could heal themselves in the stream through the power of belief.[131] The religious movement is premised on the belief in the divinity of Olumba as the seventh reincarnation of God, according to Genesis 5:24. His followers traced Olumba's lineage back to Adam. According to his story, Olumba stated that he was warned at an early age not to live an opulent life. He gave away all his clothes and belongings, wearing only a white t-shirt and shorts with no shoes. Olumba attracted a small group of believers and loyalists that formed the

---

[125] Anthony Lee, *The Baha'i Faith in Africa: Establishing a New Religious Movement, 1952–1962* (Leiden: Brill, 2011).
[126] Lee, *The Baha'i Faith in Africa*.
[127] Abdulyassar Abdulhamid, "Interesting Tales of Nigerians Who are Andians in Tongue," *Daily Trust*, May 27, 2021.
[128] Hackett, *Religion in Calabar*, 155.
[129] Rosalind I. J. Hackett, "The Spiritual Sciences in Africa," *Journal of Contemporary Religion* 3, no. 2 (1986): 8–11.
[130] Friday M. Mbon, *Brotherhood of the Cross and Star: A New Religious Movement in Nigeria* (New York: Peter Lang, 1992).
[131] G. I. S. Amadi, "Healing in 'the Brotherhood of the Cross and Star,'" *Studies in Church History* 19 (1982): 367–383.

beginning of the group's membership in 1952. In 1958, Olumba dedicated himself completely to religion, giving up his works and trade to pursue a full-time ministry, spreading religion in different places.

BCS membership included thousands of believers from Nigeria to Ghana, and others resided in Europe and the United States. Apart from Olumba's theological positioning, the BCS was influenced by African traditional beliefs. Olumba's followers considered him to be the embodiment of the holy trinity: the Father, Son, and Holy Spirit in an African body.[132] Adherents believed in the healing power of Olumba and his explanations of Christianity and the nature of God. These teachings were widely criticized by other Christians, who described the BCS as a religious sect.[133] The BCS began in Calabar in a large religious center that attracted thousands of believers to worship every Sunday. From there, the religion extended to other parts of the world, including Europe and the United States. Several zealous individuals initiated several divisions within the church. As of 2008, there were thirty-two branches in Nigeria, sixteen in other African countries, nine in North America, eight in Europe, and some in the Caribbean.[134]

Conclusion

Nigerian society had flourished as a pluralist society before the arrival of foreign religions. After the introduction of Christianity and Islam, Nigerian indigenes overcame their initial resistance and learned how to live together during the colonial era with minimal conflict. Islam, Christianity, and Indigenous beliefs have manifested in present-day Nigeria alongside minor religious movements, coexisting peacefully but also with the threat of national destruction. Today, the religions maintain fragile peace in democratic, twenty-first-century Nigeria due to fanatical insurgents.

Contemporary religious harmony is threatened by two factors. The first is the politicization of religious activities,[135] which was encouraged by colonial and postcolonial policies. Muslim converts in the North were used to conquer other parts of the North, especially non-Muslim areas, and they imposed Islam on some captured territories. The colonial government was also accused of Christianization, whereby many officials were Christians who encouraged the activities of Christian missionaries. The second threat was rooted in the colonial prohibition of evangelism in the North, which artificially delayed

---

[132] Galia Sabar and Atalia Shragai, "Olumba Olumba in Israel: Struggling on All Fronts," *African Identities* 6, no. 3 (2008): 201–225.
[133] Hackett, *Religion in Calabar*, 9.
[134] Sabar and Shragai, "Olumba Olumba in Israel."
[135] Iheanyi M. Enwerem, *A Dangerous Awakening: The Politicization of Religion in Nigeria* (Ibadan: IFRA-Nigeria, 2013).

the diffusion of religious influence across the region. People began to draw political borders along religious lines, which served as the beginning of religious discrimination and subsequent conflicts. These biases have encouraged the development and radicalization of religious terrorism, such as the various contemporary cases of violence, killings, and kidnapping.

17

Health and Medicine

Healthcare services and medicine were developed in Nigeria over four different eras, beginning with a system of traditional medicine.[1] Nigerians initially relied on the Indigenous medical systems to treat every known disease, and unexplained illnesses were regarded as afflictions from the gods or other spiritual forces. Then, and now, knowledge of plants for medical and pharmaceutical purposes was well established.

Contact with Europeans would introduce significant changes to medical practices. The next era in Nigeria's medical history was shaped by the arrival and settlement of Christian missionaries. They introduced European approaches to medicine and provided scientific explanations for many diseases. These missionaries intended to gain new converts to Christianity for the greater glory of God.[2] Their "heal the body, heal the soul" approach provided primary healthcare for Nigerians from every part of society.

After British rule was established, colonial officials imposed developmental plans and provided different healthcare facilities. The implementation of healthcare was slow, and it relied heavily on work done by Christian missionaries. Healthcare systems created by the colonial administration formed the foundation for Nigeria's postcolonial medical development.[3]

Traditional Medicine and Healthcare System

Healthcare services and medicine in Nigeria existed before either the official establishment of the colonial administration or the arrival of Christian missionaries. Africans had treatments for known illnesses, some managed by the gods that governed different aspects of their lives.[4] Indigenous African healthcare

---

[1] Osiomheyalo Idaewor, "Eboh and Traditional Medicine in Pre-Colonial Apana Social Systems," *Journal of History and Diplomatic Studies* 10, no. 1 (2014): 145–165.

[2] Felix K. Ekechi, "The Medical Factor in Christian Conversion in Africa: Observations from Southeastern Nigeria," *Missiology: An International Review* 21, no. 3 (1993): 289–309.

[3] Anna Greenwood, ed., *Beyond the State: The Colonial Medical Service in British Africa* (Manchester: Manchester University Press, 2016).

[4] Ishaq I. Omoleke, "Intergovernmental Relations and Management of Primary Health Care in Nigeria," unpublished PhD dissertation, Obafemi Awolowo University, Ile-Ife, 2000.

systems can be traced back to a distant past, and their traditions were older than colonial medical practices. The African healthcare system involved three components: spirituality, divination, and herbal remedies.[5] Spirituality was involved when sicknesses were assumed to be caused by the gods,[6] which mostly involved ailments that did not have medical or physical explanations. These were the work of local deities or other spiritual forces. Priests would be asked to conduct rituals that could appease the gods and end the afflictions.

Some healthcare providers used divination to diagnose the source of a problem and prescribed treatments to resolve the underlying issues.[7] In Yoruba society, these diviners were referred to as *Ifa* priests or *Babalawo*. There were also specialists trained to interpret symptoms and treat illnesses with herbal remedies, known as *Alagbo*. In many cases, these disciplines were combined: traditional healers could perform several of these functions. Indigenous and traditional medical systems reflected age-old beliefs from regions. Yoruba groups had *Adaunse* or *Onisegun*, who were trained to provide healing services.[8] Among the Hausa society, the *Wombai* performed similar functions, and the *Dibia* served Igbo communities.[9]

Nigeria's traditional healthcare services were influenced by the changes occurring in local societies. The spread of Islam and Christianity encouraged people to believe that these systems were ineffective and based on superstition. Many practices were dismissed as superstitions and rejected, especially by Christian converts. Some practices persisted to the end of the colonial era, but the entire system was discredited and disparaged as Christianity's influence increased.[10]

The colonial administration rejected traditional remedies as inferior to European medical knowledge. The "civilizing" process imposed by colonial officers had no intention of supporting pre-existing medical practices.[11] Instead, they replaced these services with modern allopathic procedures. However, the colonial

---

[5] Philip F. Builders, ed., *Herbal Medicine* (London: IntechOpen, 2018).
[6] Oluwafunminiyi Raheem and Mike Famiyesin, "Controlling the Boundaries of Morality: The History and Powers of Ayelala Deity," *Yoruba Studies Review* 2 no. 1 (2017): 231–247.
[7] Akinmayowa Akin-Otiko, "Ifá Divination: A Method of Diagnosing and Treating Chronic Illnesses/Àmódi among Yoruba People," in *Chronic Illness, Spirituality, and Healing: Diverse Disciplinary, Religious, and Cultural Perspectives*, ed. Michael J. Stoltzfus, Rebecca Green, and Darla Schumm (New York: Palgrave Macmillan, 2013), 239–252.
[8] Ismail A. B. Balogun, *The Place of Religion in the Development of Nigeria* (Ilorin: University of Ilorin, 1988), 225.
[9] Olanrewaju Ogunlana, "Nigeria," in *International Pharmaceutical Services: The Drug Industry and Pharmacy Practice in Twenty-Three Major Countries of the World*, ed. Richard N. Spivey, Albert I. Wertheimer, and T. Donald Rucker (New York: Pharmaceutical Products Press, 1992), 401.
[10] John D. Y. Peel, "The Pastor and the 'Babalawo': The Interaction of Religions in Nineteenth-Century Yorubaland," *Africa: Journal of the International African Institute* 60, no. 3 (1990): 338–369.
[11] Ali A. Abdullahi, "Trends and Challenges of Traditional Medicine in Africa," *African Journal of Traditional, Complementary and Alternative Medicine* 8, no. 5 (2011): 115–123.

government's haphazard approach to developing healthcare systems left people largely relying on traditional medical services. For instance, these remedies were used to treat the 1918 influenza outbreak, and Nigerians continued to practice traditional medicine and patronize its adherents.

Traditional medical services provided obstetrics and gynecological services via a comprehensive system that cared for expectant mothers through childbirth.[12] The maternal care system was popular during the colonial period, and it persists in present-day Nigeria. Midwives, often called *Agbebi* or *Baba Abiwere*, were accessible and available throughout the colonial period, especially in the hinterlands.[13]

Healthcare providers in the traditional system practiced many aspects of medicine. Healers performed the functions of doctors, nurses, pharmacists, and others in the healthcare sector. They retrieved different herbs, preserved them, and provided them to those in need. To study such a comprehensive profession, trainees were required to commit to a long-term apprenticeship involving every form of practice. Many healthcare providers adopted the practice as a family profession or business.[14] The Indigenous healthcare system provided preventive and curative services. Preventive measures included those against "spiritual attacks."[15] Traditional health providers were popular during the colonial period because of ease of access and continued belief in them.[16]

During the colonial era, the government built hospitals at a moderate pace in locations that were either close to coastal areas or had high concentrations of European settlers. Access was restricted to Europeans and privileged Nigerians, and although Christian missionaries provided similar services, their reach did not extend to every community.

The Role of Christian Missionaries

As Christian missionaries dispersed around the world, they tried to save bodies along with souls. Medicine and healthcare services created a bridge between missionaries and the people that they tried to convert, overcoming local resistance by offering something of value.[17] This was the case in Nigeria as

---

[12] A. O. Imogie, E. O. Agwubike, and K. Aluko, "Assessing the Role of Traditional Birth Attendants (TBAs) in Health Care Delivery in Edo State, Nigeria," *Africa Journal of Reproductive Health* 6, no. 2 (2002): 94–100.

[13] Omoleke I. Isola, "The Relevance of the African Traditional Medicine (Alternative Medicine) to Health Care Delivery System in Nigeria," *The Journal of Developing Areas* 47, no. 1 (2013): 319–338.

[14] Isola, "The Relevance of the African Traditional Medicine."

[15] Isola, "The Relevance of the African Traditional Medicine."

[16] Amoleke I. Odebiyi, "Social Factors in Health and Diseases," Inaugural Lecture 135, Obafemi Awolowo University, Ile-Ife, O. A. U. Press, 1999.

[17] Jan Harm Boer, *Missionary Messengers of Liberation in a Colonial Context: A Case Study of the Sudan United Mission* (Amsterdam: Rodopi, 1979).

some societies were initially hostile, but they eventually tolerated Christian missionaries, and their interactions ultimately developed into relationships and friendships.[18] Missionaries had successfully used similar approaches among Indians, East Africans, and other groups. When the Church Mission Society arrived in India, locals and their Maharaja government reacted with hostility.[19] However, the missionaries provided medical care that replaced hostility with mutual understanding and affection.[20]

Christian missionaries in Nigeria were adept at finding the best strategies for accessing different communities while spreading their religious beliefs. They created new schools and established healthcare services, activities that dated back to their first contact. The Portuguese traders who brought Roman Catholicism to the old Benin and Warri kingdoms in the fourteenth and fifteenth centuries continued with the nineteenth-century mission at Badagry in 1842.[21] Records show that a hospital was built by the Roman Catholic Mission in 1504 when they first came into contact with Nigeria.[22] The first phase of the Christian mission failed, but the second phase was largely successful. It was accompanied by the construction of additional hospitals and healthcare centers.[23]

During the second phase of Christian missionary activity in Nigeria, the missionaries introduced changes to the social structure of societies that they had successfully infiltrated. Sacred Heart Hospital was built by the Roman Catholic Mission (RCM) following their activities in Abeokuta.[24] The RCM and other missions provided education and healthcare services across the country.[25]

From 1867 to 1960, the RCM built a total of 38 hospitals in Nigeria that served every region. This amounted to 2,839 beds available to Nigerians and 73 doctors attending to patients, along with other health workers. The RCM's commitment to health and medicine meant that they had constructed three

---

[18] George T. Basden, *Among the Ibos of Nigeria* (London: Frank Cass & Company, 1966).
[19] Augustine Kanjamala, *The Future of Christian Mission in India: Toward a New Paradigm for the Third Millennium* (Eugene: Pickwick Publications, 2014), 72.
[20] Terence O. Ranger, "Godly Medicine: The Ambiguities of Medical Mission in Southeast Tanzania, 1900–1945," *Social Science and Medicine* 15, no. 3 (1981): 261–277.
[21] S. I. Okoro, "The Igbo and Educational Development in Nigeria, 1846–2015," *International Journal of History and Cultural Studies* 4, no. 1 (2018): 65–80.
[22] Ralph A. Schräm, *History of Nigerian Health Services* (Ibadan: Ibadan University Press, 1971), 340.
[23] Samson Adetunji Fatokun, "Christian Missions in South-Western Nigeria, and the Response of African Traditional Religion," *International Review of Mission* 96, no. 380-381 (2007): 105–113.
[24] Festus O. Egwaikhide, Victor A. Isumonah, and Olumide S. Ayodele, *Federal Presence in Nigeria: The "Sung" and "Unsung" Basis for Ethnic Grievance* (Dakar: CODESRIA, 2009), 93.
[25] Ikenga R. A. Ozigboh, *Roman Catholicism in Southern Nigeria 1885–1931* (Onitsha: Etukokwu Publishers, 1988).

times as many healthcare facilities as any other mission.[26] By 1960, the Church Missionary Society had built 7 hospitals with 622 beds, and the Church of Brethren Mission and Church of Scotland had built 3 and 4 hospitals, respectively. The Lutheran Mission had 1 hospital, the Methodist Missionary Society built 7 hospitals, the Nigerian Baptist Mission established 5, the Sudan Interior Mission and Sudan United Mission respectively established 12 and 13 hospitals in the North, and the Seventh Day Adventist mission constructed 3. By 1960, a total of 118 hospitals had been constructed by 13 missionary groups, providing 7,241 beds and 352 doctors.[27]

During the colonial era, Christian missionaries established more hospitals and healthcare services in the South than in the North.[28] This was due to several factors, including the general acceptance of missionaries in Southern Nigeria, especially among the Yoruba people. The Southern region received the most benefit from the presence of Christian missionaries. They were accepted with joy and celebration, especially in Abeokuta. Cooperation between missionaries and residents launched many different developmental projects.[29]

The inaccessibility of Northern regions also encouraged more missionary activity in the South. Early missionaries and traders settled at Southern ports close to the Atlantic Ocean. Local road networks were insufficient for accessing other parts of Nigeria, and missionaries feared attacks from hostile residents. Missionaries felt that residents in the South had a greater need for their evangelism.[30] By the time of Nigeria's independence in 1960, 87 of the existing 118 missionary hospitals had been built in the Southern region.[31]

Missionary activity in the North started later than in other parts. The region had a long history of Islam that had been adopted in every aspect of their lives. After the conquest of Northern Nigeria, Lugard promised the government of Sokoto that nothing would interfere with Islamic practices in the North. To keep to this promise, the colonial administration restricted missionary activities in the North,[32] seeking to avoid any antagonism that might stem from the presence of Christian missionaries.[33]

---

[26] Dennis A. Ityavyar, "Background to the Development of Health Services in Nigeria," *Social Science & Medicine* 24, no. 6 (1987): 487–499.
[27] Schräm, *History of Nigerian Health Services.*
[28] Ogechukwu Ezekwem, "Missions and the Rise of the Western Maternity among the Igbo of South-eastern Nigeria," MA. Thesis, University of Texas, 2014.
[29] Toyin Falola and Biodun Adediran, *Islam and Christianity in West Africa* (Ile-Ife: University of Ife Press Ltd. 1983), 112.
[30] Ityavyar, "Background to the Development."
[31] Schräm, *History of Nigerian Health Services.*
[32] Andrew E. Barnes, "'The Great Prohibition': The Expansion of Christianity in Colonial Northern Nigeria," *History Compass* 8, no. 6 (2010): 440–454.
[33] Emmanuel A. Ayandele, *The Missionary Impact on Modern Nigeria 1842–1914: A Political and Social Analysis, 1842–1914* (London: Longman, 1966).

Missionaries unsuccessfully attempted to change British governmental policies. By 1914, they had reached an agreement with the colonial government and gained access to the North. It was understood that missionaries would focus mainly on social development projects, such as healthcare and education. Missionaries built hospitals and used them as opportunities to preach the gospel.[34] Some of the most prominent organizations were the Sudan United Mission and Sudan Interior Mission. The Sudan United Mission built a hospital in Gongola, which was the first missionary hospital in the North.[35] Despite encountering hostility in Jos, Sokoto, Kano, and Minna, the Sudan Interior Mission built several hospitals and provided basic healthcare services. The Sudan United Mission performed similar activities in the Middle-Belt areas. By 1960, the two groups had built twenty-five medical facilities and employed up to ninety-three medical personnel.

Missionaries had to change African ideas of illness and healthcare. Although Africans understood that sickness could occur naturally, they also believed that some ailments were inflicted by the gods. Any illness that was not supernatural could be treated with effective herbal remedies, but traditional beliefs held that ailments inflicted by the gods could only be cured by the gods. These beliefs posed challenges for the missionaries.

After Christian missionaries gained access to the Northern region, they entered into constructive partnerships with Northern leaders. In 1938, the Sudan Interior Mission reached an agreement with the leaderships of Katsina, Sokoto, and Kano. Their magazine, known as *Sudan Witness*, featured pictures with the Emir of Gwandu.[36] The Emir supported the Sudan Interior Mission and their medical efforts to fight leprosy, and he also provided a place for them to settle.[37]

In 1885, the RCM arrived in the Southeast and built local support by providing healthcare services, gaining more ground than their Pentecostal counterparts who had previously struggled to establish themselves in the region.[38] The RCM's care and enthusiasm for treating illnesses gained popular support and encouraged the spread of missionary activities in the Southeast. In Onitsha, a chief fell ill and was deserted and ostracized by his people. However, Anglican missionaries cared for him with food and medical treatment, and after his recovery he became a passionate advocate for spreading the gospel.

---

[34] Ubah, "Christian Missionary Penetration."
[35] Schräm, *History of Nigerian Health Services*.
[36] Sudan Interior Mission, "Peaceful Invasion of the Northern Emirates of Nigeria," *Sudan Witness* 14, no. 1 (1938).
[37] Shobana Shankar, "Medical Missionaries and Modernizing Emirs in Colonial Hausaland: Leprosy Control and Native Authority in the 1930s," *The Journal of African History* 48, no. 1 (2007): 45–68.
[38] Felix K. Ekechi, *Missionary Enterprise and Rivalry in Igboland, 1857–1914* (London: Frank Cass, 1971).

Former subjects followed his example, increasing the social and spiritual influence of the missionaries.[39]

Early medical care provided by missionaries was curative rather than preventive because it demonstrated the effectiveness of their ideas. Instead of building infrastructure that could prevent illness, they built medical centers to treat illness and measured their success by the number of hospitals that were constructed. The Christian missionaries' lack of emphasis on preventive medicine and weak attempts to promote healthcare education limited their achievements.[40]

The Colonial State and the Development of Health Care Services

European colonizing efforts were justified by the pretext of bringing "civilization" to Africa. To support this narrative, colonizers undermined Africa's notable historical developments and technological breakthroughs.[41] Propaganda was used to gain support for foreign ideas of governance and social structure. Colonialism and missionary efforts were foundational developments for present-day Nigeria, as every sector of the country's modern economy was either established or developed during the colonial era.[42] The colonial administration developed healthcare services to cure tropical diseases and treatable conditions. Europeans also had to acclimatize themselves to the region and develop immunities to new diseases that were already familiar to Africans, as in the case of malaria.

Many Europeans who traveled to Africa, especially in the nineteenth century, died of yellow fever and malaria.[43] At first, British officials were not aware that quinine could be used to cure malaria, and their immune systems were unable to defend against these diseases.[44] Europeans described Africa as the "White man's grave." Malaria, described as the "Black man's disease," was a major impediment, as death rates were at their highest in the nineteenth century before gradually declining in the following century.[45] By 1901, the

---

[39] Ekechi, "The Medical Factor in Christian Conversion."
[40] Ityavyar, "Background to the Development."
[41] Lugard, *The Dual Mandate*.
[42] Efiong I. Utuk, "Britain's Colonial Administrations and Developments, 1861–1960: An Analysis of Britain's Colonial Administrations and Developments in Nigeria," Ph.D *diss.*, Portland State University, 1975.
[43] Mark Honigsbaum, *The Fever Trail – In Search of the Cure for Malaria* (New York: Farrar Straux and Giroux, 2002).
[44] Philip D. Curtin, "The White Man's Grave: Image and Reality, 1780–1850," *Journal of British Studies* 1, no. 1 (1961): 94–110.
[45] Olatunji E. Alao, "Britain and the Civilizing Mission in Nigeria: Revisiting Anti-Malaria Policy in Lagos Metropolis during the Colonial Era, 1861–1960," *Lagos Historical Review* 13 (2013): 85–106.

disease was fatal for 43 out of 1,000 infected Europeans, and this death rate held steady into the beginning of World War I.[46]

The British administration's first formal attempt to provide healthcare services was in Lagos. It was originally a treatment center for Royal Navy seamen that had been converted into a public hospital with forty-two beds. In 1873, the colonial administration created the Infectious Disease Hospital in Lagos specifically for treating infected Europeans.[47] In the same year, the Nigerian debtors' prison was converted into a mental and psychiatric treatment center.[48] The administration's efforts to care for the sick primarily focused on Europeans, with a secondary goal of maintaining economic continuity in the colony. The British administration built additional health facilities and hospitals to benefit its ailing officials. Most healthcare facilities were concentrated near the Atlantic coast and exclusively served Europeans. A forty-bed hospital was built on the coast of Calabar in 1879. Medical services were eventually made available, in limited amounts, to Nigerians who worked for the Europeans. This was largely due to concerns about African workers and household staff spreading infectious diseases to Europeans.[49]

Lagos was declared a colony in 1861, but the British did not develop healthcare facilities in the Northern region until much later, after their conquest was complete.[50] Healthcare facilities were built there primarily to care for Europeans and their administrative staff. In 1900, Lord Lugard declared that the Northern part of Nigeria would be the Northern Protectorate, asserting authority over the Sokoto caliphate, the Tiv, and the Kanem-Borno.[51] The Northern capital was moved to Jebba and then to Kaduna in 1914. The British administration's commercial interests led them to develop medical facilities in the region, serving British officials and employees of the colony, as seen in the case of Lokoja.

Healthcare services developed more quickly in Southern Nigeria. Many Europeans settled in Southern cities on the Atlantic coast, and most of Britain's economic activity took place in coastal regions where it was easier to import and export foreign goods. Healthcare services followed the development of new trading opportunities, which meant more facilities in the South. These facilities were intended to serve Europeans, regardless of their location, North or South, and healthcare services continued to develop in commercial areas. When mining activities were initiated in Jos, the British administration

---

[46] Curtin, "The White Man's Grave."
[47] Margaret Peil, *Lagos: The City Is the People* (London: Belhaven Press, 1991), 13.
[48] Ityavyar, "Background to the Development."
[49] Ityavyar, "Background to the Development."
[50] Robert Stock, "Health Care for Some: A Nigerian Study of Who Gets What, Where and Why?" *International Journal of Health Services* 15, no. 3 (1985): 469–484.
[51] Lugard, *The Dual Mandate*.

built a hospital that was similar to existing facilities in commercial centers like Kano and Lagos.[52]

The colonial administration eventually considered the healthcare needs of other places. Government healthcare projects were designed to increase economic output. The colonial government forced Nigerians to leave their businesses and farms to construct roads, railways, mines, and other infrastructure without adequate healthcare. These workers built railways linking Lagos and Port Harcourt with Kano and Jos in the North to move products and raw materials from the interior to Europe and the rest of the world.

Forced laborers were the first to access British healthcare services. The goal was to maintain a workforce that could build roads and railways. Ongoing construction was necessary to develop the colonial economy and export raw materials. Healthcare services complemented the colonial administration's capitalist ambitions.[53] When World War I began in 1914, healthcare services began to suffer. Doctors were redeployed to Europe to treat wounded European soldiers, which left Nigerian hospitals and healthcare facilities short of staff to meet the country's increasing medical demands. Many hospital construction projects and related facilities were left idle during the war. Hospitals like those in Opobo, Ilesa, and Badagry were derelict or abandoned due to a lack of medical staff. Thirty-six medical practitioners were deployed to Europe, but only ten returned. The rest were casualties of war.[54] These changes exposed Nigerians to diseases that claimed many lives. The outbreak of illness was so severe that the loss of life was comparable to deaths caused directly by the war.[55] After the conflict, conditions in the country worsened as many British officials returned to Nigeria carrying foreign diseases such as influenza and syphilis.[56] Nigerian immune systems were unfamiliar with these afflictions and unprepared for their spread. A similar situation also occurred after World War II.

After World War I, the British administration resumed its abandoned healthcare projects largely to extract greater value to offset the empire's losses from war. The Lagos General Hospital was built, along with facilities in Ijebu Ode, Enugu, Jos, Aba, and Mubi. Christian missionaries in Nigeria made additional efforts to construct healthcare facilities because caring for the sick was a key component of their work to spread Christianity. In the 1920s, the

---

[52] James A. Johnson, Carleen H. Stoskopf, and Leiyu Shi, eds., *Comparative Health Systems: A Global Perspective* (Burlington: Jones & Bartlett Learning, 2018), 359.
[53] Jack Wayne, "Capitalism and Colonialism in Late Nineteenth Century Europe," *Studies in Political Economy* 5, no. 1 (1981): 79–106.
[54] Ralph Schräm, *A History of the Nigerian Health Services* (Ibadan: University of Ibadan Press, 1971).
[55] Schräm, *A History of the Nigerian Health Services*.
[56] Akaayar F. Ahokegh, "Colonialism, Development of Infrastructure and Urbanization in Tiv Land of Central Nigeria," *Academia*, www.academia.edu/3875702/Colonialism_and_Infrastructure_Development_in_Nigeria.

Dispensary Attendant School was built to train health assistants who could supplement the efforts of doctors and nurses by providing support on demand.[57] The Yaba Medical School was built to train assistant doctors in Nigerian hospitals. After these institutions were created, the country's medical facilities were strengthened. World War II had a less direct effect on Nigeria, but British colonial officials remained driven by capitalist motives.

To retain its dominant position in world markets, the British Empire increased the pace at which it extracted raw materials from its colonies. Global demand increased for rubber and tin, and the British government focused its attention on Nigerian resources. The administration invested in mining activities, like the industries in Jos, and complemented those efforts with hospitals, healthcare facilities, and medical centers in areas such as Jos and Kafanchan. A sixty-two-bed hospital opened in Jos, in the Barkin-Ladi area, and other facilities were built or renovated to treat more challenging conditions. The British government continued to build healthcare centers and hospitals for people across the country. Different plans and systems were introduced to address specific healthcare requirements. Although these acts were primarily due to economic motives, Nigeria's increasingly activist nationalism pushed colonial administrators to provide better healthcare for the country.

Reactions to Diseases and Pandemics

Like every society, the Nigerian colony faced challenges that tested its medical capabilities. These included tropical diseases, sicknesses, epidemics, and pandemics that were local, regional, and global. The state of Nigeria's healthcare sector often meant that unusual epidemics or pandemics could result in high morbidity rates and other problems. The 1918–19 influenza outbreak affected a large number of Nigerians.[58] It was one of the deadliest pandemics in history, infecting 500 million, or one-third of the global population at the time. No conclusive medical explanation has identified how the virus developed, but some have linked it to a virulent A-Type, while other virologists have posited that it was the result of an H1N1 virus attributed to an avian source.[59] In 12 months, the pandemic killed 50 million people, with some of the highest morbidity rates occurring in Europe and its colonies. The illness was most

---

[57] Sonya Gill and Shirish N. Kavadi, *Health Financing and Costs: A Comparative Study of Trends in Eighteen Countries with Special Reference to India* (Mumbai: Foundation for Research in Community Health, 1999), 50.
[58] Jimoh M. Oluwasegun, "Managing Epidemic: The British Approach to 1918–1919 Influenza in Lagos," *Journal of Asian and African Studies* 52, no. 4 (2017): 412–424.
[59] Howard Phillips and David Killingray, eds., *The Spanish Influenza Pandemic of 1918–1919: New Perspectives* (London: Routledge, 2003).

prominent among the 20–40 age group, and the most vulnerable people were under the age of 5 or over 65.[60]

The influenza outbreak had a devastating effect on Nigeria, with about 500,000 deaths. The pandemic caught the world unaware as there were no medical treatments to suppress or cure the disease.[61] Remedies involved nonmedical alternatives such as quarantine and isolation. Restrictions were placed on public gatherings, curfews were imposed, and people were encouraged to maintain proper hygiene and cover their noses and mouths. Nigeria had a population of 18 million people, and 50–80 percent were infected. The illness was concentrated in densely populated areas such as Lagos.[62]

No definitive proof exists, but virologists believe that the influenza outbreak began in the United States, infecting soldiers who brought the disease to Europe and other parts of the world.[63] Other virologists have suggested that it began in Asia, and laborers from China infected the French population before it spread to the rest of Europe and worldwide.[64] The illness was first identified in August 1918 at a British port where a ship with infected people anchored in Sierra Leone and continued to Nigeria, arriving at the Gold Coast. An American ship called the S. S. *Bida* arrived in Lagos carrying infected individuals on September 14, 1918. The first case in Nigeria was officially reported on September 23, marking the beginning of the outbreak in the country.[65] On September 28, the S. S. *Batanga* brought more infected people to Calabar, and other ships continued to arrive and increase the concentration of infected individuals. Influenza spread to other parts of Nigeria, primarily through the railway system, and many of the infected people traveled to large urban centers. Initially, the virus was concentrated around ports and train stations; many ship workers and customs officers became gravely ill. On October 1 and 5, Abeokuta and Ibadan reported their first cases. The disease spread more rapidly as it infiltrated Nigerian communities.[66]

Influenza was introduced in the Eastern regions of Nigeria primarily through Forcados port. The S. S. *Ravenston*, S. S. *Benue*, and S. S. *Onitsha*

---

[60] Centre for Disease Control and Prevention, United States of America, "1918 Pandemic (H1N1 virus)," March 20, 2019, https://archive.cdc.gov/#/details?url=https://www.cdc.gov/flu/pandemic-resources/1918-pandemic-h1n1.html.

[61] Niall P. A. S. Johnson and Juergen Mueller, "Updating the Accounts: Global Mortality of the 1918–1920 'Spanish' Influenza Pandemic," *Bulletin of the History of Medicine* 76, no. 1 (2002): 105–115.

[62] Don C. Ohadike, "Diffusion and Physiological Responses to the Influenza Pandemic of 1918–19 in Nigeria," *Social Science and Medicine* 32, no. 12 (1991): 1393–1399.

[63] Richard Collier, *The Plague of the Spanish Lady: The Influenza Pandemic of 1918–1919* (New York: Atheneum, 1974).

[64] L. Hoyle, *The Influenza Viruses* (New York: Springer, 1968), 256.

[65] Oluwasegun, "Managing Epidemic."

[66] Luke Williams, "Nigeria and the Great Influenza Pandemic of 1918–1919: A Conceptual Challenge for the History of Medicine," MA Thesis, La Trobe University, 1989.

arrived carrying infected Nigerian and European patients. From Forcados, the illness spread to Warri on October 17, 1918. Once the virus arrived in Nigeria's interior, almost every family had someone to bury.[67] Initial efforts to stop the disease met with limited success. No known medicine was successful at fighting influenza before the outbreak, which contributed to high morbidity rates, especially in Nigeria. It spread quickly as people with mild symptoms refused to be quarantined and continued with their daily routines. These people traveled, visited loved ones, and brought the virus to other parts of the country unnoticed.[68]

The situation was worsened by the lack of medical staff. Ohadike observed that there were only 53 medical officers in the whole of Nigeria: 32 in the South and 21 in the North.[69] People began to panic, and almost 1,000 workers fled their jobs in Jos, seeking safety in other villages. This only exposed the virus to greater numbers of people, bringing it to rural areas that had previously been unaffected.[70] The pandemic affected almost every part of the country. The diminishing workforce affected every sector of the national economy.[71] The influenza was referred to as *Lukuluku* among Ekiti communities in the South, and was later called *Ajakale Arun*, which meant "a widely spread disease."[72]

The people had various reactions to the pandemic, and the lack of effective medicine pushed them to explore alternative solutions. Muslims in some areas soaked passages from the Quran in water and drank them for protection.[73] Christians approached the pandemic from a religious perspective, believing that it was a manifestation of God's punishment for engaging in World War I. Others described it as the holy spirit's descent to Earth. This formed the foundation of the popular *Aladura* church. People lost their faith in medicine, traditional beliefs, and orthodox religion, choosing to form a more radical Christian movement that relied on prayers and miracles.[74]

The *Aladura* church adopted spiritual approaches to healing. Sophia Odunlami, who was nineteen years old, claimed to have been healed after suffering from influenza for five days. She claimed that God spoke with her and revealed that the world and the war would be healed. Odunlami declared that

[67] Williams, "Nigeria and the Great Influenza Pandemic."
[68] Williams, "Nigeria and the Great Influenza Pandemic."
[69] Ohadike, "Diffusion and Physiological Responses."
[70] Ohadike, "Diffusion and Physiological Responses."
[71] Thomas A. Garrett, "Economic Effects of the 1918 Influenza Pandemic: Implications for a Modern-Day Pandemic," *Federal Reserve Bank of St. Louis Review* 90, no. 2 (2008): 75–93.
[72] A. Oguntuyi, *History of Ekiti from the Beginnings to 1939* (Ibadan: Bisi Books, 1979), 123–125.
[73] David Killingray, "A New 'Imperial Disease': The Influenza Pandemic of 1918–9 and Its Impact on the British Empire," *Caribbean Quarterly* 49, no. 4 (2003): 30–49.
[74] John D. Y. Peel, *Aladura: A Religious Movement among the Yoruba* (London: Oxford University Press, 1968), 60–62.

drinking rainwater while praying could cure the disease, and she asked people to refrain from either Western or traditional medical treatment. Instead, she encouraged them to read chapter 24 of the biblical Book of Zachariah.[75] Moses Orimolade was another popular Nigerian figure during the pandemic. He carried out different healing crusades, and thousands turned to him for spiritual help. Orimolade spent long periods in prayer, invoking the supernatural.[76]

The colonial government's response to Nigeria's 1918 influenza pandemic was relatively slow. The pandemic caught the world unaware, and there was no consensus regarding effective treatment. Initial public health directives were issued by the colonial office in England. Other approaches were adopted later in the course of the outbreak. Government officials were complacent when faced with a Nigerian mortality rate that was higher than 5 percent. They believed that Nigeria was generally unhealthy, and they were unsurprised by the number of deaths from the disease.[77] This mentality deterred officials from taking responsibility for the high fatality rate in Nigeria. British officials allegedly shifted the blame for Nigerian deaths onto various causes. First, they stressed that local superstitions had been responsible for the spread of the pandemic, declaring that proper preventive measures had not been taken.[78] British administrators also blamed people living in the northeast part of Ghana (at that time, the Gold Coast), chastising residents who did not regularly wear clothes.[79] Increasingly desperate measures were taken, and ridiculous claims were issued to shift responsibility away from the British administration.[80]

After seeing that Western medicine was ineffective, British officials and the colony's head of medical services invited stakeholders to a meeting to discuss ways to address the outbreak. English and Nigerian doctors attended a meeting in London that included senior medical personnel and other British officials. This was arguably the first time that practitioners of traditional medicine had been given such relevance as discriminatory colonial policies did not favor their methods. Two African medical practitioners at the conference suggested

---

[75] Samson A. Fatokun, "'I Will Pour Out My Spirit upon All Flesh': The Origin, Growth and Development of the Precious Stone Church – The Pioneering African Indigenous Pentecostal Denomination in Southwest Nigeria," *Cyber Journal for Pentecostal-Charismatic Research* 19 (2010): 1–28.

[76] Allan Anderson, *African Reformation: African Initiated Christianity in the 20th Century* (New Jersey: Africa World Press, 2001), 82.

[77] Sandra M. Tomkins, "Colonial Administration in British Africa during the Influenza Epidemic of 1918-19," *Canadian Journal of African Studies* 28, no. 1 (1994): 60–83.

[78] Great Britain. Colonial Office. Colonial Annual Reports. Annual Report, Ashanti, 1918 (London, 1919) 19.

[79] David Killingray, "The Influenza Epidemic of 1918-1919 in the Gold Coast," *Journal of African History* 24, no. 4 (1983): 485–502.

[80] Matthew Heaton and Toyin Falola, "Global Explanations Versus Local Interpretations: The Historiography of the Influenza Pandemic of 1918-19 in Africa," *History in Africa* 33 (2006): 205–230.

some efforts to help end the disease and improve preventive measures. Three courses of action were proposed: infected ships should receive special attention to prevent the virus from spreading further; in cities like Lagos, which experienced high infection rates from the virus, the government should put measures in place to contain the illness; and when the whole of Nigeria was exposed to the virus, further contact should be reduced by monitoring the ships that were admitted from heavily affected areas.[81]

The government accepted these recommendations and circulated copies of the preventive measures, printed in English and local languages, across Lagos and the surrounding communities. The government also tried to reduce panic and protect food supplies from villages and cities that shipped produce to Lagos. Additional restrictions were placed on inbound ships, and their passengers: infected individuals were to undergo a proper quarantine procedure. Special efforts were made to communicate these changes to the entire country, and Christian missionaries were instrumental in relaying important information. Individuals who were quarantined or suspected of infection were cared for by the government.[82]

The colonial government carried out decontamination exercises, using Cyllin disinfectant and sulfur fumigation, in houses and on ships to reduce the spread of the virus. However, this process was truncated due to shortages of disinfectants and workers. The individuals expected to perform the decontamination process abandoned their duties when they discovered that many of their colleagues were infected, and some lost their lives. Other laborers who had contracted the flu went into hiding to avoid quarantine, which led to the further spread of the disease. When the British administration discovered that many households were hiding infected persons from the public, it conducted raids to force infected people into quarantine.[83]

After the relative success of these measures, the British administration enacted the Health Ordinance of 1917, legally recognizing the pandemic as infectious. Under the ordinance, British officials had the power to search apartments, by force if necessary, to discover infected individuals. Nigerians reacted by fleeing their urban residences and settling in outlying villages, carrying the disease to areas that had not previously been at risk. The government later formed additional teams to search other areas, criminalizing the avoidance of quarantine and imposing compulsory medications and health regulations.[84]

---

[81] Public Record Office (PRO), London (1919) CO879/118 Report of the Influenza Epidemic in Lagos. 25 April 1919.
[82] Oluwasegun, "Managing Epidemic." See also Public Record Office (PRO), London (1919) CO879/118 Report of the Influenza Epidemic in Lagos; April 25, 1919.
[83] The African Messenger, "The Influenza Epidemic of 1918," *The African Messenger*, March 9, 1922.
[84] David Arnold, ed., *Imperial Medicine and Indigenous Societies*, Vol. 6 (Manchester: Manchester University Press, 1988).

The influenza pandemic had a dreadful effect on the Nigerian population. Kano had the highest casualty rate in the North, with around 38,288 deaths across the state.[85] The British colonial government enacted lockdowns and restrictive measures in other parts of the country, but Kano received little attention. The disease spread through the city, and victims failed to receive adequate medical attention despite the city's rising death rates. The colonial government's lax attitude was paired with increased taxation. For instance, the emir of Kano collected £100,123 in taxes, which was higher than in previous years. This insensitivity was noticed by local residents, and they detested how the emir had mirrored the unfeeling practices of the colonial government.[86] Kano also faced the challenge of sporadic price increases. Farmers were too sick either to farm or to manage the burdens of sick or deceased family members. Shortages affected every sector of the economy, and some prices doubled or even tripled. The economy had already been thrown off balance by World War I, and necessities were no longer affordable. Nigeria's transportation system suffered from neglect during the war, which affected the transportation of cattle that would normally be brought to markets and sold to generate revenue. The concern of the colonial administration was its tax income, which actually expanded by 1920.[87]

Leprosy was another disease that posed a challenge to Nigeria's healthcare system.[88] It is an infectious illness that causes progressive attrition of the skin and damage to the nerves. Leprosy had been a social problem before the advent of colonialism, and infected individuals were often stigmatized due to the belief that their disease had a supernatural cause. Lepers were considered to be a disgrace to their families and the community and were frequently exiled. Leprosy was a major problem: around 200,000 infected individuals were counted during the 1938 British Empire Leprosy Relief examination.[89] Other sources asserted that almost one million individuals were affected by 1938. Many villages, cities, and settlements, especially in the Southern part of the country, saw infection rates ranging from 2 to 30 percent.[90]

The first systematic approach for treating leprosy was conducted by the British Empire Leprosy Relief Association (BELRA), inaugurated in 1924.[91]

---

[85] KSHCB/NAK/SNP/93. P./1918, Kano Province Annual Report, 1918.

[86] Adamu Mohammed Fika, *The Kano Civil War and British Over-rule, 1882–1940* (Oxford: Oxford University Press, 1978).

[87] Muhammad Wada, "The Spread and Impact of the Great Influenza Pandemic in Kano Emirate, Northern Nigeria 1918–1920," *Humanus Discourse* 1, no. 4 (2021): 1–15.

[88] Tunde Oduwobi, "Tackling Leprosy in Colonial Nigeria, 1926–1960," *Journal of the Historical Society of Nigeria* 22 (2013): 178–205.

[89] Oduwobi, "Tackling Leprosy in Colonial Nigeria."

[90] C. E. B. Russell, "The Leprosy Problem in Nigeria," *Journal of the Royal African Society* 37, no. 146 (1938): 66–71.

[91] John Manton, "Global and Local Contexts: The Northern Ogoja Leprosy Scheme, Nigeria, 1945–1960," *História Ciências Saúde-Manguinhos* 10, no. 1 (2003): 209–223.

Christian missionaries and local officials provided financial and logistical support for BELRA's medical research, transmitting medical information and news about local discoveries across the entire country.[92] This helped educate the population, providing them with more information about the disease and giving them basic information for preventing it. BELRA faced many challenges, which was why it had to rely on support from local authorities. Over time, the organization lost its relevance and effectiveness, becoming merely a ceremonial entity. After its creation and inauguration, the only meeting it held occurred in May 1936. The group consisted of officials that formed its Executive Committee, which comprised medical practitioners and the director of the medical and sanitary service department, along with non-officials that included some members of the legislative council, the secretary, and the Bank of West Africa's representatives.

The government enacted many different policies in its early attempts to combat and contain the spread of leprosy. The 1908 Lepers Ordinances for the Southern Protectorate provided asylum for infected people under the protection of the government.[93] The 1911 Lepers Proclamation, which was made for the Northern Protectorate, established that asylum in the North would be under the control of the Native Authorities.[94] These measures were unsuccessful since the centers in the North and the South were neglected, and the lepers were abandoned there.

After the 1914 amalgamation and later in 1916, the two leprosy ordinances were repealed. The 1916 Leprosy Ordinances applied to the entirety of Nigeria while retaining the provisions from previous enactments. The new law made local administrations responsible for the maintenance of asylums, placing general restrictions on lepers while attempting to avoid unfair segregation. Lepers were not allowed to conduct activities that might expose others and spread the disease, which was reflected in the restrictions. These measures isolated many lepers from society, but they were the only effective way to address the illness. Many individuals were suffering from advanced stages of the disease that could not be cured: out of 200,000 infected people, only around 6,000 were completely healed. Later efforts improved the opportunities for medical treatment that was available, replacing the leper colonies that only imposed isolation.[95]

In Eastern Nigeria, which reported many cases of infection, the numbers kept increasing.[96] No specific actions were taken by the government, which

---

[92] Oduwobi, "Tackling Leprosy in Colonial Nigeria."
[93] Oduwobi, "Tackling Leprosy in Colonial Nigeria."
[94] Oduwobi, "Tackling Leprosy in Colonial Nigeria."
[95] Ernest Muir, "Leprosy in Nigeria. A Report on Anti-leprosy Work in Nigeria with Suggestions for Its Development," *Leprosy Review* 7 (1936): 164–166.
[96] John Manton, "Leprosy in Eastern Nigeria and the Social History of Colonial Skin," *Leprosy Review* 82 (2011): 124–134.

was concerned only with taxes and economic development to benefit the government. Christian missionaries showed the utmost concern, providing measures to address leprosy in Eastern Nigeria.[97] The government ignored increasing rates of leprosy in the East until 1941 when it created the Nigeria Leprosy Service. The service took control of the Uzuakoli and Oji River Centers that had initially been administered and maintained by the Methodist and Anglican missionaries, respectively. The Itu Center was largely ignored, despite its significance for treating leprosy.

The Igbo were especially affected, and many of the leprosy centers were not properly funded or equipped. The Church of Scotland founded the Itu Leprosy center in 1926, and local authorities were the settlement's primary sponsors, providing food and other basic amenities. These authorities advocated increased funding, but their efforts were largely unsuccessful. Funding needs became more pressing for local authorities and District Officers as other diseases and financial demands arose.[98]

The Ogoja Leprosy Settlement was another significant institution during the colonial period. Ogoja was created by the RCM, and it served as one of the largest and most prominent leprosy settlements.[99] After reaching an agreement with the government, the Catholic mission initially decided to fund the Ogoja effort and it drew global support, especially from heavily Catholic regions. International organizations provided experts to treat affected individuals. The center began treating new cases and paid more attention to rural areas. Government intervention occurred after the foundation of the Nigeria Leprosy Service in 1945, which was created to address national concerns after World War II.[100]

The management of influenza and leprosy in Nigeria might have taken a different turn without the intervention of the colonial administration. The continuous influx of new officials meant a lack of historical context and varied decisions. The colonial government consistently prioritized economic interests, ignoring the developmental goals that had been part of Lugard's highly publicized dual mandate. The insensitivity of colonial officials was evident in the skyrocketing revenue drawn from the colony during outbreaks of these diseases. African medical practitioners had put forward effective ideas for fighting influenza that were largely ignored by the colonizers. If these methods had been considered in the context of public development and national

---

[97] Warwick Anderson, *Colonial Pathologies: American Tropical Medicine, Race and Hygiene in the Philippines* (Durham: Duke University Press, 2006).

[98] Nigerian National Archives, Enugu. OGPROF 2/1/1788. Leprosy Control in Ogoja Province.

[99] John Manton, "The Roman Catholic Mission and Leprosy Control in Colonial Ogoja Province, Nigeria, 1936–1960," unpublished PhD dissertation, University of Oxford, 2005.

[100] Manton, "Global and Local Contexts."

advancement – instead of being dismissed as ineffective fetishes – Nigeria's present-day medical facilities would have benefitted from ideas from various sources.

The Medical Profession and Education

Nigeria's medical education can be traced to precolonial medical practices. In traditional societies, healthcare practices and education were acquired over a long period of apprenticeship that encompassed all aspects of medical knowledge available at the time. In some instances, entire families were involved in the medical profession, training individuals from an early age to ensure that they had adequate knowledge. The advent of globalization brought new diseases, such as the influenza which became a pandemic in 1918. Due to these new afflictions, modern orthodox methods became more relevant while traditional approaches lost prestige.

The idea of training Nigerians with modern orthodox medical practices was conceived by CMS Reverend Henry Venn, and his plan was executed in 1862. The CMS resident doctor, O. Harrison, created the first medical school in Abeokuta. The institution's original curriculum taught anatomy, botany, chemistry, physiology, and other technical courses that became too advanced for many Nigerians. One of its earliest students was Nathaniel King, who later became the first Indigenous modern medical practitioner.[101]

After the colonial government was fully established, it decided to create a medical training center and established the Yaba Medical School in 1934. The goal was to provide a more concise professional medical education for its students. The initial scope of the school's curriculum was so limited that it could not train students to meet the standards that were obtainable in Europe.[102] There were more than seventy students in the inaugural class of Yaba Medical School, with fifty-seven studying pharmacy and thirteen studying medicine. Medical studies took five years, including two years of preclinical study and three years of clinical study. The school's limited curriculum encouraged graduates to complete their medical training in England.[103]

University College Ibadan was established in 1946, and it offered a more comprehensive medical studies curriculum. Its pioneering departments included medicine, surgery, anatomy, pathology, preventive and social medicine, physiology, obstetrics, and gynecology. The university was developed to meet British medical standards, which meant that students no longer needed to complete their studies in England. From this point onward, more medical schools were developed, and the number of local medical practitioners in Nigeria began to increase.[104]

---

[101] Adelola Adeloye, *African Pioneers of Modern Medicine: Nigerian Doctors of the Nineteenth Century* (Ibadan: University Press, 1985).
[102] Aliyu B. Fafunwa, *A History of Nigerian Higher Education* (London: Macmillan, 1971).
[103] Adeloye, *African Pioneers of Modern Medicine*.
[104] Eric Ashby, *African Universities and Western Tradition* (Cambridge: Harvard University Press, 1964).

Conclusion

What this chapter has done is make sense of the development of colonial healthcare and its corollary. As a norm, all societies developed some form of healthcare program to sustain the health and well-being of the people. At the root of these programs was the availability of medicine that helped to prevent and cure various ailments. As the chapter has explained, Nigeria witnessed four epochal periods of healthcare services and medicine that changed the trajectory and phase of medical practice throughout the country.

The contributions of Christian missionaries and, subsequently, the British colonial government to the development of healthcare in Nigeria cannot be overemphasized. Although the motives of both parties were different – and in some cases were self-serving and primarily designed to serve economic ends – medical facilities (notably hospitals and dispensaries) were slowly made available for Nigerians. Not only were Nigerians trained as health assistants and doctors when diseases affected Nigeria following the global influenza pandemic, these medical facilities and personnel were also put to great use to stem the tide. A few years after World War II, more formal healthcare services were provided, while the University College Hospital was built to strengthen knowledge production in medicine and healthcare.

18

Cultures

The totality of human beliefs, customs, and other habits and practices acquired through close interaction with and observation of other members of their society constitutes culture. To this extent, culture is a factor in the development of individuals, not only because it provides the necessary material around which the younger ones build their social behaviors and habits, but also because it gives individuals an in-group perspective against which they judge, view, and evaluate various phenomena.[1] Included in the definition offered by Sir Edward Tylor is the phrase "complex whole," which is contextually suggestive of material and immaterial aspects of a culture that contribute to people's understanding of life and its meaning.[2] It asserts that cultural traditions are exclusively internalized by those within the same geographic space, as they mutually normalize a particular behavior because they identify with it. Also, we must note that in relation to different definitions of cultural studies, culture, like humans, mutates. The mutation of human culture is informed by the need to adapt to the changing dynamics of human relationships.[3] We meet humans of diverse cultural traditions, and societies must absorb their ideas and adapt to shifting practices and dynamics.

Historically, it was not until 1914 that the British initiated the making of a Nigerian state by altering the "cultural boundaries" and immediately replacing them with an artificially manufactured country that began the production of a "new" cultural society.[4] By the arrangement of the British, the various cultural traditions and groups that occupied the expanse of the geographical landscape, which would later be known as Nigeria, were neighbors with various cultural

---

[1] David B. Kronenfeld, *Culture as a System: How We Know the Meaning and Significance of What We Do and Say* (London: Routledge, 2018).
[2] Edward Burnett Tylor, *Primitive Culture: Researches into the Development of Mythology, Philosophy, Religion, Art, and Custom*, Vol. 1 (London: John Murray, 1871).
[3] Daniele Goldoni, "Cultural Mutation: What Media Do to Culture," *Citizens of Europe* 3 (2015): 381–424.
[4] Lewis H. Gann and Peter Duignan, eds., *Colonialism in Africa, 1970–1960*, 5 vols. (London: Cambridge University Press, 1969).

backgrounds and varying historical foundations.[5] Interactions between them were managed by unwritten rules of engagement that respected their physical and cultural boundaries.[6] However, things began to change following the colonial conquest. The resulting artificial boundaries did not suddenly erase the numerous cultural traditions and identities that were hitherto present. Thereafter, as each group continued to promote its established cultural identity, such as the Tiv or Ijo, weak attempts were made to create a unified country. Religion, education, and formal economies began to produce some Nigeria-wide culture in the use of language and dress. As Peter Ekeh notes, many cultural identities in Nigeria are products of colonial invention.[7]

It was, and indeed still is, difficult for colonial experiences and structures to erase older cultures, notwithstanding the political efforts made toward the unity of the peoples of Nigeria. As such, this chapter considers cultural retention during the colonial era and those aspects of the culture that were retained or carried over into the colonial period. Moving forward, we shall also examine the cultural changes that were inspired by colonial rule – in other words, the transformations that followed in the first half of the twentieth century. We will also look into the new formations and the fusion of the Indigenous and Western cultures.

Cultural Retentions

More than 250 ethnic identities occupy Nigeria.[8] These cultures are numerous, and because of their plural nature, each of them practiced what was transmitted to them from one generation to another through the agency of orality and performance.[9] The influence of colonial rule was overwhelming,[10] although the changes in culture were not simply precipitated by the fact that the contact was new, as there had been other cultural contacts before 1885, one instance being that of Islam.[11] The colonial changes affected the economy more deeply, creating cities and infrastructures that had an impact on society.

---

[5] Akinwumi Ogundiran, *Precolonial Nigeria: Essays in Honor of Toyin Falola* (Trenton: Africa World Press, 2005); and Basil Davidson, *West Africa before the Colonial Era: A History to 1850* (London: Routledge, 1998).
[6] Olayemi Akinwunmi, Okpeh O. Okpeh, and Jerry D. Gwamna, eds., *Inter-Group Relations in Nigeria During the 19th and 20th Centuries* (Makurdi: Aboki Publishers, 2006).
[7] Peter Ekeh, "Colonialism and Social Structure," An Inaugural Lecture. Ibadan: Ibadan University Press, 1983.
[8] Jacob F. A. Ajayi and Ebiegberi Alagoa, "Nigeria before 1800: Aspects of Economic Development and Inter-group Relations," in *Groundwork of Nigerian History*, ed. Obaro Ikime (Ibadan: Heinemann Books, 1980), 224–335.
[9] Ruth Finnegan, *The Limba Stories and Storytelling* (Oxford: Oxford University Press, 1970).
[10] Walter Rodney, *How Europe Underdeveloped Africa* (London: Bogle–L'Ouverture Publications, 1972).
[11] Ivan Van Sertima, *They Came Before Columbus: The African Presence in Ancient America* (New York: Random House, 1977).

It is important to understand the motivations behind certain cultural practices so that the reason(s) for preserving them are effectively communicated. Dance, for example, is generally understood to show an expression of happiness and sometimes fulfilment.[12] Its style and performance can be preserved in line with the motives of the performer. This suggests that the creation of dance corresponds with a joyous experience that has happened in one way or the other to an individual or a group. Through the activity of dance, humans express their inner feelings and emotions. However, beyond the expression of emotional conditions there are the general cultural celebrations, like festivals, traditional rites, wedding ceremonies, and even the celebration of life. For instance, the *Nkwa-Umu-Agbogho* dance of the Afikpo people of Ebonyi State is a centuries-old dance[13] that celebrates life cycles.[14] Such a traditional dance is practiced among the Igbo to honor the maidens of society who conform to cultural regulations.[15] In addition to celebrating these young women, the community has the opportunity to come together for the socialization of the younger ones through their bonding with relatives in an extended setting. In other words, it was and continues to be one of the avenues used by the people to unite themselves as a group of individuals.[16]

The *Nkwa-Umu-Agbogho* dance serves more than an entertainment function. As some practices, including dance, serve socialization purposes, this particular dance conveys the spiritual essence of the people. The interconnection of this dance with spirituality is derived from its tribute to the deceased. Apart from the above, the tradition is also a means to root out immoral sexual indulgence, especially for those who are considered underage or young.[17] Maidens in society are educated about their roles in the observation of this cultural rite as a necessary precondition for inter/intra-communal relations. This awareness of immoral sexual indulgence teaches young women acceptable social conduct and educates young males about the grave consequences of gender-based violence against women. Married women actively engage in the dance, playing a role in its composure, performance, and delivery. As such, this dance serves important purposes beyond mere entertainment.

---

[12] Roger Copeland and Marshall Cohen, eds., *What is Dance?: Readings in Theory and Criticism* (Oxford: Oxford University Press, 1983).
[13] Salome Nnoromele, *Life among the Ibo Women of Nigeria* (San Diego: Lucent Books, 1967).
[14] Kariamu Welsh–Asante, *Zimbabwe Dance: Rhythmic Forces, Ancestral Voices: An Aesthetic Analysis* (Trenton: Africa World Press, 2000), 17–38.
[15] Glory N. Nnam and Nnamdi C. Onuora–Oguno, "Elele O: An Age Long Nkwa Umuagbogho Dance of Idaw River Girls' Secondary School, Enugu," *Journal of Nigerian Music Education* 10 (2018): 134–135.
[16] Nnoromele, *Life among the Ibo Women*.
[17] Uji Charles and Awuawuer Tijime Justin, "Towards the Theories and Practice of the Dance Art," *International Journal of Humanities and Social Science* 4, no. 4 (2014): 254.

Swange music is another important form of heritage that enjoyed patronage up to colonial times. It belongs to the Tiv people, and holds cultural and political significance in their collective memory.[18] Different oral histories establish that the emergence of this music dates back to a time when songs were used for various purposes, such as entertainment, enjoyment, leisure, and education.[19] Incidentally, this music developed from the understanding that issues of social and cultural importance can be addressed and managed by rendition in song.[20] In essence, *Swange*, apart from it being a source of entertainment, was used to speak of social anomalies. It should be noted that many societies employ artistic creations to correct behaviors and engagements that are deemed morally questionable.[21] While *Swange* is deployed to shape people's social and moral behavior, especially within the Benue people of the current Niger, the songs were retained in the colonial era to serve the same purpose.

Kwagh-alom or *Kikya* are the two basic elements of *Swange*, and it is from them that the genre draws its moral trajectory, which has remained well known over time. The cultural significance of the songs has resulted in varying renditions by artists.[22] The *Swange* song is rendered for various purposes, but most importantly to embarrass or ridicule the enemy faction. *Swange* is also used to challenge individuals who have lowered their moral standards or allowed themselves to be overridden by personal greed. This means that the song seeks to expose the entrenched deficiency noticeable among some groups and has evolved carefully into something more suitable to the moral sense of the people collectively. *Swange* musicians, for example, use the song to correct the growing anomaly, moral deficiency, and heartrending value deficit that has become the order of the day.

The continued employment of music during the colonial era meant that it was strongly built into the societal system of, for instance, the Tiv people. For this reason, from being an instrument of moral correction, *Swange* music became a political tool in abuse of positions in public office for personal gain.[23] This, once again, reinforces the argument that the construction of

---

[18] Awuawuer T. Justin, "Understanding Swange Dance of the Tiv People of Central Nigeria within the Perspective of Socio-political Changes," *International Journal of Political Science and Governance* 3, no. 1 (2021): 17–23.

[19] Tim Cuttings, *The Swange Music and Dance* (Abuja: TimeXperts Publishing, 2013).

[20] Jude Terna Kur and Nicholas Sesugh Iwokwagh, "The Information Value of Traditional Tiv Music and Dance in the Age of Modern Communication Technologies," *Asian Journal of Information Technology* 10, no. 3 (2011): 101–107.

[21] Saint Gbilekaa, "Tiv Popular Music and Dance: Myth and Reality," in *The Tiv in Contemporary Nigeria*, ed. Terdoo Ahire (Zaria: Tiv Studies Project Publication, 1993), 42–48.

[22] Richard A. Tsevende, Tim C. Agber, Don S. Iorngurun, and Nancy N. Ugbagir, *Tiv Swange Music and Dance* (Abuja: TimeXperts Publishing, 2013).

[23] Justin, "Understanding Swange Dance."

a morally acceptable society in precolonial and colonial times was partly ceded to entertainers because of their social acceptability. Although the song embodied the form of ridiculing the alleged morally delinquent behavior, it challenged the accused to see why their actions were bad.[24] For example, an unskilled farmer who did not understand the ecological importance of certain plants might fail to achieve success in his agricultural engagements and could, as a result, blame someone else for his constant misfortune. A song would confront him about this, reminding him that one's success in farming is largely dependent on the ability to understand changes in ecology, soil type, the functions or significance of each plant, and the overall land conditions.

To use another example, various forms of entertainment are entrenched in the rich traditions of the Edo of Benin.[25] What is most significant about the Benin people is their art.[26] Historically, they have been identified as prominent sculptors whose creations are globally revered. Their artworks serve spiritual, social, and political purposes. To the Europeans, these artworks were initially understood as purely for entertainment or leisure purposes. Their perception, shaped by their cultural understanding of creativity, perceived that works of art were meant to fulfil an aesthetic function. However, these works, while serving an entertainment purpose as they appeal to a sense of beauty, also serve different religious purposes.[27] Given the fact that many of these sculptors, for example, lived within the king's palace, it can be understood that these artists were highly revered and regarded. The colonial conquest invaded the cultural space, but the ideas associated with artworks were retained during the colonial period.[28]

In the Benin tradition, the king is considered a linkage between the living and the dead, and his regal position was revered and celebrated by his people. In the Benin kingdom, there were many social roles associated with the king.[29] Among other things, the king was the historian and the custodian of values that have been preserved over the years. Because of this reality, he inadvertently filled the positions of teacher, policymaker, political representative, and,

---

[24] Jude Terna Kur and Nicholas Sesugh Iwokwagh, "The Information Value of Traditional Tiv Music and Dance in the Age of Modern Communication Technologies," *Asian Journal of Information Technology* 10, no. 3 (2011): 101–107.

[25] Damien Ukwandu and Benjamin Obeghare Izu, "The Ugie Festival Ceremonies as a Demonstration of Ancient Benin Culture in Nigeria," *Archiv Orientální* 84, no. 2 (2021): 249–267.

[26] Paula Ben-Amos, *Art, Innovation, and Politics in Eighteenth-Century Benin* (Indiana: Indiana University Press, 1999).

[27] Kathleen Bickford Berzock, *Benin: Royal Arts of a West African Kingdom* (Illinois: Art Institute of Chicago, 2008).

[28] Barnaby Phillips, *Loot: Britain and the Benin Bronzes* (London: Oneworld Publications, 2021).

[29] Michael Crowder and Obaro Ikime, eds., *West African Chiefs: Their Changing Status under Colonial Rule and Independence* (Ile-Ife: University of Ife Press, 1970).

equally, the one to influence the cultural direction of the people.[30] As a result of his importance, the people assigned themselves the responsibility of overseeing the king's welfare, which explains why some individuals were prepared to voluntarily dedicate their time and resources to the defense of their culture. It is undeniable that art fulfilled aesthetic functions, though it also carried important social and cultural meanings. For instance, Benin royal art, which includes brass, ivory, and coral, was culturally believed to possess sacred power to the extent that such objects could instigate an exchange between the king and the supernatural.[31] Due to the certainty that it was instrumental to their spiritual growth, the Edo attached spiritual and social values to art.

These monumental artifacts were retained because of the understanding that they continued to preserve the people's culture and philosophy. Among other reasons, the artworks were used as a means to relate to and with the greatness of the past, and the events of the past were interpreted to give fillip to the traditions of the people.[32] Because they had been educated about the methods of recreation and use from a tender age, the kings employed these artworks during the colonial period. The British attack on Benin in 1897 involved the looting of artworks.[33] Thus, Benin's artworks are now part of the understanding of cultural encounters. Quite a few African historical pieces have also been excavated by archaeologists, including some of Benin,[34] thus enabling us to write about aspects of Nigerian history.

Another Nigerian tradition that was retained with minor external influence was the Yoruba *Egungun*. Although the closest interpretation in the English language of this cultural phenomenon is "masquerading," its significance spans beyond such a basic meaning. Specifically, *Egungun* serves as a form of spiritual bonding and protection among the Yoruba.[35] They are also the symbol of warring expeditions, as they are consulted and invoked as part of wars, as in the case of Oyo. Back in the day, political leaders in the Yoruba society were checkmated by some *Egungun* cults. This is because they were understood to be spiritual designates of the ancestors who exercised no fear to confront anyone disrupting the affairs of the community, regardless of their

---

[30] Amie Jane Leavitt, *Discovering the Kingdom of Benin* (New York: Rosen Publishing, 2014), 16-21.

[31] Daniel Irabor, "The Art of the Benin People," *Journal of Advances in Social Science and Humanities* 5, no. 8 (2019): 949-974.

[32] Eckart Von Sydow, "Ancient and Modern Art in Benin City," *Africa: Journal of the International African Institute* 11, no. 1 (1938): 55-62.

[33] Philip A. Igbafe, "The Fall of Benin: A Reassessment," *The Journal of African History* 11, no. 3 (1970): 385-400.

[34] Crowder and Ikime, eds., *West African Chiefs*.

[35] Cristina Boscolo, *Odún: Discourses, Strategies, and Power in the Yorùbá Play of Transformation* (Leiden: Brill, 2009), 191-265.

social status.[36] Colorful costumes were identified with the *Egungun* to depict the value of the Yoruba cloth or dress, which emphasized beauty, wealth, and knowledge.[37]

Acrobatic displays, colorful effervescence, and majestic steps were aspects of the performances the *Egungun* were associated with.[38] They found their relevance as celestial beings that had the supernatural ability to view human engagement and, therefore, intervened when invoked. They were culturally considered supernatural beings with attributes incomparable to those of humans. And, because of this spiritual mandate, they were often referred to as "members of the celestial order."[39] The spectacles engrained in these *Egungun* performances were spiritually aligned to their ancestral characteristics, so much so that a designate of *Egungun* in the twenty-first century was required to act in accordance with establish historical practices. One of the reasons they retained their legitimacy as cultural traditions of the people was because of the awareness that they evoked a spirit of nostalgia and reawakened dormant memories.[40] *Egungun* contributed to social cohesion among the Yoruba by bringing people together and promoting peace.[41]

Eku (the costume of the *Egungun*) serves many purposes, ranging from serving as a repository of artistic beauty to offering spiritual protection against unforeseen challenges.[42] Although the choices of color could sometimes be influenced by the social trends of a particular time, it remained unchanged over time in the celebration of the *Egungun* festival. *Egungun* practices are associated with different age groups, associations, and professions in the Yoruba society.[43] An *Egungun* group specifically represents female members, suggestive of the knowledge of gender equality and investment from the group's ancestral beginning. Popularly called *Gelede*, this *Egungun* advocates

---

[36] Oluwole Famule, "Masks, Masque, and Masquerades," in *Culture and Customs of the Yorùbá*, ed. Toyin Falola and Akintunde Akinyemi (Austin: Pan African University Press, 2017).

[37] Segun Omosule, "Artistic Undercurrents of Performance: A Study of Egungun Costumes in Ode Irele," *California Linguistic Notes* XXXIV, no. 2 (2009): 1–20.

[38] Cornelius Adepegba, *Yoruba Egungun: Its Association with Ancestors and the Typology of Yoruba Masquerades by Its Costume* (Ibadan: Ibadan University Press, 1984).

[39] Oludamola Adebowale, "Significance of Egungun in Yoruba Cultural History," *Guardian*, February 9, 2020.

[40] P. S. O. Aremu, Biodun Banjo, and Yaya Olanipekun, "Egungun Tradition in Trado-Modern Society in South-Western Nigeria," *Mediterranean Journal of Social Sciences* 3, no. 1 (2012): 283.

[41] Kacke Götrick, *Apidan Theatre and Modern Drama: A Study in a Traditional Yoruba Theatre and its Influence on Modern Drama by Yoruba Playwrights* (Stockholm: Almqvist & Wiksell International, 1984), 38.

[42] Bolaji Campbell, "Eegun Ogun: War Masquerades in Ibadan in the Era of Modernization," *African Arts* 48, no. 1 (2015): 47–48.

[43] Olabisi Adekanla, *Imesi-Ile: The Ancient Kiriji Camp* (Ibadan: Peetee Nigeria Limited, 1999), 37.

for females' rights, as it stands in solidarity with demands for equality.[44] *Egungun* practiced in colonial Nigeria indicated some conscious efforts from custodians to preserve their cultural traditions. This has been done to the extent that many of these cultures were, and continue to be, inserted into some Western-induced spaces to ensure their survival.

The Hausa are a group that has continued to evolve with the world.[45] They accepted Islam and became part of an Islamic culture that was able to withstand the colonial penetration of their land. Part of the legacy of these people during colonial times was their music and songs. Like many other cultures in the country, dances, songs, and other entertainment engagements were embedded in the Hausa culture and have survived over the years.[46] Their songs were organized to include the participation of community members.[47] Marketplaces, religious gatherings, and festivals were among the places where members engaged in their songs and dances. Their musicians were considered as the memory-keepers of society, so when they sang in public, they did so in such a way that they reminded the people of their historical beginnings and the impressive accomplishments of their ancestors.[48] During the colonial period, Hausa engagements reverberated with cultural heritages. Their connection to the past was seen as a way of surviving the changing environment wherein their identity was threatened by numerous sources, like the Europeans and, sometimes, the Fulani expansionists who came to their region for economic and political reasons.

Colonial Changes and Cultural Transformations

The foregoing exploration of Nigerian cultures, even though covering only limited examples, represents an attempt to correct some errors. The data shows the existence of vibrant, established cultural practices. To say that "Africa's lack of history – and, thus, of civilization – explained why it needed European rule"[49] is fallacious. To insist, as some did when colonial rule began, that Nigeria – or Africa – does not have a history that validates their civilizations is to inadvertently conclude that the people were primitive and devoid of

---

[44] Babatunde Lawal, *The Gèlèdé Spectacle: Art, Gender, and Social Harmony in an African Culture* (Seattle: University of Washington Press, 1996).

[45] Frank A. Salamone, *The Hausa of Nigeria* (Lanham: University Press of America, 2010).

[46] David W. Ames and Anthony V. King, *Glossary of Hausa Music and its Social Contexts* (Evanston: Northwestern University Press, 1971).

[47] David W. Ames, "Sociocultural View of Hausa Musical Activity," in *The Traditional Artist in African Society*, ed. Warren d'Azevedo (Bloomington: Indiana University Press, 1973), 128–161.

[48] Sviatoslav Podstavsky, "Hausa Entertainers and their Social Status: A Reconsideration of Sociohistorical Evidence," *Ethnomusicology* 48, no. 3 (2004): 348–377.

[49] Philip S. Zachernuk, "African History and Imperial Culture in Colonial Nigerian Schools," *Journal of the International African Institute* 68, no. 4 (1998): 484–505.

reasonable thinking, as has been done very particularly, and parochially so, by Eurocentric scholars.[50] The aforementioned examination of Nigerian precolonial cultures that were retained during colonial time underpins the discussion that the cultures of the people were not only well-established but also diverse.[51] The people continued to transport and transform their cultural legacies in sync with contemporary realities.

In addition to artistic expressions of culture, colonialism impacted the daily activities of individuals, including their languages.[52] The linguistic repertoire of the people was forced to undergo modification because of the introduction of English.[53] While no major Nigerian language has become extinct, the use of English has spread. It is against this background that the numerous changes that happened to Nigerian cultures due to embracing new changes are considered.

The Western education system spread new ideas and cultural resources.[54] This is obvious because not only were the first set of Western-educated Nigerians specifically trained for menial positions, they were also earmarked for new roles such as interpreters[55] and clerical officers.[56] However, the increased enrollment of the Nigerian people meant that they would become the new elite at the cost of some of their cultural traditions. Literacy was needed to manage the new political system under colonialism.[57] Even when the existing traditional government was operating on constitutional monarchical systems, the inclusion of indigenes who acquired a formal education in the political institutions affirmed the acceptance of changes that graced the Nigerian political landscape. Simultaneously, in identifying those who acquired Western education, the Indigenous people began to attribute importance, significance, and increased value to the educated people in ways that would eventually determine their cultural traditions and trajectories. This was exemplified in the promotion of the English language, and the resultant

[50] Hugh Trevor-Roper, "The Rise of Christian in Europe," *The Listener* 70, no. 1809 (1963): 871. Also, Hugh Trevor-Roper, "The Past and Present: History and Sociology," *Past and Present*, no. 42 (1969): 6.
[51] Ilesanmi Akanmidu Paul, "The Survival of the Yorùbá Healing Systems in the Modern Age," *Yorùbá Studies Review* 2, no. 2 (2018): 1–21.
[52] Michael Omolewa, "The English Language in Colonial Nigeria, 1862–1960: A Study of the Major Factors Which Promoted the English Language," *Journal of Nigeria English Studies Association* 7, nos. 1&2 (1975): 103–117.
[53] Marystella C. Okolo-Nwakaeme, "Reassessing the Impact of Colonial Languages on the African Identity for African Development," *Africa Media Review* 13, no. 2 (2005): 85–103.
[54] Andrew E. Barnes, "Western Education in Colonial Africa," in *Africa: Colonial Africa, 1885–1939*, Vol. 3, ed. Toyin Falola (Durham: Carolina Academic Press, 2002), 139–156.
[55] Selwyn R. Cudjoe, "Some Reminiscences of a Senior Interpreter," *The Nigerian Field* XVIII, no. 4 (1953): 148–164.
[56] Jonathan Derrick, "The 'Native Clerk' in Colonial West Africa," *African Affairs* 82, no. 326 (1983): 61–74.
[57] Agneta Pallinder-Law, "Aborted Modernization in West Africa? The Case of Abeokuta," *The Journal of African History* 15, no. 1 (1974): 65–82.

reconfiguration of the people's traditional culture. This was possible even though the percentage of newly educated Nigerians was comparatively low. Consequently, political power was directed to this smaller group, who would eventually use that power to influence the direction of cultural change of the people.[58]

Western education presented another significant change to Nigerian culture under colonialism. The system introduced people to another mode of learning. Within the European context, the organization of education into a formal system was creditable because this form of education was organized via the activities of learners who were tutored and observed. Specific time was allocated to the pursuance of a diploma, after which the learners received a certificate of participation in academic engagement. Through this, individuals developed their theoretical knowledge to the extent that they became integral to the process of developing theories for the development of their society.[59] This, in turn, provided them with the opportunity to improve their economic conditions because climbing the social ladder, the reality of the period, was dictated by those who had academic experiences.

Meanwhile, the Indigenous educational systems available among Nigerians varied considerably. Precolonial cultures, for example, among the Yoruba, had nonformal educational systems to organize themselves, and which evolved in accordance with the dictates of their environment.[60] Yoruba people had a system that allowed learners to acquire education directly from their households and occupations.[61] These educational structures helped to make sculptors who would be celebrated globally, farmers who would be recognized for their farm products, and experts in other fields.

The educational systems were different but complementary. One could learn skills at home and theoretical knowledge in school.[62] There is no doubt that notable changes in infrastructural development, economic exchanges, and new knowledge were inspired by the Western education system. It is important to acknowledge that when people embrace a different language, they also adopt different ideas associated with the language, meaning that an oscillation of human cultures occurs between and among civilizations the very moment

---

[58] Magnus O. Bassey, "Higher Education and the Rise of Early Political Elites in Africa," *Review of Higher Education in Africa* 1, no. 1 (2009): 30–38.

[59] Eric Roberts J. Hussey, "Educational Policy and Political Development in Africa," *African Affairs* 45, no. 179 (1946): 72–80.

[60] Akinwale R. Ayanleke, "Yoruba Traditional Education System: A Veritable Tool for Salvaging the Crisis Laden Education System in Nigeria," *Academic Journal of Interdisciplinary Studies* 2, no. 6 (2013): 141–145.

[61] Mutiat T. Oladejo, "Empowerment of Women and Sustainable Development in the 20th Century: The Yoruba Women Example," in *Capacity Building for Sustainable Development*, ed. Valentine Udoh James (Oxfordshire: CABI, 2018), 84.

[62] Getahun Yacob Abraham, "A Post-Colonial Perspective on African Education Systems," *African Journal of Education and Practice* 6, no. 3 (2020): 47 and 51.

their languages are exchanged. For Nigerians, the attraction of the Western education system did inspire various changes; one's proficiency in the English language predisposed them to the language first as an instrument of communication and then as an agent of cultural osmosis. Many Nigerians who were educated through the British education system became influenced by Western culture because language has a way of imposing its cultural traditions on people without them always being aware of this.[63]

The influence of Western culture permeated Nigeria for several reasons. For instance, those who were exposed to British education began to take a few things from European cultures.[64] As cultural changes and modifications can also be unconscious yet steady and active, the newly educated Nigerians started creating new social institutions. It is historically difficult to pinpoint when Nigerian people became conscious of interchanging their cultural traditions with those of the British. The intermixing of these cultures set the stage for the primacy and subsequent adoption of the English dress culture, which became more popular during the tail end of colonial rule in Nigeria.[65] The establishment of Yaba College in 1947 and the creation of the University of Ibadan in 1948 contributed to the continuously accelerating transformation of Nigerian cultures.[66]

The Nigerian music industry and musical culture also experienced a change with the advent of colonization. Music held an important position within many Nigerian cultures, as Indigenous music was an instrument of entertainment and recreation. Specifically, the Northern part of the country held a vocal tradition and specialized in *goje* music, which was sung on a one-stringed percussion instrument.[67] This musical tradition survived by adapting to the new situations engendered by the colonial era.

Another instance is that of the Igbo cultural group, with its wide-ranging folk instruments such as slit drums, flutes, lyres, and others which are still used in Igbo society.[68] As such, the people's ability to use music to coordinate

---

[63] Siyan Oyeweso, "Colonial Education, Identity Construction, and Formation of Elites in Nigeria." Paper Presented at the Conference on Indigenous Epistemology, Strengthening Research and Decolonization of Education in Nigeria held at the University of Ibadan, Nigeria, February 11–14, 2020.

[64] Jacob F. A. Ajayi, *Christian Missions in Nigeria, 1841–1891: The Making of a New Elite* (London: Longman, 1965).

[65] Sarbani Sen Vengadasalam, *New Postcolonial Dialectics: An Intercultural Comparison of Indian and Nigerian English Plays* (Newcastle upon Tyne: Cambridge Scholars Publisher, 2019), 100.

[66] Tim Livsey, *Nigeria's University Age: Reframing Decolonisation and Development* (London: Palgrave Macmillan, 2017).

[67] Jacqueline Cogdell DjeDje, *Fiddling in West Africa: Touching the Spirit in Fulbe, Hausa, and Dagbamba Cultures* (Bloomington: Indiana University Press, 2008).

[68] Justin N. Lo-Bamijoko, "Classification of Igbo Musical Instruments," *African Music* 6, no. 4 (1980): 19–41.

communal affairs, and make entertainment possible highlights why it was part of their culture for a long time. The slit drums, traditionally called *ufie*, for example, were used for various social engagements such as the praise of leaders[69] and the arrival and departure of socially important figures on special occasions. There were different genres of music to signify different events, and there were even songs meant for the elite class when they carry out social actions beneficial to society. All these older instruments and songs were reworked for new uses and in new compositions.[70]

Nevertheless, contact with the European world encouraged the introduction of several styles and types of Western music in the country. Slowly but surely, concert music began to evolve in Nigeria. The development of new Nigerian musical productions became more noticeable.[71] Areas closer to the coast and centers of power were faster in creating new styles. This explains why the evolution of modern Nigerian music occurred more rapidly in Lagos[72] and Abeokuta because they were relatively close to the British colonial government. Whereas the changes in the cultural outlook of a number of these ethnic groups were facilitated by the emergence of colonialism, the fact that they immersed themselves in the colonialist cultural systems continued to influence their contemporary cultural thinking.

New Formations

When different cultural forms and perspectives were joined by the experiences of colonialism, new forms developed as a result of cross-cultural integration. Colonialism, as a determining factor in cultural change, found expression in various ways.[73] Nigerian cultures underwent a series of changes as they drew from new ways of doing things.[74] In essence, while talking about new formations, the changes and conditions of these Indigenous cultures inspired by the reality of colonization are considered. Nigerians were constantly confronted with temptations to "improve" their cultural traditions to accommodate the changes that colonization inspired. All modifications to Indigenous cultures

---

[69] Stella N. Nwobu, "The Functions and Spiritual Connotations of Traditional Music Performance with Particular Reference to Ufie Music in Igboland," *AFRREV IJAH* 2, no. 3 (2013): 210–227.
[70] Iyabode Deborah Akande, "On the Content and Form of Ìwúde Songs in Òkè–Igbó," *International Journal of Humanities and Social Science* 7, no. 1 (2017): 192–199.
[71] Bode Omojola, *Nigerian Art Music: With an Introduction Study of Ghanaian Art Music* (Bayreuth: Bayreuth African Studies, 1995).
[72] Leonard Lynn, "The Growth of Entertainment of Non–African Origin in Lagos," MA thesis, University of Ibadan, 1967.
[73] Bernd Hamm and Russell Charles Smandych, *Cultural Imperialism: Essays on the Political Economy of Cultural Domination* (Peterborough: Broadview Press, 2005).
[74] Ademola Dasylva, "'Culture Education' and the Challenge of Globalization in Modern Nigeria," *Oral Tradition* 21, no. 2 (2006): 325–341.

were based on the desire for access to power and control and to be adaptive and more creative. The connectivity of power and change in the cultural outlook may not be readily apparent at the surface level, but when considered more deeply one understands the relationship between them. For example, the adoption of an English name by colonized Nigerians suggested to them a connection to the imperial culture which, even if it did not provide a political slot for them in the corridors of power, conferred on them the social respect and regard associated with people in power.[75] It makes sense, therefore, that being connected to power and ascribing superiority to the British contributed largely to the evolution of the people's culture.

These power dynamics seeped into every practice. For example, mode of dress among Nigerians became a statement and declaration of status.[76] For a person who wore *agbada* (a paired three-piece set), the shift to wearing Western-style suits is something one cannot overlook when discussing cultural evolution. Some people have associated the adoption of European cloth with a loss of identity because of the gradual loss of the people's interests in their Indigenous attire. The fact remains, however, that changes like this were inevitable when traditional culture came into contact with westernization, especially in terms of a master–subordinate relationship. This would eventually become integral to Nigerian cultures, as the adoption of European cloth patterns cannot be dissociated from the reality of colonization. With the implementation of colonial systems and ideologies, the behaviors and mannerisms of the Indigenous people shifted, and their economic interactions experienced changes. The idea of purchasing specific styles of clothes for events, occasions, statuses, and professions generated new economic trends and cultural perceptions that influenced modern Nigerian cultures.

Gradually, the awareness that society was now delineated into formal and informal sectors started to condition people to develop dress styles for specific occasions. From there, even traditional wear acquired touches of European style, and many became emboldened to blur the cultural lines that delineated gender-based fashion identities. Predictably, the association of European dresses with specific organizations inspired people to dress in a way that would signal the relationship between the British and their social and economic systems.

Beyond the modification of the clothing culture was their adaptation of European names resulting from their colonial relationship with the British. In contemporary Nigeria, it is rare to come across individuals whose first names can be used to trace their cultural heritage. The name Samuel, for instance,

---

[75] Ihechukwu Madubuike, "Decolonization of African Names," *Présence Africaine* 98, no. 1 (1976): 42–43.

[76] Lou Taylor, *Establishing Dress History* (Manchester: Manchester University Press, 2004), 295.

does not reveal the cultural origins of the bearer. Historically, many older Nigerian cultures practiced an anthropomorphic naming culture, which enabled them to name their children based on historical antecedence, routine observations, or religious beliefs,[77] to the extent that one's first name could be used by members of the same culture to locate the history, contributions, and specialization of one's family.

Indigenous names had a form that could not be totally casually altered;[78] however, the introduction of Christianity and Islam affected this.[79] The changes began with the excision of traditional identity markers, to be replaced with European and Christian ones.[80] For example, the Yoruba names that are associated with *Ifa* or their other deities were demonized. In later years, some Pentecostal churches stigmatized older names such as *Ifa*funke and *Osu*nbunmi and changed them to *Jesu*funke and *Jesu*bunmi, respectively. For those who accepted Islamic religion and culture, there was the Arabization of their names:[81] Abdulazeez, Mohammed, Bello, Muhammed, Ibrahim, and Dhikirulah, among others, became very popular. The fact remains that the people wanted to be linked to a higher social status, and, from all indications, the conferment of an English name in colonial Nigeria was considered effective in the negotiation of power in their different societies.[82]

The British naming system has become an integral part of modern Nigerian culture. Many people are found with one or more European names attached to them, whether by their parents or by their own choice.[83] Fred, Diva, Linda, and Raymond are some common names that Nigerians answer to in contemporary times. There were times when the people argued against the use of European names, particularly when they became aware of the reasons why such names were adopted. During the nationalist struggles in Nigeria, many educated people decided to revolt against the system that repressed their Indigenous identity, and they started movements to embrace their local languages in preference to those that stemmed from British culture.[84] This was when notable Nigerian scholars such as Chinua Achebe (Albert) dropped their foreign names

---

[77] Benson O. Igboin, "Names and the Reality of Life: An Inquiry into inherent Power in Names among the Owan of Nigeria," *Ado Journal of Religions* 2, no. 1 (2004): 9–26.

[78] W. Olajide, "Existentialising Names and their Significance among the Yorùbá," *Ọpánbàtà: LASU Journal of African Studies* 6 (2012): 56–75.

[79] Reuben Olúwáfẹ́mi Ìkọ̀tún, "New Trends in Yorùbá Personal Names among Yorùbá Christians," *Linguistik Online* 59 (2013): 65–83.

[80] Ìkọ̀tún, "New Trends in Yorùbá Personal Names."

[81] Ahamad Ogunbado, "Islam and Its Impacts in Yorubaland," *Islamic Quarterly* 57, no. 1 (2003).

[82] Justina Cheang, "Choice of Foreign Names as a Strategy for Identity Management," *Intercultural Communication Studies* 17, no. 2 (2008): 197–202.

[83] Eyo O. Mensah, Idom T. Inyabri, and Benjamin O. Nyong, "Names, Naming and the Code of Cultural Denial in a Contemporary Nigerian Society: An Afrocentric Perspective," *Journal of Black Studies* 52, no. 3 (2020): 248–276.

[84] Kwame Nkrumah, *Towards Colonial Freedom* (London: Panaf Books, 1962).

in favor of their Indigenous names. Similarly, Obafemi Awolowo, a nationalist politician, exorcized the British name he was given, Jeremiah, to foreground his Indigenous identity. Irrespective of this, however, the fact that new names constitute new cultural formations in Nigeria after their experience with colonialism cannot be overemphasized.

It is helpful to note that the transformations in Nigerian cultures in the highlighted areas should be accompanied by a discussion of the entertainment industry. Especially in music, from the traditional folk songs to the creation of the musical styles named *Juju*, hip-hop, and highlife, among many others, the meeting of the colonial and the Indigenous cultures in Nigeria has produced robust hybrids. Because the economic and political center of colonialism was Lagos, the spread of these brands of music in the region was not apparent in the minds of the people, yet not a complete wonder to the locals. The new forms of music created were determined by several factors, chief of which was the religious leaning of the people. For those who are Christian, the development of *Juju* is easily traceable because it supports music and song genres that were rendered in the church,[85] while *Apala*, another brand of music, tended toward the Islamic culture.[86] Regardless of these characteristics, these new forms of music were drawn from their Indigenous backgrounds, and their inspiration, motivation, and style were encouraged through their local music.

For example, the proliferation of *Juju* music began from a generation who, during their leisure time, were influenced by the artistry and mechanics of palm-wine music.[87] *Juju* became a well-developed musical genre and remained popular for a very long time. Cuban and American styles were blended with the *Juju* vocal tradition to make *Juju* music more interesting and widely acceptable. Unlike traditional music accompanied by slit drum instruments, gongs, and other Indigenous equipment, *Juju* was played with guitar, stringed instruments, banjos, shakers, and drums, all of which were used to enhance musical performances. The tag "*Juju* music" emerged in the 1920s, and its creation has been credited to Babatunde King, who reportedly constructed the name from the onomatopoeic relationship with the sound produced by the Brazilian tambourine.[88] *Juju* artistes emerged from the growing Nigerian social network to display their accomplished music performances. Talents such as Tunde Nightingale, Speedy Araba, and Ojoge Daniel became pioneers in the musical style.[89]

---

[85] John D. Y. Peel, *Christianity, Islam, and Orisa-Religion: Three Traditions in Comparison and Interaction* (Oakland: University of California Press, 2016), 151.

[86] Abdul-Rasheed Na'Allah, *African Discourse in Islam, Oral Traditions, and Performance* (New York: Routledge, 2010), 160.

[87] Christopher Alan Waterman, *Juju: A Social History and Ethnography of an African Popular* (Chicago: University of Chicago Press, 1990).

[88] Benson Idonije, "Salute to Tunde King, Pioneer of Juju Music," *Guardian*, April 2, 2008.

[89] Afolabi Alaja-Browne, "The Origin and Development of JuJu Music," *The Black Perspective in Music* 17, nos. 1&2 (1989): 55–72.

Meanwhile, as indicated earlier, Apala developed from Muslims seeking to commemorate the primacy of fasting and the supremacy of Allah.[90] With some musical instruments at their disposal, specialists in Apala music developed their brand and made it a significant addition to the new cultural formations. The Apala maestro, Haruna Ishola, was renowned within the genre. He was a household celebrity, loved, and admired by people of various religions.[91] The general instruments that accompany the Apala style of music are talking drums, traditionally called *omele*; a rattle, called *sèkèrè*; a thumb piano, called *agidigbo*; and a bell, called *agogo*.[92] Gradually, the music began to evolve, mutating and taking different attributes from other forms to evolve with the social requirements of the period. People chose Apala music as their preferred source of inspiration and entertainment. And, because the individuals producing this music garnished it with impressive sounds and musical dexterity, it drew the attention of many and became a very popular musical style they would become attracted to. The later development of *Fuji* music has its origin in Apala music.[93]

Around the same time, the Nigerian music industry began to experience rapid development due to the influx of musical instruments imported via colonization. Among these were electric instruments, which found their way from the United States and European countries to Nigeria. Immediately, these instruments became the focus of different creative artists, and thus began the emergence of different song patterns. Rock 'n' foll, funk, and soul were new musical genres that greeted the Nigerian urban communities and received strong patronage. During this period, there were also attempts to become pioneers in different areas of music, so much so that the characteristics of songs from different backgrounds were blended to produce new styles. Consider, for example, the adoption of these imported musical materials by Isaiah K. Dairo, which gave *Juju* music the significance it deserved. Efforts such as these signaled the adoption of new ways of life and demonstrated the practice of blending aspects of both Indigenous and foreign cultures, which often resulted in innovation and change.[94]

---

[90] Stephen O. Olusoji, "Comparative Analysis of the Islam Influenced Apala, Waka and Sakara Popular Music of the Yoruba," (unpublished PhD dissertation, University of Ibadan, 2008).

[91] Rasheed O. Ajetunmobi and Adewale Adepoju, "Transforming African Nations through Indigenous Music: A Study of Haruna Ishola's Apala Music," *The Social Sciences* 8, no. 1 (2013): 29–33.

[92] Simon Broughton, Mark Ellingham, Jon Lusk, and Duncan Antony Clark, eds., *The Rough Guide to World Music: Africa and Middle East* (London: Rough Guides, 2006), 293.

[93] John Collins, "A Historical Review of Popular Entertainment in Sub-Saharan Africa," in *Africa in Contemporary Perspective: A Textbook for Undergraduate Students*, ed. Takyiwaa Manuh and Esi SutherlandAddy (Legon–Accra: Sub-Saharan Publishers, 2013), 452.

[94] Tunji Vidal, *The Institutionalization of Western Music Culture in Nigeria and the Search for National Identity* (Ile-Ife: Obafemi Awolowo University Press, 2002).

Conclusion

This chapter considers the various cultural practices – old and new – during the period of colonization. The British did not abolish local languages or many other aspects of cultural practices. However, because they were the colonizing forces, they influenced the emergence of new cultural traditions. Notwithstanding the reality that colonial rule had notable impacts, such as in the use of the English language, the majority of the colonized people did not depart from their Indigenous systems, even though they navigated those through new methods and principles. There was large-scale cultural retention during the colonial period, just as newer cultural aspects developed.

However, many cultural practices witnessed immediate transformation when new, more modern practices gained more popularity among the people. The imposition of the English language made a huge impact: its adoption meant that aspects of British traditions would equally be transmitted in the process. As we can see, this led to changes, in some places, in certain older cultural practices, such as the Indigenous clothing culture and naming systems that became transformed into a foreign style. People in areas that accepted Christianity began to give biblical and Western names to their children to navigate their way into a society that was becoming synonymous with modernity. Adaptations to modernity became major tools to access the formal economy.

19

Urbanization

Urbanization – the development of villages and towns that become cities with higher population densities, modern facilities, and opportunities for socioeconomic mobility – has garnered considerable interest from various academic disciplines.[1] Sociologists, including Kennedy Eborka and Charles Jarmon, have considered urbanization and urban development as subjects of significant interest to sociology and anthropology.[2] Authors such as Boyowa Chokor have studied the concept in relation to land planning and governance.[3] Historians have also examined the multidisciplinary concept of urbanization. Chima Korieh has studied the history of migration patterns and identity formation among the Igbo.[4] Patrick Edewor has explored the history of urbanization in Nigeria's major cities along with trends for residential segregation.[5] Many Nigerian scholars have studied their country's urban history, and this chapter builds on the efforts of their brilliant minds.[6]

---

[1] For instance, David Drakakis-Smith, *Urbanisation, Housing and the Development Process* (London: Routledge, 2012); Samuel P. Hays, "From the History of the City to the History of the Urbanized Society," *Journal of Urban History* 19, no. 1 (1993): 3–25; and Andrey Korotayev and Leonid Grini, "The Urbanization and Political Development of the World System: A Comparative Quantitative Analysis," in *History and Mathematics: Historical Dynamics and Development of Complex Societies*, Vol. 2, ed. Peter Turchin, Leonid Grinin, Andrey Korotayev, and Victor C. de Munck (Moscow: Volgograd Center for Social Research, 2006), 115–153.

[2] Kennedy Eborka, "Migration and Urbanization in Nigeria from Pre-colonial to Post-colonial Eras: A Sociological Overview," in *Migration and Urbanization in Contemporary Nigeria: Policy Issues and Challenges*, ed. John Lekan Oyefara (Lagos: University of Lagos Press and Bookshop Ltd., 2021), 15–54; and Charles Jarmon, *Nigeria: Reorganization and Development since the Mid-Twentieth Century* (Leiden: E. J. Brill, 1988).

[3] Boyowa A. Chokor, "Changing Urban Housing Form and Organization in Nigeria: Lessons for Community Planning," *Planning Perspectives* 20, no. 1 (2005): 69–96.

[4] Chima J. Korieh, "Migration Patterns and Identity Formation among the Igbo," in *Population Movements, Conflicts and Displacements in Nigeria*, ed. Toyin Falola and Okpeh Ochayi Okpeh (Trenton: Africa World Press, 2007), 107–131.

[5] Patrick Edewor, "Residential Segregation in Nigerian Cities," in *Globalizing Cities: Inequality and Segregation in Developing Countries*, ed. Ranvinder S. Sandhu and Jasmeet Sandhu (New Delhi: Rawat Publications, 2011), 29–43.

[6] Akin Mabogunje, *Urbanization in Nigeria* (London: University of London Press, 1968). See also Muritala M. Olalekan, "Urban Livelihood in Lagos 1861–1960," *Journal of the Historical Society of Nigeria* 20 (2011): 193–200.

The research methodologies and main theses of these authors are disparate, but most trace the origins of Nigerian urbanization to the same point in history: the period of colonial administration. Edewor, Korieh, and Shehu[7] have looked further into the past to link urbanization's origins with the concentration of political, commercial, and military activities in precolonial kingdoms in the Niger area. Although the precolonial cities of Lagos, Ibadan, and Kano underwent some degree of urbanization, the rapid urban development of these regions occurred in the first half of the twentieth century and spread to other places that were important to British colonial administrators. Historical studies have suggested that the British colonial administrators' activities in urbanizing these cities, which would later be described as "colonial cities," were mainly driven by political, economic, and missionary interests.[8] These interests may have been self-serving, but urban developments during the colonial administration contributed to Nigeria's national development and continued to make contributions after independence.[9]

Urbanization and Urban Development

Scholars of world history often consider the twentieth century to be a pioneering epoch for modern social, economic, and political developments.[10] It was a time of transformation shaped by the rise and fall of European imperial powers, the advent and demise of colonial authorities, the emergence of newly independent polities, modern telecommunications, and two world wars. Most countries of the world adapted to these with rapid changes to their social, political, and economic systems. The urban structure of cities, as an aspect of social life, was transformed during this period. One author has noted that urban development is pivotal for national development, which was why it garnered widespread attention during this period of monumental global change.[11]

Eborka has observed that Nigeria was not excluded from global urbanization during the twentieth century. Several other pieces of evidence corroborate that Nigeria's history of urbanization can be traced to the colonial era, and its

---

[7] Jamilu Shehu, "Trends of Urbanization in Nigeria: The Example of Gusau Town," *Polac Historical Review* 4, no. 1 (2020): 32–43

[8] Korieh, "Migration Patterns and Identity."

[9] Abiodun A. Oladiti and Ajibade S. Idowu, "The Interplay of Town Planning and Colonialism: The Contributions of Albert Thompson to Urban Development in Lagos, 1920–1945," *Social Evolution & History* 16, no. 2 (2017): 126–142. See also R. K. Home, "Town Planning and Garden Cities in the British Colonial Empire 1910–1940," *Planning Perspectives* 5, no. 1 (1990): 23–37.

[10] Daniel R. Brower and Thomas Sanders, *The World in the Twentieth Century: From Empires to Nations* (Massachusetts: Pearson, 2014).

[11] Eborka, "Migration and Urbanization in Nigeria."

development had substantial links with the political and economic activities of the colonial administration.[12] Urbanization trends in colonial Nigeria began with the establishment of centers for commerce and administration.

By the start of the twentieth century, the British colonial administration had established political and economic dominance over different parts of the territory now known as Nigeria.[13] Out of necessity, the British settled in a few territories where they oversaw economic production and political administration. These locations were chosen due to the presence of natural and economic resources that would benefit the colonial government, and for the strategic value they held for political administration. These territories – namely Lagos, Ibadan, Abeokuta, Kano, Gusau, Kaduna, Jos, Calabar, Enugu, and Port Harcourt – experienced infrastructure development over the next few decades.[14]

Lagos is currently a leading commercial hub in modern Nigeria and sub-Saharan Africa, which was not the result of an overnight expansion. The city was the first point of contact with British invaders in 1851, and the territory was thereby elevated to the status of a British Consulate and administered by the Royal Niger Company (RNC). This endured until 1861 when Lagos was recognized as the first British colony in the Niger area territory.[15] Even after it was merged into the amalgamated Colony and Protectorate of Nigeria, it was administered separately from the Protectorate of Nigeria. Lagos had the rare privilege of appointing representatives to the protectorate's legislative council as soon as the elective principle was introduced in 1922. British officials were interested in the development of Lagos due to its strategic location along the Atlantic Ocean and its prior development, in precolonial times, as a commercial center.[16]

A report by Urbanisation Research Nigeria has shown that colonial Nigeria's urbanization and urban development trends differed from precolonial trends.[17] The degree of development largely depended on the nature of political administration. In the Yoruba kingdoms of the precolonial era, urban centers, such as Oyo-Ile, were not only political and administrative headquarters but also famous settlements and war camps, like Ibadan, for leaders in conflict. In the West and

---

[12] Eborka, "Migration and Urbanization in Nigeria"; Korieh, "Migration Patterns and Identity"; and Okpeh Ochayi Okpeh, "Inter-group Migrations, Conflicts, and Displacements in Central Nigeria," in *Population Movements, Conflicts and Displacements in Nigeria*, ed. Toyin Falola and Okpeh Ochayi Okpeh (Trenton: Africa World Press, 2008), 19–85.
[13] Johnson U. J. Asiegbu, *Nigeria and its British Invaders, 1851–1920: A Thematic Documentary History* (Enugu: Nok Publishers International, 1984).
[14] Jarmon, *Nigeria: Reorganization and Development*.
[15] Asiegbu, *Nigeria and Its British Invaders*.
[16] Kristin Mann, *Slavery and the Birth of an African City: Lagos, 1760–1900* (Bloomington: Indiana University Press, 2007).
[17] See Robin Bloch, Sean Fox, Jose Monroy, and Adegbola Ojo, *Urbanisation and Urban Expansion in Nigeria: Research Report* (London: ICF International, 2015).

the North, cities were built of strong brick walls for protection and to protect the trade with the coast and across Saharan trade routes.[18]

Urbanization trends in Lagos matched the style of urbanization that would spread to other parts of Nigeria in subsequent years. Lagos was recognized as a trading port, dealing with African slaves before its 1861 annexation and changing to palm oil afterwards.[19] Access to the Atlantic and other sea routes attracted British colonial officials and later resulted in some structural developments. Government Reserved Areas (GRAs) were established to build residences for British colonial officers and other Europeans[20] while branches of European companies were opened; other developments included schools, hospitals, railways, trading centers, and churches that gave Lagos the status of a colonial city.[21]

Lagos was the first center of political administration during the colonial era, but it was not the only one.[22] The early decades of colonial administration were marked by the centralization of authority. During the administrations of Lord Lugard and Hugh Clifford, political activities were concentrated in the megacity of Lagos, where all arms of government were based. The constitutional framework allowed for a minimal degree of local administration through the indirect rule system, using local chiefs, Obas, and Emirs to enforce colonial orders.

By the late 1930s and 1940s, and especially in the years after World War II, increasing amounts of political activity spread across the country. In 1939, Bernard Bourdillon divided Nigeria into three provinces.[23] Under the 1946 Richards Constitution, the idea of regionalism became more widespread.[24] The creation of administrative commercial centers across Nigeria was instrumental in spreading urbanization beyond the city of Lagos.[25]

The Southwestern city of Ibadan began development shortly after Lagos, rapidly becoming a megacity.[26] Ibadan had a larger population than Lagos during the precolonial era and in the early years of Nigeria's colonial

---

[18] Bloch, et al., *Urbanisation and Urban Expansion*.
[19] Mann, *Slavery and the Birth*.
[20] Bright Alozie, "Space and Colonial Alterity: Interrogating British Residential Segregation in Nigeria, 1899–1919," *Ufahamu: A Journal of African Studies* 41, no. 2 (2020): 1–26.
[21] Matthew Enenche Ogwuche, "Migrants and the National Question: A Study of the Nigerian Migration Experience," *International Journal of Migration and Global Studies* 1, no. 2 (2021): 1–46.
[22] Robert Smith, "The Lagos Consulate, 1851–1861: An Outline," *The Journal of African History* 15, no. 3 (1974): 393–416.
[23] Eme O. Awa, *Federal Government in Nigeria* (Berkeley: University of California Press, 1964), 16–24.
[24] Louis J. Munoz, "Regionalism in Nigeria: The Transformation of Tradition," *Il Politico* 52, no. 2 (1987): 317–341.
[25] Bloch, et al., *Urbanisation and Urban Expansion*, 33–35.
[26] Gabriel O. Ogunremi, *Ibadan: A Historical, Cultural and Socio–Economic Study of an African City* (Ibadan: Oluyole Club, 2000).

administration. It was a larger and more developed urban center in many respects.[27] Rough estimates of population growth from 1866 to 1960 in the Nigerian megacities of Lagos, Ibadan, and Kano show that Ibadan was the largest, most populous city in colonial Nigeria. Its population in 1866 was around 100,000 people, which was four times larger than the Lagos population of 25,083. Ibadan grew six-fold by the date of Nigeria's independence, and by that time the population of Lagos had exceeded Ibadan's population by about 6.5%.[28] During the colonial period, Ibadan's successful transformation into an expanding urban center was assisted by its precolonial history as a big city that attracted people from other places.[29] Its 1946 recognition as the capital of the Western region contributed significantly to its development in the colonial period.

Kano[30] and Enugu[31] served as the capitals of the Northern and Eastern regions, respectively, while Ibadan served as the capital of the Western region during Nigeria's period of regionalism.[32] As major political and administrative centers, these settlements became significant for the colonial officials, administering the federal structure from their base in Lagos, and for the educated elites, who became regional representatives and leaders in Kano and Enugu.

Kano's development as an urban center is built on its established history. There is ample historical evidence of interactions between merchants from precolonial Yoruba kingdoms and the city of Kano.[33] Kano was a significant center for local and international trade – on a par with Lagos and Calabar – due to its close connection with the Sahara and its position as a Sahel city.[34] Kano's long precolonial history, its political and commercial relevance during the colonial period, and the site's strategic location assisted with its transformation into a major urban center. This feat was achieved by the middle of the twentieth century, when it had established itself as Nigeria's third largest city, behind Lagos and Ibadan.[35]

[27] Edewor, "Residential Segregation in Nigerian Cities."
[28] Alvan Millson, "The Yorubas Country, West Africa," *Proceedings of the Royal Geographical Society* 13, no. 10 (1891): 583.
[29] Peter C. Lloyd, Akin Mabogunje, and Bolanle Awe, ed., *The City of Ibadan: A Symposium on its Structure & Development* (London: Cambridge University Press, 1967).
[30] Michael G. Smith, *Government in Kano, 1350–1950* (Boulder: Westview Press, 1997).
[31] J. H. Jennings, "Enugu: A Geographical Outline," *The Nigerian Geographical Journal* 3, no. 1 (1959): 28–38.
[32] Akin Mabogunje, "The Growth of Residential Districts in Ibadan," *Geographical Review* 52, no. 1 (1962): 56–77.
[33] Abdulateef F. Usman and Ahmed Bako, The Integration of Yoruba Migrant Community in Kano Emirate. Paper presented at the National conference of 200 years of Uthman Danfodio Jihad, Kano, July 27–29, 2003; Edewor, "Residential Segregation in Nigerian Cities," 34
[34] Aboyade S. Ariyo, "Trade across Frontiers: An Overview of International Trade before the Advent of Modern Economic System in Nigeria," *Historia Actual Online* 35, no. 3 (2014): 53–60.
[35] Edewor, "Residential Segregation in Nigerian Cities," 37.

Most of Enugu's urban development occurred after its designation as the administrative capital of Nigeria's Eastern region. However, the city's urbanization began in 1909, when British colonizers first discovered its large coal repository. That same year, the British established a coal mining site at Udi hill, Enugu.[36] This began a series of structural improvements. As Enugu developed into a thriving economic hub, colonial officials planned the city's development to create housing areas for the British. To avoid health problems caused by local coal mining, British residential areas for Europeans were located east of Enugu, and Africans were relegated to the south.[37] Colonial officials led Enugu's growth and development, and the city's population, geographic footprint, commercial activity, and infrastructure increased over time.[38] Enugu's urban expansion meant a massive boost in employment and educational opportunities. The discovery of coal in the area, an important resource for British industry, encouraged Igbos to migrate there in search of opportunities in Enugu town and its mining industry.[39]

Other towns rapidly developed into cities. Gusau, Kaduna, Abeokuta, Calabar, Nsukka, and Port Harcourt underwent development as the pioneer cities of Lagos, Ibadan, Kano, and Enugu grew larger, but these newer centers also developed because of their relevance as emerging commercial hubs. Gusau was a former Sokoto town that became an urban center after fourteen provinces were created from the old Sokoto caliphate; the headquarters of the caliphate was established within its borders. This brought modern facilities such as schools, electricity, and modern housing to the town. The urbanization of Gusau included providing social services, establishing government residential areas, and other developments.[40] The creation of social services accelerated the urbanization of Gusau,[41] and the development of communications systems and agricultural trade led to Gusau's population increase, which accelerated its urban expansion.

The construction of railways fast-tracked urbanization in colonial Nigerian cities. The 1929 construction of a railway from Funtua to Gusau facilitated its

---

[36] Ihediwa N. Chimee, "Coal and British Colonialism in Nigeria," *RCC Perspectives* 5 (2014): 19–26.
[37] Alozie, "Space and Colonial Alterity."
[38] Jonas Eze, "Urbanization in Nigeria, Enugu (the Coal City) as an Urban Town: A Historical Review, 1918–1960," in *Urbanization, Security, and Development Issues in Nigeria 1914–2014: Festschrift in Honour of Prof. Enoch Oyedele*, ed. Patrick I. Ukase, Emmanuel O. Akubor, and Augustine I. Onoja (Zaira: Ahmadu Bello University Press, 2016), 9–20.
[39] B. E. Aduwo, Patrick Edewor, and Eziyi O. Ibem, "Urbanization and Housing for Low-income Earners in Nigeria: A Review of Features, Challenges and Prospects," *Mediterranean Journal of Social Sciences* 7, no. 3 (2016): 347–357.
[40] Shehu, "Trends of Urbanization in Nigeria," 32–43.
[41] C. A. Onyekwelu, "Urban Growth and Patterns in Nigeria," in *Issues in Urbanization and Urban Administration in Nigeria*, ed. E.O. Ezeani and N.N. Elekwa (Nsukka: Jamoe Enterprise, 2001), 47–60.

urban development. The railway was a British effort to join Nigeria's Southern and Northern territories with an effective transportation network.[42] The Gusau railway encouraged migrants from Western and Eastern Nigeria to settle there, creating trading opportunities and geographic expansion. The British policy of segregated settlements also influenced the urbanization of Gusau. Political, economic, and racial components of colonial policies, designed to control residents, led to the creation of GRAs for British settlers. Multinational companies established offices in Gusau, which drew an influx of migrants looking for work. In the twentieth century, the Igbo people were drawn to the capitalist expansion of Gusau to secure jobs with European firms.[43]

While other cities developed around industrial activities, the colonial city of Calabar became a hub for commerce and administration. Calabar's urban expansion enabled the colonial exploitation of local resources. In 1882, urbanization began with Consul Edward Hewett's relocation to the area as the establishment of a new Protectorate administration brought additional missionaries and traders.[44] European economic activity boosted Calabar's urban expansion as a thriving commercial hub.[45] The rapid population increase and the influence of colonial power brought by these developments led Calabar through a rapid social transformation.[46] The city's position on the coast served as an important link between Europeans and Africans. The British used this access to expand Nigeria's economic potential for their benefit.

In the nineteenth century, Britain was a source of enormous demand for palm oil, which was Calabar's most important natural resource. It was vital for producing industrial lubricants,[47] and the British focused on creating infrastructure to ensure its supply. This was the beginning of trading opportunities in colonial Calabar and a major factor in its urbanization. To encourage the free flow of business activities in the area, the British found it equally important to create housing settlements and recreational opportunities.[48] British developmental efforts brought a massive urban explosion to Calabar. The construction of reservation areas, hospitals, schools, and cemeteries confirmed Calabar's status as a colonial, commercial, and missionary center.[49] Technological

---

[42] Shehu, "Trends of Urbanization in Nigeria."
[43] Shehu, "Trends of Urbanization in Nigeria."
[44] Paul K. Macdonald, *Networks of Domination: The Social Foundations of Peripheral Conquest in International Politics* (New York: Oxford University Press, 2014), 149–181.
[45] Jonah Akpan Uwem and Susan Ikwo Iseyin, "Urbanization in the Lower Cross River Region: 1882–1960," *Journal of History and Diplomatic Studies* 6 (2019): 1–23.
[46] Geoffrey I. Nwaka, "Colonial Calabar: Its Administration and Development," in *Old Calabar Revisited*, ed. Solomon O. Jaja, Erim O. Erim and Bassey W. Andah (Enugu: Harrus Publishers, 1990), 63–93.
[47] Uwem and Iseyin, "Urbanization in the Lower Cross River Region."
[48] Uwem and Iseyin, "Urbanization in the Lower Cross River Region."
[49] David L. Imbua, *Intercourse and Crosscurrents in the Atlantic World: Calabar-British Experience, 17th–20th Centuries* (Durham: Carolina Academic Press, 2012).

innovations strengthened its existing transportation and communication networks – mechanical and electrical innovations were introduced to the city at the beginning of the twentieth century.[50]

Research has established that the cities of Gusau, Calabar, Port Harcourt, Kaduna, and Jos were less developed than the three capitals of Lagos, Ibadan, and Kano, but they were significant urban centers in Nigeria's colonial history. Lagos, Kano, and Ibadan had established histories as urban centers before the advent of British colonialism, but the urbanization of cities such as Kaduna, Jos, and Port Harcourt was entirely due to British colonial activity. Edewor has noted that the urbanization of Kaduna began with the colonial administration of Lord Lugard, which established it as the administrative headquarters of the Protectorate of Northern Nigeria.[51] Jos became the center of the tin mining industry in 1921, and interest in Port Harcourt was based on its proximity to the Atlantic Ocean. Port Harcourt's development as a trade route and a commercial hub was also encouraged by its substantial coal reserves.[52]

Urbanization and urban development trends did not follow the same trajectory in all regions. Lagos had grown as a commercial city for decades before the arrival of colonial officials, and Ibadan and Kano had spent centuries developing as centers for political and economic activities. Each city's pace of urban development was also affected by its significance to the British government. As a leading hub for commercial and administrative activities, Lagos was replete with modern facilities. Administrative capitals for regional governments, which had less commercial activity, developed more rapidly than places like Port Harcourt and Jos, which were exclusively commercial. Regardless of this uneven development, colonial officials made substantial contributions to the development of these colonial cities.

Land Delivery, Town Planning, and Spatial Expansion of Cities

Colonial settlements became modern cities via differing developmental paths. Common trends in these transformations included land policing, town planning, and spatial expansion. The spatial expansion of Lagos, Kano, and Ibadan led to the development of nearby suburbs, bringing the second wave of colonial cities such as Abeokuta, Onitsha, and Nsukka to life. Lamond and her coauthors have noted that the colonial period's major trends in urban development included massive migration, which led to population increases, neighborhood expansion, and annexation.[53] These cities' rapid development required land

[50] Onyekwelu, "Urban Growth and Patterns in Nigeria."
[51] Edewor, "Residential Segregation in Nigerian Cities," 35.
[52] Aduwo, Edewor, and Ibem, "Urbanization and Housing," 347–357.
[53] Jessica Lamond, Emma Lewis, Johnson B. Falade, Kwasi B. Awuah, and Robin Bloch, "Urban Land, Planning and Governance Systems in Nigeria," *Urbanisation Research Nigeria: Research Report* (2015).

usage policies and town planning regulations. As with most policies introduced by Nigeria's colonial administration, land tenure and town planning decisions mainly served British interests. They were indifferent to local requirements and gave limited consideration to urban sustainability.

In preindependence Nigeria, the British imposed their land administration system on traditional land tenure systems, effectively transferring land ownership. In Northern Nigeria, existing land tenure practices were known as the Muslim Maliki Law, implemented in 1804. This system was overruled by the British Land and Native Proclamation Ordinance of 1910, which gave the colonial government the power to claim all public land under the administration of the colonial governor, allegedly to benefit the natives.[54] Urbanization began in colonial Nigeria in Lagos in the nineteenth century, marked by the development of infrastructure and the construction of a railway in the city during the 1890s. The 1928 Planning Ordinances, which the Lagos Executive Development Board issued, included efforts to reclaim swamps, build markets, and develop estates. Similar urban activities were carried out in Calabar, Kano, Gusau, and Enugu.[55]

The earliest history of British urban development in Nigeria can be traced to the 1863 Lagos Town Improvement Ordinance,[56] which resulted in an expansion of the urbanization of Lagos. The ordinance created the traditional city of "Eko," using a design strategy that is reflected in the alignment of Lagos streets to the present day. It also created urban sanitation in the area. These changes were made for a simple reason: Lagos was a major commercial hub surrounded by water, making it easier for the continuous export of slaves by powerful networks of local slave traders (despite the ban by the British government) and creating the foundations of a booming economic enterprise.[57] Residents strongly opposed urban development, but Lagos was too valuable to be left alone. The city was declared a British Protectorate, and Captain Alfred Moloney assumed the office of Governor of Lagos in 1886. He immediately built a botanical garden in Ebute Meta,[58] followed by the creation of a railway system.

It was important for colonial officials to segregate Europeans in Lagos, which is evident in how European Reservation Areas were kept separate from native residences. In 1917, the town's physical layout had been shaped by its development plans, and Lagos was regarded as a first-class colonial city. In 1926, Apapa was created to meet the commercial needs of the British in

---

[54] Chokor, "Changing Urban Housing Form."
[55] Chokor, "Changing Urban Housing Form."
[56] Eborka, "Migration and Urbanization in Nigeria."
[57] Pearl Akunnaya Opoko and Adedapo A. Oluwatayo, "Trends in Urbanization: Implication for Planning and Low–income Housing Delivery in Lagos, Nigeria," *Architecture Research* 4, no. 1 (2014): 15–26.
[58] Opoko and Oluwatayo, "Trends in Urbanization."

Lagos.[59] As the city gradually developed into an urban environment, the colonial government planned to provide transportation and communication systems, roads, amenities, social services, and public utilities. These efforts were consolidated by the British adoption of collaborative decisions that overruled local objections to planned improvements.[60]

Lagos experienced urbanization due to its economic activities and strategic geographical location. In Kano, urbanization was influenced by geographic expansion and the influence of its fast-growing emirate, which adhered to Islamic religious values. Kano's housing system reflected the Emir's political and social authority and reflected existing cultural practices and prevailing environmental conditions.[61] Town planning in the city of Kano reflected Arab architectural influences, which the colonial officers decided to preserve. On the other hand, existing housing structures were left unchanged because colonial officers needed the Emir to exert power and authority on their behalf. Urban institutions further facilitated the expansion of Kano which was historically a big city. Overall, colonial officers were indecisive about controlling land development in the emirate.[62] Even without direct involvement in its development, Kano became a modern urban city, and it saw an influx of migrants from other parts of Nigeria who were restricted to an area known as *Sabon Gari*.[63]

Kaduna, the former administrative capital of the Northern Protectorate, was another fast-developing city in the Northern Nigerian region. Unlike Kano, Sokoto, and Gusau, colonial Kaduna did not enjoy substantial influence: the system of political authority was based on territories.[64] Town planning in the region was copied from the Arabs, which meant that the British were less involved in urban development.

Colonial officials saw Kaduna, originally known as Zaria, as a metropolitan city. The area was an economic hub for cotton processing, and it drew massive migration, especially with the city's railway transportation. The British originally had little interest in settling in Kaduna as there were no exploitable natural resources, and the Hausas eagerly exerted influence on behalf of the colonial

---

[59] Ayodeji Olukoju, "The Port of Lagos, 1850–1929: The Rise of West Africa's Leading Seaport," in *Atlantic Ports and the First Globalisation, c. 1850–1930*, ed. Miguel Suárez Bosa (London: Palgrave Macmillan, 2014), 112–129.
[60] Akpabio M. Ufot–Akpabio and Beulah I. Ofem, "Urbanization and Urban Development in Nigeria: A Perspective of Akwa Ibom State," *Journal of Agriculture, Environmental Resource Management* 4, no. 2 (2019): 369–383.
[61] Yakubu Ahmed Ilyasu, Sunday Vincent Akwashiki, and Jamila Salisu, "Socio-Political Implication of Urbanization in Nigeria: An Overview," *International Journal of Social Science and Human Research* 3, no. 7 (2020): 76–78.
[62] Ilyasu, Akwashiki, and Salisu, "Socio-Political Implication of Urbanization."
[63] David E. Allyn, "The Sabon Gari System in Northern Nigeria, 1911–1940," unpublished PhD dissertation, University of California, 1976.
[64] Elisha P. Renne, *Death and the Textile Industry in Nigeria* (London: Routledge, 2020), 19–37.

imperialists. However, British concerns over Kaduna's influx of Muslim immigrants required them to address the threat of Islamic dominance. The colonial administration eventually became more involved in the city's political and religious architecture, taking a more active role in urban planning and placing restrictions on Muslim activity.[65]

Ibadan controlled a large amount of territory before the advent of colonialism, supported by its large population and undefeated military. The city retained its influence under colonial rule, preserving traditional aspects of Yoruba urban living. Ibadan's physical size reflected its economic and political power before colonialism, but its housing settlements were haphazard due to the absence of effective town planning. Ibadan's population increase and historical status led the colonizers to urbanize the city, arguably for economic purposes. Population size was one of the main determinants of town planning during colonial rule. Ibadan experienced urban expansion due to its population increase, but it also suffered from recurring disease outbreaks due to poor sanitation. The British controlled the cocoa trade in Ibadan, exporting products to Britain, and the city had strong connections with other Yoruba communities.[66]

Lagos, Ibadan, Kano, and Kaduna were major urban centers in Western and Northern Nigeria. In the East, Enugu and Port Harcourt were leading centers of urbanization and development under the colonial administration. British interest in Enugu, which served as both an administrative center and a vital source of coal, prompted some intentional urban planning policies. The 1917 Township Ordinance formally classified cities into three categories.[67] Lagos was recognized as Nigeria's only first-class city, and Enugu and Port Harcourt were grouped with Ibadan, Kano, and Kaduna as second-class urban centers. Bloch, Fox, Monroy, and Ojo have observed that the classification of these cities seemed ambiguous. Ibadan and Kano were larger than Lagos in terms of population and geographical size, but it was essential to recognize cities like Enugu as second-class urban centers to strengthen their commercial activities.[68]

Port Harcourt was originally called Igwuocha and received its new name from Lord Lugard. Port Harcourt's territory was carved out of farmland that British colonial administrators had forcibly seized. Urban expansion in the colonial city of Port Harcourt was influenced by its main economic activity,

---

[65] Ranvinder Singh Sandhu and Jasmeet Sandhu, eds., *Globalizing Cities: Inequality and Segregation in Developing Countries* (New Delhi: Rawat Publications, 2007).

[66] Olusola A. Olufemi, "Planning and Morphology of Indigenous Towns in Nigeria," *Africa Insight* 25, no. 3 (1995): 195–200.

[67] Ola Aluko, "Functionality of the Town Planning Authorities in Effecting Urban and Regional Planning Laws and Control in Nigeria: The Case of Lagos State," *African Research Review* 5, no. 6 (2011): 159.

[68] Bloch, et al., *Urbanisation and Urban Expansion*, 33.

which was fishing. British colonial officials met Port Harcourt as a fishing settlement in 1913, and they created improvements to enhance its ability to export fish to England. The city's geographical location served the political and economic interests of the British. As they transformed Port Harcourt into a commercial city, the British developed modern transportation and communication networks. Residential areas were established for British and other European settlers to oversee the economic activities in this fast-growing colonial center, and Port Harcourt transformed into the administrative powerhouse of the Southeast.[69]

Creating Cities

Under colonialism, Nigeria's major cities – such as Lagos, Kano, and Enugu – were rapidly urbanized. Economic expansion, population increases, and the new construction of architectural masterpieces to be enjoyed by European residents all encouraged this trend. Before the arrival of the colonial government, Nigeria's residents had managed the physical planning of their territory. The British viewed some of Nigeria's largest settlements as mere villages, but they only needed to build on existing plans for these sites, which in most cases meant that no major overhauls were required. However, British input largely drove the urban expansion of these rural settlements to pursue economic gains.[70]

The colonial administration's role in the urbanization of Nigeria was centered on the colonial government's need to exert power and authority over their new protectorate. Colonial activities shaped physical plans for urban centers and identified opportunities to create urbanized institutions.[71] Rural settlements such as Enugu and Port Harcourt were transformed into distinct cities based on their historical connections. Other rural settlements also saw unprecedented migration and the growth of cosmopolitanism.

The British introduced urbanization in colonial Nigeria and facilitated the sustained development of the cities to improve the welfare of their inhabitants.[72] Urbanization was applied as a tool to strengthen the unification of Nigeria, and physical planning was necessary to build residences for European expatriates. This urbanization transformed Nigeria into a major economic power to be

---

[69] Chukudi V. Izeogu, *Problems and Prospects of Urban and Regional Planning in Nigeria: Port Harcourt Metropolis Since 1914* (New York: Page Publishing Inc, 2018).
[70] Ebenezer O. Aka, "Town and Country Planning and Administration in Nigeria," *International Journal of Public Sector Management* 6, no. 3 (1993): 47–64.
[71] Cyril Cynado and Cynado Ezeogidi, *British Conquest, Colonization and Administration in Nigeria* (Enugu: Rhyce & Kerex, 2019).
[72] Julius Olujimi and Gbenga Enisan, "The Influence of the Colonial Planning Education on Urban and Regional Planning Administration in Nigeria," *ResearchGate,* www.researchgate.net/publication/283655405_The_Influence_of_the_Colonial_Planning_Education_on_Urban_and_Regional_Planning_Administration_in_Nigeria.

exploited by the British. Despite this benefit, colonial officials viewed Nigeria's urban development unfavorably as they had little experience with the rapid urbanization seen in colonial Nigeria and had a haphazard system for city planning. A lack of coordination marked it, and there were no major attempts to integrate local planning with national objectives.[73] The development of new towns, based on the assistance of the colonial government, could mainly be seen in street designs that reflected the government's resources at the time.

Colonial administrators introduced the Lagos 1863 Town Improvement Ordinance to address the lack of urban planning in precolonial Nigeria.[74] The ordinance was intended to provide urban sanitation for the Lagos Protectorate. Lord Lugard's Land Proclamation of 1900 transferred land ownership from native authorities to British colonial officials.[75] The Cantonment Proclamation of 1904 imposed residential segregation between European settlers and native residents.[76] In 1914, Ordinance No. 9 allowed the British to use lands acquired for public use. The 1917 Township Ordinance No. 29 established a physical layout for Lagos, and this ordinance established Lagos as a first-class colonial city.[77] The British also introduced township schemes to solve population crises in native areas, which had caused an outbreak of bubonic plague in the late 1920s.[78]

The colonial administration – pursuing economic, religious, and social goals – established physical frameworks for modern town planning in colonial Nigeria. Colonial officials provided social amenities and built infrastructure, transportation, and communication systems to consolidate their authority in Nigeria. New cities were established for economic reasons, which was the case in Lagos, Calabar, and Enugu. To ensure the rapid urbanization of these sites, colonial officials built railways and seaports that exported products more easily.[79]

The urbanization of colonial Nigeria was met with reluctance. Areas marked for urban development were plagued with environmental hazards that had previously caused Nigeria to be labeled a "white man's grave."[80] Urban development required a safe environment that could prevent the outbreak of

---

[73] Olujimi, "The Influence of Colonial Planning Education."
[74] Femi Olokesusi, Femi O. Aiyegbajeje, Gora Mboup, and Dennis Mwaniki, "Smart City Foundation for Smart Economy," in *Smart Economy in Smart Cities: International Collaborative Research: Ottawa, St.Louis, Stuttgart, Bologna, Cape Town, Nairobi, Dakar, Lagos, New Delhi, Varanasi, Vijayawada, Kozhikode, Hong Kong*, ed. T. M. Vinod Kumar (Singapore: Springer Nature, 2017), 798.
[75] Hosaena Ghebru and Austen Okumo, *Land administration service delivery and its challenges in Nigeria: A Case Study of Eight States* (Washington, DC: International Food Policy Research Institute, 2016), 3.
[76] Robert K. Home, *Of Planting and Planning: The Making of British Colonial Cities* (New York: Routledge, 2013), 138.
[77] Home, *Of Planting and Planning*, 138.
[78] Opoko and Oluwatayo, "Trends in Urbanisation."
[79] Akpan and Iseyin, "Urbanisation in the Lower Cross River Region," 1–23.
[80] Aka, "Town and Country Planning."

diseases, and developing such an environment demanded a huge amount of resources that the British were unwilling to commit. Instead, colonial officials introduced policies that created segregated housing for natives.[81] The initiative behind urbanization created separate experiences for Europeans and Nigerians. Housing plans created cities exclusively designed for the British and their counterparts to enjoy luxurious accommodation. These cities were also developed under hierarchical structures based on a location's various social, political, and economic activities.

After World War II, colonial administrators focused on the need for detailed physical planning in Nigeria. Ordinances ensured that neighborhood planning mirrored the concepts applied in the United Kingdom. During this period, urban planning also implemented preventive health measures to address the population increase in rural settlements.[82] However, plans from the early 1920s mainly focused on infrastructure development, neglecting other elements of city planning. This meant that the management of growth and economic development was overlooked. Colonial officials also saw urbanism in Nigeria as a way to advertise their accomplishments to other global powers: the unusual act of creating architectural masterpieces from rural settlements. Although the European Residential Areas were originally created due to racial segregation, these reserved areas were eventually occupied by Nigerian administrators, especially after nationalist movements became more influential.[83]

Nigeria's urbanization under the colonial administration was driven by three forces: economic, political, and missionary. The British needed access to regions that could support the economic activity of British companies, including the RNC. At the political level, the British required settlement areas to facilitate their administration. And at the missionary level, these settlements supported religious activities.

Urbanization and City Life

The impacts of urbanization included sociological effects, changed land planning processes, and even changes to governance and criminal justice. There were three major consequences of urbanization trends and developments in colonial cities: migration, crime, and socioeconomic conditions. Urbanization is intrinsically linked with migration or people's movement from one place to another. Migration was a major driver of urbanization in colonial Nigeria.[84] Edewor has pointed out that the urban developments in major colonial cities

---

[81] Joseph T. Uyanga, *Towards a Nigerian National Urban Policy* (Ibadan: Ibadan University Press, 1982), 67–79.
[82] Chokor, "Changing Urban Housing Form."
[83] Eborka, "Migration and Urbanization in Nigeria."
[84] Bloch, et al., *Urbanisation and Urban Expansion*, 27.

and the availability of new jobs in the civil service encouraged a large-scale mobilization of people from neighboring towns and villages to cities.[85] Lagos quickly attracted migrants from neighboring towns such as Abeokuta and Ibadan. Ibadan's urbanization began before the advent of colonialism, but migrants from other towns contributed to its growth as an urban center during the colonial period. Similar migration patterns occurred in Kano and Enugu. In the early years of colonial Kano's urbanization, most migrants came from Kaduna, Zaria, and Sokoto. In the southeastern city of Enugu, migrants flowed in from Onitsha, Calabar, and many smaller towns and villages.

The study of Nigerian urbanization and urban development by Bloch, Fox, Monroy, and Ojo has noted that there were four migration patterns associated with urban expansion: rural to rural, rural to urban, urban to urban, and urban to rural.[86] Although rural-to-urban migration patterns had the largest impact on urbanization during its formative period in Nigeria, the other migration patterns considerably impacted urban development in the later years of colonialism. The outward expansion of cities like Kano, Lagos, and Enugu encouraged the spatial expansion of urban developments in their geographic regions. The work of Bloch and coauthors has suggested that these developments were significant for the emergence of second- and third-tier cities.[87]

Increasing populations were a direct consequence of a two-way migration in colonial cities. The demographics of Lagos changed rapidly between its annexation in 1861 and Nigeria's independence in 1960. In studying population trends for the coastal city of Lagos, Alvan Millson (cited by Fourchard) noted that Lagos had a population of about 25,000 in 1861.[88] By 1960, Millson found that the population of Lagos had expanded to more than 660,000. This growth was significantly higher than in other major cities like Kano and Ibadan, as no other Nigerian city grew six-fold during that century.[89]

Reuben Udo's assessment of migration and urbanization found that Nigerians of different ethnic and linguistic backgrounds had spread across all ninety-three of colonial Nigeria's administrative divisions by the 1950s.[90] Udo referenced the 1953 national census, which recorded a Yoruba population of 10 million, a Hausa population of 6 million, and an Igbo population of 7 million. He found that the Hausa and Igbo had spread across all the ninety-three administrative divisions, and the Yoruba had a significant presence in

---

[85] Edewor, "Residential Segregation in Nigerian Cities," 31.
[86] Bloch, et al., *Urbanisation and Urban Expansion*, 27.
[87] Bloch, et al., *Urbanisation and Urban Expansion*, 12.
[88] Laurent Fourchard, "Lagos and the Invention of Juvenile Delinquency in Nigeria," *Journal of African History* 47, no. 10 (2006): 115–137.
[89] Fourchard, "Lagos and the Invention of Juvenile."
[90] Reuben K. Udo, "Migration and Urbanization in Nigeria," in *Population Growth and Socio–economic Change in West Africa*, ed. John C. Caldwell (New York: Columbia University Press, 1975), 298–307.

eighty-nine divisions.[91] This proliferation had serious ramifications for demographic dynamics beyond the concerns of overpopulation in major cities.

Although most historical and sociological studies of migration and urbanization in colonial Nigeria limited their perspective to internal migration patterns,[92] a handful has considered the influence of international migration. Lawal[93] and Korieh[94] noted that many people without Western education who migrated to major cities like Lagos, Kano, and Enugu could not access employment opportunities as populations grew in these colonial cities. They migrated into neighboring countries like Gabon and Cameroon, and it has been suggested that there was an exchange of migrants from these countries into Nigeria, although inadequate historical evidence supports this view. Lawal claims that Cameroon was the leading destination for most of these Nigerian emigrants.

Two other factors that promoted international migration were the centuries-old trans-Saharan trade, which the Hausa states initiated with neighboring nations, and the events associated with the outbreak of World War II. The global conflict ultimately fostered lasting friendships between Africans of different nationalities.[95] Unregulated migration into colonial cities had serious impacts on housing and urban planning. The colonial administration developed housing policies that served British interests, which could be seen in the establishment of GRAs that were exclusively for European residents. Indigenes flowing into cities from rural and urban areas encouraged a trend of residential segregation to accommodate the diverse socioeconomic status of urban residents.[96] Bloch and coauthors have noted that urban residential structures became a symbol of social distinction,[97] and this pattern was predominant in Lagos.[98] Bloch and others also examined the proliferation of informal settlements in colonial cities, a major challenge for effective urban planning. Settlements arose from unplanned urbanization along transport infrastructure – mainly roads – and illegal squatting at the periphery of major urban areas. In Ibadan, informal settlements had been established in places like Elekuro, even during precolonial times.[99]

Administrators, town planners, and researchers who studied urbanization trends in colonial Nigeria focused on urban sustainability. Colonial cities had increased in population but not in physical size, which strained previously adequate

---

[91] Udo, "Migration and Urbanization."
[92] Eborka, "Migration and Urbanization in Nigeria," 3.
[93] Bayo A. Lawal, "Nigerian Migrants in the Cameroons and the Reactions of the Host Communities: 1885–1961," in *Population Movements, Conflicts and Displacements in Nigeria*, ed. Toyin Falola and Okpeh O. Okpeh (Trenton: Africa World Press, 2008), 85–105.
[94] Korieh, "Migration Patterns and Identity."
[95] Eborka, "Migration and Urbanization in Nigeria," 13.
[96] Edewor, "Residential Segregation in Nigerian Cities."
[97] Bloch, et al., *Urbanisation and Urban Expansion*, 39.
[98] Opoko and Oluwatayo, "Trends in Urbanisation."
[99] Bloch, et al., *Urbanisation and Urban Expansion*, 39.

resources. The culture of residential segregation in urban centers meant that the increasing demands on local resources resulted in the creation of slums and shanty towns,[100] which some authors categorized as "informal settlements."[101] Regardless of the differing conceptions of informal settlements and shanty towns, most authors agree that these locations introduced a host of socioeconomic challenges militating against reasonable standards of living for these new "urbanists."

Urban sustainability problems went unresolved, and residents of the colonial cities, especially in the metropolitan city of Lagos, were faced with socioeconomic crises. These problems were exacerbated by inadequate infrastructure.[102] City infrastructure failed to provide basic amenities, including water, housing, and mass transit systems, and the deployment of additional infrastructures – such as roads, railways, schools, and medical facilities – was impaired by the increasing demands on existing resources. The most debilitating socioeconomic challenge confronting Nigerians in connection with urban sustainability crises may have been the lack of employment opportunities in cities. This was a cruel irony as most people who migrated to cities from rural areas sought employment. British colonial officials could not develop effective town planning and governance strategies that could address these challenges holistically, and many migrants were emotionally devastated.

Overpopulation, unemployment, and infrastructural crises encouraged criminal activity, which has been the most carefully studied impact of urbanization and urban development. Some scholars have linked criminal behavior with social challenges. Alexander Paterson, who was commissioned by Sir Arthur Richards' colonial administration to study trends in Nigerian crime and criminality, linked increasing crime rates with unemployment, idleness, and the economic implications of wartime exigencies.[103] Increasing numbers of crimes were reported involving urban violence, thuggery, and prostitution.[104] Ojo and Adams, analyzing migration trends and urban violence, noted that urban centers were agglomerations of people from different cultural, ethnic, and linguistic backgrounds; this precipitated different forms of violence, especially intergroup crises.[105]

---

[100] Opoko and Oluwatayo, "Trends in Urbanisation."
[101] John Oucho and Linda Oucho, "Migration, Urbanisation and Health Challenges in Sub-Saharan Africa," Conference Paper: Conditions and Cultural Change, Economic and Demographic Trends in Latin America. Latin American Population Association, Havana, Cuba, 2015.
[102] Matthew Gandy, "Planning, Anti-planning and the Infrastructure Crisis Facing Metropolitan Lagos," *Urban Studies* 43, no. 2 (2006): 371–396.
[103] NAI, COMCOL 1, 2600, Social Welfare in the Colony and Protectorate of Nigeria: A Report to His Excellency, the Governor of Nigeria, 1942.
[104] Toyin Falola, "Prostitution in Ibadan,1895-1950," *The Journal of Business and Social Studies*, New Series, 6: 2, 40–54.
[105] Olusola Matthew Ojo and Timothy Adeola Adams, "Migration and Urban Violence in Nigeria: Imperative of Peace Culture," *Journal of Migration and Global Studies* 1, no. 2 (2021): 18–22.

Neither prostitution nor thuggery were identified as crimes under Nigerian law, but both were morally questionable behaviors that promoted adjacent criminal activity. Prostitution was connected to a range of female criminality, including public solicitation, brothel keeping, living on immoral earnings, and procuring. These activities were predominant in urban centers. Thuggery also became prevalent in colonial cities; scholars have observed increasing numbers of thugs, or "area boys," in urban areas.[106] These area boys, also called "*boma boys*," were found in the largest colonial cities – Lagos, Ibadan, Kano, and Enugu – where they engaged in violent criminal activities.[107] They organized into structured gangs based on age groups, streets, and neighborhoods, and their behavior was linked with pickpocketing, petty theft, plunder of public goods, and the destruction of facilities. Historians such as Hobsbawm[108] and Falola[109] have discussed the nature and activities of such groups, which qualified as antisocial elements perpetrating crime either deliberately or to satisfy their physical cravings.

Conclusion

Modern Nigeria's sociological, ecological, environmental, and economic challenges are exacerbated by ineffective urban planning, land use, and governance policies. These matters have become a source of worry for many different stakeholders. Administrative bodies have made little progress in addressing these challenges, but historians, sociologists, and other scholars have successfully traced the development of these urban challenges to urbanization and urban development trends from the colonial period.

Colonial administrators designed town planning and land delivery mechanisms to further their interests, especially maintaining residential segregation in cities. These ill-considered decisions unleashed a host of urbanization and urban development challenges, and many remain prevalent today. In revising this aspect of Nigeria's colonial history, it is hoped that concerned stakeholders can gain insights into town planning and land tenure governance. This will allow them to focus on rural and urban areas' ecological and socioeconomic sustainability.

---

[106] Simon Heap, "'Jaguda Boys': Pickpocketing in Ibadan, 1930–60," *Urban History* 24, no. 3 (1997): 324–343.

[107] Adediran Daniel Ikuomola, Rashidi Akanji Okunola, and Simon Heap, "Historical Analysis of Touts as a Deviant Subgroup in Lagos State – Nigeria," *African Journal of Arts and Humanities* 2, no. 2 (2009): 49–62.

[108] Eric J. Hobsbawm, *Primitive Rebels: Studies in Archaic Forms of Social Movement in the 19th and 20th Centuries* (Manchester: Manchester University Press, 1959).

[109] Toyin Falola, "Theft in Colonial Southwestern Nigeria Africa," *Instituto Italiano Per* 50, no. 1 (1995): 1–24.

20

Creativity and Aesthetics

Arriving at a universal definition of creativity and aesthetics might be impossible, especially because that is not what this chapter sets out to achieve. Yet, it is important to lay a good foundation for defining both terms, as understanding them is relevant to the ensuing discourse. Creativity, when traced etymologically, comes from the Latin expression "creare," which means "to create" or "to make." The word "creativity" can also be understood as "to bring value," "to innovate," "to birth," and many others that usually suggest the result of a cognitive endeavor. Therefore, as Michael Mumford opines, "over the course of the last decade, however, we seem to have reached a general agreement that creativity involves the production of novel, useful products."[1]

Iyue Tyodoo adds more perspective to Mumford's statement in his definition. He states that "creativity is the power of the human mind to create new ideas or products. Thinking creatively means looking at things from different perspectives and not being restricted by rules, customs, or norms."[2] While it is important to reiterate, as stated earlier, that no definition can adequately cater for the many meanings of creativity, Tyodoo's definition helps foreground what this chapter intends to focus on as far as creativity is concerned. This is "the mind's power of imagination and insight that creates something new, original and valuable."[3] These words describe the works and persons behind the artistic works produced in Nigeria during the colonial era. They relied on earlier works on oral tradition and the indisputable creative acumen displayed by men and women before them in different traditional African settings. During the colonial era, Nigeria's creative minds were able to evolve a new strand of creative output that would also be the foundation of a thriving and globally appreciated creative industry, especially music and theater.

---

[1] Michael D. Mumford, "Where Have We Been, Where are We Going? Taking Stock in Creativity Research," *Creativity Research Journal* 15, no. 2 (2003): 110.
[2] Iyue Tyodoo, "Creativity in Ivom Performance among Tiv People and Lessons for Democratic Practice in Nigeria," in *Theatre, Creativity and Democratic Practice in Nigeria*, ed. Ameh Akoh, AbdulRasheed Adeoye, and Osita Ezenwanebe (Maiduguri: Society of Nigeria Theatre Artists, 2014), 13.
[3] Peter Ortese, *Psychology of Creativity* (Makurdi: Aboki Publishers, 2009).

Again, defining aesthetics is not easy. Aesthetics has to do with beauty and taste and the pleasure a person derives from beholding a work of art. The aesthetics of a work of art – be it music, literature, or theater – speak of the beauty and the thoughtful and meaningful underlying principle of said work of art, which can also be perceived by its beholder. The field of aesthetics has generated issues of subjectivity on the part of the beholder of art. Of course, the influence of culture and other contexts that inform the production of a certain work of art might also be brought forward as arguments in asking about the universality of art. These are not issues to be discussed in this chapter, but it is noteworthy that they are addressed in subsequent chapters of this work as it delves into the creative works, minds, and the beauty of works of art in Nigeria during the British colonial era. The focus here will be on the works of Nigerians in the colonial era, and not the works of foreigners who lived in this region at the time.

The Root of Creativity and Aesthetics

Precolonial Nigerian people had a deep sense of art and beauty – so much so that one of the offenses still alleged against the colonizers is stealing artworks from the region to Europe.[4] The root of Nigeria's creativity and aesthetics in the colonial era goes back to oral performance and traditions. Performance and oral forms such as proverbs, chants, festivals, panegyric, and rituals are a vital part of the creative endeavors of this era. The other branch upon which creative output was established during the colonial era was Western culture and education. At the height of colonial Nigeria's developmental phase, the people enhanced their creative and aesthetic skills, producing timeless artistic forms such as those in Figure 20.1. that symbolize the greatness of the past.

The form and shape that creative endeavors such as music and theater took during colonialism were heavily influenced by Western culture, even though they evolved from traditional forms. The earlier forms found in almost all places in Nigeria are termed "oral traditions" because they were passed down verbally from one generation to another. It was after interaction with Europeans that most communities began to accommodate documentation through papers and print.[5] Besides the introduction of paper, Europeans also came with their styles of art-making and perception and did not hesitate to impose these upon their subjects, directly or indirectly, in the context of colonialism. For instance, with Europeanism came Christianity, Western music, and, of course, musical instruments. Hence, the assertion that Western culture and civilization are a vital pillar upon which Nigeria's creativity and aesthetics stood during the colonial era is justifiable.

---

[4] Dan Hicks, *The Brutish Museums: The Benin Bronzes, Colonial Violence and Cultural Restitution* (London: Pluto Press, 2020).
[5] Jacob F. A. Ajayi, "How Yoruba was Reduced to Writing," *Odu* 8 (1960): 49–58.

Figure 20.1 Creativity and aesthetics were at the height of colonial Nigeria's developmental phase as locals weaved mats, and produced ceramics, fine pots, and other traditional crafts as part of the age-long skills for economic and communal growth.

From the preceding, it is obvious that the interrelation of these cultures meant that none of them can be found in their original form in the communities of Nigeria anymore. The creation of Nigeria also signaled a change in the cultural productions of each region and community, as there were increased interactions between people and cultures. For instance, it was during this period that the Ogunde Theater, which will be discussed in more detail later in the chapter, travelled all over the country with its unique form of stage play and drama.

Apart from the influence of Western culture on the creativity of colonial Nigerians, there was also the overwhelming influence of slave returnees from the Caribbean, and especially those from Brazil.[6] The influence of these returnees on the people, especially those who lived in the big city of Lagos,

---

[6] Adedoyin Teriba, "A Return to the Motherland: Afro–Brazilians' Architecture and Societal Aims in Colonial West Africa," in *Design Dispersed: Forms of Migration and Flight*, ed. Burcu Dogramaci and Kerstin Pinther (Bielefeld: transcript Verlag, 2019), 232–247.

was so great that it was reflected in the music style that evolved around the time.[7] Although these slaves had been a part of different African communities before being sold and shipped to the New World, they had interacted with the cultures of their masters and the natives of their new abode during their enslavement, so they returned with a broadened horizon and unique skills and ideas.[8] Of course, as a product of multiculturalism and cultural syncretism, they came back with a new culture, which was a major influence on the music of native Nigerians who lived in Lagos at the time. Robert Sydney Smith opines that:

> Towards the middle of the nineteenth century, there appeared even more powerful portents of change on the Slave Coast. These were, first, the emigrants coming in search of their homeland from the colony of 'liberated Africans in Sierra Leone; then the Christian missionaries who followed in their wake, and lastly the palm-oil merchants, the "legitimate" trading rivals of the slavers.[9]

Smith further argues that:

> The first recorded emigrants left Sierra Leone in 1839 and, according to the *Memoirs* of the Reverend Henry Townsend, landed in Lagos. They were shortly followed by another group, who met a hostile reception in the great slaving port, complaining later in Abeokuta that the Lagosians had robbed them of all but their clothes before they allowed them to continue their journey inland. Despite this setback, the movement continued but it was now directed towards Badagry.[10]

Among other things, the arrival and settling of ex-slaves in Lagos also created a sense of social awakening.[11] But beyond this alone, performance art within the Nigerian context, especially in the urban areas, was already shifting away from the monopoly traditional festivals and rituals had on it. Performances began to take new homes in churches, drinking joints, nightclubs, and many other social arenas. These new homes, no doubt, gave platforms of expression to Nigeria's newly evolving music genres and theater at the time.

Through missionary schools and enforced British curricula, Nigerian children who went to school during the colonial era were introduced to Western musical instruments, Western styles of music, and Western songs. Kayode

---

[7] Arugha A. Ogisi, "The Origin of Concert Music in Nigeria, 1850–1920," *EJOTMAS: Ekpoma Journal of Theatre and Media Arts* 2, no. 1–2 (2008): 109.

[8] Nicholas Omenka, "The African–Brazilian Repatriates and the Religious and Cultural Transformation of Colonial Lagos," *Abia Journal of the Humanities and the Social Sciences* 1, no. 1 (2004): 27–45.

[9] Robert Sydney Smith, *The Lagos Consulate, 1851–1861* (Oakland: University of California Press, 2020), 12.

[10] Smith, *The Lagos Consulate*, 13.

[11] Adeyemi B. Aderibigbe, *Lagos: The Development of an African City* (Lagos: Longman, 1975).

Samuel records how a particular musical instrument was brought into the country in large quantities to engage Nigerian students in Western music:

> Propagation was further enhanced through the importation of harmonium organs used as accompaniment to the teaching of European hymns and songs. For instance, a company named Harrison and Harrison of Great Britain shipped the first pipe organ in 1897. Unfortunately, most of these songs have no link or relevance to African culture or the pupils' experience.[12]

The aim of teaching these children Western music was to achieve a bigger goal of convincing them of the inadequacies in their traditional religious practices and make them embrace Christianity. Sadly, the Europeans recorded successes in this area. Not only were they able to successfully instill their music in the consciousness of Nigerians, they also left their legacy in the minds of many people, especially those of elite social status. This is because, according to Samuel Kayode, this new style of music did not always correlate with the inherited Nigerian music style. Of course, at the time, to be associated with anything traditional meant that such a person was not properly acclimatized and perhaps could be categorized as one of the wretched of society. It was, therefore, a deliberate effort on the part of elite Nigerians to try to dissociate themselves from this traditional lifestyle. This permeated many aspects of the daily life of an average Nigerian at the core of colonialism and reflected their choices of where to live, what to wear, the language they spoke, and, of course, the art they consumed. Hence, Western music was strongly disposed to replace the different traditional music forms found in Nigeria. According to Samuel,

> The missionaries and the immigrant Africans... taught music at the established mission (primary, secondary and teacher training) schools. The aim was merely to produce catechists, priests and headmasters who could read from staff notation, play hymns and chants on the harmonium....the content of the curriculum was confined to singing, rudiments of music and local texts fitted to pre-existing English folk melodies. There was therefore a strong propagation of Western classical music between 1844 and 1890.[13]

This inevitable embrace of Western classical music featured prominently in the music outputs experienced during the colonial era. This point is further corroborated by Bode Omojola:

> The colonial period witnessed a progressive introduction of British and Western culture in Nigeria, significantly through the church and missionary schools. Indigenous musical traditions were discouraged both at

---

[12] Kayode Samuel, "The Chequered History of Music Education in Nigeria," in *Educational Theory and Practice Across Disciplines: Projecting Beyond the 21st Century*, ed. Olawale A. Moronkola, Clement O. Kolawole, Babatunde O. Asagba, Jonathan O. Osiki, and Adebola Jaiyeoba (Ibadan: University of Ibadan, 2015), 195.
[13] Samuel, "The Chequered History of Music," 194.

mission schools and churches, while many Nigerians were encouraged to develop skills in the playing of western musical instruments. British regimental bands recruited local musicians, while mission schools helped to train indigenous performers. By the early part of the twentieth century, many Nigerians had become proficient players of Western musical instruments including the organ, and brass and wind instruments. The practice of European music by Nigerian musicians had gathered significant momentum earlier in the nineteenth century when Anglican Church missionaries promoted the performance of European religious and classical music in churches and mission schools in cities like Lagos, Badagry, and Abeokuta.[14]

This led to the point of missionary churches as breeding grounds for people who would be the voices and faces of Nigerian music during the colonial era. Some of the most popular music icons of this time were well-versed in the Western classical music style. One of them was Fela Sowande, whose life and music will be given closer attention later in the chapter.

Music

One of the prominent forms of creative output during the colonial era was music. As already discussed, music did not start in Nigeria when the Europeans came to the region. Rather, it had long been a vital part of living for native Africans. What happened during the colonial era could be said to be the evolution or progression of music in the country to a new status – a status influenced by the traditional culture of the peoples of precolonial Nigeria, slave returnees' culture, and, ultimately, European culture.

Fela Sowande was typical of the teaching of music in missionary schools in Nigeria during the colonial era.[15] He was born in 1905 to an Anglican minister working at St. Andrews in Oyo. Music was a prerequisite for all who went to school at the time, so it was inevitable that Fela was surrounded by music students, music teachers, and music lovers at different points while growing up. When his father was transferred to Lagos on his ministerial journey as an Anglican priest, a new phase in Fela Sowande's musical journey began. In Lagos, he met and learned under Thomas King Ekundayo Phillips, the first Nigerian to study music in London.[16] Beyond learning under Ekundayo Phillips as a boy chorister upon graduation from Kings College and as an accomplished pianist, Sowande assumed the role of Deputy Organist to

---

[14] Bode Omojola, "Politics, Identity, and Nostalgia in Nigerian Music: A Study of Victor Olaiya's Highlife," *Ethnomusicology* 53, no. 2 (2009): 249–276.
[15] Godwin Sadoh, *The Organ Works of Fela Sowande: Cultural Perspectives* (Bloomington: iUniverse LLC, 2014).
[16] Eileen Southern, "Conversation with Fela Sowande, High Priest of Music," *The Black Perspective in Music* 4, no. 1 (1976): 90–104.

Ekundayo Phillips at the Christ Church Cathedral. He worked his way out of colonial Nigeria to England to pursue further education.[17]

Although he started out as a student of civil engineering, his love for and background in music were too strong to allow him to embrace engineering as a field of study. Hence, Sowande looked in the direction of music and followed that path. His musical taste was further influenced by the Black man's struggle as he experienced it in Europe. According to Mwatabu Okantah:

> Sowande first met jazz in the company of fellow Nigerians in 1932 listening to Duke Ellington on short wave radio. Added to this were broadcasts from France, the BBC, and from New York and Chicago, and recordings by Art Tatum, Teddy Wilson and Earl Hines. This led to his organization of the Triumph Dance Club Orchestra, in which he played piano. He was also a member of the jazz band, The Chocolate Dandies that had been organized about 1927 in Lagos.[18]

It should be noted that his relationship with Ekundayo Phillips was also an immersion into the Western style of music. Okantah believes that his work with Ekundayo Phillips gave him the necessary exposure to European music.[19] Of course, this influence would go beyond his time with Ekundayo Phillips and some of the music styles he had listened to over the radio. Sowande's works had a lot of Western flavor. A good part of his musical performances was done with white collaborations or white bands, thus earning him popularity among Europeans.[20]

According to Bode Omojola, while Sowande's works might have been predominantly European in orientation, he was the pioneer of modern music in Nigeria:

> Fela Sowande is undoubtedly the father of modern Nigerian Art Music and perhaps the most distinguished and internationally known African composer. The most significant pioneer-composer of works in the European classical idiom, his works mark the beginning of an era of modern Nigerian Art Music.[21]

As suggested earlier, Sowande had direct interactions with African Americans and their music while in London. This not only became a critical part of his musical sojourn, it also ended up being a time of reawakening for him; a period

---

[17] Southern, "Conversation with Fela Sowande."
[18] Mwatabu Okantah, "Chief Fela Sowande, Traditional African Culture and the Black Studies Movement: A Student Remembers," *Journal of Pan African Studies* 1, no. 10 (2007): 100.
[19] Okantah, "Chief Fela Sowande."
[20] Hardmod C. Nicolao, *Fela Sowande: Composer, Art Music, Jazz, Highlife, Royal College of Organists, George Gershwin, Royal College of Organists* (Beau Basin, Mauritius: Crypt Publishing, 2012).
[21] Bode Omojola, *Nigerian Art Music: With an Introduction Study of Ghanaian Art Music* (Ibadan: IFRA-Nigeria, 1995).

when he began to ask questions about his identity and heritage. After a while in foreign countries, Sowande returned to Nigeria:

> In 1953, he returned to Nigeria to head the Music Section of the Nigerian Broadcasting System ... In this post he produced weekly radio programs based on field research of Yoruba folklore, mythology and oral history presented by tribal priests ... From 1962 until 1965 he was a senior research fellow at the University of Ibadan, then becoming musicology professor at the university's Institute of African Studies ... He was a visiting scholar for the 1961 school year at Northwestern University's anthropology department. The Music Department at the University of Nigeria-Nsukka was renamed the *Sowande School of Music* in his honor in 1962.[22]

Although it has been established that Sowande's music was largely influenced by Western music and culture, there is another part of his work that cannot be overlooked: the African flavor in his creative works. Despite the predominance of his European style, his versatility and creativity on the piano were globally recognized. This was partly due to his ability to look within and engage his cultural background in some of his musical endeavors. Omojola, corroborating this, states that "Sowande's ambition as a composer and as a performer was not merely to excel in Western art music. His most important objective, as his career progressed, was to project his African identity in his compositions and performances."[23] The African side of his creativity was further apparent when he worked with the British Broadcasting Corporation (BBC) African Service. In Omojola's words:

> The *African Suite*, written in 1944, combines well-known West African music with European forces and methods. For the opening movement, "Joyful Day," Sowande uses a melody written by Ghanaian composer Ephrain Amu, as he does in the fourth movement, "Onipe." In "Nostalgia," Sowande composes a traditional slow movement to express his nostalgia for the homeland (in itself a rather European idea). At the centre of the work is a restive "Lullaby," based on a folk original. The finale of the Suite, "Akinla," traces a very singular musical history. It began as a popular Highlife tune – Highlife being a pungent, 20th-century style, combining colonial Western military and popular music with West African elements and a history of its own. Sowande then featured it as a cornerstone of his "argument" that West African music could be heard on European terms: the African Suite was originally broadcast by the BBC to the British colonies in Africa.[24]

---

[22] Okantah, "Chief Fela Sowande."
[23] Bode Omojola, *The Music of Fela Sowande: Encounters, African Identity, and Creative Ethnomusicology* (Point Richmond: Music Research Institute Press, 2009), 58.
[24] Bode Omojola, "Style in Modern Nigerian Art Music: The Pioneering Works of Fela Sowande," *Africa: Journal of the International African Institute* 68, no. 4 (1998): 455.

This tune featured prominently on CBC Radio in Canada for about forty years. Even when Sowande's style of music was slowly losing its relevance in other regions of the world, such as Europe and the United States, its mix of jazz, opera, chamber music, Broadway tunes, and African folk materials endeared it to the audience in Canada for a long time. Other organ works like *Ka Mura, Jesu Olugbala, Obangiji*, and others, though first performed in London, maintained their Yoruba roots while not losing their appeal to European audiences. This speaks of the genius of Sowande.

Another notable figure in the Nigerian music scene during the colonial era was Victor Olaiya.[25] Interestingly, Olaiya was known for a musical genre that arguably did not start in Nigeria: Highlife. Although many argue that highlife music is a West African phenomenon, there is evidence showing that it was more associated with the people of the Gold Coast (now Ghana) than Nigeria.[26] During the colonial era and beyond, however, highlife music was associated with Nigeria and became an indicator of national unity and, in fact, identity.[27]

According to Bode Omojola, while Nigerian elites had initially distanced themselves from traditional culture as they believed it did not portray a superior position, they sought to validate themselves over the underprivileged. This began to change at the moment of nationalistic awakening, a period when nationalist leaders were fervent and more intense about demanding self-governance and independence for the country.[28] One of the emphases of the time was cultural nationalism as a way of rebelling against the culture of their colonizers.[29] Hence, music genres such as highlife sufficed as a good medium to promote the culture of the people. Omojola argues that:

> The sharing of similar stylistic elements by musicians who hailed from disparate regions and ethnic groups in Nigeria underlines the significance of highlife music as an inclusive musical style that paralleled the emergence of national politics in the country. We must remember that one of the major goals of Nigeria's political leaders during the colonial era was to unite the various ethnic groups.[30]

Therefore, Victor Olaiya's music was not just another body of artistic and creative work, but one that served a nationalist end. Born on December 31, 1932, in the colonial city of Calabar, Olaiya had his early education in

---

[25] Ferdinand Ekechukwu, "Life and Times of Victor Olaiya," *Thisday*, February 15, 2020.
[26] Nate Plageman, *Highlife Saturday Night: Popular Music and Social Change in Urban Ghana* (Bloomington: Indiana University Press, 2013).
[27] John Collins, "The Early History of West African Highlife Music," *Popular Music* 8, no. 3 (1989): 221–230.
[28] Omojola, "Politics, Identity, and Nostalgia," 253.
[29] Rina Okonkwo, "Cultural Nationalism in the Colonial Period," in *African Cultural Development*, ed. Ogbu Kalu (Enugu: Fourth Dimension, 1985).
[30] Omojola, "Politics, Identity, and Nostalgia," 255.

Southeast Nigeria.[31] Besides being from a family where music was appreciated, his father was a church organist. He was also introduced to music while in school, where he learned how to play the trumpet, a musical instrument he would become widely known for, and other musical instruments such as the French horn and the B flat clarinet.[32] His relocation to Lagos in the 1950s was significant for the success of his musical career, as this period coincided with nationalist agitations for independence. As noted earlier, cultural nationalism became integral to this movement. According to Omojola:

> From the early 1950s to the 1960s, Olaiya played at different times with musicians including Bobby Benson, Victor Uwaifor, Bala Miller, Rex Lawson, and Fela Anikulapo-Kuti – some of Nigeria's greatest performers of highlife music during and immediately after the colonial era. These early collaborations effectively created the genre highlife in Nigeria, and they reflect the social and political times that contributed to that creation.[33]

The creativity in Victor Olaiya's music is found in his ability to blend European styles with his traditional heritage.[34] Indeed, this was a notable attribute among artists of this time – as noted earlier about Sowande, and as will also be noted about Ogunde, Ogunmola, and Ladipo, pioneers of the Yoruba traveling theater. It was almost impossible for those artists to adopt or adapt one form of the Western element or the other into their plays. Besides the obvious fact that European civilization emerged as an imposition and was able to exhibit a high level of relevance with the Nigerian populace at the time – especially the ones who lived in urban areas – it became imperative for these artists to find common ground for both the traditional culture of the people and European culture.

A careful study of Olaiya's music shows his adeptness at major Nigerian ethnic group features, especially in how he maneuvered with ease through their languages in his songs. Indeed, Olaiya used more of the Yoruba language than other languages in most of his songs. This can be explained by the fact that he was born into a Yoruba family and spent a substantial part of his life living among Yoruba-speaking people. Taking a closer look at the song "Omo Pupa," Olaiya explains his love for a fair-complexioned lady (translated as *omo pupa* in Yoruba), delivered in rich, almost flattering Yoruba words. The lyrics of the song, when properly arranged, establish a sense of appreciation for the highlife form of music and, more particularly, respect for the genius of Olaiya as a highlife performer. Omojola notes that:

---

[31] Ekechukwu, "Life and Times of Victor Olaiya."
[32] Ekechukwu, "Life and Times of Victor Olaiya."
[33] Omojola, "Politics, Identity, and Nostalgia," 253.
[34] Chuks Nwanne, "Dr. Victor Olaiya . . . 60 Years of Blowing on Fame and Fortune," *The Guardian*, February 15, 2020.

Omo Pupa begins with an instrumental introduction that features brass and woodwinds, moving back and forth between unisons and parallel harmonies. The guitars outline the basic patterns of the harmonic progressions, which are generally limited to the primary chords; while the agogo (bell), the wooden clappers, and the drums set the rhythmic groove that is typical of a classic highlife style. The use of the Yoruba dundun (talking drum), especially in providing rhythmic embellishments between melodic phrases, clearly provides a local accent to the music and anticipates the Yoruba text.[35]

Anyone who listens to Olaiya's music can sense and appreciate the depth and beauty of his combination of musical instruments, which are smoothly blended with his clear and distinct voice.[36] One can speak of the creative way his songs start with a mix of musical displays and the regular interjection of musical interludes within the songs. As his chosen musical instrument, Olaiya is fond of showcasing his dexterity with the trumpet in between songs.[37] Of course, the use of a local instrument in his musical compositions points to both the nature of highlife music and to his ties to his heritage, which is the Yoruba culture. In his analysis of one of Olaiya's songs, titled "Oruku Tindi," Omojola talks about his use of the dundun in particular:

> The use of the dundun talking drum at the very opening is strategic in drawing attention to the indigenous Yoruba performance tradition that Olaiya recalls in this song. As the title "Oruku Tindi" indicates, this song . . . is a nostalgic recall of the Yoruba *alo* (storytelling sessions). In the nostalgic memory of many Yoruba people, these sessions devoted to riddles are performed as a prelude to *alo*, which take place in the evening, usually under [the] moonlight and following the completion of daily chores.[38]

For the people that Olaiya represented, the art of storytelling is not taken with levity, even though it is mostly done during leisure time. Storytelling was a vital part of most African communities before colonialism.[39] Hence, the use of this technique by artistes such as Olaiya is a means to perpetuate this practice and enrich the quality of their music. Artistes such as Olaiya use storytelling techniques to ease their audience into the message of the art, first by arousing a sense of nostalgia in the people for their traditional heritage and lacing moral messages between seemingly trivial issues. This was common among traditional storytellers in the ancient culture of the Nigerian people.

---

[35] Omojola, "Politics, Identity, and Nostalgia."
[36] Emmanuel Esomnofu, "Dr. Victor Olaiya: The Man, The Music, The Maestro," *PAM*, February 17, 2020, https://pan-african-music.com/en/dr-victor-olaiya-dead-89/.
[37] Esomnofu, "Dr. Victor Olaiya."
[38] Omojola, "Politics, Identity, and Nostalgia," 265–266.
[39] Kennedy Chinyowa, "The Sarungano and Shona Storytelling: An African Theatrical Paradigm," *Studies in Theatre and Performance* 21, no. 1 (2001): 18–30.

Olaiya's creativity in music is also apparent in the thematic preoccupations of his songs. Interestingly, his songs barely concern themselves with the political realities of Nigeria at the time, which was predominantly colonial. This is instructive because African artistes were (and still are) known for their ability to accommodate the overarching realities of the people in their artistic productions. Indeed, the ability to do this creatively also determines the acceptability and popularity of such works of art. However, although Olaiya had not devoted much of his music to comments on political issues of the day, his works still enjoyed wide listenership and acceptance. Of course, he still played the role of the conscience and perhaps the arbiter of morality for his people. His works explored themes such as love, pleasure, and the need for hard work. Works like "Omo Pupa," "Mo Fe Mu Yan," "Joromi," and more exemplify Victor Olaiya's music steeped in love themes or fantasies.

One significant thing in his exploration of this theme is that, just like people of his time, words are used intentionally, and sensitive issues are treated with serious caution. Hence, whereas he uses precise words such as "oyan" (the Yoruba word for breast), he does not become more graphic or detailed than this, leaving the rest to the imagination of his audience. The point here is that even when discussing issues like love and sex in his songs, Olaiya respects the moral codes of his society and reflects these in his artistic works.

Furthermore, the tension between the native culture of colonized people of Nigerian and British foreign cultures plays out in Olaiya's music through his creative narrative technique. The songs "Omo Pupa" and "Iye Jemila" are notable examples espousing this point. As mentioned earlier, "Omo Pupa" unpacks Olaiya's desires for the fair-complexioned lady, in a respectful, moralistic way. Another important thing to note about this song is the singer's deliberateness in using a place like London as bait for the girl he desires. Part of the effect of British colonialism is its deliberate overriding of native culture, instilling in the native man a sense of the superiority of white culture. This serves as a background to understand why the singer will mention lyrically something like "ti n ba de London, ma f'owo oko ranse" (meaning he intends to send airfare to his beloved fair-complexioned lady once he gets to London). In essence, London was an aspirational location for the average Nigerian at the time. Going to London – or to any European city, for that matter – was regarded as a great achievement and a source of respect from those in Nigeria. It was lodged in the psychology of the average Nigerian that their cities – even Lagos – could, at best, play second fiddle to European cities such as London. Hence, the singer is more assured of a chance with the fair-complexioned lady with the promise of a trip to London.

"Iye Jemila" brings to the fore the inevitable involvement of parents in the affairs of their children in the African context, especially one associated with the choice of a marital partner. This song, in the Ijebu dialect of the Yoruba language, narrates the singer's preference for a girl called Jemila, whose decision on whom to marry is largely determined by her parents. In the song, the singer offers many things to win Jemila's parents over, but none of these work, including the offer of money. While Omojola commends the artistic genius found in the music of Olaiya, he also notes a salient point of divergence, such as the perception of culture in songs as in the case of "Omo Pupa" and "Iye Jemila." He comments: "The form of this song ... is cumulative in design, featuring a process of continuous variation that is reminiscent of indigenous Yoruba musical narrative. This arrangement differs conceptually from the Western-derived ternary form of 'Omo Pupa.'"[40]

While not involved in the political commentaries on Nigeria, Olaiya can be said to have been recognized as a symbol of national unity. This will not be far from the truth as Olaiya embodies other cultures in Nigeria alongside his Yoruba heritage, and this is reflected in his music. He sang songs in Pidgin, which is essentially a unifying language in a nation like Nigeria where there are more than 250 unique languages and not everyone speaks English. Furthermore, Olaiya also sang in the Igbo ("Ai Ga Na") and Hausa ("Tina Mate") languages, making it clear that he spoke and understood three major Nigerian languages. This enables him, and the message of his songs, to transcend one geographical location. The sense of national unity embedded in Olaiya's music, and perhaps the noninvolvement of his music in political issues, positioned him as an ideal symbol of national unity.[41] On this, Omojola notes:

> As one of the personalities at the core of the emerging modern popular culture in the 1950s and 1960s, Olaiya and his music thus symbolized the concept of national unity at a time when unity was a key political theme in the country. In what seemed to be an official demonstration of this belief, Victor Olaiya was chosen to perform at the independence celebrations banquet in Marina, Lagos on 1 October 1960. He was also invited to perform the same role in October 1963 during the official celebrations that commemorated the status of Nigeria as a republic. These two events illustrate the significance of highlife music within the nationalist politics of the period. The selection of performances for the October 1960 celebrations was guided by a centrally controlled deliberateness aimed at ensuring that items that were deemed inappropriate were not included.[42]

This brings to mind the works of Bernard Olabanji Benson, popularly known as Bobby Benson. Benson is accredited with being the father of highlife music in Nigeria.[43] While Benson started his musical sojourn in London,

---

[40] Omojola, "Politics, Identity, and Nostalgia," 269.
[41] Niyi Akingbe, "In Memoriam: Dr Victor Abimbola Olaiya (1930–2020)," *Journal of the Musical Arts in Africa* 17, no. 1 (2020): 121–124.
[42] Omojola, "Politics, Identity, and Nostalgia," 254.
[43] Mosunmola A. Omibiyi, "Bobby Benson: The Entertainer–Musician," *Nigerian Magazine*, 1983.

joining the band Negro Ballet and touring Europe with the same band, his notable impact was felt more when he returned to Nigeria with his Scottish-Caribbean wife, Cassandra. The duo formed the Bobby Benson and Cassandra Theatrical Party, later renamed the Bobby Benson Jam Session. The creative combination of these two saw to it that their audience was entertained with music, dance, and even comedy. This was a group that provided the people with all-around entertainment.

Benson later began to embrace the highlife genre of music and adapted it to the Nigerian musical scene.[44] His influence in the music scene is seen in evergreen works such as "Taxi Driver" and in his impact on many notable musicians such as Victor Olaiya, who came after him. Bobby Benson's musical journey helped prepare a generation of musicians whose works and creative genius would transcend the times they lived in. There were the likes of Roy Chicago, Chief Bill Friday, Eddie Okonta, Rex Jim Lawson, and many more. Like Benson himself, these musical icons incorporated cultural elements in their music, thereby being a part of the efforts of nationalism, independence, and overall decolonization of the people, albeit from the cultural angle.

Theater in Colonial Nigeria

The first truth to establish here is that drama and the accompanying theatrical components were not introduced to the African continent and Niger area; several studies have established the existence of drama before the coming of the Europeans.[45] There were both sacred and secular aspects of drama in the precolonial era. This is in tandem with the views of J. Ndukaku Amankulor and Chinyere G. Okafor on precolonial Igbo creative endeavors, who believe that "In spite of the fact that the artist in pre-colonial Igboland was an individual whose talents were special to him, he nevertheless functioned invariably to serve the spiritual and aesthetic interests of the people."[46]

Like music, drama in the Nigerian context experienced an evolution during the colonial era. This evolution birthed what is today perceived as modern

---

[44] Oghenemudiakevwe Igbi, "Nigerian Highlife Music: A Survey of the Sociopolitical Events from 1950–2005," *EJOTMAS: Ekpoma Journal of Theatre and Media Arts* 5, no. 1–2 (2005): 173.

[45] Mzo Sirayi, "Oral African Drama in South Africa: The Xhosa Indigenous Drama Forms," *South African Theatre Journal* 10, no. 1 (1996): 49–61; Idris O. O. Amali, "Indigenous Nigerian Oral Drama as an Instrument of Social Regulation: A Case of the Ogbllo Secret Society of Idoma," *Ufahamu: Journal of the African Activist Association* 20, no. 1 (1992): 56–67.

[46] James Amankulor and Chinyere G. Okafor, "Continuity and Change in Traditional Nigerian Theater Among the Igbo in the Era of Colonial Politics," *Ufahamu: A Journal of African Studies* 16, no. 3 (1988): 36.

African drama.[47] It was inevitable that traditional creative and artistic works would entertain the new introduction brought about by Western culture. Amankulor and Okafor further capture this view in their study of an Igbo festival:

> Adaptation to the new socio-political atmosphere became the key to the survival of traditional drama. This adaptation was not only at the level of membership but permeated all activities of the title societies ... In costuming, for example, brass buttons have replaced the uda/a seeds as leopard spots for the Omabe masked-player in [the] Nsukka area. Black stockings are sometimes used by the masked actors of Ekpo theater instead of the traditional blackening of the eyes with charcoal. The "whiteman" face-mask can be seen on a Ije/e mask just as his figures feature in the Mbari houses. In characterization, masked actors depicting different Western types such as the policeman, gentleman in helmet and lady with high-heeled shoes and handbag[s] became novelties in the ensemble of Okumkpa theater of Afikpo. The radio-cassette now complements traditional music in enhancing the festival atmosphere. The songs also incorporate images drawn from modem life. For example, "eletrik" (electricity) refers to the bright and agile, and "uzowaya" (tarred road) connotes the wayward woman.[48]

One of the major harms of colonialism, especially due to the predominance of the Christian religion among the native people, was the deliberate and inadvertent relegation of the people's traditional religious practices to the background, even in cases where these practices were connected to creative works such as sculpture and drama. Indeed, actions such as this affected not only the spiritual and sacred aspects but also the creative and aesthetic performance. Therefore, the death of certain festivals or spiritual activities also signaled the abrupt end of specific creative activities.[49] Little wonder that the great Yoruba dramatist, Duro Ladipo, had to find another platform for his creative abilities after the bata drum (a Yoruba traditional drum) used during the Easter Cantata in his local church assembly was frowned upon.[50] Amankulor and Okafor reiterate this line of argument:

> The destruction of many ancestral shrines and proscription of influential communal festivals and ceremonies meant that the roots of many traditional arts, including dramatic art, were mortally wounded. Those that have managed to survive, due to either innate historic sensibilities or

---

[47] Christopher F. Kamlongera, "The British and the Beginnings of Contemporary African Drama," *Africana Marburgensia* 19, no. 1 (1986): 14–28.
[48] Amankulor and Okafor, "Continuity and Change in Traditional Nigerian Theater," 43.
[49] Eli Bentor, "Challenges to Rural Festivals with the Return to Democratic Rule in Southeastern Nigeria," *African Arts* 38, no. 4 (2005): 38–45.
[50] Ulli Beier, ed., *The Return of Shango: The Theatre of Duro Ladipo* (Bayreuth: IWALEWA-Haus, 1994).

artistic diplomacy in the era of colonial politics, still face the danger of extinction from contemporary African religious zealots for whom anything traditional or cultural must be associated with heathenism and devilry.[51]

Yet, despite the unwelcome interruption of Western culture in the native people's artistic endeavors, it should also be noted that one of the seemingly positive contributions of this period was its ability to widen the scope of creative works. In theater, for instance, the need to accommodate novel stories and characters due to the presence of the white colonialists widened the scope of drama in the Nigerian area, which also birthed modern African drama, to which Nigeria is a contributor. However, during the colonial era, the traditional form of theater, known as traveling theater, gained some form of prominence and popularity.[52] Traveling theater, which has deep roots in the Yoruba culture, serves as a foundation for the theater and film industry in Nigeria today. According to Biodun Jeyifo:

> If we agree with a scholar's description of theatrical tradition as "the transmission of a code of rules (i.e. conventions) to which players, playwrights and audiences conform, and store of possible modes of representing action which accumulates over the generations," the emergence and development of modern Yoruba Travelling Theatre as a vital, many-sided theatrical tradition in just four decades of its professional existence becomes a matter of considerable interest. Clearly, the historical emergence and growth of this theatrical tradition is to be seen in terms of both its roots in the traditional religious and secular performing arts of the Yoruba people and its more direct, immediate antecedents in the performances and entertainments engendered by the contact with European Christian missions and secular forces.[53]

Indeed, this theater is also traceable to the Christian religion, as the basis of their drama was rooted in both the religion and the traditional culture of the natives. References to Christianity were inevitable because the earliest forms of theater experienced in Nigeria were from the Church.

Joel Adedeji traces this history from colonial times and as far back as the early 1900s.[54] He submits that while the African Church in Nigeria and drama became separate entities in about 1910, the church leaders still had strong control over the activities of theater at the time. The separation of active involvement of the church from theater is traceable to the activities of the

---

[51] Amankulor and Okafor, "Continuity and Change in Traditional Nigerian Theater," 47.
[52] Joachim Fiebach, "Cultural Identities, Interculturalism, and Theatre: On the Popular Yoruba Travelling Theatre," *Theatre Research International* 21, no. 1 (1996): 52–58.
[53] Biodun Jeyifo, *The Yoruba Popular Travelling Theatre of Nigeria* (Lagos: Nigerian Magazine Publications, 1984), 35–36.
[54] Joel A. Adedeji, "The Origin and Form of the Yoruba Masque Theatre," *Cahiers d'Études africaines* 46 (1972): 254–276.

Lagos Glee Singers, who made their debut performance at the Glover Memorial Hall in 1910.[55] This group maintained the tradition of theater in Nigeria for a while before also disintegrating. However, the members of this group also proceeded to play a part in promoting the cause of theater in Nigeria, mostly within the church setting. Examples include people such as Ajayi K. Ajisafe, of whom Adedeji writes:

> In 1918, the African Church Choir Union was formed at the initiative of A. K. Ajisafe. The Union "aimed to improve Native airs for divine service and popularize Native music by means of special concerts." Also, A. K. Ajisafe's creative genius [sic] in traditional music and drama had made the United African Methodist Church (Eleja), established in 1917, an outstanding African church.[56]

There were also the likes of C. B. Olumuyiwa and Isaac B. Akinyele, who were former members of the Lagos Glee Singers and managed to stay relevant in the theater through their local churches. None of their efforts, however, are as significant as that of Ajayi K. Ajisafe. Adedeji argues that the United Native African (UNA) Church, with leaders such as G. A. Williams, was very active in theatrical productions.[57] However, the end of World War I and the outbreak of the influenza epidemic affected the composition of the United Church and led to the prominence of other churches. While some did not pay as much attention to theatrical productions as it was done in UNA, others did. For instance, the Cherubim and Seraphim Church in Lagos was said to have embraced organizing concerts and playing regularly for fundraising and as a spiritual activity. Hence, "The first recorded evidence of the Cherubim and Seraphim's sally into the Theatre was found in the performance of 'The Valiant Twelve' in Lagos in 1931. The show was a 'variety entertainment' which included such items as 'dialogue,' 'recitation,' and 'sacred song.'"[58] However, the Church also took a detour from the use of cultural and native materials in their theaters, as was common earlier with the UNA. Thus, the Aladura Movement was known for de-emphasizing the use of traditional forms and materials in their theatrical operations.

Many years down the line, this would also change as there was a disruption occasioned by the Great Depression of 1948 and the Church was not left out of the changes that were happening. There was the evolution of the Native Air Opera. On this, Adedeji writes:

> Native Opera... That's how the real public native plays based on biblical stories were described in the middle of the 1930s. These years saw the birth in Nigeria of native plays composed in native airs. For the next 10

---

[55] Joel Adedeji, "The Church and the Emergence of the Nigerian Theatre: 1915–1945," *Journal of the Historical Society of Nigeria* 6, no. 4 (1973): 389.
[56] Adedeji, "The Church and the Emergence of the Nigerian Theatre," 389.
[57] Adedeji, "The Church and the Emergence of the Nigerian Theatre," 388.
[58] Adedeji, "The Church and the Emergence of the Nigerian Theatre," 390.

years that followed, the African Churches led by the United African Methodist Church 'Eleja', Oke Arin, Lagos (UAMC) had a monopoly in this field. If the play was not the "Birth of Christ" it would be "Joseph [David] and Goliath."[59]

This was the era that also saw the emergence of the iconic Hubert Ogunde. His works are fundamental to discussing theater as a creative form, especially during the colonial era. Adedeji notes that:

> The Church of the Lord, a scion of the Aladura Movement, began at Ogere in Ijebu Province in 1931 and adopted a more down-to-earth approach which distinguished it from the other Aladura churches. Its chief attraction to adherents is in its form of service which is fitted to Yoruba cultural patterns. This must have stimulated Ogunde's interest and affected his attitude to the content, style and form of the "Native Air Opera" already popularized by his contemporaries and the Church. As a live-wire, Ogunde began a design which not only revolutionized the Yoruba Operatic Theatre but also pushed the Nigerian Theatre to an outstanding height.[60]

Hubert Ogunde is regarded as a pioneer in Nigerian professional folk opera.[61] Born in 1916, he founded the Ogunde Concert Party in 1945, a group regarded as Nigeria's first professional theatrical company.[62] Ogunde set out with his theater group to reawaken the Indigenous culture of the native people despite the effects of colonialism.[63] Ironically, his first folk opera, titled *Garden of Eden and the Throne of God*, had traceable elements of Christianity. Other plays – such as *Africa and God, Israel in Egypt, Nebuchadnezzar's Reign*, among others – also have Christian themes. This is not surprising, as he was an active member of the church as well as being a pastor's son. From his primary school days, it was inevitable that he would participate in church activities, which would become a source of interest.

> I started schooling in 1926 at the Baptist School Ife where my father, in addition to being the pastor in charge of the mission, was also the headmaster of the school. He was also the school's organist. Soon I joined the school's choir. This was my second inspiration in my journey to music. The church songs of those days were soul-rendering. For me, it had its special charm.[64]

---

[59] Adedeji, "The Church and the Emergence of the Nigerian Theatre," 392.
[60] Adedeji, "The Church and the Emergence of the Nigerian Theatre," 394.
[61] Ebun Clark, *Hubert Ogunde: The Making of Nigerian Theatre* (Oxford: Oxford University Press, 1979).
[62] Clark, *Hubert Ogunde*.
[63] Joel Adedeji, "Nationalism and the Nigerian National Theatre," *Munger Africana Library Notes* 54 (1980): 5–21.
[64] Bernth Lindfors, "Ogunde on Ogunde: Two Autobiographical Statements," *Educational Theatre Journal* 28, no. 2 (1976): 241.

Furthermore, when he started working as a teacher, he was actively involved in church music as an organist because the church and its music were a fundamental part of schooling in those days. He further learned music under the school organist, Mr. G. A. Adenuga, and his father. Ogunde notes that his quest to understand theater better, even after practicing in Nigeria for a while, inspired the decision to go to London for further theater studies. This was after years of teaching in different schools and serving in the police force.

> I was, by standards obtaining in the country, doing fine as a playwright. But I knew that I had a long way to go before I could be a truly professional playwright and showman. Daily I wanted to go to Europe and study drama. I was convinced that an overseas study course would greatly add to the show talents which I already possessed. I beat my own procrastination in 1947 and went to England and was lucky to be admitted in the Buddy Bradley School of Dancing at the Piccadilly Circus, London. During my stay there I had the opportunity of visiting several theaters and film studios in the United Kingdom and later I went to Paris on a sight-seeing trip.[65]

While it is true that Ogunde's creative adventure in theater was influenced by Western culture and Christian religion, anyone who is familiar with his work can also tell how hugely traditional and rich in Yoruba culture his plays are.[66] Ogunde himself recorded that his Ghanaian tour failed because the audience could not understand his use of the Yoruba language in his stage play, Ghana being a place he had eagerly looked forward to going to before the trip.[67] Of course, he had the opportunity to redeem his image in Ghana many years later.

Ogunde's deep roots in Yoruba culture stem from his time with his maternal grandfather. His father had married a "pagan" woman who was the daughter of an *Ifa* priest in Ife, and, as fate would have it, he spent more of his early days with his mother, who also took him on trips to participate at a distance in *Ifa* worshipping. He records that while he was there, he spent some time living with his grandfather, who was fond of him. With his grandfather, he was exposed to festivals, chants, and other deep cultural activities among the Yoruba people. According to Ogunde, "It was by being constantly at the old man's side watching him pouring out his incantations and listening to the songs and drums of the pagans that I first developed interest in juju music and plays."[68]

This, therefore, explains his immersion in Yoruba culture, which added color to his performances and allowed him to stand out both within and outside the continent. His creative cachet was such that he toured European countries on more than one occasion:

[65] Lindfors, "Ogunde on Ogunde," 243–244.
[66] Ulli Beier, *Theatre in Nigeria* (New Delhi: Sangeet Natak Akademi, 1973).
[67] Lindfors, "Ogunde on Ogunde," 245.
[68] Lindfors, "Ogunde on Ogunde," 241.

I have had the opportunity of making many friends and seeing many parts of the world. At the early stage of my profession, my wife and I toured Britain, France and Italy to get acquainted with the stage set-ups. My troupe was at the 1967 Canadian Expo. In 1968–69, the military government sponsored my troupe – forty in number – to Britain and the rest of Europe. We were well received and our performances were widely acclaimed by the British and world press.[69]

There were tours to African countries like Ghana, the Ivory Coast, and Sierra Leone and even within the cities of his home country, Nigeria. Gregory Nwakunor notes that the play *Strike and Hunger*, performed in 1946, catapulted Ogunde to popularity.[70] The play dramatized the nationwide general strike of 1945, led by Michael Imoudu.[71] This started in Lagos with railway officials refusing to work, which soon spread to other government workers around the country. On this premise, Ogunde created the play *Strike and Hunger* to depict the hunger, suffering, and general injustice that the people were experiencing in the colonial nation of Nigeria at the time. Interestingly, even Ogunde did not know the impact his plays had on the people. Perhaps he only realized this after an awful encounter with the police in Jos.

According to an autobiographical account from an interview with Ogunde, presented by Bernth Lindfors, Ogunde and his troupe started their tour to Northern Nigeria to stage his play in 1946, landing in Jos, where they opened the play. While performing, he and the crew were arrested and charged with trying to incite the populace against His Majesty.[72] He was fined £125. According to Ogunde, "Before the Jos incident, I had staged the play in Kaduna, Zaria, Lagos, Ibadan, and Abeokuta without trouble. That was why I was shocked that the Jos Police took a different attitude."[73] However, his northern fans contributed to paying the fine, and he even had money left over after the settlement. Unfortunately, however, this incident was repeated in Kano, where he was not even allowed to perform before he was arrested.

The next year, Ogunde staged *Tiger's Empire*. This is recorded as the first occasion on which women were paid as professional actresses in Nigeria. Ogunde wrote and produced other politically themed plays such as *Herbert Macaulay*, which told of the life and times of the eponymous nationalist. While his plays were initially staged only within Lagos and Abeokuta, by 1948,

---

[69] Lindfors, "Ogunde on Ogunde," 246.
[70] Gregory A. Nwakunor, "Hubert Ogunde: A Centenary Birthday Dance for the Doyen of Theatre," *The Guardian*, July 16, 2016.
[71] Oliver Coates, "Hubert Ogunde's Strike and Hunger and the 1945 General Strike in Lagos: Labor and Reciprocity in the Kingdom of Ọba Yéjídé," *Research in African Literatures* 48, no. 2 (2017): 166–184.
[72] Lindfors, "Ogunde on Ogunde."
[73] Lindfors, "Ogunde on Ogunde." 244.

Ogunde's artistry was beginning to receive greater attention.[74] Consequently, he went on a tour of the Southwestern cities in Nigeria in that same year, taking his plays to places such as Ibadan, Ede, and Ogbomoso, among others. His plays are known for their inclusion of dancing and music. Their distinct traditional Yoruba flavor was well appreciated, both far and near, and he was commissioned to start a national theater group in Nigeria.

Kola Ogunmola was not so different from Hubert Ogunde and Duro Ladipo in their early days – the trio are recognized as the founding fathers of theater in Nigeria. Ogunmola started his career in a remote primary school in Ekiti.[75] He was a distinguished teacher who used music, ceremonial procession, and drama to entice more students to the schools where he taught. He promoted Western education among his people using the tools of music and drama.[76] From here, his fame as a theater practitioner began to grow. With a similar background to Ogunde and Ladipo, Ogunmola and other theater practitioners emerged, drawing influence from their roots and activities in missionary churches. This became a viable tool that they added to their traditional roots in the Yoruba culture, and which would earn them a place in the hearts of many as icons of cultural nationalism.

Despite limitations in terms of funds and professionally trained actors, Ogunmola is revered for his dexterity in producing notable dramas, and for his managerial skills in maintaining a group that helped deliver on the standards of the folk theater of the period.[77] His acting and directorial skills were once commended by Ulli Beier, who said, "Ogunmola's forte is his acting – his mime in particular . . . As an actor, and even as a director, he can reach great heights."[78] Etherton corroborates Beier's point: "It was the opinion of many who saw Ogunmola perform his plays that he was the most brilliant actor of the 1950s and 1960s."[79] Perhaps predicated on the fact that theater was still growing in Nigeria at the time, or on the fact that the traveling theater was booming in the Southwestern part of the country, or just the obvious brilliance in Ogunmola's creative output, Jeyifo, echoed in Adekola, also recognizes Ogunmola's uniqueness:

> Some famous and acclaimed actors and actresses do not of course get stuck with such a stage label derived from some particular production. Rather they attract the adulation of the audience in their own idiosyncratic

---

[74] Beier, *Theatre in Nigeria*.
[75] Ulli Beier, "Yoruba Folk Opera," *African Music* 1, no. 1 (1954): 32–34.
[76] Beier, "Yoruba Folk Opera."
[77] Philip A. Ogundeji, *Friendship, Housewife–rivalry and Human Lust in the Plays of Kola Ogunmola* (Ibadan: University of Ibadan, Department of Theatre Arts, 1991).
[78] Ulli Beier, "Yoruba Theatre," in *Introduction to African Literature: An Anthology of Critical Writing on African and Afro-American Literature and Oral Tradition*, ed. Ulli Beier (Illinois: Northwestern University Press, 1967), 247.
[79] Michael Etherton, "The Development of African Drama," *Theatre Research International* 9, no. 3 (2009), 48.

expressions from role to role. The outstanding example of this is the late Kola Ogunmola, who is justifiably and universally acclaimed to have been the greatest actor the Travelling Theatre has provided to date.[80]

Part of managing his team included finding a means to ensure that his group members stayed long enough for the cohesion needed in a team of performers. Interestingly, at some points, he had to marry female members of his group to ensure that they stayed because it was common for females to leave due to marriage or pressure from their parents. Kola Ogunmola's plays were indeed in a class of their own. This was demonstrated in his ability to dig deep into his Yoruba heritage to produce plays that appealed to the cultural sensibilities of the Yoruba people.[81] This is important because, just like Hubert Ogunde, Ogunmola emerged at the point when traditional cultural and religious beliefs were being relegated to the background to give greater prominence to Western culture brought about by colonialism. Hence, Ogunmola assumed the role of the artiste in society, who serves as the people's conscience and helps them stay abreast of important things in their culture – the Yoruba culture, in this case. Biodun Jeyifo, once again quoted in Adekola, opines that:

> For the fact that Ogunmola was born and bred within the Yoruba cultural environment, he was able to utilize effectively this knowledge and experience of the Yoruba culture he possessed for the success of his theater profession. Thus, he was able to arouse the interest of his audience and make them ponder on the adulterated Yoruba socio-cultural life with the aim of correcting the unpleasant aspects.[82]

Of course, the efforts of Ogunmola were obvious to both the people who came to be entertained by his works and to academic critics of art. Beier goes on to note that "There was sensitivity here, an attention to detail that was totally captivating. Even with virtually no knowledge of Yoruba, one could follow any tiny shade of meaning and mood. The acting was selectively realistic."[83] In other words, Ogunmola's plays were not just limited in reach to a Yoruba audience; he also had nonspeakers of the language in mind and ensured that by merely watching, an audience could decode the meaning of a play even without understanding the words. This kind of aim in theater is achievable only when the acting is skillful and well-coordinated, and this must have been the case with Ogunmola's plays, as noted by Beier.

Ogunmola's works spread across different themes and eras. As noted, he started as a teacher in a mission school, where he also began creating his

---

[80] Oyebola O. Adekola, "Kola Ogunmola: A Socio-Cultural Study of His Folkloric Plays," Master's thesis: University of Ibadan, 1991.
[81] Beier, *Theatre in Nigeria*.
[82] Adekola, "Kola Ogunmola," 26.
[83] Ulli Beier, "E. K. Ogunmola: A Personal Memoir," in *Drama and Theatre in Nigeria: A Critical Source Book*, ed. Yemi Ogunbiyi (Lagos: Nigeria Magazine Publications), 323.

theatrical practices. As expected, Ogunmola's first set of plays touched on biblical themes, albeit not with obvious traces of the Yoruba tradition. His first play was titled *Reign of the Mighty*, which highlighted the life of King Nebuchadnezzar in the Bible. Some other plays also had biblical themes. Beyond this, however, his plays addressed other pressing societal issues and mirrored the realities of his immediate society. According to Jeyifo (cited in Adekola), "Ogunmola's plays deal mostly with the mundane realities of everyday existence, sufficiently generalized in terms of the constitutive situations of the plots such that any given member of the audience can easily identify with them."[84]

While one might argue that Ogunmola's prominence came about after Independence, it is important to note that his plays were also used to address colonial activities and their effects, as noted earlier in terms of how his plays were intended to remind his Yoruba audience of their roots. Ogunmola can be referred to as a complete artiste, being a traveling theater actor and director, and his impact on the creative sector during the colonial era cannot be underestimated. The same can be said of Duro Ladipo, who makes up the trio that was the most popular of the traveling theater movements in the early postindependence periods.

Duro Ladipo's troupe did more in the early independence period. It is also imperative that his life and works are considered as creative and aesthetic endeavors in the decades after independence. This is simply because it was obvious that, despite gaining independence, Nigeria was still plagued by colonial problems, eventually leading to the first coup in 1966. Additionally, the vestiges of colonialism were very much in effect during the 1960s, and the words of creative dramatists such as Duro Ladipo and Kola Ogunmola were instrumental in cultural nationalism and eradicating colonial-inspired Western thinking.

Interestingly, Ladipo was born as an *abiku*, which in Yoruba cosmological belief is a child that is born to die again.[85] Oluseyi Ogunjobi argues that Duro Ladipo's tie to the spirit world – as an *abiku* – had a significant influence on his life and career as a dramatist.[86] He notes that after Ladipo's mother had tried all available options to make her son stay on earth – including practicing Christianity, in the search for a lasting solution – nothing worked for her. She found the solution she needed in an *Ifa* priest from her household.[87] The available record has it that this *Ifa* priest, who was also a Sango worshipper, would play a significant role in the early developmental years of Ladipo.

[84] Adekola, "Kola Ogunmola."
[85] Timothy Mobolade, "The Concept of Abiku," *African Arts* 7, no. 1 (1973): 62–64.
[86] Oluseyi Ogunjobi, "The Creative Development, Importance, and Dramaturgy of Duro Ladipo's Oba Ko So," *Cross/Cultures* 177 (2014): 291–318.
[87] Remi Raji-Oyelade, Sola Olorunyomi, and Abiodun Duro Ladipo, *Duro Ladipo: Thunder-God on Stage* (Ibadan: Institute of African Studies, University of Ibadan, 2003).

Furthermore, Ladipo was also influenced by the Christian religion embraced by his father, who refused to be involved in "pagan" worship.[88]

By 1942, Ladipo, as for the others discussed earlier in the chapter, also found himself in the teaching profession with his government Middle Two Certificate. Indeed, the mixture of all these influences prompted him to become a dramatist. According to Ogunjobi;

> Duro displayed an early interest in folk songs, traditional music and moonlight tales. As a precocious child who could imitate human actions and compose delightful songs at the briefest prompt, Duro would later use the dual advantage of Western missionary education and his innate cultural creativity to commendable effect.[89]

So far, this chapter has highlighted some of the icons that represented creativity and aesthetics in the Niger area during the colonial era. Each of these icons was renowned and unique in certain areas. Again, there is no doubt that they excelled in their respective rights, with evidence supporting their contributions to the country's musical and theatrical output. In all of the aforementioned cases, one can easily notice that these artistes were fond of incorporating materials from their cultural backgrounds, especially language.[90] Possibly because Lagos was (and still is) the center for entertainment and economic activities, the Yoruba language and Yoruba artistes seemed to have enjoyed greater visibility and privileges at the time. As noted, they made it a point of duty to engage in their crafts through the medium of their mother tongues.

One can tell that most of these artistes, even when they had been trained in the English language and had been encouraged to make their art in musical form, got to a point in their creative journey where the urge to utilize the resources made available by their African roots was paramount. In the case of Fela Sowande, Victor Olaiya, Hubert Ogunde, Kola Ogunmola, and others, their earliest works either explored Western/biblical themes or used a foreign language, just as some of their most prominent works were presented in the Yoruba language. Again, this was a deliberate effort on the part of the artistes who began to see their creative works as a medium to "fight" and decolonize the people's minds. Undoubtedly, many Nigerians regarded the English language as superior to their mother tongue during colonialism and after – so much so that some elites prevented their children from learning their mother tongue because they believed it represented what is local, inferior, and globally unrecognized.

While this is true – because the colonial world powers wanted it so – artistes such as the ones discussed herein used their craft to brilliantly reinstate the place of Indigenous languages in the world order. Consequently, the Yoruba

---

[88] Raji-Oyelade, Olorunyomi, and Duro Ladipo, *Duro Ladipo*.
[89] Ogunjobi, "The Creative Development."
[90] Oluseyi Ogunjobi, "The Visual Languages of Duro Ladipo's Theatre in Oba Moro, Oba Koso and Oba Waja," unpublished PhD dissertation, University of Leeds, 2011.

language became recognized in countries such as the United States of America and the United Kingdom partly due to the efforts of these artistes. Besides being a tool to fight imperialism, the Yoruba language also greatly enriched the quality of these artistes' productions.

For instance, the traveling theater of Duro Ladipo is believed to have replicated some of the most important historical accounts of the Yoruba people. The play, Oba Ko So (The King Did Not Hang) recounts the legend of Sango, who was believed to have been a king in the Old Oyo empire.[91] Communicating this Yoruba story in the language of the people went a long way toward keeping the people abreast of their myths, legends, and history, which served as a way of preserving cultural legacies. Although specifically commenting on Victor Olaiya's works, Omojola's submission about the use of language in his music can also be applied to other creative output from Nigeria during and even after the colonial era. He notes that "Language plays a very significant role in imparting distinctive character and accent to a musical style, and it is only to be expected that the distinctive features of Ghanaian and Nigerian Highlife derive considerably from the use of indigenous languages."[92]

Language, therefore, was not only a way for these artistes to explore their creativity and the beauty of their cultural heritage more deeply; it also became a tool for nationalism and a subtle way of revolting against the imperial hold of the English language and Western culture in its entirety. Therefore, as much as the artistes during the colonial era were stuck with European elements in their art, they were adept enough to find ways to incorporate vital elements of their traditional culture, such as the use of their Indigenous language.

Lagos: The Hub of Creativity

One of the first places the Europeans settled in the Niger area was the coastal region of Lagos; previously called *Oko* and *Eko* at different times by the inhabitants of the area, it was eventually renamed Lagos by the Portuguese traders who visited.[93] Lagos became a choice area for colonialists partly because of its closeness to the Atlantic. Consequently, the city gradually began to take shape as the Nigerian economic and entertainment hub, and, by extension, it also became regarded as the main economic/entertainment hub of Africa. Yet, before the colonial invasion, Lagos was not even among

---

[91] Abiodun Duro Ladipo and Gbóyèga Kóláwolé, "Opera in Nigeria: The Case of Duro Ladipo's "Ọba Kòso,"" *Black Music Research Journal* 17, no. 1 (1997): 101–129.

[92] Omojola, "Politics, Identity, and Nostalgia," 263.

[93] Kaye Whiteman, *Lagos: A Cultural and Literary History* (Oxford: Signal Books Limited, 2012).

the most important Yoruba kingdoms at the time. Its place as an economic hub in the Southern part of the country and the nation, as a whole, was largely not foreseen during this period. But, with the Atlantic slave trade, there was a turnaround. Robert Sydney Smith attempts to trace the different stages of development in Lagos in *The Lagos Consulate, 1851–1861*, and makes the vital point that:

> The development of overseas trade on an increasing scale, the ensuing prosperity, and the settlement of European slave traders in their midst constituted a considerable disturbance in the traditional pattern of life of the Lagosians. The growing consequence and wealth of the kingdom enabled it to play a part in the wider politics of the coast.[94]

Not only did the wealth of the city contribute to political activities in the area, but it also determined the direction of art and entertainment in the colonial era. During this period, Lagos was more or less the capital of colonial Nigeria. While other regions were grouped either under the Northern or Southern Protectorates, the colony of Lagos stood as an independent entity until it was united with the Southern Protectorate in 1906. This shows the central role the city played during colonialism. Therefore, this tended to affect other aspects of life, including the creative and entertainment sectors. Note that all the icons of creativity and aesthetics highlighted so far had, at one point or another in their lives, had to live in Lagos for a while.

As economic activities became centralized in Lagos, the city also housed notable men and women in society. Being the center of administration meant that many colonial masters lived in Lagos with their families. Although they also lived separately from their subjects, this was within the same city. Also, notable Nigerian elites were known to live in Lagos at the time, partly because some could not afford to be far from the seat of power, and also because Lagos was one of the cities that witnessed early and heavy industrialization right from the colonial era.[95] Furthermore, Lagos is also close to Ibadan, a notable administrative city during the colonial era. All of these factors ensured that the elites and, perhaps, the richest of the Nigerian society were mostly domiciled in Lagos at the time.

Of course, humans are inherently social in nature. It was only natural for the people of Lagos to crave entertainment or social interaction beyond work.[96] This, therefore, facilitated the growth of the entertainment sector in the city. As a result, there was a change in how people interacted, as Lagos was (and still is) an urban city center, which meant an irreversible synchronization between the Western culture and the people's traditional cultures was

---

[94] Smith, *The Lagos Consulate*, 11.
[95] Michael J. C. Echeruo, *Victorian Lagos: Aspects of Nineteenth Century Lagos Life* (London: Macmillan, 1977).
[96] Monsuru Muritala, *Livelihood in Colonial Lagos* (Lanham: Lexington Books, 2019), 102.

taking place. Social entertainment centers, nightclubs, modern drinking bars, banquet parties, cinemas, and other leisure/entertainment venues were already available at night times and weekends for people living in the city.[97] This meant that demand for artistic works such as music and theater was also on the rise.

According to Omojola, increased demand for these artistic works in the colonial city of Lagos became inevitable because of the rapid urbanization the city experienced during the colonial era.[98] This was due to obvious factors, such as the city's ability to play host to a mixed population comprising Europeans, returnee slaves from the New World and Europe, and even Nigerian natives. As one would expect, this also had an impact on the artistic activities happening in the city at this time:

> Lagos became an urban center with a considerable cosmopolitan population that included Europeans as well as ex-African slaves who had returned from Brazil, and those who were repatriated from Sierra Leone. ... migrants from Brazil, Cuba, the United States, and the British West Indies began to settle in Lagos from the late nineteenth century, constituting an important part of the expanding social demography of the city. These migrants introduced a host of new musical elements (including instruments, dances, and songs) that became accessible to local musicians. The performance space of musical activities expanded beyond indigenous contexts like traditional festivals and ritual ceremonies to include the church, the night club, dinner parties, and palm-wine bars. In responding to the social demands of the new environment, many musicians engaged in experimental creative forms in which African, Western, and Afro-Cuban elements were combined. These syncretic musical styles provided the antecedents for highlife music that was made popular by musicians like Bobby Benson and Victor Olaiya.[99]

Omojola is not alone on this, as his point is further corroborated by Adeogun's views on the changes in the artistic tastes of the people of Lagos following urbanization.[100] Of course, the presence of people from different groups and different cultural backgrounds was part of what facilitated urbanization in the city. In his words:

> In these urban localities, western popular dance music thrived. Europeans brought their dances such as the waltz, foxtrot, quickstep and tango. Before long, Nigerians in the urban centers caught on to this brand of

---

[97] Oladipo O. Olubomehin, "Cinema Business in Lagos, Nigeria since 1903," *Historical Research Letter* 3 (2012): 1–10.
[98] Omojola, "Politics, Identity, and Nostalgia."
[99] Omojola, "Politics, Identity, and Nostalgia."
[100] Adebowale O. Adeogun, "Music Education in Nigeria, 1842–2001: Policy and Content Evaluation, Towards a New Dispensation," unpublished PhD dissertation, University of Pretoria, 2007, 23.

music. Later, Nigerians formed their own orchestras that enabled them play the European dance steps. Subsequently, there was traditionally derived music played on Europeans instruments. In addition, out of a deliberate protest against western popular dance music, there emerged the Nigerian popular music forms. Some of the Nigerian popular music forms that emerged include highlife, juju, apala and sakara.[101]

Notably, there were creative activities in other cities and towns around the country too. Besides music and theater, for instance, many communities were also still known for their works in sculpting, fabric making, and dyeing, among other activities. However, the emphasis on Lagos is because it gave better visibility and opportunity for growth to those who operated within the city. Of course, there must have been many others also within the city whose works never made it into the limelight, but those in the city center of Lagos had a better chance of being noticed than those in other towns and cities. Moreover, besides the fact that Lagos had people who appreciated this art and could afford to access it, it also had other facilities, such as town halls, that were constructed to host artistic works. One example is the Glover Memorial Hall, which staged some of the earliest and best plays produced during the colonial era.[102]

Conclusion

The foundations for the creative and aesthetic output found in postcolonial Nigeria have deep roots in the efforts of those in the colonial era. These colonial artistes were not just all about the entertainment their art proffered, although this is important; they were also preservers of the people's cultural beliefs. Their music and theater, some examples of which have been examined herein, set the tone for what was to come immediately after independence. Of course, one cannot overlook the efforts of political nationalists who played their part in ensuring a cultural revival among the people of Nigeria after years of being under colonial rule and being given to the belief that the Western culture was superior to their Indigenous culture.

As a way of reviving people's interest in their Indigenous cultures, it became fashionable for artistes to create unique works using Indigenous languages. This was significant because, during colonialism and in the early years of independence, it was common for the social elite to embrace the use of the English language to the detriment of Indigenous languages like

---

[101] Adeogun, "Music Education in Nigeria," 23.
[102] Mufutau O. Jimoh, "A Study in Spatial Focal Points and Social Contestation of Urban Life in Lagos: A History of Glover Memorial Hall, 1889–1960," *Ife Journal of History* 8, no. 1 (2016): 124–149.

Yoruba, Hausa, and Igbo. Hence, artistic works of the colonial era were not only rich in creativity, but they were also deeply cultural and engaging. Little wonder that artists working in newer genres such as hip-hop would learn to look within their sociocultural context to make aesthetically appealing and culturally engaging music.[103]

---

[103] Oluwafunminiyi Raheem, "From the Sublime to the Ridiculous?: Contemporary Nigerian Hip-Hop, Music Consumption and the Search for Meaning (1999–2015)," in *Yoruba Arts, Culture, Entertainment & Tourism in the Age of Globalization & Uncertainty*, ed. Felix Ayoh'Omidire, Shina Alimi, and Akin Adejuwon (OAU: Institute of Cultural Studies, 2020), 172–192.

PART IV

Nationalism and Independence

21

Reform Movements Before 1940

British colonizers were challenged continuously during their arrival and occupation of Nigeria. The country's colonial history holds records of opposition from individuals and organizations that resisted the colonial administration. Many kings and chiefs initially responded with military opposition, seeing their sovereignty threatened by the establishment of a foreign colonial authority. In later years, resistance was conducted with tactics enabled by the Western education that emerging elite members of society had acquired. These elites later established strong nationalist organizations that opposed the colonial administration and its policies. These movements successfully attained independence for the country in 1960.

Gabriel Olusanya noted that nationalism in Nigeria predated the amalgamation of the colony's different parts in 1914.[1] Early resistance struggles occurred in different regions before amalgamation, but the act of amalgamation united people from different social classes, communities, ethnic groups, and religions to pursue a common civic objective. Although different individuals and organizations participated in the struggle, this chapter focuses on the roles that the educated elites played through political organizations, media outlets, and pan-African organizations. Before discussing the activities and achievements of these nationalist leaders and organizations, the concept of nationalism must be considered with respect to the way the Nigerian nationalists were attempting to behave.

The Idea of Nationalism

The concept of nationalism is controversial in most social science disciplines; different phenomena have been attached to the term.[2] One text describes the concept as a "double-edged sword," with negative and positive implications. Strong feelings of nationalism have been the basis for fighting oppression or

---

[1] Gabriel O. Olusanya, "The Nationalist Movement in Nigeria," in *Groundwork of Nigerian History*, ed. Obaro Ikime (Ibadan: Heinemann Educational Books, 1980), 545.
[2] See, for instance, Anthony D. Smith, *Nationalism: Theory, Ideology, History* (Cambridge: Polity Press, 2010).

demanding a nation's right to self-determination.[3] It has even been described as the motive for a singular ethnic group to seek to dominate an entire state. The negative conceptualization of nationalism, also described as "ethnic nationalism," often holds the same implications as concepts such as racism and discrimination, without moral justification.[4] One author has noted that usage of the term varies from state to state.[5]

Despite the various interpretations of the concept, a single idea unites all conceptualizations of nationalism: the preservation of national identity. Smith's 1991 definition of nationalism is one of the most popular descriptions: "an ideological movement for attaining and maintaining autonomy, unity and identity on behalf of a population deemed by some of its members to constitute an actual or potential nation."[6] It has also been defined as "a theory of political legitimacy, which requires that ethnic boundaries should not cut across political ones, and in particular, that ethnic boundaries within a given state ... should not separate the power holders from the rest."[7] More recent literature has adopted the definition of the term as given in the Merriam-Webster dictionary: "loyalty and devotion to a nation, especially a sense of national consciousness exalting one nation above all others and placing primary emphasis on the promotion of its culture and interests as opposed to those of other nations or supranational groups."[8] An understanding of nationalism presupposes the existence of a territory, a legal political community, and a common civic culture and ideology.

The concept of contemporary nationalism emerged in Europe in the early nineteenth century.[9] In the view of Europeans from this period, nationalism was aimed at guaranteeing self-government for those societies that desired it.[10] The nationalist struggles in Europe in the nineteenth century were rooted in the modern concept of self-determination, undertaken as deliberate actions by

---

[3] Louis L. Snyder, *The Meaning of Nationalism* (New York: Greenwood Press, 1968).
[4] Olusola Olasupo, Isaac Olajide, and E. O. C. Ijeoma, "Nationalism and Nationalist Agitation in Africa: The Nigerian Trajectory," *The Review of Black Political Economy* 44, no. 3-4 (2017), 261–283.
[5] Abubakar Abdulahi and Yahaya T. Baba, "Nationalism and National Integration in Nigeria," in *Nigerian Politics*, ed. Rotimi Ajayi Joseph and Yinka Fashagba (Cham: Springer, 2019), 307.
[6] Cited in Joep Leerssen, *National Thought in Europe: A Cultural History* (Amsterdam: Amsterdam University Press, 2006), 15.
[7] Ernest Gellner, *Nations and Nationalism* (Oxford: Basil Blackwell, 1983), 1.
[8] Kelechi C. Ubaku, Chikezie A. Emeh, and Chinenye N. Anyikwa, "Impact of Nationalist Movement on the Actualization of Nigerian Independence," *International Journal of History and Philosophical Research* 2, no.1 (2014), 54–67.
[9] Stefan Berger and Eric Storm, eds., *Writing the History of Nationalism* (London: Bloomsbury Academic, 2019).
[10] Samah Sabra, "Imaging Nations: An Anthropological Perspective," *Nexus* 20 (2007): 76–104.

citizens opposing monarchies and feudal systems of government. The citizens worked toward the institutionalization of representative government based on universal principles of democracy. One such example is the French Revolution of 1789–99, which opposed the absolutist regime of Louis XIV and eventually orchestrated a constitutional government in France.[11] Nationalist feelings have also fueled struggles for racial equality in the United States, especially between the eighteenth and twentieth centuries.[12]

Educated elite Africans who were taught the history and politics of European powers, seized the notion of nationalism to challenge the authority of those Westerners who had seized their territories under the pretext of colonialism. In African history, nationalism became associated with a sense of consciousness used by African people from different territories to assert their rights to self-government and decolonization.[13] It directly opposed the notions and practices of imperialism and colonialism instituted by European colonial powers. The different ways that nationalist notions have been applied in Europe and Africa show the complexity of the concept. Even within the same political entity, nationalist ideas differ based on the peculiarities of the period and the needs of the state.[14] In the case of Nigeria, for instance, the struggle for independence is a view of nationalism that is separate from that which characterized the struggle to preserve the country's indivisibility and national integration during the Nigerian Civil War.

In this chapter, the concept of nationalism is rooted in the agitations of Nigerians who opposed the colonial administration. It is important to define these agitations as distinct from the nationalist struggles for decolonization in most parts of Africa during the middle of the twentieth century. Early nationalist struggles resulted in anticolonialism and decolonization over the long term, but most of the nationalist movements discussed in this chapter focused on the entrenchment of a responsible colonial administration and the inclusion of Nigerians in that administration. This chapter also examines nationalist movements that operated in colonial Nigeria at different times before 1940. It will include political organizations, media outlets, and pan-African organizations based outside the Nigerian territory that contributed to the country's nationalist struggles.

---

[11] Michael Rowe, "The French Revolution, Napoleon, and Nationalism in Europe," in *The Oxford Handbook on the History of Nationalism*, ed. John Breuilly (Oxford: Oxford University Press, 2013), 127–148.

[12] Paul Finkelman, *Encyclopedia of African American History, 1896 to the Present: O–T* (Oxford: Oxford University Press, 2009).

[13] Thomas Hodgkin, *Nationalism in Colonial Africa* (New York: New York University Press, 1957).

[14] Abdulahi and Baba, "Nationalism and National Integration."

The Advent and Growth of Nationalism

Scholars of history and political science tend to address the theoretical distinctions between the appearance and evolution of nationalism in Nigeria. Abdulahi and Baba, in their discussion of the "factors responsible for nationalist movements in Nigeria," suggest that political, economic, and socioeconomic factors account for the "rise and growth" of Nigeria's nationalist movements.[15] They note that the sense of consciousness associated with the concept of nationalism is usually expressed in one of two ways. It may manifest through the attitudes of members of a nation who seek to protect their national identity, or through the actions taken by members of a nation who choose to sustain their call for self-determination. Ubaku and others, while tracing the advent of nationalism in Nigeria to the 1914 amalgamation of the Northern and Southern Protectorates, neglect to consider all the motivating factors that account for the advent of nationalism in the polity.[16] Instead, they foregrounded the internal and external factors that account for the growth of nationalism.

Two periods in Nigeria's history have been associated with the advent of nationalism. The first was the period of resistance from chiefs and kings of autonomous nation-states, opposing colonial invasion to protect their territories. The second occurred during the amalgamation of the Northern and Southern Protectorates. The tendency to attribute nationalism's origins to the amalgamation period is often based on the assumption that there was no single political state before this period.[17] Nationalist ideology presupposes the existence of a nation or other political entities seeking to pursue a common civic culture.[18]

The period of early struggles is an appropriate time-frame for identifying the advent of nationalism in Nigeria. Nationalist struggles during this period were efforts made by the political and military leaders to protect their territories from colonial invasion.[19] Notable figures such as Attahiru of Sokoto, Jaja of Opobo, Nana of Itshekiri, and Oba Ovonramwen led historic acts of resistance against the colonial invaders to protect their dignity or authority as rulers or to preserve the political autonomy of their respective communities.[20] Entire communities also led acts of resistance against colonial invasions at different

---

[15] Abdulahi and Baba, "Nationalism and National Integration."
[16] Ubaku, Emeh, and Anyikwa, "Impact of Nationalist Movement."
[17] Ubaku, Emeh, and Anyikwa, "Impact of Nationalist Movement."
[18] Sabra, "Imaging Nations."
[19] Obaro Ikime, "Colonial Conquest and Resistance in Southern Nigeria," *Journal of the Historical Society of Nigeria* 6, no. 3 (1972): 251–270.
[20] Uche U. Okonkwo, "Herbert Macaulay as the Father of Nigeria's Nationalism: A Historical Misnomer and Misogyny Regarding the Role of Igbo Women in the Decolonization Process," *Journal of International Women's Studies* 21, no. 1 (2020): 172–184.

times.[21] The Ijebu people raised an army of more than 7,000 soldiers to expel the British from their territory.[22] Although these acts of resistance failed, they were crucial to the institutionalization of nationalism. They provided a solid bedrock for the growth of nationalism across the entire political entity later known as Nigeria.

The major event responsible for the emergence of nationalism was the British invasion. The intrusion resulted in the conglomeration of different territories around the River Niger into a single nation-state. Before 1861, when the first annexation of colonies (and protectorates) took place in the country, each pre-existing community had a defined population and an autonomous government – or at least a semblance of it, in the form of a sociopolitical organization.[23] The arrival of the British ruptured these pre-existing political structures. Leaders of precolonial nation-states began their opposition with acts of resistance. They struggled to retain the autonomy of their societies and freedom from subjugation by foreign powers. Rulers who opposed the British invasion sought to protect their authority and personal dignity, along with the political sovereignty of their respective regions.

Colonialism imposed a "modernized" system of government that was not only unfamiliar to the Indigenous population but also challenged their identity and the political relevance of their communities. As they realized that their individual territories would be conglomerated into a single nation-state, the indigenes began to recognize a national identity. They had minimized their opposition to the conquest of their polities, but would continue to resist the foreign machinery through which their "new nation-state" was governed.

The Indigenous population resisted the British colonial government, its policies, and the administration of their private and public affairs, which led to the modern concept of nationalism in Nigeria. In this view, nationalism was the consciousness held by the people of the Protectorate of Nigeria, who defended their right to self-governance. For the leaders of these new political ideals, achieving total self-governance was an endless road with many detours. Complete political autonomy for Nigeria was not achieved until the country became a republic in 1963,[24] but the struggles led by these nationalists would experience several minor victories along the way.

---

[21] Dawood Egbefo, "Resistance to Colonial in Nigeria: Esanland Encounter with the British Colonialists and its Effects on Intra–Inter-Group Relations," *Academic Horizon: A Journal of the School of Postgraduate Studies* 1, no. 1 (2015): 54–70.

[22] Bamidele Badejo, *Ijebu-Ode in Perspectives* (Ijebu-Ode: Fairweather Books Publications, 1992), 11.

[23] Joseph A. Atanda, *Political Systems of Nigerian Peoples up to 1900* (Ibadan: John Archers Publisher Limited, 2006), 4–16.

[24] John de St. Jorre, *The Nigerian Civil War* (London: Hodder and Stoughton Publishers, 1972).

A study of nationalist movements underscores that the postamalgamation colonial period accounted for the most intense nationalist struggles in Nigeria's history. The only period that could arguably be seen as more intense would be the 1967–70 civil war.[25] There is some disagreement as to whether the sentiments behind the civil war were truly nationalist, and thus it may be omitted from a consideration of nationalist movements in Nigeria's political history.

Postamalgamation nationalist efforts had a much greater impact than early acts of resistance on the country's political administration. However, early resistance struggles increased awareness among pre-amalgamated Nigerian peoples, unequivocally establishing the advent of nationalism in Nigeria. The historical figures and communities that led these acts of resistance took part in a convergence different from the institutionalized structures of the postamalgamation colonial era, but both types of resistance nurtured a communal attitude of opposition to the British colonial system.[26] The factors responsible for these nationalist efforts can be viewed through the lens of the motivations of each of the historical figures and communities that led these acts of resistance.

Although the existence of a foreign government that administers a nation-state poses a threat to that nation-state's political autonomy, specific factors that transcended political considerations drove the rise and growth of Nigerian nationalism. These factors were political, economic, and sociocultural in the early resistance era, as identified by Abdulahi and Baba. As previously suggested, early acts of resistance were motivated by the desire to protect territories from colonial invasion. In some territories, for instance, acts of resistance against colonialism were motivated by economic desires. The British exploited the economic resources of most territories within the area that would later be amalgamated into the political state of Nigeria. In the case of the Ijebu, early resistance struggles were based on a need to preserve the economic independence of their political entity.[27] A noteworthy event in the Ijebu struggle against colonial invasion was their refusal to grant the request of Europeans who had asked that they open their roads to all passengers to promote commerce. The Ijebu alliance, in uniting with the Egba and other allies to protect their economic interests, is aligned with the undercurrents of modern nationalist ideologies.

Sociocultural factors motivating early nationalist struggles involved the preservation of religious and cultural heritages. Before British colonialism in

---

[25] St. Jorre, *The Nigerian Civil War*.
[26] Murtala Shittu, "Nationalist Movement's Trends in Contemporary Nigerian Government and Politics," *International Journal of Development and Sustainability* 2, no. 2 (2013): 850–860.
[27] Michael Crowder, ed., *West African Resistance: The Military Response to Colonial Occupation* (London: Hutchinson Library, 1978), 182.

Nigeria, each territory had their own religious beliefs and practices largely rooted in their Indigenous culture.[28] By the end of the nineteenth century, the arrival of European missionaries and their occupation of Nigerian territories led to the growth of Christian churches that threatened the existence of traditional religions.[29] The religious motivations for resisting colonial powers were particularly noticeable in Northern territories, where the emir held both political and religious authority.

Seeds of nationalist thought were planted by the resistance of various individuals and communities that opposed colonial powers. After the amalgamation of the Northern and Southern Protectorates in 1914, nationalistic agitations intensified. As observed by Obiakor, the residents of previously existing territories considered the creation of the Nigerian political state to be artificial.[30] This led to an alliance between traditional rulers and educated elites, who formed a common consciousness to fight for the independence of the newly created political entity known as Nigeria. The agitations that started during this period were "nationalistic" because they cut across ethnic, linguistic, cultural, and religious boundaries.

Several internal and external factors fueled the growth of Nigerian nationalism at different times between the 1914 amalgamation and the 1940s. The internal factors were political, economic and sociocultural. Politically, colonialism installed a system of government that was not only alien to traditional systems of political government but was also oppressive. Colonial policies imposed by the British government largely promoted Britain's political and economic interests with little regard for Africans. The amalgamation occurred in 1914, but British colonial powers did not introduce the elective principle into the Nigerian political system until eight years later through the Clifford Constitution.

The political system instituted in Nigeria under the Clifford Constitution was unrepresentative. The Constitution merely paid lip service to elective principles because only a minority of Nigerian representatives were allowed to participate in a British-dominated government whose franchise was determined by residence in Lagos or Calabar, requiring an economic status that was only achievable by a few elites. This conflicted with the notions of representation and legitimacy that the local population had known in their Indigenous communities before colonization. The discriminatory practices of British officials were also apparent, especially in their decisions to exclude Nigerians from appointment or promotion to top civil service offices. Nigerians were also

---

[28] See, for instance, Dominus O. Essien, "The Traditional Religion of Pre-Colonial Akwa Ibom and Its Impact," *Transafrican Journal of History* 23 (1994): 32–42.

[29] Jacob F. A. Ajayi, *Christian Mission in Nigeria 1841–1891: The Making of New Elite* (London: Longmans, 1965).

[30] Nwachukwu Obiakor, "Nation Building in Post-Colonial Nigeria," *UZU: Journal of History and International Studies* 2, no. 1 (2009): 79–88.

forbidden from entering European Reservation Areas, which were spaces reserved exclusively for British Residents.[31]

Economic factors influenced the growth of nationalism. Nigerians could not access high-paying jobs due to discriminatory practices in the civil service. This left many of them, including the educated elites, with meager financial resources. This was a severe change from the economic conditions of most households and communities before colonization. As observed by Abdulahi and Baba, most precolonial African countries engaged in communal and agrarian economic activities.[32] The advent of colonialism altered pre-existing economic systems and installed a capitalist system that many claimed impoverished the colonized people while enriching foreign firms.[33] Britain's self-serving capitalist policies in colonial Nigeria manifested in tax policies, land appropriation schemes, and an agenda for resource exploitation that added to the grievances of Nigerians.[34] The unfamiliar and unfair capitalist policies fed nationalist sentiments among many Nigerians, later escalating into the Aba Women's War of 1929 and other nationalist struggles.[35]

The major socioeconomic factors that contributed to the growth of nationalism in preindependence Nigeria are closely linked: the activities of Christian missionaries and the impact of Western education. Nigerians were offered Western education to serve in the civil service or the clergy. Ironically, following the discriminatory treatment meted out by the civil service appointments, salaries, and promotions, Nigerians used their training to organize nationalist struggles against the British colonial system. Most people who converted to Christianity noticed that although European missionaries preached brotherhood and equality in the church, they neither compelled the British government to uphold those values nor exhibited them themselves. Dissatisfaction with the church's hypocrisy was another reason for Nigerians to oppose colonialism.

External factors also intensified nationalist struggles. This included the organization of African students in London-based colleges, the actions of nationalist movements in other colonial territories, and the outbreak of World War II. Nigerian students who studied abroad, especially in colleges in the United Kingdom, collaborated with other African students to form organizations that sought the collective liberation of their respective countries. These organizations were nationalist movements based on notions of African nationalism and pan-Africanism. Their most significant impact was the model

---

[31] Michael Omolewa, *Certificate History of Nigeria* (Harlow: Longman Group, 1986), 184.
[32] Abdulahi and Baba, "Nationalism and National Integration."
[33] Abdulahi and Baba, "Nationalism and National Integration."
[34] Ubaku, Emeh and Anyikwa, "Impact of Nationalist Movement," 59.
[35] James S. Coleman, *Nigeria: Background to Nationalism* (Berkeley: University of California Press, 1958).

they provided for future nationalist leaders in African countries such as Nigeria.

Nationalist movements in other African countries and British colonies strengthened nationalist agitations in Nigeria. One of the most impactful external nationalist efforts was the Garvey movement.[36] Marcus Garvey's movement, founded in 1914 under the auspices of the Universal Negro Improvement Association (UNIA), promoted "racial solidarity and cultural nationalism" in Jamaica that later spread to Nigeria.[37] His nationalist ideas influenced Nigerian nationalist leaders such as Ernest Ikoli and Nnamdi Azikiwe.[38] The inspiration for Azikiwe's nationalist agenda was based on the ideas of "universal fatherhood, universal brotherhood and universal happiness," and his pan-African objectives have been attributed to Marcus Garvey. Garvey's impact on nationalism in Nigeria was most evident in 1920, when Patriarch James G. Campbell, the head of the African church, joined with Rev. S. M. Abiodun and Rev. W. B. Euba to found a Nigerian branch of Garvey's movement in Lagos.[39]

World War II was another major external factor that influenced the growth of nationalism in Nigeria. After fighting beside Great Britain in the war against the Axis Powers, African soldiers who returned from combat saw that the British were not superior to them and could claim no moral right to subjugate others.[40] During the war, African soldiers interacted with peoples of different colonies – especially India and Ceylon – that had developed more intense nationalist struggles and achieved greater degrees of independence. The British and other allied powers had also promised their respective colonies that they could determine their form of governance after participating in the war. This promise resulted in the Atlantic Charter of 1941, which promoted further nationalist struggles for decolonization and independence.

Agents of Reforms or Nationalist Movements

Groups that lead nationalist activities are often regarded as organizers of nationalist movements.[41] In some literature, discussions of nationalist movements only

---

[36] Toyin Falola, *History of Nigeria 3: Nigeria in the Twentieth Century* (Lagos: Longman, 1991).
[37] Yekutiel Gershoni, "Common Goals, Different Ways: The UNIA and the NCBWA in West Africa, 1920-1930," *Journal of Third World Studies* 18, no. 2 (2001): 171-185.
[38] Michael J. C. Echeruo, "Nnamdi Azikiwe and Nineteenth-Century Nigerian Thought," *Journal of Modern African Studies* 12, no. 2 (1974): 245-263.
[39] Rina Okonkwo, *Protest Movements in Lagos, 1908-1930* (Lewiston: E. Mellen Press, 1995), 55-60.
[40] Gabriel O. Olusanya, "The Role of Ex-Servicemen in Nigerian Politics," *The Journal of Modern African Studies* 6, no. 2 (1968): 221-232.
[41] Shittu, "Nationalist Movement's Trends," 854-858.

refer to political activities,[42] which is a myopic view of nationalism. Nigerian nationalism describes the struggles undertaken by the people opposing political oppression. These struggles eventually resulted in the decolonization of the political state, but during the pre-1940 colonial era of Nigerian history, decolonization was merely a long-term goal.

Labor unions, humanitarian organizations, print media outlets, and other pan-African organizations engaged in activities abroad that also influenced nationalist movements. However, this chapter only considers political organizations, print media outlets, and pan-African organizations in its discussion of nationalist movements in Nigeria. These nationalist movements had enduring demands, objectives, and struggles that were more persistent than the short-term resistance mounted by labor unions and humanitarian organizations that opposed specific policies or acts of the British government.

Political Organizations

Political organizations were the most widely recognized and impactful categories of nationalist movements in colonial Nigeria. British colonial administration was established in Nigeria during the first three decades of the twentieth century.[43] Adopting the elective principle opened the door for a handful of people who participated in government, and educated elites formed political organizations. The primary objective of these organizations was to seize control of the seats available in the Legislative Council. As subsequent constitutions increased the number of seats available, the rivalry between these organizations intensified. The organizations still collaborated on nationalistic objectives that focused on guaranteeing responsible colonial government as they worked toward the eventual decolonization of their Indigenous political state.

The Nigerian National Democratic Party is often recognized as Nigeria's first political party, but that designation belongs to the People's Union. The Lagos-based union, founded in 1908 by a leadership alliance of traditional rulers and educated elites, sought to protect the welfare of residents.[44] Key leaders were the organization's cofounders John Randle, Orisadipe Obasa, Sir Kitoye Ajasa, Dr. Richard Akinwande Savage, and Sir Adeyemo Alakija.[45] One of the union's major contributions was its resistance to the colonial government's proposal for a new system of water pipes. The construction was to be

---

[42] Olasupo, Olajide, and Ijeoma, "Nationalism and Nationalist Agitation in Africa," 275.
[43] Toyin Falola and Matthew Heaton, *A History of Nigeria* (New York: Cambridge University Press, 2008), 136.
[44] Emmanuel A. Ayandele, "The Colonial Church Question in Lagos Politics, 1905–11," *Odù: Journal of Yoruba and Related Studies* 4, no. 2 (1967): 53–73.
[45] *Lagos Weekly Record*, "The People's Union of Lagos and the Native Land Tenure Question," *Lagos Weekly Record*, August 17, 1912.

funded by Lagos residents, and the majority of the city's population opposed these plans because they involved increased taxes.[46] Ultimately, the project would only serve the interests of Europeans and a few wealthy Africans.

Ayandele has noted that the People's Union should not be treated as a political party but a political association.[47] As an association, it brought together people from various walks of life to protect their common interests. It also sought to influence government policies. Although the association fractured after some of its leaders accepted a compromise on the water project, it laid the framework for political activism in subsequent decades. The association itself later metamorphosed into a political party that mounted major opposition to the Nigerian National Democratic Party by the year 1923. As a political party, the People's Union was conservative because it favored gradual reformation rather than the radical changes advocated by the NNDP. Although the People's Union was a short-lived political party, its activism led the colonial government to replace a proposed poll tax system with an income tax system in 1927.[48]

The second political organization in colonial Nigeria's history was the Nigerian National Democratic Party (NNDP). It was formed on June 24, 1923, and is often regarded as Nigeria's first political party.[49] The NNDP was founded by Herbert Macaulay, who is often regarded as the father of Nigerian nationalism.[50] He seized on the opportunity offered by the 1922 Clifford Constitution, which allowed a few Nigerian representatives to be elected for seats in the Legislative Council. Under the Clifford Constitution, the elective principle applied only to Lagos, and the NNDP's activities were also limited to the city. However, Herbert Macaulay's leadership influenced the political consciousness and aspirations of all Nigerians.[51] The party combined its political platform with the *Lagos Daily News* newspaper, calling for economic and educational development in the country, self-government for Lagos, and the Africanization of the civil service. One of its major contributions involved pressuring the colonial government to establish the Yaba High College in 1932, laying the foundation for Nigeria's higher education system.[52]

---

[46] *Lagos Weekly Record*, "The People's Union of Lagos."
[47] Ayandele, "The Colonial Church Question."
[48] Marika Sherwood, "Two PanAfrican Political Activists Emanating from Edinburgh University: Dr. John Randle and Richard Akinwande Savage," in *Africa in Scotland, Scotland in Africa: Historical Legacies and Contemporary Hybridities*, ed. Afe Adogame and Andrew Lawrence (Leiden: Brill, 2014), 103–136.
[49] S. O. Arifalo, "The Rise and Decline of the Nigerian National Democratic Party (NNDP) 1923–1938," *Odu : A Journal of West African Studies* 24 (1983): 89–110.
[50] Tekena N. Tamuno, *Herbert Macaulay, Nigerian Patriot* (London: Heinemann Educational, 1976).
[51] Patrick Cole, *Modern and Traditional Elites in the Politics of Lagos* (New York: Cambridge University Press, 1975), 110.
[52] Coleman, *Nigeria: Background to Nationalism*, 198.

Politically, the NNDP served as a watchdog monitoring the colonial government and criticizing ill-motivated government policies. Classic examples include its criticisms of the 1927 income tax, the appointment and removal of chief ordinances, and the extension of the indirect rule system to Lagos.[53] The party elevated political consciousness among Nigerians and provided a representative government for local Nigerians. Its authority in the Legislative Council was successfully challenged by a rival political party, the Nigerian Youth Movement, in 1938.

The Nigerian Youth Movement (NYM) was founded in 1934, starting as a pressure group known as the Lagos Youth Movement.[54] It eventually expanded beyond Lagos and became a political party.[55] The NYM later replaced the NNDP as the country's foremost political party. Unlike the NNDP, which was based solely in Lagos, the NYM evolved into a political party with a national outlook. Within four years of its founding, it became the most powerful political party in Nigeria and the most impactful nationalist movement.[56]

Coleman noted that the NYM was "the nucleus of Nigeria's first genuine nationalist organization."[57] The party's major objective was to unify Nigeria's different regions. It also advocated universal adult suffrage, free education, judicial autonomy, and the Africanization of the civil service.[58] The organization's newspaper, the *Lagos Daily Service*, opposed questionable policies enacted by the colonial government and promoted nationalist consciousness among Nigerians. The NYM successfully replaced the NNDP as the political group that successfully placed Nigerian representatives on the Legislative Council through elections, and it maintained a unique position as a pioneer nationalist movement that held a national outlook. Disagreements between key members of the organization later resulted in the fragmentation of the party and the creation of a splinter group, the National Council of Nigeria and the Cameroons (NCNC).

Print Media

The print media was a major force for building nationalist sentiment during the colonial period.[59] Newspaper owners and editors criticized the colonial government's policies, raised nationalist consciousness among the readers, and

---

[53] Ubaku, Emeh, and Anyikwa, "Impact of Nationalist Movement," 62.
[54] F. O. E. Okafor, *The Nigerian Youth Movement, 1934–44: A Re-appraisal of the Historiography* (Onitsha: Eturokwu Press (Nig.) Limited, 1989).
[55] Shittu, "Nationalist Movement's Trends."
[56] Okafor, *The Nigerian Youth Movement*.
[57] Coleman, *Nigeria: Background to Nationalism*.
[58] Olusanya, "The Nationalist Movement in Nigeria," 558.
[59] Fred I. Omu, *Press and Politics in Nigeria, 1880–1937* (London: Longman Press, 1978).

disseminated vital information to audiences. Nigeria's print media became a nationalist movement in its own right, and the emergence and growth of Nigeria's media have historically been associated with nationalist sentiments.[60]

The emergence of the Nigerian press was inspired by earlier newspapers established in other British West African colonies such as Sierra Leone and Gold Coast (now Ghana), and independent Liberia. It was also enabled by the education that Anglican missionaries had provided. Anglicans started the earliest newspapers in these colonies. Nigeria's first newspaper was established in December 1859. It was founded by Henry Townsend and called the *Iwe Irohin fun Awon Ara Egba ati Yoruba*, which translates into English as "Newspaper for the Egba and Yoruba."[61]

The literature on journalism has attributed the origin of newspapers' nationalistic sentiments to publications from Sierra Leone that had infused civic awareness and raised political consciousness that resisted the oppressive nature of colonialism. Sierra Leonean returnees who later settled in Egbaland transmitted this culture to the content of *Iwe Irohin*. *Iwe Irohin* did not overtly promote anticolonialist agitation, but its outspoken criticism against the slave trade spurred nationalist consciousness in the newspapers subsequently established in Nigeria.[62] Most newspapers were owned by educated elites and associated with political parties, which meant that they supported nationalist campaigns.[63] These newspapers included the *Lagos Times*, the *Lagos Weekly Record*, the *Lagos Daily News*, *The Daily Times of Nigeria*, the *West African Pilot*, and the *Lagos Daily Service*.

The *Lagos Times* was one of Nigeria's earliest established newspapers, founded in 1880 by a wealthy Sierra Leonean businessman named Richard Beale Blaize.[64] Unlike most of its predecessors, the *Lagos Times* became Nigeria's first overtly nationalist newspaper. Due to Blaize's Lagos roots, it was also the country's first Indigenous newspaper. Its editorial mission was to safeguard public rights, and the newspaper published content in which writers and editors advocated the rights of Africans, especially its primary audience living in Lagos and the Gold Coast (Ghana).[65] The radical approach undertaken by the editors of this newspaper led to its suspension by its promoters three years later.

---

[60] Omu, *Press and Politics in Nigeria*.
[61] Fred I. Omu, "The Iwe Irohin, 1859–1867," *Journal of the Historical Society of Nigeria* 4, no. 1 (1967): 35–44.
[62] Omu, "The Iwe Irohin."
[63] Olu Akinsuroju, "The Nigerian Press, 1859–1969." A Lecture Delivered at the Third Workshop of the Western State Council of the NUJ, held in Ibadan, September 25, 1971.
[64] Ifedayo Daramola, "A Century of Mass Media and Nigeria's Development: Issues and Challenges," *Communications on Applied Electronics* 7, no. 10 (2017): 4–14.
[65] Jean H. Kopytoff, *A Preface to Modern Nigeria: The "Sierra Leonians" in Yoruba, 1830–1890* (Madison: University of Wisconsin Press, 1965), 283–284.

The *Lagos Times* resurfaced when a partnership between Blaize and John Payne Jackson, a former bookkeeper, led to the formation of a newspaper called *Lagos Weekly Times* on May 31, 1890. By November 29 of the same year, Blaize had discontinued its publication, as a dispute had developed between him and Jackson over the latter's inability to account for the newspaper's expenses. The cessation of the partnership led Blaize to resuscitate the defunct *Lagos Times*. Jackson founded his own newspaper, the *Lagos Weekly Record*, in 1890, after falling out with Blaize and it stood out as the most radical nationalist newspaper of the time.

The hostile relationship between the former business partners eventually poisoned the social relationships between the two families and led to an intense business rivalry. Jackson was determined to outsell the *Lagos Times* and force his former boss out of business, which led him to reform the newspaper that was created as *Weekly Times*, renaming it *Lagos Weekly Record*. The paper successfully developed a wider scope of coverage for topics centered on the colony's political, economic, and social issues.[66]

Shittu has described the *Lagos Weekly Record* as "virulently critical of the British government through its journalistic effort."[67] It took radical approaches to issues and policies that pertained to the colonial government. Its "fiery" editorials were greatly irritating to the British administration.[68] It was the most outspoken newspaper of the time, and set the nationalist tone for subsequent papers. Jackson's editorials were as incisive as his policies. Lord Lugard, governor of Nigeria at the time, detested Jackson. The *Lagos Weekly Record* played a vital role in early resistance efforts, not only in Nigeria but also in other African countries. It was consistently published over four decades, from 1891 to 1930, continuing for fifteen years after the death of its founder.[69]

The *Lagos Daily News* succeeded the *Lagos Weekly Record* as print media's foremost nationalist newspaper in Nigeria. It was established in 1925 by Herbert Macaulay, serving as the official newspaper for the NNDP.[70] The party used the paper to publicize its political agenda and serve its nationalistic interests. The newspaper educated the Nigerian people about their rights and built support for the party's nationalist agenda. It was a vital medium for challenging restrictive policies imposed by the colonial government.

---

[66] Nozomi Sawada, "The Educated Elite and Associational Life in Early Lagos Newspapers: In Search of Unity for the Progress of Society," unpublished PhD dissertation, University of Birmingham, 2011, 49–50.
[67] Shittu, "Nationalist Movement's Trends," 856.
[68] Michele Maringues, "The Nigerian Press: Current State, Travails and Prospects," in *Nigeria during the Abacha Years, 1993-98: The Domestic and International Politics of Democratization*, ed. Kunle Amuwo, Daniel C. Bach, and Yann Lebeau (Ibadan: IFRA, 2001), 185.
[69] Daramola, "A Century of Mass Media."
[70] Falola and Heaton, *A History of Nigeria*, xxiii and xxvii.

Three Europeans – Ronald Osborne, Leonard Archer, and Richard Barrow – established *The Daily Times* together with Adeyemo Alakija in the same year that the *Lagos Daily News* was founded. Despite the paper's joint ownership by British nationals, *The Daily Times* openly criticized the British colonial government's administration of Nigeria. Under the supervision of Ernest Ikoli, its first editor, the newspaper became a vital medium for information and an agent of nationalism.[71] Its original editorial policy promoted support for Nigerian advancement and "a strong sense of sane nationalism." *The Daily Times* did its part to explain the need for self-rule, especially after it became an outlet for the National Youth Movement.[72] The newspaper was generally considered conservative and suffered declines at three different times.

In contrast to the conservatism of *The Daily Times*, the *West African Pilot* was particularly revolutionary. It was established in 1937 by Nnamdi Azikiwe, and its motto was "show the light and the people will find the way."[73] The *West African Pilot* worked toward the mental emancipation of its Nigerian readers. Its editorials vocally rebuked the British colonial system's imperialist nature.[74] A foreign journalist, reporting on the revolutionary tendencies of the British West African press after a tour of Nigeria in 1945, described the *West African Pilot* as "pos[ing] a severe threat to the continued existence of the British Empire."[75] The *West African Pilot* would emerge as the focal point for raising nationalist consciousness and stimulating political awareness, successfully challenging the dominance of *The Daily Times*.[76] Azikiwe was influenced by Thomas H. Jackson's radical ideas, which can be seen in the language used in some of his newspaper editorials.[77]

Jackson was a fellow nationalist who influenced Azikiwe's thoughts and whose idealism informed Azikiwe's philosophy of nationalism. The *West African Pilot* would metamorphose from "Azikiwe's newspaper" to become the official newspaper of a political party after the establishment of the NCNC,

---

[71] Increase H. E. Coker, *Landmarks of the Nigerian Press: An Outline of the Origins and Development of the Newspaper Press in Nigeria, 1859 to 1965* (Apapa: Nigerian National Press, 1968).

[72] Michael J. C. Echeruo, "History of the Nigerian Press," in *The Story of the Daily Times 1926–1970*, ed. Daily Times (Lagos: Daily Times Office, 1976).

[73] Christian C. Aguolu and L. E. Aguolu, "A Force in Library Development in Nigeria," *World Libraries* 7, no. 2 (1997): 9–18.

[74] Fatmata J. Jabati, *The West African Pilot: Historical Study of a Nationalist Newspaper* (Ohio: Ohio University, 1985).

[75] C. Winchester, "Report to Lord Kemsley on the British West African Press, Typescript Document," Owerri, National Library, 1945.

[76] Daramola, "A Century of Mass Media," 8.

[77] Fred Omu, "Journalism and the Rise of Nationalism: John Payne Jackson," *Journal of the Historical Society of Nigeria* 7, no. 3 (1974): 521–539.

part of the few nationalist movements that championed the total decolonization of Nigeria.[78]

Another established nationalist newspaper was the *Lagos Daily Service*. It was created as an organ of the NYM to enlighten the public about the party's political and nationalistic agenda. Through this newspaper, the NYM advanced its struggles for universal adult suffrage, free education, judicial independence, and the Africanization of the civil service.[79] However, wrangling within the NYM led to Azikiwe's defection from the party. He accused the party of being "tribalistic" in the 1938 elections. After that, the journalistic essence of the *Lagos Daily Service* was compromised. It was used to denigrate Azikiwe's personality and leadership in response to his attacks on the Yoruba leadership of the NYM that were printed in his newspaper, the *West African Pilot*. The political organization converted its weekly publication into daily updates to keep up with the exchange.[80] After this era, the newspaper became a vital instrument of the Action Group for fighting the NCNC in the struggle for political control of the soon-to-be-independent colony.[81]

Pan-African Organizations

Pan-African associations for West African students and youths added impetus to nationalist struggles at home. Their memberships, which cut across different West African countries, gave pan-African organizations a common goal: the emancipation of the African continent. Members were largely elites from various colonies who became acquainted with one another through their educational affiliation. The origins of pan-Africanism began with an association organized by Marcus Garvey, Henry Sylvester-Williams, and W. E. B. Du Bois.[82] Its goal was to unite "people of color" from all over the world to protect Africa's cultural heritage.[83] These pan-Africanist ideals readily influenced educated elites in other parts of Africa. In Nigeria, it led to the emergence of the National Congress of British West Africa and the West African Students' Union.[84]

---

[78] Ubaku, Emeh, and Anyikwa, "Impact of Nationalist Movement," 62.
[79] Olusanya, "The Nationalist Movement in Nigeria," 558–559.
[80] Patrick Wilmot, *The Theory and Practice of Nationalism in Africa* (Lagos: Lantern Book, 1975), 10.
[81] Uma Eleazu, *Federalism and Nation-Building: The Nigerian Experience* (Devon: Stockwell Ltd., 1977), 188.
[82] Marika Sherwood, *Origins of Pan-Africanism: Henry Sylvester Williams, Africa, and the African Diaspora* (New York: Routledge, 2011).
[83] Olasupo, Olajide, and Ijeoma, "Nationalism and Nationalist Agitation in Africa," 263.
[84] Hakim Adi, "Pan-Africanism and West African Nationalism in Britain," *African Studies Review* 43, no. 1 (2000): 69–82.

The National Congress of British West Africa (NCBWA), founded in 1917, was one of the earliest nationalist movements in West Africa.[85] It advocated African emancipation, and its original membership included Gold Coast (Ghana) educated elites such as Thomas Hutton-Mills, Sr., Joseph Casely Hayford, Edward Francis Small, Henry van Hien, and Kobina Sekyi.[86] The NCBWA was inspired by a combination of regional, international, and internal factors. The major regional factor was the successful creation of similar pan-African organizations within the West Africa subcontinent. Such organizations failed to adequately meet the nationalist demands of the entire region. Similarly, efforts made by other organizations for people of African descent, particularly in the United States, inspired similar organizations at home.[87]

The educated elites who founded NCBWA formed the organization to articulate their protests against exclusion from the civil service. The colonial authority gave preferential treatment to traditional rulers in its administration. The NCBWA was a full-fledged regional nationalist organization with branches in Sierra Leone, Gambia, and Nigeria.[88] The leaders of the Nigerian branch of the Congress were Dr. Akinwande Savage, John Randle, and James G. Campbell.[89] It later admitted interested traditional rulers as members. The well-articulated demands of the NCBWA pressed for the expansion of seats allocated to indigenes in the Legislative Councils of respective British West African colonies. They also agitated for the establishment of a West African university, the creation of a West African Court of Appeal, the separation of the legislature from the judiciary, the institutionalization of freedom of the press, and the abolition of discriminatory practices in the civil service.[90]

Although some NCBWA delegates were sent to London to meet some prominent figures and voice their demands, they were not granted an audience. The colonial administration viewed the NCBWA as unrepresentative of the interests of the West African people. The unsuccessful trip led to the eventual decline of the organization.[91] However, the NCBWA brought together educated elites from different West African countries, which helped

---

[85] Gabriel I. C. Eluwa, "The National Congress of British West Africa: A Study in African Nationalism," *Présence Africaine* 77 (1971): 131–149.

[86] LaRay E. Denzer, "The Gold Coast Section of the National Congress of British West Africa," MA thesis, University of Legon, 1965.

[87] George Shepperson, "Notes on Negro American Influences on the Emergence of African Nationalism," *The Journal of African History* 1, no. 2 (1960): 299–312.

[88] Eluwa, "The National Congress of British West Africa."

[89] Gabriel O. Olusanya, "The Lagos Branch of the National Congress of British West Africa," *Journal of the Historical Society of Nigeria* 4, no. 2 (1968): 321–333.

[90] Gabriel Eluwa, "National Congress of British West Africa: A Pioneer Nationalist Movement," *Geneva Africa* 11, no. 1 (1972): 38.

[91] James S. Coleman, "Nationalism in Tropical Africa," *The American Political Science Review* 48, no. 2 (1954): 404–426.

them present a united front against the oppressive British colonial administration. Their stance influenced other pan-African and local nationalist organizations that followed.[92]

The West African Students Union (WASU) was an association of students from Nigeria and other West African colonies who studied in the United Kingdom.[93] Ladipo Solanke, a Nigerian, founded the organization in 1925, providing a platform for young West Africans to agitate for the decolonization of their respective countries. Its young members were politically conscious and actively engaged in nationalist struggles, and the organization fostered unity, nationalism, and racial pride among its members.[94] This was especially important when a majority of people of African descent faced oppression and discrimination. WASU called for several reforms in the administration of most West African states. One of the organization's major achievements was its role as a training ground for future political leaders in British West African countries. Most of its members later became leaders of nationalist movements and political parties in their respective countries.

The Impact of Nationalist Movements on Decolonization

Many nationalist movements collaborated on the long journey to actualize the decolonization of Nigeria, even when they fought over political control or trade monopolies. Examples include the NYM versus the NNDP, on the one hand, and the *Lagos Times* versus the *Lagos Weekly Record*, on the other. They were united in their criticism of the colonial administration. The primary focus of nationalist struggles before 1940 was the achievement of a responsible colonial administration. Nationalist leaders and organizations fought discrimination against Africans in the civil service, the nonrepresentative nature of British-majority Legislative Councils, and the lack of tertiary education within the country.

As these nationalist movements grew, they focused their efforts on Nigerian independence. Political organizations and newspapers played the most significant role. Political parties served as a mechanism for airing the grievances of common people who opposed the colonial administration. They also filled the governmental vacuum in Nigeria that the departing colonial administration left. Political parties used the print media that they owned and managed to sensitize the general public, raise political consciousness, and articulate nationalist agendas.[95]

---

[92] Coleman, "Nationalism in Tropical Africa."
[93] Hakim Adi, "West African Students in Britain, 1900–60: The Politics of Exile," in *Africans in Britain*, ed. David Killingray (London: Frank Cass, 1994), 114–118.
[94] Hakim Adi, *West Africans in Britain 1900–1960: Nationalism, Pan-Africanism and Communism* (London: Lawrence & Wishart, 1998).
[95] Ubaku, Emeh, and Anyikwa, "Impact of Nationalist Movement," 62.

Nationalist leaders successfully pressured Nigeria's colonial government to establish an institution for higher education, first with Yaba High College in 1934[96] and then with University College Ibadan in 1948. They also influenced the amendments of the colonial constitutions, working to secure greater participation for Nigerians. The most significant achievement of nationalist movements was their work to attain self-rule for the former colony of Nigeria. Following the incorporation of the Atlantic Charter in 1941 and after African soldiers returned from fighting alongside Great Britain in World War II, political independence became the primary objective of nationalist movements.[97] Nigeria was no exception.[98]

Conclusion

Nationalist movements had a powerful impact on the actualization of Nigeria's independence.[99] The political organizations, print media outlets, and pan-African organizations discussed in this chapter actively protected the rights of Nigerians and pressured the colonial government to make responsible policies. They criticized self-serving administrative policies and practices while leading the struggle for the decolonization of the country.[100] This was a gradual process; although most of the activities that influenced the departure of the British from Nigeria occurred within the final decade before decolonization, agitations for self-rule and decolonization date back to the amalgamation in 1914. Nationalists consistently led the British toward the cession of their imperial authority in Nigeria. The declaration of independence by 1960 was the realization of a long-term objective of the country's foremost leaders.[101]

---

[96] Toyin Falola, *Economic Reforms and Modernization in Nigeria, 1945–1965* (Kent: The Kent State University Press, 2004), 41.
[97] Abdulahi and Baba, "Nationalism and National Integration."
[98] Chima J. Korieh, *Nigeria and World War II: Colonialism, Empire, and Global Conflict* (Cambridge: Cambridge University Press, 2020).
[99] Eme Ekekwe, "Nationalist Movement and Ideology: Nigeria, 1940–1960," MA thesis, Carleton University, 1976.
[100] Ehiedu E. G. Iweriebor, *Radical Politics in Nigeria, 1945–1950: The Significance of the Zikist Movement* (Zaria: Ahmadu Bello University Press, 1996).
[101] Lev N. Pribytkovskiy, *Nigeria in the Struggle for Independence* (Annapolis: Research & Microfilm Publications, 1962).

22

World War II and Its Aftermath

Nationalism in Nigerian history has undergone several stages. The earliest nationalistic efforts date as far back as the initial resistance struggles against colonialism.[1] Different points in history have prompted a re-evaluation of the nationalist agenda or spurred an intensification of the struggle. World War II is one such event.[2] The war began as a struggle between the major European powers. Germany brokered an alliance with the Soviet Union and proceeded to attack Poland, an ally of Britain and France. The two rival Western powers, who sought to protect their ally and check Germany's growing aggression, declared war on Germany. Sixty million individuals lost their lives in the conflict that followed.[3]

As far away as the major theaters of World War II seemed to the emerging political state of colonial Nigeria, the conflict would have serious implications for the trajectory of the country's politics for decades to come. Nigeria was one of the many African colonies that got drawn into the war, and its contributions, particularly to the British army, were significant.[4] Contrary to earlier European accounts, colonial Nigeria played an active role in the war. Nigerian citizens did not participate out of compulsion or in response to some minimal incentive given to them as payment for recruitment in the British army. As will be demonstrated in this chapter, the entirety of Nigeria voluntarily provided moral, economic, and military support for their colonial masters because they identified with the "common cause" for which the Allied Powers fought the war.[5] I argue that it was the high

---

[1] James S. Coleman, *Nigeria Background to Nationalism* (Berkeley and Los Angeles: University of California Press, 1958).
[2] Chima J. Korieh, *Nigeria and World War II: Colonialism, Empire, and Global Conflict* (Cambridge: Cambridge University Press, 2020).
[3] Andrew N. Buchanan, *World War II in Global Perspective, 1931–1953: A Short History* (Hoboken: John Wiley & Sons, 2019).
[4] Oliver Coates, "New Perspectives on West Africa and World War Two," *Journal of African Military History*, 4 (2020): 5–39.
[5] Disu O. Abayomi and Oluwafunminiyi Raheem, "Fighting for Britain: Examining British Recruitment Strategies in Nigeria," in *Unknown Conflicts of the Second World War: Forgotten Fronts*, ed. Chris Murray (United Kingdom: Routledge, 2019), 2–15.

stakes that the nation had in the war that intensified the nationalist struggle in Nigeria.

What events could have warranted this significant shift in attitude toward colonialism in the country? This is the question that this chapter seeks to answer; I shall trace the history of Nigeria's participation in World War II, the effects of the outbreak of the war on Britain's colonial control and nationalist efforts in Nigeria, and how the events that generate such consequences produced the aftermath of decolonization in Nigeria.

Nigeria in a Global Conflict

Though many histories of World War II tend to downplay the roles of the British colonies, African historians have shown that this claim was incorrect. Gabriel Olusanya, a foremost Nigerian historian, is particularly concerned with studying the impacts of war on politics in Nigeria.[6] By exposing Nigerians to the war, Britain brought them into contact with external factors that would fuel nationalist efforts in the country.

The African proverb that unless the hunted elephants hire their own historians, the tale of the hunt will always favor the hunters seems apt in respect of the narration of the World Wars by both African and European historians. The effect of African historians such as Olusanya taking up the recounting of the World Wars from African perspectives has motivated European historians to follow suit. For instance, in a lecture delivered in 2019, Paul Mulvey said of World War II "it was truly a global imperial war for Britain, with British and imperial soldiers, sailors and airmen seeing action in far more locations around the world than ever before."[7] Nicholas Mansergh, who also surveyed the history of British colonies, observed that the respective colonies were self-governing and only decided to go to war in support of Great Britain.[8]

In his description of Britain's involvement in World War II, Mulvey observed that the war was a global one in two ways. First, the nature of the antagonism between the Allied Powers and the Axis Powers was cross-continental. The war was part of a regional conflict in Europe due to Germany's bloated assurance of its status as the "master race" as well as its systematic agenda to establish an imperialist domination in Europe. The localization of Germany's dominions in Europe notwithstanding, the participation of the United States also transcended European continental borders. Second, Mulvey observed that even without America's participation in the war, the war would still be global, since the battles

---

[6] Gabriel O. Olusanya, *The Second World War and Politics in Nigeria, 1939–1953* (London: Evans Brothers, 1973).

[7] Paul Mulvey, "The British Empire in World War Two (Lecture)," *Academia.edu*, September 25, 2020. www.academia.edu/444982/The_British_Empire_in_World_War_Two_lecture.

[8] Nicholas Mansergh, *Survey of British Commonwealth Affairs: Problems of Wartime Cooperation and Post-War Change, 1939–52* (London: Frank Cass, 1968), 3.

associated with the war were fought in different parts of the world, including Africa and Asia. Major African war fronts included Egypt, Libya, Tunisia, Algeria, Morocco, Sudan, Ethiopia, Somalia, Kenya, and Madagascar.[9]

With specific reference to Nigeria's involvement in World War II, even though the territory of the former British West Africa colony was not an active war front, the political state contributed to British efforts in the war.[10] As observed by Chima Korieh,[11] a Nigerian historian, Britain sought the help of Africans to win the war. In Nigeria, the citizens were proud to support the British against the Nazis, who were regarded as their common enemy. Traditional rulers such as the Oba of Benin, Omonoba Akenzua II, urged Nigerians to bury their grievances against the British and help them win the war. In 1944, Idoma chiefs also supported the British during the war. These chiefs wrote to the British to pledge economic support in the form of palm kernel production.[12]

Nigerian newspapers also advocated solidarity. They backed Britain via a journalistic spirit by writing articles and editorials in favor of the war effort. For instance, in 1939 the *West African Pilot* called on all Nigerians to render any assistance they could to the British government to prevent internal or external attacks. The *Nigerian Daily Times*, in its editorials, stated that the British declaration of war attested to an upholding of fair rule and governance.[13]

Colonial Nigeria's participation in World War II consisted not only of moral support for the British stance in the war but also of human and economic resources.[14] Several hundred thousand Nigerian men were drafted into British armies to fight a war they had no hand in creating. On the home front, the women and men who stayed behind contributed agricultural and mineral products to Britain's war supplies. One might question the reason behind such unprovoked support by Nigeria and other British African colonies and their devoted allegiance to a faraway cause. Not only did nationals of colonial Nigeria resist imperialism upon the arrival of the British, but they also continued to champion nationalist feelings from the early colonial period until their independence in 1960. The participation of African colonies in the war could be explained from two perspectives. First, Britain and other parties to the

---

[9] Mulvey, "The British Empire."
[10] Abayomi and Raheem, "Fighting for Britain."
[11] Korieh, *Nigeria and World War II.*
[12] Erin Myrice, "The Impact of the Second World War on the Decolonization of Africa." Paper presented at the Africana Studies Student Research Conference, Scholar Works, 2015, https://scholarworks.bgsu.edu/cgi/viewcontent.cgi?article=1048&context=africana_studies_conf.
[13] Nigerian Eastern Mail, "Restitution of Ex-servicemen," *Nigerian Eastern Mail*, March 23, 1946, 20.
[14] Levi O. Amadi, "The Reactions and Contributions of Nigerians during the Second World War: Agents of Political Integration in Nigeria, 1939–1945," *Transafrican Journal of History* 6, no. 7 (1977–78): 1–11.

war recruited mercenaries from different countries to aid them in the war. Britain relied heavily on its colonies in Africa and Asia.[15] Second, during the war, colonial consciousness started brewing in Nigeria. Even though nationalist struggles were promoted in the country, the outbreak of the war created a sense of solidarity among the British colonies with the British Empire. Like their counterparts in other regions, Nigerians thus "appropriated and localized the war itself and expressed their readiness to make sacrifices" to defeat the Nazis.[16]

World War II and Britain's Imperial Control

World War II ended in 1945 with victory for the Allied Powers.[17] However, no parties emerged unscathed by the effects of the war. The conflict is perhaps the most formative event of the twentieth century; its impacts are evident not only in terms of the casualties of the war but also in terms of the economic, political, and health implications it has had on the entire world.[18] Scholars who studied the economic and health outcomes of the war across Europe observed long-term effects such as lower per capita income of European economies; increased mortality rate; unbalanced sex ratios; the prevalence of hunger and abject poverty; and dispossession, persecution, and migration.[19] Persons who experience war, irrespective of socioeconomic class, tended to report a lower overall standard of health in their adulthood compared to those who did not experience war. Also, negative social conditions were observed, such as the absence of father figures or an unwillingness to marry.[20]

The scholarly literature has tended to pay greater attention to the political and macroeconomic impacts of the war than on health, social, and microeconomic factors. This is understandable, as the war itself was indeed political. As mentioned, the war was borne of Germany's political objective to establish an imperialistic dominion across Eastern Europe. Perhaps the Allied Powers would not have been bothered by this grand objective until other Western

---

[15] Rita Headrick, "African Soldiers in World War II," *Armed Forces & Society* 4, no. 3 (1978): 501–526; and Christopher A. Bayly and Ti N. Harper, *Forgotten Armies: The Fall of British Asia, 1941–1945* (Cambridge: Harvard University Press, 2005).

[16] Korieh, *Nigeria and World War II*, 2.

[17] Michael Neiberg, *Potsdam: The End of World War II and the Remaking of Europe* (New York: Basic Books, 2015).

[18] Matthias Strohn, ed., *The Long Shadow of World War II: The Legacy of the War and its Impact on Political and Military Thinking since 1945* (Oxford: Casemate Publishers, 2021).

[19] Mark Harrison, ed., *The Economics of World War II: Six Great Powers in International Comparison* (Cambridge: Cambridge University Press, 1998); and Iris Kesternich, Bettina Siflinger, James P. Smith, and Joachim K. Winter, "The Effects of World War II on Economic and Health Outcomes across Europe," *The Review of Economics and Statistics* 96, no. 1 (2014): 103–118.

[20] Kesternich, Siflinger, Smith, and Winter, "The Effects of the Second World War."

powers, such as France and Great Britain, felt threatened by Germany's untamed ambitions. Thus, the victory of the Allied Powers over the Axis Powers curtailed the monopolistic and imperialistic tendencies of Nazi Germany,[21] helped enshrine democracy in different parts of Europe and the world, guaranteed the freedom of the Jews, and also occasioned the unification of states. The establishment of the United Nations in 1945 was one of the political aftereffects of the war.[22] As hinted by the opening paragraph of the charter establishing the United Nations, the organization was established to "save future generations from the scourge of war."[23] This was pertinent, since the previously established League of Nations failed to achieve the same purpose.

While the extent of the impacts of World War II are beyond the scope of this chapter, I shall offer an evaluation of the impacts of the war on Great Britain and Nigeria and show how the advent of the conflict contributed significantly to the decolonization of Nigeria. A plethora of research has attested that the end of the war did not come without consequences.[24] The aftermath was felt greatly by both the victors and the vanquished, and Britain, one of the major parties to the war, was not spared. It immediately brought economic and political turmoil to Britain and its colonies.[25] Notably, though the impacts of the war are felt in all countries which fought, as well as in others, Britain especially backed its involvement in the war by drawing on history. As the only member of the victorious Allied Powers who had participated in the conflict since the start, Britain steered its citizens, colonial territories, and the rest of the world to interpret the war through the filter of its own experiences. Thus, the war soon became "the propaganda campaign which emphasized both the communal nature of the 'people's war' and the moral superiority of the national cause."[26] For Britain, however, there seemed to be an upsurge of emotion in its attachment to the war. Not only did Britain peddle the war as a "people's war," thus engaging the interests of ordinary civilians in war affairs, but it also used the pretext of the global war to forge a sense of unity in her collapsing empire. Ironically, the war, which the old empire sought to use to keep itself formidable, would later be the major cause of its gradual decline.[27]

---

[21] Zink Harold, *The United States in Germany 1944–1955* (Princeton: D. Van Nostrand, 1957).
[22] John E. Trent and Laura Schnurr, *A United Nations Renaissance: What the UN is, and what it could be* (Opladen: Barbara Budrich Publishers, 2018).
[23] Michael Kluger and Richard J. Evans, *Roosevelt and Churchill: The Atlantic Charter* (South Yorkshire: Frontline Books, 2020).
[24] See, for instance, Stewart Ross, *Causes and Consequences of the Second World War* (London: Evans Brothers Limited, 2003).
[25] Alasdair Blair, *Britain and the World since 1945* (London: Routledge, 2015).
[26] Mark Donnelly, *Britain in the Second World War* (London: Routledge, 1999), 1.
[27] Donny Gluckstein, *A People's History of the Second World War: Resistance Versus Empire* (London: Pluto Press, 2012).

Even though Britain had the rare privilege of recording some unique successes in the war – relatively light casualties, no invasion of the home islands, standing alone as the only major European power against Germany after the fall of France, and being the only member of the "Big Three" (the United States, the Soviet Union, and Britain) that had fought from the outset – it nonetheless paid high political, economic, and other costs. For instance, even though Britain was the only one of the Big Three which fought from the outset, it was the United States and the Soviet Union that emerged as superpowers.[28] Before the involvement of the two superpowers in the war, when only France and Britain were on the offensive against Germany and Italy, it was clear that Germany and Italy were prevailing. Their initial victory in the war has been linked to their superior armaments and the doctrine and discipline of its soldiers. By engaging the helping hands of the United States and the Soviet Union, the war transformed from a mere European war into a global one. Thus, the victory, as led by the Soviet Union and the United States, led to the end of European domination of the world.[29]

Perhaps, the most painful after-effect of World War II on Britain is the resultant collapse of its empire.[30] In *The Rise and Fall of the British Empire*, Lawrence James observes that the outbreak of the two World Wars in the twentieth century was the principal factor that prompted the imperial decline.[31] In James's view, the two wars were essentially one single war with an interlude of about two decades. Germany's confrontation with Britain exposed the weakness of the latter's army; the unprogressive nature of its working class; and the need for the citizens, the Commonwealth, and the colonies to redefine their positions before a declining former imperial power. As observed by James, the citizens responded by voting out Winston Churchill and his Conservative Party in 1945, even as members of the Commonwealth responded with divided loyalty to Britain, especially with regard to the country's ideological conflict with the Soviet Union, while nationals of the country's colonies realized that Britain was not strong enough to protect their lives and territories.[32] Thus, nationalist feelings in these colonies intensified, leading to Britain's gradual loss of political control over these territories.

Using India and Palestine as case studies, Paul Mulvey considered the outbreak of the war as the definitive event in the decline of Britain's colonial

---

[28] Ken Aldred and Martin A. Smith, *Superpowers in the Post–Cold War Era* (London: Palgrave Macmillan, 1999), 18–49.
[29] Miguel B. Jerónimo and António Costa Pinto, eds., *The Ends of European Colonial Empires: Cases and Comparisons* (London: Palgrave Macmillan, 2015).
[30] Piers Brendon, *The Decline and Fall of the British Empire, 1781–1997* (New York: Alfred A. Knopf, 2008).
[31] Lawrence James, *The Rise and Fall of the British Empire* (New York: St. Martin's Press, 1994).
[32] James, *The Rise and Fall of the British Empire*.

authority.[33] By 1945, when the war ended, India and Palestine had become dissatisfied with British colonial rule. The Indians, for one, were drafted into the war without due consultation and were forced to fight and perish in Britain's inadequate and incompetent armies. As an incentive to draw Indians into the conflict, Britain offered them the right to self-government at the end of the war. The nationalists of that country seized upon the opportunity to demand total independence.[34] With India out of the British Empire in 1947, other colonies began to decolonize.[35] Within two decades of the end of the war, Britain had lost control of more than twenty former colonies. In the case of Nigeria, even though total and complete separation from Britain's imperial control was not achieved until 1963, nationalistic events had become so intense that several political changes occurred in the country between 1945 and 1960.[36]

The Aftermath of World War II

The aftermath of the war promoted nationalism in colonial Nigeria and the eventual decolonization of the country two decades later. The mobilization of hundreds of thousands of Nigerians to fight instigated the political integration of the different parts of colonial Nigeria.[37] Before the outbreak of hostilities, the different parts of Nigeria were aware of their cultural and ethnolinguistic differences as well as the demographic imbalances of the protectorates, the Northern province being larger than the Western and Eastern provinces combined. These imbalances harmed the political integration of the different provinces. Even though the nationalist agenda was promoted around the country by newspapers and political organizations before the war, most of these efforts were regionalized in the same pattern as the newspapers and political organizations which championed nationalism. However, with the outbreak of a global war, the country witnessed the proliferation of different provinces submitting to a common national cause.

The participation of Nigerians in World War II could be said to be one of the agents of political integration in the country only if "political integration" is understood as a gradual process of association between the different peoples of Nigeria. Indeed, right from the outset, the war promoted the understanding

---

[33] Paul Mulvey, "Falling Apart: Britain Leaves India and Palestine," *Academia*, www.academia.edu/11080905/Falling_Apart_Britain_Leaves_India_and_Palestine_1947-48_lecture.
[34] Mulvey, "Falling Apart."
[35] Charles River, *Decolonization: The History and Legacy of the End of Western Imperialism in the 20th Century* (Scotts Valley: CreateSpace Independent Publishing Platform, 2017).
[36] Toyin Falola, ed., *Britain and Nigeria, 1900–1960: Exploitation or Development?* (London: Zed Books, 1987).
[37] Amadi, "The Reactions and Contributions of Nigerians."

and sentimental attachment of Nigerians to certain grand values, political ideologies, and a sense of institution that would later generate among the different peoples of colonial Nigeria a sense of unity and their view of Nigeria as a single political entity within the British Empire.[38] During the war, Nigeria played an assertive role in the empire, particularly among West African colonies. For instance, during the antecedents of World War II, when Italy invaded Ethiopia in 1935, Nigerians contributed both economic and military resources to aid Ethiopia in fending off the attack. As observed in one account of the war, Britain had assumed at the outbreak that, except for Ethiopia, on which Italy had set its eyes, Africa would be tangentially affected by the war.[39]

Contrary to this assumption, various African territories became war fronts. As the most populous political entity in British-controlled Africa, Nigeria's participation in the war became more relevant than previously thought.[40] Beyond Nigeria's expectations as regards the war, Nigeria's participation has been cited as proof of its fidelity to the empire. Nigerians viewed the war not as an ideological conflict but as a moral conflict between good and evil. This sentiment fueled their passionate attachment to the empire and an unprecedented level of cooperation rooted in loyalty to the British. As will be discussed in detail later, the sense of an advanced status within the empire is refuted by Britain's disregard for the welfare of Nigerians and its war survivors. Assured of the strength of its military force, which had become national (and indeed nationalistic), and the nonsuperiority of the military or moral strength of its colonial master, Nigeria began to shift from a colonial to a nationalist consciousness.

After the war, Nigeria saw the growth of intellectualism. The war was a conflict of political ideologies: Germany sought to proselytize fascism across Europe; Britain and France resisted. In Nigeria, the war was peddled as a fight for freedom and a moral cause. Thus, sooner rather than later, the people were exposed to political concepts and ideologies such as democracy, fascism, dictatorship, and imperialism. Different accounts of the war have given the impression that the conflict was rooted in the proliferation of propaganda campaigns. Encouraged by the propaganda of the Allied Forces, people from different parts of Nigeria, traditional rulers, middle- and lower-class people, and the intellectual elite were thus drawn into the war.[41] The result of this mass mobilization was that, while before the outbreak of the war only the educated elite and a few other groups of individuals understood these political concepts and their ramifications on the future of colonial Nigeria, by the end of the war,

---

[38] Amadi, "The Reactions and Contributions of Nigerians."
[39] John Darwin, *The Empire Project: The Rise and Fall of the British World-System, 1830–1970* (New York: Cambridge University Press, 2009), 612–613.
[40] Judith Byfield, Carolyn Brown, Timothy Parson, and Ahmad Sikainga, eds., *Africa and World War II* (Cambridge: Cambridge University Press, 2015).
[41] Korieh, *Nigeria and World War II*, 95.

every average Nigerian of adult age and with mental capacity had become politically knowledgeable.

In our discourse on the growth of intellectualism in colonial Nigeria during wartime, there are two principal groups whose roles cannot be overlooked: the traditional rulers and the mass media. As suggested earlier, the traditional rulers were particularly cooperative with the colonial government at home as well as the British government abroad. For instance, the Emir of Kano was reported to have penned a letter to the Governor of Nigeria, Sir Bernard Henry Bourdillon, wherein he stated the willingness of the emirate to stay loyal to the British king and provide aid to Britain.[42] The Oba of Benin also declared the support of his kingdom to the cause of the war in powerful words that are worthy of quotation here: "I want you to realize that it is good to maintain our military traditions and above all, I want you to be sure that Great Britain and the Empire are quite as strong as the Rock of Gibraltar."[43] These traditional rulers, like others, commanded respect from their "subjects." Thus, when the tables turned against imperialistic Britain in the postwar years, they became formidable nationalists, together with the educated elite.

While the influence of the traditional rulers helped mobilize their subjects to the British cause, the mass media spread pro-British ideology.[44] Different mass media platforms, including radio and print media, fed Nigerians information about the war. As noted in one commentary, "propaganda clearly encompass both the act of purveying certain beliefs or attitudes to a group of people in order to shape their opinions and ultimately direct their behavior toward a desired action, as well as the cultural products and texts appropriated or created to transmit those meanings and information and to incite the desired action."[45] This was the strategy employed by the different media outlets, especially the Nigerian press, in sustaining the people's interests in the war and helping to gauge continued support for and loyalty to the Allied Powers. One example was a publication by the *Lagos Standard* wherein the editors echoed the goodwill of Nigerians toward the British cause: "We want to prove ourselves men, gentlemen, and loyal citizens of not only the empire that offers us protection but citizens of the World's Republic ... *Civis Mundi Sum; Civis Mundi Sum!*"[46]

---

[42] *Nigeria Civil Servant* (Official Organ of the Civil Servant Union) 2, no. 1 (1944), 13.
[43] "Native Attitude in Nigeria," *Nigerian Eastern Mail,* December 9, 1939, 7.
[44] Emmanuel N. Mordi, "Wartime Propaganda, Devious Officialdom, and the Challenge of Nationalism during the Second World War in Nigeria," *Nordic Journal of African Studies* 18, no. 3 (2009): 235–257.
[45] Anthony W. Sheppard, "An Exotic Enemy: Anti–Japanese Musical Propaganda in World War II Hollywood," *Journal of the American Musicological Society* 54, no. 2 (2001): 303–357.
[46] *The Lagos Standard,* October 10, 1940.

Britain employed different mechanisms such as films, radio programs, posters, and exhibitions to promote its war propaganda. Newspapers were the most vibrant medium of communication in Nigeria. However, the irony was that Britain's overzealousness to project only positive views of the war led to a stultification of press freedom during wartime. As observed by Mordi, imperial Britain was in a quandary over press freedom in Nigeria during this period. Just four days before the declaration of war on Germany, the Governor of Nigeria at wartime, Sir Bernard Bourdillon, had issued the Defence Regulations under the Emergency Powers Regulations 1939, under which press censorship was formally instituted and the Chief Secretary to the Government was made the official Press Censor.[47] The regulations expressly prohibited any publication on military strategy or the conduct of the war and any article capable of lowering troops' morale or creating unrest among any section of the population in the colony.[48] The press censor's verdict on any publication that he considered to be within any of these four categories would be an order of proscription. In other cases, the press censor could not object to the publication or could state that the responsibility for the publication rested with the publisher.

Originally, the press conceded the censorship on two major considerations. First, the regulations were temporary measures that obliterated certain liberties needed during wartime.[49] Second, the press also voluntarily aligned with the British war propaganda that the war was to defend the world against fascism. Meanwhile, the challenge to the censorship of the press began in 1943 when the successive colonial administration of Sir Arthur Richards subtly employed the press censorship regulations made by his predecessor to deny the publication of any criticism against his colonial administration. This constituted a direct attack on the fundamental right to freedom of expression and posed a threat to nationalism in the country. In response, several newspapers broke free of the censorship and used their platforms to promote militant nationalism with such great force that it was to lead to the end of colonial rule within two decades.[50]

Besides the censorship, another negative repercussion of the war that contributed to the growth of nationalism in Nigeria was the resulting economic crisis.[51] Analyses of the economic history of colonial Nigeria have revealed that the destruction of the economy of the former colony, at both micro and macro

---

[47] Emmanuel N. Mordi, "Imperial Britain and the Challenge of Press Freedom in Nigeria during the Second World War," *Journal of Development and Communication Studies* 5, no. 1 (2016–2017): 98–121.

[48] Mordi, "Imperial Britain and the Challenge of Press Freedom."

[49] Akinjide Osuntokun, *Nigeria in the First World War* (London: Longman, 1979).

[50] James S. Coleman, *Nigeria: Background to Nationalism* (Berkeley: University of California Press, 1958).

[51] S. A. Shokpeka and Odigwe A. Nwaokocha, "British Colonial Economic Policy in Nigeria, the Example of Benin Province 1914–1954," *Journal of Human Ecology* 28, no. 1 (2017): 57–66.

Figure 22.1 Mrs. Funmilayo Ransome-Kuti (b. 1900) strongly advocated women's rights and was one of the strongest forces for a pan-Nigerian constitution and Nigerian independence.

levels, began with the colonial authority's introduction of cash crop production in the country.[52] This resulted in the neglect of food crops, which had provided a livelihood for low- and middle-class farmers. Before the war, the imbalances in production were still manageable. When the war broke out, the minimal quantity of food crops produced in the country was insufficient to meet the increased demands on both the home front and the war front, resulting in economic distress. Byfield used the case study of Abeokuta to underscore the consequences of the high demands made by the British for food supplies, especially on Nigerian women, and how the resulting economic distress fueled a revolt that led to the abolition of taxes on women and the removal of the traditional king, Alake of Abeokuta.[53] One of the major faces of this revolt was Mrs. Funmilayo Ransome-Kuti, as shown in Figure 22.1, who pushed for the rights of women. Not only was she part of the struggle by Nigerian nationalists for a pan-Nigerian constitution, but she was also a strong advocate who fought for the independence of the country, which was attained in 1960. Notwithstanding the country's

---

[52] John O. Aghahowa and E. E. M. Ukpebor, "The British Colonial Economic Policies and Nigeria Underdevelopment," *The Nigerian Journal of Politics and Public Policy* 3, no. 1&2 (1999): 193–210.

[53] Judith Byfield, "Women, Rice, and War: Political and Economic Crisis in Wartime Abeokuta (Nigeria)," in *Africa and the World War II*, ed. Judith Byfield, Carolyn Brown, Timothy Parson, and Ahmad Sikainga (Cambridge: Cambridge University Press, 2015).

low production of food crops, the colonial government pressured farmers to continue to produce cash crops to supply its armies. Nigerian living standards were adversely affected by the war. Even though the colonial government intervened by regulating prices and distributing food, little could be done to assuage the widespread food shortages, poverty, and inflationary trends.[54]

As a corollary to this, the outbreak of the war led to the development of railways and other transport systems in Nigeria. As observed by Ayoola, different parts of Africa were drawn into the global conflict by their European colonial masters, who mobilized resources from these colonies.[55] Following the aggression of Japan in different territories in 1940 and the loss of Britain's Southeast Asian territories to Japan's control, Africa became a strategic part of the British war effort. Thus, different transport infrastructures were developed to connect different parts of Nigeria with other countries.[56] These infrastructures became channels through which essential raw materials (cash crops) and mineral resources (tin and columbite) were transported to other British African countries or war fronts in Africa. This seemingly positive development was not without consequences. Heavy reliance on the transport systems, especially the railway networks, coupled with poor management, rendered it impossible for Nigerians to import capital goods from other countries, thereby exacerbating wartime economic distress.[57]

The combined effect of the foregoing internal events during World War II was the promotion of nationalistic struggles in Nigeria. From this perspective, Oliver Coates has argued that both familiar and unfamiliar events contributed to the promotion of nationalistic struggles after the war.[58] The major events he highlights in his discourse are the outbreaks of the two World Wars and the resulting global depressions. Beyond these factors, however, it is evident that political integration, the promotion of intellectualism and the censorship of the press produced both the awareness and the dissatisfaction needed to fuel nationalistic sentiments in the country. The interplay of these factors in promoting nationalism has been linked with the war's effects on the collapse of the British Empire and Britain's neglect of Nigerian soldiers who had participated in the war. As will be shown in the next section, the breed of nationalistic efforts championed after the war was unlike the pre-1940

[54] Wale Oyemakinde, "The Pullen Marketing Scheme: A Trial in Food Price Control in Nigeria, 1941–1947," *Journal of the Historical Society of Nigeria* 6, no. 4 (1973): 413–423.
[55] Tokunbo Ayoola, "The Second World War and Africa's Socioeconomic Infrastructures: A Case Study of the Nigerian Railroad System," in *Contemporary Africa: African Histories and Modernities*, ed. Toyin Falola and Emmanuel M. Mbah (New York: Palgrave Macmillan, 2014), 63–87.
[56] Paul Collier, "Building an African Infrastructure: Building Railways in Africa," *Finance and Development* 48, no. 4 (2011): 19–21.
[57] Ayoola, "The Second World War."
[58] Oliver Coates, "Nigeria and the World: War, Nationalism and Politics, 1914–1960," in *The Oxford Handbook of Nigerian Politics*, ed. Carl Levan and Patrick Ukata (Oxford: Oxford University Press, 2019), 699–713.

moderate nationalist struggles that only sought government responsibility. In the case of the post–World War II period, nationalist struggles became anticolonial. Africans had had enough of the imperialistic control of the British government over their territories.

Impact on Nationalism and Decolonization

As proved in the preceding sections of this chapter, World War II produced different outcomes in Nigeria, the British Empire, and the rest of the world. However, the most significant result of the war for our discourse in this book is the intensification of nationalist efforts and the eventual decolonization of Nigeria in 1960. A wealth of literature attests to the fact that the end of the war paved the way for nationalistic struggles in Nigeria. Olusanya, who studied the impacts of the war on Nigerian politics, has observed that while the Nigerian nationalist movement predated the outbreak of the war, it did not reach its maturity until later.[59] Olusanya was unequivocal in suggesting that the establishment of scanty newspapers and political organizations before the outbreak of the war was only to keep the colonial government on its toes through constant criticisms. The nationalists did not entertain the idea of independence until after the war. It was equally observed that the political integration that happened at the outbreak of the war would later lead to the expansion of nationalistic efforts. Nigerians became interested in the nationalist struggle, which, before this time, had been of interest only to the educated elite.

Different factors have been suggested for the widespread promotion of anticolonial nationalism in Nigeria after the war. The political integration of the different provinces (now regions) in Nigeria and the growth of intellectualism exposed people from different parts of the world to political ideologies and thus helped enshrine nationalistic notions. The economic distress caused by the war infuriated many Nigerians. Another cause was the general strike of 1945, which was instrumental in promoting nationalism in Nigeria. Economic distress in the country provoked intense reactions in response to the British colonial government's inability to appropriately cater to the needs of Nigerians. Similar experiences have been observed in other former colonies, particularly India, when the Bengal Famine of 1943 became one of the factors that provoked such great nationalistic efforts that Britain was left with no choice but to grant the country independence in 1947.[60] Notably, political integration, the growth of intellectualism, and the socioeconomic effects of the war were all factors that promoted anticolonial nationalism in the country. Some experiences of Nigerian soldiers, as well as particular events that either affected or were championed by Britain

---

[59] Olusanya, *The Second World War*.
[60] Mulvey, "Falling Apart."

and the Allied Forces, constituted external factors with significant impacts on the promotion of anticolonial nationalism in the country.

The experiences of Nigerian soldiers during the war were an important factor in the promotion of anticolonial nationalism in Nigeria. The exploits of these soldiers in the war fostered a new consciousness among them: the need for self-rule. Those who came back from the war realized that they had been cheated all along and that the white people were not the gods or superhumans they were perceived to be.[61] They observed that on the battlefront, white soldiers suffered the same fate as Nigerians. In some historical records, Nigerian soldiers performed better than some of their British counterparts. They then realized that, aside from the difference in the color of their skin, Europeans had no natural superiority over them.[62] The awareness of these soldiers of the frailty of the British army in the face of aggression from German, Italian, and Japanese forces also weakened their sense of loyalty to the colonizers. Thus, despite Britain's victory in World War II, a widespread campaign for the decolonization of different colonial territories in the British Empire began. This emboldened Nigerians to demand self-rule.[63]

The experiences of Nigerian soldiers during wartime triggered nationalistic feelings, which the British government sidelined. While the British government decorated its citizens who had fought in the war with victory medals, Nigerian soldiers complained that they received little (although many of them did receive medals).[64] This embarrassed and angered the Nigerian soldiers and ignited a burning passion for independence. And, for the first time in ages, Nigerians saw that they could achieve what they wanted. The *West African Pilot* conveyed the displeasure of Nigerians regarding the treatment of the ex-servicemen: "Are not thousands of these heroes still roaming about Lagos and the Provinces in search of the wherewithals of Life?"[65] As observed by Korieh, although the British tried to save face by giving out land to Nigerian veterans, not all of the latter wanted to be farmers.[66] By then, the deed was done. Britain knew that the desire for self-rule was well established, so they began – albeit slowly – to pave the way for Nigeria's independence. In a bid to address the root cause head on, Nigerian nationalists commenced the anticolonial

---

[61] Gabriel O. Olusanya, "The Role of Ex-servicemen in Nigerian Politics," *The Journal of Modern African Studies* 6, no. 2 (1968): 221–232.

[62] Timothy H. Parsons, "The Military Experience of Ordinary Africans in World War II," in *Africa and World War II*, ed. Judith Byfield, Carolyn Brown, Timothy Parson, and Ahmad Sikainga (Cambridge: Cambridge University Press, 2015), 3–16.

[63] Cheikh A. Babou, "Decolonization or National Liberation: Debating the End of British Colonial Rule in Africa," *Annals of the American Academy of Political and Social Science* 632 (2010): 42.

[64] "Africa's Forgotten Wartime Heroes," *BBC*, August 14, 2009, http://news.bbc.co.uk/1/hi/world/africa/8201717.stm.

[65] *West African Pilot*, March 23, 1949.

[66] Korieh, *Nigeria and World War II*.

nationalism movement by demanding equal rights, especially in governance and education.[67]

Another external factor that boosted nationalism in the country was the Atlantic Charter incorporated by Britain's prime minister, Winston Churchill, and the US president, Franklin Roosevelt. The Charter explicitly stated that after the Allied forces' victory, they would "respect the right of all peoples to choose the form of government under which they will live."[68] The Charter raised critical questions, such as whether it was permissible for European countries to rule African countries. One author has asserted that the draft of the Charter was a political tool by the United States to establish itself as the neutral peacekeeping agent and the focal point of democracy.[69] The eight principles of the Atlantic Charter had underlying ideological notions from which Colonial Nigerians drew nationalistic inspiration. Also, establishing the United Nations under a 1942 revised Charter helped Nigerians strengthen their vision for independence. In the United Nations, all colonies were equal, and there was a consensus among the member nations to uphold the dignity of all humans. Even though the United Nations initially merely paid lip service to the decolonization campaign, it soon took the process seriously, especially with the establishment of its Decolonization Committee.[70]

The growth of anticolonial nationalism and the wave of decolonization brewing in other countries, especially British colonies, strengthened the morale of nationalists at home. For instance, at the same time that Nigeria and most other African colonies were clamoring for nationalism, a similar event was occurring in Asia. The successes of these Asian countries in gaining independence proved encouraging to Africans in their independence struggles.[71] In the case of British African colonies, decolonization did not begin until 1957, with Ghana being the first British colony to gain independence.[72] Nevertheless, the activities of nationalist movements in other African countries also promoted nationalistic activities in Nigeria. A popular nationalist movement that influenced nationalist activities during this time was the Garvey movement.[73] Even though the Garvey movement started before World War II to advocate for the complete freedom of Africans, Nigerian nationalists such as Nnamdi Azikiwe

---

[67] Korieh, *Nigeria and World War II.*
[68] Kluger and Evans, *Roosevelt and Churchill.*
[69] Yui Hatcho, "The Atlantic Charter of 1941: A Political Tool of Non-Belligerent America," *The Japanese Journal of American Studies* 14 (2003): 123–139.
[70] Aurora Almada E. Santos, "The Role of the Decolonization Committee of the United Nations Organization in the Struggle Against Portuguese Colonialism in Africa: 1961–1974," *The Journal of Pan African Studies* 4, no. 10 (2012): 248–260.
[71] Basil Davidson, *Modern Africa: A Social and Political History* (London: Routledge, 1994), 61–65.
[72] David Birmingham, *The Decolonization of Africa* (London: UCL Press, 1995).
[73] Rina L. Okonkwo, "The Garvey Movement in British West Africa," *The Journal of African History* 21, no. 1 (1980): 105–117.

borrowed from the ideologies and writings of Marcus Garvey to pursue the ambitions of Nigeria – in this case, independence.[74]

Before the outbreak of the war, there were only a few nationalist movements in the country. The two major political organizations driving nationalist efforts were the National Youth Movement (NYM) and the Nigerian National Democratic Party (NNDP). However, a major challenge with these political parties was the apparent limitation of their operations in space and time. Both movements based their operations only in Lagos, where they sought to take control of the few legislative seats allowed to Indigenous Nigerians in the legislative council. After the outbreak of the war, however, seeds of nationalism spread across the country. A greater number of political parties clamoring for the decolonization of the country emerged. Notable nationalist movements in the country that were established during the time were the National Council of Nigerians and the Cameroons (NCNC), the Action Group (AG), and the Northern People's Congress (NPC). The impacts of each of these movements were felt not only in the particular region where they were headquartered but also throughout the country. The nationalistic efforts they advocated also outlived the granting of independence in 1960.[75]

The NCNC, an Igbo-dominated political party which was established by Nnamdi Azikiwe, demanded positive reforms from the government.[76] The NCNC was the first political party to have nationwide support. It merged with the NYM (a pre-World War II political organization), to strengthen its political structure. The party's leadership rested firmly with Nnamdi Azikiwe, the party's Secretary-General, despite the aged Herbert Macaulay being the party's president. The reason for the natural preference for Azikiwe as the leader of the organization was probably due to his arresting personality and the fact that he operated numerous newspapers wherein he advanced nationalist struggles.[77] Nnamdi Azikiwe used the platform of the political party as well as his newspaper, the *West African Pilot*, to press for constitutional reform in the country.[78] Notably, Azikiwe and the NCNC were overtly critical of the Richards Constitution in 1946, even though it brought more unity to both the Northern and Southern Protectorates. The party determinedly contested the entrenchment of a strong unitary government in the country.[79] As part of the party's press

---

[74] Mathew Mbu, "Zik and the African Revolution," in *Zik: Life and Times*, ed. E. A. Mucheazi (Abuja: National Orientation Agency (NOA) Publication, 1997).

[75] O. E. Udofia, "Nigerian Political Parties: Their Role in Modernizing the Political System, 1920–1966," *Journal of Black Studies* 11, no. 4 (1981): 435–447.

[76] Robert L. Sklar, *Nigerian Political Parties: Power in an Emergent African Nation* (Princeton: Princeton University Press, 2015), 143–189.

[77] Mbu, "Zik and the African Revolution."

[78] David Zitnak, "Imagining the Nigerian Nation through the West African Pilot 1960–1966." Master's Thesis, University of Louisville, 2016.

[79] Coleman, *Nigeria: Background to Nationalism*.

delegation to the London Constitutional Conference of 1947, Azikiwe proposed a reverse from regionalism to a unitary government which he believed would achieve the unity objectives of the failing Richards Constitution.[80] The vociferous criticisms leveled by the NCNC against the Richards Constitution yielded some constitutional reforms, which would set a landmark in the struggle for independence. This was most notably seen in the birth of the Macpherson Constitution, the first pre-independence constitution to give Nigerians the right to greater participation in politics and to introduce policies to ensure the entrenchment of a responsible colonial government.[81]

Another political organization that was created after World War II and that was to have an immense influence on the politics of Nigeria was the AG. The AG was created as a direct response to the Igbo domination of the NCNC.[82] *How can a party that supports a national cause allow no room for leadership from other ethnic groups?* Such derision led Obafemi Awolowo, the former general secretary of *Egbe Omo Oduduwa* and leader of the Nigerian Produce Traders' Association, to found the AG. The party resisted the unitary government advocated by the NCNC and instead proposed party-based regionalism. There seemed to be some strong competition between the AG and the NCNC.[83] Both parties wrestled for votes in the southern regions, and the different parties had cases of cross-carpeting due to the proximity of their respective centers of influence. Though it has been argued that the AG was more ideologically and philosophically structured than the NCNC,[84] it is pertinent to add that the foundation of the AG derived from the NCNC. Despite being tagged as a tribal group, Awolowo managed to sell the visions and missions of the party to non-Yorubas who later became members. The party was also a strong supporter of the demands of minority groups. Meanwhile, the party experienced serious challenges in gaining the same level of nationwide support garnered by the NCNC and the NPC. When the alliance of these two parties led to the emergence of a coalition government in 1960, the AG provided strong opposition in parliament.[85]

---

[80] "Zik Traces Development of Political Parties from 1922–Till Now," *West African Pilot*, October 1, 1960.
[81] L.P.M., "Nigeria under the Macpherson Constitution," *The World Today* 9, no. 1 (1953): 12–21.
[82] Sklar, *Nigerian Political Parties*, 231–283.
[83] John A. A. Ayoade, "Party and Ideology in Nigeria: A Case Study of the Action Group," *Journal of Black Studies* 16, no. 2 (1985): 169–188.
[84] Ayoade, "Party and Ideology in Nigeria."
[85] Kelechi C. Ubaku, Chikezie A. Emeh, and Chinenye N. Anyikwa, "Impact of Nationalist Movement on the Actualization of Nigerian Independence 1914–1960," *International Journal of History and Philosophical Research* 2, no. 1 (2014): 54–67.

The NPC was created in the late 1940s by a coterie of Northern Muslims who received permission from the emirs to go ahead.[86] The political party they formed counterbalanced the Southern-centric politics dominated by the NCNC and the AG. The NPC brought about major reform in the Muslim North. The most influential political figure was Sir Ahmadu Bello, the Sardauna of Sokoto, who aspired to be the Sultan of Sokoto.[87] Bello's primary interest was to protect the territorial integrity of the North and to bring economic change to the region, including those regions that were dominated by non-Muslims. Although Ahmadu Bello's ambitions were limited to the North, he still backed the NPC's efforts to leverage the voting strength in the region to control the national government. The NPC also promoted ethnic nationalism.[88]

Political figures in NPC, such as Sir Tafawa Balewa and Aminu Kano, who studied in British universities, allied with the British government to upgrade the emirates. The change in the administration of the emirates was not supported by the emirs, who believed that it reduced their authority. The other Northern leaders committed to this restructuring ensured that their traditional powers were not tampered with. To protect the interests of the party, an internal rivalry that arose between Muslim factions was concealed and public condemnation of the Muslim aristocracy was frowned upon. The NPC supported the Northern leaders' interest in independence, which was limited to the Northern territories. Support for broader national independence was secondary. The Northern leaders' reluctance to advocate for national independence was a result of fear of being marginalized due to the lack of education of the majority of the Northerners.[89]

A major challenge of the postwar nationalistic efforts championed by these parties was that it was not genuinely national, and this problem could be traced to the existing constitutional framework. The Macpherson Constitution, which replaced the Richards Constitution in 1951, did not solve the major pitfalls of the previous constitution as raised by the delegation at the 1947 Constitutional Conference. As much as the 1951 Constitution presented opportunities for Nigerians to be members of the parliament, it caused ethnic regionalism.[90] The political organizations formed during the constitution's operation emphasized regionalism. Although the emergence of these political

---

[86] Ken Post, *The Nigerian Federal Election of 1959: Politics and Administration in a Developing Political System* (Ibadan: Nigerian Institute of Social and Economic Research, 1963).
[87] John Paden, *Ahmadu Bello, Sardauna of Sokoto: Values and Leadership in Nigeria* (London: Heinemann, 1986).
[88] Billy J. Dudley, *Parties and Politics in Northern Nigeria* (London: Frank Cass, 1968).
[89] Michael Crowder, *The Story of Nigeria* (London: Faber and Faber, 1968).
[90] Louis J. Munoz, "Regionalism in Nigeria: The Transformation of Tradition," *Il Politico* 52, no. 2 (1987): 317–341.

organizations brought about a responsible government, it also fueled the rise of ethnic disunity and regional division.[91] The nationalist movements that appeared during this period were largely based on ethnicity and regionalism. This was evident during the 1951 and 1953 elections when the NPC, whose motto was "One Nigeria, One People," won the majority seats in the North, while the NCNC and AG won the majority seats in the East and West, respectively.

The British perceived the gap in the nationalist struggle as a case of ethnic nationalism. That is, nationalists promoted their ethnic consciousness instead of national consciousness. Britain thus employed a "divide and rule" tactic. This singular but destructive method was to prove damaging to national unity and consciousness in the years to come. According to Olusanya, this exercise provoked ethnic nationalism with clear consequences for postindependence politics.[92] Britain promoted Islamic identity in Northern Nigeria, which made the full integration of the Northern and the Southern Protectorates impossible.[93] The challenges that arose from the ethnic regionalism of the Macpherson Constitution led to a constitutional conference in London that saw the emergence of the 1954 Lyttleton constitution. The reason for the creation of this constitution was to make Nigeria governable irrespective of her political diversity. The constitution encouraged true federalism but, later proved to be ineffective for federalism. The major setback of the constitution was the regionalization of the civil service.[94] Despite these challenges, nationalist actors were unified and relentless in the struggle for independence, which was eventually achieved on October 1, 1960.[95]

Conclusion

This chapter discusses the significance of the participation of Nigerians during and after World War II. At the outbreak of the war, colonial consciousness had grown among the people. As such, while the incentives offered by the British – namely, the right to self-government after the end of the war – were tantalizing enough, they were largely based on volition and interest to fight for a noble cause that led Nigerians to participate in the war. Meanwhile, by the end of the war, the power dynamics in the imperial colony became threatened. Britain

---

[91] Olufemi Vaughan, "Ethno–Regionalism and the Origins of Federalism in Nigeria," *in Democracy and Prebendalism in Nigeria*, ed. Wale Adebanwi and Ebenezer Obadare (New York: Palgrave Macmillan, 2013), 227–242.
[92] Gabriel O. Olusanya, "The Nationalist Movement in Nigeria," in *Groundwork of Nigerian History*, ed. Obaro Ikime (Ibadan Heinemann Educational Books, 1980), 545–569.
[93] Olusanya, "The Nationalist Movement in Nigeria."
[94] Ian F. Nicolson, *The Administration of Nigeria, 1900–1960: Men, Methods and Myths* (Oxford: Clarendon Press, 1969).
[95] Crowder, *The Story of Nigeria*.

had suffered great losses, both economically and in human lives, which had consequences that would affect its imperial control over its colonies. In Nigeria, the harsh realities of the war altered the citizens' initial enthusiasm. Britain also added impetus to the now-brewing anticolonial nationalist struggle by its treatment of Nigerian soldiers who fought alongside British soldiers. Thus, despite being destructive, World War II was pivotal in helping Nigerians gain self-rule. Had there been no war, Africans, including Nigerians, may not at that time have had the tenacity to vehemently pursue their political freedom and independence. It was indeed a catalyst for Nigeria's freedom and independence.

23

Trade Unions and Politics

The end of colonial rule in Nigeria can be viewed from many perspectives.[1] Political movements and the radicalism of nationalist leaders are often discussed as the primary forces for attaining the nation's independence, but, although they were the major drivers of nationalist struggles in colonial Nigeria, other factors were also present. By overemphasizing the role of nationalist leaders and political organizations, literature on colonial history has encouraged the mistaken belief that the 1960 attainment of self-rule was solely the result of the radical and relentless efforts of a few people. This chapter re-evaluates that assumption by examining trade unionism and politics in colonial Nigeria. A study of the nature, organization, and activism of trade unions in the country reveals their involvement in political activity and the quest for independence.

The conventional definition provided by Sidney and Beatrice Webb in *The History of Trade Unionism* states that trade unions are "continuous associations of wage earners to maintain or improve the conditions of their employment."[2] The underlying premise of this definition is that trade unions are labor organizations focused on labor and industrial relations. Some scholars claim that such unions have little impact on political development, despite their influence over economic issues. These claims are incongruent with the reality of trade union activities. The First Industrial Revolution in Britain, continental Europe, and the United States between the late eighteenth and early nineteenth centuries is a classic example of change driven by labor unions.[3] It began as labor activism and resulted in long-lasting economic and political changes in various countries. Despite this evidence, some authors assert that colonial Africa's trade unions were merely labor organizations with no significant influence on politics.

---

[1] See, for instance, Cheikh Anta Babou, "Decolonization or National Liberation: Debating the End of British Colonial Rule in Africa," *The ANNALS of the American Academy of Political and Social Science* 632, no. 1 (2010): 41–54.

[2] Sidney Webb and Beatrice Webb, *The History of Trade Unionism* (London: Longmans, Green and Co., 1896).

[3] Keith Laybourn, *A History of British Trade Unionism, c. 1770–1990* (Wolfeboro Falls: Alan Sutton Publishing, 1992).

Scholars and popular knowledge establish that trade unions played active roles in the defense of human rights, democratization, and the exit of military rule and nation-building in postcolonial Nigeria.[4] This reality invites a return to colonial Nigeria's history for an examination of the relationship between trade unions and politics – and, more significantly, an analysis of their participation in nationalist struggles.

The Evolution of Trade Unionism

The historiography of trade unionism in Nigeria, or any part of Africa, has never been free from ambiguity. Conflicting views about the origins and evolution of trade unionism are shown in the breadth of literature written in history and related disciplines such as sociology, anthropology, political science, and political economy.[5] The multidisciplinary nature of the concept may be responsible for the difficulties encountered by scholars and historians attempting to link the origin of trade unionism with a specific event in history. Historical studies on trade unionism have been useful for understanding and appreciating critical areas of research and practice in political science and political economy.[6] Scholars and historians have traced the origins of trade unionism in most parts of Europe to the Industrial Revolution, which dominated the political and economic landscapes of most European countries in the eighteenth and nineteenth centuries.[7]

Earlier works of literature on the history of trade unionism in Africa generally trace it to one of two events: further back into the eighteenth century, when the Industrial Revolution sparked major political and economic reforms in different parts of Europe; and the imposition of colonialism in the nineteenth century.[8]

---

[4] Danièle Obono, "Trade Unions as Social Movements and Political Actors in Nigeria (1994–2004)," *Stichproben. Wiener Zeitschrift für kritische Afrikastudien* 11 (2011): 95–113.

[5] Owei Lakemfa, *A Centenary of Trade Unionism in Nigeria and the Challenge of the International Trends* (Lagos: Kolagbodi Memorial Foundation, 2014); Olusoji J. George, Oluwakemi Owoyemi, and Uche Onokala, "Trade Unions and Unionism in Nigeria: A Historical Perspective," *Research in World Economy* 3, no. 2 (2012): 68–74; David Northrup, *Trade Without Rulers: Pre-Colonial Economic Development in South-Eastern Nigeria* (Oxford: Clarendon Press, 1978); and Edmund O. Egboh, "Trade Unions in Nigeria," *African Studies* 27, no. 1 (1968): 35–40.

[6] Jon Kraus, "African Trade Unions: Progress or Poverty?" *African Studies Review* 19, no. 3 (1976): 95–108.

[7] Lenard R. Berlanstein, ed., *The Industrial Revolution and Work in Nineteenth Century Europe* (New York: Routledge, 2003); Maxine Berg and Pat Hudson, "Rehabilitating the Industrial Revolution," *The Economic History Review* 45, no. 1 (1992): 24–50; and Wolfgang J. Mommsen and Hans-Gerhard, ed., *The Development of Trade Unionism in Great Britain and Germany, 1880–1914* (London: George Allen & Unwin).

[8] Hubert Schillinger, "Trade Unions in Africa: Weak but Feared," *Occasional Papers: International Development Corporation, Friedrich-Ebert-Stiftung*, March 2005, https://library.fes.de/pdf-files/iez/02822.pdf; and Joseph E. Inikori, "Africans and the Industrial

Hubert Schillinger, in my own take, traced the history of trade unionism in Africa to the post–World War II period.[9] He asserts that there was no place for trade unions in Africa before colonialism, with the notable exceptions of Tunisia, South Africa, Sierra Leone, and the Gambia. He also declared that the formation of African trade unions owed a debt to European rule. "In the founding phase after 1945," he avers, "the setting-up of African trade unions took place with the blessing and, very often, open support of the colonial administration which saw in it a means of keeping social peace."[10] Despite his questionable authority, most literature accepts that the origin of trade unionism in Africa dates to the colonial period.[11]

Alternative accounts trace it to the First Industrial Revolution, which occurred in Great Britain, Europe, and the United States between 1760 and 1840. However, most of these works fail to show links between the Industrial Revolution and the African development of trade unionism. These perspectives also tend to ignore Africa's local history before the colonial intrusion. The Industrial Revolution did influence the evolution and development of trade unions in Africa. One author has suggested that the Industrial Revolution provided a theoretical or philosophical basis for trade unionism in Africa.[12] Beyond this, it is impossible to find relevant connections between Europe's Industrial Revolution and trade unionism in Africa, apart from references to Schillinger's postulation about its colonial origins.

Some literature traces the origin of trade unionism in Nigeria to the colonial period, while other scholars have asserted that forms of trade unions existed before the colonial intrusion.[13] The latter opinion is more popular, especially in recent historiography. Current literature has made a significant effort to explain the historical links between Nigeria's modern trade unionism and its associations of tradesmen and market women before the annexation of Lagos in 1861, the first act of colonial invasion. Isamah remarked that "in pre-colonial Nigeria, work organizations involving occupational groups as

---

Revolution in England: A Roundtable Response," *International Journal of Maritime History* 15, no. 2 (2003): 330–361.
[9] Schillinger, "Trade Unions in Africa."
[10] Schillinger, "Trade Unions in Africa," 2.
[11] Roger Scott, "Are Trade Unions Still Necessary in Africa?" *Transition* 33 (1967): 27–31.
[12] Inikori, "Africans and the Industrial Revolution in England."
[13] Kenneth Chukwuemeka Nwoko, "Trade Unionism and Governance in Nigeria: A Paradigm Shift from Labour Activism to Political Opposition," *Information, Society and Justice Journal* 2, no. 2 (2009): 139–152; Godson Okwuchukwu Okafor and Chinonye Faith Malizu, "The Media, Democracy and Trade Unionism in Nigeria: Challenges and Prospects," *New Media and Mass Communication* 17 (2013): 79–89; and Olusoji James George, Oluwakemi Owoyemi, and Uche Onokala, "Trade Unions and Unionism in Nigeria: A Historical Perspective," *Research in World Economy* 3, no. 2 (2012): 68–74.

hunters, blacksmiths, leatherworkers, etc. existed."[14] This modern perspective on the historiography of trade unionism in Nigeria observes three remarkable epochs in the history and evolution of Nigeria's trade unions. The first is the precolonial period, when organizations formed to support tradesmen and people involved in different crafts. These organizations consisted not only of hunters, blacksmiths, and leatherworkers, as Isamah has suggested, but also included carvers, weavers, and, in some cases, children and other blood relatives of such tradesmen.

Such groups were not properly called "trade unions." However, these "craft organizations" performed roles that qualified them as a form of a union since they regulated trade practices, provided mutual aid and other opportunities for members, and sought to guarantee fair prices or rates of pay for their services. In some parts of the country, these organizations could also engage in quasi-governmental functions, such as the settlement of disputes and the organization of tribute payments sent to kings or traditional rulers.[15]

The second epoch in the history and evolution of trade unions was the colonial period, which signaled the era when organized trade unions emerged and the concept of trade unionism became noticeable in literature. Egboh notes that organized trade unions did not surface in Nigerian history until civil service workers organized themselves into a trade union for the first time on August 19, 1912. The union, known as the Civil Service British Workers' Union, which became the Nigerian Civil Service Union after the country's independence, was inspired by the organization of Indigenous civil service workers in colonial Sierra Leone.[16]

Nigeria's Civil Service British Workers' Union comprised Indigenous workers of the Nigerian Civil Service. The influence of Sierra Leone's civil service did more than merely inspire Nigerian workers. Henry Libert, a Sierra Leonean, was actively involved in the formation of the union.[17] The founding leaders of the Civil Service British Workers' Union borrowed ideas from Sierra Leonean leaders to define the union's mission and to provide direction for the actualization of its aims and objectives.[18]

In the period between the emergence of precolonial "craft organizations" and Nigeria's independence from Great Britain, trade unions evolved into different forms. The most significant changes within these institutions took

---

[14] Austin Isamah, "Organized Labor Under the Military Regimes in Nigeria," *Africa Development* 15, no. 2 (1990): 81–94.
[15] Egboh, "Trade Unions in Nigeria," 35–40; and Peter Lloyd, "Craft Organization in Yoruba Towns," *Africa* 23, no. 1 (1953): 30–44.
[16] Salisu O. Paul, Timothy O. Usman, and Mohammed A. Ali, "Labor Unions and the Transformation of the Nigerian Civil Service: A Discourse," *IJPAMR* 2, no. 1 (2013): 13.
[17] Tony Akowe, "40 Years of NLC: So Far, So Fair?" *The Nation*, February 25, 2018.
[18] Rina Okonkwo, "The Nigeria Civil Service Union, 1919–1922," *The International Journal of African Historical Studies* 26, no. 3 (1993): 609–622.

place during the colonial period. By the time of the 1914 amalgamation, the local understanding of trade unions referenced the Civil Service British Workers' Union instead of the "craft organizations" that had previously existed. During its formative years, the Workers' Union was an exclusive association of first-class workers. After the outbreak of World War I, it underwent a liberalization phase that had ripple effects among Indigenous workers who were affected by surging costs of living. Trade unions in Nigeria changed their developmental trajectory, and newly formed unions broke off from the Civil Service British Workers' Union. By 1931, three major trade unions had emerged from the Civil Service British Workers' Union: The Mechanical Union, the Railway Workers' Union, and the Nigerian Union of Teachers. Legislative support, evidenced by the passing of the Nigerian Trade Union Ordinance in 1938, spurred the growth of additional trade unions in Nigeria.[19] The number of registered trade unions escalated to 91, with more than 30,000 union members registered by 1944.[20]

The philosophical underpinnings of trade unions were rooted in the protectionist goals of earlier "craft organizations." The initial objective of the Civil Service British Workers' Union was to protect the interests and welfare of its members. Following the union's liberalization after the 1914 outbreak of World War I, it agitated for a 30 percent salary increase to offset the financial difficulties imposed by the conflict.[21] The union subsequently focused its efforts on discriminatory practices in the civil service and salary disparities between European and African workers performing identical jobs.[22] While colonialism might have inspired the organization of Nigeria's trade unions, and the Industrial Revolution gave them a theoretical basis, the finer details of trade unionism in Nigeria were developed locally.[23] The trajectory of trade unionism and the later political contributions of these groups in colonial Nigeria demonstrate their independence from colonial or European influences.

Aristocratic ideologies characterized Nigeria's first generation of trade unions. Most members were senior workers in the Nigerian civil service. During this period, trade unions took an exclusionary stance regarding lower-level workers who had largely been affected by the service's discriminatory practices. Union members were not interested in defending broader groups of

---

[19] Edmund O. Egboh, "Trade Union Education in Nigeria (1940–1964)," *African Studies Review* 14, no. 1 (1971): 83–93.

[20] Nigeria Department of Labour Annual Reports. 1945.

[21] Wogu Ananaba, *The Trade Union Movement in Africa: Promise and Performance* (London: C. Hurst, 1979).

[22] George, Owoyemi, and Onokala, "Trade Unions and Unionism in Nigeria."

[23] Segun O. Osoba, "The Development of Trade Unionism in Colonial and Post-colonial Nigeria," in *Topics on Nigerian Economic and Social History*, ed. Isaac A. Akinjogbin and Segun Osoba (Ile-Ife: University of Ife Press, 1980), 185–207.

workers from harsh labor policies imposed by the British colonial government. The outbreak of war liberalized the union and transformed it into an active labor movement.

The successful 1914 protest for salary increases led the Civil Service British Workers' Union to press for better working conditions. Unlike the practice in most European territories, and even in modern-day Nigeria, the group was not only interested in improved labor practices and industrial relations; the nascent movements transformed into politically active organizations that advanced the nationalist agenda.[24] The Nigerian trade unions' transformation into nationalist institutions was the third epoch of their evolution. This unusual turn of events can only be understood in the context of the country's unique experience of social and communal justice, rather than being due to alleged philosophical or historical links with Europe.

Unionism and Politics

Trade unionism is deeply rooted in economic and labor policies; hence, most trade union studies examine labor practices and industrial relations. This has led some authors to insist that trade unions were not involved in political activism, especially in Africa. The nature of trade unions and state relations in Africa has fueled considerable debate, with each side supporting or rejecting political rhetoric in the union narrative. Berg and Butler Hudson are among the authors to launch an attack on the idea that African trade unions were involved in politics.[25] They assert that Guinea and Kenya were exceptions, but evidence generally indicated that trade unions had "limited impacts on political activities during the colonial period ... and restricted roles after independence."[26] The trade unions, "if not completely subordinate to the party (or government), are at least pliable and responsive to party pressures."[27]

By focusing on the labor relations and economic policies of such institutions, some African scholars and historians have neglected the debate over trade unions' political activism. Cohen, who wrote one of the leading books on labor and politics in Nigeria, described trade unions as political and economic institutions.[28] He considered state–trade union relations in four aspects: "party-union integration with unions subordinated; partnership, with some cooperation, state constraints, and some union autonomy; independent union movements, aligned with political oppositions; and independent,

---

[24] Edmund O. Egboh, "The Nigerian Trade-Union Movement and its Relations with World Trade-Union Internationals," *Présence Africaine* 75 (1970): 76–88.
[25] Berg and Butler Hudson, "Rehabilitating the Industrial Revolution."
[26] Berg and Butler Hudson, "Rehabilitating the Industrial Revolution."
[27] Berg and Butler Hudson, "Rehabilitating the Industrial Revolution," 340, 366.
[28] Robin Cohen, *Labour and Politics in Nigeria, 1945–1971* (London: Heinemann, 1974).

non-politically aligned unions."[29] Cohen subtly suggested that trade unions were politically active, but he neither openly opposed Berg and Butler Hudson's stance nor corroborated his position with substantial evidence. Scholars like Nwoko and Okolie have only recently begun to emphasize the political aspect of trade unions in Nigeria.[30]

Nwoko, who examined the ongoing evolution of trade unions in Nigeria as they developed from mere labor movements to becoming established political actors, identifies two periods for this radical shift: the colonial and the postcolonial periods. Contrary to earlier suggestions, the evidence of trade unions' political involvement could be found in their members' protests for higher salaries, cost-of-living allowances, and other improvements for their workers. The Civil Service British Workers' Union was the first trade union in colonial Nigeria, created and structured "along British lines," but it applied local customs and techniques to make various demands and establish its independence from British thinking.[31]

Although the organization of trade unions in Nigeria can be traced through local history via the emergence of "craft organizations" in the precolonial period and other non-European factors such as the civil service union in Sierra Leone, it is impossible to completely remove British influence from the narrative of trade unions in Nigeria. Inquiry into the nature of trade unionism in Nigeria, and especially into the state–trade union relations in colonial Nigeria, suggests that British labor practices contributed to the organization of trade unions. Conversely, the British colonial government and its labor policies were the main targets of trade union activism. Connections between trade unions and Nigerian politics can be viewed from two perspectives: the British colonial government's impact on the organization and activities of trade unions, and trade union activism's impact on politics and political development.

Some scholars tracking the evolution and development of trade unionism in Africa have declared that the British colonial government provided the impetus for the formation of trade unions in most of its African colonies.[32] This notion is inconsistent with evidence from Nigerian history. Although the major motivation for the formation of trade unions in Nigeria may have been a desire to protect senior members of the Nigerian civil service, the British were not actively involved in the formation of trade unions in Nigeria. The Civil Service British Workers' Union was largely formed through local initiatives inspired by external factors, including Britain or its colonial government.

---

[29] Cohen, *Labour and Politics in Nigeria*.
[30] For instance, see Nwoko, "Trade Unionism and Governance in Nigeria."; and Charles N. Okolie, "Trade Unionism, Collective Bargaining and Nation Building: The Nigerian Experience," *OGIRISI: A New Journal of African Studies* 7 (2010): 136–148.
[31] Nwoko, "Trade Unionism and Governance in Nigeria," 141.
[32] Schillinger, "Trade Unions in Africa," 2.

The Nigerian Civil Service British Workers' Union was modeled after the civil service union of Sierra Leone, which was also a British West African colony. The organization of Sierra Leone's civil service union was based on experiences with British labor practices and trade union activities. However, in the Nigerian context, the major and immediate role played by the British colonial government was that of a target for trade union activism. George, Owoyemi, and Onakala have observed colonial government interventions in trade union struggles.[33] The British colonial government's involvement in such conflicts can be divided into four phases. The first was between 1900 and 1920, when the labor movement consisted of workers clamoring for a better payment system to meet the economic demands of the colonial administration. The second phase was between 1921 and 1928, which was the period when trade unions were formalized. The third phase, from 1929 to 1938, was when Lord Passfield was appointed as the Colonial Secretary in Britain's first Labour government. Passfield's policies compelled colonial governments in Nigeria and other colonies "to initiate long-term labor and industrial relations policies, legislation and practice, on [the] lines of those prevailing in the United Kingdom."[34] The final phase occurred during World War II, between 1939 and 1945. The Labour Inspectorate was formed during this period, later becoming the Department of Labour, and the oppressive legislation affecting trade union activities was subsequently abolished.[35]

State–trade union relations during the colonial period were marked by intense opposition. The initial members of the Civil Service British Workers' Union were largely Indigenous senior officers in the civil service, and they benefited from labor policies introduced by the British government. The later evolution of trade unions witnessed the liberalization of trade unions and serious activism. Any unsatisfactory policy or practice introduced to the civil service would be met with strong opposition from the trade union.

The British colonial government's intervention in trade union conflicts did not promote the activities of trade unions, despite the assertions of some authors. Throughout different phases of trade union struggles, the British initiated policies and encouraged practices that opposed the aims and objectives of Nigeria's trade unions. The conflict between the colonial government's self-serving interests and the agenda of the trade unions resulted in the unions upping the ante during Lord Passfield's administration as Colonial Secretary.

Several authors have attempted to show the political impacts of Nigerian trade unions in the postindependence landscape. Nwoko stated that trade unions, represented under the umbrella of the Nigerian Trade Union

---

[33] George, Owoyemi, and Onokala, "Trade Unions and Unionism in Nigeria."
[34] Onyeka C. Nwanunobi, "Wage Labour and the Politics of Nigeria and Kenya: A Comparative Study," *African Studies Review* 17, no. 1 (1974): 77–104.
[35] George, Owoyemi, and Onokala, "Trade Unions and Unionism in Nigeria."

Congress (NTUC), played active roles in shaping some non-labor-related policies in Nigeria. Their actions included the powerful demonstrations, protests, and strikes that followed the Anglo–Nigerian Defense Agreement.[36] In 1960, the federal government saw the agreement as a "reaffirmation of the friendly and cordial ties ... between Nigeria and the United Kingdom," but the NTUC and most other citizens saw it as an insidious agenda for controlling Nigeria's political and economic landscapes.[37]

Nigerian trade unions bested the federal government such that the agreement was later abrogated due to pressures from trade unions.[38] Trade union struggles have had other, more remarkable effects on political activities in postindependence Nigeria. Other authors have extensively studied the impact of trade union activities, especially during military regimes. Harsh, undemocratic policies were introduced by dictatorial governments, and trade unions mounted the primary opposition to such draconian policies.[39]

Scholars have revisited the history of Nigerian trade unions to study their impact on politics and political development therein.[40] The political activities of trade unions transcended mere opposition to the colonial government's labor policies. Trade unions successfully advocated the reformation of the civil service with protests, demonstrations, boycotts, strikes, and other actions. This encouraged them to press for specific demands, like incremental salary increases for workers, reduced discrimination against African employees, cost-of-living allowances, and improved conditions of service. These causes gave trade unions the impetus to engage in mainstream political activity.

The Nigerian Union of Teachers (NUT) was established in 1931. In its formative years, this trade union advocated improved working conditions for its members.[41] It later became actively involved in pushing for education system reforms.[42] The colonial government's crackdown on trade union leaders, including Obafemi Awolowo and Michael Imodu, bred resentment among Nigerian workers, who adopted a holistic approach to opposing harmful labor and political policies implemented by the British colonial government.[43]

---

[36] *Daily Express*, October 28, 1961.
[37] Olasupo Ojedokun, "The Anglo–Nigerian Entente and its Demise, 1960–1962," *Journal of Commonwealth Political Studies* ix, no. 3 (1971): 210–233.
[38] Nwoko, "Trade Unionism and Governance in Nigeria," 142.
[39] Okafor and Malizu, "The Media, Democracy and Trade."
[40] Michael Oyelere, "Political Developments, Trade Union and Social Movement Unionism: A Case of Nigeria Labor Congress," *Regent's Working Papers in Business & Management*, 2014, 1–16.
[41] Edward C. I. Diogu, "Teachers and Politics in Nigeria: A Study in the Policy Influence of the Nigeria Union of Teachers," unpublished PhD dissertation, State University of New York at Buffalo, 1985.
[42] George, Owoyemi, and Onokala, "Trade Unions and Unionism in Nigeria."
[43] Rotimi Ajayi "The Politicization of Trade Unionism: The Case of Labor/NCNC Alliance in Nigeria, 1940–1960," *Ufahamu: A Journal of African Studies* 27, no. 1–3 (1999): 48–62.

Trade unions in colonial Nigeria gradually transformed into politically active groups. This process had several different phases, which Tar and George, Owoyemi, and Onakala have examined. Three important stages mark the development of political consciousness among trade unions. First, they had no interest in any form of activism. The feeble activity of trade unions during this phase was due to the contentment of members within the only existing trade union: the Civil Service British Workers' Union. The second phase began during World War I when the Workers' Union became involved in labor activism. In the final phase, trade unions fully transformed into political organizations.[44] As Ayegbusi and Rukema have observed, these trade unions outgrew their initial goals – protecting their members' interests – and began advocating for all Nigerians on national issues during the colonial period.[45]

The rise of political consciousness among colonial Nigeria's trade unions has been attributed to the leaders of political parties and nationalist organizations involved in trade union activities. Obafemi Awolowo, a leading nationalist, was a one-time national leader of Nigeria's National Union of Road Transport Workers.[46] The political consciousness of trade unions escalated after they formed coalitions with political organizations. The Trade Union Congress of Nigeria (TUCN) began promoting nationalist struggles after affiliating with the National Council of Nigeria and Cameroon (NCNC), which Nnamdi Azikiwe had founded in 1944. The TUCN leadership and the NCNC movement exposed the labor force to radical nationalism. The Zikist movement's vision, within the NCNC, was centered on "the eviction of British imperialists from the shores of Nigeria and thereafter to chase all European usurpers wherever they may be found, out of Africa."[47] By associating with the TUCN, the union embraced the energetic spirit of anticolonial consciousness. Union leaders also displayed radicalism in their agitations against oppressive and discriminatory colonial policies.

Interactions between politics and trade unionism in colonial Nigeria were not always positive. The combination of politics and trade unionism can easily engender the politicization of trade unions, creating a situation worse than the feeble stance of colonial Nigeria's original trade unions. Ideally, trade unions are professional bodies aligned to protect class interests. When union leaders intentionally blur the boundaries between themselves and political leaders, they potentially replace class interests with self-serving goals.

---

[44] Usman A. Tar, "Organised Labor and Democratic Struggles in Nigeria," *Information, Society and Justice Journal* 2, no. 2 (2009): 165–181.
[45] Talabi Rasheed Ayegbusi and Joseph Rudigi Rukema, "Labor Unions and the Nigerian Democratic Experience: An Appraisal," *Mankind Quarterly* 61, no. 4 (2021): 872–900.
[46] Ajayi, "The Politicisation of Trade Unionism."
[47] Michael C. K. Ajuluchukwu, "Zikists of the Burning Struggle," *The Guardian*, March 8, 1998.

For colonial Nigeria's trade unions, and especially for the TUCN, the affiliation with the NCNC introduced the forces of ethnic politics that characterized most of colonial Nigeria's political organizations.[48] During the colonial period, Nwoko argued that Nigerian trade unions could become the vanguard of working-class citizens, serving as a public watchdog mounting vocal opposition to oppressive governments – especially since the first generation of political parties in Nigeria were characterized by "tribalism and sectarianism."[49] The affiliation between trade unions and political organizations in Nigeria had mixed results. Trade unions were exposed to the spirit of radicalism and political activism that animated political organizations, but they were also exposed to the ethnicity, sectarianism, and nepotism of these same groups. These negative traits have remained a part of trade unions to the present day.[50]

The positive impact of trade unionism on politics and political development in Nigeria cannot be overlooked. Unions became formidable forces in Nigeria's colonial history, bringing enduring change to the country's industrial, economic, and political landscapes.[51] Aiyede notes that Nigeria's trade unions have transformed beyond labor movements to protect the interests and welfare of all workers. They became major actors in the democratization project and provided a platform for the Nigerian people to oppose government decisions.[52]

Okolie also stated that trade unions have actively been involved in nation-building since the colonial period. Labor activism techniques, such as collective bargaining by trade unions, are useful in pressing for labor reforms and compelling political action.[53] The most significant impact that trade unions had on colonial Nigeria's politics came from their involvement in nationalist struggles.

The Impact of Trade Unionism on Nationalism

Colonial Nigeria's trade unions became involved with anticolonial nationalism after working with political organizations, but a deeper inquiry into the nature of trade unions and their previous activities reveals that other factors

---

[48] Ananaba, *The Trade Union Movement in Africa*.
[49] Nwoko, "Trade Unionism and Governance in Nigeria," 143.
[50] Okolie, "Trade Unionism, Collective Bargaining and Nation Building."
[51] Adewumi D. Adebayo, "The ILO and the Political Economy of Labor Policy Making in Nigeria, 1930–1960," *The Journal of Imperial and Commonwealth History* 50, no. 2 (2022): 348–382.
[52] Remi Aiyede, "United We Stand: Labor Unions and Human Rights NGOs in the Democratization Process in Nigeria," *Development in Practice* 14, no. 1–2 (2004): 224–233.
[53] Okolie, "Trade Unionism, Collective Bargaining and Nation Building," 143–146.

contributed to their support for nationalist causes. There were four reasons for increasing nationalist consciousness: the unions' previous successes in acquiring labor-related concessions from the British colonial government; the colonialists' crackdown on local laborers, especially trade union leaders; trade unions entering into coalitions with political organizations; and increased national awareness and consciousness of nationalist efforts, especially after the outbreak of World War II.

The historiography of state–trade union relations in colonial Nigeria is a story of strong trade unions that had gained the upper hand in negotiations with the colonial government. The influence of trade unions continued to increase after their first act of labor activism, which was the protest to increase workers' salaries by 30 percent to offset rising costs of living. The Civil Service British Workers' Union later fought discrimination in the civil service since no Nigerian worker had been eligible to attain the rank of Senior Serviceman. Nigerians who were equally as qualified as their white counterparts could only rise to the post of Assistant Medical Officer. The discriminatory salary scale also favored Europeans over Africans performing identical jobs. The British colonial government abandoned these practices after successful pressure from trade unions.[54]

The disintegration of the Civil Service British Workers' Union failed to dampen the enthusiasm of the trade unions that emerged from its remains. Unions in colonial Nigeria combined British-inspired labor activism with local knowledge and tactics from precolonial craft organizations to press home their demands. However, the British colonial government's repeated capitulations were most likely because the protesting workers' roles were essential for governance. The British government needed the Nigerian labor force to maximize its economic production. The British controlled the nation's wealth, but Nigerian workers could harm economic activity through continuous strikes and boycotts.

As the British colonial government applied pressure on trade union leaders, its efforts further strengthened nationalist consciousness among trade unions.[55] Leaders such as Obafemi Awolowo of Nigeria's National Union of Road Transport Workers and Michael Imodu of the Nigerian Railway Workers' Union (NRWU) were targeted by colonial government forces. Michael Imodu was arrested after leading an NRWU protest against the low wages paid to Nigerian workers.[56] The British had hoped that arresting union leaders would deter future protests, but their oppressive efforts

---

[54] Ayegbusi and Rukema, "Labor Unions and the Nigerian Democratic Experience."
[55] Wale Oyemakinde, "Michael Imoudu and the Emergence of Militant Trade Unionism in Nigeria, 1940–1942," *Journal of the Historical Society of Nigeria* 7, no. 3 (1974): 541–561.
[56] Robin Cohen, "Nigeria's Labor Leader Number 1: Notes for a Biographical Study of M.A.O. Imoudu," *Journal of the Historical Society of Nigeria* 5, no. 2 (1970): 303.

provoked the general trade union members. By this time, they were already radical nationalists.

Under Imodu's leadership, NRWU radicalism replaced the conservative approach that had previously characterized Nigeria's labor movement. Radical action became a necessary tool for preventing further colonial oppression. The NRWU was described as the "laboratory for the development of the worker's consciousness,"[57] which was seen in its determination to confront the British government regarding more favorable working conditions. When the government began applying pressure on union leaders, this led to more strikes and boycotts that spurred the growth of radicalism in other unions, and which was later expressed through nationalist struggles.

Even before trade unions began their affiliation with political organizations, individual unions had taken radical stances against the colonial government through their labor activism. The NRWU, under the visionary leadership of Michael Imodu, has been identified as one of the main forces responsible for shifting the nature of trade union activism from conservative to radical.[58] Trade unions also developed a heightened nationalist consciousness after the outbreak of World War II. The onset of the war encouraged sentimental bonding between the British Empire and its colonies in Africa, but its lingering effects led to a surge in nationalist agitation. For trade unions, the hardships imposed by the global conflict did more to encourage nationalist consciousness than any political coalition.

The historiography of trade union involvement in nationalist efforts focuses on collaboration between trade unions and political organizations, as scholars tend to emphasize the role of groups like the NCNC. Ajuluchukwu has observed that the Zikist movement of the NCNC was a radical anticolonial nationalist organization, and its activism influenced the development of nationalist consciousness in the TUCN.[59] In 1948, the Zikist movement met the colonial administration with audacious acts of civil disobedience, labor activism, and the procurement of weaponry.[60] This unprecedented resistance resulted from an order from the Zikist movement that urged Nigerian workers and citizens to pay taxes to Nnamdi Azikiwe instead of the British government. The order would have been implemented if Azikiwe had not insisted that he was a legitimate revenue collector.[61] After this disruptive campaign, the British government clamped down on the movement's leaders.

The importance of trade unions for the anticolonial liberation struggle has transcended written historiography to become an important component of

---

[57] Ajayi, "The Politicisation of Trade Unionism."
[58] Ajayi "The Politicisation of Trade Unionism."
[59] Ajuluchukwu, "Zikists of the Burning Struggle."
[60] Ehiedu E. G. Iweriebor, *Radical Politics in Nigeria, 1945–1950: The Significance of the Zikist Movement* (Zaria: Ahmadu Bello University Press, 1996).
[61] Ajayi, "The Politicisation of Trade Unionism."

public knowledge. Ayegbusi and Rukema stated that "labor unions in Africa were an important force in the anti-colonial liberation struggle,"[62] noting that evidence could be found in Nigeria's colonial history. These authors conducted quantitative research, gathering the opinions of Nigerian citizens regarding trade unions and their contributions to Nigerian independence. One respondent remarked that "organized labor contributed significantly . . . if you look at the 1949 Enugu coal massacre, the role of the Ekmuku society of Asaba and women rioting in Abba."[63] Another respondent referred to the general strike of 1945, which was led by the NRWU in collaboration with the NCNC. The general opinion of respondents was that these strikes, along with other trade unions' actions, such as boycotts, protests, and demonstrations, made immense contributions to anticolonial nationalism.

Historical studies and other scholarly works overwhelmingly support the idea that the strikes of 1945 and 1949 were milestones in the anticolonial nationalist struggles led by Nigeria's trade unions, but other significant trade union activities also contributed to Nigeria's eventual independence. One example is the NCNC delegation that traveled to London and demanded an overhaul of the Richards Constitution.[64] The group included labor leaders such as Michael Imodu, who had become Secretary-General of TUCN. Leaders of TUCN branches in Lagos, Ibadan, and Benin also took part in the voyage to London. In addition to the trade unions' anticolonial activism, individual workers engaged in political affiliations with groups that included the Zikist movement of the NCNC.

The NCNC made immense contributions to the political and nationalist consciousness of colonial Nigeria's trade unions, especially the TUCN, but the Zikist movement also employed labor-movement methods in its nationalist struggles. The NCNC employed activist tactics, such as boycotts and strikes, to press for tax reduction in 1948. The labor movement's synchronization with the political nationalist movement was possible because of the radical nature of trade union leaders, including Imodu, Coker, and Emejulu, and also because of the overall politicization of the labor movement. The Zikist movement actively promoted doctrines that ensured the economic freedom of workers and improved their living conditions. Its coalition with trade unions strengthened the link between political radicalism and labor activism, recruiting labor leaders to become nationalist leaders for the movement.[65]

---

[62] Ayegbusi and Rukema, "Labor Unions and the Nigerian Democratic Experience," 878–880.
[63] Ayegbusi and Rukema, "Labor Unions and the Nigerian Democratic Experience," 878–880.
[64] A. O. Okon, "Nigeria and a People's Constitution: The Imperative of Democracy and Change," *The Constitution* 4, no. 1 (2004): 16.
[65] Iweriebor, *Radical Politics in Nigeria*.

Some scholars have vehemently asserted that, except in Guinea and Kenya, trade unions in Africa during the colonial period were not actively involved in nationalist struggles, but overwhelming evidence in written historiography and oral history documents trade union participation in nationalist struggles.[66] Trade unions in colonial Nigeria might have begun as passive occupational groups, but they developed into labor movements with defined objectives and powerful methods for achieving them. Their early labor activism and radical sentiment provided the impetus for a shift to radical nationalism.

The height of radical nationalism in trade union struggles may have been the Enugu coal massacre, also known as the Iva Valley massacre.[67] This began as a protest organized by coal workers who wanted incremental salaries. The Nigerian police, acting on instructions from the colonial government, opened fire on the workers and killed at least twenty-one Nigerians.[68] The event has remained contentious in the history of Nigeria's labor movement, as a testament to the violence inflicted on Nigerian workers and their unions under the colonial administration.[69] It exposed the fact that the colonial government's unjust labor policies and practices not only influenced labor relations and industrial matters but were also political. This fact encouraged Nigerian workers to confront the British colonial administration directly.

The coalition between the TUCN and the NCNC was a major force in promoting nationalist agitations in trade unions, alongside other factors specific to the nature and organization of trade unions. The TUCN–NCNC coalition was the only union–party alliance in colonial Nigeria. In 1947, right before the Enugu coal massacre, a coalition of trade unions formed the Nigerian National Federation of Labor (NNFL) to compete with the TUCN. Ohiare describes the emergence of the NNFL as the first split within Nigeria's labor movement. It was followed by failed attempts to merge the NNFL and the TUCN. Both unions came together to confront the colonial government regarding the Enugu coal massacre of 1949.[70]

Some trade union leaders were involved in the leadership of nationalist organizations outside of union–party alliances, and vice versa. Obafemi

---

[66] James Smoot Coleman and Carl Gustav Rosberg, eds., *Political Parties and National Integration in Tropical Africa* (Berkeley: University of California Press, 1966).

[67] S. O. Jaja, "The Enugu Colliery Massacre in Retrospect: An Episode in British Administration of Nigeria," *Journal of the Historical Society of Nigeria* 11, no. 3/4 (1982–1983): 86–106.

[68] Olatunji Ololade, "Sorrowful Songs from the Valley of Iva," *The Nation Newspaper*, September 15, 2015.

[69] Hyginus C. Onuegbu, "Trade Unions in Nigeria: A Contemporary Overview." Paper Presented to the distinguished guests, participants and organizers of the Trade Union Congress (TUC), Rivers State Leadership Retreat, held at NUJ Press Centre, Port Harcourt, September 20, 2016.

[70] Philip Ohiare, Interview. *Borin* (May 5, 1997).

Awolowo and Nnamdi Azikiwe – two major nationalist leaders in colonial Nigeria – were active trade union leaders. Awolowo was a motor transport worker, and Azikiwe was a revenue collector. Unfortunately, coalitions between trade unions and political organizations had their faults. For example, mistrust developed between the leaderships of the TUCN and the NCNC, affecting nationalist struggles and the fight for independence. Nationalist leaders from the NCNC called for the withdrawal of the TUCN because they believed that politics could not be merged with labor activism. However, votes from the TUCN affirmed its full participation in the NCNC's political ideologies, which led to its continued existence. The decision, made by TUCN leaders, was pivotal for ensuring the country's independence.[71]

Conclusion

This chapter has revisited Nigeria's colonial history, reviewing written historiography and pieces of oral history to examine the role of trade unions in colonial Nigeria's political development. It rebuts the notion peddled in some works – mostly by foreign authors – that trade unions were passive observers of politics in colonial Nigeria. Trade unions not only engaged in political action but were also active participants in nationalist struggles.[72] Contemporary trade unions, such as the Nigerian Labour Congress (NLC)[73] and the Academic Staff Union of Universities (ASUU),[74] have shown themselves to be powerful social movements seeking major labor and economic reforms. Their antecedents were equally active in the colonial period, participating in radical nationalism.

Studies on nationalism in colonial Nigeria often focus on nationalist leaders and political organizations, neglecting groups such as trade unions. This chapter has highlighted the involvement of trade unions in nationalist struggles. Political organizations were influential in the development of national consciousness among trade unions, but they were just one of several factors that shifted the stance of trade unions away from labor activism to become important forces for anticolonial nationalism.

---

[71] Ajayi, "The Politicisation of Trade Unionism."
[72] Chigbo Ofong, "Political Trade Unionism in Nigeria: An Historical and Socioeconomic Analysis," unpublished PhD dissertation, Johns Hopkins University, 1982.
[73] Effiong J. Ekpo, "The Nigeria Labor Congress and National Development (1993–2000)," *European Journal of Political Science Studies* 2, no. 1 (2018): 172–193.
[74] Sylvester A. Odiagbe, "Industrial Conflict in Nigerian Universities: A Case Study of the Disputes Between the Academic Staff Union of Universities (ASUU) and the Federal Government of Nigeria (FGN)," unpublished PhD dissertation, University of Glasgow, 2012.

24

Party Politics and Personalities

Colonialism brought the concept of party politics to Nigeria. Ekeh has described party politics as part of a "migrated social structure,"[1] explaining that political parties are institutions that the imperialist West transplanted directly into Asia and Africa. Ekeh and other authors assert that Western forces used colonialism to establish social, political, and economic institutions that were patterned after their own, allegedly superior, systems. As a British colony, Nigeria's legal, political, and economic systems were either patterned after or inspired by British colonial experiences, which include the concept of party politics. The history of political parties in Nigeria begins with the conceptualization and history of political parties in Western Europe.[2]

By definition, a political party is an organization with political objectives. The words "political" and "party" can be traced to their Latin origins: "polis," which refers to "city-state," and "patre," which implies "to divide." Sartori explains that the Latin "patre" was inculcated into the English political language in the seventeenth century.[3] The word "sect" had previously been used, while, in the same century, the related word "partager" had entered the French vocabulary. This implied "partaking," and it was later modified to become "party" in the English political vocabulary.

The concept of a political party has been defined by various scholars in terms of the relationship between its component words.[4] Commenting on the second volume of Edmund Burke's book, Paul Langford identified political parties as organizations of individuals promoting "the national interest, upon some particular principle in which they are all agreed."[5] Coleman and Rosberg describe

---

[1] Peter P. Ekeh, "Colonialism and Social Structure," An Inaugural Lecture. Ibadan: Ibadan University Press, 1983.
[2] Joseph LaPalombara and Myron Weiner, "The Origin and Development of Political Parties," in *Political Parties and Political Development*, ed. Joseph LaPalombara and Myron Weiner (Princeton: Princeton University Press, 1966), 3–42.
[3] LaPalombara and Weiner, "The Origin and Development."
[4] See, for instance, Gerald M. Pomper, "Concepts of Political Parties," *Journal of Theoretical Politics* 4, no. 2 (1992): 143–159.
[5] Paul Langford, ed., *The Writings and Speeches of Edmund Burke* (Oxford: Clarendon Press, 1981).

a political party as an organization of people with the explicit objective of acquiring and/or maintaining legal control of a sovereign state's government.[6] These scholars consider political parties to be individual associations or coalitions of groups, and they may be seeking to control either a prospective or an established sovereign state.

The evolution and development of nationalism in colonial Nigeria involved contributions from traditional rulers, educated elites, mass media outlets, and trade unions. These groups are collectively described as nationalist organizations promoting anticolonial nationalism and actualizing the decolonization of Nigeria.[7] Political parties were one of the primary platforms that these organizations used to express their nationalist sentiments. This chapter narrates the evolution and development of party politics in colonial Nigeria, reviewing contributions to nationalist movements documented in the extant literature and other historical evidence.

The Evolution and Development of Political Parties

The global evolution of political parties can be traced to Western Europe's political history in the seventeenth and eighteenth centuries. Absolute monarchy was arguably the predominant form of government in most parts of the world, including Western Europe, dating back to antiquity. England's monarchical system was founded on the country's strong roots in Christianity and the perceived "divine right" of its monarch.[8] The Glorious Revolution of 1688–9 terminated the reign of King James II, changing the government from an absolute monarchy to a constitutional monarchy.[9] As the monarch's power was reduced, the parliament grew stronger. Parliament had originally served as consultants on governmental matters, and it eventually ended up on the front lines of state administration. The primary political parties that emerged during this period were the Whigs, now known as the Conservative Party, and the Tories, today's Labour Party.[10]

While England was undergoing significant political reformation, similar developments were occurring in other European countries. France had been also ruled by absolute monarchs, and its first major process of democratization

---

[6] James S. Coleman and Carl Gustav Rosberg, eds., *Political Parties and National Integration in Tropical Africa* (Berkeley: University of California Press, 1966).
[7] Kelechi C. Ubaku, Chikezie A. Emeh, and Chinenye N. Anyikwa, "Impact of Nationalist Movement on the Actualization of Nigerian Independence 1914–1960," *International Journal of History and Philosophical Research* 2, no. 1 (2014): 54–67.
[8] James H. Burns, *Lordship, Kingship, and Empire: The Idea of Monarchy, 1400–1525* (Oxford: Clarendon Press, 1992).
[9] Robert P. Barnes, "Scotland and the Glorious Revolution of 1688," *Albion* 3, no. 3 (1971): 116–127.
[10] Suzanne Forbes, *Print and Party Politics in Ireland, 1689–1714* (Cham: Palgrave Macmillan, 2018), 195–227.

occurred with the adoption of republicanism in the eighteenth century.[11] This was a gradual process as the sovereign state moved from an absolute monarchy to a constitutional monarchy after the French Constitution was introduced in 1791. However, the French Revolution hastened the democratization process, and a constitutional monarchy was jettisoned in favor of republicanism. Similar developments took place in Germany, Denmark, and other European countries later in the nineteenth century.[12]

When European powers convened the Berlin Conference of 1884–5 to partition African territories, virtually every European country had adopted some form of liberal democracy that relied on party systems. These sovereign states intended not only to settle in African territories but also to control them politically and economically.[13] In asserting imperialist domination over Africa, European colonialists established economic and political controls that were based on transplanting their own systems, with little consideration for the Indigenous systems already existing in the heterogeneous territories of the African continent. France had a clear intent to assimilate the Africans into its colonies. Britain adopted a policy of "association," rather than assimilation, but it was equally imperialist. The colonization process ultimately introduced Nigeria to indirect democracy and party politics.[14]

Historical studies have traced the evolution of colonial Nigeria's political parties to 1922 and the Clifford Constitution's introduction of the elective principle.[15] Scholars like Orjinta and Ameh have tracked the origin of Nigeria's party politics to an earlier date – March 1920 – when the West African Conference was held.[16] The conference was convened by the newly established National Congress of British West Africa (NCBWA), which was West Africa's pioneer nationalist movement. The event was described as a "Conference of Africans of British West Africa," and it discussed ways to ensure the greater representation and participation of Africans in British West African colonies, which included service in the administrations and governments of their respective territories.[17] The NCBWA's contributions to the inception of nationalism and the emergence of political parties have garnered widespread acclaim in the literature. Nigerian historian Gabriel Eluwa notes that the

---

[11] Paolo Conte, Mathieu Ferradou, and Jeanne-Laure Le Quang, "The Early 'Republic of France' as a Cosmopolitan Moment," *La Révolution française* 22 (2022): 1–11.
[12] John W. Maynor, *Republicanism in the Modern World* (Cambridge: Polity Press, 2003).
[13] Melki Fatima Zohra, "The Partition of West Africa, with Reference to the British Colonies up to 1914," *Dirassat* 2, no. 1 (2013): 169–183.
[14] Ekeh, *Colonialism and Social Structure*.
[15] Peter F. Adebayo, "Political Party, Formation, Development, Performance and Prospects," *Drumspeak: International Journal of Research in the Humanities* 4, nos. 1–2 (2011): 94–113.
[16] Hillary I. Orjinta and Ngbede O. Ameh, "Political Parties and National Integration in Nigeria," *African Journal of Politics and Administrative Studies (AJPAS)* 13 (2020): 2.
[17] Orjinta and Ameh, "Political Parties and National Integration."

emergence of the new movement, in the second decade of the twentieth century, was "significant [for] a new political awakening in that part of the world."[18]

British West African elites participating in the NCBWA event were united in advocating for twelve resolutions that were passed at this landmark event. The first resolution reflected their frustration with the inadequacy of the legislative councils set up by colonial governors in British West Africa. The resolution stated that "half of the members of each of the Legislative Councils in British West Africa should be elected Africans, and that there should be in each colony a new House of Assembly consisting of all the members of the colony's Legislative Council and six other elected representatives, with control over finance."[19]

Although the colonial governors rejected the NCBWA resolutions, a precedent was set that inspired major advancements in nationalist agitation. Colonial governors eventually acquiesced to some of the demands from the 1920 conference. Hugh Clifford, colonial Governor of Nigeria (1919–25), for instance, improved the representation of Africans on his colony's legislative council by promulgating a 1922 constitution that introduced the elective principle, which afforded greater franchise to indigenes.[20]

In introducing the elective principle, the 1922 Clifford Constitution is widely seen as one of the first significant efforts to reshape colonial Nigeria's political environment.[21] Political parties emerged for the first time in Nigeria's history – the notion of party politics had been introduced to the British West African colony. Some Nigerian scholars have credited Hugh Clifford for major advancements in inclusivity, self-governance, and the gradual decolonization of Nigeria. Tamuno states that Clifford should be recognized for "a fuller representation of local interests and [for] giving a larger share in the discussion and management of public affairs to articulate members of the various Nigerian communities than are provided by existing institutions."[22] This was a significant departure from his predecessor's autocratic management of the colony's political and economic affairs. However, Tamuno's assessment also notes that, under the Clifford administration, only half of the Legislative Council's members were Nigerians, hence it failed to function as a truly representative government.[23]

---

[18] Gabriel Eluwa, "Background to the Emergence of the National Congress of British West Africa," *African Studies Review* 14, no. 2 (1971): 205–218.
[19] Gabriel Eluwa, "The National Congress of British West Africa: A Study in African Nationalism," *Présence Africaine* 77 (1971): 131–149.
[20] Orjinta and Ameh, "Political Parties and National Integration in Nigeria."
[21] Tekena Tamuno, "Governor Clifford and Representative Government," *Journal of the Historical Society of Nigeria* 4, no. 1 (1967): 117–124.
[22] Tamuno, "Governor Clifford."
[23] Tamuno, "Governor Clifford."

Scholars discussing the evolution and development of Nigeria's political parties have attempted to establish classifications based on the parties' dates of emergence, dominance, and disintegration. Ujo, in categorizing political parties throughout Nigeria's history, posited that all of Nigeria's political parties belong to one of four epochs or "generations."[24] Muhammed and Saliu cited Ujo's classifications to trace the evolution of Nigeria's political parties across four periods: the pre-1945 period, the period between 1945 and the first republic, the period of the second republic and the aborted third republic, and the present-day period of the fourth republic.[25]

Ogunnoiki has traced the history of political parties across Nigeria's four republics, which are separate from the political parties of the colonial era. He considers the colonial-era political groups to be "the first generation of political parties."[26] These classifications elicit an appreciation of Nigeria's political history, but they are unsuitable for delineating the evolution and development of political parties in colonial Nigeria. Authors who have proposed such classifications are attempting to explain the evolution of political parties from their inception to the present moment, limiting their focus to colonial-era activity and the different stages of political party development during the colonial period. However, the development of colonial Nigeria's political parties would better be delineated across two generations: the Lagos-based political parties of the 1920s and 1930s, followed by the region-based political parties of the 1940s and 1950s.

The 1922 adoption of the elective principle enabled the creation of colonial Nigeria's first generation of political parties: the NNDP and the Lagos Youth Movement (later the National Youth Movement [NYM]). The NNDP was created first, through the actions of Herbert Macaulay, on June 24, 1923. The NNDP won the 1923 elections with every available seat on the Legislative Council due to its status as the only recognized political party at the time. The NNDP retained its dominance for the following ten years, winning all three of the seats allocated to Lagos in 1928 and 1933. The Lagos Youth Movement was formed in 1934, created by Enerst Ekoli, Dr. James C. Vaughan, Samuel Akinsanya, and Hezekiah O. Davies. In 1938, it won electoral victories against the NNDP.[27] The movement

---

[24] Abdulhameed A. Ujo, *Understanding Political Parties in Nigeria* (Kaduna: Klamidas Publishers, 2000), 18–42.

[25] Hassan A. Saliu and Abdulrasheed A. Muhammad, "Growing Nigeria's Democracy through Viable Political Parties," in *Perspective on Nation-Building and Development in Nigeria: Political and Legal Issues*, ed. Hassan A. Saliu, Isah H. Jimoh, Noah Yusuf, and Emmanuel O. Ojo (Lagos: Concept Publication Ltd., 2008).

[26] Ogunnoiki, "Political Parties, Ideology and the Nigerian State."

[27] Nathaniel Danjibo and Kelvin Ashindorbe, "The Evolution and Pattern of Political Party Formation and the Search for National Integration in Nigeria," *Brazilian Journal of African Studies* 3, no. 5 (2018): 85–100; and Ogunnoiki, "Political Parties, Ideology and the Nigerian State," 124.

was an increasingly significant political force in colonial Nigeria. Its members included some of the colony's foremost nationalists, such as Nnamdi Azikiwe and Chief Obafemi Awolowo.[28] Although the group saw some success, it lost seats to the NNDP in the 1943 election, and again in 1948.

The first generation of political parties was initially based in Lagos. The Clifford Constitution introduced elections for only four seats on the colony's legislative council: three for Lagos and one for Calabar. Early political parties, especially the NNDP, had no reason to campaign outside of Lagos. The NNDP included the word "national" in its name, but not in its political outlook: most of its activities were confined to Lagos, where it held most of its influence. As colonial Nigeria's first major political party, the NNDP contested elections for all four legislative seats, winning all three seats in Lagos and losing the fourth seat to a Calabar-based political organization, the Calabar Improvement League.[29] Ultimately, the NNDP was overshadowed by the Lagos Youth Movement. This movement was also based in Lagos, especially during its inception, and it avoided NNDP's grandiose naming conventions. The Lagos Youth Movement gathered momentum over time, and it expanded to become the NYM before it eventually disintegrated in 1941.[30]

The first generation of political parties blazed a trail for party politics in colonial Nigeria, becoming a significant reference point for discourse on Nigeria's traditional political history. However, the NNDP and the NYM failed due to various challenges, including their limited outlooks, ethnic mistrust, and leadership crises that encouraged the emergence of the second generation of political parties – more intellectually and politically vibrant organizations. The NNDP wielded power for two decades, winning all of the Lagos seats on the legislative council in four out of five elections. The NYM's dissolution was gradual and occurred much earlier. Most scholars trace its difficulties to an intraparty crisis that ensued in 1941. Disagreements between Ernest Ikoli and Samuel Akinsanya, two of the founding members of the party, led to a dispute over which candidate should fill the party's vacant seat on the legislative council.[31] The leadership broke into two factions, and fierce contention led to accusations of tribally motivated sentiments. Nnamdi Azikiwe and some of his loyalists defected from the party in that same year.[32]

---

[28] Toyin Falola, *Economic Reforms and Modernization in Nigeria, 1945–1965* (Kent: Kent State University Press, 2004); and Nnamdi Azikiwe, *Zik: A Selection from the Speeches of Nnamdi Azikiwe* (Cambridge: Cambridge University Press, 1961).

[29] James S. Coleman, *Nigeria Background to Nationalism* (Berkeley: University of California Press, 1958).

[30] Adeleke Olumide Ogunnoiki, "Political Parties, Ideology and the Nigerian State." *International Journal of Advanced Academic Research* 4, no. 12 (2018): 114-150 (25).

[31] Robert L. Sklar, *Nigerian Political Parties: Power in an Emergent African Nation* (Princeton: Princeton University Press, 2015).

[32] Coleman, *Nigeria: Background to Nationalism*, 144.

The second generation of political parties developed a few years after the promulgation of the 1946 Richards Constitution, which introduced regionalism to Nigeria. The idea of regionalism was originally conceived by Bernard Bourdillon, colonial Governor of Nigeria from 1935–43. Bourdillon saw inadequacies in the Clifford Constitution that failed to ensure proper representation, and he sought to address the central government's systemic neglect of Nigeria's Northern Protectorate. In 1939, he began the gradual regionalization of Nigeria's governmental powers by creating three provinces: the Northern, Eastern, and Western provinces.[33] Bourdillon resigned in 1943, before he finalized his draft of Nigeria's constitution. Sir Arthur Richards succeeded him and took over the drafting and implementation of a new constitutional framework. The 1946 Richards Constitution created legislative councils for all three provinces, and it introduced provisions that allowed Indigenous political parties and their candidates to contest elections. The 1946 constitution also created a central legislative government with representatives from each regional assembly.[34]

Despite the criticism directed at the 1946 Richards Constitution, its cumulative contributions to the democratization and political development of Nigeria were more positive than negative. One such contribution was the proliferation of second-generation political parties. Newly formed political groups such as the National Council of Nigeria and the Cameroons (NCNC), the Northern People's Congress (NPC), and the Action Group (AG) dominated the colony's political landscape. The first of these parties was the NCNC, which was created on August 26, 1944. It was one of colonial Nigeria's foremost nationalist organizations, founded and led by Herbert Macaulay (see Figure 24.1) and Nnamdi Azikiwe.[35] The Northern Elements Progressive Union (NEPU) was formed by Mallam Aminu Kano in August 1950.[36] The following year, Chief Obafemi Awolowo created the AG and Alhaji Ahmadu Bello, the Sardauna of Sokoto, founded the NPC.[37]

Historical evidence has chronicled the strong cultural roots and regional outlooks of second-generation political parties. Most written records that document the formation of these parties, especially the AG and the NPC, discuss offshoots of ethnic-based cultural organizations.[38] The AG developed out of *Egbe Omo Oduduwa*, a pan-Yoruba cultural organization formed in

---

[33] Bernard Bourdillon and Richmond Palmer, "Nigerian Constitutional Proposals," *African Affairs* 44, no. 176 (1945): 120–124.
[34] Charas Madu Tella, Ahmed Wali Doho, and Aliyu Bapeto, "The Evolution, Development and Practice of Federalism in Nigeria," *Public Policy and Administration Review* 2, no. 4 (2014): 51–66.
[35] Sklar, *Nigerian Political Parties*, 143–189.
[36] Kayode Komolafe, "The NEPU Example," *Thisday*, August 12, 2020.
[37] Ogunnoiki, "Political Parties, Ideology and the Nigerian State," 125–126.
[38] Sklar, *Nigerian Political Parties*.

Figure 24.1 Herbert Macaulay (1864–1946), foremost politician, political activist, journalist, and architect, is regarded as Nigeria's father of modern nationalism.

1945.[39] The political party that became the Northern People's Congress began as a sociocultural organization known as *Jam'iyyar Mutanen Arewa*, which was formed in colonial Nigeria's Northern Province in 1949.[40] Another group left Arewa to form the NEPU in 1950.[41] Cultural organizations had promoted cultural consciousness and fostered social networking. The 1946 Richards Constitution triggered a metamorphosis within these cultural organizations, and they developed into political parties.

One of the major limitations of these new groups was their regional outlook. The AG and the NPC had formed from ethnic-based cultural organizations that restricted their influence and activity to the Western and Northern regions, respectively. Even the NCNC, which professed to be "national in outlook," fell short of its objective as the group's activities and momentum were limited to the Eastern Region.[42] Critics have noted that the formation of these groups ran counter to the Richards Constitution's professed objective of unification. Obafemi Awolowo (leader of the AG) stated that colonial Nigeria could no longer be called a nation but rather "a mere geographical expression."[43]

Most of the second-generation political parties outlived their first-generation predecessors, and the political landscape of the 1950s and 1960s was dominated by second-generation political parties and their coalitions. By the time Nigeria attained independence in 1960, the NNDP and the NYM had dissolved. In the 1959 general elections, none of the second-generation political parties emerged as a national party that could lead the federal government, which prompted

---

[39] S. O. Arifalo, *The Egbe Omo Oduduwa: A Study in Ethnic and Cultural Nationalism (1945–1965)* (Akure: Stebak Books, 2001).
[40] Ahmadu Bello, *My Life* (Cambridge: Cambridge University Press, 1962), 139.
[41] Komolafe, "The NEPU Example."
[42] Danjibo and Ashindorbe, "The Evolution and Pattern of Political Party Formation," 90–91.
[43] Obafemi Awolowo, *Path to Nigerian Freedom* (London: Faber and Faber, 1947).

coalitions between these groups and alliances with embryonic, less-influential political parties.[44] The NPC forged alliances with the Igala Union and the Niger Delta Congress, among others. The AG allied with the United Middle Belt Congress, while the NEPU formed a coalition with the National Council of Nigerian Citizens. The largest alliance after the 1959 election was created by coordination between the Northern People's Congress and the National Council of Nigerian Citizens.[45]

Each party's inability to establish an absolute majority led to the creation of coalitions. Like their predecessors, second-generation political parties were shaken by ethnic sentiments that fostered intraparty conflicts and led to their gradual deterioration. However, Nigeria's first military coup abruptly suspended party politics in Nigeria, definitively ending the second generation of political parties.

Party Politics, Political Ideologies, and Ethnic Nationalism

Historians and other scholars of Nigeria's political history have delivered critical appraisals of the party politics, political ideologies, and ethnic nationalism that developed during Nigeria's colonial period. In most of the recent works from the social sciences disciplines, the ideas of party politics and political ideologies are largely discussed in the context of shortcomings in Nigeria's political system and their links with the country's present challenges.[46] Terms such as "politics," "politicking," and "political marketing" are used to reference negative aspects of modern Nigeria's political or party system. However, party politics and their attendant characteristics have historical and conceptual antecedents in colonial history. These ideas have not always been linked with the worst outcomes of Nigeria's political and economic history.[47]

One author has noted that while present-day politics is rife with self-dealing and personal enrichment, early concepts of politics in Nigeria were strongly rooted in ideologies and conventions that sought to promote national consciousness, unity, and national integration, especially during the colonial period.[48] Nigeria's current political climate is unquestionably marred by ethnoreligious crises and allegations of electoral malpractice, corruption, and

---

[44] Larry R. Jackson, "Nigeria: The Politics of the First Republic," *Journal of Black Studies* 2, no. 3 (1972): 277–302.

[45] Jackson, "Nigeria: The Politics of the First Republic."

[46] See, for instance, Larry J. Diamond, "Class, Ethnicity and the Democratic State: Nigeria, 1950–1966," *Comparative Study in Society & History* 25, no. 3 (1983): 457–489.

[47] Ezekiel Major Adeyi, "Funding of Political Parties and Candidates in Nigeria: A Historical Perspective," in *Money and Politics in Nigeria*, ed. Victor Adetula (Abuja: International Foundation for Electoral Systems, 2008), 29–38.

[48] Victor Adetula, ed., *Money and Politics in Nigeria* (Abuja: International Foundation for Electoral Systems, 2008).

abuse of office.[49] Despite these current problems, some scholars have suggested that party politics in colonial Nigeria were motivated by selfless interests. There were instances of ethnoreligious crises in Nigeria's colonial past, but their root cause was not directly linked with political party activity.

Adeyi, in reviewing the funding of political parties and candidates in Nigeria from historical perspective, has examined the relationship between money and politics in colonial Nigeria's political history.[50] Ultimately, he found that money was only one of several factors that influenced party politics during that period, and concluded that money was important in establishing party dominance and winning elections, but it was not the sole driver of party politics.[51]

The clearest expression of party politics is participation in the electioneering process. With this in mind, Adeyi studied the landmark 1938 election, where the NYM won all three Lagos seats on the legislative council. This landslide victory occurred even though the NYM had less funding than their opposition. Adeyi has found that the two most important factors in colonial Nigeria's party politics were the party's ideologies and the colonial administration's influence.[52] Parties could gain power if their ideology was accepted by a majority of the voting population, although unwelcome intervention from the colonial administration could prevent this.

Historical evidence points to ideology as the most powerful weapon that political parties wielded in colonial Nigeria.[53] The concept of "political ideologies," along with related ideas like politics and political parties, was alien to people in Nigeria before the advent of colonialism. These ideas were largely introduced to educated elites through contact with foreign systems, practices, and processes. The democratic politics in Britain and other countries where elites had studied introduced the concept of political ideologies to Nigeria's political landscape.

Political ideology is described as statements accepted by political parties that bind their actions.[54] Nnoli views ideology as an important part of political activity – not only as a mental structure ordering the thought process of

---

[49] Marcin Walecki, "Political Money and Corruption: Limiting Corruption in Political Finance," in *Money and Politics in Nigeria*, ed. Victor Adetula (Abuja: International Foundation for Electoral Systems, 2008), 1–12; and Ekpenyong Nyong Akpanika, "Religious and Political Crises in Nigeria: A Historical Exploration," *IOSR Journal of Humanities and Social Science* 22, no. 9 (2017): 65–76.

[50] Adeyi, "Funding of Political Parties and Candidates in Nigeria."

[51] Adeyi, "Funding of Political Parties and Candidates in Nigeria," 29.

[52] Adeyi, "Funding of Political Parties and Candidates in Nigeria."

[53] Shola Omotola, "Nigerian Parties and Political Ideologies," *Journal of Alternative Perspectives in the Social Sciences* 1, no. 3 (2009): 612–634.

[54] V. J. Strikler and R. Davies, "Political Party Conventions," in *International Encyclopedia of Government and Politics*, ed. Frank N. Magill (London: Fitzroy Dearborn Publishers, 1996).

political personalities, but also for serving as a guide to personal actions and judgment relating to the polity.[55] The ideological belief of any party is often used as a moral compass for establishing party unity. Political ideology is the most important vehicle for any political party looking to achieve its aims and objectives.[56] This is especially true for colonial Nigeria's political parties.

A plethora of historical evidence affirms the role of political ideologies in colonial Nigeria's party politics. They served as lines of distinction between parties during the country's colonial period, especially among second-generation political parties. The AG and National Council of Nigerian Citizens leaned toward radicalism,[57] while the Northern People's Congress cleaved to conservatism that was inspired by its strong cultural roots and the Sardauna of Sokoto's leadership.[58]

Ideology was also a major factor in determining the loyalty of political party members. Various incidents of defection or "carpet crossing" took place in colonial Nigeria's political history, and they were largely inspired by ideological clashes between party leadership.[59] Underlying ethnic interests also caused political clashes. Despite their differences in ideology, the political parties and leaders of colonial Nigeria largely combined their intellectual, ideological, and political efforts to confront their common adversary: the self-serving colonial administration. The ultimate goal of these groups was Nigerian self-rule.

Historians have identified social values that were inherent in party politics during Nigeria's colonial period. Nationalistic feelings, intellectualism, charismatic leadership, and collaborative stances to oppose the self-interested colonial government were key components of colonial Nigeria's party politics. Adeyi has asserted that the educated elites leading political parties during this period did not engage in politics for personal enrichment or other selfish gains.[60] Although his assertion reflects the popular opinion of colonial Nigeria's political climate, it is undeniable that various political leaders advanced class interests or worked toward ethnic goals at different points.[61] These efforts could oppose the greater objective of their respective political parties or run counter to nationalist goals. Different ethnic crises and other challenges to political party leadership demonstrate the presence of selfish interests in preindependence Nigeria's party politics.

[55] Okwudiba Nnoli, *Introduction to Politics* (Enugu: PACREP, 2003).
[56] Giovanni Sartori, "Politics, Ideology, and Belief Systems," *The American Political Science Review* 63, no. 2 (1969): 398.
[57] John A. A. Ayoade, "Party and Ideology in Nigeria: A Case Study of the Action Group," *Journal of Black Studies* 16, no. 2 (1985): 169–188.
[58] Sklar, *Nigerian Political Parties*, 321–376.
[59] Matthew T. Mbu, *Matthew T. Mbu: Dignity in Service* (Ibadan: Safari Books, 2018), 157.
[60] Adeyi, "Funding of Political Parties and Candidates in Nigeria," 29–30
[61] S. Oyeranmi, "The Colonial Background to the Problem of Ethnicity in Nigeria: 1914–1960," *Journal of History and Diplomatic Studies* 8 (2011): 35–62.

Alongside the positive contributions made by colonial Nigeria's political parties, historical evidence associates that period's political climate with the emergence of modern Nigeria's ethnoreligious crises. Akpanika has explored the history of religious and political crises in Nigeria to link the country's present challenges with political systems established during the colonial period.[62] Akpanika cites Uka to note that the present disagreements between Nigeria's two major religions and three major ethnic groups had been instigated by the colonial administration through their conscious plans to divide, amalgamate, and govern the country.[63] Most scholars hold the colonialists responsible for Nigeria's ethnic and religious crises, but it is also true that the actions of political parties and leaders in colonial Nigeria intensified these conflicts.

Colonial Nigeria's political parties – especially its second-generation political parties – are credited with the development of ethnic nationalism.[64] This form of nationalism is based on the desire to promote a specific ethnic group's interests. Anticolonial nationalists viewed the colony as a single nation, and they sought to promote that consciousness. Pan-Africanists promoted the common identity of all African people. Ethnic nationalists define nationality and national identity in terms of an ethnic group's shared history, culture, and associations.[65] Ethnic nationalism is not intrinsically divisive, but when it is used as the basis for excluding other people, especially in a federal state like Nigeria, this can quickly lead to ethnic and political crises.[66]

Ethnic nationalism and ethnic-based politics were particularly evident in the practices and activities of Nigeria's second-generation political parties from the 1950s to the First Republic. Danjibo and Ashindorbe have noted that a major weakness of these parties was their rapid devolution into ethnicity-based groups. These sentiments prevented such groups from successfully pursuing the national integration objectives that they had espoused. Despite their shortcomings, colonial Nigeria's political parties made significant contributions to the country's political and constitutional development. Political parties spearheaded the emergence of Nigeria's mass media.[67] Political activism to support public education, and their efforts to cultivate a national consciousness, contributed to the development of

---

[62] Akpanika, "Religious and Political Crises in Nigeria," 67.
[63] Emele Mba Uka, "Perspectives on Religion, Terrorism and Development – A Critical Review of Religion, Religious Freedom, Terrorism and Development in Contemporary Context of Boko-Haram Insurgency in Nigeria," *Contemporary Journal of Inter-Disciplinary Studies* 2, no. 2 (2015): 1–34.
[64] Isiaka A. Badmus, "Under Reconstruction: Ethnicity, Ethnic Nationalism, and the Future of the Nigerian State," *Verfassung und Recht in Übersee* 42, no. 2 (2009): 212–239.
[65] Kelechi C. Ubaku, Chikezie A. Emeh, and Chinenye N. Anyikwa, "Impact of Nationalist Movement on the Actualization of Nigerian Independence, 1914–1960," *International Journal of History and Philosophical Research* 2, no. 1 (2014): 54–67.
[66] Louis Achi, "The Rise of Ethnic Nationalism," *Thisday*, June 20, 2021.
[67] Fred Omu, *Press and Politics in Nigeria, 1880–1937* (Atlantic Highlands: Humanities Press, 1978), 68–69.

trade unions in colonial Nigeria. These efforts were directly responsible for Nigeria's decolonization.[68] The most important political party achievement was the promotion of nationalist sentiment and the ultimate attainment of Nigerian self-rule.

The Contributions of Political Parties and Personalities in Nationalist Struggles

The brand of nationalism promoted by colonial Nigeria's political parties has become the most-studied form of nationalism in the country's political history. Traditional rulers such as Jaja of Opobo and Kosoko of Lagos engaged in acts of resistance.[69] In the early years of colonialism, African missionaries promoted cultural nationalism. These actions inspired nationalist sentiments in later movements, but the preindependence political parties and their leaders receive the most credit for actualizing self-governance in the former British colony.[70]

The NNDP, the NYM, the National Council of Nigerian Citizens, the AG, and the Northern People's Congress used different mechanisms to realize their objectives for self-governance. Historians consider the NYM and the National Council of Nigerian Citizens to have been the most radical, and the Northern People's Congress more conservative. The democratic socialist ideology of the AG held the middle ground.[71] Through varying mechanisms, approaches, and ideologies, these parties shared the common objective of self-government for Nigeria. They combined their efforts to pursue this goal relentlessly.

Most scholars of Nigeria's political history focus on the nationalist successes of second-generation political parties, but early advancement began with the first-generation parties, especially the NNDP. The NNDP was led by Herbert Macaulay and stood at the forefront of political nationalism in the 1920s. Macaulay was a vibrant Nigerian nationalist, described as the "Moses of our age," and his movement was supported by the *Lagos Daily News*. The NNDP championed the cause of Nigeria and Nigerians on every front, especially in socioeconomic conflicts.[72]

The NNDP's motto was "salus populi est suprema lex," which translates as "the safety of the people is the supreme law," referencing the party's ideological

---

[68] Oluwatoyin Oduntan and Kemi Rotimi, "Tensional Decolonization and Public Order in Western Nigeria, 1957–1960," *Decolonization: Indigeneity, Education & Society* 4, no. 2 (2015): 103–122.

[69] Obaro Ikime, "Colonial Conquest and Resistance in Southern Nigeria," *Journal of the Historical Society of Nigeria* 6, no. 3 (1972): 251–270.

[70] Robert L. Tignor, *Capitalism and Nationalism at the End of Empire* (Princeton: Princeton University Press, 2015), 261–290.

[71] Ogunnoiki, "Political Parties, Ideology and the Nigerian State," 126.

[72] Ubaku, Emeh, and Anyikwa, "Impact of Nationalist Movement," 54–67.

leanings. Ogunnoiki has described the party as rooted in "liberal nationalism, democracy and welfarism."[73] The party advocated the colony's economic development and demanded equal opportunities for Nigerians. The NNDP fiercely opposed the imposition of income tax in 1927, and also advocated the establishment of an institute for higher education in Nigeria. This may have been the party's most notable contribution, as the British colonial government succumbed to the party's demands and established Yaba Higher College in 1932.[74] In the late 1930s, after the establishment of the NYM, political nationalism became more widespread. Coleman describes the NYM as the "nucleus of Nigeria's first genuine nationalist organization."[75] Its clear objective was the promotion of national unity, and it was vibrant and vocal in promoting national consciousness, unification, and welfarism for Nigeria and Nigerians. Okafor states that the party was a political movement that made serious, genuine efforts at promoting real national consciousness.[76]

The NYM leadership, especially after the admission of outspoken nationalists like Nnamdi Azikiwe and Obafemi Awolowo, was progressive and radical. They vocally opposed the colonial government's ban on exporting palm kernels from the Western province and subsequently fought the promulgation of the Cocoa Pool Act.[77] The movement leveraged the *Lagos Daily Service*, its official newspaper, to advocate for free education, universal adult suffrage, improved conditions of service, and a separation of the judiciary and executive branches of government.[78] The NYM made significant contributions to promoting national consciousness and welfarism in Nigeria. However, most scholars challenge the suggestion that their unification objectives were successful. The group's intraparty crises in 1941 were marked by ethnic conflicts and led to its gradual dissolution.

Historiography – especially in studies of Nigerian political history – recognizes different forms of nationalism: civic nationalism, social nationalism, cultural nationalism, economic nationalism, political nationalism, ethnic nationalism, socialist or left-wing nationalism, ultranationalism, protonationalism, diaspora nationalism, and anticolonial nationalism. These causes are not mutually exclusive, and each type emerged in response to the specific needs of the Nigerian people in the colonial era; each form has unique features that make it distinct.

---

[73] Ogunnoiki, "Political Parties, Ideology and the Nigerian State," 124.
[74] Ubaku, Emeh, and Anyikwa, "Impact of Nationalist Movement," 61.
[75] Coleman, *Nigeria: Background to Nationalism*, 218.
[76] Samuel O. Okafor, *Indirect Rule: The Development of the Central Legislature in Nigeria* (Lagos: Nelson Africa, 1981).
[77] Ubaku, Emeh, and Anyikwa, "Impact of Nationalist Movement," 62.
[78] John H. Enemugwem, "The Impact of the Lagos Press in Nigeria, 1861–1922," *LWATI: A Journal of Contemporary Research* 6, no. 1 (2009): 106–114.

Among the most-studied nationalist causes in Nigerian political history are cultural nationalism, political nationalism, and anticolonial nationalism. However, political parties and party leaders in colonial times mounted all-out, decades-long nationalist campaigns that drew from several nationalist ideologies. The practices and activities of these parties encompass nuances and notions from different kinds of nationalism that were aggregated into a uniform nationalist agenda. Historical evidence has established the leftism of the AG and the Zikist Movement, a militant division of the National Council of Nigerian Citizens.[79] These political parties infused left-wing or socialist democratic ideology into their nationalist goals. Ethnic nationalism, which Ubaku, Emeh, and Anyikwa have described as a movement that defines a nation in terms of its ethnicity,[80] was a major focus for first-generation political parties, and for some of the second-generation parties, especially in their formative years. At different times, ethnic nationalism had either supported or threatened the anticolonial nationalist efforts of political parties and personalities.

Anticolonial nationalism was at the core of colonial Nigeria's nationalist struggles. The colony's attainment of self-rule began with the granting of internal self-government for the Western and Eastern regions in 1957. The climax of self-rule was the establishment of total political independence for Nigeria in 1963, and it is largely attributed to the agitations of anticolonial nationalists. Historians and scholars of Nigeria's political history have drawn a line between the first and second generations of political parties; it is said that while the first generation pioneered political nationalism in Nigeria, the second generation transformed it into anticolonial nationalism. Studies of colonial Nigeria's political history focus on the roles and contributions of second-generation political parties in the narrative of Nigeria's decolonization.

The National Council of Nigerian Citizens (formerly the National Council of Nigeria and the Cameroons) was a major second-generation political party. Under the leadership of Herbert Macaulay and Nnamdi Azikiwe, the NCNC made significant contributions to colonial Nigeria's constitutional and political developments.[81] Its primary objective was to establish democracy and advance the interests of the Nigerian people. The political party opposed any act or policy from the British colonial government that was seen as undemocratic or detrimental to the socioeconomic interests of Nigerian citizens.

The NCNC vocally opposed the Richards Constitution because it was drafted without adequate Nigerian consultation. NCNC leadership believed that true democracy could only be achieved by having Nigerians manage the political affairs of their own country, which justified their ongoing agitations

---

[79] NCNC Secretariat, *West African Pilot* (29 October, 1948).
[80] Ubaku, Emeh, and Anyikwa, "Impact of Nationalist Movement," 56.
[81] Orjinta and Ameh, "Political Parties and National Integration in Nigeria," 77.

for self-government. The party was a truly nationalist movement that used several newspapers to disseminate its beliefs. Its most widely read newspaper was the *West African Pilot*.[82] The party also allied with trade unions such as the Railway Workers' Union and the TUCN, to press for civil service reforms and improvements in working conditions for Nigerians. After observing the NCNC's contributions to anticolonial nationalism and the radical nature of its approach, a British journalist described the party as a threat to the British Empire's stability in Nigeria.[83]

The Zikist Movement's remarkable activities show the NCNC's significance in the rise of anticolonial nationalism and the decolonization of Nigeria.[84] As its name implies, the Zikist Movement was founded on Nnamdi Azikiwe's communist ideology – the movement was a radical, left-wing militant organization within the NCNC. Its strong ideological roots and activities as a military organization meant that the movement was actively involved in nationalist struggles. The Zikist Movement emerged in February 1946, formed by Nnamdi Azikiwe's young loyalists and admirers defending him, his leadership, and his ideology.[85] It metamorphosed into a nationalist movement, possibly due to the increasing intensity of anticolonial nationalist efforts from the NCNC and Azikiwe himself. Eluwa, Ukagwu, Nwachukwu, and Nwaubani state that the movement "sought to undermine and destroy the (colonial) administration through strike organization, boycotts and sheer violence."[86]

Zikists used the most radical means available for issuing their demands. They secretly published seditious pamphlets, instigated riots, and incited workers to strike or boycott to protest the treatment of Nigerian workers. Ubaku, Ameh, and Anyikwa have found that Zikist activity drove government reforms in virtually every arena, including constitutional proposals, political activities, and labor relations.[87] The Zikist Movement not only made significant contributions to the anticolonial nationalist movement, but also helped Nigerian workers shatter the constraints of racial discrimination.

The AG was another second-generation political party in Nigeria that was influential during the colonial period. At its founding in 1951, the AG adopted an unequivocally nationalistic perspective that was evident in the party's aims and objectives. The unification of nationalistic efforts in the Western Region

---

[82] David Zitnak, "Imagining the Nigerian Nation through the West African Pilot 1960–1966," unpublished Masters thesis, University of Louisville, 2016.

[83] C. Winchester, "Report to Lord Kemsley on the British West African Press, Typescript Document," National Library, Owerri, Imo State, 1945.

[84] Gabriel O. Olusanya, "The Zikist Movement: A Study in Political Radicalism, 1946–50," *The Journal of Modern African Studies* 4, no. 3 (1966): 323–333.

[85] Olusanya, "The Zikist Movement."

[86] Gabriel Eluwa, M. O. Ukagwu, J. U. N. Nwachukwu, and A. C. N. Nwaubani, *A History of Nigeria for Schools and Colleges* (Ibadan: African-First Publishers Limited, 1988).

[87] Ubaku, Emeh, and Anyikwa, "Impact of Nationalist Movement," 63.

was essential for its development. The AG, aided by strong leadership from key political personalities including Obafemi Awolowo and Ladoke Akintola, presented a united front for tackling anticolonialism and defending the Western Region's interests.[88] The party's nationalist agenda was limited by its deep-seated ethnic politics, but it saw success in improving the welfare of the Nigerian people and defending its interests against colonialists. The party espoused a socialist democratic ideology, and its significant achievements included educational reforms, especially in the Western Region.[89]

During the colonial period, the Northern People's Congress stood as a counterpoint to the AG in the West and the NCNC in the East. The NPC's conservative values made it unique among the period's three major political parties. However, this conservatism did not include support for the colonial administration, and the party actively contributed to nationalist agitations that resulted in the decolonization of Nigeria. The NPC worked to ensure the regional autonomy of Northern Nigeria into a unified nation, and it introduced local government reforms that upheld the traditions and customs of the Emirates. Like the AG and the NCNC, the Northern People's Congress focused on region-based politics. Each of the three parties attempted to expand outside of their initial regions, but none of them was as successful at establishing a united national platform. Despite their ethnic politics and regional influences, these parties made substantial contributions to anticolonial nationalism in Nigeria. Scholars of political history correctly describe them as nationalist movements.[90]

Historical studies have focused on the impact of colonial Nigeria's nationalist movements working as political parties to accomplish the gradual decolonization of the country. "Nationalist movements" is an all-encompassing term that includes trade unions, media organizations, political parties, and prominent individuals from that era.[91] A breadth of historical studies has noted that political parties were at the forefront of nationalist efforts, championing what is now recognized as anticolonial nationalism. Colonial Nigeria's first- and second-generation political parties used the resources at their disposal to advance the nationalist cause. Mass media organizations like the *Lagos Daily Times*, *Lagos Daily News*, *Lagos Daily Service*, *West African Pilot*, *Eastern Nigerian Guardian*, *Southern Nigerian Defender*, and the *Nigerian Tribune* were founded to raise public awareness of party activities. They were also used in promoting national

---

[88] Akin Omoboriowo, *Awoism: Select Themes on the Complex Ideology of Chief Obafemi Awolowo* (Ibadan: Evans Brothers, 1982).
[89] Simon A. Ajayi, "The Genesis of Free Education in Western Nigeria, 1951–1966," *Journal of Social Sciences* 3, no. 1 (2008): 108–122.
[90] Gabriel O. Olusanya, "The Nationalist Movement in Nigeria," in *Groundwork of Nigerian History*, ed. Obaro Ikime (Ibadan: Heinemann Educational Books, 1980), 545–569.
[91] Luke U. Uche, *Mass Media, People, and Politics in Nigeria* (New Delhi: Concept Publishing Company, 1989).

consciousness and nationalist sentiments to agitate against colonialist policies and their ongoing occupation of Nigeria.[92]

Key individuals were involved in colonial Nigeria's nationalist agitations. The educated elites were at the forefront of party leadership and nationalist efforts during the colonial period of Nigeria's political history. The lives, careers, and activist works of personalities such as Herbert Macaulay, Nnamdi Azikiwe, Obafemi Awolowo, Ahmadu Bello, Ernest Ikoli, Tafawa Balewa, Alvan Ikoku, Funmilayo Ransome-Kuti, Alimotu Pelewura, and Oyinkan Abayomi have been studied extensively in the literature. The large number of men studied as key personalities from Nigeria's political and anticolonial nationalist efforts suggests that the political arena, and especially the nationalist movement, was predominantly male. However, authors have begun correcting this misconception by highlighting the nationalist roles of female activists such as Ransome-Kuti and Pelewura.[93] Martin observes, in *Ojo Nro*, that – contrary to the portrayals from earlier works of literature – women were involved in nationalist activities.[94] Their activities and methods had different dimensions and proportions in comparison with those associated with mainstream political anticolonial nationalist movements, and such movements were largely recorded in male-dominated literature.

Political and anticolonialist nationalism was spearheaded by leaders and nationalists such as Herbert Macaulay, Nnamdi Azikiwe, Obafemi Awolowo, and Tafawa Balewa. Scholars, historians, and other admirers describe Herbert Macaulay as the father of Nigerian nationalism.[95] Lawal and Jimoh contribute to a breadth of historical studies on Macaulay's life, career, and political activism, but they emphasize the dynamics of his hostile relationship with Hugh Clifford, who was Governor of Nigeria.[96] They explore the relationship between Macaulay and Clifford as a representation of the toxic relationship between the British and the Africans. Macaulay became the "epicenter of indigenous opposition to the British (colonial administration)," dominating Nigerian politics and political nationalism from his first efforts in 1898 until his passing in 1946.[97] His ideologies and charisma also influenced nationalists such as Azikiwe, Awolowo, Balewa, and Bello.

[92] Omu, *Press and Politics in Nigeria*.
[93] Ikonnaya Osemwengie and Oghogho Oriakhi, "Nationalism and Freedom in Colonial Nigeria: A Gendered Perspective," *Lagos Historical Review* 18 (2018): 33–48; and Susan Geiger, "Women and African Nationalism," *Journal of Women's History* 2, no. 1 (1990): 227–244.
[94] Maria Martin, "Ojo Nro: An Intellectual History of Nigerian Women's Nationalism in an Umbrella Organization, 1947–1967," unpublished PhD dissertation, Michigan State University, 2018.
[95] Tekena Tamuno, *Herbert Macaulay, Nigerian Patriot* (London: Heinemann Educational, 1976).
[96] Olakunle Lawal and Olusegun M. Jimoh, "Missiles from 'Kirsten Hall': Herbert Macaulay versus Hugh Clifford, 1922–1931," *Lagos Historical Review* 12 (2012): 41–62.
[97] Lawal and Jimoh, "Missiles from 'Kirsten Hall'."

Azikiwe is one of the most thoroughly studied political party leaders and nationalists in Nigeria's history.[98] Fondly addressed as "Zik of Africa," he began as a pan-Africanist with a clear vision for Africa's emancipation from colonial and imperialist control. As a widely read member of the educated elite, Azikiwe combined intellectualism with radicalism to pursue nationalist Nigerian objectives.[99] He promoted strong ethnic nationalism among the Igbos and brokered a unification of Nigeria's different regions, promoting national consciousness across the entire country. Azikiwe published several newspapers, including the *West African Pilot*, the *Eastern Nigerian Guardian*, and the *Southern Defender*, and he was expressive and radical in opposing colonial government policies.[100] He was also strategic in building national sentiment among Nigerians – the Zikist Movement, an association of his admirers and loyalists, was the most significant manifestation of these efforts. Even without Macaulay's presence as the first nationalist in Nigeria, the accomplishments of Azikiwe represented a significant moment in the political history of colonial Nigeria.

Obafemi Awolowo, Ahmadu Bello, Ernest Ikoli, Ahmadu Kano, and other nationalists also contributed to the anticolonial struggles. Unlike the broad geographic influence of Macaulay and Azikiwe, these nationalists commanded respect within their regions. Most of them led political parties that held distinctly regional outlooks. The AG, the Northern People's Progressive Union, and the Northern People's Congress were regional organizations, as was the influence of their key leaders: Awolowo, Aminu, and Bello. However, Awolowo and Bello successfully gained some recognition at the national level. Awolowo was the first premier of the Western Region, a one-time federal commissioner for finance, and the first opposition leader of Nigeria's postindependence central parliament. Awolowo may be the most controversial of the nationalists, but his respectable personality, charisma, and ideology resonated with the Yoruba people of Western Nigeria.[101] Ahmed and Umar describe Awolowo as Nigeria's foremost federalist, a democratic socialist, and a strong advocate for colonial Nigeria's educational reforms.[102]

Awolowo espoused a staunch democratic socialist ideology and fervent support for federalism,[103] while Bello was conservative and had no appetite

---

[98] Agbafor Igwe, *Nnamdi Azikiwe: The Philosopher of our Time* (Enugu: Fourth Dimension Publisher, 1992).

[99] Nnamdi Azikiwe, *Ideology for Nigeria: Capitalism, Socialism, or Welfarism?* (Yaba: Macmillan Nigeria, 1980).

[100] John E. Flint, "'Managing Nationalism': The Colonial Office and Nnamdi Azikiwe, 1932–43," *The Journal of Imperial and Commonwealth History* 27, no. 2 (1999): 143–158.

[101] Insa Nolte, *Obafemi Awolowo and the Making of Remo: The Local Politics of a Nigerian Nationalist* (Edinburgh: Edinburgh University Press, 2009).

[102] Ahmed and Abubakar Umar, "Nationalists in Nigeria from 1914–1960," 7.

[103] Obafemi Awolowo, *The People's Republic* (Ibadan: Oxford University Press, 1968).

for federal politics.[104] This attitude may have been influenced by his traditional position as the Sardauna of Sokoto, but it set the tone for the style, politics, and ideology of the Northern People's Congress. A small group of Northerners who opposed the conservative ideology of Bello and the NPC created the association that would become the NEPU, led by Aminu Kano.[105]

In chronicling the nationalist contributions of women in colonial Nigerian politics, Oyinkan Abayomi (née Ajasa) played an important role. This British-educated music teacher, feminist, and politician established the Nigerian Women's Party (NWP) in 1944.[106] Through her organization, Abayomi advocated women's education, equal employment opportunities in the civil service, and protection for the rights of market women. The NWP's successes in pursuit of these objectives were instrumental in reshaping the gender narratives of colonial Nigeria's history and its anticolonial activities.[107]

Conclusion

The early efforts of Nigeria's nationalist political parties assumed many different dimensions and trajectories. First-generation political parties, like the Nigerian National Democratic Party and the Lagos Youth Movement, focused on including Nigerians in the political affairs of the colony. They also worked to improve social welfare, especially regarding the working conditions for members of Nigeria's civil service. The second-generation political parties, from the mid-twentieth century onward, became increasingly hostile to the colonial administration. Their activities resulted in the evolution and development of anticolonial nationalism.

Party politics took different dimensions in Nigeria as parties aligned toward different ideologies. A common attribute of second-generation political parties was the ethnic nationalism that promoted regional identities, and the inclusion of those identities in the national experience. These variations of nationalism – and the differences in each party's political ideology and approach to nationalism – made significant contributions to Nigeria's anticolonial development. Their work transitioned the country into its current status as a sovereign federal republic, independent of political and economic control exerted by outside forces.

---

[104] Bello, *My Life*.
[105] Alan Feinstein, *African Revolutionary: The Life and Times of Nigeria's Aminu Kano* (New York: The New York Times Book Co., 1973).
[106] Cheryl Johnson-Odim, "Lady Oyinkan Abayomi: A Profile," in *Nigerian Women in Historical Perspective*, ed. Bolanle Awe (Lagos: Sankore Publishers, 1992), 149–163.
[107] Folarin Coker, *A Lady: A Biography of Lady Oyinkan Abayomi* (Ibadan: Evans Brothers, 1987).

25

Constitutions and Emerging Federalism

Present-day Nigeria's political history originated with imperial Britain's act of colonization. The British gradually amalgamated hundreds of individual political units into the entity that would become known as the Nigerian federal state.[1] These units were notably diverse, including a wide range of geographies and populations. Scholars have observed that the colonization of the different territories was strategically predetermined by the British imperialists.[2] However, their administration was shaped by a preference for convenience and a desire to meet the needs of the colonizers. The territories known as the Protectorate of Northern Nigeria and the Protectorate of Southern Nigeria contained several distinct ethnic groups, which created an institutional impetus to adopt a federal structure that could consolidate them all.[3] This is often the reality for federal states in the present day. In Nigeria's case, its development of a federal structure was historically linked with political and constitutional developments from the country's colonial period.

Nigeria's political and constitutional histories are intrinsically linked. Constitutional developments changed the trajectories of political decisions, and political discourse regularly prompted constitutional developments. The evolution of nationalism and federalism shaped these components of Nigeria's colonial history. Nationalist struggles, especially after World War II, led to major constitutional and political reforms in the country's colonial history. They also encouraged the introduction of federalism. The heterogeneity of the Nigerian population motivated the adoption of a federal structure, but federalism did not emerge as a natural creation. The polities that were forcibly merged into the political entity that was Nigeria had been independent and had minimal political interactions with each other. In colonialism's early period, the administration of the Colony and Protectorate of Nigeria was more of a unitary state than a federal one. Nationalist agitations were indirectly

---

[1] Terhemba Wuam and Victor Egwemi, *The 1914 Amalgamation and a Century of Nigerian Nationhood* (Lagos: Bahiti and Dalila Publishers, 2016).

[2] John M. Carland, *The Colonial Office and Nigeria, 1898–1914* (Stanford: Hoover Press Publication, 1985).

[3] Ian F. Nicolson, *The Administration of Nigeria, 1900–1960: Men, Methods and Myths* (Oxford: Clarendon Press, 1969).

linked to the adoption of federalism because the British faced continuous demands for a government that could satisfy nationalist demands for inclusiveness.

Constitution and the Constitution-Making Process

The Nigerian state was created through the amalgamation of the Colony of Lagos and the Protectorates of Southern and Northern Nigeria, and government machinery was required to manage the newly formed political state. A breadth of historical studies has shown that early interactions between the Europeans and Nigerian indigenes were driven mainly by economic and evangelical interests.[4] The missionaries saw great potential for spreading the Christian gospel and establishing churches in the evergreen West African lands.[5] Up to the mid-nineteenth century, European interest centered on its need for human labor, through the slave trade, to drive its economic system.[6] Agitations and activism led to Britain's abolition of the slave trade in 1807, which resulted in other forms of trade being introduced to the region in subsequent years.[7]

In the second half of the nineteenth century, British forces began to arrive in the geographic territory that would later be known as Nigeria, creating the Colony and Protectorate of Nigeria in 1914. British colonial administration formally began with the annexation of Lagos as a British colony in 1861. Many scholars have noted that Britain's interest in extending its imperial authority beyond Lagos was linked with a desire to amass greater wealth by extracting raw materials from these regions.[8] Britain's Secretary of State strengthened its hold on the region by establishing full-blown political administrations in its colonies and protectorates. Sir Frederick Lord Lugard's singular act of amalgamation, fusing the Colony of Lagos with the Protectorates of Northern and Southern Nigeria, finalized the transformation of these different units as a single political entity under imperial control.[9]

After the amalgamation, a formal system of administration was necessary for the entire Colony and Protectorate of Nigeria. Rahmani has described the preliminary steps taken by the Colonial Office, which had begun as early as

---

[4] Arthur N. Cook, *British Enterprise in Nigeria* (Philadelphia: University of Pennsylvania Press, 1943).
[5] Mamman Daudu, *An Outline of the History of Christianity in West Africa* (Zaria: Micsons Press & Publishers, 2000).
[6] Mokhtaria Rahmani, "Constitutional Development in Nigeria 1945–1960," (unpublished PhD dissertation, Djillali Liabbes University, 2015).
[7] John N. Orji, *A Political Organization in Nigeria since the Late Stone Age: A History of the Igbo People* (New York: Palgrave Macmillan, 2011), 139–159.
[8] Anthony G. Hopkins, "Property Rights and Empire Building: Britain's Annexation of Lagos, 1861," *The Journal of Economic History* 40, no. 4 (1980): 777–798.
[9] Wuam and Egwemi, *The 1914 Amalgamation*.

1898. A six-member committee, known as the Selbourne Committee, was established to oversee the administration of each of the three colonized territories.[10] By the time of the amalgamation, the High Commissioner of the Northern Region, Lord Lugard, had emerged as the first Governor of Nigeria. Through the Secretary of State, Lugard proposed that the British Parliament establish three administrative bodies: an executive council for the entire territory, a legislative council for the colony, and a legislative council for the protectorate.

The executive council comprised ten officials: the two Lieutenant-Governors in charge of the Northern and Southern Protectorates, the Administrator of the Colony, the Attorney General, the Director of Railways and Works, the Commandant of Troops, the Director of Medical Services, the Treasurer, the Director of Marine, and the Controller of Customs.[11] With the approval of the British Parliament, Lord Lugard made the executive council the sole administrative and decision-making authority for the Colony and Protectorate of Nigeria. Unsurprisingly, Lugard retained the power to veto the actions of the executive council and all of the legislative councils.

Factually, law-making was a function of the executive organ, making it the single most powerful organ of the British colonial government. Legislative councils were established for the Colony of Lagos and the Protectorate of Nigeria, but they merely held advisory roles for the governor and the executive council. The structural dysfunctions of the legislative councils were evident in their unrepresentative natures and in the way that they could not make binding decisions for the executive council. Each of the legislative councils was dominated by Europeans. Only six nominated Africans were eligible to join the legislative council, and the council's European members held the more reputable portfolios of Administrator, Legal Advisor, Assistant Treasurer, Municipal Engineer, Sanitary Officer, Harbor Master, Commissioner of Lands, and Commercial Intelligence Officer for the Colony of Lagos. At the legislative council for the Protectorate, Europeans largely held secretarial functions.[12] Most executive council members sat on the legislative council, underscoring the latter's subordination to the former.

Historians, political thinkers, and other scholars have been fascinated by Lugard's system of colonial administration. Members of the British Parliament and cabinet were initially perplexed by the unique features of the Colonial Governor's proposed administration while the idea was in its embryonic state. John Anderson, Under-Secretary of State at the time, considered it anomalous. Strachy, a top official at the Colonial Office, had more to critique about the administration. He was conversant with different forms of government in

---

[10] Rahmani, "Constitutional Development in Nigeria."
[11] Rahmani, "Constitutional Development in Nigeria."
[12] Cook, *British Enterprise in Nigeria*.

sovereign and colonized territories, but he found Lugard's system of colonial administration for the Colony and Protectorate of Nigeria to be unclassifiable. Relations between the executive council and the legislative council were unusual in light of the evolution of democratic systems and the principle of separation of powers in most parts of Western Europe at the time. However, the more pressing concern was the division of colonial territory. Critics found Lugard's system of government impossible to classify as either unitary or federal. Lugard's design ultimately received approval because it seemed practicable at the time, despite its apparent defects.[13]

Lugard's introduction of the 1914 amalgamation constitution was the first attempt to create a system of legal and political administration for the newly formed country. Items of historical evidence attest to the existence of formalized and informal legal and political systems maintained in most of the independent polities that were subjugated and amalgamated by the British imperialists, but there was no uniformity or formal operation of constitutionalism in these territories. Oyediran has explained that the constitution describes the formal allocation of functions, powers, and duties between various arms and levels of government.[14] It is usually recorded in written format – although it may also be unwritten or flexible – to prevent its manipulation by those who would amend it to advance personal interests. The 1914 amalgamation constitution was written, proposed, and enacted by authorities that only Britain recognized.

The most significant shortcoming of the amalgamation constitution may have been that it was not adapted to meet the needs and aspirations of colonial Nigeria's Indigenous people. Locals were not consulted during the drafting of the constitution and the colonial administration made no significant efforts to investigate or reconcile interests within different parts of the Colony and Protectorate of Nigeria. A breadth of historical studies has noted that Lord Lugard, a former High Commissioner for the Northern Protectorate, was particularly interested in advancing the interests of the Northern Protectorate and pacifying the emirs.[15] This influenced his preferred model for partitioning the Colony and Protectorate of Nigeria.

Charles Temple, governor of Northern Nigeria from 1914 to 1917, was concerned that Lugard's plan to divide the country into three provinces would create a Northern Province that was larger than the other two provinces combined, and could spark significant ethnic mistrust and create imbalances in political authority between the regions. The unrepresentative nature of the

---

[13] Rahmani, "Constitutional Developments in Nigeria."

[14] Oyeleye Oyediran, *Nigerian Constitutional Development* (Ibadan: Oyediran Consults International, 1998).

[15] Z. O. Apata, "Lugard and the Creation of Provincial Administration in Northern Nigeria, 1900–1918," *African Study Monographs* 11, no. 3 (1989): 143–152.

legislative councils and their purely advisory powers posed further challenges to the constitutionalism of Lugard's administration. These other issues would become the main focus of Hugh Clifford, but despite the massive constitutional reforms that he introduced, some challenges were left unresolved.

Scholars of Nigeria's political and constitutional history agree that significant constitutional developments began in the 1920s in colonial Nigeria during the Clifford administration.[16] In 1919, after he was appointed Governor-General for the Colony and Protectorate of Nigeria, Clifford was concerned by the framework that his predecessor had left for the Nigerian colonial government. He then proposed major constitutional reforms that affected the mode of assumption of office, increased the membership of the legislative councils, and included Nigeria's Indigenous people in its colonial government. Scholars have noted that Clifford was the first governor to draw up a written constitution for Nigeria.[17] Under his new constitutional design, an executive council and a legislative council were established for the entire Colony and Protectorate of Nigeria, which had only minor differences from the composition of Lugard's administration.

In the manner of Lugard's administration, the executive council under the Clifford Constitution was solely composed of Europeans, and it remained responsible for the entire country's administration. However, the legislative council increased from twenty-seven to forty-six members, and it included ten Africans. Four of the African members were to be elected from Lagos and Calabar, and the remaining six were appointed by nomination.[18] Despite the significant improvements made to the legislative council's composition, no substantial changes were made to its authority.

The legislative council for the protectorate had the authority to make laws for the entire country, but its powers could be blocked by an overriding veto from the Governor. Possibly the most striking feature of the 1922 Clifford Constitution was the introduction of the elective principle. Despite the elective principle's limited coverage of the metropolitan cities of Lagos and Calabar and the restriction of franchise to adult males with substantial financial resources, most scholars have praised Clifford for beginning an era of representative governance in Nigeria's constitutional history.[19] As one author

---

[16] Onofere Princewill Okereka, "Evolution of Constitutional Governments in Nigeria: Its Implementation on National Cohesion," *Global Journal of Political Science and Administration* 3, no. 5 (2015): 1–8.

[17] Michael Ediagbonya, "Nigerian Constitutional Developments in Historical Perspective, 1914–1960," *American Journal of Humanities and Social Sciences Research (AJHSSR)* 4, no. 2 (2020): 242–248.

[18] Tekena N. Tamuno, "Governor Clifford and Representative Government," *Journal of the Historical Society of Nigeria* 4, no. 1 (1967): 117–124.

[19] C. I. Eluwa, M. O. Ukagwu, U. N. Nwachukwu, and A. C. Nwaubani, *A History of Nigeria* (Onitsha: Africana First Publishers Limited, 2005), 312.

observed, "Clifford's constitution marked a relatively fresh departure from Lugard's. It was a cautious reform based on the gradual participation of the Africans in the government, according to their age and maturity. It paved the way for steady political progress according to needs and constraints."[20]

Although a wealth of historical studies has traced the constitutional and political histories of Nigeria, with a significant focus on its constitutional developments, especially during the colonial period, only a few scholars have attempted to examine the constitution-making process in light of its colonial history. Many scholars have highlighted the significance of constitution-making for the country's political developments, especially in the postcolonial period. Attahiru Jega has noted that an effective constitution-making process must be "inclusive in character," accommodating all shades of thought and opinions, and it must only be promulgated after adequate consultation and consensus.[21] Scholars have mixed views about the inclusive nature of Nigeria's postcolonial constitutions, but a majority are likely to agree that constitution-making processes during Nigeria's earlier period of colonialism were neither made to include Nigerians in their political narrative nor fashioned to satisfy their needs and aspirations.

Nationalist movements were largely responsible for ensuring that the colonial administration was alert and responsive to the needs and aspirations of Nigeria's Indigenous people, working toward the eventual decolonization of the country in 1960.[22] These nationalist movements evolved across different stages in Nigeria's political history, beginning as structured criticism of the colonial administration and its policies, especially those associated with the civil service. These concerns were followed by demands for opportunities to participate in the colonial administration, ending with anticolonial administration efforts.

As nationalist sentiments increased in colonial Nigeria, the colony's approach to creating a constitution changed. The history of constitution-making in colonial Nigeria can be separated into two periods: before World War II, and after. Administrations before World War II, especially Lugard's administration, imposed restrictive legislation on Nigeria's residents without considering their interests. The 1922 constitution is largely credited with pioneering major political and constitutional reforms that would define the country's political trajectory for the next few decades. However, the constitutions created after World War II largely introduced the most significant contributions to Nigeria's constitutional history till the fall of the First Republic.[23]

---

[20] Penelope Hetherington, *British Paternalism and Africa, 1920–1940* (London: Frank Cass, 1978).
[21] Attahiru Jega, "Towards Restructuring of Nigeria," *Thisday*, July 10, 2020.
[22] Olusola Olasupo, Isaac Olayide Oladeji, and E. O. C. Ijeoma, "Nationalism and Nationalist Agitation in Africa: The Nigerian Trajectory," *The Review of Black Political Economy* 44 (2017): 261–283.
[23] Rahmani, *Constitutional Developments in Nigeria*.

Constitutional Developments After World War II

The period after World War II saw increased nationalist agitation in colonial Nigeria, culminating in significant political and constitutional reforms. The formative years of colonial Nigeria's constitutional development laid the foundation for the colony's political structure. However, the period after World War II saw the most significant constitutional amendments.

Educated elites and traditional rulers had rallied to the colonial administration at the onset of the war, calling for Nigerian indigenes and other Africans to support Britain and the Allied Powers. By 1944, Nigeria's educated elites had realized that Nigerians needed to be included in governance and the establishment of constitutional and political frameworks to ensure that governmental powers were fully transferred to Indigenous people. The first constitution that the colonial administration fashioned to meet these nationalist aspirations was the Richards Constitution, created in 1946 by Sir Arthur Richard.[24] Nigeria's three regions – North, West, and East – had existed since 1939,[25] although they were not allowed to legislate apart from recommending bills for issues that affected their territory. The Richards Constitution was introduced during intense discussions about ending colonial rule and upholding the dignity of every human. In an attempt to respond to criticisms, the Richards Constitution intended to correct the shortcomings of the Clifford Constitution. It established a broad legislative council, allowing deliberations from the North and the regional house of assembly.[26] Governor Richards was compelled to create this constitutional framework because of Nigeria's tense political climate. It was completed after discussions about the need for a constitution in Nigeria and an assessment of the country's diverse cultural and geographic influences.[27]

The Richards Constitution aimed to promote unity in Nigeria and include Nigerians in their governance. A wider legislative council was created to assist with this goal, attempting to include every community. The council was composed of forty-three members, which included six chiefs, nineteen officials, and eighteen unofficial members. The six chiefs included four emirs, recommended by the upper house of the Northern Province, and two chiefs from the Western Province, recommended by the Governor. The constitution also altered existing ideologies for the judicial council. The Governor proposed the existence of a single Supreme Court for the entire country. All British colonies had a single Supreme Court, and Nigeria had a protectorate court.

---

[24] Kalu Ezera, *Constitutional Developments in Nigeria* (Ibadan: University Press, 1960).
[25] Adiele E. Afigbo, "Background to Nigerian Federalism: Federal Features in the Colonial State," *Publius: The Journal of Federalism* 21, no. 4 (1991): 13–29.
[26] Rahmani, "Constitutional Development in Nigeria," 63.
[27] Jacob F. A. Ajayi, "Nineteenth Century Origins of Nigerian Nationalism," *Journal of the Historical Society of Nigeria* 2, no. 2 (1961): 196–210.

The Richards Constitution created a foundation for federalism in Nigeria; it clarified the functions of regional councils and their financial responsibilities. Each region had its own budget and managed its own costs, apart from central services run by the government.[28] The constitution created offices for regional deputies and heads of all principal departments to affirm regionalism. This ensured effective and efficient administration in each region while preventing Lagos from becoming too centralized. This constitution also established strong connections with native authorities to uphold regionalism. It is often recognized for fostering unity between the Northern and Southern Protectorates, providing the basis for nationalism in the country.[29]

Nationalists and labor movements harshly criticized the 1946 constitution. The *West African Pilot* and the *Daily Comet* launched journalistic attacks on the constitution.[30] They alleged that Governor Richards had disregarded public opinion and input from nationalists while drafting the constitution. The adoption of nomination for government offices instead of elections was also criticized for an absence of Nigerian participation in their country's affairs, along with thinly veiled measures to render the educated elites insignificant. The Nigerian Trade Union Congress (NTUC) mobilized workers to oppose the constitution, which forced a set of resolutions that were later enshrined in the constitution.[31] These resolutions included the provision of suffrage, a reduction in the Governor's powers, and the inclusion of African representatives in the legislative council. The National Council of Nigeria and Cameroons (NCNC) also advocated the constitution to grant full independence to the regions.[32] The Richards Constitution galvanized nationalist sentiment, which was indispensable for creating political consciousness and political activism in the country.

John Macpherson, who became the Governor of Nigeria in 1948, introduced additional reforms. The introduction of the 1951 Macpherson Constitution can be seen as an answer to the unyielding nationalist calls to reject the Richards Constitution.[33] Colonial agitation had also increased in West

---

[28] Aaron Tsado Gana and Samuel G. Egwu, eds., *Federalism in Africa: Framing the National Question*, Vol. 1 (Trenton: Africa World Press, 2003).

[29] James Smoot Coleman, *Nigeria: Background to Nationalism* (Berkeley: University of California Press, 1958).

[30] Attahiru Jega, "The Political Economy of Nigerian Federalism," in *Foundations of Nigerian Federalism, 1960–1995*, Vol. III, ed. Isawa J. Elaigwu and R. A. Akindele (Abuja: National Council of Intergovernmental Relation, 1996), 96.

[31] Rotimi Ajayi, "The Politicization of Trade Unionism: The Case of Labour/NCNC Alliance in Nigeria 1940–1960," *Ufahamu* 27, no. 1–3 (1999): 52.

[32] Tekena Tamuno, "Nigeria Federalism in Historical Perspective," in *Federalism and Political Restructuring in Nigeria*, ed. Adigun Agbaje, Rotimi Suberu, and G. Herault (Ibadan: Spectrum Books Ltd., 1998), 13–33.

[33] LPM, "Nigeria under the Macpherson Constitution," *The World Today* 9, no. 1 (1953): 12–21.

Africa, Southeast Asia, and South Asia, especially India.[34] The drafting of the Macpherson Constitution involved intense deliberations with Nigerians attempting to establish a federal constitution for their country. Macpherson worked to gain public acceptance for constitutional changes to avoid the backlash seen previously. His ideologies could be seen as colonial efforts to secure support from nationalists, for they were seen as integral to the transfer of power.[35]

The constitution ensured the autonomy of the regional governments. Each region advocated its own interests, and the central government deliberated on national issues. The constitution inextricably linked regional executives with the administration of regional governments.[36] It allowed for the establishment of party-parliamentary committees, where bills would be deliberated after submission to the legislative council for further debate. The constitution addressed concerns about discrimination against Nigerians by including them in the civil service. A commission was established to recruit Nigerian men and women into the civil service. However, this brought the problem of how Nigerian civil servants could abandon the system's rigid, archaic practices that undermined Nigerians' welfare and subsequent administration. The constitution also addressed discrimination in the educational system. This was coupled with deliberate efforts to develop education at different levels, although the overall educational system remained inadequate for a country the size of Nigeria.

With the constitution, Macpherson attempted to solve local government problems, which was seen in the democratization of the native authority system. Native authorities now had more autonomy to run local affairs, and the three regions enacted ordinances to reform their native authorities.[37] Macpherson's constitution represented a major development for Nigerian federalism, adopting elections to fill seats in the central legislature rather than the nomination of majorities. It established regional houses of assembly that culminated in the establishment of Nigeria's first federal system of government. The Macpherson Constitution was also unique in its measures to advance the nationalist movement.[38] A constitutional provision allowed for the establishment of regional political parties to propagate the native interests of each region, but the constitution collapsed after the Northern People's Congress (NPC) threatened secession.[39] Northerners had vehemently opposed

---

[34] Rahmani, "Constitutional Development in Nigeria," 110.

[35] LPM, "Nigeria under the Macpherson Constitution."

[36] Imuetinyan Uglagbe, "The Second Phase of Nigerian Constitution under the British Imperial Rules 1951–1959," *International Journal of Law* 4, no. 3 (2018): 27–30.

[37] Mojibayo M. Fadakinte and Musa Abdulkareem, "The Travails of Nigerian Federalism 1951–1999: A Federation in Crisis of Constitutional Engineering," *African Journal of Political Science and International Relations* 15, no. 1 (2021): 19–27.

[38] Dele Babalola, "The Origins of Nigerian Federalism: The Rikerian Theory and Beyond," *Federal Governance* 8, no. 3 (2013): 43–54.

[39] Nicolson, *The Administration of Nigeria*, 9.

the political, social, and economic changes that might be brought by Western education, which could reduce their local authority. The constitution also faltered after the Eastern regional crisis: the nonelection of Nnamdi Azikiwe in the Council of Ministers, the Kano riot, and Anthony Enahoro's presentation of a bill in 1953 that called for Nigeria's independence by 1956. Enahoro's call was rejected by Sir Ahmadu Bello, the Sardauna of Sokoto, who believed that the North was not ready for self-rule, seeking to replace "1956" with "as soon as practicable."[40]

The apparent breakdown of the 1951 constitution prompted a series of constitutional conferences, including the London Constitutional Conference of 1953 and the Lagos Constitutional Conference of 1954, headed by Sir Oliver Lyttleton.[41] These conferences discussed the major political and constitutional issues that would form the fabric of the 1954 Lyttleton Constitution.[42] The 1954 constitution made provisions for direct elections into the federal legislature, and it established an office of a Premier for each region in 1957. The constitution also established the role of the Prime Minister at the center of government. This role was first occupied by the deputy leader of the NPC, Sir Tafawa Balewa, who was not interested in giving up strong regional powers to wield a weaker central authority.

The need for regional autonomy was a recurring theme in the Lyttleton Constitution, along with the regionalization of the civil service. Natives in each region joined the service system for their local communities,[43] and the regions hastily set up training programs to facilitate the recruitment of civil service members. The Western and Eastern regions attempted to implement universal primary education and establish regional universities. Under this constitution, the regions were politically and economically stronger than the central government. Regions also had public services and judiciary branches. The Lyttleton Constitution made Nigeria a federal state, and although this was met with the further clamor for constitutional change, it fast-tracked Nigeria's independence in 1960.

The Lyttleton Constitution's federal structure favored Nigeria's three major ethnic groups, but minority groups had always existed in Nigeria. The constitution eventually collapsed because there were no provisions for the representation of these groups. Their concerns had increased after the rapid regionalization of governments. Deliberate efforts from these groups, expressing grievances and demanding centralized government decisions, proved abortive. These points of contention later culminated in the failure of the 1954 constitution.

---

[40] Christopher C. Mojekwu, "Nigerian Constitutionalism," *Nomos: American Society for Political and Legal Philosophy* 20 (1979): 163–186.
[41] Isawa J. Elaigwu, *The Politics of Federalism in Nigeria* (London: Adonis & Abbey Publishers Ltd., 2017).
[42] Ben O. Nwabueze, *A Constitutional History of Nigeria* (London: C. Hurst, 1982).
[43] Martin Lynn, "The Nigerian Self-Government Crisis of 1953 and the Colonial Office," *The Journal of Imperial and Commonwealth History* 34, no. 2 (2006): 245–261.

The Lyttleton Constitution's regional government only deepened ethnic politics and identities that had become more prominent since the attainment of self-rule.[44] The North believed Nigeria's independence would reduce its influence and political authority. These developments inhibited the creation of collective national consciousness and widened existing gaps between groups. The 1954 constitution was largely seen as the product of colonialist officials responding to Nigeria's emergent nationalism.[45] In 1953, Chief Obafemi Awolowo told Sir John Macpherson that his constitution would be the last colonial constitution accepted by Nigeria. However, The Lyttleton Constitution was the last colonial constitution accepted before Nigeria's 1960 independence. This constitution resulted from intense strategizing by officials in the Colonial Office.

Scholars have suggested that the 1951 Macpherson Constitution was mostly the outcome of British perceptions of individuals and issues within the budding state of Nigeria. The 1954 Lyttleton Constitution did not reflect nationalist desires but showed conscious British efforts to curb nationalist influence. Political scholars have suggested that colonial constitutions were a powerful strategy to defuse threats of decolonization. They encouraged Northern efforts to delay Nigeria's transition process as it attempted to catch up with the Western and Eastern regions, which preferred a more rapid independence process.[46]

Amid all its shortcomings, the 1954 constitution paved the way for Nigeria's independence. The country's newly established Federal House of Representatives was able to make an unequivocal request to the British government to grant Nigeria's independence. The Federal Prime Minister, Regional Premiers, President of the Senate, and other federal and regional representatives met with British representatives in March 1960 to discuss Nigeria's attainment of self-rule.[47]

The Evolution and Development of Federalism: Constitutional and Political Perspectives

The origin of Nigerian federalism is connected to the series of constitutions implemented by the British. Lugard's act of amalgamating the Northern and Southern Protectorates in 1914 was not intended to create a federal state.[48] However, the need to improve Nigeria's administration – and to address local

---

[44] Fadakinte and Abdulkareem, "The Travails of Nigerian Federalism."
[45] Eghosa E. Osaghae, *Crippled Giant: Nigeria since Independence* (London: Hurst and Company, 1998).
[46] Ladipo Adamolekun and S. Bamidele Ayo, "The Evolution of the Nigerian Federal Administration System," *Publius: The Journal of Federalism* 19, no. 1 (1989): 157–176.
[47] Mojekwu, "Nigerian Constitutionalism."
[48] Auwalu Musa and Ndaliman Alhaji Hassan, "An Evaluation of the Origins, Structure and Features of Nigerian Federalism," *The International Journal of Social Sciences and Humanities Invention* 1, no. 5 (2014): 314–325.

concerns about their lack of involvement in national affairs – facilitated the development of constitutions that would become the bedrock of modern-day Nigerian federalism.[49] Constitutions put forward by Richards, Macpherson, and Lyttleton did not consciously seek to establish a federal structure for the Nigerian state. The common purpose of these post–World War II constitutions was to meet the demands of Indigenous people, particularly nationalists, and include them in the national government, preparing the country for its gradual transition to a sovereign polity.

The formal establishment of the federalism principle in Nigerian constitutional law may be traced to the 1954 Lyttleton Constitution, although some assert that the 1946 Richards Constitution planted seeds for the concept in Nigerian governance.[50] The ultimate evolution of federalist tendencies in the Nigerian polity dates to the inception of colonial administration. Colonial incursion had commenced in the mid-nineteenth century and came to a head with the Berlin Conference, but full-scale colonial governance of the entity that was Nigeria did not commence until the early twentieth century.[51] Before this time, the Southern and Northern Regions were administratively distinct.

After the amalgamation, Lugard took responsibility for governing the newly created nation and adopted the system now known as Indirect Rule.[52] Lugard's experience with colonial administration in India and Burma had familiarized him with the managerial quagmires involved in governing wildly heterogeneous societies. Instead, he opted to administer governance through the traditional rulership frameworks already in place. The colonial administration implemented such systems in communities like those found in today's Eastern region, where such systems were absent.[53] Lugard cited a need for unity across public finance, trade, and communications.[54]

The early colonial administration identified two major regions: Southern and Northern Nigeria. A Lieutenant-Governor led each region. For administrative

---

[49] Osarhieme Benson Osadolor, "The Development of the Federal Idea and the Federal Framework, 1914–1960," in *Federalism and Political Restructuring in Nigeria*, ed. Adigun Agbaje, Rotimi Suberu, and Georges Herault (Ibadan: Spectrum Books Ltd., 1998).
[50] Charas Madu Tella, Ahmed Wali Doho, and Aliyu Bapeto, "The Evolution, Development and Practice of Federalism in Nigeria," *Public Policy and Administration Review* 2, no. 4 (2014): 51–66.
[51] Michael Mulligan, "Nigeria, the British Presence in West Africa and International Law in the 19th Century," *Journal of The History of International Law* 11, no. 2 (2009): 273.
[52] Obaro Ikime, "Reconsidering Indirect Rule: The Nigerian Example," *Journal of the Historical Society of Nigeria* 4, no. 3 (1968): 421–438.
[53] Ugo Pascal Onumonu, "The Development of the Kingship Institution in Oru–Igbo up to 1991," *OGIRISI: A New Journal of African Studies* 12 (2016): 68–96.
[54] Frederick J. D. Lugard, *Report by Sir FD Lugard on the Amalgamation of Northern and Southern Nigeria, and Administration 1912–1919* (London: HMSO Stationery Office, 1920).

convenience, the Southern Protectorate was further divided into three provinces, and the number of provinces in the North varied over time. Despite this apportionment of territory, there was no comparable delegation of powers as the entire legislative authority was concentrated in a central government that limited executive authority. A sizable number of central departments had no corresponding office at the regional level, with some authority delegated to the Lieutenant-Governors. At the provincial level, chiefs lacked any powers of promulgation. They mostly served as administrative tools for executing the policies established by the central government.

The entire model of early colonial administration could be identified as a mild unitary regime or a highly tempered federal governmental structure. Scholars support the federal portrayal, although they deem it an "accidental" outcome instead of a deliberate choice imposed by Lugard's politicking.[55] Obafemi Awolowo supported this assertion, noting that, "To him [Lugard] ... belongs the credit or discredit for setting Nigeria on a course which Nigerian nationalists and patriots feel obliged to pursue."[56] He referred to the path of federalism.

As more Africans received education abroad, a class of intellectuals developed who had the political savvy to understand the intricacies of governance.[57] This emerging group pressured colonial administrators to institute political reforms that involved indigenes governing themselves, making them more than passive cogs in the machinery of indirect rule. Colonial officials responded to these requests with the 1922 Clifford Constitution. This introduced elections for natives from Lagos and Calabar to serve on the central Legislative Council. At best, these were advisory roles, and allowances for greater local participation peaked with these admissions to the legislative council. There were no corresponding provisions for the involvement of indigenes in executive affairs. After introducing the elective principle and laying the foundation for participatory democracy, the Clifford Constitution made few contributions to advance the course of federalism in pre-independence Nigeria.

In some ways, the 1922 constitution slowed the development of federalism. It fused administrative departments in the North and South, expanding the central secretariat to take on additional functions. Records point to Clifford's wish to abolish the Lieutenant-Governor's roles in both regions. He at least wanted to weaken their mandate and make them subject to the central government's authority. His proposals were allegedly based on the observation that different regions in the newly created colony country were pursuing markedly different destinies.

---

[55] N. U. Akpan, "Nigerian Federalism: Accidental Foundations by Lugard," *Journal of the Historical Society of Nigeria* 9, no. 2 (1978): 1–20.

[56] Obafemi Awolowo, *The People's Republic* (Ibadan: Oxford University Press, 1968).

[57] Emmanuel A. Ayandele, *Educated Elites in the Nigerian Society* (Ibadan: University of Ibadan Press, 1974).

Clifford was particularly concerned about the status of the North. His goal was to create a "united" Nigeria, and he felt that the North must become more open to accomplish that goal. Clifford's strategy was "that the coordination of all administrative work . . . should be directed from a single center."[58] He failed to abrogate the offices of the Lieutenant-Governors, but he implemented some administrative changes to weaken their authority and transfer larger amounts of governmental power to the center.[59] The Clifford document's apparent failure to grant a constitutional devolution of powers and its feeble attempt to encourage local political involvement became focal points for political agitation from the growing community of educated Indigenous elites.[60] Subsequent colonial administrators acknowledged these shortcomings, and, over two decades, they gradually decentralized government authority. These efforts culminated in the introduction of the 1946 Richards Constitution.

By 1946, it was clear that the political landscape was ready for change. Bernard Bourdillon, who preceded Richards, had implemented a long-debated policy to divide the country into three regions under a system where some powers were shared.[61] Bourdillion's decision was supported by Colonial Office studies; these documents explained that traditional and religious leaders in the North considered their region to be distinct from the others. It was feared that efforts to unify them with the other regions could potentially fracture the yet-to-be-independent country.[62] The colonial study, led by Lord Hailey, proposed the introduction of regional councils with substantive financial and legislative authority.[63]

After assuming the office of Governor-General, Richards sought to consolidate and advance the ideas of his predecessor. He codified the new system of government in the body of the eponymous constitution he promulgated in 1946. A key feature of this constitution was the creation of a widely encompassing national legislative council, which enlisted the participation of the Northern region for the first time. Another provision was the constitutional delegation of administrative and financial powers to regional governments, shifting the locus of power away from the central government. With financial independence came the power to generate independent revenue, devoid of interference from the central government.

---

[58] Clifford to Milner, 3 Dec. 1919, CO 583/80/214.
[59] John A. Ballard, "Administrative Origins of Nigerian Federalism," *African Affairs* 70, no. 281 (1971): 333–348.
[60] Rotimi Ajayi and Joseph Y. Fashagba, eds., *Nigerian Politics. Advances in African Economic, Social and Political Development* (Cham: Springer Nature, 2021).
[61] O. Ajene, "Political Parties and Federalism," in *Foundations of Nigerian Federalism: 1900–1960*, ed. Isawa J. Elaigwu and Godfrey N. Uzoigwe (Jos: Institute of Governance and Social Research, 1996).
[62] Coleman, *Nigeria: Background to Nationalism*.
[63] Lord Hailey's report, NAK: Zarprof C2/1940.

It is worth considering the prevailing global situation that precipitated this change of administrative style: the vicious armed conflict that marked the late 1930s and the larger part of the 1940s. As one of the major powers involved in the hostilities, Britain strained its resources and partially lost the ability to exert authority over its colonial territories.[64] There was a shortage of personnel to maintain centralized control over colonial territories. Britain had also lost a great deal of its financial prowess and capital stock, severely depleting its ability to maintain administrative authority over Nigeria's local inhabitants.[65]

The 1951 Macpherson Constitution and the 1954 Lyttleton Constitution are credited with unequivocally establishing federalism's foundations in Nigeria. The 1946 Richards Constitution charted a path the latter constitutions would follow later. Most scholars describe the 1946 constitution as quasi-federal, while later constitutions included more features of federalism. The Macpherson Constitution distributed some governmental powers more broadly, but it primarily maintained the tenets established by its predecessor. The Macpherson Constitution was commendable for consultations with locals during its construction, and the resulting provisions were quite progressive. Nigerian locals were elected to the central legislature and formed an effective majority. Regional houses of assembly also had larger legislatures, with some regions operating bicameral legislative frameworks. The Macpherson Constitution provided new opportunities for indigenes to occupy executive functions, as each region was to have a premier and an associated cabinet. A Nigerian prime minister sat at the center of government, along with a council of ministers.

Despite the progress of the 1951 constitution, political officeholders in Nigeria found that most of their powers remained restricted. People still relied on the central government for all their administrative affairs. If the regions were politically demarcated in a journey toward federalism, then it was a caricature of the federalist spirit; those regions were not granted significant levels of self-governance. This state of affairs had toxic effects on the preindependent nation's political psyche, with central elements retaining power. These concerns precipitated a constitutional review, which culminated in the unveiling of the 1954 Lyttleton Constitution. Many groups heralded this document as the country's premier federal constitution. It gave full recognition to regional autonomy with a moderately powerful center, effectively establishing a quasi-confederate structure.

One of the Lyttleton Constitution's key impacts on federalism in Nigeria was its devolution of the executive and judicial arms of government. The Macpherson Constitution had initially decentralized legislative authority

---

[64] John Alewo Musa Agbonika, "Federalism and Military Rule in Nigeria," (unpublished PhD dissertation, University of London, 1991).
[65] Erin Myrice, "The Impact of the Second World War on the Decolonization of Africa," *Africana Studies Research Student Conference*, 2015.

with the creation of the central legislative council and the regional houses of assembly. The Lyttleton Constitution enhanced the federal structure by creating an executive branch for each region. This meant that Nigerians assumed comprehensive local authority over operational affairs in their regions. The executive system of these units mirrored the parliamentary framework at the center of government. Each governor was a titular head of state, and the Premier held sway as the head of government. The principle of federalism was also applied to the judicial system, establishing regional high courts to interpret legislation enacted by the regional legislative houses. Regional civil service branches were established and controlled by the regional governments, removed entirely from central oversight. In essence, regional government departments were no longer branches of the central government.

The decentralization of powers and local autonomy required significant degrees of economic independence. The Lyttleton Constitution met this need by placing regional governments in charge of the colonial economy's lifeblood: agricultural commodities.[66] This system saw moderate operational and developmental success, but it is necessary to interrogate the practicality of the federalist system that British officials transferred to the administrators of the newly independent Nigeria. Scholars disagree over the benefits of this devolution and decentralization, debating whether it was a logical route for the nation or whether this political system was imposed on residents as fulfilling a colonial power's parochial pursuits. It can be said that the nature of the amalgamated nation set it on a trajectory where only the federalist political infrastructure was practicable. The country forged by the 1914 amalgamation was extremely large, even for colonial ambitions. Lugard noted that it was their largest colonial territory in Africa in terms of human resources and geographic area.[67] An attempt to centralize legislation, policy decisions, and judicial administration for such a large population distributed over such a substantial area would have been an administrative catastrophe.

Large countries are not required to adopt a federal government framework. The People's Republic of China, the largest nation in history, now overtaken by India in recent years, is a subtle unitary state.[68] The states that comprise the United Kingdom also adopt a mono-bloc governmental system.[69] Factors other than size determine whether a country must pursue a federal solution, and one such factor is the population's heterogeneity. Nigeria's various

---

[66] Agbonika, *Federalism and Military Rule in Nigeria*.
[67] Tella, Doho, and Bapeto, "The Evolution, Development and Practice."
[68] Lok Wai Kin, "The Relationship between Central and Local Governments under the Unitary State System of China," in *One Country, Two Systems, Three Legal Orders–Perspectives of Evolution*, ed. Jorge C. Oliveira and Paulo Cardinal (Berlin: Springer, 2009), 527–540.
[69] Stephen Tierney, "Federalism in a Unitary State: A Paradox Too Far?" *Regional & Federal Studies* 19, no. 2 (2009): 237–253.

ethnicities and cultures are so wildly disparate that they had no hope of coexisting under a unified administrative structure.

The 1953 Kano riots suggested what might happen if a unitary system was imposed on the budding nation, and threatened its continued unity.[70] Even under the quasi-federal structure established in 1914, which included a unified South, it became apparent that such a framework was infeasible. Bourdillon noted that the South-East and South-West regions were not culturally homogeneous and thus needed to be separated for several reasons, including language.[71] Richards noted that the country "naturally" fell into three regions occupied by people with diverse traditions and political perspectives.[72]

World War II encouraged the British administration to seriously consider scaling back its empirical efforts. A decolonization plan was set in motion, requiring increasing amounts of self-governance in the colonies.[73] However, British authorities quickly realized that this approach could only be achieved without rancor if various units pursued their political destinies independently. The decolonization project could be framed as a noble colonialist effort to do what was best for their conquered lands, but scholars have observed that the imposition of federalism ultimately advanced the British agenda. In Nigeria, federalism was seen as the magic bullet that the British used to pacify the Northern region to integrate it with the overall Nigerian project. This explains why the South was kept under a singular government, away from the Northern administration. It also provides the rationale for successive colonial administrations refusing to include Northern representatives in their central administration until the late 1940s.[74]

Experts found it curious that the British favored a unitary approach when it suited their purposes, but they discarded it when that approach required additional material and personnel.[75] There is also a more sinister explanation for the British preference for federalism. Some critics have described it as an extension of their previous "divide-and-rule" approach: keeping various regions administratively separate prevented locals from creating a united front that could oppose their colonial overlords.[76]

---

[70] Lynn, "The Nigerian Self-Government Crisis of 1953."
[71] Lucy Mair, *The Principles of Native Administration in Nigeria: Selected Documents 1900–1947* (London: Oxford University Press, 1965).
[72] Sir Arthur Richards Proposals for the Revision of the Constitution of Nigeria (Cmd 6599) (London: HMSO, 1945).
[73] Toyin Falola and Bola Dauda, *Decolonizing Nigeria, 1945–1960: Politics, Power, and Personalities* (Austin: Pan-African University Press, 2017).
[74] Afigbo, "Background to Nigerian Federalism."
[75] Aderonke Majekodunmi, "Federalism in Nigeria: The Past, Current Peril and Future Hopes," *Journal of Policy and Development Studies* 289, no. 1850 (2015): 1–14.
[76] Richard Morrock, "Heritage of Strife: The Effects of Colonialists' 'Divide and Rule' Strategy upon the Colonized Peoples," *Science & Society* 37, no. 2 (1973): 129–151.

Conclusion

Previous chapters have examined the impact of nationalist leaders and movements, including political parties and trade unions, on the intensification of anticolonial nationalism in Nigeria. World War II was crucial for motivating educated elites and other Africans to demand inclusion in government administration, leading to the gradual transfer of power to Indigenous people. Constitutions became useful instruments for colonial administrators who sought to steer Nigeria's political trajectory.

In other respects, the evolution and development of federalism have been crucial for the former colony's political and constitutional histories. The heterogeneity of the territory formerly known as the Colony and Protectorate of Nigeria provided a sufficient motive for adopting a federal structure. Like Nigeria, federalism was largely the creation of the British in attempting to further specific policies. This chapter has shown how Nigeria's present-day federalist framework traces its roots back to the colonial period; the British and the Nigerian nationalists can be credited with institutionalizing the administrative concept. The path toward devolution was far from linear, and some constitutional tweaking and politicking were necessary for its ultimate adoption.

26

Regionalism and Ethnic Politics in the 1950s

A plethora of historical studies rightly posits that Nigeria was artificially created as a political state by the British aggregating a large number of polarized and diverse ethnolinguistic groups.[1] Diversity, fragmentation, and inequality were apparent among these groups from the beginning. Some large polities had expansive territories, remarkable military strongholds, and highly organized sociopolitical structures, but most groups were widely dispersed and had unique cultural traditions, linguistic variations, and decentralized sociopolitical structures. The region's inherent diversity made it almost impossible for the British to administer the territory it had targeted for imperialist economic and political control. Colonial Nigeria's political history began with Sir Frederick Lord Lugard's radical, frequently criticized decision to unify more than 300 ethnic groups into a single political entity: the Colony and Protectorate of Nigeria.[2]

The 1914 amalgamation of the Northern and Southern Protectorates of Nigeria is often credited as the single major act that unequivocally established the Nigerian political state.[3] However, scholars of Nigeria's political history have identified historical antecedents that proved equally relevant for the country's political development and the evolution of national identity. The creation of Nigeria as a political state began in 1861 when the transatlantic city of Lagos was annexed as a British colony.[4] In 1900, the Protectorate of Northern Nigeria and the Colony and Protectorate of Southern Nigeria was created; the latter was later divided into Western and Eastern provinces for easier administration.[5] The Colony and Protectorate of Southern Nigeria and the Protectorate of Northern Nigeria were amalgamated in 1914 following the

---

[1] Francis Z. L. Bacho and Mohammed S. Abdul-Kadir, "Artificial Creation of the State and Enduring Conflicts in Africa: Legacies of the 'Indirect Rule' Policy in the Northern Parts of Ghana and Nigeria," *Ghana Journal of Development Studies* 4, no. 1 (2007): 13–27.
[2] Lord Lugard, *The Dual Mandate in British Tropical Africa* (London: Frank Cass, 1965).
[3] Peter de Iongh, "Nigeria, Two Imperialists and their Creation," *History Today* 14 (1964): 835–843.
[4] Alan Burns, *History of Nigeria* (London: George Allen and Unwin Ltd., 1929), 95–128.
[5] Ian F. Nicolson, *The Administration of Nigeria, 1900–1960: Men, Methods and Myths* (Oxford: Clarendon Press, 1969).

Colonial Governor's decree.[6] The British viewed the country's amalgamation as a reasonable political decision, improving the administration of highly polarized and fragmented groups living in the area. The amalgamation gave birth to a new political state and made governance more convenient, but it quickly unleashed a sequence of national identity crises that were to plague the new colony's political developments in subsequent years.[7]

Previous chapters have examined the evolution and developments of nationalism and different nationalist agents in Nigeria's colonial development. The preceding chapter also touched on the evolution and impacts of ethnic nationalism in Nigerian politics. This chapter evaluates state formation and nation-building through the country's constitutional and political developments, especially the shifting centralization of governmental power and its impact on politics and nationalism in colonial Nigeria.

Regionalism and Ethnicity in Nigeria's Political and Constitutional History

Although regionalism and ethnicity are widely studied political concepts, garnering considerable attention in historical studies, they lack uniform holistic definitions. Some authors see the outcome of regionalism as producing "institutionalized practices,"[8] while also promoting "increasing population flows, multiple channels and complex social networks, spreading ideas and attitudes."[9] Ethnicity can create allegiance to one's ethnic group over a federation or state.[10] The concept of ethnicity may seem straightforward, but attempts to define it reveal the underlying complexities of both notions.[11] Regionalism and ethnicity can be understood in the context of Nigeria's political and constitutional histories, which describes the systemic division of governmental control where a central or federal government holds clearly

---

[6] Abdul Raufu Mustapha. *Ethnic Structure, Inequality and Governance of the Public Sector in Nigeria* (Geneva: United Nations Research Institute for Social Development, 2006).

[7] Terhemba Wuam and Victor Egwemi, *The 1914 Amalgamation and a Century of Nigerian Nationhood* (Lagos: Bahiti and Dalila Publishers, 2016).

[8] Peter J. Katzenstein and Takashi Shiraishi, eds., *Beyond Japan: The Dynamics of East Asian Regionalism* (Ithaca: Cornell University Press, 2006).

[9] Louise Fawcett, "Exploring Regional Domains: A Comparative History of Regionalism," *International Affairs* 80, no. 3 (2004): 429–446.

[10] Idowu William, "Ethnicity, Ethnicism and Citizenship: A Philosophical Reflection on the African Experience," *Journal of Social Sciences* 8, no. 1 (2004): 45–58.

[11] Wsevolod W. Isajiw, "Definition and Dimensions of Ethnicity: A Theoretical Framework," in *Challenges of Measuring an Ethnic World: Science, Politics and Reality: Proceedings of the Joint Canada–United States Conference on the Measurement of Ethnicity*, ed. Statistics Canada and US Bureau of the Census (Washington, DC: US Government Printing Office, 1993), 407–427.

defined authority and powers.[12] Subordinate units, called regions, also have clearly defined authority and powers.[13] Within this system, governmental authority is reinforced by the principle of noninterference. One of the best clarifications of ethnicity is provided by Nnoli:

> [Ethnicity can be regarded as a] social phenomenon associated with the identity of members of the largest possible competing communal groups (ethnic groups) seeking to protect and advance their interest in a political system. The relevant communal factor may be language, culture, race, religion and/or common history.[14]

From a certain point of view, both regionalism and ethnicity resulted from the political realities of precolonial and colonial Nigeria. Nnoli has observed that affiliation with specific ethnic identities has transcended the merely social to become a major political phenomenon over time. As Nigeria's political history indicates, ethnicity was originally a natural phenomenon. However, the institution of regionalism – and subsequent government structures based on federalism – were deliberate efforts by the British pursuing imperialist economic and political goals.[15] A single, colonial Nigeria was created from the deliberate fusion of multiple diverse groups, and its creation would fuel ethnic-based rivalries that had enduring implications for the country's constitutional and political developments.[16]

Ayatse and Iorhen observed that before the advent of colonialism, most of the individual ethnic groups within Nigeria comprised small autonomous villages and cities with populations ranging from a few hundred to thousands.[17] They all enjoyed their independence and were free to practice individual traditions and maintain independent sociopolitical systems. The incursion of the British and their need to impose a manageable administration system led to the introduction of regionalism, whose aftermath caused the gradual death of existing political institutions. Scholars investigating the origins and developments of regionalism and ethnicity in the context of the Nigerian experience have reached a consensus

---

[12] Olufemi Vaughan, "Ethno–Regionalism and the Origins of Federalism in Nigeria," in *Democracy and Prebendalism in Nigeria: Critical Interpretations*, ed. Wale Adebanwi and Ebenezar Obadare (New York: Palgrave Macmillan, 2013), 227–242.
[13] Louis J. Munoz, "Regionalism in Nigeria: The Transformation of Tradition," *The Politician* 52, no. 2 (1987): 317–341.
[14] Okwudiba Nnoli, *Ethnic Politics in Nigeria* (Enugu: Fourth Dimension Publishers, 1978), 5.
[15] Eme O. Awa, "Regionalism in Nigeria: A Study in Federalism," unpublished PhD dissertation, New York University, 1955.
[16] Wasiu M. Raheem, Oyewale I. Oyeleye, Margaret A. Adeniji, and Opeyemi C. Aladekoyi, "Regional Imbalances and Inequalities in Nigeria: Causes, Consequences and Remedies," *Research on Humanities and Social Sciences* 4, no. 18 (2014): 163–174.
[17] Felicia H. Ayatse and Isaac Iorhen Akuva, "The Origin and Development of Ethnic Politics and its Impacts on Post-Colonial Governance in Nigeria," *European Scientific Journal* 9, no. 17 (2013): 178–189.

regarding the colonial roots of both concepts. Ebegbulem notes that the history of ethnicity in Nigeria dates to the era of colonialism, specifically resulting from the "colonial transgression" of amalgamating the colony's southern and northern units in 1914.[18] The difficulties in aggregating multiple, polarized, and diverse ethnic groups were complicated by the indirect rule system that had been applied selectively to govern specific parts of Nigeria.[19]

The Northern and Southern regions of Nigeria were administered separately.[20] Indirect rule was applied in the Southern parts of the protectorate, using traditional rulers as intermediaries to serve the colonial administration. In the North, the Colonial Governor maintained direct oversight of public affairs. This arrangement allowed for a relatively peaceful and effective administration but would foster ethnocentrism in subsequent years.[21] Lord Lugard's administration divided the major ethnic groups in colonial Nigeria, which promoted inequalities. The administration's autocratic methods did not sit well with many people from different groups, especially in the South. The colonizers not only invented ideas of ethnicity through their forced amalgamation and administrative choices but also applied divisive policies that were calculated to segregate Nigeria's different regions. In the early years of Nigeria's formation as a state, during the colonial governorship of Lord Lugard, he promulgated colonial laws prohibiting non-indigenes of the Northern Protectorate – especially those affiliated with the Christian religion – from entering Northern territory. Lugard also prohibited individuals from possessing land outside their home regions, creating separate settlements, known as Sabon Gari, for non-indigene residents of the Northern Protectorate.[22] This segregation temporarily reduced the potential for ethnic crises but later undermined attempts at national integration sought by subsequent administrations.

Ethnic diversity characterized the Colony and Protectorate of Nigeria from its beginnings. Colonial policies introduced later, either motivated by the self-serving interests of colonialists or intending to promote unity among these multifaceted ethnic groups, only fanned the embers of mutual distrust. One of the major integration strategies devised by Nigeria's colonial administrators was the institution of federalism. Historians understand the concept as a system of government operating with constitutional divisions between a central government, which is usually more powerful, and its coordinating units. The coordinating units can be provinces, regions, states, or local governments. Federalism

---

[18] Joseph C. Ebegbulem, "Ethnic Politics and Conflicts in Nigeria: Theoretical Perspective," *Khazar Journal of Humanities and Social Sciences* 14, no. 3 (2011): 76–91.
[19] James S. Coleman, *Nigeria: Background to Nationalism* (Berkeley: University of California Press, 1958).
[20] Obaro Ikime, "Reconsidering Indirect Rule: The Nigerian Example," *Journal of the Historical Society of Nigeria* 4, no. 3 (1968): 421–438.
[21] Ebegbulem, "Ethnic politics and conflicts in Nigeria," 81.
[22] Ebegbulem, "Ethnic politics and conflicts in Nigeria," 82.

was introduced to Nigeria's political history by the Lyttleton Constitution of 1954,[23] although a variant known as regionalism was introduced earlier. In the 1930s, regionalism was implemented under the colonial administration of Bernard Bourdillon and his successor, Arthur Richards.[24]

Bourdillon felt that the administrative style of his predecessor, Lord Lugard, would not unify Nigeria's fragmented Colony and Protectorate after years of compartmentalization across Northern and Southern political lines. Bourdillon began drafting a constitution that would institute federalism in Nigeria, but he was unable to complete it before he left office in 1943. His successor, Arthur Richards, promulgated the final draft of the constitution in 1946 and named it after himself. One relic from the 1946 Richards Constitution was the compartmentalization of Nigeria, organized into Northern, Eastern, and Western regions (originally called "provinces").[25] Richards believed that the constitution would fashion out a "quasi-federal structure" for the colony of Nigeria. Although the structure was embryonic, it was hoped that it could promote national unity while preserving the heterogeneity and diversity of colonial Nigeria's population.[26]

Historians and scholars of Nigeria's constitutional history consider the Richards Constitution's enactment a landmark event for the country's political and constitutional development. Coleman describes the institution of regionalism as the most agreeable feature of the 1946 Constitution.[27] There had previously been some disagreement among the colony's political actors regarding the most practicable form of federalism and the division of powers. However, a compromise had been reached by the time of the constitution's promulgation as all actors recognized the value of participating in national affairs through the mechanisms described in the new constitution.[28]

The enactment of the Richards Constitution was a major political accomplishment, eliciting trust and support from political elites. During Governor Richards' administration, the colony had been divided along ideological lines. Regional separatists advocated partitioning the country into three fully autonomous regions, and staunch federalists declared that the country could only survive with a strong federal structure governing states that were organized

---

[23] M. M. Fadakinte and M. Abdulkareem, "The Travails of Nigerian Federalism 1951–1999: A Federation in Crisis of Constitutional Engineering," *African Journal of Political Science and International Relations* 15, no. 1 (2021): 19–27.

[24] Charas Madu Tella, Ahmed Wali Doho, and Aliyu Bapeto, "The Evolution, Development and Practice of Federalism in Nigeria," *Public Policy and Administration Review* 2, no. 4 (2014): 51–66.

[25] J. Flint, "Governor versus Colonial Office: An Anatomy of the Richards Constitution for Nigeria, 1939 to 1945," *Historical Papers* 16, no. 1 (1981): 124–143.

[26] Wale Adebanwi, "Contesting Multiculturalism: Ethno–regionalism and Contending Forms of Nationalism in Late Colonial Nigeria," *Commonwealth & Comparative Politics* 56, no. 1 (2018): 40–64.

[27] Coleman, *Nigeria: Background to Nationalism*.

[28] Coleman, *Nigeria: Background to Nationalism*, 276.

along ethnic lines. Others argued for secession because they considered the country's unification to be impossible. Richards identified the leaders and political parties that were most influential within these groups and leveraged the opportunity to score political points by compromising between these ideologies.

Despite the high hopes engendered by the enactment of the Richards Constitution, it failed miserably in terms of either achieving unification or promoting diversity. Colonial Nigeria's partitioning into three regions only promoted ethnic loyalty and fostered discord. The constitution was heavily criticized for implementing a poor and ineffective form of federalism. Regional assemblies were created and populated through local elections, but their roles were merely advisory. The Governor retained veto powers, and all executive administration was centralized within the office of the colonial Governor and his cabinet of European ministers.[29]

The failure of the Richards Constitution warranted its repeal in 1951, to be replaced by the Macpherson Constitution. The new constitution sought to strengthen the colony's federal structure by creating a central legislative house called the House of Representatives and vesting regional assemblies with law-making authority. The 1950s saw continuous political and constitutional improvements, reflected in the enactments of the 1951 Macpherson Constitution, the 1954 Lyttleton Constitution, and the 1959 Independence Constitution.[30] However, the country's political battles were tainted by ethnic allegiances, regional discord, and the failure of nationalist institutions in this final decade of its colonial history. These events can be traced to the ill-thought-out adoption of regionalism and the promotion of ethnic politics and ethnic nationalism among political elites.

Regionalism, Ethnic Politics, and Ethnic Nationalism in the 1950s

Party politics steered the trajectory of nationalism in colonial Nigeria, which had a significant impact on the attainment of independence.[31] The political elites who led these parties were not only conscious of the need for the country's timely decolonization, they also experienced the failures of the British indirect rule system. They had seen the impracticability of proper representation of Nigeria's Indigenous people, the self-serving nature of the colonial administration, and the accompanying British attitudes. The contributions of political elites and their parties, especially those from the second generation, have been lauded in a breadth of historical studies and works of

---

[29] Kalu Ezera, *Constitutional Developments in Nigeria* (Ibadan: University Press, 1960).
[30] Ezera, *Constitutional Developments in Nigeria*.
[31] Ademola E. Oluniyi, "Regionalism, Ideology Crises, Party Affiliation and Future of Democracy in Nigeria," *Afro Asian Journal of Social Sciences* 5, no. 5 (2014): 1–20.

literature.[32] Despite the praise they have received from many disciplines studying Nigeria's political and constitutional developments, colonial Nigeria's political parties are also linked with the emergence of ethnic politics and ethnic nationalism. These two forces have substantially damaged Nigeria's social fiber as a nation.

At the conceptual level, ethnic politics and ethnic nationalism are morally neutral phenomena. Scholars often view ethnicity as a social construct that promotes differentiation between groups of people due to their ethnic origins. This can unleash a flood of social, religious, and political conflicts,[33] but it has been suggested that ethnicity is not always explainable or visible in the practice of ethnic politics.[34] Olayode posits that ethnic politics manifest where political actors fashion a system of practices modeled on the sociocultural phenomenon of ethnicity within a country or state.[35] Other authors have observed that ethnic politics is often used by political parties to accord some degree of relevance to their activities. Adetiba notes that politicians and political parties find ethnic politics to be a useful device for garnering relevance, and, in Nigeria, ethnicity has become central to politics: "it is either you belong to the mainstream of ethnic politics or not without which one may not likely be politically relevant."[36]

Ethnic politics broadly defines the nature of political activities in any diverse polity, encapsulating a wide range of practices, tactics, and methods adopted in political systems. Ethnic nationalism is a form of nationalism that promotes national consciousness based on ethnic identity.[37] The term focuses on the objectives of political parties and actors promoting national consciousness among the masses, including how they actualize their objectives. As a corollary to ethnic politics, ethnic nationalism extends the ethnicity-based affordances of identity and relevance from political actors to ordinary citizens. Ethnic nationalism is often a useful political device for promoting a sense of "belongingness" between people of the same ethnic group, recognizing diversity in a heterogeneous society.[38] In other cases, especially where feelings of mutual

---

[32] Kia Bariledum and S. Vurasi Serebe, "Political Elites and the Challenges of National Development: The Nigeria Experience," *European Scientific Journal* 9, no. 31 (2013): 161–172.

[33] Toyin Cotties Adetiba, "Dynamics of Ethnic Politics in Nigeria: An Impediment to its Political System," *Journal of Economics and Behavioral Studies* 11, no. 2 (2019): 132–144.

[34] Bruce J. Berman, "Ethnicity, Patronage and the African State: The Politics of Uncivil Nationalism," *African Affairs* 97, no. 388 (1998): 305–341.

[35] Kehinde Olayode, "Beyond Intractability: Ethnic Identity and Political Conflicts in Africa," *International Journal of Humanities and Social Science* 6, no. 6 (2016): 242–248.

[36] Adetiba, "Dynamics of Ethnic Politics in Nigeria," 133.

[37] Bethwell A. Ogot, *Ethnicity, Nationalism, and Democracy in Africa* (Kenya: Institute of Research and Postgraduate Studies, Maseno University College, 1996).

[38] For instance, Loring M. Danforth, *The Macedonian Conflict: Ethnic Nationalism in a Transnational World* (Princeton: Princeton University Press, 1995).

distrust and discord persist between ethnic groups, ethnic nationalism may fan the embers of ethnic loyalty and disunity to incite ethnic violence and a range of political crises.[39]

A breadth of historical studies has examined the roots of ethnic violence and conflicts that have disrupted the Nigerian political system.[40] Two types of conflicts are not naturally related, but they are continually united in the Nigerian political landscape: Ethnic violence is perpetuated by ethnic groups that oppose each other, and political conflicts result from disagreements with major decisions made by political systems or governments within nations.[41] Political violence can arise from many different crises, but the Nigerian political system regularly experiences political violence developing from ethnic crises.

Uwaifo notes that power struggles between political actors may intensify ethnicity and ethnic politics in any ethnically diverse state and, unless these struggles are addressed, they can lead to ethnic and political crises. He has also noted that resource allocation and structural imbalances are major drivers of ethnic conflict in Nigeria. The country's political parties are widely recognized as promoting discord and political conflicts throughout the country's history, including disputes rooted in ethnic politics.[42] The Nigerian state's current political climate has become too complicated to attribute major political challenges to one or two factors. There are many reasons for the state's weakness, including corruption, a lack of transparency, poor electoral practices, and feeble institutions.[43] These factors directly affect political development and other aspects of national growth. However, ethnic politics was a principal challenge for nation-building during the colonial period of Nigeria's history.

Most African colonies were heterogeneous, with abundant ethnolinguistic groups, and the nationality debate became an imperative issue during the colonial era. In Nigeria, not long after the amalgamation of the Southern and Northern Protectorates, concerns were raised over the ability to foster unity among the new colony's many ethnic groups. Sklar has recorded how political thinkers, historians, and other scholars took one of two approaches to resolve

---

[39] Bogdan D. Denitch, *Ethnic Nationalism: The Tragic Death of Yugoslavia* (Minneapolis: University of Minnesota Press, 1994).

[40] Ray Ikechukwu Jacob, "A Historical Survey of Ethnic Conflict in Nigeria," *Asian Social Science* 8, no. 4 (2012):13–29.

[41] Godwin A. Vaaseh and Omolere M. Ehinmore, "Ethnic Politics and Conflicts in Nigeria's First Republic: The Misuse of Native Administrative Police Forces (NAPFS) and the Tiv Riots of Central Nigeria, 1960–1964," *Canadian Social Science* 7, no. 3 (2011): 214–222.

[42] Samuel Osaretin Uwaifo, "Ethnicity and Development of Political Parties in Nigeria," *Ethnicity* 28 (2016): 1–9.

[43] Abiodun Ajayi and Oluwafunminiyi Raheem, "The Deepening Crisis of Leadership and Accountability in Nigeria, 1999–2019," *Orirun: UNIOSUN Journal of African Studies* 2, no. 2 (2020): 1–26.

the debate over national identity.[44] Whether ethnolinguistic identity was to be the fundamental basis of nationality under the country's recognized legal and political foundations or that identity was to be fashioned from federal or national states was a major subject of discussion. The colonial administration eventually responded to the need for effective structures to promote national integration through constitutional developments in the 1940s and 1950s, but the preindependence constitutions failed to achieve national integration. Instead, the political structures established under those constitutions only promoted ethnic politics, which was an obstacle to national integration and nation-building.

Ethnic politics and ethnic nationalism developed with encouragement from political elites, their parties, and other political actors in colonial Nigeria. The extant literature has raised suspicion about the self-serving attitudes of these groups, identifying how their ideologies and acts encouraged ethnic politics during the colonial period. The second generation of political parties was based on regions, decisively suppressing other groups that could threaten their prominence within their territory. The indirect rule system of colonial administrators and their hierarchical government were primarily responsible for the rise of ethnicity in Nigeria, but political parties and their elites recognized how they could profit from ethnic division. They took advantage of various crises to solidify their political status, which promoted ethnic politics.

Ideologically, colonial Nigeria's three regions diverged in the 1950s. Each region's dominant political ideology was formed by its ruling political party: the three dominant parties were the National Council of Nigerian Citizens, the Action Group, and the Northern Peoples' Congress.[45] Most historians and scholars recognize that the political trajectory of colonial Nigeria hinged on the ethnicity-focused objectives, activities, and ideologies of these three parties,[46] which promoted ethnic politics in the country. The Action Group and the Northern Peoples' Congress promoted the interests of the Western and Northern regions, respectively.[47] They pursued ethno-nationalistic objectives, focused on improving the socioeconomic lives of people within their regions, and advocated government structures and decolonization timetables that supported those goals. These parties increased the prevalence of ethnic politics

---

[44] Richard Sklar, "Unity or Regionalism: The Nationalities Question," in *Crafting the New Nigeria: Confronting the Challenges*, ed. Robert I. Rotberg (Boulder: Lynne Rienner Publishers, 2004), 39–59.

[45] O. E. Udofia, "Nigerian Political Parties: Their Role in Modernizing the Political System, 1920–1966," *Journal of Black Studies* 11, no. 4 (1981): 435–447.

[46] Adeleke Olumide Ogunnoiki, "Political Parties, Ideology and the Nigerian State," International Journal of Advanced Academic Research 4, no. 12 (2018): 114–150.

[47] Nathaniel Danjibo and Kelvin Ashindorbe, "The Evolution and Pattern of Political Party Formation and the Search for National Integration in Nigeria," *Brazilian Journal of African Studies* 3, no. 5 (2018): 85–100.

to potentially dangerous levels, asserting exclusive political control within the regions they dominated. This offered self-serving benefits to political personalities and parties, allaying fears of marginalization among residents, which were important for ensuring the perpetuity of ethnic politics in colonial Nigeria and the early years of the postcolonial period. Ultimately, a critical review of political and constitutional developments in the country has shown that regionalism and the foregrounding of ethnic nationalism are the forms of nationalism that are most likely to safeguard the interests of the general public.

The concepts of regionalism and ethnic nationalism in preindependence Nigeria are complex. They promoted specific cultural and political identities for each region but also harnessed cultural and political identities to liberate Nigeria. During a time marked by heated calls for self-rule, regionalism gave rise to ethnic consciousness. It also brought growing ethnic mistrust that derailed early discussions about self-rule. The North contained a large population that was mostly uneducated. Northern leaders enjoyed a certain prestige under British colonialism and were especially concerned about the implications of a new country's emergence. This was evident in separate, ethnicity-based demands for better living conditions in Nigeria. The political forces of ethnic nationalism fueled strong resistance to colonial paternalism; rivalry and contention existed between the "Big Three" politicians: Obafemi Awolowo, Nnamdi Azikiwe, and Ahmadu Bello.

Obafemi Awolowo identified with Yoruba nationalism and propagated ethnolinguistic autonomy in establishing governmental institutions, which he believed would strengthen the Yoruba's influence over emerging governmental powers. Azikiwe identified with Igbo nationalism and rejected Awolowo's proposals; instead, he advocated creating a centralized Nigeria composed of eight protectorates. His arguments sought to diminish the potential for marginalization due to any region gaining dominance over the others. Ahmadu Bello identified with Hausa/Fulani nationalism and argued for the indispensability of traditional institutions within the colonial administration. These institutions would retain the existing authority that Northern leaders held over their subjects. Bello's perspective also focused on the nationality question raised by Awolowo and Azikiwe.[48] The three major politicians failed to consider a Nigerian nationality that could supersede ethnic identities. At this point, the widespread prevalence of divisive ethnonationalist sentiments threatened the future of Nigeria. Ethnic nationalism became a stumbling block halting Nigeria's socioeconomic and political growth and preventing the actualization of national consciousness among the people.[49]

---

[48] Robert L. Sklar, *Nigerian Political Parties: Power in an Emergent African Nation* (Princeton: Princeton University Press, 2015).

[49] Jacob F. A. Ajayi, "The National Question in Nigeria in Historical Perspective." Being excerpts of lecture delivered at the fifth *Guardian* Lecture, November 1992.

The earliest forms of ethnonationalism were movements to curtail British dominance over Nigerians' political and economic affairs. However, colonial decisions had allowed ethnic and regional differences to determine the execution of social, political, and economic policies – this fostered ethnoregional social, political, and educational challenges that became important components of ethnoregional identities. Colonial policies reinforced differences between the three regions, defining their relationships as a constant series of misunderstandings with each other. Colonial policies that favored population size allowed the North to assert political power on a national scale because the Northern region held 55 percent of the total population during the colonial period. These policies did little to address the negative ethnoregionalism that stoked fears of ethnic and regional domination. The Western and Eastern regions saw the North's political authority as a threat to its political hegemony.

Meanwhile, the Western and Eastern regions held an educational advantage that allowed them to seize greater numbers of employment opportunities in governmental institutions. This led the North to fear that other regions would apply their educational advantage to control government institutions. Northern leaders promoted a Northern identity, possibly as an attempt to retain political power. In response, Southern leaders advanced Southern identities. Ethnic insecurities impaired the actualization of Nigeria's independence, with a resultant failure to meet the need for an ardent national consciousness that could pursue such a goal.[50]

Minority Issues

Colonial Nigeria's political history was shaped by a series of conflicts, agitations, and deep-seated feelings of marginalization experienced by minority ethnic groups – the groups that held less territory and had smaller populations.[51] Obayemi has referred to them as "mini states," identified by sociologists who stratified Nigeria's ethnic groups based on population size.[52] This work recognized the Hausa/Fulani, Yoruba, and Igbo as major ethnic groups or megastates, and hundreds of other ethnic groups were classified as minorities. Historical evidence suggests that public discourse emphasizing these perceived differences and the promotion of ethnicity through the colonial government's regional structures generated the feelings of marginalization experienced by

---

[50] Uduma Oji Uduma, "The Challenges of Ethnonationalism for the Nigerian State," *Journal of African Studies and Development* 5, no. 3 (2013): 33–40.

[51] Paul Ilesanmi Akanmidu, "The British's Contact with Nigeria's Peoples, Amalgamation and the Question of Minority Agitation, 1914–1999," *Africology: Journal of Pan African Studies* 12, no. 1 (2018): 421–439.

[52] Ade Obayemi, "States and Peoples of the Niger–Benue Confluence Area," in *Groundwork of Nigerian History*, ed. Obaro Ikime (Ibadan: Heinemann Educational Books, 1980), 186.

most of colonial Nigeria's minority groups. Major ethnic groups seized the opportunity to wield greater power by embracing ethnic politics.

Scholars and historians have identified the colonial administration as the source of ethnic mistrust, feelings of marginalization, and agitations from minority groups in the colonial period, and these tensions have extended into present-day Nigeria. Ogbu notes that minority status is a social and conceptual construct that only finds expression in the context of a state; only when a group encounters a larger group within the same polity can the former be perceived as a minority.[53]

Before colonialism, most of Nigeria's ethnic groups had contact with each other – major in some instances, but minimal for the most part.[54] The main mega-states established during this period were the Oyo and Benin empires and the Sokoto/Kano emirates. When the British agglomerated more than 350 culturally and linguistically differentiated ethnic groups in 1914, creating the so-called Nigerian state, they rapidly brought these groups into closer contact and created the concept of minority status. Akanmidu has observed that the birth of minority status, and the rise of the minority question, were aided by the consciousness of structural and political fragmentation within the country and the creation of three major ethnic groups.[55] This resulted in perceived and actual marginalization, and it was to "constitute a clog in the wheel of the socio-economic and political developments of the Nigerian state."[56]

A wealth of historical studies has examined how the advent of colonialism and the colonial administration fostered marginalization and agitation among minority ethnic groups in colonial Nigeria. These studies point to the ill-timed and ill-conceived regional structure employed by the colony for the majority of the colonial period. Rindap and Mari have noted that the core of the minority question rests on disenchantment with the colonial administration's regional structure.[57] The British partitioned the country across geopolitical regions in a process that started with the 1914 amalgamation. The country was originally divided along Northern and Southern lines, and would later be partitioned into Northern, Eastern, and Western regions following the 1946 adoption of the Richards Constitution, which raised ethnic tensions. Efforts to remedy these mishaps with the 1951 Macpherson Constitution and the 1954 Lyttleton Constitution had negligible impact. Marginalization and minority agitation

---

[53] John U. Ogbu, "Research Currents: Cultural–Ecological Influences on Minority School Learning," *Language Arts* 62, no. 8 (1985): 860–869.
[54] Okpeh O. Okpeh, "Patterns and Dynamics of Inter-Group Relations in Nigeria, 1800–1900 AD," *Journal of the Historical Society of Nigeria* 17 (2007/2008): 123–137.
[55] Akanmidu, "The British's Contact with Nigeria's Peoples."
[56] Akanmidu, "The British's Contact with Nigeria's Peoples."
[57] Manko Rose Rindap and I. M. A. Mari, "Ethnic Minorities and the Nigerian State," *Afrrev Ijah: An International Journal of Arts and Humanities* 3, no. 3 (2014): 89–101.

remained in Nigeria's political history from the colonial period to the post-independence era.[58]

Akanmidu has observed that the country's division across three regions, enabling dominance by the Hausa/Fulani, Yoruba, and Igbo – the three major ethnic groups – led to the rise of ethnic consciousness in the Northern and Eastern regions. The Western region dealt with relatively little marginalization because people in the region were predominantly Yoruba and were familiar with centralized systems that dated back to precolonial times. Although the previous acceptance of Hausa/Fulani hegemony encouraged most of the non-Hausa and non-Fulani groups in the North to accept this development, perceptions of marginalization remained in the Middle-Belt areas of Ilorin and Kabba. These territories had been designated as part of the Northern region, despite their cultural origins among the Yoruba of the Western region.[59] Feelings of marginalization were most pronounced in the Eastern region as several groups had a substantial presence, but colonizers arbitrarily placed the Igbos on a higher pedestal. Ongoing feelings of marginalization crystallized into disruptive agitations and other forms of ethnic and political crises in the country. The enduring impact is visible to the present day.[60]

Nigeria's political history, from the early stages of colonialism to the present day, includes a series of ethnic agitations and conflicts emerging from the marginalization of ethnic groups. Usuanlele and Ibhawoh, in reviewing the plight of the minorities in Nigeria, affirm that ethnic tensions developed between Nigeria's major and minor ethnic groups.[61] Regionalization and the development of ethnicity-based political parties encouraged the major groups to develop national or regional politics that protected their interests and excluded the minority.[62] In the rare instances when minority groups had representatives in the legislative house, the dominance of major groups quickly overwhelmed their arguments. Minority groups felt excluded from nation-building, denied their chance to enjoy the "national cake."

The most common reason for ethnic violence is the unequal distribution of resources. Most extant works of literature show that unresolved minority issues in colonial Nigeria slowed the pace of decolonization and fostered deep-rooted

---

[58] Ugbana Ukpo, *Ethnic Minority Problems in Nigerian Politics* (Stockholm: LiberTryck AB, 1977).

[59] V. Egwemi, "The Amalgamation of 1914 and the North–South Divide in Nigeria: Some Comments on Contemporary Manifestation," in *Colonialism and the Transition to Modernity in Africa*, ed. Joseph Mangut (Lapai: Ibb University, 2011).

[60] Akanmidu, "The British's Contact with Nigeria's Peoples," 431.

[61] Uyilawa Usuanlele and Bonny Ibhawoh, "Introduction: Minorities and the National Question in Nigeria," in *Minority Rights and the National Question in Nigeria*, ed. Uyilawa Usuanlele and Bonny Ibhawoh (Cham: Palgrave Macmillan, 2017), 1–14.

[62] Nereus I. Nwosu and Johnson O. Olaniyi, "Colonialism and the Emergence of Party Politics in Nigeria," *Transafrican Journal of History* 25 (1996): 20–28.

feelings of ethnic mistrust that led the minority groups to withdraw from the process. This impeded efforts to overcome their common foe: the colonizers.[63] Minority agitations were expressed through minority-focused nationalist movements. Akanmidu has remarked that the festering feelings of marginalization among minority ethnic groups led to the emergence of minority movements in Nigeria's political system.[64] During the 1950s, the three most popular movements were the Calabar–Ogoja River State Movement in the East, the Benin–Delta State Movement and the Midwest in the West, and the Middle-Belt Movement in the North. These organizations intensified their agitations over the years, and later provoked action from the colonial administration.[65]

The first major attempt to address colonial Nigeria's minority issues was made by its last British Colonial Governor, Sir James Wilson Robertson, in 1957. Robertson established the Willinks Minorities Commission to examine the plight of the colony's minority ethnic groups and to propose practical solutions.[66] The commission, headed by Sir Henry Willink, identified two major causes of marginalization: the victimization of the minority groups by the dominant political groups, and the regional structure's tendency to brush aside the interests of the minority. The Commission recommended the inclusion of a Bill of Rights to address minority concerns, along with fundamental objectives of national integration in the subsequent constitution. This was a change from state creation, which was the source of minority grievances at the time.[67]

The outbreak of ethnic conflict undermined colonial Nigeria's attempts at national integration for different groups and regions. The colonial administration eventually rose to the occasion, establishing the Willinks Commission, but no significant improvements were made to address minority concerns. Neither the inclusion of fundamental human rights in the 1959 Constitution nor the attainment of independence in the following year could resolve them. Minority concerns and their reactive agitations remain prevalent in present-day Nigeria, especially in the Niger Delta region.[68] These groups have articulated objectives that include political inclusion and the protection of their socioeconomic interests. The colonial administration or the Willinks administration could possibly have addressed the most debilitating political challenges confronting present-day Nigeria if they had been able to read the signals.

---

[63] Uyilawa Usuanlele and Bonny Ibhawoh, "Introduction: Minorities and the National Question in Nigeria," in *Minority Rights and the National Question in Nigeria*, ed. Uyilawa Usuanlele and Bonny Ibhawoh (Cham, Switzerland: Palgrave Macmillan, 2017).
[64] Akanmidu, "The British's Contact with Nigeria's Peoples."
[65] Akanmidu, "The British's Contact with Nigeria's Peoples," 432.
[66] Lexington Izuagie, "The Willink Minority Commission and Minority Rights in Nigeria," *EJOTMAS: Ekpoma Journal of Theatre and Media Arts* 5, no. 1–2 (2015): 206–223.
[67] Usuanlele and Ibhawoh, "Minorities and the National Question in Nigeria," 7
[68] Eghosa E. Osaghae, "The Ogini Uprising: Oil Politics, Minority Agitation and the Future of the Nigerian State," *African Affairs* 94 (1995): 325–344.

The Impacts of Regionalism and Ethnic Politics on Anticolonial Nationalism and Political Development

Diverse narratives explore anticolonialism in preindependence Nigeria, and, although each narrative is distinctive, they can fail to capture the imprints of regionalism and ethnic nationalism in Nigeria's discussions of anticolonialism.[69] Nationalist leaders, political parties, mass media, and trade unions were instrumental in the evolution of anticolonial nationalism and Nigeria's eventual attainment of independence. External events, such as the outbreak of World War I, and other factors, including the regional structure of governmental machinery during the later period of colonialism, were also influential. Most political thinkers, historians, and general critics of Nigeria's political system accept that adopting regionalism and its aftermath and the rise of ethnic politics has produced largely negative effects. This popular perspective is essential for this chapter's argument, but it remains important to adopt a holistic and critical approach to regionalism, ethnic politics, and their effects on the country's political developments.

Although the notion of ethnic politics is not inherently perilous, it can easily be used by political actors to pursue self-serving goals. Those goals often negatively affect a country's development, and this is the distasteful reality of colonial Nigeria's political history. Political parties and political leaders in the later period of colonialism have spent decades pursuing ethnicity-oriented policies. A wealth of historical studies has described how the three major second-generation political parties did not always maintain constructive relationships. Their preference for ethnicity-based nationalism, and the regionalism that strengthened their promotion of local interests, prevented the total unification of Nigeria. Instead, it led to a breakup of the entire country based on political affiliation and geopolitical regions. This only intensified divisions based on ethnicity, limiting the pursuit of nationalism and the decolonization objectives.[70]

Babangida has observed that ethnicity is the major cause of violence in Nigeria. It also facilitates other negative events, wasting enormous quantities of human and material resources that could have improved the lives of citizens.[71] Perpetual threats to life and property encourage investors to withdraw from markets, which harms economic growth. These harsh outcomes are evident in the political, social, and economic aspects of national development in present-day Nigeria.

Ethnic violence and its aftermath can be traced to the ethnicity-based nationalism and politics of the 1950s.[72] In 1953, Anthony Enahoro of the Action Group

---

[69] Yahaya Yakubu, "Ethnicity and Nationalism in Nigeria: The Paradox of Dual Identities," *International Journal of Recent Innovations in Academic Research* 3, no. 2 (2019): 25–29.
[70] Uwaifo, "Ethnicity and Development of Political Parties in Nigeria," 6.
[71] Ibrahim Babangida, "Ethnic Nationalities and Nigeria State." Excerpts from a Lecture delivered at NIPSS, Kuru, Jos, Plateau State, 2002.
[72] Adeleke Adegbami and Charles I. Uche, "Ethnicity and Ethnic Politics: An Impediment to Political Development in Nigeria," *Public Administration Research* 4, no. 1 (2015): 59.

and a representative for the Western Region in the House of Representatives made a motion for Nigeria to attain self-government by 1956. In response, the leadership of the Northern Peoples' Congress mobilized their supporters against the initiative. They felt that the immediate decolonization of Nigeria would allow the better-educated Eastern and Western political elite to monopolize the machinery of government. Northern protests developed into the Kano Riots of 1953.[73] The riots only lasted for four days, but their outcome included the death of forty-six Nigerians, the breakdown of the 1951 Macpherson Constitution, and an alliance between the two southern regions to oppose the North.[74]

Ethnic politics have not served Nigeria's best interests. Nationalist leaders and political parties applied them to pursue their self-serving interests and to the detriment of the entire country's political system, but a critical review of the evolution and development of Nigeria's political parties suggests that they failed to serve even those groups. The adoption of ethnic politics, at various times, has damaged the reputation of individual politicians and dissolved entire political parties. Obafemi Awolowo and Ahmadu Bello, who advocated ethnic nationalism and led regionally oriented political parties, were described by various critics as "tribalistic."[75] Other political parties completely collapsed when their leaders were caught up in ethnic rivalries. A classic example can be found in the first generation of political parties when the leadership of the National Youth Movement failed to acknowledge Samuel Akinsanya as the genuine winner of an intraparty election. He was denied the presidency of the party because he was an Ijebu Yoruba, and the dispute was a catalyst for the eventual collapse of the party in the 1940s.[76]

The colonial promotion of regionalism attempted to provide equal representation among ethnic groups. This policy failed to unify ethnicities within regions, and political leaders failed to recognize how they were being manipulated by the colonizers, leading to the emergence of minority ethnonationalism. Minority groups advocated cooperation with dominant ethnic parties within regions to allay their fears of marginalization. Even with these developments, there was no assurance that minority groups were willing to be subsumed by other ethnic groups. Instead, they orchestrated plans to ally with other minority ethnic groups, attempting to influence regional powers through threats of secession. The mistrust among ethnic groups established an unfortunate legacy of interethnic rivalry in Nigeria. Nationalist movements during this period were affected by ethnic chauvinism.[77]

---

[73] Isaac O. Albert, "Urban Violence in Africa: Violence in Metropolitan Kano: A Historical Perspective," in *Urban Violence in Africa: Pilot Studies (South Africa, Côte-d'Ivoire, Nigeria)*, ed. Eghosa E. Osaghae (Ibadan: IFRA-Nigeria, 1994).

[74] Isaac Olawale, *Inter-ethnic Relations in a Nigerian City: A Historical Perspective of the Hausa-Igbo Conflicts in Kano 1953-1991* (Ibadan: IFRA-Nigeria, 1993).

[75] Iyanda Kamoru Ahmed and Abubakar Umar, "Nationalists in Nigeria from 1914-1960," *International Journal of Social Sciences and Management Review* 2, no. 5 (2019): 1-12.

[76] Coleman, "Nigeria: Background to Nationalism."

[77] Uduma Oji Uduma, "The Challenges of Ethnonationalism for the Nigerian State," *Journal of African Studies and Development* 5, no. 3 (2013): 33-40.

Fortunately, regionalism and ethnic nationalism paved the way for the colonial administration's collapse. Despite their misgivings, the ethnic groups were united behind the demand for self-rule, regardless of its format. These groups revolted against colonial policies that did nothing to alleviate their poor living conditions. The Northern and the Southern protectorates were united in their goal to permanently end the segregationist attitude of colonialists in the civil service and the legislature. Despite the seeming imbalance in political authority and educational advantages between the two protectorates, they both recognized that their people were treated as inferiors. Northern and Southern groups eventually decided that their primary focus should be independent self-governance that would allow them to resolve their difficulties with each other.[78]

Regionalization brought political parties that were based on ethnicity. The Western region had the Action Group (AG), spearheaded by Obafemi Awolowo; the Eastern Region had the National Council of Nigeria and Cameroons (NCNC), led by Nnamdi Azikiwe; and the Northern region had the Northern People's Congress (NPC), led by Ahmadu Bello and his protégé, Abubakar Tafawa Balewa as shown in Figures 26.1 and 26.2. These groups jostled for a majority of legislative seats to attain ethnic dominance. Political parties initially failed to answer the question of collective nationality, but they later embraced the idea of an overall national consciousness. Leaders acknowledged that internal competition would only perpetuate their servitude, for everyone needed to articulate the belief that they were all united as Nigerians, regardless of their ethnicity. Leading newspapers, which were regionally based and owned by political parties, propagated this belief. It was further affirmed by former British colonies, such as India, that had overcome internal rivalries to attain considerable social, political, and economic growth after independence. The unexpected solidarity among these ethnic groups offset previous arguments and arrangements based on ethnicity. This landmark development addressed imbalances that had been a major reason for promoting ethnic consciousness over national consciousness.[79] The collective struggle of the three regional blocs was major progress toward Nigerian decolonization, which could be seen in their national emphasis on education and overall development – ethnic nationalism can be viewed as the basis for national integration.

The political representation of Nigerians was inadequate in the country's legislature because most of the legislators were British. These British legislators had always supported the draconian policies of the colonialists, ignoring the real issues that affected native residents. This situation encouraged

---

[78] Vaughan, "Ethno–Regionalism and the Origins."
[79] Kelechi C. Ubaku, Chikezie A. Emeh, and Chinenye N. Anyikwa, "Impact of Nationalist Movement on the Actualization of Nigerian Independence, 1914–1960," *International Journal of History and Philosophical Research* 2, no. 1 (2014): 54–67.

Figure 26.1 Abubakar Tafawa Balewa, Northern Nigerian politician, legislator, founder of the Northern People's Party, and the first and only Prime Minister of Nigeria at independence. He was murdered in a bloody coup in 1964.

Figure 26.2 Renowned nationalists, politicians, and premiers of Nigeria's Eastern, Northern, and Western regions: Dr. Nnamdi Azikiwe, Sir Ahmadu Bello and Chief Obafemi Awolowo. Their respective roles in the struggle for independence continue to shape and impact modern Nigeria's polity.

a national movement, involving every ethnic group, to include Nigerians in national affairs. There was no clear dominance among ethnic groups, and the regionalization policy demonstrated that they would be incapable of attaining independence without a national identity. Existing frameworks for ethnic nationalism allowed individuals to translate their ethnic loyalty into national patriotism. This assisted the nationalists in fighting for political independence.[80]

[80] Paul Oluwatosin Bello, "Ethnic Nationalism and Conflicts in Africa: Lessons from Nigeria," *Bangladesh Sociological Society* 15, no. 1 (2018): 86.

The eventual convergence of ethnic groups facilitated the establishment of political parties. The emergence of the free press created media outlets such as the *Lagos Pilot*, the *Lagos Daily*, and a host of others. During the colonial administration, regionalism and ethnic nationalism led initiatives for major constitutional changes. Colonial constitutions faced strong resistance that demanded adequate representation for Nigerians, fighting against being marginalized in their own spaces. Nationalist leaders worked to create a Nigerian nation by advocating for and implementing policies that could be described as ethnically balanced to unify diverse Nigerian citizens. These policies would not solve the problems they intended to address, but they were quite useful for attaining independence.[81]

Major ethnic regions formed the basis for political, administrative, and economic policies in Nigeria, and demanded concessions and, ultimately, independence from the colonial government. The British acquiesced to this demand and slowly paved the way for independence in Nigeria. Part of this effort saw Princess Alexandra Kent as shown in Figures 26.3 and 26.4, representative of Queen Elizabeth II, during a three-week official state visit in Nigeria, announce the granting of independence to former colony and also open its new parliament.

It was a momentous period in Nigerian history which included, on the sideline, a Miss Independence contest won by little Miss Rosemary Anieze, pictured in Figure 26.5. Four years before this time, Queen Elizabeth II paid a royal visit to the Emir of Kano, Muhammadu Sanusi, and was hosted to a Grand Durbar, as seen in Figure 26.6.

To address fears of ethnic dominance during the colonial period, it was agreed by the Federal House of Representatives that Nigerians should elect Nigerians and that they should be dominant in the legislature. What would be the essence of policies for Nigerian affairs when Nigerians had little or no say in their implementation? The forces of regionalism and ethnic nationalism became an active part of Nigerian politics. It could be argued that they culminated in the nationalist movements that established the newspapers that were the foundations of the country's journalism. They also created institutions of higher learning that provided Nigerians with quality education and formed political associations and parties that energized Nigerian enthusiasm for participation in politics. These groups were also behindcriticism of inadequate colonial policies, proposals for constitutional reform, and the subsequent attainment of independence. Major gains were accompanied by regional disunity and mistrust – fostered by ethnic nationalism and regionalism – that remained in Nigeria's political space even after independence.[82]

---

[81] Abdulahi Abubakar and Yahaya T. Baba, "Nationalism and National Integration in Nigeria," in *Nigerian Politics*, ed. Rotimi Ajayi and Joseph Y. Fashagba (Cham: Springer, 2021), 305–319.

[82] Coleman, *Nigeria: Background to Nationalism*.

REGIONALISM AND ETHNIC POLITICS IN THE 1950S 567

Figure 26.3 Representative of Queen Elizabeth II, Princess Alexandra of Kent, in a friendly smile with two female hosts during her three-week official state visit where she announced the granting of independence to Nigeria and also opened the country's parliament.

Figure 26.4 Princess Alexandra of Kent and Nigerian prime minister Sir Abubakar Tafawa Balewa, together at the opening of the First Session of the First Parliament as part of the independence ceremonies in October 1960. Britain and Nigeria retain a very robust relationship in all areas of life.

Figure 26.5 Rosemary Anieze, wearing the sash, crowned Miss Independence on September 28, 1960, having beaten fifteen other contestants to the title, walks outside the National Stadium in Lagos to loud cheers from fans and supporters.

Figure 26.6 Queen Elizabeth II and Prince Philip in a royal visit to the Emir of Kano, Muhammadu Sanusi I, on February 16, 1956, where a Grand Durbar Festival was hosted in their honor.

Conclusion

The British administration of Nigeria had been conducted effectively through indirect rule, especially considering the consolidation of its power. However, the colonial administration was met with fierce criticism from Nigerians who opposed the harsh living conditions that it imposed. Discontent led to discussions about the urgent need for self-rule. British colonialists made some constitutional reforms to placate angry residents and possibly consolidate its administration further. One such reform was regionalism.

During the colonial period, regionalism involved three major parts of Nigeria: North, East, and West. These regions operated independently from one another and enjoyed political representation in the country's legislature. Although regionalism was useful for the emergence of a nascent Nigerian consciousness, the promotion of ethnic interests over national interests had toxic effects on that consciousness, such that each region was solely concerned with its own affairs. In the ensuing power struggle, regions jettisoned collective political action for ethnoregional political identities. Collective social and political actions were only harnessed to benefit local communities. These actions, and the minority groups' fears of marginalization, created additional fractures in the unity that would have assisted Nigeria's earliest movements for independence.[83]

[83] Sklar, "Unity or Regionalism."

PART V

Conclusion

27

Colonial Legacies

This book has traced how Nigeria's colonial history significantly impacted the country's political, legal, and sociocultural histories. The British colonial administration in Nigeria's history was marked by events, practices, and systems that were distinct from other periods in the country's history,[1] often grouped into precolonial, colonial, and postcolonial eras. The presence of foreign administrators – and the colonial administration's control over social, political, economic, and legal superstructures – altered Nigeria's developmental trajectories in ways that would continue after independence.[2]

Historians, sociologists, and other scholars have studied colonialism's impact on the development of different colonies after attaining independence. African countries, and those of other continents like Asia and the Americas, have been a major area of interest for scholars of colonial legacies, but others have analyzed colonialism's impact in parts of Asia. Two of the most influential works on colonialism's impact are the crossnational analyses conducted by Acemoglu, Johnson, and Robinson, which were reported in 2001[3] and 2002.[4] Most authors have chosen the 1960s as the decade of Africa's independence. The reports by Acemoglu and colleagues, and other studies of colonial legacies reported in the last two decades, have centered on colonialism's effect on the developmental trajectories in former colonies. Significant differences in development have been observed in former French and British colonies,[5] the

---

[1] Obaro Ikime, *The Fall of Nigeria: The British Conquest* (New York: Africana Publishing Company, 1977).

[2] Marco Wyss, *Postcolonial Security: Britain, France, and West Africa's Cold War* (Oxford: Oxford University Press, 2021), 95–115.

[3] Daron Acemoglu, Simon Johnson, and James Robinson, "Colonial Origins of Comparative Development: An Empirical Investigation," *American Economic Review* 91, no. 5 (2001): 1369–1401.

[4] Daron Acemoglu, Simon Johnson, and James Robinson, "Reversal of Fortune: Geography and Institutions in the Making of the Modern World Income Distribution," *The Quarterly Journal of Economics* 117, no. 4 (2002): 1231–1294.

[5] Alexander Lee and Kenneth A. Schultz, "Comparing British and French Colonial Legacies: A Discontinuity Analysis of Cameroon," *Quarterly Journal of Political Science* 7 (2012): 1–46.

African continent and elsewhere,[6] and areas where the colonizers employed either direct or indirect rule.[7]

Nigeria is often described as the giant of Africa, containing the continent's largest population, hosting its largest economy, and wielding the greatest amount of regional power in international affairs.[8] Nigeria also experienced close to a century of colonial domination under the British, if we take the Lagos Colony established in 1861 as the starting point. This colonial experience has garnered considerable attention, and most studies attempting to evaluate colonialism's impact on Nigeria's postindependence development have considered the country's developmental trajectories from sociocultural, economic, and political perspectives.[9] Scholars have examined British colonialism's impact on Nigeria's postindependence institutional developments.[10] After the country's independence, Nigeria inherited the institutions and structures created by the British. They continue to shape the educational, judicial, political, and civil service systems.[11] Lawal has linked colonialism with the presence of corruption in Nigeria's political and legal systems,[12] and a substantial amount of historical evidence has been gathered to support these views.

A Summary of the Significant Changes

Like many other African nations, Nigeria has a complicated history of colonialism, and the effects of British colonial rule are still felt today. Nigeria's current state is not only a result of colonial legacies; other elements that affect the country's growth and difficulties include postcolonial government, corruption, and regional dynamics.[13] Sensitivity is key when discussing colonial legacies, and it is crucial to recognize various viewpoints on the advantages

---

[6] Anne E. Booth, *Colonial Legacies: Economic and Social Development in East and Southeast Asia* (Honolulu: University of Hawaii Press, 2007).

[7] Matthew K. Lange, "British Colonial Legacies and Political Development," *World Development* 32, no. 6 (2004): 905–922.

[8] Peter Holmes, *Nigeria: Giant of Africa* (London: Swallow Editions, 1985).

[9] Adeyeri and Adejuwon, "The Implications of British Colonial Economic Policies," 1–16; Femi Okiremuete Shaka, "The Colonial Legacy: History and Its Impact on the Development of Modern Culture in Nigeria," *Third Text* 19, no. 3 (2005): 297–305; and Lange, "British Colonial Legacies."

[10] Toyin Falola, ed., *Britain and Nigeria: Exploitation or Development?* (London: Zed Books, 1987).

[11] Valentin Seidler, "Colonial Legacy and Institutional Development: The Cases of Botswana and Nigeria," unpublished PhD dissertation, WU Vienna University of Economics and Business, 2011.

[12] Adebayo A Lawal, "Corruption in Nigeria: A Colonial Legacy," Inaugural Lecture Series. University of Lagos, June 7, 2006.

[13] Toyin Falola, *Understanding Modern Nigeria: Ethnicity, Democracy, and Development* (Cambridge: Cambridge University Press, 2021).

and disadvantages of British colonial control in Nigeria. Nigerians and scholars agree on the changes, but they can disagree on their evaluations and impacts. Today, if you blame the British on any aspect of contemporary Nigeria, expect an objection asserting that "the past is gone!" – that is, blame Nigerians for mismanaging themselves.

Preceding chapters have detailed different aspects of the colonial era. Nigeria was a British colony from the late nineteenth century until its independence in 1960. As already demonstrated, Nigeria was subjected to British political, economic, and social institutions, which had a long-lasting effect on the nation. For administrative purposes, during the colonial administration the British split Nigeria into various territories. As a result, new borders were drawn that were not always consistent with pre-existing linguistic, cultural, or ethnic differences. These boundaries have exacerbated the ethnic tensions, religious conflicts, and a Civil War in Nigeria.

Concerning the political and administrative structures, the British introduced a centralized system of governance in Nigeria, with a hierarchical administrative system. They established systems of indirect rule, which involved using traditional rulers as intermediaries between the British authorities and the local population. The British employed a "divide and rule" policy by exploiting existing ethnic and religious tensions in Nigeria to maintain control. This policy contributed to deep-rooted ethnic and religious divisions that persist in Nigerian society, often leading to conflicts and challenges in national unity. The centralized structure of governance and the adoption of Western democratic institutions during colonial rule shaped Nigeria's political landscape after independence. This governance system influenced Nigeria's subsequent political structure after independence, shaping the relationships between the federal government and different regional entities.

The task of colonial modernization began with the provision of infrastructure, such as railways, roads, bridges, and telecommunication systems, which laid the foundation for Nigeria's future development. These infrastructures facilitated transportation, trade, and communication, contributing to economic growth in some areas. Notably, they eased the exploitation of natural resources. British colonial rule was characterized by the extraction and exploitation of natural resources, particularly minerals and agricultural products. The colonial administration facilitated the establishment of mining and agricultural industries to benefit the British Empire economically. The benefits of economic changes did not spread equally. The British colonial administration primarily focused on extracting resources from Nigeria, often at the expense of the local population. Economic disparities widened during colonial rule, as the British favored certain regions and ethnic groups over others, leading to unequal distribution of resources and opportunities.

British colonization brought significant political and economic changes to Nigerian society, including the spread of Christianity and Western education.

Missionary activities introduced Western values, education, and religious beliefs, which impacted Nigeria's cultural and religious landscape.

Sociocultural, Economic, and Political Legacies

Colonial institutions are often considered to determine the levels of sociocultural, economic, and political development in former colonies after attaining their independence.[14] Literature from several humanities and social sciences fields has examined the relationships between colonial rule and postindependence development. In Nigeria, the beginning of British colonialism in 1861 – invading precolonial city-states and kingdoms that would later form the Colony and Protectorate of Nigeria – led to the creation of institutions and systems that steered the historical course of the newly formed polity over the next century.

Historians have posited that European colonialism was rooted in notions of imperialism that led to the colonizing nation's expansion of social, cultural, political, economic, and legal systems into its colonized territories.[15] European colonialists viewed Western culture as superior, using these perspectives to justify the undermining of local cultures. Governance models, educational systems, and economic policies were largely imposed on colonies with and without local consultations. For example, France pursued this imperialist agenda, adopting a colonial policy of assimilation for some years, expecting to convert several Africans into French citizens.[16] Britain did not openly seek to convert its colonized subjects into British citizens, but the scale of the British Empire and the establishment of British-styled institutions and systems in its colonies displayed an agenda of overt expansionism.[17]

The English language was one of the most obvious transplants of British culture into the Nigerian territory. It was originally adopted as a means of communication in educational, commercial, governmental, and legal systems to facilitate contact between Nigerians and the British traders, missionaries, and colonizers.[18] English later became the *lingua franca* of the entire British Empire. Western European powers, driven by convenience and cultural superiority, perpetuated the use of their respective languages as "official" languages

---

[14] Lee and Schultz, "Comparing British and French Colonial Legacies."
[15] Frances Gouda, *Dutch Culture Overseas: Colonial Practice in the Netherlands Indies, 1900–1942* (Sheffield: Equinox Publishing, 2008); and David Strang, "Contested Sovereignty: The Social Construction of Colonial Imperialism," in *State Sovereignty as Social Construct*, ed. Thomas J. Biersteker and Cynthia Weber (Cambridge: Cambridge University Press, 1996), 22–49.
[16] Martin Thomas, ed., *The French Colonial Mind: Mental Maps of Empire and Colonial Encounters* (Lincoln: University of Nebraska Press, 2011).
[17] Peter J. Cain and Anthony G. Hopkins, *British Imperialism: 1688–2015* (London: Routledge, 2016).
[18] J. A. Mangan, ed., *"Benefits Bestowed?": Education and British Imperialism* (Manchester: Manchester University Press, 1988).

for the colonies that they occupied. This practice continued in most colonies after independence. The colonialists considered language to be an important tool for asserting dominance. Scholarly literature has already noted that language was used as a tool to produce social inequalities.[19]

As an ethnolinguistically diverse country, Nigeria can justify the retention of English as an official language because it removes barriers that might challenge interactions between people from different ethnolinguistic backgrounds. However, adopting a foreign colonial language has produced some negative consequences. Yameogo's analysis of the language policies and economies of twenty-nine African countries shows a positive correlation between industrialization and the adoption of a local language. This probably suggests that countries like Nigeria, which continue to use the language of their colonizers for official communications, would see improvements in trade, industrialization, and other economic activities if they officially embraced local languages.[20] This correlation is intriguing, but it should be noted that the informal sectors of the economy still use Indigenous languages.

Before the advent of British colonialism in Nigeria, precolonial polities had made contact with speakers of other languages, and, in some cases, they adopted them or borrowed many words. Language exchange was popularized in precolonial times also through the practice of borrowing foreign phrases or orthographies, as in the rise of Ajami, based on Arabic orthography. The Sokoto Caliphate and its vassal emirates, which were deeply rooted in Islamic traditions, adopted Arabic for worship and religious education. By the end of the nineteenth century, the Arabic language had become an essential symbol of identity and culture for the predominantly Muslim Hausa–Fulani groups.[21] The popularity of Arabic and the southward spread of Islam meant that the language would become a means of communication for trade and social interactions in many parts of Nigeria.

The imposition of the English language occurred under circumstances that were different from Arabic's acceptance in Nigeria's Northern region. Salisu and Abdullahi have asserted that the installation of English as colonial Nigeria's official language not only displaced Arabic and other local languages, it also denied their contributions to the country's history while damaging Indigenous groups' sense of identity and cultural pride.[22] This conclusion by

---

[19] Monica Heller and Bonnie McElhinny, *Language, Capitalism, Colonialism: Toward a Critical History* (Toronto: University of Toronto Press, 2017).

[20] Souleymane Yameogo, "Official Language, Ethnic Diversity and Industrialization in Africa: Language Policy Perspectives,"unpublished PhD dissertation, KDI School of Public Policy and Management, 2020.

[21] A. O. Hashim, "Arabic Language as a Source of Diplomatic Relations between Sokoto Caliphate and Its Neighbors," *Journal of History and Diplomatic Studies* 6 (2009): 175–189.

[22] Muhammed Salisu and Abdullahi Salisu Abdullahi, "Colonial Impact on the Socio-Communicative Functions of Arabic Language in Nigeria: An Overview," *Canadian Social Science* 9, no. 6 (2013): 204–209.

Salisu and Abdullahi ignores the data on the continuing use of local languages and the spread of Ajami.

The Christian missionary agenda was also related to imperialist notions of language transplantation. Historical evidence shows that Nigerians first came in contact with Portuguese missionaries in the fifteenth century,[23] although the first major Christian church was not established in the region until 1842. Christian missionaries arrived alongside European slave traders in the fifteenth century. The slave trade would later be abolished in the nineteenth century, partly due to changing economies and black resistance, but the proselytization of the Christian faith continued in colonial Africa. British colonizers who arrived at the end of the nineteenth century, directly and indirectly, promoted the spread of Christianity in colonial Nigeria.[24] These efforts focused on Nigeria's southern territories and encountered resistance in the Northern region's emirates. Despite the assumptions of the missionaries, the Indigenous people in the Southern territories were similarly committed to their traditional religious practices. European missionaries spread their Christian gospel and established churches in Southern territories.[25] One such case, shown in Figure 27.1, is the Cathedral Church of Christ located on a sprawling street in Lagos, completed in 1946.

Christianity's present popularity in Nigeria, adopted as a religion by almost half of the country's population, cannot be fully disconnected from the events of colonial rule.[26] Religion and ethnicity have become the primary symbols of identity in modern Nigeria, and the country's official language is promoted to find common ground between people of diverse religious and ethnolinguistic backgrounds.

Beyond religion and culture, colonialism also affected other aspects of social life and culture. Its influence can be seen in food, clothing, material culture, education, arts, and technology. Meanwhile, the effects of globalization have been noted in a wealth of literature.[27] Uwaezuoke states that the African continent is undergoing a cultural revolution largely attributable to

---

[23] J. O. Ijoma, "Portuguese Activities in West Africa before 1600: The Consequences," *Transafrican Journal of History* 11 (1982): 136–146.

[24] Kanayo L. Nwadialor, "Christian Missionaries and Civilization in Southern Nigeria, 1841–1960: Implications for Contemporary Christians," *UJAH: Unizik Journal of Arts and Humanities* 14, no. 2 (2013): 173–193.

[25] John G. Nengel and Chigemezi N. Wogu, "Colonial Politics, Missionary Rivalry, and the Beginnings of Seventh-Day Adventist Mission in Northern Nigeria," *Mission Studies: Journal of the International Association for Mission Studies* 3 (2021): 213–235.

[26] Bulus Y. Galadima and Yusufu Turaki, "Christianity in Nigeria: Part I," *African Journal of Evangelical Theology* 20, no. 1 (2001): 85–101.

[27] S. Ibi Ajayi, "Globalisation and Africa," *Journal of African Economies* 12, no. 1 (2003): 120–150; and N. S. Siddharthan, "Globalization: Productivity, Efficiency and Growth: An Overview," *Economic and Political Weekly* 39, no. 5 (2004): 420–422.

Figure 27.1 A sprawling street in Lagos in the 1960s hosts one of its most important and iconic colonial structures and the first cathedral building in Nigeria, the Cathedral Church of Christ, completed in 1946.

colonialism's impact.[28] In Nigeria and other African countries, the impact of colonial legacies is noticeable in social and cultural systems.

British colonialism in Nigeria was primarily motivated by economic interests. The colonizing power unequivocally expressed its interest in pursuing its economic objectives from the beginning. In the second half of the nineteenth century, when the British first arrived in Lagos, their trade was administered under the aegis of the Royal Niger Company and its royal charter.[29] The company was encouraged to exploit natural resources in the region. Raw materials would be supplied to British industries, and local markets would purchase British goods. Local products such as cocoa, groundnuts, and palm products became major export crops in Nigeria's colonial economy. The British Royal Niger Company and its corporate partners purchased these products cheaply from local farmers, exported them to Europe for processing, and sold the finished goods to Nigerians at profitable prices. The establishment

---

[28] Obioha Precious Uwaezuoke, "Globalization and the Future of African Culture," *Philosophical Papers and Review* 2, no. 1 (2010): 1–8.

[29] G. L. Baker, "Research Notes on the Royal Niger Company – Its Predecessors and Successors," *Journal of the Historical Society of Nigeria* 2, no. 1 (1960): 151–161.

of a formal colonial government in the early twentieth century consolidated the economic objectives of the import–export trade.[30]

Mapuva and Chari have noted that African countries suffered greatly during the colonial era.[31] Adeyeri and Adejuwon have suggested that the self-interested economic policies of the colonial administration were detrimental to Africa's financial and economic conditions. British colonialism facilitated Nigeria's underdevelopment, and foreign businesses extracted resources from local communities.[32] British economic policies included land tenure reforms, the creation of white-collar civil service jobs that lured workers away from farming occupations, and the monetization of the economy with the creation of banking and credit systems.[33] Ultimately, the colonial period laid the economic foundation for Nigeria's development after independence. Colonial policies introduced economic diversification and created new job opportunities, but substantial negative and positive outcomes accompanied these improvements.

The colonial administration brought opportunities for development, such as formal education, modern health facilities, and improved transportation and communication systems, but the colonization of Nigeria was not without many negative effects. The country experienced debilitating political challenges as a direct result of colonial governance. Nigeria's natural and human resources were looted, and colonial institutions nurtured a culture of corruption in organizations and the civil service. Lawal has noted that corruption in the public service in postcolonial Nigeria can trace its roots to notions of colonialism, imperialism, and capitalism that directly opposed Indigenous moral values of honesty, communal living, and responsible leadership.[34]

Britain's involvement in Nigeria's economy was motivated by a desire to develop the colonizing power at the expense of the colonized. External trade was encouraged between Britain and its so-called commonwealth of nations, but the terms of trade were grossly disproportionate and unfavorable for the colonies.[35] Capitalist economic systems introduced by Britain were not only incongruent with existing practices in most parts of Nigeria, they also failed to

---

[30] J. O. Ahazuem and Toyin Falola, "Production for the Metropolis: Agriculture and Forest Products," in *Britain and Nigeria, Exploitation or Development?* ed. Toyin Falola (London: Zed Books, 1987).

[31] Jephias Mapuva and Freeman Chari, "Colonialism No Longer an Excuse for Africa's Failure," *Journal of Sustainable Development in Africa* 12, no. 5 (2010): 22–36.

[32] Olusegun Adeyeri and Kehinde David Adejuwon, "The Implications of British Colonial Economic Policies on Nigeria's Development," *International Journal of Advanced Research in Management and Social Sciences* 1, no. 2 (2012): 5–6

[33] Chibuike U. Uche, "Foreign Banks, Africans, and Credit in Colonial Nigeria, c. 1890–1912," *The Economic History Review* 52, no. 4 (1999): 669–691.

[34] Lawal, *Corruption in Nigeria*.

[35] Claude Ake, *A Political Economy of Africa* (Lagos: Longman Nigeria Plc., 2008).

consider the interests of the majority of the indigenes, especially those without education and who lacked access to the better-paying formal economies. After gaining independence, Nigeria still suffered from a narrow economic base and unequal linkages with external markets.[36] Despite Nigeria's massive nationalization and indigenization policies introduced in the 1960s and 1970s, the country's economy remained dependent on its former colonial authority and other Western powers.[37]

The form, structure, and systems of political administration that colonialism introduced to Nigeria had lasting impacts on local political developments. Colonial political systems controlled local political and administrative systems. Colonial administrators developed political and constitutional frameworks that supported their ideas of governance, which led to the creation of constitutions, legislative assemblies, and policies that were not based on popular support. Only after World War II, when breakthroughs were achieved in nationalist agitations, were educated Nigerians meaningfully included in the emerging formal governance.

The most obvious result of excluding Nigerians from governance was the lack of adequate training for political leadership. There was no culture of democratic institutions. It was unclear what the purpose of government was: for service, or for individual aggrandizement? Some authors have established the links between colonialism, inefficiency, and corrupt governance in Nigeria. Okonkwo traced the history of corruption in Africa to precolonial times, asserting that Africans in public service sought to further their financial interests, which was a starkly different predisposition from that of the British.[38] Without debating such views, it is notable that the poor quality of political leadership and bad governance have many links with the colonial period.

British constitutional, legal, and political systems displaced local administrations. Although the indirect rule system was employed to bridge the gaps between Nigerians and colonial administrators, the system's partial failure in the Western and Eastern regions prevented aspiring politicians from receiving a proper education in politics and leadership. Most traditional rulers engaged in local administration were uneducated in the Western sense and less involved in the colonial implementation of regional and national politics. Nigerian politicians, who led political affairs in Nigeria's closing years of colonialism, were not engaged in local administration.

---

[36] Oladele Fadeiye, *A Social Studies Textbook for Colleges and Universities*, Vol. 2 (Ibadan: Akin–Johnson Press and Publishers, 2005).

[37] Patrick Chikendu, *Imperialism and Nationalism* (Enugu: Academic Publishing Company, 2004).

[38] Rina Okonkwo, "Corruption in Nigeria: A Historical Perspective (1947–2002)," in *African Humanities: Humanities and Nation Building*, ed. Francis Anyika (Nsukka: Afro–Orbis Publications, 2005).

The constitutional, legal, and political systems instituted during colonial rule also worsened relationships between different regions and ethnic groups. Beginning with Lord Lugard, the first Colonial Governor, administrators initiated several policies that favored minority elite interests. Lugard's decisions were heavily influenced by his fondness for the emirate system in the Northern region, whose ruling class actively supported his indirect rule approach. Lugard's administrative success as Governor of Northern Nigeria, coupled with his desire to maintain the support of members of its ruling class, led him to extend regional policies to the entire country. These developments were not welcomed in the Southern regions.

Agbiboa and Okem have stated that the main factor militating against nation-building in Nigeria has been the country's complex ethnoreligious configuration.[39] This challenge is nearly as old as the Nigerian state itself. However, instead of devising workable plans and policies to address this problem, colonial administrators complicated the challenges of ethnic sentiment through colonial policies and systems incompatible with their professed nation-building objectives. British colonial administrators, looking to appease a select class, largely shaped specific colonial policies. These policies included the separate administration for the Northern region during Lugard's administration, elective principles that were restricted to Lagos and Calabar during Governor Clifford's administration, the Richards Constitution that partitioned Nigeria's territory into three unequal regions, and the establishment of Regional Houses of Chiefs in the Western and Eastern regions. Most of these policies agitated the majority of Nigerians, who felt excluded or unfairly treated.

The issue of minority rights was a major cause for concern during the colonial period. However, British administrators ignored the issues that affected minority ethnic groups until the problem became harder to resolve. The ethnic groups were particularly displeased with the regional structure introduced by Arthur Richards, which systematically excluded them from political administration. Even the eventual establishment of a Minority Interests Commission would fail to provide lasting solutions to minority challenges.[40]

Nigeria inherited a political system that fostered ethnic rivalries. The country's current state of political instability has been linked to the same regional competition, unequal division of resources, and neglect of minority interests that characterized political administration during the colonial period.[41]

---

[39] Daniel Egiegba Agbiboa and Andrew Emmanuel Okem, "Unholy Trinity: Assessing the Impact of Ethnicity and Religion on National Identity in Nigeria," *Peace Research* 43, no. 2 (2011): 98–125.

[40] Lexington Izuagie, "The Willink Minority Commission and Minority Rights in Nigeria," *EJOTMAS: Ekpoma Journal of Theatre and Media Arts* 5, nos. 1–2 (2015): 206–223.

[41] Caroline Cohn, "India and Nigeria: Similar Colonial Legacies, Vastly Different Trajectories: An Examination of the Differing Fates of Two Former British Colonies," *Cornell International Affairs Review* 7, no. 1 (2013): 18–30.

The British colonial administration's influence on Nigeria's political development was particularly evident during the First Republic – a period in which the country retained a preindependence culture of political fragmentation along regional lines.

The perpetuation of British imperialist control in certain aspects of Nigerian politics was also a concern. At independence, the Queen of England remained Nigeria's head of state, although her interests were represented by an Indigene who was publicly elected. Despite adopting republicanism and indigenization policies, which were significant efforts to minimize Britain's political and economic control, Nigerian governments could not overcome neocolonial influences from their former colonizer. Over time, as Iheduru has pointed out, Nigeria's political leaders contributed to the country's underdevelopment by failing to initiate policies and strategies that could address the country's political challenges, allowing the nation to lapse into its current, miserable state.[42]

Enduring Institutional Changes

Colonialism's negative effects on Nigeria's political, economic, and sociocultural development have been widely documented in multiple academic disciplines. These negative narratives are a one-sided portrayal of the colonial experience. Colonialism's positive influence, which Nigerian historians and scholars often overlook, created the foundation for the modern Nigerian state. The colonial era was a period of large-scale cultural, economic, and political transformations. Changes in Nigeria's political dynamics and socioeconomic conditions were due to frameworks and institutions established by the colonial government. Colonial systems were a reflection of Britain's political and economic ideologies, applied to consolidate Britain's grip on Nigeria, but colonial institutions brought the Nigerian political state into the present day. Civil service, the judiciary, and educational systems were important parts of Nigeria's development.

Before colonial activities in Nigeria, its education systems were informal and structured to serve a society's immediate needs. Two precolonial education systems have been identified: Islamic education, practiced in the North,[43] and traditional informal education, implemented in most parts of the South.[44]

---

[42] Okechukwu Iheduru, "Nigeria's Comparative Politics," in *Interests, Identities, and Institutions in a Changing Global Order*, ed. Jeffrey Kopstein and Mark Lichbach (Cambridge: Cambridge University Press, 2008), 535–587.

[43] Kabir Mohammed and Binta M. Yarinchi, "The Role and Impact of Pre-Colonial Education on the People of Hausaland Prior to 1903 AD," *International Journal of Humanities and Social Science Invention* 2, no. 11 (2013): 7–13.

[44] Jacob F. A. Ajayi, "Historical Education in Nigeria," *Journal of the Historical Society of Nigeria* 8, no. 1 (1975): 3–8.

Islamic education taught Islam's principles and included memorizing the Holy Qur'an and the teachings of Prophet Muhammad (PBUH). This education was generally strict. Traditional education focused on imparting vocational skills that positively contributed to society, building students' character and socializing them to become part of existing groups.[45]

In 1842, missionaries arrived in Nigeria to spread Christianity and gain new converts.[46] They also brought early ideas for developing educational institutions in colonial Nigeria. However, residents could not understand the missionaries and held strong attachments to cultural and religious beliefs that slowed down the missionaries from accomplishing their goals.[47] The missionaries began educational work by training people to read the Bible in English so that they could work as local catechists and school administrators. The missionaries focused on promoting Western education to propagate Christianity, but they also made efforts to record the orthography of Indigenous languages.[48] Early missionary schools in Nigeria included CMS Grammar School, Badagry, established in 1845; First Girls Secondary School in Nigeria, Lagos, established in 1869; Wesleyan Primary School, Badagry, established in 1843; and Baptist Boys High School, Lagos, established in 1885.[49] Despite the early impacts of these missionary schools in colonial Nigeria, there was no coherent organization in their work. Syllabi were incongruous and haphazard, and there was no clear national vision or mission for education. Missionaries also encountered strong resistance in the North due to religious opposition.

Missionaries promoted education without much formal support from the colonial government, although there was widespread recognition that cultural education would advance the cause of colonialism. Establishing a functional educational system in a heterogeneous society like Nigeria involved massive costs that the British government was unwilling to incur. The colonial administration's first official involvement in Nigeria's educational system occurred in 1877 when three missionaries in Lagos received £200 for their services.[50] Colonialists showed concern for Nigerian education by adapting Britain's educational policies and ordinances in their fast-growing colony. The 1882 Educational Ordinance was Nigeria's first on education from the colonial

---

[45] Aliu Babatunde Fafunwa, *History of Education in Nigeria* (Oxfordshire: Routledge, 2018).
[46] Ahaotu Godwin Ndubuisi, "British Educational Management Policies in Nigeria: A Historical Overview," *Electronic Research Journal of Behavioral Sciences* 1 (2018): 1–14.
[47] Jacob F. A. Ajayi, *Christian Missions in Nigeria 1841–1891: The Making of a New Elite* (Lagos: Longman Publishers, 1965).
[48] S. W. Chianakwalam, "Educational Development in Nigeria and the Gold Coast," *Journal of Education Management* 84, no. 15 (2002): 66–89.
[49] Ndubuisi, "British Educational Management Policies."
[50] Hauwa Imam, "Educational Policy in Nigeria from the Colonial Era to the Post-Independence Period," *Italian Journal of Sociology of Education* 4, no. 1 (2012): 10–15.

administration,[51] claiming control of education in the colony and formally introducing Nigeria to Western education. It established clear requirements for Nigeria's educational system, and similar ordinances were applied in other West African colonies.[52]

The 1887 Educational Ordinance, known as the Nigerian Ordinance, issued grants to schools to ensure the rapid development of secondary education. The 1916 Educational Ordinance served Nigeria's general interests by implementing a unified education system that could facilitate the swift integration of Northern and Southern Nigeria. The educational ordinances and commissions included the 1926 Educational Ordinance, the 1943 Asquith Commission, and the Elliot Commission of 1943–4. The Minority Report of the Elliot Commission recommended the establishment of a university in Ibadan, which resulted in the creation of the University of Ibadan in 1948, enrolling 103 students.[53] University education in colonial Nigeria adopted a curriculum that featured subjects relevant to the Industrial Age, which also influenced the British education system. Emphasis was placed on engineering, mathematics, and other science-related subjects. Callaway has argued that colonial education in Nigeria and other West African colonies served British interests and prevented the subsequent modernization of indigenes.[54]

The civil service system in Nigeria was born from the need to ensure effective administration. The colonial civil service system, which Europeans initially populated, made progress in developing local infrastructure, like the railway system and other transportation networks.[55] Nigeria was a fertile ground to support the economic interests of colonial administrators. Local trade was already booming, making it possible for the British to implement a system that made administration less demanding.[56] The colonial government introduced tax payments, and the civil service saw to its implementation. The civil service was usually headed by a colonial official appointed by Nigeria's

---

[51] Folasade R. Sulaiman, "Internationalization in Education: The British Colonial Policies on Education in Nigeria 1882–1926," *Journal of Sociological Research* 3, no. 2 (2012): 84–101.

[52] Clive Whitehead, "Education in British Colonial Dependencies, 1919–39: A Re-Appraisal," *Comparative Education* 17, no. 1 (1981): 71–80.

[53] Cornelius Olaleye Taiwo, *The Nigerian Education System, Past, Present and Future* (Lagos: Thomas Nelson Nigeria Limited, 1980).

[54] Immaculata Nnenna Enwo-Irem, "Colonialism and Education: The Challenges for Sustainable Development in Nigeria," *Mediterranean Journal of Social Sciences* 4, no. 5 (2013): 163.

[55] Gabriel O. Olusanya, "The Nigerian Civil Service in the Colonial Era: A Study of Imperial Reactions to Changing Circumstances," in *Studies in Southern Nigerian History*, ed. Boniface I. Obichere (London: Routledge, 1982).

[56] Emmanuel Jude Abiodun Akinwale, "A Historical and Comparative Analysis of Colonial and Post-colonial Bureaucracy in Nigeria," *Journal of Public Administration and Governance* 4, no. 2 (2014): 1–11.

Governor-General.[57] After World War II, the colonial government specifically strengthened its civil service system to address administrative bottlenecks. The result was effectively a partnership between local Nigerians and the colonial government. The civil service also ensured that the policy of indirect rule integrated Nigeria's government workers into a single unit.

Nigeria's civil service had its flaws, and bureaucracy was a major weakness. Although the civil service was structured for efficient administration, it was rife with internal problems. There was no adequate channel for information to move through the system; officials were mainly concerned with maintaining their hierarchy of power and meeting the challenge of oversight functions within the system. The colonial government eventually recruited indigenes into its institutions, but the process was riddled with bureaucratic inequality. Although there was an element of meritocracy in the recruitment process, some scholars have noted that colonial bureaucracy in Nigeria was complicated by the failure to curb preferential treatment for specific ethnicities.[58]

The colonial government enlisted the assistance of Nigerians once its civil service began operating in earnest. The recruitment process was ostensibly merit-based, but the majority of indigenous officials were mostly from Nigeria's southern regions. Southerners had by far become the most educated Nigerians due to their adoption of Western education. Fewer educated individuals were available in the North, where the traditional elites had dismissed Western education as unsuitable for their exalted stations. The civil service was created to ease administrative burdens, and the colonial government recruited indigenes to meet the demands for trained personnel. The fact that most indigenous officials were Southerners threatened the status of Northerners and contributed to the colonial bureaucracy that the civil service was meant to address.[59] The colonial civil service system was also riddled with unchecked corruption,[60] and the exploitation of the taxation system eventually triggered many complaints and some riots. Britain's colonial government intended to have the civil service prepare Nigerians for self-rule, but the service has remained tainted by corruption that has endured into the present day.

Despite these challenges, the civil service functioned well enough during the colonial administration because its internal policies for promotion were based on merit. During the colonial era, Nigeria's civil service addressed pressing ecological issues such as a cocoa plant infection. The colonial civil

---

[57] Akinwale, "A Historical and Comparative Analysis."
[58] Eghosa Osaghae, "Explaining the Changing Patterns of Ethnic Politics in Nigeria," *Nationalism and Ethnic Politics* 9, no. 3 (2003): 54–73.
[59] Osaghae, "Explaining the Changing Patterns."
[60] Tekena Tamuno, "British Colonial Administration in Nigeria in the Twentieth Century," in *Groundwork of Nigerian History*, ed. Obaro Ikime (Ibadan: Heinemann Educational Books, 1980), 393–409.

service also worked to develop Nigeria's more remote regions. The service received funding from taxes, which were the criterion for adult suffrage at one point.

Nigeria's precolonial judicial systems were rooted in cultural and religious beliefs.[61] There was no written constitution, but affairs were organized by a well-established system of retributive justice.[62] Colonialism brought a British-styled judicial system based on common law.[63] The British rejected traditional Southern punishments, such as exile to forbidden forests or beheading in shrines, and Northern justice, which included amputating limbs from individuals caught stealing.[64]

The British government consolidated its dominance by replacing traditional justice systems with colonial institutions. In 1863, Ordinance No. 3 established Lagos as a British colony, creating replicas of British courts to formulate and implement laws within the colony. In 1876, Ordinance No. 4 empowered the courts to apply British common law.[65] This was a brazen disregard for existing local customs and the traditions that had prevailed before colonialism. The colonial government ultimately established full control of Nigeria's judicial institutions. A Supreme Court was created for the colony, but it only functioned to regulate trade. In 1866 it was replaced with the Court of Civil and Criminal Justice. The West African Court of Appeal, headquartered in Sierra Leone, functioned as the colony's Court of Appeal and conducted trials by jury. Appeal cases from this court were usually referred to the judicial committee of the Privy Council in London. In 1876, a Supreme Court was re-established to serve the colony of Lagos, carrying out judicial activities under English common law. Local customs were still observed in some aspects of life, but not implemented for criminal justice.

In 1861, a police force was established to ensure that indigenes complied with judicial activities and to impose law and order.[66] Police actions were confrontational for most Nigerians, and the police quickly transformed into symbols of oppression and violence. Colonial Nigeria's police institutions originally functioned to protect British commercial interests, eventually

---

[61] Derek Asiedu-Akrofi, "Judicial Recognition and Adoption of Customary Law in Nigeria," *American Journal of Comparative Law* 37, no. 3 (1989): 571.

[62] Oluwafunminiyi Raheem and Mike Famiyesin, "Controlling the Boundaries of Morality: The History and Powers of Ayelala Deity," *Yoruba Studies Review* 2, no. 1 (2017): 231–247.

[63] Noel Otu, "Colonialism and the Criminal Justice System in Nigeria," *International Journal of Comparative and Applied Criminal Justice* 23, no. 2 (1999): 293–306.

[64] Asiedu-Akrofi, "Judicial Recognition and Adoption."

[65] Charles Mwalimu, *The Nigerian Legal system: Public Law*, Vol. 1, (New York: Peter Lang, 2005).

[66] Akintunde Olusegun Obilade, *The Nigerian Legal System* (London: Sweet & Maxwell, 1979).

upholding law and order by curtailing petty criminal activities.[67] The colonial government expected local chiefs to cooperate with the police, but this increased the demands on the colonial administration and reduced the influence of the traditional rulers by making them subject to police authority.

British legal and police institutions were accompanied by the concept of punishment. Penalties for illegal conduct were overtly drawn from British statutory law, which involved imprisonment and confinement, increasing the frustration of many Nigerians.[68] Nigerians generally rejected judicial institutions because they saw them as incompatible with their native legal systems. In the Northern part of the country, the system of justice was influenced by the dictates of the Qur'an. Residents opposed the idea of replacing the religious Shari'a courts with a secular English legal system. The colonial administration ultimately found it necessary to acknowledge the presence of Shari'a courts, although they considered the English legal system superior. Native courts were established for indigenous interests in the Northern region,[69] and customary courts were established in the Southern regions.[70] British District Commissioners were appointed to supervise judicial matters in their respective districts.[71]

Early Postcolonial

Political, economic, and cultural studies of Nigeria's early postindependence history have repeatedly identified Britain's impact on practices in the new sovereign state. Historical evidence from these studies suggests that this influence was mainly due to the historical consciousness of Nigerians and the neocolonial agenda of the British. Nafziger defines historical consciousness as reliance on past events to inform present actions.[72] Several factors borne out of history, culture, and the historical consciousness of Nigerians triggered the need to cultivate a new sense of cultural identity in a majority of people, and this identity was rooted in the colonial past. On the other hand, deliberate neocolonial influences steered Nigeria's political and economic developmental trajectory. Nigeria's political leadership made deliberate efforts to wrest their country from ongoing neocolonial control, but only minor breakthroughs were made.

---

[67] Philip T. Ahire, "Policing and the Construction of the Colonial State in Nigeria, 1860–1960," *Journal of Third World Studies* 7, no. 2 (1990): 151–172.
[68] Gary Slapper, *The English Legal System* (London: Cavendish Publishing, 2004).
[69] Takehiko Ochiai, "The Application of Sharia and the Evolution of the Native Court System in Colonial Northern Nigeria (1900–1960)," *Asian Journal of African Studies* 49 (2020): 79–110.
[70] Asiedu–Akrofi, "Judicial Recognition and Adoption."
[71] Adolphous Godwin Karibi–Whyte, *The Relevance of the Judiciary in the Polity–In Historical Perspective* (Lagos: Nigerian Institute of Advanced Legal Studies, 1987).
[72] Rhoda Nanre Nafziger, "Decolonizing History: Historical Consciousness, Identity and Civic Engagement of Nigerian Youth," unpublished PhD dissertation, Pennsylvania State University, 2020.

Neocolonialism, or the perpetuation of colonial domination in a former colony's local affairs, has been linked with political underdevelopment. Attah has observed that, in Nigeria's case, neocolonialism was introduced by the British colonial government before decolonization.[73] Unfortunately, some Nigerian political elites collaborated with these efforts because they stood to benefit after Nigeria's independence.[74] These political elites retained the former colonial authority's political, legal, and administrative systems after independence, even when those systems were incompatible with the postcolonial aspirations of the new sovereign state. The Queen of England was recognized as Nigeria's ceremonial head of state until 1963 (when Nigeria became a republic), and the Queen's Privy Council was the highest appellate court in the Nigerian legal system.[75] Nigeria also joined the British Commonwealth of Nations, a relic of the British Empire's former imperialist agenda, and the country pursued pro-British, pro-Western foreign policies in international arenas.[76]

In the six decades that followed Nigeria's independence, various policies and strategies have been implemented by the Nigerian government in an attempt to break free from the shackles of neocolonial political control imposed by the country's former colonizers. The first significant step toward guaranteeing full and unqualified sovereignty for Nigeria's government was adopting a republican system in 1963.[77] The 1963 Constitution, called the Republican Constitution, recognized a popularly elected president as head of state to replace the British Queen. The constitution also designated the Supreme Court of Nigeria as the apex Court in the Republic of Nigeria, removing the Privy Council from the country's hierarchy of courts. Nigeria officially joined the Non-Aligned Movement in 1964 as an overt expression of its commitment to remain neutral in international affairs, especially regarding the United States and the Soviet Union – the superpowers of post–World War II.[78]

Western imperial influences retained control over Nigeria's economic activities and systems by establishing economic and financial institutions that served their interests. These institutions remained after independence, along

---

[73] Noah Echa Attah, "The Historical Conjuncture of Neo-Colonialism and Underdevelopment in Nigeria," *Journal of African Studies and Development* 5, no. 5 (2013): 70–79.

[74] Segun Osoba, "Transition to Neo-Colonialism," in *Britain and Nigeria: Exploitation or Development?* ed. Toyin Falola (London: Zed Books, 1987): 223–249.

[75] Thomas Mohr, "The Privy Council Appeal and British Imperial Policy, 1833–1939," in *Modernization, National Identity and Legal Instrumentalism*, Vol. II: Public Law, ed. Michał Gałędek and Anna Klimaszewska (Leiden: Brill, 2020), 86–112.

[76] Modupeolu Faseke, ed., *Nigeria and the Commonwealth: Reflections and Projections* (Ibadan: Macmillan Nigeria Publishers, 2009), 203–236.

[77] Larry Diamond, *Class, Ethnicity, and Democracy in Nigeria: The Failure of the First Republic* (Syracuse: Syracuse University Press, 1988).

[78] Timothy M. Shaw and Olajide Aluko, *Nigerian Foreign Policy: Alternative Perceptions and Projections* (London: Macmillan, 1983).

with their British-styled bureaucratic systems and predominantly European managers. In the first few decades of Nigeria's postcolonial history, most leading business organizations were British-owned. Companies such as Barclays Bank and Unilever monopolized key economic systems, such as monetary and credit institutions, and steered Nigeria's economy by influencing industrial and labor relations.[79]

Some have noted that foreign control over Nigeria's economic system was enabled by bilateral agreements arranged between Britain and Nigeria during the decolonization period, the importation of foreign capital into the Nigerian economy, and the retention of economic policies Britain imposed on Nigeria during colonial rule.[80] Attah points out that British colonialism laid the foundation for the neocolonial control over Nigeria's economy in the years before independence, whereby the colonial administration implemented laws and policies that were calculated to help British-owned multinational corporations.[81] These laws included the Income Tax Ordinance and the Industrial Development (Income Tax Relief) Act of 1958. Companies could evade taxes on their substantial economic activities in Nigeria, which allowed them to return capital to England at the expense of Nigeria's development.

The Nigerian government organized the indigenization and nationalization of multinational corporations to address economic threats from foreign influences.[82] In the 1960s, the federal legislature reformed the Nigerian economic system, establishing institutions, facilities, and policies to achieve the country's goal of becoming a fast-developing economy. Key economic systems were overhauled, including banking, insurance, industrial development, and labor unions. However, most of the reforms that reshaped Nigeria's economy were implemented by the military regimes of the 1970s. The oil boom of the same decade enabled Nigeria's economic development, which placed the country alongside leading global economies. If the momentum of this decade had been maintained, Nigeria could have met the optimistic projections of political economists that the country would develop at the same rate as Brazil and India. Unfortunately, a culture of corruption and poor leadership had eaten deep into the fabric of the country's political class, preventing such hopes from materializing.[83]

---

[79] Chibuike U. Uche, "British Government, British Businesses, and the Indigenization Exercise in Post–Independence Nigeria," *The Business History Review* 86, no. 4 (2012): 745–771.
[80] Olakunle A. Lawal, "British Commercial Interests and the Decolonization Process in Nigeria, 1950–60," *African Economic History* no. 22 (1994): 93–110.
[81] Attah, "The Historical Conjuncture of Neo-Colonialism," 70–79.
[82] Christopher Ide, "Indigenization Policy: The Case of Nigeria 1960–1980, 1983," unpublished PhD dissertation, Atlanta University, 1983.
[83] Brian Pinto, "Nigeria During and After the Oil Boom: A Policy Comparison with Indonesia," *The World Bank Economic Review* 1, no. 3 (1987): 419–445.

An ongoing, postindependence cultural revolution has become the single most important colonial legacy that has been retained as a lasting impact of neocolonialism in Nigeria. In modern times, Western culture has diffused throughout African countries, including Nigeria. Scholars have offered different explanations for this phenomenon, including Nigeria's aforementioned historical consciousness. The country's cultural changes also have links to the spread of external influences between the late twentieth century and the early twenty-first century. Iyorza has noted that global media in the twentieth century – bringing improved communication methods and increased opportunities for global cultural exchange – has enabled a media revolution in Nigeria, and the entire African continent, impacting cultural neocolonialism.[84] The effects of this media revolution and its interactions with cultural neocolonialism are seen in the changing attitudes toward arts, clothing, music, and sports among Nigerian people.

Scholars studying Nigeria's cultural revolution and the effects of cultural neocolonialism have been particularly interested in Western culture's impact on young Nigerians and their clothing, music, and sports preferences. Shonekan[85] and Adedeji[86] have examined emerging manifestations of new cultural formations among Nigerian youths, driven by Western culture and its impact on their cultural identity. American hip-hop music, deeply associated with the black community in the United States, has been recognized as the most popular music genre among Nigerians. However, Adedeji asserts that political consciousness was already reflected in Nigerian music before the popularization of hip-hop music in Nigeria, and that hip-hop's appeal came from its ability to allow Nigerian youths to identify as black citizens of a global world, experiencing culturally based challenges similar to those faced by other people of African origin.

Is Nigeria's new cultural revolution having a positive effect on the country's development? Iyorza states that the phenomena of globalization – media revolution, and cultural neocolonialism – negatively impact Nigeria's national culture and development.[87] Industrial development in the country continues to suffer setbacks because of local preferences for foreign products, such as clothes, paintings, music, and movies, and the devaluation of the country's

---

[84] Stanislaus Iyorza, "Global Media and Neo-Colonialism in Africa: The Socio-Ecological Model Solution to Nigeria's Development Efforts," in *Freedom, Self-Determination and Growth in Africa*, ed. Kingsly Owete, Monica Emmanuel, Umar H. D. Danfulani, Sati Fwatshak, and Anthony Agwuele (Berlin: Media Team IT Education Centre, 2014), 1–18.
[85] Stephanie Shonekan, "The Blueprint: The Gift and The Curse of American Hip Hop Culture for Nigeria's Millennial Youth," *The Journal of Pan African Studies* 6, no. 3 (2013): 181–198.
[86] Wale Adedeji, "African Popular Culture and the Path of Consciousness: Hip Hop and the Culture of Resistance in Nigeria," *Postcolonial Text* 8, no. 3 & 4 (2013): 1–18.
[87] Iyorza, "Global Media and Neo-Colonialism in Africa," 5–6.

currency. The lifestyles and attitudes of many Western-educated Nigerians are patterned after foreign modes of thinking and learning, which are more relevant for white-collar jobs and other systems that are either not present in Nigeria's economy or not suited to the country's needs and aspirations. Although strategies are being implemented to decolonize the country's political and economic systems, little has been done to address cultural neocolonialism. Neocolonial forces have continued to exert influence over major elements of Nigeria's national culture, which adds to the challenge of underdevelopment.

Conclusion

British colonizers arriving in Lagos in the mid-nineteenth century marked a significant turning point for the city and the neighboring regions, later amalgamated into the Colony and Protectorate of Nigeria. The British occupied Nigeria in pursuit of economic, political, and missionary interests. However, to consolidate their economic control over the region, they established a political administration in the Colony and Protectorate of Nigeria that was typical for every British colony. The establishment of colonial rule introduced formal, Western-styled political administration and instigated a significant period in Nigeria's political history.

Historians, sociologists, political scientists, and other scholars have established that colonialism's presence in Nigeria left monumental political, sociocultural, and economic legacies. After Nigeria attained independence in 1960, neocolonialism and postcolonialism continued to influence the country's political, economic, and sociocultural systems. Neocolonialism is linked with Nigeria's present underdevelopment, together with misrule and mismanagement by Nigerian leaders.

BIBLIOGRAPHY

Abayomi, Disu O., and Oluwafunminiyi Raheem. "Fighting for Britain: Examining British Recruitment Strategies in Nigeria." In *Unknown Conflicts of the Second World War: Forgotten Fronts*, ed. Chris Murray. London: Routledge, 2019, 2–15.

Abba, Alkasum. *History of Yola, 1809–1914: The Establishment and Evolution of a Metropolis*. Zaria: Ahmadu Bello University, 2003.

Abdulahi, Abubakar, and Yahaya T. Baba. "Nationalism and National Integration in Nigeria." In *Nigerian Politics*, ed. Rotimi Ajayi Joseph and Yinka Fashagba. Cham: Springer, 2019, 307.

Abdulhamid, Abdulyassar. "Interesting Tales of Nigerians Who Are Indians in Tongue." *Daily Trust*, May 27, 2021.

Abdulkadir, Mohammed S. "Colonial Conquest and African Resistance: The Case of Idah and Ankpa in Igalaland (1864–1904)." *History Department Seminar*, Bayero University, Kano, 1987, 16–21.

——— "An Economic History of Igalaland: 1896–1939." Unpublished PhD dissertation, Bayero University, Kano, 1990.

——— "Islam in the Non-Muslim Areas of Northern Nigeria, c. 1600–1960." *Ilorin Journal of Religious Studies* 1, no. 1 (2011): 1–20.

Abdullahi, Ali A. "Trends and Challenges of Traditional Medicine in Africa." *African Journal of Traditional, Complementary and Alternative Medicine* 8, no. 5 (2011): 115–123.

Abdulrahman, Ajibola A. "Nationalism and Decolonization in Africa, 1918–1975." In *Africa in Global History: A Handbook*, ed. Toyin Falola and Mohammed Bashir Salau. Berlin: De Gruyter Oldenbourg, 2021, 185–202.

Abimbola, Wande. *Ifa: An Exposition of Ifa Literary Corpus*. Ibadan: Oxford University Press. 1976.

——— *Ifá Will Mend Our Broken World: Thoughts on Yoruba Religion and Culture in Africa and the Diaspora*. Canton: Aim Books, 1997.

——— *Yoruba Oral Tradition*. Ile-Ife: University of Ife, 1975.

Abioye, Abiola. "Fifty Years of Archives Administration in Nigeria: Lessons for the Future." *Records Management Journal* 17, no. 1 (2007): 52–62.

Abo, M. E., O. A. Fademi, G. O. Olaniyan, A. A. Ochigbo, O. I. Fatoba, and S. M. Misari. "Evolution of Extension Strategies towards Sustainable Agriculture in Nigeria." *Journal of Agricultural & Food Information* 4, no. 4 (2002): 65–80.

Abodunde, Ayodeji. *A Heritage of Faith: A History of Christianity in Nigeria*. Lagos: Pierce Watershed, 2016.

Abraham, Getahun Yacob. "A Post-Colonial Perspective on African Education Systems." *African Journal of Education and Practice* 6, no. 3 (2020): 47, 51.

Abrahams, Sidney. "The Colonial Legal Service and the Administration of Justice in Colonial Dependencies." *Journal of Comparative Legislation and International Law* 30, no. 3/4 (1948): 10.

Abubakar, Abdulahi, and Yahaya T. Baba. "Nationalism and National Integration in Nigeria." In *Nigerian Politics*, ed. Rotimi Ajayi and Joseph Y. Fashagba. Cham: Springer, 2021, 305–319.

Abubakar, Sa'ad. "The Emirate-Type of Government in the Sokoto Caliphate." *Journal of the Historical Society of Nigeria* 7, no. 2 (1974): 211–229.

The Lamibe of Fombina: A Political History of Adamawa 1809–1901. Zaria: Ahmadu Bello University Press, 1977.

"Pre-colonial Government and Administration among the Jukun." Inaugural Lecture, University of Maiduguri, March 26, 1986.

Acemoglu, Daron, Simon Johnson, and James Robinson. "Colonial Origins of Comparative Development: An Empirical Investigation." *American Economic Review* 91, no. 5 (2001): 1369–1401.

"Reversal of Fortune: Geography and Institutions in the Making of the Modern World Income Distribution." *The Quarterly Journal of Economics* 117, no. 4 (2002): 1231–1294.

Achebe, Nwando. *Farmers, Traders, Warriors, and Kings: Female Power and Authority in Northern Igboland, 1900–1960*. Portsmouth: New Hampshire, 2005.

Achi, Louis. "The Rise of Ethnic Nationalism." *Thisday*, June 20, 2021.

Achinewhu-Nworgu, Elizabeth, Queen C. Nworgu, Shade Babalola, Chinuru C. Achinewhu, and Charles Nna Dikeh. "Exploring Land Ownership and Inheritance in Nigeria." In *Education Provision to Every One: Comparing Perspectives from Around the World*, ed. James Ogunleye. Sofia: Bulgarian Comparative Education Society, 2014, 354–361.

Acholonu, Rose. "Igbo Women in Political Limbo." In *The Igbo and the Tradition of Politics*, ed. Ukachukwu D. Anyanwu and Jude C. U. Aguwa. Enugu: Fourth Dimension, 1993, 289–297.

Achunonu, Anthony Okwudili. *Poverty and the Church in Igboland, Nigeria*. Bloomington: Xlibris Corporation, 2012.

Adamolekun, Ladipo, and S. Bamidele Ayo. "The Evolution of the Nigerian Federal Administration System." *Publius: The Journal of Federalism* 19, no. 1 (1989): 157–176.

Adamu, Mahdi. "The Hausa and Their Neighbors in the Central Sudan." In *General History of Africa, 4: Africa from the Twelfth to Sixteenth Century*, ed. Djibril T. Niane. Paris: UNESCO, 1984, 266–300.

The Hausa Factor in West African History. Zaria: Ahmadu Bello University Press, 1978.

Adebanwi, Wale, ed. "Contesting Multiculturalism: Ethno-regionalism and Contending Forms of Nationalism in Late Colonial Nigeria." *Commonwealth & Comparative Politics* 56, no. 1 (2018): 40–64.

The Political Economy of Everyday Life in Africa: Beyond the Margins. London: James Currey, 2017.

Adebayo, Adewumi D. "The ILO and the Political Economy of Labor Policy Making in Nigeria, 1930–1960." *The Journal of Imperial and Commonwealth History* 50, no. 2 (2022): 348–382.

Adebayo, Akanmu G. "Iwo: The Case Study of a Non-belligerent Yoruba State in the 19th Century." In *War and Peace in Yorubaland, 1793–1893*, ed. Adeagbo Akinjogbin. Ibadan: Heinemann Educational Books, 1998, 91–98.

"The Production and Export of Hides and Skins in Colonial Northern Nigeria, 1900–1945." *The Journal of African History* 33, no. 2 (1992): 273–300.

Adebayo, Peter F. "Political Party, Formation, Development, Performance and Prospects." *Drumspeak: International Journal of Research in the Humanities* 4, nos. 1–2 (2011): 94–113.

Adebowale, Oludamola. "Significance of Egungun in Yoruba Cultural History." *Guardian*, February 9, 2020.

Adeboye, Olufunke A. "Christianity and Traditional Life in Ibadan 1853–1940." In *Readings in Nigerian History and Culture: Essays in Memory of J. A. Atanda*, ed. Dare Oguntomisin and Samuel A. Ajayi. Ibadan: Hope Publications, 2002, 106–115.

"J. F. Ade Ajayi, 1929–2014." *Africa* 85, no. 4 (2015): 741–744.

Adedeji, Joel A. "The Church and the Emergence of the Nigerian Theatre: 1915–1945." *Journal of the Historical Society of Nigeria* 6, no. 4 (1973): 389.

"Nationalism and the Nigerian National Theatre." *Munger Africana Library Notes* 54 (1980): 5–21.

"The Origin and Form of the Yoruba Masque Theatre." *Cahiers d'Études africaines* 46 (1972): 254–276.

Adedeji, Wale. "African Popular Culture and the Path of Consciousness: Hip Hop and the Culture of Resistance in Nigeria." *Postcolonial Text* 8, no. 3 & 4 (2013): 1–18.

Adefemi, Jare, eds. *The History of the Cathedral of St. Peter, Ake, Abeokuta, 1843–1986.* Abeokuta: The Standing Committee, 1986.

Adefulu, Razaq A. "*Reflections on Politics, Democratic Governance and Development in Post-colonial Nigeria.*" Faculty of Management and Social Sciences, Babcock University, 2003.

Adefuye, Ade, Babatunde Agiri, and Akinjide Osuntokun. *History of the Peoples of Lagos State.* Ikeja: Lantern Books, 1987.

Adefuye, Ade, John Gershion, and Joshua Ricketts. "Jamaican Contribution to the Socio-Economic Development of the Colony Province." In *Studies in Yoruba History and Culture*, ed. Gabriel O. Olusanya. Ibadan: Ibadan University Press, 1983.

Adegbami, Adeleke, and Charles I. Uche. "Ethnicity and Ethnic Politics: An Impediment to Political Development in Nigeria." *Public Administration Research* 4, no. 1 (2015): 59.

Adegbola, Adelegan. *Ile-Ife: The Source of Yoruba Civilization.* Ketu: Oduduwa International Communications, 2009.

Adejuwon, Akin. "'Art' of War: Analysis of Weapons of the 19th Century Yoruba Civil Wars." *Revista Universitaria de Historia Militar* 8, no. 17 (2019): 183.

Adekanla, Olabisi. *Imesi-Ile: The Ancient Kiriji Camp*. Ibadan: Peetee Nigeria Limited, 1999.

Adekola, Oyebola O. "Kola Ogunmola: A Socio-Cultural Study of His Folkloric Plays." Masters Thesis, University of Ibadan, 1991.

Adekoya, Preye. "The Succession Dispute to the Throne of Lagos and the British Conquest and Occupation of Lagos." *African Research Review* 10, no. 42 (2016): 207–226.

Adekunle, Julius O. "Yoruba Factor in Nigerian Politics." In *Yoruba Identity and Power Politics*, ed. Toyin Falola and Ann Genova. Rochester: University of Rochester Press, 2006, 273–276.

Adeleye, Rowland A. "Mahdist Triumph and British Revenge in Northern Nigeria: Satiru 1906." *Journal of the Historical Society of Nigeria* 6, no. 2 (1972): 193–214.

Power and Diplomacy in Northern Nigeria, 1804–1906: The Sokoto Caliphate and its Enemies. London: Longman, 1971.

"The Sokoto Caliphate in the 19th Century." In *History of West Africa*. Vol. II, ed. Jacob F. A. Ajayi and Michael Crowther. London: Longman, 1974, 60–69.

Adeloye, Adelola. *African Pioneers of Modern Medicine: Nigerian Doctors of the Nineteenth Century*. Ibadan: University Press, 1985.

Ademola, Adetokunbo. "Personnel Problems in the Administration of Justice in Nigeria." *Law and Contemporary Problems* 27, no. 4 (1962): 578.

Ademowo, Adeyemi J., and Adedapo Adekunle. "*Law in Traditional Yoruba Philosophy: A Critical Appraisal*. *Caribbean Journal of Philosophy* 2, no. 1 (2013): 345–354.

Adeniran, Adekunle. "Personalities and Policies in the Establishment of English in Northern Nigeria During the British Colonial Administration, 1900–1943." *Journal of the Historical Society of Nigeria* 9, no. 2 (1978): 109–113.

Adeogun, Adebowale O. "Music Education in Nigeria, 1842–2001: Policy and Content Evaluation, Towards a New Dispensation." Unpublished PhD dissertation, University of Pretoria, 2007.

Adeoti, Ezekiel O. *Alayande as Educationist 1948–1983: A Study of Alayande's Contribution to Education and Social Change*. Ibadan: Heinemann Educational Books, 1997.

Adepegba, Cornelius. *Yoruba Egungun: Its Association with Ancestors and the Typology of Yoruba Masquerades by Its Costume*. Ibadan: Ibadan University Press, 1984.

Aderibigbe, Adeyemi B. "Expansion of the Lagos Protectorate 1863–1900." Unpublished PhD dissertation, University of London, 1959.

"The Ijebu Expedition, 1892: An Episode in the British Penetration of Nigeria Reconsidered." *Proceedings of the Leverhalme Inter-Collegiate History Conference*, University College of Rhodesia and Nyasaland, 1960, 267–282.

Lagos: The Development of an African City. Lagos: Longman, 1975.

Aderinto, Adeyinka A. "Patriarchy and Culture: The Position of Women in a Rural Yoruba Community, Nigeria." *The Anthropologist* 3, no. 4 (2001): 225-230.
Adesina, Olutayo C. "*The Future of the Past.*" An Inaugural Lecture. Ibadan: Ibadan University Press, 2012.
Adesina, Oluwakemi. "Women, Shari'ah, and Zina in Northern Nigeria." *African Nebula* 2 (2010): 43-56.
Adetiba, Toyin Cotties. "Dynamics of Ethnic Politics in Nigeria: An Impediment to its Political System." *Journal of Economics and Behavioral Studies* 11, no. 2 (2019): 132-144.
Adetugbo, Abiodun. "The Development of English in Nigeria up to 1914: A Socio-Historical Appraisal." *Journal of the Historical Society of Nigeria* 9, no. 2 (1978): 89-96.
Adewale, S. A. "The Role of Ifa in the Work of the 19th Century Missionaries." *Orita – Ibadan Journal of Religious Studies* 12, no. 1 (1978): 26.
Adeyeri, Olusegun, and Kehinde David Adejuwon. "The Implications of British Colonial Economic Policies on Nigeria's Development." *International Journal of Advanced Research in Management and Social Sciences* 1, no. 2 (2012): 1-16.
Adeyi, Ezekiel Major. "Funding of Political Parties and Candidates in Nigeria: A Historical Perspective." In *Money and Politics in Nigeria*, ed. Victor Adetula. Abuja: International Foundation for Electoral Systems, 2008.
Adi, Hakim. "Pan-Africanism and West African Nationalism in Britain." *African Studies Review* 43, no. 1 (2000): 69-82.
"West African Students in Britain, 1900-60: The Politics of Exile." In *Africans in Britain*, ed. David Killingray. London: Frank Cass, 1994, 114-118.
West Africans in Britain 1900-1960: Nationalism, Pan-Africanism and Communism. London: Lawrence & Wishart, 1998.
Aduwo, B. E., Patrick Edewor, and Eziyi O. Ibem. "Urbanization and Housing for Low-income Earners in Nigeria: A Review of Features, Challenges and Prospects." *Mediterranean Journal of Social Sciences* 7, no. 3 (2016): 347-357.
Afe, Adedayo E. "Indigenous Judicial System and Governance in the Old Ondo Province, Southwestern Nigeria." *Journal of Law, Policy and Globalization* 20 (2013): 100-105.
Afigbo, Adiele E. *The Abolition of the Slave Trade in Southeastern Nigeria 1885-1950*. New York: University of Rochester Press, 2006.
"Anthropology and Colonial Administration in South-Eastern Nigeria, 1891-1939." *Journal of the Historical Society of Nigeria* 8, no. 1 (1975): 19-35.
"Background to Nigerian Federalism: Federal Features in the Colonial State." *Publius: The Journal of Federalism* 21, no. 4 (1991): 13-29.
"The Consolidation of British Imperial Administration in Nigeria: 1900-1918." *Civilizations* 21, no. 4 (1971): 436-459.
"The Eclipse of the Aro Slaving Oligarchy of South-Eastern Nigeria 1901-1927." *Journal of the Historical Society of Nigeria* 6, no. 1 (1971): 3-24.
"The Flame of History Blazing at Ibadan." *Journal of The Historical Society of Nigeria* 7, no. 4 (1975): 715-720.

"Oral Tradition and History in Eastern Nigeria." *African Notes: Bulletin of the Institute of African Studies* 3, no. 3 (1966): 12–20.

"Revolution and Reaction in Eastern Nigeria: 1900–1929: The Background to the Women's Riot of 1929." *Journal of the Historical Society of Nigeria* 3, no. 3 (1966): 539–557.

Ropes of Sand: Studies in Igbo History. Nsukka: AP Express Publishers, 1981.

The Warrant Chiefs: Indirect Rule in Southeastern Nigeria, 1891–1929. London: Longman, 1972.

"The Warrant Chief System in Eastern Nigeria: Direct or Indirect Rule?" *Journal of the Historical Society of Nigeria* 3, no. 4 (1967): 449.

Afigbo, Adiele E., Emmanuel A. Ayandele, Robert J. Gavin, and Robin Plamer, eds. *The Making of Modern Africa*. Vol. 2: *The Twentieth Century*. London: Longman Group, 1992.

Afolabi, Abiodun. "The Colonial Taxation Policy among the Yoruba of Southwestern Nigeria and Its Implications for Socio-Economic Development." *Journal of the Historical Society of Nigeria* 19 (2010): 63–92.

Afolayan, Adeshina. *Identities, Histories and Values in Postcolonial Nigeria*. Lanham: Rowman & Littlefield, 2021.

Agbiboa, Daniel Egiegba, and Andrew Emmanuel Okem. "Unholy Trinity: Assessing the Impact of Ethnicity and Religion on National Identity in Nigeria." *Peace Research* 43, no. 2 (2011): 98–125.

Agbo, Njideka. "Funmilayo Anikulapo-Kuti: The Education Game-Changer." *The Guardian*, October 25, 2018.

Agbonika, John Alewo Musa. "Federalism and Military Rule in Nigeria." Unpublished PhD dissertation. University of London, 1991.

Agboola, C. O. O. "The Jihad and the Islamization Ideal: A Reconsideration of the Case of Ilorin Emirate, c. 1823–1900." *Global Journal of Humanities* 6, no. 1&2 (2007): 45–49.

Aghahowa, John O., and E. E. M. Ukpebor. "The British Colonial Economic Policies and Nigeria Underdevelopment." *The Nigerian Journal of Politics and Public Policy* 3, nos. 1&2 (1999): 193–210.

Aghalino, Samuel Ovete. "British Colonial Policies and the Oil Palm Industry in the Niger Delta Region of Nigeria, 1900–1960." *African Study Monographs* 21, no. 1 (2000): 19–33.

Agunbiade, Tayo. "Remembering Margaret Ekpo and the Enugu Strike Massacre." *Aljazeera*, December 12, 2020. www.aljazeera.com/features/2020/12/12/remembering-margaret-ekpo-and-enugu-strike-massacre.

Aguolu, Christian C., and L. E. Aguolu. "A Force in Library Development in Nigeria." *World Libraries* 7, no. 2 (1997): 9–18.

Aguwa, Jude C. "Religious Conflict in Nigeria: Impact on Nation Building." *Dialectical Anthropology* 22, nos. 3–4 (1997): 335–351.

Ahazuem, J. O., and Toyin Falola. "Production for the Metropolis: Agriculture and Forest Products." In *Britain and Nigeria. Exploitation or Development?* ed. Toyin Falola. London: Zed Books, 1987.

Ahire, Philip T. "Policing and Construction of Colonial State in Nigeria State, 1860–1960." *Journal of Third World Studies* 7, no. 2 (1990): 151–172.

The Tiv in Contemporary Nigeria. Zaria: Tiv Studies Project, 1993.

Ahmed, A. "Jos: Class and Ethnicity." *The Analyst* III, no. 3 (1988).

Ahmed, Iyanda Kamoru, and Abubakar Umar. "Nationalists in Nigeria from 1914–1960." *International Journal of Social Sciences and Management Review* 02, no. 05 (2019): 1–12.

Ahokegh, Akaayar F. "Colonialism, Development of Infrastructure and Urbanization in Tiv Land of Central Nigeria." *Academia*. www.academia.edu/3875702/Colonialism_and_Infrastructure_Development_in_Nigeria.

Aisien, Ebiuwa, and Felix O. U. Oriakhi. "Great Benin on the World Stage: Re-assessing Portugal-Benin Diplomacy in the 15th and 16th Centuries." *IOSR Journal of Humanities and Social Science* 11, no. 1 (2013): 107–115.

Aiyede, Remi. "United we Stand: Labor Unions and Human Rights NGOs in the Democratization Process in Nigeria." *Development in Practice* 14, no. 1–2 (2004): 224–233.

Ajayi, Abiodun, and Oluwafunminiyi Raheem. "The Deepening Crisis of Leadership and Accountability in Nigeria, 1999–2019." *Orirun: UNIOSUN Journal of African Studies* 2, no. 2 (2020): 1–26.

Ajayi, Dickson 'Dare. "Recent Trends and Patterns of Nigeria's Industrial Development." *African Journal for the Psychological Study of Social Issues* 9, no. 2 (2006): 135–151.

Ajayi, Ibi S. "Globalization and Africa." *Journal of African Economies* 12, no. 1 (2003): 120–150.

Ajayi, Johnson O. "Nigeria Prisons and the Dispensation of Justice." *AFRREV IJAH: An International Journal of Arts and Humanities*, 1, no. 3 (2012): 208–233.

Ajayi, Jacob F. A. "Africa at the Beginning of the Nineteenth Century: Issues and Prospects." In *General History of Africa – VI: Africa in the Nineteenth Century until the 1880s*, ed. Jacob F. A. Ajayi. Oxford: Heinemann Educational Publishers, 1995, 1–22.

"The British Occupation of Lagos, 1851–61: A Critical Review." *Nigeria Magazine*, no. 69 (1961): 96–105.

Christian Missions in Nigeria 1841–1891: The Making of a New Elite. London: Longman, 1965.

"The Development of Secondary Grammar School Education in Nigeria." *Journal of the Historical Society of Nigeria* 2, no. 4 (1963): 522.

ed. *General History of Africa: VI Africa in the Nineteenth Century until the 1880s*. Paris: UNESCO Publishing, 1998.

"Henry Venn and the Policy of Development." *Journal of the Historical Society of Nigeria* 1, no. 4 (1959): 340.

"Higher Education in Nigeria." *African Affairs* 74, no. 297 (1975): 420–426.

"Historical Education in Nigeria." *Journal of the Historical Society of Nigeria* 8, no. 1 (1975): 3–8.

History and the Nation and Other Address. Ibadan: Spectrum Books, 1991.
"How Yoruba was Reduced to Writing." *Odu* 8 (1960): 49–58.
Milestones in Nigerian History. Ibadan: University of Ibadan Press, 1962.
"The National Question in Nigeria in Historical Perspective." Being excerpts of lecture delivered at the fifth *Guardian* Lecture, November 1992.
"Nineteenth Century Origins of Nigerian Nationalism." *Journal of the Historical Society of Nigeria* 2, no. 2 (1961): 196–210.
"Towards a More Enduring Sense of History." Being a Tribute to K. O. Dike on Behalf of the Historical Society of Nigeria, October, 1983.
"Towards an African Economic Community: A Historical Perspective." Lecture Presented at the Discussion of the Lagos Plan of Action, 1970.
Ajayi, Jacob F. A., and Stephen A. Akintoye. "Yorubaland in the Nineteenth Century." In *Groundwork of Nigerian History*, ed. Obaro Ikime. Ibadan: Heinemann Educational Books, 1999, 276–290.
Ajayi, Jacob F. A., and Ebiegberi Alagoa. "Nigeria before 1800: Aspects of Economic Development and Inter-group Relations." In *Groundwork of Nigerian History*, ed. Obaro Ikime. Ibadan: Heinemann Books, 1980, 224–335.
Ajayi, Jacob F. A., and Abednego E. Ekoko. "Transfer of Power in Nigeria: Its Origin and Consequences." In *Decolonization and African Independence: The Transfer of Power, 1960–1980*. London: Yale University Press, 1988, 245–270.
Ajayi, Jacob F. A., and Michael Crowder. *History of West Africa*, Vol. 1. New York: Columbia University Press, 1972.
Ajayi, Jacob F. A., and Robert S. Smith. *Yoruba Warfare in the 19th Century*. London: Cambridge University Press, 1964.
Ajayi, Rotimi. "The Politicization of Trade Unionism: The Case of Labor/NCNC Alliance in Nigeria, 1940–1960." *Ufahamu: A Journal of African Studies* 27, nos. 1–3 (1999): 48–62.
Ajayi, Rotimi, and Joseph Y. Fashagba. eds. *Nigerian Politics. Advances in African Economic, Social and Political Development.* Cham: Springer Nature, 2021.
Ajayi, Simon A. *Emmanuel Oyewole Akingbala: The Adventures of a Nigerian Baptist Pastor.* Ibadan: Hope Publications, 1999.
"The Genesis of Free Education in Western Nigeria, 1951–1966." *Journal of Social Sciences* 3, no. 1 (2008): 108–122.
Ajene, O. "Political Parties and Federalism." In *Foundations of Nigerian Federalism: 1900–1960*, ed. Isawa J. Elaigwu and Godfrey N. Uzoigwe. Jos: Institute of Governance and Social Research, 1996.
Ajetunmobi, Rasheed O. *The Evolution and Development of Lagos State.* Lagos: A-Triad Associates, 2003.
"Theories and Concepts in Migration and Settlement Studies: The Case of the Coastal Yoruba." *The Social Sciences*, 7, no. 2 (2012): 289–296.
Ajetunmobi, Rasheed O., and Adewale Adepoju. "Transforming African Nations through Indigenous Music: A Study of Haruna Ishola's Apala Music." *The Social Sciences* 8, no. 1 (2013): 29–33.

Ajisafe, Ajayi K. *History of Abeokuta*. Abeokuta: Fola Bookshops, 1924.
Ajuluchukwu, Michael C. K. "Zikists of the Burning Struggle." *The Guardian*, March 8, 1998.
Aka, Ebenezer O. "Town and Country Planning and Administration in Nigeria." *International Journal of Public Sector Management* 6, no. 3 (1993): 47–64.
Akande, Iyabode Deborah. "On the Content and Form of Ìwúde Songs in Òkè-Igbó." *International Journal of Humanities and Social Science* 7, no. 1 (2017): 192–199.
Akano, Ezekiel Kehinde, and Jacob Olusola Bamigbose. "The Role of African Traditional Religion in Conflict Management in Nigeria." *Journal of Living Together* 6, no. 1 (2019): 246–258.
Ake, Claude. *A Political Economy of Africa*. Lagos: Longman Nigeria Plc, 2008.
Revolutionary Pressures in Africa. London: Zed Press, 1978.
Akinade, Akintunde E. "New Religious Movements in Contemporary Nigeria: Aladura Churches as a Case Study." *Asia Journal of Theology* 10, no. 2 (1996): 316–332.
Akingbe, Niyi. "In Memoriam: Dr Victor Abimbola Olaiya (1930–2020)." *Journal of the Musical Arts in Africa* 17, no. 1 (2020): 121–124.
Akinjogbin, Isaac A. "Dahomey and its Neighbors 1708–1818." Unpublished PhD dissertation. University of London 1963.
Dahomey and Its Neighbors 1708–1818. New York: Cambridge University Press, 1967.
"Dahomey and Yoruba in the Nineteenth Century." In *Africa in the Nineteenth and Twentieth Centuries*, ed. Joseph C. Anene and Godfrey N. Brown. Ibadan: Ibadan University Press, 1966, 255–269.
"Ife Years of Travail 1793–1893." In *The Cradle of a Race: Ife from the Beginning to 1980*, ed. Isaac. A. Akinjogbin. Port Harcourt: Sunray Publications Ltd., 1978, 153.
"The Growth of Ife from Oduduwa to 1800." In *The Cradle of a Race: Ife from the Beginning to 1980*, ed. Isaac A. Akinjogbin. Port Harcourt: Sunray Publications Ltd., 1978, 112.
"The Oyo Empire in the 18th Century – A Reassessment." *Journal of the Historical Society of Nigeria* 3, no. 3 (1966): 449–460.
War and Peace in Yorubaland, 1793–1893. Ibadan: Heinemann Educational Books, 1998.
Akinola, Gabriel A. "The Origin of the Eweka Dynasty of Benin: A Study in the Use and Abuse of Oral Traditions." *Journal of the Historical Society of Nigeria* 8, no. 3 (1976): 21–36.
Akin-Otiko, Akinmayowa. "Ifá Divination: A Method of Diagnosing and Treating Chronic Illnesses/Àmódi among Yoruba People." In *Chronic Illness, Spirituality, and Healing: Diverse Disciplinary, Religious, and Cultural Perspectives*, ed. Michael J. Stoltzfus, Rebecca Green and Darla Schumm. New York: Palgrave Macmillan, 2013, 239–252.

Akinpelu, Jones A. "Values in Nigerian Society." In *New Perspectives in Moral Education*, ed. Otonti A. Nduka and E. O. Iheoma. Ibadan: Evans Bros, 1983, 33–56.

Akinsanya, Adeoye A., and Rafiu A. Akindele. "Legitimate Trade, Annexation and Cession of Lagos and International Law." *Journal of Management and Social Sciences* 7, no. 1 (2018): 266–278.

Akinsuroju, Olu. "The Nigerian Press, 1859–1969." A Lecture Delivered at the Third Workshop of the Western State Council of the NUJ held in Ibadan, September 25, 1971.

Akintola, Akinbowale. *Reformed Ogboni Fraternity (ROF): Its Origin and Interpretation of its Doctrines and Symbolism*. Ogbomoso: Ogunniyi Printing Works, 1992.

Akintonde, Moses Akintunde, and Margaret Olugbemisola Areo. "Art and Craft of Old Oyo: It's Manifestation in the Present Oyo." *Journal of Humanities and Social Science* 15, no. 5 (2013): 50–59.

Akintoye, Stephen A. "The North-Eastern Yoruba Districts and the Benin Kingdom." *Journal of the Historical Society of Nigeria* IV, no. 4 (1969): 539–553.

Revolution and Power Politics in Yorubaland 1840–1893: Ibadan Expansion and the Rise of Ekitiparapo. Ibadan: Longman, 1971.

Akinwale, Emmanuel Jude Abiodun. "A Historical and Comparative Analysis of Colonial and Post-Colonial Bureaucracy in Nigeria." *Journal of Public Administration and Governance* 4, no. 2 (2014): 1–11.

Akinwunmi, Olayemi, Okpeh O. Okpeh, and Jerry D. Gwamna, eds. *Inter-Group Relations in Nigeria During the 19th and 20th Centuries*. Makurdi: Aboki Publishers, 2006.

Akinwunmi, Tunde M. "Oral Traditions and the Reconstruction of Yoruba Dress." In *Yoruba Identity and Power Politics*, ed. Toyin Falola and Ann Genova. Rochester: Rochester University Press, 2006, 49–73.

Akowe, Tony. "40 Years of NLC: So Far, So Fair?" *The Nation*, February 25, 2018.

Akpan, N. U. "Nigerian Federalism: Accidental Foundations by Lugard." *Journal of the Historical Society of Nigeria* 9, no. 2 (1978): 1–20.

Akpanika, Ekpenyong Nyong. "Religious and Political Crises in Nigeria: A Historical Exploration." *IOSR Journal of Humanities and Social Science* 22, no. 9 (2017): 65–76.

Akubor, Emmanuel O. "From Hinterland Trade to International Commerce: Historicizing Nigeria's Contributions to World Economy from 1914." *JORAS–Nigerian Journal of Religion and Society* 4 (2014): 134–151.

Akwara, Azalahu Francis, and Benedict O. Ojomah. "Religion, Politics and Democracy in Nigeria." *Canadian Social Science* 9, no. 2 (2013): 48–61.

Akwara, Azalahu Francis, Joseph Effiong Udaw, and Gerald E. Ezirim. "Adapting Colonial Legacy to Modernism: A Focus on Rail Transport Development in Nigeria." *Mediterranean Journal of Social Sciences* 5, no. 6 (2014): 465.

Alabi, Aliyu S. "Voices After the Maxim Gun: Intellectual and Literary Opposition to Colonial Rule in Northern Nigeria." In *Resurgent Nigeria: Issues in Nigerian Intellectual History: A Festschrift in Honour of Dahiru Yahya*, ed. Sa'idu Babura Ahmad and Ibrahim Khaleel Abdussalam. Ibadan: University Press, 2011, 124–146.

Aládésanmí, Omọ́bọ́lá A., and Ìbùkún B. Ògúnjìnmí. "Yorùbá Thoughts and Beliefs in Child Birth and Child Moral Upbringing: A Cultural Perspective." *Advances in Applied Sociology* 9 (2019): 569–585.

Alaja-Browne, Afolabi. "The Origin and Development of JuJu Music." *The Black Perspective in Music* 17, no. 1/2 (1989): 55–72.

Alao, Olatunji E. "Britain and the Civilizing Mission in Nigeria: Revisiting Anti-Malaria Policy in Lagos Metropolis during the Colonial Era, 1861–1960." *Lagos Historical Review* 13 (2013): 85–106.

Albasu, S. A. "The Jihad in Hausaland and the Kano Fulani." *Nigeria Magazine* 53, no. 1 (1985): 52–54.

Albert, Isaac O. "Urban Violence in Africa: Violence in Metropolitan Kano: A Historical Perspective." In *Urban Violence in Africa: Pilot Studies (South Africa, Côte–d'Ivoire, Nigeria)*, ed. Eghosa E. Osaghae. Ibadan: IFRA-Nigeria, 1994.

Albertini, Rudolf von. "The Impact of Two World Wars on the Decline of Colonialism." *Journal of Contemporary History* 4, no. 1 (1969): 17–35.

Aldred, Ken, and Martin A. Smith. *Superpowers in the Post-Cold War Era*. London: Palgrave Macmillan, 1999.

Alegbeleye, Gabriel B. O. "Archives Administration and Records Management in Nigeria: Up the Decades from Amalgamation." *Information Management* 22, no. 3 (1998): 26.

Alemika, Etannibi E. O., and Emily I. Alemika. "Penal Crisis and Prison Management in Nigeria." *Lawyers Bi-Annual* 1, no. 2 (1995): 62–80.

Ali, Merima, Odd-Helge Fjeldstad, Boqian Jiang, and Abdulaziz B Shifa. "Colonial Legacy, State-Building and the Salience of Ethnicity in Sub-Saharan Africa." *The Economic Journal* 129, no. 619 (2019): 1048–1081.

Aliyu, Idrees. "Collaboration and the British Conquest of Bida in 1798: The Role and Achievement of the Indigenous Interest Groups." *African Study Monographs* 10, no. 2 (1989): 69–82.

Allen, Judith Van. "'Sitting on a Man': Colonialism and the Lost Political Institutions of Igbo Women." *Canadian Journal of African Studies* 6, no. 2 (1972): 165–181.

Alli, Adekunle. *Lagos from the Earliest Times to British Occupation*. Festac-Town: Adeniran Ogunsanya College of Education, 2002.

Allsworth-Jones, Philip, Katerina Harvati, and Christopher Stringer. "Archaeological Context of the Iwo Eleru Cranium from Nigeria and Preliminary Results of New Morphometric Studies." In *West African Archaeology: New Developments, New Perspectives*, ed. Philip Allsworth-Jones. Oxford: Archaeopress, 2010, 29–42.

Allyn, David E. "The Sabon Gari System in Northern Nigeria, 1911–1940." Unpublished PhD dissertation. University of California, 1976.

Alozie, Bright. "Space and Colonial Alterity: Interrogating British Residential Segregation in Nigeria, 1899–1919." *Ufahamu: A Journal of African Studies* 41, no. 2 (2020): 1–26.

Alpern, Stanley B. "What Africans Got for Their Slaves: A Master List of European Trade Goods." *History in Africa* 22 (1995): 10.

Altbach, Philip G., and Gail Paradise Kelly. *Education and the Colonial Experience*. New York: Advent Books, 1991.

Altick, Richard D. *The Weaker Sex: Victorian People and Ideas*. New York: W. W. Norton & Company, 1973.

Aluko, Ola. "Functionality of the Town Planning Authorities in Effecting Urban and Regional Planning Laws and Control in Nigeria: The Case of Lagos State." *African Research Review* 5, no. 6 (2011): 159.

Amadi, G. I. S. "Healing in 'the Brotherhood of the Cross and Star.'" *Studies in Church History* 19 (1982): 367–383.

Amadi, Levi O. "The Reactions and Contributions of Nigerians during the Second World War: Agents of Political Integration in Nigeria, 1939–1945." *Transafrican Journal of History* 6, no. 7 (1977–8): 1–11.

Amadiume, Ifi. *Male Daughters, Female Husbands: Gender and Sex in an African Society*. London: Zed Books Ltd., 2015.

Amaechi, Chidi M., and Edwin U. Amaechi. "Precolonial African Gender Cosmology and the Gender Equality Nexus: The Road Not Taken in Igboland, Nigeria." *Asian Women* 35, no. 3 (2019): 93–113.

Amali, Idris O. O. "Indigenous Nigerian Oral Drama as an Instrument of Social Regulation: A Case of the Ogbllo Secret Society of Idoma." *Ufahamu: Journal of the African Activist Association* 20, no 1 (1992): 56–67.

Amankulor, James, and Chinyere G. Okafor. "Continuity and Change in Traditional Nigerian Theater among the Igbo in the Era of Colonial Politics." *Ufahamu: A Journal of African Studies* 16, no. 3 (1988): 36.

Ames, David W. "Sociocultural View of Hausa Musical Activity." In *The Traditional Artist in African Society*, ed. Warren d'Azevedo. Bloomington: Indiana University Press, 1973, 128–161.

Ames, David W., and Anthony V. King. *Glossary of Hausa Music and its Social Contexts*. Evanston: Northwestern University Press, 1971.

Amin, Samir. *Eurocentrism: Modernity, Religion, and Democracy: A Critique of Eurocentrism and Culturalism*, trans. Russel Moore and James Membrez. New York: Monthly Review Press, 1989.

Amutabi, Maurice, ed. *Development from Below and Above in Africa*. Nairobi: Centre for Democracy, Research and Development, 2018.

Ananaba, Wogu. *The Trade Union Movement in Nigeria*. Benin City: Ethiope Publishing, 1969.

The Trade Union Movement in Africa: Promise and Performance. London: C. Hurst, 1979.

Anderson, Allan. *African Reformation: African Initiated Christianity in the 20th Century.* New Jersey: Africa World Press, 2001.
Anderson, Richard, and Henry B. Lovejoy, eds. *Liberated Africans and the Abolition of the Slave Trade, 1807–1896.* New York: University of Rochester Press, 2020.
Anderson, Richard. "The Diaspora of Sierra Leone's Liberated Africans: Enlistment, Forced Migration, and 'Liberation' at Freetown, 1808–1863." *African Economic History* 41 (2013): 101–138.
Anderson, Warwick. *Colonial Pathologies: American Tropical Medicine, Race and Hygiene in the Philippines.* Durham: Duke University Press, 2006.
Anene, Joseph C. *Southern Nigeria in Transition, 1885–1906: Theory and Practice in a Colonial Protectorate.* Cambridge: Cambridge University Press, 1966.
Anikwenze, Chinenye. "The Long Walk to Equality: Historical Influences on Women in Igbo Society." *The Republic*, January 20, 2021. www.republic.com.ng/december-20-january-21/the-long-walk-to-equality/.
Animashaun, Bashir O. "Benin Imperialism and the Transformation of Idejo Chieftaincy Institution in Lagos, 1603–1850." *Journal of the Historical Society of Nigeria* 25 (2016): 37–52.
Anjorin, A. O. "The Background to the Amalgamation of Nigeria in 1914." *Odù: Journal of Yoruba and Related Studies* 3, no. 2 (1967): 72–86.
Anstey, Roger. *The Atlantic Slave Trade and British Abolition, 1760–1810.* London: Macmillan, 1975.
Anyanwu, Ogechi E. *The Making of Mbano: British Colonialism, Resistance, and Diplomatic Engagements in Southeastern Nigeria, 1906–1960.* Lanham: Lexington Books, 2021.
Anyanwu, Ukachukwu D. "Gender Question in Igbo Politics." In *The Igbo and the Tradition of Politics*, ed. Ukachukwu D. Anyanwu and Jude C. U. Aguwa. Enugu: Fourth Dimension, 1993, 113–120.
Apata, Z. O. "Lugard and the Creation of Provincial Administration in Northern Nigeria, 1900–1918." *African Study Monographs* 11, no. 3 (1989): 143–152.
Apter, David E. *Ghana in Transition.* Princeton: Princeton University Press, 2015.
Aremu, Johnson O. "Administration of British West African Colonies and the Furtherance of Nigeria–Gold Coast Relations, 1885–1960." *International Journal of Humanities and Cultural Studies* 1, no. 4 (2015): 3.
Aremu, P. S. O., Biodun Banjo, and Yaya Olanipekun. "Egungun Tradition in Trado-Modern Society in South-Western." *Mediterranean Journal of Social Sciences* 3, no. 1 (2012): 283.
Arifalo, Samuel O. *The Egbe Omo Oduduwa: A Study in Ethnic and Cultural Nationalism (1945–1965).* Akure: Stebak Books, 2001.
"The Rise and Decline of the Nigerian National Democratic Party (NNDP) 1923–1938." *Odu: A Journal of West African Studies* 24 (1983): 89–110.
"The Rise and Decline of the Nigerian Youth Movement, 1934–1941." *The African Review: Journal of African Politics, Development and International Affairs* 13, no. 1 (1986): 59–76.

Arinze, Francis A. *Sacrifice in Igbo Religion*. Ibadan: University Press, 1974.
Ariyo, Aboyade S. "Trade across Frontiers: An Overview of International Trade before the Advent of Modern Economic System in Nigeria." *Historia Actual Online* 35, no. 3 (2014): 53–60.
Armitage, David, and Michael J. Braddick, eds. *The British Atlantic World, 1500–1800*. New York: Palgrave Macmillan, 2002.
Armstrong, Alice, Chaloka Beyani, Chuma Himonga, et al. "Uncovering Reality: Excavating Women's Rights in African Family Law." *International Journal of Law, Policy and the Family* 7, no. 3 (1993): 314–369.
Arnold, David, ed. *Imperial Medicine and Indigenous Societies*. Vol. 6. Manchester: Manchester University Press, 1988.
Arowolo, Dare. "The Effects of Western Civilization and Culture on Africa." *Afro Asian Journal of Social Sciences* 1, no. 1 (2010): 1–13.
Asein, John O. *Introduction to Nigerian Legal System*. Lagos: Ababa Press Ltd., 2005.
Ashby, Eric. *African Universities and Western Tradition*. Cambridge: Harvard University Press, 1964.
Asiedu-Akrofi, Derek. "Judicial Recognition and Adoption of Customary Law in Nigeria." *The American Journal of Comparative Law* 37, no. 3 (1989): 578.
Asiegbu, Johnson U. J. *Nigeria and Its British Invaders, 1851–1920: A Thematic Documentary History*. Enugu: Nok Publishers International, 1984.
Asiwaju, Anthony I. "The Cooperative Movement in the Colonial Context: A Comparison of the French and British Rural West African Experience to 1960." *Journal of the Historical Society of Nigeria* 11, no. 1/2 (1981–1982): 89–108.
   "Dahomey, Yorubaland, Borgu and Benin in the Nineteenth Century." In *General History of Africa- VI: Africa in the Nineteenth Century until the 1880s*, ed. Jacob F. A. Ajayi. Berkeley: University of California, 1989, 716.
   "Political Motivation and Oral Historical Traditions in Africa: The Case of Yoruba Crowns, 1900–1960." *Journal of the International African Institute* 46, no. 2 (1976): 116–121.
   "The Western Provinces under Colonial Rule." In *Groundwork of Nigerian History*, ed. Obaro Ikime. London: Heinemann Educational Book, 1980, 429–445.
   Western Yorubaland Under European Rule 1889–1945: A Comparative Analysis of French and British Colonialism. London: Longman Group Limited, 1976.
Asiwaju, Anthony I., and Ogunsola John Igue, ed. *The Nigeria–Benin Transborder Cooperation. Proceedings of a Bilateral Workshop, Topo, Badagry, May 1988*. Lagos: University of Lagos Press, 1994.
Atanda, Joseph A. "The Fall of the Old Ọyọ Empire: A Re-Consideration of Its Cause." *Journal of the Historical Society of Nigeria* 5, no. 4 (1971): 477–490.
   "Government of Yorubaland in the Pre-Colonial Period." *Tarikh* 4, no. 2 (1971): 1–12.
   "Indirect Rule in Yorubaland." *Tarikh* 3, no. 3 (1970): 16–28.

"Kings in Nigerian Society Through the Ages." Inaugural Lecture. Ibadan: University of Ibadan, 1991.

"The New Oyo Empire: A Study of British Indirect Rule in Oyo Province, 1894–1934." Unpublished PhD dissertation, University of Ibadan, 1967.

The New Oyo Empire: Indirect Rule and Change in Western Nigeria 1894-1934. London: Longman, 1973.

Political Systems of Nigerian Peoples up to 1900. Ibadan: John Archers Publishers Limited, 2006.

Attah, Noah Echa. "The Historical Conjuncture of Neo-colonialism and Underdevelopment in Nigeria." *Journal of African Studies and Development* 5, no. 5 (2013): 70–79.

Ausman, John L. "The Disturbances in Abeokuta in 1918." *Canadian Journal of African Studies* 5, no. 1 (1971): 45–60.

Awa, Eme O. "Regionalism in Nigeria: A Study in Federalism." Unpublished PhD dissertation. New York University, 1955.

Federal Government in Nigeria. Berkeley: University of California Press, 1964.

Awa, Omiko. "Lady Oyinkansola Abayomi: An Amazon, Trailblazer." *The Guardian*, February 16, 2020.

Awe, Bolanle, ed. "The Ajele System: A Study of Ibadan Imperialism in the Nineteenth Century." *Journal of the Historical Society of Nigeria* 3, no. 1 (1964): 47–60.

Nigerian Women in Historical Perspective. Ibadan: Bookcraft, 1992.

The Rise of Ibadan as a Yoruba Power in the Nineteenth Century. Oxford: Oxford University Press, 1964.

Awolalu, Joseph Omosade. *Yoruba Beliefs and Sacrificial Rites.* London: Longman, 1979.

Awolowo, Obafemi. *Path to Nigerian Freedom.* London: Faber and Faber, 1947.

The People's Republic. Ibadan: Oxford University Press, 1968.

Ayandele, Emmanuel A. "The Colonial Church Question in Lagos Politics, 1905–11." *Odù: Journal of Yoruba and Related Studies* 4, no. 2 (1967): 53–73.

Educated Elites in the Nigerian Society. Ibadan: University of Ibadan Press, 1974.

"The Missionary Factor in Northern Nigeria, 1870–1918." *Journal of the Historical Society of Nigeria* 3, no. 3 (1966): 514–522.

The Ijebu of Yorubaland 1850–1950: Politics, Economy, and Society. Ibadan: Heinemann Educational Books Plc., 1992.

The Missionary Impact on Modern Nigeria 1842–1914. London: Longmans, 1966.

Nigerian Historical Studies. London: Frank Cass, 1979.

Ayanleke, Akinwale R. "Yoruba Traditional Education System: A Veritable Tool for Salvaging the Crisis Laden Education System in Nigeria." *Academic Journal of Interdisciplinary Studies* 2, no. 6 (2013): 141–145.

Ayantuga, Obafemi Oladimomi. *Ijebu and its Neighbors, 1851–1914.* London: University of London, 1965.

Ayatse, Felicia H., and Isaac Iorhen Akuva. "The Origin and Development of Ethnic Politics and its Impacts on Post-colonial Governance in Nigeria." *European Scientific Journal* 9, no. 17 (2013): 178–189.

Ayegbusi, Talabi Rasheed, and Joseph Rudigi Rukema. "Labor Unions and the Nigerian Democratic Experience: An Appraisal." *Mankind Quarterly* 61, no. 4 (2021): 872–900.

Ayeni, Bola. *Spatial Dimension of Manufacturing Activities in Nigeria*. Ibadan: Technical Report, Department of Geography, University of Ibadan, 1981.

Ayoade, John A. A. "Party and Ideology in Nigeria: A Case Study of the Action Group." *Journal of Black Studies* 16, no. 2 (1985): 169–188.

Ayoola, Tokunbo. "Colonial Inheritance, Postcolonial Neglect, and the Management of Nigerian Railway by Rail India Technical and Economic Services (RITES)." *Lagos Notes and Records* 14, no. 1 (2008): 60–85.

"The Second World War and Africa's Socioeconomic Infrastructures: A Case Study of the Nigerian Railroad System." In *Contemporary Africa: African Histories and Modernities*, ed. Toyin Falola and Emmanuel M. Mbah. New York: Palgrave Macmillan, 2014, 63–87.

Azevedo, Mario J. *Historical Perspectives on the State of Health and Health Systems in Africa*. Vol. I. Switzerland: Palgrave Macmillan, 2017.

Azikiwe, Nnamdi. *Ideology for Nigeria: Capitalism, Socialism, or Welfarism?* Yaba: Macmillan Nigeria, 1980.

My Odyssey: An Autobiography. London: C. Hurst and Company, 1970.

Zik: A Selection from the Speeches of Nnamdi Azikiwe. Cambridge: Cambridge University Press, 1961.

Azumah, John Allembillah. *The Legacy of Arab-Islam in Africa: A Quest for Inter-Religious Dialogue*. Oxford: Oneworld, 2001.

Azumah, John, and Lamin Sanneh, eds. *The African Christian and Islam*. Carlisle: Langham Publishing, 2013.

Babalola, Dele. "The Origins of Nigerian Federalism: The Rikerian Theory and Beyond." *Federal Governance* 8, no. 3 (2013): 43–54.

Babalola, Emmanuel T. "Newspaper as Instrument for Building Literate Communities: The Nigerian Experience." *Nordic Journal of African Studies* 11, no. 3 (2002): 403–410.

Babalola, F. O. "The Future of Arabic Manuscripts in Nigeria." *The Nigerian Archives* 1, no. 4 (1993): 9–26.

Babangida, Ibrahim. "Ethnic Nationalities and Nigeria State." Excerpts from a Lecture delivered at NIPSS, Kuru, Jos, Plateau State, 2002.

Babawale, Tunde. *Nigeria in the Crisis of Governance and Development: A Retrospective and Prospective Analyses of Selected Issues and Events*, Vol. 2. Lagos: Political and Administrative Resource Center, 2007.

Babou, Cheikh Anta. "Decolonization or National Liberation: Debating the End of British Colonial Rule in Africa." *The ANNALS of the American Academy of Political and Social Science* 632, no. 1 (2010): 41–54.

Bacho, Francis Z. L., and Mohammed S. Abdul-Kadir. "Artificial Creation of the State and Enduring Conflicts in Africa: Legacies of the 'Indirect Rule' Policy in the Northern Parts of Ghana and Nigeria." *Ghana Journal of Development Studies* 4, no. 1 (2007): 13–27.

Badejo, Bamidele. *Ijebu-Ode in Perspectives.* Ijebu-Ode: Fairweather Books Publications, 1992.

Badmus, Isiaka A. "Under Reconstruction: Ethnicity, Ethnic Nationalism, and the Future of the Nigerian State." *Verfassung und Recht in Übersee* 42, no. 2 (2009): 212–239.

Bahati, Kuumba M. "African Women, Resistance Cultures and Cultural Resistances." *Agenda: Empowering Women for Gender Equity* 68 (2006): 112–121.

Bailkin, Jordanna. "Where Did the Empire Go? Archives and Decolonization in Britain." *The American Historical Review* 120, no. 3 (2015): 884–899.

Baker, G. L. "Research Notes on the Royal Niger Company – Its Predecessors and Successors." *Journal of the Historical Society of Nigeria* 2, no. 1 (1960): 151–161.

Bala, Umaru Abubakar. "Colonialism and the Development in Nigeria: Effects and Challenges." *International Affairs and Global Strategy* 70 (2019): 9–20.

Ballard, John A. "Administrative Origins of Nigerian Federalism." *African Affairs* 70, no. 281 (1971): 333–348.

Balogun, Ismail A. B. *The Place of Religion in the Development of Nigeria.* Ilorin: University of Ilorin, 1988.

Banton, Mandy. "Destroy? 'Migrate'? Conceal? British Strategies for the Disposal of Sensitive Records of Colonial Administrations at Independence." *Journal of Imperial and Commonwealth History* 40, no. 2 (2012): 321–335.

——. "'Expatriate' or 'Migrated' Archives: The Role of the UK Archivist." *Archives* 34, no. 121 (2009): 14–24.

Bappa, S., J. Ibarahim, A. M. Imam, and F. J. A. Kamara, eds. *Women in Nigeria Today.* London: Zed Books, 1985.

Barcia, Manuel. *West African Warfare in Bahia and Cuba: Soldier Slaves in the Atlantic World 1807–1844.* London: Oxford University Press, 2016.

Bariledum, Kia, and S. Vurasi Serebe. "Political Elites and the Challenges of National Development: The Nigeria Experience." *European Scientific Journal* 9, no. 31 (2013): 161–172.

Barnes, Andrew E. "'Evangelization Where It Is Not Wanted': Colonial Administrators and Missionaries in Northern Nigeria during the First Third of the Twentieth Century." *Journal of Religion in Africa* 25, no. 4 (1995): 412–441.

——. "'The Great Prohibition': The Expansion of Christianity in Colonial Northern Nigeria." *History Compass* 8, no. 6 (2010): 440–454.

——. "Western Education in Colonial Africa." In *Africa. Vol. 3: Colonial Africa, 1885–1939,* ed. Toyin Falola. Durham: Carolina Academic Press, 2002, 139–156.

Barnes, Robert P. "Scotland and the Glorious Revolution of 1688." *Albion* 3, no. 3 (1971): 116–127

Barnes, Sandra T., ed. *Africa's Ogun: Old World and New.* Indianapolis: Indiana University Press, 1997.

——. *Patrons and Power: Creating a Political Community in Metropolitan Lagos.* Indianapolis: Indiana University Press, 1986.

Barth, Henry. *Travels and Discoveries in North and Central Africa: Including Accounts of Tripoli, The Sahara, The Remarkable Kingdom of Bornu, and the Countries Around Lake Chad.* London: Ward, Lock, 1890.
Bascom, William. "Urbanization among the Yoruba." *American Journal of Sociology* 60, no. 5 (1955): 446–454.
Basden, George T. *Among the Ibos of Nigeria.* London: Frank Cass & Company, 1966.
Bassey, Magnus O. "Higher Education and the Rise of Early Political Elites in Africa." *Review of Higher Education in Africa* 1, no. 1 (2009): 30–38.
   Missionary Rivalry and Educational Expansion in Nigeria, 1885-1945. Lewston: E. Mellen Press, 1999.
Bastian, Misty L. "'Vultures of the Marketplace': Southeastern Nigeria Women and Discourses of the Ogu Umunwanyi (Women's War) of 1929." In *Women in African Colonial Histories*, ed. Jean Allman, Susan Geiger, and Nakanyike Musisi. Bloomington: Indiana University Press, 2002, 260–281.
Batran, Aziz A. "The Nineteenth Century Islamic Revolution in West Africa." In *General History of Africa VI: Africa in the Nineteenth Century until the 1880s*, ed. Jacob F. A. Ajayi. Berkeley: University of California, 1989, 539–554.
Bayly, Christopher A., and Ti N. Harper. *Forgotten Armies: The Fall of British Asia, 1941-1945.* Cambridge: Harvard University Press, 2005.
Beier, Ulli. "E. K. Ogunmola: A Personal Memoir," in *Drama and Theatre in Nigeria: A Critical Source Book*, ed. Yemi Ogunbiyi (Lagos: Nigeria Magazine Publications), 323.
   The Return of Shango: The Theatre of Duro Ladipo. Bayreuth: IWALEWA-Haus, 1994.
   "Yoruba Folk Opera." *African Music* 1, no. 1 (1954): 32–34.
   "Yoruba Theatre." In *Introduction to African Literature: An Anthology of Critical Writing on African and Afro-American Literature and Oral Tradition* ed. Ulli Beier. Illinois: Northwestern University Press, 1967, 247.
Bello, Ahmadu. *My Life.* Cambridge: Cambridge University Press, 1962.
Bello, Paul Oluwatosin. "Ethnic Nationalism and Conflicts in Africa: Lessons from Nigeria." *Bangladesh Sociological Society* 15, no. 1 (2018): 86.
Bello, Umar. "Colonial Essentialism in Lord Lugard's 'The Dual Mandate,' a Critical Textual Analysis." *Advances in Social Sciences Research Journal* 4, no. 6 (2017): 73–90.
Ben-Amos, Paula. *Art, Innovation, and Politics in Eighteenth-Century Benin.* Indiana: Indiana University Press, 1999.
Bentor, Eli. "Challenges to Rural Festivals with the Return to Democratic Rule in Southeastern Nigeria." *African Arts* 38, no. 4 (2005): 38–45.
Berg, Maxine, and Pat Hudson. "Rehabilitating the Industrial Revolution." *The Economic History Review* 45, no. 1 (1992): 24–50.
Berg, Robert J., and Jennifer S. Whitaker, eds. *Strategies for African Development.* Berkeley: University of California Press, 1986.
Berger, Stefan, and Eric Storm, eds. *Writing the History of Nationalism.* London: Bloomsbury Academic, 2019.

Bergstrom, Kari. "Legacies of Colonialism and Islam for Hausa Women: An Historical Analysis, 1804–1960." Working Paper, Michigan State University, 2002.

Berlanstein, Lenard R. ed. *The Industrial Revolution and Work in Nineteenth Century Europe*. New York: Routledge, 2003.

Berman, Bruce J. "Ethnicity, Patronage and the African State: The Politics of Uncivil Nationalism." *African Affairs* 97, no. 388 (1998): 305–341.

Berman, Edward H. "American Influence on African Education: The Role of the Phelps-Stokes Commissions." *Comparative Education Review* 15, no. 2 (1971): 135–138.

Bernstein, Gail Lee, and Haruhiro Fukui, eds. *Japan and the World: Essays on Japanese History and Politics in Honour of Ishida Takeshi*. London: Macmillan Press, 1998.

Berzock, Kathleen Bickford. *Benin: Royal Arts of a West African Kingdom*. Illinois: Art Institute of Chicago, 2008.

Bickers, Robert A., and Rosemary Seton, eds. *Missionary Encounters: Sources and Issues*. London: Curzon Press, 1996.

Bimberg, Thomas, and Stephen Resnick. *Colonial Development: An Econometric Study*. New Haven: Yale University Press, 1975.

Bingel, Baba Thomas. "Understanding Trade Unionism in Nigeria: Historical Evolution and Prospects for Future Development." In *Trade Unionism in Nigeria: Challenges for the 21st Century*, ed. Funmi Adewumi. Lagos: Frederick Ebert Foundation, 1997.

Biobaku, Saburi O. "The Egba Council, 1899–1918." *ODU: Journal of Yoruba and Related Studies* 22, no. 2 (1952): 35–49.

The Egba and Their Neighbors 1842–1872. London: Oxford University Press, 1965.

The First 150 Years of the Egba at Abeokuta (1830–1980). Ibadan: Institute of African Studies, 1983.

"Historical Sketch of Egba Traditional Authorities." *Africa: Journal of the International African Institute* 22, no. 1 (1952): 35–49.

Birmingham, David. *The Decolonization of Africa*. London: UCL Press, 1995.

Black, Jeremy, and Philip Woodfine. *The British Navy and the Use of Naval Power in the Eighteenth Century*. Leicester: Leicester University Press, 1988.

Blackett, Richard J. M. "Return to the Motherland: Robert Campbell, a Jamaican in Early Colonial Lagos." *Journal of the Historical Society of Nigeria* 8, no. 1 (1975): 133–143.

Blair, Alasdair. *Britain and the World since 1945*. London: Routledge, 2015.

Bloch, Robin, Sean Fox, Jose Monroy, and Adegbola Ojo. *Urbanisation and Urban Expansion in Nigeria: Research Report*. London: ICF International, 2015.

Blouin Jr., Francis X., and William G. Rosenberg, eds. *Archives, Documentation, and Institutions of Social Memory: Essays from the Sawyer Seminar*. Ann Arbor: University of Michigan Press, 2006.

Boahen, Albert A. *General History of Africa: VII Africa Under Colonial Domination 1880–1935*. Paris: UNESCO, 1990.

"New Trends and Processes in Africa in the Nineteenth Century." In *General History of Africa: VI Africa in the Nineteenth Century until the 1880s*, ed. Jacob F. A. Ajayi. Paris: UNESCO Publishing, 1998, 55–56.

Bobboyi, Hamidu. "The Ulama of Borno: A Study of the Relations between Scholars and State under the Sayfawa, 1470–1808." Unpublished PhD dissertation. Northwestern University, 1992.

Boer, Jan Harm. *Missionary Messengers of Liberation in a Colonial Context: A Case Study of the Sudan United Mission*. Amsterdam: Rodopi, 1979.

Bondarev, Dmitry. "Multiglossia in West African Manuscripts: The Case of Borno, Nigeria." In *Manuscript Cultures: Mapping the Field*, ed. Jörg B. Quenzer, Dmitry Bondarev, and Jan-Ulrich Sobisch. Berlin: De Gruyter, 2014, 113–158.

Booth, Anne E. *Legacies: Economic and Social Development in East and Southeast Asia*. Honolulu: University of Hawaii Press, 2007.

Boscolo, Cristina. *Odún: Discourses, Strategies, and Power in the Yorùbá Play of Transformation*. Leiden: Brill, 2009.

Boserup, Ester. *Women's Role in Economic Development*. London: Allen & Unwin, 1970.

Boston, John S. "Oral Tradition and the History of Igala." *The Journal of African History* 10, no. 1 (1969): 29–43.

Bourdillon, Bernard, and Richmond Palmer. "Nigerian Constitutional Proposals." *African Affairs* 44, no. 176 (1945): 120–124.

Boxer, Charles. *The Portuguese Seaborne Empire, 1415–1825*. New York: A. A. Knopf, 1969.

Bradbury, Robert E. "The Kingdom of Benin." In *West African Kingdoms in the Nineteenth Century*, ed. Robert E. Bradbury. Oxford: Oxford University Press, 1967, 7.

Braun, Klaus, and Jacqueline Passon, eds. *Across the Sahara: Tracks, Trade and Cross-Cultural Exchange in Libya*. Cham: Springer, 2020.

Brendon, Piers. *The Decline and Fall of the British Empire, 1781–1997*. New York: Alfred A. Knopf, 2008.

Brennan, James R. "The First Victory: The Second World War and the East Africa Campaign by Andrew Stewart." *Canadian Journal of History* 53, no. 1 (2018): 180–182.

Brennan, Vicki. *Singing Yoruba Christianity: Music, Media and Morality*. Bloomington: Indiana University Press, 2018.

Brooke-Smith, Robin, ed. *The Scramble for Africa*. London: Macmillan International Higher Education, 1987.

Brooks, George. "The Signares of Saint-Louis and Goree: Women Entrepreneurs in Eighteenth-Century Senegal." In *Women in Africa, Studies in Social and Economic Change*, ed. Nancy Hafkin and Edna Bay. Stanford, Stanford University Press, 1976, 19–44.

Broughton, Simon, Mark Ellingham, Jon Lusk, and Duncan Antony Clark, eds. *The Rough Guide to World Music: Africa and Middle East*. London: Rough Guides, 2006.

Brower, Daniel R., and Thomas Sanders. *The World in the Twentieth Century: From Empires to Nations*. Boston: Pearson, 2014.

Brown, G. M., and T. B. Michael. "Traditional Forms of Entertainment and Their Implication on Socio-Economic Development in the Niger Delta: The Experience of Odual Kingdom in Rivers State, 1600–2015." *South–South Journal of Humanities and International Studies* 1, no. 3 (2015): 313–331.

Brown, Godfrey N. "British Educational Policy in West and Central Africa." *Journal of Modern African Studies* 2, no. 3 (1964): 365–377.

Buchanan, Andrew N. *World War II in Global Perspective, 1931–1953: A Short History*. Hoboken: John Wiley & Sons, 2019.

Buell, Raymond L. *The Native Problem in Africa*. New York: The Macmillan Company, 1928.

Builders, Philip F., ed. *Herbal Medicine*. London: IntechOpen, 2018.

Bull, Mary. "Indirect Rule in Northern Nigeria, 1906–1911." In *Essays in Imperial Government*, ed. Kenneth Robinson and Frederick Madden. Oxford: Basil Blackwell, 1963, 47–87.

Bunza, Mukhtar U. "The Application of Islamic Law and the Legacies of Good Governance in the Sokoto Caliphate, Nigeria (1804–1903): Lessons for the Contemporary Period." *Electronic Journal of Islamic and Middle Eastern Law* 1 (2013): 84–101.

"Arabic Manuscripts as Alternative Sources in the Reconstruction of Northern Nigeria." In *Arabic/Ajami Manuscripts: Resources for the Development of New Knowledge in Nigeria*, ed. Yakubu Y. Ibrahim, I. M. Jumare, Mahomoud Hamman, and Salisu Bala. Kaduna: Arewa House Centre for Historical Documentation and Research, 2010.

Burnham, Philip. "Raiders and Traders in Adamawa: Slavery as a Regional System." In *Asian and African Systems of Slavery*, ed. James L. Watson. Oxford: Blackwell, 1980, 43–72.

Burns, Alan. *History of Nigeria*. London: George Allen and Unwin Ltd., 1929.

Burns, James. *Lordship, Kingship, and Empire: The Idea of Monarchy, 1400–1525*. Oxford: Clarendon Press, 1992.

Byfield, Judith A. "Innovation and Conflict: Cloth Dyers and the Interwar Depression in Abeokuta, Nigeria." *The Journal of African History* 38, no. 1 (1997): 77–99.

"Taxation, Women, and the Colonial State: Egba Women's Tax Revolt." *Meridians: Feminism, Race, Transnationalism* 3, no. 2 (2003): 250–277.

"Women, Rice, and War: Political and Economic Crisis in Wartime Abeokuta (Nigeria)." In *Africa and the World War II*, ed. Judith Byfield, Carolyn Brown, Timothy Parson, and Ahmad Sikainga. Cambridge: Cambridge University Press, 2015, 147–165.

Byfield, Judith, Carolyn Brown, Timothy Parson, and Ahmad Sikainga, eds. *Africa and World War II*. Cambridge: Cambridge University Press, 2015.

Cain, Peter J., and Anthony G. Hopkins. *British Imperialism: 1688–2015*. London: Routledge, 2016.

Callaway, Helen. *Gender, Culture and Empire: European Women in Colonial Nigeria*. London: Macmillan Press, 1987.
Campbell, Bolaji. "Eegun Ogun: War Masquerades in Ibadan in the Era of Modernization." *African Arts* 48, no. 1 (2015): 47–48.
Candido, Mariana P., and Adam Jones. *African Women in the Atlantic World: Property, Vulnerability and Mobility, 1660–1880*. Rochester: James Currey, 2019.
Carland, John M. *The Colonial Office and Nigeria, 1898–1914*. Stanford: Hoover Institution Press, 1985).
Centre for Disease Control and Prevention, United States of America. "1918 Pandemic (H1N1 virus)." March 20, 2019. https://archive.cdc.gov/#/details?url=https://www.cdc.gov/flu/pandemic-resources/1918-pandemic-h1n1.html.
Césaire, Aimé. *Discourse on Colonialism*. Trans. Joan Pinkham. New York: Monthly Review Press, 1972.
Chamberlain, M. E. *The Scramble for Africa*. London: Routledge, 2013.
Chanock, Martin. "Making Customary Law: Men, Women and Courts in Colonial Northern Rhodesia." In *African Women and the Law: Historical Perspectives*, ed. Margaret. J. Hay and Marcia Wright. Boston: Boston University, 1982, 53–67.
Charle Jr., Edwin G. "English Colonial Policy and the Economy of Nigeria." *The American Journal of Economics and Sociology* 26, no. 1 (1967): 79–92.
Charles, Uji, and Awuawuer Tijime Justin. "Towards the Theories and Practice of the Dance Art." *International Journal of Humanities and Social Science* 4, no. 4 (2014): 254.
Cheang, Justina. "Choice of Foreign Names as a Strategy for Identity Management." *Intercultural Communication Studies* 17, no. 2 (2008): 197–202.
Chianakwalam, S. W. "Educational Development in Nigeria and the Gold Coast." *Journal of Education Management* 84, no. 15 (2002): 66–89.
Chikendu, Patrick. *Imperialism and Nationalism*. Enugu: Academic Publishing Company, 2004.
Chimee, Ihediwa N. "Coal and British Colonialism in Nigeria." *RCC Perspectives* 5 (2014): 19–26.
Chinyowa, Kennedy. "The Sarungano and Shona Storytelling: An African Theatrical Paradigm." *Studies in Theatre and Performance* 21, no. 1 (2001): 18–30.
Chokor, Boyowa A. "Changing Urban Housing Form and Organization in Nigeria: Lessons for Community Planning." *Planning Perspectives* 20, no. 1 (2005): 69–96.
Christopher, A. J. *The British Empire at Its Zenith*. London: Croom Helm, 1988.
Chuku, Gloria Ifeoma. "From Petty Traders to International Merchants: A Historical Account of Three Igbo Women of Nigeria in Trade and Commerce, 1886 to 1970." *African Economic History* 27 (1999): 1–22.
Chukwu, Dan O. "The Economic Impact of Pioneer Indigenous Banks in Colonial Nigeria, 1920–1960." *Journal of the Historical Society of Nigeria* 19 (2010): 93–100.
Clapperton, Hugh. *Hugh Clapperton into the Interior of Africa: Records of the Second Expedition, 1825–1827*. Leiden: Brill, 2005.

Clark, Ebun. *Hubert Ogunde: The Making of Nigerian Theatre*. Oxford: Oxford University Press, 1979.
Clarke, William H. *Travels and Explorations in Yorubaland, 1856–1858*, ed. Joseph A. Atanda. Ibadan: Ibadan University Press, 1972.
Coates, Oliver. "Hubert Ogunde's Strike and Hunger and the 1945 General Strike in Lagos: Labor and Reciprocity in the Kingdom of Ọba Yéjídé." *Research in African Literatures* 48, no. 2 (2017): 166–184.
"New Perspectives on West Africa and World War Two." *Journal of African Military History*, 4 (2020): 5–39.
"Nigeria and the World Wars." In *The Oxford Handbook of Nigerian History*, ed. Toyin Falola and Matthew M. Heaton. Oxford: Oxford University Press, 2022.
"Nigeria and the World: War, Nationalism and Politics, 1914–1960." In *The Oxford Handbook of Nigerian Politics*, ed. Carl Levan and Patrick Ukata. Oxford Handbooks Online, 2018, 699–713.
Cohen, Abner. *The Politics of Elite Culture: Explorations in the Dramaturgy of Power in a Modern African Society*. Berkeley: University of California Press, 1981.
Cohen, Robin. "Nigeria's Labor Leader Number 1: Notes for a Biographical Study of M. A. O. Imoudu." *Journal of the Historical Society of Nigeria* 5, no. 2 (1970): 303.
Labor and Politics in Nigeria, 1945–1971. London: Heinemann, 1974.
Cohn, Caroline. "India and Nigeria: Similar Colonial Legacies, Vastly Different Trajectories: An Examination of the Differing Fates of Two Former British Colonies." *Cornell International Affairs Review* 7, no. 1 (2013): 18–30.
Coker, Folarin. *A Lady: A Biography of Lady Oyinkan Abayomi*. Ibadan: Evans Brothers, 1987.
Coker, Increase H. E. *Landmarks of the Nigerian Press: An Outline of the Origins and Development of the Newspaper Press in Nigeria, 1859 to 1965*. Apapa: Nigerian National Press, 1968.
Coker, Maurice Ayodele. "Law and Politics in Nigeria: The Political Functioning of the Judiciary in Colonial Nigeria, 1940–1960." *Mediterranean Journal of Social Sciences* 5, no. 20 (2014): 2085.
Cole, Patrick. *Modern and Traditional Elites in the Politics of Lagos*. New York: Cambridge University Press, 1975.
Coleman, James S. "Nationalism in Tropical Africa." *The American Political Science Review* 48, no. 2 (1954): 404–426.
Nigeria: Background to Nationalism. Berkeley: University of California Press, 1958.
Coleman, James S., and Carl Gustav Rosberg, eds. *Political Parties and National Integration in Tropical Africa*. Berkeley: University of California Press, 1966.
Coles, Catherine, and Beverley Mack. "Women in the Twentieth Century Hausa Society." In *Hausa Women in the Twentieth Century*, ed. Catherine Coles and Beverley Mack. Madison: The University of Wisconsin Press, 1991.

Collier, Paul. "Building an African Infrastructure: Building Railways in Africa." *Finance and Development* 48, no. 4 (2011): 19–21.
Collier, Richard. *The Plague of the Spanish Lady: The Influenza Pandemic of 1918–1919.* New York: Atheneum, 1974.
Collins, John. "The Early History of West African Highlife Music." *Popular Music* 8, no. 3 (1989): 221–230.
 "A Historical Review of Popular Entertainment in Sub-Saharan Africa." In *Africa in Contemporary Perspective: A Textbook for Undergraduate Students*, ed. Takyiwaa Manuh and Esi Sutherland-Addy. Legon-Accra: Sub-Saharan Publishers, 2013, 452.
Collins, Robert O. ed. *African History: Text and Readings.* New York: Random House, 1971.
Conrad, David C. *Empires of Medieval West Africa: Ghana, Mali, and Songhay.* New York: Chelsea House, 2010.
Conte, Paolo, Mathieu Ferradou, and Jeanne-Laure Le Quang. "The Early 'Republic of France' as a Cosmopolitan Moment." *La Révolution française* 22 (2022): 1–11.
Cook, Arthur Norton. *British Enterprise in Nigeria.* Philadelphia: Oxford University Press, 1943.
Copeland, Roger, and Marshall Cohen, eds. *What is Dance?: Readings in Theory and Criticism.* Oxford: Oxford University Press, 1983.
Coquery-Vidrovitch, Catherine. *Africa and the Africans in the Nineteenth Century: A Turbulent History.* London: Routledge, 2009.
Coulson, Noel James. *A History of Islamic Law.* London: Routledge, 2017.
Crampton, Edmund P. T. *Christianity in Northern Nigeria.* London: Geoffrey Chapman, 1979.
Crouzet, François. "Outside the Walls of Europe – The Pax Britannica." *European Review* 7, no. 4 (1999): 447–453.
Crowder, Michael, and Obaro Ikime, eds. *West African Chiefs: Their Changing Status under Colonial Rule and Independence.* Ile-Ife: University of Ife Press, 1970.
Crowder, Michael, ed. *Colonial West Africa: Collected Essays.* New York: Routledge, 2012.
 "Indirect Rule: French and British Style." *Africa: Journal of the International African Institute* 34, no. 3 (1964): 197–205.
 The Story of Nigeria. London: Faber and Faber, 1968.
 West Africa under Colonial Rule. London: Hutchinson, 1976.
 West African Resistance: The Military Response to Colonial Occupation. London: Hutchinson Library, 1978.
Crowe, Sybil E. *The Berlin West African Conference, 1884–1885.* New York: Longman, 1942.
Cudjoe, Selwyn R. "Some Reminiscences of a Senior Interpreter." *The Nigerian Field* XVIII, no. 4 (1953): 148–164.
Cunha, George M., Frazer G. Poole, and Clyde C. Walton. "The Conservation and Preservation of Historical Records." *The American Archivist* 40, no. 3 (1977): 321–324.

Cuoco, Alex. *African Narratives of Orishas, Spirits and other Deities: Stories from West Africa and the African Diaspora: A Journey into the Realm of Deities, Spirits, Mysticism, Spiritual Roots and Ancestral Wisdom.* Parker: Outskirts Press, 2014.

Curtin, Philip D. "The Archives of Tropical Africa: A Reconnaissance." *The Journal of African History* 1, no. 1 (1960): 129–147.

Africa Remembered: Narratives by West Africans from the Era of the Slave Trade. Madison: The University of Wisconsin Press, 1967.

The Atlantic Slave Trade: A Census. Madison: The University of Wisconsin Press, 1967.

"The End of the 'White Man's Grave'? Nineteenth-Century Mortality in West Africa." *The Journal of Interdisciplinary History* 21, no. 1 (1990): 63–88.

The Image of Africa: British Ideas and Action, 1780–1850. London: Palgrave Macmillan, 1964.

"The White Man's Grave: Image and Reality, 1780–1850." *Journal of British Studies* 1, no. 1 (1961): 94–110.

Cuttings, Tim. *The Swange Music and Dance.* Abuja: TimeXperts Publishing, 2013.

Cynado, Cyril, and Cynado Ezeogidi. *British Conquest, Colonization and Administration in Nigeria.* Enugu: Rhyce & Kerex, 2019.

da Costa, Emilia Viotti. "The Portuguese-African Slave Trade: A Lesson in Colonialism." *Latin American Perspectives* 12, no. 1 (1985): 41–61.

Dada, S. A. *A History of the African Church.* Ibadan: Aowa Printers, 1986.

Dalrymple-Smith, Angus E. *Commercial Transitions and Abolition in West Africa 1630–1860.* Leiden: Brill, 2020.

Danforth, Loring M. *The Macedonian Conflict: Ethnic Nationalism in a Transnational World.* Princeton: Princeton University Press, 1995.

Danjibo, Nathaniel and Kelvin Ashindorbe. "The Evolution and Pattern of Political Party Formation and the Search for National Integration in Nigeria." *Brazilian Journal of African Studies* 3, no. 5 (2018): 85–100.

Danmole, Hakeem O. A. "The Frontier Emirate: A History of Islam in Ilorin." Unpublished PhD dissertation. University of Birmingham, 1981.

Danmole, Hakeem O., and Toyin Falola. "Ibadan–Ilorin Relations in the Nineteenth Century: A Study in Imperial Struggles in Yorubaland." *Transafrican Journal of History* 14 (1985): 21–35.

Daramola, Ifedayo. "A Century of Mass Media and Nigeria's Development: Issues and Challenges." *Communications on Applied Electronics* 7, no. 10 (2017): 4–14.

Dasylva, Ademola. "'Culture Education' and the Challenge of Globalization in Modern Nigeria." *Oral Tradition* 21, no. 2 (2006): 325–341.

Dauda, Bola and Toyin Falola. *Wole Soyinka: Literature, Activism, and African Transformation.* New York: Bloomsbury Academic, 2021.

Daudu, Mamman. *An Outline of the History of Christianity in West Africa.* Zaria: Micsons Press & Publishers, 2000.

Davidson, Basil. *Modern Africa: A Social and Political History.* London: Routledge, 1994.

West Africa before the Colonial Era: A History to 1850. London: Routledge, 1998.

Davies, Lanre. "The Political Economy of the Egba Nation: A Study in Modernization and Diversification, 1830-1960." *African Nebula* no. 7 (2014): 87.

Davis, David B. *Inhuman Bondage: The Rise and Fall of Slavery in the New World.* Oxford: Oxford University Press, 2006.

Dawson, Samuel Edward. *The Lines of Demarcation of Pope Alexander VI and the Treaty of Tordesillas AD 1493 and 1494.* Ottawa: Hope & Sons, 1899.

Deaville Walker, F. A. *A Hundred Years in Nigeria: The Story of the Methodist Mission in the Western Nigeria District 1842-1942.* London: Cargate Press, 1943.

Decker, Babatunde J. "Aini – An African Indigenous Template of Poverty and the Task for Neo-Monetary Modules of Interventions." In *Development from Below and Above in Africa*, ed. Maurice Amutabi. Nairobi: Centre for Democracy, Research and Development, 2018, 83-91.

A History of Aviation in Nigeria, 1925-2005. Lagos: Dele-Davis Publishers, 2008.

"A History of the Poor in Lagos, 1861-1960," (unpublished PhD dissertation. University of Lagos, 2012).

"Colonial Memories and Emotions in Southwestern Nigeria: How 'Good' Were the 'Bad' Old Days?" *Ife Journal of History* 8, no. 1 (2016/2017): 5-25.

"Social Welfare Strategies in Colonial Lagos." *African Nebula* 1, no. 1 (2010): 56-62.

Denitch, Bogdan D. *Ethnic Nationalism: The Tragic Death of Yugoslavia.* Minnealpolis: University of Minnesota Press, 1994.

Denzer, LaRay E. "The Gold Coast Section of the National Congress of British West Africa." MA Thesis, University of Legon, 1965.

"Yoruba Women: A Historiographical Study." *The International Journal of African Historical Studies* 27, no. 1 (1994): 2-3.

Derrick, Jonathan. "The 'Native Clerk' in Colonial West Africa." *African Affairs* 82, no. 326 (1983): 61-74.

Diamond, Larry J. "Class, Ethnicity and the Democratic State: Nigeria, 1950-1966." *Comparative Study in Society & History* 25, no. 3 (1983): 457-489

Class, Ethnicity, and Democracy in Nigeria: The Failure of the First Republic. Syracuse: Syracuse University Press, 1988.

Diara, Benjamin, Johnson C. Diara, and Nche G. Christian. "The 19th Century European Missionaries and the Fight Against Malaria in Africa." *Mediterranean Journal of Social Sciences* 4, no. 16 (2013): 89-96.

Dike, Chike P. ed. *The Women's Revolt of 1929: Proceedings of a National Symposium to Mark the Sixtieth Anniversary of the Women's Uprising in South-Eastern Nigeria.* Lagos: Nelag & Co., 1995.

Dike, Kenneth O. "African History and Self-Government." *West Africa*, February 28, 1953, 177-178; March 14, 225-226; and March 21, 251.

"African History Twenty-Five Years Ago and Today." *Journal of The Historical Society of Nigeria* 10, no. 3 (1980): 13–22.

"John Beecroft, 1790–1854: Her Britannic Majesty's Consul to the Bight of Benin and Biafra, 1849–1854." *Journal of the Historical Society of Nigeria* 1, no. 1 (1956): 5–14.

Origins of the Niger Mission 1841–1891. Ibadan: Ibadan University Press, 1962.

Report on the Preservation and Administration of Historical Records and the Establishment of a Public Record Office in Nigeria. South Africa: Government Printer, 1954.

Trade and Politics in the Niger Delta 1830–1835: An Introduction to the Economic and Political History of Nigeria. London: Oxford University Press, 1955.

Dike, Paul C. *Confluence Nigerians: Man, History & Culture in the Niger/Benue Confluence Region.* Abuja: National Gallery of Art, Nigeria, 2005.

Dike, Victor E. "The Osu Caste System in Igboland: Discrimination Based on Descent." A paper presented to the Committee on Elimination of Racial Discrimination, 61st session of the International Dalit Solidarity Network, 2002, 5–23.

Diogu, Edward C. I. "Teachers and Politics in Nigeria: A Study in the Policy Influence of the Nigeria Union of Teachers." Unpublished PhD dissertation. State University of New York at Buffalo, 1985.

Dirks, Nichola. "Annals of the Archive: Ethnographic Notes on the Sources of History." In *From the Margins: Historical Anthropology and Its Future*, ed. Brian K. Axel. Durham: Duke University Press, 2002, 47–65.

DjeDje, Jacqueline Cogdell. *Fiddling in West Africa: Touching the Spirit in Fulbe, Hausa, and Dagbamba Cultures.* Bloomington: Indiana University Press, 2008.

Docherty, Paddy. *Blood and Bronze: The British Empire and the Sack of Benin.* London: Hurst, 2021.

Doi, Abdur Rahman I. "*Islam in Ibo land.*" 7, no. 1 (1974): 3.

Islam in Multi-Religious Society. Nigeria: A Case Study. Kuala Lumpur: A. S. Noordeen, 1984.

Islam in Nigeria. Zaria: Gaskiya Corporation, 1984.

Donnelly, Mark. *Britain in the Second World War.* London: Routledge, 1999.

Drakakis-Smith, David. *Urbanisation, Housing and the Development Process.* London: Routledge, 2012.

Drescher, Seymour. *Pathways from Slavery: British and Colonial Mobilizations in Global Perspective.* New York: Routledge, 2018.

Du Bois, William E. B. "The Realities in Africa: European Profit or Negro Development?" *Foreign Affairs* 21, no. 4 (1943): 721–732.

Dubois, Laurent. *Avengers of the New World: The Story of the Haitian Revolution.* Cambridge: The Belknap Press, 2004.

Dudley, Billy J. *Parties and Politics in Northern Nigeria.* London: Frank Cass, 1968.

Duncan, Graham A. "Ethiopianism in Pan-African Perspective, 1880–1920." *Studia Historiae Ecclesiasticae* 41, no. 2 (2015): 198–218.

Duranti, Luciana. "The Concept of Appraisal and Archival Theory." *The American Archivist* 57, no. 2 (1994): 328–344.

Duro Ladipo, Abiodun, and Gbóyèga Kóláwolé. "Opera in Nigeria: The Case of Duro Ladipo's 'Ọba Kòso.'" *Black Music Research Journal* 17, no. 1 (1997): 101–129.

Ebegbulem, Joseph C. "Ethnic Politics and Conflicts in Nigeria: Theoretical Perspective." *Khazar Journal of Humanities and Social Sciences* 14, no. 3 (2011): 76–91.

Eborka, Kennedy. "Migration and Urbanization in Nigeria from Pre-colonial to Post-colonial Eras: A Sociological Overview." In *Migration and Urbanization in Contemporary Nigeria: Policy Issues and Challenges*, ed. John Lekan Oyefara. Lagos: University of Lagos Press and Bookshop Ltd., 2021, 15–54.

Echeruo, Michael J. C. "History of the Nigerian Press." In *The Story of the Daily Times 1926–1970*, ed. Daily Times. Lagos: Daily Times Office, 1976.

"The Lagos Scene in the 19th Century." *Présence Africaine* no. 82 (1972): 77–93.

"Nnamdi Azikiwe and Nineteenth-century Nigerian Thought." *Journal of Modern African Studies* 12, no. 2 (1974): 245–263.

Victorian Lagos: Aspects of Nineteenth Century Lagos Life. London: Macmillan, 1977.

Edewor, Patrick. "Residential Segregation in Nigerian Cities." In *Globalizing Cities: Inequality and Segregation in Developing Countries*, ed. Ranvinder S. Sandhu and Jasmeet Sandhu. New Delhi: Rawat Publications, 2011, 29–43.

Ediagbonya, Michael. "Nigerian Constitutional Developments in Historical Perspective, 1914–1960." *American Journal of Humanities and Social Sciences Research (AJHSSR)* 4, no. 2 (2020): 242–248.

Edo, Victor O. "The Practice of Democracy in Nigeria: The Pre-Colonial Antecedent." *Lumina: An Inter-disciplinary Research Journal* 21, no. 2 (2010): 1–7.

Effah-Attoe, Stella A., and Solomon O. Jaja. *Margaret Ekpo: Lioness in Nigerian Politics*. Abeokuta: ALF Publications, 1993.

Egbe, Enyi J. "Native Authorities and Local Government Reforms in Nigeria since 1914." *IOSR Journal of Humanities and Social Science* 19, no. 3 (2014): 118.

Egbefo, Dawood O., and Hadizat A. Salihu. "The Impact of Trade and Commercial Activities in Pre-Colonial Esan Economy up to 1900." *SAU Journal of Humanities* 2, nos. 1&2 (2014): 164–175.

Egbefo, Dawood. "Resistance to Colonial in Nigeria: Esanland Encounter with the British Colonialists and Its Effects on Intra-Inter-Group Relations." *Academic Horizon: A Journal of the School of Postgraduate Studies* 1, no. 1 (2015): 54–70.

Egboh, Edmund O. "The Beginning of the End of Traditional Religion in Iboland, South-Eastern Nigeria." *Civilisations* 21, no. 2/3 (1971): 269–279.

"Polygamy in Iboland (South-Eastern Nigeria) with Special Reference to Polygamy Practice among Christian Ibos." *Civilisations* 22, no. 3 (1972): 431–444.

"The Nigerian Trade-Union Movement and Its Relations with World Trade-Union Internationals." *Présence Africaine* 75 (1970): 76–88.

"Trade Union Education in Nigeria (1940–1964)." *African Studies Review* 14, no. 1 (1971): 83–93.

"Trade Unions in Nigeria." *African Studies* 27, no. 1 (1968): 35–40.

Egbokhare, Francis O., and S. Oluwole Oyetade. *Harmonization and Standardization of Nigerian Languages*. Cape Town: CASAS, 2002.

Egharevba, Jacob. *A Short History of Benin*. Ibadan: Ibadan University Press, 1968.

Egharevba, Matthew E. "Constitutional Development and Inter-Group Relations in Nigeria: The Unending Dilemma." *Biudiscourse Journal of Arts & Education* 2, no. 1 (2007): 174–187.

Egwaikhide, Festus O., Victor A. Isumonah, and Olumide S. Ayodele. *Federal Presence in Nigeria. The "Sung" and "Unsung" Basis for Ethnic Grievance*. Dakar: CODESRIA, 2009.

Egwemi, Victor. "The Amalgamation of 1914 and the North–South Divide in Nigeria: Some Comments on Contemporary Manifestation." In *Colonialism and the Transition to Modernity in Africa*, ed. J. Mangut. Lapai: Ibb University, 2011.

Eisenstadt, Shmuel N. "Religious Organizations and Political Process in Centralized Empires." *The Journal of Asian Studies* 21, no. 3 (1962): 271–294.

Ejimofor, Cornelius O. *British Colonial Objectives and Policies in Nigeria: The Roots of Conflict*. Onitsha: Africana-FEP, 1987.

Ejiogu, E. C., and Adaoma Igwedibia. "The World Wars and Their Legacies in Africa and in the Affairs of Africans: The Case of East Africa – Kenya." *Journal of Asian and African Studies* 57, no. 1 (2022): 113–130.

Ejiogu, E. C., and Nneka L. Umego. "Africans and the Two Great Wars: A General Overview." *Journal of Asian and African Studies* 57, no. 1 (2022): 3–10.

Ekechi, F. K. "Historical Women in the Fight for Liberation." In *The Feminization of Development Processes in Africa: Current and Future Perspectives*, ed. Valentine Udoh James and James S. Etim. New York: Praeger Publishers, 1999.

"The Holy Ghost Fathers in Eastern Nigeria, 1885–1920: Observations on Missionary Strategy." *African Studies Review* 15, no. 2 (1972): 217–239.

"The Medical Factor in Christian Conversion in Africa: Observations from Southeastern Nigeria." *Missiology: An International Review* 21, no. 3 (1993): 289–309.

Missionary Enterprise and Rivalry in Igboland 1857–1914. London: Frank Cass, 1972.

Ekechukwu, Ferdinand. "Life and Times of Victor Olaiya." *Thisday*, February 15, 2020.

Ekeh, Peter P. "Colonialism and Social Structure." An Inaugural Lecture. Ibadan: Ibadan University Press, 1983.

"Nigerian Political History and the Foundations of Nigerian Federalism." Being a paper presented as Keynote Address to a Conference on the National Question Organised by the Programme of Ethnic and Federal Studies of the University of Ibadan, Nigeria, 2000.

Ekekwe, Eme. "Nationalist Movement and Ideology: Nigeria, 1940–1960." MA thesis, Carleton University, 1976.

Ekpo, Effiong J. "The Nigeria Labor Congress and National Development (1993–2000)." *European Journal of Political Science Studies* 2, no. 1 (2018): 172–193.

Ekpo, Margaret. *Breaking Barriers: An Autobiography*. Calabar: Profiles & Biographies, 2003.

Ekundare, Richard Olufemi. *An Economic History of Nigeria 1860–1960*. London: Methuen & Co Ltd., 1973.

Elaigwu, Jonah Isawa, Erim O. Erim, and Godfrey N. Uzoigwe, eds. *Foundations of Nigerian Federalism: Pre-colonial Antecedents*. Abuja: National Council on Intergovernmental Relations, 1996.

Elaigwu, Isawa J. *The Politics of Federalism in Nigeria*. London: Adonis & Abbey Publishers Ltd., 2017.

Eleazu, Uma. *Federalism and Nation-Building: The Nigerian Experience*. Devon: Stockwell Ltd., 1977.

Elfasi, M., and I. Hrbek. *General History of Africa III: Africa from the Seventh to the Eleventh Century*. Oxford: Heinemann Publishers, 1995.

Elias, Taslim O., Samuel N. Nwabara, and Chuma O. Akpamgbo. *African Indigenous Laws*. Enugu: Government Printer, 1975.

Elliott, Kit. *Benin: An African Kingdom and Culture*. Minneapolis: Lerner Publications Company, 1979.

Ellis, Alfred B. *The Yoruba Speaking Peoples of the Slave Coast of West Africa: Their Religion, Manners, Customs, Laws, Language, etc*. Lagos: Pilgrims Books, 1974.

Eltantawi, Sarah. *Shari'ah on Trial: Northern Nigeria's Islamic Revolution*. Berkeley: University of California Press, 2017.

Eluemunor, Tony. "Ekumeku War: Anioma Uprising against British Rule." *Vanguard*, March 30, 2019.

Eluwa, C. I., M. O. Ukagwu, U. N. Nwachukwu, and A. C. Nwaubani. *A History of Nigeria*. Onitsha: Africana First Publishers Limited, 2005.

Eluwa, G. I. C. "Background to the Emergence of the National Congress of British West Africa." *African Studies Review* 14, no. 2 (1971): 205–218.

A History of Nigeria for Schools and Colleges. Ibadan: Africana, 1988.

"National Congress of British West Africa: A Pioneer Nationalist Movement." *Geneva Africa* 11, no. 1 (1972): 38.

"The National Congress of British West Africa: A Study in African Nationalism." *Présence Africaine* 77 (1971): 131–149.

Enemugwem, John H. "The Impact of the Lagos Press in Nigeria, 1861–1922." *LWATI: A Journal of Contemporary Research* 6, no. 1 (2009): 106–114.

Enwerem, Iheanyi M. *A Dangerous Awakening: The Politicization of Religion in Nigeria*. Ibadan: IFRA-Nigeria, 1995.

Enwo-Irem, Immaculata Nnenna. "Colonialism and Education: The Challenges for Sustainable Development in Nigeria." *Mediterranean Journal of Social Sciences* 4, no. 5 (2013): 163.

Esedebe, Olisanwuche P. "The Educated Elite in Nigeria Reconsidered." *Journal of the Historical Society of Nigeria* 10, no. 3 (1980): 111–130.
Esomnofu, Emmanuel. "Dr. Victor Olaiya: The Man, The Music, The Maestro." *PAM*, February 17, 2020. https://pan-african-music.com/en/dr-victor-olaiya-dead-89/.
Essien, Dominus O. "The Traditional Religion of Pre-Colonial Akwa Ibom and its Impact." *Transafrican Journal of History* 23 (1994): 32–42.
Etherton, Michael. "The Development of African Drama." *Theatre Research International* 9, no. 3 (2009): 48.
Eze, Jonas. "Urbanization in Nigeria, Enugu (the Coal City) as an Urban Town: A Historical Review, 1918-1960." In *Urbanization, Security, and Development Issues in Nigeria 1914-2014: Festschrift in Honour of Prof. Enoch Oyedele*, ed. Patrick I. Ukase, Emmanuel O. Akubor, and Augustine I. Onoja. Zaira: Ahmadu Bello University Press, 2016, 9–20.
Ezeh, Godwin C. *Contemporary Issues in Nigerian History*. Nsukka: Mike Social Publishers, 2004.
Ezekwem, Ogechukwu. "Missions and the Rise of the Western Maternity among the Igbo of South-eastern Nigeria." MA thesis, University of Texas, 2014.
Ezera, Kalu. "Nigeria's Constitutional Road to Independence." *The Political Quarterly* 30, no. 2 (1959): 131–140.
Constitutional Developments in Nigeria. Ibadan: University Press, 1960.
Fabunmi, M. A. *An Anthology of Historical Notes on Ifẹ City*. Lagos: John West Publications, 1985.
Fadakinte, Mojibayo. M., and Musa Abdulkareem. "The Travails of Nigerian Federalism 1951-1999: A Federation in Crisis of Constitutional Engineering." *African Journal of Political Science and International Relations* 15, no. 1 (2021): 19–27.
Fadeiye, Oladele. *A Social Studies Textbook for Colleges and Universities*. Vol. 2. Ibadan: Akin- Johnson Press and Publishers, 2005.
Fafunwa, Aliyu B. *History of Education in Nigeria*. London: Allen & Unwin, 1974.
A History of Nigerian Higher Education. London: Macmillan, 1971.
Fagbule, Fola, and Feyi Fawehinmi. *Formation: The Making of Nigeria from Jihad to Amalgamation*. Abuja: Cassava Republic Press, 2021.
Fage, Kamilu S., and David O. Alabi. *Political and Constitutional Development in Nigeria: From Pre-colonial to Post-Colonial Era*. Kano: Northern Printers Limited, 2003.
Fahm, AbdulGafar O. "Ijebu Ode's Ojude Oba Festival: Cultural and Spiritual Significance." *SAGE Open* 5, no. 1 (2015): 1–11.
Fajana, Ade. "Colonial Control and Education: The Development of Higher Education in Nigeria 1900-1950." *Journal of the Historical Society of Nigeria* 6, no. 3 (1972): 323–340.
"The Nigerian Union of Teachers: A Decade of Growth, 1931–40." *West African Journal of Education* 3 (1973): 383.
Faleye, Olukayode A. "Plague and Trade in Lagos, 1924–1931." *The International Journal of Maritime History* 30, no. 2 (2018): 287–301.

Falola, Toyin. ed. *Britain and Nigeria, 1900–1960: Exploitation or Development?* London: Zed Books, 1987.

Colonialism and Violence in Nigeria. Bloomington: Indiana University Press, 2009.

Cultural Modernity in a Colonized World: The Writings of Chief Isaac Oluwole Delano. Texas: Pan-African University Press, 2020.

Economic Reforms and Modernization in Nigeria, 1945–1965. Kent: Kent State University Press, 2004.

History of Nigeria 3: Nigeria in the Twentieth Century. Lagos: Longman Nigeria Plc, 1991.

"The Ibadan Conference of 1885: Diplomacy and Conflict Resolution in Mid-Nineteenth Century Yorubaland." *Geneva-Africa* 23, no. 2 (1985): 37–56.

"Indigenous Knowledge and Oral Traditions in Nigeria." In *The Oxford Handbook of Nigerian History*, ed. Toyin Falola and Mathew Heaton. Oxford: Oxford University Press, 2022, 28.

"'Manufacturing Trouble': Currency Forgery in Colonial Southwestern Nigeria." *African Economic History* 25 (1997): 124.

The Power of African Culture. New York: University of Rochester Press, 2003.

"Theft in Colonial Southwestern Nigeria Africa." *Instituto Italiano Per* 50, no. 1 (1995): 1–24.

ed. *Tradition and Change in Africa: The Essays of J. F. Ade Ajayi.* Trenton: Africa World Press, 2000.

Violence in Nigeria: The Crisis of Religious Politics and Secular Ideologies. New York: University Rochester Press, 1998.

Yoruba Gurus: Indigenous Production of Knowledge in Africa. Trenton: Africa World Press Inc., 1999.

"The Yoruba Caravan System of the Nineteenth Century." *The International Journal of African Historical Society of Nigeria* 24, no. 1 (1991): 111–132.

Falola, Toyin, and Biodun Adediran. *Islam and Christianity in West Africa.* Ile-Ife: University of Ife Press Ltd. 1983.

Falola, Toyin, and Matt D. Child, eds. *The Yoruba Diaspora in the Atlantic World.* Indianapolis: Indiana University Press, 2005.

Falola, Toyin, and Bola Dauda. *Decolonizing Nigeria, 1945–1960: Politics, Power, and Personalities.* Texas: Pan-African University Press, 2017.

Falola, Toyin, and Mathew M. Heaton. *A History of Nigeria.* Cambridge: Cambridge University Press, 2008.

Falola, Toyin, and Christian Jennings, eds. *Africanizing Knowledge: African Studies Across Disciplines.* New Brunswick: Transaction Publishers, 2002.

Falola, Toyin, and Mike Odey. *Poverty Reduction Strategies in Africa.* New York: Routledge, 2018.

Falola, Toyin, and Dare Oguntomisin. *The Military in Nineteenth Century Yoruba Politics.* Ile-Ife: University of Ife Press, 1984.

Falola, Toyin, and Adam Paddock. *The Women's War of 1929: A History of Anti-Colonial Resistance in Eastern Nigeria.* Durham: Carolina Academic Press, 2011.

Familusi, M. M. *Methodism in Nigeria (1842–1992)*. Ibadan: N. P. S. Educational Publishers, 1992.

Famule, Oluwole. "Masks, Masque, and Masquerades." In *Culture and Customs of the Yorùbá*, ed. Toyin Falola and Akintunde Akinyemi. Austin: Pan African University Press, 2017.

Fanon, Frantz. *Black Skin, White Masks*. England: Pluto Press, 1967.

Farias, Paulo D. M. "History and Consolation: Royal Yorùbá Bards Comment on their Craft." *History in Africa* 19 (1992): 263–297.

Faseke, Modupeolu M. *Nigeria and the Commonwealth: Reflections and Projections*. Ibadan: Macmillan Nigeria Publishers, 2009.

"Oral History in Nigeria: Issues, Problems, and Prospects." *The Oral History Review* 18, no. 1 (1990): 77–92.

Fasinro, Hassan A. B. *Ahmadiyya Achievements and Conflicts: As I See It*. Lagos: Irede Printers, 1995.

Fatokun, Samson A. "Christian Missions in South-Western Nigeria, and the Response of African Traditional Religion." *International Review of Mission* 96, no. 380–381 (2007): 105–113.

"'I Will Pour Out My Spirit upon All Flesh': The Origin, Growth and Development of the Precious Stone Church – The Pioneering African Indigenous Pentecostal Denomination in Southwest Nigeria." *Cyber Journal for Pentecostal-Charismatic Research* 19 (2010): 1–28.

Fawcett, Louise. "Exploring Regional Domains: A Comparative History of Regionalism." *International Affairs* 80, no. 3 (2004): 429–446.

Feinberg, H. M. Review of "Benin and the Europeans 1485–1897." *African Historical Studies* 4, no.2 (1971): 405–410.

Feinstein, Alan. *African Revolutionary: The Life and Times of Nigeria's Aminu Kano*. New York: The New York Times Book Co., 1973.

Fiebach, Joachim. "Cultural Identities, Interculturalism, and Theatre: On the Popular Yoruba Travelling Theatre." *Theatre Research International* 21, no. 1 (1996): 52–58.

Fieldhouse, David K. *The Colonial Empires: A Comparative Survey from the Eighteenth Century*. London: Macmillan Press, 1966.

Merchant Capital and Economic Decolonization: The United Africa Company 1929–1987. Oxford: Clarendon Press, 1994.

Fika, Adamu Mohammed. *The Kano Civil War and British Over-Rule, 1882–1940*. Oxford: Oxford University Press, 1978.

Finkelman, Paul. *Encyclopedia of African American History, 1896 to the Present: O–T*. Oxford: Oxford University Press, 2009.

Finnegan, Ruth. *The Limba Stories and Storytelling*. Oxford: Oxford University Press, 1970.

Fisher, Humphrey J. "Conversion Reconsidered: Some Historical Aspects of Religious Conversion in Black Africa." *Africa* 43, no. 1 (1973): 27–40.

Fisher, Michael H. *Indirect Rule in India: Residents and the Residency System, 1764–1858*. New York: Oxford University Press, 1991.

Flint, J. "Chartered Companies and the Scramble for Africa." In *Africa in the Nineteenth and Twentieth Centuries*, ed. Joseph C. Anene and Godfrey N. Brown. Ibadan: Ibadan University Press, 1966, 110–117.

"Governor versus Colonial Office: An Anatomy of the Richards Constitution for Nigeria, 1939 to 1945." *Historical Papers* 16, no. 1 (1981): 124–143.

"'Managing Nationalism': The Colonial Office and Nnamdi Azikiwe, 1932–43." *The Journal of Imperial and Commonwealth History* 27, no. 2 (1999): 143–158.

"Nigeria: The Colonial Experience from 1880 to 1914." In *Colonialism in Africa 1870–1960. Vol. 1: The History and Politics of Colonialism 1870–1914*, ed. Lewis H. Gann and Peter Duignan. New York: Cambridge University Press, 1969, 220–260.

Flint, John. *Sir George Goldie and the Making of Nigeria*. London: Oxford University Press, 1960.

Flint, John E. J., and Robert Cornevin. "Lettres Aux Éditeurs/Correspondence." *Canadian Journal of African Studies* 9, no. 1 (1975): 157–159.

Fodiye, 'Abd Allah b. Muhammad. *Diya' al-ta'wil*. 2 vols., 1815.

Folami, Takiu. *A History of Lagos, Nigeria: The Shaping of an African City*. New York: Exposition Press, 1982.

Forbes, Suzanne. *Print and Party Politics in Ireland, 1689–1714*. Cham: Palgrave Macmillan, 2018.

Forde, Daryll, and G. I. Jones. *The Ibo and Ibibio Speaking Peoples of Southeastern Nigeria*. London: Oxford University Press, 1950.

Forde, Daryll, and Phyllis M. Kaberry, eds. *West African Kingdoms in the Nineteenth Century*. London: Oxford University Press, 1967.

Fourchard, Laurent. "Lagos and the Invention of Juvenile Delinquency in Nigeria." *Journal of African History* 47, no. 10 (2006): 115–137.

Fuglestad, Finn. "A Reconsideration of Hausa History before the Jihad." *The Journal of African History* 19, no. 3 (1978): 319–339.

Fwatshak, Sati U. "Reconstructing the Origins of the People of Plateau State: Questioning the 'We Are All Settlers' Theory." *Journal of the Historical Society of Nigeria* 16 (2005/2006): 122–140.

Fyfe, Christopher. "The Emergence and Evolution of African Studies in the United Kingdom.' In *Out of One, Many Africas: Reconstructing the Study and Meaning of Africa*, ed. William G. Martin and Michael O. West. Chicago: University of Illinois Press, 1999, 54–61.

Fyle, Magbialy C. "The Yoruba Diaspora in Sierra Leon's Krio Society." In *The Yoruba in the Atlantic World*, ed. Toyin Falola and Matt D. Child. Indianapolis: Indiana University Press, 2005, 367–369.

Gailey, Harry A. *Lugard and the Abeokuta Uprising: The Demise of Egba Independence*. New York: Routledge, 1982.

Galadima, Bulus Y., and Yusufu Turaki. "Christianity in Nigeria: Part I." *African Journal of Evangelical Theology* 20 no. 1 (2001): 85–101.

Gana, Aaron Tsado, and Samuel G. Egwu, eds. *Federalism in Africa: Framing the National Question*. Vol. 1. Trenton: Africa World Press, 2003.

Gandy, Matthew. "Planning, Anti-planning and the Infrastructure Crisis Facing Metropolitan Lagos." *Urban Studies* 43, no. 2 (2006): 371-396.

Gann, Lewis H., and Peter Duignan, eds. *Colonialism in Africa, 1870-1960: The History and Politics of Colonialism, 1914-1960*. Vol. 2. Cambridge: Cambridge University Press, 1970.

Colonialism in Africa, 1970-1960, 5 Vols. London: Cambridge University Press, 1969.

Garba, Hamza A., Hafiz Jibril, Khalil A. Abba, and Tasiu A. Sani. "Role of Nigerian Educated Elites Towards Anti-Colonial Struggle in Nigeria, 1930s-1960." *International Journal for Social Studies* 3, no. 6 (2017): 83-98.

Gardner, Leigh. *Taxing Colonial Africa: The Political Economy of British Imperialism*. Oxford: Oxford University, 2012.

Garrett, Thomas A. "Economic Effects of the 1918 Influenza Pandemic: Implications for a Modern-Day Pandemic." *Federal Reserve Bank of St. Louis Review* 90, no. 2 (2008): 75-93.

Gavin, Robert J., and Wale Oyemakinde. "Economic Development in Nigeria Since 1800." In *Groundwork of Nigerian History*, ed. Obaro Ikime. Ibadan: Heinemann, 1980, 482-517.

Gbadamosi, Gbadebo O. "The Establishment of Western Education among Muslims in Nigeria 1896-1926." *Journal of the Historical Society of Nigeria* 4, no. 1 (1967): 89-115.

The Growth of Islam among the Yoruba, 1841-1908. New Jersey: Humanities Press, 1978.

Gbadamosi, Tajudeen G. O., and Jacob F. A. Ajayi. "Islam and Christianity in Nigeria." In *Groundwork of Nigerian History*, ed. Obaro Ikime. Ibadan: Heinemann Educational Books, 1980, 152-161.

Gbilekaa, Saint. "Tiv Popular Music and Dance: Myth and Reality." In *The Tiv in Contemporary Nigeria*, ed. Terdoo Ahire. Zaria: Tiv Studies Project Publication, 1993, 42-48.

Geary, Sir William. *Nigeria Under British Rule*. London: Frank Cass, 1965.

Geiger, Susan. "Women and African Nationalism." *Journal of Women's History* 2, no. 1 (1990): 227-244.

Gellner, Ernest. *Nations and Nationalism*. Oxford: Basil Blackwell, 1983.

Genzlinger, Neil. "The Problem with Memoirs." *New York Times*, January 28, 2011.

George, Olusoji J. Oluwakemi Owoyemi, and Uche Onokala. "Trade Unions and Unionism in Nigeria: A Historical Perspective." *Research in World Economy* 3, no. 2 (2012): 68-74.

Gerring, John, Daniel Ziblatt, Johan Van Gorp, and Julián Arévalo. "An Institutional Theory of Direct and Indirect Rule." *World Politics* 63, no. 3 (2011): 377-433.

Gershoni, Yekutiel. "Common Goals, Different Ways: The UNIA and the NCBWA in West Africa, 1920-1930." *Journal of Third World Studies* 18, no. 2 (2001): 171-185.

Ghebru, Hosaena, and Austen Okumo. *Land Administration Service Delivery and its Challenges in Nigeria: A Case Study of Eight States*. Washington, DC: International Food Policy Research Institute, 2016.

Ghosh, Durba. "Gender and Colonialism: Expansion or Marginalization?" *The Historical Journal* 47, no. 3 (2004): 737–755.

Gifford, Prosser, and William Roger Louis. *Decolonization and African Independence: The Transfer of Power, 1960–1980*. London: Yale University Press, 1988.

France and Britain in Africa: Imperial Rivalry and Colonial Rule. New Haven: Yale University Press, 1971.

Gill, Sonya, and Shirish N. Kavadi. *Health Financing and Costs: A Comparative Study of Trends in Eighteen Countries with Special Reference to India*. Mumbai: Foundation for Research in Community Health, 1999.

Gilliland, Dean Stewart. "African Traditional Religion in Transition: The Influence of Islam on African Traditional Religion in North Nigeria." Unpublished PhD dissertation. Hartford Seminary, 1971.

Girshick, Paula, Ben-Amos Girshick, and John Thornton. "Civil War in the Kingdom of Benin, 1689–1721: Continuity or Political Change?" *The Journal of African History* 42, no. 3 (2001): 365.

Gluckman, Max. "The Utility of the Equilibrium Model in the Study of Social Change." *American Anthropologist* 70, no. 2 (1968): 219–237.

Gluckstein, Donny. *A People's History of the Second World War: Resistance Versus Empire*. London: Pluto Press, 2012.

Gofwen, Rotgak I. *Religious Conflicts in Northern Nigeria and Nation Building: The Throes of Two Decades 1980–2000*. Kaduna: Human Rights Monitor, 2004.

Goldoni, Daniele. "Cultural Mutation: What Media Do to Culture." *Citizens of Europe* 3 (2015): 381–424.

Goldstone, Jack A. "Comparative Historical Analysis and Knowledge Accumulation in the Study of Revolutions." In *Comparative Historical Analysis in the Social Sciences*, ed. James Mahoney and Dietrich Rueschemeyer. Cambridge: Cambridge University Press, 2003, 41–90.

Goltzsche, Margherita. *Gesellschaft und Politik bei den Ibo um 1900: die Rolle völkerkundlicher Studien als Quellen zur afrikanischen Geschichte*. Bern: Herbert Lang, 1976.

Good, Kenneth. "Settler Colonialism: Economic Development and Class Formation." *The Journal of Modern African Studies* 14, no. 4 (1976): 597–620.

Götrick, Kacke. *Apidan Theatre and Modern Drama: A Study in a Traditional Yoruba Theatre and Its Influence on Modern Drama by Yoruba Playwrights*. Stockholm: Almqvist & Wiksell International, 1984.

Gouda, Frances. *Dutch Culture Overseas: Colonial Practice in the Netherlands Indies, 1900–1942*. Sheffield: Equinox Publishing, 2008.

Graham, James D. "The Slave Trade, Depopulation and Human Sacrifice in Benin History: The General Approach." *Cahiers d'Études Africaines* 5, no. 18 (1965): 317–334.

Greenwood, Anna, ed. *Beyond the State: The Colonial Medical Service in British Africa*. Manchester: Manchester University Press, 2016.

Gueye, M'baye, and Albert Adu Boahen. "African Initiatives and Resistance in West Africa, 1880-1914." In *General History of Africa: VII Africa Under Colonial Domination 1880-1935*, ed. Albert Adu Boahen. Paris: UNESCO, 1990, 147.

Gusau, Sule A. "Economic Ideas of Shehu Usman Dan Fodio." *Journal Institute of Muslim MinorityAffairs* 10, no. 1 (1989): 139-151.

Hackett, Rosalind I. J. *Religion in Calabar: The Religious Life and History of a Nigerian Town*. Berlin: Mouton De Gruyter, 1989.

"The Spiritual Sciences in Africa." *Journal of Contemporary Religion* 3, no. 2 (1986): 8-11.

Hallett, Robin. ed. *The Niger Journal of Richard and John Lander*. London: Routledge & Kegan Paul, 1965.

Hamm, Bernd, and Russell Charles Smandych. *Cultural Imperialism: Essays on the Political Economy of Cultural Domination*. Peterborough: Broadview Press, 2005.

Hanna, Judith Lynne. "Dance and Women's Protest in Nigeria and the United States." In *Women and Social Protest*, ed. Guida West and Rhoda Lois Blumberg. New York: Oxford University Press, 1990, 333-345.

Harari, Yuval Noah. *Sapiens: A Brief History of Humankind*. London: Hervill Secker, 2014.

Hargreaves, John D. "The Making of the Boundaries: Focus on West Africa." In *Partitioned Africans: Ethnic Relations Across Africa's International Boundaries 1884-1984*, ed. Anthony I. Asiwaju. Lagos: Lagos University Press, 1984, 19-28.

"West African States and the European Conquest." In *Colonialism in Africa 1870-1960. Vol. One: The History and Politics of Colonialism 1870-1914*, ed. Lewis H. Gann and Peter Duignan. New York: Cambridge University Press, 1969, 199-219.

Harlow, Barbara, and Mia Carter. *Archives of Empire: Vol. 2. The Scramble for Africa*. New York: Duke University Press, 2003.

Imperialism and Orientalism: A Documentary Sourcebook. Boston: Blackwell Publishers, 1999.

Harneit-Sievers, Axel. "African Business, 'Economic Nationalism,' and British Colonial Policy: Southern Nigeria, 1935-1954." *African Economic History* 24 (1996): 25-68.

Harold, Evans. "Studies in War-time Organization: The Resident Ministry of West Africa." *African Affairs*, 173, no. 43 (1944): 52-58.

Harold, Zink. *The United States in Germany 1944-1955*. Princeton: D. Van Nostrand, 1957.

Harper, Jim C. *Western-Educated Elites in Kenya, 1900-1963: The African American Factor*. New York: Routledge, 2016.

Harrison, Mark, ed. *The Economics of World War II: Six Great Powers in International Comparison*. Cambridge: Cambridge University Press, 1998.

Harry, Celestina I. "Development of Primary/Secondary Schools in Colonial Times and the Need for Sustainable Innovations, Growth and Value Creation: A Comparative Analysis." *International Journal of Humanities Social Sciences and Education* 7, no. 3 (2020): 80–89.

Harunah, Hakeem B. *Nigeria's Defunct Slave Ports: Their Cultural Legacies and Touristic Value.* Lagos: First Academic Publishers, 2000.

——— "Sodeke: Hero and Statesman of the Egba." *Journal of the Historical Society of Nigeria* 12, no. 1/2 (1984): 109–131.

Hashim, A. O. "Arabic Language as a Source of Diplomatic Relations between Sokoto Caliphate and Its Neighbors." *Journal of History and Diplomatic Studies* 6 (2009): 175–189.

Hassett, Dónal, and Michelle Moyd. "Introduction: Writing the History of Colonial Veterans of the Great War." *First World War Studies* 10, no. 1 (2019): 1–11.

Hatcho, Yui. "The Atlantic Charter of 1941: A Political Tool of Non-belligerent America." *The Japanese Journal of American Studies*, no. 14 (2003): 123–139.

Hawkins, Edward K. *Road Transportation in Nigeria: A Study of an African Enterprise.* London: Africana University Press, 1958.

Hay, Margaret Jen, and Sharon Stichter. *African Women South of the Sahara.* New York: Longman, 1995.

Hays, Samuel P. "From the History of the City to the History of the Urbanized Society." *Journal of Urban History* 19, no. 1 (1993): 3–25.

Headrick, Daniel. *The Tools of Empire: Technology and European Imperialism in the Nineteenth Century.* New York: Oxford University Press, 1981.

Headrick, Rita. "African Soldiers in World War II." *Armed Forces & Society* 4, no. 3 (1978): 501–526.

Heap, Simon. "'Jaguda Boys': Pickpocketing in Ibadan, 1930–60." *Urban History* 24, no. 3 (1997): 324–343.

——— "The Nigerian National Archives, Ibadan: An Introduction for Users and a Summary of Holdings." *History in Africa* 18 (1991): 159–172.

——— "Transport and Liquor in Colonial Nigeria." *Journal of Transport History* 21, no. 1 (2001): 28–53.

Heaton, Matthew, and Toyin Falola. "Global Explanations Versus Local Interpretations: The Historiography of the Influenza Pandemic of 1918–19 in Africa." *History in Africa* 33 (2006): 205–230.

Helleiner, Gerald K. *Peasant Agriculture, Government, and Economic Growth in Nigeria.* Homewood: R. D. Irwin, 1966.

Heller, Monica, and Bonnie McElhinny. *Language, Capitalism, Colonialism: Toward a Critical History.* Toronto: University of Toronto Press, 2017.

Henige, David P. "Oral Tradition and Chronology." *The Journal of African History*, 12, no. 3 (1971): 371–389.

Hermann, Robin. "Empire Builders and Mushroom Gentlemen: The Meaning of Money in Colonial Nigeria." *The International Journal of African Historical Studies* 44, no. 3 (2011): 393–413.

Herskovits, Jean. "Liberated Africans and the History of Lagos Colony to 1886." Unpublished PhD dissertation. University of Oxford, 1960.
Herskovits, Melville J., and Mitchell Harwits. *Economic Transition in West Africa*. London: Routledge, 1964.
Hetherington, Penelope. *British Paternalism and Africa, 1920-1940*. London: Frank Cass, 1978.
Hicks, Dan. *The Brutish Museums: The Benin Bronzes, Colonial Violence and Cultural Restitution*. London: Pluto Press, 2020.
Hiribarren, Vincent. "A European and African Joint-Venture: Writing a Seamless History of Borno (1902-1960)." *History in Africa* 40 (2013): 77-98.
Hiskett, Mervyn. *The Course of Islam in Africa*. Edinburgh: Edinburgh University Press, 1994.
Hobsbawm, Eric J. *Primitive Rebels: Studies in Archaic Forms of Social Movement in the 19th and 20th Centuries*. Manchester: Manchester University Press, 1959.
Hodgkin, Thomas. "Islam and National Movements in West Africa." *The Journal of African History* 3, no. 2 (1962): 323-327.
Nationalism in Colonial Africa. New York: New York University Press, 1957.
"Prevail or Perish: Anglo-German Naval Competition at the Beginning of the Twentieth Century." *European Security* 20, no. 1 (2011): 65-79.
Hoffman, Philip T. *Why Did Europe Conquer the World?* Princeton: Princeton University Press, 2017.
Holmes, Peter. *Nigeria: Giant of Africa*. London: Swallow Editions, 1985.
Home, R. K. *Of Planting and Planning: The Making of British Colonial Cities*. New York: Routledge, 2013.
"Town Planning and Garden Cities in the British Colonial Empire 1910-1940." *Planning Perspectives* 5, no. 1 (1990): 23-37.
Honigsbaum, Mark. *The Fever Trail: In Search of the Cure for Malaria*. New York: Farrar Straux and Giroux, 2002.
Hopen, Edward C. *The Pastoral Fulbe Family in Gwandu*. London: Routledge, 2018.
Hopkins, Anthony G. "The Currency Revolution in South-West Nigeria in the Late Nineteenth Century." *Journal of the Historical Society of Nigeria* 3, no. 3 (1966): 471-483.
"An Economic History of Lagos, 1880-1914." Unpublished PhD dissertation. University of London, 1964.
An Economic History of West Africa. New York: Routledge, 2020.
"Property Rights and Empire Building: Britain's Annexation of Lagos, 1861." *The Journal of Economic History* 40, no. 4 (1980): 777-798.
Horton, Robin. "Stateless Societies in the History of West Africa." In *History of West Africa*. Vol. 1, edited by Jacob F. A. Ajayi and Michael Crowder. London: Longman, 1976, 72-113.
Hoyle, L. *The Influenza Viruses*. New York: Springer, 1968.
Hunt, Nancy Rose. "Placing African Women's History and Locating Gender." *Social History* 14, no. 3 (1989): 359-379.

Hunwick, John. "The Arabic Literary Tradition of Nigeria." *Research in African Literatures* 28, no. 3 (1997): 210–223.

"A Historical Whodunit: The So-Called 'Kano Chronicle' and Its Place in the Historiography of Kano." *History in Africa* 21 (1994): 127–146.

Hussey, Eric Roberts J. "Educational Policy and Political Development in Africa." *African Affairs* 45, no. 179 (1946): 72–80.

Hutson, Alaine S. "Women, Men, and Patriarchal Bargaining in an Islamic Sufi Order: The Tijaniyya in Kano, Nigeria, 1937 to the Present." *Gender & Society* 15, no. 5 (2001): 734–753.

Ibenekwu, Ikpechukwuka E. "Igbo Traditional Political System and the Crisis of Governance in Nigeria." *Ikoro: Journal of the Institute of African Studies* 9 (2010): 3–10.

Ibrahim, Bashir O. "Agitation and Protest against the British Colonial Policies in Ilorin 1923-1936." *Alore: Ilorin Journal of the Humanities* 13 (2003): 142–154.

Ibuot, Emmanuel Johnson, Cletus Johnson Ibuot, and Ibia E. Ibia. "Education, Ideology and Social Transformation." *Journal of the Historical Society of Nigeria* 27 (2018): 24–47.

Idaewor, Osiomheyalo. "Eboh and Traditional Medicine in Pre-Colonial Apana Social Systems." *Journal of History and Diplomatic Studies* 10, no. 1 (2014): 145–165.

Ide, Christopher. "Indigenization Policy: The Case of Nigeria 1960–1980, 1983." Unpublished PhD dissertation. Atlanta University, 1983.

Idonije, Benson. "Salute to Tunde King, Pioneer of Juju Music." *Guardian*, April 2, 2008.

Idowu, Bolaji E. *African Traditional Religion: A Definition*. London: S. C. M Press, 1973.

Olodumare: God in Yoruba Belief. London: Longmans, 1962.

Towards an Indigenous Church. London: Oxford University Press, 1965.

Idress, Aliyu A. "Ilorin Factor in the 19th Century Nupe Politics: A Study in the Inter-Emirate Relations within Sokoto Caliphate, Nigeria." *Transafrican Journal of History* 20 (1991): 181–189.

Ifeka-Moller, Caroline. "Female Militancy and Colonial Revolt: The Women's War of 1929, Eastern Nigeria." In *Perceiving Women*, ed. Shirley Ardener. New York: John Wiley and Sons, Inc., 1975, 127–57.

"'Sitting on a Man': Colonialism and the Lost Political Institution of Igbo Women: A Reply to Judith Van Allen." *Canadian Journal of African Studies* 7, no. 2 (1973): 317–318.

Igbafe, Philip A. *Benin Under British Administration, 1897–1938: The Impact of Colonial Rule on an African Kingdom*. London: Longman, 1979.

"British Rule in Benin 1897–1920: Direct or Indirect?" *Journal of the Historical Society of Nigeria* 3, no. 4 (1967): 701–717.

"The Fall of Benin: A Reassessment." *The Journal of African History* 11, no. 3 (1970): 385–400.

"Slavery and Emancipation in Benin, 1897-1945." *The Journal of African History* 16, no. 3 (1975): 409-429.

"Western Ibo Society and Its Resistance to British Rule: The Ekumeku Movement 1898-1911." *The Journal of African History* 12, no. 3 (1971): 441-459.

Igbi, Oghenemudiakevwe. "Nigerian Highlife Music: A Survey of the Sociopolitical Events from 1950-2005." *EJOTMAS: Ekpoma Journal of Theatre and Media Arts* 5, no. 1-2 (2005): 173.

Igboin, Benson O. "Names and the Reality of Life: An Inquiry into inherent Power in Names among the Owan of Nigeria." *Ado Journal of Religions* 2, no. 1 (2004) 9-26.

Ige, Bola. *People, Politics and Politicians of Nigeria (1940-1979)*. Ibadan: Heinemann Educational Books, 1995.

Igwe, Agbafor. *Nnamdi Azikiwe: The Philosopher of Our Time*. Enugu: Fourth Dimension Publisher, 1992.

Iheduru, Okechukwu. "Nigeria's Comparative Politics." In *Interests, Identities, and Institutions in a Changing Global Order*, 3rd ed., ed. Jeffrey Kopstein and Mark Lichbach. Cambridge: Cambridge University Press, 2008, 535-587.

Iheoma, Eugene O. "Moral Education in Nigeria: Problems and Prospects." *Journal of Moral Education* 14, no. 3 (1985): 183-193.

Ihonvbere, Julius O., and Timothy M. Shaw. *Illusions of Power: Nigeria in Transition*. New Jersey: Africa World Press, 1998.

Ijoma, J. O. "Portuguese Activities in West Africa before 1600: The Consequences." *Transafrican Journal of History* 11 (1982): 136-146.

Ikeanyibe, Okechukwu. "History of Pre-colonial Southern Nigeria." In *Nigerian Peoples and Culture*, ed. S. A. Idahosa et al. Benin City: Benson Idahosa University, 2007, 44-62.

Ikenga-Metuh, Emefie. "Two Decades of Religious Conflicts in Nigeria: A Recipe for Peace." *Bulletin of Ecumenical Theology* 6, no. 1 (1994): 69-93.

Ikime, Obaro. "The British and Native Administration Finance in Northern Nigeria, 1900-1934." *Journal of the Historical Society of Nigeria* 7, no. 4 (1975): 673-692.

Can Anything Good Come Out of History? Ibadan: Bookcraft, 2018.

"Colonial Conquest and Resistance in Southern Nigeria." *Journal of the Historical Society of Nigeria* 6, no. 3 (1972): 267-268.

"The Establishment of Indirect Rule in Northern Nigeria." *Tarikh* 3, no. 3 (1971): 1-15.

The Fall of Nigeria: The British Conquest. London: Heinemann, 1977.

Niger Delta Rivalry: Itsekiri-Urhobo Relations and the European Presence, 1884-1926. London: Longmans, 1969.

"Reconsidering Indirect Rule: The Nigerian Example." *Journal of the Historical Society of Nigeria* 4, no. 3 (1968): 421-438.

Ìkọ̀tún, Reuben Olúwáfẹ́mi. "New Trends in Yorùbá Personal Names among Yorùbá Christians." *Linguistik Online* 59 (2013): 65-83.

Ikuomola, Adediran Daniel, Rashidi Akanji Okunola, and Simon Heap. "Historical Analysis of Touts as a Deviant Subgroup in Lagos State – Nigeria." *African Journal of Arts and Humanities* 2, no. 2 (2009): 49–62.

Ilyasu, Yakubu Ahmed, Sunday Vincent Akwashiki, and Jamila Salisu. "Socio-Political Implication of Urbanization in Nigeria: An Overview." *International Journal of Social Science and Human Research* 3, no. 7 (2020): 76–78.

Imam, Hauwa. "Educational Policy in Nigeria from the Colonial Era to the Post-Independence Period." *Italian Journal of Sociology of Education* 4, no. 1 (2012): 10–15.

Imbua, David L. *Intercourse and Crosscurrents in the Atlantic World: Calabar-British Experience, 17th–20th Centuries*. Durham: Carolina Academic Press, 2012.

Imbua, David, Otoabasi Akpan, Ikechukwu Amadi, and Yakubu Ochefu, eds. *History, Culture, Diasporas and Nation Building: The Collected Works of Okon Edet Uya*. Bethesda: Arbi Press, 2012.

Imhonopi, David, Ugochukwu M. Urim, and Charles T. Iruonagbe. "Colonialism, social Structure and Class Formation: Implication for Development in Nigeria." In *A Panoply of Readings in Social Sciences: Lessons for and from Nigeria*, ed. David Imhonopi and Ugochukwu M. Urim. Otta: Covenant University, 2013, 107–122.

Imogie, A. O., E. O. Agwubike, and K. Aluko. "Assessing the Role of Traditional Birth Attendants (TBAs) in Health Care Delivery in Edo State, Nigeria." *Africa Journal of Reproductive Health* 6, no. 2 (2002): 94–100.

Imoh-Itah, Imoh, Luke Amadi, and Roger Akpan. "Colonialism and the Post-Colonial Nigeria: Complexities and Contradictions 1960–2015: A Post-Development Perspective." *International Journal of Political Science* 2, no. 3 (2016): 9–21.

Ingyoroko, Margaret, Elizabeth T. Sugh, and Terfa T. Alkali. "The Nigerian Woman and the Reformation of the Political System: A Historical Perspective." *Journal of Socialomics* 6, no. 2 (2017): 2–8.

Inikori, Joseph E. "Africans and the Industrial Revolution in England: A Roundtable Response." *International Journal of Maritime History* 15, no. 2 (2003): 330–361.

Inyang, Anietie A., and Manasseh E. Bassey. "Imperial Treaties and the Origins of British Colonial Rule in Southern Nigeria, 1860–1890," *Mediterranean Journal of Social Sciences* 5, no. 20 (2014): 1946–1953.

Iongh, Peter de. "Nigeria, Two Imperialists and their Creation." *History Today* 14 (1964): 835–843.

Irabor, Daniel. "The Art of the Benin People." *Journal of Advances in Social Science and Humanities* 5, no. 8 (2019): 949–974.

Isajiw, Wsevolod W. "Definition and Dimensions of Ethnicity: A Theoretical Framework." In *Challenges of Measuring an Ethnic World: Science, Politics and Reality: Proceedings of the Joint Canada-United States Conference on the*

Measurement of Ethnicity, ed. Statistics Canada and US Bureau of the Census. Washington, DC: US Government Printing Office, 1993, 407–427.
Isamah, Austin. "Organized Labor under the Military Regimes in Nigeria." *Africa Development* 15, no. 2 (1990): 81–94.
Isichei, Elizabeth Allo. "Colonialism Resisted," in *Studies in The History of Plateau State, Nigeria*, ed. Elisabeth Isichei (London: Macmillan Press, 1982), 207.
A History of the Igbo People. London: Macmillan, 1976.
Isola, Akinwunmi. "Making Culture Memorable: The Literary Contributions of Isaac Oluwole Delano." Lecture Delivered at the Isaac Oluwole Delano Inaugural Memorial Lecture, Muson Centre, December 20, 2004.
Isola, Omoleke I. "The Relevance of the African Traditional Medicine (Alternative Medicine) to Health Care Delivery System in Nigeria." *The Journal of Developing Areas* 47, no. 1 (2013): 319–338.
Ityavyar, Dennis A. "Background to the Development of Health Services in Nigeria." *Social Science & Medicine* 24, no. 6 (1987): 487–499.
Iweriebor, Ehiedu E. G. *Radical Politics in Nigeria, 1945–1950: The Significance of the Zikist Movement*. Zaria: Ahmadu Bello University Press, 1996.
"State Systems in Pre-Colonial, Colonial and Post-Colonial Nigeria: An Overview." *Africa: Rivista Trimestrale Di Studi e Documentazione Dell'Istituto Italiano per l'Africa e l'Oriente* 37, no. 4 (1982): 507–513.
Iyanya, Victor. "Traditional Rulers and Crisis of Legitimacy in the Post-colonial Nigeria: The Case of the Igede of Central Nigeria." Paper read at the ASAUK 2018 Conference, Aston Webb – Senate Chamber, University of Birmingham, 12 September, 2018.
Iyer, Lakshmi. "Direct Versus Indirect Colonial Rule in India: Long-term Consequences." *The Review of Economics and Statistics* 92, no. 4 (2010): 693–713.
Iyorza, Stanislaus. "Global Media and Neo-Colonialism in Africa: The Socio-Ecological Model Solution to Nigeria's Development Efforts." In *Freedom, Self-Determination and Growth in Africa*, ed. Kingsly Owete, Monica Emmanuel, Umar H. D. Danfulani, Sati Fwatshak, and Anthony Agwuele. Berlin: Media Team IT Education Centre, 2014, 1–18.
Izeogu, Chukudi V. *Problems and Prospects of Urban and Regional Planning in Nigeria: Port Harcourt Metropolis Since 1914*. New York: Page Publishing Inc, 2018.
Izuagie, Lexington. "The Willink Minority Commission and Minority Rights in Nigeria." *EJOTMAS: Ekpoma Journal of Theatre and Media Arts* 5, no. 1–2 (2015): 206–223.
Jabati, Fatmata J. *The West African Pilot: Historical Study of a Nationalist Newspaper*. Ohio: Ohio University, 1985.
Jackson, Larry R. "Nigeria: The Politics of the First Republic." *Journal of Black Studies* 2, no. 3 (1972): 277–302.
Jacob, Audu. "Precolonial Political Administration in the North Central Nigeria: A Study of the Igala Political Kingdom." *European Scientific Journal* 10, no. 19 (2014): 401.

Jacob, Ray Ikechukwu. "A Historical Survey of Ethnic Conflict in Nigeria." *Asian Social Science* 8, no. 4 (2012):13–29.
Jaekel, Francis. *The History of the Nigerian Railway. Vol. 2: Network and Infrastructures*. Ibadan: Spectrum Books Ltd., 1997.
Jaiyeola, Emmanuel O., and Isaac Aladegbola. "Patriarchy and Colonization: The 'Brooder House' for Gender Inequality in Nigeria." *Journal of Research on Women and Gender* 10 (2020): 9–10.
Jaja, Emmanuel Adagogo. *King Jaja of Opobo (1821–1891): A Sketch History of the Development and Expansion of Opobo*. Lagos: Opobo Action Council, 1977.
Jaja, Solomon O. "The Enugu Colliery Massacre in Retrospect: An Episode in British Administration of Nigeria." *Journal of the Historical Society of Nigeria* 11, no. 3/4 (1982–1983): 86–106.
 Opobo Since 1870: A Documentary Record with an Introduction. Ibadan: University of Ibadan, 1991.
James, Lawrence. *The Rise and Fall of the British Empire*. New York: St. Martin's Press, 1994.
Jarmon, Charles. *Nigeria: Reorganization and Development since the Mid-Twentieth Century*. Leiden: E. J. Brill, 1988.
Jega, Attahiru. "The Political Economy of Nigerian Federalism." In *Foundations of Nigerian Federalism, 1960–1995*. Vol. III. ed. Isawa J. Elaigwu and R. A. Akindele. Abuja: National Council of Intergovernmental Relation, 1996, 96.
 "Towards Restructuring of Nigeria." *Thisday*, July 10, 2020.
Jekayinfa, Biodun. *History of Hierarchy of Great Kings of Yorubaland*. Lagos: Lichfield Nigeria Limited, 2001.
Jennings, J. H. "Enugu: A Geographical Outline." *The Nigerian Geographical Journal* 3, no. 1 (1959): 28–38.
Jerónimo, Miguel B., and António Costa Pinto, eds. *The Ends of European Colonial Empires: Cases and Comparisons*. London: Palgrave Macmillan, 2015.
Jeyifo, Biodun. *The Yoruba Popular Travelling Theatre of Nigeria*. Lagos: Nigerian Magazine Publications, 1984.
Jimada, Idris S. *The Historical Background to the Establishment of Patigi Emirate: c1810–1898*. Zaria: Ahmadu Bello University, 2016.
 The Nupe and the Origins and Evolution of Yoruba c.1275–1897. Zaria: The Abdullahi Smith Centre for Historical Research, 2005.
Jimoh, Mufutau Oluwasegun. "A Study in Spatial Focal Points and Social Contestation of Urban Life in Lagos: A History of Glover Memorial Hall, 1889–1960." *Ife Journal of History* 8, no. 1 (2016/2017): 124–149.
Johnson, Cheryl J. "'For their Freedoms': The Anti-Imperialist and International Feminist Activity of Funmilayo Ransome-Kuti of Nigeria." *Women's Studies International Forum* 32 (2009): 51–59.
 "Grass Roots Organizing: Women in Anticolonial Activity in Southwestern Nigeria." *African Studies Review* 25, no. 2/3 (1982): 148–155.
 "Madam Alimotu Pelewura and the Lagos Market Women." *Tarikh* 7, no. 1 (1981): 1–10.

"Nigerian Women and British Colonialism: The Yoruba Example with Selected Biographies." Unpublished PhD dissertation. Northwestern University, 1978.

Johnson, James A., Carleen H. Stoskopf, and Leiyu Shi, eds. *Comparative Health Systems: A Global Perspective*. Burlington: Jones & Bartlett Learning, 2018.

Johnson, Kofi. "Aladura: The Search for Authenticity an Impetus for African Christianity." *AJPS* 14, no. 1 (2011): 149–165.

Johnson, Niall P. A. S., and Juergen Mueller. "Updating the Accounts: Global Mortality of the 1918–1920 'Spanish' Influenza Pandemic." *Bulletin of the History of Medicine* 76, no. 1 (2002): 105–115.

Johnson, Richard W. "Forever on the Wrong Side." *London Review of Books*, September 27, 2012.

Johnson, Samuel. *The History of the Yorubas from the Earliest Times to the Beginning of the British Protectorate*. Lagos: CSS Press, 1921.

Johnson-Odim, Cheryl, and Nina Emma Mba. *For Women and the Nation: Funmilayo Ransome-Kuti of Nigeria*. Urbana: University of Illinois Press, 1997.

Johnson-Odim, Cheryl. "Lady Oyinkan Abayomi: A Profile." In *Nigerian Women in Historical Perspective*, ed. Bolanle Awe. Lagos: Sankore Press, 1993, 149–163.

Johnson-Odim, Cheryl. "On Behalf of Women and the Nation: Funmilayo Ransome-Kuti and the Struggles for Nigerian Independence." In *Expanding the Boundaries of Women's History: Essays on Women in the Third World*, ed. Cheryl Johnson-Odim and Margaret Strobel. Bloomington: Indiana University Press, 1992, 144–157.

"Pelewura, Alimotu (188?-1951)." In *The Oxford Encyclopedia of Women in World History*. Vol. 1. ed. Bonnie G. Smith. Oxford: Oxford University Press, 2008, 429.

"Women and Gender in the History of Sub-Saharan Africa." In *Women's History in Global Perspective: Women and Gender in the History of Sub-Saharan Africa*. Vol. 3. ed. Bonnie G. Smith. Urbana: University of Illinois Press, 2005, 54.

Johnston, William R. *Great Britain Great Empire: An Evaluation of the British Imperial Experience*. Queensland: University of Queensland Press, 1981.

Jones, Gwilym Iwan. "From Direct to Indirect Rule in Eastern Nigeria." *Odù: Journal of Yoruba and Related Studies* 2, no. 2 (1965): 72–80.

July, Robert W. *The Origins of Modern African Thought: Its Development in West Africa During the Nineteenth and Twentieth Centuries*. Trenton: Africa World Press, 2004.

Jumare, Ibrahim M. "Colonial Taxation in the Capital of Northern Nigeria." *African Economic History* 26 (1998): 83–97.

Justin, Awuawuer T. "Understanding Swange Dance of the Tiv People of Central Nigeria within the Perspective of Socio-Political Changes." *International Journal of Political Science and Governance* 3, no. 1 (2021): 17–23.

Kahn, Andrew, and Jamelle Bouie. "The Atlantic Slave Trade in Two Minutes." *Slate*, September 16, 2021. www.slate.com/news-and-politics/2021/09/atlantic-slave-trade-history-animated-interactive.html.

Kakembo, Robert. *An African Soldier Speaks*. London: Edinburgh House Press, 1946.
Kalu, Ogbu U. *Christianity in West Africa: The Nigerian Story*. Ibadan: Daystar, 1978.
"Primitive Methodists on the Railroad Junctions of Igboland." *Journal of Religion in Africa* 16, no. 1 (1986): 44–66.
Kamlongera, Christopher F. "The British and the Beginnings of Contemporary African Drama." *Africana Marburgensia* 19, no. 1 (1986): 14–28.
Kaniki, Martin H. Y. "The Colonial Economy: The Former British Zones." In *General History of Africa: VII Africa Under Colonial Domination 1880–1935*, ed. Albert Adu Boahen. Paris: UNESCO, 1990, 382–419.
Kanjamala, Augustine. *The Future of Christian Mission in India: Toward a New Paradigm for the Third Millenium*. Eugene: Pickwick Publications, 2014.
Kaplan, Elisabeth. "We Are What We Collect, We Collect What We Are: Archives and the Construction of Identity." *American Archivist* 63 (2000): 126–151.
Karibi-Whyte, Adolphous Godwin. *The Relevance of the Judiciary in the Polity-In Historical Perspective*. Lagos: Nigerian Institute of Advanced Legal Studies, 1987.
Kariya, Kota. "Muwālāt and Apostasy in the Early Sokoto Caliphate." *Islamic Africa* 9, no. 2 (2018): 179–208.
Kastfelt, Niels. "Christianity, Colonial Legitimacy and the Rise of Nationalist Politics in Northern Nigeria." In *Legitimacy and the State in Twentieth-Century Africa*, ed. Terence Ranger and Olufemi Vaughan. London: Palgrave Macmillan, 1993, 191–209.
Katzenstein, Peter J., and Takashi Shiraishi, eds. *Beyond Japan: The Dynamics of East Asian Regionalism*. Ithaca: Cornell University Press, 2006.
Kay, Stafford, and Bradley Nystrom. "Education and Colonialism in Africa: An Annotated Bibliography." *Comparative Education Review* 15, no. 2 (1971): 240–259.
Kelly, Gail P., and Philip G. Altbach, eds. *Education and the Colonial Experience*. New Brunswick: Transaction, 1984.
Kesternich, Iris, Bettina Siflinger, James P. Smith, and Joachim K. Winter. "The Effects of World War II on Economic and Health Outcomes across Europe." *The Review of Economics and Statistics* 96, no. 1 (2014): 103–118.
Killingray, David, and James Matthews. "Beasts of Burden: British West African Carriers in the First World War." *Canadian Journal of African Studies* 13, nos. 1–2 (1979): 5–23.
Killingray, David, and Martin Plaut. *Fighting for Britain: African Soldiers in the Second World War*. London; Boydell & Brewer Ltd., 2012.
Killingray, David. "The Influenza Epidemic of 1918–1919 in the Gold Coast." *Journal of African History* 24, no. 4 (1983): 485–502.
"A New 'Imperial Disease': The Influenza Pandemic of 1918–9 and Its Impact on the British Empire." *Caribbean Quarterly* 49, no. 4 (2003): 30–49.
"The Maintenance of Law and Order in British Colonial Africa." *African Affairs* 85, no. 340 (1986): 411–437.

Kilson, Martin L. "Nationalism and Social Classes in British West Africa." *The Journal of Politics* 20, no. 2 (1968): 368-387.

Kin, Lok Wai. "The Relationship between Central and Local Governments under the Unitary State System of China." In *One Country, Two Systems, Three Legal Orders-Perspectives of Evolution*, ed. Jorge C. Oliveira and Paulo Cardinal. Berlin: 2009, 527-540.

Kingdom, D., ed. *The Laws of Nigeria*. Lagos: Government Printers 1923.

Kingsley, Mary. *West African Studies*. Cambridge: Cambridge University Press, 2010.

Kirk-Greene, Anthony H. M. "The Thin White Line: The Size of the British Colonial Service in Africa." *African Affairs* 79, no. 314 (1980): 25-44.

Kirk-Greene, Anthony H. M., and Margery Perham, *The Principles of Native Administration in Nigeria: Selected Documents, 1900-1947*. London: Oxford University Press, 1965.

Kirk-Greene, Anthony. *Britain's Imperial Administrators, 1858-1966*. London: Palgrave Macmillan Press, 1999.

Symbol of Authority: The British District Officer in Africa. London: I. B. Tauris, 2006.

Klein, Martin A. "Review of The Decolonization of West African History." *The Journal of Interdisciplinary History* 6, no. 1 (1975): 111-125.

Kluger, Michael, and Richard J. Evans. *Roosevelt and Churchill: The Atlantic Charter*. South Yorkshire: Frontline Books, 2020.

Kolapo, Femi J. *Christian Missionary Engagement in Central Nigeria, 1857-1891: The Church Missionary Society's All-African Mission on the Upper Niger*. Cham: Palgrave Macmillan, 2019.

"The Dynamics of Early 19th Century Nupe Wars." *Scientia Militaria - South African Journal of Military Studies* 31, no. 2 (2012): 14-35.

"Military Turbulence, Population Displacement and Commerce on a Southern Frontier of the Sokoto Caliphate: Nupe c.1810-1857." Unpublished PhD dissertation. York University, 1999.

Komolafe, Kayode. "The NEPU Example." *Thisday*, August 12, 2020.

Kopytoff, Jean H. *A Preface to Modern Nigeria: The "Sierra Leonians" in Yoruba, 1830-1890*. Madison: University of Wisconsin Press, 1965.

Korieh, Chima J. "Migration Patterns and Identity Formation among the Igbo." In *Population Movements, Conflicts and Displacements in Nigeria*, ed. Toyin Falola and Okpeh Ochayi Okpeh. Trenton: Africa World Press, 2007, 107-131.

Nigeria and World War II: Colonialism, Empire, and Global Conflict. Cambridge: Cambridge University Press, 2020.

Korotayev, Andrey, and Leonid Grini. "The Urbanization and Political Development of the World System: A Comparative Quantitative Analysis." In *History & Mathematics: Historical Dynamics and Development of Complex Societies*. Vol. 2. ed. Peter Turchin, Leonid Grinin, Andrey Korotayev, and Victor C. de Munck. Moscow: Volgograd Center for Social Research, 2006, 115-153.

Korsah, K. A. "Indirect Rule – A Means to an End." *African Affairs* 43, no. 173 (1944): 177-182.

Kraus, Jon. "African Trade Unions: Progress or Poverty?" *African Studies Review* 19, no. 3 (1976): 95–108.

Kronenfeld, David B. *Culture as a System: How We Know the Meaning and Significance of What We Do and Say*. London: Routledge, 2018.

Kubicek, Robert V. "The Colonial Steamer and the Occupation of West Africa by the Victorian State, 1840-1900." *The Journal of Imperial and Commonwealth History* 18, no. 1 (1990): 9–32.

Kur, Jude Terna, and Nicholas Sesugh Iwokwagh. "The Information Value of Traditional Tiv Music and Dance in the Age of Modern Communication Technologies," *Asian Journal of Information Technology* 10, no. 3 (2011): 101–107.

Lafinhan, A. H. "1st January and the Birth of a Nation." *Nigerian Tribune*, January 1, 2008.

Lakemfa, Owei. *A Centenary of Trade Unionism in Nigeria and the Challenge of the International Trends*. Lagos: Kolagbodi Memorial Foundation, 2014.

Lambrecht, Frank L. "The Pastoral Nomads of Nigeria." *Expedition Magazine* 18, no. 3 (1976): 26–31.

Laminu, Hamsatu Z. *Scholars and Scholarship in the History of Borno*. Zaria: Open Press, 1993.

Lamond, Jessica, Emma Lewis, Johnson B. Falade, Kwasi B. Awuah, and Robin Bloch. "Urban Land, Planning and Governance Systems in Nigeria." *Urbanisation Research Nigeria: Research Report* (2015).

Lange, Matthew K. "British Colonial Legacies and Political Development." *World Development* 32, no. 6 (2004): 905–922.

LPM. "Nigeria under the Macpherson Constitution." *The World Today* 9, no. 1 (1953): 12–21.

Langford, Paul, ed. *The Writings and Speeches of Edmund Burke*. Oxford: Clarendon Press, 1981.

"The Eighteenth Century (1688–1789)." In *The Oxford Illustrated History of Britain*, ed. Kenneth O. Morgan. New York: Oxford University Press, 1984, 352–418.

LaPalombara, Joseph, and Myron Weiner. "The Origin and Development of Political Parties." In *Political Parties and Political Development*, ed. Joseph LaPalombara and Myron Weiner. Princeton: Princeton University Press, 1966, 3–42.

Last, Murray. "Historical Metaphors in the Intellectual History of Kano before 1800." *History in Africa* 7 (1980): 161–178.

"The Nature of Knowledge in Northern Nigeria." In *The Trans-Saharan Book Trade, Manuscript Culture, Arabic Literacy and Intellectual History in Muslim Africa*, ed. Graziano Krätli and Ghislaine Lydon. Leiden: Brill, 2011, 178–211.

"The Sokoto Caliphate and Borno." In *General History of Africa- VI: Africa in the Nineteenth Century until the 1880s*, ed. Jacob F. A. Ajayi. Paris: UNESCO Publishing, 1998, 558.

The Sokoto Caliphate. London: Longmans, Green and Co. Ltd., 1967.

"Some Economic Aspects of Conversion in Hausaland (Nigeria)" In *Conversion to Islam*, ed. Nehemiah Levtzion. New York: Holmes & Meier, 1979, 237.

Lattimer, John E. "The Ottawa Trade Agreements." *Journal of Farm Economics* 16, no. 4 (1934): 565–581.

Law, Robin C. C. "The Career of Adele at Lagos and Badagry." *Journal of the Historical Society of Nigeria* III, no. 2 (1978): 37.

"The Constitutional Troubles in Oyo in the Eighteenth Century." *The Journal of African History* 12, no. 1 (1971): 25–44.

Contemporary Source Material for The History of the Old Oyo Empire, 1627–1824. Toronto: York University, 2001.

From Slave Trade to "Legitimate" Commerce: The Commercial Transition in Nineteenth-Century West Africa. Cambridge: Cambridge University Press, 1995.

"Horses, Firearms, and Political Power in Pre-colonial West Africa." *Past & Present* 72, no. 1 (1976): 112–132.

"A Lagoonside Port on the Eighteenth-Century Slave Coast: The Early History of Badagri." *Canadian Journal of African Studies* 28, no. 1 (1994): 32–59.

"Making Sense of a Traditional Narrative: Political Disintegration in the Kingdom of Oyo." *Cahiers d'Études Africaines* 22, no. 87/88 (1982): 387–401.

The Oyo Empire c.1600–c.1836: A West African Imperialism in the Era of the Atlantic Slave Trade. London: Oxford University Press, 1977.

"A West African Cavalry State: The Kingdom of Oyo." *The Journal of African History* 16, no. 1 (1975): 1–15.

"Trade and Politics Behind the Slave Coast: The Lagoon Traffic and the Ruse of Lagos, 1500–1800." *Journal of African History* 24, no. 3 (1983): 321–348.

Lawal, Adebayo A. "Corruption in Nigeria: A Colonial Legacy." Inaugural Lecture Series. University of Lagos, June 7, 2006.

Nigeria Culture, Politics, Governance and Development. Ibadan: Connel Publications, 2015.

Lawal, Babatunde. *The Gèlèdé Spectacle: Art, Gender, and Social Harmony in an African Culture*. Seattle: University of Washington Press, 1996.

Lawal, Bayo A. "Nigerian Migrants in the Cameroons and the Reactions of the Host Communities: 1885–1961." In *Population Movements, Conflicts and Displacements in Nigeria*, ed. Toyin Falola and Okpeh O. Okpeh. Trenton: Africa World Press, 2008, 85–105.

Lawal, Olakunle A. "British Commercial Interests and the Decolonization Process in Nigeria, 1950–60." *African Economic History* 22 (1994): 93–110.

Lawal, Olakunle A., and Oluwasegun M. Jimoh. "Missiles from 'Kirsten Hall': Herbert Macaulay versus Hugh Clifford, 1922–1931." *Lagos Historical Review* 12 (2012): 41–62.

Laybourn, Keith. *A History of British Trade Unionism c.1770–1990*. Wolfeboro Falls: Alan Sutton Publishing, 1992.

Lea, John, and Jock Young. *What Is to Be Done about Law and Order?* Harmondsworth: Penguin Books, 1984.

Leavitt, Amie Jane. *Discovering the Kingdom of Benin*. New York: Rosen Publishing, 2014, 16–21.

Lee, Alexander, and Kenneth A. Schultz. "Comparing British and French Colonial Legacies: A Discontinuity Analysis of Cameroon." *Quarterly Journal of Political Science* 7 (2012): 1–46.

Lee, Anthony. *The Baha'i Faith in Africa: Establishing a New Religious Movement, 1952–1962*. Leiden: Brill, 2011.

Leerssen, Joep. *National Thought in Europe: A Cultural History*. Amsterdam: Amsterdam University Press, 2006.

Leith-Ross, Sylvia. *African Women: A Study of the Ibo of Nigeria*. London: Faber & Faber, 1939.

Liebl, Vernie. "The Caliphate." *Middle Eastern Studies* 45, no. 3 (2009): 373–391.

Linden, Mieke van der. *The Acquisition of Africa (1870–1914): The Nature of International Law*. Leiden: Brill, 1987.

Lindfors, Bernth. "Ogunde on Ogunde: Two Autobiographical Statements." *Educational Theatre Journal* 28, no. 2 (1976): 241.

Lindsay, Lisa A. "'To Return to the Bosom of Their Fatherland': Brazilian Immigrants in Nineteenth-Century Lagos." *Slavery & Abolition* 15, no. 1 (1994): 26–27.

Livsey, Tim. *Nigeria's University Age: Reframing Decolonisation and Development*. London: Palgrave Macmillan, 2017.

——— "Open Secrets: The British 'Migrated Archives,' Colonial History, and Postcolonial History." *History Workshop Journal* 93, no. 1 (2022): 95–116.

Lloyd, Alan. *The Drums of Kumasi: The Story of the Ashanti Wars*. London: Longmans, 1964.

Lloyd, Peter C. "Class Consciousness Among the Yoruba." In *The New Elites of Tropical Africa*, ed. Peter C. Lloyd. London: Oxford University Press, 1966, 330.

——— "Osifekunde of Ijebu." In *Africa Remembered: Narratives by West Africans from the Era of the Slave Trade*, ed. Phillip D. Curtin. Madison: University of Wisconsin Press, 1967, 217–288.

Lloyd, Peter C., ed. *The New Elites of Tropical Africa*. London: Oxford University Press, 1966.

——— "Craft Organization in Yoruba Towns." *Africa* 23, no. 1 (1953): 30–44.

Lloyd, Peter C., Akin Mabogunje, and Bolanle Awe, ed. *The City of Ibadan: A Symposium on Its Structure and Development*. London: Cambridge University Press, 1967.

Lo-Bamijoko, Justin N. "Classification of Igbo Musical Instruments." *African Music* 6, no. 4 (1980): 19–41.

Lobban, Michael. *Imperial Incarceration: Detention without Trial in the Making of British Colonial Africa*. Cambridge: Cambridge University Press, 2021, 198–237.

Lockhart, Jamie, and Paul Lovejoy, eds. *Hugh Clapperton into the Interior of Africa: Records of the Second Expedition, 1825–1827*. Leiden: Brill, 2005.

Lovejoy, Henry. *Prieto: Yoruba Kingship in Colonial Cuba during the Age of Revolutions*. Chapel Hill: University of North Carolina Press, 2019.
Lovejoy, Paul E. "The Ibadan School of Historiography and its Critics." In *African Historiography: Essays in Honour of Jacob Ade Ajayi*, ed. Toyin Falola. Harlow: Longman, 1993, 195–202.
"Plantations in the Economy of the Sokoto Caliphate." *The Journal of African History* 19, no. 3 (1978): 341–368.
Lovejoy, Paul E., and Jan S. Hogendorn, *Slow Death for Slavery: The Course of Abolition in Northern Nigeria, 1897–1936*. New York: Cambridge University Press, 1993.
Lovejoy, Paul E., and Toyin Falola, *Pawnship in Africa: Debt Bondage in Historical Perspective*. Boulder: Westview Press, 1994.
Pawnship, Slavery, and Colonialism in Africa. Trenton: Africa World Press, 2003.
Lugard, Lord. *The Dual Mandate in British Tropical Africa*. London: Frank Cass, 1970.
Political Memoranda: Revision of Instructions to Political Officers on Subjects Chiefly Political and Administrative 1913–1918. London: Frank Cass, 1970.
Report by Sir FD Lugard on the Amalgamation of Northern and Southern Nigeria, and Administration 1912–1919. London: HMSO Stationery Office, 1920.
Lydon, Ghislaine. *On Trans-Saharan Trails: Islamic Law, Trade Networks, and Cross-Cultural Exchange in Nineteenth-Century Western Africa*. New York: Cambridge University Press, 2009.
Lynn, Leonard. "The Growth of Entertainment of Non-African Origin in Lagos." MA thesis, University of Ibadan, 1967.
Lynn, Martin. "Change and Continuity in the British Palm Oil Trade with West Africa, 1830–55." *The Journal of African History* 22, no. 3 (1981): 331–348.
Commerce and Economic Change in West Africa: The Palm Oil Trade in the Nineteenth Century. Cambridge: Cambridge University Press, 1997.
"The Nigerian Self-government Crisis of 1953 and the Colonial Office." *The Journal of Imperial and Commonwealth History* 34, no. 2 (2006): 245–261.
Mabogunje, Akin. "The Growth of Residential Districts in Ibadan." *Geographical Review* 52, no. 1 (1962): 56–77.
"Lagos: A Study in Urban Geography." Unpublished PhD dissertation. University of London, 1962.
Urbanization in Nigeria. London: University of London Press, 1968.
Macdonald, Paul K. *Networks of Domination: The Social Foundations of Peripheral Conquest in International Politics*. New York: Oxford University Press, 2014.
Mackenzie, John M. *The Partition of Africa*. London: Methuen, 1983.
Madubuike, Ihechukwu. "Decolonization of African Names." *Présence Africaine* 98, no. 1 (1976): 42–43.
Mafeje, Archie. "Culture and Development in Africa: The Missing Link." *CODESRIA Bulletin* 3, no. 4 (2008): 61.

Maiangwa, Benjamin, Muhammad Dan Suleiman, and Chigbo A. Anyaduba. "The Nation as Corporation: British Colonialism and the Pitfalls of Postcolonial Nationhood in Nigeria." *Peace and Conflict Studies* 25, no. 1 (2018): 2–23.
Maiangwa, Benjamin. "How the Colonial Enterprise Hard-wired Violence into Nigeria's Governance." *Quartz Africa*, 21 October, 2020. www.qz.com/africa/1920769/the-british-colonial-enterprise-wired-violence-into-nigeria/.
Mair, Lucy. *The Principles of Native Administration in Nigeria: Selected Documents 1900–1947*. London: Oxford University Press, 1965.
Maishanu, Hamza M., and Isa M. Maishanu. "The Jihad and the Formation of the Sokoto Caliphate." *Islamic Studies* 38, no. 1 (1999): 119–131.
Majekodunmi, Aderonke. "Federalism in Nigeria: The Past, Current Peril and Future Hopes." *Journal of Policy and Development Studies* 289, no. 1850 (2015): 1–14.
Makar, Tesemchi. *The History of Political Change Among the Tiv in the 19th and 20th Centuries*. Enugu: Fourth Dimension Publishers, 1994.
Maliki, Abdul. "Islam in Nigeria." *Islamic Quarterly* 9, no. 1 (1965): 30.
Mamdani, Mahmood, Thandika Mkandawire, and Wamba-dia-Wamba. *Citizens and Subjects: Contemporary Africa and the Legacy of Late Colonialism*. Princeton: Princeton University Press, 1996.
"Indirect Rule, Civil Society, and Ethnicity: The African Dilemma." *Social Justice* 23, no. 1/2 (1996): 145–150.
Define and Rule: Native as Political Identity. Cambridge: Harvard University Press, 2012.
Neither Settler Nor Native: The Making and Unmaking of Permanent Minorities. London: Harvard University Press, 2020.
Politics and Class Formation in Uganda. New York: Monthly Review Press, 1976.
"Social Movements, Social Transformation and Struggle for Democracy in Africa." *Economic and Political Weekly* 23, no. 19 (1988): 973–981.
Mangan, J. A. ed. *"Benefits Bestowed"? Education and British Imperialism*. Manchester: Manchester University Press, 1988.
Mangvwat, Yakiban. *A History of Class Formation in the Plateau Province of Nigeria, 1902–1960: The Genesis of a Ruling Class*. Durham: Carolina Academic Press, 2013.
Mann, Kristin. "Gendered Authority, Gendered Violence: Family, Household and Identity in the Life and Death of Brazilian Freed Woman in Lagos." In *African Women in the Atlantic World: Property, Vulnerability and Mobility, 1660–1880*, ed. Mariana P. Candido and Adam Jones. London: James Currey, 2019, 148–170.
Marrying Well: Marriage, Status and Social Change among the Educated Elite in Colonial Lagos. Cambridge: Cambridge University Press, 1985.
Slavery and the Birth of an African City: Lagos 1760–1900. Bloomington and Indianapolis: Indiana University Press, 1997.
Manserg, Nicholas. *Survey of British Commonwealth Affairs: Problems of Wartime Cooperation and Post-War Change, 1939–52*. London: Frank Cass, 1968.

Manton, John. "Global and Local Contexts: The Northern Ogoja Leprosy Scheme, Nigeria, 1945-1960." *História Ciências Saúde-Manguinhos* 10, no. 1 (2003): 209-223.

"Leprosy in Eastern Nigeria and the Social History of Colonial Skin." *Leprosy Review* 82 (2011): 124-134.

"The Roman Catholic Mission and Leprosy Control in Colonial Ogoja Province, Nigeria, 1936-1960." Unpublished PhD dissertation. University of Oxford, 2005.

Mapuva, Jephias, and Freeman Chari. "Colonialism No Longer an Excuse for Africa's Failure." *Journal of Sustainable Development in Africa* 12, no. 5 (2010): 22-36.

Maringues, Michele. "The Nigerian Press: Current State, Travails and Prospects." In *Nigeria during the Abacha Years, 1993-98: The Domestic and International Politics of Democratization*, ed. Kunle Amuwo, Daniel C. Bach and Yann Lebeau. Ibadan: IFRA, 2001, 185.

Martin, Maria. "Ojo Nro: An Intellectual History of Nigerian Women's Nationalism in an Umbrella Organization, 1947-1967." unpublished PhD dissertationMichigan State University, 2018.

Martin, William G. "The Rise of African Studies (USA) and the Transnational Study of Africa." *African Studies Review* 54, no. 1 (2011): 59-83.

Mason, Michael. "Captive and Client Labor and the Economy of the Bida Emirate: 1857-1901." *The Journal of African History* 14, no. 3 (1973): 453-471.

Matera, Marc, Misty L. Bastian, and Susan Kingsley. *The Women's War of 1929: Gender and Violence in Colonial Nigeria*. London: Palgrave Macmillan, 2011.

Matthews, James K. "World War I and the Rise of African Nationalism: Nigerian Veterans as Catalysts of Change." *The Journal of Modern African Studies* 20, no. 3 (1982): 493-502.

Maughan, Steven. "'Mighty England Do Good': The Major English Denominations and Organisation for the Support of Foreign Missions in the Nineteenth Century." In *Missionary Encounters: Sources and Issues*, ed. Robert A. Bickers and Rosemary Seton. London: Curzon Press, 1996, 11-37.

Mayer, Adam. *Naija Marxisms: Revolutionary Thought in Nigeria*. London: Pluto Press, 2016.

Maynor, John W. *Republicanism in the Modern World*. Cambridge: Polity Press, 2003.

Mazrui, Ali A., Patrick M. Dikirr, Robert Ostergard Jr., Michael Toler, and Paul Macharia, eds. *Africa's Islamic Experiences: History, Culture, and Politics*. New Delhi: Sterling Publishers Private Ltd., 2009.

Mazrui, Ali, and C. Wondji. *History of Africa. Vol. VIII: Africa Since 1935*. Berkeley: University of California Press, 1993.

Mba, Nina. *Nigerian Women Mobilized: Women's Political Activity in Southern Nigeria, 1900-1965*. Berkeley: Institute of International Studies, 1982.

Mbaeyi, Paul Mmegha. *British Military and Naval Forces in West African History 1807-1874*. New York: NOK Publishers, 1978.

Mbembe, Achille. *On the Post-Colony.* London: University of California Press, 2001.

"The Power of the Archive and Its Limits." In *Refiguring the Archive*, ed. Carolyn Hamilton, Verne Harris, Michèle Pickover, Graeme Reid, Jane Taylora, and Razia Saleh. Dordrecht: Kluwer Academic Publishers, 2002, 19–27.

Mbon, Friday M. *Brotherhood of the Cross and Star: A New Religious Movement in Nigeria.* New York: P. Lang, 1992.

Mbu, Mathew. "Zik and the African Revolution." In *Zik: Life and Times*, ed. E. A Mucheazi. Abuja: National Orientation Agency Publication, 1997.

McEwan, Peter J. M. ed. *Africa from Early Times to 1800.* London: Oxford University Press, 1968.

Meillassoux, Claude, ed. *The Development of Indigenous Trade and Markets in West Africa.* Oxford: Oxford University Press, 1971.

Mejida, Maiyaki M. "Anthropological and Ethnographical Work on Bassa and Her Neighbors in the Nigeria Benue Valley: A Critical Assessment of Historical Reconstruction." *Journal of the Historical Society of Nigeria* 25 (2016): 61–79.

Mellanby, Kenneth. *The Birth of Nigeria's University.* London: Methuen and Company Limited, 1958.

Mensah, Eyo O., Idom T. Inyabri, and Benjamin O. Nyong. "Names, Naming and the Code of Cultural Denial in a Contemporary Nigerian Society: An Afrocentric Perspective." *Journal of Black Studies* 52, no. 3 (2020): 248–276.

Mianda, Gertrude. "Colonialism, Education, and Gender Relations in the Belgian Congo: The Evolue Case." In *Women in African Colonial Histories*, ed. Jean Allman, Susan Geiger, and Nakanyike Musisi. Bloomington: Indiana University Press, 2002, 144–163.

Middleton, John, and David Tait, eds. *Tribes Without Rulers: Studies in African Segmentary Systems.* London: Routledge & Kegan Paul, 1958.

Miller, Joseph C. "History and Africa/Africa and History." *The American Historical Review* 104, no. 1 (1999): 1–32.

Millson, Alvan. "The Yorubas Country, West Africa." *Proceedings of the Royal Geographical Society* 13, no. 10 (1891): 583.

Mobolade, Timothy. "The Concept of Abiku." *African Arts* 7, no. 1 (1973): 62–64.

Mohammed, Ahmed Modibbo. *European Trade, Imperialism and Under Development in Northern Nigeria 19th and 20th Centuries.* Zaria: Ahmadu Bello University Press Limited, 2016.

Mohammed, Ahmed Rufai. *History of the Spread of Islam in the Niger-Benue Confluence Area: Igalaland, Ebiraland and Lokoja c. 1900–1960.* Ibadan: Ibadan University Press, 2014.

"Lokoja as a Center of Islamic Scholarship and Radiation in the Niger–Benue Confluence Area: c.1970–1960s." *Kano Studies* 3, no. 1 (1987/88): 19–42.

Mohammed, Kabir, and Binta M. Yarinch. "The Role and Impact of Pre-Colonial Education on the People of Hausaland Prior to 1903 AD." *International Journal of Humanities and Social Science Invention* 2, no. 11 (2013): 7–13.

Mohr, Thomas. "The Privy Council Appeal and British Imperial Policy, 1833–1939." In *Modernization, National Identity and Legal Instrumentalism*. Vol. II: Public Law. ed. Michał Gałędek and Anna Klimaszewska. Netherlands: Brill, 2020, 86–112.
Mojekwu, Christopher C. "Nigerian Constitutionalism." *Nomos: American Society for Political and Legal Philosophy* 20 (1979): 163–186.
Mommsen, Wolfgang J., and Hans-Gerhard Husung, eds. *The Development of Trade Unionism in Great Britain and Germany, 1880–1914*. London: George Allen & Unwin.
Montclos, Marc-Antoine Pérouse de. "Boko Haram and "Sahelistan" Terrorism Narratives: A Historical Perspective." *Afrique Contemporaine* 255, no. 3 (2015): 18–39.
"The Spread of Jihadist Insurrections in Niger and Nigeria: An Analysis Based on the Case of Boko Haram." In *Transnational Islam: Circulation of Religious Ideas, Actors and Practices between Niger and Nigeria*, ed. Elodie Apar. Ibadan: IFRA-Nigeria, 2020, 152–179.
Moore, Barrington. *Social Origins of Dictatorship and Democracy: Lord and Peasant in the Making of the Modern World*. Boston: Beacon Press, 1993.
Moore, Wilbert E. *Social Change*. Englewood Cliffs: Prentice-Hall, 1963.
Mordi, Emmanuel N. "Imperial Britain and the Challenge of Press Freedom in Nigeria during the Second World War." *Journal of Development and Communication Studies* 5, no. 1 (2016–2017): 98–121.
"Wartime Propaganda, Devious Officialdom, and the Challenge of Nationalism during the Second World War in Nigeria." *Nordic Journal of African Studies* 18, no. 3 (2009): 235–257.
Morrock, Richard. "Heritage of Strife: The Effects of Colonialists' 'Divide and Rule' Strategy upon the Colonized Peoples." *Science & Society* 37, no. 2 (1973): 129–151.
Morton-Williams, Peter. "The Oyo and the Atlantic Trade 1670–1830." *Journal of the Historical Society of Nigeria* III, no. 1 (1964): 25–45.
Mucizz, Goriawala. "Maguzawa: The Influence of the Hausa Muslims on the Beliefs and Practices of the Maguzawa, The Traditional Religionists of Kano and Katsina." In *The Gods in Retreat: Continuity and Change in African Religions*, ed. Emefie I. Metuh. Enugu: Fourth Dimension Publishers Co. Ltd., 1985, 47–58.
Mudimbe, Valentin-Yves. *The Invention of Africa: Gnosis, Philosophy, and the Order of Knowledge*. Bloomington: Indiana University Press, 1998.
Muir, Ernest. "Leprosy in Nigeria. A Report on Anti-leprosy Work in Nigeria with Suggestions for its Development." *Leprosy Review* 7 (1936): 164–166.
Mulligan, Michael. "Nigeria, the British Presence in West Africa and International Law in the 19th Century." *Journal of The History of International Law* 11, no. 2 (2009): 273.
Mulvey, Paul. "Falling Apart: Britain Leaves India and Palestine." *Academia*. www.academia.edu/11080905/Falling_Apart_Britain_Leaves_India_and_Palestine_1947-48_lecture.

"The British Empire in World War Two (Lecture)." Academia, September 25, 2020. www.academia.edu/444982/The_British_Empire_in_World_War_Two_lecture.

Mumford, Michael D. "Where Have We Been, Where Are We Going? Taking Stock in Creativity Research." *Creativity Research Journal* 15, no. 2 (2003): 110.

Munoz, Louis J. "Regionalism in Nigeria: The Transformation of Tradition." *Il Politico* 52, no. 2 (1987): 317–341.

Muritala, Monsuru. *Livelihood in Colonial Lagos*. Lanham: Lexington Books, 2019.

Murray, K. C. "Arts and Crafts of Nigeria: Their Past and Future." *Africa: Journal of the International African Institute* 14, no. 4 (1943): 155–164.

Murray, Leslye M. "Indirect Rule: Lugardian Style." MA Thesis, Morehead State University, 1973.

Musa, Auwalu, and Ndaliman Alhaji Hassan. "An Evaluation of the Origins, Structure and Features of Nigerian Federalism." *The International Journal of Social Sciences and Humanities Invention* 1, no. 5 (2014): 314–325.

Mustapha, Abdul Raufu. *Ethnic Structure, Inequality and Governance of the Public Sector in Nigeria*. Geneva: United Nations Research Institute for Social Development, 2006.

Mwalimu, Charles. *The Nigerian legal system: Public Law*. Vol. 1. New York: Peter Lang, 2005.

Myrdal, Gunnar. *An American Dilemma: The Negro Problem and Modern Democracy*. New York: Harper, 1944.

Myrice, Erin. "The Impact of the Second World War on the Decolonization of Africa." Paper presented at the Africana Studies Student Research Conference, *Scholar Works*, 2015. https://scholarworks.bgsu.edu/cgi/viewcontent.cgi?article=1048&context=africana_studies_conf.

Na'Allah, Abdul-Rasheed. *African Discourse in Islam, Oral Traditions, and Performance*. New York: Routledge, 2010.

Nadel, Siegfried Frederick. *Nupe Religion*. London: Routledge, 2018.

Nafziger, Rhoda Nanre. "Decolonizing History: Historical Consciousness, Identity and Civic Engagement of Nigerian Youth." Unpublished PhD dissertation. Pennsylvania State University, 2020.

Ndimele, Ozo-Mekuri, ed. *Nigerian Languages, Literatures, Culture and Reforms: A Festschrift for Ayo Bamgbose*. Port Harcourt: M & J Grand Orbit Communications, 2016.

Ndlovu-Gatsheni, Sabelo J. "Decoloniality as the Future of Africa." *History Compass* 13, no. 10 (2015): 485–496.

Ndubuisi, Ahaotu Godwin. "British Educational Management Policies in Nigeria: A Historical Overview." *Electronic Research Journal of Behavioral Sciences* 1 (2018): 1–14.

Nduka, Otonti. "Moral Education in the Changing Traditional Societies of Sub-Saharan Africa." *International Review of Education* 26, no. 2 (1980): 153–170.

Neiberg, Michael. *Potsdam: The End of World War II and the Remaking of Europe*. New York: Basic Books, 2015.

Nengel, John G., and Chigemezi N. Wogu. "Colonial Politics, Missionary Rivalry, and the Beginnings of Seventh-Day Adventist Mission in Northern Nigeria." *Mission Studies: Journal of the International Association for Mission Studies* 3 (2021): 213–235.

Neumark, Solomon D. "Transportation in Sub-Saharan Africa." In *An Economic History of Tropical Africa*, ed. Zbigniew A. Konczacki and Janina M. Konczacki. New Jersey: Frank Cass, 1977, 40.

Newbury, Colin W. "Accounting for Power in Northern Nigeria." *The Journal of African History* 45, no. 2 (2004): 257–277.

"Trade and Technology in West Africa: The Case of the Niger Company, 1900–1920." *The Journal of African History* 19, no. 4 (1978): 551–575.

The Western Slave Coast and its Rulers: European Trade and Administration among Adja-Speaking Peoples of South-Western Nigeria, Southern Dahomey, and Togo. London: Oxford University Press, 1961.

Newell, Stephanie. "Life Writing in the Colonial Archives: The Case of Nnamdi Azikiwe (1904–1996) of Nigeria." *Life Writing* 13, no. 3 (2016): 307–321.

The Power to Name: A History of Anonymity in Colonial West Africa. Athens: Ohio University Press, 2013.

Ngu, Sylva M. "The Amalgamation of Northern and Southern Protectorates of Nigeria: Issues and Challenges." *JORAS* 4 (2014): 1–13.

Nicolao, Hardmod C. *Fela Sowande: Composer, Art Music, Jazz, Highlife, Royal College of Organists, George Gershwin, Royal College of Organists.* Beau Basin, Mauritius: Crypt Publishing, 2012.

Nicolson, Ian F. *The Administration of Nigeria, 1900–1960: Men, Methods and Myths.* Oxford: Clarendon Press, 1969.

Nimako, Kwame and Glenn Willemsen. *The Dutch Atlantic: Slavery, Abolition and Emancipation.* London: Pluto Press, 2011.

Njoku, Ndu L. "The Dual Image of the Aro in Igbo Development History: An Aftermath of their Role in the Slave Trade." *Journal of Retracing Africa* 2, no. 1 (2016): 29–48.

Njoku, Onwuka N. "Export Production Drive in Nigeria during the Second World War." *Transafrican Journal of History* 10, no. 1/2 (1981): 11–27.

Njung, George N. "Victims of Empire: WWI Ex-servicemen and the Colonial Economy of Wartime Sacrifices in Postwar British Nigeria." *First World War Studies* 10, no. 1 (2019): 49–67.

Nkrumah, Kwame. *Towards Colonial Freedom.* London: Panaf Books, 1962.

Nmah, Patrick E., and Chukwudi Ani Amunnadi. "Christianity in Northern Nigeria from 1841–2012: A Church under Persecution." *LWATI: A Journal of Contemporary Research* 9, no. 1 (2012): 309–324.

Nnaemeka, Obioma, and Chima Korieh. "Long Journeys of Impediments and Triumphs." In *Shaping our Struggles: Nigerian Women in History, Culture and Social Change*, ed. Obioma Nnaemeka and Chima Korieh. Trenton: Africa World Press, 2010, vii–xxv.

Nnam, Glory N., and Nnamdi C. Onuora-Oguno. "Elele O: An Age Long Nkwa Umuagbogho Dance of Idaw River Girls' Secondary School, Enugu." *Journal of Nigerian Music Education* 10 (2018): 134–135.

Nnoli, Okwudiba. *Ethnic Politics in Nigeria*. Enugu: Fourth Dimension Publishers, 1978.

Introduction to Politics. Enugu: PACREP, 2003.

"A Short History of Nigeria Underdevelopment." In *Path to Nigeria Development*, ed. Okwudiba Nnoli. Dakar: CODESRIA, 1981.

Nnoromele, Salome. *Life among the Ibo Women of Nigeria*. San Diego: Lucent Books, 1967.

Noah, Monday E. "Aba Women's Riot: Need for a Re-Definition." In *The Women's Revolt of 1929: Proceedings of a National Symposium*, ed. C. Dike. Lagos: Nelag, 1995, 105–124.

Nolte, Insa. *Obafemi Awolowo and the Making of Remo: The Local Politics of a Nigerian Nationalist*. Edinburgh: Edinburgh University Press, 2009.

Northrup, David. *Trade Without Rulers: Pre-Colonial Economic Development in South-Eastern Nigeria*. Oxford: Clarendon Press, 1978.

Nottelman, Dirk. "From Ironclads to Dreadnoughts: The Development of the German Navy 1864–1918." *Warship international* 49, no. 4 (2012): 317–355.

Novak, Andrew. *The Death Penalty in Africa: Foundations and Future Prospects*. New York: Palgrave Pivot, 2014.

Nunn, Patrick. *The Edge of Memory: Ancient Stories, Oral Tradition and the Post-Glacial World*. New York: Bloomsbury Sigma, 2019.

Nwabara, Samuel N. "The Fulani Conquest and Rule of the Hausa Kingdom of Northern Nigeria (1804–1900)." *Journal des Africanistes* 33, no. 2 (1963): 231–242.

Iboland: A Century of Contact with Britain 1860–1960. London: Hodder and Stoughton, 1977.

Nwabueze, Benjamin O. *A Constitutional History of Nigeria*. London: C. Hurst & Company, 1982.

Nwabughuogu, Anthony I. *Problems of Nation Building in Africa*. Okigwe: Fasman Educational and Research Publications, 2009.

Nwadialor, Kanayo L. "Christian Missionaries and Civilization in Southern Nigeria, 1841–1960: Implications for Contemporary Christians." *UJAH: Unizik Journal of Arts and Humanities* 14, no. 2 (2013): 173–193.

"Christian Missionary Enterprise in Nigeria in Historical Perspective." In *Issues in Nigerian History and Socioeconomic Development*, ed. Nwachukwu J. Obiakor, Kanayo L. Nwadialor, and Bakky N. Adirika. Awka: Rity Printz, 2016, 1–22.

Nwadialor, Kanayo L., and Nwachukwu J. Obiakor. "The Gospel and the Flag: The Missionary Strands in the British Colonial Enterprise in Nigeria, 1841–1960." *Academic Journal of Interdisciplinary Studies* 4, no. 3 (2015): 249–258.

Nwaka, Geoffrey I. "Colonial Calabar: Its Administration and Development." In *Old Calabar Revisited*, ed. Solomon O. Jaja, Erim O. Erim, and Bassey W. Andah. Enugu: Harrus Publishers, 1990, 63–93.

Nwakunor, Gregory A. "Hubert Ogunde: A Centenary Birthday Dance for the Doyen of Theatre." *The Guardian*, July 16, 2016.

Nwangwu, George. "The Influence of Companies on the Legal, Political and Economic History of Nigeria." *Journal of Economics and Sustainable Development* 9, no. 12 (2018): 118.

Nwankwo, N. "Women and a Challenge Dated in History (1914–2003)." In *Gender Audit 2003 Election; and Issues in Women's Political Participation*, ed. Abiola Akiyode Afolabi and Lanre Arogundade. Lagos: WARDC, 2006, 7–20.

Nwankwor, Chiedo. "Women's Protests in the Struggle for Independence." In *The Oxford Handbook of Nigerian Politics*, ed. Carl LeVan and Patrick Ukata. Oxford: Oxford University Press, 2018, 108.

Nwanne, Chuks. "Dr. Victor Olaiya . . . 60 Years of Blowing on Fame and Fortune." *The Guardian*, February 15, 2020.

Nwanunobi, Onyeka C. "Wage Labour and the Politics of Nigeria and Kenya: A Comparative Study." *African Studies Review* 17, no. 1 (1974): 77–104.

Nwaubani, E. "Igbo Political Systems." *Lagos Notes and Records* 12, no. 1 (2006): 1–27.

Nwauwa, Apollos O. "The Foundation of the Aro Confederacy: A Theoretical Analysis of State Formation in Southeastern Nigeria." *ITAN: Bensu Journal of Historical Studies* 1 (1990): 93–108.

Nweke, Innocent O. "Ozo Title Institution in Igbo land in Relation to Politics in Nigeria: A Comparative Analysis." *OGIRISI: A New Journal of African Studies* 15, no. 1 (2019): 96–108.

Nwobu, Stella N. "The Functions and Spiritual Connotations of Traditional Music Performance with Particular Reference to Ufie Music in Igboland." *AFRREV IJAH* 2, no. 3 (2013): 210–227.

Nwoko, Kenneth Chukwuemeka. "Trade Unionism and Governance in Nigeria: A Paradigm Shift from Labour Activism to Political Opposition." *Information, Society and Justice Journal* 2, no. 2 (2009): 139–152.

Nwosu, Nereus I., and Johnson O. Olaniyi. "Colonialism and the Emergence of Party Politics in Nigeria." *Transafrican Journal of History* 25 (1996): 20–28.

Nwoye, Chinwe. "Igbo Cultural and Religious Worldview: An Insider's Perspective." *International Journal of Sociology and anthropology* 3, no. 9 (2011): 304–317.

Nzala, Albert T., I. I. Potekhin, and Aleksandr Z. Zusmanovich. *Forced Labour in Colonial Africa*. London: Zed Press. 1977.

Nzimiro, Ikenna. *Family and Kinship in Ibo Land: A Study in Acculturation Process*. Cologne: Druck: G. Wasmund, 1962.

— *Studies in Ibo Political Systems: Chieftaincy and Politics in Four Niger States*. London: Frank Cass. 1972.

O'Hear, Ann. "The Enslavement of Yoruba." In *The Yoruba in the Atlantic World*, ed. Toyin Falola and Matt D. Child. Bloomington: Indiana University Press, 2005, 56–76.

Obasi, Cletus O., and Rebecca G. Nnamani. "The Role of Umuada Igbo in Conflict Management and Development in Nigeria." *Open Journal of Political Science* 5, no. 4 (2015): 256–263.

Obata, E. Z. "Patterns of Political System in Pre-colonial Nigeria." In *Foundations of Nigerian Federalism: Pre-Colonial Antecedents*, ed. Jonah I. Elaigu and Erim O. Erim. Abuja: National Council on Intergovernmental Relations, 1996.

Obayemi, Ade. "States and Peoples of the Niger–Benue Confluence Area." In *Groundwork of Nigerian History*, ed. Obaro Ikime. Ibadan: Heinemann Educational Books, 1980, 186.

"The Sokoto Jihad and the 'O-kun' Yoruba: A Review." *Journal of the Historical Society of Nigeria* 9, no. 2 (1978): 61–87.

Obi, Celestina A., ed. *A Hundred Years of the Catholic Church in Eastern Nigeria 1885–1985*. Onitsha: Africana-Fep Publishers, 1985.

Obiakor, Nwachukwu. "Nation Building in Post-Colonial Nigeria." *UZU: Journal of History and International Studies* 2, no 1 (2009): 79–88.

Obienusi, Ihuoma Elizabeth. "Aba Women Protest and the Aftermath 1929 till 1960." *COOU International Journal of Humanity, Social Sciences and Global Affairs* 1, no. 1 (2019): 126–145.

Obilade, Akintunde Olusegun. *The Nigerian Legal System*. Ibadan: Sweet & Maxwell, 1979.

Obono, Danièle. "Trade Unions as Social Movements and Political Actors in Nigeria (1994–2004)." *Stichproben. Wiener Zeitschrift für kritische Afrikastudien* 11 (2011): 95–113.

Ochiai, Takehiko. "The Application of Sharia and the Evolution of the Native Court System in Colonial Northern Nigeria (1900–1960)." *Asian Journal of African Studies* 49 (2020): 77–110.

Ochonu, Moses E. "African Colonial Economies: Land, Labor, and Livelihoods." *History Compass* 11, no. 2 (2013): 91–103.

Colonial Meltdown: Northern Nigeria in the Great Depression. Athens: Ohio University Press, 2009.

"Conjoined to Empire: The Great Depression and Nigeria." *African Economic History* 34 (2006): 103–145.

"Elusive History: Fractured Archives, Politicized Orality, and Sensing the Postcolonial Past." *History in Africa* 42 (2015): 287–298.

Odebiyi, Amoleke I. "Social Factors in Health and Diseases." Inaugural Lecture 135. Obafemi Awolowo University, Ile-Ife, O. A. U. Press, 1999.

Odeleye, Joshua A. "Politics of Rail Transport Development in Developing Countries: Case of Nigeria." *Journal of Civil Engineering and Architecture* 6, no. 12 (2012): 1695–1702.

Odiagbe, Sylvester A. "Industrial Conflict in Nigerian Universities: A Case Study of the Disputes Between the Academic Staff Union of Universities (ASUU) and the Federal Government of Nigeria (FGN)." Unpublished PhD dissertation. University of Glasgow, 2012.

Odidi, Martin. "The Church and Social Responsibilities: A Case Study of the Development of Church Schools in the Diocese of Kaduna, Church of Nigeria, Anglican Communion." Unpublished PhD dissertation. University of the South, 2019.

Odubajo, Tola, and Bamidele Alabi. "The Elite Factor in Nigeria's Political-Power Dynamics." *Journal of Studies in Social Sciences* 8, no. 1 (2014): 121–139.

Odunbaku, James B. "Importance of Cowrie Shells in Pre-Colonial Yoruba land South Western Nigeria: Orile- Keesi as a Case Study." *International Journal of Humanities and Social Science* 2, no. 18 (2012): 234–241.

Oduntan, Oluwatoyin, and Kemi Rotimi. "Tensional Decolonization and Public Order in Western Nigeria, 1957–1960." *Decolonization: Indigeneity, Education & Society* 4, no. 2 (2015): 103–122.

Oduntan, Oluwatoyin B. "Iwe Irohin and the Representation of the Universal in Nineteenth-Century Egbaland." *History in Africa* 32 (2005): 295–305.

Power, Culture and Modernity in Nigeria: Beyond the Colony. New York: Routledge, 2018.

Oduwobi, Tunde. "From Conquest to Independence: The Nigerian Colonial Experience." *Historia Actual Online* 25 (2011): 19–29.

"Tackling Leprosy in Colonial Nigeria, 1926–1960." *Journal of the Historical Society of Nigeria* 22 (2013): 178–205.

Ijebu Under Colonial Rule, 1892–1960: An Administrative and Political Analysis. Lagos: First Academic Publishers, 2004.

Oduyoye, Modupe. *The Planting of Christianity in Yorubaland*. Ibadan: Day Star Press, 1969.

Ofcansky, Thomas P. "Margery Perham: A Bibliography of Published Work." *History in Africa* 15 (1988): 339–350.

Ofoego, Obioma, and Toyin Falola, *Funmilayo Ransome-Kuti and the Women's Union of Abeokuta*. Paris: UNESCO Publishing, 2015.

Ofonagoro, Walter I. "An Aspect of British Colonial Policy in Southern Nigeria: The Problems of Forced Labor and Slavery, 1895–1928." In *Studies in Southern Nigerian History*, ed. Boniface I. Obichere. London: Frank Cass, 1982, 219–243.

"The Currency Revolution in Southern Nigeria 1880–1948." Occasional Paper No. 14, African Studies Center: University of California, Los Angeles, 1976, 4.

"From Traditional to British Currency in Southern Nigeria: Analysis of a Currency Revolution, 1880–1948." *The Journal of Economic History* 39, no. 3 (1979): 623–654.

"Notes on the Ancestry of Mbanaso Okwaraozurumba otherwise known as King Jaja of Opobo, 1821–1891." *Journal of the Historical Society of Nigeria* 9, no. 3 (1978): 145–156.

Ofong, Chigbo. "Political Trade Unionism in Nigeria: An Historical and Socioeconomic Analysis." Unpublished PhD dissertation. Johns Hopkins University, 1982.

Ogbogbo, Christopher B. N. "Historical Society of Nigeria: The Study of History and the Nigerian Nation. Address by the President of the Historical Society of Nigeria." *Journal of The Historical Society of Nigeria* 24 (2015): 4.

Ogbu, John U. "Research Currents: Cultural-ecological Influences on Minority School Learning." *Language Arts* 62, no. 8 (1985): 860–869.

Ogen, Olukoya. "Exploring the Potential of Praise Poems for Historical Reconstruction among the Idepe-Ikale in Southeastern Yorubaland." *History in Africa* 39 (2012): 77–96.

Ogisi, Arugha A. "The Origin of Concert Music in Nigeria, 1850–1920." *EJOTMAS: Ekpoma Journal of Theatre and Media Arts* 2, no. 1–2 (2008): 109.

Ogot, Bethwell A. *Ethnicity, Nationalism, and Democracy in Africa*. Kenya: Institute of Research and Postgraduate Studies, Maseno University College, 1996.

General History of Africa – V: Africa from the Sixteenth to the Eighteenth Century. Paris: UNESCO Publishing, 2000.

Ogunbado, Ahamad Faosiy. "Impacts of Colonialism on Religions: An Experience of South-western Nigeria." *IOSR Journal of Humanities and Social Science* 5, no. 6 (2012): 51–57.

"Islam and its Impacts in Yorubaland." *Islamic Quarterly* 57, no. 1 (2003).

Ogundari, Kolawole, and Adebayo B. Aromolaran. "Impact of Education on Household Welfare in Nigeria." *International Economic Journal* 28, no. 2 (2014): 345–364.

Ogundeji, Philip. *Friendship, Housewife-Rivalry and Human Lust in the Plays of Kola Ogunmola*. Ibadan: University of Ibadan, Department of Theatre Arts, 1991.

Ogundiran, Akinwumi. "Material Life and Domestic Economy in a Frontier of the Oyo Empire During the Mid-Atlantic Age." *International Journal of African Historical Studies* 42, no. 3 (2009): 351–385.

"Of Small Things Remembered: Beads, Cowries, and Cultural Translations of the Atlantic Experience in Yorubaland." *The International Journal of African Historical Studies* 35, no. 2/3 (2002): 427–457.

Precolonial Nigeria: Essays in Honor of Toyin Falola. Trenton: Africa World Press, 2005.

The Yoruba: A New History. Bloomington: Indiana University Press, 2020.

Ogunjobi, Oluseyi. "The Creative Development, Importance, and Dramaturgy of Duro Ladipo's Oba Ko So." *Cross/Cultures* 177 (2014): 291–318.

"The Visual Languages of Duro Ladipo's Theatre in *Oba Moro, Oba Koso* and *Oba Waja*." Unpublished PhD dissertation. University of Leeds, 2011.

Ogunlade, F. O. "Education and Politics in Colonial Nigeria: The Case of King's College Lagos (1906–1911)." *Journal of Historical Society of Nigeria* 7, no. 2 (1974): 325–345.

"Post-Secondary Education Years, 1947–1958." In *J. F. Ade Ajayi: His Life and Career*, ed. Michael Omolewa and Akinjide Osuntokun. Ibadan: Bookcraft, 2014, 58.

Ogunlana, Olanrewaju. "Nigeria." In *International Pharmaceutical Services: The Drug Industry and Pharmacy Practice in Twenty-Three Major Countries of the World*, ed. Richard N. Spivey, Albert I. Wertheimer and T. Donald Rucker. New York: Pharmaceutical Products Press, 1992, 401.

Ogunnoiki, Adeleke Olumide. "Political Parties, Ideology and the Nigerian State." *International Journal of Advanced Academic Research* 4, no. 12 (2018): 114–150.

Ogunode, Sunday Abraham. "Kingship and Power Politics in Akokoland, 1900–1999." Unpublished PhD dissertation. University of Ibadan, 2021.

Ogunremi, Gabriel O. *Counting the Camels: The Economics of Transportation in Pre-Industrial Nigeria*. New York: Nok Publishers International, 1982.

Ibadan: A Historical, Cultural and Socio-Economic Study of an African City. Ibadan: Oluyole Club, 2000.

Ogunsuyi, Steve. *African Theatre Aesthetics and Television Drama in Nigeria*. Abuja: Roots Books and Journal limited, 2007, 31.

Oguntomisin, Gabriel O. "The Impact of the Ijebu Expedition of 1892 on Politics in Epe, 1892–1925." *African Notes: Bulletin of the Institute of African Studies* 19, nos. 1–2 (1995): 1–12.

"Political Change and Adaptation in Yorubaland in the Nineteenth Century." *Canadian Journal of African Studies* 15, no. 2 (1981): 225–228

Oguntuyi, A. *History of Ekiti from the Beginnings to 1939*. Ibadan: Bisi Books, 1979.

Ogwuche, Matthew Enenche. "Migrants and the National Question: A Study of the Nigerian Migration Experience." *International Journal of Migration and Global Studies* 1, no. 2 (2021): 1–46.

Ohadike, Don C. "Diffusion and Physiological Responses to the Influenza Pandemic of 1918–19 in Nigeria." *Social Science and Medicine* 32, no. 12 (1991): 1393–1399.

The Ekumeku Movement: Western Igbo Resistance to the British Conquest of Nigeria, 1883–1914. Athens: Ohio University Press, 1991.

Ojedokun, Olasupo. "The Anglo-Nigerian Entente and Its Demise, 1960–1962." *Journal of Commonwealth Political Studies* ix, no. 3 (1971): 210–233.

Ojiakor, Ngozi E. *Igbo Women in Nigerian Politics, 1929–1999*. New York: The Edwin Mellen Press, 2008.

Ojo, Emmanuel O. "Nigeria, 1914–2014: From Creation to Cremation?" *Journal of the Historical Society of Nigeria* 23 (2014): 67–91.

Ojo, Idahosa O. "The Nature of Laws and Law Making in Precolonial Benin." *POLAC Historical Review* 4, no. 1 (2020): 89–103.

Ojo, Olatunji. "The Organization of the Atlantic Slave Trade in Yorubaland, Ca. 1777 to Ca. 1856." *The International Journal of African Historical Studies* 41, no. 1 (2008): 77–100.

"The Slave Ship Manuelita and the Story of a Yoruba Community, 1833–1834." *Revista Tempo* 23, no. 2 (2017): 361–382.

Ojo, Olusola Matthew, and Timothy Adeola Adams. "Migration and Urban Violence in Nigeria: Imperative of Peace Culture." *Journal of Migration and Global Studies* 1, no. 2 (2021): 18–224.

Okafor, Emeka Emmanuel, and Monica Ewomazino Akokuwebe. "Women and leadership in Nigeria: Challenges and Prospects." *Developing Country Studies* 5, no. 4 (2015): 1–11.

Okafor, F. O. E. *The Nigerian Youth Movement, 1934–44: A Re-Appraisal of the Historiography*. Onitsha: Etukokwu Publishers, 1989.

Okafor, Godson Okwuchukwu and Chinonye Faith Malizu. "The Media, Democracy and Trade Unionism in Nigeria: Challenges and Prospects." *New Media and Mass Communication* 17 (2013): 79–89.

Okafor, Samuel O. *Indirect Rule: The Development of the Central Legislature in Nigeria*. Lagos: Nelson Africa, 1981.

Okantah, Mwatabu. "Chief Fela Sowande, Traditional African Culture and the Black Studies Movement: A Student Remembers." *Journal of Pan African Studies* 1, no. 10 (2007): 100.

Okeke, Chukwuma O., Christopher N. Ibenwa, and Gloria Tochukwu Okeke. "Conflicts Between African Traditional Religion and Christianity in Eastern Nigeria: The Igbo Example." *SAGE Open* 7, no. 2 (2017): 1–10.

Okene, Adam A. "Colonial Conquest and Resistance: The Case of Ebiraland 1886–1917 AD." *Kano Studies* 1, no. 1 (2000): 23.

Okereka, Onofere Princewill. "Evolution of Constitutional Governments in Nigeria: Its Implementation on National Cohesion." *Global Journal of Political Science and Administration* 3, no. 5 (2015): 1–8.

Okereke, Okoro. *Co-Operatives and the Nigerian Economy*. Nsukka: University of Nigeria Press, 1986.

Okolie, Charles N. "Trade Unionism, Collective Bargaining and Nation Building: The Nigerian Experience." *OGIRISI: A New Journal of African Studies* 7 (2010): 136–148.

Okolo-Nwakaeme, Marystella C. "Reassessing the Impact of Colonial Languages on the African Identity for African Development." *Africa Media Review* 13, no. 2 (2005): 85–103.

Okome, Onookome. "The Context of Film Production in Nigeria: The Colonial Heritage." *Ufahamu: A Journal of African Studies* 24, no. 2–3 (1996): 42–62.

Okon, A. O. "Nigeria and a People's Constitution: The Imperative of Democracy and Change." *The Constitution* 4, no. 1 (2004): 16.

Okonjo, Kamene. "The Dual-Sex Political System in Operation: Igbo Women and Community Politics in Midwestern Nigeria." In *Women in Africa: Studies in Social and Economic Change*, ed. Nancy J. Hafkin and Edna G. Bay. Stanford: Standford University Press, 1976, 45–58.

"Sex Roles in Nigerian Politics." In *Female and Male in West Africa*, ed. Christine Oppong. London: George Allen and Unwin Ltd., 1983, 211–222.

Okonkwo, R. L. "The Garvey Movement in British West Africa." *The Journal of African History* 21, no. 1 (1980): 105–117.

Okonkwo, Rina. "Corruption in Nigeria: A Historical Perspective (1947–2002)." In *African Humanities: Humanities and Nation Building*, ed. Francis Anyika. Nsukka: Afro-Orbis Publications, 2005.

"Cultural Nationalism in the Colonial Period." In *African Cultural Development*, ed. Ogbu Kalu. Enugu: Fourth Dimension, 1985.

"The Nigeria Civil Service Union, 1919–1922." *The International Journal of African Historical Studies* 26, no. 3 (1993): 609–622.

Protest Movements in Lagos, 1908–1930. Lewiston: E. Mellen Press, 1995.

Okonkwo, Uche U. "Herbert Macaulay as the Father of Nigeria's Nationalism: A Historical Misnomer and Misogyny Regarding the Role of Igbo Women in the Decolonization Process." *Journal of International Women's Studies* 21, no 1 (2020): 172–184.

Okonta, Ike, and Oronto Douglas. *Where Vultures Feast: Shell, Human Rights, and Oil in the Niger Delta*. London: Verso, 2003.

Okoro, S. I. "The Igbo and Educational Development in Nigeria, 1846–2015." *International Journal of History and Cultural Studies* 4, no. 1 (2018): 65–80.

Okoye, Chukwuemeka, and Amon Okpala. "The History of Community Banking and its Role in Nigerian Rural Economic Development." *The Review of Black Political Economy* 28, no. 3 (2001): 73–87.

Okoye, Dozie. "Things Fall Apart? Missions, Institutions, and Interpersonal Trust." *Journal of Development Economics* 148 (2021): 1–78.

Okoye, Mokwugo. *African Responses*. London: Arthur H. Stockwell, 1964.

Okpeh, Okpeh O. "Inter-Group Migrations, Conflicts, and Displacements in Central Nigeria." In *Population Movements, Conflicts and Displacements in Nigeria*, ed. Toyin Falola and Okpeh Ochayi Okpeh. Trenton: Africa World Press, 2008, 19–85.

"Patterns and Dynamics of Inter-Group Relations in Nigeria, 1800–1900 AD." *Journal of the Historical Society of Nigeria* 17 (2007/2008): 123–137.

Okpevra, Uwomano Benjamin. "The Dynamics of Intergroup Relations in Pre-Colonial Nigeria up to 1800: A Reappraisal of a Lopsided Historiography." *LWATI: A Journal of Contemporary Research* 11, no. 1 (2014): 126–143.

Oladejo, Mutiat T. "Empowerment of Women and Sustainable Development in the 20th Century: The Yoruba Women Example." In *Capacity Building for Sustainable Development*, ed. Valentine Udoh James. Oxfordshire: CABI, 2018, 84.

Women, Politics and Social Development in Colonial Yorubaland: Thematic Analysis of Selected Yoruba Women." *Journal of International Politics and Development* 8, nos. 1&2 (2012): 113–127.

The Women Went Radical: Petition Writing and Colonial State in Southwestern Nigeria, 1900–1953. Ibadan: BookBuilders, 2018.

Oladiti, Abiodun A. "Religion and Politics in Pre-Colonial Nigeria." *Cogito: Multidisciplinary Research Journal* 2 (2014): 72–84.

Oladiti, Abiodun A. and Ajibade S. Idowu. "The Interplay of Town Planning and Colonialism: The Contributions of Albert Thompson to Urban Development in Lagos, 1920–1945." *Social Evolution & History* 16, no. 2 (2017): 126–142.

Olajide, W. "Existentialising Names and Their Significance among the Yorùbá." *Ọpánbàtà: LASU Journal of African Studies* 6 (2012): 56–75.

Olalekan, Muritala M. "Urban Livelihood in Lagos 1861–1960." *Journal of the Historical Society of Nigeria* 20 (2011): 193–200.

Olaoba, Olufemi B. "The Traditional Judicial Organization and Procedure in Ekiti Palaces with Particular Reference to Ekiti North, 1830–1930." Unpublished PhD dissertation. University of Ibadan, 1992.

Olasupo, Olusola, Isaac Olajide, and E. O. C. Ijeoma. "Nationalism and Nationalist Agitation in Africa: The Nigerian Trajectory." *The Review of Black Political Economy* 44, no. 3-4 (2017): 261-283.

Olatunde, Diane. "Women's Participation and Representation in Nigeria's Politics in the Last Decade (1999-2009)." Unpublished PhD dissertation. University of the Witwatersrand, 2010.

Olatunji, O. "Sorrowful Songs from the Valley of Iva." *The Nation Newspaper*, September 15, 2015.

Ọlátúnjí, Ọlátúndé O. *Features of Yoruba Oral Poetry*. Ibadan: University Press, 1984.

Olawale, Isaac. *Inter-Ethnic Relations in a Nigerian City: A Historical Perspective of the Hausa-Igbo Conflicts in Kano 1953-1991*. Ibadan: IFRA-Nigeria, 1993.

Olayera, Michael Oluwaleke. "Religion, Politics and Insecurity in Nigeria: Impact and Way Forward." *Trinitarian: International Journal of Arts and Humanities* 1, no. 1 (2021): 1-11.

Olayode, Kehinde. "Beyond Intractability: Ethnic Identity and Political Conflicts in Africa." *International Journal of Humanities and Social Science* 6, no. 6 (2016): 242-248.

Oliver, Roland, and Anthony Atmore, *Africa Since 1800*. Cambridge: Cambridge University Press, 2005.

Olokesusi, Femi, Femi O. Aiyegbajeje, Gora Mboup, and Dennis Mwaniki. "Smart City Foundation for Smart Economy." In *Smart Economy in Smart Cities: International Collaborative Research: Ottawa, St.Louis, Stuttgart, Bologna, Cape Town, Nairobi, Dakar, Lagos, New Delhi, Varanasi, Vijayawada, Kozhikode, Hong Kong*, ed. T. M. Vinod Kumar. Singapore: Springer Nature, 2017, 798.

Oloruntimehin, Benjamin O. "African Politics and Nationalism, 1919-35." In *General History of Africa: VII Africa Under Colonial Domination 1880-1935*, ed. Albert Adu Boahen. Paris: UNESCO, 1990. 565-579.

Olubomehin, Oladipo O. "Cinema Business in Lagos, Nigeria since 1903." *Historical Research Letter* 3 (2012): 1-10.

——— "Road Transportation as Lifeline of the Economy in Western Nigeria, 1920 to 1952." *African Journal of History and Culture* 4, no. 3 (2012): 37-45.

Olubomehin, Oladipo O. *Road Transportation in South Western Nigeria, 1900-1960*. Saarbrücken: Lambert Academic Publishing, 2011.

Olufemi, Olusola A. "Planning and Morphology of Indigenous Towns in Nigeria." *Africa Insight* 25, no. 3 (1995): 195-200.

Olujimi, Julius and Gbenga Enisan. "The Influence of the Colonial Planning Education on Urban and Regional Planning Administration in Nigeria." *ResearchGate*. www.researchgate.net/publication/283655405_The_Influence_of_the_ Colonial_Planning_Education_on_Urban_and_Regional_Planning_Administr ation_in_Nigeria, November, 2015.

Olukoju, Ayodeji O. "'Buy British, Sell Foreign': External Trade Control Policies in Nigeria during World War II and its Aftermath, 1939-1950." *The International Journal of African Historical Studies* 35, no. 2/3 (2002): 363-384.

"Elder Dempster and the Shipping Trade of Nigeria during the First World War." *The Journal of African History* 33, no. 2 (1992): 255–271.

"Making Sense of the Yoruba Littoral." *Yoruba Studies Review* 2, no. 1 (2017): 45–60.

"The Port of Lagos, 1850–1929: The Rise of West Africa's Leading Seaport." In *Atlantic Ports and the First Globalisation, c. 1850–1930*, ed. Miguel Suárez Bosa. London: Palgrave Macmillan, 2014, 112–129.

"Self-Help Criminality as Resistance? Currency Counterfeiting in Colonial Nigeria." *International Review of Social History* 45, no. 3 (2000): 385–407.

"Transportation in Colonial West Africa." In *An Economic History of West Africa since 1750*, ed. Gabriel O. Ogunremi and E. K. Faluyi. Ibadan: Rex Charles Publishers, 1996, 144–156.

Oluniyi, Ademola E. "Regionalism, Ideology Crises, Party Affiliation and Future of Democracy in Nigeria." *Afro Asian Journal of Social Sciences* 5, no. 5 (2014): 1–20.

Olusanya, Gabriel O. "The Lagos Branch of the National Congress of British West Africa." *Journal of the Historical Society of Nigeria* 4, no. 2 (1968): 321–333.

"Nationalist Movements in Nigeria." In *Groundwork of Nigerian History*, ed. Obaro Ikime. Ibadan: Heinemann Educational Books, 1980, 545–569.

"The Nigerian Civil Service in the Colonial Era: A Study of Imperial Reactions to Changing Circumstances." In *Studies in Southern Nigerian History*, ed. Boniface I. Obichere. London: Routledge, 1982.

"The Role of Ex-Servicemen in Nigerian Politics." *The Journal of Modern African Studies* 6, no. 2 (1968): 221–232.

"The Zikist Movement: A Study in Political Radicalism, 1946–50." *The Journal of Modern African Studies* 4, no. 3 (1966): 323–333.

The Second World War and Politics in Nigeria, 1939–1953. London: Evans Brothers, 1973.

Olusoji, Stephen O. "Comparative Analysis of the Islam Influenced Apala, Waka and Sakara Popular Music of the Yoruba." Unpublished PhD dissertation, University of Ibadan, 2008.

Oluwasegun, Jimoh M. "Managing Epidemic: The British Approach to 1918–1919 Influenza in Lagos." *Journal of Asian and African Studies* 52, no. 4 (2017): 412–424.

Omasanjuwa, Akpojevbe, and Junisa Phebean. "Acrimony in Colonial Liberia," *Journal of Universal History Studies* 3, no. 1 (2020): 1–38.

Omenka, Nicholas. "The African-Brazilian Repatriates and the Religious and Cultural Transformation of Colonial Lagos." *Abia Journal of the Humanities and the Social Sciences* 1, no. 1 (2004): 27–45.

Omenukwa, Kanu. "The National Council of Nigeria and the Cameroons (NCNC) and the British Administration, 1944–1960: A Study of Responses to Changing Political Situations." BA project, University of Birmingham, 1967.

Omer-Cooper, John D. "The Contribution of the University of Ibadan to the Spread of the Study and Teaching of African History within Africa." *Journal of the Historical Society of Nigeria* 10, no. 3 (1980): 23–31.

Omibiyi, Mosunmola A. "Bobby Benson: The Entertainer-Musician." *Nigerian Magazine*, 1983.

Omoboriowo, Akin. *Awoism: Select Themes on the Complex Ideology of Chief Obafemi Awolowo*. Ibadan: Evans Brothers, 1982.

Omojola, Bode. *The Music of Fela Sowande: Encounters, African Identity, and Creative Ethnomusicology*. Point Richmond: Music Research Institute Press, 2009.

——. *Nigerian Art Music: With an Introduction Study of Ghanaian Art Music*. Bayreuth: Bayreuth African Studies, 1995.

——. "Politics, Identity, and Nostalgia in Nigerian Music: A Study of Victor Olaiya's Highlife." *Ethnomusicology* 53, no. 2 (2009): 249–276.

——. "Style in Modern Nigerian Art Music: The Pioneering Works of Fela Sowande." *Africa: Journal of the International African Institute* 68, no. 4 (1998): 455.

Omoleke, Ishaq I. "Intergovernmental Relations and Management of Primary Health Care in Nigeria." Unpublished PhD dissertation Obafemi Awolowo University, Ile-Ife, 2000.

Omolewa, Michael. "The Cambridge University Local Examinations Syndicate and the Development of Secondary Education in Nigeria, 1910–1926." *Journal of the Historical Society of Nigeria* 8, no. 4 (1977): 111–130.

——. *Certificate History of Nigeria*. Harlow: Longman Group, 1986.

——. "Educating the 'Native': A Study of the Education Adaptation Strategy in British Colonial Africa, 1910–1936." *Journal of African American History* 91, no. 3 (2006): 267–287

——. "The Education Factor in the Emergence of the Modern Profession of Historian in Nigeria, 1926–1956." *Journal of The Historical Society of Nigeria* 10, no. 3 (1980): 41–62.

——. "The English Language in Colonial Nigeria, 1862–1960: A Study of the Major Factors Which Promoted the English Language." *Journal of Nigeria English Studies Association* 7, nos. 1 & 2 (1975): 103–117.

Omosini, Olufemi. "Background to Railway Policy in Nigeria, 1877–1901." In *Topics on Nigerian Economic and Social History*, ed. Isaac A. Akinjogbin and Segun O. Osoba. Ife: University of Ife Press, 1980, 147.

Omosule, Segun. "Artistic Undercurrents of Performance: A Study of Egungun Costumes in Ode Irele." *California Linguistic Notes* XXXIV, no. 2 (2009): 1–20.

Omotola, Shola J. "Nigerian Parties and Political Ideology." *Journal of Alternative Perspectives in the Social Sciences* 1, no. 3 (2009): 612–634.

Omoyajowo, Joseph Akinyele. *Cherubim and Seraphim: The History of an African Independent Church*. New York: NOK Publishers Int., 1982.

Omu, Fred I. A. "The Iwe Irohin, 1859–1867." *Journal of the Historical Society of Nigeria* 4, no. 1 (1967): 35–44.

"Journalism and the Rise of Nationalism: John Payne Jackson." *Journal of the Historical Society of Nigeria* 7, no. 3 (1974): 521–539.

Press and Politics in Nigeria, 1880–1937. Atlantic Highlands: Humanities Press, 1978.

Omuojine, E. "The Land Use Act and the English Doctrine of Estate." *Journal of the Nigerian Institute of Surveyors and Valuers* 22, no. 3 (1999): 54–56.

Onagbesan, Adewale. "Account for the Life and Times of Oba Akinsemoyin." *Academia.* www.academia.edu/30839962/ACCOUNT_OF_OBA_AKINSEMOYIN.

Onuegbu, Hyginus C. "Trade Unions in Nigeria: A Contemporary Overview." Paper Presented to the distinguished guests, participants and organizers of the Trade Union Congress (TUC), Rivers State Leadership Retreat, held at NUJ Press Centre, Port Harcourt, September 20, 2016.

Onumonu, Ugo Pascal. "The Development of the Kingship Institution in Oru-Igbo up to 1991." *OGIRISI: A New Journal of African Studies* 12 (2016): 68–96.

Onuoha, Jonah, and Tochukwu J. Omenma. "The Seniority Ideology and Governance in Igbo Culture." *Ikenga International Journal of African Studies* 9, no. 1&2 (2007): 145–153.

Onuora-Oguno, Azubike C. *Development and the Right to Education in Africa.* Cham, Switzerland: Palgrave Macmillan, 2019.

Onwubiko, K. B. C. *School Certificate History of West Africa. Book II: 1800–Present Day.* Onitsha: Africana, 1973.

Onyekwelu, C. A. "Urban Growth and Patterns in Nigeria." In *Issues in Urbanization and Urban Administration in Nigeria*, ed. E. O. Ezeani and N. N. Elekwa. Nsukka: Jamoe Enterprise, 2001, 47–60.

Onyemelukwe, J. O. C. "Structural and Locational Characteristics of Manufacturing." In *A Geography of Nigerian Development*, 2nd ed., ed. J. S. Oguntoyinbo, O. O. Areola, and M. Filani. Ibadan: Heinemann Educational Books Ltd., 1983, 296–310.

Onyeozili, Emmanuel C., and Obi N. I. Ebbe. "Social Control in Precolonial Igboland of Nigeria." *African Journal of Criminology and Justice Studies* 6, nos. 1 & 2 (2012): 40.

Opoko, Pearl Akunnaya, and Adedaopo A. Oluwatayo. "Trends in Urbanization: Implication for Planning and Low-Income Housing Delivery in Lagos, Nigeria." *Architecture Research* 4, no. 1 (2014): 15–26.

Oriji, John N. *A Political Organization in Nigeria since the Late Stone Age: A History of the Igbo People.* New York: Palgrave Macmillan, 2011.

"Sacred Authority in Igbo Society." *Archives de sciences sociales des religions* 68, no. 1 (1989): 113–123.

"The Slave Trade, Warfare and Aro Expansion in the Igbo Hinterland." *Transafrican Journal of History* 16 (1987): 151–166.

Traditions of Igbo Origin: A Study of Pre-Colonial Population Movements in Africa. New York: Peter Lang, 1990.

Orjinta, Hillary I., and Ngbede O. Ameh. "Political Parties and National Integration in Nigeria." *African Journal of Politics and Administrative Studies (AJPAS)* 13 (2020): 2.

Ortese, Peter. *Psychology of Creativity*. Makurdi: Aboki Publishers, 2009.

Orugbani, Adaye. *Nigeria Since the 19th Century*. Port Harcourt: Paragraphics, 2005.

Osadolor, Osarhieme Benson. "The Development of the Federal Idea and the Federal Framework, 1914–1960." In *Federalism and Political Restructuring in Nigeria*, ed. Adigun Agbaje, Rotimi Suberu, and Georges Herault. Ibadan. Spectrum Books Ltd., 1998.

Osaghae, Eghosa E. *Crippled Giant: Nigeria since Independence*. London: Hurst and Company, 1998.

——— "Explaining the Changing Patterns of Ethnic Politics in Nigeria." *Nationalism and Ethnic Politics* 9, no. 3 (2003): 54–73.

——— "The Ogini Uprising: Oil Politics, Minority Agitation and the Future of the Nigerian State" *African Affairs* 94 (1995): 325–344.

Osanyin, Ajike F. *Early Childhood Education in Nigeria*. Shomolu: Conccpt Pub. Limited, 2002.

Osemwengie, Ikonnaya, and Oghogho Oriakhi. "Nationalism and Freedom in Colonial Nigeria: A Gendered Perspective." *Lagos Historical Review* 18 (2018): 33–48.

Oshin, Olasiji. "Road Transport and the Declining Fortunes of the Nigerian Railway, 1901–1950." *The Journal of Transport History* 12, no. 1 (1991): 11–36.

Osifodunrin, Paul. *Escapee Criminals and Crime Control in Colonial Southwestern Nigeria, 1861–1945*. Ibadan: IFRA-Nigeria, 2005.

Oso, Lai, and Umaru Pate, eds. *Mass Media and Society in Nigeria*. Lagos: Malthouse Press, 2011.

Oso, Lai. "The Commercialization of the Nigerian Press: Development and Implications." *Africa Media Review* 5, no. 3 (1991): 41–51.

Osoba, Segun O. "The Development of Trade Unionism in Colonial and Post-Colonial Nigeria." In *Topics on Nigerian Economic and Social History*, ed. Isaac A. Akinjogbin and Segun Osoba. Ile-Ife: University of Ife Press, 1980, 185–207.

——— "The Phenomenon of Labour Migration in the Era of British Colonial Rule: A Neglected Aspect of Nigeria's Social History." *Journal of the Historical Society of Nigeria* 4, no. 4 (1969): 515–538.

——— "Transition to Neo-Colonialism." In *Britain and Nigeria: Exploitation or Development?* ed. Toyin Falola. London: Zed Books, 1987, 223–249.

Osterhammel, Jurgen. *Colonialism: A Theoretical Overview*. Princeton: Markus Wiener and Kingston Ian Randle Publishers, 1997.

Osunlakin, Damilola. "Rethinking Cultural Diversity and Sustainable Development in Africa." In *Imagining Vernacular Histories: Essays in Honor of Toyin Falola*, ed. Mobolanle Ebunoluwa Sotunsa and Abikal Borah. Lanham: Rowman and Littlefield, 2020, 47–70.

Osuntokun, Akinjide, and Tunji Oloruntimehin. "J. F. Ade Ajayi and His Intellectual Contribution to the Study of History." In *J. F. Ade Ajayi: His Life and Career*, ed. Michael Omolewa and Akinjide Osuntokun. Ibadan: Bookcraft, 2014, 300.

Osuntokun, Akinjide. "Disaffection and Revolts in Nigeria during the First World War, 1914–1918." *Canadian Journal of African Studies* 5, no. 2 (1971): 171–192.

"Post-First World War Economic and Administrative Problems in Nigeria and the Response of the Clifford Administration." *Journal of the Historical Society of Nigeria* 7, no. 1 (1973): 35–48.

"Professor Jacob F. Ade Ajayi and the Ibadan School of History." In *J. F. Ade Ajayi: His Life and Career*, ed. Michael Omolewa and Akinjide Osuntokun. Ibadan: Bookcraft, 2014, 300.

Nigeria in the First World War. London: Longman, 1979.

Ottenberg, Simon. "A Moslem Ibo Village." *Cahiers d'etudes Africaines* 11, no. 2 (1971): 231–243.

Otu, Noel. "Colonialism and the Criminal Justice System in Nigeria." *International Journal of Comparative and Applied Criminal Justice* 23, no. 2 (1999): 293–306.

Oucho, John, and Linda Oucho. "Migration, Urbanisation and Health Challenges in Sub-Saharan Africa." Conference Paper: Conditions and Cultural Change, Economic and Demographic Trends in Latin America. Latin American Population Association, Havana, Cuba, 2015.

Oyediran, Oyeleye. *Nigerian Constitutional Development*. Ibadan: Oyediran Consults International, 1998.

Oyelere, Michael. "Political Developments, Trade Union and Social Movement Unionism: A Case of Nigeria Labor Congress." Regent's Working Papers in Business & Management, 2014, 1–16.

Oyemakinde, Wale. "The Chiefs Law and the Regulation of Traditional Chieftaincy in Yorubaland." *Journal of the Historical Society of Nigeria* 9, no. 1 (1977): 63–74.

"Michael Imoudu and the Emergence of Militant Trade Unionism in Nigeria, 1940–1942." *Journal of the Historical Society of Nigeria* 7, no. 3 (1974): 541–561.

"The Pullen Marketing Scheme: A Trial in Food Price Control in Nigeria, 1941–1947." *Journal of the Historical Society of Nigeria* 6, no. 4 (1973): 413–423.

"Railway Construction and Operation in Nigeria, 1895–1911: Labour Problems and Socio-Economic Impact." *Journal of the Historical Society of Nigeria* 7, no. 2 (1974): 303–324.

"The Railway Workers and Modernization in Colonial Nigeria." *Journal of the Historical Society of Nigeria* 10, no. 1 (1979): 113–124.

Oyeranmi, S. "The Colonial Background to the Problem of Ethnicity in Nigeria: 1914–1960." *Journal of History and Diplomatic Studies* 8 (2011): 35–62.

Oyeweso, Siyan, and Olasiji Oshin. "British Conquest and Administration of Yoruba." In *Culture and Society in Yorubaland*, ed. Deji Ogunremi and Biodun Adediran. Ibadan: Rex Charles, 1998, 31–35.

Oyeweso, Siyan, and Olutayo C. Adesina, eds. *Oyo: History, Tradition and Royalty*. Ibadan: Ibadan University Press, 2021.

Oyeweso, Siyan. "Colonial Education, Identity Construction, and Formation of Elites in Nigeria." Paper Presented at the Conference on Indigenous Epistemology, Strengthening Research and Decolonization of Education in Nigeria held at the University of Ibadan, Nigeria, February 11-14, 2020.

Oyewumi, Oyeronke. "Making History, Creating Gender: Some Methodological and Interpretive Questions in the Writing of Oyo Oral Traditions." In *African Gender Studies: A Reader*, ed. Oyeronke Oyewumi. New York: Palgrave Macmillan, 2005, 169-206.

Oyovbaire, Sam E. "Structural Change and Political Processes in Nigeria." *African Affairs* 82, no. 326 (1983): 3-28.

Ozigboh, Ikenga R. A. *Roman Catholicism in Southern Nigeria 1885-1931*. Onitsha: Etukokwu Publishers, 1988.

Paden, John N. *Ahmadu Bello, Sardauna of Sokoto: Values and Leadership in Nigeria*. London: Heinemann, 1986.

Religion and Political Culture in Kano. Berkeley: University of California Press, 2020.

Page, Willie F., ed. *Encyclopedia of African History and Culture. Vol. 1: Ancient Africa*. New York: Facts on File Inc., 2005.

Pakenham, Thomas. *Scramble for Africa: The White Man's Conquest of the Dark Continent from 1876-1912*. New York: Random House, 1991.

Pallinder-Law, Agneta. "Aborted Modernization in West Africa? The Case of Abeokuta." *The Journal of African History* 15, no. 1 (1974): 65-82.

Panata, Sara. "Campaigning for Political Rights in Nigeria: The Women Movement in the 1950s." *Clio. Women, Gender, History*. 43 (2016): 175-185.

"'Dear Readers . . .': Women's Rights and Duties through Letters to the Editor in the Nigerian Press (1940s-1950s)." *Numéros* 1 (2020): 141-198.

"Nigeria on the Move: The Place of Women's and Feminist Movements in National Socio-Political Struggles (1944-1994)." Unpublished PhD dissertation. University of Paris 1 Panthéon-Sorbonne, 2020.

Park, Mungo. *The Journal of a Mission to the Interior of Africa: In the Year 1805*. Philadelphia: Edward Earle, 1815.

Travels in the Interior of Africa. London: Eland, 2012.

Parrinder, Geoffrey. *Religion in an African City*. London: Oxford University Press, 1953.

Parsons, Timothy H. "The Military Experience of Ordinary Africans in World War II." In *Africa and World War II*, ed. Judith Byfield, Carolyn Brown, Timothy Parson, and Ahmad Sikainga. Cambridge: Cambridge University Press, 2015, 3-16.

Paul, Ilesanmi Akanmidu. "The British's Contact with Nigeria's Peoples, Amalgamation and the Question of Minority Agitation, 1914-1999." *Africology: Journal of Pan African Studies* 12, no. 1 (2018): 421-439.

"The Survival of the Yorùbá Healing Systems in the Modern Age." *Yorùbá Studies Review* 2, no. 2 (2018): 1-21.

Paul, Salisu O., Timothy O. Usman, and Mohammed A. Ali. "Labor Unions and the Transformation of the Nigerian Civil Service: A Discourse." *IJPAMR* 2, no. 1 (2013): 13.

Payne, John Augustus Otunba. *Table of Principal Events in Yoruba History: With Certain Other Matters of General Interest, Compiled Principally for use in the Court within the British Colony of Lagos, West Africa.* Lagos: Andrew M. Thomas, 1883, 6.

Pearce, Robert D. *The Turning Point in Africa: British Colonial Policy 1938-48.* London: Frank Cass, 1982.

Pearce-Moses, Richard. *A Glossary of Archival and Records Terminology.* Illinois: The Society of American Archivists, 2005.

Pecoud, Antoine, and Paul de Guchteneire. *Migration Without Borders: Essays on the Free Movement of People.* New York: Berghahn Books, 2007.

Peel, John D. Y. *Aladura: A Religious Movement among the Yoruba.* London: Oxford University Press, 1968, 60-62.

Christianity, Islam and Orisa Religion: Three Traditions in Comparison and Interaction. Oakland: University of California Press, 2016.

"The Pastor and the 'Babalawo': The Interaction of Religions in Nineteenth-Century Yorubaland." *Africa: Journal of the International African Institute* 60, no. 3 (1990): 338-369.

"Problems and Opportunities in an Anthropologist's Use of a Missionary Archive." In *Missionary Encounters: Sources and Issues*, ed. Robert A. Bickers and Rosemary Seton. Hove: Psychology Press, 1996, 75.

Religious Encounter and the Making of the Yoruba. Bloomington: Indiana University Press, 2003.

Peil, Margaret. *Lagos: The City Is the People.* London: Belhaven Press, 1991.

Pereira, Charmaine. "Domesticating Women? Gender, Religion and the State in Nigeria under Colonial and Military Rule." *African Identities* 3, no. 1 (2005): 69-94.

Perham, Margery, and May Bull, eds. *The Diaries of Lord Lugard*, Vols. I-III. London: Faber and Faber, 1958.

Perham, Margery. "The British Problem in Africa." *Foreign Affairs* 29, no. 4 (1951): 637-650.

Lugard: A Maker of Modern Africa - The Years of Adventure, 1858-1898. London: Collins, 1956/1960.

Lugard: The Years of Authority, 1898-1945. London: Collins, 1956.

Native Administration in Nigeria. London: Oxford University Press, 1937.

"A Re-Statement of Indirect Rule." *Africa* 7, no. 3 (1934): 321-334.

Peshkin, Alan. "Education and National Integration in Nigeria." *The Journal of Modern African Studies* 5, no. 3 (1967): 323-334.

Peterson, Derek R., Emma Hunter, and Stephanie Newell, eds. *African Print Cultures: Newspapers and Their Publics in the Twentieth Century.* Ann Arbor: University of Michigan Press, 2016.

Phillips, Barnaby. *Loot: Britain and the Benin Bronzes.* London: Oneworld Publications, 2021.

Phillips, Howard, and David Killingray, eds. *The Spanish Influenza Pandemic of 1918–1919: New Perspectives.* London: Routledge, 2003.

Pierce, Steven. "Pointing to Property: Colonialism and Knowledge about Land Tenure in Northern Nigeria." *Africa* 83, no. 1 (2013): 142–163.

Pinto, Brian. "Nigeria during and after the Oil Boom: A Policy Comparison with Indonesia." *The World Bank Economic Review* 1, no. 3 (1987): 419–445.

Plageman, Nate. *Highlife Saturday Night: Popular Music and Social Change in Urban Ghana.* Bloomington: Indiana University Press, 2013.

Podstavsky, Sviatoslav. "Hausa Entertainers and Their Social Status: A Reconsideration of Sociohistorical Evidence." *Ethnomusicology* 48, no. 3 (2004): 348–377.

Pomper, Gerald M. "Concepts of Political Parties." *Journal of Theoretical Politics* 4, no. 2 (1992): 143–159.

Porter, Philip W. *Benin to Bahia: Portuguese Empire in the South Atlantic.* Saint Paul: North Central Publishing, 1959.

Post, Ken. *The Nigerian Federal Election of 1959: Politics and Administration in a Developing Political System.* Ibadan: Nigerian Institute of Social and Economic Research, 1963.

Poynor, Robin. "Ako Figures of Owo and Second Burials in Southern Nigeria." *African Arts* 21, no. 1 (1987): 82–90.

Pratten, David. *The Man-Leopard Murders: History and Society in Colonial Nigeria.* London: Edinburgh University Press, 2007.

Pribytkovskiy, Lev N. *Nigeria in the Struggle for Independence.* Annapolis: Research & Microfilm Publications, 1962.

Probst, Peter. "The Letter and the Spirit: Literacy and Religious Authority in the History of the Aladura Movement in Western Nigeria." *Africa* 59, no. 4 (1989): 478–495.

Quarcoopome, Theophilus N. O. *West African Traditional Religion.* Ibadan: African Universities Press, 1987.

Raheem, Oluwafunminiyi. "From the Sublime to the Ridiculous?: Contemporary Nigerian Hip-Hop, Music Consumption and the Search for Meaning (1999–2015)." In *Yoruba Arts, Culture, Entertainment & Tourism in the Age of Globalization & Uncertainty*, ed. Felix Ayoh'Omidire, Shina Alimi, and Akin Adejuwon. Kajola: Institute of Cultural Studies, 2020, 172–192.

"Martin Luther versus Us: Assessing the Reformation through the Perspectives of an African Class." *African Diaspora Discourse – ADD* 2, no. 2 (2020): 49–72.

Raheem, Oluwafunminiyi, and Mike Famiyesin. "Controlling the Boundaries of Morality: The History and Powers of Ayelala Deity." *Yoruba Studies Review* 2, no. 1 (2017): 231–247.

Raheem, Wasiu M., Oyewale I. Oyeleye, Margaret A. Adeniji, and Opeyemi C. Aladekoyi. "Regional Imbalances and Inequalities in Nigeria: Causes,

Consequences and Remedies." *Research on Humanities and Social Sciences* 4, no. 18 (2014): 163–174.

Rahmani, Mokhtaria. "Constitutional Development in Nigeria 1945–1960." Unpublished PhD dissertation. Djillali Liabbes University, 2015.

Raji, A. O. Y., and T .S. Abejide. "The Guild System and its Role in the Economy of Precolonial Yorubaland." *Arabian Journal of Business and Management Review* 3, no. 3 (2013): 14–22.

Raji, Adesina A. "Revisiting Oyo Empire within the Confine of the Atlantic Age." *Humanus Discourse* 1, no 4 (2021): 1–17.

Raji-Oyelade, Remi, Sola Olorunyomi, and Abiodun Duro-Ladipo, *Duro Ladipo: Thunder-God on Stage*. Ibadan: Institute of African Studies, University of Ibadan, 2003.

Ranger, Terence, and Olufemi Vaughan, eds. *Legitimacy and the State in Twentieth Century Africa: Essays in Honour of A. H. M. Kirk-Greene*. Oxford: Palgrave Macmillan, 1993.

Ranger, Terence O. "Godly Medicine: The Ambiguities of Medical Mission in Southeast Tanzania, 1900–1945." *Social Science and Medicine* 15, no. 3 (1981): 261–277.

"Making Northern Rhodesia Imperial: Variations on a Royal Theme, 1924–1938." *African Affairs* 79, no. 316 (1980): 349–373.

Ratcliffe, Barrie. "The Economics of the Partition of Africa: Methods and Recent Research Trends." *Canadian Journal of African Studies* 15, no. 1 (1981): 3–31.

Rathbone, Richard. "World War I and Africa: Introduction." *The Journal of African History* 19, no. 1 (1978): 1–9.

Reichmuth, Stefan. "Education and the Growth of Religious Associations among Yoruba Muslims: The Ansar-Ud-Deen Society of Nigeria." *Journal of Religion in Africa* 26 (1996): 367–368.

Reid, Richard J. "Africa's Revolutionary Nineteenth Century and the Idea of the 'Scramble.'" *The American Historical Review* 126, no. 4 (2021): 1424–1447.

A History of Modern Africa: 1800 to the Present. London: Blackwell Publishing Ltd., 2009.

Reis, Joao J., Flavio dos Santos Gomes, and Marcus J. M. de Carvalho. trans. by H. Sabrina Gledhill, *The Story of Rufino: Slavery, Freedom, and Islam in the Black Atlantic*. New York: Oxford University Press, 2020.

Reis, Joao Jose. "Slave Resistance in Brazil: Bahia, 1807–1835." *Luso-Brazilian Review* 25, no. 1 (1988): 111–144.

Renne, Elisha P. *Death and the Textile Industry in Nigeria*. London: Routledge, 2020.

Resnick, Daniel P. "The Societe des Amis des Noirs and the Abolition of Slavery." *French Historical Studies* 7, no. 4 (1972): 558–569.

Reynolds, Jonathan. "Good and Bad Muslims: Islam and Indirect Rule in Northern Nigeria." *The International Journal of African Historical Studies* 34, no. 3 (2001): 601–618.

Rich, Vernon. *Law and the Administration of Justice.* New York: Wiley & Sons, 1979.

Richards, Thomas. *The Imperial Archive: Knowledge and the Fantasy of Empire.* London: Verso, 1993.

Richardson, David. *Principles and Agents: The British Slave Trade and Its Abolition.* Yale: Yale University Press, 2022.

Rindap, Manko Rose, and I. M. A. Mari. "Ethnic Minorities and the Nigerian State." *Afrrev Ijah: An International Journal of Arts and Humanities* 3, no. 3 (2014): 89–101.

River, Charles. *Decolonization: The History and Legacy of the End of Western Imperialism in the 20th Century.* Scotts Valley: CreateSpace Independent Publishing Platform, 2017.

Rodney, Walter I. *How Europe Underdeveloped Africa.* London: Bogle-L'Ouverture Publications, 1972.

Rönnbäck, Klas. *Labour and Living Standards in Pre-Colonial West Africa: The Case of the Gold Coast.* New York: Routledge, 2016.

Rosenberg, Diana. "Ibo Resistance to British Colonial Power." *Ufahamu* 19, no. 1 (1991): 3–21.

Rosenfeld, Susan A. C. "Apparitions of the Atlantic: Mobility, Kinship, and Freedom among Afro-Brazilian Emigrants from Bahia to Lagos, 1850–1900." Unpublished PhD dissertation. University of California, 2020.

Ross, Stewart. *Causes and Consequences of the Second World War.* London: Evans Brothers Limited, 2003.

Rotberg, Robert I. *Africa and Its Explorers: Motives, Methods, and Impact.* Cambridge: Harvard University Press, 1970.

Rothbard, Murray N. *America's Great Depression.* Auburn: The Ludwig von Mises Institute, 2000.

Rowe, Michael. "The French Revolution, Napoleon, and Nationalism in Europe." In *The Oxford Handbook on the History of Nationalism*, ed. John Breuilly. Oxford: Oxford University Press, 2013, 127–148.

Rubenstein, Joseph. "On Nigerian Pop Culture." *Dialectical Anthropology* 3 (1978): 261–267.

Rufai, Saheed Ahmad. "A Foreign Faith in a Christian Domain: Islam among the Igbos of Southeastern Nigeria." *Journal of Muslim Minority Affairs* 32, no. 3 (2012): 372–383.

Russell, C. E. B. "The Leprosy Problem in Nigeria." *Journal of the Royal African Society* 37, no. 146 (1938): 66–71.

Ryder, Alan F. C. *Benin and the Europeans 1485–1897.* London: Longmans, 1969.

"The Benin Missions." *Journal of the Historical Society of Nigeria* 2, no. 2 (1961): 231–259.

"Missionary Activity in the Kingdom of Warri to the Early Nineteenth Century." *Journal of the Historical Society of Nigeria* 2, no. 1 (1960): 1–26.

"A Reconsideration of the Ife-Benin Relationship." *Journal of African History* 6, no. 1 (1965): 25–37.

Saad, Abubakar. "The Northern Province Under Colonial Rule." In *Groundwork of Nigeria History*, ed. Obaro Ikime. London: Heinemann Educational Books, 1980.
Sabar, Galia, and Atalia Shragai. "Olumba Olumba in Israel: Struggling on all Fronts." *African Identities* 6, no. 3 (2008): 201–225.
Sabra, Samah. "Imaging Nations: An Anthropological Perspective." *Nexus* 20 (2007): 76–104.
Sadoh, Godwin. *The Organ Works of Fela Sowande: Cultural Perspectives*. Bloomington: iUniverse LLC, 2014.
Salami, Olawale B. "Slaves, Government and Politics in Ibadan, 1835–1893." *IOSR Journal of Humanities and Social Science* 3, no. 6 (2012): 13–17.
Salami, Yunusa K. "The Democratic Structure of Yoruba Political–Cultural Heritage." *The Journal of Pan African Studies* 1, no. 6 (2006): 67–78.
Salamone, Frank A. *The Hausa of Nigeria*. Lanham: University Press of America, 2010.
Salau, Mohammed B. "Ribats and the Development of Plantations in the Sokoto Caliphate: A Case Study of Fanisau." *African Economic History* 34 (2006): 23–43.
Salawu, Mohammed L. "Slave Factor in the Development of Bida Emirate: 1857–1900." *African Research Review* 11, no. 47 (2017): 13–22.
Saleh-Hanna, Viviane, and Chukwuma Ume. "An Evolution of the Penal System: Criminal Justice in Nigeria." In *Colonial Systems of Control: Criminal Justice in Nigeria*, ed. Viviane Saleh-Hanna. Ottawa: University of Ottawa Press, 2008, 58.
Salewa, Olawoye-Mann. "Towards a Harmonious View of Money: The Nigerian Experience." *Journal of African Studies and Development* 13, no. 4 (2021): 115–123.
Salisu, Muhammed, and Abdullahi Salisu Abdullahi. "Colonial Impact on the Socio-Communicative Functions of Arabic Language in Nigeria: An Overview." *Canadian Social Science* 9, no. 6 (2013): 204–209.
Saliu, Hassan A., and Abdulrasheed A. Muhammad. "Growing Nigeria's Democracy through Viable Political Parties." In *Perspective on Nation-Building and Development in Nigeria: Political and Legal Issues*, ed. Hassan A. Saliu, Isah H. Jimoh, Noah Yusuf, and Emmanuel O. Ojo. Lagos: Concept Publication Ltd., 2008.
Samson, Anne. *World War I in Africa: The Forgotten Conflict among the European Powers*. London: I. B. Tauris, 2013.
Samuel, Kayode. "The Chequered History of Music Education in Nigeria." In *Educational Theory and Practice Across Disciplines: Projecting Beyond the 21st Century*, ed. Olawale A. Moronkola, Clement O. Kolawole, Babatunde O. Asagba, Jonathan O. Osiki, and Adebola Jaiyeoba. Ibadan: University of Ibadan, 2015, 195.
Sandhu, Ranvinder Singh, and Jasmeet Sandhu, eds. *Globalizing Cities: Inequality and Segregation in Developing Countries*. New Delhi: Rawat Publications, 2007.

Sangode, Iya Afin Ayobunmi. *Sango: The Cult of Kingship*. Scotts Valley: CreateSpace Publishing, 2014.

Santos, Aurora Almada E. "The Role of the Decolonization Committee of the United Nations Organization in the Struggle Against Portuguese Colonialism in Africa: 1961–1974." *The Journal of Pan African Studies* 4, no. 10 (2012): 284–260.

Sartori, Giovanni. "Politics, Ideology, and Belief Systems." *The American Political Science Review* 63, no. 2 (1969): 398.

Sawada, Nozomi. "The Educated Elite and Associational Life in Early Lagos Newspapers: In Search of Unity for the Progress of Society." Unpublished PhD dissertation. University of Birmingham, 2011, 49–50.

Schaff, Adam. "The Marxist Theory of Social Development." In *Readings in Social Evolution and Development*, ed. Shmuel N. Eisenstadt. New York, Pergamon Press, 1970, 71–94.

Schillinger, Hubert. "Trade Unions in Africa: Weak but Feared." Occasional Papers: International Development Corporation, *Friedrich-Ebert-Stiftung*, March 2005. https://library.fes.de/pdf-files/iez/02822.pdf.

Schräm, Ralph. *A History of the Nigerian Health Services*. Ibadan: University of Ibadan Press, 1971.

Schumaker, Lyn. *Africanizing Anthropology: Fieldwork, Networks, and the Making of Cultural Knowledge*. Durham: Duke University Press, 2001.

Schwartz, Joan M., and Terry Cook. "Archives, Records, and Power: The Making of Modern Memory." *Archival Science* 2, no. 1 (2002): 1–19.

Schwartz, Stuart B. *Slaves, Peasants, and Rebels: Reconsidering Brazilian Slavery*. Urbana: University of Illinois Press, 1992.

Scott, Roger. "Are Trade Unions Still Necessary in Africa?" *Transition* 33 (1967): 27–31.

Seidler, Valentin. "Colonial Legacy and Institutional Development: The Cases of Botswana and Nigeria." Unpublished PhD dissertation. WU Vienna University of Economics and Business, 2011.

Semmel, Bernard. *The Methodist Revolution*. London: Heinemann Educational Books, 1974.

Sertima, Ivan Van. *They Came Before Columbus: The African Presence in Ancient America*. New York: Random House, 1977.

Shack, William A., and Elliot P. Skinner, eds. *Strangers in African Societies*. Berkeley: University of California Press, 1979.

Shaka, Femi Okiremuete. "The Colonial Legacy: History and Its Impact on the Development of Modern Culture in Nigeria." *Third Text* 19, no. 3 (2005): 297–305.

Shankar, Shobana. *Who Shall Enter Paradise?: Christian Origins in Muslim Northern Nigeria, c. 1890–1975* Athens: Ohio University Press, 2014.

Shankar, Shobana. "Medical Missionaries and Modernizing Emirs in Colonial Hausaland: Leprosy Control and Native Authority in the 1930s." *The Journal of African History* 48, no. 1 (2007): 45–68.

Shaw, Timothy M., and Olajide Aluko. *Nigerian Foreign Policy: Alternative Perceptions and Projections.* London: Macmillan, 1983.
Shehu, Jamilu. "Trends of Urbanization in Nigeria: The Example of Gusau Town." *Polac Historical Review* 4, no. 1 (2020): 32-43.
Sheppard, Anthony W. "An Exotic Enemy: Anti-Japanese Musical Propaganda in World War II Hollywood." *Journal of the American Musicological Society* 54, no. 2 (2001): 303-357.
Shepperson, George. "Notes on Negro American Influences on the Emergence of African Nationalism." *The Journal of African History* 1, no. 2 (1960): 299-312.
Sherwood, Marika. "Elder Dempster and West Africa 1891-c.1940: The Genesis of Underdevelopment?" *The International Journal of African Historical Studies* 30, no. 2 (1997): 253-276.
Sherwood, Marika. "Two Pan-African Political Activists Emanating from Edinburgh University: Dr. John Randle and Richard Akinwande Savage." In *Africa in Scotland, Scotland in Africa: Historical Legacies and Contemporary Hybridities*, ed. Afe Adogame and Andrew Lawrence. Leiden: Brill, 2014, 103-136.
Origins of Pan-Africanism: Henry Sylvester Williams, Africa, and the African Diaspora. New York: Routledge, 2011.
Shitta Bey, Olanrewaju Abdul. "The Family as Basis of Social Order: Insights from the Yoruba Traditional Culture." *International Letters of Social and Humanistic Sciences* 23 (2014): 79-89.
Shittu, Murtala. "Nationalist Movement's Trends in Contemporary Nigerian Government and Politics." *International Journal of Development and Sustainability* 2, no. 2 (2013): 850-860.
Shokpeka, S. A., and Odigwe A. Nwaokocha. "British Colonial Economic Policy in Nigeria, the Example of Benin Province 1914-1954." *Journal of Human Ecology* 28, no. 1 (2017): 57-66.
Shonekan, Stephanie. "The Blueprint: The Gift and The Curse of American Hip Hop Culture for Nigeria's Millennial Youth." *The Journal of Pan African Studies* 6, no. 3 (2013): 181-198.
"Fela's Foundation: Examining the Revolutionary Songs of Funmilayo Ransome-Kuti and the Abeokuta Market Women's Movement in 1940s Western Nigeria." *Black Music Research Journal* 29, no. 1 (2009): 127-144.
Short, Giles D. "Blood and Treasure: The Reduction of Lagos, 1851." *ANU Historical Journal* 13 (1977): 11-19.
Shyllon, Folarin. "The Poverty of Documentary Heritage Management in Nigeria." *International Journal of Cultural Property* 9, no. 1 (2000): 23-48.
Siddharthan, N. S. "Globalization: Productivity, Efficiency and Growth: An Overview." *Economic and Political Weekly* 39, no. 5 (2004): 420-422.
Sifawa, Attahiru A. "The Role of Kanem Borno "Ulama" in the 20 Intellectual Development of the Bilad al-Sudan." Paper Presented at a Conference on Impact of "Ulama" in the Central Bilad al-Sudan, organized by the Centre for Trans-Saharan Studies, University of Maiduguri, 1991.

Siollun, Max. *What Britain Did to Nigeria: A Short History of Conquest and Rule.* London: C. Hurst Publishers Limited, 2021.

Sirayi, Mzo. "Oral African Drama in South Africa: The Xhosa Indigenous Drama Forms." *South African Theatre Journal* 10, no. 1 (1996): 49–61.

Sklar, Richard L. *Nigerian Political Parties: Power in an Emergent African Nation.* Princeton: Princeton University Press, 2015

    "Unity or Regionalism: The Nationalities Question." In *Crafting the New Nigeria: Confronting the Challenges*, ed. Robert I. Rotberg. Boulder: Lynne Rienner Publishers, 2004, 39–59.

Slapper, Gary. *The English Legal System.* London: Cavendish Publishing, 2004.

Smaldone, Joseph P. *Warfare in the Sokoto Caliphate: Historical and Sociological Perspectives.* London: Cambridge University Press, 1977.

Smith, Abdullahi. "A Little New Light on the Collapse of the Alafinate of Yoruba." In *Studies in Yoruba History and Culture*, ed. Gabriel O. Olusanya. Ibadan: University Press, 1983, 42–71.

Smith, Anthony D. *Nationalism: Theory, Ideology, History.* Cambridge: Polity Press, 2010.

Smith, Linda Tuhiwai. *Decolonizing Methodologies: Research and Indigenous Peoples.* London: Zed Books, 2012.

Smith, Michael G. *Government in Kano, 1350–1950.* Boulder: Westview Press, 1997.

Smith, Robert Sydney. "The Alafin in Exile: A Study of the Igboho Period in Oyo History." *The Journal of African History* 6, no. 1 (1965): 57–77.

    Kingdoms of the Yoruba. Madison: The University of Wisconsin Press, 1988.

    The Lagos Consulate, 1851–1861. Berkeley: University of California Press, 1979.

    "The Lagos Consulate, 1851–1861: An Outline." *The Journal of African History* 15, no. 3 (1974): 393–416.

    "Nigeria-Ijebu." In *West African Resistance: The Military Response to Colonial Occupation*, ed. Michael Crowder. London: Hutchinson & Co., 1971, 175–184.

Snyder, Louis L. *The Meaning of Nationalism.* New York: Greenwood Press, 1968.

Sofola, Jafotito A. *African Culture and the African Personality.* Ibadan: African Resources Publ. Co., 1973.

Soll, Jacob. *The Information Master: Jean-Baptiste Colbert's Secret State Intelligence System.* Ann Arbor: University of Michigan Press, 2009.

Solomon, Amodu O. "National Archives Ibadan and Archival Management in Nigeria: Challenges and Prospects." *Kashere Journal of Humanities, Management and Social Sciences* 3, no. 2 (2019): 47–62.

Somervell, David C. *The British Empire.* London: Christophers, 1945.

Somotan, Halimat T. "Lagos Women in Colonial History: A Biographical Sketch of Alimotu Pelewura." *Vestiges: Traces of Record* 4 (2018): 72–74.

Southern, Eileen. "Conversation with Fela Sowande, High Priest of Music." *The Black Perspective in Music* 4, no. 1 (1976): 90–104.

Sowoolu, S. O. "The Problem of Archival Development in Nigeria." Paper Presented at the Seminar for Directors of Archival Institutions from Developing Countries, Moscow, August 28–September 5, 1972.

Soyinka, Wole. *Ake: The Years of Childhood*. New York: Random House, 1981.
St. Jorre, John de. *The Nigerian Civil War*. London: Hodder and Stoughton Publishers, 1972.
Stein, Robert L. *The French Slave Trade in the Eighteenth Century: An Old Regime Business*. Madison: University of Wisconsin Press, 1979.
Stenning, Derrick J. "Transhumance, Migratory Drift, Migration: Patterns of Pastoral Fulani Nomadism." *The Journal of the Royal Anthropological Institute of Great Britain and Ireland* 87, no. 1 (1957): 57–73.
Stewart, Marjorie H. "The Borgu People of Nigeria and Benin: The Disruptive Effect of Partition on Traditional Political and Economic Relations." *Journal of the Historical Society of Nigeria* 12, no. 3/4 (1985): 95–120.
Stock, Robert. "Health Care for Some: A Nigerian Study of Who Gets What, Where and Why?" *International Journal of Health Services* 15, no. 3 (1985): 469–484.
Stoler, Ann L. *Along the Archival Grain: Epistemic Anxieties and Colonial Common Sense*. New Jersey: Princeton University Press, 2010.
Strang, David. "Contested Sovereignty: The Social Construction of Colonial Imperialism." In *State Sovereignty as Social Construct*, ed. Thomas J. Biersteker and Cynthia Weber. Cambridge: Cambridge University Press, 1996, 22–49.
Strayer, Joseph R. "The State and Religion: An Exploratory Comparison in Different Cultures." *Comparative Studies in Society and History* 1, no. 1 (1958): 38–43.
———. "The State and Religion: Greece and Rome, the West, Islam." In *The Decline of Empires*, ed. Samuel. N. Eisenstadt. Englewood Cliffs: Prentice-Hall, 1967, 129.
Strikler, V. J., and R. Davies. "Political Party Conventions." In *International Encyclopedia of Government and Politics*, ed. Frank N. Magill. London: Fitzroy Dearborn Publishers, 1996.
Strohn, Matthias, ed. *The Long Shadow of World War II: The Legacy of the War and its Impact on Political and Military Thinking since 1945*. Oxford: Casemate Publishers, 2021.
Sulaiman, Folasade R. "Internationalization in Education: The British Colonial Policies on Education in Nigeria 1882–1926." *Journal of Sociological Research* 3, no. 2 (2012): 84–101.
Sulaiman, Ibraheem. *A Revolution in History: The Jihad of Usman Dan Fodio*. London: Mansell Publishing, 1987.
Sundkler, Bengt, and Christopher Steed. *A History of the Church in Africa*. Cambridge: Cambridge University Press, 2000.
Suret-Canale, J. "Les Sociétés Traditionnelles En Afrique Noire ET Le Concept De Mode De Production Asiatique'." *La Pensée* no. 117 (1964): 19–42.
Suret-Canale, Jean, and Albert Adu Boahen. "West Africa 1945–60." In *Africa Since 1935*, ed. Ali A. Mazrui and C. Wondji. Paris: UNESCO Publishing, 1999, 161–191.

Sweet, David W. "The Baltic in British Diplomacy before the First World War." *The Historical Journal* 13, no. 3 (1970): 451–490.
Sydow, Eckart Von. "Ancient and Modern Art in Benin City." *Africa: Journal of the International African Institute* 11, no. 1 (1938): 55–62.
Taiwo, Cornelius Olaleye. *The Nigerian Education System, Past, Present and Future*. Lagos: Thomas Nelson Nigeria Limited, 1980.
Tamuno, Tekena N. "British Colonial Administration in Nigeria in the Twentieth Century." In *Groundwork of Nigerian History*, ed. Obaro Ikime. Ibadan: Heinemann Educational Books, 1980, 393–409.
  The Evolution of the Nigerian State: The Southern Phase, 1898–1914. London: Longman, 1972.
  "Governor Clifford and Representative Government." *Journal of the Historical Society of Nigeria* 4, no. 1 (1967): 117–124.
  "Introduction: The Search for Viable Policies." In *Nigeria Since Independence: The First Twenty-Five Years. Vol. IV: Government and Public Policy*, ed. Tekena Tamuno and Jospeh A. Atanda. Ibadan: Heinemann Educational Books Ltd., 1989, 3.
  Herbert Macaulay, Nigerian Patriot. London: Heinemann Educational, 1976.
  "Nigeria Federalism in Historical Perspective." In *Federalism and Political Restructuring in Nigeria*, ed. Adigun Agbaje, Rotimi Suberu, and G. Herault (Ibadan: Spectrum Books Ltd., 1998), 13–33.
Tar, Usman A. "Organised Labor and Democratic Struggles in Nigeria." *Information, Society and Justice Journal* 2, no. 2 (2009): 165–181.
Tarus, Isaac. "A History of the Direct Taxation of the African Peoples of Kenya, 1895–1973." Unpublished PhD dissertation. Rhodes University, Grahamstown, 2004.
Taylor, Lou. *Establishing Dress History*. Manchester: Manchester University Press, 2004.
Taylor, William H. *Mission to Educate: A History of the Educational Work of the Scottish Presbyterian Mission in East Nigeria 1846–1960*. Leiden: E. J. Brill, 1996.
Tella, Charas Madu, Ahmed Wali Doho, and Aliyu Bapeto. "The Evolution, Development and Practice of Federalism in Nigeria." *Public Policy and Administration Review* 2, no. 4 (2014): 51–66.
Temperley, Howard. *White Dreams, Black Africa: The Antislavery Expeditions to the River Niger 1841–1842*. New Haven: Yale University Press, 1991.
Teriba, Adedoyin. "A Return to the Motherland: Afro-Brazilians' Architecture and Societal Aims in Colonial West Africa." In *Design Dispersed: Forms of Migration and Flight*, ed. Burcu Dogramaci and Kerstin Pinther. Bielefeld: transcript Verlag, 2019, 232–247.
Teriba, O., E. C. Edosien, and M. O. Kayode. *The Structure of Manufacturing Industry in Nigeria*. Ibadan: University of Ibadan Press, 1981.
Thackeray, Frank W., and John E. Findling, ed. *Events That Changed the World in the Eighteenth Century*. Santa Barbara: ABC-CLIO, 1998.
Theimer, Kate. "Archives in Context and as Context." *Journal of Digital Humanities* 1, no. 2 (2012): 1–2.

Thiaw, Ibrahima, and Deborah L. Mack. "Atlantic Slavery and the Making of the Modern World: Experiences, Representations, and Legacies." *Current Anthropology* 61, no. S22 (2020): 145–158.
Thiong'o, Ngugi wa. *Decolonising the Mind: The Politics of Language in African Literature*. Harare: Zimbabwe Publishing House, 1981.
Thomas, Lindon. "Oriki Orisa: The Yoruba Prayer of Praise." *Journal of Religion in Africa* 20, no. 2 (1990): 205–224.
Thomas, Martin, ed. *The French Colonial Mind: Mental Maps of Empire and Colonial Encounters*. Lincoln: University of Nebraska Press, 2011.
Thurston, Alexander. "Islamic Modernism and Colonial Education in Northern Nigeria: Na'ibi Sulaiman Wali (1927–2013)." *Religion & Education* 44, no. 1 (2017): 101–117.
Tibenderana, Peter K. "The Administration of Sokoto, Gwandu and Argungu Emirates under British Rule, 1900–1946." Unpublished PhD dissertation. University of Ibadan, 1974.
"The Beginnings of Girls' Education in the Native Administration Schools in Northern Nigeria, 1930–1945." *The Journal of African History* 26, no. 1 (1985): 93–109.
"The Irony of Indirect Rule in Sokoto Emirate, Nigeria, 1903–1944." *African Studies Review* 31, no. 1 (1988): 67–92.
Tierney, Stephen. "Federalism in a Unitary State: A Paradox too Far?" *Regional & Federal Studies* 19, no. 2 (2009): 237–253.
Tignor, Robert L. *Capitalism and Nationalism at the End of Empire: State and Business in Decolonizing Egypt, Nigeria, and Kenya, 1945–1963*. Princeton: Princeton University Press, 2015.
Tomkins, Sandra M. "Colonial Administration in British Africa during the Influenza Epidemic of 1918–19." *Canadian Journal of African Studies* 28, no. 1 (1994): 60–83.
Torday, E. "Gazetteer of Ilorin Province." *Africa* 3, no. 3 (1930): 378.
Trent, John E., and Laura Schnurr. *A United Nations Renaissance: What the UN Is, and What It Could Be*. Opladen: Barbara Budrich Publishers, 2018.
Trevor-Roper, Hugh. "The Past and Present: History and Sociology." *Past and Present*, 42 (1969): 6.
"The Rise of Christian in Europe." *The Listener* 70, no. 1809 (1963): 871.
Triandis, Harry C., Xiao Ping Chen, and Darius K-S. Chan. "Scenarios for the Measurement of Collectivism and Individualism." *Journal of Cross-cultural Psychology* 29, no. 2 (1998): 275–289.
Tsevende, Richard A., Tim C. Agber, Don S. Iorngurun, and Nancy N. Ugbagir. *Tiv Swange Music and Dance*. Abuja: TimeXperts Publishing, 2013.
Tukur, Mahmud M. *British Colonisation of Northern Nigeria, 1897–1914: A Reinterpretation of Colonial Sources*. Dakar: Amalion Publishing, 2016.
Twitchett, Kenneth. "Colonialism: An Attempt at Understanding Imperial, Colonial and Neo-colonial Relationships." *Political Studies* 13, no. 3 (1965): 300–323.

Tylor, Edward Burnett. *Primitive Culture: Researches into the Development of Mythology, Philosophy, Religion, Art, and Custom.* Vol. 1. London: John Murray, 1871.

Tyodoo, Iyue. "Creativity in Ivom Performance among Tiv People and Lessons for Democratic Practice in Nigeria." In *Theatre, Creativity and Democratic Practice in Nigeria*, ed. Ameh Akoh, AbdulRasheed Adeoye, and Osita Ezenwanebe. Maiduguri: Society of Nigeria Theatre Artists, 2014, 13.

Ubah, C. N. "The British Occupation of the Sokoto Caliphate: The Military Dimension, 1897–1906." *Paideuma* 40 (1994): 81–97.

——— "Changing Patterns of Leadership among the Igbo, 1900 – 1960." *Transafrican Journal of History* 16 (1987): 167–184.

——— "Christian Missionary Penetration of the Nigerian Emirates, with Special Reference to the Medical Missions Approach." *Muslim World* 77, no. 1 (1987): 16–27.

——— "Problems of Christian Missionaries in the Muslim Emirates of Nigeria, 1900–1928." *Journal of African Studies* 3, no. 3 (1976): 351–371.

——— "Religious Change among the Igbo during the Colonial Period." *Journal of Religion in Africa* 18, no. 1 (1988): 71–91.

Ubaku, Kelechi C., Chikezie A. Emeh, and Chinenye N. Anyikwa. "Impact of Nationalist Movement on the Actualization of Nigerian Independence, 1914–1960." *International Journal of History and Philosophical Research* 2, no. 1 (2014): 54–67.

Ubi, Otu Abam. *Yakurr of the Middle Cross River Region (Nigeria)*. Lulu.com, 2019.

Uche, Chibuike U. "British Government, British Businesses, and the Indigenization Exercise in Post-Independence Nigeria." *The Business History Review* 86, no. 4 (2012): 745–771.

——— "Foreign Banks, Africans, and Credit in Colonial Nigeria, c.1890–1912." *The Economic History Review Series* 52, no. 4 (1999): 669–691.

Uche, Luke U. *Mass Media, People, and Politics in Nigeria.* New Delhi: Concept Publishing Company, 1989.

Uchendu, Egodi. "Evidence for Islam in Southeast Nigeria." *The Social Science Journal* 47, no. 1 (2010): 172–188.

Udo, Edet A. "The Missionary Scramble for Spheres of Influence in Eastern Nigeria, 1900–1952." *Ikenga: Journal of African Studies* 1, no. 2 (1972): 22–36.

Udo, Reuben K. *Geographical Regions of Nigeria.* Berkeley: University of California Press, 2020.

——— "Migration and Urbanization in Nigeria." In *Population Growth and Socio-economic Change in West Africa*, ed. John C. Caldwell. New York: Columbia University Press, 1975, 298–307.

Udoekanem, Namnso B., David O. Adoga, and Victor O. Onwumere. "Land Ownership in Nigeria: Historical Development, Current Issues and Future Expectations." *Journal of Environment and Earth Science* 4, no. 2 (2014): 182–187.

Udofia, O. E. "Nigerian Political Parties: Their Role in Modernizing the Political System, 1920–1966." *Journal of Black Studies* 11, no. 4 (1981): 435–447.

Udomisor, Israel W. "Management of Radio and Television Stations in Nigeria." *New Media and Mass Communication* 10 (2013): 2.

Uduma, Uduma Oji. "The Challenges of Ethnonationalism for the Nigerian State." *Journal of African studies and development* 5, no. 3 (2013): 33–40.

Ufot-Akpabio, Akpabio M., and Beulah I. Ofem. "Urbanization and Urban Development in Nigeria: A Perspective of Akwa Ibom State." *Journal of Agriculture, Environmental Resource Management* 4, no. 2 (2019): 369–383.

Ugboajah, Paul K. N. "Culture-Conflict and Delinquency: A Case Study of Colonial Lagos." *Eras Edition* 10 (2008): 1–24.

Uglagbe, Imuetinyan. "The Second Phase of Nigerian Constitution under the British Imperial Rules 1951–1959." *International Journal of Law* 4, no. 3 (2018): 27–30.

Ugobude, Franklin. "Orompoto, the First Female Alaafin of Oyo." *The Guardian*, December 15, 2019.

Ugwuja, Alex A., and Jude E. Onyishi. "Female Political Protests in Colonial and Post-colonial Nigeria: The Abeokuta Women's Revolt as a Framework, 1945–1999." *PREORC Journal of Gender and Sexuality Studies* 1 (2020): 52–78.

Ujo, Abdulhameed A. *Understanding Political Parties in Nigeria*. Kaduna: Klamidas Publishers, 2000.

Uka, Emele Mba. "Perspectives on Religion, Terrorism and Development – A Critical Review of Religion, Religious Freedom, Terrorism and Development in Contemporary Context of Boko-Haram Insurgency in Nigeria." *Contemporary Journal of Inter-Disciplinary Studies* 2, no. 2 (2015): 1–34.

Ukpabi, S. C. "The Beginning of the British Conquest of Northern Nigeria." *Bulletin de l'Institut Fondamental d'Afrique Noire* 35, no. 3 (1973): 593–613.

———. "The Origins of the West African Frontier Force." *Journal of the Historical Society of Nigeria* 3, no. 3 (1966): 485–501.

Ukpo, Ugbana. *Ethnic Minority Problems in Nigerian Politics*. Stockholm: LiberTryck AB, 1977.

Ukwandu, Damien, and Benjamin Obeghare Izu. "The Ugie Festival Ceremonies as a Demonstration of Ancient Benin Culture in Nigeria." *Archiv Orientální* 84, no. 2 (2021): 249–267.

Ukwu, C. A. "The Archives in Nigeria: Its Mission and Vision." *The Nigerian Archives* 2, no. 1 (1995): 1–44.

Umar, A. O. "The Origin, Development and Utilization of Arabic Manuscripts in the National Archives, Kaduna." Paper Presented at the 'Workshop on Exploring Nigeria's Arabic/Ajami Manuscript Resources for the Development of New Knowledge, held at Arewa House, Kaduna, Nigeria, May 7–8, 2009.

Umar, Muhammad Sani. "Muslims' Intellectual Responses to British Colonialism in Northern Nigeria, 1903–1945." Unpublished PhD dissertation. Northwestern University, 1997.

Urvoy, Par Y. *Histoire de l'Empire du Bornou*. Paris: Larose, 1949.
Usman, Abdulateef F., and Ahmed Bako. The Integration of Yoruba Migrant Community in Kano Emirate. Paper presented at the National conference of 200 years of Uthman Danfodio Jihad, Kano, July 27-29, 2003.
Usman, Aribidesi, and Toyin Falola. *The Yoruba from Prehistory to the Present*. Cambridge: Cambridge University Press, 2019.
Usman, Yusuf B. *The Transformation of Katsina, 1400-1883: The Emergence and Overthrow of the Sarauta System and Establishment of the Emirate*. Zaria: Ahmadu Bello University Press, 1981.
Usoro, Eno J. "Colonial Economic Development Strategy in Nigeria 1919-1939: An Appraisal." *The Nigerian Journal of Economic and Social Studies* 19, no. 1 (1977): 121-141.
 The Nigerian Oil Palm Industry: Government Policy and Export Production, 1906-1965. Ibadan: Ibadan University Press, 1974.
Usuanlele, Uyilawa, and Bonny Ibhawoh. "Introduction: Minorities and the National Question in Nigeria." In *Minority Rights and the National Question in Nigeria*, ed. Uyilawa Usuanlele and Bonny Ibhawoh. Cham: Palgrave Macmillan, 2017, 1-14.
 "Pawnship in Edo Society: From Benin Kingdom to Benin Province Under Colonial Rule." In *Pawnship, Slavery, and Colonialism in Africa*, ed. Paul E. Lovejoy and Toyin Falola. Trenton: Africa World Press, 2003, 232.
Utuk, Efiong I. "Britain's Colonial Administrations and Developments, 1861-1960: An Analysis of Britain's Colonial Administrations and Developments in Nigeria." Unpublished PhD dissertation. Portland State University, 1975.
Uwaezuoke, Obioha Precious. "Globalization and the Future of African Culture." *Philosophical Papers and Review* 2, no. 1 (2010): 1-8.
Uwaifo, Samuel Osaretin. "Ethnicity and Development of Political Parties in Nigeria." *Ethnicity* 28 (2016): 1-9.
Uwem, Jonah Akpan, and Susan Ikwo Iseyin. "Urbanization in the Lower Cross River Region: 1882-1960." *Journal of History and Diplomatic Studies* 6 (2019): 1-23.
Uyanga, Joseph T. *Towards a Nigerian National Urban Policy*. Ibadan: Ibadan University Press, 1982.
Uzoigwe, Godfrey N. *Britain and the Conquest of Africa: The Age of Salisbury*. Ann Arbor: University of Michigan Press, 1974.
 "Evolution and Relevance of Autonomous Communities in Precolonial Igboland." *Journal of Third World Studies* 21, no. 1 (2004): 139-150.
 "The Niger Committee of 1898: Lord Selbourn's Report." *Journal of the Historical Society of Nigeria* 4, no. 3 (1968): 467-476.
Vaaseh, Godwin A., and Omolere M. Ehinmore. "Ethnic Politics and Conflicts in Nigeria's First Republic: The Misuse of Native Administrative Police Forces (NAPFS) and the Tiv Riots of Central Nigeria, 1960-1964." *Canadian Social Science* 7, no. 3 (2011): 214-222.
Vandervort, Bruce. *Wars of Imperial Conquest*. London: Routledge, 1998, 189-191.

Vansina, Jan M. *Oral Tradition as History*. Oxford: James Currey, 1985.
Vansina, Jan, Hope M. Wright, Selma Leydesdorff, and Elizabeth Tonkin. *Oral Tradition: A Study in Historical Methodology*. New York: Routledge, 2017.
Vassilakaki, Evgenia, and Valentini Moniarou-Papaconstantinou. "Beyond Preservation: Investigating the Roles of Archivist." *Library Review* 66, no. 3 (2017): 110–126.
Vaughan, Olufemi. "Ethno-Regionalism and the Origins of Federalism in Nigeria." In *Democracy and Prebendalism in Nigeria: Critical Interpretations*, ed. Wale Adebanwi and Ebenezar Obadare. New York: Palgrave Macmillan, 2013, 227–242.
Nigerian Chiefs: Traditional Power in Modern Politics, 1890s–1990s. Rochester: University of Rochester Press, 2006.
Religion and the Making of Nigeria. Durham: Duke University Press, 2017.
Veal, Michael E. *Fela: Life and Times of an African Musical Icon*. Philadelphia: Temple University Press, 2000.
Vengadasalam, Sarbani Sen. *New Postcolonial Dialectics: An Intercultural Comparison of Indian and Nigerian English Plays*. Newcastle upon Tyne: Cambridge Scholars Publisher, 2019.
Verger, Pierre. "Oral Tradition in the Cult of the Orishas and Its Connection with the History of the Yoruba." *Journal of the Historical Society of Nigeria* 1, no. 1 (1956): 61–63.
Vidal, Tunji. *The Institutionalization of Western Music Culture in Nigeria and the Search for National Identity*. Ile-Ife: Obafemi Awolowo University Press, 2002.
Villa, Juan C., Maria Boile, and Sotirios Theofanis. *International Trade and Transportation Infrastructure Development: Experiences in North America and Europe*. Amsterdam: Elsevier, 2020.
Vlach, John Michael. "Affecting Architecture of the Yoruba." *African Arts* 10, no. 1 (1976): 48–55.
Vries, Jan De. "The Industrial Revolution and the Industrious Revolution." *The Journal of Economic History* 54, no. 2 (1994): 249–270.
Wach, Joachim. *The Comparative Study of Religions*. New York: Columbia University Press, 1958.
Wada, Muhammad. "The Spread and Impact of the Great Influenza Pandemic in Kano Emirate, Northern Nigeria 1918–1920." *Humanus Discourse* 1, no. 4 (2021): 1–15.
Walecki, Marcin. "Political Money and Corruption: Limiting Corruption in Political Finance." In *Money and Politics in Nigeria*, ed. Victor Adetula. Abuja: International Foundation for Electoral Systems, 2008.
Walker, Frank D. *The Romans of the Black River: The Story of the CMS Nigeria Mission*. London: CMS, 1931.
Walkowitz, Judith R. *Prostitution and Victorian Society: Women, Class, and the State*. Cambridge: Cambridge University Press, 1980.

Wall, A. F. "Crowther, Samuel Ajayi: 1807–1891." *International Bulletin of Missionary Research* 16, no. 1 (1992): 15–21.

Walsh, William H. *An Introduction to Philosophy of History.* London: Hutchinson, 1967.

Waniko, S. S. *Arrangement and Classification of Nigerian Archives.* Lagos: Nigerian Archives Services, 1958.

Warren, W. M. "Urban Real Wages and the Nigerian Trade Union Movement, 1939–60: Rejoinder." *Economic Development and Cultural Change* 17, no. 4 (1969): 618–633.

Waterman, Christopher Alan. *Juju: A Social History and Ethnography of an African Popular.* Chicago: University of Chicago Press, 1990.

Watt, Michael. *Silent Violence: Food, Famine and Peasantry in Northern Nigeria.* London: Berkley 1983.

Watt, Robert, and Francis Johns. *Concise Legal Research.* Annandale: Federation Press, 2009.

Wayne, Jack. "Capitalism and Colonialism in Late Nineteenth Century Europe." *Studies in Political Economy* 5, no. 1 (1981): 79–106.

Webb, Sidney, and Beatrice Webb. *The History of Trade Unionism.* London: Longmans, Green and Co., 1896.

Webster, John B., and Albert A. Boahen. *The Revolutionary Years: West Africa Since 1800.* London: Longman, 1967.

Welsh-Asante, Kariamu. *Zimbabwe Dance: Rhythmic Forces, Ancestral Voices: An Aesthetic Analysis.* Trenton: Africa World Press, 2000.

West, Francis. Review of Oral Tradition: A Study in Historical Methodology." *History and Theory* 5, no. 3 (1966): 348–352.

White, Jeremy J. *Central Administration in Nigeria, 1914–1948.* Dublin: Irish Academy Press, 1981.

Whitehead, Clive. "Education in British Colonial Dependencies, 1919–39: A Re-Appraisal." *Comparative Education* 17, no. 1 (1981): 71–80.

Whiteman, Kaye. *Lagos: A Cultural and Literary History.* Oxford: Signal Books Limited, 2012.

Wiener, Martin J. *An Empire on Trial: Race, Murder, and Justice Under British Rule, 1870–1935.* New York: Cambridge University Press, 2009.

Wilkie, A. W., and J. K. Macgregor. "Industrial Training in Africa." *International Review of Mission* 3, no. 4 (1914): 742–747.

William, Idowu. "Ethnicity, Ethnicism and Citizenship: A Philosophical Reflection on the African Experience." *Journal of Social Sciences* 8, no. 1 (2004): 45–58.

Williams, Eric. *Capitalism and Slavery.* North Carolina: University of North Carolina Press Books, 2021.

Williams, Luke. "Nigeria and the Great Influenza Pandemic of 1918–1919: A Conceptual Challenge for the History of Medicine." MA thesis, La Trobe University, 1989.

Wilmot, Patrick. *The Theory and Practice of Nationalism in Africa.* Lagos: Lantern Book, 1975.

Wilson-Haffenden, James R. "Ethnological Notes on the Kwottos of Toto (Panda) District, Keffi Division, Benue Province, Northern Nigeria." *Journal of the Royal African Society* 27, no. 108 (1928): 380-393.

Winnett, Ren, Rich Furman, Douglas Epps, and Greg Lamphear, eds. *Health Care Social Work: A Global Perspective*. Oxford: Oxford University Press, 2019.

Wobasi, O. O. "Traditional System of Government and Justice in Ikwerre." In *Studies in Ikwerre History and Culture*, ed. O. Nduka. Lagos, Nigeria: Kraft Books, 1993, 38-60.

Women In Nigeria. *Margaret Ekpo: A Political Biography*. Nigeria: Women in Nigeria, 1996.

Wrigley, Edward Anthony. *Energy and the English Industrial Revolution*. Cambridge: Cambridge University Press, 2010.

Wuam, Terhemba, and Victor Egwemi. *The 1914 Amalgamation and a Century of Nigerian Nationhood*. Lagos: Bahiti and Dalila Publishers, 2016.

Wyman-McCarthy, Matthew. "British Abolitionism and Global Empire in the Late 18th Century: A Historiographic Overview." *History Compass* 16, no. 10 (2018): 1-12.

Wyss, Marco. *Postcolonial Security: Britain, France, and West Africa's Cold War*. Oxford: Oxford University Press, 2021.

Yakubu, A. M. "The Demise of Indirect Rule in the Emirates of Northern Nigeria." In *Legitimacy and the State in Twentieth-Century Africa*, ed. Terence Ranger and Olufemi Vaughan. London: Palgrave Macmillan, 1993, 162-190.

Yakubu, Oboh M. "Arts, Crafts and Indigenous Industries in Nigeria." *Journal of Cultural Studies* 4, no. 1 (2002): 215-234.

Yakubu, Yahaya. "Ethnicity and Nationalism in Nigeria: The Paradox of Dual Identities." *International Journal of Recent Innovations in Academic Research* 3, no. 2 (2019): 25-29.

Yameogo, Souleymane. "Official Language, Ethnic Diversity and Industrialization in Africa: Language Policy Perspectives." Unpublished PhD dissertation. KDI School of Public Policy and Management, 2020.

Yandaki, Aminu I. *The State in Africa: A Critical Study in Historiography and Political Philosophy*. Zaria: Gaskiya Corporation, 2015.

Yearwood, Peter J. "The Expatriate Firms and the Colonial Economy of Nigeria in the First World War." *The Journal of Imperial and Commonwealth History* 26, no. 1 (1998): 49-71.

Yeld, Rachel E. "Islam and Social Stratification in Northern Nigeria." *The British Journal of Sociology* 11, no. 2 (1960): 112-128.

Zachernuk, Philip S. "African History and Imperial Culture in Colonial Nigerian Schools." *Journal of the International African Institute* 68, no. 4 (1998): 484-505.

Colonial Subjects: An African Intelligentsia and Atlantic Ideas. Charlottesville: University of Virginia Press, 2000.

Zehnle, Stephanie. *A Geography of Jihad: Sokoto Jihadism and the Islamic Frontier in West Africa*. Berlin: De Gruyter, 2020.

Zeleza, Paul T. "Reckoning with the Past and Reimagining the Futures of African Studies for the 21st Century." Africa Peacebuilding Network Lecture Series No. 4. Keynote Address at the Social Science Research Council Training Workshop, United States International University–Africa, Nairobi, January 7, 2019, 7–8.

———. "The Political Economy of British Colonial Development and Welfare in Africa." *Transafrican Journal of History* 14 (1985): 139–161.

Zitnak, David. "Imagining the Nigerian Nation through the West African Pilot 1960–1966." MA thesis, The University of Louisville, 2016.

Zohra, Melki Fatima. "The Partition of West Africa, with Reference to the British Colonies up to 1914." *Dirassat* 2, no. 1 (2013): 169–183.

INDEX

1494 Treaty of Tordesillas, 120
1817 Muslim uprising, 56
1901 Slave Proclamation, 153
1903 Roads and Creeks Proclamation, 154
1904 Land Revenue Proclamation, 274
1911 Lepers Proclamation, 384
1922 Clifford Constitution, 32, 465, 513, 534, 542
1926 Phelps–Stokes Commission, 281
1946 Richards Constitution, 32, 42, 408, 516–517, 541, 543–544, 552

Aba Township Women's Association, 344
Aba Women's War of 1929, 32, 228, 319, 332
Abayomi, Oyinkan, 344, 527, 529
Abeewala, Ooni, 63
Abeokuta, 7, 20, 27, 50, 61–62, 65, 70, 84, 89–91, 96, 101, 109, 118, 126, 131, 150, 155, 188–191, 201–202, 242, 263, 277, 284, 287, 290, 313, 337–339, 341–342, 358, 360, 362–363, 372–373, 379, 386, 399, 407, 410, 412, 419, 426, 428, 442, 484
Abeokuta Grammar School, 290, 342
Abeokuta Women's Union, 131, 339, 341–342
Abiodun, S.M., 20, 59–60, 365, 463
Aboh, 111, 259
Abolition Act, 112–114, 121–122
Achebe, Chinua, 401
Adamu, Mahdi, 78, 148
Adedeji, Joel, 438–440, 591

Adeleye, Rowland A., 13
Afigbo, Adiele, 137, 148, 154, 227, 240, 248, 259, 296, 323, 333–334, 337
Afikpo people, 390
Afolayan, Kunle, 22
Afonja, 59–61, 90–91
African Banking Corporation, 81
African Christianity, 94
African Church, 94, 365, 438–439
African Continental Bank, 15
African Steam Navigation Company, 81, 262
African World, 270
Africanism, 25, 462, 470
AG (Action Group), 212, 489–492, 516–517
Agbebi, Mojola, 94, 125
Age of Atlanticism, 255
Ajasa, Chief Kitoye, 301, 529
Ajayi, Jacob F. Ade, 10–11, 13, 50, 93–94, 197, 214, 255, 277, 280, 286, 296, 298, 300, 354, 360
Ajisafe, Ajayi K., 336, 338, 439
Akenzua II, Omonoba, 476
Akinsanya, Samuel, 207, 210, 514, 515, 563
Akinsemoyin, 101–103, 105–107
Akintola, Ladoke, 526
Akinyele, I. B., 439
Akitoye, King, 9, 27–28, 64, 91–92, 113–114, 116, 123, 145, 148, 222
Akoko, 51, 63, 236
Akure, 7, 51, 180
Alaafin, 29, 31, 52, 59–61, 103, 189, 220, 226–227, 232, 304, 329, 350, 352
Alaafin of Oyo, 21, 29, 352

683

Aladura Movement, 439–440
Alagoa, Ebiegberi J., 12–13
Alake, 150, 187–189, 229, 336, 338, 340, 342, 484
Alakija, Adeyemo, 464, 469
ALC (Abeokuta Ladies Club), 339
Algeria, 216, 476
Alimi, 60–61, 451
Allada, 98
Alladah, 100, 103
Allah, Abd, 19
Allied Powers, 474–475, 477–478, 482, 536
Aloma, Mai Idris, 19
al-Qadi, Abd, 54
Amakiri of Kalabari, 29
Amala, 221
Amankulor, J. Ndukaku, 436–437
American Colonization Society, 78
AMORC (Rosicrucian), 366
Amu, Ephrain, 430
Anderson, John, 532
Anene, Joseph C., 13
Anglo-Aro War, 30
Angola, 216
Anikulapo-Kuti, Fela, 432
antislavery, 26, 109, 113, 132
Apa, 101, 103
Araba, Speedy, 402
Archer, Leonard, 469
Aro, 21, 30, 68, 138, 141, 231, 241, 248–249, 333
Asiku, J.U., 276
Asipa, 100, 105
Asquith Commission, 282, 585
ASUU (Academic Staff Union of Universities), 509
Attah of Idah, 51
Attahiru II, Muhammad, 224
Australia, 130, 249
AWAM (Association of West African Merchants), 207
Awolowo, Chief Obafemi, 179, 207, 212, 402, 490, 502–503, 505, 509, 515–517, 523, 526–528, 540, 542, 557, 563–564
Awori, 101
Ayandele, Emmanuel A., 13, 78, 90, 92, 296, 465

Azikiwe, Nnamdi, 15–17, 42, 179, 212, 316, 463, 469–470, 488–490, 503, 506, 509, 515–516, 523–525, 527–528, 539, 557, 564

Badagry, 27, 70, 84, 89–90, 98–101, 103, 107, 111, 117, 263, 348, 360, 362, 372, 377, 426, 428, 584
Baháʼí Faith, 366
Baituma Native Treasury, 225
Bale, 31, 226
Balewa, Tafawa, 43, 491, 527, 539, 564
Banfield, A. W., 93
Barabara, Arinmokunrin, 189
Bargoy, G. P., 93
Bariba, 83, 220
Bariba merchants, 83
Barkin-Ladi area, 378
Baro–Kano rail lines, 36
Barrow, Richard, 469
Bauchi, 37, 139, 180, 260
BBC (British Broadcasting Corporation), 429–430
BCS (Brotherhood of the Cross and Star), 366–367
Beecroft, John, 27–28, 66, 115, 123, 148, 222, 236
Beier, Ulli, 443
Belgium, 126, 174, 181, 269
Bello, Muhammad, 19, 38, 57, 160, 401, 491, 516, 527–529, 539, 557, 563–564
BELRA (British Empire Leprosy Relief Association), 383–384
Benin, 7, 27, 49–50, 52–53, 59, 64, 66, 68, 73, 78, 82–83, 87–88, 90, 98–101, 103–117, 121, 123, 126, 130, 133, 137, 140, 147–148, 152–153, 157, 159–161, 163, 180, 205, 209, 236, 238, 241, 277, 285, 304, 312, 318, 359, 372, 392–393, 476, 482, 507, 559, 561
Benson, Bobby, 432, 435–436, 449
Benue–Niger, 130, 134
Berlin Conference, 27, 175, 236–237, 512, 541
Biafra, 27, 66, 83, 98, 100, 103, 106, 108, 110, 115–116, 123, 126, 137, 145,

147–148, 152–153, 157, 236, 238, 285, 358
Bida Emirate, 133–134
Bight of Benin, 83, 100, 103, 107, 113, 115, 126, 148, 152, 236
Biobaku, S. O., 10, 13
Bonny, 9, 29, 64, 70, 72–74, 78, 81–82, 84, 93, 95, 114, 125, 145, 148, 236, 290, 300–301
Borgu, 52, 104, 200, 223
Borno, 19, 21, 50, 52, 55–57, 65, 74, 94, 104, 127, 219, 223, 313, 357
Bourdillon, Bernard, 210, 213, 408, 482–483, 516, 543, 546, 552
Boutillier, Jean-Louis, 13
Bowen, Thomas Jefferson, 325
Boyd, Alan Lennox, 43
Brazil, 67, 70, 76–77, 84, 86, 425, 449, 590
Britain, 9–10, 14, 26, 28, 30, 34, 38–40, 69, 75, 77–78, 82, 85, 88, 91, 97, 112–113, 115–117, 123, 126, 137, 143, 148–149, 156, 174–175, 204, 206, 211, 215, 222, 250, 265, 268, 271–272, 275, 286, 289, 292, 295, 306, 308, 311, 376, 411, 415, 427, 442, 461–463, 473–483, 485–488, 492, 494, 496–497, 500–501, 512, 519, 530–531, 533, 536, 544, 574, 576, 580, 583–584, 586, 588, 590
British & Foreign Bible Society, 93, 487
British Chambers of Commerce, 266, 268
British colonial administration, 5, 25, 36, 40, 216, 226, 248, 251, 306, 311, 407, 464, 472, 508, 531, 573, 575, 583
British colonial government, 25, 27, 29, 114, 139, 142, 189, 193, 205, 252, 277, 322, 355, 383, 387, 399, 459, 469, 486, 499–502, 505, 523–524, 532, 589
British colonial rule, xiii, 120, 317, 480, 574–575
British Empire, 26–27, 30, 38, 40, 77, 81, 88, 91, 114–115, 127, 133, 185, 211, 226, 237, 264, 266, 378, 383, 469, 479–481, 486, 506, 525, 575–576, 589
British House of Commons, 269

British imperialists, 25, 503, 530, 533
British West African colony, 84, 206, 250, 273, 501, 513
Burdon, A., 223
Burke, Edmund, 510
Burundi, 216
BWAEGC (British West Africa Educated Girl's Club), 345

CMS (Church Missionary Society), 278–279, 293
Calabar, 7, 64, 70, 72–74, 78, 82, 90, 93, 95, 114, 124, 129, 153, 159, 179–180, 182, 190, 236, 244, 284, 287, 311, 343, 357, 360, 366–367, 376, 379, 407, 409–413, 417, 419, 431, 461, 515, 534, 542, 561, 582
Callaway, Hellen, 246
Cameroon, 42, 420
Campbell, Benjamin, 116
Campbell, James G., 316, 463, 471
Canada, 269, 431
Caretaker Committee of the Urban District Council, 344
Caribbean, 75–76, 86, 104, 131, 149, 174, 367, 425, 436
Carnegie, D.W., 223
Carr, Henry, 280, 292, 302
Carter, Sir Gilbert Thomas, 29
Catholicism, 87, 372
Cavendish-Bentinck, Henry, 266
Chamberlain, Joseph, 195
China, 379, 545
Chokor, Boyowa, 405
Christian marriage, 307, 319
Christian missionaries, 25, 27, 37–38, 44, 55, 65–66, 70, 72, 75–76, 114, 116, 129, 131, 149, 239, 284, 295, 299, 306, 308, 315–319, 330, 360–363, 367, 369, 371–375, 377, 382, 384–385, 387, 426, 462, 578
Christian Science Monitor, 272
Christianity, xiv, 27, 37, 75, 87–88, 94–95, 97, 235, 257, 277, 291, 295, 307–308, 314, 319, 348, 350–355, 357–364, 367, 369–370, 377, 381, 401, 404, 424, 427, 438, 440, 445, 462, 511, 575, 578, 584
Christianization, 87, 367

Chuku, Gloria, 110
Chukwu, Aro, 231
Church of Scotland, 90, 360, 373, 385
Churchill, Winston, 479, 488
Civil law, 239
Civil Service British Workers' Union, 497–501, 503, 505
Clapperton, Hugh, 325, 349
Clarke, William F., 325
Clifford Constitution, 252, 320, 461, 465, 512, 515–516, 536, 542
Clifford, Hugh, 178, 309, 408, 513, 527, 534
CMS (Anglican Church Missionary Society), 90, 94, 211, 354, 360–361, 363–364, 386, 584
Coates, Oliver, 485
Cole, Abayomi, 292
Colonial Judicial Service, 243
Colonial Law Validation Act of 1865, 232
Colonial Office, 5–6, 8, 14, 16, 136, 156–158, 182, 184–185, 203, 206, 210, 235, 264, 269–272, 294, 301, 531–532, 540, 543
colonialism, 8, 11–12, 17, 26, 30–31, 36, 40, 44, 47, 50, 190, 217–218, 220, 223, 228, 303, 305–307, 311, 314, 321–325, 327, 330–332, 340, 349–351, 354, 375, 383, 396–397, 399, 402, 412, 415–416, 419, 424, 427, 433–434, 437, 440, 444–446, 448, 450, 457, 459–462, 467, 474–475, 495, 498, 510, 519, 522, 526, 530, 535, 550, 557, 559–560, 562, 573–574, 576–581, 583–584, 587, 589–592
colonization, xiii, 4, 8–9, 27, 87, 97, 101, 122, 125, 133, 135, 140–141, 149, 152, 162, 175, 183, 213, 222, 239, 323, 398–400, 403–404, 461–462, 512, 530, 575, 580
Committee on Development of Empire Resources, 269
Committee on Edible and Oil Producing Nuts and Seeds, 269, 272
Commonwealth of Nations, 249–250, 589
Conservative Party/ Whigs, 479, 511

Council of Elders, 222, 350
Court of the Alaafin, 227
Crown law, 239–241
Crowther, Samuel Ajayi, 93–94, 277, 296, 300, 354, 360
Cuba, 77, 86, 449
Cumming, H., 223
Curtin, Philip, 12

Dahomey, 82–84, 90, 91, 98, 99, 128
Dairo, Isaiah K., 403
Daniel, Ojoge, 402
Dappo, Prince, 29
Davies, Hezekiah O., 212, 514
decolonization, 17, 195, 197, 212, 214, 301, 325, 340, 436, 457, 463–464, 470, 472–473, 475, 478, 480, 486–489, 511, 513, 522, 524–526, 535, 540, 546, 553, 556, 560, 562–564, 589–590
Dempster, Elder, 191–192, 207, 250, 261
Denmark, 512
Dike, Kenneth, 6–11, 13–14, 23, 34, 50, 148, 197, 298
Doherty, Theophilus A., 208
Du Bois, W. E. B., 470

Earl of Selbourne, 222
East Indies, 216
Eastern House of Assembly, 344
Eastern Nigerian Guardian, 526, 528
Eborka, Kennedy, 405
Edewor, Patrick, 405
Edo, 218, 348, 371, 392–393
Edun, Adegboyega, 65, 188, 229
Egba, 27, 50, 62, 65, 89–91, 100–101, 109, 150, 155, 188–189, 229, 242, 319–320, 324, 336–339, 341, 362, 460, 467
Egbaland, 229, 337, 339, 362, 467
Egerton, Governor, 37, 158, 162
Egypt, 133, 357, 440, 476
Eje, Abutu, 20
Ekiti, 31, 49, 63, 100, 226, 260, 380, 443
Ekitiparapo War, 148
Eko, 111, 413, 447
Ekoli, Enerst, 514
Ekpo, Margaret, 343

Elder Dempster Shipping Company, 192, 207
Elliot Commission, 585
Emeruwa, Mark, 334
Emir of Kano, 383
Enugu, 7, 36, 159, 180–181, 313, 316, 356–357, 377, 407, 409–410, 413, 415–417, 419–420, 422, 507–508
Epe, 28–29, 111, 116, 123, 134
Ethiopia, 476, 481
Etsu Masaba, 58
Euba, W. B., 463
EUG (Egba United Government), 338

Fafunwa, Babs, 277
Fajana, Ade, 281
Falola, Toyin, 298, 422
Federalism, xv, 540, 550–551
Fieldhouse, David, 149
FNWS (Federation of Nigerian Women's Societies), 343
Fodio, Usman Dan, 19, 21, 35, 51–59, 61, 219, 232, 304, 348, 352, 355
Fombina, 57
Foreign Board of London, 96
France, 77, 88, 90, 95, 112, 115, 127, 134, 174–175, 265, 429, 442, 457, 474, 478–479, 481, 511–512, 576
Freedman, Thomas Birch, 276, 362
French Constitution, 512
French Revolution, 88, 512
Fulani, 18, 21, 48, 54, 59–61, 64, 79, 90, 134, 147, 155, 159, 355, 395, 557–558, 560, 577
Furtuwa, Ahmad B., 19
Futa Jallon region, 54

Gaha, Basorun, 59, 220
Gambia, 222, 278, 285, 471, 496
Garvey, Marcus, 463, 470, 489
Gbadamosi, Gbadebo O., 279
Geertz, Clifford, 207
Germany, 84, 120, 127, 174–175, 272, 474–475, 477, 479, 483, 512
Ghana, 42, 203, 206, 209, 211, 278, 367, 381, 431, 441–442, 467, 471, 488
Glover Memorial Hall, 439
Gobir, 54, 56, 58, 69

Gold Coast, 39, 67, 85, 118, 206, 222, 261, 266, 278, 288–289, 296, 379, 381, 431, 467, 471
Goldie, George Taubman, 30, 33, 126, 133–134, 136–138, 145, 237–238
Goldsmith, Herbert Symonds, 177
GRAs (Government Reserved Areas), 408, 420
Great Depression, 184, 191, 199, 205, 207–208, 263
Gusau, 37, 313, 407, 410, 412–414
Guyer, Jane, 255
Gwam, Lloyd C., 7–8
Gwandu, 56, 61, 84, 133–134, 374

H1N1 virus, 378
Haiti, 76–77, 88
Hausa, 12, 21, 34, 48–50, 52, 54–56, 60–61, 63, 68–69, 78, 83–84, 86, 90, 94, 99–100, 110, 125, 132, 145, 154, 203, 218, 238, 262, 297, 309, 323, 329, 355, 370, 395, 398, 419–420, 435, 451, 557–558, 560, 577
Hausa women, 323
Hausaland, 55, 84, 107, 121
Hayford, J. Casely, 471
Hinderer, Anna, 325
Hitler, Adolf, 40
Hobsbawm, Eric J., 422
Hopkins, Anthony, 78
Howby, W. P., 223
Hudson, Butler, 495, 499–500
Hutchinson, T.J., 123
Hutton-Mills, Thomas, 471

Ibadan, 7, 11–13, 15, 23, 31, 36–37, 50, 61–63, 79, 84, 90, 93, 101, 110, 118, 132, 167, 180, 182, 190–191, 197, 202, 210, 214, 226, 242, 282, 301, 312, 316, 363, 379, 386, 398, 406–410, 412, 415, 419–420, 422, 430, 442–443, 445, 448, 455, 507, 526, 533, 585
Ibadan School of History, 11–13, 23, 197
Ibibio, 68, 150, 209, 218, 228, 231, 239, 241, 248, 312
Ibolo, 63

Ibrahim, Alhaji, 357
Idoma from Wukari, 51
Ife Kingdom, 318, 328
Igalaland, 58, 355
Igbo, 20, 30, 32, 35, 49, 51, 68, 79, 133, 138, 140, 150, 154, 186, 190, 199, 203, 218, 220–221, 227, 231, 239, 241, 256, 304–305, 312, 317, 320, 326–328, 333, 335, 337, 347–348, 350, 353–354, 356–357, 360–361, 370, 385, 390, 398, 405, 411, 419, 435–437, 451, 489–490, 557–558, 560
Igbo women, 79, 190, 320, 326–327, 337
Igboland, 68, 138, 141, 150, 152, 155, 158, 163–164, 237, 248, 257, 361, 436
Igbomina, 63, 190
Ijaiye, 61–62, 90
Ijaiye war, 62
Ijebu, 29, 61–62, 67, 90, 97, 99–101, 103, 110, 118, 127–128, 131–133, 147, 180, 188, 201–202, 268, 313, 319–320, 363, 434, 440, 459–460, 563
Ijebu Ode, 29, 377
Ijemo, 65, 96, 188–189, 229, 248
Ijo, 110, 150, 348, 389
Ikime, Obaro, 13, 30, 49, 213
Ikoku, Alvan, 527
Ikoli, Ernest, 212, 463, 469, 515, 527–528
Ikorodu, 111, 313
Ikosi, 111
Ile-Ife, 328
Ilorin, 7, 29, 36, 49–50, 52, 58, 60–63, 86, 91, 93, 110, 125, 127, 131, 134–136, 155, 180, 229–231, 236, 313, 358, 560
Imagbo War, 363
Imodu, Michael, 502, 505–507
India, 155, 216, 348, 372, 463, 479–480, 486, 538, 541, 564, 590
Indigenous systems, 317, 321, 343, 404, 512
indirect rule system, 31–32, 151–154, 157, 177, 190, 215–217, 222–225, 229–230, 232–234, 245, 332, 350, 358, 361, 363, 408, 466, 551, 553, 556, 581

Industrial Revolution, 33, 88, 305–306, 494–496, 498
International Maritime and Colonial Exhibition, 181
Ishola, Haruna, 403
Islam, xiv, 19, 21, 54–57, 60–61, 68–69, 77, 90, 92–93, 114, 160–161, 219, 279, 307, 319, 323, 329, 348, 351, 353–358, 367, 370, 373, 389, 395, 401, 577, 584
Islamic law, 239, 241, 323, 351
Islamization, 12, 356
Isoko, 190, 218
Italy, 174, 442, 479, 481
Itsekeri, 73, 93
Iwe Iroyin, 299, 315
Iwo Eleru, 218

Jackson, John Payne, 468
Jakin, 103
Japan, 250, 265, 289, 485
Jarmon, Charles, 405
Jayeola-Omoyeni, M.S, 281
Jebba, 134, 180, 230, 259–260, 313, 376
Jeffries, Sir Charles, 185
Jenkinson, Hilary, 6
Jeyifo, Biodun, 438, 444
Jihad, 31, 51, 53, 57–58, 60–62, 64, 69, 76–77, 84, 110, 130, 219, 232, 323, 329, 348, 350–352, 355
Jihadists, 56, 58–61, 64, 68, 86
Johnson, James, 94, 125, 281
Johnson, Samuel, 325
Johnston, H.H., 149
Jos, 7, 37, 180, 260, 356, 374, 376–378, 380, 407, 412, 442
Jukun, 50, 218

Kaduna, 7, 39, 159, 180, 260, 316, 356, 376, 407, 410, 412, 414–415, 419, 442
Kafanchan–Kaduna, 37
Kanem-Borno, 18, 348, 376
Kano, 19, 24, 36–37, 49, 52, 56, 58, 69, 78, 92, 95, 97, 104, 118, 129, 131, 134–136, 139, 180, 182, 202, 219, 223, 242, 268, 300, 309, 357, 364, 374, 377, 383, 406–407, 409–410, 412–416, 419–420, 422, 442, 482, 491, 516, 528–529, 539, 546, 559, 563

INDEX

Kano Chronicles, 19, 24
Kano civil war, 58
Katakamarbe, Mai Idris, 19
Katsina, 51–52, 56, 69, 79, 180, 300, 309, 357, 374
Kebbi, 56, 58
Kekere, Eletu, 107
Kemball, G.B., 223
Kenya, 43, 476, 499, 508
King James II, 511
King Leopold I, 126
King Nebuchadnezzar, 445
Kitoye Ajasa, Sir, 464
Klein, Martin, 11
Korieh, Chima, 405, 476
Kosoko, King, 9, 27–28, 64, 91–92, 109, 113, 116, 132, 222, 228, 522
Koton Karfe, 58
Kutere, Ologun, 102, 107, 109
Kuti, Erelu, 102
Kuti, Funmilayo Ransome, 336, 339, 341, 344, 484, 527
Kwara, 19, 304
Kyadiya, 134

L'Ouverture, Toussaint, 76
Labour party/Tories, 511
Ladipo, Duro, 41, 206, 432, 437, 443, 445–447
Lafiagi, 58
Lagos, x, xiv, 9, 16, 27–30, 33, 36–37, 39, 41, 64–66, 70, 74, 80–85, 91–92, 95, 99–118, 123, 126, 131–132, 134, 138, 142, 145, 147–148, 150, 155, 157–159, 163, 177–180, 187–189, 204, 207–211, 222, 226, 229, 236–237, 239, 242–244, 250–251, 256–257, 261, 263, 268, 270–271, 273–274, 277–278, 282, 284–285, 287, 290, 292–296, 299, 301, 306, 313, 315–316, 328, 338–340, 344–346, 357–358, 360, 363, 376–377, 379, 382, 399, 402, 406–410, 412–417, 419–422, 425–426, 428–429, 432, 434–435, 439–440, 442, 446–450, 461, 463–470, 472, 482, 487, 489, 496, 514–515, 519, 522–523, 526, 529, 531–532, 534, 537, 539, 542, 548, 566, 578–579, 582, 584, 587, 592
Lagos Daily News, 41, 316, 465, 467–469, 522, 526
Lagos Observer, 293, 316
Lagos Times, 467–468
Lagos Treaty of Cession in 1861, 222
Lagos Weekly Note Record, 270
Lagos Weekly Record, 290, 467–468, 472
Lagos Youth Movement, 41, 211, 345, 466, 514–515, 529
Lagos–Ibadan railway, 36
Laird, Macgregor, 10
Lake Chad, 48, 51, 74, 93, 134
Lake Chad basin, 48
Lander brothers, 9, 89, 137
Langford, Paul, 510
Las Palmas, 262
Law, Bonar, 264
Law, Robin, 105
Lawson, Rex, 432
League of Nations, 185, 195, 250, 478
legend of Ògún, 21
Leigh, J.S., 282
Leonard, A.G., 273
Leprosy, 383–385
Liberia, 78, 88, 125, 262, 284, 467
Libya, 476
Little Adra, 98
Little Popo, 103
Lokoja, ix, 58, 130, 135, 180, 230, 242, 353, 356, 376
Louis XIV, 457
LPC (Ladies Progressive Club), 345
Lucumi revolt, 86
Lugard, Frederick, 6, 10, 280
Lugard, Lord, 6, 31, 131, 136, 138, 143, 145, 148, 150, 155–156, 158–159, 162–163, 168, 177, 184–188, 190, 195, 214–217, 222–227, 239, 241, 259, 273–274, 280–281, 298–299, 304, 319, 322, 337, 351–352, 355, 364, 373, 376, 385, 408, 412, 415, 417, 468, 531–535, 540–542, 545, 548, 551–552, 582
Lugard's Native Authority system, 148
Lyttelton Constitution, 43
Lyttleton Constitution, 42, 539–541, 544–545, 553

Macaulay, Herbert, 41–42, 65, 177, 208, 309, 315, 442, 465, 468, 489, 514, 516, 522, 524, 527
Macaulay, Thomas, 40, 279
Macdonald, Sir Claude, 148
MacGregor, William, 226
Macpherson Constitution, 42, 490–492, 537–538, 540, 544
Macpherson, John, 537, 540
Madagascar, 476
Maghreb, 68, 97–98
Maharaja government, 372
Mahin, 111–112, 117
Maiduguri, 7, 180, 313
Maku, 111
Malaria, 375
Malayan Report on Nigeria, 14, 16
Male revolt, 78, 86
Mali, 54, 68, 348, 358
Mali Empire, 54
Maliki, Etsu, 134
Mamdani, 30, 85, 97, 203, 205, 239
Mann, Kristin, 100, 105
Mansergh, Nicholas, 475
Market Women's Association, 339–340
Marxism, 13, 306
Maximus, Pontifex, 219
Maybin, J.A.M., 6
Mazrui, Ali, 197
McCallum, Henry E., 226
Mecca, 21, 56
Mechanical Union, 498
Methodist Revolution in England, 88
Miller, Bala, 432
Miller, Thomas, 116
Minna, 104, 180, 313, 374
Minority Commission, 15, 43
Mirror, 316
Modakeke, 63
modernization, 247, 312
Moloney, Alfred, 413
Monogamy, 317
Moor, Governor, 36, 156, 161, 282
Moore, Barrington, 303
Morocco, 476
Mozambique, 216
Mulvey, Paul, 475, 479–480
Muslim Students Society, 358

Nana of Itshekiri, 458
National Council of Nigerian Citizens, 42, 212, 518, 520, 522, 524, 556
nationalism, ix, xv, 40–41, 177–178, 214, 281, 309, 378, 431–432, 436, 445, 447, 455–465, 469, 472, 480, 483, 485–489, 491–492, 503–504, 507–509, 511–512, 518, 521–530, 537, 540, 547, 549, 553–554, 556–558, 562–566
Native Authority Ordinance of 1916, 31, 224
Native Baptist Church, 94
Native Councils Ordinance of 1901, 31, 226
Native Court Ordinance of 1914, 225
Native Court Proclamation of 1906, 225
Native Revenue Ordinance, 162–163, 167, 182, 185, 193
Native Revenue Proclamation of 1906, 271
Nazi Germany, 478
Nazis, 476–477
NBN (National Bank of Nigeria), 208–209
NCBWA (National Congress for British West Africa), 41, 471, 512–513
NCNC (National Council of Nigerian Citizens), 42, 212, 344, 346, 489–492, 503, 506–509, 516–517, 524–526, 537, 564
NEPU (Northern Elements Progressive Union), 516–517
Netherlands, 174
Niger Basin, 52, 58, 63
Niger Coast Protectorate, 66, 117, 126, 161, 236, 256
Niger Delta, 9–12, 33, 106, 127, 158, 163–164, 194, 199, 256–257, 314, 366, 518, 561
Niger Expedition, 88–89
Niger River, 49, 58, 65, 69, 72, 74, 110–111, 130, 259, 295
Niger Valley, 10
Niger–Benue area, 122, 126
Nigeria
  British colonization of, 8

British colony, 9, 157
colonial, xiii, xv, 8, 14, 25, 332, 436, 476, 504, 521, 526, 548, 553, 558, 587
Eastern, 24, 32, 35–36, 40, 227, 231, 233, 320, 323, 384–385, 411
governance, 26, 541
Indigenous nations, 25
Nigeria's Civil Service British Workers' Union, 497
Nigerian Civil War, 8, 457
Nigerian Daily Times, 316, 476
Nigerian history, xiii, xvii, 11, 23–25, 196, 318, 393, 464, 474, 497, 500
Nigerian Motor Transport Union, 194
Nigerian National Archives, 4
Nigerian National Democratic Party, 41, 178, 251, 275, 315, 340, 464–466, 468, 472, 489, 514–515, 517, 522, 529
Nigerian Pioneer, 316
Nigerian Railway Worker Union, 194
Nigerian Tribune, 526
Nigerian Union of Railwaymen, 194
Nigerian Union of Teachers, 193, 343, 498, 502
Nigerian Women's Party, 339, 345, 529
Nigerian Youth Movement, 211, 251, 315, 345, 466
Nightingale, Tunde, 402
Niyas, Ibrahim, 357
NLC (Nigerian Labour Congress), 509
NNDP (Nigerian National Democratic Party), 178–179, 208, 210–211, 251, 315, 340, 465–466, 514–515, 522–523
Non-Aligned Movement, 589
Northern Elements Progressive Union, 145, 516, 518, 529
Northern People's Congress, 42, 315, 489, 516–517, 520, 522, 526, 528–529, 538, 564
Northern People's Progressive Union, 528
Northern Protectorate, 10, 30, 136, 145, 155, 157, 159, 225, 280–281, 304, 376, 384, 414, 516, 533
Nupe, 49–50, 52–53, 58–61, 83, 92, 99–100, 107, 110, 126–127, 131, 133–136, 145, 220, 238, 304, 355–356
NUT (Nigerian Union of Teachers), 343, 502
NTUC (Nigerian Trade Union Congress), 537
Nwaji, Chief Ike, 362
Nwanyiukwu of Oloko, 320
Nwaobiala Dance movement, 332
NWU (Nigerian Women's Union), 343
NYM (Nigerian Youth Movement), 211–212, 251, 466, 470, 489, 514–515, 519, 523

Oba Akintoye, 9, 277
Obasa, Orisadipe, 301, 464
Ochonu, Moses, 15
Ode Omi, 111
Odim, Johnson, 342
Odubanjo, David, 365
Offra, 103
Ogbomoso, 61, 260, 277, 443
Ogoja, 150, 385, 561
Ogot, Bethwell A., 197
Ogunbiyi, Rev. T. A. J., 363–364
Ogunde, Hubert, 440, 443–444, 446
Ogunmola, Kola, 443–444, 446
Oguta women, 110, 259
Oha-na-Eze, 221
Oheme, Garba, 357
Oil Rivers Protectorate, 117, 126, 137–138, 236
Okafor, Chinyere G., 436–437, 523
Okrika, 121
Olaiya, Victor, 431–432, 434–436, 446–447, 449
Old Oyo Empire, 51–52, 74, 77, 79, 90, 101, 109, 114, 128, 132
Olomu, Nana, 92
Oloruntimehin, B.O., 13
Olumuyiwa, C. B., 439
Olusanya, Gabriel, 455, 475
Omojola, Bode, 427, 429, 431
Onitsha, 110, 180, 209, 211, 259, 308, 311, 326–327, 354, 360, 374, 379, 412, 419
Opobo, 81, 92, 95, 121, 127, 131, 147–148, 228, 377, 458, 522
Oro cult, 343

Osborne, Ronald, 469
Oshitelu, Josiah, 365
Osogbo, 62, 180, 202, 260
Ossomari, 111, 259
Ottawa agreements, 250
Ouidah, 103, 109
Owerri, 7, 182, 190, 358, 361
Owo, 51, 236, 242
Oxford Delegacy for Local Examinations in 1929, 294
Oyo, 29, 31, 49–53, 55, 59–65, 67, 69–70, 72, 74, 76–79, 82–84, 86, 90, 99–101, 103–104, 108–109, 114, 118, 128, 132, 159–160, 167, 182, 189, 219–221, 225–227, 232, 312–313, 328, 348, 358, 393, 407, 428, 447, 559
Oyo Empire, 29, 100, 167, 219–221, 226–227, 232
Oyo Mesi council, 220

Palmer, Herbert R., 19
Pan-Africanism, 25
Park, Mungo, 89, 121
Paterson, Alexander, 421
Pax Britannica, 96, 117, 125, 147, 161, 235, 238, 247–248, 275, 284, 293, 295
Payne, Otunba, 100, 117, 282
Pelewura, Madam Alimotu, 340, 345, 527
Pepple, Dappa, 9, 29, 81
Perham, Margery, 8–9, 335
Phillips, Ekundayo, 428–429
Plateau–Benue, 130, 140
Po, Fernando, 29
Poland, 410
Port Harcourt, 7, 39, 180, 313, 356, 377, 380, 407, 412, 415–416
Portugal, 98, 112, 126, 174
Pratten, David, 240
Princess Alexandra of Kent, 43, 566
Prison Ordinance of 1884, 242
Protectorate of Lagos, 117, 278

Queen Amina of Zazzau, 318, 329
Queen Elizabeth II, 43, 97, 115–116, 566, 583, 589
Queen Idia, 318
Queen Moremi, 318

Qur'an, 225, 279, 584, 588

racism, 456
Railway Workers' Union, 498, 505–506, 525
Randle, John, 464, 471
Ransome-Kuti, Israel Oludotun, 342
RCM (Roman Catholic Mission), 354, 362, 372, 374
regionalism, xv, 408–409, 490–492, 516, 537, 548–550, 552–553, 557–558, 562–564, 566, 569
Renton, Sir Wood, 39
Richards Constitution, 489, 491, 507, 516–517, 524, 536–537, 552–553, 582
Richards, Arthur, 421, 483, 516, 552, 582
River Niger, 89, 93, 96, 99, 459
Robertson, James Wilson, 561
Rock of Gibraltar, 482
Ross, William Alston, 226
Rossiter, Edward, 76
Royal Navy, 306, 376
Royal Niger Company (RNC), 30, 33–34, 65–66, 125, 133, 136, 138, 191, 237, 355–356, 407, 418, 579
Royal Order in Council, 222
Rwanda, 216

Salih, Shaykh Ibrahim, 19
Samuel, Kayode, 427
Sango, 70, 347, 353, 445, 447
Santo Domingo, 76–77
Savage, Richard Akinwande, 464
Schillinger, Hubert, 496
Schon, S. F., 93
Sekondi Axim, 262
Sekyi, Kobina, 471
Senegambia, 54, 68
Shari'a law, 57
Shonga, 58
Sierra Leone, 51, 62, 68, 73, 78, 81, 84–85, 89, 94, 149, 222, 262, 278, 284, 288, 292, 295, 300–301, 379, 426, 442, 449, 467, 471, 496–497, 500–501, 587
Sir Henry Willink Commission, 43
Slave Coast, 98, 426

slave labor, 49, 67, 79, 83, 112, 124, 129, 257
slave merchants, 61, 67, 113
slave trade, 9, 12, 26–28, 33, 51, 55, 64, 66–67, 69, 73, 75–77, 81, 83–84, 86, 88, 95, 99–100, 103, 105, 107–108, 110–113, 116–117, 121, 132, 137, 153, 174, 195, 236, 249, 285, 360, 448, 467, 531, 578
Slave Trade Act, 77
slavery abolishment, 26
Sloop, H. M., 116
Small, Edward Francis, 471
Smith, Abdullahi, 12
Smith, Henry F. C., 13
Smith, Robert Sydney, 426, 448
Sodeke, 62, 362
Sokoto, 7, 19, 21, 35, 51, 57, 65, 76–77, 92, 115, 127, 130–131, 133–134, 136, 139, 145, 147, 152, 159, 162, 179, 205, 219, 221, 223–225, 230, 233, 304, 309, 350, 352, 355, 357, 373–374, 376, 410, 414, 419, 458, 491, 516, 520, 529, 539, 559, 577
Sokoto Caliphate, 19, 21, 35, 133, 147, 152, 159, 219, 221, 223–225, 230, 233, 304, 355, 376
Solagberu, 60
Solanke, Ladipo, 41, 206, 472
Somalia, 476
Songhai, 220, 348
Songhai Empire, 220
Southern Baptist Convention, 90, 277
Southern Nigerian Defender, 526
Southern Protectorate, 10, 30, 32, 137, 142, 145, 151, 155–156, 158, 163–164, 222, 241, 279–281, 284, 350, 384, 542
Soviet Union, 474, 479, 589
Sowande, Fela, 428–432, 446
Sowoolu, S. O., 8
Spain, 98, 112, 174
Subair, H. A., 208
Sudan, 12, 54, 156, 373–374, 476
Sudan Interior Mission, 373–374
Sudan United Mission, 373–374
Sudan Witness, 374
Suka, Abd Allah, 19

Suret-Canale, Jean, 13
Sylvester-Williams, Henry, 470

Tamuno, Tekena, 13, 213, 513
Tanzania, 197
Tete-Ansa, Winifred, 206, 250
The Chronicle, 316
the Native Question, 215, 222
Tiv, 50, 63, 218, 353, 376, 389, 391, 555
Tordesillia treaty of 1494, 112
Toulmin, George, 270, 272
Townsend, Henry, 65, 89, 277, 299, 315, 360, 362, 426, 467
Trade Union Congress of Nigeria, 503–504, 525
Traditional medical services, 371
Transatlantic slavers, 12
Transatlantic trade, 50, 67, 88
trans-Saharan trade, 5, 18, 21, 98, 420
TUCN (Trade Union Congress of Nigeria), 503, 506–509
Tunisia, 216, 476, 496
Tylor, Sir Edward, 388
Tyodoo, Iyue, 423

UAC (United African Company), 34
Ukeje, Oneyerisara, 276
UNA (United Native African Church), 439
UNIA (Universal Negro Improvement Association), 463
United African Company, 34, 191–192, 205, 207, 250
United Kingdom, 16, 37, 206, 282, 418, 441, 447, 462, 472, 501–502, 545
United Middle Belt Congress, 518
United Nations, 120, 195, 478, 488
United Native African Church, 94
United States of America, 76, 78, 90, 113, 206, 211, 250, 292, 301, 367, 379, 403, 431, 447, 449, 457, 471, 475, 479, 488, 494, 496, 589, 591
University College Ibadan, 7, 23, 292, 298, 386, 473
Urhobo, 73, 190, 218
Urbanization, 407, 418
Uwaifor, Victor, 432
Uya, Okon, 13

694 INDEX

van Hien, Henry, 471
Vaughan, James C., 514

Wachukwu, Jaja, 43
Waddell, Hope, 73, 287
Wallace, William, 223
Waniko, S.S., 5
Warri, 59, 87–88, 90, 92, 95, 110–111, 114, 148, 182, 190, 209, 236, 244, 260, 359, 372, 380
WASU (West African Students Union), 41, 206, 209–210, 472
Waziri, 31, 224, 352
Weekly Times, 468
Weme, 98
West Africa, 11–13, 27, 29, 33, 41, 51–54, 62, 64, 69, 74, 78, 81, 83–85, 89, 100–101, 103, 107, 114–115, 121–122, 127, 134, 202, 206, 210, 216, 220, 235, 266, 272–273, 278, 281, 331, 345, 358, 384, 414, 470–471, 476, 512–513, 538
West African Pilot, 16, 42, 212, 299, 316, 467, 469–470, 476, 487, 489, 525–526, 528, 537
West Indies, 80, 127, 285, 288, 449
Western civilization, 22, 72, 88, 93, 95, 115, 121, 149, 151, 239–241, 244, 257, 264, 284, 286, 305
white supremacy, 40, 235
Whydah, 100, 109
Williams, G. A., 300, 439
Wilson, J. W., 272
World War I, xiv, 33, 39, 141, 173–176, 178, 185, 195, 201, 239, 243, 248, 251, 260, 262–264, 266, 269, 271–272, 275, 288, 376–377, 380, 383, 439, 487, 498, 503, 562
World War II, xv, 32, 35, 40, 141, 176–180, 183, 193–196, 204–206, 209–210, 213, 244, 250, 252, 262, 275, 286, 292, 310–311, 318, 320, 336, 345, 377–378, 385, 387, 408, 418, 420, 462–463, 473–481, 485–486, 488, 490, 492–493, 496, 501, 505–506, 530, 535–536, 541, 546–547, 581, 586, 589

Yaba College, 37–38, 211, 282, 293, 398
Yaba Medical School, 378, 386
Yesu, prophet, 179
Yola, 57, 130, 180
Yoruba, 9, 19–21, 23, 28–29, 31, 36, 50, 58–62, 67, 69–70, 72, 79, 83–84, 86, 90, 100–101, 103, 108, 110, 118, 125–127, 131–132, 134, 137, 140, 155, 164, 189, 202–203, 217, 218–220, 225, 227, 232, 236, 267, 300, 304–305, 315–316, 320, 325, 328, 337, 339, 342, 346–348, 350, 352–355, 358, 360, 362–365, 370, 373, 393–394, 397, 401, 407, 409, 415, 419, 424, 430–435, 437–438, 440–441, 443–448, 451, 467, 470, 497, 516, 528, 557–558, 560, 563
Yoruba women, 70, 320, 328
Yorubaland, 29, 49, 61, 63, 65, 69–70, 72–74, 91–92, 94, 99–100, 110, 114, 121, 131–133, 137, 150, 152, 154–155, 159–160, 162–163, 167, 183, 187, 194, 205, 209, 226, 236, 241, 244, 257, 350, 358

Zakat, 35, 161
Zamfara, 56
Zaria, 19, 37, 56, 92, 130, 180, 313, 318, 414, 419, 442
Zazzau, 69
Zikist movement, 503, 506–507

Printed in the United States
by Baker & Taylor Publisher Services